Fourth Edition

Building Java Programs

A Back to Basics Approach

Stuart Reges
University of Washington

Marty Stepp
Stanford University

PEARSON

Boston Columbus Indianapolis New York San Francisco Hoboken
Amsterdam Cape Town Dubai London Madrid Milan Munich Paris Montreal Toronto
Delhi Mexico City Sao Paulo Sydney Hong Kong Seoul Singapore Taipei Tokyo

Vice President, Editorial Director: Marcia Horton
Acquisitions Editor: Matt Goldstein
Editorial Assistant: Kristy Alaura
VP of Marketing: Christy Lesko
Director of Field Marketing: Tim Galligan
Product Marketing Manager: Bram Van Kempen
Field Marketing Manager: Demetrius Hall
Marketing Assistant: Jon Bryant
Director of Product Management: Erin Gregg
Team Lead, Program and Project Management: Scott Disanno
Program Manager: Carole Snyder
Project Manager: Lakeside Editorial Services L.L.C.
Senior Specialist, Program Planning and Support: Maura Zaldivar-Garcia
Cover Design: Joyce Wells
R&P Manager: Rachel Youdelman
R&P Project Manager: Timothy Nicholls
Inventory Manager: Meredith Maresca
Cover Art: Matt Walford/Cultura/Getty Images
Full-Service Project Management: Apoorva Goel/Cenveo Publisher Services
Composition: Cenveo® Publisher Services
Printer/Binder: Edwards Brothers Malloy
Cover Printer: Phoenix Color
Text Font: Monotype

Library of Congress Cataloging-in-Publication Data
Names: Reges, Stuart, author. | Stepp, Martin, author.
Title: Building Java programs : a back to basics approach / Stuart Reges, University of Washington; Marty Stepp, Stanford University.
Description: Fourth Edition. | Hoboken, NJ : Pearson, 2016.
Identifiers: LCCN 2015049340 | ISBN 9780134322766 (alk. paper)
Subjects: LCSH: Java (Computer program language)
Classification: LCC QA76.73.J38 R447 2016 | DDC 005.13/3—dc23 LC record available at http://lccn.loc.gov/2015049340

10 9 8 7 6 5 4 3 2 1

ISBN 10: 0-13-432276-2
ISBN 13: 978-0-13-432276-6

Preface

The newly revised fourth edition of our *Building Java Programs* textbook is designed for use in a two-course introduction to computer science. We have class-tested it with thousands of undergraduates, most of whom were not computer science majors, in our CS1-CS2 sequence at the University of Washington. These courses are experiencing record enrollments, and other schools that have adopted our textbook report that students are succeeding with our approach.

Introductory computer science courses are often seen as "killer" courses with high failure rates. But as Douglas Adams says in *The Hitchhiker's Guide to the Galaxy*, "Don't panic." Students can master this material if they can learn it gradually. Our textbook uses a layered approach to introduce new syntax and concepts over multiple chapters.

Our textbook uses an "objects later" approach where programming fundamentals and procedural decomposition are taught before diving into object-oriented programming. We have championed this approach, which we sometimes call "back to basics," and have seen through years of experience that a broad range of scientists, engineers, and others can learn how to program in a procedural manner. Once we have built a solid foundation of procedural techniques, we turn to object-oriented programming. By the end of the course, students will have learned about both styles of programming.

Here are some of the changes that we have made in the fourth edition:

- **New chapter on functional programming with Java 8.** As explained below, we have introduced a chapter that uses the new language features available in Java 8 to discuss the core concepts of functional programming.
- **New section on images and 2D pixel array manipulation.** Image manipulation is becoming increasingly popular, so we have expanded our `DrawingPanel` class to include features that support manipulating images as two-dimensional arrays of pixel values. This extra coverage will be particularly helpful for students taking an AP/CS A course because of the heavy emphasis on two-dimensional arrays on the AP exam.
- **Expanded self-checks and programming exercises.** Many chapters have received new self-check problems and programming exercises. There are roughly fifty total problems and exercises per chapter, all of which have been class-tested with real students and have solutions provided for instructors on our web site.

Since the publication of our third edition, Java 8 has been released. This new version supports a style of programming known as functional programming that is gaining in popularity because of its ability to simply express complex algorithms that are more easily executed in parallel on machines with multiple processors. ACM and IEEE have released new guidelines for undergraduate computer science curricula, including a strong recommendation to cover functional programming concepts.

We have added a new Chapter 19 that covers most of the functional concepts from the new curriculum guidelines. The focus is on concepts, not on language features. As a result, it provides an introduction to several new Java 8 constructs but not a comprehensive coverage of all new language features. This provides flexibility to instructors since functional programming features can be covered as an advanced independent topic, incorporated along the way, or skipped entirely. Instructors can choose to start covering functional constructs along with traditional constructs as early as Chapter 6. See the dependency chart at the end of this section.

The following features have been retained from previous editions:

- **Focus on problem solving.** Many textbooks focus on language details when they introduce new constructs. We focus instead on problem solving. What new problems can be solved with each construct? What pitfalls are novices likely to encounter along the way? What are the most common ways to use a new construct?
- **Emphasis on algorithmic thinking.** Our procedural approach allows us to emphasize algorithmic problem solving: breaking a large problem into smaller problems, using pseudocode to refine an algorithm, and grappling with the challenge of expressing a large program algorithmically.
- **Layered approach.** Programming in Java involves many concepts that are difficult to learn all at once. Teaching Java to a novice is like trying to build a house of cards. Each new card has to be placed carefully. If the process is rushed and you try to place too many cards at once, the entire structure collapses. We teach new concepts gradually, layer by layer, allowing students to expand their understanding at a manageable pace.
- **Case studies.** We end most chapters with a significant case study that shows students how to develop a complex program in stages and how to test it as it is being developed. This structure allows us to demonstrate each new programming construct in a rich context that can't be achieved with short code examples. Several of the case studies were expanded and improved in the second edition.
- **Utility as a CS1+CS2 textbook.** In recent editions, we added chapters that extend the coverage of the book to cover all of the topics from our second course in computer science, making the book usable for a two-course sequence. Chapters 12–19 explore recursion, searching and sorting, stacks and queues, collection implementation, linked lists, binary trees, hash tables, heaps, and more. Chapter 12 also

received a section on recursive backtracking, a powerful technique for exploring a set of possibilities for solving problems such as 8 Queens and Sudoku.

Layers and Dependencies

Many introductory computer science books are language-oriented, but the early chapters of our book are layered. For example, Java has many control structures (including for-loops, while-loops, and if/else-statements), and many books include all of these control structures in a single chapter. While that might make sense to someone who already knows how to program, it can be overwhelming for a novice who is learning how to program. We find that it is much more effective to spread these control structures into different chapters so that students learn one structure at a time rather than trying to learn them all at once.

The following table shows how the layered approach works in the first six chapters:

Chapter	Control Flow	Data	Programming Techniques	Input/Output
1	methods	`String` literals	procedural decomposition	`println`, `print`
2	definite loops (`for`)	variables, expressions, `int`, `double`	local variables, class constants, pseudocode	
3	return values	using objects	parameters	console input, 2D graphics (optional)
4	conditional (`if/else`)	`char`	pre/post conditions, throwing exceptions	`printf`
5	indefinite loops (`while`)	`boolean`	assertions, robust programs	
6		`Scanner`	token/line-based file processing	file I/O

Chapters 1–6 are designed to be worked through in order, with greater flexibility of study then beginning in Chapter 7. Chapter 6 may be skipped, although the case study in Chapter 7 involves reading from a file, a topic that is covered in Chapter 6.

The following is a dependency chart for the book:

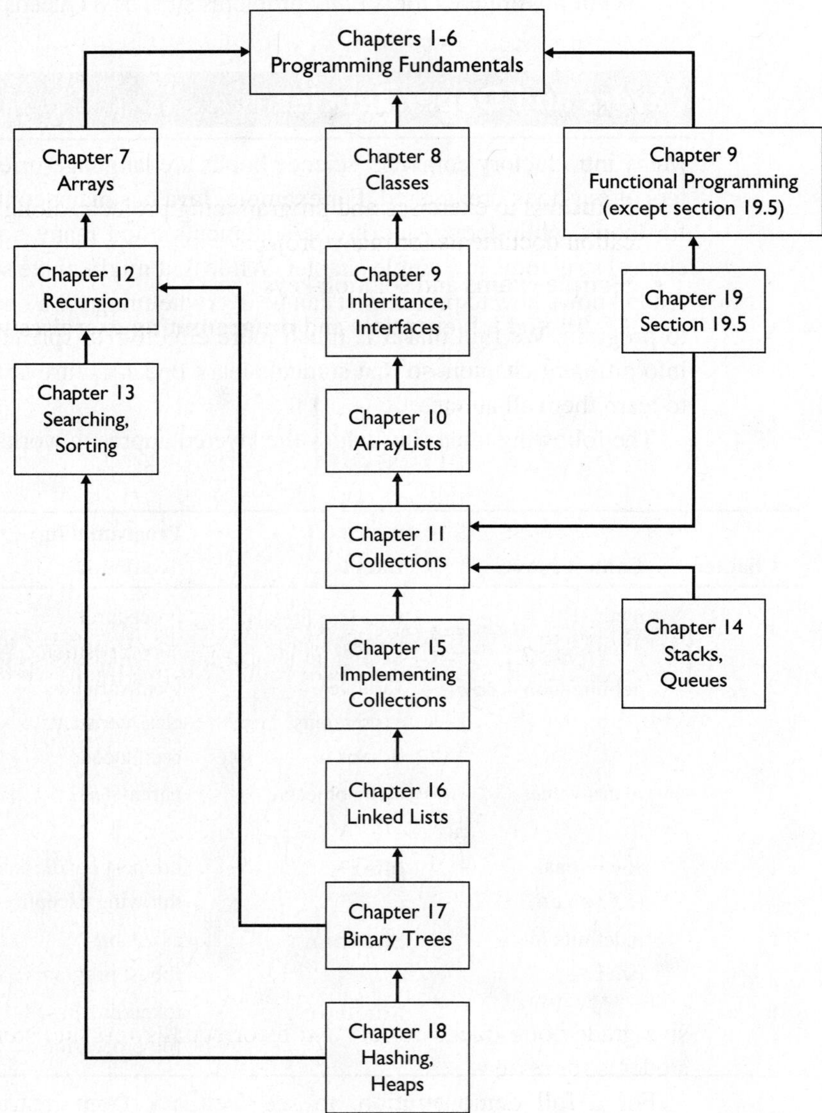

Supplements

http://www.buildingjavaprograms.com/

Answers to all self-check problems appear on our web site and are accessible to anyone. Our web site has the following additional resources for students:

- **Online-only supplemental chapters**, such as a chapter on creating Graphical User Interfaces

- **Source code and data files** for all case studies and other complete program examples
- The **`DrawingPanel` class** used in the optional graphics Supplement 3G

Our web site has the following additional resources for teachers:

- **PowerPoint slides** suitable for lectures
- **Solutions** to exercises and programming projects, along with homework specification documents for many projects
- **Sample exams** and solution keys
- **Additional lab exercises** and **programming exercises** with solution keys
- **Closed lab creation tools** to produce lab handouts with the instructor's choice of problems integrated with the textbook

To access protected instructor resources, contact us at authors@buildingjavaprograms.com. The same materials are also available at http://www.pearsonhighered.com/cs-resources. To receive a password for this site or to ask other questions related to resources, contact your Pearson sales representative.

MyProgrammingLab

MyProgrammingLab is an online practice and assessment tool that helps students fully grasp the logic, semantics, and syntax of programming. Through practice exercises and immediate, personalized feedback, MyProgrammingLab improves the programming competence of beginning students who often struggle with basic concepts and paradigms of popular high-level programming languages. A self-study and homework tool, the MyProgrammingLab course consists of hundreds of small practice exercises organized around the structure of this textbook. For students, the system automatically detects errors in the logic and syntax of code submissions and offers targeted hints that enable students to figure out what went wrong, and why. For instructors, a comprehensive grade book tracks correct and incorrect answers and stores the code inputted by students for review.

For a full demonstration, to see feedback from instructors and students, or to adopt MyProgrammingLab for your course, visit the following web site: http://www.myprogramminglab.com/

VideoNotes

VideoNote

We have recorded a series of instructional videos to accompany the textbook. They are available at the following web site: www.pearsonhighered.com/cs-resources

Roughly 3–4 videos are posted for each chapter. An icon in the margin of the page indicates when a VideoNote is available for a given topic. In each video, we spend

5–15 minutes walking through a particular concept or problem, talking about the challenges and methods necessary to solve it. These videos make a good supplement to the instruction given in lecture classes and in the textbook. Your new copy of the textbook has an access code that will allow you to view the videos.

Acknowledgments

First, we would like to thank the many colleagues, students, and teaching assistants who have used and commented on early drafts of this text. We could not have written this book without their input. Special thanks go to Hélène Martin, who pored over early versions of our first edition chapters to find errors and to identify rough patches that needed work. We would also like to thank instructor Benson Limketkai for spending many hours performing a technical proofread of the second edition.

Second, we would like to thank the talented pool of reviewers who guided us in the process of creating this textbook:

- Greg Anderson, Weber State University
- Delroy A. Brinkerhoff, Weber State University
- Ed Brunjes, Miramar Community College
- Tom Capaul, Eastern Washington University
- Tom Cortina, Carnegie Mellon University
- Charles Dierbach, Towson University
- H.E. Dunsmore, Purdue University
- Michael Eckmann, Skidmore College
- Mary Anne Egan, Siena College
- Leonard J. Garrett, Temple University
- Ahmad Ghafarian, North Georgia College & State University
- Raj Gill, Anne Arundel Community College
- Michael Hostetler, Park University
- David Hovemeyer, York College of Pennsylvania
- Chenglie Hu, Carroll College
- Philip Isenhour, Virginia Polytechnic Institute
- Andree Jacobson, University of New Mexico
- David C. Kamper, Sr., Northeastern Illinois University
- Simon G.M. Koo, University of San Diego
- Evan Korth, New York University
- Joan Krone, Denison University
- John H.E.F. Lasseter, Fairfield University

- Eric Matson, Wright State University
- Kathryn S. McKinley, University of Texas, Austin
- Jerry Mead, Bucknell University
- George Medelinskas, Northern Essex Community College
- John Neitzke, Truman State University
- Dale E. Parson, Kutztown University
- Richard E. Pattis, Carnegie Mellon University
- Frederick Pratter, Eastern Oregon University
- Roger Priebe, University of Texas, Austin
- Dehu Qi, Lamar University
- John Rager, Amherst College
- Amala V.S. Rajan, Middlesex University
- Craig Reinhart, California Lutheran University
- Mike Scott, University of Texas, Austin
- Alexa Sharp, Oberlin College
- Tom Stokke, University of North Dakota
- Leigh Ann Sudol, Fox Lane High School
- Ronald F. Taylor, Wright State University
- Andy Ray Terrel, University of Chicago
- Scott Thede, DePauw University
- Megan Thomas, California State University, Stanislaus
- Dwight Tuinstra, SUNY Potsdam
- Jeannie Turner, Sayre School
- Tammy VanDeGrift, University of Portland
- Thomas John VanDrunen, Wheaton College
- Neal R. Wagner, University of Texas, San Antonio
- Jiangping Wang, Webster University
- Yang Wang, Missouri State University
- Stephen Weiss, University of North Carolina at Chapel Hill
- Laurie Werner, Miami University
- Dianna Xu, Bryn Mawr College
- Carol Zander, University of Washington, Bothell

Finally, we would like to thank the great staff at Pearson who helped produce the book. Michelle Brown, Jeff Holcomb, Maurene Goo, Patty Mahtani, Nancy Kotary, and Kathleen Kenny did great work preparing the first edition. Our copy editors and the staff of Aptara Corp, including Heather Sisan, Brian Baker, Brendan Short, and Rachel Head, caught many errors and improved the quality of the writing. Marilyn Lloyd and Chelsea Bell served well as project manager and editorial assistant respectively on prior editions. For their help with the third edition we would like to thank Kayla Smith-Tarbox, Production Project Manager, and Jenah Blitz-Stoehr, Computer Science Editorial Assistant. Mohinder Singh and the staff at Aptara, Inc., were also very helpful in the final production of the third edition. For their great work on production of the fourth edition, we thank Louise Capulli and the staff of Lakeside Editorial Services, along with Carole Snyder at Pearson. Special thanks go to our lead editor at Pearson, Matt Goldstein, who has believed in the concept of our book from day one. We couldn't have finished this job without all of their hard work and support.

Stuart Reges
Marty Stepp

BREAKTHROUGH
To improving results

MyProgrammingLab™

Through the power of practice and immediate personalized feedback, MyProgrammingLab helps improve your students' performance.

PROGRAMMING PRACTICE

With MyProgrammingLab, your students will gain first-hand programming experience in an interactive online environment.

IMMEDIATE, PERSONALIZED FEEDBACK

MyProgrammingLab automatically detects errors in the logic and syntax of their code submission and offers targeted hints that enables students to figure out what went wrong and why.

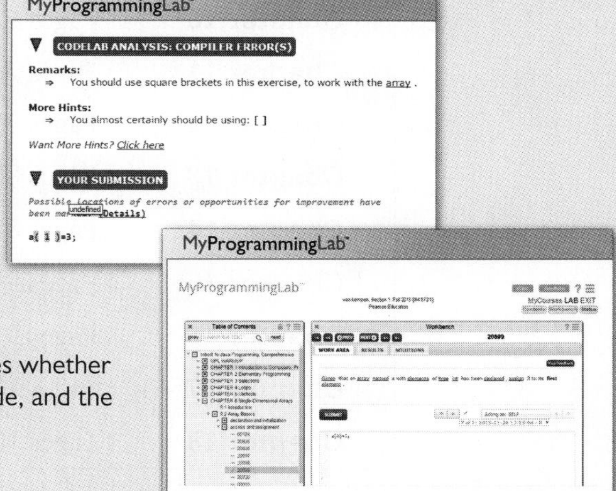

GRADUATED COMPLEXITY

MyProgrammingLab breaks down programming concepts into short, understandable sequences of exercises. Within each sequence the level and sophistication of the exercises increase gradually but steadily.

DYNAMIC ROSTER

Students' submissions are stored in a roster that indicates whether the submission is correct, how many attempts were made, and the actual code submissions from each attempt.

PEARSON eTEXT

The Pearson eText gives students access to their textbook anytime, anywhere

STEP-BY-STEP VIDEONOTE TUTORIALS

These step-by-step video tutorials enhance the programming concepts presented in select Pearson textbooks.

For more information and titles available with **MyProgrammingLab**, please visit **www.myprogramminglab.com**.

LOCATION OF VIDEO NOTES IN THE TEXT
www.pearsonhighered.com/cs-resources

VideoNote

Brief Contents

Contents

Chapter 1

Introduction to Java Programming

Introduction

This chapter begins with a review of some basic terminology about computers and computer programming. Many of these concepts will come up in later chapters, so it will be useful to review them before we start delving into the details of how to program in Java.

We will begin our exploration of Java by looking at simple programs that produce output. This discussion will allow us to explore many elements that are common to all Java programs, while working with programs that are fairly simple in structure.

After we have reviewed the basic elements of Java programs, we will explore the technique of procedural decomposition by learning how to break up a Java program into several methods. Using this technique, we can break up complex tasks into smaller subtasks that are easier to manage and we can avoid redundancy in our program solutions.

1.1 Basic Computing Concepts

Computers are pervasive in our daily lives, and, thanks to the Internet, they give us access to nearly limitless information. Some of this information is essential news, like the headlines at cnn.com. Computers let us share photos with our families and map directions to the nearest pizza place for dinner.

Lots of real-world problems are being solved by computers, some of which don't much resemble the one on your desk or lap. Computers allow us to sequence the human genome and search for DNA patterns within it. Computers in recently manufactured cars monitor each vehicle's status and motion. Digital music players such as Apple's iPod actually have computers inside their small casings. Even the Roomba vacuum-cleaning robot houses a computer with complex instructions about how to dodge furniture while cleaning your floors.

But what makes a computer a computer? Is a calculator a computer? Is a human being with a paper and pencil a computer? The next several sections attempt to address this question while introducing some basic terminology that will help prepare you to study programming.

Why Programming?

At most universities, the first course in computer science is a programming course. Many computer scientists are bothered by this because it leaves people with the impression that computer science is programming. While it is true that many trained computer scientists spend time programming, there is a lot more to the discipline. So why do we study programming first?

A Stanford computer scientist named Don Knuth answers this question by saying that the common thread for most computer scientists is that we all in some way work with *algorithms*.

> **Algorithm**
> A step-by-step description of how to accomplish a task.

Knuth is an expert in algorithms, so he is naturally biased toward thinking of them as the center of computer science. Still, he claims that what is most important is not the algorithms themselves, but rather the thought process that computer scientists employ to develop them. According to Knuth,

> It has often been said that a person does not really understand something until after teaching it to someone else. Actually a person does not *really* understand something until after teaching it to a *computer*, i.e., expressing it as an algorithm.[1]

[1]Knuth, Don. *Selected Papers on Computer Science*. Stanford, CA: Center for the Study of Language and Information, 1996.

Knuth is describing a thought process that is common to most of computer science, which he refers to as *algorithmic thinking*. We study programming not because it is the most important aspect of computer science, but because it is the best way to explain the approach that computer scientists take to solving problems.

The concept of algorithms is helpful in understanding what a computer is and what computer science is all about. The Merriam-Webster dictionary defines the word "computer" as "one that computes." Using that definition, all sorts of devices qualify as computers, including calculators, GPS navigation systems, and children's toys like the Furby. Prior to the invention of electronic computers, it was common to refer to humans as computers. The nineteenth-century mathematician Charles Peirce, for example, was originally hired to work for the U.S. government as an "Assistant Computer" because his job involved performing mathematical computations.

In a broad sense, then, the word "computer" can be applied to many devices. But when computer scientists refer to a computer, we are usually thinking of a universal computation device that can be programmed to execute any algorithm. Computer science, then, is the study of computational devices and the study of computation itself, including algorithms.

Algorithms are expressed as computer programs, and that is what this book is all about. But before we look at how to program, it will be useful to review some basic concepts about computers.

Hardware and Software

A computer is a machine that manipulates data and executes lists of instructions known as *programs*.

Program

A list of instructions to be carried out by a computer.

One key feature that differentiates a computer from a simpler machine like a calculator is its versatility. The same computer can perform many different tasks (playing games, computing income taxes, connecting to other computers around the world), depending on what program it is running at a given moment. A computer can run not only the programs that exist on it currently, but also new programs that haven't even been written yet.

The physical components that make up a computer are collectively called *hardware*. One of the most important pieces of hardware is the central processing unit, or *CPU*. The CPU is the "brain" of the computer: It is what executes the instructions. Also important is the computer's *memory* (often called random access memory, or *RAM*, because the computer can access any part of that memory at any time). The computer uses its memory to store programs that are being executed, along with their data. RAM is limited in size and does not retain its contents when the computer is turned off. Therefore, computers generally also use a *hard disk* as a larger permanent storage area.

Computer programs are collectively called *software*. The primary piece of software running on a computer is its operating system. An *operating system* provides an environment in which many programs may be run at the same time; it also provides a bridge between those programs, the hardware, and the *user* (the person using the computer). The programs that run inside the operating system are often called *applications*.

When the user selects a program for the operating system to run (e.g., by double-clicking the program's icon on the desktop), several things happen: The instructions for that program are loaded into the computer's memory from the hard disk, the operating system allocates memory for that program to use, and the instructions to run the program are fed from memory to the CPU and executed sequentially.

The Digital Realm

In the last section, we saw that a computer is a general-purpose device that can be programmed. You will often hear people refer to modern computers as *digital* computers because of the way they operate.

> **Digital**
> Based on numbers that increase in discrete increments, such as the integers 0, 1, 2, 3, etc.

Because computers are digital, everything that is stored on a computer is stored as a sequence of integers. This includes every program and every piece of data. An MP3 file, for example, is simply a long sequence of integers that stores audio information. Today we're used to digital music, digital pictures, and digital movies, but in the 1940s, when the first computers were built, the idea of storing complex data in integer form was fairly unusual.

Not only are computers digital, storing all information as integers, but they are also *binary*, which means they store integers as *binary numbers*.

> **Binary Number**
> A number composed of just 0s and 1s, also known as a base-2 number.

Humans generally work with *decimal* or base-10 numbers, which match our physiology (10 fingers and 10 toes). However, when we were designing the first computers, we wanted systems that would be easy to create and very reliable. It turned out to be simpler to build these systems on top of binary phenomena (e.g., a circuit being open or closed) rather than having 10 different states that would have to be distinguished from one another (e.g., 10 different voltage levels).

From a mathematical point of view, you can store things just as easily using binary numbers as you can using base-10 numbers. But since it is easier to construct a physical device that uses binary numbers, that's what computers use.

This does mean, however, that people who aren't used to computers find their conventions unfamiliar. As a result, it is worth spending a little time reviewing how binary numbers work. To count with binary numbers, as with base-10 numbers, you start with 0 and count up, but you run out of digits much faster. So, counting in binary, you say

```
0
1
```

And already you've run out of digits. This is like reaching 9 when you count in base-10. After you run out of digits, you carry over to the next digit. So, the next two binary numbers are

```
10
11
```

And again, you've run out of digits. This is like reaching 99 in base-10. Again, you carry over to the next digit to form the three-digit number 100. In binary, whenever you see a series of ones, such as 111111, you know you're just one away from the digits all flipping to 0s with a 1 added in front, the same way that, in base-10, when you see a number like 999999, you know that you are one away from all those digits turning to 0s with a 1 added in front.

Table 1.1 shows how to count up to the base-10 number 8 using binary.

Table 1.1 Decimal vs. Binary

Decimal	Binary
0	0
1	1
2	10
3	11
4	100
5	101
6	110
7	111
8	1000

We can make several useful observations about binary numbers. Notice in the table that the binary numbers 1, 10, 100, and 1000 are all perfect powers of 2 (2^0, 2^1, 2^2, 2^3). In the same way that in base-10 we talk about a ones digit, tens digit, hundreds digit, and so on, we can think in binary of a ones digit, twos digit, fours digit, eights digit, sixteens digit, and so on.

Computer scientists quickly found themselves needing to refer to the sizes of different binary quantities, so they invented the term *bit* to refer to a single binary digit and the term *byte* to refer to 8 bits. To talk about large amounts of memory, they invented the terms "kilobytes" (KB), "megabytes" (MB), "gigabytes" (GB), and so on. Many people think that these correspond to the metric system, where "kilo" means 1000, but that is only approximately true. We use the fact that 2^{10} is approximately equal to 1000 (it actually equals 1024). Table 1.2 shows some common units of memory storage:

Table 1.2 Units of Memory Storage

Measurement	Power of 2	Actual Value	Example
kilobyte (KB)	2^{10}	1024	500-word paper (3 KB)
megabyte (MB)	2^{20}	1,048,576	typical book (1 MB) or song (5 MB)
gigabyte (GB)	2^{30}	1,073,741,824	typical movie (4.7 GB)
terabyte (TB)	2^{40}	1,099,511,627,776	20 million books in the Library of Congress (20 TB)
petabyte (PB)	2^{50}	1,125,899,906,842,624	10 billion photos on Facebook (1.5 PB)

The Process of Programming

The word *code* describes program fragments ("these four lines of code") or the act of programming ("Let's code this into Java"). Once a program has been written, you can *execute* it.

Program Execution

The act of carrying out the instructions contained in a program.

The process of execution is often called *running*. This term can also be used as a verb ("When my program runs it does something strange") or as a noun ("The last run of my program produced these results").

A computer program is stored internally as a series of binary numbers known as the *machine language* of the computer. In the early days, programmers entered numbers like these directly into the computer. Obviously, this is a tedious and confusing way to program a computer, and we have invented all sorts of mechanisms to simplify this process.

Modern programmers write in what are known as high-level programming languages, such as Java. Such programs cannot be run directly on a computer: They first have to be translated into a different form by a special program known as a *compiler*.

Compiler

A program that translates a computer program written in one language into an equivalent program in another language (often, but not always, translating from a high-level language into machine language).

A compiler that translates directly into machine language creates a program that can be executed directly on the computer, known as an *executable*. We refer to such compilers as *native compilers* because they compile code to the lowest possible level (the native machine language of the computer).

This approach works well when you know exactly what computer you want to use to run your program. But what if you want to execute a program on many different computers? You'd need a compiler that generates different machine language output for each of them. The designers of Java decided to use a different approach. They cared a lot about their programs being able to run on many different computers, because they wanted to create a language that worked well for the Web.

Instead of compiling into machine language, Java programs compile into what are known as *Java bytecodes*. One set of bytecodes can execute on many different machines. These bytecodes represent an intermediate level: They aren't quite as high-level as Java or as low-level as machine language. In fact, they are the machine language of a theoretical computer known as the *Java Virtual Machine (JVM).*

Java Virtual Machine

A theoretical computer whose machine language is the set of Java bytecodes.

A JVM isn't an actual machine, but it's similar to one. When we compile programs to this level, there isn't much work remaining to turn the Java bytecodes into actual machine instructions.

To actually execute a Java program, you need another program that will execute the Java bytecodes. Such programs are known generically as *Java runtimes*, and the standard environment distributed by Oracle Corporation is known as the *Java Runtime Environment (JRE).*

Java Runtime

A program that executes compiled Java bytecodes.

Most people have Java runtimes on their computers, even if they don't know about them. For example, Apple's Mac OS X includes a Java runtime, and many Windows applications install a Java runtime.

Why Java?

When Sun Microsystems released Java in 1995, it published a document called a "white paper" describing its new programming language. Perhaps the key sentence from that paper is the following:

> Java: A simple, object-oriented, network-savvy, interpreted, robust, secure, architecture neutral, portable, high-performance, multithreaded, dynamic language.[2]

This sentence covers many of the reasons why Java is a good introductory programming language. For starters, Java is reasonably simple for beginners to learn, and it embraces object-oriented programming, a style of writing programs that has been shown to be very successful for creating large and complex software systems.

[2]http://www.oracle.com/technetwork/java/langenv-140151.html

Java also includes a large amount of prewritten software that programmers can utilize to enhance their programs. Such off-the-shelf software components are often called *libraries*. For example, if you wish to write a program that connects to a site on the Internet, Java contains a library to simplify the connection for you. Java contains libraries to draw graphical user interfaces (GUIs), retrieve data from databases, and perform complex mathematical computations, among many other things. These libraries collectively are called the *Java class libraries*.

Java Class Libraries

The collection of preexisting Java code that provides solutions to common programming problems.

The richness of the Java class libraries has been an extremely important factor in the rise of Java as a popular language. The Java class libraries in version 1.7 include over 4000 entries.

Another reason to use Java is that it has a vibrant programmer community. Extensive online documentation and tutorials are available to help programmers learn new skills. Many of these documents are written by Oracle, including an extensive reference to the Java class libraries called the *API Specification* (API stands for Application Programming Interface).

Java is extremely platform independent; unlike programs written in many other languages, the same Java program can be executed on many different operating systems, such as Windows, Linux, and Mac OS X.

Java is used extensively for both research and business applications, which means that a large number of programming jobs exist in the marketplace today for skilled Java programmers. A sample Google search for the phrase "Java jobs" returned around 180,000,000 hits at the time of this writing.

The Java Programming Environment

You must become familiar with your computer setup before you start programming. Each computer provides a different environment for program development, but there are some common elements that deserve comment. No matter what environment you use, you will follow the same basic three steps:

1. Type in a program as a Java class.
2. Compile the program file.
3. Run the compiled version of the program.

The basic unit of storage on most computers is a *file*. Every file has a name. A file name ends with an *extension*, which is the part of a file's name that follows the period. A file's extension indicates the type of data contained in the file. For example, files with the extension `.doc` are Microsoft Word documents, and files with the extension `.mp3` are MP3 audio files.

The Java program files that you create must use the extension `.java`. When you compile a Java program, the resulting Java bytecodes are stored in a file with the same name and the extension `.class`.

Most Java programmers use what are known as Integrated Development Environments, or IDEs, which provide an all-in-one environment for creating, editing, compiling, and executing program files. Some of the more popular choices for introductory computer science classes are Eclipse, jGRASP, DrJava, BlueJ, and TextPad. Your instructor will tell you what environment you should use.

Try typing the following simple program in your IDE (the line numbers are not part of the program but are used as an aid):

```
public class Hello {
    public static void main(String[] args) {
        System.out.println("Hello, world!");
    }
}
```

Don't worry about the details of this program right now. We will explore those in the next section.

Once you have created your program file, move to step 2 and compile it. The command to compile will be different in each development environment, but the process is the same (typical commands are "compile" or "build"). If any errors are reported, go back to the editor, fix them, and try to compile the program again. (We'll discuss errors in more detail later in this chapter.)

Once you have successfully compiled your program, you are ready to move to step 3, running the program. Again, the command to do this will differ from one environment to the next, but the process is similar (the typical command is "run"). The diagram in Figure 1.1 summarizes the steps you would follow in creating a program called `Hello.java`.

In some IDEs (most notably Eclipse), the first two steps are combined. In these environments the process of compiling is more incremental; the compiler will warn you about errors as you type in code. It is generally not necessary to formally ask such an environment to compile your program because it is compiling as you type.

When your program is executed, it will typically interact with the user in some way. The `Hello.java` program involves an onscreen window known as the *console*.

Console Window

A special text-only window in which Java programs interact with the user.

The console window is a classic interaction mechanism wherein the computer displays text on the screen and sometimes waits for the user to type responses. This is known as *console* or *terminal interaction*. The text the computer prints to the console window is known as the *output* of the program. Anything typed by the user is known as the console *input*.

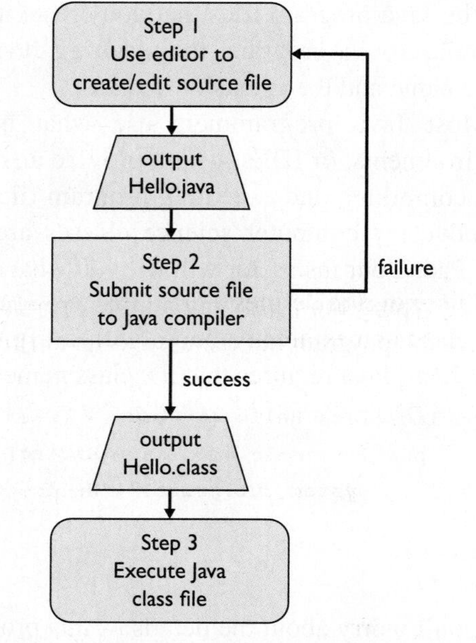

Figure 1.1 Creation and execution of a Java program

To keep things simple, most of the sample programs in this book involve console interaction. Keeping the interaction simple will allow you to focus your attention and effort on other aspects of programming.

1.2 And Now—Java

It's time to look at a complete Java program. In the Java programming language, nothing can exist outside of a *class*.

Class

A unit of code that is the basic building block of Java programs.

The notion of a class is much richer than this, as you'll see when we get to Chapter 8, but for now all you need to know is that each of your Java programs will be stored in a class.

It is a tradition in computer science that when you describe a new programming language, you should start with a program that produces a single line of output with the words, "Hello, world!" The "hello world" tradition has been broken by many authors of Java books because the program turns out not to be as short and simple when it is written in Java as when it is written in other languages, but we'll use it here anyway.

Here is our "hello world" program:

```
public class Hello {
    public static void main(String[] args) {
        System.out.println("Hello, world!");
    }
}
```

This program defines a class called `Hello`. Oracle has established the convention that class names always begin with a capital letter, which makes it easy to recognize them. Java requires that the class name and the file name match, so this program must be stored in a file called `Hello.java`. You don't have to understand all the details of this program just yet, but you do need to understand the basic structure.

The basic form of a Java class is as follows:

```
public class <name> {
    <method>
    <method>
    ...
    <method>
}
```

This type of description is known as a *syntax template* because it describes the basic form of a Java construct. Java has rules that determine its legal *syntax* or grammar. Each time we introduce a new element of Java, we'll begin by looking at its syntax template. By convention, we use the less-than (<) and greater-than (>) characters in a syntax template to indicate items that need to be filled in (in this case, the name of the class and the methods). When we write "..." in a list of elements, we're indicating that any number of those elements may be included.

The first line of the class is known as the *class header*. The word `public` in the header indicates that this class is available to anyone to use. Notice that the program code in a class is enclosed in curly brace characters (`{ }`). These characters are used in Java to group together related bits of code. In this case, the curly braces are indicating that everything defined within them is part of this public class.

So what exactly can appear inside the curly braces? What can be contained in a class? All sorts of things, but for now, we'll limit ourselves to *methods*. Methods are the next-smallest unit of code in Java, after classes. A method represents a single action or calculation to be performed.

Method

A program unit that represents a particular action or computation.

Simple methods are like verbs: They command the computer to perform some action. Inside the curly braces for a class, you can define several different methods.

At a minimum, a complete program requires a special method that is known as the `main` method. It has the following syntax:

```
public static void main(String[] args) {
    <statement>;
    <statement>;
    ...
    <statement>;
}
```

Just as the first line of a class is known as a class header, the first line of a method is known as a *method header*. The header for `main` is rather complicated. Most people memorize this as a kind of magical incantation. You want to open the door to Ali Baba's cave? You say, "Open Sesame!" You want to create an executable Java program? You say, `public static void main(String[] args)`. A group of Java teachers make fun of this with a website called publicstaticvoidmain.com.

Just memorizing magical incantations is never satisfying, especially for computer scientists who like to know everything that is going on in their programs. But this is a place where Java shows its ugly side, and you'll just have to live with it. New programmers, like new drivers, must learn to use something complex without fully understanding how it works. Fortunately, by the time you finish this book, you'll understand every part of the incantation.

Notice that the `main` method has a set of curly braces of its own. They are again used for grouping, indicating that everything that appears between them is part of the `main` method. The lines in between the curly braces specify the series of actions the computer should perform when it executes the method. We refer to these as the *statements* of the method. Just as you put together an essay by stringing together complete sentences, you put together a method by stringing together statements.

Statement

An executable snippet of code that represents a complete command.

Each statement is terminated by a semicolon. The sample "hello world" program has just a single statement that is known as a `println` statement:

```
System.out.println("Hello, world!");
```

Notice that this statement ends with a semicolon. The semicolon has a special status in Java; it is used to terminate statements in the same way that periods terminate sentences in English.

In the basic "hello world" program there is just a single command to produce a line of output, but consider the following variation (called `Hello2`), which has four lines of code to be executed in the `main` method:

```
public class Hello2 {
    public static void main(String[] args) {
        System.out.println("Hello, world!");
        System.out.println();
        System.out.println("This program produces four");
        System.out.println("lines of output.");
    }
}
```

Notice that there are four semicolons in the `main` method, one at the end of each of the four `println` statements. The statements are executed in the order in which they appear, from first to last, so the `Hello2` program produces the following output:

```
Hello, world!

This program produces four
lines of output.
```

Let's summarize the different levels we just looked at:

- A Java program is stored in a class.
- Within the class, there are methods. At a minimum, a complete program requires a special method called `main`.
- Inside a method like `main`, there is a series of statements, each of which represents a single command for the computer to execute.

It may seem odd to put the opening curly brace at the end of a line rather than on a line by itself. Some people would use this style of indentation for the program instead:

```
public class Hello3
{
    public static void main(String[] args)
    {
        System.out.println("Hello, world!");
    }
}
```

Different people will make different choices about the placement of curly braces. The style we use follows Oracle's official Java coding conventions, but the other style has its advocates too. Often people will passionately argue that one way is much better than the other, but it's really a matter of personal taste because each choice has some advantages and some disadvantages. Your instructor may require a particular style; if not, you should choose a style that you are comfortable with and then use it consistently.

Now that you've seen an overview of the structure, let's examine some of the details of Java programs.

Did You Know?

Hello, World!

The "hello world" tradition was started by Brian Kernighan and Dennis Ritchie. Ritchie invented a programming language known as C in the 1970s and, together with Kernighan, coauthored the first book describing C, published in 1978. The first complete program in their book was a "hello world" program. Kernighan and Ritchie, as well as their book *The C Programming Language*, have been affectionately referred to as "K & R" ever since.

Many major programming languages have borrowed the basic C syntax as a way to leverage the popularity of C and to encourage programmers to switch to it. The languages C++ and Java both borrow a great deal of their core syntax from C.

Kernighan and Ritchie also had a distinctive style for the placement of curly braces and the indentation of programs that has become known as "K & R style." This is the style that Oracle recommends and that we use in this book.

String Literals (Strings)

When you are writing Java programs (such as the preceding "hello world" program), you'll often want to include some literal text to send to the console window as output. Programmers have traditionally referred to such text as a *string* because it is composed of a sequence of characters that we string together. The Java language specification uses the term *string literals*.

In Java you specify a string literal by surrounding the literal text in quotation marks, as in

```
"This is a bunch of text surrounded by quotation marks."
```

You must use double quotation marks, not single quotation marks. The following is not a valid string literal:

```
'Bad stuff here.'
```

The following is a valid string literal:

```
"This is a string even with 'these' quotes inside."
```

String literals must not span more than one line of a program. The following is not a valid string literal:

```
"This is really
bad stuff
right here."
```

System.out.println

As you have seen, the `main` method of a Java program contains a series of statements for the computer to carry out. They are executed sequentially, starting with the first statement, then the second, then the third, and so on until the final statement has been executed. One of the simplest and most common statements is `System.out.println`, which is used to produce a line of output. This is another "magical incantation" that you should commit to memory. As of this writing, Google lists around 8,000,000 web pages that mention `System.out.println`. The key thing to remember about this statement is that it's used to produce a line of output that is sent to the console window.

The simplest form of the `println` statement has nothing inside its parentheses and produces a blank line of output:

```
System.out.println();
```

You need to include the parentheses even if you don't have anything to put inside them. Notice the semicolon at the end of the line. All statements in Java must be terminated with a semicolon.

More often, however, you use `println` to output a line of text:

```
System.out.println("This line uses the println method.");
```

The above statement commands the computer to produce the following line of output:

```
This line uses the println method.
```

Each `println` statement produces a different line of output. For example, consider the following three statements:

```
System.out.println("This is the first line of output.");
System.out.println();
System.out.println("This is the third, below a blank line.");
```

Executing these statements produces the following three lines of output (the second line is blank):

```
This is the first line of output.

This is the third, below a blank line.
```

Escape Sequences

Any system that involves quoting text will lead you to certain difficult situations. For example, string literals are contained inside quotation marks, so how can you include a quotation mark inside a string literal? String literals also aren't allowed to break across lines, so how can you include a line break inside a string literal?

The solution is to embed what are known as *escape sequences* in the string literals. Escape sequences are two-character sequences that are used to represent special characters. They all begin with the backslash character (\). Table 1.3 lists some of the more common escape sequences.

Table 1.3 Common Escape Sequences

Sequence	Represents
`\t`	tab character
`\n`	new line character
`\"`	quotation mark
`\\`	backslash character

Keep in mind that each of these two-character sequences actually stands for just a single character. For example, consider the following statement:

```
System.out.println("What \"characters\" does this \\ print?");
```

If you executed this statement, you would get the following output:

```
What "characters" does this \ print?
```

The string literal in the `println` has three escape sequences, each of which is two characters long and produces a single character of output.

While string literals themselves cannot span multiple lines (that is, you cannot use a carriage return within a string literal to force a line break), you can use the `\n` escape sequence to embed new line characters in a string. This leads to the odd situation where a single `println` statement can produce more than one line of output.

For example, consider this statement:

```
System.out.println("This\nproduces 3 lines\nof output.");
```

If you execute it, you will get the following output:

```
This
produces 3 lines
of output.
```

The `println` itself produces one line of output, but the string literal contains two new line characters that cause it to be broken up into a total of three lines of output. To produce the same output without new line characters, you would have to issue three separate `println` statements.

This is another programming habit that tends to vary according to taste. Some people (including the authors) find it hard to read string literals that contain `\n` escape sequences, but other people prefer to write fewer lines of code. Once again, you should make up your own mind about when to use the new line escape sequence.

print versus println

Java has a variation of the `println` command called `print` that allows you to produce output on the current line without going to a new line of output. The `println` command really does two different things: It sends output to the current line, and then it moves to the beginning of a new line. The `print` command does only the first of these. Thus, a series of `print` commands will generate output all on the same line. Only a `println` command will cause the current line to be completed and a new line to be started. For example, consider these six statements:

```
System.out.print("To be ");
System.out.print("or not to be.");
System.out.print("That is ");
System.out.println("the question.");
System.out.print("This is");
System.out.println(" for the whole family!");
```

These statements produce two lines of output. Remember that every `println` statement produces exactly one line of output; because there are two `println` statements here, there are two lines of output. After the first statement executes, the current line looks like this:

```
To be
      ^
```

The arrow below the output line indicates the position where output will be sent next. We can simplify our discussion if we refer to the arrow as the *output cursor*. Notice that the output cursor is at the end of this line and that it appears after a space. The reason is that the command was a `print` (doesn't go to a new line) and the string literal in the `print` ended with a space. Java will not insert a space for you unless you specifically request it. After the next `print`, the line looks like this:

```
To be or not to be.
                   ^
```

There's no space at the end now because the string literal in the second `print` command ends in a period, not a space. After the next `print`, the line looks like this:

```
To be or not to be.That is
                           ^
```

There is no space between the period and the word "That" because there was no space in the `print` commands, but there is a space at the end of the string literal in the third statement. After the next statement executes, the output looks like this:

```
To be or not to be.That is the question.

^
```

Because this fourth statement is a `println` command, it finishes the output line and positions the cursor at the beginning of the second line. The next statement is another `print` that produces this:

```
To be or not to be.That is the question.
This is ^
```

The final `println` completes the second line and positions the output cursor at the beginning of a new line:

```
To be or not to be.That is the question.
This is for the whole family!

^
```

These six statements are equivalent to the following two single statements:

```
System.out.println("To be or not to be.That is the question.");
System.out.println("This is for the whole family!");
```

Using the `print` and `println` commands together to produce lines like these may seem a bit silly, but you will see that there are more interesting applications of `print` in the next chapter.

Remember that it is possible to have an empty `println` command:

```
System.out.println();
```

Because there is nothing inside the parentheses to be written to the output line, this command positions the output cursor at the beginning of the next line. If there are `print` commands before this empty `println`, it finishes out the line made by those `print` commands. If there are no previous `print` commands, it produces a blank line. An empty `print` command is meaningless and illegal.

Identifiers and Keywords

The words used to name parts of a Java program are called *identifiers*.

Identifier

A name given to an entity in a program, such as a class or method.

Identifiers must start with a letter, which can be followed by any number of letters or digits. The following are all legal identifiers:

```
first              hiThere        numStudents    TwoBy4
```

The Java language specification defines the set of letters to include the underscore and dollar-sign characters (_ and $), which means that the following are legal identifiers as well:

```
two_plus_two       _count        $2donuts       MAX_COUNT
```

The following are illegal identifiers:

```
two+two            hi there      hi-There       2by4
```

Java has conventions for capitalization that are followed fairly consistently by programmers. All class names should begin with a capital letter, as with the `Hello`, `Hello2`, and `Hello3` classes introduced earlier. The names of methods should begin with lowercase letters, as in the `main` method. When you are putting several words together to form a class or method name, capitalize the first letter of each word after the first. In the next chapter we'll discuss constants, which have yet another capitalization scheme, with all letters in uppercase and words separated by underscores. These different schemes might seem like tedious constraints, but using consistent capitalization in your code allows the reader to quickly identify the various code elements.

For example, suppose that you were going to put together the words "all my children" into an identifier. The result would be

- `AllMyChildren` for a class name (each word starts with a capital)
- `allMyChildren` for a method name (starts with a lowercase letter, subsequent words capitalized)
- `ALL_MY_CHILDREN` for a constant name (all uppercase, with words separated by underscores; described in Chapter 2)

Java is case sensitive, so the identifiers `class`, `Class`, `CLASS`, and `cLASs` are all considered different. Keep this in mind as you read error messages from the compiler. People are good at understanding what you write, even if you misspell words or make little mistakes like changing the capitalization of a word. However, mistakes like these cause the Java compiler to become hopelessly confused.

Don't hesitate to use long identifiers. The more descriptive your names are, the easier it will be for people (including you) to read your programs. Descriptive identifiers are worth the time they take to type. Java's `String` class, for example, has a method called `compareToIgnoreCase`.

Be aware, however, that Java has a set of predefined identifiers called *keywords* that are reserved for particular uses. As you read this book, you will learn many of these keywords and their uses. You can only use keywords for their intended purposes. You must be careful to avoid using these words in the names of identifiers. For example, if you name a method `short` or `try`, this will cause a problem, because `short` and `try` are reserved keywords. Table 1.4 shows the complete list of reserved keywords.

Table 1.4 List of Java Keywords

`abstract`	`continue`	`for`	`new`	`switch`
`assert`	`default`	`goto`	`package`	`synchronized`
`boolean`	`do`	`if`	`private`	`this`
`break`	`double`	`implements`	`protected`	`throw`
`byte`	`else`	`import`	`public`	`throws`
`case`	`enum`	`instanceof`	`return`	`transient`
`catch`	`extends`	`int`	`short`	`try`
`char`	`final`	`interface`	`static`	`void`
`class`	`finally`	`long`	`strictfp`	`volatile`
`const`	`float`	`native`	`super`	`while`

A Complex Example: `DrawFigures1`

The `println` statement can be used to draw text figures as output. Consider the following more complicated program example (notice that it uses two empty `println` statements to produce blank lines):

```
public class DrawFigures1 {
    public static void main(String[] args) {
        System.out.println("   /\\");
        System.out.println("  /  \\");
        System.out.println(" /    \\");
        System.out.println(" \\    /");
        System.out.println("  \\  /");
        System.out.println("   \\/");
        System.out.println();
        System.out.println(" \\    /");
        System.out.println("  \\  /");
        System.out.println("   \\/");
        System.out.println("   /\\");
        System.out.println("  /  \\");
        System.out.println(" /    \\");
        System.out.println();
        System.out.println("   /\\");
        System.out.println("  /  \\");
        System.out.println(" /    \\");
        System.out.println("+------+");
        System.out.println("|      |");
        System.out.println("|      |");
        System.out.println("+------+");
        System.out.println("|United|");
        System.out.println("|States|");
        System.out.println("+------+");
        System.out.println("|      |");
```

```
        System.out.println("|      |");
        System.out.println("+------+");
        System.out.println("   /\\");
        System.out.println("  /  \\");
        System.out.println(" /    \\");
    }
}
```

The following is the output the program generates. Notice that the program includes double backslash characters (\\), but the output has single backslash characters. This is an example of an escape sequence, as described previously.

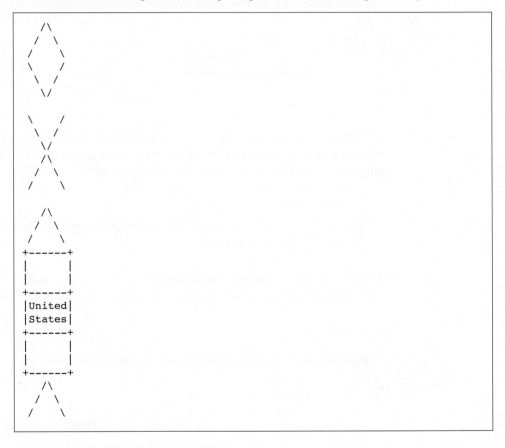

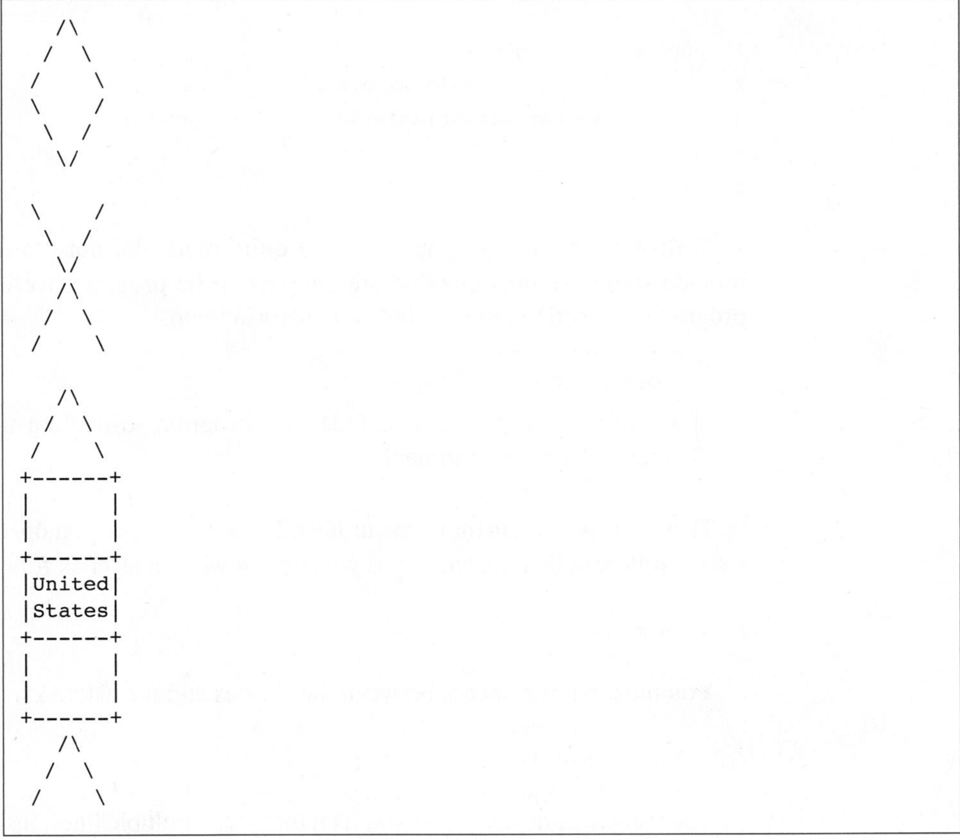

```
   /\
  /  \
 /    \
 \    /
  \  /
   \/

 \    /
  \  /
   \/
   /\
  /  \
 /    \

   /\
  /  \
 /    \
+------+
|      |
|      |
+------+
|United|
|States|
+------+
|      |
|      |
+------+
   /\
  /  \
 /    \
```

Comments and Readability

Java is a free-format language. This means you can put in as many or as few spaces and blank lines as you like, as long as you put at least one space or other punctuation mark between words. However, you should bear in mind that the layout of a program can enhance (or detract from) its readability. The following program is legal but hard to read:

```
public class Ugly{public static void main(String[] args)
{System.out.println("How short I am!");}}
```

Here are some simple rules to follow that will make your programs more readable:

- Put class and method headers on lines by themselves.
- Put no more than one statement on each line.
- Indent your program properly. When an opening brace appears, increase the indentation of the lines that follow it. When a closing brace appears, reduce the indentation. Indent statements inside curly braces by a consistent number of spaces (a common choice is four spaces per level of indentation).
- Use blank lines to separate parts of the program (e.g., methods).

Using these rules to rewrite the `Ugly` program yields the following code:

```
public class Ugly {
    public static void main(String[] args) {
        System.out.println("How short I am!");
    }
}
```

Well-written Java programs can be quite readable, but often you will want to include some explanations that are not part of the program itself. You can annotate programs by putting notes called *comments* in them.

Comment

Text that programmers include in a program to explain their code. The compiler ignores comments.

There are two comment forms in Java. In the first form, you open the comment with a slash followed by an asterisk and you close it with an asterisk followed by a slash:

```
/* like this */
```

You must not put spaces between the slashes and the asterisks:

```
/ * this is bad * /
```

You can put almost any text you like, including multiple lines, inside the comment:

```
/* Thaddeus Martin
   Assignment #1
   Instructor: Professor Walingford
   Grader:     Bianca Montgomery      */
```

The only things you aren't allowed to put inside a comment are the comment end characters. The following code is not legal:

```
/* This comment has an asterisk/slash /*/ in it,
   which prematurely closes the comment. This is bad. */
```

Java also provides a second comment form for shorter, single-line comments. You can use two slashes in a row to indicate that the rest of the current line (everything to the right of the two slashes) is a comment. For example, you can put a comment after a statement:

```
System.out.println("You win!"); // Good job!
```

Or you can create a comment on its own line:

```
// give an introduction to the user
System.out.println("Welcome to the game of blackjack.");
System.out.println();
System.out.println("Let me explain the rules.");
```

You can even create blocks of single-line comments:

```
// Thaddeus Martin
// Assignment #1
// Instructor:  Professor Walingford
// Grader:      Bianca Montgomery
```

Some people prefer to use the first comment form for comments that span multiple lines but it is safer to use the second form because you don't have to remember to close the comment. It also makes the comment stand out more. This is another case in which, if your instructor does not tell you to use a particular comment style, you should decide for yourself which style you prefer and use it consistently.

Don't confuse comments with the text of `println` statements. The text of your comments will not be displayed as output when the program executes. The comments are there only to help readers examine and understand the program.

It is a good idea to include comments at the beginning of each class file to indicate what the class does. You might also want to include information about who you are, what course you are taking, your instructor and/or grader's name, the date, and so on. You should also comment each method to indicate what it does.

Commenting becomes more useful in larger and more complicated programs, as well as in programs that will be viewed or modified by more than one programmer. Clear comments are extremely helpful to explain to another person, or to yourself at a later time, what your program is doing and why it is doing it.

In addition to the two comment forms already discussed, Java supports a particular style of comments known as *Javadoc comments*. Their format is more complex, but they have the advantage that you can use a program to extract the comments to make HTML files suitable for reading with a web browser. Javadoc comments are useful in more advanced programming and are discussed in more detail in Appendix B.

1.3 Program Errors

In 1949, Maurice Wilkes, an early pioneer of computing, expressed a sentiment that still rings true today:

> As soon as we started programming, we found out to our surprise that it wasn't as easy to get programs right as we had thought. Debugging had to be discovered. I can remember the exact instant when I realized that a large part of my life from then on was going to be spent in finding mistakes in my own programs.

You also will have to face this reality as you learn to program. You're going to make mistakes, just like every other programmer in history, and you're going to need strategies for eliminating those mistakes. Fortunately, the computer itself can help you with some of the work.

There are three kinds of errors that you'll encounter as you write programs:

- *Syntax errors* occur when you misuse Java. They are the programming equivalent of bad grammar and are caught by the Java compiler.
- *Logic errors* occur when you write code that doesn't perform the task it is intended to perform.
- *Runtime errors* are logic errors that are so severe that Java stops your program from executing.

Syntax Errors

Human beings tend to be fairly forgiving about minor mistakes in speech. For example, we might find it to be odd phrasing, but we generally understand Master Yoda when he says, "Unfortunate that you rushed to face him . . . that incomplete was your training. Not ready for the burden were you."

The Java compiler will be far less forgiving. The compiler reports syntax errors as it attempts to translate your program from Java into bytecodes if your program breaks any of Java's grammar rules. For example, if you misplace a single semicolon in your program, you can send the compiler into a tailspin of confusion. The compiler may report several error messages, depending on what it thinks is wrong with your program.

A program that generates compilation errors cannot be executed. If you submit your program to the compiler and the compiler reports errors, you must fix the errors and resubmit the program. You will not be able to proceed until your program is free of compilation errors.

Some development environments, such as Eclipse, help you along the way by underlining syntax errors as you write your program. This makes it easy to spot exactly where errors occur.

It's possible for you to introduce an error before you even start writing your program, if you choose the wrong name for its file.

Common Programming Error

File Name Does Not Match Class Name

As mentioned earlier, Java requires that a program's class name and file name match. For example, a program that begins with `public class Hello` must be stored in a file called `Hello.java`.

If you use the wrong file name (for example, saving it as `WrongFileName.java`), you'll get an error message like this:

```
WrongFileName.java:1: error: class Hello is public,
    should be declared in a file named Hello.java
public class Hello {
       ^
1 error
```

The file name is just the first hurdle. A number of other errors may exist in your Java program. One of the most common syntax errors is to misspell a word. You may have punctuation errors, such as missing semicolons. It's also easy to forget an entire word, such as a required keyword.

The error messages the compiler gives may or may not be helpful. If you don't understand the content of the error message, look for the caret marker (^) below the line, which points at the position in the line where the compiler became confused. This can help you pinpoint the place where a required keyword might be missing.

Common Programming Error

Misspelled Words

Java (like most programming languages) is very picky about spelling. You need to spell each word correctly, including proper capitalization. Suppose, for example, that you were to replace the `println` statement in the "hello world" program with the following:

```
System.out.pruntln("Hello, world!");
```

When you try to compile this program, it will generate an error message similar to the following:

```
Hello.java:3: error: cannot find symbol
symbol  : method pruntln(java.lang.String)
```

Continued on next page

Continued from previous page

```
location: variable out of type PrintStream
        System.out.pruntln("Hello, world!");
                          ^
1 error
```

The first line of this output indicates that the error occurs in the file `Hello.java` on line 3 and that the error is that the compiler cannot find a symbol. The second line indicates that the symbol it can't find is a method called `pruntln`. That's because there is no such method; the method is called `println`. The error message can take slightly different forms depending on what you have misspelled. For example, you might forget to capitalize the word `System`:

```
system.out.println("Hello, world!");
```

You will get the following error message:

```
Hello.java:3: error: package system does not exist
        system.out.println("Hello, world!");
                  ^
1 error
```

Again, the first line indicates that the error occurs in line 3 of the file `Hello.java`. The error message is slightly different here, though, indicating that it can't find a package called `system`. The second and third lines of this error message include the original line of code with an arrow (caret) pointing to where the compiler got confused. The compiler errors are not always very clear, but if you pay attention to where the arrow is pointing, you'll have a pretty good sense of where the error occurs.

If you still can't figure out the error, try looking at the error's line number and comparing the contents of that line with similar lines in other programs. You can also ask someone else, such as an instructor or lab assistant, to examine your program.

Common Programming Error

Forgetting a Semicolon

All Java statements must end with semicolons, but it's easy to forget to put a semicolon at the end of a statement, as in the following program:

```
public class MissingSemicolon {
    public static void main(String[] args) {
        System.out.println("A rose by any other name")
```

Continued on next page

Continued from previous page

```
4        System.out.println("would smell as sweet");
5    }
6 }
```

In this case, the compiler produces output similar to the following:

```
MissingSemicolon.java:3: error: ';' expected
        System.out.println("would smell as sweet");
        ^
1 error
```

Some versions of the Java compiler list line 4 as the cause of the problem, not line 3, where the semicolon was actually forgotten. This is because the compiler is looking forward for a semicolon and isn't upset until it finds something that isn't a semicolon, which it does when it reaches line 4. Unfortunately, as this case demonstrates, compiler error messages don't always direct you to the correct line to be fixed.

Common Programming Error

Forgetting a Required Keyword

Another common syntax error is to forget a required keyword when you are typing your program, such as `static` or `class`. Double-check your programs against the examples in the textbook to make sure you haven't omitted an important keyword.

The compiler will give different error messages depending on which keyword is missing, but the messages can be hard to understand. For example, you might write a program called `Bug4` and forget the keyword `class` when writing its class header. In this case, the compiler will provide the following error message:

```
Bug4.java:1: error: class, interface, or enum expected
public Bug4 {
       ^
1 error
```

However, if you forget the keyword `void` when declaring the main method, the compiler generates a different error message:

```
Bug5.java:2: error: invalid method declaration; return type required
    public static main(String[] args) {
                  ^
1 error
```

Yet another common syntax error is to forget to close a string literal.

A good rule of thumb to follow is that the first error reported by the compiler is the most important one. The rest might be the result of that first error. Many programmers don't even bother to look at errors beyond the first, because fixing that error and recompiling may cause the other errors to disappear.

Logic Errors (Bugs)

Logic errors are also called *bugs*. Computer programmers use words like "bug-ridden" and "buggy" to describe poorly written programs, and the process of finding and eliminating bugs from programs is called *debugging*.

The word "bug" is an old engineering term that predates computers; early computing bugs sometimes occurred in hardware as well as software. Admiral Grace Hopper, an early pioneer of computing, is largely credited with popularizing the use of the term in the context of computer programming. She often told the true story of a group of programmers at Harvard University in the mid-1940s who couldn't figure out what was wrong with their programs until they opened up the computer and found an actual moth trapped inside.

The form that a bug takes may vary. Sometimes your program will simply behave improperly. For example, it might produce the wrong output. Other times it will ask the computer to perform some task that is clearly a mistake, in which case your program will have a runtime error that stops it from executing. In this chapter, since your knowledge of Java is limited, generally the only type of logic error you will see is a mistake in program output from an incorrect `println` statement or method call.

We'll look at an example of a runtime error in the next section.

1.4 Procedural Decomposition

Brian Kernighan, coauthor of *The C Programming Language*, has said, "Controlling complexity is the essence of computer programming." People have only a modest capacity for detail. We can't solve complex problems all at once. Instead, we structure our problem solving by dividing the problem into manageable pieces and conquering each piece individually. We often use the term *decomposition* to describe this principle as applied to programming.

> **Decomposition**
>
> A separation into discernible parts, each of which is simpler than the whole.

With procedural programming languages like C, decomposition involves dividing a complex task into a set of subtasks. This is a very verb- or action-oriented approach, involving dividing up the overall action into a series of smaller actions. This technique is called *procedural decomposition*.

Common Programming Error

Not Closing a String Literal or Comment

Every string literal has to have an opening quote and a closing quote, but it's easy to forget the closing quotation mark. For example, you might say:

```
System.out.println("Hello, world!);
```

This produces three different error messages, even though there is only one underlying syntax error:

```
Hello.java:3: error: unclosed string literal
        System.out.println("hello world);
                           ^
Hello.java:3: error: ';' expected
        System.out.println("hello world);
                                   ^
Hello.java:5: error: reached end of file while parsing

    }
    ^
3 errors
```

In this case, the first error message is quite clear, including an arrow pointing at the beginning of the string literal that wasn't closed. The second error message was caused by the first. Because the string literal was not closed, the compiler didn't notice the right parenthesis and semicolon that appear at the end of the line.

A similar problem occurs when you forget to close a multiline comment by writing `*/`, as in the first line of the following program:

```
/* This is a bad program.

public class Bad {
    public static void main(String[] args){
        System.out.println("Hi there.");
    }
} /* end of program */
```

The preceding file is not a program; it is one long comment. Because the comment on the first line is not closed, the entire program is swallowed up.

Luckily, many Java editor programs color the parts of a program to help you identify them visually. Usually, if you forget to close a string literal or comment, the rest of your program will turn the wrong color, which can help you spot the mistake.

Java was designed for a different kind of decomposition that is more noun- or object-oriented. Instead of thinking of the problem as a series of actions to be performed, we think of it as a collection of objects that have to interact.

As a computer scientist, you should be familiar with both types of problem solving. This book begins with procedural decomposition and devotes many chapters to mastering various aspects of the procedural approach. Only after you have thorougly practiced procedural programming will we turn our attention back to object decomposition and object-oriented programming.

As an example of procedural decomposition, consider the problem of baking a cake. You can divide this problem into the following subproblems:

- Make the batter.
- Bake the cake.
- Make the frosting.
- Frost the cake.

Each of these four tasks has details associated with it. To make the batter, for example, you follow these steps:

- Mix the dry ingredients.
- Cream the butter and sugar.
- Beat in the eggs.
- Stir in the dry ingredients.

Thus, you divide the overall task into subtasks, which you further divide into even smaller subtasks. Eventually, you reach descriptions that are so simple they require no further explanation (i.e., primitives).

A partial diagram of this decomposition is shown in Figure 1.2. "Make cake" is the highest-level operation. It is defined in terms of four lower-level operations called "Make batter," "Bake," "Make frosting," and "Frost cake." The "Make batter" operation is defined in terms of even lower-level operations, and the same could be done for the other three operations. This diagram is called a structure diagram and is intended to show how a problem is broken down into subproblems. In this diagram, you can also tell in what order operations are performed by reading from left to right. That is not true of most structure diagrams. To determine the actual order in which subprograms are performed, you usually have to refer to the program itself.

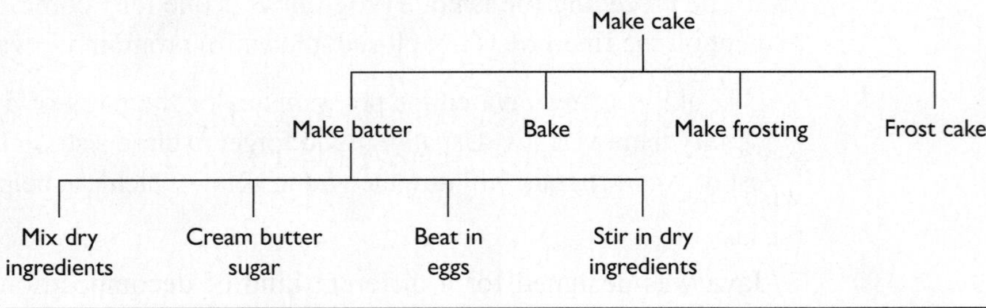

Figure 1.2 Decomposition of "Make cake" task

One final problem-solving term has to do with the process of programming. Professional programmers develop programs in stages. Instead of trying to produce a complete working program all at once, they choose some piece of the problem to implement first. Then they add another piece, and another, and another. The overall program is built up slowly, piece by piece. This process is known as *iterative enhancement* or *stepwise refinement*.

Iterative Enhancement

The process of producing a program in stages, adding new functionality at each stage. A key feature of each iterative step is that you can test it to make sure that piece works before moving on.

Now, let's look at a construct that will allow you to iteratively enhance your Java programs to improve their structure and reduce their redundancy: static methods.

Static Methods

VideoNote

Java is designed for objects, and programming in Java usually involves decomposing a problem into various objects, each with methods that perform particular tasks. You will see how this works in later chapters, but for now, we are going to explore procedural decomposition. We will postpone examining some of Java's details while we discuss programming in general.

Consider the following program, which draws two text boxes on the console:

```
public class DrawBoxes {
    public static void main(String[] args) {
        System.out.println("+------+");
        System.out.println("|      |");
        System.out.println("|      |");
        System.out.println("+------+");
        System.out.println();
        System.out.println("+------+");
        System.out.println("|      |");
        System.out.println("|      |");
        System.out.println("+------+");
    }
}
```

The program works correctly, but the four lines used to draw the box appear twice. This redundancy is undesirable for several reasons. For example, you might wish to change the appearance of the boxes, in which case you'll have to make all of the edits twice. Also, you might wish to draw additional boxes, which would require you to type additional copies of (or copy and paste) the redundant lines.

A preferable program would include a Java command that specifies how to draw the box and then executes that command twice. Java doesn't have a "draw a box" command, but you can create one. Such a named command is called a *static method.*

Static Method

A block of Java statements that is given a name.

Static methods are units of procedural decomposition. We typically break a class into several static methods, each of which solves some piece of the overall problem. For example, here is a static method to draw a box:

```
public static void drawBox() {
    System.out.println("+------+");
    System.out.println("|      |");
    System.out.println("|      |");
    System.out.println("+------+");
}
```

You have already seen a static method called `main` in earlier programs. Recall that the `main` method has the following form:

```
public static void main(String[] args) {
    <statement>;
    <statement>;
    ...
    <statement>;
}
```

The static methods you'll write have a similar structure:

```
public static void <name>() {
    <statement>;
    <statement>;
    ...
    <statement>;
}
```

The first line is known as the method header. You don't yet need to fully understand what each part of this header means in Java; for now, just remember that you'll need to write `public static void`, followed by the name you wish to give the method, followed by a set of parentheses. Briefly, here is what the words in the header mean:

- The keyword `public` indicates that this method is available to be used by all parts of your program. All methods you write will be public.
- The keyword `static` indicates that this is a static (procedural-style, not object-oriented) method. For now, all methods you write will be static, until you learn about defining objects in Chapter 8.
- The keyword `void` indicates that this method executes statements but does not produce any value. (Other methods you'll see later compute and return values.)
- `<name>` (e.g., `drawBox`) is the name of the method.
- The empty parentheses specify a list (in this case, an empty list) of values that are sent to your method as input; such values are called *parameters* and will not be included in your methods until Chapter 3.

Including the keyword `static` for each method you define may seem cumbersome. Other Java textbooks often do not discuss static methods as early as we do here; instead, they show other techniques for decomposing problems. But even though static methods require a bit of work to create, they are powerful and useful tools for improving basic Java programs.

After the header in our sample method, a series of `println` statements makes up the body of this static method. As in the `main` method, the statements of this method are executed in order from first to last.

By defining the method `drawBox`, you have given a simple name to this sequence of `println` statements. It's like saying to the Java compiler, "Whenever I tell you to 'drawBox,' I really mean that you should execute the `println` statements in the `drawBox` method." But the command won't actually be executed unless our `main` method explicitly says that it wants to do so. The act of executing a static method is called a *method call*.

Method Call

A command to execute another method, which causes all of the statements inside that method to be executed.

To execute the `drawBox` command, include this line in your program's `main` method:

```
drawBox();
```

Since we want to execute the `drawBox` command twice (to draw two boxes), the `main` method should contain two calls to the `drawBox` method. The following program uses the `drawBox` method to produce the same output as the original `DrawBoxes` program:

```
public class DrawBoxes2 {
    public static void main(String[] args) {
        drawBox();
        System.out.println();
        drawBox();
    }

    public static void drawBox() {
        System.out.println("+------+");
        System.out.println("|      |");
        System.out.println("|      |");
        System.out.println("+------+");
    }
}
```

Flow of Control

The most confusing thing about static methods is that programs with static methods do not execute sequentially from top to bottom. Rather, each time the program encounters a static method call, the execution of the program "jumps" to that static method, executes each statement in that method in order, and then "jumps" back to the point where the call began and resumes executing. The order in which the statements of a program are executed is called the program's *flow of control.*

> **Flow of Control**
>
> The order in which the statements of a Java program are executed.

Let's look at the control flow of the `DrawBoxes2` program shown previously. It has two methods. The first method is the familiar `main` method, and the second is `drawBox`. As in any Java program, execution starts with the `main` method:

```
public static void main(String[] args) {
    drawBox();
    System.out.println();
    drawBox();
}
```

In a sense, the execution of this program is sequential: Each statement listed in the `main` method is executed in turn, from first to last.

But this `main` method includes two different calls on the `drawBox` method. This program will do three different things: execute `drawBox`, execute a `println`, then execute `drawBox` again.

The diagram below indicates the flow of control produced by this program.

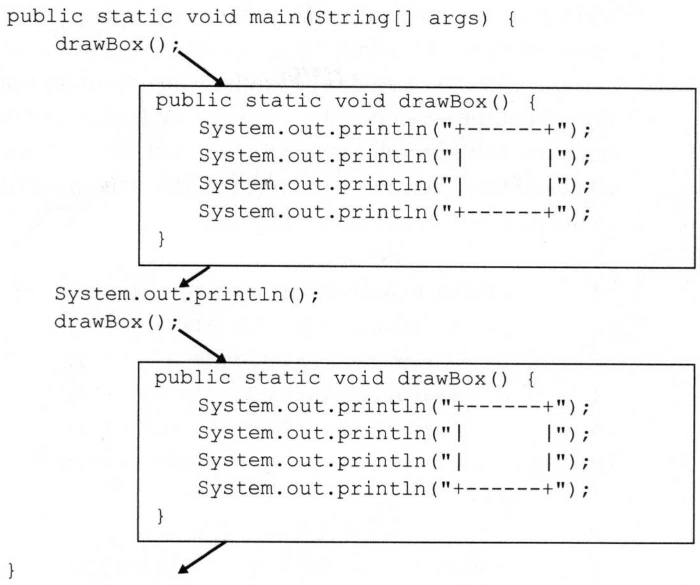

```
public static void main(String[] args) {
    drawBox();
        public static void drawBox() {
            System.out.println("+------+");
            System.out.println("|      |");
            System.out.println("|      |");
            System.out.println("+------+");
        }
    System.out.println();
    drawBox();
        public static void drawBox() {
            System.out.println("+------+");
            System.out.println("|      |");
            System.out.println("|      |");
            System.out.println("+------+");
        }
}
```

Following the diagram, you can see that nine `println` statements are executed. First you transfer control to the `drawBox` method and execute its four statements. Then you return to `main` and execute its `println` statement. Then you transfer control a second time to `drawBox` and once again execute its four statements. Making these method calls is almost like copying and pasting the code of the method into the `main` method. As a result, this program has the exact same behavior as the nine-line `main` method of the `DrawBoxes` program:

```
public static void main(String[] args) {
    System.out.println("+------+");
    System.out.println("|      |");
    System.out.println("|      |");
    System.out.println("+------+");
    System.out.println();
    System.out.println("+------+");
    System.out.println("|      |");
    System.out.println("|      |");
    System.out.println("+------+");
}
```

This version is simpler in terms of its flow of control, but the first version avoids the redundancy of having the same `println` statements appear multiple times. It also gives a better sense of the structure of the solution. In the original version, it is clear that there is a subtask called `drawBox` that is being performed twice. Also, while the last version of the `main` method contains fewer lines of code than the `DrawBoxes2` program, consider what would happen if you wanted to add a third box to the output. You would have to add the five requisite `println` statements again, whereas in the programs that use the `drawBox` method you can simply add one more `println` and a third method call.

Java allows you to define methods in any order you like. It is a common convention to put the `main` method as either the first or last method in the class. In this textbook we will generally put `main` first, but the programs would behave the same if we switched the order. For example, the following modified program behaves identically to the previous `DrawBoxes2` program:

```
public class DrawBoxes3 {
    public static void drawBox() {
        System.out.println("+------+");
        System.out.println("|      |");
        System.out.println("|      |");
        System.out.println("+------+");
    }

    public static void main(String[] args) {
        drawBox();
        System.out.println();
        drawBox();
    }
}
```

The `main` method is always the starting point for program execution, and from that starting point you can determine the order in which other methods are called.

Methods That Call Other Methods

The `main` method is not the only place where you can call another method. In fact, any method may call any other method. As a result, the flow of control can get quite complicated. Consider, for example, the following rather strange program. We use nonsense words ("foo," "bar," "baz," and "mumble") on purpose because the program is not intended to make sense.

```
public class FooBarBazMumble {
    public static void main(String[] args) {
        foo();
        bar();
        System.out.println("mumble");
    }

    public static void foo() {
        System.out.println("foo");
    }
```

```

    public static void bar() {
        baz();
        System.out.println("bar");
    }

    public static void baz() {
        System.out.println("baz");
    }
}
```

You can't tell easily what output this program produces, so let's explore in detail what the program is doing. Remember that Java always begins with the method called `main`. In this program, the `main` method calls the `foo` method and the `bar` method and then executes a `println` statement:

```
public static void main(String[] args) {
    foo();
    bar();
    System.out.println("mumble");
}
```

Each of these two method calls will expand into more statements. Let's first expand the calls on the `foo` and `bar` methods:

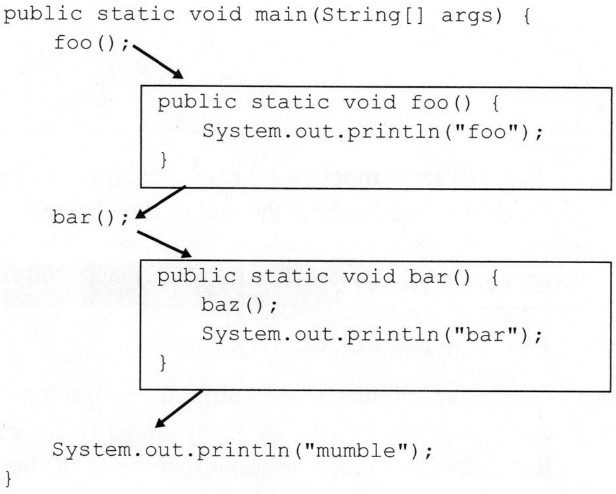

```
public static void main(String[] args) {
    foo();
        public static void foo() {
            System.out.println("foo");
        }
    bar();
        public static void bar() {
            baz();
            System.out.println("bar");
        }
    System.out.println("mumble");
}
```

This helps to make our picture of the flow of control more complete, but notice that `bar` calls the `baz` method, so we have to expand that as well.

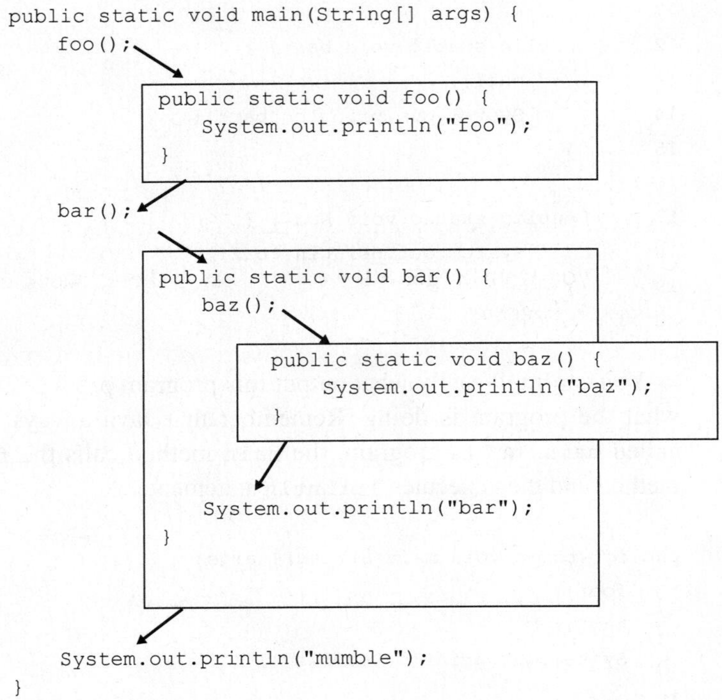

```
public static void main(String[] args) {
    foo();
        public static void foo() {
            System.out.println("foo");
        }
    bar();
        public static void bar() {
            baz();
                public static void baz() {
                    System.out.println("baz");
                }
            System.out.println("bar");
        }
    System.out.println("mumble");
}
```

Finally, we have finished our picture of the flow of control of this program. It should make sense, then, that the program produces the following output:

```
foo
baz
bar
mumble
```

We will see a much more useful example of methods calling methods when we go through the case study at the end of the chapter.

Did You Know?

The New Hacker's Dictionary

Computer scientists and computer programmers use a lot of jargon that can be confusing to novices. A group of software professionals spearheaded by Eric Raymond have collected together many of the jargon terms in a book called *The New Hacker's Dictionary*. You can buy the book, or you can browse it online at Eric's website: http://catb.org/esr/jargon/html/frames.html.

For example, if you look up *foo*, you'll find this definition: "Used very generally as a sample name for absolutely anything, esp. programs and files." In

Continued on next page

Continued from previous page

other words, when we find ourselves looking for a nonsense word, we use "foo."

The New Hacker's Dictionary contains a great deal of historical information about the origins of jargon terms. The entry for *foo* includes a lengthy discussion of the combined term *foobar* and how it came into common usage among engineers.

If you want to get a flavor of what is there, check out the entries for *bug, hacker, bogosity,* and *bogo-sort.*

An Example Runtime Error

Runtime errors occur when a bug causes your program to be unable to continue executing. What could cause such a thing to happen? One example is if you asked the computer to calculate an invalid value, such as 1 divided by 0. Another example would be if your program tries to read data from a file that does not exist.

We haven't discussed how to compute values or read files yet, but there is a way you can "accidentally" cause a runtime error. The way to do this is to write a static method that calls itself. If you do this, your program will not stop running, because the method will keep calling itself indefinitely, until the computer runs out of memory. When this happens, the program prints a large number of lines of output, and then eventually stops executing with an error message called a `StackOverflowError`. Here's an example:

```
public class Infinite {
    public static void main(String[] args) {
        oops();
    }

    public static void oops() {
        System.out.println("Make it stop!");
        oops();
    }
}
```

This ill-fated program produces the following output (with large groups of identical lines represented by "..."):

```
Make it stop!
Make it stop!
Make it stop!
Make it stop!
Make it stop!
Make it stop!
Make it stop!
```

```
Make it stop!
Make it stop!
...
Make it stop!
Exception in thread "main" java.lang.StackOverflowError
        at sun.nio.cs.SingleByteEncoder.encodeArrayLoop(Unknown Source)
        at sun.nio.cs.SingleByteEncoder.encodeLoop(Unknown Source)
        at java.nio.charset.CharsetEncoder.encode(Unknown Source)
        at sun.nio.cs.StreamEncoder$CharsetSE.implWrite(Unknown Source)
        at sun.nio.cs.StreamEncoder.write(Unknown Source)
        at java.io.OutputStreamWriter.write(Unknown Source)
        at java.io.BufferedWriter.flushBuffer(Unknown Source)
        at java.io.PrintStream.newLine(Unknown Source)
        at java.io.PrintStream.println(Unknown Source)
        at Infinite.oops(Infinite.java:7)
        at Infinite.oops(Infinite.java:8)
        at Infinite.oops(Infinite.java:8)
        at Infinite.oops(Infinite.java:8)
        at ...
```

Runtime errors are, unfortunately, something you'll have to live with as you learn to program. You will have to carefully ensure that your programs not only compile successfully, but do not contain any bugs that will cause a runtime error. The most common way to catch and fix runtime errors is to run the program several times to test its behavior.

1.5 Case Study: `DrawFigures`

Earlier in the chapter, you saw a program called `DrawFigures1` that produced the following output:

```
   /\
  /  \
 /    \
 \    /
  \  /
   \/

 \    /
  \  /
   \/
   /\
  /  \
 /    \
```

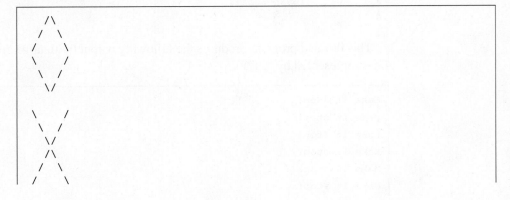

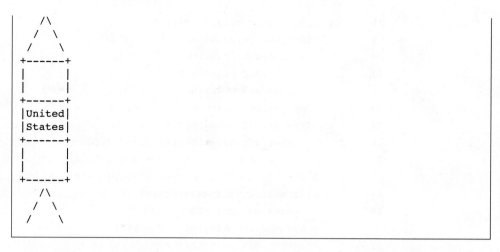

It did so with a long sequence of `println` statements in the `main` method. In this section you'll improve the program by using static methods for procedural decomposition to capture structure and eliminate redundancy. The redundancy might be more obvious, but let's start by improving the way the program captures the structure of the overall task.

Structured Version

If you look closely at the output, you'll see that it has a structure that would be desirable to capture in the program structure. The output is divided into three subfigures: the diamond, the X, and the rocket.

You can better indicate the structure of the program by dividing it into static methods. Since there are three subfigures, you can create three methods, one for each subfigure. The following program produces the same output as `DrawFigures1`:

```
public class DrawFigures2 {
    public static void main(String[] args) {
        drawDiamond();
        drawX();
        drawRocket();
    }

    public static void drawDiamond() {
        System.out.println("   /\\");
        System.out.println("  /  \\");
        System.out.println(" /    \\");
        System.out.println(" \\    /");
        System.out.println("  \\  /");
        System.out.println("   \\/");
        System.out.println();
    }

```

```
    public static void drawX() {
        System.out.println(" \\    /");
        System.out.println("  \\  /");
        System.out.println("   \\/");
        System.out.println("   /\\");
        System.out.println("  /  \\");
        System.out.println(" /    \\");
        System.out.println();
    }

    public static void drawRocket() {
        System.out.println("   /\\");
        System.out.println("  /  \\");
        System.out.println(" /    \\");
        System.out.println("+------+");
        System.out.println("|      |");
        System.out.println("|      |");
        System.out.println("+------+");
        System.out.println("|United|");
        System.out.println("|States|");
        System.out.println("+------+");
        System.out.println("|      |");
        System.out.println("|      |");
        System.out.println("+------+");
        System.out.println("   /\\");
        System.out.println("  /  \\");
        System.out.println(" /    \\");
    }
}
```

The program appears in a class called `DrawFigures2` and has four static methods defined within it. The first static method is the usual `main` method, which calls three methods. The three methods called by `main` appear next.

Figure 1.3 is a structure diagram for this version of the program. Notice that it has two levels of structure. The overall problem is broken down into three subtasks.

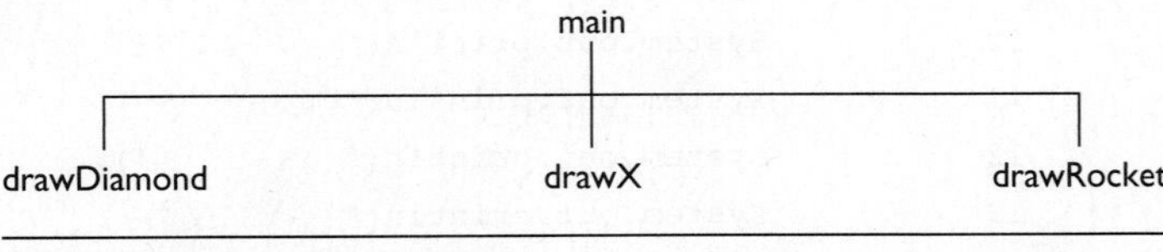

Figure 1.3 Decomposition of `DrawFigures2`

Final Version without Redundancy

The program can still be improved. Each of the three subfigures has individual elements, and some of those elements appear in more than one of the three subfigures. The program prints the following redundant group of lines several times:

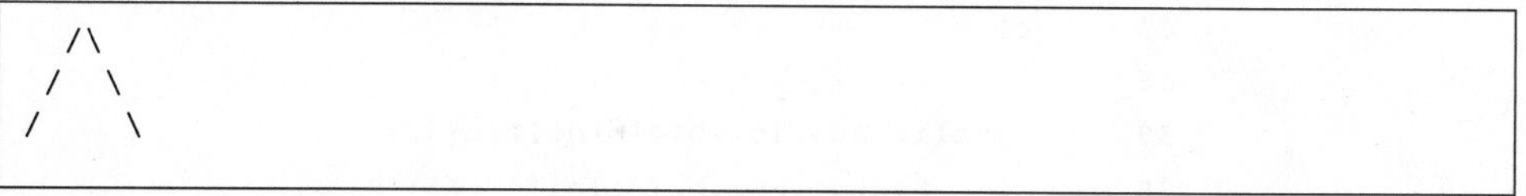

A better version of the preceding program adds an additional method for each redundant section of output. The redundant sections are the top and bottom halves of the diamond shape and the box used in the rocket. Here is the improved program:

```
public class DrawFigures3 {
    public static void main(String[] args) {
        drawDiamond();
        drawX();
        drawRocket();
    }

    public static void drawDiamond() {
        drawCone();
        drawV();
        System.out.println();
    }

    public static void drawX() {
        drawV();
        drawCone();
        System.out.println();
    }

    public static void drawRocket() {
        drawCone();
        drawBox();
        System.out.println("|United|");
        System.out.println("|States|");
        drawBox();
        drawCone();
        System.out.println();
    }

```

```
    public static void drawBox() {
        System.out.println("+------+");
        System.out.println("|      |");
        System.out.println("|      |");
        System.out.println("+------+");
    }

    public static void drawCone() {
        System.out.println("   /\\");
        System.out.println("  /  \\");
        System.out.println(" /    \\");
    }

    public static void drawV() {
        System.out.println(" \\    /");
        System.out.println("  \\  /");
        System.out.println("   \\/");
    }
}
```

This program, now called `DrawFigures3`, has seven static methods defined within it. The first static method is the usual `main` method, which calls three methods. These three methods in turn call three other methods, which appear next.

Analysis of Flow of Execution

The structure diagram in Figure 1.4 shows which static methods `main` calls and which static methods each of them calls. As you can see, this program has three levels of structure and two levels of decomposition. The overall task is split into three subtasks, each of which has two subtasks.

A program with methods has a more complex flow of control than one without them, but the rules are still fairly simple. Remember that when a method is called, the computer executes the statements in the body of that method. Then the computer proceeds to the next statement after the method call. Also remember that the computer always starts with the `main` method, executing its statements from first to last.

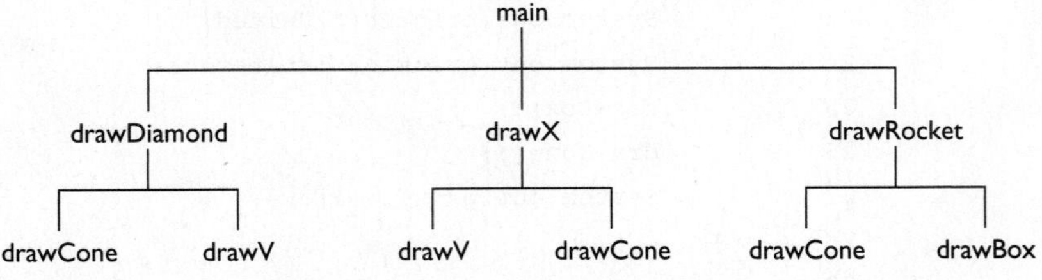

Figure 1.4 Decomposition of `DrawFigures3`

So, to execute the `DrawFigures3` program, the computer first executes its `main` method. That, in turn, first executes the body of the method `drawDiamond`. `drawDiamond` executes the methods `drawCone` and `drawV` (in that order). When `drawDiamond` finishes executing, control shifts to the next statement in the body of the `main` method: the call to the `drawX` method.

A complete breakdown of the flow of control from static method to static method in `DrawFigures3` follows:

```
1st   main
2nd       drawDiamond
3rd           drawCone
4th           drawV
5th       drawX
6th           drawV
7th           drawCone
8th       drawRocket
9th           drawCone
10th          drawBox
11th          drawBox
12th          drawCone
```

Recall that the order in which you define methods does not have to parallel the order in which they are executed. The order of execution is determined by the body of the `main` method and by the bodies of methods called from `main`. A static method declaration is like a dictionary entry—it defines a word, but it does not specify how the word will be used. The body of this program's `main` method says to first execute `drawDiamond`, then `drawX`, then `drawRocket`. This is the order of execution, regardless of the order in which the methods are defined.

Java allows you to define methods in any order you like. Starting with `main` at the top and working down to lower and lower-level methods is a popular approach to take, but many people prefer the opposite, placing the low-level methods first and `main` at the end. Java doesn't care what order you use, so you can decide for yourself and do what you think is best. Consistency is important, though, so that you can easily find a method later in a large program.

It is important to note that the programs `DrawFigures1`, `DrawFigures2`, and `DrawFigures3` produce exactly the same output to the console. While `DrawFigures1` may be the easiest program for a novice to read, `DrawFigures2` and particularly `DrawFigures3` have many advantages over it. For one, a well-structured solution is easier to comprehend, and the methods themselves become a means of explaining the program. Also, programs with methods are more flexible and can more easily be adapted to similar but different tasks. You can take the seven methods defined in `DrawFigures3` and write a new program to produce a larger and more complex output. Building static methods to create new commands increases your flexibility without adding unnecessary complication. For example, you could replace the `main` method with a version that calls the other methods in the following new order. What output would it produce?

```
public static void main(String[] args) {
    drawCone();
    drawCone();
    drawRocket();
    drawX();
    drawRocket();
    drawDiamond();
    drawBox();
    drawDiamond();
    drawX();
    drawRocket();
}
```

Chapter Summary

Computers execute sets of instructions called programs. Computers store information internally as sequences of 0s and 1s (binary numbers).

Programming and computer science deal with algorithms, which are step-by-step descriptions for solving problems.

Java is a modern object-oriented programming language developed by Sun Microsystems, now owned by Oracle Corporation, that has a large set of libraries you can use to build complex programs.

A program is translated from text into computer instructions by another program called a compiler. Java's compiler turns Java programs into a special format called Java bytecodes, which are executed using a special program called the Java Runtime Environment.

Java programmers typically complete their work using an editor called an Integrated Development Environment (IDE). The commands may vary from environment to environment, but the same three-step process is always involved:

1. Type in a program as a Java class.
2. Compile the program file.
3. Run the compiled version of the program.

Java uses a command called `System.out.println` to display text on the console screen.

Written words in a program can take different meanings. Keywords are special reserved words that are part of the language. Identifiers are words defined by the programmer to name entities in the program. Words can also be put into strings, which are pieces of text that can be printed to the console.

Java programs that use proper spacing and layout are more readable to programmers. Readability is also improved by writing notes called comments inside the program.

The Java language has a syntax, or a legal set of commands that can be used. A Java program that does not follow the proper syntax will not compile. A program that does compile but that is written incorrectly may still contain errors called exceptions that occur when the program runs. A third kind of error is a logic or intent error. This kind of error occurs when the program runs but does not do what the programmer intended.

Commands in programs are called statements. A class can group statements into larger commands called static methods. Static methods help the programmer group code into reusable pieces. An important static method that must be part of every program is called `main`.

Iterative enhancement is the process of building a program piece by piece, testing the program at each step before advancing to the next.

Complex programming tasks should be broken down into the major tasks the computer must perform. This process is called procedural decomposition. Correct use of static methods aids procedural decomposition.

Self-Check Problems

Section 1.1: Basic Computing Concepts

1. Why do computers use binary numbers?

2. Convert each of the following decimal numbers into its equivalent binary number:

   a. 6
   b. 44
   c. 72
   d. 131

3. What is the decimal equivalent of each of the following binary numbers?

   a. 100
   b. 1011
   c. 101010
   d. 1001110

4. In your own words, describe an algorithm for baking cookies. Assume that you have a large number of hungry friends, so you'll want to produce several batches of cookies!

5. What is the difference between the file `MyProgram.java` and the file `MyProgram.class`?

Section 1.2: And Now—Java

6. Which of the following can be used in a Java program as identifiers?

```
println          first-name    AnnualSalary    "hello"    ABC
42isTheAnswer    for           sum_of_data     _average   B4
```

7. Which of the following is the correct syntax to output a message?

   a. `System.println(Hello, world!);`
   b. `System.println.out('Hello, world!');`
   c. `System.println("Hello, world!");`

d. `System.out.println("Hello, world!");`

e. `Out.system.println"(Hello, world!)";`

8. What is the output produced from the following statements?

```
System.out.println("\"Quotes\"");
System.out.println("Slashes \\//");
System.out.println("How '\"confounding' \"\\\" it is!");
```

9. What is the output produced from the following statements?

```
System.out.println("name\tage\theight");
System.out.println("Archie\t17\t5'9\"");
System.out.println("Betty\t17\t5'6\"");
System.out.println("Jughead\t16\t6'");
```

10. What is the output produced from the following statements?

```
System.out.println("Shaq is 7'1");
System.out.println("The string \"\" is an empty message.");
System.out.println("\\'\"\"");
```

11. What is the output produced from the following statements?

```
System.out.println("\ta\tb\tc");
System.out.println("\\\\");
System.out.println("'");
System.out.println("\"\"\"");
System.out.println("C:\nin\the downward spiral");
```

12. What is the output produced from the following statements?

```
System.out.println("Dear \"DoubleSlash\" magazine,");
System.out.println();
System.out.println("\tYour publication confuses me. Is it");
System.out.println("a \\\\ slash or a //// slash?");
System.out.println("\nSincerely,");
System.out.println("Susan \"Suzy\" Smith");
```

13. What series of `println` statements would produce the following output?

```
"Several slashes are sometimes seen,"
said Sally. "I've said so." See?
\ / \\ // \\\ ///
```

14. What series of `println` statements would produce the following output?

```
This is a test of your
knowledge of "quotes" used
in 'string literals.'

You're bound to "get it right"
if you read the section on
''quotes.''
```

15. Write a `println` statement that produces the following output:

```
/ \ // \\ /// \\\
```

16. Rewrite the following code as a series of equivalent `System.out.println` statements (i.e., without any `System.out.print` statements):

```
System.out.print("Twas ");
System.out.print("brillig and the");
System.out.println(" ");
System.out.print(" slithy toves did");
System.out.print(" ");
System.out.println("gyre and");
System.out.println("gimble");
System.out.println();
System.out.println( "in the wabe.");
```

17. What is the output of the following program? Note that the program contains several comments.

```
public class Commentary {
    public static void main(String[] args) {
        System.out.println("some lines of code");
        System.out.println("have // characters on them");
        System.out.println("which means "); // that they are comments
        // System.out.println("written by the programmer.");

        System.out.println("lines can also");
        System.out.println("have /* and */ characters");
        /* System.out.println("which represents");
        System.out.println("a multi-line style");
        */ System.out.println("of comment.");
    }
}
```

Section 1.3: Program Errors

18. Name the three errors in the following program:

```
public MyProgram {
    public static void main(String[] args) {
        System.out.println("This is a test of the")
        System.out.Println("emergency broadcast system.");
    }
}
```

19. Name the four errors in the following program:

```
public class SecretMessage {
    public static main(string[] args) {
        System.out.println("Speak friend");
```

```
        System.out.println("and enter);

}
```

20. Name the four errors in the following program:

```
public class FamousSpeech
    public static void main(String[]) {
        System.out.println("Four score and seven years ago,");
        System.out.println("our fathers brought forth on");
        System.out.println("this continent a new nation");
        System.out.println("conceived in liberty,");
        System.out.println("and dedicated to the proposition");
        System.out.println("that");    /* this part should
        System.out.println("all");        really say,
        System.out.println("men");        "all PEOPLE!" */
        System.out.println("are";
        System.out.println("created");
        System.out.println("equal");
    }
}
```

Section 1.4: Procedural Decomposition

21. Which of the following method headers uses the correct syntax?

a. `public static example() {`
b. `public static void example() {`
c. `public void static example() {`
d. `public static example void[] {`
e. `public void static example{} (`

22. What is the output of the following program? (You may wish to draw a structure diagram first.)

```
public class Tricky {
    public static void main(String[] args) {
        message1();
        message2();
        System.out.println("Done with main.");
    }

    public static void message1() {
        System.out.println("This is message1.");
    }

    public static void message2() {
        System.out.println("This is message2.");
        message1();
```

```
        System.out.println("Done with message2.");
    }
}
```

23. What is the output of the following program? (You may wish to draw a structure diagram first.)

```
public class Strange {
    public static void first() {
        System.out.println("Inside first method");
    }

    public static void second() {
        System.out.println("Inside second method");
        first();
    }

    public static void third() {
        System.out.println("Inside third method");
        first();
        second();
    }

    public static void main(String[] args) {
        first();
        third();
        second();
        third();
    }
}
```

24. What would have been the output of the preceding program if the `third` method had contained the following statements?

```
public static void third() {
    first();
    second();
    System.out.println("Inside third method");
}
```

25. What would have been the output of the `Strange` program if the `main` method had contained the following statements? (Use the original version of `third`, not the modified version from the most recent exercise.)

```
public static void main(String[] args) {
    second();
    first();
    second();
    third();
}
```

26. What is the output of the following program? (You may wish to draw a structure diagram first.)

```
public class Confusing {
    public static void method2() {
        method1();
        System.out.println("I am method 2.");
    }

    public static void method3() {
        method2();
        System.out.println("I am method 3.");
        method1();
    }

    public static void method1() {
        System.out.println("I am method 1.");
    }

    public static void main(String[] args) {
        method1();
        method3();
        method2();
        method3();
    }
}
```

27. What would have been the output of the preceding program if the `method3` method had contained the following statements?

```
public static void method3() {
    method1();
    method2();
    System.out.println("I am method 3.");
}
```

28. What would have been the output of the `Confusing` program if the `main` method had contained the following statements? (Use the original version of `method3`, not the modified version from the most recent exercise.)

```
public static void main(String[] args) {
    method2();
    method1();
    method3();
    method2();
}
```

29. The following program contains at least 10 syntax errors. What are they?

```
public class LotsOf Errors {
    public static main(String args) {
        System.println(Hello, world!);
```

```
        message()
    }

    public static void message {
        System.out println("This program surely cannot ";
        System.out.println("have any "errors" in it");
    }
```

30. Consider the following program, saved into a file named `Example.java`:

```
1  public class Example {
2      public static void displayRule() {
3          System.out.println("The first rule ");
4          System.out.println("of Java Club is,");
5          System.out.println();
6          System.out.println("you do not talk about Java Club.");
7      }
8
9      public static void main(String[] args) {
10         System.out.println("The rules of Java Club.");
11         displayRule();
12         displayRule();
13     }
14 }
```

What would happen if each of the following changes were made to the `Example` program? For example, would there be no effect, a syntax error, or a different program output? Treat each change independently of the others.

a. Change line 1 to: `public class Demonstration`

b. Change line 9 to: `public static void MAIN(String[] args) {`

c. Insert a new line after line 11 that reads: `System.out.println();`

d. Change line 2 to: `public static void printMessage() {`

e. Change line 2 to: `public static void showMessage() {` and change lines 11 and 12 to: `showMessage();`

f. Replace lines 3–4 with: `System.out.println("The first rule of Java Club is,");`

31. The following program is legal under Java's syntax rules, but it is difficult to read because of its layout and lack of comments. Reformat it using the rules given in this chapter, and add a comment header at the top of the program.

```
   public
class GiveAdvice{ public static
void main (String[]args){ System.out.println (

"Programs can be easy or");  System.out.println(
  "difficult to read, depending"
);  System.out.println("upon their format.")
            ;System.out.println();System.out.println(
"Everyone, including yourself,");
System.out.println
("will be happier if you choose");
```

```
            System.out.println("to format your programs."
);      }
    }
```

32. The following program is legal under Java's syntax rules, but it is difficult to read because of its layout and lack of comments. Reformat it using the rules given in this chapter, and add a comment header at the top of the program.

```
public
class Messy{public
static void main(String[]args){message ()
  ;System.out.println()    ; message ( );}   public static void
message() { System.out.println(
    "I really wish that"
    );System.out.println
("I had formatted my source")
;System.out.println("code correctly!");}}
```

Exercises

1. Write a complete Java program called `Stewie` that prints the following output:

```
//////////////////////
|| Victory is mine! ||
\\\\\\\\\\\\\\\\\\\\\\
```

2. Write a complete Java program called `Spikey` that prints the following output:

```
  \/
 \\//
\\\///
///\\\
 //\\
  /\
```

3. Write a complete Java program called `WellFormed` that prints the following output:

```
A well-formed Java program has
a main method with { and }
braces.

A System.out.println statement
has ( and ) and usually a
String that starts and ends
with a " character.
(But we type \" instead!)
```

4. Write a complete Java program called `Difference` that prints the following output:

```
What is the difference between
a ' and a "? Or between a " and a \"?

One is what we see when we're typing our program.
The other is what appears on the "console."
```

5. Write a complete Java program called `MuchBetter` that prints the following output:

```
A "quoted" String is
'much' better if you learn
the rules of "escape sequences."
Also, "" represents an empty String.
Don't forget: use \" instead of " !
'' is not the same as "
```

6. Write a complete Java program called `Meta` whose output is the text that would be the source code of a Java program that prints "Hello, world!" as its output.

7. Write a complete Java program called `Mantra` that prints the following output. Use at least one static method besides `main`.

```
There's one thing every coder must understand:
The System.out.println command.

There's one thing every coder must understand:
The System.out.println command.
```

8. Write a complete Java program called `Stewie2` that prints the following output. Use at least one static method besides `main`.

```
//////////////////////
|| Victory is mine! ||
\\\\\\\\\\\\\\\\\\\\\\
|| Victory is mine! ||
\\\\\\\\\\\\\\\\\\\\\\
|| Victory is mine! ||
\\\\\\\\\\\\\\\\\\\\\\
|| Victory is mine! ||
\\\\\\\\\\\\\\\\\\\\\\
|| Victory is mine! ||
\\\\\\\\\\\\\\\\\\\\\\
```

9. Write a program called `Egg` that displays the following output:

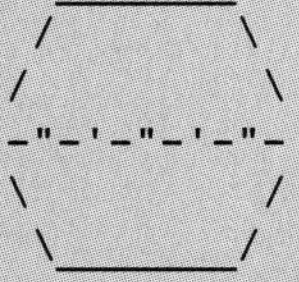

10. Modify the program from the previous exercise to become a new program `Egg2` that displays the following output. Use static methods as appropriate.

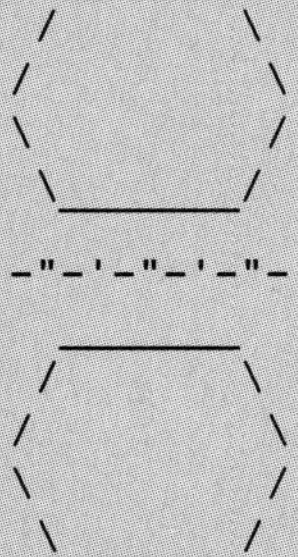

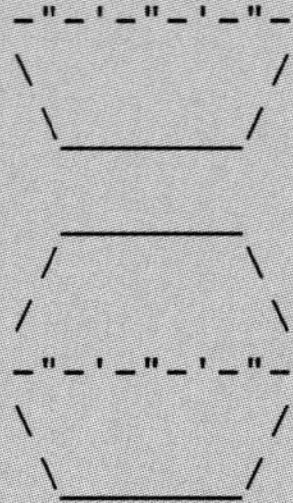

11. Write a Java program called `TwoRockets` that generates the following output. Use static methods to show structure and eliminate redundancy in your solution. Note that there are two rocket ships next to each other. What redundancy can you eliminate using static methods? What redundancy cannot be eliminated?

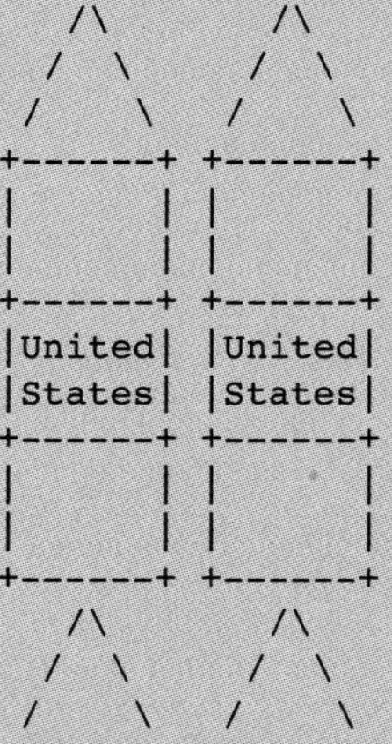

12. Write a program called `FightSong` that produces this output. Use at least two static methods to show structure and eliminate redundancy in your solution.

```
Go, team, go!
You can do it.

Go, team, go!
You can do it.
You're the best,
In the West.
Go, team, go!
You can do it.

Go, team, go!
You can do it.
You're the best,
in the West.
Go, team, go!
You can do it.

Go, team, go!
You can do it.
```

13. Write a Java program called `StarFigures` that generates the following output. Use static methods to show structure and eliminate redundancy in your solution.

```
*****
*****
 * *
  *
 * *

*****
*****
 * *
  *
 * *
*****
*****

  *
  *
  *
*****
*****
 * *
  *
 * *
```

14. Write a Java program called `Lanterns` that generates the following output. Use static methods to show structure and eliminate redundancy in your solution.

```
    *****
  *********
*************

    *****
  *********
*************
* | | | | | *
*************
    *****
  *********
*************

    *****
  *********
*************
    *****
* | | | | | *
* | | | | | *
    *****
    *****
```

15. Write a Java program called `EggStop` that generates the following output. Use static methods to show structure and eliminate redundancy in your solution.

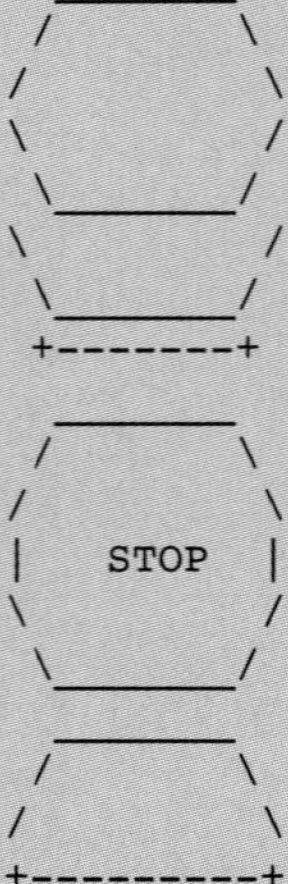

16. Write a program called `Shining` that prints the following line of output 1000 times:

```
All work and no play makes Jack a dull boy.
```

You should not write a program that uses 1000 lines of source code; use methods to shorten the program. What is the shortest program you can write that will produce the 1000 lines of output, using only the material from this chapter?

Programming Projects

1. Write a program to spell out MISSISSIPPI using block letters like the following (one per line):

```
M     M    IIIII     SSSSS     PPPPPP
MM   MM      I     S     S     P     P
M M M M      I     S           P     P
M  M  M      I      SSSSS      PPPPPP
M     M      I           S     P
M     M      I     S     S     P
M     M    IIIII    SSSSS      P
```

2. Sometimes we write similar letters to different people. For example, you might write to your parents to tell them about your classes and your friends and to ask for money; you might write to a friend about your love life, your classes, and your hobbies; and you might write to your brother about your hobbies and your friends and to ask for money. Write a program that prints similar letters such as these to three people of your choice. Each letter should have at least one paragraph in common with each of the other letters. Your main program should have three method calls, one for each of the people to whom you are writing. Try to isolate repeated tasks into methods.

3. Write a program that produces as output the following lyrics, which are similar to the song, "There Was an Old Lady Who Swallowed a Fly," by Simms Taback. Use methods for each verse and the refrain. Here are the complete lyrics to print:

```
There was an old lady who swallowed a fly.
I don't know why she swallowed that fly,
Perhaps she'll die.
```

```
There was an old lady who swallowed a spider,
That wriggled and iggled and jiggled inside her.
She swallowed the spider to catch the fly,
I don't know why she swallowed that fly,
Perhaps she'll die.

There was an old lady who swallowed a bird,
How absurd to swallow a bird.
She swallowed the bird to catch the spider,
She swallowed the spider to catch the fly,
I don't know why she swallowed that fly,
Perhaps she'll die.

There was an old lady who swallowed a cat,
Imagine that to swallow a cat.
She swallowed the cat to catch the bird,
She swallowed the bird to catch the spider,
She swallowed the spider to catch the fly,
I don't know why she swallowed that fly,
Perhaps she'll die.

There was an old lady who swallowed a dog,
What a hog to swallow a dog.
She swallowed the dog to catch the cat,
She swallowed the cat to catch the bird,
She swallowed the bird to catch the spider,
She swallowed the spider to catch the fly,
I don't know why she swallowed that fly,
Perhaps she'll die.

There was an old lady who swallowed a horse,
She died of course.
```

4. Write a program that produces as output the words of "The Twelve Days of Christmas." (Static methods simplify this task.) Here are the first two verses and the last verse of the song:

```
On the first day of Christmas,
my true love sent to me
a partridge in a pear tree.

On the second day of Christmas,
my true love sent to me
two turtle doves, and
a partridge in a pear tree.
...

On the twelfth day of Christmas,
my true love sent to me
Twelve drummers drumming,
eleven pipers piping,
ten lords a-leaping,
nine ladies dancing,
eight maids a-milking,
seven swans a-swimming,
six geese a-laying,
```

```
five golden rings,
four calling birds,
three French hens,
two turtle doves, and
a partridge in a pear tree.
```

5. Write a program that produces as output the words of "The House That Jack Built." Use methods for each verse and for repeated text. Here are lyrics to use:

```
This is the house that Jack built.

This is the malt
That lay in the house that Jack built.

This is the rat,
That ate the malt
That lay in the house that Jack built.

This is the cat,
That killed the rat,
That ate the malt
That lay in the house that Jack built.

This is the dog,
That worried the cat,
That killed the rat,
That ate the malt
That lay in the house that Jack built.

This is the cow with the crumpled horn,
That tossed the dog,
That worried the cat,
That killed the rat,
That ate the malt
That lay in the house that Jack built.

This is the maiden all forlorn
That milked the cow with the crumpled horn,
That tossed the dog,
That worried the cat,
That killed the rat,
That ate the malt
That lay in the house that Jack built.
```

6. Write a program that produces as output the words of "Bought Me a Cat." Use methods for each verse and for repeated text. Here are the song's complete lyrics:

```
Bought me a cat and the cat pleased me,
I fed my cat under yonder tree.
Cat goes fiddle-i-fee.

Bought me a hen and the hen pleased me,
I fed my hen under yonder tree.
```

```
Hen goes chimmy-chuck, chimmy-chuck,
Cat goes fiddle-i-fee.

Bought me a duck and the duck pleased me,
I fed my duck under yonder tree.
Duck goes quack, quack,
Hen goes chimmy-chuck, chimmy-chuck,
Cat goes fiddle-i-fee.

Bought me a goose and the goose pleased me,
I fed my goose under yonder tree.
Goose goes hissy, hissy,
Duck goes quack, quack,
Hen goes chimmy-chuck, chimmy-chuck,
Cat goes fiddle-i-fee.

Bought me a sheep and the sheep pleased me,
I fed my sheep under yonder tree.
Sheep goes baa, baa,
Goose goes hissy, hissy,
Duck goes quack, quack,
Hen goes chimmy-chuck, chimmy-chuck,
Cat goes fiddle-i-fee.
```

7. Write a program that produces as output the words of the following silly song. Use methods for each verse and for repeated text. Here are the song's complete lyrics:

```
I once wrote a program that wouldn't compile
I don't know why it wouldn't compile,
My TA just smiled.

My program did nothing
So I started typing.
I added System.out.println("I <3 coding"),
I don't know why it wouldn't compile,
My TA just smiled.

"Parse error," cried the compiler
Luckily I'm such a code baller.
I added a backslash to escape the quotes,
I added System.out.println("I <3 coding"),
I don't know why it wouldn't compile,
My TA just smiled.

Now the compiler wanted an identifier
And I thought the situation was getting dire.
I added a main method with its String[] args,
I added a backslash to escape the quotes,
I added System.out.println("I <3 coding"),
I don't know why it wouldn't compile,
My TA just smiled.
```

```
Java complained it expected an enum
Boy, these computers really are dumb!
I added a public class and called it Scum,
I added a main method with its String[] args,
I added a backslash to escape the quotes,
I added System.out.println("I <3 coding"),
I don't know why it wouldn't compile,
My TA just smiled.
```

Chapter 2

Primitive Data and Definite Loops

Introduction

Now that you know something about the basic structure of Java programs, you are ready to learn how to solve more complex problems. For the time being we will still concentrate on programs that produce output, but we will begin to explore some of the aspects of programming that require problem-solving skills.

The first half of this chapter fills in two important areas. First, it examines expressions, which are used to perform simple computations in Java, particularly those involving numeric data. Second, it discusses program elements called variables that can change in value as the program executes.

The second half of the chapter introduces your first control structure: the `for` loop. You use this structure to repeat actions in a program. This is useful whenever you find a pattern in a task such as the creation of a complex figure, because you can use a `for` loop to repeat the action to create that particular pattern. The challenge is finding each pattern and figuring out what repeated actions will reproduce it.

The `for` loop is a flexible control structure that can be used for many tasks. In this chapter we use it for *definite loops*, where you know exactly how many times you want to perform a particular task. In Chapter 5 we will discuss how to write *indefinite loops*, where you don't know in advance how many times to perform a task.

2.1 Basic Data Concepts

Programs manipulate information, and information comes in many forms. Java is a *type-safe* language, which means that it requires you to be explicit about what kind of information you intend to manipulate and it guarantees that you manipulate the data in a reasonable manner. Everything that you manipulate in a Java program will be of a certain *type,* and you will constantly find yourself telling Java what types of data you intend to use.

Data Type

A name for a category of data values that are all related, as in type `int` in Java, which is used to represent integer values.

A decision was made early in the design of Java to support two different kinds of data: primitive data and objects. The designers made this decision purely on the basis of performance, to make Java programs run faster. Unfortunately, it means that you have to learn two sets of rules about how data works, but this is one of those times when you simply have to pay the price if you want to use an industrial-strength programming language. To make things a little easier, we will study the primitive data types first, in this chapter; in the next chapter, we will turn our attention to objects.

Primitive Types

There are eight primitive data types in Java: `boolean`, `byte`, `char`, `double`, `float`, `int`, `long`, and `short`. Four of these are considered fundamental: `boolean`, `char`, `double`, and `int`. The other four types are variations that exist for programs that have special requirements. The four fundamental types that we will explore are listed in Table 2.1.

The type names (`int`, `double`, `char`, and `boolean`) are Java keywords that you will use in your programs to let the compiler know that you intend to use that type of data.

It may seem odd to use one type for integers and another type for real numbers. Isn't every integer a real number? The answer is yes, but these are fundamentally different types of numbers. The difference is so great that we make this distinction even in English. We don't ask, "How much sisters do you have?" or "How many do you weigh?" We realize that sisters come in discrete integer quantities (0 sisters, 1 sister, 2 sisters, 3 sisters, and so on), and we use the word "many" for integer quantities ("How

Table 2.1 Commonly Used Primitive Types in Java

Type	Description	Examples
`int`	integers (whole numbers)	`42, –3, 18, 20493, 0`
`double`	real numbers	`7.35, 14.9, –19.83423`
`char`	single characters	`'a', 'X', '!'`
`boolean`	logical values	`true, false`

many sisters do you have?"). Similarly, we realize that weight can vary by tiny amounts (175 pounds versus 175.5 pounds versus 175.25 pounds, and so on), and we use the word "much" for these real-number quantities ("How much do you weigh?").

In programming, this distinction is even more important, because integers and reals are represented in different ways in the computer's memory: Integers are stored exactly, while reals are stored as approximations with a limited number of digits of accuracy. You will see that storing values as approximations can lead to round-off errors when you use real values.

The name `double` for real values is not very intuitive. It's an accident of history in much the same way that we still talk about "dialing" a number on our telephones even though modern telephones don't have dials. The C programming language introduced a type called `float` (short for "floating-point number") for storing real numbers. But `float`s had limited accuracy, so another type was introduced, called `double` (short for "double precision," meaning that it had double the precision of a simple `float`). As memory became cheaper, people began using `double` as the default for floating-point values. In hindsight, it might have been better to use the word `float` for what is now called `double` and a word like "half" for the values with less accuracy, but it's tough to change habits that are so ingrained. So, programming languages will continue to use the word `double` for floating-point numbers, and people will still talk about "dialing" people on the phone even if they've never touched a telephone dial.

Expressions

VideoNote

When you write programs, you will often need to include values and calculations. The technical term for these elements is *expressions.*

> **Expression**
> A simple value or a set of operations that produces a value.

The simplest expression is a specific value, like `42` or `28.9`. We call these "literal values," or *literals.* More complex expressions involve combining simple values. Suppose, for example, that you want to know how many bottles of water you have. If you have two 6-packs, four 4-packs, and two individual bottles, you can compute the total number of bottles with the following expression:

```
(2 * 6) + (4 * 4) + 2
```

Notice that we use an asterisk to represent multiplication and that we use parentheses to group parts of the expression. The computer determines the value of an expression by *evaluating* it.

> **Evaluation**
> The process of obtaining the value of an expression.

The value obtained when an expression is evaluated is called the *result.* Complex expressions are formed using *operators.*

Operator

A special symbol (like + or *) that is used to indicate an operation to be performed on one or more values.

The values used in the expression are called *operands.* For example, consider the following simple expressions:

```
3 + 29
4 * 5
```

The operators here are the + and *, and the operands are simple numbers.

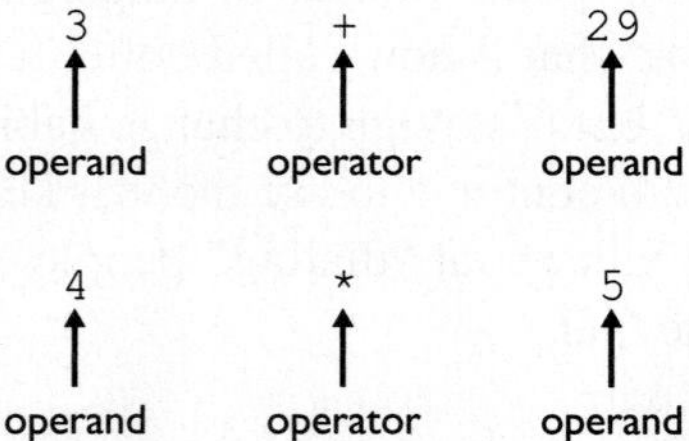

When you form complex expressions, these simpler expressions can in turn become operands for other operators. For example, the expression

```
(3 + 29) – (4 * 5)
```

has two levels of operators.

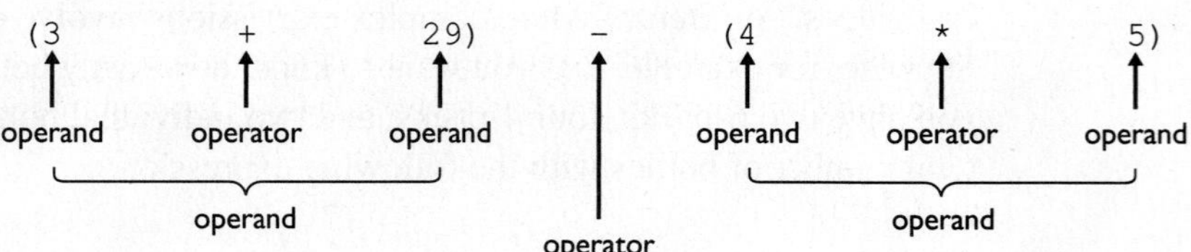

The addition operator has simple operands of `3` and `29` and the multiplication operator has simple operands of `4` and `5`, but the subtraction operator has operands that are each parenthesized expressions with operators of their own. Thus, complex expressions can be built from smaller expressions. At the lowest level, you have simple numbers. These are used as operands to make more complex expressions, which in turn can be used as operands in even more complex expressions.

There are many things you can do with expressions. One of the simplest things you can do is to print the value of an expression using a `println` statement. For example, if you say:

```
System.out.println(42);
System.out.println(2 + 2);
```

you will get the following two lines of output:

```
42
4
```

Notice that for the second `println`, the computer evaluates the expression (adding 2 and 2) and prints the result (in this case, 4).

You will see many different operators as you progress through this book, all of which can be used to form expressions. Expressions can be arbitrarily complex, with as many operators as you like. For that reason, when we tell you, "An expression can be used here," we mean that you can use arbitrary expressions that include complex expressions as well as simple values.

Literals

The simplest expressions refer to values directly using what are known as *literals.* An integer literal (considered to be of type `int`) is a sequence of digits with or without a leading sign:

```
3    482    −29434    0    92348    +9812
```

A floating-point literal (considered to be of type `double`) includes a decimal point:

```
298.4    0.284    207.    .2843    −17.452    −.98
```

Notice that `207.` is considered a `double` even though it coincides with an integer, because of the decimal point. Literals of type `double` can also be expressed in scientific notation (a number followed by `e` followed by an integer):

```
2.3e4    1e-5    3.84e92    2.458e12
```

The first of these numbers represents 2.3 times 10 to the 4th power, which equals 23,000. Even though this value happens to coincide with an integer, it is considered to be of type `double` because it is expressed in scientific notation. The second number represents 1 times 10 to the –5th power, which is equal to 0.00001. The third number represents 3.84 times 10 to the 92nd power. The fourth number represents 2.458 times 10 to the 12th power.

We have seen that textual information can be stored in literal strings that store a sequence of characters. In later chapters we will explore how to process a string character by character. Each such character is of type `char`. A character literal is enclosed in single quotation marks and includes just one character:

```
'a'    'm'    'X'    '!'    '3'    '\\'
```

All of these examples are of type `char`. Notice that the last example uses an escape sequence to represent the backslash character. You can even refer to the single quotation character using an escape sequence:

```
'\''
```

Finally, the primitive type `boolean` stores logical information. We won't be exploring the use of type `boolean` until we reach Chapter 4 and see how to introduce logical tests into our programs, but for completeness, we include the `boolean` literal values here. Logic deals with just two possibilities: true and false. These two Java keywords are the two literal values of type `boolean`:

```
true    false
```

Arithmetic Operators

The basic arithmetic operators are shown in Table 2.2. The addition and subtraction operators will, of course, look familiar to you, as should the asterisk as a multiplication operator and the forward slash as a division operator. However, as you'll see, Java has two different division operations. The remainder or mod operation may be unfamiliar.

Division presents a problem when the operands are integers. When you divide 119 by 5, for example, you do not get an integer result. Therefore, the results of integer division are expressed as two different integers, a quotient and a remainder:

$$\frac{119}{5} = 23 \text{ (quotient) with } 4 \text{ (remainder)}$$

In terms of the arithmetic operators:

`119 / 5` evaluates to `23`
`119 % 5` evaluates to `4`

Table 2.2 Arithmetic Operators in Java

Operator	Meaning	Example	Result
+	addition	2 + 2	4
–	subtraction	53 – 18	35
*	multiplication	3 * 8	24
/	division	4.8 / 2.0	2.4
%	remainder or mod	19 % 5	4

These two division operators should be familiar if you recall how long-division calculations are performed:

```
       31
  34)1079
      102
       59
       34
       25
```

Here, dividing 1079 by 34 yields 31 with a remainder of 25. Using arithmetic operators, the problem would be described like this:

`1079 / 34` evaluates to `31`
`1079 % 34` evaluates to `25`

It takes a while to get used to integer division in Java. When you are using the division operator (`/`), the key thing to keep in mind is that it truncates anything after the decimal point. So, if you imagine computing an answer on a calculator, just think of ignoring anything after the decimal point:

- `19/5` is `3.8` on a calculator, so `19/5` evaluates to `3`
- `207/10` is `20.7` on a calculator, so `207/10` evaluates to `20`
- `3/8` is `0.375` on a calculator, so `3/8` evaluates to `0`

The remainder operator (`%`) is usually referred to as the "mod operator," or simply "mod." The mod operator lets you know how much was left unaccounted for by the truncating division operator. For example, given the previous examples, you'd compute the mod results as shown in Table 2.3.

In each case, you figure out how much of the number is accounted for by the truncating division operator. The mod operator gives you any excess (the remainder). When you put this into a formula, you can think of the mod operator as behaving as follows:

```
x % y = x  (x / y) * y
```

Table 2.3 Examples of Mod Operator

Mod problem	First divide	What does division account for?	How much is left over?	Answer
`19 % 5`	19/5 is 3	3 * 5 is 15	19 − 15 is 4	4
`207 % 10`	207/10 is 20	20 * 10 is 200	207 − 200 is 7	7
`3 % 8`	3/8 is 0	0 * 8 is 0	3 − 0 is 3	3

It is possible to get a result of `0` for the mod operator. This happens when one number divides evenly into another. For example, each of the following expressions evaluates to `0` because the second number goes evenly into the first number:

```
28 % 7
95 % 5
44 % 2
```

A few special cases are worth noting because they are not always immediately obvious to novice programmers:

- **Numerator smaller than denominator:** In this case division produces 0 and mod produces the original number. For example, `7 / 10` is `0` and `7 % 10` is `7`.
- **Numerator of 0:** In this case both division and mod return 0. For example, both `0 / 10` and `0 % 10` evaluate to `0`.
- **Denominator of 0:** In this case, both division and mod are undefined and produce a runtime error. For example, a program that attempts to evaluate either `7 / 0` or `7 % 0` will throw an `ArithmeticException` error.

The mod operator has many useful applications in computer programs. Here are just a few ideas:

- Testing whether a number is even or odd (`number % 2` is `0` for evens, `number % 2` is `1` for odds).
- Finding individual digits of a number (e.g., `number % 10` is the final digit).
- Finding the last four digits of a social security number (`number % 10000`).

The remainder operator can be used with `doubles` as well as with integers, and it works similarly: You consider how much is left over when you take away as many "whole" values as you can. For example, the expression `10.2 % 2.4` evaluates to `0.6` because you can take away four `2.4`s from `10.2`, leaving you with `0.6` left over.

For floating-point values (values of type `double`), the division operator does what we consider "normal" division. So, even though the expression `119 / 5` evaluates to `23`, the expression `119.0 / 5.0` evaluates to `23.8`.

Precedence

Java expressions are like complex noun phrases in English. Such phrases are subject to ambiguity. For example, consider the phrase "the man on the hill by the river with the telescope." Is the river by the hill or by the man? Is the man holding the telescope, or is the telescope on the hill, or is the telescope in the river? We don't know how to group the various parts together.

You can get the same kind of ambiguity if parentheses aren't used to group the parts of a Java expression. For example, the expression `2 + 3 * 4` has two operators. Which operation is performed first? You could interpret this two ways:

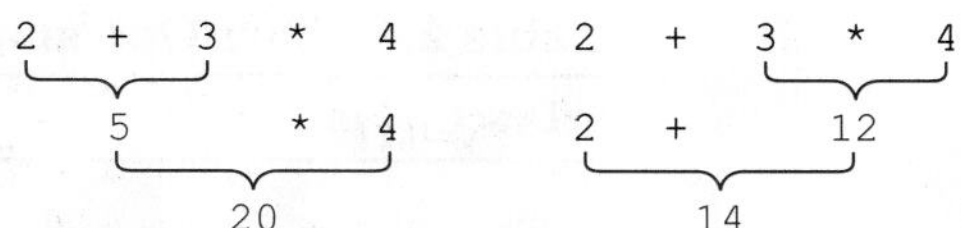

The first of these evaluates to `20` while the second evaluates to `14`. To deal with the ambiguity, Java has rules of *precedence* that determine how to group together the various parts.

> **Precedence**
>
> The binding power of an operator, which determines how to group parts of an expression.

The computer applies rules of precedence when the grouping of operators in an expression is ambiguous. An operator with high precedence is evaluated first, followed by operators of lower precedence. Within a given level of precedence the operators are evaluated in one direction, usually left to right.

For arithmetic expressions, there are two levels of precedence. The multiplicative operators (`*`, `/`, `%`) have a higher level of precedence than the additive operators (+, –). Thus, the expression `2 + 3 * 4` is interpreted as

```
2 + 3 * 4
    12
2 +   12
   14
```

Within the same level of precedence, arithmetic operators are evaluated from left to right. This often doesn't make a difference in the final result, but occasionally it does. Consider, for example, the expression

```
40 – 25 – 9
```

which evaluates as follows:

```
40 - 25 - 9
  15    - 9
     6
```

You would get a different result if the second subtraction were evaluated first.

You can always override precedence with parentheses. For example, if you really want the second subtraction to be evaluated first, you can force that to happen by introducing parentheses:

```
40 – (25 – 9)
```

Table 2.4 Java Operator Precedence

Description	Operators
unary operators	+, –
multiplicative operators	*, /, %
additive operators	+, –

The expression now evaluates as follows:

```
40  -  (25  -  9)
40  -      16
      24
```

Another concept in arithmetic is *unary* plus and minus, which take a single operand, as opposed to the binary operators we have seen thus far (e.g., *, /, and even binary + and –), all of which take two operands. For example, we can find the negation of `8` by asking for `–8`. These unary operators have a higher level of precedence than the multiplicative operators. Consequently, we can form expressions like the following:

```
12 * –8
```

which evaluates to `–96`.

We will see many types of operators in the next few chapters. Table 2.4 is a precedence table that includes the arithmetic operators. As we introduce more operators, we'll update this table to include them as well. The table is ordered from highest precedence to lowest precedence and indicates that Java will first group parts of an expression using the unary operators, then using the multiplicative operators, and finally using the additive operators.

Before we leave this topic, let's look at a complex expression and see how it is evaluated step by step. Consider the following expression:

```
13 * 2 + 239 / 10 % 5 – 2 * 2
```

It has a total of six operators: two multiplications, one division, one mod, one subtraction, and one addition. The multiplication, division, and mod operations will be performed first, because they have higher precedence, and they will be performed from left to right because they are all at the same level of precedence:

```
13 * 2  +  239 / 10 % 5  -  2 * 2
  26    +  239 / 10 % 5  -  2 * 2
  26    +     23    % 5  -  2 * 2
  26    +        3       -  2 * 2
  26    +     3          -    4
```

Now we evaluate the additive operators from left to right:

```
26 + 3  -  4
\_____/
  29    -  4
  \_________/
      25
```

Mixing Types and Casting

You'll often find yourself mixing values of different types and wanting to convert from one type to another. Java has simple rules to avoid confusion and provides a mechanism for requesting that a value be converted from one type to another.

Two types that are frequently mixed are `ints` and `doubles`. You might, for example, ask Java to compute `2 * 3.6`. This expression includes the `int` literal `2` and the `double` literal `3.6`. In this case, Java converts the `int` into a `double` and performs the computation entirely with `double` values; this is always the rule when Java encounters an `int` where it was expecting a `double`.

This becomes particularly important when you form expressions that involve division. If the two operands are both of type `int`, Java will use integer (truncating) division. If either of the two operands is of type `double`, however, it will do real-valued (normal) division. For example, `23 / 4` evaluates to `5`, but all of the following evaluate to `5.75`:

```
23.0 / 4
23. / 4
23 / 4.0
23 / 4.
23. / 4.
23.0 / 4.0
```

Sometimes you want Java to go the other way, converting a `double` into an `int`. You can ask Java for this conversion with a *cast*. Think of it as "casting a value in a different light." You request a cast by putting the name of the type you want to cast to in parentheses in front of the value you want to cast. For example,

```
(int) 4.75
```

will produce the `int` value `4`. When you cast a `double` value to an `int`, it simply truncates anything after the decimal point.

If you want to cast the result of an expression, you have to be careful to use parentheses. For example, suppose that you have some books that are each 0.15 feet wide and you want to know how many of them will fit in a bookshelf that is 2.5 feet wide. You could do a straight division of `2.5 / 0.15`, but that evaluates to a `double` result that is between 16 and 17. Americans use the phrase "16 and change" as a way to express the idea that a value is larger than 16 but not as big as 17. In this case, we don't care about the "change"; we only want to compute the 16 part. You might form the following expression:

```
(int) 2.5 / 0.15
```

Unfortunately, this expression evaluates to the wrong answer because the cast is applied to whatever comes right after it (here, the value `2.5`). This casts `2.5` into the integer `2`, divides by `0.15`, and evaluates to `13` and change, which isn't an integer and isn't the right answer. Instead, you want to form this expression:

```
(int) (2.5 / 0.15)
```

This expression first performs the division to get 16 and change, and then casts that value to an `int` by truncating it. It thus evaluates to the `int` value `16`, which is the answer you're looking for.

2.2 Variables

VideoNote

Primitive data can be stored in the computer's memory in a *variable.*

> **Variable**
>
> A memory location with a name and a type that stores a value.

Think of the computer's memory as being like a giant spreadsheet that has many cells where data can be stored. When you create a variable in Java, you are asking it to set aside one of those cells for this new variable. Initially the cell will be empty, but you will have the option to store a value in the cell. And as with a spreadsheet, you will have the option to change the value in that cell later.

Java is a little more picky than a spreadsheet, though, in that it requires you to tell it exactly what kind of data you are going to store in the cell. For example, if you want to store an integer, you need to tell Java that you intend to use type `int`. If you want to store a real value, you need to tell Java that you intend to use a `double`. You also have to decide on a name to use when you want to refer to this memory location. The normal rules of Java identifiers apply (the name must start with a letter, which can be followed by any combination of letters and digits). The standard convention in Java is to start variable names with a lowercase letter, as in `number` or `digits`, and to capitalize any subsequent words, as in `numberOfDigits`.

To explore the basic use of variables, let's examine a program that computes an individual's *body mass index* (BMI). Health professionals use this number to advise people about whether or not they are overweight. Given an individual's height and weight, we can compute that person's BMI. A simple BMI program, then, would naturally have three variables for these three pieces of information. There are several details that we need to discuss about variables, but it can be helpful to look at a complete program first to see the overall picture. The following program computes and prints the BMI for an individual who is 5 feet 10 inches tall and weighs 195 pounds:

```
public class BMICalculator {
    public static void main(String[] args) {
        // declare variables
        double height;
        double weight;
        double bmi;

        // compute BMI
        height = 70;
        weight = 195;
        bmi = weight / (height * height) * 703;

        // print results
        System.out.println("Current BMI:");
        System.out.println(bmi);
    }
}
```

Notice that the program includes blank lines to separate the sections and comments to indicate what the different parts of the program do. It produces the following output:

```
Current BMI:
27.976530612244897
```

Let's now examine the details of this program to understand how variables work. Before variables can be used in a Java program, they must be declared. The line of code that declares the variable is known as a variable *declaration.*

> **Declaration**
> A request to set aside a new variable with a given name and type.

Each variable is declared just once. If you declare a variable more than once, you will get an error message from the Java compiler. Simple variable declarations are of the form

```
<type> <name>;
```

as in the three declarations at the beginning of our sample program:

```
double height;
double weight;
double bmi;
```

Notice that a variable declaration, like a statement, ends with a semicolon. These declarations can appear anywhere a statement can occur. The declaration indicates the type and the name of the variable. Remember that the name of each primitive type is a keyword in Java (`int`, `double`, `char`, `boolean`). We've used the keyword `double` to define the type of these three variables.

Once a variable is declared, Java sets aside a memory location to store its value. However, with the simple form of variable declaration used in our program, Java does not store initial values in these memory locations. We refer to these as *uninitialized* variables, and they are similar to blank cells in a spreadsheet:

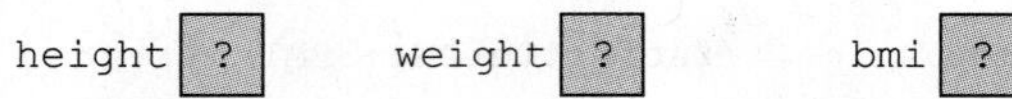

So how do we get values into those cells? The easiest way to do so is using an *assignment statement.* The general syntax of the assignment statement is

```
<variable> = <expression>;
```

as in

```
height = 70;
```

This statement stores the value `70` in the memory location for the variable `height`, indicating that this person is 70 inches tall (5 feet 10 inches). We often use the phrase "gets" or "is assigned" when reading a statement like this, as in "`height` gets `70`" or "`height` is assigned `70`."

When the statement executes, the computer first evaluates the expression on the right side; then, it stores the result in the memory location for the given variable. In this case the expression is just a simple literal value, so after the computer executes this statement, the memory looks like this:

height 70.0   weight ?   bmi ?

Notice that the value is stored as `70.0` because the variable is of type `double`. The variable `height` has now been initialized, but the variables `weight` and `bmi` are still uninitialized. The second assignment statement gives a value to `weight`:

```
weight = 195;
```

After executing this statement, the memory looks like this:

height 70.0   weight 195.0   bmi ?

The third assignment statement includes a formula (an expression to be evaluated):

```
bmi = weight / (height * height) * 703;
```

To calculate the value of this expression, the computer divides the weight by the square of the height and then multiplies the result of that operation by the literal value `703`. The result is stored in the variable `bmi`. So, after the computer has executed the third assignment statement, the memory looks like this:

```
height [70.0]     weight [195.0]     bmi [27.976530612244897]
```

The last two lines of the program report the BMI result using `println` statements:

```
System.out.println("Current BMI:");
System.out.println(bmi);
```

Notice that we can include a variable in a `println` statement the same way that we include literal values and other expressions to be printed.

As its name implies, a variable can take on different values at different times. For example, consider the following variation of the BMI program, which computes a new BMI assuming the person lost 15 pounds (going from 195 pounds to 180 pounds).

```
public class BMICalculator2 {
    public static void main(String[] args) {
        // declare variables
        double height;
        double weight;
        double bmi;

        // compute BMI
        height = 70;
        weight = 195;
        bmi = weight / (height * height) * 703;

        // print results
        System.out.println("Previous BMI:");
        System.out.println(bmi);

        // recompute BMI
        weight = 180;
        bmi = weight / (height * height) * 703;

        // report new results
        System.out.println("Current BMI:");
        System.out.println(bmi);
    }
}
```

The program begins the same way, setting the three variables to the following values and reporting this initial value for BMI:

height	70.0	weight	195.0	bmi	27.976530612244897

But the new program then includes the following assignment statement:

```
weight = 180;
```

This changes the value of the `weight` variable:

height	70.0	weight	180.0	bmi	27.976530612244897

You might think that this would also change the value of the `bmi` variable. After all, earlier in the program we said that the following should be true:

```
bmi = weight / (height * height) * 703;
```

This is a place where the spreadsheet analogy is not as accurate. A spreadsheet can store formulas in its cells and when you update one cell it can cause the values in other cells to be updated. The same is not true in Java.

You might also be misled by the use of an equals sign for assignment. Don't confuse this statement with a statement of equality. The assignment statement does not represent an algebraic relationship. In algebra, you might say

$x = y + 2$

In mathematics you state definitively that x is equal to y plus two, a fact that is true now and forever. If x changes, y will change accordingly, and vice versa. Java's assignment statement is very different.

The assignment statement is a command to perform an action at a particular point in time. It does not represent a lasting relationship between variables. That's why we usually say "gets" or "is assigned" rather than saying "equals" when we read assignment statements.

Getting back to the program, resetting the variable called `weight` does not reset the variable called `bmi`. To recompute `bmi` based on the new value for `weight`, we must include the second assignment statement:

```
weight = 180;
bmi = weight / (height * height) * 703;
```

Otherwise, the variable `bmi` would store the same value as before. That would be a rather depressing outcome to report to someone who's just lost 15 pounds. By including both of these statements, we reset both the `weight` and `bmi` variables so that memory looks like this:

height	70.0	weight	180.0	bmi	25.82448979591837

The output of the new version of the program is

```
Previous BMI:
27.976530612244897
Current BMI:
25.82448979591837
```

One very common assignment statement that points out the difference between algebraic relationships and program statements is:

```
x = x + 1;
```

Remember not to think of this as "`x` equals `x + 1`." There are no numbers that satisfy that equation. We use a word like "gets" to read this as "`x` gets the value of `x` plus one." This may seem a rather odd statement, but you should be able to decipher it given the rules outlined earlier. Suppose that the current value of `x` is `19`. To execute the statement, you first evaluate the expression to obtain the result `20`. The computer stores this value in the variable named on the left, `x`. Thus, this statement adds one to the value of the variable. We refer to this as *incrementing* the value of `x`. It is a fundamental programming operation because it is the programming equivalent of counting (1, 2, 3, 4, and so on). The following statement is a variation that counts down, which we call *decrementing* a variable:

```
x = x – 1;
```

We will discuss incrementing and decrementing in more detail later in this chapter.

Assignment/Declaration Variations

Java is a complex language that provides a lot of flexibility to programmers. In the last section we saw the simplest form of variable declaration and assignment, but there are many variations on this theme. It wouldn't be a bad idea to stick with the simplest form while you are learning, but you'll come across other forms as you read other people's programs, so you'll want to understand what they mean.

The first variation is that Java allows you to provide an initial value for a variable at the time that you declare it. The syntax is as follows:

```
<type> <name> = <expression>;
```

as in

```
double height = 70;
double weight = 195;
double bmi = weight / (height * height) * 703;
```

This variation combines declaration and assignment in one line of code. The first two assignments have simple numbers after the equals sign, but the third has a complex expression after the equals sign. These three assignments have the same effect as providing three declarations followed by three assignment statements:

```
double height;
double weight;
double bmi;
height = 70;
weight = 195;
bmi = weight / (height * height) * 703;
```

Another variation is to declare several variables that are all of the same type in a single statement. The syntax is

```
<type> <name>, <name>, <name>, ..., <name>;
```

as in

```
double height, weight;
```

This example declares two different variables, both of type `double`. Notice that the type appears just once, at the beginning of the declaration.

The final variation is a mixture of the previous two forms. You can declare multiple variables all of the same type, and you can initialize them at the same time. For example, you could say

```
double height = 70, weight = 195;
```

This statement declares the two `double` variables `height` and `weight` and gives them initial values (`70` and `195`, respectively). Java even allows you to mix initializing and not initializing, as in

```
double height = 70, weight = 195, bmi;
```

This statement declares three `double` variables called `height`, `weight`, and `bmi` and provides initial values to two of them (`height` and `weight`). The variable `bmi` is uninitialized.

Common Programming Error

Declaring the Same Variable Twice

One of the things to keep in mind as you learn is that you can declare any given variable just once. You can assign it as many times as you like once you've declared it, but the declaration should appear just once. Think of variable declaration as being like checking into a hotel and assignment as being like going in

Continued on next page

Continued from previous page

and out of your room. You have to check in first to get your room key, but then you can come and go as often as you like. If you tried to check in a second time, the hotel would be likely to ask you if you really want to pay for a second room.

If you declare a variable more than once, Java generates a compiler error. For example, say your program contains the following lines:

```
int x = 13;
System.out.println(x);
int x = 2;          // this line does not compile
System.out.println(x);
```

The first line is okay. It declares an integer variable called `x` and initializes it to `13`. The second line is also okay, because it simply prints the value of `x`. But the third line will generate an error message indicating that "`x` is already defined." If you want to change the value of `x` you need to use a simple assignment statement instead of a variable declaration:

```
int x = 13;
System.out.println(x);
x = 2;
System.out.println(x);
```

We have been referring to the "assignment statement," but in fact assignment is an operator, not a statement. When you assign a value to a variable, the overall expression evaluates to the value just assigned. That means that you can form expressions that have assignment operators embedded within them. Unlike most other operators, the assignment operator evaluates from right to left, which allows programmers to write statements like the following:

```
int x, y, z;
x = y = z = 2 * 5 + 4;
```

Because the assignment operator evaluates from right to left, this statement is equivalent to:

```
x = (y = (z = 2 * 5 + 4));
```

The expression `2 * 5 + 4` evaluates to `14`. This value is assigned to `z`. The assignment is itself an expression that evaluates to `14`, which is then assigned to `y`. The assignment to `y` evaluates to `14` as well, which is then assigned to `x`. The result is that all three variables are assigned the value `14`.

String Concatenation

You saw in Chapter 1 that you can output string literals using `System.out.println`. You can also output numeric expressions using `System.out.println`:

```
System.out.println(12 + 3 – 1);
```

This statement causes the computer first to evaluate the expression, which yields the value `14`, and then to write that value to the console window. You'll often want to output more than one value on a line, but unfortunately, you can pass only one value to `println`. To get around this limitation, Java provides a simple mechanism called *concatenation* for putting together several pieces into one long string literal.

> **String Concatenation**
>
> Combining several strings into a single string, or combining a string with other data into a new, longer string.

The addition (+) operator concatenates the pieces together. Doing so forms an expression that can be evaluated. Even if the expression includes both numbers and text, it can be evaluated just like the numeric expressions we have been exploring. Consider, for example, the following:

```
"I have " + 3 + " things to concatenate"
```

You have to pay close attention to the quotation marks in an expression like this to keep track of which parts are "inside" a string literal and which are outside. This expression begins with the text `"I have "` (including a space at the end), followed by a plus sign and the integer literal `3`. Java converts the integer into a textual form (`"3"`) and concatenates the two pieces together to form `"I have 3"`. Following the `3` is another plus and another string literal, `" things to concatenate"` (which starts with a space). This piece is glued onto the end of the previous string to form the string `"I have 3 things to concatenate"`.

Because this expression produces a single concatenated string, we can include it in a `println` statement:

```
System.out.println("I have " + 3 + " things to concatenate");
```

This statement produces a single line of output:

```
I have 3 things to concatenate
```

String concatenation is often used to report the value of a variable. Consider, for example, the following program that computes the number of hours, minutes, and seconds in a standard year:

```
public class Time {
    public static void main(String[] args) {
        int hours = 365 * 24;
```

```
        int minutes = hours * 60;
        int seconds = minutes * 60;
        System.out.println("Hours in a year = " + hours);
        System.out.println("Minutes in a year = " + minutes);
        System.out.println("Seconds in a year = " + seconds);
    }
}
```

Notice that the three `println` commands at the end each have a string literal concatenated with a variable. The program produces the following output:

```
Hours in a year = 8760
Minutes in a year = 525600
Seconds in a year = 31536000
```

You can use concatenation to form arbitrarily complex expressions. For example, if you had variables `x`, `y`, and `z` and you wanted to write out their values in coordinate format with parentheses and commas, you could say:

```
System.out.println("(" + x + ", " + y + ", " + z + ")");
```

If `x`, `y`, and `z` had the values `8`, `19`, and `23`, respectively, this statement would output the string `"(8, 19, 23)"`.

The + used for concatenation has the same level of precedence as the normal arithmetic + operator, which can lead to some confusion. Consider, for example, the following expression:

```
2 + 3 + " hello " + 7 + 2 * 3
```

This expression has four addition operators and one multiplication operator. Because of precedence, we evaluate the multiplication first:

```
2 + 3 + " hello " + 7 + 2 * 3
                        \___/
2 + 3 + " hello " + 7 +   6
```

This grouping might seem odd, but that's what the precedence rule says to do: We don't evaluate any additive operators until we've first evaluated all of the multiplicative operators. Once we've taken care of the multiplication, we're left with the four addition operators. These will be evaluated from left to right.

The first addition involves two integer values. Even though the overall expression involves a string, because this little subexpression has just two integers we perform integer addition:

```
2 + 3 + " hello " + 7 + 6
\___/
  5   + " hello " + 7 + 6
```

The next addition involves adding the integer `5` to the string literal `" hello "`. If either of the two operands is a string, we perform concatenation. So, in this case, we convert the integer into a text equivalent (`"5"`) and glue the pieces together to form a new string value:

```
5  +  " hello "  +  7  +  6
\_______________/
  "5 hello "        +  7  +  6
```

You might think that Java would add together the `7` and `6` the same way it added the `2` and `3` to make `5`. But it doesn't work that way. The rules of precedence are simple, and Java follows them with simple-minded consistency. Precedence tells us that addition operators are evaluated from left to right, so first we add the string `"5 hello "` to `7`. That is another combination of a string and an integer, so Java converts the integer to its textual equivalent (`"7"`) and concatenates the two parts together to form a new string:

```
"5 hello "  +  7  +  6
\_______________/
  "5 hello 7"     +  6
```

Now there is just a single remaining addition to perform, which again involves a string/integer combination. We convert the integer to its textual equivalent (`"6"`) and concatenate the two parts together to form a new string:

```
"5 hello 7"  +  6
\_______________/
  "5 hello 76"
```

Clearly, such expressions can be confusing, but you wouldn't want the Java compiler to have to try to guess what you mean. Our job as programmers is easier if we know that the compiler is going to follow simple rules consistently. You can make the expression clearer, and specify how it is evaluated, by adding parentheses. For example, if we really did want Java to add together the `7` and `6` instead of concatenating them separately, we could have written the original expression in the following much clearer way:

```
(2 + 3) + " hello " + (7 + 2 * 3)
```

Because of the parentheses, Java will evaluate the two numeric parts of this expression first and then concatenate the results with the string in the middle. This expression evaluates to `"5 hello 13"`.

Increment/Decrement Operators

In addition to the standard assignment operator, Java has several special operators that are useful for a particular family of operations that are common in programming. As we mentioned earlier, you will often find yourself increasing the value of a variable by a particular amount, an operation called *incrementing*. You will also often find yourself decreasing the value of a variable by a particular amount, an operation called *decrementing*. To accomplish this, you write statements like the following:

```
x = x + 1;
y = y - 1;
z = z + 2;
```

Likewise, you'll frequently find yourself wanting to double or triple the value of a variable or to reduce its value by a factor of 2, in which case you might write code like the following:

```
x = x * 2;
y = y * 3;
z = z / 2;
```

Java has a shorthand for these situations. You glue together the operator character (+, –, *, etc.) with the equals sign to get a special assignment operator (+=, –=, *=, etc.). This variation allows you to rewrite assignment statements like the previous ones as follows:

```
x += 1;
y -= 1;
z += 2;

x *= 2;
y *= 3;
z /= 2;
```

This convention is yet another detail to learn about Java, but it can make the code easier to read. Think of a statement like `x += 2` as saying, "add `2` to `x`." That's more concise than saying `x = x + 2`.

Java has an even more concise way of expressing the particular case in which you want to increment by 1 or decrement by 1. In this case, you can use the increment and decrement operators (++ and --). For example, you can say

```
x++;
y--;
```

There are actually two different forms of each of these operators, because you can also put the operator in front of the variable:

```
++x;
--y;
```

The two versions of ++ are known as the preincrement (`++x`) and postincrement (`x++`) operators. The two versions of -- are similarly known as the predecrement

Table 2.5 Java Operator Precedence

Description	Operators
unary operators	`++, --, +, -`
multiplicative operators	`*, /, %`
additive operators	`+, -`
assignment operators	`=, +=, -=, *=, /=, %=`

(`--x`) and postdecrement (`x--`) operators. The pre- versus post- distinction doesn't matter when you include them as statements by themselves, as in these two examples. The difference comes up only when you embed these statements inside more complex expressions, which we don't recommend.

Now that we've seen a number of new operators, it is worth revisiting the issue of precedence. Table 2.5 shows an updated version of the Java operator precedence table that includes the assignment operators and the increment and decrement operators. Notice that the increment and decrement operators are grouped with the unary operators and have the highest precedence.

Did You Know?

++ and --

The ++ and -- operators were first introduced in the C programming language. Java has them because the designers of the language decided to use the syntax of C as the basis for Java syntax. Many languages have made the same choice, including C++ and C#. There is almost a sense of pride among C programmers that these operators allow you to write extremely concise code, but many other people feel that they can make code unnecessarily complex. In this book we always use these operators as separate statements so that it is obvious what is going on, but in the interest of completeness we will look at the other option here.

The pre- and post- variations both have the same overall effect—the two increment operators increment a variable and the two decrement operators decrement a variable—but they differ in terms of what they evaluate to. When you increment or decrement, there are really two values involved: the original value that the variable had before the increment or decrement operation, and the final value that the variable has after the increment or decrement operation. The post- versions evaluate to the original (older) value and the pre- versions evaluate to the final (later) value.

Consider, for example, the following code fragment:

```
int x = 10;
int y = 20;
int z = ++x * y--;
```

Continued on next page

Continued from previous page

What value is `z` assigned? The answer is `220`. The third assignment increments `x` to 11 and decrements `y` to 19, but in computing the value of `z`, it uses the new value of `x` (`++x`) times the old value of `y` (`y--`), which is 11 times 20, or 220.

There is a simple mnemonic to remember this: When you see `x++`, read it as "give me `x`, then increment," and when you see `++x`, read it as "increment, then give me `x`." Another memory device that might help is to remember that C++ is a bad name for a programming language. The expression "C++" would be interpreted as "evaluate to the old value of C and then increment C." In other words, even though you're trying to come up with something new and different, you're really stuck with the old awful language. The language you want is ++C, which would be a new and improved language rather than the old one. Some people have suggested that perhaps Java is ++C.

Variables and Mixing Types

You already know that when you declare a variable, you must tell Java what type of value it will be storing. For example, you might declare a variable of type `int` for integer values or of type `double` for real values. The situation is fairly clear when you have just integers or just reals, but what happens when you start mixing the types? For example, the following code is clearly okay:

```
int x;
double y;
x = 2 + 3;
y = 3.4 * 2.9;
```

Here, we have an integer variable that we assign an integer value and a `double` variable that we assign a `double` value. But what if we try to do it the other way around?

```
int x;
double y;
x = 3.4 * 2.9; // illegal
y = 2 + 3;     // okay
```

As the comments indicate, you can't assign an integer variable a `double` value, but you can assign a `double` variable an integer value. Let's consider the second case first. The expression `2 + 3` evaluates to the integer `5`. This value isn't a `double`, but every integer is a real value, so it is easy enough for Java to convert the integer into a `double`. The technical term is that Java *promotes* the integer into a `double`.

The first case is more problematic. The expression `3.4 * 2.9` evaluates to the `double` value `9.86`. This value can't be stored in an integer because it isn't an integer. If you want to perform this kind of operation, you'll have to tell Java to convert this value into an integer. As described earlier, you can cast a `double` to an `int`, which will truncate anything after the decimal point:

```
x = (int) (3.4 * 2.9);  // now legal
```

This statement first evaluates `3.4 * 2.9` to get `9.86` and then truncates that value to get the integer `9`.

Common Programming Error

Forgetting to Cast

We often write programs that involve a mixture of `ints` and `doubles`, so it is easy to make mistakes when it comes to combinations of the two. For example, suppose that you want to compute the percentage of correctly answered questions on a student's test, given the total number of questions on the test and the number of questions the student got right. You might declare the following variables:

```
int totalQuestions;
int numRight;
double percent;
```

Suppose the first two are initialized as follows:

```
totalQuestions = 73;
numRight = 59;
```

How do you compute the percentage of questions that the student got right? You divide the number right by the total number of questions and multiply by 100 to turn it into a percentage:

```
percent = numRight / totalQuestions * 100; // incorrect
```

Unfortunately, if you print out the value of the variable `percent` after executing this line of code, you will find that it has the value `0.0`. But obviously the student got more than 0% correct.

The problem comes from integer division. The expression you are using begins with two `int` values:

```
numRight / totalQuestions
```

which means you are computing

```
59 / 73
```

Continued on next page

Continued from previous page

This evaluates to `0` with integer division. Some students fix this by changing the types of all the variables to `double`. That will solve the immediate problem, but it's not a good choice from a stylistic point of view. It is best to use the most appropriate type for data, and the number of questions on the test will definitely be an integer. You could try to fix this by changing the value `100` to `100.0`:

```
percent = numRight / totalQuestions * 100.0; // incorrect
```

but this doesn't help because the division is done first. However, it does work if you put the `100.0` first:

```
percent = 100.0 * numRight / totalQuestions;
```

Now the multiplication is computed before the division, which means that everything is converted to `double`.

Sometimes you can fix a problem like this through a clever rearrangement of the formula, but you don't want to count on cleverness. This is a good place to use a cast. For example, returning to the original formula, you can cast each of the `int` variables to `double`:

```
percent = (double) numRight / (double) totalQuestions * 100.0;
```

You can also take advantage of the fact that once you have cast one of these two variables to `double`, the division will be done with doubles. So you could, for example, cast just the first value to `double`:

```
percent = (double) numRight / totalQuestions * 100.0;
```

2.3 The `for` Loop

Programming often involves specifying redundant tasks. The `for` loop helps to avoid such redundancy by repeatedly executing a sequence of statements over a particular range of values. Suppose you want to write out the squares of the first five integers. You could write a program like this:

```
public class WriteSquares {
    public static void main(String[] args) {
        System.out.println(1 + " squared = " + (1 * 1));
        System.out.println(2 + " squared = " + (2 * 2));
        System.out.println(3 + " squared = " + (3 * 3));
        System.out.println(4 + " squared = " + (4 * 4));
        System.out.println(5 + " squared = " + (5 * 5));
    }
}
```

which would produce the following output:

```
1 squared = 1
2 squared = 4
3 squared = 9
4 squared = 16
5 squared = 25
```

But this approach is tedious. The program has five statements that are very similar. They are all of the form:

```
System.out.println(number + " squared = " + (number * number));
```

where `number` is either `1`, `2`, `3`, `4`, or `5`. The `for` loop avoids such redundancy. Here is an equivalent program using a `for` loop:

```
public class WriteSquares2 {
    public static void main(String[] args) {
        for (int i = 1; i <= 5; i++) {
            System.out.println(i + " squared = " + (i * i));
        }
    }
}
```

This program initializes a variable called `i` to the value `1`. Then it repeatedly executes the `println` statement as long as the variable `i` is less than or equal to `5`. After each `println`, it evaluates the expression `i++` to increment `i`.

The general syntax of the `for` loop is as follows:

```
for (<initialization>; <continuation test>; <update>) {
    <statement>;
    <statement>;
    ...
    <statement>;
}
```

You always include the keyword `for` and the parentheses. Inside the parentheses are three different parts, separated by semicolons: the initialization, the continuation test, and the update. Then there is a set of curly braces that encloses a set of statements. The `for` loop controls the statements inside the curly braces. We refer to the controlled statements as the *body* of the loop. The idea is that we execute the body multiple times, as determined by the combination of the other three parts.

The diagram in Figure 2.1 indicates the steps that Java follows to execute a `for` loop. It performs whatever initialization you have requested once before the loop begins executing. Then it repeatedly performs the continuation test you have provided.

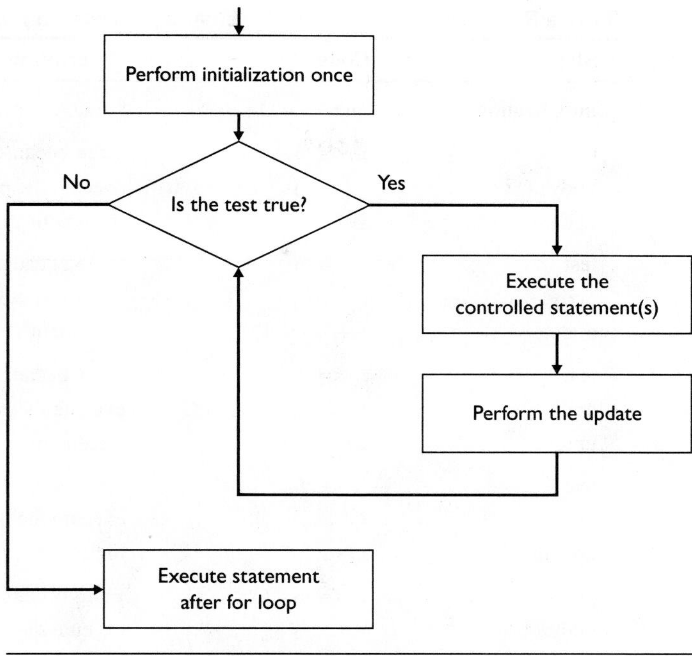

Figure 2.1 Flow of `for` loop

If the continuation test evaluates to `true`, it executes the controlled statements once and executes the update part. Then it performs the test again. If it again evaluates to `true`, it executes the statements again and executes the update again. Notice that the update is performed after the controlled statements are executed. When the test evaluates to `false`, Java is done executing the loop and moves on to whatever statement comes after the loop.

The `for` loop is the first example of a *control structure* that we will study.

Control Structure

A syntactic structure that controls other statements.

You should be careful to use indentation to indicate controlled statements. In the case of the `for` loop, all of the statements in the body of the loop are indented as a way to indicate that they are "inside" the loop.

Tracing for Loops

Let's examine the `for` loop of the `WriteSquares2` program in detail:

```
for (int i = 1; i <= 5; i++) {
    System.out.println(i + " squared = " + (i * i));
}
```

Table 2.6 Trace of for `(int i = 1; i <= 5; i++)`

Step	Code	Description
initialization	`int i = 1;`	variable `i` is created and initialized to `1`
test	`i <= 5`	`true` because `1 <= 5`, so we enter the loop
body	`{...}`	execute the `println` with `i` equal to `1`
update	`i++`	increment `i`, which becomes `2`
test	`i <= 5`	`true` because `2 <= 5`, so we enter the loop
body	`{...}`	execute the `println` with `i` equal to `2`
update	`i++`	increment `i`, which becomes `3`
test	`i <= 5`	`true` because `3 <= 5`, so we enter the loop
body	`{...}`	execute the `println` with `i` equal to `3`
update	`i++`	increment `i`, which becomes `4`
test	`i <= 5`	`true` because `4 <= 5`, so we enter the loop
body	`{...}`	execute the `println` with `i` equal to `4`
update	`i++`	increment `i`, which becomes `5`
test	`i <= 5`	`true` because `5 <= 5`, so we enter the loop
body	`{...}`	execute the `println` with `i` equal to `5`
update	`i++`	increment `i`, which becomes `6`
test	`i <= 5`	`false` because `6 > 5`, so we are finished

In this loop, the initialization (`int i = 1`) declares an integer variable `i` that is initialized to `1`. The continuation test (`i <= 5`) indicates that we should keep executing as long as `i` is less than or equal to `5`. That means that once `i` is greater than `5`, we will stop executing the body of the loop. The update (`i++`) will increment the value of `i` by one each time, bringing `i` closer to being larger than `5`. After five executions of the body and the accompanying five updates, `i` will be larger than 5 and the loop will finish executing. Table 2.6 traces this process in detail.

Java allows great flexibility in deciding what to include in the initialization part and the update, so we can use the `for` loop to solve all sorts of programming tasks. For now, though, we will restrict ourselves to a particular kind of loop that declares and initializes a single variable that is used to control the loop. This variable is often referred to as the *control variable* of the loop. In the test we compare the control variable against some final desired value, and in the update we change the value of the control variable, most often incrementing it by `1`. Such loops are very common in programming. By convention, we often use names like `i`, `j`, and `k` for the control variables.

Each execution of the controlled statement of a loop is called an *iteration* of the loop (as in, "The loop finished executing after four iterations"). Iteration also refers to looping in general (as in, "I solved the problem using iteration").

Consider another `for` loop:

```
for (int i = 100; i <= 100; i++) {
    System.out.println(i + " squared = " + (i * i));
}
```

This loop executes a total of 201 times, producing the squares of all the integers between `-100` and `+100` inclusive. The values used in the initialization and the test, then, can be any integers. They can, in fact, be arbitrary integer expressions:

```
for (int i = (2 + 2); i <= (17 * 3); i++) {
    System.out.println(i + " squared = " + (i * i));
}
```

This loop will generate the squares of all the integers between `4` and `51` inclusive. The parentheses around the expressions are not necessary but improve readability. Consider the following loop:

```
for (int i = 1; i <= 30; i++) {
    System.out.println("+--------+");
}
```

This loop generates 30 lines of output, all exactly the same. It is slightly different from the previous one because the statement controlled by the `for` loop makes no reference to the control variable. Thus,

```
for (int i = -30; i <= -1; i++) {
    System.out.println("+--------+");
}
```

generates exactly the same output. The behavior of such a loop is determined solely by the number of iterations it performs. The number of iterations is given by

```
<ending value> - <starting value> + 1
```

It is much simpler to see that the first of these loops iterates 30 times, so it is better to use that loop.

Now let's look at some borderline cases. Consider this loop:

```
for (int i = 1; i <= 1; i++) {
    System.out.println("+--------+");
}
```

According to our rule it should iterate once, and it does. It initializes the variable `i` to `1` and tests to see if this is less than or equal to `1`, which it is. So it executes the `println`, increments `i`, and tests again. The second time it tests, it finds that `i` is no longer less than or equal to `1`, so it stops executing. Now consider this loop:

```
for (int i = 1; i <= 0; i++) {
    System.out.println("+--------+"); // never executes
}
```

This loop performs no iterations at all. It will not cause an execution error; it just won't execute the body. It initializes the variable to `1` and tests to see if this is less than or equal to `0`. It isn't, so rather than executing the statements in the body, it stops there.

When you construct a `for` loop, you can include more than one statement inside the curly braces. Consider, for example, the following code:

```
for (int i = 1; i <= 20; i++) {
    System.out.println("Hi!");
    System.out.println("Ho!");
}
```

This will produce 20 pairs of lines, the first of which has the word "Hi!" on it and the second of which has the word "Ho!"

When a `for` loop controls a single statement, you don't have to include the curly braces. The curly braces are required only for situations like the previous one, where you have more than one statement that you want the loop to control. However, the Java coding convention includes the curly braces even for a single statement, and we follow this convention in this book. There are two advantages to this convention:

- Including the curly braces prevents future errors. Even if you need only one statement in the body of your loop now, your code is likely to change over time. Having the curly braces there ensures that, if you add an extra statement to the body later, you won't accidentally forget to include them. In general, including curly braces in advance is cheaper than locating obscure bugs later.
- Always including the curly braces reduces the level of detail you have to consider as you learn new control structures. It takes time to master the details of any new control structure, and it will be easier to master those details if you don't have to also be thinking about when to include and when not to include the braces.

Common Programming Error

Forgetting Curly Braces

You should use indentation to indicate the body of a `for` loop, but indentation alone is not enough. Java ignores indentation when it is deciding how different statements are grouped. Suppose, for example, that you were to write the following code:

```
for (int i = 1; i <= 20; i++)
    System.out.println("Hi!");
    System.out.println("Ho!");
```

The indentation indicates to the reader that both of the `println` statements are in the body of the `for` loop, but there aren't any curly braces to indicate that to Java. As a result, this code is interpreted as follows:

Continued on next page

Continued from previous page

```
for (int i = 1; i <= 20; i++) {
    System.out.println("Hi!");
}
System.out.println("Ho!");
```

Only the first `println` is considered to be in the body of the `for` loop. The second `println` is considered to be outside the loop. So, this code would produce 20 lines of output that all say "Hi!" followed by one line of output that says "Ho!" To include both `println`s in the body, you need curly braces around them:

```
for (int i = 1; i <= 20; i++) {
    System.out.println("Hi!");
    System.out.println("Ho!");
}
```

`for` Loop Patterns

In general, if you want a loop to iterate exactly *n* times, you will use one of two standard loops. The first standard form looks like the ones you have already seen:

```
for (int <variable> = 1; <variable> <= n; i++) {
    <statement>;
    <statement>;
    ...
    <statement>;
}
```

It's pretty clear that this loop executes *n* times, because it starts at `1` and continues as long as it is less than or equal to *n*. For example, this loop prints the numbers 1 through 10:

```
for (int i = 1; i <= 10; i++) {
    System.out.print(i + " ");
}
```

Because it uses a `print` instead of a `println` statement, it produces a single line of output:

```
1 2 3 4 5 6 7 8 9 10
```

Often, however, it is more convenient to start our counting at `0` instead of `1`. That requires a change in the loop test to allow you to stop when *n* is one less:

```
for (int <variable> = 0; <variable> < n; i++) {
    <statement>;
    <statement>;
    ...
    <statement>;
}
```

Notice that in this form when you initialize the variable to `0`, you test whether it is strictly less than *n*. Either form will execute exactly *n* times, although there are some situations where the zero-based loop works better. For example, this loop executes 10 times just like the previous loop:

```
for (int i = 0; i < 10; i++) {
    System.out.print(i + " ");
}
```

Because it starts at `0` instead of starting at `1`, it produces a different sequence of 10 values:

```
0 1 2 3 4 5 6 7 8 9
```

Most often you will use the loop that starts at `0` or `1` to perform some operation a fixed number of times. But there is a slight variation that is also sometimes useful. Instead of running the loop in a forward direction, we can run it backward. Instead of starting at `1` and executing until you reach *n*, you instead start at *n* and keep executing until you reach `1`. You can accomplish this by using a decrement rather than an increment, so we sometimes refer to this as a decrementing loop.

Here is the general form of a decrementing loop:

```
for (int <variable> = n; <variable> >= 1; <variable>—) {
    <statement>;
    <statement>;
    ...
    <statement>;
}
```

For example, here is a decrementing loop that executes 10 times:

```
for (int i = 10; i >= 1; i--) {
    System.out.print(i + " ");
}
```

Because it runs backward, it prints the values in reverse order:

```
10 9 8 7 6 5 4 3 2 1
```

Nested for Loops

VideoNote

The for loop controls a statement, and the for loop is itself a statement, which means that one for loop can control another for loop. For example, you can write code like the following:

```
for (int i = 1; i <= 10; i++) {
    for (int j = 1; j <= 5; j++) {
        System.out.println("Hi there.");
    }
}
```

This code is probably easier to read from the inside out. The println statement produces a single line of output. The inner j loop executes this statement five times, producing five lines of output. The outer i loop executes the inner loop 10 times, which produces 10 sets of 5 lines, or 50 lines of output. The preceding code, then, is equivalent to

```
for (int i = 1; i <= 50; i++) {
    System.out.println("Hi there.");
}
```

This example shows that a for loop can be controlled by another for loop. Such a loop is called a *nested loop*. This example wasn't very interesting, though, because the nested loop can be eliminated.

Now that you know how to write for loops, you will want to be able to produce complex lines of output piece by piece using the print command. Recall from Chapter 1 that the print command prints on the current line of output without going to a new line of output. For example, if you want to produce a line of output that has 80 stars on it, you can use a print command to print one star at a time and have it execute 80 times rather than using a single println.

Let's look at a more interesting nested loop that uses a print command:

```
for (int i = 1; i <= 6; i++) {
    for (int j = 1; j <= 3; j++) {
        System.out.print(j + " ");
    }
}
```

We can once again read this from the inside out. The inner loop prints the value of its control variable j as it varies from 1 to 3. The outer loop executes this six different times. As a result, we get six occurrences of the sequence 1 2 3 as output:

```
1 2 3 1 2 3 1 2 3 1 2 3 1 2 3 1 2 3
```

This code prints all of its output on a single line of output. Let's look at some code that includes a combination of `print` and `println` to produce several lines of output:

```
for (int i = 1; i <= 6; i++) {
    for (int j = 1; j <= 10; j++) {
        System.out.print("*");
    }
    System.out.println();
}
```

When you write code that involves nested loops, you have to be careful to indent the code correctly to make the structure clear. At the outermost level, the preceding code is a simple `for` loop that executes six times:

```
for (int i = 1; i <= 6; i++) {
    ...
}
```

We use indentation for the statements inside this `for` loop to make it clear that they are the body of this loop. Inside, we find two statements: another `for` loop and a `println`. Let's look at the inner `for` loop:

```
for (int j = 1; j <= 10; j++) {
    System.out.print("*");
}
```

This loop is controlled by the outer `for` loop, which is why it is indented, but it itself controls a statement (the `print` statement), so we end up with another level of indentation. The indentation thus indicates that the `print` statement is controlled by the inner `for` loop, which in turn is controlled by the outer `for` loop. So what does this inner loop do? It prints 10 stars on the current line of output. They all appear on the same line because we are using a `print` instead of a `println`. Notice that after this loop we perform a `println`:

```
System.out.println();
```

The net effect of the `for` loop followed by the `println` is that we get a line of output with 10 stars on it. But remember that these statements are contained in an outer loop that executes six times, so we end up getting six lines of output, each with 10 stars:

```
**********
**********
**********
**********
**********
**********
```

Let's examine one more variation. In the code above, the inner `for` loop always does exactly the same thing: It prints exactly 10 stars on a line of output. But what happens if we change the test for the inner `for` loop to make use of the outer `for` loop's control variable (`i`)?

```
for (int i = 1; i <= 6; i++) {
    for (int j = 1; j <= i; j++) {
        System.out.print("*");
    }
    System.out.println();
}
```

In the old version the inner loop always executes 10 times, producing 10 stars on each line of output. With the new test (`j <= i`), the inner loop will execute `i` times with each iteration. But `i` is changing: It takes on the values `1`, `2`, `3`, `4`, `5`, and `6`. On the first iteration of the outer loop, when `i` is `1`, the test `j <= i` is effectively testing `j <= 1`, and it generates a line with one star on it. On the second iteration of the outer loop, when `i` is `2`, the test is effectively testing `j <= 2`, and it generates a line with two stars on it. On the third iteration of the outer loop, when `i` is `3`, the test is effectively testing `j <= 3`, and it generates a line with three stars on it. This continues through the sixth iteration.

In other words, this code produces a triangle as output:

```
*
**
***
****
*****
******
```

2.4 Managing Complexity

You've learned about several new programming constructs in this chapter, and it's time to put the pieces together to solve some complex tasks. As we pointed out in Chapter 1, Brian Kernighan, one of the coauthors of *The C Programming Language*, has said that "Controlling complexity is the essence of computer programming." In this section we will examine several techniques that computer scientists use to solve complex problems without being overwhelmed by complexity.

Scope

As programs get longer, it is increasingly likely that different parts of the program will interfere with each other. Java helps us to manage this potential problem by enforcing rules of *scope*.

Scope

The part of a program in which a particular declaration is valid.

As you've seen, when it comes to declaring static methods, you can put them in any order whatsoever. The scope of a static method is the entire class in which it appears. Variables work differently. The simple rule is that the scope of a variable declaration extends from the point where it is declared to the right curly brace that encloses it. In other words, find the pair of curly braces that directly encloses the variable declaration. The scope of the variable is from the point where it is declared to the closing curly brace.

This scope rule has several implications. Consider first what it means for different methods. Each method has its own set of curly braces to indicate the statements to be executed when the method is called. Any variables declared inside a method's curly braces won't be available outside the method. We refer to such variables as *local variables,* and we refer to the process of limiting their scope as *localizing* variables.

Local Variable

A variable declared inside a method that is accessible only in that method.

Localizing Variables

Declaring variables in the innermost (most local) scope possible.

In general, you will want to declare variables in the most local scope possible. You might wonder why we would want to localize variables to just one method. Why not just declare everything in one outer scope? That certainly seems simpler, but there are some important drawbacks. Localizing variables leads to some duplication (and possibly confusion) but provides more security. As an analogy, consider the use of refrigerators in dormitories. Every dorm room can have its own refrigerator, but if you are outside a room, you don't know whether it has a refrigerator in it. The contents of the room are hidden from you.

Java programs use variables to store values just as students use refrigerators to store beer, ice cream, and other valuables. The last time we were in a dorm we noticed that most of the individual rooms had refrigerators in them. This seems terribly redundant, but the reason is obvious. If you want to guarantee the security of something, you put it where nobody else can get it. You will use local variables in your programs in much the same way. If each individual method has its own local variables to use, you don't have to consider possible interference from other parts of the program.

Let's look at a simple example involving two methods:

```
// This program does not compile.
public class ScopeExample {
    public static void main(String[] args) {
```

```
        int x = 3;
        int y = 7;
        computeSum();
    }

    public static void computeSum() {
        int sum = x + y; // illegal, x/y are not in scope
        System.out.println("sum = " + sum);
    }
}
```

In this example, the `main` method declares local variables `x` and `y` and gives them initial values. Then it calls the method `computeSum`. Inside this method, we try to use the values of `x` and `y` to compute a sum. However, because the variables `x` and `y` are local to the `main` method and are not visible inside of the `computeSum` method, this doesn't work. (In the next chapter, we will see a technique for allowing one method to pass a value to another.)

The program produces error messages like the following:

```
ScopeExample.java:10: error: cannot find symbol
symbol  : variable x
location: class ScopeExample
        int sum = x + y;   // illegal, x/y are not in scope
                  ^
ScopeExample.java:10: error: cannot find symbol
symbol  : variable y
location: class ScopeExample
         int sum = x + y;   // illegal, x/y are not in scope
                       ^
```

It's important to understand scope in discussing the local variables of one method versus another. Scope also has implications for what happens inside a single method. You have seen that curly braces are used to group together a series of statements. But you can have curly braces inside curly braces, and this leads to some scope issues. For example, consider the following code:

```
for (int i = 1; i <= 5; i++) {
    int squared = i * i;
    System.out.println(i + " squared = " + squared);
}
```

This is a variation of the code we looked at earlier in the chapter to print out the squares of the first five integers. In this version, a variable called `squared` is used to keep track of the square of the `for` loop control variable. This code works fine, but consider this variation:

```
for (int i = 1; i <= 5; i++) {
    int squared = i * i;
    System.out.println(i + " squared = " + squared);
}
System.out.println("Last square = " + squared); // illegal
```

This code generates a compiler error. The variable `squared` is declared inside the `for` loop. In other words, the curly braces that contain it are the curly braces for the loop. It can't be used outside this scope, so when you attempt to refer to it outside the loop, you'll get a compiler error.

If for some reason you need to write code like this that accesses the variable after the loop, you have to declare the variable in the outer scope before the loop:

```
int squared = 0;   // declaration is now in outer scope
for (int i = 1; i <= 5; i++) {
    squared = i * i;   // change this to an assignment statement
    System.out.println(i + " squared = " + squared);
}
System.out.println("Last square = " + squared); // now legal
```

There are a few special cases for scope, and the `for` loop is one of them. When a variable is declared in the initialization part of a `for` loop, its scope is just the `for` loop itself (the three parts in the `for` loop header and the statements controlled by the `for` loop). That means you can use the same variable name in multiple `for` loops:

```
for (int i = 1; i <= 10; i++) {
    System.out.println(i + " squared = " + (i * i));
}
for (int i = 1; i <= 10; i++) {
    System.out.println(i + " cubed = " + (i * i * i));
}
```

The variable `i` is declared twice in the preceding code, but because the scope of each variable is just the `for` loop in which it is declared, this isn't a problem. (It's like having two dorm rooms, each with its own refrigerator.) Of course, you can't do this with nested `for` loops. The following code, for example, will not compile:

```
for (int i = 1; i <= 5; i++) {
    for (int i = 1; i <= 10; i++) { // illegal
        System.out.println("hi there.");
    }
}
```

When Java encounters the inner `for` loop, it will complain that the variable `i` has already been declared within this scope. You can't declare the same variable twice within the same scope. You have to come up with two different names to distinguish between them, just as when there are two Carls in the same family they tend to be called "Carl Junior" and "Carl Senior" to avoid any potential confusion.

A control variable that is used in a `for` loop doesn't have to be declared in the initialization part of the loop. You can separate the declaration of the `for` loop control variable from the initialization of the variable, as in the following code:

```
int i;
for (i = 1; i <= 5; i++) {
    System.out.println(i + " squared = " + (i * i));
}
```

Doing so extends the variable's scope to the end of the enclosing set of curly braces. One advantage of this approach is that it enables you to refer to the final value of the control variable after the loop. Normally you wouldn't be able to do this, because the control variable's scope would be limited to the loop itself. However, declaring the control variable outside the loop is a dangerous practice, and it provides a good example of the problems you can encounter when you don't localize variables. Consider the following code, for example:

```
int i;
for (i = 1; i <= 5; i++) {
    for (i = 1; i <= 10; i++) {
        System.out.println("hi there.");
    }
}
```

As noted earlier, you shouldn't use the same control variable when you have nested loops. But unlike the previous example, this code compiles, because here the variable declaration is outside the outer `for` loop. So, instead of getting a helpful error message from the Java compiler, you get a program with a bug in it. You'd think from reading these loops that the code will produce 50 lines of output, but it actually produces just 10 lines of output. The inner loop increments the variable `i` until it becomes `11`, and that causes the outer loop to terminate after just one iteration. It can be even worse if you reverse the order of these loops:

```
int i;
for (i = 1; i <= 10; i++) {
    for (i = 1; i <= 5; i++) {
        System.out.println("hi there.");
    }
}
```

This code has an *infinite loop.*

Infinite Loop
A loop that never terminates.

This loop is infinite because no matter what the outer loop does to the variable `i`, the inner loop always sets it back to `1` and iterates until it becomes `6`. The outer loop then increments the variable to `7` and finds that `7` is less than or equal to `10`, so it always goes back to the inner loop, which once again sets the variable back to `1` and iterates up to `6`. This process goes on indefinitely. These are the kinds of interference problems you can get when you fail to localize variables.

Common Programming Error

Referring to the Wrong Loop Variable

The following code is intended to print a triangle of stars. However, it has a subtle bug that causes it to print stars infinitely:

```
for (int i = 1; i <= 6; i++) {
    for (int j = 1; j <= i; i++){
        System.out.print("*");
    }
    System.out.println();
}
```

The problem is in the second line, in the inner `for` loop header's update statement. The programmer meant to write `j++` but instead accidentally wrote `i++`. A trace of the code is shown in Table 2.7.

Table 2.7 Trace of Nested `for` Loop

Step	Code	Description
initialization	`int i = 1;`	variable `i` is created and initialized to `1`
initialization	`int j = 1;`	variable `j` is created and initialized to `1`
test	`j <= i`	`true` because `1 <= 1`, so we enter the inner loop
body	`{...}`	execute the `print` with `j` equal to `1`
update	`i++`	increment `i`, which becomes `2`
test	`j <= i`	`true` because `1 <= 2`, so we enter the inner loop
body	`{...}`	execute the `print` with `j` equal to `1`
update	`i++`	increment `i`, which becomes `3`
...	...	...

The variable `j` should be increasing, but instead `i` is increasing. The effect of this mistake is that the variable `j` is never incremented in the inner loop, and therefore the test of `j <= i` never fails, so the inner loop doesn't terminate.

Continued on next page

Continued from previous page

Here's another broken piece of code. This one tries to print a 6 × 4 box of stars, but it also prints infinitely:

```
for (int i = 1; i <= 6; i++) {
    for (int j = 1; i <= 4; j++) {
        System.out.print("*");
    }
    System.out.println();
}
```

The problem is on the second line, this time in the inner `for` loop header's test. The programmer meant to write `j <= 4` but instead accidentally wrote `i <= 4`. Since the value of `i` is never incremented in the inner loop, the test of `i <= 4` never fails, so the inner loop again doesn't terminate.

Pseudocode

As you write more complex algorithms, you will find that you can't just write the entire algorithm immediately. Instead, you will increasingly make use of the technique of writing *pseudocode.*

Pseudocode

English-like descriptions of algorithms. Programming with pseudocode involves successively refining an informal description until it is easily translated into Java.

For example, you can describe the problem of drawing a box as

```
draw a box with 50 lines and 30 columns of asterisks.
```

While this statement describes the figure, it does not give specific instructions about how to draw it (that is, what algorithm to use). Do you draw the figure line by line or column by column? In Java, figures like these must be generated line by line, because once a `println` has been performed on a line of output, that line cannot be changed. There is no command for going back to a previous line in the output. Therefore, you must output the first line in its entirety, then the second line in its entirety, and so on. As a result, your decompositions for figures such as these will be line-oriented at the top level. Thus, a version of the statement that is closer to Java is

```
for (each of 50 lines) {
    draw a line of 30 asterisks.
}
```

This instruction can be made more specific by introducing the idea of repeatedly writing a single character on the output line and then moving to a new line of output:

```
for (each of 50 lines) {
    for (each of 30 columns) {
        write one asterisk on the output line.
    }
    go to a new output line.
}
```

Using pseudocode, you can gradually convert an English description into something that is easily translated into a Java program. The simple examples we've looked at so far are hardly worth the application of pseudocode, so we will now examine the problem of generating a more complex figure:

```
*********
 *******
  *****
   ***
    *
```

This figure must also be generated line by line:

```
for (each of 5 lines) {
    draw one line of the triangle.
}
```

Unfortunately, each line is different. Therefore, you must come up with a general rule that fits all the lines. The first line of this figure has a series of asterisks on it with no leading spaces. Each of the subsequent lines has a series of spaces followed by a series of asterisks. Using your imagination a bit, you can say that the first line has 0 spaces on it followed by a series of asterisks. This allows you to write a general rule for making this figure:

```
for (each of 5 lines) {
    write some spaces (possibly 0) on the output line.
    write some asterisks on the output line.
    go to a new output line.
}
```

In order to proceed, you must determine a rule for the number of spaces and a rule for the number of asterisks. Assuming that the lines are numbered 1 through 5, looking at the figure, you can fill in Table 2.8.

You want to find a relationship between line number and the other two columns. This is simple algebra, because these columns are related in a linear way. The second

Table 2.8 Analysis of Figure

Line	Spaces	Asterisks
1	0	9
2	1	7
3	2	5
4	3	3
5	4	1

column is easy to get from the line number. It equals `(line – 1)`. The third column is a little tougher. Because it goes down by 2 every time and the first column goes up by 1 every time, you need a multiplier of –2. Then you need an appropriate constant. The number 11 seems to do the trick, so you can make the third column equal `(11 – 2 * line)`. You can improve your pseudocode, then, as follows:

```
for (line going 1 to 5) {
    write (line – 1) spaces on the output line.
    write (11 – 2 * line) asterisks on the output line.
    go to a new output line.
}
```

This pseudocode is simple to turn into a program:

```
public class DrawV {
    public static void main(String[] args) {
        for (int line = 1; line <= 5; line++) {
            for (int i = 1; i <= (line – 1); i++) {
                System.out.print(" ");
            }
            for (int i = 1; i <= (11 – 2 * line); i++) {
                System.out.print("*");
            }
            System.out.println();
        }
    }
}
```

Sometimes we manage complexity by taking advantage of work that we have already done. For example, how would you produce this figure?

```
    *
   ***
  *****
 *******
*********
```

You could follow the same process you did before and find new expressions that produce the appropriate number of spaces and asterisks. However, there is an easier way. This figure is the same as the previous one, except the lines appear in reverse order. This is a good place to use a decrementing loop to run the `for` loop backward: Instead of starting at `1` and going up to `5` with a ++ update, you can start at `5` and go down to `1` using a –– update.

The simple way to produce the upward-pointing triangle, then, is with the following code:

```
public class DrawCone {
    public static void main(String[] args) {
        for (int line = 5; line >= 1; line--) {
            for (int i = 1; i <= (line - 1); i++) {
                System.out.print(" ");
            }
            for (int i = 1; i <= (11 - 2 * line); i++) {
                System.out.print("*");
            }
            System.out.println();
        }
    }
}
```

Class Constants

The `DrawCone` program in the last section draws a cone with five lines. How would you modify it to produce a cone with three lines? Your first thought might be to simply change the `5` in the code to a `3`. However, that would cause the program to produce the following output:

```
  *****
 *******
*********
```

which is obviously wrong. If you work through the geometry of the figure, you will discover that the problem is with the use of the number `11` in the expression that calculates the number of asterisks to print. The number `11` comes from this formula:

```
2 * (number of lines) + 1
```

Thus, when the number of lines is five, the appropriate value is `11`, but when the number of lines is three, the appropriate value is `7`. Programmers call numbers like these *magic numbers*. They are magic in the sense that they seem to make the program work, but their definition is not always obvious. Glancing at the `DrawCone` program, one is apt to ask, "Why 5? Why 11? Why 3? Why 7? Why me?"

To make programs more readable and more adaptable, you should try to avoid magic numbers whenever possible. You do so by storing the magic numbers. You can use variables to store these values, but that is misleading, given that you are trying to represent values that don't change. Fortunately, Java offers an alternative: You can declare values that are similar to variables but that are guaranteed to have constant values. Not surprisingly, they are called *constants*. We most often define *class constants,* which can be accessed throughout the entire class.

Class Constant

A named value that cannot be changed. A class constant can be accessed anywhere in the class (i.e., its scope is the entire class).

You can choose a descriptive name for a constant that explains what it represents. You can then use that name instead of referring to the specific value to make your programs more readable and adaptable. For example, in the `DrawCone` program, you might want to introduce a constant called `LINES` that represents the number of lines (recall from Chapter 1 that we use all uppercase letters for constant names). You can use that constant in place of the magic number `5` and as part of an expression to calculate a value. This approach allows you to replace the magic number `11` with the formula from which it is derived (`2 * LINES + 1`).

Constants are declared with the keyword `final`, which indicates the fact that their values cannot be changed once assigned, as in

```
final int LINES = 5;
```

You can declare a constant anywhere you can declare a variable, but because constants are often used by several different methods, we generally declare them outside methods. This causes another run-in with our old pal, the `static` keyword. If you want your static methods to be able to access your constants, the constants themselves must be static. Likewise, just as we declare our methods to be public, we usually declare our constants to be public. The following is the general syntax for constant definitions:

```
public static final <type> <name> = <expression>;
```

For example, here are definitions for two constants:

```
public static final int HEIGHT = 10;
public static final int WIDTH = 20;
```

These definitions create constants called `HEIGHT` and `WIDTH` that will always have the values `10` and `20`, respectively. These are known as class constants, because we declare them in the outermost scope of the class, along with the methods of the class. That way, they are visible in each method of the class.

We've already mentioned that we can avoid using a magic number in the `DrawCone` program by introducing a constant for the number of lines. Here's what the constant definition looks like:

```
public static final int LINES = 5;
```

We can now replace the `5` in the outer loop with this constant and replace the `11` in the second inner loop with the expression `2 * LINES + 1`. The result is the following program:

```
public class DrawCone2 {
    public static final int LINES = 5;

    public static void main(String[] args) {
        for (int line = LINES; line >= 1; line--) {
            for (int i = 1; i <= (line - 1); i++) {
                System.out.print(" ");
            }
            int stars = 2 * LINES + 1 - 2 * line;
            for (int i = 1; i <= stars; i++) {
                System.out.print("*");
            }
            System.out.println();
        }
    }
}
```

Notice that in this program the expression for the number of stars has become sufficiently complex that we've introduced a local variable called `stars` to store the value. The advantage of this program is that it is more readable and more adaptable. A simple change to the constant `LINES` will make it produce a figure with a different number of lines.

2.5 Case Study: Hourglass Figure

VideoNote

Now we'll consider an example that is even more complex. To solve it, we will follow three basic steps:

1. Decompose the task into subtasks, each of which will become a static method.
2. For each subtask, make a table for the figure and compute formulas for each column of the table in terms of the line number.
3. Convert the tables into actual `for` loop code for each method.

The output we want to produce is the following:

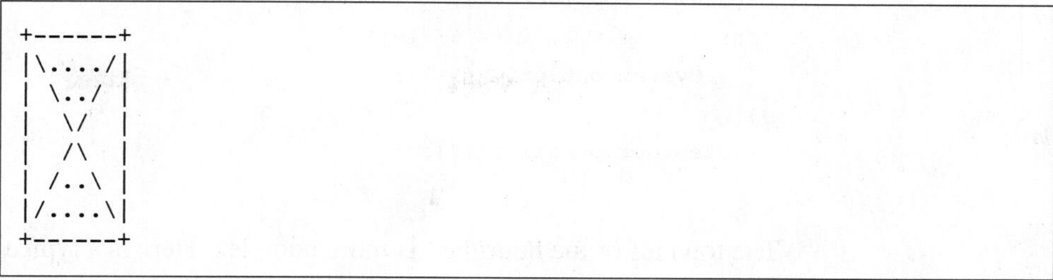

```
+------+
|\..../|
| \../ |
|  \/  |
|  /\  |
| /..\ |
|/....\|
+------+
```

Problem Decomposition and Pseudocode

To generate this figure, you have to first break it down into subfigures. In doing so, you should look for lines that are similar in one way or another. The first and last lines are exactly the same. The three lines after the first line all fit one pattern, and the three lines after that fit another:

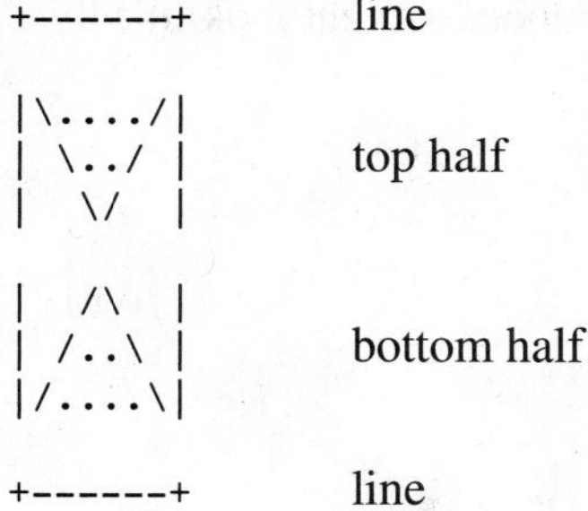

```
+------+     line

|\..../|
| \../ |     top half
|  \/  |

|  /\  |
| /..\ |     bottom half
|/....\|

+------+     line
```

Thus, you can break down the overall problem as follows:

```
draw a solid line.
draw the top half of the hourglass.
draw the bottom half of the hourglass.
draw a solid line.
```

You should solve each subproblem independently. Eventually you'll want to incorporate a class constant to make the program more flexible, but let's first solve the problem without worrying about the use of a constant.

The solid line task can be further specified as

```
write a plus on the output line.
write 6 dashes on the output line.
write a plus on the output line.
go to a new output line.
```

This set of instructions translates easily into a static method:

```
public static void drawLine() {
    System.out.print("+");
    for (int i = 1; i <= 6; i++) {
        System.out.print("-");
    }
    System.out.println("+");
}
```

The top half of the hourglass is more complex. Here is a typical line:

```
| \../ |
```

There are four individual characters, separated by spaces and dots.

```
|        \      . .      /        |
bar  spaces  backslash  dots  slash  spaces  bar
```

Thus, a first approximation in pseudocode might look like this:

```
for (each of 3 lines) {
    write a bar on the output line.
    write some spaces on the output line.
    write a backslash on the output line.
    write some dots on the output line.
    write a slash on the output line.
    write some spaces on the output line.
    write a bar on the output line.
    go to a new line of output.
}
```

Again, you can make a table to figure out the required expressions. Writing the individual characters will be easy enough to translate into Java, but you need to be more specific about the spaces and dots. Each line in this group contains two sets of spaces and one set of dots. Table 2.9 shows how many to use.

The two sets of spaces fit the rule `(line – 1)`, and the number of dots is `(6 – 2 * line)`. Therefore, the pseudocode should read

```
for (line going 1 to 3) {
    write a bar on the output line.
    write (line – 1) spaces on the output line.
    write a backslash on the output line.
    write (6 – 2 * line) dots on the output line.
    write a slash on the output line.
    write (line – 1) spaces on the output line.
    write a bar on the output line.
    go to a new line of output.
}
```

Table 2.9 Analysis of Figure

Line	Spaces	Dots	Spaces
1	0	4	0
2	1	2	1
3	2	0	2

Initial Structured Version

The pseudocode for the top half of the hourglass is easily translated into a static method called `drawTop`. A similar solution exists for the bottom half of the hourglass. Put together, the program looks like this:

```
public class DrawFigure {
    public static void main(String[] args) {
        drawLine();
        drawTop();
        drawBottom();
        drawLine();
    }

    // produces a solid line
    public static void drawLine() {
        System.out.print("+");
        for (int i = 1; i <= 6; i++) {
            System.out.print("-");
        }
        System.out.println("+");
    }

    // produces the top half of the hourglass figure
    public static void drawTop() {
        for (int line = 1; line <= 3; line++) {
            System.out.print("|");
            for (int i = 1; i <= (line - 1); i++) {
                System.out.print(" ");
            }
            System.out.print("\\");
            for (int i = 1; i <= (6 - 2 * line); i++) {
                System.out.print(".");
            }
            System.out.print("/");
            for (int i = 1; i <= (line - 1); i++) {
                System.out.print(" ");
            }
```

```
            System.out.println("|");
        }
    }

    // produces the bottom half of the hourglass figure
    public static void drawBottom() {
        for (int line = 1; line <= 3; line++) {
            System.out.print("|");
            for (int i = 1; i <= (3  line); i++) {
                System.out.print(" ");
            }
            System.out.print("/");
            for (int i = 1; i <= 2 * (line  1); i++) {
                System.out.print(".");
            }
            System.out.print("\\");
            for (int i = 1; i <= (3  line); i++) {
                System.out.print(" ");
            }
            System.out.println("|");
        }
    }
}
```

Adding a Class Constant

The DrawFigure program produces the desired output, but it is not very flexible. What if we wanted to produce a similar figure of a different size? The original problem involved an hourglass figure that had three lines in the top half and three lines in the bottom half. What if we wanted the following output, with four lines in the top half and four lines in the bottom half?

```
+--------+
|\....../|
| \..../ |
|  \../  |
|   \/   |
|   /\   |
|  /..\  |
| /....\ |
|/......\|
+--------+
```

Obviously the program would be more useful if we could make it flexible enough to produce either output. We do so by eliminating the magic numbers with the introduction of a class constant. You might think that we need to introduce two constants—one for the height and one for the width—but because of the regularity of this

Table 2.10 Analysis of Different Height Figures

Subheight	Dashes in `drawLine`	Spaces in `drawTop`	Dots in `drawTop`	Spaces in `drawBottom`	Dots in `drawBottom`
3	6	`line – 1`	`6 – 2 * line`	`3 – line`	`2 * (line – 1)`
4	8	`line – 1`	`8 – 2 * line`	`4 – line`	`2 * (line – 1)`

figure, the height is determined by the width and vice versa. Consequently, we only need to introduce a single class constant. Let's use the height of the hourglass halves:

```
public static final int SUB_HEIGHT = 4;
```

We've called the constant `SUB_HEIGHT` rather than `HEIGHT` because it refers to the height of each of the two halves, rather than the figure as a whole. Notice how we use the underscore character to separate the different words in the name of the constant.

So, how do we modify the original program to incorporate this constant? We look through the program for any magic numbers and insert the constant or an expression involving the constant where appropriate. For example, both the `drawTop` and `drawBottom` methods have a `for` loop that executes 3 times to produce 3 lines of output. We change this to 4 to produce 4 lines of output, and more generally, we change it to `SUB_HEIGHT` to produce `SUB_HEIGHT` lines of output.

In other parts of the program we have to update our formulas for the number of dashes, spaces, and dots. Sometimes we can use educated guesses to figure out how to adjust such a formula to use the constant. If you can't guess a proper formula, you can use the table technique to find the appropriate formula. Using this new output with a subheight of 4, you can update the various formulas in the program. Table 2.10 shows the various formulas.

We then go through each formula and figure out how to replace it with a new formula involving the constant. The number of dashes increases by 2 when the subheight increases by 1, so we need a multiplier of 2. The expression `2 * SUB_HEIGHT` produces the correct values. The number of spaces in `drawTop` does not change with the subheight, so the expression does not need to be altered. The number of dots in `drawTop` involves the number 6 for a subheight of 3 and the number 8 for a subheight of 4. Once again we need a multiplier of 2, so we use the expression `2 * SUB_HEIGHT – 2 * line`. The number of spaces in `drawBottom` involves the value 3 for a subheight of 3 and the value 4 for a subheight of 4, so the generalized expression is `SUB_HEIGHT – line`. The number of dots in `drawBottom` does not change when subheight changes.

Here is the new version of the program with a class constant for the subheight. It uses a `SUB_HEIGHT` value of `4`, but we could change this to `3` to produce the smaller version or to some other value to produce yet another version of the figure.

```
public class DrawFigure2 {
    public static final int SUB_HEIGHT = 4;

    public static void main(String[] args) {
        drawLine();
```

```
        drawTop();
        drawBottom();
        drawLine();
    }

    // produces a solid line
    public static void drawLine() {
        System.out.print("+");
        for (int i = 1; i <= (2 * SUB_HEIGHT); i++) {
            System.out.print("-");
        }
        System.out.println("+");
    }

    // produces the top half of the hourglass figure
    public static void drawTop() {
        for (int line = 1; line <= SUB_HEIGHT; line++) {
            System.out.print("|");
            for (int i = 1; i <= (line - 1); i++) {
                System.out.print(" ");
            }
            System.out.print("\\");
            int dots = 2 * SUB_HEIGHT - 2 * line;
            for (int i = 1; i <= dots; i++) {
                System.out.print(".");
            }
            System.out.print("/");
            for (int i = 1; i <= (line - 1); i++) {
                System.out.print(" ");
            }
            System.out.println("|");
        }
    }

    // produces the bottom half of the hourglass figure
    public static void drawBottom() {
        for (int line = 1; line <= SUB_HEIGHT; line++) {
            System.out.print("|");
            for (int i = 1; i <= (SUB_HEIGHT - line); i++) {
                System.out.print(" ");
            }
            System.out.print("/");
            for (int i = 1; i <= 2 * (line - 1); i++) {
                System.out.print(".");
            }
```

```
            System.out.print("\\");
            for (int i = 1; i <= (SUB_HEIGHT  line); i++) {
                System.out.print(" ");
            }
            System.out.println("|");
        }
    }
}
```

Notice that the `SUB_HEIGHT` constant is declared with class-wide scope, rather than locally in the individual methods. While localizing variables is a good idea, the same is not true for constants. We localize variables to avoid potential interference, but that argument doesn't hold for constants, since they are guaranteed not to change. Another argument for using local variables is that it makes static methods more independent. That argument has some merit when applied to constants, but not enough. It is true that class constants introduce dependencies between methods, but often that is what you want. For example, the three methods in `DrawFigure2` should not be independent of each other when it comes to the size of the figure. Each subfigure has to use the same size constant. Imagine the potential disaster if each method had its own `SUB_HEIGHT`, each with a different value—none of the pieces would fit together.

Further Variations

The solution we have arrived at may seem cumbersome, but it adapts more easily to a new task than does our original program. For example, suppose that you want to generate the following output:

```
+----------+
|\......../|
| \....../ |
|  \..../  |
|   \../   |
|    \/    |
|    /\    |
|   /..\   |
|  /....\  |
| /......\ |
|/........\|
+----------+
|    /\    |
|   /..\   |
|  /....\  |
| /......\ |
|/........\|
|\......../|
| \....../ |
|  \..../  |
|   \../   |
|    \/    |
+----------+
```

This output uses a subheight of 5 and includes both a diamond pattern and an X pattern. You can produce this output by changing the `SUB_HEIGHT` constant to `5`:

```
public static final int SUB_HEIGHT = 5;
```

and rewriting the `main` method as follows to produce both the original X pattern and the new diamond pattern, which you get simply by reversing the order of the calls on the two halves:

```
public static void main(String[] args) {
    drawLine();
    drawTop();
    drawBottom();
    drawLine();
    drawBottom();
    drawTop();
    drawLine();
}
```

Chapter Summary

Java groups data into types. There are two major categories of data types: primitive data and objects. Primitive types include `int` (integers), `double` (real numbers), `char` (individual text characters), and `boolean` (logical values).

Values and computations are called expressions. The simplest expressions are individual values, also called literals. Some example literals are: `42`, `3.14`, `'Q'`, and `false`. Expressions may contain operators, as in `(3 + 29) – 4 * 5`. The division operation is odd in that it's split into quotient (`/`) and remainder (`%`) operations.

Rules of precedence determine the order in which multiple operators are evaluated in complex expressions. Multiplication and division are performed before addition and subtraction. Parentheses can be used to force a particular order of evaluation.

Data can be converted from one type to another by an operation called a cast.

Variables are memory locations in which values can be stored. A variable is declared with a name and a type. Any data value with a compatible type can be stored in the variable's memory and used later in the program.

Primitive data can be printed on the console using the `System.out.println` method, just like text strings. A string can be connected to another value (concatenated) with the + operator to produce a larger string. This feature allows you to print complex expressions including numbers and text on the console.

A loop is used to execute a group of statements several times. The `for` loop is one kind of loop that can be used to apply the same statements over a range of numbers or to repeat statements a specified number of times. A loop can contain another loop, called a nested loop.

A variable exists from the line where it is declared to the right curly brace that encloses it. This range, also called the scope of the variable, constitutes the part of the program where the variable can legally be used. A variable declared inside a method or loop is called a local variable. A local variable can only be used inside its method or loop.

An algorithm can be easier to write if you first write an English description of it. Such a description is also called pseudocode.

Important constant values written into a program should be declared as class constants, both to explain their names and values and to make it easier to change their values later.

Self-Check Problems

Section 2.1: Basic Data Concepts

1. Which of the following are legal `int` literals?

```
22    1.5    -1    2.3    10.0    5.    -6875309    '7'
```

2. What is the result of the following expression?

```
1 + 2 * 3 + 7 * 2 % 5
```

a. `1` b. `2` c. `5` d. `11` e. `21`

3. Trace the evaluation of the following expressions, and give their resulting values:

a. `2 + 3 * 4 - 6`
b. `14 / 7 * 2 + 30 / 5 + 1`
c. `(12 + 3) / 4 * 2`
d. `(238 % 10 + 3) % 7`
e. `(18 - 7) * (43 % 10)`
f. `2 + 19 % 5 - (11 * (5 / 2))`
g. `813 % 100 / 3 + 2.4`
h. `26 % 10 % 4 * 3`
i. `22 + 4 * 2`
j. `23 % 8 % 3`
k. `12 - 2 - 3`
l. `6/2 + 7/3`
m. `6 * 7 % 4`
n. `3 * 4 + 2 * 3`
o. `177 % 100 % 10 / 2`
p. `89 % (5 + 5) % 5`
q. `392 / 10 % 10 / 2`
r. `8 * 2 - 7 / 4`
s. `37 % 20 % 3 * 4`
t. `17 % 10 / 4`

4. Trace the evaluation of the following expressions, and give their resulting values:

a. `4.0 / 2 * 9 / 2`
b. `2.5 * 2 + 8 / 5.0 + 10 / 3`
c. `12 / 7 * 4.4 * 2 / 4`
d. `4 * 3 / 8 + 2.5 * 2`
e. `(5 * 7.0 / 2 – 2.5) / 5 * 2`
f. `41 % 7 * 3 / 5 + 5 / 2 * 2.5`
g. `10.0 / 2 / 4`
h. `8 / 5 + 13 / 2 / 3.0`
i. `(2.5 + 3.5) / 2`
j. `9 / 4 * 2.0 – 5 / 4`
k. `9 / 2.0 + 7 / 3 – 3.0 / 2`
l. `813 % 100 / 3 + 2.4`
m. `27 / 2 / 2.0 * (4.3 + 1.7) – 8 / 3`
n. `53 / 5 / (0.6 + 1.4) / 2 + 13 / 2`
o. `2 * 3 / 4 * 2 / 4.0 + 4.5 – 1`
p. `89 % 10 / 4 * 2.0 / 5 + (1.5 + 1.0 / 2) * 2`

5. Trace the evaluation of the following expressions, and give their resulting values:

a. `2 + 2 + 3 + 4`
b. `"2 + 2" + 3 + 4`
c. `2 + " 2 + 3 " + 4`
d. `3 + 4 + " 2 + 2"`
e. `"2 + 2 " + (3 + 4)`
f. `"(2 + 2) " + (3 + 4)`
g. `"hello 34 " + 2 * 4`
h. `2 + "(int) 2.0" + 2 * 2 + 2`
i. `4 + 1 + 9 + "." + (-3 + 10) + 11 / 3`
j. `8 + 6 * –2 + 4 + "0" + (2 + 5)`
k. `1 + 1 + "8 – 2" + (8 – 2) + 1 + 1`
l. `5 + 2 + "(1 + 1)" + 4 + 2 * 3`
m. `"1" + 2 + 3 + "4" + 5 * 6 + "7" + (8 + 9)`

Section 2.2: Variables

6. Which of the following choices is the correct syntax for declaring a real number variable named `grade` and initializing its value to `4.0`?

a. `int grade : 4.0;`
b. `grade = double 4.0;`
c. `double grade = 4.0;`
d. `grade = 4;`
e. `4.0 = grade;`

7. Imagine you are writing a personal fitness program that stores the user's age, gender, height (in feet or meters), and weight (to the nearest pound or kilogram). Declare variables with the appropriate names and types to hold this information.

8. Imagine you are writing a program that stores a student's year (Freshman, Sophomore, Junior, or Senior), the number of courses the student is taking, and his or her GPA on a 4.0 scale. Declare variables with the appropriate names and types to hold this information.

9. Suppose you have an `int` variable called `number`. What Java expression produces the last digit of the number (the 1s place)?

10. The following program contains 9 mistakes! What are they?

```
public class Oops2 {
    public static void main(String[] args) {
        int x;
        System.out.println("x is" x);

        int x = 15.2;    // set x to 15.2
        System.out.println("x is now + x");

        int y;           // set y to 1 more than x
        y = int x + 1;
        System.out.println("x and y are " + x + and + y);
    }
}
```

11. Suppose you have an `int` variable called `number`. What Java expression produces the second-to-last digit of the number (the 10s place)? What expression produces the third-to-last digit of the number (the 100s place)?

12. What is the value of variable x after the following code executes?

```
int x = 3;
x = x + 2;
x = x + x;
```

a. 3 b. 5 c. 7 d. 10 e. 12

13. What are the values of `a`, `b`, and `c` after the following statements?

```
int a = 5;
int b = 10;
int c = b;

a = a + 1;
b = b - 1;
c = c + a;
```

14. What are the values of `first` and `second` at the end of the following code? How would you describe the net effect of the code statements in this exercise?

```
int first = 8;
int second = 19;
first = first + second;
second = first – second;
first = first – second;
```

15. Rewrite the code from the previous exercise to be shorter, by declaring the variables together and by using the special assignment operators (e.g., `+=` , `-=`, `*=`, and `/=`) as appropriate.

16. What are the values of `i`, `j`, and `k` after the following statements?

```
int i = 2;
int j = 3;
int k = 4;
int x = i + j + k;


i = x - i - j;
j = x - j - k;
k = x - i - k;
```

17. What is the output from the following code?

```
int max;
int min = 10;
max = 17 - 4 / 10;
max = max + 6;
min = max - min;
System.out.println(max * 2);
System.out.println(max + min);
System.out.println(max);
System.out.println(min);
```

18. Suppose you have a real number variable *x*. Write a Java expression that computes the following value *y* while using the `*` operator only four times:

$$y = 12.3x^4 - 9.1x^3 + 19.3x^2 - 4.6x + 34.2$$

19. The following program redundantly repeats the same expressions many times. Modify the program to remove all redundant expressions using variables of appropriate types.

```
public class ComputePay {
    public static void main(String[] args) {
        // Calculate pay at work based on hours worked each day
        System.out.println("My total hours worked:");
        System.out.println(4 + 5 + 8 + 4);

        System.out.println("My hourly salary:");
        System.out.println("$8.75");

        System.out.println("My total pay:");
        System.out.println((4 + 5 + 8 + 4) * 8.75);
```

```

        System.out.println("My taxes owed:");  // 20% tax
        System.out.println((4 + 5 + 8 + 4) * 8.75 * 0.20);
    }
}
```

20. The following program redundantly repeats the same expressions many times. Modify the program to remove all redundant expressions using variables of appropriate types.

```
// This program computes the total amount owed for a meal,
// assuming 8% tax and a 15% tip.
public class Receipt {
    public static void main(String[] args) {
        System.out.println("Subtotal:");
        System.out.println(38 + 40 + 30);
        System.out.println("Tax:");
        System.out.println((38 + 40 + 30) * .08);
        System.out.println("Tip:");
        System.out.println((38 + 40 + 30) * .15);
        System.out.println("Total:");
        System.out.println(38 + 40 + 30 +
                           (38 + 40 + 30) * .08 +
                           (38 + 40 + 30) * .15);
    }
}
```

Section 2.3: The `for` Loop

21. Complete the following code, replacing the "FINISH ME" parts with your own code:

```
public class Count2 {
    public static void main(String[] args) {
        for (int i = /* FINISH ME */) {
            System.out.println(/* FINISH ME */);
        }
    }
}
```

to produce the following output:

```
2 times 1 = 2
2 times 2 = 4
2 times 3 = 6
2 times 4 = 8
```

22. Assume that you have a variable called `count` that will take on the values `1, 2, 3, 4`, and so on. You are going to formulate expressions in terms of `count` that will yield different sequences. For example, to get the sequence `2, 4, 6, 8, 10, 12, ...`, you would use the expression `(2 * count)`. Fill in the following table, indicating an expression that will generate each sequence.

Sequence	Expression
a. 2, 4, 6, 8, 10, 12, . . .	
b. 4, 19, 34, 49, 64, 79, . . .	
c. 30, 20, 10, 0, 10, 20, . . .	
d. 7, 3, 1, 5, 9, 13, . . .	
e. 97, 94, 91, 88, 85, 82, . . .	

23. Complete the code for the following `for` loop:

```
for (int i = 1; i <= 6; i++) {
    // your code here
}
```

so that it prints the following numbers, one per line:

```
-4
14
32
50
68
86
```

24. What is the output of the following `oddStuff` method?

```
public static void oddStuff() {
    int number = 4;
    for (int count = 1; count <= number; count++) {
        System.out.println(number);
        number = number / 2;
    }
}
```

25. What is the output of the following loop?

```
int total = 25;
for (int number = 1; number <= (total / 2); number++) {
    total = total – number;
    System.out.println(total + " " + number);
}
```

26. What is the output of the following loop?

```
System.out.println("+---+");
for (int i = 1; i <= 3; i++) {
    System.out.println("\\   /");
    System.out.println("/   \\");
}
System.out.println("+---+");
```

27. What is the output of the following loop?

```
for (int i = 1; i <= 3; i++)
    System.out.println("How many lines");
    System.out.println("are printed?");
```

28. What is the output of the following loop?

```
System.out.print("T-minus ");
for (int i = 5; i >= 1; i––) {
    System.out.print(i + ", ");
}
System.out.println("Blastoff!");
```

29. What is the output of the following sequence of loops?

```
for (int i = 1; i <= 5; i++) {
    for (int j = 1; j <= 10; j++) {
        System.out.print((i * j) + " ");
    }
    System.out.println();
}
```

30. What is the output of the following sequence of loops?

```
for (int i = 1; i <= 10; i++) {
    for (int j = 1; j <= 10 – i; j++) {
        System.out.print(" ");
    }
    for (int j = 1; j <= 2 * i – 1; j++) {
        System.out.print("*");
    }
    System.out.println();
}
```

31. What is the output of the following sequence of loops?

```
for (int i = 1; i <= 2; i++) {
    for (int j = 1; j <= 3; j++) {
        for (int k = 1; k <= 4; k++) {
            System.out.print("*");
        }
        System.out.print("!");
    }
    System.out.println();
}
```

32. What is the output of the following sequence of loops? Notice that the code is the same as that in the previous exercise, except that the placement of the braces has changed.

```
for (int i = 1; i <= 2; i++) {
    for (int j = 1; j <= 3; j++) {
        for (int k = 1; k <= 4; k++) {
            System.out.print("*");
        }
    }
    System.out.print("!");
    System.out.println();
}
```

33. What is the output of the following sequence of loops? Notice that the code is the same as that in the previous exercise, except that the placement of the braces has changed.

```
for (int i = 1; i <= 2; i++) {
    for (int j = 1; j <= 3; j++) {
        for (int k = 1; k <= 4; k++) {
            System.out.print("*");
            System.out.print("!");
        }
        System.out.println();
    }
}
```

Section 2.4: Managing Complexity

34. Suppose that you are trying to write a program that produces the following output:

```
1 3 5 7 9 11 13 15 17 19 21
1 3 5 7 9 11
```

The following program is an attempt at a solution, but it contains four major errors. Identify them all.

```
public class BadNews {
    public static final int MAX_ODD = 21;

    public static void writeOdds() {
```

```
        // print each odd number
        for (int count = 1; count <= (MAX_ODD  2); count++) {
            System.out.print(count + " ");
            count = count + 2;
        }

        // print the last odd number
        System.out.print(count + 2);
    }

    public static void main(String[] args) {
        // write all odds up to 21
        writeOdds();

        // now, write all odds up to 11
        MAX_ODD = 11;
        writeOdds();
    }
}
```

35. What is the output of the following `unknown` method?

```
public class Strange {
    public static final int MAX = 5;

    public static void unknown() {
        int number = 0;

        for (int count = MAX; count >= 1; count--) {
            number += (count * count);
        }

        System.out.println("The result is: " + number);
    }

    public static void main(String[] args) {
        unknown();
    }
}
```

36. Suppose that you have a variable called `line` that will take on the values `1, 2, 3, 4,` and so on, and a class constant named `SIZE` that takes one of two values. You are going to formulate expressions in terms of `line` and `SIZE` that will yield different sequences of numbers of characters. Fill in the table below, indicating an expression that will generate each sequence.

`line` value	constant `SIZE` value	Number of characters	Expression
a. 1, 2, 3, 4, 5, 6, ...	1	4, 6, 8, 10, 12, 14, ...	
1, 2, 3, 4, 5, 6, ...	2	6, 8, 10, 12, 14, 16, ...	
b. 1, 2, 3, 4, 5, 6, ...	3	13, 17, 21, 25, 29, 33, ...	
1, 2, 3, 4, 5, 6, ...	5	19, 23, 27, 31, 35, 39, ...	
c. 1, 2, 3, 4, 5, 6, ...	4	10, 9, 8, 7, 6, 5, ...	
1, 2, 3, 4, 5, 6, ...	9	20, 19, 18, 17, 16, 15, ...	

37. Write a table that determines the expressions for the number of each type of character on each of the 6 lines in the following output.

```
!!!!!!!!!!!!!!!!!!!!!!
\\!!!!!!!!!!!!!!!!!!//
\\\\!!!!!!!!!!!!!!////
\\\\\\!!!!!!!!!!//////
\\\\\\\\!!!!!!////////
\\\\\\\\\\!!//////////
```

38. Suppose that a program has been written that produces the output shown in the previous problem. Now the author wants the program to be scalable using a class constant called `SIZE`. The previous output used a constant height of 6, since there were 6 lines. The following is the output for a constant height of 4. Create a new table that shows the expressions for the character counts at this new size of 4, and compare these tables to figure out the expressions for any size using the `SIZE` constant.

```
!!!!!!!!!!!!!!
\\!!!!!!!!!!//
\\\\!!!!!!////
\\\\\\!!//////
```

Exercises

1. In physics, a common useful equation for finding the position s of a body in linear motion at a given time t, based on its initial position s_0, initial velocity v_0, and rate of acceleration a, is the following:

$$s = s_0 + v_0 t + \frac{1}{2}at^2$$

Write code to declare variables for s_0, v_0, a, and t, and then write the code to compute s on the basis of these values.

2. Write a `for` loop that produces the following output:

```
1 4 9 16 25 36 49 64 81 100
```

For added challenge, try to modify your code so that it does not need to use the * multiplication operator. (It can be done! Hint: Look at the differences between adjacent numbers.)

3. The Fibonacci numbers are a sequence of integers in which the first two elements are 1, and each following element is the sum of the two preceding elements. The mathematical definition of each kth Fibonacci number is the following:

$$F(k) = \begin{cases} F(k-1) + F(k-2), & k > 2 \\ 1, & k \leq 2 \end{cases}$$

The first 12 Fibonacci numbers are

```
1 1 2 3 5 8 13 21 34 55 89 144
```

Write a `for` loop that computes and prints the first 12 Fibonacci numbers.

4. Write nested `for` loops to produce the following output:

```
*****
*****
*****
*****
```

5. Write nested `for` loops to produce the following output:

```
*
**
***
****
*****
```

6. Write nested `for` loops to produce the following output:

```
1
22
333
4444
55555
666666
7777777
```

7. Write nested `for` loops to produce the following output:

```
    1
   2
  3
 4
5
```

8. Write nested `for` loops to produce the following output:

```
    1
   22
  333
 4444
55555
```

9. Write nested `for` loops to produce the following output, with each line 40 characters wide:

```
----------------------------------------
_-^-_-^-_-^-_-^-_-^-_-^-_-^-_-^-_-^-_-^-
1122334455667788990011223344556677889900
----------------------------------------
```

10. It's common to print a rotating, increasing list of single-digit numbers at the start of a program's output as a visual guide to number the columns of the output to follow. With this in mind, write nested `for` loops to produce the following output, with each line 60 characters wide:

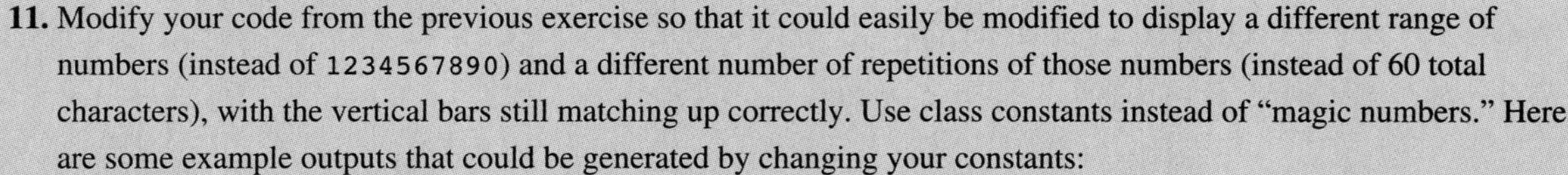

```
         |         |         |         |         |         |
123456789012345678901234567890123456789012345678901234567890
```

11. Modify your code from the previous exercise so that it could easily be modified to display a different range of numbers (instead of `1234567890`) and a different number of repetitions of those numbers (instead of 60 total characters), with the vertical bars still matching up correctly. Use class constants instead of "magic numbers." Here are some example outputs that could be generated by changing your constants:

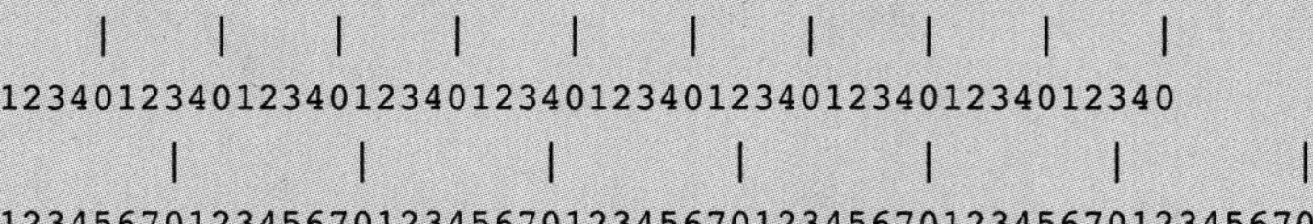

```
    |    |    |    |    |    |    |    |    |    |
12340123401234012340123401234012340123401234012340
       |       |       |       |       |       |       |
12345670123456701234567012345670123456701234567012345670
```

12. Write nested `for` loops that produce the following output:

```
000111222333444555666777888999
000111222333444555666777888999
000111222333444555666777888999
```

13. Modify the code so that it now produces the following output:

```
99999888887777766666555554444433333222221111100000
99999888887777766666555554444433333222221111100000
99999888887777766666555554444433333222221111100000
99999888887777766666555554444433333222221111100000
99999888887777766666555554444433333222221111100000
```

14. Modify the code so that it now produces the following output:

```
999999999888888887777777666666555554444333221
999999999888888887777777666666555554444333221
999999999888888887777777666666555554444333221
999999999888888887777777666666555554444333221
```

15. Write a method called `printDesign` that produces the following output. Use nested `for` loops to capture the structure of the figure.

```
-----1-----
----333----
---55555---
--7777777--
-999999999-
```

16. Write a Java program called `SlashFigure` that produces the following output. Use nested `for` loops to capture the structure of the figure. (See also Self-Check Problems 34 and 35.)

```
!!!!!!!!!!!!!!!!!!!!!!
\\!!!!!!!!!!!!!!!!!!//
\\\\!!!!!!!!!!!!!!////
\\\\\\!!!!!!!!!!//////
\\\\\\\\!!!!!!////////
\\\\\\\\\\!!//////////
```

17. Modify your `SlashFigure` program from the previous exercise to become a new program called `SlashFigure2` that uses a global constant for the figure's height. (You may want to make loop tables first.) The previous output used a constant height of 6. The following are the outputs for constant heights of 4 and 8:

Height 4	Height 8
!!!!!!!!!!!!!!	!!!!!!!!!!!!!!!!!!!!!!!!!!!!!!
\\!!!!!!!!!!//	\\!!!!!!!!!!!!!!!!!!!!!!!!!!//
\\\\!!!!!!////	\\\\!!!!!!!!!!!!!!!!!!!!!!////
\\\\\\!!//////	\\\\\\!!!!!!!!!!!!!!!!!!//////
	\\\\\\\\!!!!!!!!!!!!!!////////
	\\\\\\\\\\!!!!!!!!!!//////////
	\\\\\\\\\\\\!!!!!!////////////
	\\\\\\\\\\\\\\!!//////////////

18. Write a pseudocode algorithm that will produce the following figure as output:

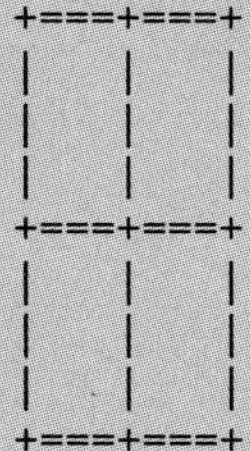

```
+===+===+
|   |   |
|   |   |
|   |   |
+===+===+
|   |   |
|   |   |
|   |   |
+===+===+
```

19. Use your pseudocode from the previous exercise to write a Java program called `Window` that produces the preceding figure as output. Use nested `for` loops to print the repeated parts of the figure. Once you get it to work, add a class constant so that the size of the figure can be changed simply by changing the constant's value.

20. Write a Java program called `StarFigure` that produces the following output. Use nested for loops to capture the structure of the figure.

```
////////////////\\\\\\\\\\\\\\\\
////////////********\\\\\\\\\\\\
////////****************\\\\\\\\
////************************\\\\
********************************
```

21. Modify your `StarFigure` program from the previous exercise to become a new program named `StarFigure2` that uses a global constant for the figure's height. (You may want to make loop tables first.) The previous output used a constant height of 5. The following are the outputs for constant heights of 3 and 6:

Height 3	Height 6
////////\\\\\\\\	////////////////////\\\\\\\\\\\\\\\\\\\\
////********\\\\	////////////////********\\\\\\\\\\\\\\\\
****************	////////////****************\\\\\\\\\\\\
	////////************************\\\\\\\\
	////********************************\\\\
	**

22. Write a Java program called `DollarFigure` that produces the following output. Use nested `for` loops to capture the structure of the figure.

```
$$$$$$$**************$$$$$$$
**$$$$$$************$$$$$$**
****$$$$$**********$$$$$****
******$$$$********$$$$******
********$$$******$$$********
**********$$****$$**********
************$**$************
```

23. Modify your `DollarFigure` program from the previous exercise to become a new program called `DollarFigure2` that uses a global constant for the figure's height. (You may want to make loop tables first.) The previous output used a constant height of 7.

Programming Projects

1. Write a program that produces the following output using nested `for` loops:

```
****** //////////// ******
*****  //////////\\  *****
****   ////////\\\\   ****
***    //////\\\\\\    ***
**     ////\\\\\\\\     **
*      //\\\\\\\\\\      *
       \\\\\\\\\\\\
```

2. Write a program that produces the following output using nested `for` loops:

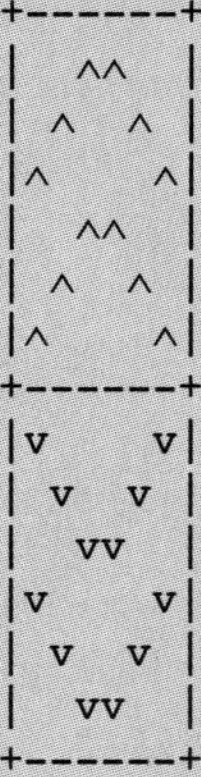

```
+------+
|  ^^  |
| ^  ^ |
|^    ^|
|  ^^  |
| ^  ^ |
|^    ^|
+------+
|v    v|
| v  v |
|  vv  |
|v    v|
| v  v |
|  vv  |
+------+
```

3. Write a program that produces the following output using nested `for` loops:

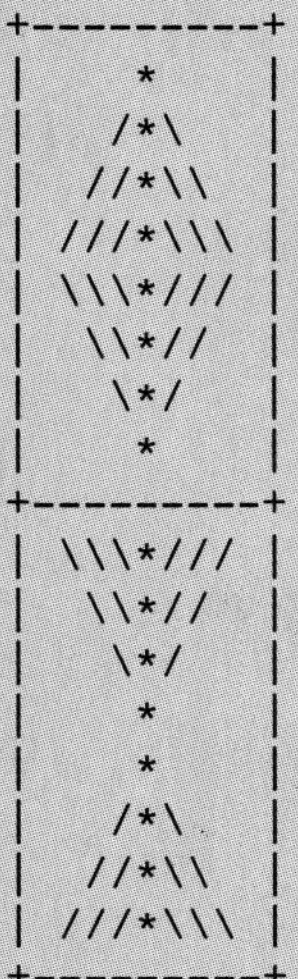

```
+---------+
|    *    |
|   /*\   |
|  //*\\  |
| ///*\\\ |
| \\\*/// |
|  \\*//  |
|   \*/   |
|    *    |
+---------+
| \\\*/// |
|  \\*//  |
|   \*/   |
|    *    |
|    *    |
|   /*\   |
|  //*\\  |
| ///*\\\ |
+---------+
```

4. Write a program that produces the following hourglass figure as its output using nested `for` loops:

```
|""""""""""|
 \::::::::/
  \::::::/
   \::::/
    \::/
     ||
    /::\
   /::::\
  /::::::\
 /::::::::\
|""""""""""|
```

5. Write a program that produces the following output using nested `for` loops. Use a class constant to make it possible to change the number of stairs in the figure.

```
                      o  *******
                     /|\ *     *
                     / \ *     *
                 o  ******     *
                /|\ *          *
                / \ *          *
            o  ******          *
           /|\ *               *
           / \ *               *
       o  ******               *
      /|\ *                    *
      / \ *                    *
  o  ******                    *
 /|\ *                         *
 / \ *                         *
********************************
```

6. Write a program that produces the following rocket ship figure as its output using nested `for` loops. Use a class constant to make it possible to change the size of the rocket (the following output uses a size of 3).

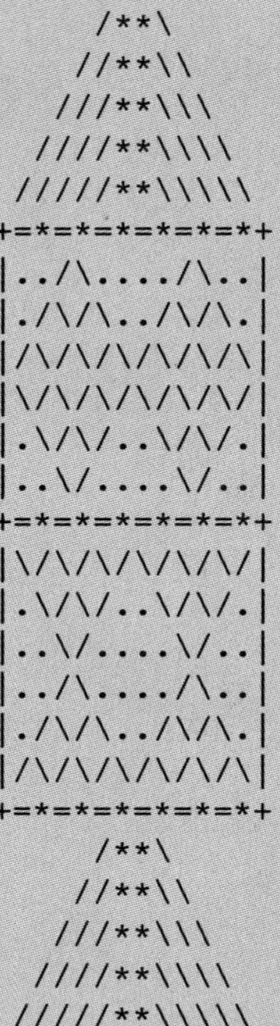

```
     /**\
    //**\\
   ///**\\\
  ////**\\\\
 /////**\\\\\
+=*=*=*=*=*=*+
|../\..../\..|
|./\/\../\/\.|
|/\/\/\/\/\/\|
|\/\/\/\/\/\/|
|.\/\/..\/\/.|
|..\/....\/..|
+=*=*=*=*=*=*+
|\/\/\/\/\/\/|
|.\/\/..\/\/.|
|..\/....\/..|
|../\..../\..|
|./\/\../\/\.|
|/\/\/\/\/\/\|
+=*=*=*=*=*=*+
     /**\
    //**\\
   ///**\\\
  ////**\\\\
 /////**\\\\\
```

7. Write a program that produces the following figure (which vaguely resembles the Seattle Space Needle) as its output using nested `for` loops. Use a class constant to make it possible to change the size of the figure (the following output uses a size of 4).

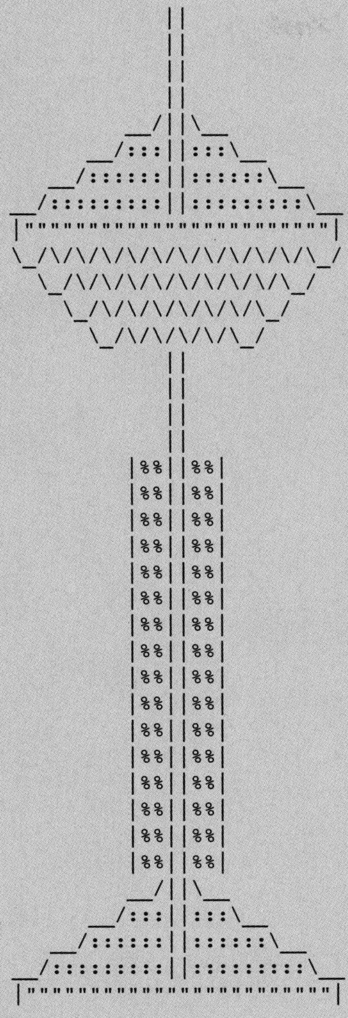

8. Write a program that produces the following figure (which vaguely resembles a textbook) as its output using nested `for` loops. Use a class constant to make it possible to change the size of the figure (the following output uses a size of 10).

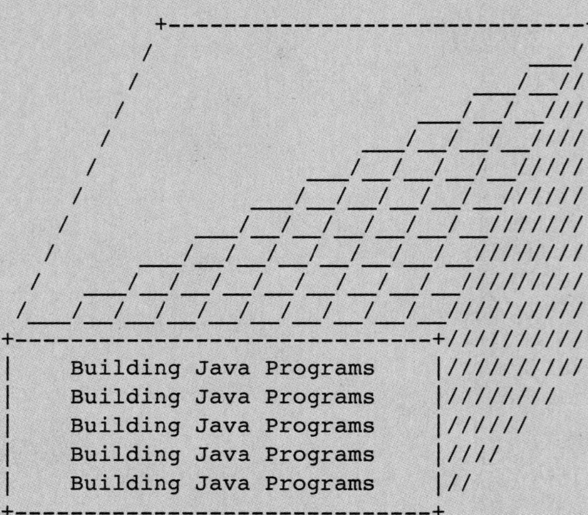

Chapter 3

Introduction to Parameters and Objects

Introduction

Chapter 2 introduced techniques for managing complexity, including the use of class constants, which make programs more flexible. This chapter explores a more powerful technique for obtaining such flexibility. Here, you will learn how to use parameters to create methods that solve not just single tasks, but whole families of tasks. Creating such methods requires you to generalize, or look beyond a specific task to find the more general category of task that it exemplifies. The ability to generalize is one of the most important qualities of a good software engineer, and the generalization technique you will study in this chapter is one of the most powerful techniques programmers use. After exploring parameters, we'll discuss some other issues associated with methods, such as the ability of a method to return a value.

This chapter then introduces the idea of objects and how to use them in Java programs. We aren't going to explore the details of defining objects for a while, but we want to begin using objects early. One of the most attractive features of Java is that it comes with a rich library of predefined objects that can be used to solve many common programming tasks.

The chapter concludes with an exploration of a very important kind of object known as a `Scanner`. Using a `Scanner` object, you can write programs that obtain values from the user. This feature will allow you to write interactive programs that prompt for input as well as producing output.

3.1 Parameters

Humans are very good at learning new tasks. When we learn, we often develop a single generalized solution for a family of related tasks. For example, someone might ask you to take 10 steps forward or 20 steps forward. These are different tasks, but they both involve taking a certain number of steps forward. We think of this action as a single task of taking steps forward, and we understand that the number of steps will vary from one task to another. In programming terms, we refer to the number of steps as a *parameter* that allows us to generalize the task.

> **Parameter (Parameterize)**
>
> Any of a set of characteristics that distinguish different members of a family of tasks. To parameterize a task is to identify a set of its parameters.

For a programming example, let's return to the `DrawFigure2` program of Chapter 2. It performs its task adequately, but there are several aspects of this program that we can improve. For example, there are many different places where a `for` loop writes out spaces. This approach is redundant and can be consolidated into a single method that performs all space-writing tasks.

Each space-writing task requires a different number of spaces, so you need some way to tell the method how many spaces to write. The methods you've written so far have a simple calling mechanism where you say:

```
writeSpaces();
```

One approach might be to set a variable to a particular value before the method is called:

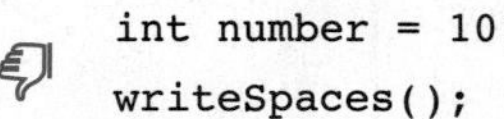

```
int number = 10;
writeSpaces();
```

Then the method could look at the value of the variable `number` to see how many spaces to write. Unfortunately, this approach won't work. Recall from Chapter 2 that scope rules determine where variables can be accessed. Following those rules, the variable `number` would be a local variable in `main` that could not be seen inside `writeSpaces`.

Instead, you can specify one or more parameters to a method. The idea is that instead of writing a method that performs just one version of a task, you write a more flexible version that solves a family of related tasks that all differ by one or more parameters. In the case of the `writeSpaces` method, the parameter is the number of spaces to write.

The following is the definition of `writeSpaces` with a parameter for the number of spaces to write:

```
public static void writeSpaces(int number) {
    for (int i = 1; i <= number; i++) {
        System.out.print(" ");
    }
}
```

The parameter appears in the method header, after the name and inside the parentheses that you have, up to this point, been leaving empty. The `writeSpaces` method uses a parameter called `number` of type `int`. As we indicated earlier, you can no longer call the parameterized method by using just its name:

```
writeSpaces();
```

You must now say something like

```
writeSpaces(10);
```

When a call like this is made, the value `10` is used to initialize the `number` parameter. You can think of this as information flowing into the method from the call:

```
writeSpaces(10);

public static void writeSpaces(int number) {
    ...
}
```

The parameter `number` is a local variable, but it gets its initial value from the call. Calling this method with the value `10` is equivalent to including the following declaration at the beginning of the `writeSpaces` method:

```
int number = 10;
```

Of course, this mechanism is more flexible than a specific variable declaration, because you can instead say

```
writeSpaces(20);
```

and it will be as if you had said

```
int number = 20;
```

at the beginning of the method. You can even use an integer expression for the call:

```
writeSpaces(3 * 4 – 5);
```

In this case, Java evaluates the expression to get the value `7` and then calls `writeSpaces`, initializing `number` to `7`.

Computer scientists use the word "parameter" broadly to mean both what appears in the method header (the *formal parameter*) and what appears in the method call (the *actual parameter*).

Formal Parameter

A variable that appears inside parentheses in the header of a method that is used to generalize the method's behavior.

Actual Parameter

A specific value or expression that appears inside parentheses in a method call.

The term "formal parameter" does not describe its purpose. A better name would be "generalized parameter." In the `writeSpaces` method, `number` is the generalized parameter that appears in the method declaration. It is a placeholder for some unspecified value. The values appearing in the method calls are the actual parameters, because each call indicates a specific task to perform. In other words, each call provides an actual value to fill the placeholder.

The word "argument" is often used as a synonym for "parameter," as in "These are the arguments I'm passing to this method." Some people prefer to reserve the word "argument" for actual parameters and the word "parameter" for formal parameters.

Let's look at an example of how you might use this `writeSpaces` method. Remember that the `DrawFigure2` program had the following method, called `drawTop`:

```
// produces the top half of the hourglass figure
public static void drawTop() {
    for (int line = 1; line <= SUB_HEIGHT; line++) {
        System.out.print("|");
        for (int i = 1; i <= (line - 1); i++) {
            System.out.print(" ");
        }
        System.out.print("\\");
        int dots = 2 * SUB_HEIGHT - 2 * line;
        for (int i = 1; i <= dots; i++) {
            System.out.print(".");
        }
        System.out.print("/");
        for (int i = 1; i <= (line - 1); i++) {
            System.out.print(" ");
        }
        System.out.println("|");
    }
}
```

Using the `writeSpaces` method, you can rewrite this as follows:

```
public static void drawTop() {
    for (int line = 1; line <= SUB_HEIGHT; line++) {
        System.out.print("|");
        writeSpaces(line - 1);
        System.out.print("\\");
        int dots = 2 * SUB_HEIGHT - 2 * line;
        for (int i = 1; i <= dots; i++) {
            System.out.print(".");
        }
        System.out.print("/");
        writeSpaces(line - 1);
        System.out.println("|");
    }
}
```

Notice that `writeSpaces` is called two different times, specifying how many spaces are required in each case. You could modify the `drawBottom` method from the `DrawFigure2` program similarly to simplify it.

The Mechanics of Parameters

VideoNote

When Java executes a call on a method, it initializes the method's parameters. For each parameter, it first evaluates the expression passed as the actual parameter and then uses the result to initialize the local variable whose name is given by the formal parameter. Let's use an example to clarify this process:

```
public class ParameterExample {
    public static void main(String[] args) {
        int spaces1 = 3;
        int spaces2 = 5;

        System.out.print("*");
        writeSpaces(spaces1);
        System.out.println("*");

        System.out.print("!");
        writeSpaces(spaces2);
        System.out.println("!");

        System.out.print("'");
        writeSpaces(8);
        System.out.println("'");
```

```

        System.out.print("<");
        writeSpaces(spaces1 * spaces2 - 5);
        System.out.println(">");
    }

    // writes "number" spaces on the current output line
    public static void writeSpaces(int number) {
        for (int i = 1; i <= number; i++) {
            System.out.print(" ");
        }
    }
}
```

In the first two lines of the `main` method, the computer finds instructions to allocate and initialize two variables:

The next three lines of code produce an output line with three spaces bounded by asterisks on either side:

```
System.out.print("*");
writeSpaces(spaces1);
System.out.println("*");
```

You can see where the asterisks come from, but look at the method call that produces the spaces. When Java executes the call on `writeSpaces`, it must set up its parameter. To set up the parameter, Java first evaluates the expression being passed as the actual parameter. The expression is simply the variable `spaces1`, which has the value `3`. Therefore, the expression evaluates to `3`. Java uses this result to initialize a local variable called `number`.

The following diagram indicates how the computer's memory would look as the `writeSpaces` method is entered the first time. Because there are two methods involved (`main` and `writeSpaces`), the diagram indicates which variables are local to `main` (`spaces1` and `spaces2`) and which are local to `writeSpaces` (the parameter `number`):

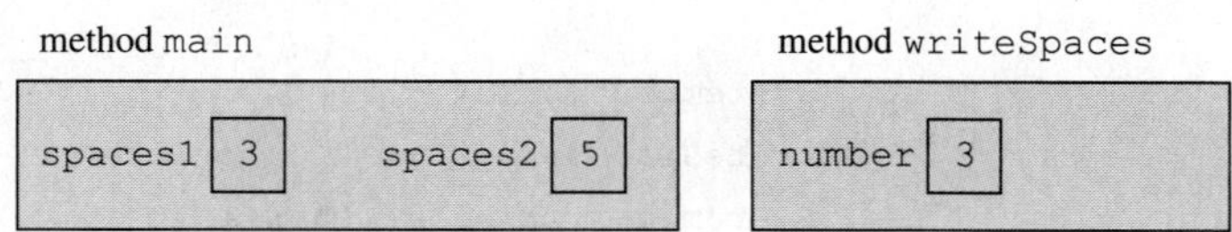

The net effect of this process is that the `writeSpaces` method has a local copy of the value stored in the variable `spaces1` from the `main` method. The `println` that comes after the call on `writeSpaces` puts an asterisk at the end of the line and then completes the line of output.

Let's now trace the next three lines of code:

```
System.out.print("!");
writeSpaces(spaces2);
System.out.println("!");
```

The first line prints an exclamation mark on the second line of output, then calls `writeSpaces` again, this time with the variable `spaces2` as its actual parameter. The computer evaluates this expression, obtaining the result `5`. This value is used to initialize `number`. Thus, this time it creates a copy of the value stored in the variable `spaces2` from the `main` method:

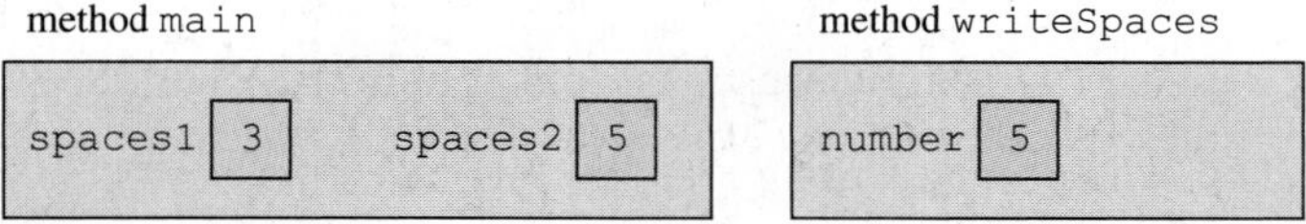

Because `number` has a different value this time (`5` instead of `3`), the method produces a different number of spaces. After the method executes, the `println` finishes the line of output with a second exclamation mark.

Here are the next three lines of code:

```
System.out.print("'");
writeSpaces(8);
System.out.println("'");
```

This code writes a single quotation mark at the beginning of the third line of output and then calls `writeSpaces` again. This time it uses the integer literal `8` as the expression, which means that it initializes the parameter `number` as a copy of the number 8:

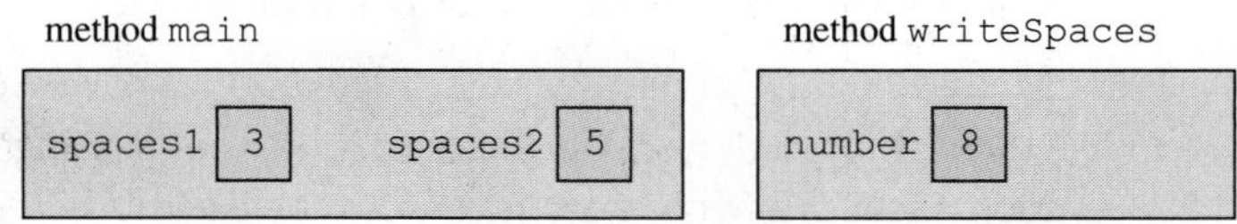

Again, the method will behave differently because of the different value of `number`. It prints eight spaces on the line and finishes executing. Then the `println` completes the line of output by printing another single quotation mark at the end of the line.

Finally, the last three lines of code in the `main` method are:

```
System.out.print("<");
writeSpaces(spaces1 * spaces2 – 5);
System.out.println(">");
```

This code prints a less-than character at the beginning of the fourth line of output and then makes a final call on the `writeSpaces` method. This time the actual parameter is an expression, not just a variable or literal value. Thus, before the call is made, the computer evaluates the expression to determine its value:

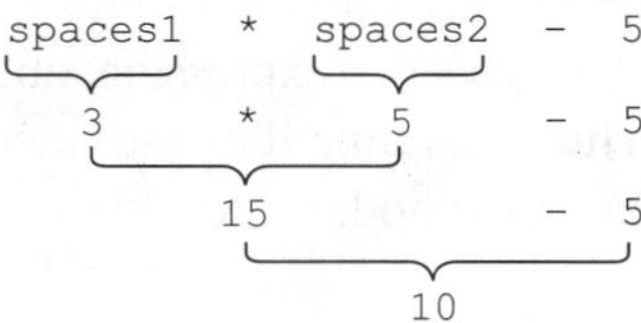

The computer uses this result to initialize `number`:

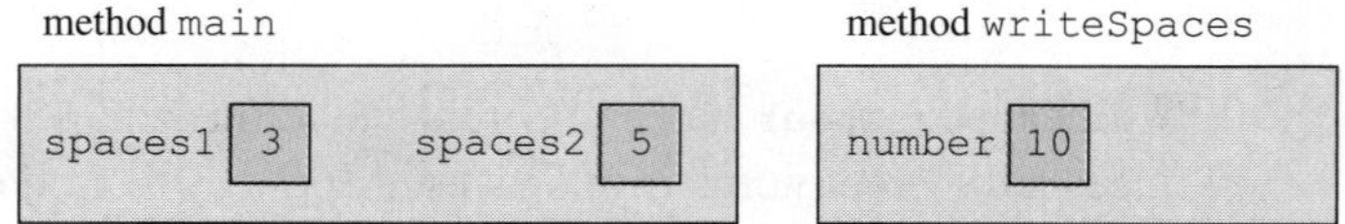

Now `number` is a copy of the value described by this complex expression. Therefore, the total output of this program is

```
*    *
!      !
'         '
<          >
```

Common Programming Error

Confusing Actual and Formal Parameters

Many students get used to seeing declarations of formal parameters and mistakenly believe that their syntax is identical to that for passing actual parameters. It's a common mistake to write the type of a variable as it's being passed to a parameter:

```
writeSpaces(int spaces1); // this doesn't work
```

Continued on next page

Continued from previous page

This confusion is due to the fact that parameters' types are written in the declaration of the method, like this:

```
public static void writeSpaces(int number)
```

Types must be written when variables or parameters are declared, but when variables are used, such as when the code calls a method and passes the variables as actual parameters, their types are not written. Actual parameters are not declarations; therefore, types should not be written before them:

```
writeSpaces(spaces1); // much better!
```

Limitations of Parameters

We've seen that a parameter can be used to provide input to a method. But while you can use a parameter to send a value into a method, you can't use a parameter to get a value out of a method.

When a parameter is set up, a local variable is created and is initialized to the value being passed as the actual parameter. The net effect is that the local variable is a copy of the value coming from the outside. Since it is a local variable, it can't influence any variables outside the method. Consider the following sample program:

```
public class ParameterExample2 {
    public static void main(String[] args) {
        int x = 17;
        doubleNumber(x);
        System.out.println("x = " + x);
        System.out.println();

        int number = 42;
        doubleNumber(number);
        System.out.println("number = " + number);
    }

    public static void doubleNumber(int number) {
        System.out.println("Initial value = " + number);
        number = number * 2;
        System.out.println("Final value = " + number);
    }
}
```

This program begins by declaring and initializing an integer variable called `x` with the value `17`:

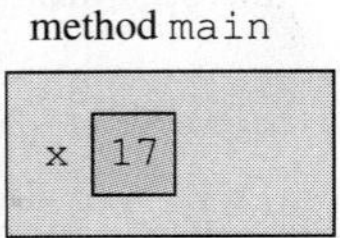

It then calls the method `doubleNumber`, passing `x` as a parameter. The value of `x` is used to initialize the parameter `number` as a local variable of the method called `doubleNumber`:

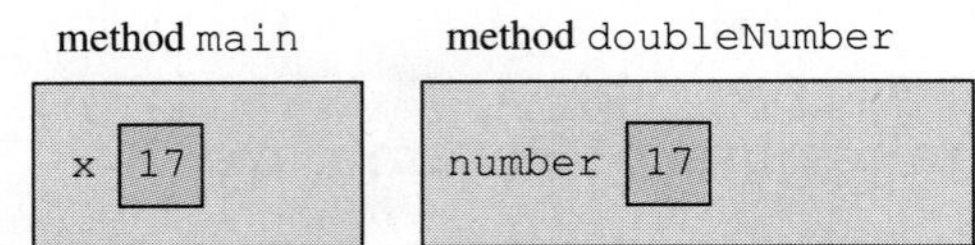

The program then executes the statements inside of `doubleNumber`. First, `doubleNumber` prints the initial value of `number` (`17`). Then it doubles `number`:

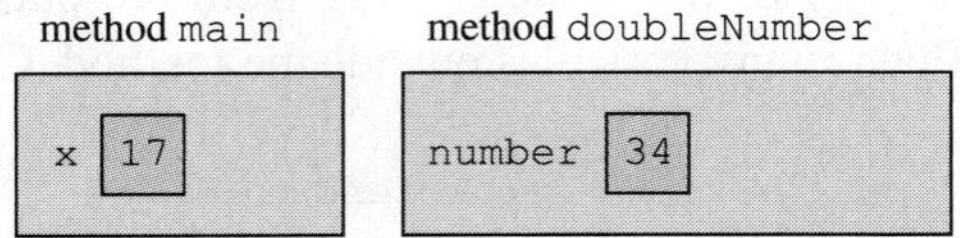

Notice that this has no effect on the variable `x`. The parameter called `number` is a copy of `x`, so even though they started out the same, changing the value of `number` does not affect `x`. Next, `doubleNumber` reports the new value of `number` (`34`).

At this point, `doubleNumber` finishes executing and we return to `main`:

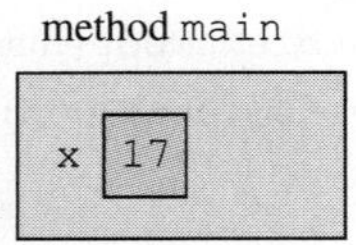

The next statement in the `main` method reports the value of `x`, which is `17`. Then it declares and initializes a variable called `number` with the value `42`:

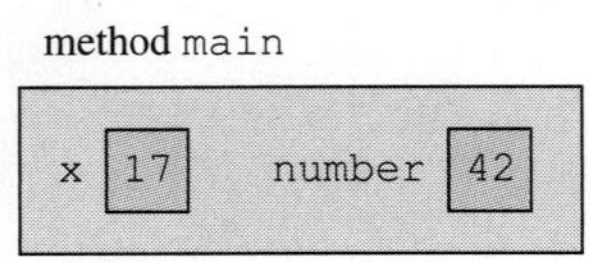

The following statement calls `doubleNumber` again, this time passing it the value of `number`. This is an odd situation because the parameter has the same name as the variable in `main`, but Java doesn't care. It always creates a new local variable for the `doubleNumber` method:

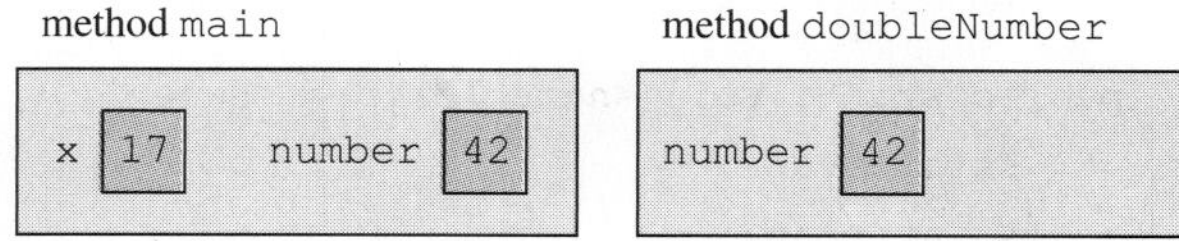

So, at this point there are two different variables called `number`, one in each method. Now it's time to execute the statements of `doubleNumber` again. It first reports the value of `number` (`42`), then doubles it:

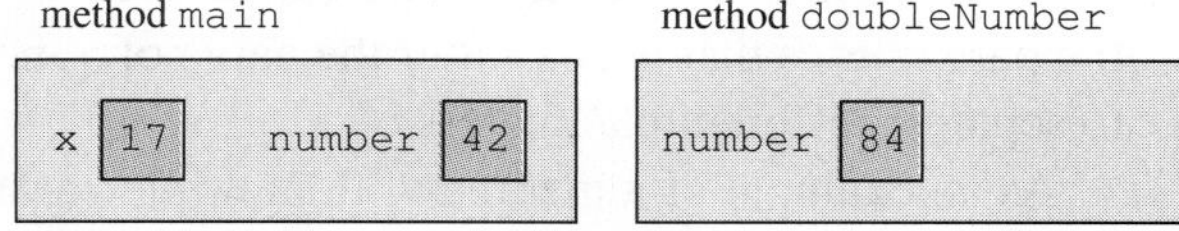

Again, notice that doubling `number` inside `doubleNumber` has no effect on the original variable `number` in `main`. These are separate variables. The method then reports the new value of `number` (`84`) and returns to `main`:

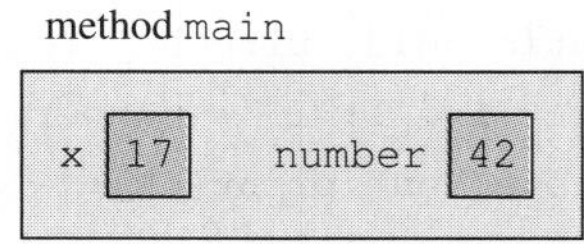

The program then reports the value of `number` and terminates. So, the overall output of the program is as follows:

```
Initial value = 17
Final value = 34
x = 17

Initial value = 42
Final value = 84
number = 42
```

The local manipulations of the parameter do not change these variables outside the method. The fact that variables are copied is an important aspect of parameters. On the positive side, we know that the variables are protected from change because the parameters are copies of the originals. On the negative side, it means that although parameters will allow us to send values into a method, they will not allow us to get values back out of a method.

Multiple Parameters

So far, our discussion of parameter syntax has been informal. It's about time that we wrote down more precisely the syntax we use to declare static methods with parameters. Here it is:

```
public static void <name>(<type> <name>, ..., <type> <name>) {
    <statement>;
    <statement>;
    ...
    <statement>;
}
```

This template indicates that we can declare as many parameters as we want inside the parentheses that appear after the name of a method in its header. We use commas to separate different parameters.

As an example of a method with multiple parameters, let's consider a variation of `writeSpaces`. It is convenient that we can use the method to write different numbers of spaces, but it always writes spaces. What if we want 18 asterisks or 23 periods or 17 question marks? We can generalize the task even further by having the method take two parameters—a character and a number of times to write that character:

```
public static void writeChars(char ch, int number) {
    for (int i = 1; i <= number; i++) {
        System.out.print(ch);
    }
}
```

The character to be printed is a parameter of type `char`, which we will discuss in more detail in the next chapter. Recall that character literals are enclosed in single quotation marks.

The syntax template for calling a method that accepts parameters is the following:

```
<method name>(<expression>, <expression>, ..., <expression>);
```

By calling the `writeChars` method you can write code like the following:

```
writeChars('=', 20);
System.out.println();
for (int i = 1; i <= 10; i++) {
    writeChars('>', i);
    writeChars(' ', 20 – 2 * i);
    writeChars('<', i);
    System.out.println();
}
```

This code produces the following output:

```
====================
>                  <
>>                <<
>>>              <<<
>>>>            <<<<
>>>>>          <<<<<
>>>>>>        <<<<<<
>>>>>>>      <<<<<<<
>>>>>>>>    <<<<<<<<
>>>>>>>>>  <<<<<<<<<
>>>>>>>>>><<<<<<<<<<
```

Using the `writeChars` method we can write an even better version of the `drawTop` method from the `DrawFigure2` program of Chapter 2. We saw earlier that using `writeChars` we could eliminate two of the inner loops, but this left us with the inner loop to print dots. Now we can eliminate all three of the inner loops and produce a much more readable version of the method:

```
public static void drawTop() {
    for (int line = 1; line <= SUB_HEIGHT; line++) {
        System.out.print("|");
        writeChars(' ', line - 1);
        System.out.print("\\");
        writeChars('.', 2 * SUB_HEIGHT - 2 * line);
        System.out.print("/");
        writeChars(' ', line - 1);
        System.out.println("|");
    }
}
```

You can include as many parameters as you want when you define a method. Each method call must provide exactly that number of parameters, in the same order. For example, consider the first call on `writeChars` in the preceding code fragment and the header for `writeChars`. Java lines up the parameters in sequential order (with the first actual parameter going into the first formal parameter and the second actual parameter going into the second formal parameter):

```
writeChars('=', 20);

public static void writeChars(char ch, int number) {
    ...
}
```

We've seen that methods can call other methods; this is equally true of methods that take parameters. For example, here is a method for drawing a box of a given height and width that calls the `writeChars` method:

```
public static void drawBox(int height, int width) {
    // draw top of box
    writeChars('*', width);
    System.out.println();

    // draw middle lines
    for (int i = 1; i <= height - 2; i++) {
        System.out.print('*');
        writeChars(' ', width - 2);
        System.out.println("*");
    }

    // draw bottom of box
    writeChars('*', width);
    System.out.println();
}
```

Notice that `drawBox` is passed values for its parameters called `height` and `width` and that these parameters are used to form expressions that are passed as values to `writeChars`. For example, inside the `for` loop we call `writeChars` asking it to produce `width - 2` spaces. (We subtract 2 because we print a star at the beginning and the end of the line.) Here is a sample call on the method:

```
drawBox(5, 10);
```

This code produces the following output:

```
**********
*        *
*        *
*        *
**********
```

When you're writing methods that accept many parameters, the method header can become very long. It is common to *wrap* long lines (ones that exceed roughly 80 characters in length) by inserting a line break after an operator or parameter and indenting the line that follows by twice the normal indentation width:

```
// this method's header is too long, so we'll wrap it
public static void printTriangle(int xCoord1, int yCoord1,
        int xCoord2, int yCoord2, int xCoord3, int yCoord3) {
    ...
}
```

Parameters versus Constants

In Chapter 2, you saw that class constants are a useful mechanism to increase the flexibility of your programs. By using such constants, you can make it easy to modify a program to behave differently. Parameters provide much of the same flexibility, and more. Consider the `writeSpaces` method. Suppose you wrote it using a class constant:

```
public static final int NUMBER_OF_SPACES = 10;
```

This approach would give you the flexibility to produce a different number of spaces, but it has one major limitation: The constant can change only from execution to execution; it cannot change within a single execution. In other words, you can execute the program once with one value, edit the program, recompile, and then execute it again with a different value, but you can't use different values in a single execution of the program using a class constant.

Parameters are more flexible. Because you specify the value to be used each time you call the method, you can use several different values in a single program execution. As you have seen, you can call the method many different times within a single program execution and have it behave differently every time. However, using parameters involves more work for the programmer than using class constants. It makes your method headers and method calls more tedious, not to mention making the execution (and, thus, the debugging) more complex.

Therefore, you will probably find occasion to use each technique. The basic rule is to use a class constant when you only want to change the value from execution to execution. If you want to use different values within a single execution, use a parameter.

Overloading of Methods

You'll often want to create slight variations of the same method, passing different parameters. For example, you could have a `drawBox` method that allows you to specify a particular height and width, but you might also want to have a version that draws a box of default size. In other words, sometimes you want to specify these values, as in

```
drawBox(8, 10);
```

and other times you want to just draw a box with the standard height and width:

```
drawBox();
```

Some programming languages require you to come up with different names for these versions, such as `drawBox` and `drawDefaultBox`. As you can imagine, coming up with new names for each variation becomes tedious. Fortunately, Java allows you to have more than one method with the same name, as long as they have different parameters. This is called *overloading*. The primary requirement for overloading is that the different methods that you define must have different *method signatures*.

Method Overloading

The ability to define two or more different methods with the same name but different method signatures.

Method Signature

The name of a method, along with its number and type of parameters.

The two example `drawBox` versions clearly have different method signatures, because one has two parameters and the other has zero parameters. It would be obvious from any call on the method which version to use: If you see two parameters, you execute the version with two parameters; if you see zero parameters, you execute the version with zero parameters.

The situation gets more complicated when overloading involves the same number of parameters, but this turns out to be one of the most useful applications of overloading. For example, the `println` method is actually a series of overloaded methods. We can call `println` passing it a `String`, an `int`, a `double`, and so on. This flexibility is implemented as a series of different methods, all of which take one parameter: One version takes a `String`, another version takes an `int`, another version takes a `double`, and so on. Obviously, you do slightly different things to print one of these kinds of data versus another, which is why it's useful to have these different versions of the method.

3.2 Methods That Return Values

The last few methods we've looked at have been action-oriented methods that perform some specific task. You can think of them as being like commands that you could give someone, as in "Draw a box" or "Draw a triangle." Parameters allow these commands to be more flexible, as in "Draw a box that is 10 by 20."

You will also want to be able to write methods that compute values. These methods are more like questions, as in "What is the square root of 2.5?" or "What do you get when you carry 2.3 to the 4th power?" Consider, for example, a method called `sqrt` that would compute the square root of a number.

It might seem that the way to write such a method would be to have it accept a parameter of type `double` and `println` its square root to the console. But you may want to use the square root as part of a larger expression or computation, such as solving a quadratic equation or computing the distance between points on an *x*/*y* plane.

A better solution would be a square root command that passes the number of interest as a parameter and returns its square root back to the program as a result. You could then use the result as part of an expression, store it in a variable, or print it to the console. Such a command is a new type of method that is said to *return* a value.

> **Return**
> To send a value out as the result of a method that can be used in an expression in your program. Void methods do not return any value.

If you had such a method, you could ask for the square root of 2.5 by writing code like this:

```
// assuming you had a method named sqrt
double answer = sqrt(2.5);
```

The `sqrt` method has a parameter (the number whose square root you want to find), and it also returns a value (the square root). The actual parameter `2.5` goes "into" the method, and the square root comes out. In the preceding code, the returned result is stored in a variable called `answer`.

You can tell whether or not a method returns a value by looking at its header. All the methods you've written so far have begun with `public static void`. The word `void` is known as the *return type* of the method.

The `void` return type is a little odd because, as its name implies, the method returns nothing. A method can return any legal type: an `int`, a `double`, or any other type. In the case of the `sqrt` method, you want it to return a `double`, so you would write its header as follows:

```
public static double sqrt(double n)
```

As in the previous case, the word that comes after `public static` is the return type of the method:

```
public static double sqrt(double n)
              └──┬──┘
             return type
```

Fortunately, you don't actually need to write a method for computing the square root of a number, because Java has one that is built in. The method is included in a class known as `Math` that includes many useful computing methods. So, before we discuss the details of writing methods that return values, let's explore the `Math` class and what it has to offer.

The `Math` Class

In Chapter 1 we mentioned that a great deal of predefined code, collectively known as the Java class libraries, has been written for Java. One of the most useful classes is `Math`. It includes predefined mathematical constants and a large number of common mathematical functions. The `Math` class should be available on any machine on which Java is properly installed.

As we noted in the previous section, the `Math` class has a method called `sqrt` that computes the square root of a number. The method has the following header:

```
public static double sqrt(double n)
```

This header says that the method is called `sqrt`, that it takes a parameter of type `double`, and that it returns a value of type `double`.

Unfortunately, you can't just call this method directly by referring to it as `sqrt` because it is in another class. Whenever you want to refer to something declared in another class, you use *dot notation:*

```
<class name>.<element>
```

So you would refer to this method as `Math.sqrt`. Here's a sample program that uses the method:

```
public class WriteRoots {
    public static void main(String[] args) {
        for (int i = 1; i <= 20; i++) {
            double root = Math.sqrt(i);
            System.out.println("sqrt(" + i + ") = " + root);
        }
    }
}
```

This program produces the following output:

```
sqrt(1) = 1.0
sqrt(2) = 1.4142135623730951
sqrt(3) = 1.7320508075688772
sqrt(4) = 2.0
sqrt(5) = 2.23606797749979
sqrt(6) = 2.449489742783178
sqrt(7) = 2.6457513110645907
sqrt(8) = 2.8284271247461903
sqrt(9) = 3.0
sqrt(10) = 3.1622776601683795
sqrt(11) = 3.3166247903554
sqrt(12) = 3.4641016151377544
sqrt(13) = 3.605551275463989
sqrt(14) = 3.7416573867739413
sqrt(15) = 3.872983346207417
sqrt(16) = 4.0
sqrt(17) = 4.123105625617661
sqrt(18) = 4.242640687119285
sqrt(19) = 4.358898943540674
sqrt(20) = 4.47213595499958
```

Table 3.1 Math Constants

Constant	Description
`E`	base used in natural logarithms (2.71828 . . .)
`PI`	ratio of circumference of a circle to its diameter (3.14159 . . .)

Notice that we passed a value of type `int` to `Math.sqrt`, but the header says that it expects a value of type `double`. Remember that if Java is expecting a `double` and gets an `int`, it converts the `int` into a corresponding `double`.

The `Math` class also defines two frequently used constants: *e* and π (see Table 3.1). Following the Java convention, we use all uppercase letters for their names and refer to them as `Math.E` and `Math.PI`.

Table 3.2 lists some of the most useful static methods from the `Math` class. You can see a complete list of methods defined in the `Math` class by checking out the API

Table 3.2 Useful Static Methods in the `Math` Class

Method	Description	Example
`abs`	absolute value	`Math.abs(-308)` returns `308`
`ceil`	ceiling (rounds upward)	`Math.ceil(2.13)` returns `3.0`
`cos`	cosine (radians)	`Math.cos(Math.PI)` returns `-1.0`
`exp`	exponent base *e*	`Math.exp(1)` returns `2.7182818284590455`
`floor`	floor (rounds downward)	`Math.floor(2.93)` returns `2.0`
`log`	logarithm base *e*	`Math.log(Math.E)` returns `1.0`
`log10`	logarithm base 10	`Math.log10(1000)` returns `3.0`
`max`	maximum of two values	`Math.max(45, 207)` returns `207`
`min`	minimum of two values	`Math.min(3.8, 2.75)` returns `2.75`
`pow`	power (general exponentiation)	`Math.pow(3, 4)` returns `81.0`
`random`	random value	`Math.random()` returns a random `double` value *k* such that $0.0 \leq k < 1.0$
`round`	round real number to nearest integer	`Math.round(2.718)` returns `3`
`sin`	sine (radians)	`Math.sin(0)` returns `0.0`
`sqrt`	square root	`Math.sqrt(2)` returns `1.4142135623730951`
`toDegrees`	converts from radians to degrees	`Math.toDegrees(Math.PI)` returns `180.0`
`toRadians`	converts from degrees to radians	`Math.toRadians(270.0)` returns `4.71238898038469`

documentation for your version of Java. The API describes how to use the standard libraries that are available to Java programmers. It can be a bit overwhelming, because the Java libraries are vast. Wander around a bit if you are so inclined, but don't be dismayed that there are so many libraries to choose from in Java.

If you do look into the `Math` API, you'll notice that the `Math` class has several overloaded methods. For example, there is a version of the absolute value method (`Math.abs`) for integers and another for `doubles`. The rules that govern which method is called are complex, so we won't cover them here. The basic idea, though, is that Java tries to find the method that is the best fit. For the most part, you don't have to think much about this issue; you can just let Java choose for you, and it will generally make the right choice.

Defining Methods That Return Values

You can write your own methods that return values by using a special statement known as a `return` statement. For example, we often use a method that returns a value to express an equation. There is a famous story about the mathematician Carl Friedrich Gauss that illustrates the use of such a method. When Gauss was a boy, his teacher asked the class to add up the integers 1 through 100, thinking that it would take a while for them to complete the task. Gauss immediately found a formula and presented his answer to the teacher. He used a simple trick of adding two copies of the series together, one in forward order and one in backward order. This method allowed him to pair up values from the two copies so that their sum was the same:

First series	Second series	Sum
1	100	101
2	99	101
3	98	101
4	97	101
...	...	...
100	1	101

Every entry in the right-hand column is equal to 101 and there are 100 rows in this table, so the overall sum is $100 \times 101 = 10{,}100$. Of course, that's the sum of two copies of the sequence, so the actual answer is half that. Using this approach, Gauss determined that the sum of the first 100 integers is 5050. When the series goes from 1 to n, the sum is $(n + 1) \times n / 2$.

We can use Gauss' formula to write a method that computes the sum of the first n integers:

```
public static int sum(int n) {
    return (n + 1) * n / 2;
}
```

The sum method could be used by the main method in code such as the following:

```
int answer = sum(100);
System.out.println("The sum of 1 through 100 is " + answer);
```

A diagram of what happens when this code is executed follows. The method is invoked with the parameter n being initialized to 100. Plugging this value into the formula, we get a value of 5050, which is sent back to be stored in the variable called answer:

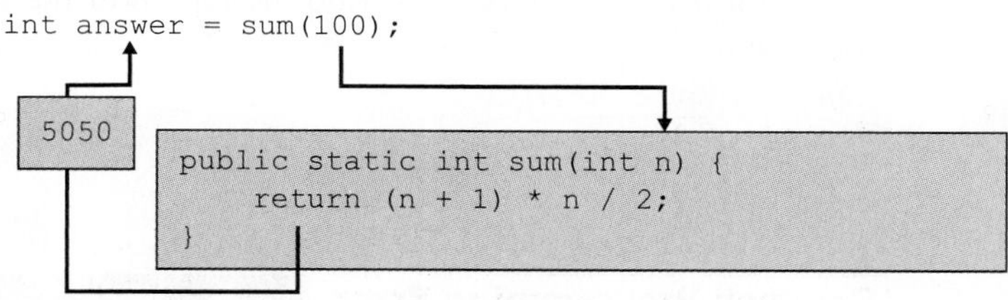


```
System.out.println("The sum of 1 through 100 is " + answer);
```

Notice once again that in the header for the method the familiar word void (indicating no return value) has been replaced with the word int. Remember that when you declare a method that returns a value, you have to tell Java what kind of value it will return. Thus, we can update our syntax template for static methods once more to clarify that the header includes a return type (void for none):

```
public static <type> <name>(<type> <name>, ..., <type> <name>) {
    <statement>;
    <statement>;
    ...
    <statement>;
}
```

The syntax of the return statement is:

```
return <expression>;
```

When Java encounters a return statement, it evaluates the given expression and immediately terminates the method, returning the value it obtained from the expression. As a result, it's not legal to have any other statements after a return statement; the return must be the last statement in your method. It is also an error for a Java method with a return type other than void to terminate without a return.

There are exceptions to the previous rules, as you'll see later. For example, it is possible for a method to have more than one return statement; this will come up in the next chapter, when we discuss conditional execution using if and if/else statements.

Let's look at another example method that returns a value. In *The Wizard of Oz*, the Scarecrow after being given a diploma demonstrates his intelligence by saying, "The sum of the square roots of any two sides of an isosceles triangle is equal to the square root of the remaining side. Oh, joy, oh, rapture. I've got a brain!" Probably he was trying to state the Pythagorean theorem, although it's not clear whether the writers were bad at math or whether they were making a comment about the value of a diploma. In an episode of *The Simpsons,* Homer repeats the Scarecrow's mistaken formula after putting on a pair of Henry Kissinger's glasses that he finds in a bathroom at the Springfield nuclear power plant.

The correct Pythagorean theorem refers only to right triangles and says that the length of the hypotenuse of a right triangle is equal to the square root of the sums of the squares of the two remaining sides. If you know the lengths of two sides a and b of a right triangle and want to find the length of the third side c, you compute it as follows:

$$c = \sqrt{a^2 + b^2}$$

Common Programming Error

Ignoring the Returned Value

When you call a method that returns a value, the expectation is that you'll do something with the value that's returned. You can print it, store it in a variable, or use it as part of a larger expression. It is legal (but unwise) to simply call the method and ignore the value being returned from it:

```
sum(1000);    // doesn't do anything
```

The preceding call doesn't print the sum or have any noticeable effect. If you want the value printed, you must include a `println` statement:

```
int answer = sum(1000);     // better
System.out.println("Sum up to 1000 is " + answer);
```

A shorter form of the fixed code would be the following:

```
System.out.println("Sum up to 1000 is " + sum(1000));
```

Say you want to print out the lengths of the hypotenuses of two right triangles, one with side lengths of 5 and 12, and the other with side lengths of 3 and 4. You could write code such as the following:

```
double c1 = Math.sqrt(Math.pow(5, 2) + Math.pow(12, 2));
System.out.println("hypotenuse 1 = " + c1);
double c2 = Math.sqrt(Math.pow(3, 2) + Math.pow(4, 2));
System.out.println("hypotenuse 2 = " + c2);
```

The preceding code is correct, but it's a bit hard to read, and you'd have to duplicate the same complex math a third time if you wanted to include a third triangle. A better solution would be to create a method that computes and returns the hypotenuse length when given the lengths of the two other sides as parameters. Such a method would look like this:

```
public static double hypotenuse(double a, double b) {
    double c = Math.sqrt(Math.pow(a, 2) + Math.pow(b, 2));
    return c;
}
```

This method can be used to craft a more concise and readable `main` method, as shown here.

```
public class Triangles {
    public static void main(String[] args) {
        System.out.println("hypotenuse 1 = " + hypotenuse(5, 12));
        System.out.println("hypotenuse 2 = " + hypotenuse(3, 4));
    }

    public static double hypotenuse(double a, double b) {
        double c = Math.sqrt(Math.pow(a, 2) + Math.pow(b, 2));
        return c;
    }
}
```

A few variations of this program are possible. For one, it isn't necessary to store the `hypotenuse` method's return value into the variable `c`. If you prefer, you can simply compute and return the value in one line. In this case, the body of the `hypotenuse` method would become the following:

```
return Math.sqrt(Math.pow(a, 2) + Math.pow(b, 2));
```

Also, some programmers avoid using `Math.pow` for low powers such as 2 and just manually do the multiplication. Using that approach, the body of the hypotenuse method would look like this:

```
return Math.sqrt(a * a + b * b);
```

Common Programming Error

Statement after Return

It's illegal to place other statements immediately after a `return` statement, because those statements can never be reached or executed. New programmers often accidentally do this when trying to print the value of a variable after returning. Say you've written the `hypotenuse` method but have accidentally written the parameters to `Math.pow` in the wrong order, so the method is not producing the right answer. You would try to debug this by printing the value of `c` that is being returned. Here's the faulty code:

```
// trying to find the bug in this buggy version of hypotenuse
public static double hypotenuse(double a, double b) {
    double c = Math.sqrt(Math.pow(2, a) + Math.pow(2, b));
    return c;
    System.out.println(c);  // this doesn't work
}
```

The compiler complains about the `println` statement being unreachable, since it follows a `return` statement. The compiler error output looks something like this:

```
Triangles.java:10: error: unreachable statement
        System.out.println(c);
        ^
Triangles.java:11: error: missing return statement
    }
    ^
2 errors
```

The fix is to move the `println` statement earlier in the method, before the `return` statement:

```
public static double hypotenuse(double a, double b) {
    double c = Math.sqrt(Math.pow(2, a) + Math.pow(2, b));
    System.out.println(c);   // better
    return c;
}
```

3.3 Using Objects

We've spent a considerable amount of time discussing the primitive types in Java and how they work, so it's about time that we started talking about objects and how they work.

The idea for objects came from the observation that as we start working with new kinds of data (integers, reals, characters, text, etc.), we find ourselves writing a lot of methods that operate on that data. Rather than completely separating the basic operations from the data, it seemed to make sense to include them together. This packaging of data and operations into one entity is the central idea behind objects. An *object* stores some data and has methods that act on its data.

> **Object**
> A programming entity that contains state (data) and behavior (methods).

As we said in Chapter 1, classes are the basic building blocks of Java programs. But classes also serve another purpose: to describe new types of objects.

> **Class**
> A category or type of object.

When it is used this way, a class is like a blueprint of what the object looks like. Once you've given Java the blueprint, you can ask it to create actual objects that match that blueprint. We sometimes refer to the individual objects as *instances* of the class. We tend to use the words "instance" and "object" interchangeably.

This concept is difficult to understand in the abstract. To help you come to grips with what it means and how it works, we'll look at several different classes. In keeping with our idea of focusing on fundamental concepts first, in this chapter we'll study how to use existing objects that are already part of Java, but we aren't going to study how to define our own new types of objects just yet. We'll get to that in Chapter 8, after we've had time to practice using objects.

Using objects differs from using primitive types, so we'll have to introduce some new syntax and concepts. It would be nice if Java had a consistent model for using all types of data, but it doesn't. Consequently, if you want to understand how your programs operate, you'll have to learn two sets of rules: one for primitives and one for objects.

`String` Objects

VideoNote

`String` objects are one of the most useful and most commonly used types of objects in Java, so they make a good starting point. They aren't the best example of objects, though, because there are a lot of special rules that apply only to `strings`. In the next section, we'll look at a more typical kind of object.

One special property of `String` objects is that there are literals that represent them (string literals). We've been using them in `println` statements since Chapter 1. What we haven't discussed is that these literal values represent objects of type `String` (instances of the `String` class). For example, in the same way that you can say

```
int x = 8;
```

you can say

```
String s = "hello there";
```

You can declare variables of type `String` and use the assignment statement to give values to these variables. You can also write code that involves `String` expressions:

```
String s1 = "hello";
String s2 = "there";
String combined = s1 + " " + s2;
```

This code defines two `Strings` that each represent a single word and a third `String` that represents the concatenation of the two words with a space in between. You'll notice that the type `String` is capitalized (as are the names of all object types in Java), unlike the primitive types such as `double` and `int`.

These examples haven't shown what's special about `String` objects, but we're getting there. Remember that the idea behind objects was to include basic operations with the data itself, the way we make cars that have controls built in. The data stored in a `String` is a sequence of characters. There are all sorts of operations you might want to perform on this sequence of characters. For example, you might want to know how many characters there are in the `String`. `String` objects have a `length` method that returns this information.

If the `length` method were static, you would call it by saying something like

```
length(s)     // this isn't legal
```

But when you perform operations on objects, you use a different syntax. Objects store data and methods, so the method to report a `String`'s length actually exists inside that `String` object itself. To call an object's method, you write the name of the variable first, followed by a dot, and then the name of the method:

```
s.length()
```

Think of it as talking to the `String` object. When you ask for `s.length()`, you're saying, "Hey, `s`. I'm talking to you. What's your length?" Of course, different `String` objects have different lengths, so you will get different answers when you communicate with different `String` objects.

The general syntax for calling a method of an object is the following:

```
<variable>.<method name>(<expression>, <expression>, ..., <expression>)
```

For example, suppose that you have initialized two `String` variables as follows:

```
String s1 = "hello";
String s2 = "how are you?";
```

You can use a `println` to examine the length of each `String`:

```
System.out.println("Length of s1 = " + s1.length());
System.out.println("Length of s2 = " + s2.length());
```

This code produces the following output:

```
Length of s1 = 5
Length of s2 = 12
```

What else might you want to do with a `String` object? With the `length` method, you can figure out how many characters there are in a `String`, but what about getting the individual characters themselves? There are several ways to do this, but one of the most common is to use a method called `charAt` that returns the character at a specific location in the string.

This leads us to the problem of how to specify locations in a sequence. Obviously there is a first character, a second character, and so on, so it makes sense to use an integer to refer to a specific location. We call this the *index*.

Index

An integer used to specify a location in a sequence of values. Java generally uses zero-based indexing (with 0 as the first index value, followed by 1, 2, 3, and so on).

Each character of a `String` object is assigned an index value, starting with 0. For example, for the variable `s1` that refers to the string `"hello"`, the indexes are:

0	1	2	3	4
h	e	l	l	o

It may seem intuitive to consider the letter "h" to be at position 1, but there are advantages to starting with an index of 0. It's a convention that was adopted by the designers of the C language and that has been followed by the designers of C++ and Java, so it's a convention you'll have to learn to live with.

For the longer `String s2`, the positions are:

0	1	2	3	4	5	6	7	8	9	10	11
h	o	w		a	r	e		y	o	u	?

Notice that the spaces in this `String` have positions as well (here, positions 3 and 7). Also notice that the indexes for a given string always range from 0 to one less than the length of the string.

Using the `charAt` method, you can request specific characters of a string. The return type is `char`. For example, if you ask for `s1.charAt(1)` you'll get `'e'` (the 'e' in "hello"). If you ask for `s2.charAt(5)`, you'll get `'r'` (the 'r' in "how are you?"). For any `String`, if you ask for `charAt(0)`, you'll get the first character of the string.

When you are working with `String` objects, you'll often find it useful to write a `for` loop to handle the different characters of the `String`. Because `Strings` are indexed starting at 0, this task is easier to write with `for` loops that start with `0` rather than `1`. Consider, for example, the following code that prints out the individual characters of `s1`:

```
String s1 = "hello";
for (int i = 0; i < s1.length(); i++) {
    System.out.println(i + ": " + s1.charAt(i));
}
```

This code produces the following output:

```
0: h
1: e
2: l
3: l
4: o
```

Remember that when we start loops at 0, we usually test with less than (<) rather than less than or equal to (<=). The string `s1` has five characters in it, so the call on `s1.length()` will return `5`. But because the first index is 0, the last index will be one less than 5, or 4. This convention takes a while to get used to, but zero-based indexing is used throughout Java, so you'll eventually get the hang of it.

Another useful `String` method is the `substring` method. It takes two integer arguments representing a starting and ending index. When you call the `substring` method, you provide two of these indexes: the index of the first character you want and the index just past the last index that you want.

Recall that the `String s2` has the following positions:

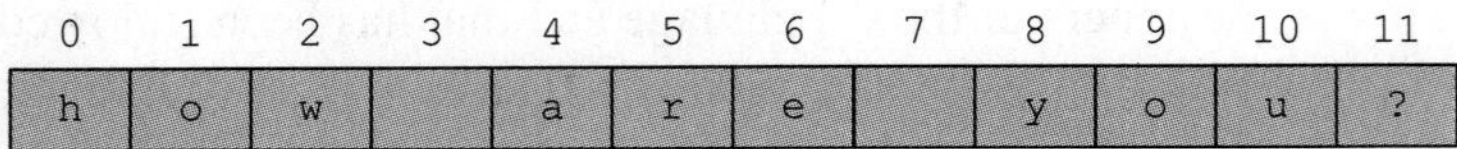

If you want to pull out the individual word "how" from this string, you'd ask for

```
s2.substring(0, 3)
```

Remember that the second value that you pass to the `substring` method is supposed to be one beyond the end of the substring you are forming. So, even though there is a space at position 3 in the original string, it will not be part of what you get from the call on `substring`. Instead, you'll get all the characters just before position 3.

Following this rule means that sometimes you will give a position to a substring at which there is no character. For instance, the last character in the string to which `s2` refers is at index 11 (the question mark). If you want to get the substring "you?" including the question mark, you'd ask for

```
s2.substring(8, 12)
```

There is no character at position 12 in `s2`, but this call asks for characters starting at position 8 that come before position 12, so this actually makes sense.

You have to be careful about what indexes you use, though. With the `substring` method you can ask for the position just beyond the end of the `String`, but you can't ask for anything beyond that. For example, if you ask for

```
s2.substring(8, 13)     // out of bounds!
```

your program will generate an execution error. Similarly, if you ask for the `charAt` at a nonexistent position, your program will generate an execution error. These errors are known as *exceptions.*

Exceptions are runtime errors as mentioned in Chapter 1.

Exception

A runtime error that prevents a program from continuing its normal execution.

We say that an exception is *thrown* when an error is encountered. When an exception is thrown, Java looks to see if you have written code to handle it. If not, program execution is halted and you will see what is known as a *stack trace* or *back trace.* The stack trace shows you the series of methods that have been called, in reverse order. In the case of bad `String` indexes, the exception prints a message such as the following to the console:

```
Exception in thread "main"
        java.lang.StringIndexOutOfBoundsException:
        String index out of range: 13
        at java.lang.String.substring(Unknown Source)
        at ExampleProgram.main(ExampleProgram.java:3)
```

You can use `Strings` as parameters to methods. For example, the following program uses `String` parameters to eliminate some of the redundancy in a popular children's song:

```
public class BusSong {
    public static void main(String[] args) {
        verse("wheels", "go", "round and round");
        verse("wipers", "go", "swish, swish, swish");
        verse("horn", "goes", "beep, beep, beep");
    }

    public static void verse(String item, String verb, String sound) {
        System.out.println("The " + item + " on the bus " +
                           verb + " " + sound + ",");
```

```
        System.out.println(sound + ",");
        System.out.println(sound + ".");
        System.out.println("The " + item + " on the bus " +
                           verb + " " + sound + ",");
        System.out.println("All through the town.");
        System.out.println();
    }
}
```

It produces the following output:

```
The wheels on the bus go round and round,
round and round,
round and round.
The wheels on the bus go round and round,
All through the town.

The wipers on the bus go swish, swish, swish,
swish, swish, swish,
swish, swish, swish.
The wipers on the bus go swish, swish, swish,
All through the town.

The horn on the bus goes beep, beep, beep,
beep, beep, beep,
beep, beep, beep.
The horn on the bus goes beep, beep, beep,
All through the town.
```

Table 3.3 lists some of the most useful methods that you can call on `String` objects. `Strings` in Java are *immutable,* which means that once they are constructed, their values can never be changed.

Immutable Object

An object whose value cannot be changed.

It may seem odd that `Strings` are immutable and yet have methods like `toUpperCase` and `toLowerCase`. But if you read the descriptions in the table carefully, you'll see that these methods don't actually change a given `String` object; instead they return a new string. Consider the following code:

```
String s = "Hello, Maria";
s.toUpperCase();
System.out.println(s);
```

Table 3.3 Useful Methods of `String` Objects

Method	Description	Example (assuming `s` is `"hello"`)
`charAt(index)`	character at a specific index	`s.charAt(1)` returns `'e'`
`endsWith(text)`	whether or not the string ends with some text	`s.endsWith("llo")` returns `true`
`indexOf(text)`	index of a particular character or `String` (`–1` if not present)	`s.indexOf("o")` returns `4`
`length()`	number of characters in the string	`s.length()` returns `5`
`replace(s1, s2)`	replace all occurrences of one substring with another	`s.replace("l", "y")` returns `"heyyyyo"`
`startsWith(text)`	whether or not the string starts with some text	`s.startsWith("hi")` returns `false`
`substring(start, stop)`	characters from start index to just before stop index	`s.substring(1, 3)` returns `"el"`
`toLowerCase()`	a new string with all lowercase letters	`s.toLowerCase()` returns `"hello"`
`toUpperCase()`	a new string with all uppercase letters	`s.toUpperCase()` returns `"HELLO"`

You might think that this will turn the string `s` into its uppercase equivalent, but it doesn't. The second line of code constructs a new string that has the uppercase equivalent of the value of `s`, but we don't do anything with this new value. In order to turn the string into uppercase, the key is to either store this new string in a different variable or reassign the variable `s` to point to the new string:

```
String s = "Hello, Maria";
s = s.toUpperCase();
System.out.println(s);
```

This version of the code produces the following output:

```
HELLO, MARIA
```

The `toUpperCase` and `toLowerCase` methods are particularly helpful when you want to perform string comparisons in which you ignore the case of the letters involved.

Another useful method found in String objects is the `replace` method. It accepts two parameters: a string to search for, and a new string to replace all occurrences of it with.

```
String s = "Tweedle Dee";
```

Interactive Programs and `Scanner` Objects

VideoNote

As you've seen, you can easily produce output in the console window by calling `System.out.println` and `System.out.print`. You can also write programs that pause and wait for the user to type a response. Such programs are known as *interactive* programs, and the responses typed by the user are known as *console input.*

> **Console Input**
>
> Responses typed by the user when an interactive program pauses for input.

When you refer to `System.out`, you are accessing an object in the `System` class known as the standard output stream, or "standard out" for short. There is a corresponding object for standard input known as `System.in`, but Java wasn't designed for console input, and `System.in` has never been particularly easy to use for this purpose. Fortunately for us, there is an easier way to read console input: `Scanner` objects.

Most objects have to be explicitly constructed by calling a special method known as a *constructor.*

> **Constructor (Construct)**
>
> A method that creates and initializes an object. Objects in Java programs must be constructed before they can be used.

Remember that a class is like a blueprint for a family of objects. Calling a constructor is like sending an order to the factory asking it to follow the blueprint to get you an actual object that you can manipulate. When you send in your order to the factory, you sometimes specify certain parameters (e.g., what color you want the object to be).

In Java, constructors are called using the special keyword `new`, followed by the object's type and any necessary parameters. For example, to construct a specific `Scanner` object, you have to pass information about the source of input. In particular, you have to provide an input stream. To read from the console window, pass it `System.in`:

```
Scanner console = new Scanner(System.in);
```

Once you've constructed the `Scanner`, you can ask it to return a value of a particular type. A number of methods, all beginning with the word "next," are available to obtain the various types of values. Table 3.4 lists them.

Typically, you will use variables to keep track of the values returned by these methods. For example, you might say:

```
int n = console.nextInt();
```

Table 3.4 Scanner Methods

Method	Description
`next()`	reads and returns the next token as a `String`
`nextDouble()`	reads and returns a `double` value
`nextInt()`	reads and returns an `int` value
`nextLine()`	reads and returns the next line of input as a `String`

The call on the `console` object's `nextInt` method pauses for user input. Whenever the computer pauses for input, it will pause for an entire line of input. In other words, it will wait until the user hits the Enter key before continuing to execute the program.

You can use the `Scanner` class to read input line by line using the `nextLine` method, although we won't be using `nextLine` very much for now. The other "next" methods are all *token*-based (that is, they read single elements of input rather than entire lines).

Token

A single element of input (e.g., one word, one number).

By default, the `Scanner` uses *whitespace* to separate tokens.

Whitespace

Spaces, tab characters, and new line characters.

A `Scanner` object looks at what the user types and uses the whitespace on the input line to break it up into individual tokens. For example, the line of input

```
hello     there. "how are"          "you?"  all-one-token
```

would be split into six tokens:

```
hello
there.
"how
are"
"you?"
all-one-token
```

Notice that the `Scanner` includes punctuation characters such as periods, question marks, and quotation marks in the tokens it generates. It also includes dashes, so because there is no whitespace in the middle to break it up into different tokens, we get just one token for "all-one-token." It's possible to control how a `Scanner` turns things into tokens (a process called *tokenizing* the input), but we won't be doing anything that fancy.

It is possible to read more than one value from a `Scanner`, as in:

```
double x = console.nextDouble();
double y = console.nextDouble();
```

Because there are two different calls on the `console` object's `nextDouble` method, this code will cause the computer to pause until the user has entered two numeric values. The values can be entered on the same line or on separate lines. In general, the computer continues to pause for user input until it has obtained whatever values you have asked the `Scanner` to obtain.

If a user types something that isn't an integer when you call `nextInt`, such as `XYZZY`, the `Scanner` object generates an exception. Recall from the section on `String` objects that exceptions are runtime errors that halt program execution. In this case, you'll see runtime error output such as the following:

```
Exception in thread "main" java.util.InputMismatchException
        at java.util.Scanner.throwFor(Unknown Source)
        at java.util.Scanner.next(Unknown Source)
        at java.util.Scanner.nextInt(Unknown Source)
        at Example.main(Example.java:13)
```

You will see in a later chapter how to test for user errors. In the meantime, we will assume that the user provides appropriate input.

Sample Interactive Program

Using the `Scanner` class, we can write a complete interactive program that performs a useful computation for the user. If you ever find yourself buying a house, you'll want to know what your monthly mortgage payment is going to be. The following is a complete program that asks for information about a loan and prints the monthly payment:

```
// This program prompts for information about a loan and
// computes the monthly mortgage payment.

import java.util.*;    // for Scanner

public class Mortgage {
    public static void main(String[] args) {
        Scanner console = new Scanner(System.in);

        // obtain values
        System.out.println("This program computes monthly " +
                           "mortgage payments.");
        System.out.print("loan amount     : ");
        double loan = console.nextDouble();
        System.out.print("number of years : ");
        int years = console.nextInt();
        System.out.print("interest rate   : ");
        double rate = console.nextDouble();
        System.out.println();

        // compute result and report
        int n = 12 * years;
        double c = rate / 12.0 / 100.0;
```

```
        double payment = loan * c * Math.pow(1 + c, n) /
                              (Math.pow(1 + c, n) - 1);
        System.out.println("payment = $" + (int) payment);
    }
}
```

The following is a sample execution of the program (user input is in bold):

```
This program computes monthly mortgage payments.
loan amount      : 275000
number of years : 30
interest rate    : 4.25

payment = $1352
```

The first thing we do in the program is construct a `Scanner` object, which we will use for console input. Next, we explain what the program is going to do, printing a description to the console. This is essential for interactive programs. You don't want a program to pause for user input until you've explained to the user what is going to happen.

Below the `println`, you'll notice several pairs of statements like these:

```
System.out.print("loan amount      : ");
double loan = console.nextDouble();
```

The first statement is called a *prompt,* a request for information from the user. We use a `print` statement instead of a `println` so that the user will type the values on the same line as the prompt (i.e., to the right of the prompt). The second statement calls the `nextDouble` method of the `console` object to read a value of type `double` from the user. This value is stored in a variable called `loan`. This pattern of prompt/read statements is common in interactive programs.

After prompting for values, the program computes several values. The formula for computing monthly mortgage payments involves the loan amount, the total number of months involved (a value we call `n`), and the monthly interest rate (a value we call `c`). The payment formula is given by the following equation:

$$payment = loan \frac{c(1 + c)^n}{(1 + c)^n - 1}$$

You will notice in the program that we use the `Math.pow` method for exponentiation to translate this formula into a Java expression.

The final line of the program prints out the monthly payment. You might imagine that we would simply say:

```
System.out.println("payment = $" + payment);
```

However, because the payment is stored in a variable of type `double`, such a statement would print all the digits of the number. For example, for the log listed above, it would print the following:

```
payment = $1352.8347004685593
```

That is a rather strange-looking output for someone who is used to dollars and cents. For the purposes of this simple program, it's easy to cast the `double` to an `int` and report just the dollar amount of the payment:

```
System.out.println("payment = $" + (int) payment);
```

Most people trying to figure out their mortgage payments aren't that interested in the pennies, so the program is still useful. In the next section, we will see how to round a `double` to two decimal places.

There is something new at the beginning of this class file called an *import declaration.* Remember that Java has a large number of classes included in what are collectively known as the Java class libraries. To help manage these classes, Java provides an organizational unit known as a *package.* Related classes are combined together into a single package. For example, the `Scanner` class is stored in a package known as `java.util`. Java programs don't normally have access to a package unless they include an import declaration.

Package

A collection of related Java classes.

Import Declaration

A request to access a specific Java package.

We haven't needed an `import` declaration yet because Java automatically imports every class stored in a package called `java.lang`. The `java.lang` package includes basic classes that most Java programs are likely to use (e.g., `System`, `String`, `Math`). Because Java does not automatically import `java.util`, you have to do it yourself.

Java allows you to use an asterisk to import all classes from a package:

```
import java.util.*;
```

But some people prefer to specifically mention each class they import. The import declaration allows you to import just a single class from a package, as in

```
import java.util.Scanner;
```

The problem is that once you start importing one class from a package, you're likely to want to import others as well. We will use the asterisk version of `import` in this book to keep things simple.

3.4 Case Study: Projectile Trajectory

It's time to pull together the threads of this chapter with a more complex example that will involve parameters, methods that return values, mathematical computations, and the use of a `Scanner` object for console input.

Physics students are often asked to calculate the trajectory that a projectile will follow, given its initial velocity and its initial angle relative to the horizontal. For example, the projectile might be a football that someone has kicked. We want to compute the path it follows given Earth's gravity. To keep the computation reasonable, we will ignore air resistance.

There are several questions relating to this problem that we might want to answer:

- When does the projectile reach its highest point?
- How high does it reach?
- How long does it take to come back to the ground?
- How far does it land from where it was launched?

There are several ways to answer these questions. One simple approach is to provide a table that displays the trajectory step by step, indicating the *x* position, *y* position, and elapsed time.

To make such a table, we need to obtain three values from the user: the initial velocity, the angle relative to the horizontal, and the number of steps to include in the table we will produce. We could ask for the velocity in either meters/second or feet/second, but given that this is a physics problem, we'll stick to the metric system and ask for meters/second.

We also have to think about how to specify the angle. Unfortunately, most of the Java methods that operate on angles require angles in radians rather than degrees. We could request the angle in radians, but that would be highly inconvenient for the user, who would be required to make the conversion. Instead, we can allow the user to enter the angle in degrees and then convert it to radians using the built-in method `Math.toRadians`.

So, the interactive part of the program will look like this:

```
Scanner console = new Scanner(System.in);
System.out.print("velocity (meters/second)? ");
double velocity = console.nextDouble();
System.out.print("angle (degrees)? ");
double angle = Math.toRadians(console.nextDouble());
System.out.print("number of steps to display? ");
int steps = console.nextInt();
```

Notice that for the velocity and angle we call the `nextDouble` method of the `console` object, because we want to let the user specify any number (including one with a decimal point), but for the number of steps we call `nextInt`, because the number of lines in our table needs to be an integer.

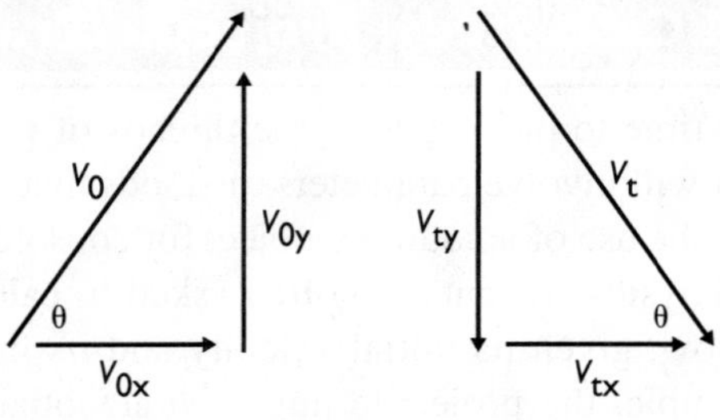

Figure 3.1 Initial and Final Velocity of Projectile

Look more closely at this line of code:

```
double angle = Math.toRadians(console.nextDouble());
```

Some beginners would write this as two separate steps:

```
double angleInDegrees = console.nextDouble();
double angle = Math.toRadians(angleInDegrees);
```

Both approaches work and are reasonable, but keep in mind that you don't need to divide this operation into two separate steps. You can write it in the more compact form as a single line of code.

Once we have obtained these values from the user, we are ready to begin the computations for the trajectory table. The *x*/*y*-position of the projectile at each time increment is determined by its velocity in each dimension and by the acceleration on the projectile due to gravity. Figure 3.1 shows the projectile's initial velocity v_0 and angle θ just as it is thrown and final velocity v_t just as it hits the ground.

We need to compute the *x* component of the velocity versus the *y* component of the velocity. From physics, we know that these can be computed as follows:

```
double xVelocity = velocity * Math.cos(angle);
double yVelocity = velocity * Math.sin(angle);
```

Because we are ignoring the possibility of air resistance, the *x*-velocity will not change. The *y*-velocity, however, is subject to the pull of gravity. Physics tells us that on the surface of the Earth, acceleration due to gravity is approximately 9.81 meters/second^2. This is an appropriate value to define as a class constant:

```
public static final double ACCELERATION = –9.81;
```

Notice that we define gravity acceleration as a negative number because it decreases the *y*-velocity of an object (pulling it down as opposed to pushing it away).

Our goal is to display *x*, *y*, and elapsed time as the object goes up and comes back down again. The *y*-velocity decreases steadily until it becomes 0. From physics, we know that the graph of the projectile will be symmetrical. The projectile will go upward until its *y*-velocity reaches 0, and then it will follow a similar path back down that takes an equal amount of time. Thus, the total time involved in seconds can be computed as follows:

```
double totalTime = -2.0 * yVelocity / ACCELERATION;
```

Now, how do we compute the values of *x*, *y*, and elapsed time to include in our table? It is relatively simple to compute two of these. We want steady time increments for each entry in the table, so we can compute the time increment by dividing the total time by the number of steps we want to include in our table:

```
double timeIncrement = totalTime / steps;
```

As noted earlier, the *x*-velocity does not change, so for each of these time increments, we move the same distance in the *x*-direction:

```
double xIncrement = xVelocity * timeIncrement;
```

The tricky value to compute here is the *y*-position. Because of acceleration due to gravity, the *y*-velocity changes over time. But from physics, we have the following general formula for computing the displacement of an object given the velocity v, time t, and acceleration a:

$$\text{displacement} = vt + \frac{1}{2}at^2$$

In our case, the velocity we want is the *y*-velocity and the acceleration is from the Earth's gravity constant. Here, then, is a pseudocode description of how to create the table:

```
set all of x, y, and t to 0.
for (given number of steps) {
    add timeIncrement to t.
    add xIncrement to x.
    reset y to yVelocity * t + 0.5 * ACCELERATION * t * t.
    report step #, x, y, t.
}
```

We are fairly close to having real Java code here, but we have to think about how to report the values of `x`, `y`, and `t` in a table. They will all be of type `double`, which means they are likely to produce a large number of digits after the decimal point. But we aren't interested in seeing all those digits, because they aren't particularly relevant and because our computations aren't that accurate.

Before we try to complete the code for the table, let's think about the problem of displaying only some of the digits of a number. The idea is to truncate the digits so that we don't see all of them. One way to truncate is to cast a `double` to an `int`, which truncates all of the digits after the decimal point. We could do that, but we probably want at least some of those digits. Say, for example, that we want to report two digits after the decimal point. The trick is to bring the two digits we want to the other side of the decimal point. We can do that by multiplying by 100 and then casting to `int`:

```
(int) (n * 100.0)
```

This expression gets us the digits we want, but now the decimal point is in the wrong place. For example, if `n` is initially `3.488834`, the preceding expression will give us `348`. We have to divide this result by 100 to turn it back into the number 3.48:

```
(int) (n * 100.0) / 100.0
```

While we're at it, we can make one final improvement. Notice that the original number was `3.488834`. If we do simple truncation we get `3.48`, but really this number is closer to `3.49`. We can round to the nearest digit by calling the `Math.round` method on the number instead of casting it:

```
Math.round(n * 100.0) / 100.0
```

This is an operation that we are likely to want to perform on more than one number, so it deserves to be included in a method:

```
public static double round2(double n) {
    return Math.round(n * 100.0) / 100.0;
}
```

Getting back to our pseudocode for the table, we can incorporate calls on the `round2` method to get a bit closer to actual Java code:

```
set all of x, y, and t to 0.
for (given number of steps) {
    add timeIncrement to t.
    add xIncrement to x.
    reset y to yVelocity * t + 0.5 * ACCELERATION * t * t.
    report step #, round2(x), round2(y), round2(t).
}
```

It would be nice if the values in the table were aligned. To get numbers that line up nicely, we would have to use formatted output, which we will discuss in Chapter 4. For now, we can at least get the numbers to line up in columns by separating them with tab characters. Remember that the escape sequence `\t` represents a single tab.

If we're going to have a table with columns, it also makes sense to have a header for the table. And we probably want to include a line in the table showing the initial condition, where x, y, and time are all equal to 0. So we can expand our pseudocode into the following Java code:

```
double x = 0.0;
double y = 0.0;
double t = 0.0;
System.out.println("step\tx\ty\ttime");
System.out.println("0\t0.0\t0.0\t0.0");
for (int i = 1; i <= steps; i++) {
    t += timeIncrement;
    x += xIncrement;
    y = yVelocity * t + 0.5 * ACCELERATION * t * t;
    System.out.println(i + "\t" + round2(x) + "\t" +
                       round2(y) + "\t" + round2(t));
}
```

Unstructured Solution

We can put all of these pieces together to form a complete program. Let's first look at an unstructured version that includes most of the code in `main`. This version also includes some new `println` statements at the beginning that give a brief introduction to the user:

```
// This program computes the trajectory of a projectile.

import java.util.*; // for Scanner

public class Projectile {
    // constant for Earth acceleration in meters/second^2
    public static final double ACCELERATION = -9.81;

    public static void main(String[] args) {
        Scanner console = new Scanner(System.in);

        System.out.println("This program computes the");
        System.out.println("trajectory of a projectile given");
        System.out.println("its initial velocity and its");
        System.out.println("angle relative to the");
        System.out.println("horizontal.");
        System.out.println();

        System.out.print("velocity (meters/second)? ");
        double velocity = console.nextDouble();
        System.out.print("angle (degrees)? ");
        double angle = Math.toRadians(console.nextDouble());
```

```
        System.out.print("number of steps to display? ");
        int steps = console.nextInt();
        System.out.println();

        double xVelocity = velocity * Math.cos(angle);
        double yVelocity = velocity * Math.sin(angle);
        double totalTime = -2.0 * yVelocity / ACCELERATION;
        double timeIncrement = totalTime / steps;
        double xIncrement = xVelocity * timeIncrement;

        double x = 0.0;
        double y = 0.0;
        double t = 0.0;
        System.out.println("step\tx\ty\ttime");
        System.out.println("0\t0.0\t0.0\t0.0");
        for (int i = 1; i <= steps; i++) {
            t += timeIncrement;
            x += xIncrement;
            y = yVelocity * t + 0.5 * ACCELERATION * t * t;
            System.out.println(i + "\t" + round2(x) + "\t" +
                               round2(y) + "\t" + round2(t));
        }
    }

    public static double round2(double n) {
        return Math.round(n * 100.0) / 100.0;
    }
}
```

The following is a sample execution of the program:

```
This program computes the
trajectory of a projectile given
its initial velocity and its
angle relative to the
horizontal.

velocity (meters/second)? 30
angle (degrees)? 50
number of steps to display? 10

step    x       y       time
0       0.0     0.0     0.0
1       9.03    9.69    0.47
```

```
2       18.07   17.23   0.94
3       27.1    22.61   1.41
4       36.14   25.84   1.87
5       45.17   26.92   2.34
6       54.21   25.84   2.81
7       63.24   22.61   3.28
8       72.28   17.23   3.75
9       81.31   9.69    4.22
10      90.35   0.0     4.69
```

From the log of execution, you can see that the projectile reaches a maximum height of 26.92 meters after 2.34 seconds (the fifth step) and that it lands 90.35 meters from where it began after 4.69 seconds (the tenth step).

This version of the program works, but we don't generally want to include so much code in the `main` method. The next section explores how to break up the program into smaller pieces.

Structured Solution

There are three major blocks of code in the `main` method of the `Projectile` program: a series of `println` statements that introduce the program to the user, a series of statements that prompt the user for the three values used to produce the table, and then the code that produces the table itself.

So, in pseudocode, the overall structure looks like this:

```
give introduction.
prompt for velocity, angle, and number of steps.
produce table.
```

The first and third steps are easily turned into methods, but not the middle step. This step prompts the user for values that we need to produce the table. If we turned it into a method, it would have to somehow return three values back to `main`. A method can return only a single value, so unfortunately we can't turn this step into a method. We could turn it into three different methods, one for each of the three values, but each of those methods would be just two lines long, so it's not clear that doing so would improve the overall structure.

The main improvement we can make, then, is to split off the introduction and the table into separate methods. Another improvement we can make is to turn the physics displacement formula into its own method. It is always a good idea to turn equations into methods. Introducing those methods, we get the following structured version of the program:

```
// This program computes the trajectory of a projectile.

import java.util.*;      // for Scanner

public class Projectile2 {
```

```
    // constant for Earth acceleration in meters/second^2
    public static final double ACCELERATION = −9.81;

    public static void main(String[] args) {
        Scanner console = new Scanner(System.in);
        giveIntro();

        System.out.print("velocity (meters/second)? ");
        double velocity = console.nextDouble();
        System.out.print("angle (degrees)? ");
        double angle = Math.toRadians(console.nextDouble());
        System.out.print("number of steps to display? ");
        int steps = console.nextInt();
        System.out.println();

        printTable(velocity, angle, steps);
    }

    // prints a table showing the trajectory of an object given
    // its initial velocity and angle and including the given
    // number of steps in the table
    public static void printTable(double velocity,
                                  double angle, int steps) {
        double xVelocity = velocity * Math.cos(angle);
        double yVelocity = velocity * Math.sin(angle);
        double totalTime = −2.0 * yVelocity / ACCELERATION;
        double timeIncrement = totalTime / steps;
        double xIncrement = xVelocity * timeIncrement;

        double x = 0.0;
        double y = 0.0;
        double t = 0.0;
        System.out.println("step\tx\ty\ttime");
        System.out.println("0\t0.0\t0.0\t0.0");
        for (int i = 1; i <= steps; i++) {
            t += timeIncrement;
            x += xIncrement;
            y = displacement(yVelocity, t, ACCELERATION);
            System.out.println(i + "\t" + round2(x) + "\t" +
                               round2(y) + "\t" + round2(t));
        }
    }

    // gives a brief introduction to the user
```

```
    public static void giveIntro() {
        System.out.println("This program computes the");
        System.out.println("trajectory of a projectile given");
        System.out.println("its initial velocity and its");
        System.out.println("angle relative to the");
        System.out.println("horizontal.");
        System.out.println();
    }

    // returns the vertical displacement for a body given
    // initial velocity v, elapsed time t, and acceleration a
    public static double displacement(double v, double t,
                                      double a) {
        return v * t + 0.5 * a * t * t;
    }

    // rounds n to 2 digits after the decimal point
    public static double round2(double n) {
        return Math.round(n * 100.0) / 100.0;
    }
}
```

This version executes the same way as the earlier version.

Chapter Summary

Methods may be written to accept parameters, which are sets of characteristics that distinguish different members of a family of tasks. Parameters allow data values to flow into a method, which can change the way the method executes. A method declared with a set of parameters can perform an entire family of similar tasks instead of exactly one task.

When primitive values such as those of type `int` or `double` are passed as parameters, their values are copied into the method. Primitive parameters send values into a method but not out of it; the method can use the data values but cannot affect the value of any variables outside it.

Two methods can have the same name if they declare different parameters. This is called overloading.

Methods can be written to return values to the calling code. This feature allows a method to perform a complex computation and then provide its result back to the calling code. The type of the return value must be declared in the method's header and is called the method's return type.

Java has a class called `Math` that contains several useful static methods that you can use in your programs, such as powers, square roots, and logarithms.

An object is an entity that combines data and operations. Some objects in Java include `String`s, which are sequences of text characters, and `Scanner`s, which read user input.

Objects contain methods that implement their behavior. To call a method on an object, write its name, followed by a dot, followed by the method name.

A `String` object holds a sequence of characters. The characters have indexes, starting with 0 for the first character.

An exception is an error that occurs when a program has performed an illegal action and is unable to continue executing normally.

Some programs are interactive and respond to input from the user. These programs should print a message to the user, also called a prompt, asking for the input.

Java has a class called `Scanner` that reads input from the keyboard. A `Scanner` can read various pieces of input (also called tokens) from an input source. It can read either one token at a time or an entire line at a time.

Self-Check Problems

Section 3.1: Parameters

1. Which of the following is the correct syntax for a method header with parameters?

a. `public static void example(x, y) {`
b. `public static (int x, int y) example() {`
c. `public static void example(int x,y) {`
d. `public static void example(x: int, y: int) {`
e. `public static void example(int x, int y) {`

2. What output is produced by the following program?

```
public class MysteryNums {
    public static void main(String[] args) {
        int x = 15;
        sentence(x, 42);

        int y = x - 5;
        sentence(y, x + y);
    }

    public static void sentence(int num1, int num2) {
        System.out.println(num1 + " " + num2);
    }
}
```

3. The following program has 9 mistakes. What are they?

```
public class Oops3 {
    public static void main() {
        double bubble = 867.5309;
        double x = 10.01;
        printer(double x, double y);
```

```
        printer(x);
        printer("barack", "obama");
        System.out.println("z = " + z);
    }

    public static void printer(x, y double) {
        int z = 5;
        System.out.println("x = " + double x + " and y = " + y);
        System.out.println("The value from main is: " + bubble);
    }
}
```

4. What output is produced by the following program?

```
public class Odds {
    public static void main(String[] args) {
        printOdds(3);
        printOdds(17 / 2);

        int x = 25;
        printOdds(37 - x + 1);
    }

    public static void printOdds(int n) {
        for (int i = 1; i <= n; i++) {
            int odd = 2 * i - 1;
            System.out.print(odd + " ");
        }
        System.out.println();
    }
}
```

5. What is the output of the following program?

```
public class Weird {
    public static void main(String[] args) {
        int number = 8;
        halfTheFun(11);
        halfTheFun(2 - 3 + 2 * 8);
        halfTheFun(number);
        System.out.println("number = " + number);
    }

    public static void halfTheFun(int number) {
        number = number / 2;
        for (int count = 1; count <= number; count++) {
            System.out.print(count + " ");
```

```
        }
        System.out.println();
    }
}
```

6. What is the output of the following program?

```
public class MysteryNumbers {
    public static void main(String[] args) {
        String one = "two";
        String two = "three";
        String three = "1";
        int number = 20;

        sentence(one, two, 3);
        sentence(two, three, 14);
        sentence(three, three, number + 1);
        sentence(three, two, 1);
        sentence("eight", three, number / 2);
    }

    public static void sentence(String three, String one, int number) {
        System.out.println(one + " times " + three + " = " + (number * 2));
    }
}
```

7. What output is produced by the following program?

```
public class MysteryWho {
    public static void main(String[] args) {
        String whom = "her";
        String who = "him";
        String it = "who";
        String he = "it";
        String she = "whom";

        sentence(he, she, it);
        sentence(she, he, who);
        sentence(who, she, who);
        sentence(it, "stu", "boo");
        sentence(it, whom, who);
    }

    public static void sentence(String she, String who, String whom) {
        System.out.println(who + " and " + whom + " like " + she);
    }
}
```

8. What output is produced by the following program?

```
public class MysteryTouch {
    public static void main(String[] args) {
        String head = "shoulders";
        String knees = "toes";
        String elbow = "head";
        String eye = "eyes and ears";
        String ear = "eye";

        touch(ear, elbow);
        touch(elbow, ear);
        touch(head, "elbow");
        touch(eye, eye);
        touch(knees, "Toes");
        touch(head, "knees " + knees);
    }

    public static void touch(String elbow, String ear) {
        System.out.println("touch your " + elbow + " to your " + ear);
    }
}
```

9. What output is produced by the following program?

```
public class MysterySoda {
    public static void main(String[] args) {
        String soda = "Coke";
        String pop = "Pepsi";
        String Coke = "pop";
        String Pepsi = "soda";
        String say = pop;

        carbonated(Coke, soda, pop);
        carbonated(pop, Pepsi, Pepsi);
        carbonated("pop", pop, "Kool-Aid");
        carbonated(say, "say", pop);
    }
    public static void carbonated(String Coke, String soda, String pop) {
        System.out.println("say " + soda + " not " + pop + " or " + Coke);
    }
}
```

10. Write a method called `printStrings` that accepts a `String` and a number of repetitions as parameters and prints that `String` the given number of times with a space after each time. For example, the call

```
printStrings("abc", 5);
```

will print the following output:

```
abc abc abc abc abc
```

11. The `System.out.println` command works on many different types of values, such as integers or `doubles`. What is the term for such a method?

Section 3.2: Methods That Return Values

12. What is wrong with the following program?

```
public class Temperature {
    public static void main(String[] args) {
        double tempf = 98.6;
        double tempc = 0.0;
        ftoc(tempf, tempc);
        System.out.println("Body temp in C is: " + tempc);
    }

    // converts Fahrenheit temperatures to Celsius
    public static void ftoc(double tempf, double tempc) {
        tempc = (tempf – 32) * 5 / 9;
    }
}
```

13. Evaluate the following expressions:

a. `Math.abs(–1.6)`
b. `Math.abs(2 + –4)`
c. `Math.pow(6, 2)`
d. `Math.pow(5 / 2, 6)`
e. `Math.ceil(9.1)`
f. `Math.ceil(115.8)`
g. `Math.max(7, 4)`
h. `Math.min(8, 3 + 2)`
i. `Math.min(–2, –5)`
j. `Math.sqrt(64)`
k. `Math.sqrt(76 + 45)`
l. `100 + Math.log10(100)`
m. `13 + Math.abs(–7) – Math.pow(2, 3) + 5`
n. `Math.sqrt(16) * Math.max(Math.abs(–5), Math.abs(–3))`
o. `7 – 2 + Math.log10(1000) + Math.log(Math.pow(Math.E, 5))`
p. `Math.max(18 – 5, Math.ceil(4.6 * 3))`

14. What output is produced by the following program?

```
public class MysteryReturn {
    public static void main(String[] args) {
        int x = 1, y = 2, z = 3;
        z = mystery(x, z, y);
        System.out.println(x + " " + y + " " + z);
```

```java
        x = mystery(z, z, x);
        System.out.println(x + " " + y + " " + z);
        y = mystery(y, y, z);
        System.out.println(x + " " + y + " " + z);
    }

    public static int mystery(int z, int x, int y) {
        z--;
        x = 2 * y + z;
        y = x - 1;
        System.out.println(y + " " + z);
        return x;
    }
}
```

15. Write the result of each expression. Note that a variable's value changes only if you reassign it using the = operator.

```java
double grade = 2.7;
Math.round(grade);                              // grade =
grade = Math.round(grade);                      // grade =

double min = Math.min(grade, Math.floor(2.9));  //   min =

double x = Math.pow(2, 4);                      //     x =
x = Math.sqrt(64);                              //     x =

int count = 25;
Math.sqrt(count);                               // count =
count = (int) Math.sqrt(count);                 // count =

int a = Math.abs(Math.min(-1, -3));             //     a =
```

16. Write a method called `min` that takes three integers as parameters and returns the smallest of the three values; for example, a call of `min(3, -2, 7)` would return `-2`, and a call of `min(19, 27, 6)` would return `6`. Use `Math.min` to write your solution.

17. Write a method called `countQuarters` that takes an `int` representing a number of cents as a parameter and returns the number of quarter coins represented by that many cents. Don't count any whole dollars, because those would be dispensed as dollar bills. For example, `countQuarters(64)` would return 2, because 64 cents is equivalent to 2 quarters with 14 cents left over. A call of `countQuarters(1278)` would return 3, because after the 12 dollars are taken out, 3 quarters remain in the 78 cents that are left.

Section 3.3: Using Objects

18. What output is produced by the following code?

```java
String first = "James";
String last = "Kirk";
String middle = "T.";
System.out.println(last);
System.out.println("My name is " + first);
System.out.println(first + " " + last);
```

```
System.out.println(last + ", " + first + " " + middle);
System.out.println(middle + " is for Tiberius");
```

19. Assuming that the following variables have been declared:

```
//        index 0123456789012345
String str1 = "Frodo Baggins";
String str2 = "Gandalf the GRAY";
```

evaluate the following expressions:

a. `str1.length()`
b. `str1.charAt(7)`
c. `str2.charAt(0)`
d. `str1.indexOf("o")`
e. `str2.toUpperCase()`
f. `str1.toLowerCase().indexOf("B")`
g. `str1.substring(4)`
h. `str2.substring(3, 14)`
i. `str2.replace("a", "oo")`
j. `str2.replace("gray", "white")`
k. `"str1".replace("r", "range")`

20. Assuming that the following variables have been declared:

```
String str1 = "Q.E.D.";
String str2 = "Arcturan Megadonkey";
String str3 = "Sirius Cybernetics Corporation";
```

evaluate the following expressions:

a. `str1.length()`
b. `str2.length()`
c. `str1.toLowerCase()`
d. `str2.toUpperCase()`
e. `str1.substring(2, 4)`
f. `str2.substring(10, 14)`
g. `str1.indexOf("D")`
h. `str1.indexOf(".")`
i. `str2.indexOf("donkey")`
j. `str3.indexOf("X")`
k. `str2 + str3.charAt(17)`
l. `str3.substring(9, str3.indexOf("e"))`
m. `str3.substring(7, 12)`
n. `str2.toLowerCase().substring(9, 13) + str3.substring(18, str3.length() – 7)`

21. Consider the following `String`:

```
String quote = "Four score and seven years ago";
```

What expression produces the new `String` `"SCORE"`? What expression produces `"four years"`?

22. Write a program that outputs "The Name Game," where the user inputs a first and last name and a song in the following format is printed about their first, then last, name. Use a method to avoid redundancy.

```
What is your name? Fifty Cent
Fifty Fifty, bo-Bifty
Banana-fana fo-Fifty
Fee-fi-mo-Mifty
FIFTY!
Cent, Cent, bo-Bent
Banana-fana fo-Fent
Fee-fi-mo-Ment
CENT!
```

23. Consider the following code fragment:

```
Scanner console = new Scanner(System.in);
System.out.print("How much money do you have? ");
double money = console.nextDouble();
```

Describe what will happen when the user types each of the following values. If the code will run successfully, describe the value that will be stored in the variable `money`.

a. `34.50`
b. `6`
c. `$25.00`
d. `million`
e. `100*5`
f. `600x000`
g. `none`
h. `645`

24. Write Java code to read an integer from the user, then print that number multiplied by 2. You may assume that the user types a valid integer.

25. Consider the following program. Modify the code to use a `Scanner` to prompt the user for the values of `low` and `high`.

```
public class SumNumbers {
    public static void main(String[] args) {
        int low = 1;
        int high = 1000;
        int sum = 0;
        for (int i = low; i <= high; i++) {
            sum += i;
        }
        System.out.println("sum = " + sum);
    }
}
```

Below is a sample execution in which the user asks for the sum of the values 1 through 10:

```
low? 1
high? 10
sum = 55
```

26. Write Java code that prompts the user for a phrase and a number of times to repeat it, then prints the phrase the requested number of times. Here is an example dialogue with the user:

```
What is your phrase? His name is Robert Paulson.
How many times should I repeat it? 3
His name is Robert Paulson.
His name is Robert Paulson.
His name is Robert Paulson.
```

Exercises

1. Write a method called `printNumbers` that accepts a maximum number as an argument and prints each number from `1` up to that maximum, inclusive, boxed by square brackets. For example, consider the following calls:

```
printNumbers(15);
printNumbers(5);
```

These calls should produce the following output:

```
[1] [2] [3] [4] [5] [6] [7] [8] [9] [10] [11] [12] [13] [14] [15]
[1] [2] [3] [4] [5]
```

You may assume that the value passed to `printNumbers` is `1` or greater.

2. Write a method called `printPowersOf2` that accepts a maximum number as an argument and prints each power of 2 from 2^0 (1) up to that maximum power, inclusive. For example, consider the following calls:

```
printPowersOf2(3);
printPowersOf2(10);
```

These calls should produce the following output:

```
1 2 4 8
1 2 4 8 16 32 64 128 256 512 1024
```

You may assume that the value passed to `printPowersOf2` is `0` or greater. (The `Math` class may help you with this problem. If you use it, you may need to cast its results from `double` to `int` so that you don't see a `.0` after each number in your output. Also try to write this program without using the `Math` class.)

3. Write a method called `printPowersOfN` that accepts a base and an exponent as arguments and prints each power of the base from $base^0$ (1) up to that maximum power, inclusive. For example, consider the following calls:

```
printPowersOfN(4, 3);
printPowersOfN(5, 6);
printPowersOfN(−2, 8);
```

These calls should produce the following output:

```
1 4 16 64
1 5 25 125 625 3125 15625
1 −2 4 −8 16 −32 64 −128 256
```

You may assume that the exponent passed to `printPowersOfN` has a value of `0` or greater. (The `Math` class may help you with this problem. If you use it, you may need to cast its results from `double` to `int` so that you don't see a `.0` after each number in your output. Also try to write this program without using the `Math` class.)

4. Write a method called `printSquare` that accepts a minimum and maximum integer and prints a square of lines of increasing numbers. The first line should start with the minimum, and each line that follows should start with the next-higher number. The sequence of numbers on a line wraps back to the minimum after it hits the maximum. For example, the call

```
printSquare(3, 7);
```

should produce the following output:

```
34567
45673
56734
67345
73456
```

If the maximum passed is less than the minimum, the method produces no output.

5. Write a method called `printGrid` that accepts two integers representing a number of rows and columns and prints a grid of integers from `1` to (rows * columns) in column major order. For example, the call

```
printGrid(4, 6);
```

should produce the following output:

```
1 5 9 13 17 21
2 6 10 14 18 22
3 7 11 15 19 23
4 8 12 16 20 24
```

6. Write a method called `largerAbsVal` that takes two integers as parameters and returns the larger of the two absolute values. A call of `largerAbsVal(11, 2)` would return `11`, and a call of `largerAbsVal(4, –5)` would return `5`.

7. Write a variation of the `largestAbsVal` method from the last exercise that takes three integers as parameters and returns the largest of their three absolute values. For example, a call of `largestAbsVal(7, –2, –11)` would return `11`, and a call of `largestAbsVal(−4, 5, 2)` would return `5`.

8. Write a method called `quadratic` that solves quadratic equations and prints their roots. Recall that a quadratic equation is a polynomial equation in terms of a variable x of the form $ax^2 + bx + c = 0$. The formula for solving a quadratic equation is

$$x = \frac{-b \pm \sqrt{b^2 - 4ac}}{2a}$$

Here are some example equations and their roots:

$x^2 - 7x + 12$: $x = 4, x = 3$

$x^2 - 3x + 2$: $x = -2, x = -1$

Your method should accept the coefficients a, b, and c as parameters and should print the roots of the equation. You may assume that the equation has two real roots, though mathematically this is not always the case.

9. Write a method called `lastDigit` that returns the last digit of an integer. For example, `lastDigit(3572)` should return `2`. It should work for negative numbers as well. For example, `lastDigit(-947)` should return `7`.

10. Write a method called `area` that accepts as a parameter the radius of a circle and that returns the area of the circle. For example, the call `area(2.0)` should return `12.566370614359172`. Recall that area can be computed as pi (π) times the radius squared and that Java has a constant called `Math.PI`.

11. Write a method called `distance` that accepts four integer coordinates x_1, y_1, x_2, and y_2 as parameters and computes the distance between points (x_1, y_1) and (x_2, y_2) on the Cartesian plane. The equation for the distance is

$$d = \sqrt{(x_2 - x_1)^2 + (y_2 - y_1)^2}$$

For example, the call of `distance(1, 0, 4, 4)` would return `5.0` and the call of `distance(10, 2, 3, 15)` would return `14.7648230602334`.

12. Write a method called `scientific` that accepts a real number base and an exponent as parameters and computes the base times 10 to the exponent, as seen in scientific notation. For example, the call of `scientific(6.23, 5)` would return `623000.0` and the call of `scientific(1.9, –2)` would return `0.019`.

13. Write a method called `pay` that accepts two parameters: a real number for a TA's salary, and an integer for the number of hours the TA worked this week. The method should return how much money to pay the TA. For example, the call `pay(5.50, 6)` should return `33.0`. The TA should receive "overtime" pay of $1^1/_2$ times the normal salary for any hours above 8. For example, the call `pay(4.00, 11)` should return (4.00 * 8) + (6.00 * 3) or `50.0`.

14. Write a method called `cylinderSurfaceArea` that accepts a radius and height as parameters and returns the surface area of a cylinder with those dimensions. For example, the call `cylinderSurfaceArea(3.0, 4.5)` should return `141.3716694115407`. The formula for the surface area of a cylinder with radius r and height h is the following:

surface area $= 2\pi r^2 + 2\pi rh$

15. Write a method called `sphereVolume` that accepts a radius as a parameter and returns the volume of a sphere with that radius. For example, the call `sphereVolume(2.0)` should return `33.510321638291124`. The formula for the volume of a sphere with radius r is the following:

volume $= {}^4/_3\, \pi r^3$

16. Write a method called `triangleArea` that accepts the three side lengths of a triangle as parameters and returns the area of a triangle with those side lengths. For example, the call `triangleArea(8, 5.2, 7.1)` should return `18.151176098258745`. To compute the area, use Heron's formula, which states that the area of a triangle whose three sides have lengths a, b, and c, is the following. The formula is based on the computed value s, a length equal to half the perimeter of the triangle:

$$area = \sqrt{s(s - a)(s - b)(s - c)}$$

$$s = \frac{a + b + c}{2}$$

17. Write a method called `padString` that accepts two parameters: a string and an integer representing a length. The method should pad the parameter string with spaces until its length is the given length. For example, `padString("hello", 8)` should return `"hello   "`. (This sort of method is useful when trying to print output that lines up horizontally.) If the string's length is already at least as long as the length parameter, your method should return the original string. For example, `padString("congratulations", 10)` should return `"congratulations"`.

18. Write a method called `vertical` that accepts a string as its parameter and prints each letter of the string on separate lines. For example, a call of `vertical("hey now")` should produce the following output:

```
h
e
y

n
o
w
```

19. Write a method called `printReverse` that accepts a string as its parameter and prints the characters in opposite order. For example, a call of `printReverse("hello there!")` should print `"!ereht olleh"`. If the empty string is passed, the method should produce no output.

20. Write a method called `inputBirthday` that accepts a `Scanner` for the console as a parameter and prompts the user to enter a month, day, and year of birth, then prints the birthdate in a suitable format. Here is an example dialogue with the user:

```
On what day of the month were you born? 8
What is the name of the month in which you were born? May
During what year were you born? 1981
You were born on May 8, 1981. You're mighty old!
```

21. Write a method called `processName` that accepts a `Scanner` for the console as a parameter and prompts the user to enter a full name, then prints the name in reverse order (i.e., last name, first name). Here is an example dialogue with the user:

```
Please enter your full name: Sammy Jankis
Your name in reverse order is Jankis, Sammy
```

22. Write a program that outputs "The Name Game," where the user inputs a first and last name and a song in the following format is printed about their first, then last, name. Use a method to avoid redundancy.

```
What is your name? Fifty Cent


Fifty Fifty, bo-Bifty
Banana-fana fo-Fifty
Fee-fi-mo-Mifty
FIFTY!

Cent, Cent, bo-Bent
Banana-fana fo-Fent
Fee-fi-mo-Ment
CENT!
```

Programming Projects

1. Write a program that produces images of Christmas trees as output. It should have a method with two parameters: one for the number of segments in the tree and one for the height of each segment. For example, the tree shown here on the left has three segments of height 4 and the one on the right has two segments of height 5:

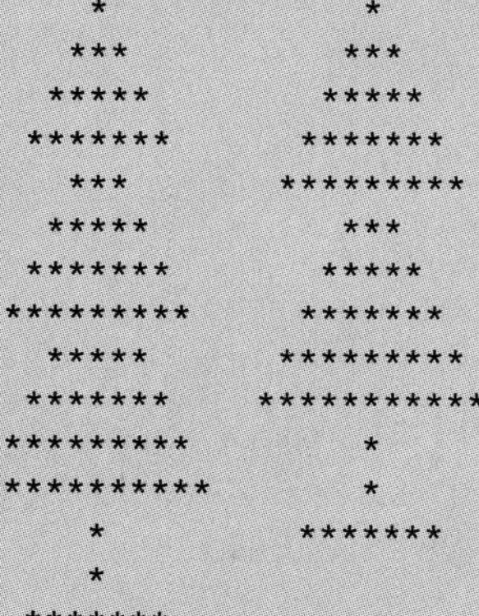

2. A certain bank offers 6.5% interest on savings accounts, compounded annually. Create a table that shows how much money a person will accumulate over a period of 25 years, assuming that the person makes an initial investment of \$1000 and deposits \$100 each year after the first. Your table should indicate for each year the current balance, the interest, the new deposit, and the new balance.
3. Write a program that shows the total number of presents that the person in the song "The Twelve Days of Christmas" received on each day, as indicated in Table 3.5.

Table 3.5 Twelve Days of Christmas

Day	Presents Received	Total Presents
1	1	1
2	2	3
3	3	6
4	4	10
5	5	15
. . .	. . .	. . .

4. Write a program that prompts for the lengths of the sides of a triangle and reports the three angles.
5. Write a program that computes the spherical distance between two points on the surface of the Earth, given their latitudes and longitudes. This is a useful operation because it tells you how far apart two cities are if you multiply the distance by the radius of the Earth, which is roughly 6372.795 km.

   Let φ_1, λ_1, and φ_2, λ_2 be the latitude and longitude of two points, respectively. $\Delta\lambda$, the longitudinal difference, and $\Delta\sigma$, the angular difference/distance in radians, can be determined as follows from the spherical law of cosines:

   $$\Delta\sigma = \arccos(\sin \varphi_1 \sin \varphi_2 + \cos \varphi_1 \cos \varphi_2 \cos \Delta\lambda)$$

   For example, consider the latitude and longitude of two major cities:

   - Nashville, TN: N 36°7.2′, W 86°40.2′
   - Los Angeles, CA: N 33°56.4′, W 118°24.0′

   You must convert these coordinates to radians before you can use them effectively in the formula. After conversion, the coordinates become

   - Nashville: $\varphi_1 = 36.12° = 0.6304$ rad, $\Delta_1 = -86.67° = -1.5127$ rad
   - Los Angeles: $\varphi_2 = 33.94° = 0.5924$ rad, $\Delta_2 = -118.40° = -2.0665$ rad

   Using these values in the angular distance equation, you get

   $r\Delta\sigma = 6372.795 \times 0.45306 = 2887.259$ km

   Thus, the distance between these cities is about 2887 km, or 1794 miles. (Note: To solve this problem, you will need to use the `Math.acos` method, which returns an arccosine angle in radians.)
6. Write a program that produces calendars as output. Your program should have a method that outputs a single month's calendar like the one below, given parameters to specify how many days are in the month and what the date of the first Sunday is in that month. In the month shown below, these values are 31 and 6, respectively.

```
  Sun    Mon    Tue    Wed    Thu    Fri    Sat
+------+------+------+------+------+------+------+
|      |      |    1 |    2 |    3 |    4 |    5 |
|    6 |    7 |    8 |    9 |   10 |   11 |   12 |
|   13 |   14 |   15 |   16 |   17 |   18 |   19 |
|   20 |   21 |   22 |   23 |   24 |   25 |   26 |
|   27 |   28 |   29 |   30 |   31 |      |      |
+------+------+------+------+------+------+------+
```

One tricky part of this program is making the various columns line up properly with proper widths. We will learn better ways of formatting output in the next chapter. For now, you may copy the following `helper` method into your program and call it to turn a number into a left-padded string of a given exact width. For example, the call `System.out.print(padded(7, 5));` prints `"    7"` (the number 7 with four leading spaces).

```
// Returns a string of the number n, left-padded
// with spaces until it is at least the given width.
public static String padded(int n, int width) {
    String s = "" + n;
    for (int i = s.length(); i < width; i++) {
        s = " " + s;
    }
    return s;
}
```

Supplement 3G

Graphics (Optional)

Introduction

One of the most compelling reasons to learn about using objects is that they allow us to draw graphics in Java. Graphics are used for games, computer animations, and modern graphical user interfaces (GUIs), and to render complex images. Graphics are also a good way to practice the use of parameters as discussed in the previous chapter.

In this optional supplement we will examine a few of the basic classes from Java's graphical framework and use them to draw patterned two-dimensional figures of shapes and text onto the screen.

3G.1 Introduction to Graphics

VideoNote

Java's original graphical tools were collectively known as the Abstract Window Toolkit (AWT). The classes associated with the AWT reside in the package `java.awt`. In order to create graphical programs like the ones you'll see in this section, you'll need to include the following `import` declaration at the top of your programs:

```
import java.awt.*;   // for graphics
```

To keep things simple, we'll use a custom class called `DrawingPanel` that was written by the authors of this textbook to simplify some of the more esoteric details of Java graphics. Its core code is less than a page long, so we aren't hiding much. You won't need to import `DrawingPanel`, but you will need to place the file `DrawingPanel.java` in the same folder as your program.

The drawing panel keeps track of the overall image, but the actual drawing will be done with an object of type `Graphics`. The `Graphics` class is also part of the `java.awt` library.

DrawingPanel

You can create a graphical window on your screen by constructing a `DrawingPanel` object. You must specify the width and height of the drawing area. When the following line executes, a window appears immediately on the screen:

```
DrawingPanel <name> = new DrawingPanel(<width>, <height>);
```

`DrawingPanel` objects have two public methods, listed in Table 3G.1.

The typical way that you'll use `DrawingPanel` will be to construct a panel of a particular height and width, set its background color (if you don't want the default white background), and then draw something on it using its `Graphics` object. The `DrawingPanel` appears on the screen at the time that you construct it.

All coordinates are specified as integers. Each (*x*, *y*) position corresponds to a different pixel on the computer screen. The word *pixel* is shorthand for "picture element" and represents a single dot on the computer screen.

> **Pixel**
> A single small dot on a computer screen.

Table 3G.1 Useful Methods for `DrawingPanel`

Method	Description
`getGraphics()`	returns a `Graphics` object that can be used to draw onto the panel
`setBackground(color)`	sets the background color of the panel to the given color (the default is white)

The coordinate system assigns the upper-left corner of a panel the position (0, 0). As you move to the right of this position, the x value increases. As you move down from this position, the y value increases. For example, suppose that you construct a `DrawingPanel` object with a width of 200 pixels and a height of 100 pixels. The upper-left corner will have the coordinates (0, 0), and the lower-right corner will have the coordinates (199, 99) as shown in Figure 3G.1.

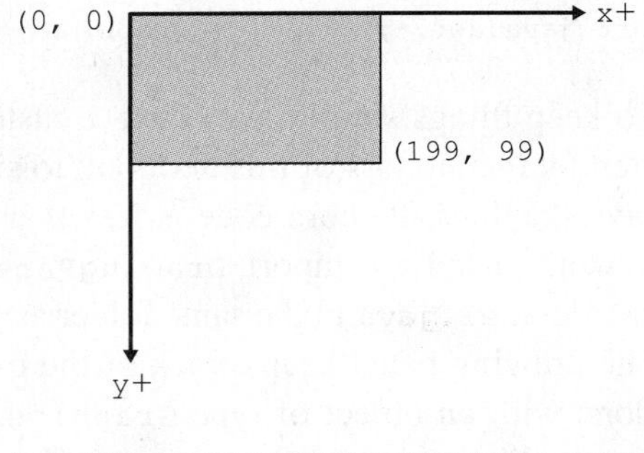

Figure 3G.1 The (x, y) Coordinate Space

This is likely to be confusing at first, because you're probably used to coordinate systems where y values decrease as you move down. However, you'll soon get the hang of it.

Drawing Lines and Shapes

So, how do you actually draw something? To draw shapes and lines, you don't talk directly to the `DrawingPanel`, but rather to a related object of type `Graphics`. Think of the `DrawingPanel` as a canvas and the `Graphics` object as the paintbrush. The `DrawingPanel` class has a method called `getGraphics` that returns its `Graphics` object:

```
Graphics g = <panel>.getGraphics();
```

One of the simplest drawing commands is `drawLine`, which takes four integer arguments.

For example, the method:

```
g.drawLine(<x1>, <y1>, <x2>, <y2>);
```

draws a line from the point $(x1, y1)$ to the point $(x2, y2)$. The `drawLine` method is just one of many commands a `Graphics` object understands; see Table 3G.2 for others. The `Graphics` object has many more methods in addition to the ones discussed here. You can read about them in the Java API documentation.

Here is a sample program that puts these pieces together:

```
// Draws a line onto a DrawingPanel.

import java.awt.*;    // for graphics

```

Table 3G.2 Some Useful Methods of `Graphics` Objects

Method	Description
`drawLine(x1, y1, x2, y2)`	draws a line between the points (*x*1, *y*1) and (*x*2, *y*2)
`drawOval(x, y, width, height)`	draws the outline of the largest oval that fits within the specified rectangle
`drawRect(x, y, width, height)`	draws the outline of the specified rectangle
`drawString(message, x, y)`	draws the given text with its lower-left corner at (*x*, *y*)
`fillOval(x, y, width, height)`	fills the largest oval that fits within the specified rectangle using the current color
`fillRect(x, y, width, height)`	fills the specified rectangle using the current color
`setColor(color)`	sets this graphics context's current color to the specified color (all subsequent graphics operations using this graphics context use this specified color)
`setFont(font)`	sets this graphics context's current font to the specified font (all subsequent strings drawn using this graphics context use this specified font)

```
public class DrawLine1 {
    public static void main(String[] args) {
        // create the drawing panel
        DrawingPanel panel = new DrawingPanel(200, 100);

        // draw a line on the panel using
        // the Graphics paintbrush
        Graphics g = panel.getGraphics();
        g.drawLine(25, 75, 175, 25);
    }
}
```

When you run this program, the window shown in Figure 3G.2 appears. Though it isn't text on the console, as in previous chapters, we'll still refer to this as the "output" of the program.

(Java can be run on a variety of systems. Depending on your operating system, your output may differ slightly from the screenshots in this chapter.)

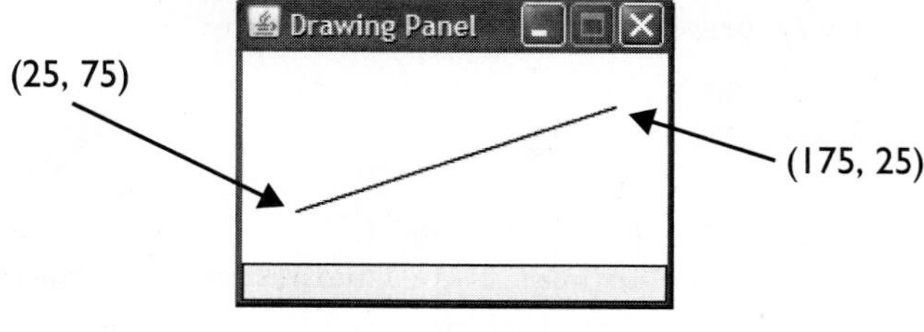

Figure 3G.2 Output of `DrawLine1`

The first statement in `main` constructs a `DrawingPanel` with a width of 200 and a height of 100. Once it has been constructed, the window will pop up on the screen. The second statement draws a line from (25, 75) to (175, 25). The first point is in the lower-left part of the window (25 over from the left, 75 down from the top). The second point is in the upper-right corner (175 over from the left, 25 down from the top).

Notice these particular lines of code:

```
Graphics g = panel.getGraphics();
g.drawLine(25, 75, 175, 25);
```

You might wonder why you can't just say:

```
panel.drawLine(25, 75, 175, 25);   // this is illegal
```

The problem is that there are two different objects involved in this program: the `DrawingPanel` itself (the canvas) and the `Graphics` object associated with the panel (the paintbrush). The panel doesn't know how to draw a line; only the `Graphics` object knows how to do this. You have to be careful to make sure that you are talking to the right object when you give a command.

This requirement can be confusing, but it is common in Java programs. In fact, in a typical Java program, there are hundreds (if not thousands) of objects interacting with each other. These interactions aren't so unlike interactions between people. If you want to schedule a meeting, a busy corporate executive might tell you, "Talk to my secretary about that." Or if you're asking difficult legal questions, a person might tell you, "Talk to my lawyer about that." In this case, the `DrawingPanel` doesn't know how to draw, so if it could talk it would say, "Talk to my `Graphics` object about that."

It's also legal to use the `Graphics` object without storing it in a variable, like this:

```
panel.getGraphics().drawLine(25, 75, 175, 25);    // also legal
```

But you'll often want to send several commands to the `Graphics` object, so it's more convenient to give it a name and store it in a variable.

Let's look at a more complicated example:

```
// Draws three lines to make a triangle.

import java.awt.*;

public class DrawLine2 {
    public static void main(String[] args) {
        DrawingPanel panel = new DrawingPanel(200, 100);

```

```
        // draw a triangle on the panel
        Graphics g = panel.getGraphics();
        g.drawLine(25, 75, 100, 25);
        g.drawLine(100, 25, 175, 75);
        g.drawLine(25, 75, 175, 75);
    }
}
```

This program draws three different lines to form a triangle, as shown in Figure 3G.3. The lines are drawn between three different points. In the lower-left corner we have the point (25, 75). In the middle at the top we have the point (100, 25). And in the lower-right corner we have the point (175, 75). The various calls on `drawLine` simply draw the lines that connect these three points.

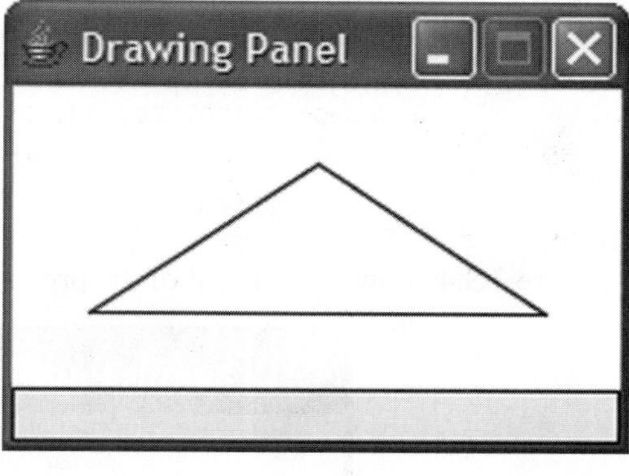

Figure 3G.3 Output of `DrawLine2`

The `Graphics` object also has methods for drawing particular shapes. For example, you can draw rectangles with the `drawRect` method:

```
g.drawRect(<x>, <y>, <width>, <height>);
```

This draws a rectangle with upper-left coordinates (x, y) and the given height and width.

Another figure you'll often want to draw is a circle or, more generally, an oval. But how do you specify where it appears and how big it is? What you actually specify is what is known as the "bounding rectangle" of the circle or oval. Java will draw the largest oval possible that fits inside that rectangle. So, the method:

```
g.drawOval(<x>, <y>, <width>, <height>);
```

draws the largest oval that fits within the rectangle with upper-left coordinates (x, y) and the given height and width.

Notice that the first two values passed to `drawRect` and `drawOval` are coordinates, while the next two values are a width and a height. For example, here is a short program that draws two rectangles and two ovals:

```
// Draws several shapes.

import java.awt.*;

public class DrawShapes1 {
    public static void main(String[] args) {
        DrawingPanel panel = new DrawingPanel(200, 100);

        Graphics g = panel.getGraphics();
        g.drawRect(25, 50, 20, 20);
        g.drawRect(150, 10, 40, 20);
        g.drawOval(50, 25, 20, 20);
        g.drawOval(150, 50, 40, 20);
    }
}
```

Figure 3G.4 shows the output of the program.

Figure 3G.4 Output of `DrawShapes1`

The first rectangle has its upper-left corner at the coordinates (25, 50). Its width and height are each 20, so this is a square. The coordinates of its lower-right corner would be (45, 70), or 20 more than the (*x*, *y*) coordinates of the upper-left corner. The program also draws a rectangle with its upper-left corner at (150, 10) that has a width of 40 and a height of 20 (wider than it is tall). The bounding rectangle of the first oval has upper-left coordinates (50, 25) and a width and height of 20. In other words, it's a circle. The bounding rectangle of the second oval has upper-left coordinates (150, 50), a width of 40, and a height of 20 (it's an oval that is wider than it is tall).

Sometimes you don't just want to draw the outline of a shape; you want to paint the entire area with a particular color. There are variations of the `drawRect` and `drawOval` methods known as `fillRect` and `fillOval` that do exactly that, drawing a rectangle or oval and filling it in with the current color of paint (the default is black). Let's change two of the calls in the previous program to be "fill" operations instead of "draw" operations:

```
// Draws and fills several shapes.

import java.awt.*;

public class DrawShapes2 {
    public static void main(String[] args) {
        DrawingPanel panel = new DrawingPanel(200, 100);

        Graphics g = panel.getGraphics();
        g.fillRect(25, 50, 20, 20);
        g.drawRect(150, 10, 40, 20);
        g.drawOval(50, 25, 20, 20);
        g.fillOval(150, 50, 40, 20);
    }
}
```

Now we get the output shown in Figure 3G.5 instead.

Figure 3G.5 Output of `DrawShapes2`

Colors

All of the shapes and lines drawn by the preceding programs were black, and all of the panels had a white background. These are the default colors, but you can change the background color of the panel, and you can change the color being used by the `Graphics` object as many times as you like. To change these colors, you use the standard `Color` class, which is part of the `java.awt` package.

Table 3G.3 `Color` Constants

Color.BLACK	Color.GREEN	Color.RED
Color.BLUE	Color.LIGHT_GRAY	Color.WHITE
Color.CYAN	Color.MAGENTA	Color.YELLOW
Color.DARK_GRAY	Color.ORANGE	
Color.GRAY	Color.PINK	

There are a number of predefined colors that you can refer to directly. They are defined as class constants in the `Color` class (a lot like the constants we used in Chapter 2). The names of these constants are all in uppercase and are self-explanatory. To refer to one of these colors, you have to precede it with the class name and a dot, as in `Color.GREEN` or `Color.BLUE`. The predefined `Color` constants are listed in Table 3G.3.

As mentioned earlier, the `DrawingPanel` object has a method that can be used to change the background color that covers the entire panel:

```
<panel>.setBackground(<color>);
```

Likewise, the `Graphics` object has a method that can be used to change the current color that draws or fills shapes and lines:

```
g.setColor(<color>);
```

Calling `setColor` is like dipping your paintbrush in a different color of paint. From that point on, all drawing and filling will be done in the specified color. For example, here is another version of the previous program that uses a cyan (light blue) background color and fills in the oval and square with white instead of black:

```
// Draws and fills shapes in different colors.

import java.awt.*;

public class DrawColoredShapes {
    public static void main(String[] args) {
        DrawingPanel panel = new DrawingPanel(200, 100);
        panel.setBackground(Color.CYAN);

        Graphics g = panel.getGraphics();
        g.drawRect(150, 10, 40, 20);
        g.drawOval(50, 25, 20, 20);
        g.setColor(Color.WHITE);
        g.fillOval(150, 50, 40, 20);
        g.fillRect(25, 50, 20, 20);
    }
}
```

This program produces the output shown in Figure 3G.6. (The figures shown in this textbook may not match the colors you would see on your screen.)

Figure 3G.6 Output of `DrawColoredShapes`

Notice that you tell the panel to set the background color, while you tell the `Graphics` object to set the foreground color. The reasoning is that the background color is a property of the entire window, while the foreground color affects only the particular shapes that you draw.

Notice also that the order of the calls has been rearranged. The two drawing commands appear first, then the call on `setColor` that changes the color to white, then the two filling commands. This ensures that the drawing is done in black and the filling is done in white. The order of operations is very important in these drawing programs, so you'll have to keep track of what your current color is each time you give a new command to draw or fill something.

Common Programming Error

Misunderstanding Draw vs. Fill

Some new programmers think that a shape must be drawn (such as with `drawRect`) before it can be filled in (such as with `fillRect`). This is not the case. In fact, when you are trying to draw an outlined shape, this is exactly the wrong thing to do. Suppose you want to draw a 60×30 green rectangle with a black border at (20, 50). You might write the following code:

```
g.setColor(Color.BLACK);    // incorrect code
g.drawRect(20, 50, 60, 30);
g.setColor(Color.GREEN);
g.fillRect(20, 50, 60, 30);
```

Continued on next page

Continued from previous page

However, the fill command covers the same pixels as the draw command, and the green interior will be drawn over the black outline, leading to the following appearance:

Instead, the code should fill the interior of the rectangle first, then draw the black outline, to make sure that the outline shows on top of the filling. The following is the correct code and its output:

```
g.setColor(Color.GREEN);    // corrected code
g.fillRect(20, 50, 60, 30);
g.setColor(Color.BLACK);
g.drawRect(20, 50, 60, 30);
```

Drawing with Loops

In each of the preceding examples we used simple constants for the drawing and filling commands, but it is possible to use expressions. For example, suppose that we stick with our `DrawingPanel` size of 200 pixels wide and 100 pixels tall and we want to produce a diagonal series of four rectangles that extend from the upper-left corner to the lower-right corner, each with a white oval inside. In other words, we want to produce the output shown in Figure 3G.7.

The overall width of 200 and overall height of 100 are divided evenly into four rectangles, which means that they must all be 50 pixels wide and 25 pixels high. So, width and height values for the four rectangles are the same, but the positions of their

Figure 3G.7 Desired Output of `DrawLoop1`

upper-left corners are different. The first rectangle's upper-left corner is at (0, 0), the second is at (50, 25), the third is at (100, 50), and the fourth is at (150, 75). We need to write code to generate these different coordinates.

This is a great place to use a `for` loop. Using the techniques introduced in Chapter 2, we can make a table and develop a formula for the coordinates. In this case it is easier to have the loop start with 0 rather than 1, which will often be the case with drawing programs. Here is a program that makes a good first stab at generating the desired output:

```
// Draws boxed ovals using a for loop (flawed version).

import java.awt.*;

public class DrawLoop1 {
    public static void main(String[] args) {
        DrawingPanel panel = new DrawingPanel(200, 100);
        panel.setBackground(Color.CYAN);

        Graphics g = panel.getGraphics();
        for (int i = 0; i < 4; i++) {
            g.drawRect(i * 50, i * 25, 50, 25);
            g.setColor(Color.WHITE);
            g.fillOval(i * 50, i * 25, 50, 25);
        }
    }
}
```

This program produces the output shown in Figure 3G.8.

The coordinates and sizes are right, but not the colors. Instead of getting four black rectangles with white ovals inside, we're getting one black rectangle and three white rectangles. That's because we only have one call on `setColor` inside the loop. Initially the color will be set to black, which is why the first rectangle comes out

Figure 3G.8 Output of `DrawLoop1`

black. But once we make a call on `setColor` changing the color to white, every subsequent drawing and filling command is done in white, including the second, third, and fourth rectangles.

So, we need to include calls to set the color to black, to draw the rectangles, and to set the color to white to draw the filled ovals. While we're at it, it's a good idea to switch the order of these tasks. The rectangles and ovals overlap slightly, and we would rather have the rectangle drawn over the oval than the other way around. The following program produces the correct output:

```
// Draws boxed ovals using a for loop.

import java.awt.*;

public class DrawLoop2 {
    public static void main(String[] args) {
        DrawingPanel panel = new DrawingPanel(200, 100);
        panel.setBackground(Color.CYAN);

        Graphics g = panel.getGraphics();
        for (int i = 0; i < 4; i++) {
            g.setColor(Color.WHITE);
            g.fillOval(i * 50, i * 25, 50, 25);
            g.setColor(Color.BLACK);
            g.drawRect(i * 50, i * 25, 50, 25);
        }
    }
}
```

It's also possible to create custom `Color` objects of your own, rather than using the constant colors provided in the `Color` class. Computer monitors use red, green, and blue (RGB) as their primary colors, so when you construct a `Color` object you pass your own parameter values for the redness, greenness, and blueness of the color:

```
new Color(<red>, <green>, <blue>)
```

The red/green/blue components should be integer values between `0` and `255`. The higher the value, the more of that color is mixed in. All `0` values produce black, and all `255` values produce white. Values of `(0, 255, 0)` produce a pure green, while values of `(128, 0, 128)` make a dark purple color (because red and blue are mixed). Search for "RGB table" in your favorite search engine to find tables of many common colors.

The following program demonstrates the use of custom colors. It uses a class constant for the number of rectangles to draw and produces a blend of colors from black to white:

```
// Draws a smooth color gradient from black to white.

import java.awt.*;

public class DrawColorGradient {
    public static final int RECTS = 32;

    public static void main(String[] args) {
        DrawingPanel panel = new DrawingPanel(256, 256);
        panel.setBackground(new Color(255, 128, 0)); // orange

        Graphics g = panel.getGraphics();

        // from black to white, top left to bottom right
        for (int i = 0; i < RECTS; i++) {
            int shift = i * 256 / RECTS;
            g.setColor(new Color(shift, shift, shift));
            g.fillRect(shift, shift, 20, 20);
        }
    }
}
```

This program produces the output shown in Figure 3G.9.

It is also legal to store a `Color` object into a variable or pass it as a parameter. For example, we could have written the coloring code in the preceding program as follows:

```
Color c = new Color(shift, shift, shift);
g.setColor(c);
...
```

We will use this idea later when parameterizing colors in this chapter's Case Study.

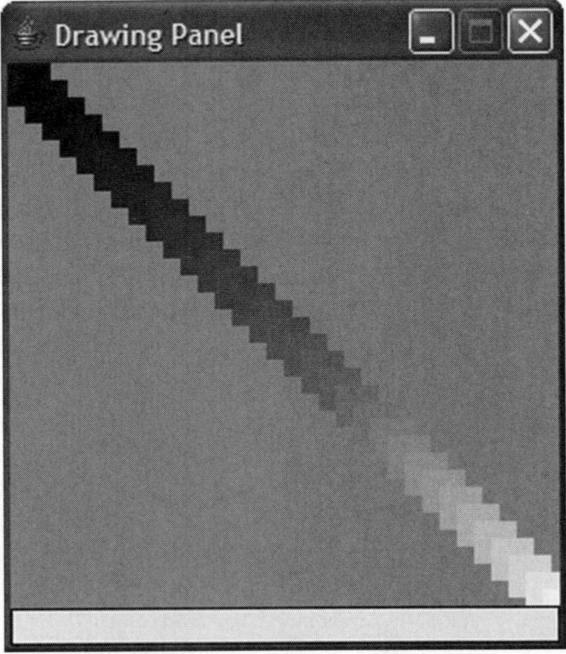

Figure 3G.9 Output of `DrawColorGradient`

Text and Fonts

Another drawing command worth mentioning can be used to include text in your drawings. The `drawString` method of the `Graphics` object draws the given `String` with its lower-left corner at coordinates (*x*, *y*):

```
g.drawString(<message>, <x>, <y>);
```

This is a slightly different convention than we used for `drawRect`. With `drawRect`, we specified the coordinates of the upper-left corner. Here we specify the coordinates of the lower-left corner. By default, text is drawn approximately 10 pixels high. Here is a sample program that uses a loop to draw a particular `String` 10 different times, each time indenting it 5 pixels to the right and moving it down 10 pixels from the top:

```
// Draws a message several times.

import java.awt.*;

public class DrawStringMessage1 {
    public static void main(String[] args) {
        DrawingPanel panel = new DrawingPanel(200, 100);
```

```
        panel.setBackground(Color.YELLOW);

        Graphics g = panel.getGraphics();
        for (int i = 0; i < 10; i++) {
            g.drawString("There is no place like home",
                         i * 5, 10 + i * 10);
        }
    }
}
```

This program produces the output shown in Figure 3G.10.

Figure 3G.10 Output of `DrawStringMessage`

Fonts are used to describe different styles for writing characters on the screen. If you'd like to change the style or size of the onscreen text, you can use the `setFont` method of the `Graphics` object.

> **Font**
>
> An overall design for a set of text characters, including the style, size, weight, and appearance of each character.

This method changes the text size and style in which strings are drawn.

The parameter to `setFont` is a `Font` object. A `Font` object is constructed by passing three parameters—the font's name as a `String`, its style (such as bold or italic), and its size as an integer:

```
new Font(<name>, <style>, <size>)
```

Common font styles such as bold are implemented as constants in the `Font` class. The available constants and some popular font names are listed in Tables 3G.4 and 3G.5.

Table 3G.4 Useful Constants of the `Font` Class

Constant	Displays
`Font.BOLD`	**Bold text**
`Font.ITALIC`	*Italic text*
`Font.BOLD + Font.ITALIC`	***Bold/Italic text***
`Font.PLAIN`	Plain text

Table 3G.5 Common Font Names

Name	Description
`"Monospaced"`	a typewriter font, such as `Courier New`
`"SansSerif"`	a font without curves (serifs) at letter edges, such as Arial
`"Serif"`	a font with curved edges, such as Times New Roman

As in the case of colors, setting the font affects only strings that are drawn after the font is set. The following program sets several fonts and uses them to draw strings:

```
// Draws several messages using different fonts.

import java.awt.*;

public class DrawFonts {
    public static void main(String[] args) {
        DrawingPanel panel = new DrawingPanel(200, 100);
        panel.setBackground(Color.PINK);

        Graphics g = panel.getGraphics();
        g.setFont(new Font("Monospaced",
                  Font.BOLD + Font.ITALIC, 36));
        g.drawString("Too big", 20, 40);

        g.setFont(new Font("SansSerif", Font.PLAIN, 10));
        g.drawString("Too small", 30, 60);

        g.setFont(new Font("Serif", Font.ITALIC, 18));
        g.drawString("Just right", 40, 80);
    }
}
```

This program produces the output shown in Figure 3G.11.

Figure 3G.11 Output of `DrawFonts`

Images

The `DrawingPanel` is also capable of displaying images loaded from files in formats such as JPEG, PNG, and GIF. To display an image, first you must find an image file (such as one on the internet or on your computer) and place it into the same directory as your code project. Images are displayed in two steps: first the image must be loaded from the hard drive into an `Image` object, and then your panel's `Graphics` object can display the image.

```
Image <name> = <panel>.loadImage("<filename>");
g.drawImage(<name>, <x>, <y>, <panel>);
```

The *x* and *y* coordinates passed when drawing the image represent its top/left corner pixel position.

There are a few quirks to the syntax. One is that we use the `DrawingPanel` to load the image, while you use the `Graphics` object to draw it. It's easy to accidentally get the two mixed up. Also, unlike the other drawing commands, `drawImage` requires you to pass the `DrawingPanel` as a last parameter to the method. This is required by Java's `Graphics` class in order for the code to compile.

For example, the following program loads an image that looks like a drawing of a rainbow and draws it onto the `DrawingPanel` with a text string underneath it.

```
// This program displays a rainbow from an image file.
import java.awt.*;

public class DrawRainbow {
    public static void main(String[] args) {
```

```
        DrawingPanel panel = new DrawingPanel(280, 200);
        Image rainbow = panel.loadImage("rainbow.png");
        Graphics g = panel.getGraphics();
        g.drawImage(rainbow, 0, 0, panel);
        g.drawString("Somewhere over the rainbow...", 10, 180);
    }
}
```

The program produces the output shown in Figure 3G.12.

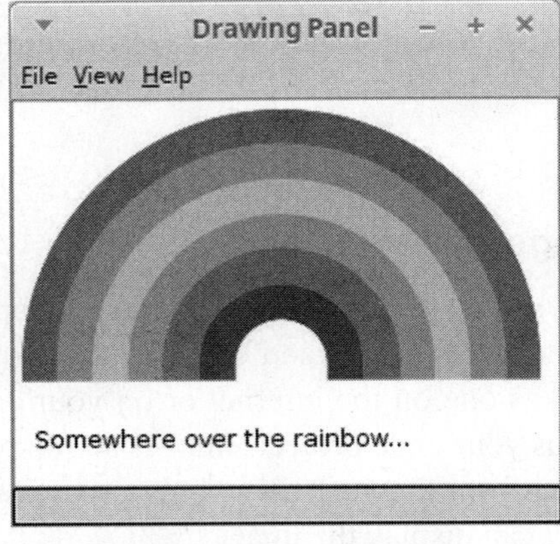

Figure 3G.12 Output of `DrawRainbow`

If you want to draw the same image multiple times on the panel, you don't need to repeat the `loadImage` part of the process. It is much more efficient to load the image a single time and then draw it as many times as you like. The following code would draw several copies of an image in a file named `smiley.png`, which is 100 × 100 pixels in size. The output of this code is shown in Figure 3G.13.

```
Image smileyFace = panel.loadImage("smiley.png");
Graphics g = panel.getGraphics();
for (int i = 0; i < 4; i++) {
    g.drawImage(smileyFace, i * 110 + 10, 10, panel);
}
```

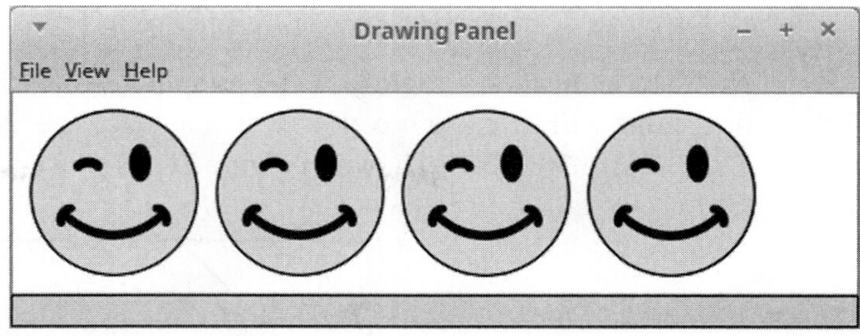

Figure 3G.13 Smiley face output

3G.2 Procedural Decomposition with Graphics

VideoNote

If you write complex drawing programs, you will want to break them down into several static methods to structure the code and to remove redundancy. When you do this, you'll have to pass the `Graphics` object to each static method that you introduce. For a quick example, the `DrawStringMessage1` program from the previous section could be split into a `main` method and a `drawText` method, as follows:

```
// Draws a message several times using a static method.

import java.awt.*;

public class DrawStringMessage2 {
    public static void main(String[] args) {
        DrawingPanel panel = new DrawingPanel(200, 100);
        panel.setBackground(Color.YELLOW);

        Graphics g = panel.getGraphics();
        drawText(g);
    }

    public static void drawText(Graphics g) {
        for (int i = 0; i < 10; i++) {
            g.drawString("There is no place like home",
                         i * 5, 10 + i * 10);
        }
    }
}
```

This program produces the same output as the original program (Figure 3G.10).

The program wouldn't compile without passing `Graphics g` to the `drawText` method, because `g` is needed to call drawing methods such as `drawString` and `fillRect`.

A Larger Example: DrawDiamonds

Now let's consider a slightly more complicated task: drawing the largest diamond figure that will fit into a box of a particular size. The largest diamond that can fit into a box of size 50 × 50 is shown in Figure 3G.14.

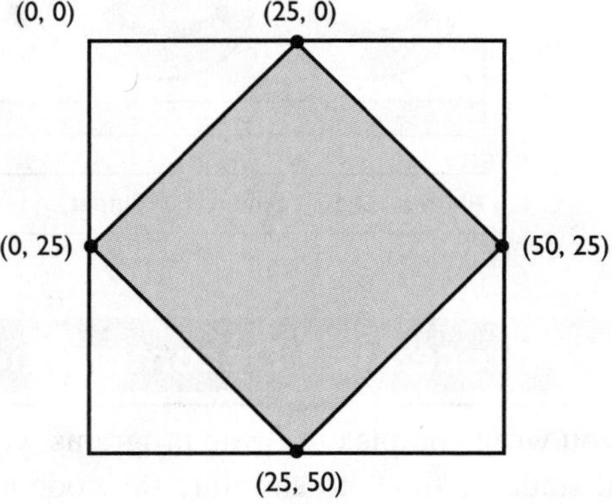

Figure 3G.14 Diamond

The code to draw such a diamond would be the following:

```
g.drawRect(0, 0, 50, 50);
g.drawLine(0, 25, 25, 0);
g.drawLine(25, 0, 50, 25);
g.drawLine(50, 25, 25, 50);
g.drawLine(25, 50, 0, 25);
```

Now imagine that we wish to draw three such 50 × 50 diamonds at different locations. We can turn our diamond-drawing code into a `drawDiamond` method that we'll call three times. Since each diamond will be in a different position, we can pass the *x*- and *y*-coordinates as parameters to our `drawDiamond` method.

A diamond enclosed by a box with top-left corner at the location (78, 22) is shown in Figure 3G.15.

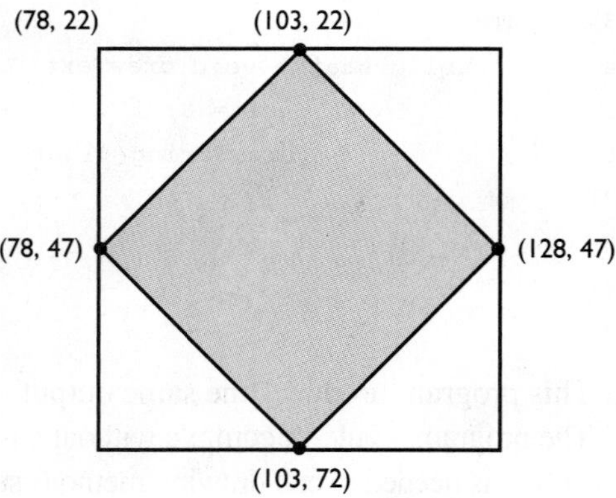

Figure 3G.15 Diamond at (78, 22)

The code to draw this diamond would be the following:

```
g.drawRect(78, 22, 50, 50);
g.drawLine(78, 47, 103, 22);
g.drawLine(103, 22, 128, 47);
g.drawLine(128, 47, 103, 72);
g.drawLine(103, 72, 78, 47);
```

As you can see, the parameter values passed to the `drawRect` and `drawLine` methods are very similar to those of the first diamond, except that they're shifted by 78 in the *x*-direction and 22 in the *y*-direction (except for the third and fourth parameters to `drawRect`, since these are the rectangle's width and height). This (78, 22) shift is called an *offset*.

We can generalize the coordinates to pass to `Graphics g`'s drawing commands so that they'll work with any diamond if we pass that diamond's top-left *x*- and *y*-offset. For example, we'll generalize the line from (0, 25) to (25, 0) in the first diamond and from (78, 47) to (103, 22) in the second diamond by saying that it is a line from $(x, y + 25)$ to $(x + 25, y)$, where (x, y) is the offset of the given diamond.

The following program uses the `drawDiamond` method to draw three diamonds without redundancy:

```
// This program draws several diamond figures of size 50x50.

import java.awt.*;

public class DrawDiamonds {
    public static void main(String[] args) {
        DrawingPanel panel = new DrawingPanel(250, 150);
        Graphics g = panel.getGraphics();

        drawDiamond(g, 0, 0);
        drawDiamond(g, 78, 22);
        drawDiamond(g, 19, 81);
    }

    // draws a diamond in a 50x50 box
    public static void drawDiamond(Graphics g, int x, int y) {
        g.drawRect(x, y, 50, 50);
        g.drawLine(x, y + 25, x + 25, y);
        g.drawLine(x + 25, y, x + 50, y + 25);
        g.drawLine(x + 50, y + 25, x + 25, y + 50);
        g.drawLine(x + 25, y + 50, x, y + 25);
    }
}
```

This program produces the output shown in Figure 3G.16.

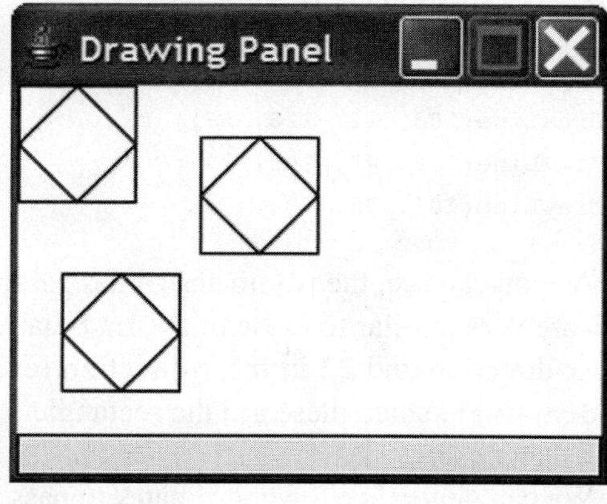

Figure 3G.16 Output of `DrawDiamonds`

It's possible to draw patterned figures in loops and to have one drawing method call another. For example, if we want to draw five diamonds, starting at (12, 15) and spaced 60 pixels apart, we just need a `for` loop that repeats five times and shifts the *x*-coordinate by 60 each time. Here's an example loop:

```
for (int i = 0; i < 5; i++) {
    drawDiamond(g, 12 + 60 * i, 15);
}
```

If we created another method to draw the line of five diamonds, we could call it from `main` to draw many lines of diamonds. Here's a modified version of the `DrawDiamonds` program with two graphical methods:

```
// This program draws several diamond figures of size 50x50.

import java.awt.*;

public class DrawDiamonds2 {
    public static void main(String[] args) {
        DrawingPanel panel = new DrawingPanel(360, 160);
        Graphics g = panel.getGraphics();

        drawManyDiamonds(g, 12, 15);
        g.setColor(Color.RED);
        drawManyDiamonds(g, 55, 100);
    }

    // draws five diamonds in a horizontal line
```

```
    public static void drawManyDiamonds(Graphics g,
                                        int x, int y) {
        for (int i = 0; i < 5; i++) {
            drawDiamond(g, x + 60 * i, y);
        }
    }

    // draws a diamond in a 50x50 box
    public static void drawDiamond(Graphics g, int x, int y) {
        g.drawRect(x, y, 50, 50);
        g.drawLine(x, y + 25, x + 25, y);
        g.drawLine(x + 25, y, x + 50, y + 25);
        g.drawLine(x + 50, y + 25, x + 25, y + 50);
        g.drawLine(x + 25, y + 50, x, y + 25);
    }
}
```

This program produces the output shown in Figure 3G.17.

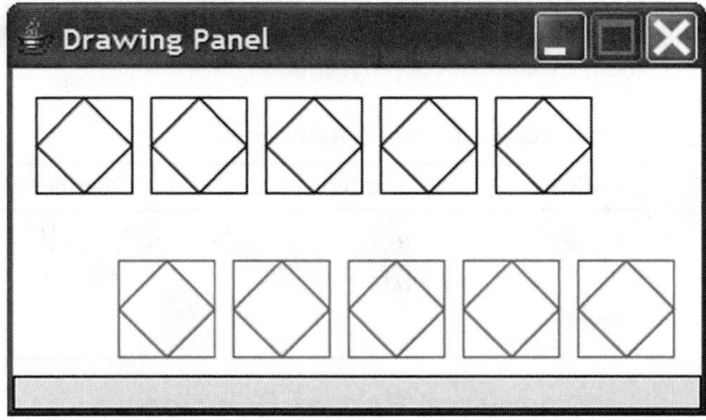

Figure 3G.17 Output of `DrawDiamonds2`

3G.3 Case Study: Pyramids

Imagine that you've been asked to write a program that will draw the images in Figure 3G.18 onto a `DrawingPanel`.

The overall drawing panel has a size of 350 × 250. Each pyramid is 100 pixels high and 100 pixels wide. The pyramids consist of centered flights of colored stairs

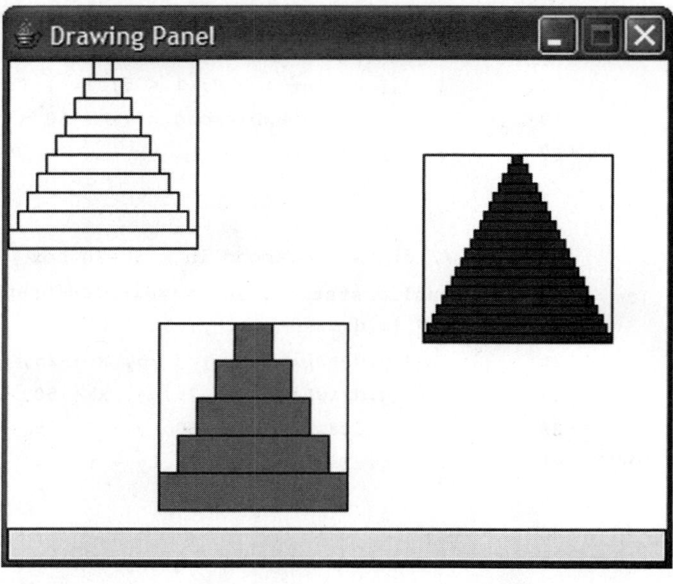

Figure 3G.18 Desired Pyramids Output

that widen toward the bottom, with black outlines around each stair. Table 3G.6 lists the attributes of each pyramid.

Table 3G.6 Pyramid Attributes

Fill color	Top-left corner	Number of stairs	Height of each stair
white	(0, 0)	10 stairs	10 pixels
red	(80, 140)	5 stairs	20 pixels
blue	(220, 50)	20 stairs	5 pixels

Unstructured Partial Solution

When trying to solve a larger and more complex problem like this, it's important to tackle it piece by piece and make iterative enhancements toward a final solution. Let's begin by trying to draw the top-left white pyramid correctly.

Each stair is centered horizontally within the pyramid. The top stair is 10 pixels wide. Therefore, it is surrounded by $\frac{90}{2}$ or 45 pixels of empty space on either side. That means that the 10×10 rectangle's top-left corner is at (45, 0). The second stair is 20 pixels wide, meaning that it's surrounded by $\frac{80}{2}$ or 40 pixels on each side:

(0, 0)
← 45 → 10 ← 45 →
← 40 → 20 ← 40 →

The following program draws the white pyramid in the correct position:

```
import java.awt.*;

// Draws the first pyramid only, with a lot of redundancy.
public class Pyramids1 {
    public static void main(String[] args) {
        DrawingPanel panel = new DrawingPanel(350, 250);
        Graphics g = panel.getGraphics();

        // draws the border rectangle
        g.drawRect(0, 0, 100, 100);

        // draws the 10 "stairs" in the white pyramid
        g.drawRect(45,  0,  10, 10);
        g.drawRect(40, 10,  20, 10);
        g.drawRect(35, 20,  30, 10);
        g.drawRect(30, 30,  40, 10);
        g.drawRect(25, 40,  50, 10);
        g.drawRect(20, 50,  60, 10);
        g.drawRect(15, 60,  70, 10);
        g.drawRect(10, 70,  80, 10);
        g.drawRect( 5, 80,  90, 10);
        g.drawRect( 0, 90, 100, 10);
    }
}
```

Looking at the code, it's clear that there's a lot of redundancy among the 10 lines to draw the stairs. Examining the patterns of numbers in each column reveals that the *x* value decreases by 5 each time, the *y* value increases by 10 each time, the width increases by 10 each time, and the height stays the same.

Another way of describing a stair's *x* value is to say that it is half of the overall 100 minus the stair's width. With that in mind, the following `for` loop draws the 10 stairs without the previous redundancy:

```
for (int i = 0; i < 10; i++) {
    int stairWidth = 10 * (i + 1);
    int stairHeight = 10;
    int stairX = (100 – stairWidth) / 2;
    int stairY = 10 * i;
    g.drawRect(stairX, stairY, stairWidth, stairHeight);
}
```

Generalizing the Drawing of Pyramids

Next let's add code to draw the bottom (red) pyramid. Its (*x*, *y*) position is (80, 140) and it has only five stairs. That means each stair is twice as tall and wide as those in the white pyramid.

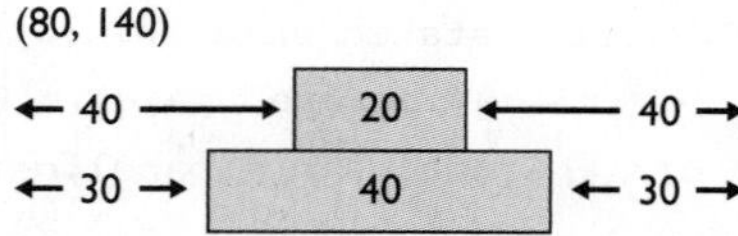

Given this information, we can determine that the top stair's upper-left corner is at (120, 140) and its size is 20 × 20, the second stair's upper-left corner is at (110, 160) and its size is 40 × 20, and so on.

For the moment, let's focus on getting the coordinates of the stairs right and not worry about the red fill color. Here is a redundant bit of code to draw the red pyramid's stairs, without the coloring:

```
// draws the border rectangle
g.drawRect(80, 140, 100, 100);
// draws the 5 "stairs" of the red pyramid
g.drawRect(120, 140, 20, 20);
g.drawRect(110, 160, 40, 20);
g.drawRect(100, 180, 60, 20);
g.drawRect( 90, 200, 80, 20);
g.drawRect( 80, 220, 100, 20);
```

Again we have redundancy among the five lines to draw the stairs, so let's look for a pattern. We'll use a loop to eliminate the redundancy like we did for the last pyramid, but with appropriate modifications. Each stair's height is now 20 pixels, and each stair's width is now 20 times the number for that stair. The *x*- and *y*-coordinates are a bit trickier. The *x*-coordinate formula is similar to the `(100 – stairWidth) / 2` from before, but this time it must be shifted right by 80 to account for the position of its bounding box's top-left corner. The *y*-coordinate must similarly be shifted downward by 140 pixels. Here's the correct loop:

```
// draws the 5 "stairs" of the red pyramid
for (int i = 0; i < 5; i++) {
    int stairWidth = 20 * (i + 1);
    int stairHeight = 20;
    int stairX = 80 + (100 – stairWidth) / 2;
    int stairY = 140 + 20 * i;
    g.drawRect(stairX, stairY, stairWidth, stairHeight);
}
```

Can you spot the pattern between the two `for` loops used to draw the stairs of the pyramids? The *x*- and *y*-coordinates differ only in the addition of the offset from (0, 0) in the second loop. The stairs' widths and heights differ only in that one pyramid's stairs are 20 pixels tall and the other pyramid's stairs are 10 pixels tall (the result of dividing the overall size of 100 by the number of stairs).

Using the preceding information, let's turn the code for drawing a pyramid into a method that we can call three times to avoid redundancy. The parameters will be the (*x*, *y*) coordinates of the top-left corner of the pyramid's bounding box and the number of stairs in the pyramid. We'll also need to pass `Graphics g` as a parameter so that we can draw onto the `DrawingPanel`. We'll modify the `for` loop to compute the stair height first, then use the height to compute the stair width, and finally use the width and height to help compute the (*x*, *y*) coordinates of the stair. Here's the code:

```
public static void drawPyramid(Graphics g, int x,
                               int y, int stairs) {
    // draws the border rectangle
    g.drawRect(x, y, 100, 100);

    // draws the stairs of the pyramid
    for (int i = 0; i < stairs; i++) {
        int stairHeight = 100 / stairs;
        int stairWidth = stairHeight * (i + 1);
        int stairX = x + (100 – stairWidth) / 2;
        int stairY = y + stairHeight * i;
        g.drawRect(stairX, stairY, stairWidth, stairHeight);
    }
}
```

The preceding code is now generalized to draw a pyramid at any location with any number of stairs. But one final ingredient is missing: the ability to give a different color to each pyramid.

Complete Structured Solution

The preceding code is correct except that it doesn't allow us to draw the pyramids in the proper colors. Let's add an additional parameter, a `Color`, to our method and use it to fill the pyramid stairs as needed. We'll pass `Color.WHITE` as this parameter's value for the first white pyramid; it'll fill the stairs with white, even though this isn't necessary.

The way to draw a filled shape with an outline of a different color is to first fill the shape, then use the outline color to draw the same shape. For example, to get red rectangles with black outlines, first we'll use `fillRect` with red, then we'll use `drawRect` with black with the same parameters.

Here's the new version of the `drawPyramid` method that uses the fill color as a parameter:

```
public static void drawPyramid(Graphics g, Color c,
                                   int x, int y, int stairs) {
    g.drawRect(x, y, 100, 100);

    for (int i = 0; i < stairs; i++) {
        int stairHeight = 100 / stairs;
        int stairWidth = stairHeight * (i + 1);
        int stairX = x + (100 - stairWidth) / 2;
        int stairY = y + stairHeight * i;

        g.setColor(c);
        g.fillRect(stairX, stairY, stairWidth, stairHeight);
        g.setColor(Color.BLACK);
        g.drawRect(stairX, stairY, stairWidth, stairHeight);
    }
}
```

Using this method, we can now draw all three pyramids easily by calling `drawPyramid` three times with the appropriate parameters:

```
drawPyramid(g, Color.WHITE, 0, 0, 10);
drawPyramid(g, Color.RED, 80, 140, 5);
drawPyramid(g, Color.BLUE, 220, 50, 20);
```

One last improvement we can make to our `Pyramids` program is to turn the overall pyramid size of 100 into a constant, so there aren't so many 100s lying around in the code. Here is the complete program:

```
// This program draws three colored pyramid figures.

import java.awt.*;

public class Pyramids {
    public static final int SIZE = 100;

    public static void main(String[] args) {
        DrawingPanel panel = new DrawingPanel(350, 250);
        Graphics g = panel.getGraphics();

        drawPyramid(g, Color.WHITE, 0, 0, 10);
        drawPyramid(g, Color.RED, 80, 140, 5);
        drawPyramid(g, Color.BLUE, 220, 50, 20);
    }

    // draws one pyramid figure with the given
```

```
    // number of stairs at the given (x, y) position
    // with the given color
    public static void drawPyramid(Graphics g, Color c,
                                   int x, int y, int stairs) {

        // draws the border rectangle
        g.drawRect(x, y, SIZE, SIZE);

        // draws the stairs of the pyramid
        for (int i = 0; i < stairs; i++) {
            int stairHeight = SIZE / stairs;
            int stairWidth = stairHeight * (i + 1);
            int stairX = x + (SIZE – stairWidth) / 2;
            int stairY = y + stairHeight * i;

            // fills the rectangles with the fill colors
            g.setColor(c);
            g.fillRect(stairX, stairY, stairWidth, stairHeight);

            // draws the black rectangle outlines
            g.setColor(Color.BLACK);
            g.drawRect(stairX, stairY, stairWidth, stairHeight);
        }
    }
}
```

Chapter Summary

`DrawingPanel` is a custom class provided by the authors to easily show a graphical window on the screen. A `DrawingPanel` contains a `Graphics` object that can be used to draw lines, text, and shapes on the screen using different colors.

A `Graphics` object has many useful methods for drawing shapes and lines, such as `drawLine`, `fillRect`, and `setColor`. Shapes can be "drawn" (drawing only the outline) or "filled" (coloring the entire shape).

The `Graphics` object can write text on the screen with its `drawString` method. You can specify different font styles and sizes with the `setFont` method.

Graphical programs that are decomposed into methods must pass appropriate parameters to those methods (for example, the `Graphics` object, as well as any (*x*, *y*) coordinates, sizes, or other values that guide the figures to be drawn).

Self-Check Problems

Section 3G.1: Introduction to Graphics

1. Which of the following is the correct syntax to draw a rectangle?

a. `Graphics g.drawRect(10, 20, 50, 30);`

b. `g.drawRect(10, 20, 50, 30);`

c. `g.draw.rectangle(10, 20, 50, 30);`

d. `Graphics.drawRect(10, 20, 50, 30);`

e. `g.drawRect(x = 10, y = 20, width = 50, height = 30);`

2. There are two mistakes in the following code, which attempts to draw a line from coordinates (50, 86) to (20, 35). What are they?

```
DrawingPanel panel = new DrawingPanel(200, 200);
panel.drawLine(50, 20, 86, 35);
```

3. The following code attempts to draw a black-filled outer rectangle with a white-filled inner circle inside it:

```
DrawingPanel panel = new DrawingPanel(200, 100);
Graphics g = panel.getGraphics();
g.setColor(Color.WHITE);
g.fillOval(10, 10, 50, 50);
g.setColor(Color.BLACK);
g.fillRect(10, 10, 50, 50);
```

However, the graphical output looks like Figure 3G.19 instead. What must be changed for it to look as intended?

Figure 3G.19 Graphical output of Self-Check 3G.3

4. The following code attempts to draw a black rectangle from (10, 20) to (50, 40) with a line across its diagonal:

```
DrawingPanel panel = new DrawingPanel(200, 100);
Graphics g = panel.getGraphics();
g.drawRect(10, 20, 50, 40);
g.drawLine(10, 20, 50, 40);
```

However, the graphical output looks like Figure 3G.20 instead. What must be changed for it to look as intended?

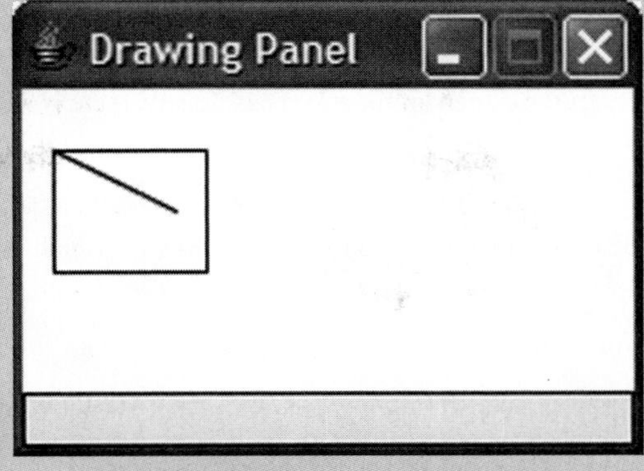

Figure 3G.20 Graphical output of Self-Check 3G.4

5. What sort of figure will be drawn by the following program? Can you draw a picture that will approximately match its appearance without running it first?

```
import java.awt.*;

public class Draw7 {
    public static void main(String[] args) {
        DrawingPanel panel = new DrawingPanel(200, 200);
        Graphics g = panel.getGraphics();
        for (int i = 0; i < 20; i++) {
            g.drawOval(i * 10, i * 10, 200 - (i * 10), 200 - (i * 10));
        }
    }
}
```

Exercises

1. Write a program that uses the `DrawingPanel` to draw Figure 3G.21.

Figure 3G.21 Expected graphical output of Exercise 3G.1

The window is 220 pixels wide and 150 pixels tall. The background is yellow. There are two blue ovals of size 40 × 40 pixels. They are 80 pixels apart, and the left oval's top-left corner is located at position (50, 25). There is a red square whose top two corners exactly intersect the centers of the two ovals. Lastly, there is a black horizontal line through the center of the square.

2. Modify your program from the previous exercise to draw the figure by a method called `drawFigure`. The method should accept three parameters: the `Graphics g` of the `DrawingPanel` on which to draw, and a pair of (*x*, *y*) coordinates specifying the location of the top-left corner of the figure. Use the following heading for your method:

```
public static void drawFigure(Graphics g, int x, int y)
```

Set your `DrawingPanel`'s size to 450 × 150 pixels, and use your `drawFigure` method to place two figures on it, as shown in Figure 3G.22. One figure should be at position (50, 25) and the other should be at position (250, 45).

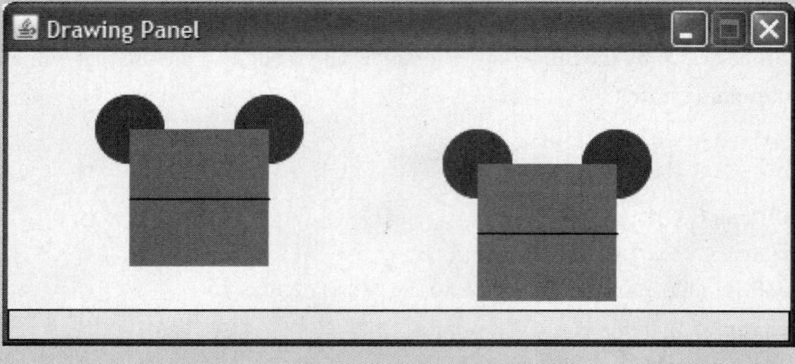

Figure 3G.22 Expected graphical output of Exercise 3G.2

3. Suppose you have the following existing program called `Face` that uses the `DrawingPanel` to draw the face figure shown in Figure 3G.23. Modify the program to draw the modified output shown in Figure 3G.24. Do so by writing a parameterized method that draws a face at different positions. The window size should be changed to 320 × 180 pixels, and the two faces' top-left corners are at (10, 30) and (150, 50).

Figure 3G.23 Initial graphical output of Exercise 3G.3

```
public class Face {
    public static void main(String[] args) {
        DrawingPanel panel = new DrawingPanel(220, 150);
```

```
        Graphics g = panel.getGraphics();

        g.setColor(Color.BLACK);
        g.drawOval(10, 30, 100, 100);    // face outline

        g.setColor(Color.BLUE);
        g.fillOval(30, 60, 20, 20);      // eyes
        g.fillOval(70, 60, 20, 20);

        g.setColor(Color.RED);           // mouth
        g.drawLine(40, 100, 80, 100);
    }
}
```

Figure 3G.24 Expected graphical output of Exercise 3G.3

4. Modify your previous `Face` program to draw the new output shown in Figure 3G.25. The window size should be changed to 520 × 180 pixels, and the faces' top-left corners are at (10, 30), (110, 30), (210, 30), (310, 30), and (410, 30).

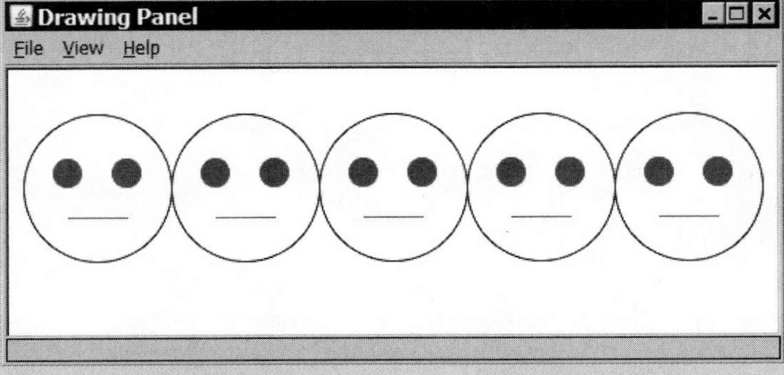

Figure 3G.25 Expected graphical output of Exercise 3G.4

5. Write a program called `ShowDesign` that uses the `DrawingPanel` to draw Figure 3G.26.

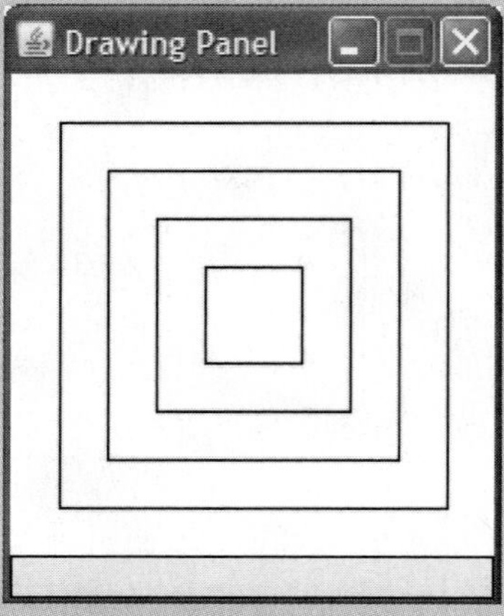

Figure 3G.26 Expected graphical output of Exercise 3G.5

The window is 200 pixels wide and 200 pixels tall. The background is white and the foreground is black. There are 20 pixels between each of the four rectangles, and the rectangles are concentric (their centers are at the same point). Use a loop to draw the repeated rectangles.

6. Modify your `ShowDesign` program from the previous exercise so that it has a method that accepts parameters for the window width and height and displays the rectangles at the appropriate sizes. For example, if your method was called with values of 300 and 100, the window would look like Figure 3G.27.

Figure 3G.27 Expected graphical output of Exercise 3G.6

7. Write a program called `Squares` that uses the `DrawingPanel` to draw the shape shown in Figure 3G.28.

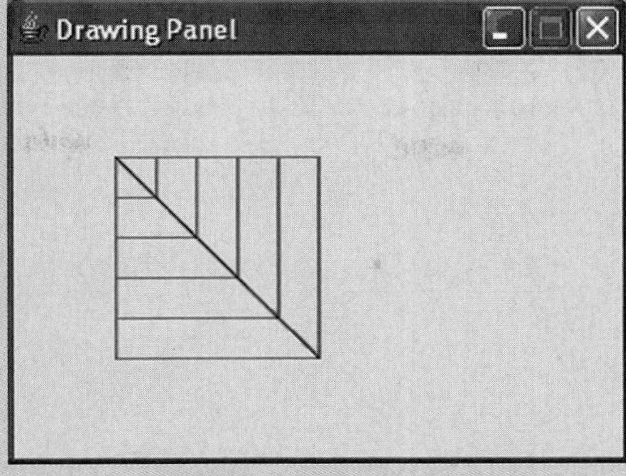

Figure 3G.28 Expected graphical output of Exercise 3G.7

The `DrawingPanel` is 300 pixels wide by 200 pixels high. Its background is cyan. The horizontal and vertical lines are drawn in red and the diagonal line is drawn in black. The upper-left corner of the diagonal line is at (50, 50). Successive horizontal and vertical lines are spaced 20 pixels apart.

8. Modify your code from the previous exercise to produce the pattern shown in Figure 3G.29.

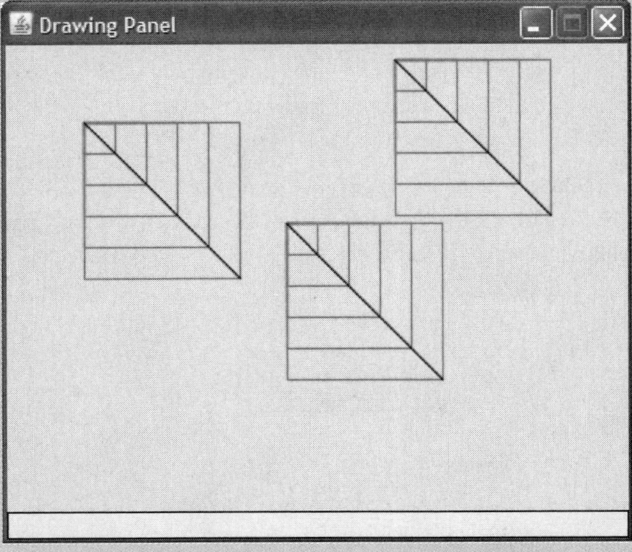

Figure 3G.29 Expected graphical output of Exercise 3G.8

The `DrawingPanel` is now 400 × 300 pixels in size. The first figure is at the same position, (50, 50). The other figures are at positions (250, 10) and (180, 115), respectively. Use one or more parameterized static methods to reduce the redundancy of your solution.

9. Modify your code from the previous exercise to produce the pattern shown in Figure 3G.30.

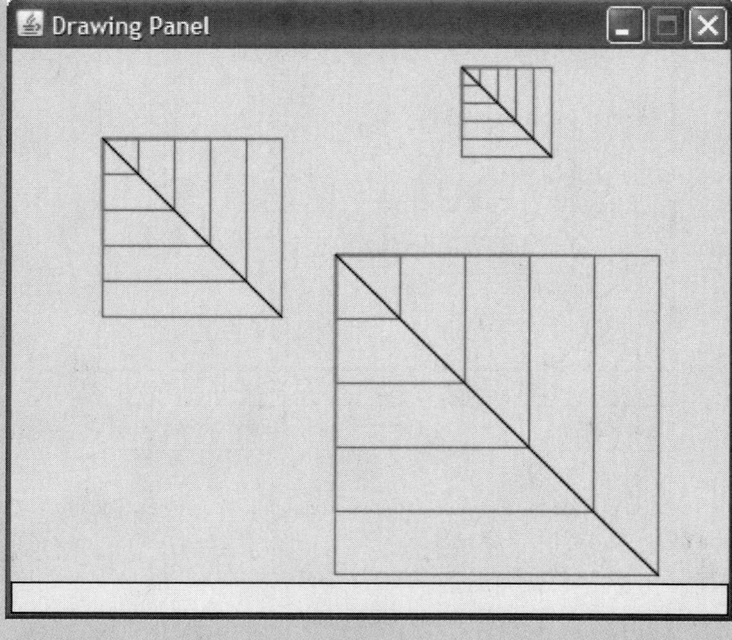

Figure 3G.30 Expected graphical output of Exercise 3G.9

The `DrawingPanel` is the same except that now each figure has a different size. The left figure has its original size of 100, the top-right figure has a size of 50, and the bottom-right figure has a size of 180. Use parameterized static methods to reduce the redundancy of your solution.

10. Write a program called `Stairs` that uses the `DrawingPanel` to draw the figure shown in Figure 3G.31. The first stair's top-left corner is at position (5, 5). The first stair is 10 × 10 pixels in size. Each stair is 10 pixels wider than the one above it. Make a table with the (*x*, *y*) coordinates and (*width* × *height*) sizes of the first five stairs. Note which values change and which ones stay the same.

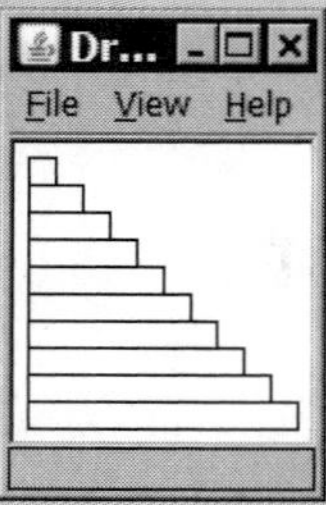

Figure 3G.31 Expected graphical output of Exercise 3G.10

11. Modify your previous `Stairs` program to draw each of the outputs shown in Figure 3G.32. Modify only the body of your loop. (You may want to make a new table to find the expressions for *x*, *y*, *width*, and *height* for each new output.)

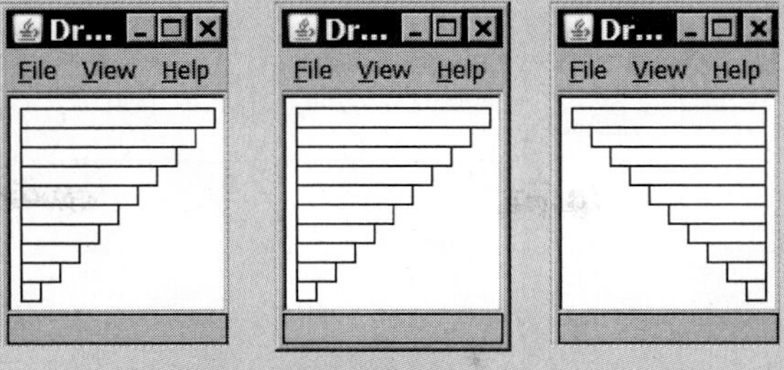

Figure 3G.32 Expected graphical outputs of Exercise 3G.11

12. Write a program called `Triangle` that uses the `DrawingPanel` to draw the figure shown in Figure 3G.33.

Figure 3G.33 Expected graphical output of Exercise 3G.12

The window is 600 × 200 pixels in size. The background is yellow and the lines are blue. The lines are 10 pixels apart vertically, and the diagonal lines intersect at the bottom of the figure in its horizontal center.

13. Write a program called `Football` that uses the `DrawingPanel` to draw the figure shown in Figure 3G.34. Though the figure looks to contain curves, it is entirely made of straight lines.

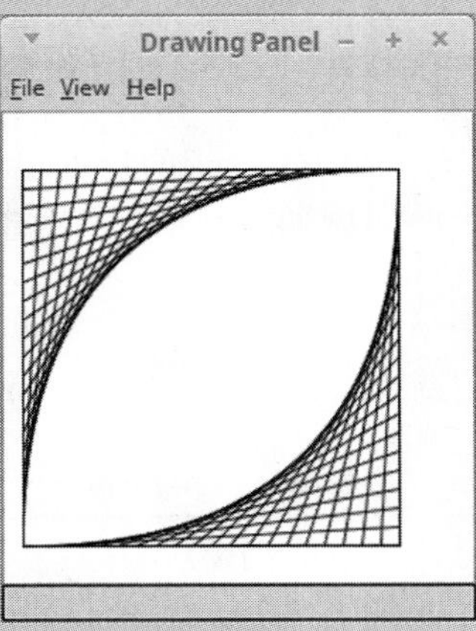

Figure 3G.34 Expected graphical output of Exercise 3G.13

The window is 250 × 250 pixels in size. There is an outer rectangle from (10, 30) to (210, 230), and a set of black lines drawn around the edges every 10 pixels. For example, along the top-left there is a line from (10, 200) to (20, 30), a line from (10, 190) to (30, 30), a line from (10, 180) to (40, 30), . . . and along the bottom-right there is a line from (20, 210) to (210, 200), a line from (30, 210) to (210, 190), and so on.

Programming Projects

1. Write a program that draws the patterns shown in Figure 3G.35 onto a `DrawingPanel`.

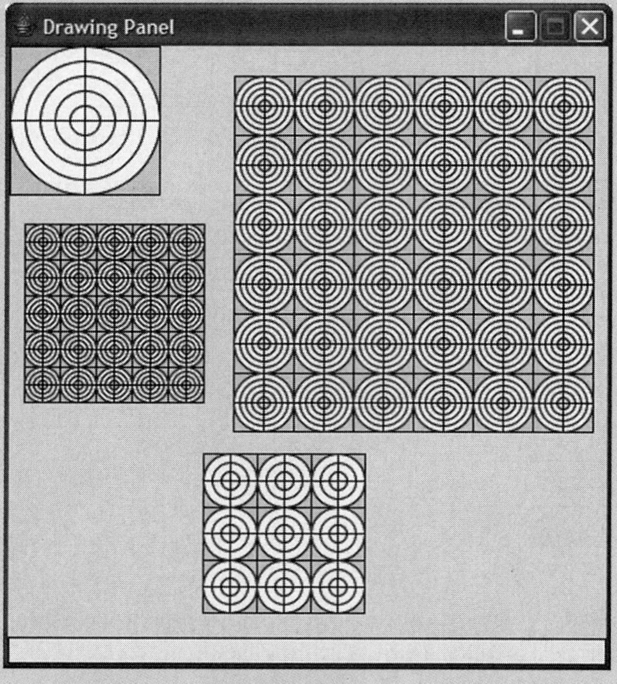

Figure 3G.35 Expected graphical output of Programming Project 3G.1

The `DrawingPanel`'s size is 400 × 400 pixels and its background color is cyan. It contains four figures of concentric yellow circles with black outlines, all surrounded by a green rectangle with a black outline. The four figures on your `DrawingPanel` should have the properties shown in Table 3G.7.

Table 3G.7 Circle Figure Properties

Description	(*x*, *y*) position	Size of subfigures	Number of circles	Number of rows/cols
top left	(0, 0)	100 × 100	5	1 × 1
bottom left	(10, 120)	24 × 24	4	5 × 5
top right	(150, 20)	40 × 40	5	6 × 6
bottom right	(130, 275)	36 × 36	3	3 × 3

Break down your program into methods for drawing one subfigure as well as larger grids of subfigures, such as the 5 × 5 grid at (10, 120).

2. Write a program that draws the image shown in Figure 3G.36 onto a `DrawingPanel` of size 200 × 200. Each stamp is 50 × 50 pixels in size.

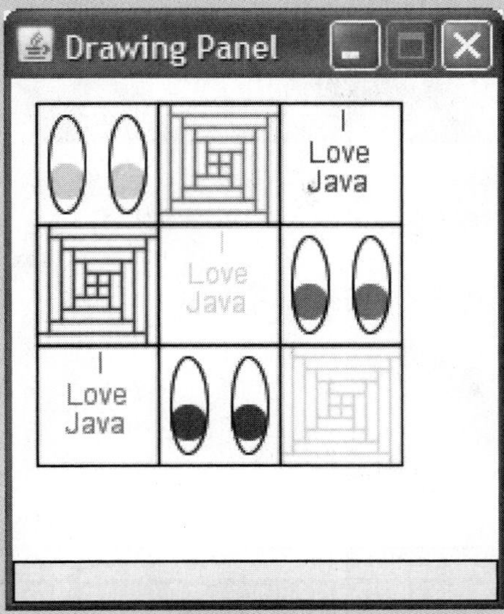

Figure 3G.36 Expected graphical output of Programming Project 3G.2

3. Write a program that draws checkerboards like these shown in Figure 3G.37 onto a `DrawingPanel` of size 420 × 300.

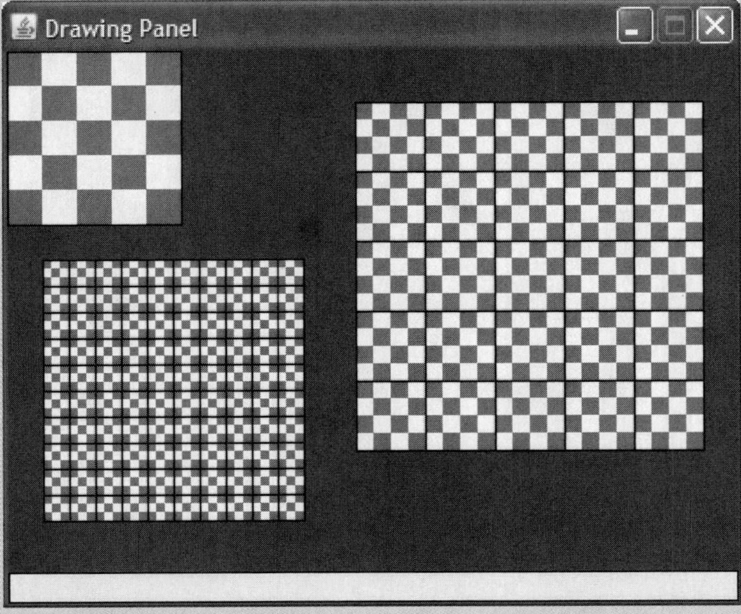

Figure 3G.37 Expected graphical output of Programming Project 3G.3

4. Write a modified version of the `Projectile` case study program from Chapter 3 that draws a graph of the projectile's flight onto a `DrawingPanel` of size 420 × 220. For example, the panel shown in Figure 3G.38 draws a projectile with an initial velocity of 30 meters per second, an angle of 50 degrees, and 10 steps.

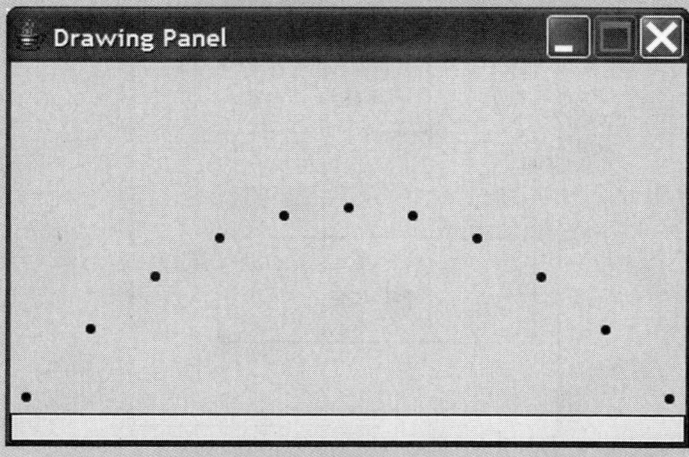

Figure 3G.38 Expected graphical output of Programming Project 3G.4

5. Write a program that draws the image shown in Figure 3G.39 onto a `DrawingPanel` of size 650 × 400. The image represents a famous optical illusion called the "Cafe Wall," in which a series of straight squares appears to be slanted.

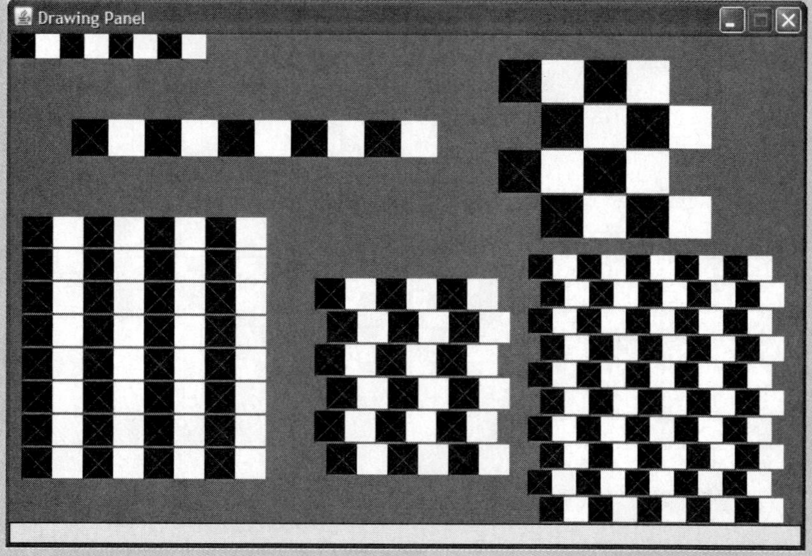

Figure 3G.39 Expected graphical output of Programming Project 3G.5

The image has a gray background and many rows of black and white squares with a blue X drawn through each black square. The two free-standing rows in the diagram have the following properties:

Table 3G.8 Cafe Wall Row Properties

Description	(*x*, *y*) position	Number of pairs	Size of each box
upper-left	(0, 0)	4	20
mid-left	(50, 70)	5	30

The diagram has four grids of rows of squares, with 2 pixels of vertical space between adjacent rows. A key aspect of the optical illusion is that every other row is shifted horizontally by a particular offset. The four grids have the following properties:

Table 3G.9 Cafe Wall Grid Properties

Description	(*x*, *y*) position	Number of pairs	Size of each box	2nd row offset
lower-left	(10, 150)	4	25	0
lower-middle	(250, 200)	3	25	10
lower-right	(425, 180)	5	20	10
upper-right	(400, 20)	2	35	35

Chapter 4

Conditional Execution

Introduction

In the last few chapters, you've seen how to solve complex programming problems using `for` loops to repeat certain tasks many times. You've also seen how to introduce some flexibility into your programs by using class constants and how to read values input by the user with a `Scanner` object. Now we are going to explore a much more powerful technique for writing code that can adapt to different situations.

In this chapter, we'll look at *conditional execution* in the form of a control structure known as the `if/else` statement. With `if/else` statements, you can instruct the computer to execute different lines of code depending on whether certain conditions are true. The `if/else` statement, like the `for` loop, is so powerful that you will wonder how you managed to write programs without it.

This chapter will also expand your understanding of common programming situations. It includes an exploration of loop techniques that we haven't yet examined and includes a discussion of text-processing issues. Adding conditional execution to your repertoire will also require us to revisit methods, parameters, and return values so that you can better understand some of the fine points. The chapter concludes with several rules of thumb that help us to design better procedural programs.

4.1 if/else Statements

You will often find yourself writing code that you want to execute some of the time but not all of the time. For example, if you are writing a game-playing program, you might want to print a message each time the user achieves a new high score and store that score. You can accomplish this by putting the required two lines of code inside an if statement:

```
if (currentScore > maxScore) {
    System.out.println("A new high score!");
    maxScore = currentScore;
}
```

The idea is that you will sometimes want to execute the two lines of code inside the if statement, but not always. The test in parentheses determines whether or not the statements inside the if statement are executed. In other words, the test describes the conditions under which we want to execute the code.

The general form of the if statement is as follows:

```
if (<test>) {
    <statement>;
    <statement>;
    ...
    <statement>;
}
```

The if statement, like the for loop, is a control structure. Notice that we once again see a Java keyword (if) followed by parentheses and a set of curly braces enclosing a series of controlled statements.

The diagram in Figure 4.1 indicates the flow of control for the simple if statement. The computer performs the test, and if it evaluates to true, the computer executes the controlled statements. If the test evaluates to false, the computer skips the controlled statements.

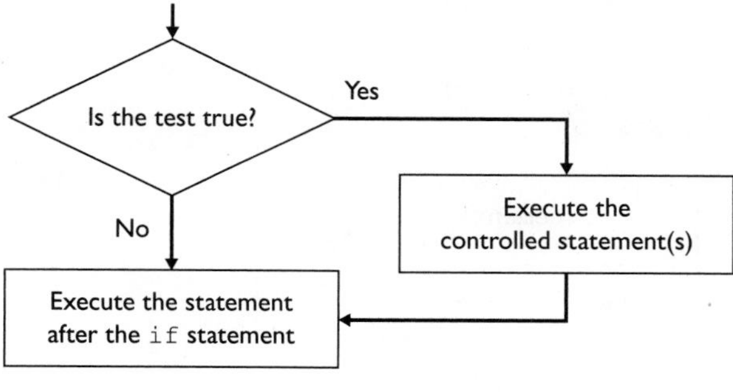

Figure 4.1 Flow of if statement

You'll use the simple `if` statement when you have code that you want to execute sometimes and skip other times. Java also has a variation known as the `if/else` statement that allows you to choose between two alternatives. Suppose, for example, that you want to set a variable called `answer` to the square root of a number:

```
answer = Math.sqrt(number);
```

You don't want to ask for the square root if the number is negative. To avoid this potential problem, you could use a simple `if` statement:

```
if (number >= 0) {
    answer = Math.sqrt(number);
}
```

This code will avoid asking for the square root of a negative number, but what value will it assign to `answer` if `number` is negative? In this case, you'll probably want to give a value to `answer` either way. Suppose you want `answer` to be `–1` when `number` is negative. You can express this pair of alternatives with the following `if/else` statement:

```
if (number >= 0) {
    answer = Math.sqrt(number);
} else {
    answer = –1;
}
```

The `if/else` statement provides two alternatives and executes one or the other. So, in the code above, you know that `answer` will be assigned a value regardless of whether `number` is positive or negative.

The general form of the `if/else` statement is:

```
if (<test>) {
    <statement>;
    <statement>;
    ...
    <statement>;
} else {
    <statement>;
    <statement>;
    ...
    <statement>;
}
```

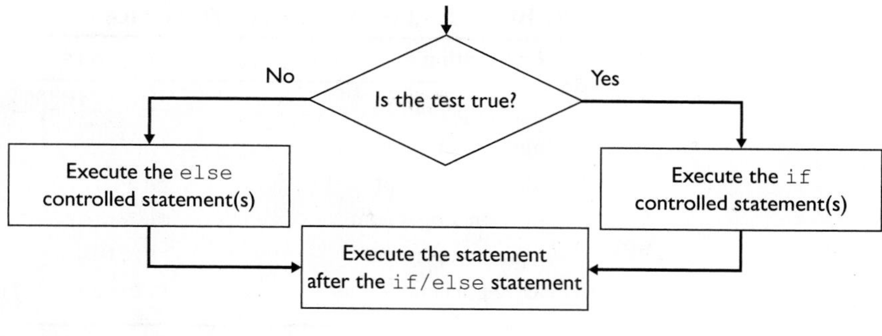

Figure 4.2 Flow of if/else statement

This control structure is unusual in that it has two sets of controlled statements and two different keywords (`if` and `else`). Figure 4.2 indicates the flow of control. The computer performs the test and, depending upon whether the code evaluates to `true` or `false`, executes one or the other group of statements.

As in the case of the `for` loop, if you have a single statement to execute, you don't need to include curly braces. However, the Java convention is to include the curly braces even if you don't need them, and we follow that convention in this book.

Relational Operators

An `if/else` statement is controlled by a test. Simple tests compare two expressions to see if they are related in some way. Such tests are themselves expressions of the following form and return either `true` or `false`:

```
<expression> <relational operator> <expression>
```

To evaluate a test of this form, first evaluate the two expressions and then see whether the given relation holds between the value on the left and the value on the right. If the relation holds, the test evaluates to `true`. If not, the test evaluates to `false`.

The relational operators are listed in Table 4.1. Notice that the equality operator consists of two equals signs (==), to distinguish it from the assignment operator (=).

Table 4.1 Relational Operators

Operator	Meaning	Example	Value
`==`	equal to	`2 + 2 == 4`	`true`
`!=`	not equal to	`3.2 != 4.1`	`true`
`<`	less than	`4 < 3`	`false`
`>`	greater than	`4 > 3`	`true`
`<=`	less than or equal to	`2 <= 0`	`false`
`>=`	greater than or equal to	`2.4 >= 1.6`	`true`

Table 4.2 Java Operator Precedence

Description	Operators
unary operators	`++, --, +, -`
multiplicative operators	`*, /, %`
additive operators	`+, -`
relational operators	`<, >, <=, >=`
equality operators	`==, !=`
assignment operators	`=, +=, -=, *=, /=, %=`

Because we use the relational operators as a new way of forming expressions, we must reconsider precedence. Table 4.2 is an updated version of Table 2.5 that includes these new operators. You will see that, technically, the equality comparisons have a slightly different level of precedence than the other relational operators, but both sets of operators have lower precedence than the arithmetic operators.

Let's look at an example. The following expression is made up of the constants `3`, `2`, and `9` and contains addition, multiplication, and equality operations:

```
3 + 2 * 2 == 9
```

Which of the operations is performed first? Because the relational operators have a lower level of precedence than the arithmetic operators, the multiplication is performed first, then the addition, then the equality test. In other words, Java will perform all of the "math" operations first before it tests any relationships. This precedence scheme frees you from the need to place parentheses around the left and right sides of a test that uses a relational operator. When you follow Java's precedence rules, the sample expression is evaluated as follows:

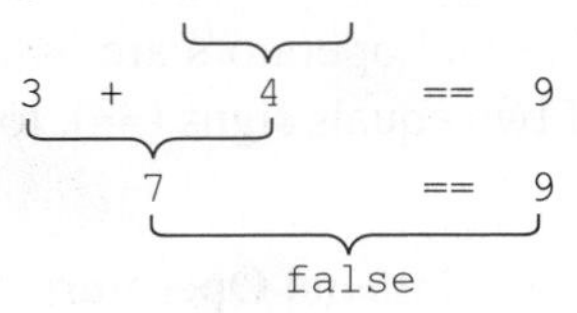

```
3 + 2 * 2 == 9
    └─┬─┘
3 +   4   == 9
└──┬──┘
   7      == 9
   └────┬────┘
      false
```

You can put arbitrary expressions on either side of the relational operator, as long as the types are compatible. Here is a test with complex expressions on either side:

```
(2 - 3 * 8) / (435 % (7 * 2)) <= 3.8 - 4.5 / (2.2 * 3.8)
```

One limitation of the relational operators is that they should be used only with primitive data. Later in this chapter we will talk about how to compare objects for equality, and in a later chapter we'll discuss how to perform less-than and greater-than comparisons on objects.

Nested if/else Statements

VideoNote

Many beginners write code that looks like this:

```
if (<test1>) {
    <statement1>;
}
if (<test2>) {
    <statement2>;
}
if (<test3>) {
    <statement3>;
}
```

This sequential structure is appropriate if you want to execute any combination of the three statements. For example, you might write this code in a program for a questionnaire with three optional parts, any combination of which might be applicable for a given person.

Figure 4.3 shows the flow of the sequential `if` code. Notice that it's possible for the computer to execute none of the controlled statements (if all tests are false), just one of them (if only one test happens to be true), or more than one of them (if multiple tests are true).

Often, however, you only want to execute one of a series of statements. In such cases, it is better to *nest* the `if` statements, stacking them one inside another:

```
if (<test1>) {
    <statement1>;
} else {
    if (<test2>) {
        <statement2>;
    } else {
        if (<test3>) {
            <statement3>;
        }
    }
}
```

When you use this construct, you can be sure that the computer will execute at most one statement: the statement corresponding to the first test that evaluates to `true`. If no tests evaluate to `true`, no statement is executed. If executing at most

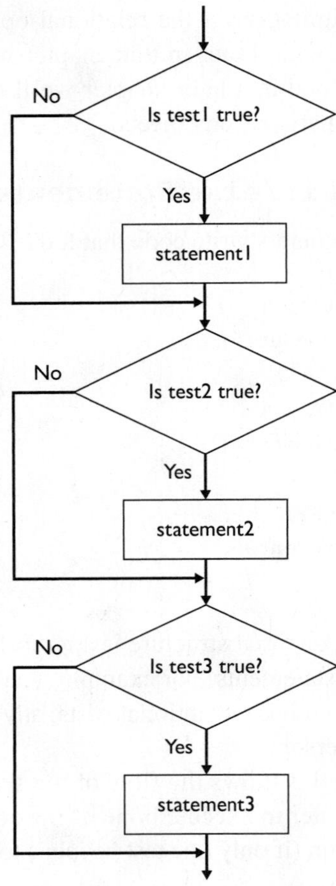

Figure 4.3 Flow of sequential `if`s

one statement is your objective, this construct is more appropriate than the sequential `if` statements. It reduces the likelihood of errors and simplifies the testing process.

As you can see, nesting `if` statements like this leads to a lot of indentation. The indentation isn't very helpful, because this construct is really intended to allow the choice of one of a number of alternatives. K&R style has a solution for this as well. If an `else` is followed by an `if`, we put them on the same line:

```
if (<test1>) {
    <statement1>;
} else if (<test2>) {
    <statement2>;
} else if (<test3>) {
    <statement3>;
}
```

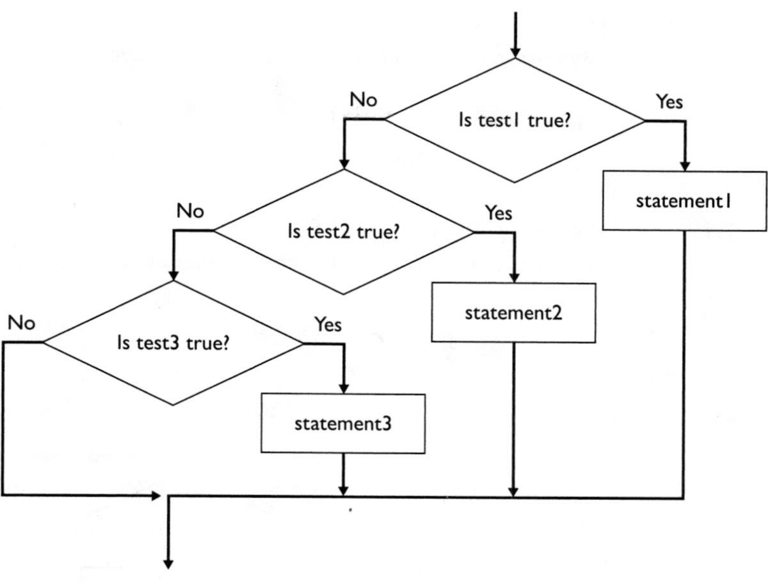

Figure 4.4 Flow of nested `if`s ending in test

When you follow this convention, the various statements all appear at the same level of indentation. We recommend that nested `if/else` statements be indented in this way.

Figure 4.4 shows the flow of the nested `if/else` code. Notice that it is possible to execute one of the controlled statements (the first one that evaluates to `true`) or none (if no tests evaluate to `true`).

In a variation of this structure, the final statement is controlled by an `else` instead of a test:

```
if (<test1>) {
    <statement1>;
} else if (<test2>) {
    <statement2>;
} else {
    <statement3>;
}
```

In this construct, the computer will always select the final branch when all the tests fail, and thus the construct will always execute exactly one of the three statements. Figure 4.5 shows the flow of this modified nested `if/else` code.

To explore these variations, consider the task of having the computer state whether a number is positive, negative, or zero. You could structure this task as three simple `if` statements as follows:

```
if (number > 0) {
    System.out.println("Number is positive.");
}
if (number == 0) {
    System.out.println("Number is zero.");
}
if (number < 0) {
    System.out.println("Number is negative.");
}
```

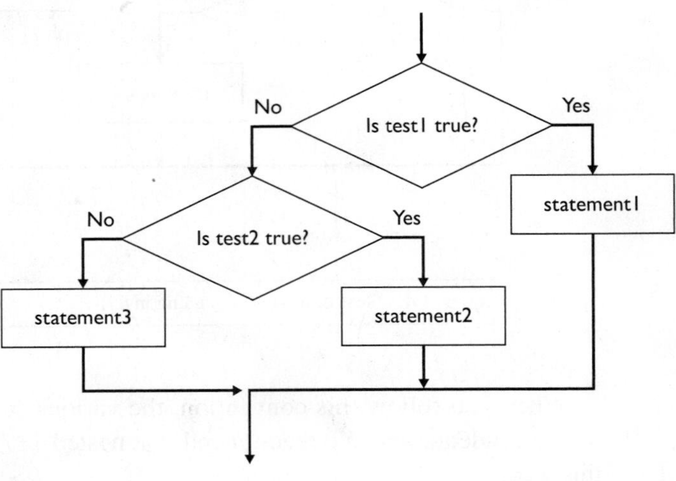

Figure 4.5 Flow of nested ifs ending in else

To determine how many of the printlns are potentially executed, you have to stop and think about the tests being performed. But you shouldn't have to put that much effort into understanding this code. The code is clearer if you nest the if statements:

```
if (number > 0) {
    System.out.println("Number is positive.");
} else if (number == 0) {
    System.out.println("Number is zero.");
} else if (number < 0) {
    System.out.println("Number is negative.");
}
```

This solution has a problem, however. You know that you want to execute one and only one println statement, but this nested structure does not preclude the possibility of no statement being executed (which would happen if all three tests failed). Of course, with these particular tests that will never happen: If a number is neither positive nor zero, it must be negative. Thus, the final test here is unnecessary and misleading. You must think about the tests to determine whether or not it is possible for all three tests to fail and all three branches to be skipped.

In this case, the best solution is the nested `if/else` approach with a final branch that is always taken if the first two tests fail:

```
if (number > 0) {
    System.out.println("Number is positive.");
} else if (number == 0) {
    System.out.println("Number is zero.");
} else {
    System.out.println("Number is negative.");
}
```

You can glance at this construct and see immediately that exactly one `println` will be executed. You don't have to look at the tests being performed in order to realize this; it is a property of this kind of nested `if/else` structure. If you want, you can include a comment to make it clear what is going on:

```
if (number > 0) {
    System.out.println("Number is positive.");
} else if (number == 0) {
    System.out.println("Number is zero.");
} else { // number must be negative
    System.out.println("Number is negative.");
}
```

One final benefit of this approach is efficiency. When the code includes three simple `if` statements, the computer will always perform all three tests. When the code uses the nested `if/else` approach, the computer carries out tests only until a match is found, which is a better use of resources. For example, in the preceding code we only need to perform one test for positive numbers and at most two tests overall.

When you find yourself writing code to choose among alternatives like these, you have to analyze the particular problem to figure out how many of the branches you potentially want to execute. If it doesn't matter what combination of branches is taken, use sequential `if` statements. If you want one or none of the branches to be taken, use nested `if/else` statements with a test for each statement. If you want exactly one branch to be taken, use nested `if/else` statements with a final branch controlled by an `else` rather than by a test. Table 4.3 summarizes these choices.

Table 4.3 if/else Options

Situation	Construct	Basic form

You want to execute any combination of controlled statements	Sequential ifs	if (<test1>) {
		    <statement1>;
		}
		if (<test2>) {
		    <statement2>;
		}
		if (<test3>) {
		    <statement3>;
		}

You want to execute zero or one of the controlled statements	Nested ifs ending in test	if (<test1>) {
		    <statement1>;
		} else if (<test2>) {
		    <statement2>;
		} else if (<test3>) {
		    <statement3>;
		}

You want to execute exactly one of the controlled statements	Nested ifs ending in else	if (<test1>) {
		    <statement1>;
		} else if (<test2>) {
		    <statement2>;
		} else {
		    <statement3>;
		}

Common Programming Error

Choosing the Wrong if/else Construct

Suppose that your instructor has told you that grades will be determined as follows:

A for scores ≥ 90
B for scores ≥ 80
C for scores ≥ 70
D for scores ≥ 60
F for scores < 60

You can translate this scale into code as follows:

```
String grade;
if (score >= 90) {
    grade = "A";
```

Continued on next page

Continued from previous page

```
}
if (score >= 80) {
    grade = "B";
}
if (score >= 70) {
    grade = "C";
}
if (score >= 60) {
    grade = "D";
}
if (score < 60) {
    grade = "F";
}
```

However, if you then try to use the variable `grade` after this code, you'll get this error from the compiler:

```
variable grade might not have been initialized
```

This is a clue that there is a problem. The Java compiler is saying that it believes there are paths through this code that will leave the variable `grade` uninitialized. In fact, the variable will always be initialized, but the compiler cannot figure this out. We can fix this problem by giving an initial value to `grade`:

```
String grade = "no grade";
```

This change allows the code to compile. But if you compile and run the program, you will find that it gives out only two grades: D and F. Anyone who has a score of at least 60 ends up with a D and anyone with a grade below 60 ends up with an F. And even though the compiler complained that there was a path that would allow `grade` not to be initialized, no one ever gets a grade of "no grade."

The problem here is that you want to execute exactly one of the assignment statements, but when you use sequential `if` statements, it's possible for the program to execute several of them sequentially. For example, if a student has a score of 95, that student's `grade` is set to `"A"`, then reset to `"B"`, then reset to `"C"`, and finally reset to `"D"`. You can fix this problem by using a nested `if/else` construct:

```
String grade;
if (score >= 90) {
    grade = "A";
} else if (score >= 80) {
```

Continued on next page

Continued from previous page

```
    grade = "B";
} else if (score >= 70) {
    grade = "C";
} else if (score >= 60) {
    grade = "D";
} else { // score < 60
    grade = "F";
}
```

You don't need to set `grade` to `"no grade"` now because the compiler can see that no matter what path is followed, the variable `grade` will be assigned a value (exactly one of the branches will be executed).

Object Equality

You saw earlier in the chapter that you can use the `==` and `!=` operators to test for equality and nonequality of primitive data, respectively. Unfortunately, these operators do not work the way you might expect when you test for equality of objects like strings. You will have to learn a new way to test objects for equality.

For example, you might write code like the following to read a token from the console and to call one of two different methods depending on whether the user responded with "yes" or "no." If the user types neither word, this code is supposed to print an error message:

```
System.out.print("yes or no? ");
String s = console.next();
if (s == "yes") {
    processYes();
} else if (s == "no") {
    processNo();
} else {
    System.out.println("You didn't type yes or no");
}
```

Unfortunately, this code does not work. No matter what the user enters, this program always prints "You didn't type yes or no". We will explore in detail in Chapter 8 why this code doesn't work. For now the important thing to know is that Java provides a second way of testing for equality that is intended for use with objects. Every Java object has a method called `equals` that takes another object as an argument. You can use this method to ask an object whether it equals another object. For example, we can fix the previous code as follows:

```
System.out.print("yes or no? ");
String s = console.next();
```

```
if (s.equals("yes")) {
    processYes();
} else if (s.equals("no")) {
    processNo();
} else {
    System.out.println("You didn't type yes or no");
}
```

Remember when you're working with strings that you should always call the `equals` method rather than using ==.

The `String` class also has a special variation of the `equals` method called `equalsIgnoreCase` that ignores case differences (uppercase versus lowercase letters). For example, you could rewrite the preceding code as follows to recognize responses like "Yes," "YES," "No," "NO," yES", and so on:

```
System.out.print("yes or no? ");
String s = console.next();
if (s.equalsIgnoreCase("yes")) {
    processYes();
} else if (s.equalsIgnoreCase("no")) {
    processNo();
} else {
    System.out.println("You didn't type yes or no");
}
```

Factoring if/else Statements

VideoNote

Suppose you are writing a program that plays a betting game with a user and you want to give different warnings about how much cash the user has left. The nested `if/else` construct that follows distinguishes three different cases: funds less than $500, which is considered low; funds between $500 and $1000, which is considered okay; and funds over $1000, which is considered good. Notice that the user is given different advice in each case:

```
if (money < 500) {
    System.out.println("You have $" + money + " left.");
    System.out.print("Cash is dangerously low. Bet carefully.");
    System.out.print("How much do you want to bet? ");
    bet = console.nextInt();
} else if (money < 1000) {
    System.out.println("You have $" + money + " left.");
    System.out.print("Cash is somewhat low. Bet moderately.");
    System.out.print("How much do you want to bet? ");
    bet = console.nextInt();
} else {
```

```
        System.out.println("You have $" + money + " left.");
        System.out.print("Cash is in good shape. Bet liberally.");
        System.out.print("How much do you want to bet? ");
        bet = console.nextInt();
}
```

This construct is repetitious and can be made more efficient by using a technique called *factoring*. Using this simple technique, you factor out common pieces of code from the different branches of the `if/else` construct. In the preceding program, three different branches can execute, depending on the value of the variable `money`. Start by writing down the series of actions being performed in each branch and comparing them, as in Figure 4.6.

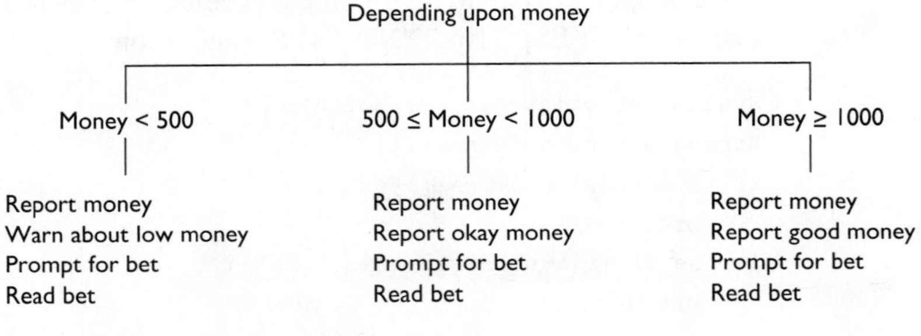

Figure 4.6 `if/else` branches before factoring

You can factor at both the top and the bottom of a construct like this. If you notice that the top statement in each branch is the same, you factor it out of the branching part and put it before the branch. Similarly, if the bottom statement in each branch is the same, you factor it out of the branching part and put it after the loop. You can factor the top statement in each of these branches and the bottom two statements, as in Figure 4.7.

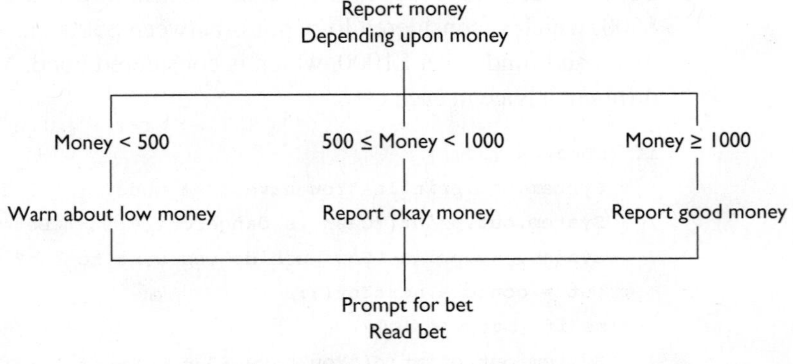

Figure 4.7 `if/else` branches after factoring

Thus, the preceding code can be reduced to the following more succinct version:

```
System.out.println("You have $" + money + " left.");
if (money < 500) {
```

```
    System.out.print("Cash is dangerously low. Bet carefully.");
} else if (money < 1000) {
    System.out.print("Cash is somewhat low. Bet moderately.");
} else {
    System.out.print("Cash is in good shape. Bet liberally.");
}
System.out.print("How much do you want to bet? ");
bet = console.nextInt();
```

Testing Multiple Conditions

When you are writing a program, you often find yourself wanting to test more than one condition. For example, suppose you want the program to take a particular course of action if a number is between 1 and 10. You might say:

```
if (number >= 1) {
    if (number <= 10) {
        doSomething();
    }
}
```

In these lines of code, you had to write two statements: one testing whether the number was greater than or equal to 1 and one testing whether the number was less than or equal to 10.

Java provides an efficient alternative: You can combine the two tests by using an operator known as the logical AND operator, which is written as two ampersands with no space in between (`&&`). Using the AND operator, we can write the preceding code more simply:

```
if (number >= 1 && number <= 10) {
    doSomething();
}
```

As its name implies, the AND operator forms a test that requires that both parts of the test evaluate to `true`. There is a similar operator known as logical OR that evaluates to `true` if either of two tests evaluates to `true`. The logical OR operator is written using two vertical bar characters (`||`). For example, if you want to test whether a variable `number` is equal to 1 or 2, you can say:

```
if (number == 1 || number == 2) {
    processNumber(number);
}
```

We will explore the logical AND and logical OR operators in more detail in the next chapter.

4.2 Cumulative Algorithms

The more you program, the more you will find that certain patterns emerge. Many common algorithms involve accumulating an answer step by step. In this section, we will explore some of the most common *cumulative algorithms*.

> **Cumulative Algorithm**
>
> An operation in which an overall value is computed incrementally, often using a loop.

For example, you might use a cumulative algorithm over a set of numbers to compute the average value or to find the largest number.

Cumulative Sum

You'll often want to find the sum of a series of numbers. One way to do this is to declare a different variable for each value you want to include, but that would not be a practical solution: If you have to add a hundred numbers together, you won't want to declare a hundred different variables. Fortunately, there is a simpler way.

The trick is to keep a running tally of the result and process one number at a time. For example, to add to a variable called `sum`, you would write the following line of code:

```
sum = sum + next;
```

Alternatively, you could use the shorthand assignment operator:

```
sum += next;
```

The preceding statement takes the existing value of `sum`, adds the value of a variable called `next`, and stores the result as the new value of `sum`. This operation is performed for each number to be summed. Notice that when you execute this statement for the first time `sum` does not have a value. To get around this, you initialize `sum` to a value that will not affect the answer: `0`.

Here is a pseudocode description of the cumulative sum algorithm:

```
sum = 0.
for (all numbers to sum) {
    obtain "next".
    sum += next.
}
```

To implement this algorithm, you must decide how many times to go through the loop and how to obtain a `next` value. Here is an interactive program that prompts the user for the number of numbers to add together and for the numbers themselves:

```java
// Finds the sum of a sequence of numbers.

import java.util.*;

public class ExamineNumbers1 {
    public static void main(String[] args) {
        System.out.println("This program adds a sequence of");
        System.out.println("numbers.");
        System.out.println();

        Scanner console = new Scanner(System.in);

        System.out.print("How many numbers do you have? ");
        int totalNumber = console.nextInt();

        double sum = 0.0;
        for (int i = 1; i <= totalNumber; i++) {
            System.out.print("    #" + i + "? ");
            double next = console.nextDouble();
            sum += next;
        }
        System.out.println();

        System.out.println("sum = " + sum);
    }
}
```

The program's execution will look something like this (as usual, user input is boldface):

```
This program adds a sequence of
numbers.

How many numbers do you have? 6
    #1? 3.2
    #2? 4.7
    #3? 5.1
    #4? 9.0
    #5? 2.4
    #6? 3.1

sum = 27.5
```

Let's trace the execution in detail. Before we enter the `for` loop, we initialize the variable `sum` to `0.0`:

sum 0.0

On the first execution of the for loop, we read in a value of 3.2 from the user and add this value to sum:

sum [3.2] next [3.2]

The second time through the loop, we read in a value of 4.7 and add this to the value of sum:

sum [7.9] next [4.7]

Notice that the sum now includes both of the numbers entered by the user, because we have added the new value, 4.7, to the old value, 3.2. The third time through the loop, we add in the value 5.1:

sum [13.0] next [5.1]

Notice that the variable sum now contains the sum of the first three numbers (3.2 + 4.7 + 5.1). Now we read in 9.0 and add it to the sum:

sum [22.0] next [9.0]

Then we add in the fifth value, 2.4:

sum [24.4] next [2.4]

Finally, we add in the sixth value, 3.1:

sum [27.5] next [3.1]

We then exit the for loop and print the value of sum.

There is an interesting scope issue in this particular program. Notice that the variable sum is declared outside the loop, while the variable next is declared inside the loop. We have no choice but to declare sum outside the loop because it needs to be initialized and it is used after the loop. But the variable next is used only inside the loop, so it can be declared in that inner scope. It is best to declare variables in the innermost scope possible.

The cumulative sum algorithm and variations on it will be useful in many of the programming tasks you solve. How would you do a cumulative product? Here is the pseudocode:

```
product = 1.
for (all numbers to multiply) {
    obtain "next".
    product = product * next.
}
```

Min/Max Loops

Another common programming task is to keep track of the maximum and/or minimum values in a sequence. For example, consider the task of deciding whether it will be viable to build a living area on the Moon inhabited by humans. One obstacle is that the average daily surface temperature on the Moon is a chilly −50 degrees Fahrenheit. But a much more daunting problem is the wide range of values; it ranges from a minimum of −240 degrees to a maximum of 250 degrees.

To compute the maximum of a sequence of values, you can keep track of the largest value you've seen so far and use an `if` statement to update the maximum if you come across a new value that is larger than the current maximum. This approach can be described in pseudocode as follows:

```
initialize max.
for (all numbers to examine) {
    obtain "next".
    if (next > max) {
        max = next.
    }
}
```

Initializing the maximum isn't quite as simple as it sounds. For example, novices often initialize `max` to `0`. But what if the sequence of numbers you are examining is composed entirely of negative numbers? For example, you might be asked to find the maximum of this sequence:

−84, −7, −14, −39, −410, −17, −41, −9

The maximum value in this sequence is –7, but if you've initialized `max` to `0`, the program will incorrectly report `0` as the maximum.

There are two classic solutions to this problem. First, if you know the range of the numbers you are examining, you can make an appropriate choice for `max`. In that case, you can set `max` to the lowest value in the range. That seems counterintuitive because normally we think of the maximum as being large, but the idea is to set `max` to the smallest possible value it could ever be so that anything larger will cause `max` to be reset to that value. For example, if you knew that the preceding sequence of numbers consisted of temperatures in degrees Fahrenheit, you would know that they temperatures could never be smaller than absolute zero (around −460 degrees Fahrenheit), so you could initialize `max` to that value.

The second possibility is to initialize `max` to the first value in the sequence. That won't always be convenient because it means obtaining one of the numbers outside the loop.

When you combine these two possibilities, the pseudocode becomes:

```
initialize max either to lowest possible value or to first value.
for (all numbers to examine) {
    obtain "next".
    if (next > max) {
        max = next;
    }
}
```

The pseudocode for computing the minimum is a slight variation of this code:

```
initialize min either to highest possible value or to first value.
for (all numbers to examine) {
    obtain "next".
    if (next < min) {
        min = next.
    }
}
```

To help you understand this better, let's put the pseudocode into action with a real problem. In mathematics, there is an open problem that involves what are known as *hailstone sequences.* These sequences of numbers often rise and fall in unpredictable patterns, which is somewhat analogous to the process that forms hailstones.

A hailstone sequence is a sequence of numbers in which each value x is followed by:

$(3x + 1)$, if x is odd

$\left(\frac{x}{2}\right)$ if x is even

For example, if you start with 7 and construct a sequence of length 10, you get the sequence:

7, 22, 11, 34, 17, 52, 26, 13, 40, 20

In this sequence, the maximum and minimum values are 52 and 7, respectively. If you extend this computation to a sequence of length 20, you get the sequence:

7, 22, 11, 34, 17, 52, 26, 13, 40, 20, 10, 5, 16, 8, 4, 2, 1, 4, 2, 1

In this case, the maximum and minimum values are 52 and 1, respectively.

You will notice that once 1, 2, or 4 appears in the sequence, the sequence repeats itself. It is conjectured that all integers eventually reach 1, like hailstones that fall to the ground. This is an unsolved problem in mathematics. Nobody has been able to disprove it, but nobody has proven it either.

Let's write a method that takes a starting value and a sequence length and prints the maximum and minimum values obtained in a hailstone sequence formed with that starting value and of that length. Our method will look like this:

```
public static void printHailstoneMaxMin(int value, int length) {
    ...
}
```

We can use the starting value to initialize `max` and `min`:

```
int min = value;
int max = value;
```

We then need a loop that will generate the other values. The user will input a parameter telling us how many times to go through the loop, but we don't want to execute the loop body `length` times: Remember that the starting value is part of the sequence, so if we want to use a sequence of the given length, we have to make sure that the number of iterations is one less than `length`. Combining this idea with the `max/min` pseudocode, we know the loop will look like this:

```
for (int i = 1; i <= length - 1; i++) {
    compute next number.
    if (value > max) {
        max = value.
    } else if (value < min) {
        min = value.
    }
}
print max and min.
```

To fill out the pseudocode for "compute next number," we need to translate the hailstone formula into code. The formula is different, depending on whether the current value is odd or even. We can use an `if/else` statement to solve this task. For the test, we can use a "mod 2" test to see what remainder we get when we divide by 2. Even numbers have a remainder of 0 and odd numbers have a remainder of 1. So the test should look like this:

```
if (value % 2 == 0) {
    do even computation.
} else {
    do odd computation.
}
```

Translating the hailstone mathematical formulas into Java, we get the following code:

```
if (value % 2 == 0) {
    value = value / 2;
} else {
    value = 3 * value + 1;
}
```

The only part of our pseudocode that we haven't filled in yet is the part that prints the result. This part comes after the loop and is fairly easy to complete. Here is the complete method:

```
public static void printHailstoneMaxMin(int value, int length) {
    int min = value;
    int max = value;
```

```
        for (int i = 1; i <= length - 1; i++) {
            if (value % 2 == 0) {
                value = value / 2;
            } else {
                value = 3 * value + 1;
            }
            if (value > max) {
                max = value;
            } else if (value < min) {
                min = value;
            }
        }
        System.out.println("max = " + max);
        System.out.println("min = " + min);
    }
```

Cumulative Sum with `if`

Let's now explore how you can use `if/else` statements to create some interesting variations on the cumulative sum algorithm. Suppose you want to read a sequence of numbers and compute the average. This task seems like a straightforward variation of the cumulative sum code. You can compute the average as the sum divided by the number of numbers:

```
double average = sum / totalNumber;
System.out.println("average = " + average);
```

But there is one minor problem with this code. Suppose that when the program asks the user how many numbers to process, the user enters `0`. Then the program will not enter the cumulative sum loop, and your code will try to compute the value of `0` divided by `0`. Java will then print that the average is `NaN`, a cryptic message that is short for "Not a Number." It would be better for the program to print out some other kind of message which indicates that there aren't any numbers to average. You can use an `if/else` statement for this purpose:

```
if (totalNumber <= 0) {
    System.out.println("No numbers to average");
} else {
    double average = sum / totalNumber;
    System.out.println("average = " + average);
}
```

Another use of `if` statements would be to count how many negative numbers the user enters. You will often want to count how many times something occurs in a program.

This goal is easy to accomplish with an `if` statement and an integer variable called a *counter*. You start by initializing the counter to `0`:

```
int negatives = 0;
```

You can use any name you want for the variable. Here we used `negatives` because that is what you're counting. The other essential step is to increment the counter inside the loop if it passes the test of interest:

```
if (next < 0) {
    negatives++;
}
```

When you put this all together and modify the comments and introduction, you end up with the following variation of the cumulative sum program:

```
// Finds the average of a sequence of numbers as well as
// reporting how many of the user-specified numbers were negative.

import java.util.*;

public class ExamineNumbers2 {
    public static void main(String[] args) {
        System.out.println("This program examines a sequence");
        System.out.println("of numbers to find the average");
        System.out.println("and count how many are negative.");
        System.out.println();

        Scanner console = new Scanner(System.in);

        System.out.print("How many numbers do you have? ");
        int totalNumber = console.nextInt();

        int negatives = 0;
        double sum = 0.0;
        for (int i = 1; i <= totalNumber; i++) {
            System.out.print("    #" + i + "? ");
            double next = console.nextDouble();
            sum += next;
            if (next < 0) {
                negatives++;
            }
        }
        System.out.println();

        if (totalNumber <= 0) {
```

```
            System.out.println("No numbers to average");
        } else {
            double average = sum / totalNumber;
            System.out.println("average = " + average);
        }
        System.out.println("# of negatives = " + negatives);
    }
}
```

The program's execution will look something like this:

```
This program examines a sequence
of numbers to find the average
and count how many are negative.

How many numbers do you have? 8
    #1? 2.5
    #2? 9.2
    #3? −19.4
    #4? 208.2
    #5? 42.3
    #6? 92.7
    #7? −17.4
    #8? 8

average = 40.7625
# of negatives = 2
```

Roundoff Errors

As you explore cumulative algorithms, you'll discover a particular problem that you should understand. For example, consider the following execution of the previous `ExamineNumbers2` program with different user input:

```
This program examines a sequence
of numbers to find the average
and count how many are negative.

How many numbers do you have? 4
    #1? 2.1
    #2? -3.8
    #3? 5.4
    #4? 7.4

average = 2.7750000000000004
# of negatives = 1
```

If you use a calculator, you will find that the four numbers add up to 11.1. If you divide this number by 4, you get 2.775. Yet Java reports the result as `2.7750000000000004`. Where do all of those zeros come from, and why does the number end in 4? The answer is that floating-point numbers can lead to *roundoff errors.*

Roundoff Error

A numerical error that occurs because floating-point numbers are stored as approximations rather than as exact values.

Roundoff errors are generally small and can occur in either direction (slightly high or slightly low). In the previous case, we got a roundoff error that was slightly high.

Floating-point numbers are stored in a format similar to scientific notation, with a set of digits and an exponent. Consider how you would store the value one-third in scientific notation using base-10. You would state that the number is 3.33333 (repeating) times 10 to the –1 power. We can't store an infinite number of digits on a computer, though, so we'll have to stop repeating the 3s at some point. Suppose we can store 10 digits. Then the value for one-third would be stored as 3.333333333 times 10 to the –1. If we multiply that number by 3, we don't get back 1. Instead, we get 9.999999999 times 10 to the –1 (which is equal to 0.9999999999).

You might wonder why the numbers we used in the previous example caused a problem when they didn't have any repeating digits. You have to remember that the computer stores numbers in base-2. Numbers like 2.1 and 5.4 might look like simple numbers in base-10, but they have repeating digits when they are stored in base-2.

Roundoff errors can lead to rather surprising outcomes. For example, consider the following short program:

```
public class Roundoff {
    public static void main(String[] args) {
        double n = 1.0;
        for (int i = 1; i <= 10; i++) {
            n += 0.1;
            System.out.println(n);
        }
    }
}
```

This program presents a classic cumulative sum with a loop that adds 0.1 to the number `n` each time the loop executes. We start with `n` equal to `1.0` and the loop iterates 10 times, which we might expect to print the numbers 1.1, 1.2, 1.3, and so on through 2.0. Instead, it produces the following output:

```
1.1
1.2000000000000002
1.3000000000000003
```

```
1.4000000000000004
1.5000000000000004
1.6000000000000005
1.7000000000000006
1.8000000000000007
1.9000000000000008
2.000000000000001
```

The problem occurs because 0.1 cannot be stored exactly in base-2 (it produces a repeating set of digits, just as one-third does in base-10). Each time through the loop the error is compounded, which is why the roundoff error gets worse each time.

As another example, consider the task of adding together the values of a penny, a nickel, a dime, and a quarter. If we use variables of type `int`, we will get an exact answer regardless of the order in which we add the numbers:

```
int cents1 = 1 + 5 + 10 + 25;
int cents2 = 25 + 10 + 5 + 1;
System.out.println(cents1);
System.out.println(cents2);
```

The output of this code is as follows:

```
41
41
```

Regardless of the order, these numbers always add up to 41 cents. But suppose that instead of thinking of these values as whole cents, we think of them as fractions of a dollar that we store as `double`s:

```
double dollars1 = 0.01 + 0.05 + 0.10 + 0.25;
double dollars2 = 0.25 + 0.10 + 0.05 + 0.01;
System.out.println(dollars1);
System.out.println(dollars2);
```

This code has surprising output:

```
0.41000000000000003
0.41
```

Even though we are adding up exactly the same numbers, the fact that we add them in a different order makes a difference. The reason is roundoff errors.

There are several lessons to draw from this:

- Be aware that when you store floating-point values (e.g., `double`s), you are storing approximations and not exact values. If you need to store an exact value, store it using type `int`.

- Don't be surprised when you see numbers that are slightly off from the expected values.
- Don't expect to be able to compare variables of type `double` for equality.

To follow up on the third point, consider what the preceding code would lead to if we were to perform the following test:

```
if (dollars1 == dollars2) {
    ...
}
```

The test would evaluate to `false` because the values are very close, but not close enough for Java to consider them equal. We rarely use a test for exact equality when we work with `doubles`. Instead, we can use a test like this to see if numbers are close to one another:

```
if (Math.abs(dollars1 – dollars2) < 0.001) {
    ...
}
```

We use the absolute value (`abs`) method from the `Math` class to find the magnitude of the difference and then test whether it is less than some small amount (in this case, `0.001`).

Later in this chapter, we'll introduce a variation on `print`/`println` called `printf` that will make it easier to print numbers like these without all of the extra digits.

4.3 Text Processing

Programmers commonly face problems that require them to create, edit, examine, and format text. Collectively, we call these tasks *text processing*.

> **Text Processing**
> Editing and formatting strings of text.

In this section, we'll look in more detail at the `char` primitive type and introduce a new command called `System.out.printf`. Both of these tools are very useful for text-processing tasks.

The char Type

The primitive type `char` represents a single character of text. It's legal to have variables, parameters, and return values of type `char` if you so desire. Literal values of type `char` are expressed by placing the character within single quotes:

```
char ch = 'A';
```

Table 4.4 Differences between char and String

	char	String
Type of value	primitive	object
Memory usage	2 bytes	depends on length
Methods	none	`length`, `toUpperCase`, . . .
Number of letters	exactly 1	0 to many
Surrounded by	apostrophes: `'c'`	quotes: `"Str"`
Comparing	<, >=, ==, . . .	`equals`

It is also legal to create a `char` value that represents an escape sequence:

```
char newline = '\n';
```

In the previous chapter, we discussed `String` objects. The distinction between `char` and `String` is a subtle one that confuses many new Java programmers. The main difference is that a `String` is an object, but a `char` is a primitive value. A `char` occupies a very small amount of memory, but it has no methods. Table 4.4 summarizes several of the differences between the types.

Why does Java have two types for such similar data? The `char` type exists primarily for historical reasons; it dates back to older languages such as C that influenced the design of Java.

So why would a person ever use the `char` type when `String` is available? It's often necessary to use `char` because some methods in Java's API use it as a parameter or return type. But there are also a few cases in which using `char` can be more useful or simpler than using `String`.

The characters of a `String` are stored inside the object as values of type `char`. You can access the individual characters through the object's `charAt` method, which accepts an integer index as a parameter and returns the character at that index. We often loop over a string to examine or change its characters. For example, the following method prints each character of a string on its own line:

```
public static void printVertical(String message) {
    for (int i = 0; i < message.length(); i++) {
        char ch = message.charAt(i);
        System.out.println(ch);
    }
}
```

char versus int

Values of type `char` are stored internally as 16-bit integers. A standard encoding scheme called Unicode determines which integer value represents each character. (Unicode will be covered in more detail later in this chapter.) Since characters are really integers, Java automatically converts a value of type `char` into an `int` whenever it is expecting an `int`:

```
char letter = 'a' + 2; // stores 'c'
```

It turns out that the integer value for `'a'` is `97`, so the expression's result is `99`, which is stored as the character `'c'`. An `int` can similarly be converted into a `char` using a type cast. (The cast is needed as a promise to the compiler, because not every possible `int` value corresponds to a valid character.) Below is an example of a code segment that uses a type cast to convert an `int` value to a value of type `char`:

```
int code = 66;
char grade = (char) code; // stores 'B'
```

Because values of type `char` are really integers, they can also be compared by using relational operators such as < or ==. In addition, they can be used in loops to cover ranges of letters. For example, the following code prints every letter of the alphabet:

```
for (char letter = 'a'; letter <= 'z'; letter++) {
    System.out.print(letter);
}
if (c == '8') {... // true
```

You can learn more about the character-to-integer equivalences by searching the web for Unicode tables.

Cumulative Text Algorithms

Strings of characters are often used in cumulative algorithms as discussed earlier in this chapter. For example, you might loop over the characters of a string searching for a particular letter. The following method accepts a string and a character and returns the number of times the character occurs in the string:

```
public static int count(String text, char c) {
    int found = 0;
    for (int i = 0; i < text.length(); i++) {
        if (text.charAt(i) == c) {
            found++;
        }
    }
    return found;
}
```

A `char` can be concatenated with a `String` using the standard + operator. Using this idea, a `String` can be built using a loop, starting with an empty string and

Table 4.5 Useful Methods of the `Character` Class

Method	Description	Example
`getNumericValue(ch)`	Converts a character that looks like a number into that number	`Character.getNumericValue('6')` returns `6`
`isDigit(ch)`	Whether or not the character is one of the digits `'0'` through `'9'`	`Character.isDigit('X')` returns `false`
`isLetter(ch)`	Whether or not the character is in the range `'a'` to `'z'` or `'A'` to `'Z'`	`Character.isLetter('f')` returns `true`
`isLowerCase(ch)`	Whether or not the character is a lowercase letter	`Character.isLowerCase('Q')` returns `false`
`isUpperCase(ch)`	Whether or not the character is an uppercase letter	`Character.isUpperCase('Q')` returns `true`
`toLowerCase(ch)`	The lowercase version of the given letter	`Character.toLowerCase('Q')` returns `'q'`
`toUpperCase(ch)`	The uppercase version of the given letter	`Character.toUpperCase('x')` returns `'X'`

concatenating individual characters in the loop. This is called a *cumulative concatenation*. The following method accepts a string and returns the same characters in the reverse order:

```
public static String reverse(String phrase) {
    String result = "";
    for (int i = 0; i < phrase.length(); i++) {
        result = phrase.charAt(i) + result;
    }
    return result;
}
```

For example, the call of `reverse("Tin man")` returns `"nam niT"`.

Several useful methods can be called to check information about a character or convert one character into another. Remember that `char` is a primitive type, which means that you can't use the dot syntax used with `Strings`. Instead, the methods are static methods in a class called `Character`; the methods accept `char` parameters and return appropriate values. Some of the most useful `Character` methods are listed in Table 4.5.

The following method counts the number of letters A–Z in a `String`, ignoring all nonletter characters such as punctuation, numbers, and spaces:

```
public static int countLetters(String phrase) {
    int count = 0;
    for (int i = 0; i < phrase.length(); i++) {
        char ch = phrase.charAt(i);
```

```
        if (Character.isLetter(ch)) {
            count++;
        }
    }
    return count;
}
```

For example, the call of `countLetters("gr8 JoB!")` returns 5.

System.out.printf

So far we've used `System.out.println` and `System.out.print` for console output. There's a third method, `System.out.printf`, which is a bit more complicated than the others but gives us some useful new abilities. The "f" in `printf` stands for "formatted," implying that `System.out.printf` gives you more control over the format in which your output is printed.

Imagine that you'd like to print a multiplication table from 1 to 10. The following code prints the correct numbers, but it doesn't look very nice:

```
for (int i = 1; i <= 10; i++) {
    for (int j = 1; j <= 10; j++) {
        System.out.print(i * j + " ");
    }
    System.out.println();
}
```

The output is the following. Notice that the numbers don't line up vertically:

```
1 2 3 4 5 6 7 8 9 10
2 4 6 8 10 12 14 16 18 20
3 6 9 12 15 18 21 24 27 30
4 8 12 16 20 24 28 32 36 40
5 10 15 20 25 30 35 40 45 50
6 12 18 24 30 36 42 48 54 60
7 14 21 28 35 42 49 56 63 70
8 16 24 32 40 48 56 64 72 80
9 18 27 36 45 54 63 72 81 90
10 20 30 40 50 60 70 80 90 100
```

We could separate the numbers by tabs, which would be better. But this separation doesn't give us very much control over the appearance of the table. Every number would be exactly eight spaces apart on the screen, and the numbers would appear left-aligned. It would be a pain to try to right-align the numbers manually, because you'd have to use `if/else` statements to check whether a given number was in a certain range and, if necessary, pad it with a given number of spaces.

Did You Know?

ASCII and Unicode

We store data on a computer as binary numbers (sequences of 0s and 1s). To store textual data, we need an encoding scheme that will tell us what sequence of 0s and 1s to use for any given character. Think of it as a giant secret decoder ring that says things like, "If you want to store a lowercase 'a,' use the sequence 01100001."

In the early 1960s, IBM developed an encoding scheme called *EBCDIC* that worked well with the company's punched cards, which had been in use for decades before computers were even invented. But it soon became clear that EBCDIC wasn't a convenient encoding scheme for computer programmers. There were gaps in the sequence that made characters like `'i'` and `'j'` appear far apart even though they follow one directly after the other.

In 1967, the American Standards Association published a scheme known as *ASCII* (pronounced "AS-kee") that has been in common use ever since. The acronym is short for "American Standard Code for Information Interchange." In its original form, ASCII defined 128 characters that each could be stored with 7 bits of data.

The biggest problem with ASCII is that it is an *American* code. There are many characters in common use in other countries that were not included in ASCII. For example, the British pound (£) and the Spanish variant of the letter n (ñ) are not included in the standard 128 ASCII characters. Various attempts have been made to extend ASCII, doubling it to 256 characters so that it can include many of these special characters. However, it turns out that even 256 characters is simply not enough to capture the incredible diversity of human communication.

Around the time that Java was created, a consortium of software professionals introduced a new standard for encoding characters known as *Unicode*. They decided that the 7 bits of standard ASCII and the 8 bits of extended ASCII were simply not big enough and chose not to set a limit on how many bits they might use for encoding characters. At the time of this writing, the consortium has identified over 110,000 characters, which require a little over 16 bits to store. Unicode includes the characters used in most modern languages and even some ancient languages. Egyptian hieroglyphs were added in 2007, although it still does not include Mayan hieroglyphs, and the consortium has rejected a proposal to include Klingon characters.

The designers of Java used Unicode as the standard for the type `char`, which means that Java programs are capable of manipulating a full range of characters. Fortunately, the Unicode Consortium decided to incorporate the ASCII encodings, so ASCII can be seen as a subset of Unicode. If you are curious about the actual ordering of characters in ASCII, type "ASCII table" into your favorite search engine and you will find millions of hits to explore.

A much easier way to print values aligned in fixed-width fields is to use the `System.out.printf` command. The `printf` method accepts a specially written `String` called a *format string* that specifies the general appearance of the output, followed by any parameters to be included in the output:

```
System.out.printf(<format string>, <parameter>, ..., <parameter>);
```

A format string is like a normal `String`, except that it can contain placeholders called *format specifiers* that allow you to specify a location where a variable's value should be inserted, along with the format you'd like to give that value. Format specifiers begin with a `%` sign and end with a letter specifying the kind of value, such as `d` for decimal integers (`int`) or `f` for floating-point numbers (real numbers of type `double`). Consider the following `printf` statement:

```
int x = 38, y = -152;
System.out.printf("location: (%d, %d)\n", x, y);
```

This statement produces the following output:

```
location: (38, -152)
```

The `%d` is not actually printed but is instead replaced with the corresponding parameter written after the format string. The number of format specifiers in the format string must match the number of parameters that follow it. The first specifier will be replaced by the first parameter, the second specifier by the second parameter, and so on. `System.out.printf` is unusual because it can accept a varying number of parameters.

The `printf` command is like `System.out.print` in that it doesn't move to a new line unless you explicitly tell it to do so. Notice that in the previous code we ended our format string with `\n` to complete the line of output.

Since a format specifier uses `%` as a special character, if you want to print an actual `%` sign in a `printf` statement, instead write two `%` characters in a row. For example:

```
int score = 87;
System.out.printf("You got %d%% on the exam!\n", score);
```

The code produces the following output:

```
You got 87% on the exam!
```

A format specifier can contain information after its `%` sign to specify the width, precision, and alignment of the value being printed. For example, `%8d` specifies an integer right-aligned in an 8-space-wide area, and `%12.4f` specifies a `double` value right-aligned in a 12-space-wide area, rounded to four digits past the decimal point. Table 4.6 lists some common format specifiers that you may wish to use in your programs.

Table 4.6 Common Format Specifiers

Specifier	Result
`%d`	Integer
`%8d`	Integer, right-aligned, 8-space-wide field
`%-6d`	Integer, left-aligned, 6-space-wide field
`%f`	Floating-point number
`%12f`	Floating-point number, right-aligned, 12-space-wide field
`%.2f`	Floating-point number, rounded to nearest hundredth
`%16.3f`	Floating-point number, rounded to nearest thousandth, 16-space-wide field
`%s`	String
`%8s`	String, right-aligned, 8-space-wide field
`%-9s`	String, left-aligned, 9-space-wide field

As a comprehensive example, suppose that the following variables have been declared to represent information about a student:

```
int score = 87;
double gpa = 3.18652;
String name = "Jessica";
```

The following code sample prints the preceding variables with several format specifiers:

```
System.out.printf("student name: %10s\n", name);
System.out.printf("exam score   : %10d\n", score);
System.out.printf("GPA          : %10.2f\n", gpa);
```

The code produces the following output:

```
student name:    Jessica
exam score   :        87
GPA          :      3.19
```

The three values line up on their right edge, because we print all of them with a width of 10. The `printf` method makes it easy to line up values in columns in this way. Notice that the student's GPA rounds to 3.19, because of the `2` in that variable's format specifier. The specifier `10.2` makes the value fit into an area 10 characters wide with exactly 2 digits after the decimal point.

Let's return to our multiplication table example. Now that we know about `printf`, we can print the table with right-aligned numbers relatively easily. We'll right-align the numbers into fields of width 5:

```
for (int i = 1; i <= 10; i++) {
    for (int j = 1; j <= 10; j++) {
```

```
            System.out.printf("%5d", i * j);
        }
        System.out.println();
    }
```

This code produces the following output:

```
    1    2    3    4    5    6    7    8    9   10
    2    4    6    8   10   12   14   16   18   20
    3    6    9   12   15   18   21   24   27   30
    4    8   12   16   20   24   28   32   36   40
    5   10   15   20   25   30   35   40   45   50
    6   12   18   24   30   36   42   48   54   60
    7   14   21   28   35   42   49   56   63   70
    8   16   24   32   40   48   56   64   72   80
    9   18   27   36   45   54   63   72   81   90
   10   20   30   40   50   60   70   80   90  100
```

The `printf` method can also solve the problem with the `Roundoff` program introduced earlier in this chapter. Fixing the precision of the `double` value ensures that it will be rounded to avoid the tiny roundoff mistakes that result from `double` arithmetic. Here is the corrected program:

```
// Uses System.out.printf to correct roundoff errors.
public class Roundoff2 {
    public static void main(String[] args) {
        double n = 1.0;
        for (int i = 1; i <= 10; i++) {
            n += 0.1;
            System.out.printf("%3.1f\n", n);
        }
    }
}
```

The program produces the following output:

```
1.1
1.2
1.3
1.4
1.5
1.6
1.7
1.8
1.9
2.0
```

4.4 Methods with Conditional Execution

We introduced a great deal of information about methods in Chapter 3, including how to use parameters to pass values into a method and how to use a `return` statement to have a method return a value. Now that we've introduced conditional execution, we need to revisit these issues so that you can gain a deeper understanding of them.

Preconditions and Postconditions

Every time you write a method you should think about exactly what that method is supposed to accomplish. You can describe how a method works by describing the *preconditions* that must be true before it executes and the *postconditions* that will be true after it has executed.

Precondition

A condition that must be true before a method executes in order to guarantee that the method can perform its task.

Postcondition

A condition that the method guarantees will be true after it finishes executing, as long as the preconditions were true before the method was called.

For example, if you are describing the task of a person on an automobile assembly line, you might use a postcondition like, "The bolts that secure the left front tire are on the car and tight." But postconditions are not the whole story. Employees on an assembly line depend on one another. A line worker can't add bolts and tighten them if the left tire isn't there or if there are no bolts. So, the assembly line worker might have preconditions like, "The left tire is mounted properly on the car, there are at least eight bolts in the supply box, and a working wrench is available." You describe the task fully by saying that the worker can make the postcondition(s) true if the precondition(s) are true before starting.

Like workers on an assembly line, methods need to work together, each solving its own portion of the task in order for them all to solve the overall task. The preconditions and postconditions describe the dependencies between methods.

Throwing Exceptions

We have seen several cases in which Java might throw an exception. For example, if we have a console `Scanner` and we call `nextInt`, the program will throw an exception if the user types something that isn't an `int`. In Appendix C, we examine how you can handle exceptions. For now, we just want to explore some of the ways in which exceptions can occur and how you might want to generate them in your own code.

Ideally programs execute without generating any errors, but in practice various problems arise. If you ask the user for an integer, the user may accidentally or perhaps even maliciously type something that is not an integer. Or your code might have a bug in it.

The following program always throws an exception because it tries to compute the value of 1 divided by 0, which is mathematically undefined:

```
1 public class CauseException {
2     public static void main(String[] args) {
3         int x = 1 / 0;
4         System.out.println(x);
5     }
6 }
```

When you run the program, you get the following error message:

```
Exception in thread "main" java.lang.ArithmeticException: / by zero
        at CauseException.main(CauseException.java:3)
```

The problem occurs in line 3, when you ask Java to compute a value that can't be stored as an `int`. What is Java supposed to do with that value? It throws an exception that stops the program from executing and warns you that an arithmetic exception occurred while the program was executing that specific line of code.

It is worth noting that division by zero does not always produce an exception. You won't get an exception if you execute this line of code:

```
double x = 1.0 / 0.0;
```

In this case, the program executes normally and produces the output `Infinity`. This is because floating-point numbers follow a standard from the Institute of Electrical and Electronics Engineers (IEEE) that defines exactly what should happen in these cases, and there are special values representing infinity and `"NaN"` (not a number).

You may want to throw exceptions yourself in the code you write. In particular, it is a good idea to throw an exception if a precondition fails. For example, suppose that you want to write a method for computing the factorial of an integer. The factorial is defined as follows:

$n!$ (which is read as "n factorial") $= 1 * 2 * 3 * \ldots * n$

You can write a Java method that uses a cumulative product to compute this result:

```
public static int factorial(int n) {
    int product = 1;
    for (int i = 2; i <= n; i++) {
```

```
        product = product * i;
    }
    return product;
}
```

You can then test the method for various values with a loop:

```
for (int i = 0; i <= 10; i++) {
    System.out.println(i + "! = " + factorial(i));
}
```

The loop produces the following output:

```
0! = 1
1! = 1
2! = 2
3! = 6
4! = 24
5! = 120
6! = 720
7! = 5040
8! = 40320
9! = 362880
10! = 3628800
```

It seems odd that the `factorial` method should return `1` when it is asked for 0!, but that is actually part of the mathematical definition of the factorial function. It returns `1` because the local variable `product` in the `factorial` method is initialized to `1`, and the loop is never entered when the parameter `n` has the value `0`. So, this is actually desirable behavior for 0!.

But what if you're asked to compute the factorial of a negative number? The method returns the same value, `1`. The mathematical definition of factorial says that the function is undefined for negative values of `n`, so it actually shouldn't even compute an answer when `n` is negative. Accepting only numbers that are zero or positive is a precondition of the method that can be described in the documentation:

```
// pre : n >= 0
// post: returns n factorial (n!)
```

Adding comments about this restriction is helpful, but what if someone calls the `factorial` method with a negative value anyway? The best solution is to throw an exception. The general syntax of the `throw` statement is:

```
throw <exception>;
```

In Java, exceptions are objects. Before you can throw an exception, you have to construct an exception object using `new`. You'll normally construct the object as you are throwing the exception, because the exception object includes information about what was going on when the error occurred. Java has a class called `IllegalArgumentException` that is meant to cover a case like this where someone has passed an inappropriate value as an argument. You can construct the exception object and include it in a `throw` statement as follows:

```
throw new IllegalArgumentException();
```

Of course, you'll want to do this only when the precondition fails, so you need to include the code inside an `if` statement:

```
if (n < 0) {
    throw new IllegalArgumentException();
}
```

You can also include some text when you construct the exception that will be displayed when the exception is thrown:

```
if (n < 0) {
    throw new IllegalArgumentException("negative n: " + n);
}
```

Incorporating the `pre/post` comments and the exception code into the method definition, you get the following code:

```
// pre : n >= 0
// post: returns n factorial (n!)
public static int factorial(int n) {
    if (n < 0) {
        throw new IllegalArgumentException("negative n: " + n);
    }
    int product = 1;
    for (int i = 2; i <= n; i++) {
        product = product * i;
    }
    return product;
}
```

You don't need an `else` after the `if` that throws the exception, because when an exception is thrown, it halts the execution of the method. So, if someone calls the `factorial` method with a negative value of `n`, Java will never execute the code that follows the `throw` statement.

You can test this code with the following `main` method:

```
public static void main(String[] args) {
    System.out.println(factorial(-1));
}
```

When you execute this program, it stops executing and prints the following message:

```
Exception in thread "main"
java.lang.IllegalArgumentException: negative n: -1
        at Factorial2.factorial(Factorial2.java:8)
        at Factorial2.main(Factorial2.java:3)
```

The message indicates that the program `Factorial2` stopped running because an `IllegalArgumentException` was thrown with a negative `n` of `-1`. The system then shows you a backward trace of how it got there. The illegal argument appeared in line 8 of the `factorial` method of the `Factorial2` class. It got there because of a call in line 3 of the `main` of the `Factorial2` class. This kind of information is very helpful when you want to find the bugs in your programs.

Throwing exceptions is an example of *defensive programming*. We don't intend to have bugs in the programs we write, but we're only human, so we want to build in mechanisms that will give us feedback when we make mistakes. Writing code that will test the values passed to methods and throw an `IllegalArgumentException` when a value is not appropriate is a great way to provide that feedback.

Revisiting Return Values

VideoNote

In Chapter 3 we looked at some examples of simple calculating methods that return a value, as in this method for finding the sum of the first *n* integers:

```
public static int sum(int n) {
    return (n + 1) * n / 2;
}
```

Now that you know how to write `if/else` statements, we can look at some more interesting examples involving return values. For example, earlier in this chapter you saw that the `Math` class has a method called `max` that returns the larger of two values. There are actually two different versions of the method, one that finds the larger of two integers and one that finds the larger of two `doubles`. Recall that when two methods have the same name (but different parameters), it is called overloading.

Let's write our own version of the `max` method that returns the larger of two integers. Its header will look like this:

```
public static int max(int x, int y) {
    ...
}
```

We want to return either `x` or `y`, depending on which is larger. This is a perfect place to use an `if/else` construct:

```
public static int max(int x, int y) {
    if (x > y) {
        return x;
    } else {
        return y;
    }
}
```

This code begins by testing whether `x` is greater than `y`. If it is, the computer executes the first branch by returning `x`. If it is not, the computer executes the `else` branch by returning `y`. But what if `x` and `y` are equal? The preceding code executes the `else` branch when the values are equal, but it doesn't actually matter which `return` statement is executed when `x` and `y` are equal.

Remember that when Java executes a `return` statement, the method stops executing. It's like a command to Java to "get out of this method right now." That means that this method could also be written as follows:

```
public static int max(int x, int y) {
    if (x > y) {
        return x;
    }
    return y;
}
```

This version of the code is equivalent in behavior because the statement `return x` inside the `if` statement will cause Java to exit the method immediately and Java will not execute the `return` statement that follows the `if`. On the other hand, if we don't enter the `if` statement, we proceed directly to the statement that follows it (`return y`).

Whether you choose to use the first form or the second in your own programs depends somewhat on personal taste. The `if/else` construct makes it more clear that the method is choosing between two alternatives, but some people prefer the second alternative because it is shorter.

As another example, consider the `indexOf` method of the `String` class. We'll define a variable `s` that stores the following `String`:

```
String s = "four score and seven years ago";
```

Now we can write expressions like the following to determine where a particular character appears in the `String`:

```
int r = s.indexOf('r');
int v = s.indexOf('v');
```

This code sets `r` to `3` because 3 is the index of the first occurrence of the letter `'r'` in the `String`. It sets `v` to `17` because that is the index of the first occurrence of the letter `'v'` in the `String`.

The `indexOf` method is part of the `String` class, but let's see how we could write a different method that performs the same task. Our method would be called differently because it is a static method outside the `String` object. We would have to pass it both the `String` and the letter:

```
int r = indexOf('r', s);
int v = indexOf('v', s);
```

So, the header for our method would be:

```
public static int indexOf(char ch, String s) {
    ...
}
```

Remember that when a method returns a value, we must include the return type after the words `public static`. In this case, we have indicated that the method returns an `int` because the index will be an integer.

This task can be solved rather nicely with a `for` loop that goes through each possible index from first to last. We can describe this in pseudocode as follows:

```
for (each index i in the string) {
    if the char is at position i, we've found it.
}
```

To flesh this out, we have to think about how to test whether the character at position `i` is the one we are looking for. Remember that `String` objects have a method called `charAt` that allows us to pull out an individual character from the `String`, so we can refine our pseudocode as follows:

```
for (int i = 0; i < s.length(); i++) {
    if (s.charAt(i) == ch) {
        we've found it.
    }
}
```

To complete this code, we have to refine what to do when "we've found it." If we find the character, we have our answer: the current value of the variable `i`. And if that is the answer we want to return, we can put a `return` statement there:

```
for (int i = 0; i < s.length(); i++) {
    if (s.charAt(i) == ch) {
        return i;
    }
}
```

To understand this code, you have to understand how the `return` statement works. For example, if the `String s` is the one from our example ("four score...") and we are searching for the character `'r'`, we know that when `i` is equal to `3` we will find that `s.charAt(3)` is equal to `'r'`. That case causes our code to execute the `return` statement, effectively saying:

```
return 3;
```

When a `return` statement is executed, Java immediately exits the method, which means that we break out of the loop and return `3` as our answer. Even though the loop would normally increment `i` to `4` and keep going, our code doesn't do that because we hit the `return` statement.

There is only one thing missing from our code. If we try to compile it as it is, we get this error message from the Java compiler:

```
missing return statement
```

This error message occurs because we haven't told Java what to do if we never find the character we are searching for. In that case, we will execute the `for` loop in its entirety and reach the end of the method without having returned a value. This is not acceptable. If we say that the method returns an `int`, we have to guarantee that every path through the method will return an `int`.

If we don't find the character, we want to return some kind of special value to indicate that the character was not found. We can't use the value `0`, because `0` is a legal index for a `String` (the index of the first character). So, the convention in Java is to return `–1` if the character is not found. It is easy to add the code for this `return` statement after the `for` loop:

```
public static int indexOf(char ch, String s) {
    for (int i = 0; i < s.length(); i++) {
        if (s.charAt(i) == ch) {
            return i;
        }
    }
    return –1;
}
```

Common Programming Error

String Index Out of Bounds

It's very easy to forget that the last index of a `String` of length n is actually $n - 1$. Forgetting this fact can cause you to write incorrect text-processing loops like this one:

```
// This version of the code has a mistake!
// The test should be i < s.length()
public static int indexOf(char ch, String s) {
    for (int i = 0; i <= s.length(); i++) {
        if (s.charAt(i) == ch) {
            return i;
        }
    }
    return -1;
}
```

The program will throw an exception if the loop runs past the end of the `String`. On the last pass through the loop, the value of the variable `i` will be equal to `s.length()`. When it executes the `if` statement test, the program will throw the exception. The error message will resemble the following:

```
Exception in thread "main"
  java.lang.StringIndexOutOfBoundsException:
  String index out of range: 11
      at java.lang.String.charAt(Unknown Source)
      at OutOfBoundsExample.indexOf(OutOfBoundsExample.java:9)
      at OutOfBoundsExample.main(OutOfBoundsExample.java:4)
```

An interesting thing about the bug in this example is that it only occurs if the `String` does not contain the character `ch`. If `ch` is contained in the `String`, the `if` test will be `true` for one of the legal indexes in `s`, so the code will return that index. Only if all the characters from `s` have been examined without finding `ch` will the loop attempt its last fatal pass.

It may seem strange that we don't have a test for the final `return` statement that returns `-1`, but remember that the `for` loop tries every possible index of the `String` searching for the character. If the character appears anywhere in the `String`, the `return` statement inside the loop will be executed and we'll never get to the `return` statement after the loop. The only way to get to the `return` statement after the loop is to find that the character appears nowhere in the given `String`.

Reasoning about Paths

The combination of `if/else` and `return` is powerful. It allows you to solve many complex problems in the form of a method that accepts some input and computes a result. But you have to be careful to think about the different paths that exist in the code that you write. At first this process might seem annoying, but when you get the hang of it, you will find that it allows you to simplify your code.

For example, suppose that we want to convert scores on the SAT into a rating to be used for college admission. Each of the three components of the SAT ranges from 200 to 800, so the overall total ranges from 600 to 2400. Suppose that a hypothetical college breaks up this range into three subranges with totals below 1200 considered not competitive, scores of at least 1200 but less than 1800 considered competitive, and scores of 1800 to 2400 considered highly competitive.

Let's write a method called `rating` that will take the total SAT score as a parameter and will return a string with the appropriate text. We can use the AND operator described earlier to write an `if/else` construct that has tests for each of these ranges:

```
public static String rating(int totalSAT) {
    if (totalSAT >= 600 && totalSAT < 1200) {
        return "not competitive";
    } else if (totalSAT >= 1200 && totalSAT < 1800) {
        return "competitive";
    } else if (totalSAT >= 1800 && totalSAT <= 2400) {
        return "highly competitive";
    }
}
```

This method has been written in a logical manner with specific tests for each of the three cases, but it doesn't compile. The compiler indicates at the end of the method that there was a "missing return statement." That seems odd because there are three different `return` statements in this method. We have included a `return` for each of the different cases, so why is there a compiler error?

When the compiler encounters a method that is supposed to return a value, it computes every possible path through the method and makes sure that each path ends with a call on `return`. The method we have written has four paths through it. If the first test succeeds, then the method returns `"not competitive"`. Otherwise, if the second test succeeds, then the method returns `"competitive"`. If both of those tests fail but the third test succeeds, then the method returns `"highly competitive"`. But what if all three tests fail? That case would constitute a fourth path that doesn't have a `return` statement associated with it. Instead, we would reach the end of the method without having returned a value. That is not acceptable, which is why the compiler produces an error message.

It seems annoying that we have to deal with a fourth case because we know that the total SAT score will always be in the range of 600 to 2400. Our code covers all of the cases that we expect for this method, but that isn't good enough. Java insists that we cover every possible case.

Understanding this idea can simplify the code you write. If you think in terms of paths and cases, you can often eliminate unnecessary code. For our method, if we really want to return just one of three different values, then we don't need a third test. We can make the final branch of the nested `if/else` be a simple `else`:

```
public static String rating(int totalSAT) {
    if (totalSAT >= 600 && totalSAT < 1200) {
        return "not competitive";
    } else if (totalSAT >= 1200 && totalSAT < 1800) {
        return "competitive";
    } else {  // totalSAT >= 1800
        return "highly competitive";
    }
}
```

This version of the method compiles and returns the appropriate string for each different case. We were able to eliminate the final test because we know that we want only three paths through the method. Once we have specified two of the paths, then everything else must be part of the third path.

We can carry this idea one step further. We've written a method that compiles and computes the right answer, but we can make it even simpler. Consider the first test, for example. Why should we test for the total being greater than or equal to 600? If we expect that it will always be in the range of 600 to 2400, then we can simply test whether the total is less than 1200. Similarly, to test for the highly competitive range, we can simply test whether the score is at least 1800. Of the three ranges, these are the two simplest to test for. So we can simplify this method even further by including tests for the first and third subranges and assume that all other totals are in the middle range:

```
public static String rating(int totalSAT) {
    if (totalSAT < 1200) {
        return "not competitive";
    } else if (totalSAT >= 1800) {
        return "highly competitive";
    } else {  // 1200 <= totalSAT < 1800
        return "competitive";
    }
}
```

Whenever you write a method like this, you should think about the different cases and figure out which ones are the simplest to test for. This will allow you to avoid writing an explicit test for the most complex case. As in these examples, it is a good idea to include a comment on the final `else` branch to describe that particular case in English.

Before we leave this example, it is worth thinking about what happens when the method is passed an illegal SAT total. If it is passed a total less than 600, then it classifies it as not competitive and if it passed a total greater than 2400, it will classify it as highly competitive. Those aren't bad answers for the program to give, but the right thing to do is to document the fact that there is a precondition on the total. In addition, we can add an extra test for this particular case and throw an exception if the precondition is violated. Testing for the illegal values is a case in which the logical OR is appropriate because illegal values will either be too low or too high (but not both):

```
// pre: 600 <= totalSAT <= 2400 (throws IllegalArgumentException if not)
public static String rating(int totalSAT) {
    if (totalSAT < 600 || totalSAT > 2400) {
        throw new IllegalArgumentException("total: " + totalSAT);
    } else if (totalSAT < 1200) {
        return "not competitive";
    } else if (totalSAT >= 1800) {
        return "highly competitive";
    } else {  // 1200 <= totalSAT < 1800
        return "competitive";
    }
}
```

4.5 Case Study: Body Mass Index

Individual body mass index has become a popular measure of overall health. The Centers for Disease Control and Prevention (CDC) website about body mass index (http://www.cdc.gov/healthyweight/assessing/bmi/index.html) explains:

> Body Mass Index (BMI) is a number calculated from a person's weight and height. BMI provides a reliable indicator of body fatness for most people and is used to screen for weight categories that may lead to health problems.

It has also become popular to compare the statistics for two or more individuals who are pitted against one another in a "fitness challenge," or to compare two sets of numbers for the same person to get a sense of how that person's BMI will vary if a person loses weight. In this section, we will write a program that prompts the user for the height and weight of two individuals and reports the overall results for the two people. Here is a sample execution for the program we want to write:

```
This program reads data for two
people and computes their body
mass index and weight status.
```

```
Enter next person's information:
height (in inches)? 73.5
weight (in pounds)? 230

Enter next person's information:
height (in inches)? 71
weight (in pounds)? 220.5

Person #1 body mass index = 29.93
overweight
Person #2 body mass index = 30.75
obese
```

In Chapter 1 we introduced the idea of *iterative enhancement,* in which you develop a complex program in stages. Every professional programmer uses this technique, so it is important to learn to apply it yourself in the programs you write.

In this case, we eventually want our program to explain to the user what it does and compute BMI results for two different people. We also want the program to be well structured. But we don't have to do everything at once. In fact, if we try to do so, we are likely to be overwhelmed by the details. In writing this program, we will go through three different stages:

1. First, we'll write a program that computes results for just one person, without an introduction. We won't worry about program structure yet.
2. Next, we'll write a complete program that computes results for two people, including an introduction. Again, we won't worry about program structure at this point.
3. Finally, we will put together a well-structured and complete program.

One-Person Unstructured Solution

Even the first version of the program will prompt for user input, so we will need to construct a `Scanner` object to read from the console:

```
Scanner console = new Scanner(System.in);
```

To compute the BMI for an individual, we will need to know the height and weight of that person. This is a fairly straightforward "prompt and read" task. The only real decision here is with regard to the type of variable to use for storing the height and weight. People often talk about height and weight in whole numbers, but the question to ask is whether or not it makes sense for people to use fractions. Do people ever describe their heights using half-inches? The answer is yes. Do people ever describe their weights using half-pounds? Again the answer is yes. So it makes sense to store the values as doubles, to allow people to enter either integer values or fractions:

```
System.out.println("Enter next person's information:");
System.out.print("height (in inches)? ");
```

```
double height1 = console.nextDouble();
System.out.print("weight (in pounds)? ");
double weight1 = console.nextDouble();
```

Once we have the person's height and weight, we can compute the person's BMI. The CDC website gives the following BMI formula for adults:

$$\frac{\text{weight (lb)}}{[\text{height (in)}]^2} \times 703$$

This formula is fairly easy to translate into a Java expression:

```
double bmi1 = weight1 / (height1 * height1) * 703;
```

If you look closely at the sample execution, you will see that we want to print blank lines to separate different parts of the user interaction. The introduction ends with a blank line, then there is a blank line after the "prompt and read" portion of the interaction. So, after we add an empty `println` and put all of these pieces together, our `main` method looks like this:

```
public static void main(String[] args) {
    Scanner console = new Scanner(System.in);
    System.out.println("Enter next person's information:");
    System.out.print("height (in inches)? ");
    double height1 = console.nextDouble();
    System.out.print("weight (in pounds)? ");
    double weight1 = console.nextDouble();
    double bmi1 = weight1 / (height1 * height1) * 703;
    System.out.println();
    ...
}
```

This program prompts for values and computes the BMI. Now we need to include code to report the results. We could use a `println` for the BMI:

```
System.out.println("Person #1 body mass index = " + bmi1);
```

This would work, but it produces output like the following:

```
Person #1 body mass index = 29.930121708547368
```

The long sequence of digits after the decimal point is distracting and implies a level of precision that we simply don't have. It is more appropriate and more appealing to the user to list just a few digits after the decimal point. This is a good place to use a `printf`:

```
System.out.printf("Person #1 body mass index = %5.2f\n", bmi1);
```

Table 4.7 Weight Status by BMI

BMI	Weight status
below 18.5	underweight
18.5–24.9	normal
25.0–29.9	overweight
30.0 and above	obese

In the sample execution we also see a report of the person's weight status. The CDC website includes the information shown in Table 4.7. There are four entries in this table, so we need four different `println` statements for the four possibilities. We will want to use `if` or `if/else` statements to control the four `println` statements. In this case, we know that we want to print exactly one of the four possibilities. Therefore, it makes most sense to use a nested `if/else` construct that ends with an `else`.

But what tests do we use for the nested `if/else`? If you look closely at Table 4.7, you will see that there are some gaps. For example, what if your BMI is 24.95? That number isn't between 18.5 and 24.9 and it isn't between 25.0 and 29.9. It seems clear that the CDC intended its table to be interpreted slightly differently. The range is probably supposed to be 18.5–24.999999 (repeating), but that would look rather odd in a table. In fact, if you understand nested `if/else` statements, this is a case in which a nested `if/else` construct expresses the possibilities more clearly than a table like the CDC's. The nested `if/else` construct looks like this:

```
if (bmi1 < 18.5) {
    System.out.println("underweight");
} else if (bmi1 < 25) {
    System.out.println("normal");
} else if (bmi1 < 30) {
    System.out.println("overweight");
} else {  // bmi1 >= 30
    System.out.println("obese");
}
```

So, putting all this together, we get a complete version of the first program:

```
import java.util.*;

public class BMI1 {
    public static void main(String[] args) {
        Scanner console = new Scanner(System.in);

        System.out.println("Enter next person's information:");
        System.out.print("height (in inches)? ");
```

```
        double height1 = console.nextDouble();
        System.out.print("weight (in pounds)? ");
        double weight1 = console.nextDouble();
        double bmi1 = weight1 / (height1 * height1) * 703;
        System.out.println();

        System.out.printf("Person #1 body mass index = %5.2f\n", bmi1);
        if (bmi1 < 18.5) {
            System.out.println("underweight");
        } else if (bmi1 < 25) {
            System.out.println("normal");
        } else if (bmi1 < 30) {
            System.out.println("overweight");
        } else {  // bmi1 >= 30
            System.out.println("obese");
        }
    }
}
```

Here is a sample execution of the program:

```
Enter next person's information:
height (in inches)? 73.5
weight (in pounds)? 230

Person #1 body mass index = 29.93
overweight
```

Two-Person Unstructured Solution

Now that we have a program that computes one person's BMI and weight status, let's expand it to handle two different people. Experienced programmers would probably begin by adding structure to the program before trying to make it handle two sets of data, but novice programmers will find it easier to consider the unstructured solution first.

To make this program handle two people, we can copy and paste a lot of the code and make slight modifications. For example, instead of using variables called `height1`, `weight1`, and `bmi1`, for the second person we will use variables `height2`, `weight2`, and `bmi2`.

We also have to be careful to do each step in the right order. Looking at the sample execution, you'll see that the program prompts for data for both individuals first and then reports results for both. Thus, we can't copy the entire program and simply paste a second copy; we have to rearrange the order of the statements so that all of the prompting happens first and all of the reporting happens later.

We've also decided that when we move to this second stage, we will add code for the introduction. This code should appear at the beginning of the program and should include an empty `println` to produce a blank line to separate the introduction from the rest of the user interaction.

We now combine these elements into a complete program:

```
// This program finds the body mass index (BMI) for two
// individuals.

import java.util.*;

public class BMI2 {
    public static void main(String[] args) {
        System.out.println("This program reads data for two");
        System.out.println("people and computes their body");
        System.out.println("mass index and weight status.");
        System.out.println();

        Scanner console = new Scanner(System.in);

        System.out.println("Enter next person's information:");
        System.out.print("height (in inches)? ");
        double height1 = console.nextDouble();
        System.out.print("weight (in pounds)? ");
        double weight1 = console.nextDouble();
        double bmi1 = weight1 / (height1 * height1) * 703;
        System.out.println();

        System.out.println("Enter next person's information:");
        System.out.print("height (in inches)? ");
        double height2 = console.nextDouble();
        System.out.print("weight (in pounds)? ");
        double weight2 = console.nextDouble();
        double bmi2 = weight2 / (height2 * height2) * 703;
        System.out.println();

        System.out.printf("Person #1 body mass index = %5.2f\n", bmi1);
        if (bmi1 < 18.5) {
            System.out.println("underweight");
        } else if (bmi1 < 25) {
            System.out.println("normal");
        } else if (bmi1 < 30) {
            System.out.println("overweight");
        } else {  // bmi1 >= 30
```

```
            System.out.println("obese");
        }

        System.out.printf("Person #2 body mass index = %5.2f\n", bmi2);
        if (bmi2 < 18.5) {
            System.out.println("underweight");
        } else if (bmi2 < 25) {
            System.out.println("normal");
        } else if (bmi2 < 30) {
            System.out.println("overweight");
        } else {  // bmi2 >= 30
            System.out.println("obese");
        }
    }
}
```

This program compiles and works. When we execute it, we get exactly the interaction we wanted. However, the program lacks structure. All of the code appears in `main`, and there is significant redundancy. That shouldn't be a surprise, because we created this version by copying and pasting. Whenever you find yourself using copy and paste, you should wonder whether there isn't a better way to solve the problem. Usually there is.

Two-Person Structured Solution

Let's explore how static methods can improve the structure of the program. Looking at the code, you will notice a great deal of redundancy. For example, we have two code segments that look like this:

```
System.out.println("Enter next person's information:");
System.out.print("height (in inches)? ");
double height1 = console.nextDouble();
System.out.print("weight (in pounds)? ");
double weight1 = console.nextDouble();
double bmi1 = weight1 / (height1 * height1) * 703;
System.out.println();
```

The only difference between these two code segments is that the first uses variables `height1`, `weight1`, `bmi1`, and the second uses variables `height2`, `weight2`, and `bmi2`. We eliminate redundancy by moving code like this into a method that we can call twice. So, as a first approximation, we can turn this code into a more generic form as the following method:

```
public static void getBMI(Scanner console) {
    System.out.println("Enter next person's information:");
    System.out.print("height (in inches)? ");
```

```
    double height = console.nextDouble();
    System.out.print("weight (in pounds)? ");
    double weight = console.nextDouble();
    double bmi = weight / (height * height) * 703;
    System.out.println();
}
```

We have to pass in the Scanner from main. Otherwise we have made all the variables local to this method. From main we can call this method twice:

```
getBMI(console);
getBMI(console);
```

Unfortunately, introducing this change breaks the rest of the code. If we try to compile and run the program, we find that we get error messages in main whenever we refer to the variables bmi1 and bmi2.

The problem is that the method computes a bmi value that we need later in the program. We can fix this by having the method return the bmi value that it computes:

```
public static double getBMI(Scanner console) {
    System.out.println("Enter next person's information:");
    System.out.print("height (in inches)? ");
    double height = console.nextDouble();
    System.out.print("weight (in pounds)? ");
    double weight = console.nextDouble();
    double bmi = weight / (height * height) * 703;
    System.out.println();
    return bmi;
}
```

Notice that the method header now lists the return type as double. We also have to change main. We can't just call the method twice the way we would call a void method. Because each call returns a BMI result that the program will need later, for each call we have to store the result coming back from the method in a variable:

```
double bmi1 = getBMI(console);
double bmi2 = getBMI(console);
```

Study this change carefully, because this technique can be one of the most challenging for novices to master. When we write the method, we have to make sure that it returns the BMI result. When we write the call, we have to make sure that we store the result in a variable so that we can access it later.

After this modification, the program will compile and run properly. But there is another obvious redundancy in the main method: The same nested if/else construct appears twice. The only difference between them is that in one case we use the variable `bmi1`, and in the other case we use the variable `bmi2`. The construct is easily generalized with a parameter:

```
public static void reportStatus(double bmi) {
    if (bmi < 18.5) {
        System.out.println("underweight");
    } else if (bmi < 25) {
        System.out.println("normal");
    } else if (bmi < 30) {
        System.out.println("overweight");
    } else {  // bmi >= 30
        System.out.println("obese");
    }
}
```

Using this method, we can replace the code in `main` with two calls:

```
System.out.printf("Person #1 body mass index = %5.2f\n", bmi1);
reportStatus(bmi1);
System.out.printf("Person #2 body mass index = %5.2f\n", bmi2);
reportStatus(bmi2);
```

That change takes care of the redundancy in the program, but we can still use static methods to improve the program by better indicating structure. It is best to keep the `main` method short if possible, to reflect the overall structure of the program. The problem breaks down into three major phases: introduction, the computation of the BMI, and the reporting of the results. We already have a method for computing the BMI, but we haven't yet introduced methods for the introduction and reporting of results. It is fairly simple to add these methods.

There is one other method that we should add to the program. We are using a formula from the CDC website for calculating the BMI of an individual given the person's height and weight. Whenever you find yourself programming a formula, it is a good idea to introduce a method for that formula so that it is easy to spot and so that it has a name.

Applying all these ideas, we end up with the following version of the program:

```
// This program finds the body mass index (BMI) for two
// individuals. This variation includes several methods
// other than main.

import java.util.*;

public class BMI3 {
    public static void main(String[] args) {
        giveIntro();
```

```
        Scanner console = new Scanner(System.in);
        double bmi1 = getBMI(console);
        double bmi2 = getBMI(console);
        reportResults(bmi1, bmi2);
    }

    // introduces the program to the user
    public static void giveIntro() {
        System.out.println("This program reads data for two");
        System.out.println("people and computes their body");
        System.out.println("mass index and weight status.");
        System.out.println();
    }

    // prompts for one person's statistics, returning the BMI
    public static double getBMI(Scanner console) {
        System.out.println("Enter next person's information:");
        System.out.print("height (in inches)? ");
        double height = console.nextDouble();
        System.out.print("weight (in pounds)? ");
        double weight = console.nextDouble();
        double bmi = BMIFor(height, weight);
        System.out.println();
        return bmi;
    }

    // this method contains the body mass index formula for
    // converting the given height (in inches) and weight
    // (in pounds) into a BMI
    public static double BMIFor(double height, double weight) {
        return weight / (height * height) * 703;
    }

    // reports the overall bmi values and weight status
    public static void reportResults(double bmi1, double bmi2) {
        System.out.printf("Person #1 body mass index = %5.2f\n", bmi1);
        reportStatus(bmi1);
        System.out.printf("Person #2 body mass index = %5.2f\n",bmi2);
        reportStatus(bmi2);
    }

    // reports the weight status for the given BMI value
    public static void reportStatus(double bmi) {
        if (bmi < 18.5) {
```

```
                System.out.println("underweight");
            } else if (bmi < 25) {
                System.out.println("normal");
            } else if (bmi < 30) {
                System.out.println("overweight");
            } else {  // bmi >= 30
                System.out.println("obese");
            }
        }
    }
```

This solution interacts with the user the same way and produces the same results as the unstructured solution, but it has a much nicer structure. The unstructured program is in a sense simpler, but the structured solution is easier to maintain if we want to expand the program or make other modifications. These structural benefits aren't so important in short programs, but they become essential as programs become longer and more complex.

Procedural Design Heuristics

There are often many ways to divide (decompose) a problem into methods, but some sets of methods are better than others. Decomposition is often vague and challenging, especially for larger programs that have complex behavior. But the rewards are worth the effort, because a well-designed program is more understandable and more modular. These features are important when programmers work together or when revisiting a program written earlier to add new behavior or modify existing code. There is no single perfect design, but in this section we will discuss several *heuristics* (guiding principles) for effectively decomposing large programs into methods.

Consider the following alternative poorly structured implementation of the single-person BMI program. We'll use this program as a counterexample, highlighting places where it violates our heuristics and giving reasons that it is worse than the previous complete version of the BMI program.

```
// A poorly designed version of the BMI case study program.

import java.util.*;

public class BadBMI {
    public static void main(String[] args) {
        System.out.println("This program reads data for one");
        System.out.println("person and computes his/her body");
        System.out.println("mass index and weight status.");
        System.out.println();

        Scanner console = new Scanner(System.in);
        person(console);
```

```
    }

    public static void person(Scanner console) {
        System.out.println("Enter next person's information:");
        System.out.print("height (in inches)? ");
        double height = console.nextDouble();
        getWeight(console, height);
    }

    public static void getWeight(Scanner console, double height) {
        System.out.print("weight (in pounds)? ");
        double weight = console.nextDouble();
        reportStatus(console, height, weight);
    }

    public static void reportStatus(Scanner console, double height,
                                    double weight) {
        double bmi = weight / (height * height) * 703;
        System.out.println("Person #1 body mass index = " + bmi);
        if (bmi < 18.5) {
            System.out.println("underweight");
        } else if (bmi < 25) {
            System.out.println("normal");
        } else if (bmi < 30) {
            System.out.println("overweight");
        } else {
            System.out.println("obese");
        }
    }
}
```

The methods of a program are like workers in a company. The author of a program acts like the director of a company, deciding what employee positions to create, how to group employees together into working units, which work to task to which group, and how groups will interact. Suppose a company director were to divide work into three major departments, two of which are overseen by middle managers:

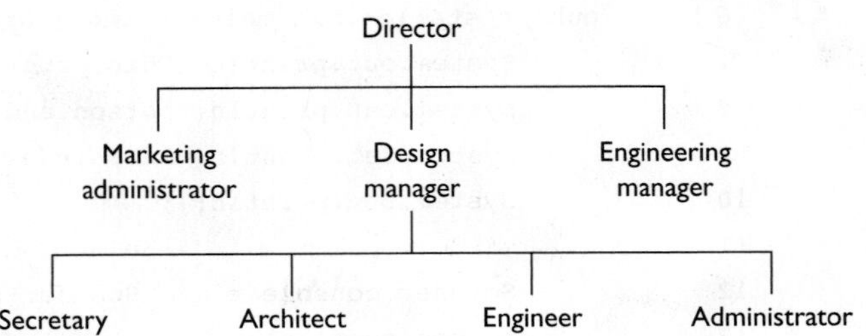

A good structure gives each group clear tasks to complete, avoids giving any particular person or group too much work, and provides a balance between workers and management. These guidelines lead to the first of our procedural design heuristics.

1. Each method should have a coherent set of responsibilities. In our analogy to a company, each group of employees must have a clear idea of what work it is to perform. If any of the groups does not have clear responsibilities, it's difficult for the company director to keep track of who is working on what task. When a new job comes in, two departments might both try to claim it, or a job might go unclaimed by any department.

The analogous concept in programming is that each method should have a clear purpose and set of responsibilities. This characteristic of computer programs is called *cohesion*.

Cohesion

A desirable quality in which the responsibilities of a method or process are closely related to each other.

A good rule of thumb is that you should be able to summarize each of your methods in a single sentence such as "The purpose of this method is to ... ." Writing a sentence like this is a good way to develop a comment for a method's header. It's a bad sign when you have trouble describing the method in a single sentence or when the sentence is long and uses the word "and" several times. Those indications can mean that the method is too large, too small, or does not perform a cohesive set of tasks.

The methods of the `BadBMI` example have poor cohesion. The `person` method's purpose is vague, and `getWeight` is probably too trivial to be its own method. The `reportStatus` method would be more readable if the computation of the BMI were its own method, since the formula is complex.

A subtler application of this first heuristic is that not every method must produce output. Sometimes a method is more reusable if it simply computes a complex result and returns it rather than printing the result that was computed. This format leaves the caller free to choose whether to print the result or to use it to perform further computations. In the `BadBMI` program, the `reportStatus` method both computes and prints the user's BMI. The program would be more flexible if it had a method to simply compute and return the BMI value, such as `BMIFor` in the `BMI3` version of the code. Such a method might seem trivial because its body is just one line in length, but it has a clear, cohesive purpose: capturing a complex expression that is used several times in the program.

2. No one method should do too large a share of the overall task. One subdivision of a company cannot be expected to design and build the entire product line for the year. This system would overwork that subdivision and would leave the other divisions without enough work to do. It would also make it difficult for the subdivisions to communicate effectively, since so much important information and responsibility would be concentrated among so few people.

Similarly, one method should not be expected to comprise the bulk of a program. This principle follows naturally from our first heuristic regarding cohesion, because a method that does too much cannot be cohesive. We sometimes refer to methods like these as "do-everything" methods because they do nearly everything involved in solving the problem. You may have written a "do-everything" method if one of your methods is much longer than the others, hoards most of the variables and data, or contains the majority of the logic and loops.

In the `BadBMI` program, the `person` method is an example of a do-everything method. This fact may seem surprising, since the method is not very many lines long. But a single call to `person` leads to several other calls that collectively end up doing all of the work for the program.

3. Coupling and dependencies between methods should be minimized. A company is more productive if each of its subdivisions can largely operate independently when completing small work tasks. Subdivisions of the company do need to communicate and depend on each other, but such communication comes at a cost. Interdepartmental interactions are often minimized and kept to meetings at specific times and places.

When we are programming, we try to avoid methods that have tight *coupling*.

Coupling

An undesirable state in which two methods or processes rigidly depend on each other.

Methods are coupled if one cannot easily be called without the other. One way to determine how tightly coupled two methods are is to look at the set of parameters one passes to the other. A method should accept a parameter only if that piece of data needs to be provided from outside and only if that data is necessary to complete the method's task. In other words, if a piece of data could be computed or gathered inside the method, or if the data isn't used by the method, it should not be declared as a parameter to the method.

An important way to reduce coupling between methods is to use `return` statements to send information back to the caller. A method should return a result value if it computes something that may be useful to later parts of the program. Because it is desirable for methods to be cohesive and self-contained, it is often better for the program to return a result than to call further methods and pass the result as a parameter to them.

None of the methods in the `BadBMI` program returns a value. Each method passes parameters to the next methods, but none of them returns the value. This is a lost opportunity because several values (such as the user's height, weight, or BMI) would be better handled as `return` values.

4. The `main` method should be a concise summary of the overall program. The top person in each major group or department of our hypothetical company reports to the group's director. If you look at the groups that are directly connected to the director at the top level of the company diagram, you can see a summary of the overall work: design, engineering, and marketing. This structure helps the director stay aware of what each group is doing. Looking at the top-level structure can also help the employees get a quick overview of the company's goals.

A program's `main` method is like the director in that it begins the overall task and executes the various subtasks. A `main` method should read as a summary of the overall program's behavior. Programmers can understand each other's code by looking at `main` to get a sense of what the program is doing as a whole.

A common mistake that prevents `main` from being a good program summary is the inclusion of a "do-everything" method. When the `main` method calls it, the do-everything method proceeds to do most or all of the real work.

Another mistake is setting up a program in such a way that it suffers from *chaining*.

Chaining

An undesirable design in which a "chain" of several methods call each other without returning the overall flow of control to `main`.

A program suffers from chaining if the end of each method simply calls the next method. Chaining often occurs when a new programmer does not fully understand returns and tries to avoid using them by passing more and more parameters down to the rest of the program. Figure 4.8 shows a hypothetical program with two designs. The flow of calls in a badly chained program might look like the diagram on the left.

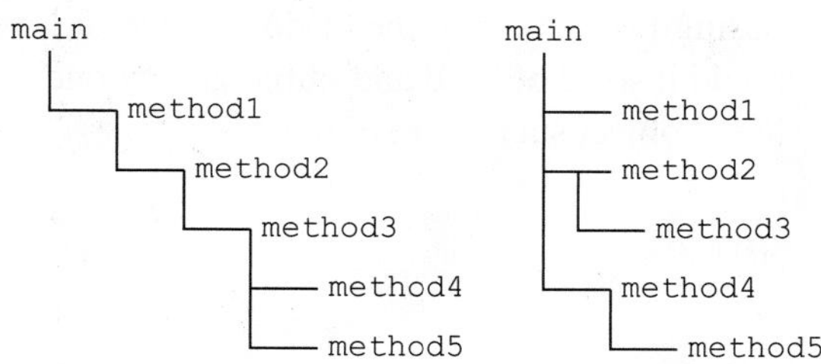

Figure 4.8 Sample code with chaining (left) and without chaining (right)

The `BadBMI` program suffers heavily from chaining. Each method does a small amount of work and then calls the next method, passing more and more parameters down the chain. The `main` method calls `person`, which calls `getWeight`, which calls `reportStatus`. Never does the flow of execution return to `main` in the middle of the computation. So when you read `main`, you don't get a very clear idea of what computations will be made.

One method should not call another simply as a way of moving on to the next task. A more desirable flow of control is to let `main` manage the overall execution of tasks in the program, as shown in the `BMI3` program and on the right side of Figure 4.8. This guideline doesn't mean that it is always bad for one method to call another method; it is okay for one method to call another when the second is a subtask within the overall task of the first, such as in `BMI3` when the `reportResults` method calls `reportStatus`.

5. Data should be "owned" at the lowest level possible. Decisions in a company should be made at the lowest possible level in the organizational hierarchy. For example, a low-level administrator can decide how to perform his or her own work without needing to constantly consult a manager for approval. But the administrator does not have enough information or expertise to design the entire product line; this design task goes to a higher authority such as the manager. The key principle is that each work task should be given to the lowest person in the hierarchy who can correctly handle it.

This principle has two applications in computer programs. The first is that the `main` method should avoid performing low-level tasks as much as possible. For example, in an interactive program `main` should not read the majority of the user input or contain lots of `println` statements.

The second application is that variables should be declared and initialized in the narrowest possible scope. A poor design is for `main` (or another high-level method) to read all of the input, perform heavy computations, and then pass the resulting data as parameters to the various low-level methods. A better design uses low-level methods to read and process the data, and return data to `main` only if they are needed by a later subtask in the program.

It is a sign of poor data ownership when the same parameter must be passed down several method calls, such as the `height` variable in the `BadBMI` program. If you are passing the same parameter down several levels of calls, perhaps that piece of data should instead be read and initialized by one of the lower-level methods (unless it is a shared object such as a `Scanner`).

Chapter Summary

An `if` statement lets you write code that will execute only if a certain condition is met. An `if/else` statement lets you execute one piece of code if a condition is met, and another if the condition is not met. Conditions are Boolean expressions and can be written using relational operators such as <, >= , and `!=` . You can test multiple conditions using the `&&` and `||` operators.

You can nest `if/else` statements to test a series of conditions and execute the appropriate block of code on the basis of whichever condition is true.

The == operator that tests primitive data for equality doesn't behave the way we would expect with objects, so we test objects for equality by calling their `equals` method instead.

Common code that appears in every branch of an `if/else` statement should be factored out so that it is not replicated multiple times in the code.

Cumulative algorithms compute values incrementally. A cumulative sum loop declares a sum variable and incrementally adds to that variable's value inside the loop.

Since the `double` type does not store all values exactly, small roundoff errors can occur when the computer performs calculations on real numbers. Avoid these errors by providing a small amount of tolerance in your code for values near the values that you expect.

The `char` type represents individual characters of text. Each letter of a `String` is stored internally as a `char` value, and you can use the `String`'s `charAt` method to access these characters with an index.

The `System.out.printf` method prints formatted text. You can specify complex format strings to control the width, alignment, and precision by which values are printed.

You can "throw" (generate) exceptions in your own code. This technique can be useful if your code ever reaches an unrecoverable error condition, such as the passing of an invalid argument value to a method.

Self-Check Problems

Section 4.1: `if/else` Statements

1. Translate each of the following English statements into logical tests that could be used in an `if/else` statement. Write the appropriate `if` statement with your logical test. Assume that three `int` variables, `x`, `y`, and `z`, have been declared.
   a. `z` is odd.
   b. `z` is not greater than `y`'s square root.
   c. `y` is positive.
   d. Either `x` or `y` is even, and the other is odd.
   e. `y` is a multiple of `z`.
   f. `z` is not zero.
   g. `y` is greater in magnitude than `z`.
   h. `x` and `z` are of opposite signs.
   i. `y` is a nonnegative one-digit number.

j. `z` is nonnegative.

k. `x` is even.

l. `x` is closer in value to `y` than `z` is.

2. Given the variable declarations

```
int x = 4;
int y = -3;
int z = 4;
```

what are the results of the following relational expressions?

a. `x == 4`

b. `x == y`

c. `x == z`

d. `y == z`

e. `x + y > 0`

f. `x - z != 0`

g. `y * y <= z`

h. `y / y == 1`

i. `x * (y + 2) > y - (y + z) * 2`

3. Which of the following `if` statement headers uses the correct syntax?

a. `if x = 10 then {`

b. `if [x == 10] {`

c. `if (x => y) {`

d. `if (x equals 42) {`

e. `if (x == y) {`

4. The following program contains 7 mistakes! What are they?

```
public class Oops4 {
    public static void main(String[] args) {
        int a = 7, b = 42;
        minimum(a, b);
        if {smaller = a} {
            System.out.println("a is the smallest!");
        }
    }

    public static void minimum(int a, int b) {
        if (a < b) {
            int smaller = a;
        } else (a => b) {
            int smaller = b;
        }
        return int smaller;
    }
}
```

5. Consider the following method:

```
public static void ifElseMystery1(int x, int y) {
    int z = 4;
    if (z <= x) {
        z = x + 1;
    } else {
        z = z + 9;
    }
    if (z <= y) {
        y++;
    }
    System.out.println(z + " " + y);
}
```

What output is produced for each of the following calls?

a. `ifElseMystery1(3, 20);`
b. `ifElseMystery1(4, 5);`
c. `ifElseMystery1(5, 5);`
d. `ifElseMystery1(6, 10);`

6. Consider the following method:

```
public static void ifElseMystery2(int a, int b) {
    if (a * 2 < b) {
        a = a * 3;
    } else if (a > b) {
        b = b + 3;
    }
    if (b < a) {
        b++;
    } else {
        a--;
    }
    System.out.println(a + " " + b);
}
```

What output is produced for each of the following calls?

a. `ifElseMystery2(10, 2);`
b. `ifElseMystery2(3, 8);`
c. `ifElseMystery2(4, 4);`
d. `ifElseMystery2(10, 30);`

7. Write Java code to read an integer from the user, then print `even` if that number is an even number or `odd` otherwise. You may assume that the user types a valid integer.

8. The following code contains a logic error:

```
Scanner console = new Scanner(System.in);
System.out.print("Type a number: ");
int number = console.nextInt();
if (number % 2 == 0) {
    if (number % 3 == 0) {
        System.out.println("Divisible by 6.");
    } else {
        System.out.println("Odd.");
    }
}
```

Examine the code and describe a case in which the code would print something that is untrue about the number that was entered. Explain why. Then correct the logic error in the code.

9. Describe a problem with the following code:

```
Scanner console = new Scanner(System.in);
System.out.print("What is your favorite color?");
String name = console.next();
if (name == "blue") {
    System.out.println("Mine, too!");
}
```

10. Factor out redundant code from the following example by moving it out of the `if/else` statement, preserving the same output.

```
if (x < 30) {
    a = 2;
    x++;
    System.out.println("Java is awesome! " + x);
} else {
    a = 2;
    System.out.println("Java is awesome! " + x);
}
```

11. The following code is poorly structured:

```
int sum = 1000;
Scanner console = new Scanner(System.in);
System.out.print("Is your money multiplied 1 or 2 times? ");
int times = console.nextInt();
if (times == 1) {
    System.out.print("And how much are you contributing? ");
    int donation = console.nextInt();
    sum = sum + donation;
    count1++;
    total = total + donation;
}
```

```
if (times == 2) {
    System.out.print("And how much are you contributing? ");
    int donation = console.nextInt();
    sum = sum + 2 * donation;
    count2++;
    total = total + donation;
}
```

Rewrite it so that it has a better structure and avoids redundancy. To simplify things, you may assume that the user always types `1` or `2`. (How would the code need to be modified to handle any number that the user might type?)

12. The following code is poorly structured:

```
Scanner console = new Scanner(System.in);
System.out.print("How much will John be spending? ");
double amount = console.nextDouble();
System.out.println();
int numBills1 = (int) (amount / 20.0);
if (numBills1 * 20.0 < amount) {
    numBills1++;
}
System.out.print("How much will Jane be spending? ");
amount = console.nextDouble();
System.out.println();
int numBills2 = (int) (amount / 20.0);
if (numBills2 * 20.0 < amount) {
    numBills2++;
}
System.out.println("John needs " + numBills1 + " bills");
System.out.println("Jane needs " + numBills2 + " bills");
```

Rewrite it so that it has a better structure and avoids redundancy. You may wish to introduce a method to help capture redundant code.

13. Write a piece of code that reads a shorthand text description of a color and prints the longer equivalent. Acceptable color names are `B` for `Blue`, `G` for `Green`, and `R` for `Red`. If the user types something other than `B`, `G`, or `R`, the program should print an error message. Make your program case-insensitive so that the user can type an uppercase or lowercase letter. Here are some example executions:

```
What color do you want? B
You have chosen Blue.

What color do you want? g
You have chosen Green.

What color do you want? Bork
Unknown color: Bork
```

14. Write a piece of code that reads a shorthand text description of a playing card and prints the longhand equivalent. The shorthand description is the card's rank (`2` through `10`, `J`, `Q`, `K`, or `A`) followed by its suit (`C`, `D`, `H`, or `S`). You should expand the shorthand into the form "<Rank> of <Suit>". You may assume that the user types valid input. Here are two sample executions:

```
Enter a card: 9 S
Nine of Spades
```

```
Enter a card: K C
King of Clubs
```

Section 4.2: Cumulative Algorithms

15. What is wrong with the following code, which attempts to add all numbers from 1 to a given maximum? Describe how to fix the code.

```
public static int sumTo(int n) {
    for (int i = 1; i <= n; i++) {
        int sum = 0;
        sum += i;
    }
    return sum;
}
```

16. What is wrong with the following code, which attempts to return the number of factors of a given integer *n*? Describe how to fix the code.

```
public static int countFactors(int n) {
    for (int i = 1; i <= n; i++) {
        if (n % i == 0) {   // factor
            return i;
        }
    }
}
```

17. Write code to produce a cumulative product by multiplying together many numbers that are read from the console.

18. The following expression should equal `6.8`, but in Java it does not. Why not?

```
0.2 + 1.2 + 2.2 + 3.2
```

19. The following code was intended to print a message, but it actually produces no output. Describe how to fix the code to print the expected message.

```
double gpa = 3.2;
if (gpa * 3 == 9.6) {
   System.out.println("You earned enough credits.");
}
```

Section 4.3: Text Processing

20. What output is produced by the following program?

```
public class CharMystery {
    public static void printRange(char startLetter, char endLetter) {
        for (char letter = startLetter; letter <= endLetter; letter++) {
            System.out.print(letter);
        }
        System.out.println();
    }

    public static void main(String[] args) {
        printRange('e', 'g');
        printRange('n', 's');
        printRange('z', 'a');
        printRange('q', 'r');
    }
}
```

21. Write an `if` statement that tests to see whether a `String` begins with a capital letter.

22. What is wrong with the following code, which attempts to count the number occurrences of the letter `'e'` in a `String`, case-insensitively?

```
int count = 0;
for (int i = 0; i < s.length(); i++) {
    if (s.charAt(i).toLowerCase() == 'e') {
        count++;
    }
}
```

23. Consider a `String` stored in a variable called `name` that stores a person's first and last name (e.g., "Marla Singer"). Write the expression that would produce the last name followed by the first initial (e.g., "Singer, M.").

24. Write code to examine a `String` and determine how many of its letters come from the second half of the alphabet (that is, have values of `'n'` or subsequent letters). Compare case-insensitively, such that values of `'N'` through `'Z'` also count. Assume that every character in the `String` is a letter.

Section 4.4: Methods with Conditional Execution

25. Consider a method `printTriangleType` that accepts three integer arguments representing the lengths of the sides of a triangle and prints the type of triangle that these sides form. The three types are equilateral, isosceles, and scalene. An equilateral triangle has three sides of the same length, an isosceles triangle has two sides that are the same length, and a scalene triangle has three sides of different lengths.

However, certain integer values (or combinations of values) would be illegal and could not represent the sides of an actual triangle. What are these values? How would you describe the precondition(s) of the `printTriangleType` method?

26. Consider a method `getGrade` that accepts an integer representing a student's grade percentage in a course and returns that student's numerical course grade. The grade can be between `0.0` (failing) and `4.0` (perfect). What are the preconditions of such a method?

27. The following method attempts to return the median (middle) of three integer values, but it contains logic errors. In what cases does the method return an incorrect result? How can the code be fixed?

```
public static int medianOf3(int n1, int n2, int n3) {
    if (n1 < n2) {
        if (n2 < n3) {
            return n2;
        } else {
            return n3;
        }
    } else {
        if (n1 < n3) {
            return n1;
        } else {
            return n3;
        }
    }
}
```

28. One of the exercises in Chapter 3 asked you to write a method that would find the roots of a quadratic equation of the form $ax^2 + bx + c = 0$. The quadratic method was passed `a`, `b`, and `c` and then applied the following quadratic formula:

$$x = \frac{-b \pm \sqrt{b^2 - 4ac}}{2a}$$

Under what conditions would this formula fail? Modify the quadratic method so that it will reject invalid values of `a`, `b`, or `c` by throwing an exception. (If you did not complete the exercise in the previous chapter, just write the method's header and the exception-throwing code.)

29. Consider the following Java method, which is written incorrectly:

```
// This method should return how many of its three
// arguments are odd numbers.
public static void printNumOdd(int n1, int n2, int n3) {
    int count = 0;
    if (n1 % 2 != 0) {
        count++;
    } else if (n2 % 2 != 0) {
        count++;
```

```
    } else if (n3 % 2 != 0) {
        count++;
    }
    System.out.println(count + " of the 3 numbers are odd.");
}
```

Under what cases will the method print the correct answer, and when will it print an incorrect answer? What should be changed to fix the code? Can you think of a way to write the code correctly without any `if/else` statements?

Exercises

1. Write a method called `fractionSum` that accepts an integer parameter n and returns as a `double` the sum of the first n terms of the sequence

$$\sum_{i=1}^{n} \frac{1}{i}$$

In other words, the method should generate the following sequence:

$$1 + \frac{1}{2} + \frac{1}{3} + \frac{1}{4} + \frac{1}{5} + \ldots$$

You may assume that the parameter n is nonnegative.

2. Write a method called `repl` that accepts a `String` and a number of repetitions as parameters and returns the `String` concatenated that many times. For example, the call `repl("hello", 3)` should return `"hellohellohello"`. If the number of repetitions is zero or less, the method should return an empty string.

3. Write a method called `season` that takes as parameters two integers representing a month and day and returns a `String` indicating the season for that month and day. Assume that the month is specified as an integer between 1 and 12 (1 for January, 2 for February, and so on) and that the day of the month is a number between 1 and 31. If the date falls between 12/16 and 3/15, the method should return `"winter"`. If the date falls between 3/16 and 6/15, the method should return `"spring"`. If the date falls between 6/16 and 9/15, the method should return `"summer"`. And if the date falls between 9/16 and 12/15, the method should return `"fall"`.

4. Write a method called `daysInMonth` that takes a month (an integer between 1 and 12) as a parameter and returns the number of days in that month in this year. For example, the call `daysInMonth(9)` would return `30` because September has 30 days. Assume that the code is not being run during a leap year (that February always has 28 days). The following table lists the number of days in each month:

Month	1 Jan	2 Feb	3 Mar	4 Apr	5 May	6 Jun	7 Jul	8 Aug	9 Sep	10 Oct	11 Nov	12 Dec
Days	31	28	31	30	31	30	31	31	30	31	30	31

5. Write a method called `pow` that accepts a base and an exponent as parameters and returns the base raised to the given power. For example, the call `pow(3, 4)` should return `3 * 3 * 3 * 3`, or `81`. Assume that the base and exponent are nonnegative.

6. Write a method called `printRange` that accepts two integers as arguments and prints the sequence of numbers between the two arguments, separated by spaces. Print an increasing sequence if the first argument is smaller than the second; otherwise, print a decreasing sequence. If the two numbers are the same, that number should be printed by itself. Here are some sample calls to `printRange`:

```
printRange(2, 7);
printRange(19, 11);
printRange(5, 5);
```

The output produced from these calls should be the following sequences of numbers:

```
2 3 4 5 6 7
19 18 17 16 15 14 13 12 11
5
```

7. Write a static method called `xo` that accepts an integer *size* as a parameter and prints a square of *size* by *size* characters, where all characters are "o" except that an "x" pattern of "x" characters has been drawn from the corners of the square. On the first line, the first and last characters are "x"; on the second line, the second and second-from-last characters are "x"; and so on. Here are two example outputs:

xo(5);	**xo(6);**
xooox	xoooox
oxoxo	oxooxo
ooxoo	ooxxoo
oxoxo	ooxxoo
xooox	oxooxo
	xoooox

8. Write a method called `smallestLargest` that accepts a `Scanner` for the console as a parameter and asks the user to enter numbers, then prints the smallest and largest of all the numbers supplied by the user. You may assume that the user enters a valid number greater than `0` for the number of numbers to read. Here is a sample execution:

```
How many numbers do you want to enter? 4
Number 1: 5
Number 2: 11
Number 3: −2
Number 4: 3
Smallest = −2
Largest = 11
```

9. Write a method called `evenSumMax` that accepts a `Scanner` for the console as a parameter. The method should prompt the user for a number of integers, then prompt the integer that many times. Once the user has entered all the integers, the method should print the sum of all the even numbers the user typed, along with the largest even number typed. You may assume that the user will type at least one nonnegative even integer. Here is an example dialogue:

```
How many integers? 4
Next integer? 2
```

```
Next integer? 9
Next integer? 18
Next integer? 4
Even sum = 24, Even max = 18
```

10. Write a method called `printGPA` that accepts a `Scanner` for the console as a parameter and calculates a student's grade point average. The user will type a line of input containing the student's name, then a number that represents the number of scores, followed by that many integer scores. Here are two example dialogues:

```
Enter a student record: Maria 5 72 91 84 89 78
Maria's grade is 82.8

Enter a student record: Jordan 4 86 71 62 90
Jordan's grade is 77.25
```

Maria's grade is 82.8 because her average of (72 + 91 + 84 + 89 + 78) / 5 equals 82.8.

11. Write a method called `longestName` that accepts a `Scanner` for the console and an integer *n* as parameters and prompts for *n* names, then prints the longest name (the name that contains the most characters) in the format shown below, which might result from a call of `longestName(console, 4)`:

```
name #1? Roy
name #2? DANE
name #3? sTeFaNiE
name #4? Mariana
Stefanie's name is longest
```

12. Write the method called `printTriangleType` referred to in Self-Check Problem 25. This method accepts three integer arguments representing the lengths of the sides of a triangle and prints the type of triangle that these sides form. Here are some sample calls to `printTriangleType`:

```
printTriangleType(5, 7, 7);
printTriangleType(6, 6, 6);
printTriangleType(5, 7, 8);
printTriangleType(2, 18, 2);
```

The output produced by these calls should be

```
isosceles
equilateral
scalene
isosceles
```

Your method should throw an `IllegalArgumentException` if passed invalid values, such as ones where one side's length is longer than the sum of the other two, which is impossible in a triangle. For example, the call of `printTriangleType(2, 18, 2);` should throw an exception.

13. Write a method called `average` that takes two integers as parameters and returns the average of the two integers.

14. Modify your pow method from Exercise 5 to make a new method called `pow2` that uses the type `double` for the first parameter and that works correctly for negative numbers. For example, the call `pow2(−4.0, 3)` should return `−4.0 * −4.0 * −4.0`, or `−64.0`, and the call `pow2(4.0, −2)` should return `1 / 16`, or `0.0625`.

15. Write a method called `getGrade` that accepts an integer representing a student's grade in a course and returns that student's numerical course grade. The grade can be between `0.0` (failing) and `4.0` (perfect). Assume that scores are in the range of `0` to `100` and that grades are based on the following scale:

Score	Grade
< 60	0.0
60–62	0.7
63	0.8
64	0.9
65	1.0
. . .	
92	3.7
93	3.8
94	3.9
>= 95	4.0

For an added challenge, make your method throw an `IllegalArgumentException` if the user passes a grade lower than `0` or higher than `100`.

16. Write a method called `printPalindrome` that accepts a `Scanner` for the console as a parameter, prompts the user to enter one or more words, and prints whether the entered `String` is a palindrome (i.e., reads the same forward as it does backward, like `"abba"` or `"racecar"`).

For an added challenge, make the code case-insensitive, so that words like "Abba" and "Madam" will be considered palindromes.

17. Write a method called `stutter` that accepts a string parameter and returns that string with its characters repeated twice. For example, `stutter("Hello!")` returns `"HHeelllloo!!"`

18. Write a method called `wordCount` that accepts a `String` as its parameter and returns the number of words in the `String`. A word is a sequence of one or more nonspace characters (any character other than `' '`). For example, the call `wordCount("hello")` should return `1`, the call `wordCount("how are you?")` should return `3`, the call `wordCount(" this  string  has  wide  spaces ")` should return `5`, and the call `wordCount(" ")` should return `0`.

19. Write a method called `quadrant` that accepts as parameters a pair of `double` values representing an (*x*, *y*) point and returns the quadrant number for that point. Recall that quadrants are numbered as integers from 1 to 4 with the upper-right quadrant numbered 1 and the subsequent quadrants numbered in a counterclockwise fashion:

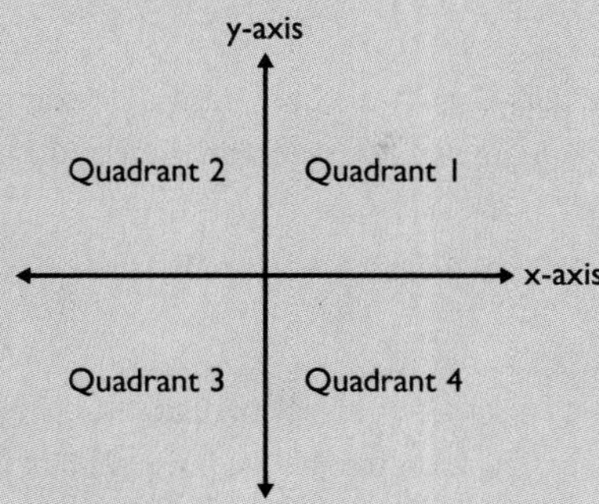

Notice that the quadrant is determined by whether the *x* and *y* coordinates are positive or negative numbers. Return `0` if the point lies on the *x*- or *y*-axis. For example, the call of `quadrant(-2.3, 3.5)` should return `2` and the call of `quadrant(4.5, -4.5)` should return `4`.

20. Write a method called `numUnique` that takes three integers as parameters and returns the number of unique integers among the three. For example, the call `numUnique(18, 3, 4)` should return `3` because the parameters have three different values. By contrast, the call `numUnique(6, 7, 6)` should return `2` because there are only two unique numbers among the three parameters: `6` and `7`.

21. Write a method called `perfectNumbers` that accepts an integer maximum as its parameter and prints all "perfect numbers" up to and including that maximum. A perfect number is an integer that is equal to the sum of its proper factors, that is, all numbers that evenly divide it other than 1 and itself. For example, 28 is a perfect number because 1 + 2 + 4 + 7 + 14 = 28. The call `perfectNumbers(500);` should produce the following output:

```
Perfect numbers up to 500: 6 28 496
```

Programming Projects

1. Write a program that prompts for a number and displays it in Roman numerals.
2. Write a program that prompts for a date (month, day, year) and reports the day of the week for that date. It might be helpful to know that January 1, 1601, was a Monday.
3. Write a program that compares two college applicants. The program should prompt for each student's GPA, SAT, and ACT exam scores and report which candidate is more qualified on the basis of these scores.
4. Write a program that prompts for two people's birthdays (month and day), along with today's month and day. The program should figure out how many days remain until each user's birthday and which birthday is sooner. Hint: It is much easier to solve this problem if you convert each date into an "absolute day" of year, from 1 through 365.

5. Write a program that computes a student's grade in a course. The course grade has three components: homework assignments, a midterm exam, and a final exam. The program should prompt the user for all information necessary to compute the grade, such as the number of homework assignments, the points earned and points possible for each assignment, the midterm and final exam scores, and whether each exam was curved (and, if so, by how much).

   Consider writing a variation of this program that reports what final exam score the student needs to get a certain course grade.

6. A useful technique for catching typing errors is to use a check digit. For example, suppose that a school assigns a six-digit number to each student. A seventh digit can be determined from the other digits with the use of the following formula:

   7th digit = (1 * (1st digit) + 2 * (2nd digit) + . . . + 6 * (6th digit)) % 10

   When a user types in a student number, the user types all seven digits. If the number is typed incorrectly, the check digit will fail to match in 90% of the cases. Write an interactive program that prompts for a six-digit student number and reports the check digit for that number, using the preceding formula.

7. Write a program that displays Pascal's triangle:

```
                    1
                  1   1
                1   2   1
              1   3   3   1
            1   4   6   4   1
          1   5  10  10   5   1
        1   6  15  20  15   6   1
      1   7  21  35  35  21   7   1
    1   8  28  56  70  56  28   8   1
  1   9  36  84 126 126  84  36   9   1
1  10  45 120 210 252 210 120  45  10   1
```

   Use `System.out.printf` to format the output into fields of width 4.

8. Write a program that produces a Caesar cipher of a given message string. A Caesar cipher, or rotation cipher, is formed by rotating each letter of a message by a given amount. For example, if you rotate by 3, every A becomes D; every B becomes E; and so on. Toward the end of the alphabet, you wrap around: X becomes A; Y becomes B; and Z becomes C. Your program should prompt for a message and an amount by which to rotate each letter and should output the encoded message.

```
Your message? Attack zerg at dawn
Encoding key? 3
Your message: DWWDFN CHUJ DW GDZQ
```

Chapter 5

Program Logic and Indefinite Loops

Introduction

The chapter begins by examining a new construct called a `while` loop that allows you to loop an indefinite number of times. The `while` loop will allow you to solve a new class of programming problems in which you don't know in advance how many times you want a loop to execute. For example, game-playing programs often involve `while` loops because it is not possible to know beforehand how the user will play the game. Because we will be exploring game programs, we will also explore how to generate random numbers inside a Java program. We will also explore another class of algorithms known as fencepost algorithms that occur often in loop-programming tasks.

The chapter then discusses the fourth primitive type that we are going to examine in detail, `boolean`. The `boolean` type is used to store logical (true/false) information. Once you understand the details of the `boolean` type, you will be able to write complex loops involving multiple tests.

Next, we'll briefly examine the important topic of handling user errors.

The chapter concludes with a discussion of assertions. Using assertions, you can reason about the formal properties of programs (what is true at different points in program execution).

5.1 The `while` Loop

The `for` loops we have been writing since Chapter 2 are fairly simple loops that execute a predictable number of times. Recall that we call them *definite* loops because we know before the loops begin executing exactly how many times they will execute. Now we want to turn our attention to *indefinite* loops, which execute an unknown number of times. Indefinite loops come up often in interactive programs and file processing. For example, you don't know in advance how many times a user might want to play a game, and you won't know before you look at a file exactly how much data it stores.

The `while` loop is the first indefinite loop we will study. It has the following syntax:

```
while (<test>) {
    <statement>;
    <statement>;
     ...
    <statement>;
}
```

The diagram in Figure 5.1 indicates the flow of control for the `while` loop. The loop performs its test and, if the test evaluates to `true`, executes the controlled statements. It repeatedly tests and executes if the test evaluates to `true`. Only when the test evaluates to `false` does the loop terminate.

As Figure 5.1 indicates, the `while` loop performs its test at the top of the loop, before the body of the loop is executed. A `while` loop will not execute its controlled statements if its test evaluates to `false` the first time it is evaluated.

Here is an example of a `while` loop:

```
int number = 1;
while (number <= 200) {
    number = number * 2;
}
```

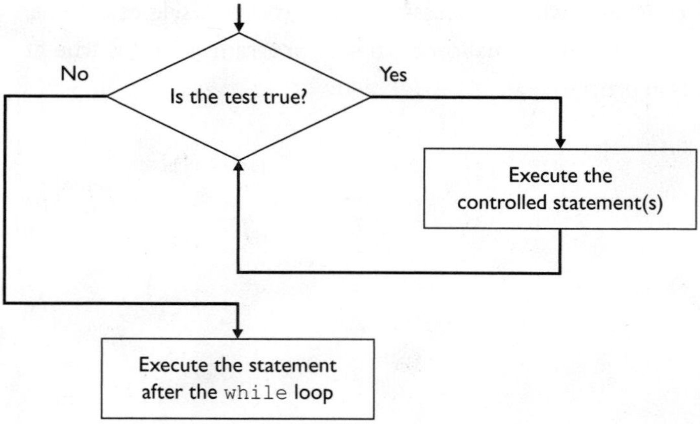

Figure 5.1 Flow of `while` loop

This loop initializes an integer variable called number to 1 and then doubles it while it is less than or equal to 200. On the surface, this operation is similar to using an if statement:

```
int number = 1;
if (number <= 200) {
    number = number * 2;
}
```

The difference between the two forms is that the while loop executes multiple times, looping until the test evaluates to false. The if statement executes the doubling statement only once, leaving number equal to 2. The while loop executes the doubling statement repeatedly, with number taking on the values 1, 2, 4, 8, 16, 32, 64, 128, and 256. The loop doesn't stop executing until the test evaluates to false. It executes the assignment statement eight times and terminates when number is set to the value 256 (the first power of 2 that is greater than 200).

Here is a while loop containing two statements:

```
int number = 1;
while (number <= max) {
    System.out.println("Hi there");
    number++;
}
```

This while loop is almost the same as the following for loop:

```
for (int number = 1; number <= max; number++) {
    System.out.println("Hi there");
}
```

The only difference between these two loops is the scope of the variable number. In the while loop, number is declared in the scope outside the loop. In the for loop, number is declared inside the loop.

A Loop to Find the Smallest Divisor

Suppose you want to find the smallest divisor of a number other than 1. Table 5.1 gives examples of what you are looking for.

Here is a pseudocode description of how you might find this value:

```
start divisor at 2.
while (the current value of divisor does not work) {
    increase divisor.
}
```

Table 5.1 Examples of Factors

Number	Factors	Smallest divisor
10	2 * 5	2
15	3 * 5	3
25	5 * 5	5
31	31	31
77	7 * 11	7

You don't start `divisor` at `1` because you are looking for the first divisor greater than `1`. To refine this pseudocode, you must be more explicit about what makes a divisor work. A divisor of a number has no remainder when the number is divided by that divisor. You can rewrite this rule as the following pseudocode:

```
start divisor at 2.
while (the remainder of number/divisor is not 0) {
    increase divisor.
}
```

This exercise is a use for the mod operator, which gives the remainder for integer division. The following `while` loop performs the task:

```
int divisor = 2;
while (number % divisor != 0) {
    divisor++;
}
```

One problem you will undoubtedly encounter when you write `while` loops is the infamous infinite loop. Consider the following code:

```
int number = 1;
while (number > 0) {
    number++;
}
```

Because `number` begins as a positive value and the loop makes it larger, this loop will continue indefinitely. You must be careful when you formulate your `while` loops to avoid situations in which a piece of code will never finish executing. Every time you write a `while` loop, you should consider when and how it will finish executing.

Common Programming Error

Infinite Loop

It is relatively easy to write a `while` loop that never terminates. One reason it's so easy to make this mistake is that a `while` loop doesn't have an update step in its header like a `for` loop does. It's crucial for the programmer to include a correct update step because this step is needed to eventually cause the loop's test to fail.

Consider the following code, which is intended to prompt the user for a number and repeatedly print that number divided in half until 0 is reached. This first attempt doesn't compile:

```
Scanner console = new Scanner(System.in);
System.out.print("Type a number: ");

// this code does not compile
while (number > 0) {
    int number = console.nextInt();
    System.out.println(number / 2);
}
```

The problem with the preceding code is that the variable `number` needs to be in scope during the loop's test, so it cannot be declared inside the loop. An incorrect attempt to fix this compiler error would be to cut and paste the line initializing `number` outside the loop:

```
// this code has an infinite loop
int number = console.nextInt(); // moved out of loop

while (number > 0) {
    System.out.println(number / 2);
}
```

This version of the code has an infinite loop; if the loop is entered, it will never be exited. This problem arises because there is no update inside the `while` loop's body to change the value of `number`. If `number` is greater than `0`, the loop will keep printing its value and checking the loop test, and the test will evaluate to `true` every time.

Continued on next page

Continued from previous page

The following version of the code solves the infinite loop problem. The loop contains an update step on each pass that divides the integer in half and stores its new value. If the integer hasn't reached 0, the loop repeats:

```
// this code behaves correctly
int number = console.nextInt(); // moved out of loop
while (number > 0) {
    number = number / 2; // update step: divide in half
    System.out.println(number);
}
```

The key idea is that every `while` loop's body should contain code to update the terms that are tested in the loop test. If the `while` loop test examines a variable's value, the loop body should potentially reassign a meaningful new value to that variable.

Random Numbers

We often want our programs to exhibit apparently random behavior. For example, we want game-playing programs to make up a number for the user to guess, shuffle a deck of cards, pick a word from a list for the user to guess, and so on. Programs are, by their very nature, predictable and nonrandom. But we can produce values that seem to be random. Such values are called *pseudorandom* because they are produced algorithmically.

Pseudorandom Numbers

Numbers that, although they are derived from predictable and well-defined algorithms, mimic the properties of numbers chosen at random.

Java provides several mechanisms for obtaining pseudorandom numbers. One option is to call the `random` method from the `Math` class to obtain a random value of type `double` that has the following property:

0.0 ≤ `Math.random()` < 1.0

This method provides a quick and easy way to get a random number, and you can use multiplication to change the range of the numbers the method produces. Java also provides a class called `Random` that can be easier to use. It is included in the `java.util` package, so you have to include an import declaration at the beginning of your program to use it.

`Random` objects have several useful methods that are related to generating pseudorandom numbers, listed in Table 5.2. Each time you call one of these methods, Java will generate and return a new random number of the requested type.

Table 5.2 Useful Methods of Random Objects

Method	Description
`nextInt()`	Random integer between -2^{31} and $(2^{31} - 1)$
`nextInt(max)`	Random integer between 0 and (max – 1)
`nextDouble()`	Random real number between 0.0 (inclusive) and 1.0 (exclusive)
`nextBoolean()`	Random logical value of true or false

To create random numbers, you first construct a `Random` object:

```
Random r = new Random();
```

You can then call its `nextInt` method, passing it a maximum integer. The number returned will be between 0 (inclusive) and the maximum (exclusive). For example, if you call `nextInt(100)`, you will get a number between 0 and 99. You can add 1 to the number to have a range between 1 and 100.

Let's look at a simple program that picks numbers between 1 and 10 until a particular number comes up. We'll use the `Random` class to construct an object for generating our pseudorandom numbers.

Our loop should look something like this (where `number` is the value the user has asked us to generate):

```
int result;
while (result != number) {
    result = r.nextInt(10) + 1; // random number from 1–10
    System.out.println("next number = " + result);
}
```

Notice that we have to declare the variable `result` outside the `while` loop, because `result` appears in the `while` loop test. The preceding code has the right approach, but Java won't accept it. The code generates an error message that the variable `result` might not be initialized. This is an example of a loop that needs *priming*.

Priming a Loop

Initializing variables before a loop to "prime the pump" and guarantee that the loop is entered.

We want to set the variable `result` to something that will cause the loop to be entered, but the value isn't important as long as it gets us into the loop. We do want to be careful not to set it to a value the user wants us to generate, though. We are dealing with values between 1 and 10 in this program, so we could set `result` to a value such as `-1` that is clearly outside this range of numbers. We sometimes refer to this as a “dummy” value because we don’t actually process it. Later in this chapter we will see a variation of the `while` loop that doesn’t require this kind of priming.

The following is the complete program solution:

```
import java.util.*;

public class Pick {
    public static void main(String[] args) {
        System.out.println("This program picks numbers from");
        System.out.println("1 to 10 until a particular");
        System.out.println("number comes up.");
        System.out.println();

        Scanner console = new Scanner(System.in);
        Random r = new Random();

        System.out.print("Pick a number between 1 and 10--> ");
        int number = console.nextInt();

        int result = -1; // set to -1 to make sure we enter the loop
        int count = 0;
        while (result != number) {
            result = r.nextInt(10) + 1; // random number from 1-10
            System.out.println("next number = " + result);
            count++;
        }
        System.out.println("Your number came up after " +
                           count + " times");
    }
}
```

Depending on the sequence of numbers returned by the `Random` object, the program might end up picking the given number quickly, as in the following sample execution:

```
This program picks numbers from
1 to 10 until a particular
number comes up.

Pick a number between 1 and 10--> 2
next number = 7
next number = 8
next number = 2
Your number came up after 3 times
```

It's also possible that the program will take a while to pick the number, as in the following sample execution:

```
This program picks numbers from
1 to 10 until a particular
number comes up.

Pick a number between 1 and 10--> 10
next number = 9
next number = 7
next number = 7
next number = 5
next number = 8
next number = 8
next number = 1
next number = 5
next number = 1
next number = 9
next number = 7
next number = 10
Your number came up after 12 times
```

Common Programming Error

Misusing the Random Object

A `Random` object chooses a new random integer every time the `nextInt` method is called. When students are trying to produce a constrained random value, such as one that is odd, sometimes they mistakenly write code such as the following:

```
// this code contains a bug
Random r = new Random();

if (r.nextInt() % 2 == 0) {
    System.out.println("Even number: " + r.nextInt());
} else {
    System.out.println("Odd number: " + r.nextInt());
}
```

The preceding code fails in many cases because the `Random` object produces one random integer for use in the `if/else` test, then another for use in whichever `println` statement is chosen to execute. For example, the `if` test might retrieve a random value of `47` from the `Random` object. The test would find

Continued on next page

Continued from previous page

that `47 % 2` does not equal `0`, so the code would proceed to the `else` statement. The `println` statement would then execute another call on `nextInt`, which would return a completely different number (say, `128`). The output of the code would then be the following bizarre statement:

```
Odd number: 128
```

The solution to this problem is to store the randomly chosen integer in a variable and call `nextInt` again only if another random integer is truly needed. The following code accomplishes this task:

```
// this code behaves correctly
Random r = new Random();
int n = r.nextInt(); // save random number into a variable
if (n % 2 == 0) {
    System.out.println("Even number: " + n);
} else {
    System.out.println("Odd number: " + n);
}
```

Simulations

VideoNote

Traditional science and engineering involve a lot of real-world interaction. Scientists run experiments to test their hypotheses and engineers build prototypes to test their designs. But increasingly scientists and engineers are turning to computers as a way to increase their productivity by running simulations first to explore possibilities before they go out and run an actual experiment or build an actual prototype. A famous computer scientist named Jeanette Wing has argued that this increased use of computation by scientists and engineers will lead to computational thinking being viewed as fundamental in the same way that reading, writing, and arithmetic are considered fundamental today.

From a programming perspective, the two key ingredients in a simulation are pseudorandom numbers and loops. Some simulations can be written using `for` loops, but more often than not we use a `while` loop because the simulation should be run indefinitely until some condition is met.

As a simple example, let's look at how we would simulate the rolling of two dice until the sum of the dice is 7. We can use a `Random` object to simulate the dice, calling it once for each of the two dice. We want to loop until the sum is equal to 7 and we can print the various rolls that come up as we run the simulation. Here is a good first attempt:

```
Random r = new Random();
while (sum != 7) {
    // roll the dice once
    int roll1 = r.nextInt(6) + 1;
    int roll2 = r.nextInt(6) + 1;
    int sum = roll1 + roll2;
    System.out.println(roll1 + " + " + roll2 + " = " + sum);
}
```

The preceding code produces the following compiler error:

```
Dice.java:7: error: cannot find symbol
symbol : variable sum
location: class Dice
    while (sum != 7) {
           ^
1 error
```

The problem is that the `while` loop test refers to the variable `sum`, but the variable is declared inside the body of the loop. We can't declare the variable in the inner scope because we need to refer to it in the loop test. So we have to move the variable declaration before the loop. We also have to give the variable an initial value to guarantee that it enters the loop. This code is another example of a time when we need to prime the loop:

```
Random r = new Random();
int sum = 0; // set to 0 to make sure we enter the loop
while (sum != 7) {
    // roll the dice once
    int roll1 = r.nextInt(6) + 1;
    int roll2 = r.nextInt(6) + 1;
    sum = roll1 + roll2;
    System.out.println(roll1 + " + " + roll2 + " = " + sum);
}
```

This version of the code compiles and works properly. A sample execution follows:

```
1 + 4 = 5
5 + 6 = 11
1 + 3 = 4
4 + 3 = 7
```

do/while Loop

The `while` loop is the standard indefinite loop, but Java provides several alternatives. This section presents the `do/while` loop. Other variations are included in Appendix C.

As we have seen, the `while` loop tests at the "top" of the loop, before it executes its controlled statement. Java has an alternative known as the `do/while` loop that tests at the "bottom" of the loop. The `do/while` loop has the following syntax:

```
do {
    <statement>;
    ...
    <statement>;
} while (<test>);
```

Here is some sample code using a `do/while` loop:

```
int number = 1;
do {
    number *= 2;
} while (number <= 200);
```

This loop produces the same result as the corresponding `while` loop, doubling the variable `number` until its value reaches `256`, which is the first power of `2` greater than `200`. But unlike the `while` loop, the `do/while` loop always executes its controlled statements at least once. The diagram in Figure 5.2 shows the flow of control in a `do/while` loop.

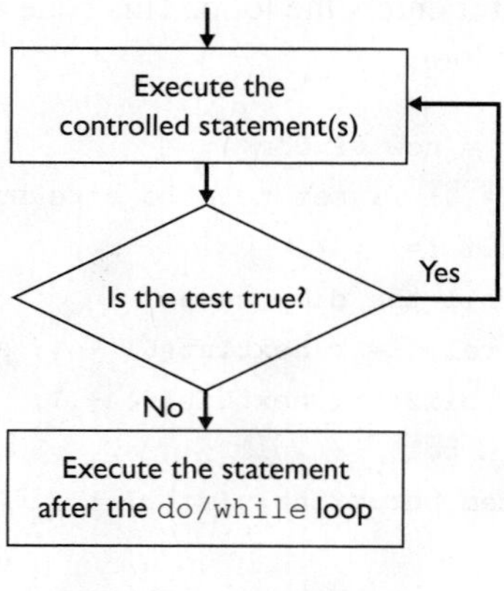

Figure 5.2 Flow of `do/while` loop

The `do/while` loop is most useful in situations in which you know you have to execute the loop at least once. For example, in the last section we wrote the following code that simulates the rolling of two dice until you get a sum of 7:

```
Random r = new Random();
int sum = 0; // set to 0 to make sure we enter the loop
while (sum != 7) {
    // roll the dice once
    int roll1 = r.nextInt(6) + 1;
```

```
    int roll2 = r.nextInt(6) + 1;
    sum = roll1 + roll2;
    System.out.println(roll1 + " + " + roll2 + " = " + sum);
}
```

We had to prime the loop by setting `sum` to 0 so that the computer would enter the loop. With a `do/while` loop, we can eliminate the priming:

```
Random r = new Random();
int sum;
do {
    // roll the dice once
    int roll1 = r.nextInt(6) + 1;
    int roll2 = r.nextInt(6) + 1;
    sum = roll1 + roll2;
    System.out.println(roll1 + " + " + roll2 + " = " + sum);
} while (sum != 7);
```

In this version, we always execute the body of the loop at least once, which ends up giving a value to the variable `sum` *before* it reaches the loop test that now appears at the bottom of the loop.

There are many programming problems in which using `do/while` loops is appropriate. These loops are often useful in interactive programs where you know you want to do something at least once. For example, you might have a loop that allows a user to play a game multiple times; you can be fairly sure that the user will want to play at least once. Likewise, if you are playing a guessing game with the user, you will always have to obtain at least one guess.

5.2 Fencepost Algorithms

A common programming problem involves a particular kind of loop known as a *fencepost loop*. Consider the following problem: You want to put up a fence that is 100 yards long, and you want to install a post every 10 yards. How many posts do you need? If you do a quick division in your head, you might think that you need 10 posts, but actually you need 11 posts. That's because fences begin and end with posts. In other words, a fence looks like Figure 5.3.

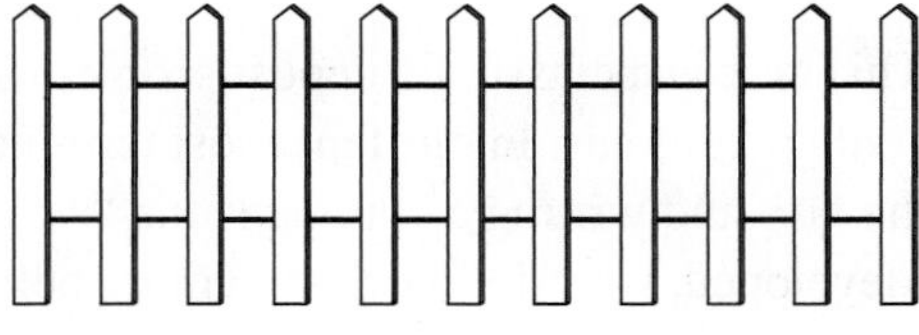

Figure 5.3 A typical fence

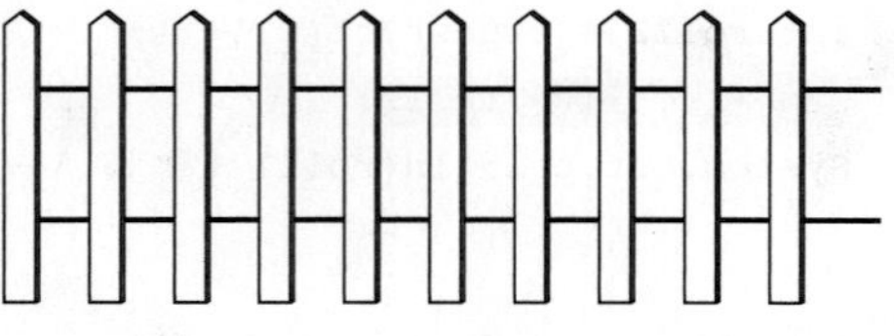

Figure 5.4 A flawed fence

Because you want posts on both the far left and the far right, you can't use the following simple loop (it doesn't plant the final post):

```
for (the length of the fence) {
    plant a post.
    attach some wire.
}
```

If you use the preceding loop, you'll get a fence that looks like Figure 5.4.

Switching the order of the two operations doesn't help, because then you miss the first post. The problem with this loop is that it produces the same number of posts as sections of wire, but we know we need an extra post. That's why this problem is also sometimes referred to as the "loop and a half" problem—we want to execute one half of this loop (planting a post) one additional time.

One solution is to plant one of the posts either before or after the loop. The usual solution is to do it before:

```
plant a post.
for (the length of the fence) {
    attach some wire.
    plant a post.
}
```

Notice that the order of the two operations in the body of the loop is now reversed because the initial post is planted before the loop is entered.

As a simple example, consider the problem of writing out the integers between 1 and 10, separated by commas. In other words, we want to get the following output:

```
1, 2, 3, 4, 5, 6, 7, 8, 9, 10
```

This task is a classic fencepost problem because we want to write out 10 numbers but only 9 commas. In our fencepost terminology, writing a number is the "post" part of the task and writing a comma is the "wire" part. So, implementing the pseudocode we developed, we print the first number before the loop:

```
System.out.print(1);
for (int i = 2; i <= 10; i++) {
```

```
    System.out.print(", " + i);
}
System.out.println();
```

Sentinel Loops

VideoNote

Suppose you want to read a series of numbers from the user and compute their sum. You could ask the user in advance how many numbers to read, as we did in the last chapter, but that isn't always convenient. What if the user has a long list of numbers to enter and hasn't counted them? One way around asking for the number is to pick some special input value that will signal the end of input. We call this a *sentinel value.*

> **Sentinel**
> A special value that signals the end of input.

For example, you could tell the user to enter the value `-1` to stop entering numbers. But how do you structure your code to use this sentinel? In general, you'll want to use the following approach:

```
sum = 0.
while (we haven't seen the sentinel) {
    prompt and read.
    add it to the sum.
}
```

This approach doesn't quite work. Suppose, for example, that the user enters the numbers `10`, `42`, `5`, and `-1`. As the pseudocode indicates, we'll prompt for and read each of these four values and add them to our sum until we encounter the sentinel value of `-1`. We initialize the sum to `0`, so this computes `(10 + 42 + 5 + -1)`, which is `56`. But the right answer is `57`. The sentinel value of `-1` isn't supposed to be included in the sum.

This problem is a classic fencepost or "loop-and-a-half" problem: You want to prompt for and read a series of numbers, including the sentinel, and you want to add up most of the numbers, but you don't want to add the sentinel to the sum.

The usual fencepost solution works: We insert the first prompt-and-read instruction before the loop and reverse the order of the two steps in the body of the loop:

```
sum = 0.
prompt and read.
while (we haven't seen the sentinel) {
    add it to the sum.
    prompt and read.
}
```

You can then refine this pseudocode by introducing a variable for the number that is read from the user:

```
sum = 0.
prompt and read a value into n.
while (n is not the sentinel) {
    add n to the sum.
    prompt and read a value into n.
}
```

This pseudocode translates fairly easily into Java code:

```
Scanner console = new Scanner(System.in);
int sum = 0;
System.out.print("next integer (-1 to quit)? ");
int number = console.nextInt();
while (number != -1) {
    sum += number;
    System.out.print("next integer (-1 to quit)? ");
    number = console.nextInt();
}
System.out.println("sum = " + sum);
```

When the preceding code is executed, the interaction might look like this:

```
next integer (-1 to quit)? 34
next integer (-1 to quit)? 19
next integer (-1 to quit)? 8
next integer (-1 to quit)? 0
next integer (-1 to quit)? 17
next integer (-1 to quit)? 204
next integer (-1 to quit)? -1
sum = 282
```

Fencepost with `if`

Many of the fencepost loops that you write will require conditional execution. In fact, the fencepost problem itself can be solved with an `if` statement. Remember that the classic solution to the fencepost is to handle the first post before the loop begins:

```
plant a post.
for (the length of the fence) {
    attach some wire.
    plant a post.
}
```

This solution solves the problem, but it can be confusing because inside the loop the steps are apparently in reverse order. You can use an `if` statement and keep the original order of the steps:

```
for (the length of the fence) {
    plant a post.
    if (this isn't the last post) {
        attach some wire.
    }
}
```

This variation isn't used as often as the classic solution because it involves both a loop test and a test inside the loop. Often these tests are nearly identical, so it is inefficient to test the same thing twice each time the loop executes. But there will be situations in which you might use this approach. For example, in the classic approach, the lines of code that correspond to planting a post are repeated. If you were writing a program in which this step required a lot of code, you might decide that putting the `if` statement inside the loop was a better approach, even if it led to some extra testing.

As an example, consider writing a method called `multiprint` that will print a string a particular number of times. Suppose that you want the output on a line by itself, inside square brackets, and separated by commas. Here are two example calls:

```
multiprint("please", 4);
multiprint("beetlejuice", 3);
```

You would expect these calls to produce the following output:

```
[please, please, please, please]
[beetlejuice, beetlejuice, beetlejuice]
```

Your first attempt at writing this method might be a simple loop that prints square brackets outside the loop and prints the string and a comma inside the loop:

```
public static void multiprint(String s, int times) {
    System.out.print("[");
    for (int i = 1; i <= times; i++) {
        System.out.print(s + ", ");
    }
    System.out.println("]");
}
```

Unfortunately, this code produces an extraneous comma after the last value:

```
[please, please, please, please, ]
[beetlejuice, beetlejuice, beetlejuice, ]
```

Because the commas are separators, you want to print one more string than comma (e.g., two commas to separate the three occurrences of "beetlejuice"). You can use the classic solution to the fencepost problem to achieve this effect by printing one string outside the loop and reversing the order of the printing inside the loop:

```
public static void multiprint(String s, int times) {
    System.out.print("[" + s);
    for (int i = 2; i <= times; i++) {
        System.out.print(", " + s);
    }
    System.out.println("]");
}
```

Notice that because you're printing one of the strings before the loop begins, you have to modify the loop so that it won't print as many strings as it did before. Adjusting the loop variable `i` to start at `two` accounts for the first value that is printed before the loop.

Unfortunately, this solution does not work properly either. Consider what happens when you ask the method to print a string zero times, as in:

```
multiprint("please don't", 0);
```

This call produces the following incorrect output:

```
[please don't]
```

You want it to be possible for a user to request zero occurrences of a string, so the method shouldn't produce that incorrect output. The problem is that the classic solution to the fencepost problem involves printing one value before the loop begins. To get the method to behave correctly for the zero case, you can include an `if/else` statement:

```
public static void multiprint(String s, int times) {
    if (times == 0) {
        System.out.println("[]");
    } else {
        System.out.print("[" + s);
        for (int i = 2; i <= times; i++) {
            System.out.print(", " + s);
        }
        System.out.println("]");
    }
}
```

Alternatively, you can include an if statement inside the loop (the double-test approach):

```
public static void multiprint(String s, int times) {
    System.out.print("[");
    for (int i = 1; i <= times; i++) {
        System.out.print(s);
        if (i < times) {
            System.out.print(", ");
        }
    }
    System.out.println("]");
}
```

Although the preceding version of the code performs a similar test twice on each iteration, it is simpler than using the classic fencepost solution and its special case. Neither solution is better than the other, as there is a tradeoff involved. If you think that the code will be executed often and that the loop will iterate many times, you might be more inclined to use the efficient solution. Otherwise, you might choose the simpler code.

5.3 The boolean Type

George Boole was such a good logician that Java has a data type named after him. The Java type boolean is used to describe logical true/false relationships. Recall that boolean is one of the primitive types, like int, double, and char.

Novices often wonder why computer scientists are so interested in logic. The answer is that logic is fundamental to computing in the same way that physics is fundamental to engineering. Engineers study physics because they want to build real-world artifacts that are governed by the laws of physics. If you don't understand physics, you're likely to build a bridge that will collapse. Computer scientists build artifacts as well, but in a virtual world that is governed by the laws of logic. If you don't understand logic, you're likely to build computer programs that collapse.

Without realizing it, you have already used booleans. All of the control structures we have looked at—if/else statements, for loops, and while loops—are controlled by expressions that specify tests. For example, the expression

```
number % 2 == 0
```

is a test for divisibility by 2. It is also a Boolean expression. Boolean expressions are meant to capture the concepts of truth and falsity, so it is not surprising that the domain of type `boolean` has only two values: `true` and `false`. The words `true` and `false` are reserved words in Java. They are the literal values of type `boolean`. All Boolean expressions, when evaluated, will return one or the other of these literals. Don't confuse these special values with the string literals `"true"` and `"false"`. You don't need quotes to refer to the Boolean literals.

When you write a program that manipulates numerical values, you'll often want to compute a value and store it in a variable or write a method that captures some complex formula. We end up doing the same thing with type `boolean`. We might want to record a Boolean value in a variable and we often write methods that return Boolean results. For example, we have seen that the `String` class has methods that return a Boolean result, including `startsWith`, `endsWith`, `equals`, and `equalsIgnoreCase`.

To understand this better, remember what these terms mean for the type `int`. The literals of type `int` include `0`, `1`, `2`, and so on. Because these are literals of type `int`, you can write expressions like the following ones with them:

```
int number1 = 1;
int number2 = 0;
```

Consider what you can do with variables of type `boolean`. Suppose you define two `boolean` variables, `test1` and `test2`. These variables can take on only two possible values: `true` and `false`. You can say:

```
boolean test1 = true;
boolean test2 = false;
```

You can also write a statement that copies the value of one `boolean` variable to another, as with variables of any other type:

```
test1 = test2;
```

Furthermore, you know that the assignment statement can use expressions like:

```
number1 = 2 + 2;
```

and that the simple tests you have been using are Boolean expressions. That means you can write statements like the following ones:

```
test1 = (2 + 2 == 4);
test2 = (3 * 100 < 250);
```

These assignment statements say, in effect, "Set this `boolean` variable according to the truth value returned by the following test." The first statement sets the variable `test1` to `true`, because the test evaluates to `true`. The second sets the variable `test2` to `false`, because the second test evaluates to `false`. You don't need to include parentheses, but they make the statements more readable.

Obviously, then, assignment is one of the operations you can perform on variables of type `boolean`.

Logical Operators

In Java, you can form complicated Boolean expressions using what are known as the *logical operators,* shown in Table 5.3.

Table 5.3 Logical Operators

Operator	Meaning	Example	Value
`&&`	AND (conjunction)	`(2 == 2) && (3 < 4)`	`true`
`||`	OR (disjunction)	`(1 < 2) || (2 == 3)`	`true`
`!`	NOT (negation)	`!(2 == 2)`	`false`

The NOT operator (`!`) reverses the truth value of its operand. If an expression evaluates to `true`, its negation evaluates to `false`, and vice versa. You can express this relationship in a truth table. The truth table that follows has two columns, one for a variable and one for its negation. For each value of the variable, the table shows the corresponding value of the negation.

Truth Table for NOT (`!`)

p	!p
`true`	`false`
`false`	`true`

In addition to the negation operator, there are two logical connectives you will use, AND (`&&`) and OR (`||`). You use these connectives to tie together two Boolean expressions, creating a new Boolean expression. The following truth table shows that the `AND` operator evaluates to `true` only when both of its individual operands are `true`.

Truth Table for AND (`&&`)

p	q	p && q
`true`	`true`	`true`
`true`	`false`	`false`
`false`	`true`	`false`
`false`	`false`	`false`

The following truth table shows that the `OR` operator evaluates to `true` except when both operands are `false`.

Truth Table for OR (||)

p	q	p || q
true	true	true
true	false	true
false	true	true
false	false	false

The Java OR operator has a slightly different meaning from the English word "or." In English you say, "I'll study tonight or I'll go to a movie." One or the other will be true, but not both. The OR operator is more like the English expression "and/or": If one or both operands are `true`, the overall proposition is `true`.

You generally use logical operators when what you have to say cannot be reduced to a single test. For example, as we saw in the previous chapter, if you want to do a particular operation when a number is between 1 and 10, you might say,

```
if (number >= 1) {
    if (number <= 10) {
        doSomething();
    }
}
```

But you can say this more easily using logical `AND`:

```
if (number >= 1 && number <= 10) {
    doSomething();
}
```

People use the words "and" and "or" all the time, but Java only allows you to use them in the strict logical sense. Be careful not to write code like the following:

```
// this does not compile
if (x == 1 || 2 || 3) {
    doSomething();
}
```

In English, we would read this as "`x` equals `1` or `2` or `3`," which makes sense to us, but it doesn't make sense to Java. You might also be tempted to write code like the following:

```
// this does not compile
if (1 <= x <= 10) {
    doSomethingElse();
}
```

In mathematics, this expression would make sense and would test whether x is between 1 and 10 inclusive. However, the expression doesn't make sense in Java.

You can only use the logical AND and OR operators to combine a series of Boolean expressions. Otherwise, the computer will not understand what you mean. To express the "1 or 2 or 3" idea, combine three different Boolean expressions with logical ORs:

```
if (x == 1 || x == 2 || x == 3) {
    doSomething();
}
```

To express the "between 1 and 10 inclusive" idea, combine two Boolean expressions with a logical AND:

```
if (1 <= x && x <= 10) {
    doSomethingElse();
}
```

Now that we've introduced the AND, OR, and NOT logical operators, it's time to revisit our precedence table. The NOT operator appears at the top, with the highest level of precedence. The other two logical operators have fairly low precedence, lower than the arithmetic and relational operators but higher than the assignment operators. The AND operator has a slightly higher level of precedence than the OR operator. Table 5.4 includes these new operators.

According to these rules of precedence, when Java evaluates an expression like the following one, the computer will evaluate the NOT first, the AND second, and then the OR.

```
if (test1 || !test2 && test3) {
    doSomething();
}
```

Table 5.4 Java Operator Precedence

Description	Operators
unary operators	!, ++, --, +, -
multiplicative operators	*, /, %
additive operators	+, -
relational operators	<, >, <=, >=
equality operators	==, !=
logical AND	&&
logical OR	||
assignment operators	=, +=, -=, *=, /=, %=, &&=, ||=

Short-Circuited Evaluation

In this section we will explore the use of the logical operators to solve a complex programming task, and we'll introduce an important property of these operators. We will write a method called `firstWord` that takes a `String` as a parameter and returns the first word in the string. To keep things simple, we will adopt the convention that a `String` is broken up into individual words by spaces. If the `String` has no words at all, the method should return an empty string. Here are a few example calls:

Method Call	Value Returned
`firstWord("four score and seven years")`	`"four"`
`firstWord("all-one-word-here")`	`"all-one-word-here"`
`firstWord("   lots   of   space here")`	`"lots"`
`firstWord(" ")`	`""`

Remember that we can call the `substring` method to pull out part of a string. We pass two parameters to the `substring` method: the starting index of the substring and the index one beyond the end of the substring. If the string is stored in a variable called `s`, our task basically reduces to the following steps:

```
set start to the first index of the word.
set stop to the index just beyond the word.
return s.substring(start, stop).
```

As a first approximation, let's assume that the starting index is 0. This starting index won't work for strings that begin with spaces, but it will allow us to focus on the second step in the pseudocode. Consider a string that begins with `"four score"`. If we examine the individual characters of the string and their indexes, we find the following pattern:

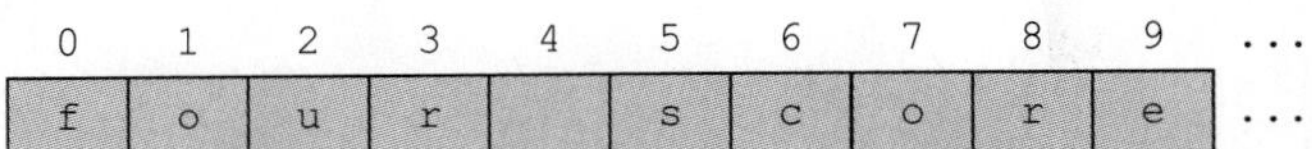

We set `start` to `0`. We want to set the variable `stop` to the index just beyond the end of the first word. In this example, the word we want is `"four"`, and it extends from indexes 0 through 3. So, if we want the variable `stop` to be one beyond the end of the desired substring, we want to set it to index 4, the location of the first space in the string.

So how do we find the first space in the string? We use a `while` loop. We simply start at the front of the string and loop until we get to a space:

```
set stop to 0.
while (the character at index stop is not a space) {
    increase stop by 1.
}
```

This is easily converted into Java code. Combining it with our assumption that `start` will be `0`, we get:

```
public static String firstWord(String s) {
    int start = 0;
    int stop = 0;
    while (s.charAt(stop) != ' ') {
        stop++;
    }
    return s.substring(start, stop);
}
```

This version of the method works for many cases, including our sample string, but it doesn't work for all strings. It has two major limitations. We began by assuming that the string did not begin with spaces, so we know we have to fix that limitation.

The second problem is that this version of `firstWord` doesn't work on one-word strings. For example, if we execute it with a string like `"four"`, it generates a `StringIndexOutOfBoundsException` indicating that `4` is not a legal index. The exception occurs because our code assumes that we will eventually find a space, but there is no space in the string `"four"`. So `stop` is incremented until it becomes equal to `4`, and an exception is thrown because there is no character at index 4. This is sometimes referred to as "running off the end of the string."

To address this problem, we need to incorporate a test that involves the length of the string. Many novices attempt to do this by using some combination of `while` and `if`, as in the following code:

```
int stop = 0;
while (stop < s.length()) {
    if (s.charAt(stop) != ' ') {
        stop++;
    }
}
```

This code works for one-word strings like `"four"` because as soon as `stop` becomes equal to the length of the string, we break out of the loop. However, it doesn't work for the original multiword cases like `"four score"`. We end up in an infinite loop because once `stop` becomes equal to `4`, we stop incrementing it, but we get trapped inside the loop because the test says to continue as long as `stop` is less than the length of the string. This approach of putting an `if` inside a `while` led to a world-famous bug on December 31, 2008, when Zune music players all over the world stopped working (see Self-Check Problem 21 for more details).

The point to recognize is that in this case we need to use two different conditions in controlling the loop. We want to continue incrementing `stop` only if we know that we haven't seen a space *and* that we haven't reached the end of the string. We can express that idea using the logical AND operator:

```
int stop = 0;
while (s.charAt(stop) != ' ' && stop < s.length()) {
    stop++;
}
```

Unfortunately, even this test does not work. It expresses the two conditions properly, because we want to make sure that we haven't reached a space and we want to make sure that we haven't reached the end of the string. But think about what happens just as we reach the end of a string. Suppose that s is "four" and stop is equal to 3. We see that the character at index 3 is not a space and we see that stop is less than the length of the string, so we increment one more time and stop becomes 4. As we come around the loop, we test whether s.charAt(4) is a space. This test throws an exception. We also test whether stop is less than 4, which it isn't, but that test comes too late to avoid the exception.

Java offers a solution for this situation. The logical operators && and || use *short-circuited evaluation.*

Short-Circuited Evaluation

The property of the logical operators && and || that prevents the second operand from being evaluated if the overall result is obvious from the value of the first operand.

In our case, we are performing two different tests and asking for the logical AND of the two tests. If either test fails, the overall result is false, so if the first test fails, it's not necessary to perform the second test. Because of short-circuited evaluation—that is, because the overall result is obvious from the first test—we don't perform the second test at all. In other words, the performance and evaluation of the second test are prevented (short-circuited) by the fact that the first test fails.

This means we need to reverse the order of our two tests:

```
int stop = 0;
while (stop < s.length() && s.charAt(stop) != ' ') {
    stop++;
}
```

If we run through the same scenario again with stop equal to 3, we pass both of these tests and increment stop to 4. Then, as we come around the loop again, we first test to see if stop is less than s.length(). It is not, which means the test evaluates to false. As a result, Java knows that the overall expression will evaluate to false and never evaluates the second test. This order of events prevents the exception from occurring, because we never test whether s.charAt(4) is a space.

This solution gives us a second version of the method:

```
public static String firstWord(String s) {
    int start = 0;
    int stop = 0;
    while (stop < s.length() && s.charAt(stop) != ' ') {
        stop++;
    }
    return s.substring(start, stop);
}
```

But remember that we assumed that the first word starts at position 0. That won't necessarily be the case. For example, if we pass a string that begins with several spaces, this method will return an empty string. We need to modify the code so that it skips any leading spaces. Accomplishing that goal requires another loop. As a first approximation, we can write the following code:

```
int start = 0;
while (s.charAt(start) == ' ') {
    start++;
}
```

This code works for most strings, but it fails in two important cases. The loop test assumes we will find a nonspace character. What if the string is composed entirely of spaces? In that case, we'll simply run off the end of the string, generating a `StringIndexOutOfBoundsException`. And what if the string is empty to begin with? We'll get an error immediately when we ask about `s.charAt(0)`, because there is no character at index `0`.

We could decide that these cases constitute errors. After all, how can you return the first word if there is no word? So, we could document a precondition that the string contains at least one nonspace character, and throw an exception if we find that it doesn't. Another approach is to return an empty string in these cases.

To deal with the possibility of the string being empty, we need to modify our loop to incorporate a test on the length of the string. If we add it at the end of our `while` loop test, we get the following code:

```
int start = 0;
while (s.charAt(start) == ' ' && start < s.length()) {
    start++;
}
```

But this code has the same flaw we saw before. It is supposed to prevent problems when `start` becomes equal to the length of the string, but when this situation occurs, a `StringIndexOutOfBoundsException` will be thrown before the computer reaches the test on the length of the string. So these tests also have to be reversed to take advantage of short-circuited evaluation:

```
int start = 0;
while (start < s.length() && s.charAt(start) == ' ') {
    start++;
}
```

To combine these lines of code with our previous code, we have to change the initialization of `stop`. We no longer want to search from the front of the string. Instead, we need to initialize `stop` to be equal to `start`. Putting these pieces together, we get the following version of the method:

```
public static String firstWord(String s) {
    int start = 0;
    while (start < s.length() && s.charAt(start) == ' ') {
        start++;
    }
    int stop = start;
    while (stop < s.length() && s.charAt(stop) != ' ') {
        stop++;
    }
    return s.substring(start, stop);
}
```

This version works in all cases, skipping any leading spaces and returning an empty string if there is no word to return.

boolean Variables and Flags

All `if/else` statements are controlled by Boolean tests. The tests can be `boolean` variables or Boolean expressions. Consider, for example, the following code:

```
if (number > 0) {
    System.out.println("positive");
} else {
    System.out.println("not positive");
}
```

This code could be rewritten as follows:

```
boolean positive = (number > 0);
if (positive) {
    System.out.println("positive");
} else {
    System.out.println("not positive");
}
```

Using `boolean` variables adds to the readability of your programs because it allows you to give names to tests. Consider the kind of code you would generate for a dating program. You might have some integer variables that describe certain attributes of a person: `looks`, to store a rough estimate of physical beauty (on a scale of 1–10); `IQ`, to store intelligence quotient; `income`, to store gross annual income; and `snothers`, to track intimate friends ("snother" is short for "significant other"). Given these variables to specify a person's attributes, you can develop various tests of suitability. As you are writing the program, you can use `boolean` variables to give names to those tests, adding greatly to the readability of the code:

```
boolean cute = (looks >= 9);
boolean smart = (IQ > 125);
boolean rich = (income > 100000);
boolean available = (snothers == 0);
boolean awesome = cute && smart && rich && available;
```

You might find occasion to use a special kind of `boolean` variable called *a flag*. Typically we use flags within loops to record error conditions or to signal completion. Different flags test different conditions. As an analogy, consider a referee at a sports game who watches for a particular illegal action and throws a flag if it happens. You sometimes hear an announcer saying, "There is a flag down on the play."

Let's introduce a flag into the cumulative sum code we saw in the previous chapter:

```
double sum = 0.0;
for (int i = 1; i <= totalNumber; i++) {
    System.out.print("    #" + i + "? ");
    double next = console.nextDouble();
    sum += next;
}
System.out.println("sum = " + sum);
```

Suppose we want to know whether the sum ever goes negative at any point. Notice that this situation isn't the same as the situation in which the sum ends up being negative. Like a bank account balance, the sum might switch back and forth between positive and negative. As you make a series of deposits and withdrawals, the bank will keep track of whether you overdraw your account along the way. Using a `boolean` flag, we can modify the preceding loop to keep track of whether the sum ever goes negative and report the result after the loop:

```
double sum = 0.0;
boolean negative = false;
for (int i = 1; i <= totalNumber; i++) {
    System.out.print("    #" + i + "? ");
    double next = console.nextDouble();
```

```
        sum += next;
        if (sum < 0.0) {
            negative = true;
        }
    }
    System.out.println("sum = " + sum);
    if (negative) {
        System.out.println("Sum went negative");
    } else {
        System.out.println("Sum never went negative");
    }
```

Boolean Zen

In 1974, Robert Pirsig started a cultural trend with his book *Zen and the Art of Motorcycle Maintenance: An Inquiry into Values.* A slew of later books copied the title with *Zen and the Art of X,* where *X* was Poker, Knitting, Writing, Foosball, Guitar, Public School Teaching, Making a Living, Falling in Love, Quilting, Stand-up Comedy, the SAT, Flower Arrangement, Fly Tying, Systems Analysis, Fatherhood, Screenwriting, Diabetes Maintenance, Intimacy, Helping, Street Fighting, Murder, and on and on. There was even a book called *Zen and the Art of Anything.*

We now join this cultural trend by discussing Zen and the art of type `boolean`. It seems to take a while for many novices to get used to Boolean expressions. Novices often write overly complex expressions involving `boolean` values because they don't grasp the simplicity that is possible when you "get" how the `boolean` type works.

For example, suppose that you are writing a game-playing program that involves two-digit numbers, each of which is composed of two different digits. In other words, the program will use numbers like 42 that are composed of two distinct digits, but not numbers like 6 (only one digit), 394 (more than two digits), or 22 (both digits are the same). You might find yourself wanting to test whether a given number is legal for use in the game. You can restrict yourself to two-digit numbers with a test like the following one:

```
n >= 10 && n <= 99
```

You also have to test to make sure that the two digits aren't the same. You can get the digits of a two-digit number with the expressions `n / 10` and `n % 10`. So you can expand the test to ensure that the digits aren't the same:

```
n >= 10 && n <= 99 && (n / 10 != n % 10)
```

This test is a good example of a situation in which you could use a method to capture a complex Boolean expression. Returning a `boolean` will allow you to call the method as many times as you want without having to copy this complex expression each time, and you can give a name to this computation to make the program more readable.

Suppose you want to call the method `isTwoUniqueDigits`. You want the method to take a value of type `int` and return `true` if the `int` is composed of two unique digits and `false` if it is not. So, the method would look like the following:

```
public static boolean isTwoUniqueDigits(int n) {
    ...
}
```

How would you write the body of this method? We've already written the test, so we just have to figure out how to incorporate it into the method. The method has a `boolean` return type, so you want it to return the value `true` when the test succeeds and the value `false` when it fails. You can write the method as follows:

```
public static boolean isTwoUniqueDigits(int n) {
    if (n >= 10 && n <= 99 && (n % 10 != n / 10)) {
        return true;
    } else {
        return false;
    }
}
```

This method works, but it is more verbose than it needs to be. The preceding code evaluates the test that we developed. That expression is of type `boolean`, which means that it evaluates to either `true` or `false`. The `if/else` statement tells the computer to return `true` if the expression evaluates to `true` and to return `false` if it evaluates to `false`. But why use this construct? If the method is going to return `true` when the expression evaluates to `true` and return `false` when it evaluates to `false`, you can just return the value of the expression directly:

```
public static boolean isTwoUniqueDigits(int n) {
    return (n >= 10 && n <= 99 && (n % 10 != n / 10));
}
```

Even the preceding version can be simplified, because the parentheses are not necessary (although they make it clearer exactly what the method will return). This code evaluates the test that we developed to determine whether a number is composed of two unique digits and returns the result (`true` when it does, `false` when it does not).

Consider an analogy to integer expressions. To someone who understands Boolean Zen, the `if/else` version of this method looks as odd as the following code:

```
if (x == 1) {
    return 1;
} else if (x == 2) {
    return 2;
} else if (x == 3) {
    return 3;
```

```
} else if (x == 4) {
    return 4;
} else if (x == 5) {
    return 5;
}
```

If you always want to return the value of `x`, you should just say:

```
return x;
```

A similar confusion can occur when students use `boolean` variables. In the last section we looked at a variation of the cumulative sum algorithm that used a `boolean` variable called `negative` to keep track of whether or not the sum ever goes negative. We then used an `if/else` statement to print a message reporting the result:

```
if (negative) {
    System.out.println("Sum went negative");
} else {
    System.out.println("Sum never went negative");
}
```

Some novices would write this code as follows:

```
if (negative == true) {
    System.out.println("Sum went negative");
} else {
    System.out.println("Sum never went negative");
}
```

The comparison is unnecessary because the `if/else` statement expects an expression of type `boolean` to appear inside the parentheses. A `boolean` variable is already of the appropriate type, so we don't need to test whether it equals `true`; it either *is* `true` or it isn't (in which case it is `false`). To someone who understands Boolean Zen, the preceding test seems as redundant as saying:

```
if ((negative == true) == true) {
    ...
}
```

Novices also often write tests like the following:

```
if (negative == false) {
    ...
}
```

This makes some sense because the test is doing something useful, in that it switches the meaning of the `boolean` variable (evaluating to `true` if the variable is `false` and evaluating to `false` if the variable is `true`). But the negation operator is designed to do this kind of switching of `boolean` values, so this test is better written as follows:

```
if (!negative) {
    ...
}
```

You should get used to reading the exclamation mark as "not", so this test would be read as "if not negative." To those who understand Boolean Zen, that is a more concise way to express the test than to test whether `negative` is equal to `false`.

Negating Boolean Expressions

Programmers often find themselves needing to form the negation of a complex Boolean expression. For example, it is often easiest to reason about a loop in terms of an exit condition that would make us want to stop the loop, but the `while` loop requires us to express the code in terms of a continuation condition. Suppose that you want to write a loop that keeps prompting the user for an integer until that integer is a two-digit number. Because two-digit numbers range from 10 to 99, you can use the following lines of code to test whether a number has exactly two digits:

```
number >= 10 && number <= 99
```

To put this in a `while` loop, we have to turn the test around because the `while` loop test is a continuation test. In other words, we want to stay in the loop while this is *not* true (while the user has not yet given us a two-digit number). One approach is to use the logical NOT operator to negate this expression:

```
while (!(number >= 10 && number <= 99))
```

Notice that we need to parenthesize the entire Boolean expression and then put the NOT operator in front of it. While this approach works, it is generally considered bad style. It is best to simplify this expression.

A general approach to simplifying such expressions was formalized by the British logician Augustus De Morgan. We can apply one of two rules that are known as *De Morgan's laws*.

Table 5.5 shows De Morgan's laws. Notice that when you negate a Boolean expression, each operand is negated (`p` becomes `!p` and `q` becomes `!q`) and the logical operator flips. Logical OR becomes logical AND and vice versa when you compute the negation.

Table 5.5 De Morgan's Laws

Original expression	Negated expression	Simplified negation
`p || q`	`!(p || q)`	`!p && !q`
`p && q`	`!(p && q)`	`!p || !q`

We can use the first De Morgan's law for our two-digit number program because we are trying to find the negation of an expression that involves the logical OR operator. Instead of writing:

```
while (!(number >= 10 && number <= 99))
```

we can say:

```
while (number < 10 || number > 99)
```

Each individual test has been negated and the AND operator has been replaced with an OR operator.

Let's look at a second example that involves the other De Morgan's law. Suppose that you want to ask the user a question and you want to force the user to answer either "yes" or "no". If you have a `String` variable called `response`, you can use the following test to describe what you want to be true:

```
response.equals("yes") || response.equals("no")
```

If we're writing a loop to keep reading a response until this expression evaluates to `true`, then we want to write the loop so that it uses the negation of this test. So, once again, we could use the NOT operator for the entire expression:

```
while (!(response.equals("yes") || response.equals("no")))
```

Once again it is best to simplify the expression using De Morgan's law:

```
while (!response.equals("yes") && !response.equals("no"))
```

5.4 User Errors

In the previous chapter, you learned that it is good programming practice to think about the preconditions of a method and to mention them in the comments for the method. You also learned that in some cases your code can throw exceptions if preconditions are violated.

When you are writing interactive programs, the simplest approach is to assume that the user will provide good input. You can then document your preconditions and throw exceptions when the user input isn't what was expected. In general, though, it's better to write programs that don't make assumptions about user input. You've seen, for example, that the `Scanner` object can throw an exception if the user enters the wrong kind of data. It's preferable to write programs that can deal with user errors. Such programs are referred to as being *robust.*

Robust

Ability of a program to execute even when presented with illegal data.

In this section we will explore how to write robust interactive programs. Before you can write robust code, though, you have to understand some special functionality of the `Scanner` class.

Scanner Lookahead

The `Scanner` class has methods that allow you to perform a test before you read a value. In other words, it allows you to look before you leap. For each of the "next" methods of the `Scanner` class, there is a corresponding "has" method that tells you whether or not you can perform the given operation.

For example, you will often want to read an `int` using a `Scanner` object. But what if the user types something other than an `int`? `Scanner` has a method called `hasNextInt` that tells you whether or not reading an `int` is currently possible. To determine whether it is possible, the `Scanner` object looks at the next token and checks whether it can be interpreted as an integer.

We tend to interpret certain sequences of characters as particular types of data, but when we read tokens, they can be interpreted in different ways. The following program will allow us to explore this concept:

```
import java.util.*;

public class ExamineInput1 {
    public static void main(String[] args) {
        System.out.println("This program examines the ways");
        System.out.println("a token can be read.");
        System.out.println();

        Scanner console = new Scanner(System.in);

        System.out.print("token? ");
        System.out.println("  hasNextInt = " +
                           console.hasNextInt());
        System.out.println("  hasNextDouble = " +
                           console.hasNextDouble());
```

```
        System.out.println("   hasNext = " + console.hasNext());
    }
}
```

Let's look at a few sample executions. Here is the output of the program when we enter the token 348:

```
This program examines the ways
a token can be read.

token? 348
  hasNextInt = true
  hasNextDouble = true
  hasNext = true
```

As you'd expect, the call on hasNextInt returns true, which means that we could interpret this token as an integer. The Scanner would also allow us to interpret this token as a double, so hasNextDouble also returns true. But notice that hasNext() returns true as well. That result means that we could call the next method to read in this token as a String.

Here's another execution, this time for the token 348.2:

```
This program examines the ways
a token can be read.

token? 348.2
  hasNextInt = false
  hasNextDouble = true
  hasNext = true
```

This token cannot be interpreted as an int, but it can be interpreted as a double or a String. Finally, consider this execution for the token hello:

```
This program examines the ways
a token can be read.

token? hello
  hasNextInt = false
  hasNextDouble = false
  hasNext = true
```

The token hello can't be interpreted as an int or double; it can only be interpreted as a String.

Handling User Errors

Consider the following code fragment:

```
Scanner console = new Scanner(System.in);
System.out.print("How old are you? ");
int age = console.nextInt();
```

What if the user types something that is not an integer? If that happens, the Scanner will throw an exception on the call to nextInt. We saw in the previous section that we can test whether or not the next token can be interpreted as an integer by using the hasNextInt method. So, we can test before reading an int whether the user has typed an appropriate value.

If the user types something other than an integer, we want to discard the input, print out some kind of error message, and prompt for a second input. We want this code to execute in a loop so that we keep discarding input and generating error messages as necessary until the user enters legal input.

Here is a first attempt at a solution in pseudocode:

```
while (user hasn't given us an integer) {
    prompt.
    discard input.
    generate an error message.
}
read the integer.
```

This reflects what we want to do, in general. We want to keep prompting, discarding, and generating error messages as long as the input is illegal, and when a legal value is entered, we want to read the integer. Of course, in that final case we don't want to discard the input or generate an error message. In other words, the last time through the loop we want to do just the first of these three steps (prompting, but not discarding and not generating an error message). This is another classic fencepost problem, and we can solve it in the usual way by putting the initial prompt before the loop and changing the order of the operations within the loop:

```
prompt.
while (user hasn't given us an integer) {
    discard input.
    generate an error message.
    prompt.
}
read the integer.
```

This pseudocode is fairly easy to turn into actual Java code:

```
Scanner console = new Scanner(System.in);
System.out.print("How old are you? ");
while (!console.hasNextInt()) {
    console.next(); // to discard the input
    System.out.println("Not an integer; try again.");
    System.out.print("How old are you? ");
}
int age = console.nextInt();
```

In fact, this is such a common operation that it is worth turning into a static method:

```
// prompts until a valid number is entered
public static int getInt(Scanner console, String prompt) {
    System.out.print(prompt);
    while (!console.hasNextInt()) {
        console.next(); // to discard the input
        System.out.println("Not an integer; try again.");
        System.out.print(prompt);
    }
    return console.nextInt();
}
```

Using this method, we can rewrite our original code as follows:

```
Scanner console = new Scanner(System.in);
int age = getInt(console, "How old are you? ");
```

When you execute this code, the interaction looks like this:

```
How old are you? what?
Not an integer; try again.
How old are you? 18.4
Not an integer; try again.
How old are you? ten
Not an integer; try again.
How old are you? darn!
Not an integer; try again.
How old are you? help
Not an integer; try again.
How old are you? 19
```

5.5 Assertions and Program Logic

Logicians concern themselves with declarative statements called *assertions.*

Assertion

A declarative sentence that is either true or false.

The following statements are all assertions:

- 2 + 2 equals 4.
- The sun is larger than the Earth.
- $x > 45$.
- It was raining.
- The rain in Spain falls mainly on the plain.

The following statements are not assertions (the first is a question and the second is a command):

- How much do you weigh?
- Take me home.

Some assertions are true or false depending upon their context:

- $x > 45$. (The validity of this statement depends on the value of x.)
- It was raining. (The validity of this statement depends on the time and location.)

You can pin down whether they are true or false by providing a context:

- When $x = 13$, $x > 45$.
- On July 4, 1776, in Philadelphia, it was raining.

To write programs correctly and efficiently, you must learn to make assertions about your programs and to understand the contexts in which those assertions will be true. For example, if you are trying to obtain a nonnegative number from the user, you want the assertion "Number is nonnegative" to be true. You can use a simple prompt and read:

```
System.out.print("Please give me a nonnegative number--> ");
double number = console.nextDouble();
// is number nonnegative?
```

But the user can ignore your request and input a negative number anyway. In fact, users often input values that you don't expect, usually because they are confused. Given the uncertainty of user input, this particular assertion may sometimes be true and sometimes false. But something later in the program may depend on the assertion being true. For example, if you are going to take the square root of that number, you must be sure the number is nonnegative. Otherwise, you might end up with a bad result.

Using a loop, you can guarantee that the number you get is nonnegative:

```
System.out.print("Please give me a nonnegative number--> ");
double number = console.nextDouble();
while (number < 0.0) {
    System.out.print("That is a negative number. Try again--> ");
    number = console.nextDouble();
}
// is number nonnegative?
```

You know that `number` will be nonnegative after the loop; otherwise, the program would not exit the `while` loop. As long as a user gives negative values, your program stays in the `while` loop and continues to prompt for input.

This doesn't mean that `number` *should* be nonnegative after the loop. It means that `number` *will* be nonnegative. By working through the logic of the program, you can see that this is a certainty, an assertion of which you are sure. You could even prove it if need be. Such an assertion is called a *provable assertion.*

Provable Assertion

An assertion that can be proven to be true at a particular point in program execution.

Provable assertions help to identify unnecessary bits of code. Consider the following statements:

```
int x = 0;
if (x == 0) {
    System.out.println("This is what I expect.");
} else {
    System.out.println("How can that be?");
}
```

The `if/else` construct is not necessary. You know what the assignment statement does, so you know that it sets `x` to `0`. Testing whether `x` is `0` is as unnecessary as saying, "Before I proceed, I'm going to check that 2 + 2 equals 4." Because the `if` part of this `if/else` statement is always executed, you can prove that the following lines of code always do the same thing as the preceding lines:

```
int x = 0;
System.out.println("This is what I expect.");
```

This code is simpler and, therefore, better. Programs are complex enough without adding unnecessary code.

The concept of assertions has become so popular among software practitioners that many programming languages provide support for testing assertions. Java added support for testing assertions starting with version 1.4 of the language. You can read more about Java's `assert` statement in Appendix C.

Reasoning about Assertions

The focus on assertions comes out of a field of computer science known as *formal verification.*

> **Formal Verification**
>
> A field of computer science that involves reasoning about the formal properties of programs to prove the correctness of a program.

For example, consider the properties of the simple `if` statement:

```
if (<test>) {
    // test is always true here
    ...
}
```

You enter the body of the `if` statement only if the test is true, which is why you know that the test must be true if that particular line is reached in program execution. You can draw a similar conclusion about what is true in an `if/else` statement:

```
if (<test>) {
    // test is always true here
    ...
} else {
    // test is never true here
    ...
}
```

You can draw a similar conclusion about what is true inside the body of a `while` loop:

```
while (<test>) {
    // test is always true here
    ...
}
```

But in the case of the `while` loop, you can draw an even stronger conclusion. You know that as long as the test evaluates to `true`, you'll keep going back into the loop.

Thus, you can conclude that after the loop is done executing, the test can no longer be true:

```
while (<test>) {
    // test is always true here
    ...
}
// test is never true here
```

The test can't be true after the loop because if it had been true, the program would have executed the body of the loop again.

These observations about the properties of `if` statements, `if/else` statements, and `while` loops provide a good start for proving certain assertions about programs. But often, proving assertions requires a deeper analysis of what the code actually does. For example, suppose you have a variable `x` of type `int` and you execute the following `if` statement:

```
if (x < 0) {
    // x < 0 is always true here
    x = -x;
}
// but what about x < 0 here?
```

You wouldn't normally be able to conclude anything about `x` being less than `0` after the `if` statement, but you can draw a conclusion if you think about the different cases. If `x` was greater than or equal to `0` before the `if` statement, it will still be greater than or equal to `0` after the `if` statement. And if `x` was less than `0` before the `if` statement, it will be equal to –x after. When `x` is less than `0`, –x is greater than `0`. Thus, in either case, you know that after the `if` statement executes, `x` will be greater than or equal to `0`.

Programmers naturally apply this kind of reasoning when writing programs. Computer scientists are trying to figure out how to do this kind of reasoning in a formal, verifiable way.

A Detailed Assertions Example

VideoNote

To explore assertions further, let's take a detailed look at a code fragment and a set of assertions we might make about the fragment. Consider the following method:

```
public static void printCommonPrefix(int x, int y) {
    int z = 0;
    // Point A
    while (x != y) {
        // Point B
        z++;
```

```
            // Point C
            if (x > y) {
                // Point D
                x = x / 10;
            } else {
                // Point E
                y = y / 10;
            }
            // Point F
        }
        // Point G
        System.out.println("common prefix = " + x);
        System.out.println("digits discarded = " + z);
    }
```

This method finds the longest sequence of leading digits that two numbers have in common. For example, the numbers 32845 and 328929343 each begin with the prefix 328. This method will report that prefix and will also report the total number of digits that follow the common prefix and that are discarded.

We will examine the program to check whether various assertions are always true, never true, or sometimes true and sometimes false at various points in program execution. The comments in the method indicate the points of interest. The assertions we will consider are:

```
x > y
x == y
z == 0
```

Normally computer scientists write assertions in mathematical notation, as in `z = 0`, but we will use a Java expression to distinguish this assertion of equality from the practice of assigning a value to the variable.

We can record our answers in a table with the words "always," "never," or "sometimes." Our table will look like the following one:

	x > y	**x == y**	**z == 0**
Point A			
Point B			
...	...	...	...

Let's start at point A, which appears near the beginning of the method's execution:

```
public static void printCommonPrefix(int x, int y) {
    int z = 0;
    // Point A
```

The variables x and y are parameters and get their values from the call to the method. Many calls are possible, so we don't really know anything about the values of x and y. Thus, the assertion x > y could be true but doesn't have to be. The assertion is sometimes true, sometimes false at point A. Likewise, the assertion x == y could be true depending on what values are passed to the method, but it doesn't have to be true. However, we initialize the local variable z to 0 just before point A, so the assertion z == 0 will always be true at that point in execution. So, we can fill in the first line of the table as follows:

	x > y	x == y	z == 0
Point A	sometimes	sometimes	always

Point B appears just inside the while loop:

```
while (x != y) {
    // Point B
    z++;
    ...
}
```

We get to point B only by entering the loop, which means that the loop test must have evaluated to true. In other words, at point B it will always be true that x is not equal to y, so the assertion x == y will never be true at that point. But we don't know which of the two is larger. Therefore, the assertion x > y is sometimes true and sometimes false.

You might think that the assertion z == 0 would always be true at point B because we were at point A just before we were at point B, but that is not the right answer. Remember that point B is inside a while loop. On the first iteration of the loop we will have been at point A just before reaching point B, but on later iterations of the loop we will have been inside the loop just before reaching point B. And if you look at the line of code just after point B, you will see that it increments z. There are no other modifications to the variable z inside the loop. Therefore, each time the body of the loop executes, z will increase by 1. So, z will be 0 at point B the first time through the loop, but it will be 1 on the second iteration, 2 on the third iteration, and so forth. Therefore, the right answer for the assertion z == 0 at point B is that it is sometimes true, sometimes false. So, the second line of the table should look like this:

	x > y	x == y	z == 0
Point B	sometimes	never	sometimes

Point C is right after the increment of the variable z. There are no changes to the values of x and y between point B and point C, so the same answers apply at point C for the assertions `x > y` and `x == y`. The assertion `z == 0` will never be true after the increment, even though `z` starts at `0` before the loop begins and there are no other manipulations of the variable inside the loop; once it is incremented, it will never be `0` again. Therefore, we can fill in the table for point C as follows:

	x > y	x == y	z == 0
Point C	sometimes	never	never

Points D and E are part of the `if/else` statement inside the `while` loop, so we can evaluate them as a pair. The `if/else` statement appears right after point C:

```
// Point C
if (x > y) {
    // Point D
    x = x / 10;
} else {
    // Point E
    y = y / 10;
}
```

No variables are changed between point C and points D and E. Java performs a test and branches in one of two directions. The `if/else` test determines whether `x` is greater than `y`. If the test is `true`, we go to point D. If not, we go to point E. So, for the assertion `x > y`, we know it is always true at point D and never true at point E. The assertion `x == y` is a little more difficult to work out. We know it can never be true at point D, but could it be true at point E? Solely on the basis of the `if/else` test, the answer is yes. But remember that at point C the assertion could never be true. The values of `x` and `y` have not changed between point C and point E, so it still can never be true.

As for the assertion `z == 0`, the variable `z` hasn't changed between point C and points D and E, and `z` is not included in the test. So whatever we knew about `z` before still holds. Therefore, the right answers to fill in for points D and E are as follows:

	x > y	x == y	z == 0
Point D	always	never	never
Point E	never	never	never

Point F appears after the `if/else` statement. To determine the relationship between `x` and `y` at point F, we have to look at how the variables have changed. The `if/else` statement either divides `x` by 10 (if it is the larger value) or divides `y` by 10 (if it is the larger value). So, we have to ask whether it is possible for the assertion `x > y` to be true at point F. The answer is yes. For example, `x` might have been `218` and `y` might have been `6` before the `if/else` statement. In that case, `x` would now be `21`, which is still larger than `y`. But does it have to be larger than `y`? Not necessarily. The values might have been reversed, in which case `y` will be larger than `x`. So, that assertion is sometimes true and sometimes false at point F.

What about the assertion `x == y`? We know it doesn't have to be true because we have seen cases in which `x` is greater than `y` or `y` is greater than `x`. Is it possible for it to be true? Are there any values of `x` and `y` that would lead to this outcome? Consider the case in which `x` is `218` and `y` is `21`. Then we would divide `x` by 10 to get `21`, which would equal `y`. So, this assertion also is sometimes true and sometimes false.

There was no change to `z` between points D and E and point F, so we simply carry our answer down from the previous columns. So we would fill in the table as follows for point F:

	`x > y`	`x == y`	`z == 0`
Point F	sometimes	sometimes	never

Point G appears after the `while` loop:

```
while (x != y) {
    ...
}
// Point G
```

We can escape the `while` loop only if `x` becomes equal to `y`. So, at point G we know that the assertion `x == y` is always true. That means that the assertion `x > y` can never be true. The assertion `z == 0` is a little tricky. At point F it was never true, so you might imagine that at point G it can never be true. But we weren't necessarily at point F just before we reached point G. We might never have entered the `while` loop at all, in which case we would have been at point A just before point G. At point A the variable `z` was equal to `0`. Therefore, the right answer for this assertion is that it is sometimes true, sometimes false at point G. The final row of our table thus looks like this:

	`x > y`	`x == y`	`z == 0`
Point G!	never	always	sometimes

When we combine this information, we can fill in our table as follows:

	`x > y`	`x == y`	`z == 0`
Point A	sometimes	sometimes	always
Point B	sometimes	never	sometimes
Point C	sometimes	never	never
Point D	always	never	never
Point E	never	never	never
Point F	sometimes	sometimes	never
Point G	never	always	sometimes

5.6 Case Study: NumberGuess

If we combine indefinite loops, the ability to check for user errors, and random number generation, it's possible for us to create guessing games in which the computer thinks of random numbers and the user tries to guess them. Let's consider an example game with the following rules. The computer thinks of a random two-digit number but keeps it secret from the player. We'll allow the program to accept positive numbers only, so the acceptable range of numbers is `00` through `99` inclusive. The player will try to guess the number the computer picked. If the player guesses correctly, the program will report the number of guesses that the player made.

To make the game more interesting, the computer will give the player a hint each time the user enters an incorrect guess. Specifically, the computer will tell the player how many digits from the guess are contained in the correct answer. The order of the digits doesn't affect the number of digits that match. For example, if the correct number is `57` and the player guesses `73`, the computer will report one matching digit, because the correct answer contains a `7`. If the player next guesses `75`, the computer will report two matching digits. At this point the player knows that the computer's number must be `57`, because `57` is the only two-digit number whose digits match those of `75`.

Since the players will be doing a lot of console input, it's likely that they will type incorrect numbers or nonnumeric tokens by mistake. We'd like our guessing-game program to be robust against user input errors.

Initial Version without Hinting

In previous chapters, we've talked about the idea of iterative enhancement. Since this is a challenging program, we'll tackle it in stages. One of the hardest parts of the program is giving correct hints to the player. For now, we'll simply write a game that tells players whether they are correct or incorrect on each guess and, once the game is done, reports the number of guesses the players made. The program won't be robust against user input errors yet; that can be added later. To further simplify the game, rather than having the computer choose a random number, we'll choose a known value for the number so that the code can be tested more easily.

Since we don't know how many tries a player will need before correctly guessing the number, it seems that the main loop for this game will have to be a `while` loop. It might be tempting to write the code to match the following pseudocode:

```
// flawed number guess pseudocode
think of a number.
while (user has not guessed the number) {
    prompt and read a guess.
    report whether the guess was correct or incorrect.
}
```

But the problem with this pseudocode is that you can't start the `while` loop if you don't have a `guess` value from the player yet. The following code doesn't compile, because the variable `guess` isn't initialized when the loop begins:

```
// this code doesn't compile
int numGuesses = 0;
int number = 42; // computer always picks same number
int guess;

while (guess ! = number) {
    System.out.print("Your guess? ");
    guess = console.nextInt();
    numGuesses++;
    System.out.println("Incorrect.");
}

System.out.println("You got it right in " + numGuesses + " tries.");
```

It turns out that the game's main guess loop is a fencepost loop, because after each incorrect guess the program must print an "Incorrect" message (and later a hint). For *n* guesses, there are *n* – 1 hints. Recall the following general pseudocode for fencepost loops:

```
plant a post.
for (the length of the fence) {
    attach some wire.
    plant a post.
}
```

This particular problem is an indefinite fencepost using a `while` loop. Let's look at some more specific pseudocode. The "posts" are the prompts for guesses, and the "wires" are the "Incorrect" messages:

```
// specific number guess pseudocode
think of a number.
ask for the player's initial guess.
while (the guess is not the correct number) {
    inform the player that the guess was incorrect.
    ask for another guess.
}

report the number of guesses needed.
```

This pseudocode leads us to write the following Java program. Note that the computer always picks the value 42 in this version of the program:

```
import java.util.*;

public class NumberGuess1 {
    public static void main(String[] args) {
        Scanner console = new Scanner(System.in);
        int number = 42; // always picks the same number

        System.out.print("Your guess? ");
        int guess = console.nextInt();
        int numGuesses = 1;

        while (guess != number) {
            System.out.println("Incorrect.");
            System.out.print("Your guess? ");
            guess = console.nextInt();
            numGuesses++;
        }

        System.out.println("You got it right in " +
                           numGuesses + " tries.");
    }
}
```

We can test our initial program to verify the code we've written so far. A sample dialogue looks like this:

```
Your guess? 65
Incorrect.
Your guess? 12
Incorrect.
Your guess? 34
Incorrect.
Your guess? 42
You got it right in 4 tries.
```

Randomized Version with Hinting

Now that we've tested the code to make sure our main game loops, let's make the game random by choosing a random value between `00` and `99` inclusive. To do so, we'll create a `Random` object and call its `nextInt` method, specifying the maximum value. Remember that the value passed to `nextInt` should be one more than the desired maximum, so we'll pass `100`:

```
// pick a random number between 00 and 99 inclusive
Random rand = new Random();
int number = rand.nextInt(100);
```

The next important feature our game should have is to give a hint when the player makes an incorrect guess. The tricky part is figuring out how many digits of the player's guess match the correct number. Since this code is nontrivial to write, let's make a method called `matches` that does the work for us. To figure out how many digits match, the `matches` method needs to use the guess and the correct number as parameters. It will return the number of matching digits. Therefore, its header should look like this:

```
public static int matches(int number, int guess) {
    ...
}
```

Our algorithm must count the number of matching digits. Either digit from the guess can match either digit from the correct number. Since the digits are somewhat independent—that is, whether the ones digit of the guess matches is independent of whether the tens digit matches—we should use sequential `if` statements rather than an `if/else` statement to represent these conditions.

The digit-matching algorithm has one special case. If the player guesses a number such as `33` that contains two of the same digit, and if that digit is contained in the correct answer (say the correct answer is `37`), it would be misleading to report that two digits match. It makes more sense for the program to report one matching digit. To handle this case, our algorithm must check whether the guess contains two of the same digit and consider the second digit of the guess to be a match only if it is different from the first.

Here is the pseudocode for the algorithm:

```
matches = 0.
if (the first digit of the guess matches
      either digit of the correct number) {
    we have found one match.
}

if (the second digit of the guess is different from the first digit,
      AND it matches either digit of the correct number) {
    we have found another match.
}
```

We need to be able to split the correct number and the guess into the two digits that compose each so that we can compare them. Recall from the Boolean Zen section that we can use the division and remainder operators to express the digits of any two-digit number `n` as `n / 10` for the tens digit and `n % 10` for the ones digit.

Let's write the statement that compares the tens digit of the guess against the correct answer. Since the tens digit of the guess can match either of the correct number's digits, we'll use an OR test with the `||` operator:

```
int matches = 0;

// check the first digit for a match
if (guess / 10 == number / 10 || guess / 10 == number % 10) {
    matches++;
}
```

Writing the statement that compares the ones digit of the guess against the correct answer is slightly trickier, because we have to take into consideration the special case described previously (in which both digits of the guess are the same). We'll account for this by counting the second digit as a match only if it is unique *and* matches a digit from the correct number:

```
// check the second digit for a match
if (guess / 10 ! = guess % 10 &&
        (guess % 10 == number / 10 || guess % 10 == number % 10)) {
    matches++;
}
```

The following version of the program uses the hinting code we've just written. It also adds the randomly chosen number and a brief introduction to the program:

```
// Two-digit number-guessing game with hinting.
import java.util.*;

public class NumberGuess2 {
    public static void main(String[] args) {
        System.out.println("Try to guess my two-digit");
        System.out.println("number, and I'll tell you how");
        System.out.println("many digits from your guess");
        System.out.println("appear in my number.");
        System.out.println();

        Scanner console = new Scanner(System.in);

        // pick a random number from 0 to 99 inclusive
```

```
        Random rand = new Random();
        int number = rand.nextInt(100);

        // get first guess
        System.out.print("Your guess? ");
        int guess = console.nextInt();
        int numGuesses = 1;

        // give hints until correct guess is reached
        while (guess != number) {
            int numMatches = matches(number, guess);
            System.out.println("Incorrect (hint: " +
                               numMatches + " digits match)");
            System.out.print("Your guess? ");
            guess = console.nextInt();
            numGuesses++;
        }

        System.out.println("You got it right in " +
                           numGuesses + " tries.");
    }

    // returns how many digits from the given
    // guess match digits from the given correct number
    public static int matches(int number, int guess) {
        int numMatches = 0;

        if (guess / 10 == number / 10 ||
            guess / 10 == number % 10) {
            numMatches++;
        }

        if (guess / 10 ! = guess % 10 &&
                (guess % 10 == number / 10 ||
                guess % 10 == number % 10)) {
            numMatches++;
        }

        return numMatches;
    }
}
```

The following is a sample log of the program execution:

```
Try to guess my two-digit
number, and I'll tell you how
many digits from your guess
appear in my number.

Your guess? 13
Incorrect (hint: 0 digits match)
Your guess? 26
Incorrect (hint: 0 digits match)
Your guess? 78
Incorrect (hint: 1 digits match)
Your guess? 79
Incorrect (hint: 1 digits match)
Your guess? 70
Incorrect (hint: 2 digits match)
Your guess? 7
You got it right in 6 tries.
```

Final Robust Version

The last major change we'll make to our program is to make it robust against invalid user input. There are two types of bad input that we may see:

1. Nonnumeric tokens.
2. Numbers outside the range of 0–99.

Let's deal with these cases one at a time. Recall the `getInt` method that was discussed earlier in this chapter. It repeatedly prompts the user for input until an integer is typed. Here is its header:

```
public static int getInt(Scanner console, String prompt)
```

We can make use of `getInt` to get an integer between 0 and 99. We'll repeatedly call `getInt` until the integer that is returned is within the acceptable range. The postcondition we require before we can stop prompting for guesses is:

```
guess >= 0 && guess <= 99
```

To ensure that this postcondition is met, we can use a `while` loop that tests for the opposite condition. Using De Morgan's law, we know that the opposite of the previous test would be the following:

```
guess < 0 || guess > 99
```

The reversed test is used in our new `getGuess` method to get a valid guess between 0 and 99. Now whenever we want to read user input in the main program, we'll call `getGuess`. It's useful to separate the input prompting in this way, to make sure that we don't accidentally count invalid inputs as guesses.

The final version of our code is the following:

```
// Robust two-digit number-guessing game with hinting.
import java.util.*;

public class NumberGuess3 {
    public static void main(String[] args) {
        giveIntro();
        Scanner console = new Scanner(System.in);

        // pick a random number from 0 to 99 inclusive
        Random rand = new Random();
        int number = rand.nextInt(100);

        // get first guess
        int guess = getGuess(console);
        int numGuesses = 1;

        // give hints until correct guess is reached
        while (guess != number) {
            int numMatches = matches(number, guess);
            System.out.println("Incorrect (hint: " +
                               numMatches + " digits match)");
            guess = getGuess(console);
            numGuesses++;
        }

        System.out.println("You got it right in " +
                           numGuesses + " tries.");
    }

    public static void giveIntro() {
        System.out.println("Try to guess my two-digit");
        System.out.println("number, and I'll tell you how");
        System.out.println("many digits from your guess");
        System.out.println("appear in my number.");
        System.out.println();
    }

    // returns # of matching digits between the two numbers
```

```
    // pre: number and guess are unique two-digit numbers
    public static int matches(int number, int guess) {
        int numMatches = 0;

        if (guess / 10 == number / 10 ||
                guess / 10 == number % 10) {
            numMatches++;
        }

        if (guess / 10 != guess % 10 &&
                (guess % 10 == number / 10 ||
                guess % 10 == number % 10)) {
            numMatches++;
        }

        return numMatches;
    }

    // prompts until a number in proper range is entered
    // post: guess is between 0 and 99
    public static int getGuess(Scanner console) {
        int guess = getInt(console, "Your guess? ");
        while (guess < 0 || guess >= 100) {
            System.out.println("Out of range; try again.");
            guess = getInt(console, "Your guess? ");
        }

        return guess;
    }

    // prompts until a valid number is entered
    public static int getInt(Scanner console, String prompt) {
        System.out.print(prompt);
        while (!console.hasNextInt()) {
            console.next(); // to discard the input
            System.out.println("Not an integer; try again.");
            System.out.print(prompt);
        }
        return console.nextInt();
    }
}
```

The following sample log of execution demonstrates the new input robustness of this program:

```
Try to guess my two-digit
number, and I'll tell you how
many digits from your guess
appear in my number.

Your guess? 12
Incorrect (hint: 0 digits match)
Your guess? okay
Not an integer; try again.
Your guess? 34
Incorrect (hint: 1 digits match)
Your guess? 35
Incorrect (hint: 1 digits match)
Your guess? 67
Incorrect (hint: 0 digits match)
Your guess? 89
Incorrect (hint: 0 digits match)
Your guess? 3
Incorrect (hint: 2 digits match)
Your guess? 300
Out of range; try again.
Your guess? 30
You got it right in 7 tries.
```

Notice that we're careful to comment our code to document relevant preconditions and postconditions of our methods. The precondition of the `matches` method is that the two parameters are unique two-digit numbers. The postcondition of our new `getGuesses` method is that it returns a guess between 0 and 99 inclusive. Also, note that the program does not count invalid input (`okay` and `300` in the previous sample log of execution) as guesses.

Chapter Summary

Java has a `while` loop in addition to its `for` loop. The `while` loop can be used to write indefinite loops that keep executing until some condition fails.

Priming a loop means setting the values of variables that will be used in the loop test, so that the test will be sure to succeed the first time and the loop will execute.

Java can generate pseudorandom numbers using objects of the `Random` class.

The `do/while` loop is a variation on the `while` loop that performs its loop test at the end of the loop body. A `do/while` loop is guaranteed to execute its body at least once.

A fencepost loop executes a "loop-and-a-half" by executing part of a loop's body once before the loop begins.

A sentinel loop is a kind of fencepost loop that repeatedly processes input until it is passed a particular value, but does not process the special value.

The `boolean` primitive type represents logical values of either `true` or `false`. Boolean expressions are used as tests in `if` statements and loops. Boolean expressions can use relational operators such as < or `!=` as well as logical operators such as `&&` or `!`.

Complex Boolean tests with logical operators such as `&&` or `||` are evaluated lazily: If the overall result is clear from evaluating the first part of the expression, later parts are not evaluated. This is called short-circuited evaluation.

`Boolean` variables (sometimes called "flags") can store Boolean values and can be used as loop tests.

A complex Boolean expression can be negated using a set of rules known as De Morgan's laws, in which each sub-expression is negated and all AND and OR operations are swapped.

A robust program checks for errors in user input. Better robustness can be achieved by looping and reprompting the user to enter input when he or she types bad input. The `Scanner` class has methods like `hasNextInt` that you can use to "look ahead" for valid input.

Assertions are logical statements about a particular point in a program. Assertions are useful for proving properties about how a program will execute. Two useful types of assertions are preconditions and postconditions, which are claims about what will be true before and after a method executes.

Self-Check Problems

Section 5.1: The `while` Loop

1. For each of the following `while` loops, state how many times the loop will execute its body. Remember that "zero," "infinity," and "unknown" are legal answers. Also, what is the output of the code in each case?

a.
```
int x = 1;
while (x < 100) {
     System.out.print(x + " ");
     x += 10;
}
```

b.
```
int max = 10;
while (max < 10) {
     System.out.println("count down: " + max);
     max--;
}
```

c.
```
int x = 250;
while (x % 3 != 0) {
     System.out.println(x);
}
```

d.
```
int x = 2;
while (x < 200) {
     System.out.print(x + " ");
     x *= x;
}
```
e.
```
String word = "a";
while (word.length() < 10) {
     word = "b" + word + "b";
}
System.out.println(word);
```
f.
```
int x = 100;
while (x > 0) {
     System.out.println(x / 10);
     x = x / 2;
}
```

2. Convert each of the following `for` loops into an equivalent `while` loop:

a.
```
for (int n = 1; n <= max; n++) {
     System.out.println(n);
 }
```
b.
```
int total = 25;
for (int number = 1; number <= (total / 2); number++) {
     total = total – number;
     System.out.println(total + " " + number);
}
```
c.
```
for (int i = 1; i <= 2; i++) {
     for (int j = 1; j <= 3; j++) {
          for (int k = 1; k <= 4; k++) {
               System.out.print("*");
          }
          System.out.print("!");
     }
     System.out.println();
}
```
d.
```
int number = 4;
for (int count = 1; count <= number; count++) {
     System.out.println(number);
     number = number / 2;
}
```

3. Consider the following method:

```
public static void mystery(int x) {
     int y = 1;
     int z = 0;
     while (2 * y <= x) {
          y = y * 2;
```

```
        z++;
    }
    System.out.println(y + " " + z);
}
```

For each of the following calls, indicate the output that the preceding method produces:

```
mystery(1);
mystery(6);
mystery(19);
mystery(39);
mystery(74);
```

4. Consider the following method:

```
public static void mystery(int x) {
    int y = 0;
    while (x % 2 == 0) {
        y++;
        x = x / 2;
    }
    System.out.println(x + " " + y);
}
```

For each of the following calls, indicate the output that the preceding method produces:

```
mystery(19);
mystery(42);
mystery(48);
mystery(40);
mystery(64);
```

5. Consider the following code:

```
Random rand = new Random();
int a = rand.nextInt(100);
int b = rand.nextInt(20) + 50;
int c = rand.nextInt(20 + 50);
int d = rand.nextInt(100) – 20;
int e = rand.nextInt(10) * 4;
```

What range of values can each variable (`a`, `b`, `c`, `d`, and `e`) have?

6. Write code that generates a random integer between `0` and `10` inclusive.

7. Write code that generates a random odd integer (not divisible by `2`) between `50` and `99` inclusive.

8. For each of the `do/while` loops that follow, state the number of times that the loop will execute its body. Remember that "zero," "infinity," and "unknown" are legal answers. Also, what is the output of the code in each case?

a.
```
int x = 1;
do {
```

```
        System.out.print(x + " ");
        x = x + 10;
    } while (x < 100);
```

b.
```
int max = 10;
do {
    System.out.println("count down: " + max);
    max--;
} while (max < 10);
```

c.
```
int x = 250;
do {
    System.out.println(x);
} while (x % 3 != 0);
```

d.
```
int x = 100;
do {
    System.out.println(x);
    x = x / 2;
} while (x % 2 == 0);
```

e.
```
int x = 2;
do {
    System.out.print(x + " ");
    x *= x;
} while (x < 200);
```

f.
```
String word = "a";
do {
    word = "b" + word + "b";
} while (word.length() < 10);
System.out.println(word);
```

g.
```
int x = 100;
do {
    System.out.println(x / 10);
    x = x / 2;
} while (x > 0);
```

h.
```
String str = "/\\";
do {
    str += str;
} while (str.length() < 10);
System.out.println(str);
```

9. Write a `do/while` loop that repeatedly prints a certain message until the user tells the program to stop. The `do/while` is appropriate because the message should always be printed at least one time, even if the user types `n` after the first message appears. The message to be printed is as follows:

```
She sells seashells by the seashore.
Do you want to hear it again? y
She sells seashells by the seashore.
Do you want to hear it again? y
```

```
She sells seashells by the seashore.
Do you want to hear it again? n
```

10. Write a method called `zeroDigits` that accepts an integer parameter and returns the number of digits in the number that have the value `0`. For example, the call `zeroDigits(5024036)` should return `2`, and `zeroDigits(743)` should return `0`. The call `zeroDigits(0)` should return `1`. (We suggest you use a `do/while` loop in your solution.)

11. Write a `do/while` loop that repeatedly prints random numbers between `0` and `1000` until a number above `900` is printed. At least one line of output should always be printed, even if the first random number is above `900`. Here is a sample execution:

```
Random number: 235
Random number: 15
Random number: 810
Random number: 147
Random number: 915
```

Section 5.2: Fencepost Algorithms

12. Consider the flawed method `printLetters` that follows, which accepts a `String` as its parameter and attempts to print the letters of the `String`, separated by dashes. For example, the call of `printLetters("Rabbit")` should print `R-a-b-b-i-t`. The following code is incorrect:

```
public static void printLetters(String text) {
    for (int i = 0; i < text.length(); i++) {
        System.out.print(text.charAt(i) + "-");
    }
    System.out.println(); // to end the line of output
}
```

What is wrong with the code? How can it be corrected to produce the desired behavior?

13. Write a sentinel loop that repeatedly prompts the user to enter a number and, once the number `-1` is typed, displays the maximum and minimum numbers that the user entered. Here is a sample dialogue:

```
Type a number (or -1 to stop): 5
Type a number (or -1 to stop): 2
Type a number (or -1 to stop): 17
Type a number (or -1 to stop): 8
Type a number (or -1 to stop): -1
Maximum was 17
Minimum was 2
```

If `-1` is the first number typed, no maximum or minimum should be printed. In this case, the dialogue would look like this:

```
Type a number (or -1 to stop): -1
```

Section 5.3: The `boolean` Type

14. Consider the following variable declarations:

```
int x = 27;
int y = -1;
```

```
int z = 32;
boolean b = false;
```

What is the value of each of the following Boolean expressions?

a. `!b`
b. `b || true`
c. `(x > y) && (y > z)`
d. `(x == y) || (x <= z)`
e. `!(x % 2 == 0)`
f. `(x % 2 != 0) && b`
g. `b && !b`
h. `b || !b`
i. `(x < y) == b`
j. `!(x / 2 == 13) || b || (z * 3 == 96)`
k. `(z < x) == false`
l. `!((x > 0) && (y < 0))`

15. Write a method called `isVowel` that accepts a character as input and returns `true` if that character is a vowel (a, e, i, o, or u). For an extra challenge, make your method case-insensitive.

16. The following code attempts to examine a number and return whether that number is prime (i.e., has no factors other than 1 and itself). A flag named `prime` is used. However, the Boolean logic is not implemented correctly, so the method does not always return the correct answer. In what cases does the method report an incorrect answer? How can the code be changed so that it will always return a correct result?

```
public static boolean isPrime(int n) {
    boolean prime = true;
    for (int i = 2; i < n; i++) {
        if (n % i == 0) {
            prime = false;
        } else {
            prime = true;
        }
    }

    return prime;
}
```

17. The following code attempts to examine a `String` and return whether it contains a given letter. A flag named `found` is used. However, the Boolean logic is not implemented correctly, so the method does not always return the correct answer. In what cases does the method report an incorrect answer? How can the code be changed so that it will always return a correct result?

```
public static boolean contains(String str, char ch) {
    boolean found = false;
    for (int i = 0; i < str.length(); i++) {
        if (str.charAt(i) == ch) {
            found = true;
```

```
        } else {
            found = false;
        }
    }
    return found;
}
```

18. Using "Boolean Zen," write an improved version of the following method, which returns whether the given `String` starts and ends with the same character:

```
public static boolean startEndSame(String str) {
    if (str.charAt(0) == str.charAt(str.length() – 1)) {
        return true;
    } else {
        return false;
    }
}
```

19. Using "Boolean Zen," write an improved version of the following method, which returns whether the given number of cents would require any pennies (as opposed to being an amount that could be made exactly using coins other than pennies):

```
public static boolean hasPennies(int cents) {
    boolean nickelsOnly = (cents % 5 == 0);
    if (nickelsOnly == true) {
        return false;
    } else {
        return true;
    }
}
```

20. Consider the following method:

```
public static int mystery(int x, int y) {
    while (x != 0 && y != 0) {
        if (x < y) {
            y –= x;
        } else {
            x –= y;
        }
    }
    return x + y;
}
```

For each of the following calls, indicate the value that is returned:

```
mystery(3, 3)
mystery(5, 3)
mystery(2, 6)
```

```
mystery(12, 18)
mystery(30, 75)
```

21. The following code is a slightly modified version of actual code that was in the Microsoft Zune music player in 2008. The code attempts to calculate today's date by determining how many years and days have passed since 1980. Assume the existence of methods for getting the total number of days since 1980 and for determining whether a given year is a leap year:

```
int days = getTotalDaysSince1980();
year = 1980;
while (days > 365) { // subtract out years
    if (isLeapYear(year)) {
        if (days > 366) {
            days -= 366;
            year += 1;
        }
    } else {
        days -= 365;
        year += 1;
    }
}
```

Thousands of Zune players locked up on January 1, 2009, the first day after the end of a leap year since the Zune was released. (Microsoft quickly released a patch to fix the problem.) What is the problem with the preceding code, and in what cases will it exhibit incorrect behavior? How can it be fixed?

22. Which of the following is a properly reversed version of the following Boolean expression, according to De Morgan's Laws?

```
(2 == 3) && (-1 < 5) && isPrime(n)
```

a. `(2 != 3) && (-1 > 5) && isPrime(n)`
b. `(2 == 3) || (-1 < 5) || isPrime(n)`
c. `!(2 == 3) && !(-1 < 5) && !isPrime(n)`
d. `(2 != 3) || (-1 >= 5) || !isPrime(n)`
e. `!(2 != 3) || !(-1 < 5) || isNotPrime(n)`

Section 5.4: User Errors

23. The following code is not robust against invalid user input. Describe how to change the code so that it will not proceed until the user has entered a valid age and grade point average (GPA). Assume that any `int` is a legal age and that any `double` is a legal GPA.

```
Scanner console = new Scanner(System.in);
System.out.print("Type your age: ");
int age = console.nextInt();
System.out.print("Type your GPA: ");
double gpa = console.nextDouble();
```

For an added challenge, modify the code so that it rejects invalid ages (for example, numbers less than 0) and GPAs (say, numbers less than 0.0 or greater than 4.0).

24. Consider the following code:

```
Scanner console = new Scanner(System.in);
System.out.print("Type something for me! ");
if (console.hasNextInt()) {
   int number = console.nextInt();
   System.out.println("Your IQ is " + number);
} else if (console.hasNext()) {
   String token = console.next();
   System.out.println("Your name is " + token);
}
```

What is the output when the user types the following values?

a. `Jane`   b. `56`   c. `56.2`

25. Write a piece of code that prompts the user for a number and then prints a different message depending on whether the number was an integer or a real number. Here are two sample dialogues:

```
Type a number: 42.5
You typed the real number 42.5

Type a number: 3
You typed the integer 3
```

26. Write code that prompts for three integers, averages them, and prints the average. Make your code robust against invalid input. (You may want to use the `getInt` method discussed in this chapter.)

Section 5.5: Assertions and Program Logic

27. Identify the various assertions in the following code as being always true, never true, or sometimes true and sometimes false at various points in program execution. The comments indicate the points of interest:

```
public static int mystery(Scanner console, int x) {
    int y = console.nextInt();
    int count = 0;

    // Point A
    while (y < x) {
        // Point B
        if (y == 0) {
            count++;
            // Point C
        }
        y = console.nextInt();
        // Point D
    }

    // Point E
    return count;
}
```

Categorize each assertion at each point with ALWAYS, NEVER, or SOMETIMES:

	`y < x`	`y == 0`	`count > 0`
Point A			
Point B			
Point C			
Point D			
Point E			

28. Identify the various assertions in the following code as being always true, never true, or sometimes true and sometimes false at various points in program execution. The comments indicate the points of interest:

```
public static int mystery(int n) {
    Random r = new Random();
    int a = r.nextInt(3) + 1;
    int b = 2;
    // Point A
    while (n > b) {
        // Point B
        b = b + a;
        if (a > 1) {
            n--;
            // Point C
            a = r.nextInt(b) + 1;
        } else {
            a = b + 1;

            // Point D
        }
    }
    // Point E
    return n;
}
```

Categorize each assertion at each point with ALWAYS, NEVER, or SOMETIMES:

	`n > b`	`a > 1`	`b > a`
Point A			
Point B			
Point C			
Point D			
Point E			

29. Identify the various assertions in the following code as being always true, never true, or sometimes true and sometimes false at various points in program execution. The comments indicate the points of interest:

```
public static int mystery(Scanner console) {
    int prev = 0;
    int count = 0;
    int next = console.nextInt();
    // Point A
    while (next != 0) {
        // Point B
        if (next == prev) {
            // Point C
            count++;
        }
        prev = next;
        next = console.nextInt();
        // Point D
    }
    // Point E
    return count;
}
```

Categorize each assertion at each point with ALWAYS, NEVER, or SOMETIMES:

	`next == 0`	`prev == 0`	`next == prev`
Point A			
Point B			
Point C			
Point D			
Point E			

Exercises

1. Write a method called `showTwos` that shows the factors of 2 in a given integer. For example, consider the following calls:

```
showTwos(7);
showTwos(18);
showTwos(68);
showTwos(120);
```

These calls should produce the following output:

```
7 = 7
18 = 2 * 9
68 = 2 * 2 * 17
120 = 2 * 2 * 2 * 15
```

2. Write a method called `gcd` that accepts two integers as parameters and returns the greatest common divisor (GCD) of the two numbers. The GCD of two integers `a` and `b` is the largest integer that is a factor of both `a` and `b`.

One efficient way to compute the GCD of two numbers is to use Euclid's algorithm, which states the following:

GCD (a, b) = GCD $(b, a \% b)$

GCD $(a, 0)$ = Absolute value of a

3. Write a method called `toBinary` that accepts an integer as a parameter and returns a `String` containing that integer's binary representation. For example, the call of `printBinary(44)` should return `"101100"`.

4. Write a method called `randomX` that prints a lines that contain a random number of "x" characters (between 5 and 20 inclusive) until it prints a line that contains 16 or more characters. For example, the output might look like the following:

```
xxxxxxx
xxxxxxxxxxxxxxx
xxxxxxxxxxxx
xxxxxxxxxxxxxx
xxxxxx
xxxxxxxxxxx
xxxxxxxxxxxxxxxxx
```

5. Write a method called `randomLines` that prints between 5 and 10 random strings of letters (between "a" and "z"), one per line. Each string should have random length of up to 80 characters.

6. Write a method called `makeGuesses` that guesses numbers between `1` and `50` inclusive until it makes a guess of at least `48`. It should report each guess and at the end should report the total number of guesses made. Here is a sample execution:

```
guess = 43
guess = 47
guess = 45
guess = 27
guess = 49
total guesses = 5
```

7. Write a method called `diceSum` that accepts a `Scanner` for the console as a parameter and prompts for a desired sum, then repeatedly simulates the rolling of 2 six-sided dice until their sum is the desired sum. Here is a sample dialogue with the user:

```
Desired dice sum: 9
4 and 3 = 7
3 and 5 = 8
5 and 6 = 11
5 and 6 = 11
1 and 5 = 6
6 and 3 = 9
```

8. Write a method called `randomWalk` that performs steps of a random one-dimensional walk. The random walk should begin at position 0. On each step, you should either increase or decrease the position by 1 (each with equal probability). Your code should continue making steps until a position of 3 or −3 is reached, and then report the maximum position that was reached during the walk. The output should look like the following:

```
position = 1
position = 0
position = -1
position = -2
position = -1
position = -2
position = -3
max position = 1
```

9. Write a method called `printFactors` that accepts an integer as its parameter and uses a fencepost loop to print the factors of that number, separated by the word `"and"`. For example, the factors of the number 24 should print as the following:

```
1 and 2 and 3 and 4 and 6 and 8 and 12 and 24
```

You may assume that the parameter's value is greater than `0`, or you may throw an exception if it is `0` or negative. Your method should print nothing if the empty string (`""`) is passed.

10. Write a method called `hopscotch` that accepts an integer number of "hops" as its parameter and prints a pattern of numbers that resembles a hopscotch board. A "hop" is a three-number sequence where the output shows two numbers on a line, followed by one number on its own line. 0 hops is a board up to 1; one hop is a board up to 4; two hops is a board up to 7; and so on. For example, the call of `hopscotch(3);` should print the following output:

```
   1
2     3
   4
5     6
   7
8     9
  10
```

A call of `hopscotch(0);` should print only the number 1. If it is passed a negative value, the method should produce no output.

11. Write a method called `threeHeads` that repeatedly flips a coin until the results of the coin toss are three heads in a row. You should use a `Random` object to make it equally likely that a head or a tail will appear. Each time the coin is flipped, display H for heads or T for tails. When three heads in a row are flipped, the method should print a congratulatory message. Here is a possible output of a call to the method:

```
T T H T T T H T H T H H H
Three heads in a row!
```

12. Write a method called `printAverage` that uses a sentinel loop to repeatedly prompt the user for numbers. Once the user types any number less than zero, the method should display the average of all nonnegative numbers typed. Display the average as a `double`. Here is a sample dialogue with the user:

```
Type a number: 7
Type a number: 4
Type a number: 16
Type a number: -4
Average was 9.0
```

If the first number that the user types is negative, do not print an average:

```
Type a number: -2
```

13. Write a method called `consecutive` that accepts three integers as parameters and returns `true` if they are three consecutive numbers—that is, if the numbers can be arranged into an order such that, assuming some integer `k`, the parameters' values are `k`, `k + 1`, and `k + 2`. Your method should return `false` if the integers are not consecutive. Note that order is not significant; your method should return the same result for the same three integers passed in any order.

    For example, the calls `consecutive(1, 2, 3)`, `consecutive(3, 2, 4)`, and `consecutive(-10, -8, -9)` would return `true`. The calls `consecutive(3, 5, 7)`, `consecutive(1, 2, 2)`, and `consecutive(7, 7, 9)` would return `false`.

14. Write a method called `hasMidpoint` that accepts three integers as parameters and returns `true` if one of the integers is the midpoint between the other two integers; that is, if one integer is exactly halfway between them. Your method should return `false` if no such midpoint relationship exists. For example, the call `hasMidpoint(7, 4, 10)` should return `true` because 7 is halfway between 4 and 10. By contrast, the call `hasMidpoint(9, 15, 8)` should return `false` because no integer is halfway between the other two. The integers could be passed in any order; the midpoint could be the 1st, 2nd, or 3rd. You must check all cases. If your method is passed three of the same value, return `true`.

15. Write a method called `dominant` that accepts three integers as parameters and returns `true` if any one of the three integers is larger than the sum of the other two integers. The integers might be passed in any order, so the largest value could be any of the three. For example, the call `dominant(4, 9, 2)` returns `true` because 9 is larger than 4 + 2. Assume that none of the numbers is negative.

16. Write a method called `anglePairs` that accepts three angles (integers), measured in degrees, as parameters and returns whether or not there exist both complementary and supplementary angles among the three angles passed. Two angles are complementary if their sum is exactly 90 degrees; two angles are supplementary if their sum is exactly 180 degrees. Therefore, the method should return `true` if any two of the three angles add up to 90 degrees and also any two of the three angles add up to 180 degrees. For example, the call `anglePairs(120, 60, 30)` returns `true`. Assume that each angle passed is nonnegative.

17. Write a method called `monthApart` that accepts four integer parameters, *m1*, *d1*, *m2*, and *d2*, representing two calendar dates. Each date consists of a month (1 through 12) and a day (1 through the number of days in that month [28–31]). Assume that all parameter values passed are valid. The method should return `true` if the dates are at least a month apart and `false` otherwise. For example, the call of `monthApart(4, 15, 5, 22)` would return `true` while the call of `monthApart(9, 19, 10, 17)` would return `false`. Assume that all the dates in this problem occur during the same year. Note that the first date could come before or after the second date.

18. Write a method called `digitSum` that accepts an integer as a parameter and returns the sum of the digits of that number. For example, the call `digitSum(29107)` returns 2 + 9 + 1 + 0 + 7 or `19`. For negative numbers, return the same value that would result if the number were positive. For example, `digitSum(-456)` returns 4 + 5 + 6 or `15`. The call `digitSum(0)` returns `0`.

19. Write a method called `firstDigit` that returns the first (most significant) digit of an integer. For example, `firstDigit(3572)` should return `3`. It should work for negative numbers as well; `firstDigit(-947)` should return `9`.

20. Write a method called `digitRange` that accepts an integer as a parameter and returns the range of values of its digits. The range is defined as 1 more than the difference between the largest and smallest digit value. For example, the call of `digitRange(68437)` would return `6` because the largest digit value is 8 and the smallest is 3, so $8 - 3 + 1 = 6$. If the number contains only one digit, return `1`. You should solve this problem without using a `String`.

21. Write a method called `swapDigitPairs` that accepts an integer *n* as a parameter and returns a new integer whose value is similar to *n*'s but with each pair of digits swapped in order. For example, the call of `swapDigitPairs(482596)` would return `845269`. Notice that the 9 and 6 are swapped, as are the 2 and 5, and the 4 and 8. If the number contains an odd number of digits, leave the leftmost digit in its original place. For example, the call of `swapDigitPairs(1234567)` would return `1325476`. You should solve this problem without using a `String`.

22. Write a method called `allDigitsOdd` that returns whether every digit of a positive integer is odd. Return `true` if the number consists entirely of odd digits (1, 3, 5, 7, 9) and `false` if any of its digits are even (0, 2, 4, 6, 8). For example, the call `allDigitsOdd(135319)` returns `true` but `allDigitsOdd(9145293)` returns `false`.

23. Write a method called `hasAnOddDigit` that returns whether a given positive integer has at least one digit whose value is odd. Return `true` if the number has at least one odd digit and `false` if none of its digits are odd. For example, the call `hasAnOddDigit(4822116)` should return `true` and `hasAnOddDigit(2448)` should return `false`.

24. Write a method called `isAllVowels` that returns whether a string consists entirely of vowels (a, e, i, o, or u, case-insensitively). If and only if every character of the string is a vowel, your method should return `true`. For example, the call `isAllVowels("eIEiO")` returns `true` and `isAllVowels("oink")` returns `false`. You should return `true` if passed the empty string, since it does not contain any non-vowel characters.

Programming Projects

1. Write an interactive program that reads lines of input from the user and converts each line into "Pig Latin." Pig Latin is English with the initial consonant sound moved to the end of each word, followed by "ay." Words that begin with vowels simply have an "ay" appended. For example, the phrase

```
The deepest shade of mushroom blue
```

would have the following appearance in Pig Latin:

```
e-Thay eepest-day ade-shay of-ay ushroom-may ue-blay
```

Terminate the program when the user types a blank line.

2. Write a reverse Hangman game in which the user thinks of a word and the computer tries to guess the letters in that word. The user tells the computer how many letters the word contains.

3. Write a program that plays a guessing game with the user. The program should generate a random number between `1` and some maximum (such as `100`), then prompt the user repeatedly to guess the number. When the user guesses incorrectly, the game should give the user a hint about whether the correct answer is higher or lower than the guess. Once the user guesses correctly, the program should print a message showing the number of guesses that the user made.

Consider extending this program by making it play multiple games until the user chooses to stop and then printing statistics about the player's total and average number of guesses.

4. Write a program that plays a reverse guessing game with the user. The user thinks of a number between `1` and `10`, and the computer repeatedly tries to guess it by guessing random numbers. It's fine for the computer to guess the same random number more than once. At the end of the game, the program reports how many guesses it made. Here is a sample execution:

```
This program has you, the user, choose a number
between 1 and 10. Then I, the computer, will try
my best to guess it.
Is it 8? (y/n) n
Is it 7? (y/n) n
Is it 5? (y/n) n
Is it 1? (y/n) n
Is it 8? (y/n) n
Is it 1? (y/n) n
Is it 9? (y/n) y
I got your number of 9 correct in 7 guesses.
```

For an added challenge, consider having the user hint to the computer whether the correct number is higher or lower than the computer's guess. The computer should adjust its range of random guesses on the basis of the hint.

5. Write a game that plays many rounds of Rock Paper Scissors. The user and computer will each choose between three items: rock (defeats scissors, but loses to paper), paper (defeats rock, but loses to scissors), and scissors (defeats paper, but loses to rock). If the player and computer choose the same item, the game is a tie.

You could extend this program to include different algorithmic strategies for choosing the best item. Should the computer pick randomly? Should it always pick a particular item or a repeating pattern of items? Should it count the number of times the opponent chooses various items and base its strategy on this history?

6. Write a program that draws a graphical display of a 2D random walk using a `DrawingPanel`. Start a pixel walker in the middle of the panel. On each step, choose to move 1 pixel up, down, left, or right, then redraw the pixel. (You can draw a single pixel by drawing a rectangle of size 1×1.)

7. Write a program that plays the dice game "Pig." Pig is a two-player game where the players take turns repeatedly rolling a single 6-sided die; a player repeatedly rolls the die until one of two events occurs. Either the player chooses to stop rolling, in which case the sum of that player's roll are added to his/her total points; or if the player rolls a 1 at any time, all points for that turn are lost and the turn ends immediately. The first player to reach a score of at least 100 points wins.

Chapter 6

File Processing

Introduction

In Chapter 3 we discussed how to construct a `Scanner` object to read input from the console. Now we will look at how to construct `Scanner` objects to read input from files. The idea is fairly straightforward, but Java does not make it easy to read from input files. This is unfortunate because many interesting problems can be formulated as file-processing tasks. Many introductory computer science classes have abandoned file processing altogether and left the topic for the second course because it is considered too advanced for novices.

There is nothing intrinsically complex about file processing, but Java was not designed for it and the designers of Java have not been particularly eager to provide a simple solution. They did, however, introduce the `Scanner` class as a way to simplify some of the details associated with reading files. The result is that file reading is still awkward in Java, but at least the level of detail is manageable.

Before we start writing file-processing programs, we have to explore some issues related to Java exceptions. Remember that exceptions are errors that halt the execution of a program. In the case of file processing, trying to open a file that doesn't exist or trying to read beyond the end of a file generates an exception.

6.1 File-Reading Basics

In this section, we'll look at the most basic issues related to file processing. What are files and why do we care about them? What are the most basic techniques for reading files in a Java program? Once you've mastered these basics, we'll move on to a more detailed discussion of the different techniques you can use to process files.

Data, Data Everywhere

People are fascinated by data. When the field of statistics emerged in the nineteenth century, there was an explosion of interest in gathering and interpreting large amounts of data. Mark Twain reported that the British statesman Benjamin Disraeli complained to him, "There are three kinds of lies: lies, damn lies, and statistics."

The advent of the Internet has only added fuel to the fire. Today, every person with an Internet connection has access to a vast array of databases containing information about every facet of our existence. Here are just a few examples:

- If you visit http://www.landmark-project.com and click on the link for "Raw Data," you will find data files about earthquakes, air pollution, baseball, labor, crime, financial markets, U.S. history, geography, weather, national parks, a "world values survey," and more.
- At http://www.gutenberg.org you'll find thousands of online books, including the complete works of Shakespeare and works by Sir Arthur Conan Doyle, Jane Austen, H.G. Wells, James Joyce, Albert Einstein, Mark Twain, Lewis Carroll, T.S. Eliot, Edgar Allan Poe, and many others.
- A wealth of genomic data is available from sites like http://www.ncbi.nlm.nih.gov/guide/. Biologists have decided that the vast quantities of data describing the human genome and the genomes of other organisms should be publicly available to everyone to study.
- Many popular web sites, such as the Internet Movie Database, make their data available for download as simple data files (see http://www.imdb.com/interfaces).
- The U.S. government produces reams of statistical data. The web site http://www.fedstats.gov provides a lengthy list of available downloads, including maps and statistics on employment, climate, manufacturing, demographics, health, crime, and more.

Files and File Objects

When you store data on your own computer, you store it in a *file*.

> **File**
>
> A collection of information that is stored on a computer and assigned a particular name.

As we have just noted, every file has a name. For example, if you were to download the text of *Hamlet* from the Gutenberg site, you might store it on your computer

Did You Know?

Origin of Data Processing

The field of data processing predates computers by over half a century. It is often said that necessity is the mother of invention, and the emergence of data processing is a good example of this principle. The crisis that spawned the industry came from a requirement in Article 1, Section 2, of the U.S. Constitution, which indicates that each state's population will determine how many representatives that state gets in the House of Representatives. To calculate the correct number, you need to know the population, so the Constitution says, "The actual Enumeration shall be made within three Years after the first Meeting of the Congress of the United States, and within every subsequent Term of ten Years, in such Manner as they shall by Law direct."

The first census was completed relatively quickly in 1790. Since then, every 10 years the U.S. government has had to perform another complete census of the population. This process became more and more difficult as the population of the country grew larger. By 1880 the government discovered that using old-fashioned hand-counting techniques, it barely completed the census within the 10 years allotted to it. So the government announced a competition for inventors to propose machines that could be used to speed up the process.

Herman Hollerith won the competition with a system involving punched cards. Clerks punched over 62 million cards that were then counted by 100 counting machines. This system allowed the 1890 tabulation to be completed in less than half the time it had taken to hand-count the 1880 results, even though the population had increased by 25 percent.

Hollerith struggled for years to turn his invention into a commercial success. His biggest problem initially was that he had just one customer: the U.S. government. Eventually he found other customers, and the company that he founded merged with competitors and grew into the company we now know as International Business Machines Corporation, or IBM.

We think of IBM as a computer company, but it sold a wide variety of data-processing equipment involving Hollerith cards long before computers became popular. Later, when it entered the computer field, IBM used Hollerith cards for storing programs and data. These cards were still being used when one of this book's authors took his freshman computer programming class in 1978.

in a file called `hamlet.txt`. A file name often ends with a special suffix that indicates the kind of data it contains or the format in which it has been stored. This suffix is known as a *file extension.* Table 6.1 lists some common file extensions.

Table 6.1 Common File Extensions

Extension	Description
`.txt`	text file
`.java`	Java source code file
`.class`	compiled Java bytecode file
`.doc`	Microsoft Word file
`.xls`	Microsoft Excel file
`.pdf`	Adobe Portable Document File
`.mp3`	audio file
`.jpg`	image file
`.zip`	compressed archive
`.html`	hypertext markup language files (most often web pages)
`.exe`	executable file

Files can be classified into text files and binary files depending on the format that is used. Text files can be edited using simple text editors. Binary files are stored using an internal format that requires special software to process. Text files are often stored using the `.txt` extension, but other file formats are also text formats, including `.java` and `.html` files.

To access a file from inside a Java program, you need to construct an internal object that will represent the file. The Java class libraries include a class called `File` that performs this duty.

You construct a `File` object by passing in the name of a file, as in the following line of code:

```
File f = new File("hamlet.txt");
```

Once you've constructed the object, you can call a number of methods to manipulate the file. For example, the following program calls a method that determines whether a file exists, whether it can be read, what its length is (i.e., how many characters are in the file), and what its absolute path is (i.e., where it is stored on the computer):

```
// Report some basic information about a file.

import java.io.*; // for File

public class FileInfo {
    public static void main(String[] args) {
        File f = new File("hamlet.txt");
```

```
        System.out.println("exists returns " + f.exists());
        System.out.println("canRead returns " + f.canRead());
        System.out.println("length returns " + f.length());
        System.out.println("getAbsolutePath returns "
                           + f.getAbsolutePath());
    }
}
```

Notice that the program includes an import from the package `java.io`, because the `File` class is part of that package. The term "io" (or I/O) is jargon used by computer science professionals to mean "input/output." Assuming you have stored the file `hamlet.txt` in the same directory as the program, you'll get output like the following when you run the program:

```
exists returns true
canRead returns true
length returns 191734
getAbsolutePath returns C:\data\hamlet.txt
```

The fact that we use a call on `new` to construct a `File` object can be misleading. We aren't constructing an actual file by constructing this object. The `File` object is an internal object that allows us to access files that already exist on the computer. Later in the chapter we will see how to write a program that creates a file as output.

Table 6.2 lists some useful methods for `File` objects.

Reading a File with a `Scanner`

The `Scanner` class that we have been using since Chapter 3 is flexible in that `Scanner` objects can be attached to many different kinds of input (see Figure 6.1).

Table 6.2 Useful Methods of `File` Objects

Method	Description
`canRead()`	Whether or not this file exists and can be read
`delete()`	Deletes the given file
`exists()`	Whether or not this file exists on the system
`getAbsolutePath()`	The full path where this file is located
`getName()`	The name of this file as a `String`, without any path attached
`isDirectory()`	Whether this file represents a directory/folder on the system
`isFile()`	Whether this file represents a file (nonfolder) on the system
`length()`	The number of characters in this file
`renameTo(file)`	Changes this file's name to the given file's name

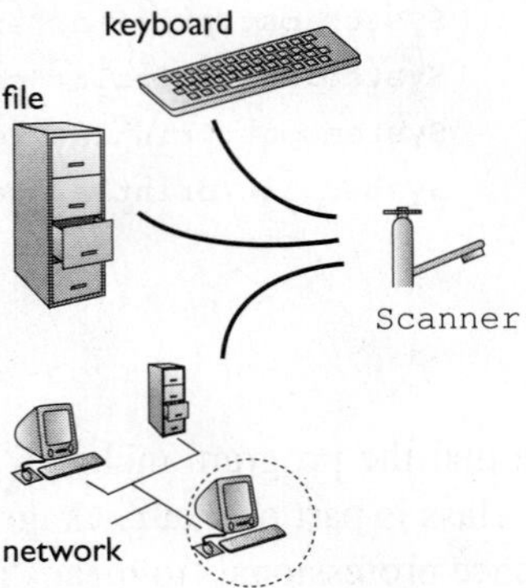

Figure 6.1 Scanners can be connected to many input sources.

You can think of a `Scanner` object as being like a faucet that you can attach to a pipe that has water flowing through it. The water can come from various sources. For example, in a house you'd attach a faucet to a pipe carrying water from the city water supply or from a well, but faucets in places like mobile homes and airplanes have different sources of water.

Thus far, we have been constructing `Scanner` objects by passing `System.in` to the `Scanner` constructor:

```
Scanner console = new Scanner(System.in);
```

This line of code instructs the computer to construct a `Scanner` that reads from the console (i.e., pauses for input from the user).

Instead of passing `System.in` to the constructor, you can pass a `File` object:

```
File f = new File("hamlet.txt");
Scanner input = new Scanner(f);
```

In this case the variable `f` is not necessary, so we can shorten this code to the following:

```
Scanner input = new Scanner(new File("hamlet.txt"));
```

This line of code, or something like it, will appear in all of your file-processing programs. When we were reading from the console window, we called our `Scanner` variable `console`. When you read from an input file, you may want to call the variable `input`. Of course, you can name the variable anything you want, as long as you refer to it in a consistent way.

Unfortunately, when you try to compile a program that constructs a `Scanner` in this manner, you'll run into a snag. Say you write a `main` method that begins by opening a `Scanner` as follows:

```
// flawed method--does not compile
public static void main(String[] args) {
    Scanner input = new Scanner(new File("hamlet.txt"));
    ...
}
```

This program does not compile. It produces a message like the following:

```
CountWords.java:8:
unreported exception java.io.FileNotFoundException;
must be caught or declared to be thrown
        Scanner input = new Scanner(new File(hamlet.txt));
                                ^
1 error
```

The issue involves exceptions, which were described in Chapter 3. Remember that exceptions are errors that prevent a program from continuing normal execution. In this case the compiler is worried that it might not be able to find a file called `hamlet.txt`. What is it supposed to do if that happens? It won't have a file to read from, so it won't have any way to continue executing the rest of the code.

If the program is unable to locate the specified input file, it will generate an error by throwing what is known as a `FileNotFoundException`. This particular exception is known as a *checked exception*.

Checked Exception

An exception that *must* be caught or specifically declared in the header of the method that might generate it.

Because `FileNotFoundException` is a checked exception, you can't just ignore it. Java provides a construct known as the `try/catch` statement for handling such errors (described in Appendix C), but it allows you to avoid handling this error as long as you clearly indicate the fact that you aren't handling it. All you have to do is include a *`throws` clause* in the header for the `main` method to clearly state the fact that your `main` method might generate this exception.

`throws` Clause

A declaration that a method will not attempt to handle a particular type of exception.

Here's how to modify the header for the `main` method to include a `throws` clause indicating that it may throw a `FileNotFoundException`:

```
public static void main(String[] args)
        throws FileNotFoundException {
    Scanner input = new Scanner(new File("hamlet.txt"));
    ...
}
```

With the `throws` clause, the line becomes so long that we have to break it into two lines to allow it to fit in the margins of the textbook. On your own computer, you will probably include all of it on a single line.

After this modification, the program compiles. Once you've constructed the `Scanner` so that it reads from the file, you can manipulate it like any other `Scanner`. Of course, you should always prompt before reading from the console to give the user an indication of what kind of data you want, but when reading from a file, you don't need to prompt because the data is already there, stored in the file. For example, you could write a program like the following to count the number of words in *Hamlet*:

```
// Counts the number of words in Hamlet.

import java.io.*;
import java.util.*;

public class CountWords {
    public static void main(String[] args)
            throws FileNotFoundException {
        Scanner input = new Scanner(new File("hamlet.txt"));
        int count = 0;
        while (input.hasNext()) {
            String word = input.next();
            count++;
        }
        System.out.println("total words = " + count);
    }
}
```

Note that you have to include an import from `java.util` for the `Scanner` class and an import from `java.io` for the `File` class. The program generates the following output:

```
total words = 31956
```

Common Programming Error

Reading Beyond the End of a File

As you learn how to process input files, you are likely to write programs that accidentally attempt to read data when there is no data left to read. For example, the `CountWords` program we just saw uses a `while` loop to keep reading words from the file as long as there are still words left to read. After the `while` loop, you might include an extra statement to read a word:

```
while (input.hasNext()) {
    String word = input.next();
    count++;
}
String extra = input.next(); // illegal, no more input
```

This new line of code causes the computer to try to read a word when there is no word to read. Java throws an exception when this occurs:

```
Exception in thread "main" java.util.NoSuchElementException
        at java.util.Scanner.throwFor(Scanner.java:817)
        at java.util.Scanner.next(Scanner.java:1317)
        at CountWords.main(CountWords.java:15)
```

As usual, the most important information appears at the end of this list of line numbers. The exception indicates that the error occurred in line 15 of `CountWords`. The other line numbers come from the `Scanner` class and aren't helpful.

If you find yourself getting a `NoSuchElementException`, it is probably because you have somehow attempted to read beyond the end of the input. The `Scanner` is saying, "You've asked me for some data, but I don't have any such value to give you."

Common Programming Error

Forgetting "`new File`"

Suppose that you intend to construct a `Scanner` the way we've learned:

```
Scanner input = new Scanner(new File("hamlet.txt"));
```

But you accidentally forget to include the `File` object and instead write this line of code:

```
Scanner input = new Scanner("hamlet.txt"); // not right
```

Continued on next page

Continued from previous page

The line of code may seem correct because it mentions the name of the file, but it won't work because it doesn't include the `File` object.

Normally, when you make a mistake like this Java warns you that you have done something illegal. In this case, however, you'll get no warning from Java. This is because, as you'll see later in this chapter, it is possible to construct a `Scanner` from a `String`, in which case Java reads from the `String` itself.

If you were to make this mistake in the `CountWords` program, you would get the following output:

```
total words = 1
```

The program would report just one word because the `String "hamlet.txt"` looks like a single word to the `Scanner`. So, whenever you construct a `Scanner` that is supposed to read from an input file, make sure that you include the call on `new File` to construct an appropriate `File` object.

6.2 Details of Token-Based Processing

VideoNote

Now that we've introduced some of the basic issues involved in reading an input file, let's explore reading from a file in more detail. One way to process a file is token by token.

Token-Based Processing

Processing input token by token (i.e., one word at a time or one number at a time).

Recall from Chapter 3 the primary token-reading methods for the `Scanner` class:

- `nextInt` for reading an `int` value
- `nextDouble` for reading a `double` value
- `next` for reading the next token as a `String`

For example, you might want to create a file called `numbers.dat` with the following content:

```
308.2 14.9 7.4
2.8


3.9 4.7 -15.4
2.8
```

You can create such a file with an editor like Notepad on a Windows machine or TextEdit on a Macintosh. Then you might write a program that processes this input file and produces some kind of report. For example, the following program reads the first five numbers from the file and reports their sum:

```
// Program that reads five numbers and reports their sum.

import java.io.*;
import java.util.*;

public class ShowSum1 {
    public static void main(String[] args)
            throws FileNotFoundException {
        Scanner input = new Scanner(new File("numbers.dat"));

        double sum = 0.0;
        for (int i = 1; i <= 5; i++) {
            double next = input.nextDouble();
            System.out.println("number " + i + " = " + next);
            sum += next;
        }
        System.out.println("Sum = " + sum);
    }
}
```

This program uses a variation of the cumulative sum code from Chapter 4. Remember that you need a `throws` clause in the header for `main` because there is a potential `FileNotFoundException`. The program produces the following output:

```
number 1 = 308.2
number 2 = 14.9
number 3 = 7.4
number 4 = 2.8
number 5 = 3.9
Sum = 337.19999999999993
```

Notice that the reported sum is not 337.2. This result is another example of a roundoff error (also described in Chapter 4).

The preceding program reads exactly five numbers from the file. More typically, you'll continue to read numbers as long as there are more numbers to read while a `while` loop is executing. Remember that the `Scanner` class includes a series of `hasNext` methods that parallel the various `next` methods. In this case, `nextDouble` is being used to read a value of type `double`, so you can use `hasNextDouble` to test whether there is such a value to read:

```
// Reads an input file of numbers and prints the numbers and
// their sum.

import java.io.*;
import java.util.*;

public class ShowSum2 {
    public static void main(String[] args)
            throws FileNotFoundException {
        Scanner input = new Scanner(new File("numbers.dat"));

        double sum = 0.0;
        int count = 0;
        while (input.hasNextDouble()) {
            double next = input.nextDouble();
            count++;
            System.out.println("number " + count + " = " + next);
            sum += next;
        }
        System.out.println("Sum = " + sum);
    }
}
```

This program would work on an input file with any number of numbers; `numbers.dat` happens to contain eight. This version of the program produces the following output:

```
number 1 = 308.2
number 2 = 14.9
number 3 = 7.4
number 4 = 2.8
number 5 = 3.9
number 6 = 4.7
number 7 = -15.4
number 8 = 2.8
Sum = 329.29999999999995
```

Structure of Files and Consuming Input

We think of text as being two-dimensional, like a sheet of paper, but from the computer's point of view, each file is just a one-dimensional sequence of characters. For example, consider the file `numbers.dat` that we used in the previous section:

```
308.2 14.9 7.4
2.8


3.9 4.7 -15.4
2.8
```

We think of this as a six-line file with text going across and down and two blank lines in the middle. However, the computer views the file differently. When you typed the text in this file, you hit the Enter key to go to a new line. This key inserts special "new line" characters in the file. You can annotate the file with `\n` characters to indicate the end of each line:

```
308.2 14.9 7.4\n
2.8\n
\n
\n
3.9 4.7 -15.4\n
2.8\n
```

Common Programming Error

Reading the Wrong Kind of Token

It's easy to write code that accidentally reads the wrong kind of data. For example, the `ShowSum1` program always reads exactly five `doubles` from the input file `numbers.dat`. But suppose that the input file has some extraneous text in it:

```
308.2 14.9 7.4
hello
2.8

3.9 4.7 –15.4
2.8
```

The first line of the file contains three numbers that the program will read properly. But when it attempts to read a fourth number, the computer finds that the next token in the file is the text "hello". This token cannot be interpreted as a `double`, so the program generates an exception:

```
number 1 = 308.2
number 2 = 14.9
number 3 = 7.4
Exception in thread "main" java.util.InputMismatchException
```

Continued on next page

Continued from previous page

```
        at java.util.Scanner.throwFor(Scanner.java:819)
        at java.util.Scanner.next(Scanner.java:1431)
        at java.util.Scanner.nextDouble(Scanner.java:2335)
        at ShowSum1.main(ShowSum1.java:13)
```

Once again, the useful line number appears at the bottom of this list. The last line indicates that the exception occurred in line 13 of the `ShowSum1` class. The other line numbers are from the `Scanner` class and aren't helpful.

You saw earlier that when you attempt to read beyond the end of a file, the `Scanner` throws a `NoSuchElementException`. In the case of this program that attempts to read the wrong kind of token, the `Scanner` throws an `InputMismatchException`. By paying attention to the kind of exception the `Scanner` throws, you can get better feedback about what the problem is.

When you mark the end of each line in your program, you no longer need to use a two-dimensional representation. You can collapse this text to a one-dimensional sequence of characters:

```
308.2 14.9 7.4\n2.8\n\n\n3.9 4.7 -15.4\n2.8\n
```

This sequence is how the computer views the file: as a one-dimensional sequence of characters including special characters that represent "new line". On some systems, including Windows machines, there are two different "new line" characters, but we'll use just `\n` here—objects like `Scanner` handle these differences for you, so you can generally ignore them. (For those who are interested, the brief explanation is that Windows machines end each line with a `\r` followed by a `\n`.)

When it is processing a file, the `Scanner` object keeps track of the current position in the file. You can think of this as an *input cursor* or pointer into the file.

Input Cursor

A pointer to the current position in an input file.

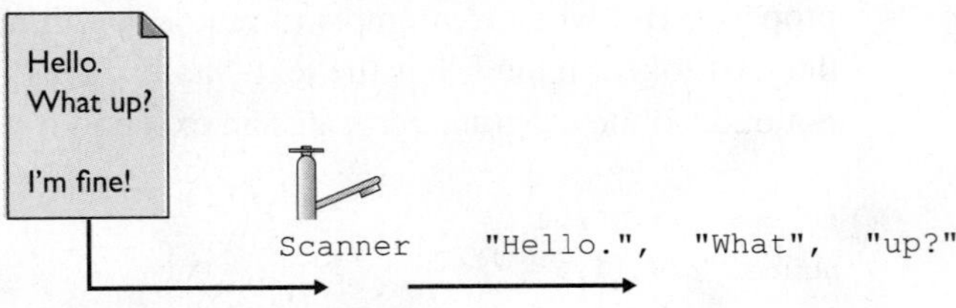

Figure 6.2 Scanners treat files as one-dimensional strings of characters and convert their contents into a series of whitespace-separated tokens.

When a `Scanner` object is first constructed, the cursor points to the beginning of the file. But as you perform various next operations, the cursor moves forward. The `ShowSum2` program from the last section processes the file through a series of calls on `nextDouble`. Let's take a moment to examine in detail how that works. Again, when the `Scanner` is first constructed, the input cursor will be positioned at the beginning of the file (indicated with an up-arrow pointing at the first character):

```
308.2 14.9 7.4\n2.8\n\n\n3.9 4.7 -15.4\n2.8\n
↑
input
cursor
```

After the first call on `nextDouble` the cursor will be positioned in the middle of the first line, after the token "308.2":

```
308.2 14.9 7.4\n2.8\n\n\n3.9 4.7 -15.4\n2.8\n
     ↑
     input
     cursor
```

We refer to this process as *consuming input.*

Consuming Input
Moving the input cursor forward past some input.

The process of consuming input doesn't actually change the file, it just changes the corresponding `Scanner` object so that it is positioned at a different point in the file.

The first call on `nextDouble` consumes the text "308.2" from the input file and leaves the input cursor positioned at the first character after this token. Notice that this leaves the input cursor positioned at a space. When the second call is made on `nextDouble`, the `Scanner` first skips past this space to get to the next token, then consumes the text "14.9" and leaves the cursor positioned at the space that follows it:

```
308.2 14.9 7.4\n2.8\n\n\n3.9 4.7 -15.4\n2.8\n
          ↑
          input
          cursor
```

The third call on `nextDouble` skips that space and consumes the text "7.4":

```
308.2 14.9 7.4\n2.8\n\n\n3.9 4.7 -15.4\n2.8\n
              ↑
              input
              cursor
```

At this point, the input cursor is positioned at the new line character at the end of the first line of input. The fourth call on `nextDouble` skips past this new line character and consumes the text "2.8":

```
308.2 14.9 7.4\n2.8\n\n\n3.9 4.7 -15.4\n2.8\n
                   ↑
                   input
                   cursor
```

Notice that when it skipped past the first new line character, the input cursor moved into data stored on the second line of input. At this point, the input cursor is positioned at the end of the second line of input, because it has consumed the "2.8" token. When a fifth call is made on `nextDouble`, the `Scanner` finds three new line characters in a row. This isn't a problem for the `Scanner`, because it simply skips past any leading whitespace characters (spaces, tabs, new line characters) until it finds an actual token. So, it skips all three of these new line characters and consumes the text "3.9":

```
308.2 14.9 7.4\n2.8\n\n\n3.9 4.7 -15.4\n2.8\n
                            ↑
                            input
                            cursor
```

At this point the input cursor is positioned in the middle of the fifth line of input. (The third and fourth lines were blank). The program continues reading in this manner, consuming the remaining three numbers in the input file. After it reads the final token, "2.8", the input cursor is positioned at the new line character at the end of the file:

```
308.2 14.9 7.4\n2.8\n\n\n3.9 4.7 -15.4\n2.8\n
                                           ↑
                                           input
                                           cursor
```

If you attempted to call `nextDouble` again, it would throw a `NoSuchElementException` because there are no more tokens left to process. But remember that the `ShowSum2` program has a `while` loop that calls `hasNextDouble` before it calls `nextDouble`. When you call methods like `hasNextDouble`, the `Scanner` looks ahead in the file to see whether there is a next token and whether it is of the specified type (in this case, a `double`). So, the `ShowSum2` program will continue executing until it reaches the end of the file or until it encounters a token that cannot be interpreted as a `double`.

When the input cursor reaches the new line character at the end of the file, the `Scanner` notices that there are no more `double` values to read and returns `false` when `hasNextDouble` is called. That return stops the `while` loop from executing and causes the program to exit.

Scanner objects are designed for file processing in a forward manner. They provide a great deal of flexibility for looking ahead in an input file, but no support for reading the input backward. There are no "previous" methods, and there's no mechanism for resetting a Scanner back to the beginning of the input. Instead, you would have to construct a new Scanner object that would be positioned at the beginning of the file. We will see an example of this technique in the case study at the end of the chapter.

Scanner Parameters

Novices are sometimes surprised that the input cursor for a Scanner does not reset to the beginning of the file when it is passed as a parameter to a method. For example, consider the following variation of the ShowSum1 program. It has a method that takes a Scanner as input and an integer specifying how many numbers to process:

```
// Demonstrates a Scanner as a parameter to a method that
// can consume an arbitrary number of tokens.

import java.io.*;
import java.util.*;

public class ShowSum3 {
    public static void main(String[] args)
            throws FileNotFoundException {
        Scanner input = new Scanner(new File("numbers.dat"));
        processTokens(input, 2);
        processTokens(input, 3);
        processTokens(input, 2);
    }

    public static void processTokens(Scanner input, int n) {
        double sum = 0.0;
        for (int i = 1; i <= n; i++) {
            double next = input.nextDouble();
            System.out.println("number " + i + " = " + next);
            sum += next;
        }
        System.out.println("Sum = " + sum);
        System.out.println();
    }
}
```

The main method creates a Scanner object that is tied to the numbers.dat file. It then calls the processTokens method several times, indicating the number of tokens to process. The first call instructs the method to process two tokens. It operates on the first two tokens of the file, generating the following output:

```
number 1 = 308.2
number 2 = 14.9
Sum = 323.09999999999997
```

The second call on the method indicates that three tokens are to be processed. Some people expect the method to process the first three tokens of the file, but that's not what happens. Remember that the `Scanner` keeps track of where the input cursor is positioned. After the first call on the method, the input cursor is positioned beyond the first two tokens. So the second call on the method processes the next three tokens from the file, producing the following output:

```
number 1 = 7.4
number 2 = 2.8
number 3 = 3.9
Sum = 14.1
```

The final call on the method asks the `Scanner` to process the next two tokens from the file, so it ends up processing the sixth and seventh numbers from the file:

```
number 1 = 4.7
number 2 = −15.4
Sum = −10.7
```

The program then terminates, never having processed the eighth number in the file.

The key point to remember is that a `Scanner` keeps track of the position of the input cursor, so you can process an input file piece by piece in a very flexible manner. Even when the `Scanner` is passed as a parameter to a method, it remembers how much of the input file has been processed so far.

Paths and Directories

Files are grouped into *folders*, also called *directories*. Directories are organized in a hierarchy, starting from a root directory at the top. For example, most Windows machines have a disk drive known as `C:`. At the top level of this drive is the *root* directory, which we can describe as `C:\`. This root directory will contain various top-level directories. Each top-level directory can have subdirectories, each of which also has subdirectories, and so on. All files are stored in one of these directories. The description of how to get from the top-level directory to the particular directory that stores a file is known as the *path* of the file.

File Path

A description of a file's location on a computer, starting with a drive and including the path from the root directory to the directory where the file is stored.

We read the path information from left to right. For example, if the path to a file is `C:\school\data\hamlet.txt`, we know that the file is on the `C:` drive in a folder called `school` and in a subfolder called `data`.

In the previous section, the program used the file name `numbers.dat`. When Java encounters a simple name like that (also called a *relative* file path), it looks in the *current directory* to find the file.

> **Current Directory (a.k.a. Working Directory)**
>
> The directory that Java uses as the default when a program uses a simple file name.

The default directory varies with the Java environment you are using. In most environments, the current directory is the one in which your program appears. We'll assume that this is the case for the examples in this textbook.

You can also use a *fully qualified*, or complete, file name (sometimes called an *absolute file path*). However, this approach works well only when you know exactly where your file is going to be stored on your system. For example, if you are on a Windows machine and you have stored the file in the `C:\data` directory, you could use a file name like the following:

```
Scanner input = new Scanner(new File("C:/data/numbers.dat"));
```

Notice that the path is written with forward-slash characters rather than backslash characters. On Windows you would normally use a backslash, but Java allows you to use a forward slash instead. If you wanted to use a backslash, you would have to use a `\\` escape sequence. Most programmers choose the simpler approach of using forward-slash characters because Java does the appropriate translation on Windows machines.

You can also specify a file using a *relative path*. To write a relative path you omit the drive specification at the beginning of the string. You can still specify subdirectory relationships that will be relative to the current directory. For example, the relative path `"data/numbers.dat"` indicates a file called `numbers.dat` in a subdirectory of the working directory called `data`.

Sometimes, rather than writing a file's path name in the code yourself, you'll ask the user for a file name. For example, here is a variation of `ShowSum2` that prompts the user for the file name:

```
// Variation of ShowSum2 that prompts for a file name.

import java.io.*;
import java.util.*;

public class ShowSum4 {
    public static void main(String[] args)
            throws FileNotFoundException {
```

```
        System.out.println("This program will add a series");
        System.out.println("of numbers from a file.");
        System.out.println();

        Scanner console = new Scanner(System.in);
        System.out.print("What is the file name? ");
        String name = console.nextLine();
        Scanner input = new Scanner(new File(name));
        System.out.println();

        double sum = 0.0;
        int count = 0;
        while (input.hasNextDouble()) {
            double next = input.nextDouble();
            count++;
            System.out.println("number " + count + " = " + next);
            sum += next;
        }
        System.out.println("Sum = " + sum);
    }
}
```

Notice that the program has two different `Scanner` objects: one for reading from the console and one for reading from the file. We read the file name using a call on `nextLine` to read an entire line of input from the user, which allows the user to type in file names that have spaces in them. Notice that we still need the `throws FileNotFoundException` in the header for `main` because even though we are prompting the user to enter a file name, there won't necessarily be a file of that name.

If we have this program read from the file `numbers.dat` used earlier, it will produce the following output:

```
This program will add a series
of numbers from a file.

What is the file name? numbers.dat

number 1 = 308.2
number 2 = 14.9
number 3 = 7.4
number 4 = 2.8
number 5 = 3.9
number 6 = 4.7
number 7 = -15.4
number 8 = 2.8
Sum = 329.29999999999995
```

The user also has the option of specifying a full file path:

```
This program will add a series
of numbers from a file.

What is the file name? C:\data\numbers.dat

number 1 = 308.2
number 2 = 14.9
number 3 = 7.4
number 4 = 2.8
number 5 = 3.9
number 6 = 4.7
number 7 = -15.4
number 8 = 2.8
Sum = 329.29999999999995
```

Notice that the user doesn't have to type two backslashes to get a single backslash. The `Scanner` object that reads the user's input is able to read it without escape sequences.

A More Complex Input File

Suppose an input file contains information about how many hours each employee of a company has worked. It might look like the following:

```
Erica 7.5 8.5 10.25 8 8.5
Erin 10.5 11.5 12 11 10.75
Simone 8 8 8
Ryan 6.5 8 9.25 8
Kendall 2.5 3
```

Suppose you want to find out the total number of hours worked by each individual. You can construct a `Scanner` object linked to this file to solve this task. As you start writing more complex file-processing programs, you will want to divide the program into methods to break up the code into logical subtasks. In this case, you can open the file in `main` and write a separate method to process the file.

Most file processing will involve `while` loops, because you won't know in advance how much data the file contains. You'll need to write different tests, depending on the particular file being processed, but they will almost all be calls on the various `hasNext` methods of the `Scanner` class. You basically want to say, "While you have more data for me to process, let's keep reading."

In this case, the data is a series of input lines that each begins with a name. For this program you can assume that names are simple, with no spaces in the middle.

That means you can read them with a call on the `next` method. As a result, the `while` loop test involves seeing whether there is another name in the input file:

```
while (input.hasNext()) {
    process next person.
}
```

So, how do you process each person? You have to read that person's name and then read that person's list of hours. If you look at the sample input file, you will see that the list of hours is not always the same length. For example, some employees worked on five days, while others worked only two or three days. This unevenness is a common occurrence in input files. You can deal with it by using a nested loop. The outer loop will handle one person at a time and the inner loop will handle one number at a time. The task is a fairly straightforward cumulative sum:

```
double sum = 0.0;
while (input.hasNextDouble()) {
    sum += input.nextDouble();
}
```

When you put the parts of the program together, you end up with the following complete program:

```
// This program reads an input file of hours worked by various
// employees and reports the total hours worked by each.

import java.io.*;
import java.util.*;

public class HoursWorked {
    public static void main(String[] args)
            throws FileNotFoundException {
        Scanner input = new Scanner(new File("hours.dat"));
        process(input);
    }

    public static void process(Scanner input) {
        while (input.hasNext()) {
            String name = input.next();
            double sum = 0.0;
            while (input.hasNextDouble()) {
                sum += input.nextDouble();
            }
            System.out.println("Total hours worked by " + name
                               + " = " + sum);
```

```
        }
    }
}
```

Notice that you need to put the `throws FileNotFoundException` in the header for `main`. You don't need to include it in the `process` method because the code to open the file appears in method `main`.

If you put the input data into a file called `hours.dat` and execute the program, you get the following result:

```
Total hours worked by Erica = 42.75
Total hours worked by Erin = 55.75
Total hours worked by Simone = 24.0
Total hours worked by Ryan = 31.75
Total hours worked by Kendall = 5.5
```

6.3 Line-Based Processing

VideoNote

So far we have been looking at programs that process input token by token. However, you'll often find yourself working with input files that are line-based: Each line of input represents a different case, to be handled separately from the rest. These types of files lend themselves to a second style of file processing called *line-based processing.*

Line-Based Processing

The practice of processing input line by line (i.e., reading in entire lines of input at a time).

Most file processing involves a combination of line- and token-based styles, and the `Scanner` class is flexible enough to allow you to write programs that include both styles of processing. For line-based processing, you'll use the `nextLine` and `hasNextLine` methods of the `Scanner` object. For example, here is a program that echoes an input file in uppercase:

```
// Reads a file and echoes it in uppercase.

import java.io.*;
import java.util.*;

public class EchoUppercase {
    public static void main(String[] args)
            throws FileNotFoundException {
        Scanner input = new Scanner(new File("poem.txt"));
        while (input.hasNextLine()) {
```

```
                String text = input.nextLine();
                System.out.println(text.toUpperCase());
            }
        }
}
```

This loop reads the input line by line and prints each line in uppercase until it runs out of lines to process. It reads from a file called `poem.txt`. Suppose that the file has the following contents:

```
My candle burns at both ends
It will not last the night;
But ah, my foes, and oh, my friends -
It gives a lovely light.

   --Edna St. Vincent Millay
```

If you run the preceding program on this input, it will produce the following output:

```
MY CANDLE BURNS AT BOTH ENDS
IT WILL NOT LAST THE NIGHT;
BUT AH, MY FOES, AND OH, MY FRIENDS -
IT GIVES A LOVELY LIGHT.

   --EDNA ST. VINCENT MILLAY
```

Notice that you could not have accomplished the same task with token-based processing. In this example, the line breaks are significant because they are part of the poem. Also, when you read a file token by token, you lose the spacing within the line because the `Scanner` skips any leading whitespace when it reads a token. The final line of this input file is indented because it is the name of the author and not part of the poem. That spacing would be lost if the file was read as a series of tokens.

String Scanners and Line/Token Combinations

In the last section we looked at a program called `HoursWorked` that processed the following data file:

```
Erica 7.5 8.5 10.25 8 8.5
Erin 10.5 11.5 12 11 10.75
Simone 8 8 8
Ryan 6.5 8 9.25 8
Kendall 2.5 3
```

The data are line-oriented, each employee's information appearing on a different line of input, but this aspect of the data wasn't incorporated into the program. The program processed the file in a token-based manner. However, that approach won't always work. For example, consider a slight variation in the data in which each line of input begins with an employee ID rather than just a name:

```
101 Erica 7.5 8.5 10.25 8 8.5
783 Erin 10.5 11.5 12 11 10.75
114 Simone 8 8 8
238 Ryan 6.5 8 9.25 8
156 Kendall 2.5 3
```

This addition seems like a fairly simple change that shouldn't require major changes to the code. Recall that the program uses a method to process the file:

```
public static void process(Scanner input) {
    while (input.hasNext()) {
        String name = input.next();
        double sum = 0.0;
        while (input.hasNextDouble()) {
            sum += input.nextDouble();
        }
        System.out.println("Total hours worked by " + name +
                           " = " + sum);
    }
}
```

Suppose you add a line of code to read the employee ID and modify the `println` to report it:

```
public static void process(Scanner input) {
    while (input.hasNext()) {
        int id = input.nextInt();
        String name = input.next();
        double sum = 0.0;
        while (input.hasNextDouble()) {
            sum += input.nextDouble();
        }
        System.out.println("Total hours worked by " + name +
                           " (id#" + id + ") = " + sum);
    }
}
```

When you run this new version of the program on the new input file, you'll get one line of output and then Java will throw an exception:

```
Total hours worked by Erica (id#101) = 825.75
Exception in thread "main" java.util.InputMismatchException
        at java.util.Scanner.throwFor(Scanner.java:819)
        at java.util.Scanner.next(Scanner.java:1431)
        at java.util.Scanner.nextInt(Scanner.java:2040)
        ...
```

The program correctly reads Erica's employee ID and reports it in the `println` statement, but then it crashes. Also, notice that the program reports Erica's total hours worked as 825.75, when the number should be 42.75. Where did it go wrong?

If you compute the difference between the reported sum of 825.75 hours and the correct sum of 42.75 hours, you'll find it is equal to 783. That number appears in the data file: It's the employee ID of the second employee, Erin. When the program was adding up the hours for Erica, it accidentally read Erin's employee ID as more hours worked by Erica and added this number to the sum. That's also why the exception occurs—on the second iteration of the loop, the program tries to read an employee ID for Erin when the next token in the file is her name, not an integer.

The solution is to somehow get the program to stop reading when it gets to the end of an input line. Unfortunately, there is no easy way to do this with a token-based approach. The loop asks whether the `Scanner` has a next `double` value to read, and the employee ID looks like a `double` that can be read. You might try to write a complex test that looks for a `double` that is not also an integer, but even that won't work because some of the hours are integers.

To make this program work, you need to write a more sophisticated version that pays attention to the line breaks. The program must read an entire line of input at a time and process that line by itself. Recall the `main` method for the program:

```
public static void main(String[] args)
        throws FileNotFoundException {
    Scanner input = new Scanner(new File("hours2.dat"));
    process(input);
}
```

If you incorporate a line-based loop, you'll end up with the following method:

```
public static void main(String[] args)
        throws FileNotFoundException {
    Scanner input = new Scanner(new File("hours2.dat"));
    while (input.hasNextLine()) {
```

```
        String text = input.nextLine();
        processLine(text);
    }
}
```

Reading the file line by line guarantees that you don't accidentally combine data for two employees. The downside to this approach is that you have to write a method called `processLine` that takes a `String` as a parameter, and you have to pull apart that `String`. It contains the employee ID, followed by the employee name, followed by the numbers indicating how many hours the employee worked on different days. In other words, the input line is composed of several pieces (tokens) that you want to process piece by piece. It's much easier to process this data in a token-based manner than to have it in a `String`.

Fortunately, there is a convenient way to do this. You can construct a `Scanner` object from an individual `String`. Remember that just as you can attach a faucet to different sources of water (a faucet in a house attached to city or well water versus a faucet on an airplane attached to a tank of water), you can attach a `Scanner` to different sources of input. You've seen how to attach it to the console (`System.in`) and to a file (passing a `File` object). You can also attach it to an individual `String`. For example, consider the following line of code:

```
Scanner input = new Scanner("18.4 17.9 8.3 2.9");
```

This code constructs a `Scanner` that gets its input from the `String` used to construct it. This `Scanner` has an input cursor just like a `Scanner` linked to a file. Initially the input cursor is positioned at the first character in the `String`, and it moves forward as you read tokens from the `Scanner`.

The following short program demonstrates this solution:

```
// Simple example of a Scanner reading from a String.

import java.util.*;

public class StringScannerExample {
    public static void main(String[] args) {
        Scanner input = new Scanner("18.4 17.9 8.3 2.9");
        while (input.hasNextDouble()) {
            double next = input.nextDouble();
            System.out.println(next);
        }
    }
}
```

This program produces the following output:

```
18.4
17.9
8.3
2.9
```

Notice that the program produces four lines of output because there are four numbers in the `String` used to construct the `Scanner`.

When a file requires a combination of line-based and token-based processing, you can construct a `String`-based `Scanner` for each line of the input file. Using this approach, you end up with a lot of `Scanner` objects. You have a `Scanner` object that is keeping track of the input file, and you use that `Scanner` to read entire lines of input. In addition, each time you read a line of text from the file, you construct a mini-`Scanner` for just that line of input. You can then use token-based processing for these mini-`Scanner` objects, because each contains just a single line of data.

This combination of line-based and token-based processing is powerful. You will find that you can use this approach (and slight variations on it) to process a large variety of input files. To summarize, this approach involves a two-step process:

1. Break the file into lines with a `Scanner` using calls on `hasNextLine` and `nextLine`.
2. Break apart each line by constructing a `Scanner` just for that line of input and making calls on token-based methods like `hasNext` and `next`.

Following this approach, if you have a file composed of n lines of input, you end up constructing $n + 1$ different `Scanner` objects–one for each of the n individual lines (step 2) and one extra `Scanner` that is used to process the overall file line by line (step 1).

In the `HoursWorked` program, each input line contains information for a single employee. Processing the input line involves making a `Scanner` for the line and then reading its various parts (employee ID, name, hours) in a token-based manner. You can put this all together into a new version of the program:

```
// Variation of HoursWorked that includes employee IDs.

import java.io.*;
import java.util.*;

public class HoursWorked2 {
    public static void main(String[] args)
            throws FileNotFoundException {
        Scanner input = new Scanner(new File("hours2.dat"));
```

```
        while (input.hasNextLine()) {
            String text = input.nextLine();
            processLine(text);
        }
    }

    // processes the given String (ID, name, and hours worked)
    public static void processLine(String text) {
        Scanner data = new Scanner(text);
        int id = data.nextInt();
        String name = data.next();
        double sum = 0.0;
        while (data.hasNextDouble()) {
            sum += data.nextDouble();
        }
        System.out.println("Total hours worked by " + name +
                           " (id#" + id + ") = " + sum);
    }
}
```

Notice that the `main` method includes line-based processing to read entire lines of input from the file. Each such line is passed to the `processLine` method. Each time the program calls `processLine`, it makes a mini-`Scanner` for just that line of input and uses token-based processing (calling the methods `nextInt`, `next`, and `nextDouble`).

This new version of the program produces the following output:

```
Total hours worked by Erica (id#101) = 42.75
Total hours worked by Erin (id#783) = 55.75
Total hours worked by Simone (id#114) = 24.0
Total hours worked by Ryan (id#238) = 31.75
Total hours worked by Kendall (id#156) = 5.5
```

While this version of the program is a little more complex than the original, it is much more flexible because it pays attention to line breaks.

6.4 Advanced File Processing

In this section, we'll explore two advanced topics related to file processing: producing output files and guaranteeing that files can be read.

Output Files with `PrintStream`

All of the programs we've studied so far have sent their output to the console window by calling `System.out.print` or `System.out.println`. But just as you can read input from a file instead of reading from the console, you can write output to a file instead of writing it to the console. There are many ways to accomplish this task. The simplest approach is to take advantage of what you already know. You've already learned all about how `print` and `println` statements work, and you can leverage that knowledge to easily create output files.

If you look at the Java documentation, you will find that `System.out` is a variable that stores a reference to an object of type `PrintStream`. The `print` and `println` statements you've been writing are calls on methods that are part of the `PrintStream` class. The variable `System.out` stores a reference to a special `PrintStream` object that is tied to the console window. However, you can construct other `PrintStream` objects that send their output to other places. Suppose, for example, that you want to send output to a file called `results.txt`. You can construct a `PrintStream` object as follows:

```
PrintStream output = new PrintStream(new File("results.txt"));
```

This line of code looks a lot like the one we used to construct a `Scanner` tied to an input file. In this case, the computer is creating an output file. If no such file already exists, the program creates it. If such a file does exist, the computer overwrites the current version. Initially, the file will be empty. It will end up containing whatever output you tell it to produce through calls on `print` and `println`.

The line of code that constructs a `PrintStream` object can generate an exception if Java is unable to create the file you've described. There are many reasons that this might happen: You might not have permission to write to the directory, or the file might be locked because another program is using it. Like the line of code that creates a file-based `Scanner`, this line of code potentially throws a `FileNotFoundException`. Therefore, Java requires you to include the `throws` clause in whatever method contains this line of code. The simplest approach is to put this line in `main`. In fact, it is common practice to have the `main` method begin with the lines of code that deal with the input and output files.

Once you have constructed a `PrintStream` object, how do you use it? You should already have a good idea of what to do. We have been making calls on `System.out.print` and `System.out.println` since Chapter 1. If you recall everything you know about `System.out` you'll have a good idea of what to do, but for this program, you will call `output.print` instead of `System.out.print` and `output.println` instead of `System.out.println`.

As a simple example, remember that in Chapter 1 we looked at the following variation of the simple "hello world" program that produces several lines of output:

```
public class Hello2 {
    public static void main(String[] args) {
        System.out.println("Hello, world!");
        System.out.println();
```

```
        System.out.println("This program produces four");
        System.out.println("lines of output.");
    }
}
```

Here is a variation that sends its output to a file called `hello.txt`:

```
// Variation of Hello2 that prints to a file.

import java.io.*;

public class Hello4 {
    public static void main(String[] args)
            throws FileNotFoundException {
        PrintStream output =
            new PrintStream(new File("hello.txt"));
        output.println("Hello, world.");
        output.println();
        output.println("This program produces four");
        output.println("lines of output.");
    }
}
```

When you run this new version of the program, a curious thing happens. The program doesn't seem to do anything; no output appears on the console at all. You're so used to writing programs that send their output to the console that this might seem confusing at first. We don't see any output in the console window when we run this program because the output was directed to a file instead. After the program finishes executing, you can open up the file called `hello.txt` and you'll find that it contains the following:

```
Hello, world.

This program produces four
lines of output.
```

The main point is that everything you've learned to do with `System.out`, you can also do with `PrintStream` objects that are tied to files.

You can also write methods that take `PrintStream` objects as parameters. For example, consider the task of fixing the spacing for a series of words. Say that you have a line of text with erratic spacing, like the following line:

```
a       new  nation,     conceived  in     liberty
```

Suppose that you want to print this text with exactly one space between each pair of words:

```
a new nation, conceived in liberty
```

How do you do that? Assume that you are writing a method that is passed a `String` to echo and a `PrintStream` object to which the output should be sent:

```
public static void echoFixed(String text, PrintStream output) {
    ...
}
```

You can construct a `Scanner` from the `String` and then use the `next` method to read one word at a time. Recall that the `Scanner` class ignores whitespace, so you'll get just the individual words without all of the spaces between them. As you read words, you'll need to echo them to the `PrintStream` object. Here's a first attempt:

```
Scanner data = new Scanner(text);
while (data.hasNext()) {
    output.print(data.next());
}
```

This code does a great job of deleting the long sequences of spaces from the `String`, but it goes too far: It eliminates all of the spaces. To get one space between each pair of words, you'll have to include some spaces:

```
Scanner data = new Scanner(text);
while (data.hasNext()) {
    output.print(data.next() + " ");
}
```

This method produces results that look pretty good, but it prints an extra space at the end of the line. To get rid of that space so that you truly have spaces appearing only between pairs of words, you'll have to change the method slightly. This is a classic fencepost problem; you want to print one more word than you have spaces. You can use the typical solution of processing the first word before the loop begins and swapping the order of the other two operations inside the loop (printing a space and then the word):

```
Scanner data = new Scanner(text);
output.print(data.next());
while (data.hasNext()) {
    output.print(" " + data.next());
}
```

This version of the program works well for almost all cases, but by including the fencepost solution, which echoes the first word before the loop begins, you've introduced an assumption that there is a first word. If the `String` has no words at all, this call on `next` will throw an exception. So, you need a test for the case in which the `String` doesn't contain any words. If you also want this program to produce a complete line of output, you'll have to include a call on `println` to complete the line of output after printing the individual words. Incorporating these changes, you get the following code:

```
public static void echoFixed(String text, PrintStream output) {
    Scanner data = new Scanner(text);
    if (data.hasNext()) {
         output.print(data.next());
         while (data.hasNext()) {
             output.print(" " + data.next());
         }
    }
    output.println();
}
```

Notice that you're now calling `output.print` and `output.println` instead of calling `System.out.print` and `System.out.println`. An interesting aspect of this method is that it can be used not only to send output to an output file, but also to send it to `System.out`. The method header indicates that it works on any `PrintStream`, so you can call it to send output either to a `PrintStream` object tied to a file or to `System.out`.

The following complete program uses this method to fix the spacing in an entire input file of text. To underscore the flexibility of the method, the program sends its output both to a file (`words2.txt`) and to the console:

```
// This program removes excess spaces in an input file.

import java.io.*;
import java.util.*;

public class FixSpacing {
    public static void main(String[] args)
             throws FileNotFoundException {
        Scanner input = new Scanner(new File("words.txt"));
        PrintStream output =
            new PrintStream(new File("words2.txt"));
        while (input.hasNextLine()) {
            String text = input.nextLine();
            echoFixed(text, output);
```

```
            echoFixed(text, System.out);
        }
    }

    public static void echoFixed(String text,
                                 PrintStream output) {
        Scanner data = new Scanner(text);
        if (data.hasNext()) {
            output.print(data.next());
            while (data.hasNext()) {
                output.print(" " + data.next());
            }
        }
        output.println();
    }
}
```

Consider the following input file:

```
   four          score     and
seven    years ago    our
   fathers brought  forth on this    continent
a     new nation,     conceived  in    liberty
  and dedicated  to  the  proposition    that
   all   men   are    created    equal
```

Using this input, the program produces the following output file, called `words2.txt`:

```
four score and
seven years ago our
fathers brought forth on this continent
a new nation, conceived in liberty
and dedicated to the proposition that
all men are created equal
```

The output also appears in the console window.

Guaranteeing That Files Can Be Read

The programs we have studied so far assume that the user will provide a legal file name. But what if the user accidentally types in the name of a file that doesn't exist or that can't be read for some reason? In this section we explore how to guarantee that a file can be read.

Let's explore how you might handle the task of prompting the user for a file name in the console window. If the user does not input a legal file name, you can keep prompting until the user does enter a legal name. The `File` class has a method called `canRead` that you can use to test whether a file exists and can be read. You can print an error message each time the file can't be read, until you get a good file name. This situation turns out to be a fencepost problem. If you end up prompting the user n times, you'll want to produce $n - 1$ error messages. You can use the classic fencepost solution of prompting for the file name once before the loop:

```
System.out.print("input file name? ");
File f = new File(console.nextLine());
while (!f.canRead()) {
    System.out.println("File not found. Try again.");
    System.out.print("input file name? ");
    f = new File(console.nextLine());
}
```

This code could be included in your `main` method, but there is enough code here that it makes sense to put it in its own method. Because it is prompting the user for input, the code requires a `Scanner` for reading from the console. It can return a `Scanner` that is tied to the input file to process.

When you try to create a method that includes this code, you again run into the problem of checked exceptions. Even though we are being very careful to make sure that the file exists and can be read, the Java compiler doesn't know that. From its point of view, this code might throw an exception. You still need to include a `throws` clause in the method header, just as you've been doing with `main`:

```
public static Scanner getInput(Scanner console)
        throws FileNotFoundException {
    System.out.print("input file name? ");
    File f = new File(console.nextLine());
    while (!f.canRead()) {
        System.out.println("File not found. Try again.");
        System.out.print("input file name? ");
        f = new File(console.nextLine());
    }
    // now we know that f is a file that can be read
    return new Scanner(f);
}
```

Here is a variation of the `CountWords` program that prompts for a file name:

```
// Variation of CountWords that prompts for a file name.

import java.io.*;
import java.util.*;
```

```

public class CountWords2 {
    public static void main(String[] args)
            throws FileNotFoundException {
        Scanner console = new Scanner(System.in);
        Scanner input = getInput(console);

        // and count words
        int count = 0;
        while (input.hasNext()) {
            String word = input.next();
            count++;
        }
        System.out.println("total words = " + count);
    }

    // Prompts the user for a legal file name; creates and
    // returns a Scanner tied to the file
    public static Scanner getInput(Scanner console)
            throws FileNotFoundException {
        System.out.print("input file name? ");
        File f = new File(console.nextLine());
        while (!f.canRead()) {
            System.out.println("File not found. Try again.");
            System.out.print("input file name? ");
            f = new File(console.nextLine());
        }
        // now we know that f is a file that can be read
        return new Scanner(f);
    }
}
```

The following log of execution shows what happens when the user types in some illegal file names, ending with a legal file name:

```
input file name? amlet.txt
File not found. Try again.
input file name? hamlet.dat
File not found. Try again.
input file name? humlet.txt
File not found. Try again.
input file name? hamlet.txt
Total words = 31956
```

The code for opening a file is fairly standard and could be used without modification in many programs. We refer to this as *boilerplate code*.

Boilerplate Code

Code that tends to be the same from one program to another.

The `getInput` method is a good example of the kind of boilerplate code that you might use in many different file-processing programs.

6.5 Case Study: Zip Code Lookup

VideoNote

Knowing the distance between two locations turns out to be extremely helpful and valuable. For example, many popular Internet dating sites allow you to search for people on the basis of a target location. On Match.com, you can search for potential matches within a particular radius of a given city or zip code (5 miles, 10 miles, 15 miles, 25 miles, and so on). Obviously this is an important feature for a dating site because people are most interested in dating other people who live near them.

There are many other applications of this kind of proximity search. In the 1970s and 1980s there was an explosion of interest in what is known as direct mail marketing that has produced what we now call junk mail. Proximity searches are very important in direct mail campaigns. A local store, for example, might decide to mail out a brochure to all residents who live within 5 miles of the store. A political candidate might pay a membership organization like The Sierra Club or the National Rifle Association a fee to get the mailing addresses of all its members who live within a certain distance of a town or a city district.

Massive databases keep track of potential customers and voters. Direct-mail marketing organizations often want to find the distance between one of these individuals and some fixed location. The distance calculations are done almost exclusively with zip codes. There are over 40,000 five-digit zip codes in the United States. Some zip codes cover rural areas that are fairly large, but more often a zip code determines your location in a city or town to within a fraction of a mile. If you use the more specific Zip + 4 database, you can often pinpoint a location to within a few city blocks.

If you do a web search for "zip code database" or "zip code software" you will find that there are many people selling the data and the software to interpret the data. There are also some free databases, although the data aren't quite as accurate. The U.S. Census Bureau is the source of much of the free data.

To explore this application, let's write a program that finds all the zip codes within a certain proximity of another zip code. A web site like Match.com could use the logic of this program to find potential dates within a certain radius. You'd simply start with the zip code of interest, find all the other zip codes within a particular distance, and then find all the customers who have those zip codes. We don't have access to a massive dating database like Match.com, so we'll be working on just the first part of this task, finding the zip codes that are within a specified distance.

As we noted earlier, some free zip code databases are available online. Our sample program uses data compiled by software developer Schuyler Erle, whose data are distributed free through a Creative Commons license (obtained from http://www.boutell.com/zipcodes/).

We have reformatted the data to make it more convenient for us to work with it (a process known as *data munging*). We will be working with a file called `zipcode.txt` that has a series of 3-line entries, one for each zip code. The first line contains the zip code, the second line contains the city and state, and the third line contains two numbers that represent the latitude and longitude of the zip code. For example, the following is an entry for one of the authors' home zip codes:

```
98104
Seattle, WA
47.60252 -122.32855
```

The overall task is to prompt the user for a target zip code and a proximity and to show all zip codes within the given proximity of the target. Here is a first attempt at pseudocode for the overall task:

```
introduce program to user.
prompt for target zip code and proximity.
display matching zip codes from file.
```

This approach doesn't quite work. To display a match, you have to compare the target location to each of the different zip codes in the data file. You'll need the latitude and longitude information to make this comparison. But when you prompt the user, you're just asking for a zip code and proximity. You could alter the program to prompt for a latitude and longitude, but that wouldn't be a very friendly program for the user. Imagine if Match.com required you to know your latitude and longitude in order for you to search for people who live near you.

Instead, you can use the zip code data to find the latitude and longitude of the target zip code. As a result, you'll have to search the data twice. The first time through you will be looking for the target zip code, so that you can find its coordinates. The second time through you will display all the zip codes that are within the distance specified by the user. Here is a new version of the pseudocode:

```
introduce program to user.
prompt for target zip code and proximity.
find coordinates for target zip code.
display matching zip codes from file.
```

Introducing the program and prompting for the target zip code and proximity are fairly straightforward tasks that don't require detailed explanation. The real work of the program involves solving the third and fourth steps in this pseudocode. Each of these steps is sufficiently complex that it deserves to be included in a static method.

First consider the problem of finding the coordinates for the target zip code. You need to set up a `Scanner` to read from the file, and then you need to call the method that will do the search. But what information should the searching method return? You want the coordinates of the target zip code (the latitude and longitude). Your method can't return two different values, but these coordinates appear on a single line of input, so you can return that line of input as a `String`. That means that your main method will include the following code:

```
Scanner input = new Scanner(new File("zipcode.txt"));
String targetCoordinates = find(target, input);
```

The method should read the input file line by line, searching for the target zip code. Remember that each entry in the file is composed of three different lines. As a result, you need a slight variation of the standard line-processing loop that reads three lines each time through the loop:

```
public static String find(String target, Scanner input) {
    while (input.hasNextLine()) {
        String zip = input.nextLine();
        String city = input.nextLine();
        String coordinates = input.nextLine();
        ...
    }
    ...
}
```

As you read various zip code entries, you want to test each to see whether it matches the target. Remember that you need to use the `equals` method to compare strings for equality. If you find a match, you can print it and return the coordinates:

```
public static String find(String target, Scanner input) {
    while (input.hasNextLine()) {
        String zip = input.nextLine();
        String city = input.nextLine();
        String coordinates = input.nextLine();
        if (zip.equals(target)) {
            System.out.println(zip + ": " + city);
            return coordinates;
        }
    }
    ...
}
```

This method isn't complete because you have to consider the case in which the target zip code doesn't appear in the file. In that case, you exit the loop without having returned a value. There are many things the program could do at this point, such as printing an error message or throwing an exception. To keep things simple, let's instead return a set of fake coordinates. If the program returns a latitude and longitude of (0, 0), there won't be any matches unless the user asks for an outrageously high proximity (over 4,000 miles):

```
public static String find(String target, Scanner input) {
    while (input.hasNextLine()) {
        String zip = input.nextLine();
        String city = input.nextLine();
        String coordinates = input.nextLine();
        if (zip.equals(target)) {
            System.out.println(zip + ": " + city);
            return coordinates;
        }
    }
    // at this point we know the zip code isn't in the file
    // we return fictitious (no match) coordinates
    return "0 0";
}
```

This method completes the first of the two file-processing tasks. In the second task, you have to read the file and search for zip codes within the given proximity. The `Scanner` doesn't have a reset option for going back to the beginning of the file. Instead, you have to construct a second `Scanner` object that will be used for the second pass. Thus, your code in `main` will look like the following:

```
input = new Scanner(new File("zipcode.txt"));
showMatches(targetCoordinates, input, miles);
```

The code for finding matches involves a similar file-processing loop that reads three lines of input at a time, printing matches as it finds them:

```
public static void showMatches(String targetCoordinates,
                               Scanner input, double miles) {
    // compute lat1 and long1
    System.out.println("zip codes within " + miles + " miles:");
    while (input.hasNextLine()) {
        String zip = input.nextLine();
        String city = input.nextLine();
        String coordinates = input.nextLine();
        // compute lat2 and long2
        double distance = distance(lat1, long1, lat2, long2);
```

```
        if (distance <= miles) {
            // print zip code
        }
    }
}
```

Again, this is an incomplete version of the method. It indicates that before the loop begins you will compute two values known as `lat1` and `long1` that represent the latitude and longitude of the target coordinates. Inside the loop you compute values for `lat2` and `long2` that represent the latitude and longitude of the next entry from the data file. The latitude and longitude are stored in a `String`. You can construct a `Scanner` for each `String` that can be used to pull out the individual tokens. You also need to fill in the details of printing. This is a good place to use a `printf` to format the output:

```
public static void showMatches(String targetCoordinates,
                               Scanner input, double miles) {
    Scanner data = new Scanner(targetCoordinates);
    double lat1 = data.nextDouble();
    double long1 = data.nextDouble();
    System.out.println("zip codes within " + miles + " miles:");
    while (input.hasNextLine()) {
        String zip = input.nextLine();
        String city = input.nextLine();
        String coordinates = input.nextLine();
        data = new Scanner(coordinates);
        double lat2 = data.nextDouble();
        double long2 = data.nextDouble();
        double distance = distance(lat1, long1, lat2, long2);
        if (distance <= miles) {
            System.out.printf("    %s %s, %3.2f miles\n",
                              zip, city, distance);
        }
    }
}
```

This addition almost completes the program. The preceding code calls a method called `distance` that is intended to compute the distance between two points, given their latitude and longitude. This problem was included as Programming Project 5 in Chapter 3. You can use the following standard formula:

Let φ_1, λ_1, and φ_2, λ_2 be the latitude and longitude of two points, respectively. $\Delta\lambda$, the longitudinal difference, and $\Delta\sigma$, the angular difference/distance in radians, can be determined from the spherical law of cosines as:

$$\Delta\sigma = \arccos(\sin \varphi_1 \sin \varphi_2 + \cos \varphi_1 \cos \varphi_2 \cos \Delta\lambda)$$

We won't dwell on the math involved here, but a short explanation might be helpful. Imagine forming a triangle by connecting two points with the North Pole. From the two latitudes, you can compute the distance from each point to the North Pole. The difference between the two longitudes tells you the angle formed by these two sides of the triangle. You may recall from geometry class that if you know two sides and the angle between them, then you can compute the third side. We are using a special version of the law of cosines that works for spheres to compute the length of the third side of the triangle (which is the line connecting the two points on our sphere). We have to convert from degrees into radians and we have to include the radius of our sphere (in this case the Earth). The resulting calculation is included in the final version of the program.

Here is the complete version of the program:

```
// This program uses a file of zip code information to allow a user
// to find zip codes within a certain distance of another zip code.

import java.util.*;
import java.io.*;

public class ZipLookup {
    // radius of sphere. Here it's the Earth, in miles
    public static final double RADIUS = 3956.6;

    public static void main(String[] args)
            throws FileNotFoundException {
        giveIntro();
        Scanner console = new Scanner(System.in);

        System.out.print("What zip code are you interested in? ");
        String target = console.next();
        System.out.print("And what proximity (in miles)? ");
        double miles = console.nextDouble();
        System.out.println();

        Scanner input = new Scanner(new File("zipcode.txt"));
        String targetCoordinates = find(target, input);
        input = new Scanner(new File("zipcode.txt"));
        showMatches(targetCoordinates, input, miles);
    }

    // introduces the program to the user
    public static void giveIntro() {
        System.out.println("Welcome to the zip code database.");
        System.out.println("Give me a 5-digit zip code and a");
```

```
        System.out.println("proximity, and I'll tell you where");
        System.out.println("that zip code is located, along");
        System.out.println("with a list of other zip codes");
        System.out.println("within the given proximity.");
        System.out.println();
    }

    // Searches for the given string in the input file; if found,
    // returns the coordinates; otherwise returns (0, 0)
    public static String find(String target, Scanner input) {
        while (input.hasNextLine()) {
            String zip = input.nextLine();
            String city = input.nextLine();
            String coordinates = input.nextLine();
            if (zip.equals(target)) {
                System.out.println(zip + ": " + city);
                return coordinates;
            }
        }
        // at this point we know the zip code isn't in the file
        // we return fictitious (no match) coordinates
        return "0 0";
    }

    // Shows all matches for the given coordinates within the
    // given number of miles
    public static void showMatches(String targetCoordinates,
                                   Scanner input, double miles) {
        Scanner data = new Scanner(targetCoordinates);
        double lat1 = data.nextDouble();
        double long1 = data.nextDouble();
        System.out.println("zip codes within " + miles + " miles:");
        while (input.hasNextLine()) {
            String zip = input.nextLine();
            String city = input.nextLine();
            String coordinates = input.nextLine();
            data = new Scanner(coordinates);
            double lat2 = data.nextDouble();
            double long2 = data.nextDouble();
            double distance = distance(lat1, long1, lat2, long2);
            if (distance <= miles) {
                System.out.printf("    %s %s, %3.2f miles\n",
                                   zip, city, distance);
            }
```

```
        }
    }

    // Returns spherical distance in miles given the latitude
    // and longitude of two points (depends on constant RADIUS)
    public static double distance(double lat1, double long1,
                                  double lat2, double long2) {
        lat1 = Math.toRadians(lat1);
        long1 = Math.toRadians(long1);
        lat2 = Math.toRadians(lat2);
        long2 = Math.toRadians(long2);
        double theCos = Math.sin(lat1) * Math.sin(lat2) +
            Math.cos(lat1) * Math.cos(lat2) * Math.cos(long1 - long2);
        double arcLength = Math.acos(theCos);
        return arcLength * RADIUS;
    }
}
```

Here is a sample execution:

```
Welcome to the zip code database.
Give me a 5-digit zip code and a
proximity, and I'll tell you where
that zip code is located, along
with a list of other zip codes
within the given proximity.

What zip code are you interested in? 98104
And what proximity (in miles)? 1

98104: Seattle, WA
zip codes within 1.0 miles:
    98101 Seattle, WA, 0.62 miles
    98104 Seattle, WA, 0.00 miles
    98154 Seattle, WA, 0.35 miles
    98164 Seattle, WA, 0.29 miles
    98174 Seattle, WA, 0.35 miles
```

There is an old saying that you get what you pay for, and these zip code data are no exception. There are several web sites that list zip codes within a mile of 98104, and they include many zip codes not included here. That's because the free zip code information is incomplete. Each of those web sites gives you the option of obtaining a better database for a small fee.

Chapter Summary

Files are represented in Java as `File` objects. The `File` class is found in the `java.io` package.

A `Scanner` object can read input from a file rather than from the keyboard. This task is achieved by passing `new File(`*filename*`)` to the `Scanner`'s constructor, rather than passing `System.in`.

A checked exception is a program error condition that must be caught or declared in order for the program to compile. For example, when constructing a `Scanner` that reads a file, you must write the phrase `throws FileNotFoundException` in the `main` method's header.

The `Scanner` treats an input file as a one-dimensional stream of data that is read in order from start to end. The input cursor consumes (moves past) input tokens as they are read and returns them to your program.

A `Scanner` that reads a file makes use of the various `hasNext` methods to discover when the file's input has been exhausted.

`Scanners` can be passed as parameters to methods to read part or all of a file, since they are objects and therefore use reference semantics.

A file name can be specified as a relative path such as `data/text/numbers.dat`, which refers to a file called `numbers.dat` that exists in the `data/text/` subfolder of the current directory. Alternatively, you can specify a full file path such as `C:/Documents and Settings/user/My Documents/data/text/numbers.dat`.

In many files, input is structured by lines, and it makes sense to process those files line by line. In such cases, it is common to use nested loops: an outer loop that iterates over each line of the file and an inner loop that processes the tokens in each line.

Output to a file can be achieved with a `PrintStream` object, which is constructed with a `File` and has the same methods as `System.out`, such as `println` and `print`.

Self-Check Problems

Section 6.1: File-Reading Basics

1. What is a file? How can we read data from a file in Java?

2. What is wrong with the following line of code?

```
Scanner input = new Scanner("test.dat");
```

3. Which of the following is the correct syntax to declare a `Scanner` to read the file `example.txt` in the current directory?

```
a. Scanner input = new Scanner("C:\example.txt");
b. Scanner input = new Scanner(new File("example.txt"));
c. Scanner input = new File("\\example.txt");
d. File input = new Scanner("/example.txt");
e. Scanner input = new Scanner("C:/example.txt");
```

4. Write code to construct a `Scanner` object to read the file `input.txt`, which exists in the same folder as your program.

Section 6.2: Details of Token-Based Processing

5. Given the following line of input, what tokens does a `Scanner` break the line apart into?

```
welcome...to the matrix.
```

   a. `"welcome", "to", "the", "matrix"`
   b. `"welcome...to the matrix."`
   c. `"welcome...to", "the", "matrix."`
   d. `"welcome...", "to", "the matrix."`
   e. `"welcome", "to the matrix"`

6. Given the following lines of input, what tokens does a `Scanner` break the line apart into?

```
in fourteen-hundred 92
columbus sailed the ocean blue :)
```

   a. `"in", "fourteen-hundred", "92"`
   b. `"in", "fourteen-hundred", "92", "columbus", "sailed", "the", "ocean", "blue", ":)"`
   c. `"in", "fourteen", "hundred", "92", "columbus", "sailed", "the", "ocean", "blue"`
   d. `"in", "fourteen-hundred", "92\ncolumbus", "sailed", "the", "ocean", "blue :)"`
   e. `"in fourteen-hundred 92", "columbus sailed the ocean blue :)"`

7. How many tokens are there in the following input, and what `Scanner` method(s) can be used to read each of the tokens?

```
Hello there,how are you?
I am "very well", thank you.
12 34 5.67 (8 + 9) "10"
```

8. What is wrong with the following line of code?

```
Scanner input = new Scanner(new File("C:\temp\new files\test.dat"));
```

   (Hint: Try printing the `String` in this line of code.)

9. Answer the following questions about a Java program located on a Windows machine in the folder `C:\Documents and Settings\amanda\My Documents\programs`:
   a. What are two legal ways you can refer to the file `C:\Documents and Settings\amanda\My Documents\programs\numbers.dat`?
   b. How can you refer to the file `C:\Documents and Settings\amanda\My Documents\programs\data\homework6\input.dat`?
   c. How many, and in what legal, ways can you refer to the file `C:\Documents and Settings\amanda\My Documents\homework\data.txt`?

10. Answer the following questions about a Java program located on a Linux machine in the folder `/home/amanda/Documents/hw6`:
    a. What are two legal ways you can refer to the file `/home/amanda/Documents/hw6/names.txt`?
    b. How can you refer to the file `/home/amanda/Documents/hw6/data/numbers.txt`?
    c. How many legal ways can you refer to the file `/home/amanda/download/saved.html`?

11. The following program contains 6 mistakes! What are they?

```
public class Oops6 {
    public static void main(String[] args) {
        Scanner in = new Scanner("example.txt");
        countWords(in);
    }

    // Counts total lines and words in the input scanner.
    public static void countWords(Scanner input) {
        Scanner input = new Scanner("example.txt");
        int lineCount = 0;
        int wordCount = 0;

        while (input.nextLine()) {
            String line = input.line();    // read one line
            lineCount++;
            while (line.next()) {          // tokens in line
                String word = line.hasNext;
                wordCount++;
            }
        }
    }
}
```

Section 6.3: Line-Based Processing

12. For the next several questions, consider a file called `readme.txt` that has the following contents:

```
6.7         This file has
        several input lines.


  10 20          30   40


test
```

What would be the output from the following code when it is run on the `readme.txt` file?

```
Scanner input = new Scanner(new File("readme.txt"));
int count = 0;
while (input.hasNextLine()) {
     System.out.println("input: " + input.nextLine());
     count++;
}
System.out.println(count + " total");
```

13. What would be the output from the code in the previous exercise if the calls to `hasNextLine` and `nextLine` were replaced by calls to `hasNext` and `next`, respectively?

14. What would be the output from the code in the previous exercise if the calls to `hasNextLine` and `nextLine` were replaced by calls to `hasNextInt` and `nextInt`, respectively? How about `hasNextDouble` and `nextDouble`?

15. Given the following file contents, what will be the output from each of the following code fragments?

```
the quick brown
   fox   jumps

       over
the lazy    dog
```

a.

```
Scanner input = new Scanner(new File("brownfox.txt"));
while (input.hasNextLine()) {
    String line = input.nextLine();
    System.out.println(line);
}
```

b.

```
Scanner input = new Scanner(new File("brownfox.txt"));
while (input.hasNext()) {
    String token = input.next();
    System.out.println(token);
}
```

16. Write a program that prints itself to the console as output. For example, if the program is stored in `Example.java`, it will open the file `Example.java` and print its contents to the console.

17. Write code that prompts the user for a file name and prints the contents of that file to the console as output. Assume that the file exists. You may wish to place this code into a method called `printEntireFile`.

18. Write a program that takes as input lines of text like the following:

```
This is some
text here.
```

The program should produce as output the same text inside a box, as in the following:

```
+--------------+
| This is some |
| text here.   |
+--------------+
```

Your program will have to assume some maximum line length (e.g., 12 in this case).

Section 6.4: Advanced File Processing

19. What object is used to write output to a file? What methods does this object have available for you to use?

20. Write code to print the following four lines of text into a file named `message.txt`:

```
Testing,
1, 2, 3.

This is my output file.
```

21. Write code that repeatedly prompts the user for a file name until the user types the name of a file that exists on the system. You may wish to place this code into a method called `getFileName`, which will return that file name as a `String`.

22. In Problem 16, you wrote a piece of code that prompted the user for a file name and printed that file's contents to the console. Modify your code so that it will repeatedly prompt the user for the file name until the user types the name of a file that exists on the system.

Exercises

1. Write a method called `boyGirl` that accepts a `Scanner` that is reading its input from a file containing a series of names followed by integers. The names alternate between boys' names and girls' names. Your method should compute the absolute difference between the sum of the boys' integers and the sum of the girls' integers. The input could end with either a boy or girl; you may not assume that it contains an even number of names. For example, if the input file contains the following text:

```
Erik 3 Rita 7 Tanner 14 Jillyn 13 Curtis 4 Stefanie 12 Ben 6
```

Then the method should produce the following console output, since the boys' sum is 27 and the girls' sum is 32:

```
4 boys, 3 girls
Difference between boys' and girls' sums: 5
```

2. Write a method called `evenNumbers` that accepts a `Scanner` reading input from a file with a series of integers, and report various statistics about the integers to the console. Report the total number of numbers, the sum of the numbers, the count of even numbers and the percent of even numbers. For example, if the input file contains the following text:

```
5 7 2 8 9 10 12 98 7 14 20 22
```

Then the method should produce the following console output:

```
12 numbers, sum = 214
8 evens (66.67%)
```

3. Write a method called `negativeSum` that accepts a `Scanner` reading input from a file containing a series of integers, and print a message to the console indicating whether the sum starting from the first number is ever negative. You should also return `true` if a negative sum can be reached and `false` if not. For example, suppose the file contains the following text:

```
38 4 19 -27 -15 -3 4 19 38
```

Your method would consider the sum of just one number (38), the first two numbers (38 + 4), the first three numbers (38 + 4 + 19), and so on to the end. None of these sums is negative, so the method would produce the following output and return `false`:

```
no negative sum
```

If the file instead contains the following numbers:

```
14 7 -10 9 -18 -10 17 42 98
```

The method finds that a negative sum of −8 is reached after adding the first six numbers. It should output the following to the console and return `true`:

```
sum of -8 after 6 steps
```

4. Write a method called `countCoins` that accepts a `Scanner` representing an input file whose data is a series of pairs of tokens, where each pair begins with an integer and is followed by the type of coin, which will be "pennies" (1 cent each), "nickels" (5 cents each), "dimes" (10 cents each), or "quarters" (25 cents each), case-insensitively. Add up the cash values of all the coins and print the total money. For example, if the input file contains the following text:

```
3 pennies 2 quarters 1 Pennies 23 NiCkeLs 4 DIMES
```

For the input above, your method should produce the following output:

```
Total money: $2.09
```

5. Write a method called `collapseSpaces` that accepts a `Scanner` representing an input file as its parameter, then reads that file and outputs it with all its tokens separated by single spaces, collapsing any sequences of multiple spaces into single spaces. For example, consider the following text:

```
many    spaces    on    this    line!
```

If this text were a line in the file, the same line should be output as follows:

```
many spaces on this line!
```

6. Write a method called `readEntireFile` that accepts a `Scanner` representing an input file as its parameter, then reads that file and returns its entire text contents as a `String`.

7. Write a method called `flipLines` that accepts a `Scanner` for an input file and writes to the console the same file's contents with each pair of lines reversed in order. If the file contains an odd number of lines, leave the last line unmodified. For example, if the file contains:

```
Twas brillig and the slithy toves
did gyre and gimble in the wabe.
All mimsey were the borogroves,
and the mome raths outgrabe.
```

your method should produce the following output:

```
did gyre and gimble in the wabe.
Twas brillig and the slithy toves
and the mome raths outgrabe.
All mimsey were the borogroves,
```

8. Write a method called `doubleSpace` that accepts a `Scanner` for an input file and a `PrintStream` for an output file as its parameters, writing into the output file a double-spaced version of the text in the input file. You can achieve this task by inserting a blank line between each line of output.

9. Write a method called `wordWrap` that accepts a `Scanner` representing an input file as its parameter and outputs each line of the file to the console, word-wrapping all lines that are longer than 60 characters. For example, if a line contains 112 characters, the method should replace it with two lines: one containing the first 60 characters and another containing the final 52 characters. A line containing 217 characters should be wrapped into four lines: three of length 60 and a final line of length 37.

10. Modify the preceding `wordWrap` method so that it outputs the newly wrapped text back into the original file. (Be careful—don't output into a file while you are reading it!) Also, modify it to use a class constant for the maximum line length rather than hard-coding 60.

11. Modify the preceding `wordWrap` method so that it only wraps whole words, never chopping a word in half. Assume that a word is any whitespace-separated token and that all words are under 60 characters in length.

12. Write a method called `stripHtmlTags` that accepts a `Scanner` representing an input file containing an HTML web page as its parameter, then reads that file and prints the file's text with all HTML tags removed. A tag is any text between the characters < and >. For example, consider the following text:

```
<html>
<head>
<title>My web page</title>
</head>
<body>
<p>There are many pictures of my cat here,
as well as my <b>very cool</b> blog page,
which contains <font color="red">awesome
stuff about my trip to Vegas.</p>

Here's my cat now:<img src="cat.jpg">
</body>
</html>
```

If the file contained these lines, your program should output the following text:

```
My web page

There are many pictures of my cat here,
as well as my very cool blog page,
which contains awesome
stuff about my trip to Vegas.

Here's my cat now:
```

You may assume that the file is a well-formed HTML document and that there are no < or > characters inside tags.

13. Write a method called `stripComments` that accepts a `Scanner` representing an input file containing a Java program as its parameter, reads that file, and then prints the file's text with all comments removed. A comment is any text on a line from `//` to the end of the line, and any text between `/*` and `*/` characters. For example, consider the following text:

```
import java.util.*;

/* My program
by Suzy Student */
public class Program {
    public static void main(String[] args) {
        System.out.println("Hello, world!"); // a println
    }
```

```
    public static /* Hello there */ void foo() {
        System.out.println("Goodbye!"); // comment here
    } /* */
}
```

If the file contained this text, your program should output the following text:

```
import java.util.*;

public class Program {
    public static void main(String[] args) {
        System.out.println("Hello, world!");
    }

    public static  void foo() {
        System.out.println("Goodbye!");
    }
}
```

14. Write a method called `printDuplicates` that takes as a parameter a `Scanner` containing a series of lines. Your method should examine each line looking for consecutive occurrences of the same token on the same line and print each duplicated token, along with the number of times that it appears consecutively. Nonrepeated tokens are not printed. You may ignore the case of repetition across multiple lines (such as if a line ends with a given token and the next line starts with the same token). You may assume that each line of the file contains at least 1 token of input. For example, consider the following input:

```
hello how how are you you you you
I I I am Jack's Jack's smirking smirking smirking smirking revenge
bow wow wow yippee yippee  yo yippee  yippee yay yay yay
one fish two fish red fish blue fish
It's the Muppet Show, wakka wakka wakka
```

Your method should produce the following output:

```
how*2 you*4
I*3 Jack's*2 smirking*4
wow*2 yippee*2 yippee*2 yay*3

wakka*3
```

15. Write a method called `coinFlip` that accepts a `Scanner` representing an input file of coin flips that are heads (H) or tails (T). Consider each line to be a separate set of coin flips and output the number and percentage of heads in that line. If it is more than 50%, print "You win!". Consider the following file:

```
H T H H T
T t   t  T h  H
```

For the input above, your method should produce the following output:

```
3 heads (60.0%)
You win!

2 heads (33.3%)
```

16. Write a method called `mostCommonNames` that accepts a `Scanner` representing an input file with names on each line separated by spaces. Some names appear multiple times in a row on the same line. For each line, print the most commonly occurring name. If there's a tie, use the first name that had that many occurrences; if all names are unique, print the first name on the line. For example, if the file has this input:

```
Benson Eric   Eric  Kim  Kim Kim   Jenny  Nancy Nancy  Paul  Paul
Ethan  Jamie Jamie Alyssa Alyssa Helene  Helene Jessica Jessica
```

For the input above, your method should produce the following output:

```
Most common: Kim
Most common: Jamie
```

17. Write a method called `inputStats` that accepts a `Scanner` representing an input file and reports the number of lines, the longest line, the number of tokens on each line, and the length of the longest token on each line. If the file contains the following text:

```
Beware the Jabberwock, my son,
the jaws that bite, the claws that catch,
Beware the JubJub bird and shun
the frumious bandersnatch.
```

For the input above, your method should produce the following output:

```
Line 1 has 5 tokens (longest = 11)
Line 2 has 8 tokens (longest = 6)
Line 3 has 6 tokens (longest = 6)
Line 4 has 3 tokens (longest = 13)
Longest line: the jaws that bite, the claws that catch,
```

18. Write a method called `plusScores` that accepts a `Scanner` representing an input file containing a series of lines that represent student records. Each student record takes up two lines of input. The first line has the student's name and the second line has a series of plus and minus characters. Below is a sample input:

```
Kane, Erica
--+-+
Chandler, Adam
++-+
Martin, Jake
+++++++
```

For each student you should produce a line of output with the student's name followed by a colon followed by the percent of plus characters. For the input above, your method should produce the following output:

```
Kane, Erica: 40.0% plus
Chandler, Adam: 75.0% plus
Martin, Jake: 100.0% plus
```

19. Write a method called `leetSpeak` that accepts two parameters: a `Scanner` representing an input file, and a `PrintStream` representing an output file. Convert the input file's text to "leet speak," where various letters are replaced by other letters/numbers, and output the new text to the given output file. Replace `"o"` with `"0"`, `"l"` (lowercase "L") with `"1"` (the number one), `"e"` with `"3"`, `"a"` with `"4"`, `"t"` with `"7"`, and an `"s"` at the end of a word with `"Z"`. Preserve the original line breaks from the input. Also wrap each word of input in parentheses. For example, if the input file contains the following text:

```
four score and
seven years ago our
fathers brought forth on this continent
a new nation
```

For the input above, your method should produce the following in the output file:

```
(f0ur) (sc0r3) (4nd)
(s3v3n) (y34rZ) (4g0) (0ur)
(f47h3rZ) (br0ugh7) (f0r7h) (0n) (7hiZ) (c0n7in3n7)
(4) (n3w) (n47i0n)
```

Programming Projects

1. Students are often asked to write term papers containing a certain number of words. Counting words in a long paper is a tedious task, but the computer can help. Write a program that counts the number of words, lines, and total characters (not including whitespace) in a paper, assuming that consecutive words are separated either by spaces or end-of-line characters.

2. Write a program that compares two files and prints information about the differences between them. For example, consider a file `data1.txt` with the following contents:

```
This file has a great deal of
text in it which needs to

be processed.
```

Consider another file `data2.txt` that exists with the following contents:

```
This file has a grate deal of
text in it which needs to

bee procesed.
```

A dialogue with the user running your program might look like the following:

```
Enter a first file name: data1.txt
Enter a second file name: data2.txt
Differences found:
Line 1:
< This file has a great deal of
> This file has a grate deal of

Line 4:
< be processed.
> bee procesed.
```

3. Write a program that prompts the user for a file name, assuming that the file contains a Java program. Your program should read the file and print its contents properly indented. When you see a left-brace character (`{`) in the file, increase your indentation level by four spaces. When you see a right-brace character (`}`), decrease your indentation level by four spaces. You may assume that the file has only one opening or closing brace per line, that every block statement (such as `if` or `for`) uses braces rather than omitting them, and that every relevant occurrence of a `{` or `}` character in the file occurs at the end of a line. Consider using a class constant for the number of spaces to indent (4), so that it can easily be changed later.

4. Write a program that reads a file containing data about the changing popularity of various baby names over time and displays the data about a particular name. Each line of the file stores a name followed by integers representing the name's popularity in each decade: 1900, 1910, 1920, and so on. The rankings range from 1 (most popular) to 1000 (least popular), or 0 for a name that was less popular than the 1000th name. The following lines are a sample of the file format:

```
Sally 0 0 0 0 0 0 0 0 0 0 886
Sam 58 69 99 131 168 236 278 380 467 408 466
Samantha 0 0 0 0 0 0 272 107 26 5 7
Samir 0 0 0 0 0 0 0 0 920 0 798
```

Your program should prompt the user for a name and search the file for that name:

```
This program allows you to search through the
data from the Social Security Administration
to see how popular a particular name has been
since 1900.

Name? Sam
```

If the name is found, the program should display data about the name on the screen:

```
Statistics on name "Sam"
     1900: 58
     1910: 69
```

```
1920: 99
1930: 131
...
```

This program is more fun and challenging if you also draw the name's popularity on a `DrawingPanel` as a line graph. Plot the decades on the *x*-axis and the popularity on the *y*-axis.

5. Write a program that plays a game where a player is asked to fill in various words of a mostly complete story without being able to see the rest. Then the user is shown his/her story, which is often funny. The input for your program is a set of story files, each of which contains "placeholder" tokens surrounded by < and >, such as:

```
One of the most <adjective> characters in fiction is named
"Tarzan of the <plural-noun> ." Tarzan was raised by a/an
<noun> and lives in the <adjective> jungle in the
heart of darkest <place> .
```

The user is prompted to fill in each of the placeholders in the story, and then a resulting output file is created with the placeholders filled in. For example:

```
Input file name? story1.txt
Please enter an adjective: silly
Please enter a plural noun: socks
Please enter a noun: tree
Please enter an adjective: tiny
Please enter a place: Canada
```

The resulting output story would be:

```
One of the most silly characters in fiction is named
"Tarzan of the socks ." Tarzan was raised by a/an
tree and lives in the tiny jungle in the
heart of darkest Canada .
```

Chapter 7
Arrays

Introduction

The sequential nature of files severely limits the number of interesting things that you can do easily with them. The algorithms we have examined so far have all been sequential algorithms: algorithms that can be performed by examining each data item once, in sequence. An entirely different class of algorithms can be performed when you can access the data items multiple times and in an arbitrary order.

This chapter examines a new object called an array that provides this more flexible kind of access. The concept of arrays is not complex, but it can take a while for a novice to learn all of the different ways that an array can be used. The chapter begins with a general discussion of arrays and then moves into a discussion of common array manipulations as well as advanced array techniques. The chapter also includes a discussion of special rules known as reference semantics that apply only to objects like arrays and strings.

7.1 Array Basics

An *array* is a flexible structure for storing a sequence of values that are all of the same type.

> **Array**
>
> An indexed structure that holds multiple values of the same type.

The values stored in an array are called *elements*. The individual elements are accessed using an integer *index*.

> **Index**
>
> An integer indicating the position of a particular value in a data structure.

As an analogy, consider post office boxes. The boxes are indexed with numbers, so you can refer to an individual box by using a description like "P.O. Box 884." You already have experience using an index to indicate positions within a `String`; recall the methods `charAt` and `substring`. Like `String` indexes, array indexes start with 0. This is a convention known as *zero-based indexing*.

> **Zero-Based Indexing**
>
> A numbering scheme used throughout Java in which a sequence of values is indexed starting with 0 (element 0, element 1, element 2, and so on).

It might seem more natural to start indexes with 1 instead of 0, but Java uses the same indexing scheme that is used in C and C++.

Constructing and Traversing an Array

Suppose you want to store some different temperature readings. You could keep them in a series of variables:

```
double temperature1;
double temperature2;
double temperature3;
```

This isn't a bad solution if you have just 3 temperatures, but suppose you need to store 3000 temperatures. Then you would want a more flexible way to store the values. You can instead store the temperatures in an array.

When you use an array, you first need to declare a variable for it, so you have to know what type to use. The type will depend on the type of elements you want to have in your array. To indicate that you are creating an array, follow the type name with a set of square brackets: `[]`. If you are storing temperature values, you want a sequence of values of type `double`, so you use the type `double[]`. Thus, you can declare a variable for storing your array as follows:

```
double[] temperature;
```

Arrays are objects, which means that they must be constructed. Simply declaring a variable isn't enough to bring the object into existence. In this case you want an array of three `double` values, which you can construct as follows:

```
double[] temperature = new double[3];
```

This is a slightly different syntax than you've used previously to create a new object. It is a special syntax for arrays only. Notice that on the left-hand side you don't put anything inside the square brackets, because you're describing a type. The variable `temperature` can refer to any array of `double` values, no matter how many elements it has. On the right-hand side, however, you have to mention a specific number of elements because you are asking Java to construct an actual array object and it needs to know how many elements to include.

The general syntax for declaring and constructing an array is as follows:

```
<element type>[] <name> = new <element type>[<length>];
```

You can use any type as the element type, although the left and right sides of this statement have to match. For example, any of the following lines of code would be legal ways to construct an array:

```
int[] numbers = new int[10];          // an array of 10 ints
char[] letters = new char[20];        // an array of 20 chars
boolean[] flags = new boolean[5];     // an array of 5 booleans
String[] names = new String[100];     // an array of 100 Strings
Color[] colors = new Color[50];       // an array of 50 Colors
```

Some special rules apply when you construct an array of objects such as an array of `Strings` or an array of `Colors`, but we'll discuss those later in the chapter.

When it executes the line of code to construct the array of temperatures, Java will construct an array of three `double` values, and the variable `temperature` will refer to the array:

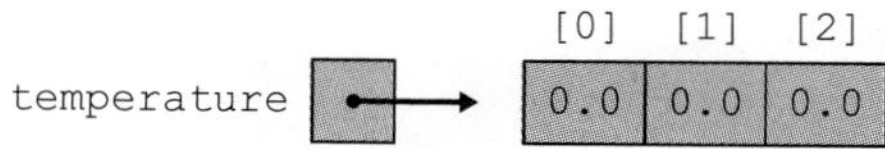

As you can see, the variable `temperature` is not itself the array. Instead, it stores a reference to the array. The array indexes are indicated in square brackets. To refer to an individual element of the array, you combine the name of the variable that

Table 7.1 Zero-Equivalent Auto-Initialization Values

Type	Value
`int`	`0`
`double`	`0.0`
`char`	`'\0'`
`boolean`	`false`
objects	`null`

refers to the array (`temperature`) with a specific index (`[0]`, `[1]`, or `[2]`). So, there is an element known as `temperature[0]`, an element known as `temperature[1]`, and an element known as `temperature[2]`.

In the `temperature` array diagram, each of the array elements has the value `0.0`. This is a guaranteed outcome when an array is constructed. Each element is initialized to a default value, a process known as *auto-initialization.*

Auto-Initialization

The initialization of variables to a default value, such as on an array's elements when it is constructed.

When Java performs auto-initialization, it always initializes to the zero-equivalent for the type. Table 7.1 indicates the zero-equivalent values for various types. The special value `null` will be explained later in this chapter.

Notice that the zero-equivalent for type `double` is `0.0`, which is why the array elements were initialized to that value. Using the indexes, you can store the specific temperature values that are relevant to this problem:

```
temperature[0] = 74.3;
temperature[1] = 68.4;
temperature[2] = 70.3;
```

This code modifies the array to have the following values:

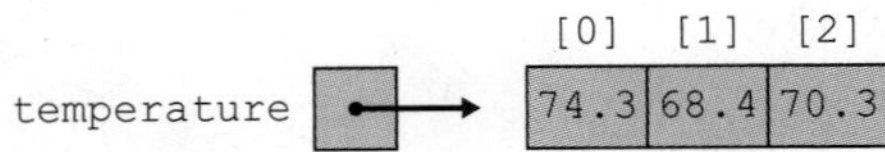

Obviously an array isn't particularly helpful when you have just three values to store, but you can request a much larger array. For example, you could request an array of 100 temperatures by writing the following line of code:

```
double[] temperature = new double[100];
```

This is almost the same line of code you executed before. The variable is still declared to be of type `double[]`, but in constructing the array, you requested 100 elements instead of 3, which constructs a much larger array:

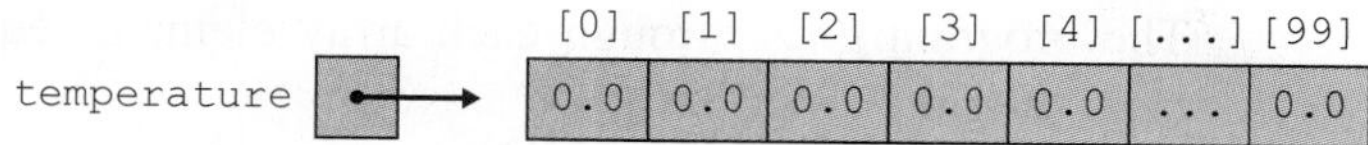

Notice that the highest index is 99 rather than 100 because of zero-based indexing.

You are not restricted to using simple literal values inside the brackets. You can use any integer expression. This flexibility allows you to combine arrays with loops, which greatly simplifies the code you write. For example, suppose you want to read a series of temperatures from a `Scanner`. You could read each value individually:

```
temperature[0] = input.nextDouble();
temperature[1] = input.nextDouble();
temperature[2] = input.nextDouble();
...
temperature[99] = input.nextDouble();
```

But since the only thing that changes from one statement to the next is the index, you can capture this pattern in a `for` loop with a control variable that takes on the values `0` to `99`:

```
for (int i = 0; i < 100; i++) {
    temperature[i] = input.nextDouble();
}
```

This is a very concise way to initialize all the elements of the array. The preceding code works when the array has a length of 100, but you can change this to accommodate an array of a different length. Java provides a useful mechanism for making this code more general. Each array keeps track of its own length. You're using the variable `temperature` to refer to your array, which means you can ask for `temperature.length` to find out the length of the array. By using `temperature.length` in the `for` loop test instead of the specific value 100, you make your code more general:

```
for (int i = 0; i < temperature.length; i++) {
    temperature[i] = input.nextDouble();
}
```

Notice that the array convention is different from the `String` convention. When you are working with a `String` variable `s`, you ask for the length of the `String` by referring to `s.length()`. When you are working with an array variable, you don't include the parentheses after the word "length." This is another one of those unfortunate inconsistencies that Java programmers just have to memorize.

The previous code provides a pattern that you will see often with array-processing code: a `for` loop that starts at 0 and that continues while the loop variable is less than the length of the array, doing something with element `[i]` in the body of the loop. The program goes through each array element sequentially, which we refer to as *traversing* the array.

> **Array Traversal**
> Processing each array element sequentially from the first to the last.

This pattern is so useful that it is worth including it in a more general form:

```
for (int i = 0; i < <array>.length; i++) {
    <do something with array[i]>;
}
```

We will see this traversal pattern repeatedly as we explore common array algorithms.

Accessing an Array

As we discussed in the last section, we refer to array elements by combining the name of the variable that refers to the array with an integer index inside square brackets:

```
<array variable>[<integer expression>]
```

Notice in this syntax description that the index can be an arbitrary integer expression. To explore this feature, let's examine how we would access particular values in an array of integers. Suppose that we construct an array of length 5 and fill it up with the first five odd integers:

```
int[] list = new int[5];
for (int i = 0; i < list.length; i++) {
    list[i] = 2 * i + 1;
}
```

The first line of code declares a variable `list` of type `int[]` that refers to an array of length 5. The array elements are auto-initialized to `0`:

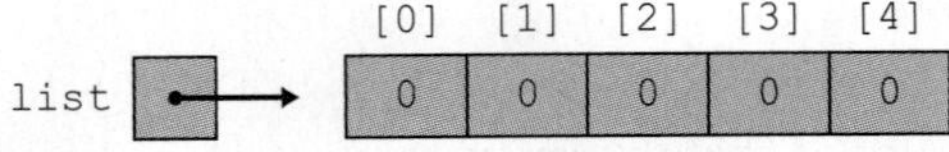

Then the code uses the standard traversing loop to fill in the array with successive odd numbers:

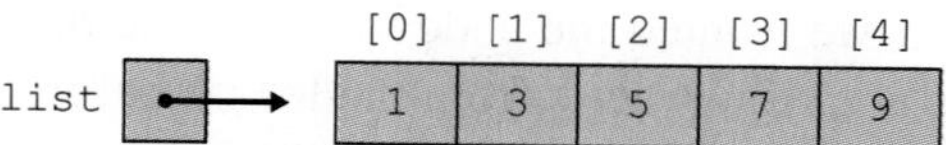

Suppose that we want to report the first, middle, and last values in the list. From an examination of the preceding diagram, we can see that these values occur at indexes 0, 2, and 4, which means we could write the following code:

```
// works only for an array of length 5
System.out.println("first = " + list[0]);
System.out.println("middle = " + list[2]);
System.out.println("last = " + list[4]);
```

This technique works when the array is of length 5, but suppose that we use an array of a different length? If the array has a length of 10, for example, this code will report the wrong values. We need to modify it to incorporate `list.length`, just as we modified the standard traversing loop.

The first element of the array will always be at index 0, so the first line of code doesn't need to change. You might at first think that we could fix the third line of code by replacing the `4` with `list.length`:

```
// doesn't work
System.out.println("last = " + list[list.length]);
```

However, this code doesn't work. The culprit is zero-based indexing. In our example, the last value is stored at index 4, not index 5, when `list.length` is 5. More generally, the last value will be at index `list.length – 1`. We can use this expression directly in our `println` statement:

```
// this one works
System.out.println("last = " + list[list.length – 1]);
```

Notice that what appears inside the square brackets is an integer expression (the result of subtracting 1 from `list.length`).

A simple approach to finding the middle value is to divide the length of the list in half:

```
// is this right?
System.out.println("middle = " + list[list.length / 2]);
```

When `list.length` is 5, this expression evaluates to `2`, which prints the correct value. But what about when `list.length` is 10? In that case the expression evaluates to `5`, and we would print `list[5]`. But when the list has an even length, there are actually two values in the middle. For a list of length 10, the two values are at `list[4]` and `list[5]`. In general, the preceding expression always returns the second of the two values in the middle when the list is of even length.

If we wanted the code to return the first of the two values in the middle instead, we could subtract 1 from the length before dividing it in half. Here is a complete set of `println` statements that follows this approach:

```
System.out.println("first = " + list[0]);
System.out.println("middle = " + list[(list.length - 1) / 2]);
System.out.println("last = " + list[list.length - 1]);
```

As you learn how to use arrays, you will find yourself wondering what types of operations you can perform on an array element that you are accessing. For example, for the array of integers called `list`, what exactly can you do with `list[i]`? The answer is that you can do anything with `list[i]` that you would normally do with any variable of type `int`. For example, if you have a variable called `x` of type `int`, any of the following expressions are valid:

```
x = 3;
x++;
x *= 2;
x--;
```

That means that the same expressions are valid for `list[i]` if `list` is an array of integers:

```
list[i] = 3;
list[i]++;
list[i] *= 2;
list[i]--;
```

From Java's point of view, because `list` is declared to be of type `int[]`, an array element like `list[i]` is of type `int` and can be manipulated as such. For example, to increment every value in the array, you could use the standard traversing loop:

```
for (int i = 0; i < list.length; i++) {
    list[i]++;
}
```

This code would increment each value in the array, turning the array of odd numbers into an array of even numbers.

It is possible to refer to an illegal index of an array, in which case Java throws an exception. For example, for an array of length 5, the legal indexes are from 0 to 4. Any number less than 0 or greater than 4 is outside the bounds of the array:

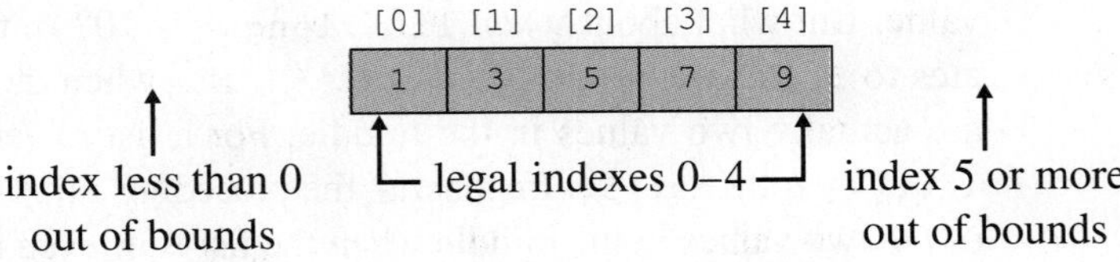

When you are working with this sample array, if you attempt to refer to `list[-1]` or `list[5]`, you are attempting to access an array element that does not exist. If your code makes such an illegal reference, Java will halt your program with an `ArrayIndexOutOfBoundsException`.

A Complete Array Program

Let's look at a program in which an array allows you to solve a problem that you couldn't solve before. If you tune in to any local news broadcast at night, you'll hear them report the high temperature for that day. It is usually reported as an integer, as in, "It got up to 78 today."

Suppose you want to examine a series of daily high temperatures, compute the average high temperature, and count how many days were above that average temperature. You've been using `Scanner`s to solve problems like this, and you can almost solve the problem that way. If you just wanted to know the average, you could use a `Scanner` and write a cumulative sum loop to find it:

```
// Reads a series of high temperatures and reports the average.

import java.util.*;

public class Temperature1 {
    public static void main(String[] args) {
        Scanner console = new Scanner(System.in);
        System.out.print("How many days' temperatures? ");
        int numDays = console.nextInt();
        int sum = 0;
        for (int i = 1; i <= numDays; i++) {
            System.out.print("Day " + i + "'s high temp: ");
            int next = console.nextInt();
            sum += next;
        }
        double average = (double) sum / numDays;
        System.out.println();
        System.out.println("Average = " + average);
    }
}
```

Did You Know?

Buffer Overruns

One of the earliest and still most common sources of computer security problems is a *buffer overrun* (also known as a *buffer overflow*). A buffer overrun is similar

Continued on next page

Continued from previous page

to an array index out of bounds exception. It occurs when a program writes data beyond the bounds of the buffer that is set aside for that data.

For example, you might have space allocated for the `String` "James T Kirk", which is 12 characters long, counting the spaces:

Suppose that you tell the computer to overwrite this buffer with the `String` "Jean Luc Picard". There are 15 letters in Picard's name, so if you write all of those characters into the buffer, you "overrun" it by writing three extra characters:

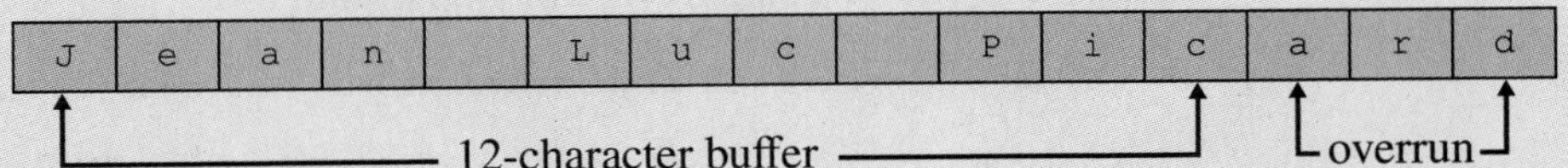

The last three letters of Picard's name ("ard") are being written to a part of memory that is beyond the end of the buffer. This is a very dangerous situation, because it will overwrite any data that is already there. An analogy would be a fellow student grabbing three sheets of paper from you and erasing anything you had written on them. You are likely to have had useful information written on those sheets of paper, so the overrun is likely to cause a problem.

When a buffer overrun happens accidentally, the program usually halts with some kind of error condition. However, buffer overruns are particularly dangerous when they are done on purpose by a malicious program. If the attacker can figure out just the right memory location to overwrite, the attacking software can take over your computer and instruct it to do things you haven't asked it to do.

Three of the most famous Internet worms were built on buffer overruns: the 1988 Morris worm, the 2001 Code Red worm, and the 2003 SQLSlammer worm.

Buffer overruns are often written as array code. You might wonder how such a malicious program could be written if the computer checks the bounds when you access an array. The answer is that older programming languages like C and C++ do not check bounds when you access an array. By the time Java was designed in the early 1990s, the danger of buffer overruns was clear and the designers of the language decided to include array-bounds checking so that Java would be more secure. Microsoft included similar bounds checking when it designed the language C# in the late 1990s.

The preceding program does a pretty good job. Here is a sample execution:

```
How many days' temperatures? 5
Day 1's high temp: 78
Day 2's high temp: 81
Day 3's high temp: 75
Day 4's high temp: 79
Day 5's high temp: 71
Average = 76.8
```

But how do you count how many days were above average? You could try to incorporate a comparison to the average temperature into the loop, but that won't work. The problem is that you can't figure out the average until you've gone through all of the data. That means you'll need to make a second pass through the data to figure out how many days were above average. You can't do that with a `Scanner`, because a `Scanner` has no "reset" option that allows you to see the data a second time. You'd have to prompt the user to enter the temperature data a second time, which would be silly.

Fortunately, you can solve the problem with an array. As you read numbers in and compute the cumulative sum, you can fill up an array that stores the temperatures. Then you can use the array to make the second pass through the data.

In the previous temperature example you used an array of `double` values, but here you want an array of `int` values. So, instead of declaring a variable of type `double[]`, declare a variable of type `int[]`. You're asking the user how many days of temperature data to include, so you can construct the array right after you've read that information:

```
int numDays = console.nextInt();
int[] temps = new int[numDays];
```

Here is the old loop:

```
for (int i = 1; i <= numDays; i++) {
    System.out.print("Day " + i + "'s high temp: ");
    int next = console.nextInt();
    sum += next;
}
```

Because you're using an array, you'll want to change this to a loop that starts at 0 to match the array indexing. But just because you're using zero-based indexing inside the program doesn't mean that you have to confuse the user by asking for "Day 0's high temp." You can modify the `println` to prompt for day `(i + 1)`. Furthermore, you no longer need the variable `next` because you'll be storing the values in the array instead. So, the loop code becomes

```
for (int i = 0; i < numDays; i++) {
    System.out.print("Day " + (i + 1) + "'s high temp: ");
```

```
    temps[i] = console.nextInt();
    sum += temps[i];
}
```

Notice that you're now testing whether the index is strictly less than `numDays`. After this loop executes, you compute the average as we did before. Then you write a new loop that counts how many days were above average using our standard traversing loop:

```
int above = 0;
for (int i = 0; i < temps.length; i++) {
    if (temps[i] > average) {
        above++;
    }
}
```

In this loop the test involves `temps.length`. You could instead have tested whether the variable is less than `numDays`; either choice works in this program because they should be equal to each other.

If you put these various code fragments together and include code to report the number of days that had an above-average temperature, you get the following complete program:

```
// Reads a series of high temperatures and reports the
// average and the number of days above average.

import java.util.*;

public class Temperature2 {
    public static void main(String[] args) {
        Scanner console = new Scanner(System.in);
        System.out.print("How many days' temperatures? ");
        int numDays = console.nextInt();
        int[] temps = new int[numDays];

        // record temperatures and find average
        int sum = 0;
        for (int i = 0; i < numDays; i++) {
            System.out.print("Day " + (i + 1) + "'s high temp: ");
            temps[i] = console.nextInt();
            sum += temps[i];
        }
        double average = (double) sum / numDays;

        // count days above average
        int above = 0;
```

```
        for (int i = 0; i < temps.length; i++) {
            if (temps[i] > average) {
                above++;
            }
        }

        // report results
        System.out.println();
        System.out.println("Average = " + average);
        System.out.println(above + " days above average");
    }
}
```

Here is a sample execution of the program:

```
How many days' temperatures? 9
Day 1's high temp: 75
Day 2's high temp: 78
Day 3's high temp: 85
Day 4's high temp: 71
Day 5's high temp: 69
Day 6's high temp: 82
Day 7's high temp: 74
Day 8's high temp: 80
Day 9's high temp: 87

Average = 77.88888888888889
5 days above average
```

Random Access

Most of the algorithms we have seen so far have involved *sequential access.*

> **Sequential Access**
> Manipulating values in a sequential manner from first to last.

A `Scanner` object is often all you need for a sequential algorithm, because it allows you to access data by moving forward from the first element to the last. But as we have seen, there is no way to reset a `Scanner` back to the beginning. The sample program we just studied uses an array to allow a second pass through the data, but even this is fundamentally a sequential approach because it involves two forward passes through the data.

An array is a powerful data structure that allows a more flexible kind of access known as *random access:*

Random Access

Manipulating values in any order whatsoever to allow quick access to each value.

An array can provide random access because it is allocated as a contiguous block of memory. The computer can quickly compute exactly where a particular value will be stored, because it knows how much space each element takes up in memory and it knows that all the elements are allocated right next to one another in the array.

When you work with arrays, you can jump around in the array without worrying about how much time it will take. For example, suppose that you have constructed an array of temperature readings that has 10,000 elements and you find yourself wanting to print a particular subset of the readings with code like the following:

```
System.out.println("#1394 = " + temps[1394]);
System.out.println("#6793 = " + temps[6793]);
System.out.println("#72 = " + temps[72]);
```

This code will execute quickly even though you are asking for array elements that are far apart from one another. Notice also that you don't have to ask for them in order. You can jump to element 1394, then jump ahead to element 6793, and then jump back to element 72. You can access elements in an array in any order that you like, and you will get fast access.

Later in the chapter we will explore several algorithms that would be difficult to implement without fast random access.

Common Programming Error

Off-by-One Bug

When you converted the `Temperature1` program to one that uses an array, you modified the `for` loop to start with an index of 0 instead of 1. The original `for` loop was written the following way:

```
for (int i = 1; i <= numDays; i++) {
    System.out.print("Day " + i + "'s high temp: ");
    int next = console.nextInt();
    sum += next;
}
```

Because you were storing the values into an array rather than reading them into a variable called `next`, you replaced `next` with `temps[i]`:

```
// wrong loop bounds
for (int i = 1; i <= numDays; i++) {
```

Continued on next page

Continued from previous page

```
    System.out.print("Day " + i + "'s high temp: ");
    temps[i] = console.nextInt();
    sum += temps[i];
}
```

Because the array is indexed starting at 0, you changed the bounds of the `for` loop to start at `0` and adjusted the `print` statement. Suppose those were the only changes you made:

```
// still wrong loop bounds
for (int i = 0; i <= numDays; i++) {
    System.out.print("Day " + (i + 1) + "'s high temp: ");
    temps[i] = console.nextInt();
    sum += temps[i];
}
```

This loop generates an error when you run the program. The loop asks for an extra day's worth of data and then throws an exception. Here's a sample execution:

```
How many days' temperatures? 5
Day 1's high temp: 82
Day 2's high temp: 80
Day 3's high temp: 79
Day 4's high temp: 71
Day 5's high temp: 75
Day 6's high temp: 83
Exception in thread "main"
    java.lang.ArrayIndexOutOfBoundsException: 5
        at Temperature2.main(Temperature2.java:18)
```

The problem is that if you're going to start the `for` loop variable at `0`, you need to do a test to ensure that it is strictly less than the number of iterations you want. You changed the `1` to a `0` but left the <= test. As a result, the loop is performing an extra iteration and trying to make a reference to an array element `temps[5]` that doesn't exist.

This is a classic off-by-one error. The fix is to change the loop bounds to use a strictly less-than test:

```
// correct bounds
for (int i = 0; i < numDays; i++) {
    System.out.print("Day " + (i + 1) + "'s high temp: ");
    temps[i] = console.nextInt();
    sum += temps[i];
}
```

Arrays and Methods

VideoNote

You will find that when you pass an array as a parameter to a method, the method has the ability to change the contents of the array. We'll examine in detail later in the chapter why this occurs, but for now, the important point is simply to understand that methods can alter the contents of arrays that are passed to them as parameters.

Let's explore a specific example to better understand how to use arrays as parameters and return values for a method. Earlier in the chapter, we saw the following code for constructing an array of odd numbers and incrementing each array element:

```
int[] list = new int[5];
for (int i = 0; i < list.length; i++) {
    list[i] = 2 * i + 1;
}
for (int i = 0; i < list.length; i++) {
    list[i]++;
}
```

Let's see what happens when we move the incrementing loop into a method. It will need to take the array as a parameter. We'll rename it `data` instead of `list` to make it easier to distinguish it from the original array variable. Remember that the array is of type `int[]`, so we would write the method as follows:

```
public static void incrementAll(int[] data) {
    for (int i = 0; i < data.length; i++) {
        data[i]++;
    }
}
```

You might think this method will have no effect whatsoever, or that we have to return the array to cause the change to be remembered. But when we use an array as a parameter, this approach actually works. We can replace the incrementing loop in the original code with a call on our method:

```
int[] list = new int[5];
for (int i = 0; i < list.length; i++) {
    list[i] = 2 * i + 1;
}
incrementAll(list);
```

This code produces the same result as the original.

The key lesson to draw from this is that when we pass an array as a parameter to a method, that method has the ability to change the contents of the array. We don't need to return the array to allow this to happen.

To continue with this example, let's define a method for the initializing code that fills the array with odd numbers. We can accomplish this by moving the initializing loop into a method that takes the array as a parameter:

```
public static void fillWithOdds(int[] data) {
    for (int i = 0; i < data.length; i++) {
        data[i] = 2 * i + 1;
    }
}
```

We would then change our `main` method to call this `fillWithOdds` method:

```
int[] list = new int[5];
fillWithOdds(list);
incrementAll(list);
```

Like the `incrementAll` method, this method would change the array even though it does not return it. But this isn't the best approach to use in this situation. It seems odd that the `fillWithOdds` method requires you to construct an array and pass it as a parameter. Why doesn't `fillWithOdds` construct the array itself? That would simplify the call to the method, particularly if we ended up calling it multiple times.

If `fillWithOdds` is going to construct the array, it will have to return a reference to it. Otherwise, only the method will have a reference to the newly constructed array. In its current form, the `fillWithOdds` method assumes that the array has already been constructed, which is why we wrote the following two lines of code in `main`:

```
int[] list = new int[5];
fillWithOdds(list);
```

If the method is going to construct the array, it doesn't have to be passed as a parameter, but it will have to be returned by the method. Thus, we can rewrite these two lines of code from `main` as a single line:

```
int[] list = fillWithOdds();
```

Now, however, we have a misleading method name. The method isn't just filling an existing array, it is constructing one. Also notice that we can make the method more flexible by telling it how large to make the array. So if we rename it and pass the size as a parameter, then we'd call it this way:

```
int[] list = buildOddArray(5);
```

We can then rewrite the `fillWithOdds` method so that it constructs and returns the array:

```
public static int[] buildOddArray(int size) {
    int[] data = new int[size];
    for (int i = 0; i < data.length; i++) {
        data[i] = 2 * i + 1;
    }
    return data;
}
```

Pay close attention to the header of the preceding method. It no longer has the array as a parameter, and its return type is `int[]` rather than `void`. It also ends with a `return` statement that returns a reference to the array that it constructs.

Putting this all together along with some code to print the contents of the array, we end up with the following complete program:

```
// Sample program with arrays passed as parameters

public class IncrementOdds {
    public static void main(String[] args) {
        int[] list = buildOddArray(5);
        incrementAll(list);
        for (int i = 0; i < list.length; i++) {
            System.out.print(list[i] + " ");
        }
        System.out.println();
    }

    // returns array of given size composed of consecutive odds
    public static int[] buildOddArray(int size) {
        int[] data = new int[size];
        for (int i = 0; i < data.length; i++) {
            data[i] = 2 * i + 1;
        }
        return data;
    }

    // adds one to each array element
    public static void incrementAll(int[] data) {
        for (int i = 0; i < data.length; i++) {
            data[i]++;
        }
    }
}
```

The program produces the following output:

```
2 4 6 8 10
```

The For-Each Loop

Java has a loop construct that simplifies certain array loops. It is known as the enhanced `for` loop, or the for-each loop. You can use it whenever you want to examine each value in an array. For example, the program `Temperature2` had an array variable called `temps` and the following loop:

```
for (int i = 0; i < temps.length; i++) {
    if (temps[i] > average) {
        above++;
    }
}
```

We can rewrite this as a for-each loop:

```
for (int n : temps) {
    if (n > average) {
        above++;
    }
}
```

This loop is normally read as, "For each `int n` in `temps`. . . ." The basic syntax of the for-each loop is

```
for (<type> <name> : <array>) {
    <statement>;
    <statement>;
    ...
    <statement>;
}
```

There is nothing special about the variable name, as long as you keep it consistent within the body of the loop. For example, the previous loop could be written with the variable `x` instead of the variable `n`:

```
for (int x : temps) {
    if (x > average) {
        above++;
    }
}
```

The for-each loop is most useful when you simply want to examine each value in sequence. There are many situations in which a for-each loop is not appropriate. For example, the following loop would double every value in an array called `list`:

```
for (int i = 0; i < list.length; i++) {
    list[i] *= 2;
}
```

Because the loop is changing the array, you can't replace it with a for-each loop:

```
for (int n : list) {
    n *= 2; // changes only n, not the array
}
```

As the comment indicates, the preceding loop doubles the variable `n` without changing the array elements.

In some cases, the for-each loop isn't the most convenient choice even when the code involves examining each array element in sequence. Consider, for example, the following loop that prints each array index along with the array value separated by a tab character:

```
for (int i = 0; i < data.length; i++) {
    System.out.println(i + "\t" + data[i]);
}
```

A for-each loop could be used to replace the array access:

```
for (int n : data) {
    System.out.println(i + "\t" + n); // not quite legal
}
```

However, this loop would cause a problem. We want to print the value of `i`, but we eliminated `i` when we converted the array access to a for-each loop. We would have to add extra code to keep track of the value of `i`:

```
// legal but clumsy
int i = 0;
for (int n : data) {
    System.out.println(i + "\t" + n);
    i++;
}
```

In this case, the for-each loop doesn't really simplify things, and the original version is probably clearer.

Initializing Arrays

Java has a special syntax for initializing an array when you know exactly what you want to put into it. For example, you could write the following code to initialize an array of integers to keep track of the number of days that are in each month ("Thirty days hath September . . .") and an array of `Strings` to keep track of the abbreviations for the days of the week:

```
int[] daysIn = new int[12];
daysIn[0] = 31;
daysIn[1] = 28;
daysIn[2] = 31;
daysIn[3] = 30;
daysIn[4] = 31;
daysIn[5] = 30;
daysIn[6] = 31;
daysIn[7] = 31;
daysIn[8] = 30;
daysIn[9] = 31;
daysIn[10] = 30;
daysIn[11] = 31;
String[] dayNames = new String[7];
dayNames[0] = "Mon";
dayNames[1] = "Tue";
dayNames[2] = "Wed";
dayNames[3] = "Thu";
dayNames[4] = "Fri";
dayNames[5] = "Sat";
dayNames[6] = "Sun";
```

This code works, but it's a rather tedious way to declare these arrays. Java provides a shorthand:

```
int[] daysIn = {31, 28, 31, 30, 31, 30, 31, 31, 30, 31, 30, 31};
String[] dayNames = {"Mon", "Tue", "Wed", "Thu", "Fri", "Sat", "Sun"};
```

The general syntax for array initialization is as follows:

```
<element type>[] <name> = {<value>, <value>, ..., <value>};
```

You use the curly braces to enclose a series of values that will be stored in the array. The order of the values is important. The first value will go into index 0, the second value will go into index 1, and so on. Java counts how many values you include and constructs an array that is just the right size. It then stores the various values into the appropriate spots in the array.

This is one of only two examples we have seen in which Java will construct an object without the `new` keyword. The other place we saw this was with `String` literals, in which Java constructs `String` objects without your having to call `new`. Both of these techniques are conveniences for programmers. These tasks are so common that the designers of the language wanted to make it easy to do them.

The `Arrays` Class

Arrays have some important limitations that you should understand. Over the years Java has attempted to remedy these limitations by providing various utility methods in a class called `Arrays`. This class provides many methods that make it easier to work with arrays. The `Arrays` class is part of the `java.util` package, so you would have to include an `import` declaration in any program that uses it.

The first limitation you should be aware of is that you can't change the size of an array in the middle of program execution. Remember that arrays are allocated as a contiguous block of memory, so it is not easy for the computer to expand the array. If you find that you need a larger array, you should construct a new array and copy the values from the old array to the new array. The method `Arrays.copyOf` provides exactly this functionality. For example, if you have an array called `data`, you can create a copy that is twice as large with the following line of code:

```
int[] newData = Arrays.copyOf(data, 2 * data.length);
```

If you want to copy only a portion of an array, there is a similar method called `Arrays.copyOfRange` that accepts an array, a starting index, and an ending index as parameters.

The second limitation is that you can't print an array using a simple `print` or `println` statement. You will get odd output when you do so. The `Arrays` class once again offers a solution: The method `Arrays.toString` returns a conveniently formatted version of an array. Consider, for example, the following three lines of code:

```
int[] primes = {2, 3, 5, 7, 11, 13, 17, 19, 23};
System.out.println(primes);
System.out.println(Arrays.toString(primes));
```

It produces the following output:

```
[I@fee4648
[2, 3, 5, 7, 11, 13, 17, 19, 23]
```

Notice that the first line of output is not at all helpful. The second line, however, allows us to see the list of prime numbers in the array because we called `Arrays.toString` to format the array before printing it.

Table 7.2 Useful Methods of the Arrays Class

Method	Description
copyOf(array, newSize)	returns a copy of the array with the given size
copyOfRange(array, startIndex, endIndex)	returns a copy of the given subportion of the given array from startIndex (inclusive) to endIndex (exclusive)
equals(array1, array2)	returns true if the arrays contain the same elements
fill(array, value)	sets every element of the array to be the given value
sort(array)	rearranges the elements so that they appear in sorted (nondecreasing) order
toString(array)	returns a String representation of the array, as in [3, 5, 7]

The third limitation is that you can't compare arrays for equality using a simple == test. We saw that this was true of Strings as well. If you want to know whether two arrays contain the same set of values, you should call the Arrays.equals method:

```
int[] data1 = {1, 1, 2, 3, 5, 8, 13, 21};
int[] data2 = {1, 1, 2, 3, 5, 8, 13, 21};
if (Arrays.equals(data1, data2)) {
    System.out.println("They store the same data");
}
```

This code prints the message that the arrays store the same data. It would not do so if we used a direct comparison with ==.

The Arrays class provides other useful methods as well, including methods for sorting the array and for filling it up with a specific value. Table 7.2 contains a list of some of the most useful methods in the Arrays class.

7.2 Array-Traversal Algorithms

VideoNote

The previous section presented two standard patterns for manipulating an array. The first is the traversing loop, which uses a variable of type int to index each array value:

```
for (int i = 0; i < <array>.length; i++) {
    <do something with array[i]>;
}
```

The second is the for-each loop:

```
for (<type> <name> : <array>) {
    <statement>;
    <statement>;
```

```
    ...
    <statement>;
}
```

In this section we will explore some common array algorithms that can be implemented with these patterns. Of course, not all array operations can be implemented this way—the section ends with an example that requires a modified version of the standard code.

We will implement each operation as a method. Java does not allow you to write generic array code, so we have to pick a specific type. We'll assume that you are operating on an array of `int` values. If you are writing a program to manipulate a different kind of array, you'll have to modify the code for the type you are using (e.g., changing `int[]` to `double[]` if you are manipulating an array of `double` values).

Printing an Array

Suppose you have an array of `int` values like the following:

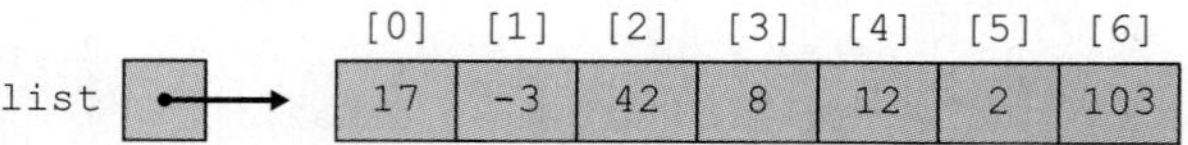

How would you go about printing the values in the array? For other types of data, you can use a `println` statement:

```
System.out.println(list);
```

Unfortunately, as mentioned in the `Arrays` class section of this chapter, with an array the `println` statement produces strange output like the following:

```
[I@6caf43
```

This is not helpful output, and it tells us nothing about the contents of the array. We saw that Java provides a solution to this problem in the form of a method called `Arrays.toString` that converts the array into a convenient text form. You can rewrite the `println` as follows to include a call on `Arrays.toString`:

```
System.out.println(Arrays.toString(list));
```

This line of code produces the following output:

```
[17, -3, 42, 8, 12, 2, 103]
```

This is a reasonable way to show the contents of the array, and in many situations it will be sufficient. However, for situations in which you want something different, you can write your own method.

Suppose that you want to write each number on a line by itself. In that case, you can use a for-each loop that does a `println` for each value:

```
public static void print(int[] list) {
    for (int n : list) {
        System.out.println(n);
    }
}
```

You can then call this method with the variable `list`:

```
print(list);
```

This call produces the following output:

```
17
-3
42
8
12
2
103
```

In some cases, the for-each loop doesn't get you quite what you want, though. For example, consider how the `Arrays.toString` method must be written. It produces a list of values that are separated by commas, which is a classic fencepost problem (e.g., seven values separated by six commas). To solve the fencepost problem, you'd want to use an indexing loop instead of a for-each loop so that you can print the first value before the loop:

```
System.out.print(list[0]);
for (int i = 1; i < list.length; i++) {
    System.out.print(", " + list[i]);
}
System.out.println();
```

Notice that `i` is initialized to `1` instead of `0` because `list[0]` is printed before the loop. This code produces the following output for the preceding sample array:

```
17, -3, 42, 8, 12, 2, 103
```

Even this code is not correct, though, because it assumes that there is a `list[0]` to print. It is possible for arrays to be empty, with a length of 0, in which case this code will generate an `ArrayIndexOutOfBoundsException`. The version of the method that follows produces output that matches the `String` produced by

`Arrays.toString`. The printing statements just before and just after the loop have been modified to include square brackets, and a special case has been included for empty arrays:

```
public static void print(int[] list) {
    if (list.length == 0) {
        System.out.println("[]");
    } else {
        System.out.print("[" + list[0]);
        for (int i = 1; i < list.length; i++) {
            System.out.print(", " + list[i]);
        }
        System.out.println("]");
    }
}
```

Searching and Replacing

Often you'll want to search for a specific value in an array. For example, you might want to count how many times a particular value appears in an array. Suppose you have an array of `int` values like the following:

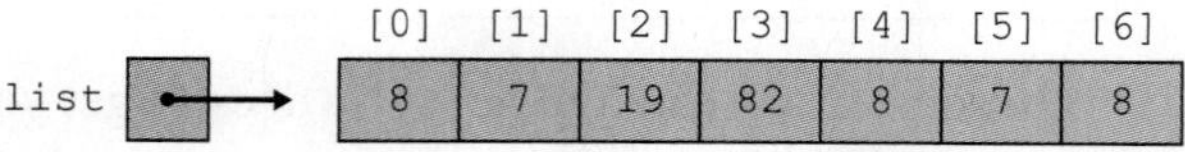

Counting occurrences is the simplest search task, because you always examine each value in the array and you don't need to change the contents of the array. You can accomplish this task with a for-each loop that keeps a count of the number of occurrences of the value for which you're searching:

```
public static int count(int[] list, int target) {
    int count = 0;
    for (int n : list) {
        if (n == target) {
            count++;
        }
    }
    return count;
}
```

You can use this method in the following call to figure out how many 8s are in the list:

```
int number = count(list, 8);
```

This call would set `number` to `3` for the sample array, because there are three occurrences of `8` in the list. If you instead made the call

```
int number = count(list, 2);
```

`number` would be set to `0`, because there are no occurrences of `2` in the list.

Sometimes you want to find out where a value is in a list. You can accomplish this task by writing a method that will return the index of the first occurrence of the value in the list. Because you don't know exactly where you'll find the value, you might try including this method in a `while` loop, as in the following pseudocode:

```
int i = 0;
while (we haven't found it yet) {
    i++;
}
```

However, there is a simpler approach. Because you're writing a method that returns a value, you can return the appropriate index as soon as you find a match. That means you can use the standard traversal loop to solve this problem:

```
for (int i = 0; i < list.length; i++) {
    if (list[i] == target) {
        return i;
    }
}
```

Remember that a `return` statement terminates a method, so you'll break out of this loop as soon as the target value is found. But what if the value isn't found? What if you traverse the entire array and find no matches? In that case, the `for` loop will finish executing without ever returning a value.

There are many things you can do if the value is not found. The convention used throughout the Java class libraries is to return the value `-1` to indicate that the value is not anywhere in the list. So you can add an extra `return` statement after the loop that will be executed only when the target value is not found. Putting all this together, you get the following method:

```
public static int indexOf(int[] list, int target) {
    for (int i = 0; i < list.length; i++) {
        if (list[i] == target) {
            return i;
        }
    }
    return -1;
}
```

You can use this method in the following call to find the first occurrence of the value `7` in the list:

```
int position = indexOf(list, 7);
```

This call would set `position` to `1` for the sample array, because the first occurrence of `7` is at index 1. There is another occurrence of `7` later in the array, at index 5, but this code terminates as soon as it finds the first match.

If you instead made the call

```
int position = indexOf(list, 42);
```

`position` would be set to `-1` because there are no occurrences of `42` in the list.

As a final variation, consider the problem of replacing all the occurrences of a value with some new value. This is similar to the counting task. You'll want to traverse the array looking for a particular value and replace the value with something new when you find it. You can't accomplish that task with a for-each loop, because changing the loop variable has no effect on the array. Instead, use a standard traversing loop:

```
public static void replaceAll(int[] list, int target, int replacement) {
    for (int i = 0; i < list.length; i++) {
        if (list[i] == target) {
            list[i] = replacement;
        }
    }
}
```

Notice that even though the method is changing the contents of the array, you don't need to return it in order to have that change take place.

As we noted at the beginning of this section, these examples involve an array of integers, and you would have to change the type if you were to manipulate an array of a different type (for example, changing `int[]` to `double[]` if you had an array of `double` values). But the change isn't quite so simple if you have an array of objects, such as `String`s. In order to compare `String` values, you must make a call on the `equals` method rather than using a simple == comparison. Here is a modified version of the `replaceAll` method that would be appropriate for an array of `String`s:

```
public static void replaceAll(String[] list, String target,
                              String replacement) {
    for (int i = 0; i < list.length; i++) {
        if (list[i].equals(target)) {
            list[i] = replacement;
        }
    }
}
```

Testing for Equality

Because arrays are objects, testing them for equality is more complex than testing primitive values like integers and doubles for equality. Two arrays are equivalent in value if they have the same length and store the same sequence of values. The method Arrays.equals performs this test:

```
if (Arrays.equals(list1, list2)) {
    System.out.println("The arrays are equal");
}
```

Like the Arrays.toString method, often the Arrays.equals method will be all you need. But sometimes you'll want slight variations, so it's worth exploring how to write the method yourself.

The method will take two arrays as parameters and will return a boolean result indicating whether or not the two arrays are equal. So, the method will look like this:

```
public static boolean equals(int[] list1, int[] list2) {
    ...
}
```

When you sit down to write a method like this, you probably think in terms of defining equality: "The two arrays are equal if their lengths are equal and they store the same sequence of values." But this isn't the easiest approach. For example, you could begin by testing that the lengths are equal, but what would you do next?

```
public static boolean equals(int[] list1, int[] list2) {
    if (list1.length == list2.length) {
        // what do we do?
        ...
    }
    ...
}
```

Methods like this one are generally easier to write if you think in terms of the opposite condition: What would make the two arrays *unequal?* Instead of testing for the lengths being equal, start by testing whether the lengths are unequal. In that case, you know exactly what to do. If the lengths are not equal, the method should return a value of false, and you'll know that the arrays are not equal to each other:

```
public static boolean equals(int[] list1, int[] list2) {
    if (list1.length != list2.length) {
        return false;
    }
    ...
}
```

If you get past the `if` statement, you know that the arrays are of equal length. Then you'll want to check whether they store the same sequence of values. Again, test for inequality rather than equality, returning `false` if there's a difference:

```
public static boolean equals(int[] list1, int[] list2) {
    if (list1.length != list2.length) {
        return false;
    }
    for (int i = 0; i < list1.length; i++) {
        if (list1[i] != list2[i]) {
            return false;
        }
    }
    ...
}
```

If you get past the `for` loop, you'll know that the two arrays are of equal length and that they store exactly the same sequence of values. In that case, you'll want to return the value `true` to indicate that the arrays are equal. This addition completes the method:

```
public static boolean equals(int[] list1, int[] list2) {
    if (list1.length != list2.length) {
        return false;
    }
    for (int i = 0; i < list1.length; i++) {
        if (list1[i] != list2[i]) {
            return false;
        }
    }
    return true;
}
```

This is a common pattern for a method like `equals`: You test all of the ways that the two objects might not be equal, returning `false` if you find any differences, and returning `true` at the very end so that if all the tests are passed the two objects are declared to be equal.

Reversing an Array

As a final example of common operations, let's consider the task of reversing the order of the elements stored in an array. For example, suppose you have an array that stores the following values:

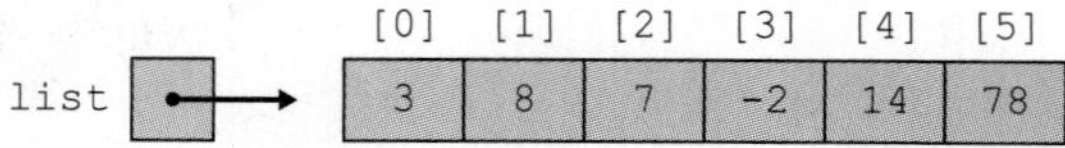

One approach would be to create a new array and to store the values from the first array into the second array in reverse order. Although that approach would be reasonable, you should be able to solve the problem without constructing a second array. Another approach is to conduct a series of exchanges or swaps. For example, the value `3` at the front of the list and the value `78` at the end of the list need to be swapped:

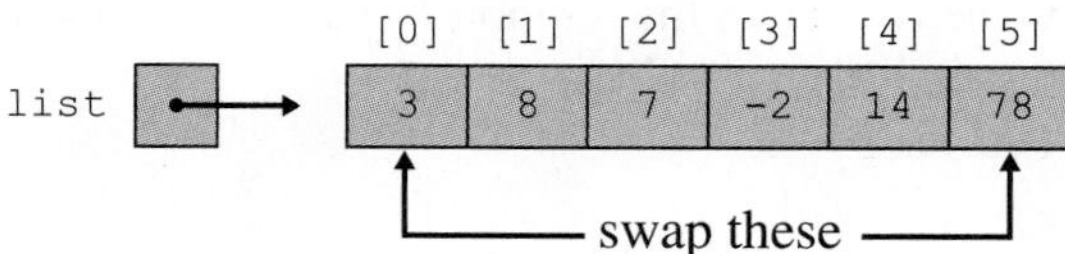

After swapping that pair, you can swap the next pair in (the values at indexes 1 and 4):

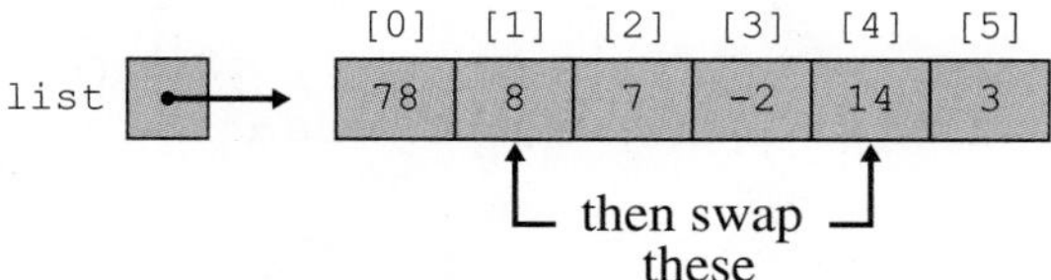

You can continue swapping until the entire list has been reversed. Before we look at the code that will perform this reversal, let's consider the general problem of swapping two values.

Suppose you have two integer variables `x` and `y` that have the values `3` and `78`:

```
int x = 3;
int y = 78;
```

How would you swap these values? A naive approach is to simply assign the values to one another:

```
// will not swap properly
x = y;
y = x;
```

Unfortunately, this doesn't work. You start out with the following:

x 3 y 78

When the first assignment statement is executed, you copy the value of `y` into `x`:

x 78 y 78

You want `x` to eventually become equal to `78`, but if you attempt to solve the problem this way, you lose the old value of `x` as soon as you assign the value of `y` to it. The second assignment statement then copies the new value of `x`, `78`, back into `y`, which leaves you with two variables equal to `78`.

The standard solution is to introduce a temporary variable that you can use to store the old value of `x` while you're giving `x` its new value. You can then copy the old value of `x` from the temporary variable into `y` to complete the swap:

```
int temp = x;
x = y;
y = temp;
```

You start by copying the old value of `x` into `temp`:

Then you put the value of `y` into `x`:

x 78 y 78 temp 3

Next, you copy the old value of `x` from `temp` to `y`:

x 78 y 3 temp 3

At this point you have successfully swapped the values of `x` and `y`, so you don't need `temp` anymore.

In some programming languages, you can define this as a `swap` method that can be used to exchange two `int` values:

```
// this method won't work
public static void swap(int x, int y) {
    int temp = x;
    x = y;
    y = temp;
}
```

As you've seen, this kind of method won't work in Java because the `x` and `y` that are swapped will be copies of any integer values passed to them. But because arrays are stored as objects, you can write a variation of this method that takes an array and two indexes as parameters and swaps the values at those indexes:

```
public static void swap(int[] list, int i, int j) {
    int temp = list[i];
```

```
    list[i] = list[j];
    list[j] = temp;
}
```

The code in this method matches the code in the previous method, but instead of using `x` and `y` it uses `list[i]` and `list[j]`. This method will work because, instead of changing simple `int` variables, the method is changing the contents of the array.

Given this `swap` method, you can fairly easily write a reversing method. You just have to think about what combinations of values to swap. Start by swapping the first and last values. The sample array has a length of 6, which means that you will be swapping the values at indexes 0 and 5. But you want to write the code so that it works for an array of any length. In general, the first swap you'll want to perform is to swap element 0 with element `(list.length – 1)`:

```
swap(list, 0, list.length – 1);
```

Then you'll want to swap the second value with the second-to-last value:

```
swap(list, 1, list.length – 2);
```

Then you'll swap the third value with the third-to-last value:

```
swap(list, 2, list.length – 3);
```

There is a pattern to these swaps that you can capture with a loop. If you use a variable `i` for the first parameter of the call on `swap` and introduce a local variable `j` to store an expression for the second parameter to `swap`, each of these calls will take the following form:

```
int j = list.length – i – 1;
swap(list, i, j);
```

To implement the reversal, you could put the method inside the standard traversal loop:

```
// doesn't quite work
for (int i = 0; i < list.length; i++) {
    int j = list.length – i – 1;
    swap(list, i, j);
}
```

If you were to test this code, though, you'd find that it seems to have no effect whatsoever. The list stores the same values after executing this code as it stores initially. The problem is that this loop does too much swapping. Here is a trace of the six swaps that are performed on the list [3, 8, 7, –2, 14, 78], with an indication of the values of `i` and `j` for each step:

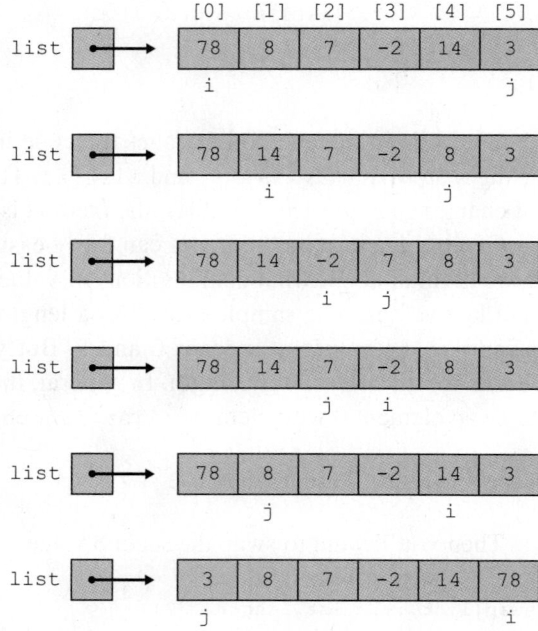

The values of i and j cross halfway through this process. As a result, the first three swaps successfully reverse the array, and then the three swaps that follow undo the work of the first three. To fix this problem, you need to stop it halfway through the process. This task is easily accomplished by changing the test:

```
for (int i = 0; i < list.length / 2; i++) {
    int j = list.length – i – 1;
    swap(list, i, j);
}
```

In the sample array, `list.length` is `6`. Half of that is `3`, which means that this loop will execute exactly three times. That is just what you want in this case (the first three swaps), but you should be careful to consider other possibilities. For example, what if `list.length` were `7`? Half of that is also `3`, because of truncating division. Is three the correct number of swaps for an odd-length list? The answer is yes. If there are an odd number of elements, the value in the middle of the list does not need to be swapped. So, in this case, a simple division by 2 turns out to be the right approach.

Including this code in a method, you end up with the following overall solution:

```
public static void reverse(int[] list) {
    for (int i = 0; i < list.length / 2; i++) {
        int j = list.length – i – 1;
        swap(list, i, j);
    }
}
```

String Traversal Algorithms

In Java we often think of a string as chunk of text, but you can also think of it as a sequence of individual characters. Viewed in this light, a string is a lot like an array. Recall that the individual elements of a string are of type `char` and that you can access the individual character values by calling the `charAt` method.

The same techniques we have used to write array traversal algorithms can be used to write string traversal algorithms. The syntax is slightly different, but the logic is the same. Our array traversal template looks like this:

```
for (int i = 0; i < <array>.length; i++) {
    <do something with array[i]>;
}
```

The corresponding string algorithm template looks like this:

```
for (int i = 0; i < <string>.length(); i++) {
    <do something with string.charAt(i)>;
}
```

Notice that with arrays you refer to `length` without using parentheses, but with a string you do use parentheses. Notice also that the array square bracket notation is replaced with a call on the `charAt` method.

For example, you can count the number of occurrences of the letter “i” in “Mississippi” with this code:

```
String s = "Mississippi";
int count = 0;
for (int i = 0; i < s.length(); i++) {
    if (s.charAt(i) == 'i') {
        count++;
    }
}
```

This code would correctly compute that there are four occurrences of “i” in the string. For another example, consider the task of computing the reverse of a string. You can traverse the string building up a new version that has the letters in reverse order by putting each new character at the front of string you are building up. Here is a complete method that uses this approach:

```
public static String reverse(String text) {
    String result = "";
    for (int i = 0; i < text.length(); i++) {
        result = text.charAt(i) + result;
    }
```

```
    return result;
}
```

If you make the call `reverse("Mississippi")`, the method returns `"ippississiM"`.

Functional Approach

Chapter 19 describes a different approach to manipulating arrays that leads to code that looks quite different than the examples in this section. It relies on features added to the Java programming language starting with version 8 that allow you to manipulate arrays and other data structures in a more declarative manner. Instead of specifying exactly how to traverse an array, you can instead tell Java what you want to do with the array elements and allow Java to figure out how to do the traversal. The addition of the for-each loop starting with version 5 of Java was an initial move in this direction, but the new features go much further.

Suppose, for example, that you have an array of values defined as follows:

```
int[] numbers = {8, 3, 2, 17};
```

Let's look at the code you would write for two simple tasks: finding the sum and printing the values. Using the standard traversal loops, you would write the following code.

```
// sum an array of numbers and print them (for loop)
int sum = 0;
for (int i = 0; i < numbers.length; i++) {
    sum += numbers[i];
}
System.out.println("sum = " + sum);
for (int i = 0; i < numbers.length; i++) {
    System.out.println(numbers[i]);
}
```

This code produces the following output.

```
sum = 30
8
3
2
17
```

The for-each loop simplifies this code by specifying that you want to manipulate each of the different values in the array in sequence, but it doesn't require you to include an indexing variable to say exactly how that is done.

```
// sum an array of numbers and print them (for-each loop)
int sum = 0;
for (int n : numbers) {
    sum += n;
}
System.out.println("sum = " + sum);
for (int n : numbers) {
    System.out.println(n);
}
```

With the new Java 8 features, this becomes even simpler. The task of finding the sum of a sequence of values is so common that there is a built-in method that does it for you. And the task of printing each value with a call on the `println` method of `System.out` can also be expressed in a very concise manner.

```
// sum an array of numbers and print them (functional)
int sum = Arrays.stream(numbers).sum();
System.out.println("sum = " + sum);
Arrays.stream(numbers).forEach(System.out::println);
```

This code doesn't at all describe how the traversal is to be performed. Instead, you tell Java the operations you want to have performed on the values in the array and leave it up to Java to perform the traversal. See Chapter 19 for a more complete explanation of this approach.

7.3 Reference Semantics

In Java, arrays are objects. We have been using objects since Chapter 3 but we haven't yet discussed in detail how they are stored. It's about time that we explored the details. Objects are stored in the computer's memory in a different way than primitive data are stored. For example, when we declare the integer variable

```
int x = 8;
```

the variable stores the actual data. So, we've drawn pictures like the following:

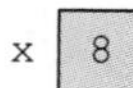

The situation is different for arrays and other objects. With regard to objects, the variable doesn't store the actual data. Instead, the data are stored in an object and the variable stores a reference to the location at which the object is stored. So, we have two different elements in the computer's memory: the variable and the object. Thus, when we construct an array object such as

```
int[] list = new int[5];
```

we end up with the following:

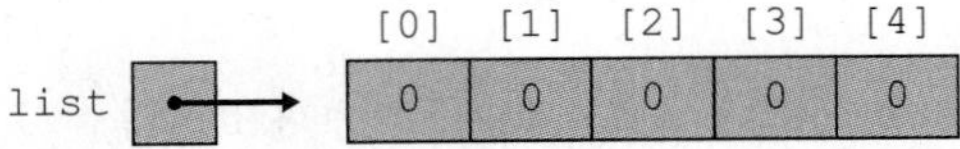

As the diagram indicates, two different values are stored in memory: the array itself, which appears on the right side of the diagram, and a variable called `list`, which stores a reference to the array (represented in this picture as an arrow). We say that `list` *refers* to the array.

It may take some time for you to get used to the two different approaches to storing data, but these approaches are so common that computer scientists have technical terms to describe them. The system for the primitive types like `int` is known as *value semantics,* and those types are often referred to as *value types.* The system for arrays and other objects is known as *reference semantics,* and those types are often referred to as *reference types.*

Value Semantics (Value Types)

A system in which values are stored directly and copying is achieved by creating independent copies of values. Types that use value semantics are called value types.

Reference Semantics (Reference Types)

A system in which references to values are stored and copying is achieved by copying these references. Types that use reference semantics are called reference types.

It will take us a while to explore all of the implications of this difference. The key thing to remember is that when you are working with objects, you are always working with references to data rather than the data itself.

At this point you are probably wondering why Java has two different systems. Java was designed for object-oriented programming, so the first question to consider is why Sun decided that objects should have reference semantics. There are two primary reasons:

- **Efficiency.** Objects can be complex, which means that they can take up a lot of space in memory. If we made copies of such objects, we would quickly run out of memory. A `String` object that stores a large number of characters might take up a lot of space in memory. But even if the `String` object is very large, a reference to it can be fairly small, in the same way that even a mansion has a simple street address. As another analogy, think how we use cell phones to communicate with people. The phones can be very tiny and easy to transport because cell phone numbers don't take up much space. Imagine that, instead of carrying around a set of cell phone numbers, you tried to carry around the actual people!

- **Sharing.** Often, having a copy of something is not good enough. Suppose that your instructor tells all of the students in the class to put their tests into a certain box. Imagine how pointless and confusing it would be if each student made a copy of the box. The obvious intent is that all of the students use the same box. Reference semantics allows you to have many references to a single object, which allows different parts of your program to share a certain object.

Without reference semantics, Java programs would be more difficult to write. Then why did Sun also decide to include primitive types that have value semantics? The reasons are primarily historical. Sun wanted to leverage the popularity of C and C++, which had similar types, and to guarantee that Java programs would run quickly, which was easier to accomplish with the more traditional primitive types. If Java's designers had a chance to redesign Java today, the company might well get rid of the primitive types and use a consistent object model with just reference semantics.

Multiple Objects

In the previous section, you saw how to manipulate a single array object. In this section, we will delve deeper into the implications of reference semantics by considering what happens when there are multiple objects and multiple references to the same object.

Consider the following code:

```
int[] list1 = new int[5];
int[] list2 = new int[5];
for (int i = 0; i < list1.length; i++) {
    list1[i] = 2 * i + 1;
    list2[i] = 2 * i + 1;
}
int[] list3 = list2;
```

Each call on `new` constructs a new object and this code has two calls on `new`, so that means we have two different objects. The code is written in such a way that `list2` will always have the exact same length and sequence of values as `list1`. After the two arrays are initialized, we define a third array variable that is assigned to `list2`. This step creates a new reference but not a new object. After the computer executes the code, memory would look like this:

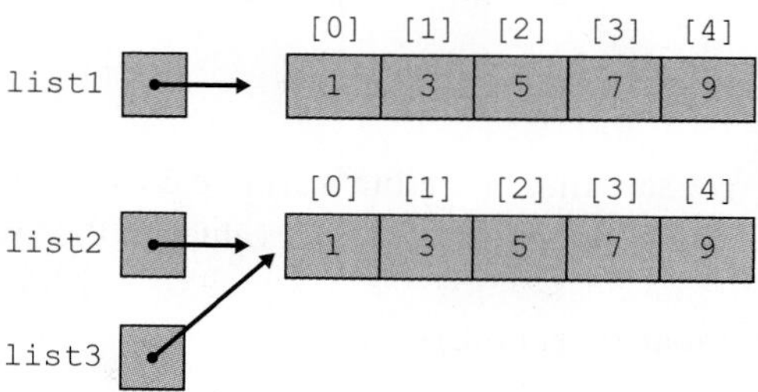

We have three variables but only two objects. The variables `list2` and `list3` both refer to the same array object. Using the cell phone analogy, you can think of this as two people who both have the cell phone number for the same person. That means that either one of them can call the person. Or, as another analogy, suppose that both you and a friend of yours know how to access your bank information online. That means that you both have access to the same account and that either one of you can make changes to the account.

The implication of this method is that `list2` and `list3` are in some sense both equally able to modify the array to which they refer. The line of code

```
list2[2]++;
```

will have exactly the same effect as the line

```
list3[2]++;
```

Since both variables refer to the same array object, you can access the array through either one.

Reference semantics help us to understand why a simple == test does not give us what we might expect. When this test is applied to objects, it determines whether two *references* are the same (not whether the objects to which they refer are somehow equivalent). In other words, when we test whether two references are equal, we are testing whether they refer to exactly the same object.

The variables `list2` and `list3` both refer to the same array object. As a result, if we ask whether `list2 == list3`, the answer will be yes (the expression evaluates to `true`). But if we ask whether `list1 == list2`, the answer will be no (the expression evaluates to `false`) even though we think of the two arrays as somehow being equivalent.

Sometimes you want to know whether two variables refer to exactly the same object, and for those situations, the simple == comparison will be appropriate. But you'll also want to know whether two objects are somehow equivalent in value, in which case you should call methods like `Arrays.equals` or the string `equals` method.

Understanding reference semantics also allows you to understand why a method is able to change the contents of an array that is passed to it as a parameter. Remember that earlier in the chapter we considered the following method:

```
public static void incrementAll(int[] data) {
    for (int i = 0; i < data.length; i++) {
        data[i]++;
    }
}
```

We saw that when our variable `list` was initialized to an array of odd numbers, we could increment all of the values in the array by means of the following line:

```
incrementAll(list);
```

When the method is called, we make a copy of the variable `list`. But the variable `list` is not itself the array; rather, it stores a reference to the array. So, when we make a copy of that reference, we end up with two references to the same object:

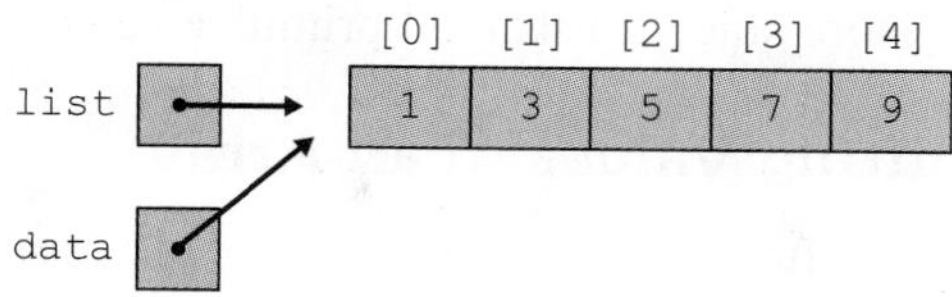

Because `data` and `list` both refer to the same object, when we change `data` by saying `data[i]++`, we end up changing the object to which `list` refers. That's why, after the loop increments each element of data, we end up with the following:

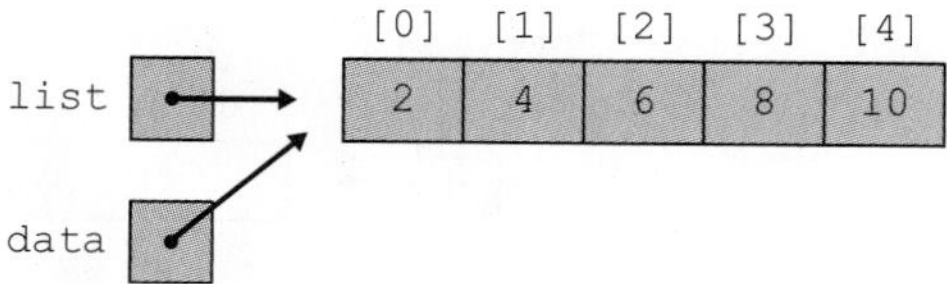

The key lesson to draw from this discussion is that when we pass an array as a parameter to a method, that method has the ability to change the contents of the array.

Before we leave the subject of reference semantics, we should describe in more detail the concept of the special value `null`. It is a special keyword in Java that is used to represent "no object".

> **null**
> A Java keyword signifying no object.

The concept of null doesn't have any meaning for value types like `int` and `double` that store actual values. But it can make sense to set a variable that stores a reference to `null`. This is a way of telling the computer that you want to have the variable, but you haven't yet come up with an object to which it should refer. So you can use `null` for variables of any object type, such as a `String` or array:

```
String s = null;
int[] list = null;
```

There is a difference between setting a variable to an empty string and setting it to `null`. When you set a variable to an empty string, there is an actual object to which your variable refers (although not a very interesting object). When you set a variable to `null`, the variable doesn't yet refer to an actual object. If you try to use the variable to access the object when it has been set to `null`, Java will throw a `NullPointerException`.

7.4 Advanced Array Techniques

VideoNote

In this section we'll discuss some advanced uses of arrays, such as algorithms that cannot be solved with straightforward traversals. We'll also see how to create arrays that store objects instead of primitive values.

Shifting Values in an Array

You'll often want to move a series of values in an array. For example, suppose you have an array of integers that stores the sequence of values [3, 8, 9, 7, 5] and you want to send the value at the front of the list to the back and keep the order of the other values the same. In other words, you want to move the 3 to the back, yielding the list [8, 9, 7, 5, 3]. Let's explore how to write code to perform that action.

Suppose you have a variable of type `int[]` called `list` of length 5 that stores the values [3, 8, 9, 7, 5]:

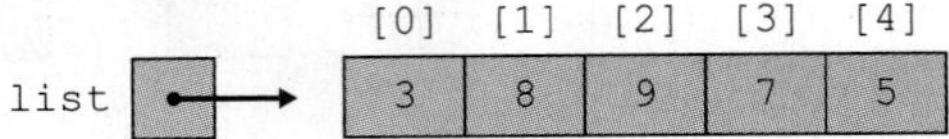

The shifting operation is similar to the swap operation discussed in the previous section, and you'll find that it is useful to use a temporary variable here as well. The 3 at the front of the list is supposed to go to the back of the list, and the other values are supposed to rotate forward. You can make the task easier by storing the value at the front of the list (3, in this example) into a local variable:

```
int first = list[0];
```

With that value safely tucked away, you now have to shift the other four values to the left by one position:

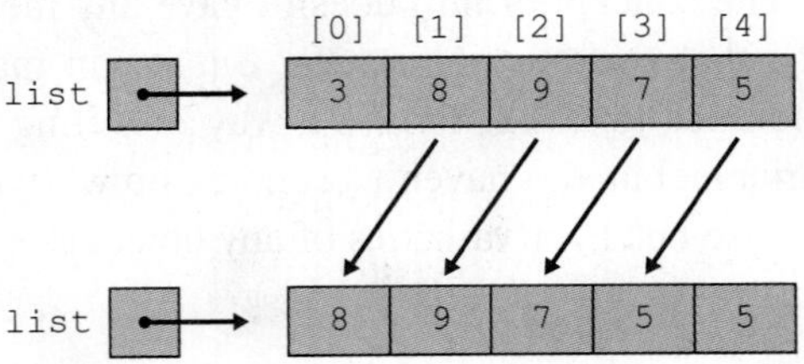

The overall task breaks down into four different shifting operations, each of which is a simple assignment statement:

```
list[0] = list[1];
list[1] = list[2];
list[2] = list[3];
list[3] = list[4];
```

Obviously you'd want to write this as a loop rather than writing a series of individual assignment statements. Each of the preceding statements is of the form

```
list[i] = list[i + 1];
```

You'll replace list element `[i]` with the value currently stored in list element `[i + 1]`, which shifts that value to the left. You can put this line of code inside a standard traversing loop:

```
for (int i = 0; i < list.length; i++) {
    list[i] = list[i + 1];
}
```

This loop is almost the right answer, but it has an off-by-one bug. This loop will execute five times for the sample array, but you only want to shift four values (you want to do the assignment for `i` equal to `0`, `1`, `2`, and `3`, but not for `i` equal to `4`). So, this loop goes one too many times. On the last iteration of the loop, when `i` is equal to `4`, the loop executes the following line of code:

```
list[i] = list[i + 1];
```

This line becomes:

```
list[4] = list[5];
```

There is no value `list[5]` because the array has only five elements, with indexes 0 through 4. So, this code generates an `ArrayIndexOutOfBoundsException`. To fix the problem, alter the loop so that it stops one iteration early:

```
for (int i = 0; i < list.length – 1; i++) {
    list[i] = list[i + 1];
}
```

In place of the usual `list.length`, use `(list.length – 1)`. You can think of the minus one in this expression as offsetting the plus one in the assignment statement.

Of course, there is one more detail you must address. After shifting the values to the left, you've made room at the end of the list for the value that used to be at the front of the list (which is currently stored in a local variable called `first`). When the loop has finished executing, you have to place this value at index 4:

```
list[list.length – 1] = first;
```

Here is the final method:

```
public static void rotateLeft(int[] list) {
    int first = list[0];
    for (int i = 0; i < list.length – 1; i++) {
        list[i] = list[i + 1];
    }
```

```
    list[list.length – 1] = first;
}
```

An interesting variation on this method is to rotate the values to the right instead of rotating them to the left. To perform this inverse operation, you want to take the value that is currently at the end of the list and bring it to the front, shifting the remaining values to the right. So, if a variable called `list` initially stores the values [3, 8, 9, 7, 5], it should bring the 5 to the front and store the values [5, 3, 8, 9, 7].

Begin by tucking away the value that is being rotated into a temporary variable:

```
int last = list[list.length – 1];
```

Then shift the other values to the right:

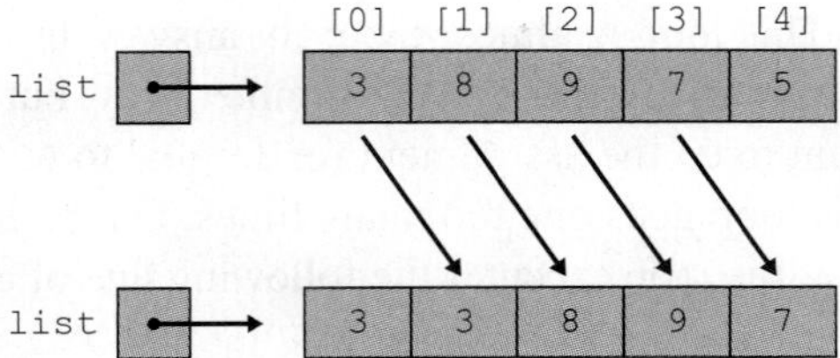

In this case, the four individual assignment statements would be the following:

```
list[1] = list[0];
list[2] = list[1];
list[3] = list[2];
list[4] = list[3];
```

A more general way to write this is the following line of code:

```
list[i] = list[i – 1];
```

If you put this code inside the standard `for` loop, you get the following:

```
// doesn't work
for (int i = 0; i < list.length; i++) {
    list[i] = list[i – 1];
}
```

There are two problems with this code. First, there is another off-by-one bug. The first assignment statement you want to perform would set `list[1]` to contain the value that is currently in `list[0]`, but this loop sets `list[0]` to `list[–1]`. Java generates an `ArrayIndexOutOfBoundsException` because there is no value `list[–1]`. You want to start `i` at `1`, not `0`:

```
// still doesn't work
for (int i = 1; i < list.length; i++) {
    list[i] = list[i – 1];
}
```

However, this version of the code doesn't work either. It avoids the exception, but think about what it does. The first time through the loop it assigns `list[1]` to what is in `list[0]`:

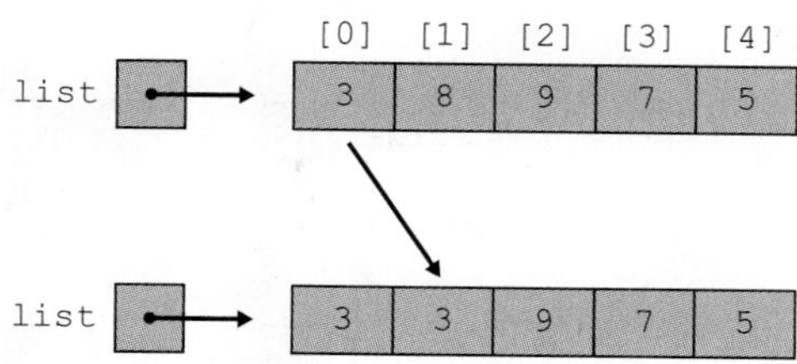

What happened to the value `8`? It's overwritten with the value `3`. The next time through the loop `list[2]` is set to be `list[1]`:

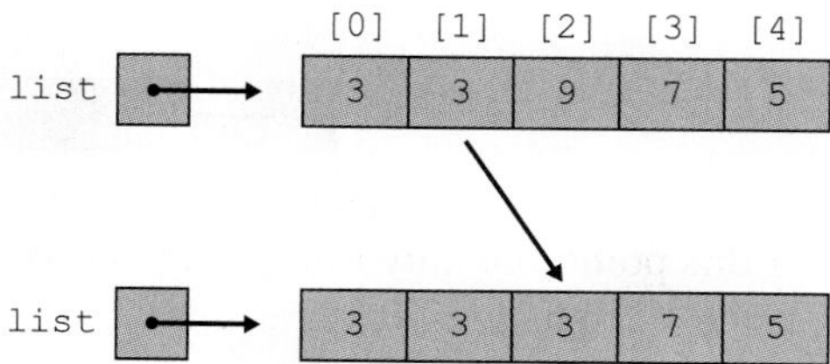

You might say, "Wait a minute . . . `list[1]` isn't a `3`, it's an `8`." It was an `8` when you started, but the first iteration of the loop replaced the `8` with a `3`, and now the `3` has been copied into the spot where `9` used to be.

The loop continues in this way, putting `3` into every cell of the array. Obviously, that's not what you want. To make this code work, you have to run the loop in reverse order (from right to left instead of left to right). So let's back up to where we started:

	[0]	[1]	[2]	[3]	[4]
list →	3	8	9	7	5

We tucked away the final value of the list into a local variable. That frees up the final array position. Now, assign `list[4]` to be what is in `list[3]`:

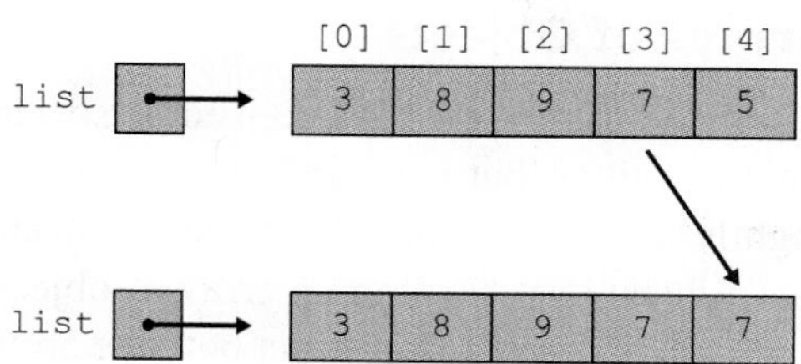

This wipes out the 5 that was at the end of the list, but that value is safely stored away in a local variable. And once you've performed this assignment statement, you free up `list[3]`, which means you can now set `list[3]` to be what is currently in `list[2]`:

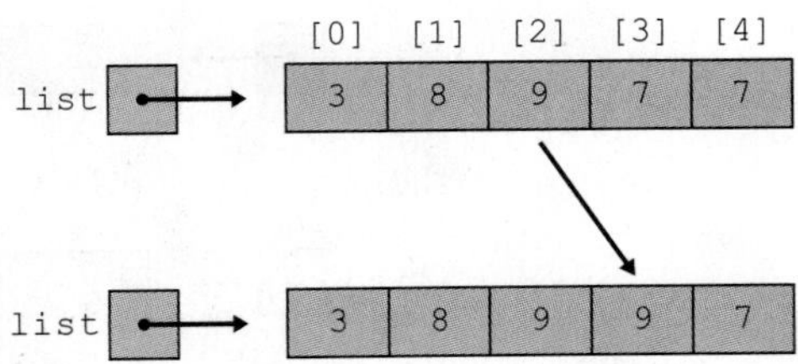

The process continues in this manner, copying the 8 from index 1 to index 2 and copying the 3 from index 0 to index 1, leaving you with the following:

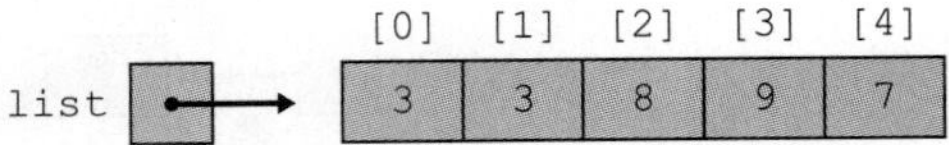

At this point, the only thing left to do is to put the 5 stored in the local variable at the front of the list:

	[0]	[1]	[2]	[3]	[4]
list →	5	3	8	9	7

You can reverse the `for` loop by changing the `i++` to `i--` and adjusting the initialization and test. The final method is as follows:

```
public static void rotateRight(int[] list) {
    int last = list[list.length - 1];
    for (int i = list.length - 1; i >= 1; i--) {
        list[i] = list[i - 1];
    }
    list[0] = last;
}
```

Arrays of Objects

All of the arrays we have looked at so far have stored primitive values like simple `int` values, but you can have arrays of any Java type. Arrays of objects behave slightly differently, though, because objects are stored as references rather than as data values. Constructing an array of objects is usually a two-step process, because you normally have to construct both the array and the individual objects.

As an example, Java has a `Point` class as part of its `java.awt` package. Each `Point` object is used for storing the (*x*, *y*) coordinates of a point in two-dimensional space. (We will discuss this class in more detail in the next chapter, but for now we will just construct a few objects from it.) Suppose that you want to construct an array of `Point` objects. Consider the following statement:

```
Point[] points = new Point[3];
```

This statement declares a variable called `points` that refers to an array of length 3 that stores references to `Point` objects. Using the `new` keyword to construct the array doesn't construct any actual `Point` objects. Instead it constructs an array of length 3, each element of which can store a reference to a `Point`. When Java constructs the array, it auto-initializes these array elements to the zero-equivalent for the type. The zero-equivalent for all reference types is the special value `null`, which indicates "no object":

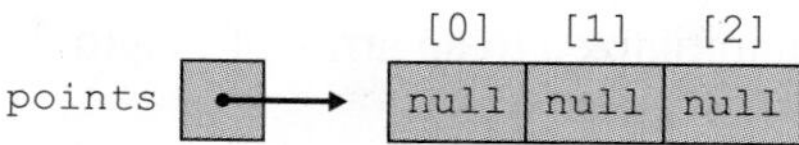

The actual `Point` objects must be constructed separately with the `new` keyword, as in the following code:

```
Point[] points = new Point[3];
points[0] = new Point(3, 7);
points[1] = new Point(4, 5);
points[2] = new Point(6, 2);
```

After these lines of code execute, your program will have created individual `Point` objects referred to by the various array elements:

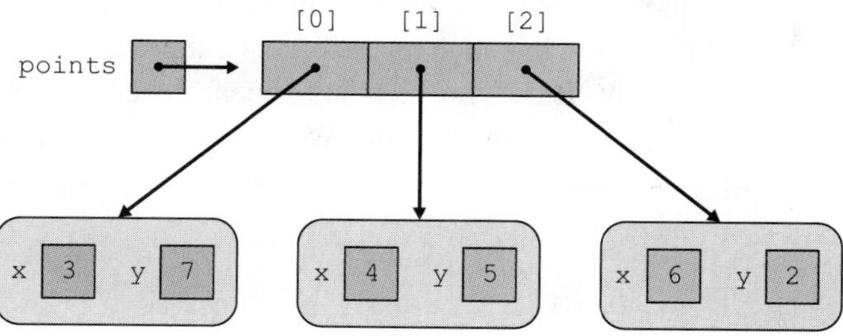

Notice that the `new` keyword is required in four different places, because there are four objects to be constructed: the array itself and the three individual `Point` objects. You could also use the curly brace notation for initializing the array, in which case you don't need the `new` keyword to construct the array itself:

```
Point[] points = {new Point(3, 7), new Point(4, 5), new Point(6, 2)};
```

Command-Line Arguments

As you've seen since Chapter 1, whenever you define a `main` method, you're required to include as its parameter `String[] args`, which is an array of `String` objects. Java itself initializes this array if the user provides what are known as *command-line arguments* when invoking Java. For example, the user could execute a Java class called `DoSomething` from a command prompt or terminal by using a command like:

```
java DoSomething
```

The user has the option to type extra arguments, as in the following:

```
java DoSomething temperature.dat temperature.out
```

In this case the user has specified two extra arguments that are file names that the program should use (e.g., the names of an input and output file). If the user types these extra arguments when starting up Java, the `String[] args` parameter to `main` will be initialized to an array of length 2 that stores these two `strings`:

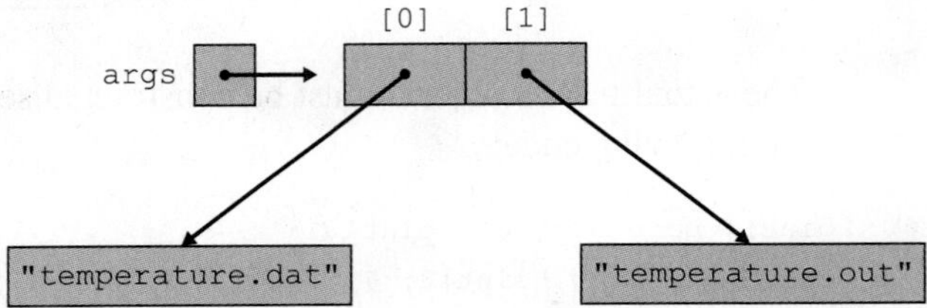

Nested Loop Algorithms

All of the algorithms we have seen have been written with a single loop. But many computations require nested loops. For example, suppose that you were asked to print all inversions in an array of integers. An inversion is defined as a pair of numbers in which the first number in the list is greater than the second number.

In a sorted list such as [1, 2, 3, 4], there are no inversions at all and there is nothing to print. But if the numbers appear instead in reverse order, [4, 3, 2, 1], then there are many inversions to print. We would expect output like the following:

```
(4, 3)
(4, 2)
(4, 1)
(3, 2)
(3, 1)
(2, 1)
```

Notice that any given number (e.g., 4 in the list above) can produce several different inversions, because it might be followed by several smaller numbers (1, 2, and

3 in the example). For a list that is partially sorted, as in [3, 1, 4, 2], there are only a few inversions, so you would produce output like this:

```
(3, 1)
(3, 2)
(4, 2)
```

This problem can't be solved with a single traversal because we are looking for pairs of numbers. There are many possible first values in the pair and many possible second values in the pair. Let's develop a solution using pseudocode.

We can't produce all pairs with a single loop, but we can use a single loop to consider all possible first values:

```
for (every possible first value) {
    print all inversions that involve this first value.
}
```

Now we just need to write the code to find all the inversions for a given first value. That requires us to write a second, nested loop:

```
for (every possible first value) {
    for (every possible second value) {
        if (first value > second value) {
            print(first, second).
        }
    }
}
```

This problem is fairly easy to turn into Java code, although the loop bounds turn out to be a bit tricky. For now, let's use our standard traversal loop for each:

```
for (int i = 0; i < data.length; i++) {
    for (int j = 0; j < data.length; j++) {
        if (data[i] > data[j]) {
            System.out.println("(" + data[i] + ", " + data[j] + ")");
        }
    }
}
```

The preceding code isn't quite right. Remember that for an inversion, the second value has to appear *after* the first value in the list. In this case, we are computing all possible combinations of a first and second value. To consider only values that come after the given first value, we have to start the second loop at `i + 1` instead of starting at `0`. We can also make a slight improvement by recognizing that because an inversion requires a pair of values, there is no reason to include the last number of the list as a possible first value. So the outer loop involving `i` can end one iteration earlier:

```
for (int i = 0; i < data.length - 1; i++) {
    for (int j = i + 1; j < data.length; j++) {
        if (data[i] > data[j]) {
            System.out.println("(" + data[i] + ", " + data[j] + ")");
        }
    }
}
```

When you write nested loops like these, it is a common convention to use `i` for the outer loop, `j` for the loop inside the outer loop, and `k` if there is a loop inside the `j` loop.

7.5 Multidimensional Arrays

The array examples in the previous sections all involved what are known as one-dimensional arrays (a single row or a single column of data). Often, you'll want to store data in a multidimensional way. For example, you might want to store a two-dimensional grid of data that has both rows and columns. Fortunately, you can form arrays of arbitrarily many dimensions:

- `double`: one `double`
- `double[]`: a one-dimensional array of `doubles`
- `double[][]`: a two-dimensional grid of `doubles`
- `double[][][]`: a three-dimensional collection of `doubles`
- `...`

Arrays of more than one dimension are called *multidimensional arrays.*

Multidimensional Array

An array of arrays, the elements of which are accessed with multiple integer indexes.

Rectangular Two-Dimensional Arrays

The most common use of a multidimensional array is a two-dimensional array of a certain width and height. For example, suppose that on three separate days you took a series of five temperature readings. You can define a two-dimensional array that has three rows and five columns as follows:

```
double[][] temps = new double[3][5];
```

Notice that on both the left and right sides of this assignment statement, you have to use a double set of square brackets. When you are describing the type on the left, you have to make it clear that this is not just a one-dimensional sequence of values, which would be of type `double[]`, but instead a two-dimensional grid of values, which is of type `double[][]`. On the right, when you construct the array, you must specify the dimensions of the grid. The normal convention is to list the row first followed by the column. The resulting array would look like this:

temps →

	[0]	[1]	[2]	[3]	[4]
[0]	0.0	0.0	0.0	0.0	0.0
[1]	0.0	0.0	0.0	0.0	0.0
[2]	0.0	0.0	0.0	0.0	0.0

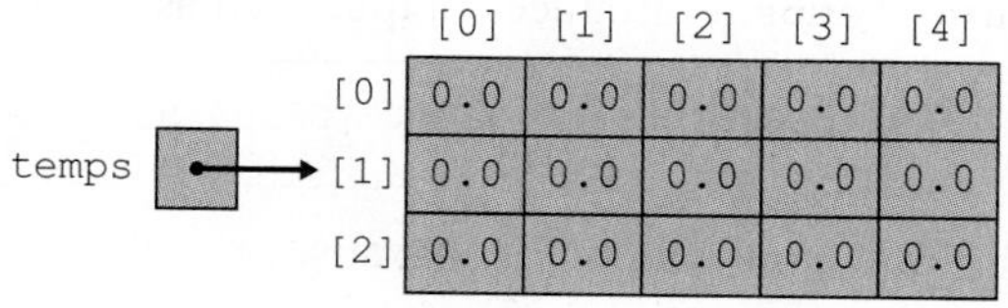

As with one-dimensional arrays, the values are initialized to `0.0` and the indexes start with 0 for both rows and columns. Once you've created such an array, you can refer to individual elements by providing specific row and column numbers (in that order). For example, to set the fourth value of the first row to `98.3` and to set the first value of the third row to `99.4`, you would write the following code:

```
temps[0][3] = 98.3;   // fourth value of first row
temps[2][0] = 99.4;   // first value of third row
```

After the program executes these lines of code, the array would look like this:

temps →

	[0]	[1]	[2]	[3]	[4]
[0]	0.0	0.0	0.0	98.3	0.0
[1]	0.0	0.0	0.0	0.0	0.0
[2]	99.4	0.0	0.0	0.0	0.0

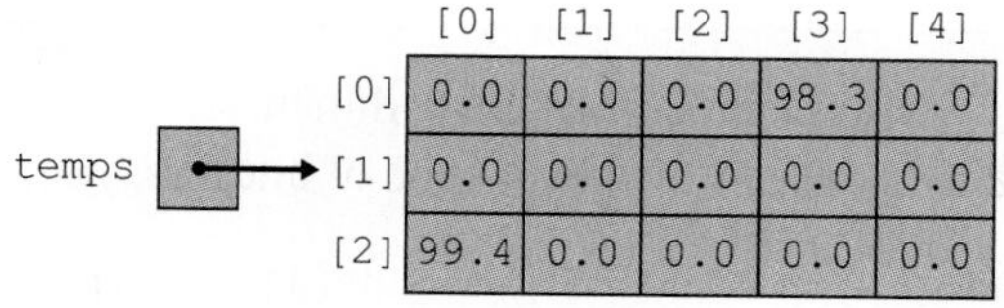

It is helpful to think of referring to individual elements in a stepwise fashion, starting with the name of the array. For example, if you want to refer to the first value of the third row, you obtain it through the following steps:

`temps`	the entire grid
`temps[2]`	the entire third row
`temps[2][0]`	the first element of the third row

You can pass multidimensional arrays as parameters just as you pass one-dimensional arrays. You need to be careful about the type, though. To pass the temperature grid, you would have to use a parameter of type `double[][]` (with both sets of brackets). For example, here is a method that prints the grid:

```
public static void print(double[][] grid) {
    for (int i = 0; i < grid.length; i++) {
        for (int j = 0; j < grid[i].length; j++) {
            System.out.print(grid[i][j] + " ");
        }
```

```
        System.out.println();
    }
}
```

Notice that to ask for the number of rows you ask for `grid.length` and to ask for the number of columns you ask for `grid[i].length`.

The `Arrays.toString` method mentioned earlier in this chapter does work on multidimensional arrays, but it produces a poor result. When used with the preceding array `temps`, it produces output such as the following:

```
[[D@14b081b, [D@1015a9e, [D@1e45a5c]
```

This poor output is because `Arrays.toString` works by concatenating the `String` representations of the array's elements. In this case the elements are arrays themselves, so they do not convert into `Strings` properly. To correct the problem you can use a different method called `Arrays.deepToString` that will return better results for multidimensional arrays:

```
System.out.println(Arrays.deepToString(temps));
```

The call produces the following output:

```
[[0.0, 0.0, 0.0, 98.3, 0.0], [0.0, 0.0, 0.0, 0.0, 0.0],
[99.4, 0.0, 0.0, 0.0, 0.0]]
```

Arrays can have as many dimensions as you want. For example, if you want a three-dimensional 4 by 4 by 4 cube of integers, you would write the following line of code:

```
int[][][] numbers = new int[4][4][4];
```

The normal convention for the order of values is the plane number, followed by the row number, followed by the column number, although you can use any convention you want as long as your code is written consistently.

Jagged Arrays

The previous examples have involved rectangular grids that have a fixed number of rows and columns. It is also possible to create a jagged array in which the number of columns varies from row to row.

To construct a jagged array, divide the construction into two steps: Construct the array for holding rows first, and then construct each individual row. For example, to construct an array that has two elements in the first row, four elements in the second row, and three elements in the third row, you can write the following lines of code:

```
int[][] jagged = new int[3][];
jagged[0] = new int[2];
jagged[1] = new int[4];
jagged[2] = new int[3];
```

This code would construct an array that looks like this:

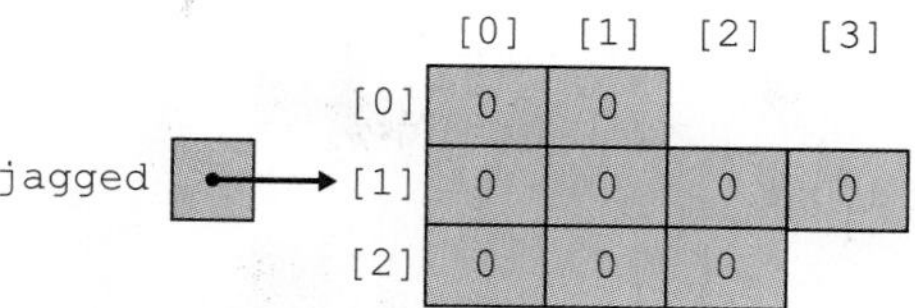

We can explore this technique by writing a program that produces the rows of what is known as *Pascal's triangle.* The numbers in the triangle have many useful mathematical properties. For example, row n of Pascal's triangle contains the coefficients obtained when you expand the equation:

$(x + y)^n$

Here are the results for n between 0 and 4:

$(x + y)^0 = 1$
$(x + y)^1 = x + y$
$(x + y)^2 = x^2 + 2xy + y^2$
$(x + y)^3 = x^3 + 3x^2y + 3xy^2 + y^3$
$(x + y)^4 = x^4 + 4x^3y + 6x^2y^2 + 4xy^3 + y^4$

If you pull out just the coefficients, you get the following values:

```
        1
      1   1
    1   2   1
  1   3   3   1
1   4   6   4   1
```

These rows of numbers form a five-row Pascal's triangle. One of the properties of the triangle is that if you are given any row, you can use it to compute the next row. For example, let's start with the last row from the preceding triangle:

```
1 4 6 4 1
```

We can compute the next row by adding adjacent pairs of values together. So, we add together the first pair of numbers (1 + 4), then the second pair of numbers (4 + 6), and so on:

```
5 10 10 5
```

```
(1 + 4)  (4 + 6)  (6 + 4)  (4 + 1)
   5        10       10       5
```

Then we put a 1 at the front and back of this list of numbers, and we end up with the next row of the triangle:

```
          1
        1   1
      1   2   1
    1   3   3   1
  1   4   6   4   1
1   5  10  10   5   1
```

This property of the triangle provides a technique for computing it. We can construct it row by row, computing each new row from the values in the previous row. In other words, we write the following loop (assuming that we have a two-dimensional array called `triangle` in which to store the answer):

```
for (int i = 0; i < triangle.length; i++) {
    construct triangle[i] using triangle[i - 1].
}
```

We just need to flesh out the details of how a new row is constructed. This is a jagged array because each row has a different number of elements. Looking at the triangle, you'll see that the first row (row 0) has one value in it, the second row (row 1) has two values in it, and so on. In general, row `i` has `(i + 1)` values, so we can refine our pseudocode as follows:

```
for (int i = 0; i < triangle.length; i++) {
    triangle[i] = new int[i + 1];
    fill in triangle[i] using triangle[i - 1].
}
```

We know that the first and last values in each row should be `1`:

```
for (int i = 0; i < triangle.length; i++) {
    triangle[i] = new int[i + 1];
    triangle[i][0] = 1;
    triangle[i][i] = 1;
    fill in the middle of triangle[i] using triangle[i - 1].
}
```

And we know that the middle values come from the previous row. To figure out how to compute them, let's draw a picture of the array we are attempting to build:

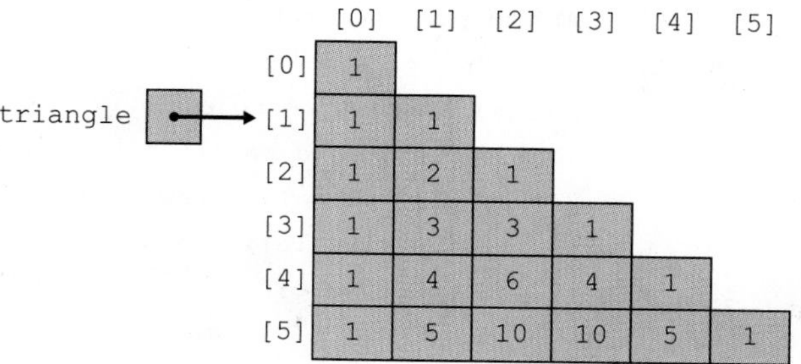

We have already written code to fill in the `1` that appears at the beginning and end of each row. We now need to write code to fill in the middle values. Look at row 5 for an example. The value `5` in column 1 comes from the sum of the values `1` in column 0 and `4` in column 1 in the previous row. The value `10` in column 2 comes from the sum of the values in columns 1 and 2 in the previous row.

More generally, each of these middle values is the sum of the two values from the previous row that appear just above and to the left of it. In other words, for column `j` the values are computed as follows:

```
triangle[i][j] = (value above and left) + (value above).
```

We can turn this into actual code by using the appropriate array indexes:

```
triangle[i][j] = triangle[i – 1][j – 1] + triangle[i – 1][j];
```

We need to include this statement in a `for` loop so that it assigns all of the middle values. The `for` loop is the final step in converting our pseudocode into actual code:

```
for (int i = 0; i < triangle.length; i++) {
    triangle[i] = new int[i + 1];
    triangle[i][0] = 1;
    triangle[i][i] = 1;
    for (int j = 1; j < i; j++) {
        triangle[i][j] = triangle[i – 1][j – 1] + triangle[i – 1][j];
    }
}
```

If we include this code in a method along with a printing method similar to the grid-printing method described earlier, we end up with the following complete program:

```
// This program constructs a jagged two-dimensional array
// that stores Pascal's Triangle. It takes advantage of the
// fact that each value other than the 1s that appear at the
// beginning and end of each row is the sum of two values
```

```
// from the previous row.

public class PascalsTriangle {
    public static void main(String[] args) {
        int[][] triangle = new int[11][];
        fillIn(triangle);
        print(triangle);
    }

    public static void fillIn(int[][] triangle) {
        for (int i = 0; i < triangle.length; i++) {
            triangle[i] = new int[i + 1];
            triangle[i][0] = 1;
            triangle[i][i] = 1;
            for (int j = 1; j < i; j++) {
                triangle[i][j] = triangle[i - 1][j - 1]
                                 + triangle[i - 1][j];
            }
        }
    }

    public static void print(int[][] triangle) {
        for (int i = 0; i < triangle.length; i++) {
            for (int j = 0; j < triangle[i].length; j++) {
                System.out.print(triangle[i][j] + " ");
            }
            System.out.println();
        }
    }
}
```

This program produces the following output:

```
1
1 1
1 2 1
1 3 3 1
1 4 6 4 1
1 5 10 10 5 1
1 6 15 20 15 6 1
1 7 21 35 35 21 7 1
1 8 28 56 70 56 28 8 1
1 9 36 84 126 126 84 36 9 1
1 10 45 120 210 252 210 120 45 10 1
```

7.6 Arrays of Pixels

Recall from Supplement 3G that images are stored on computers as a two-dimensional grid of colored dots known as *pixels*. One of the most common applications of two-dimensional (2D) arrays is for manipulating the pixels of an image. Popular apps like Instagram provide filters and options for modifying images by applying algorithms to their pixels; for example, you can make an image black-and-white, sharpen it, enhance the colors and contrast, or make it look like an old faded photograph. The two-dimensional rectangular nature of an image makes a 2D array a natural way to represent for its pixel data.

Supplement 3G introduced the `DrawingPanel` class that we use to represent a window for drawing 2D shapes and colors. Recall that an image is composed of pixels whose locations are specified with integer coordinates starting from the top-left corner of the image at (0, 0). The various drawing commands of the panel's `Graphics` object, such as `drawRect` and `fillOval`, change the color of regions of pixels. Colors are usually specified by `Color` objects, but the full range of colors comes from mixtures of red, green, and blue elements specified by integers that range from 0 to 255 inclusive. Each combination of three integers specifies a particular color and is known as an *RGB value*.

The `DrawingPanel` includes several methods for getting and setting the color of pixels, listed in Table 7.3. You can interact with a single pixel, or you can grab all of the pixels of the image as a 2D array and manipulate the entire array. The array is in row-major order; that is, the first index of the array is the *y*-coordinate and the second is the *x*-coordinate. For example, `a[r][c]` represents the pixel at position (*x*=*c*, *y*=*r*). For efficiency it is generally recommended to use the array-based versions of the methods; the individual-pixel methods run slowly when applied repeatedly over all pixels of a large image.

The following `DrawPurpleTriangle` example program uses `getPixels` and `setPixels` to fill a triangular region of the panel with a purple color. Figure 7.1 shows the graphical output of the program. Notice that you must call `setPixels` at the end to see the updated image; changing the array will not produce any effect on the screen until you tell the panel to update itself using the new contents of the array.

Table 7.3 `DrawingPanel` methods related to pixels

Method	Description
`getPixel(x, y)`	returns a pixel's color as a `Color` object
`getPixels()`	returns all pixels' colors as a 2D array of `Color` objects, in row-major order *(first index is row or y, second index is column or x)*
`setPixel(x, y, color)`	sets a pixel's color to the given `Color` object's color
`setPixels(pixels)`	sets all pixels' colors from given 2D array of `Color` objects, resizing the panel if necessary to match the array's dimensions

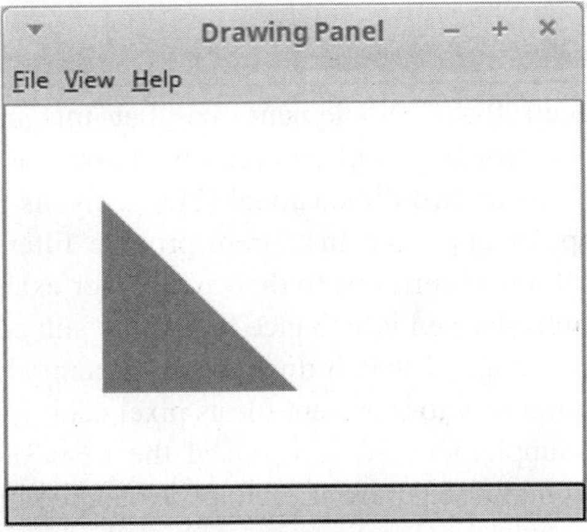

Figure 7.1 Output of `DrawPurpleTriangle`

```java
// This program demonstrates the DrawingPanel's
// getPixels and setPixels methods for
// manipulating pixels of an image.

import java.awt.*;

public class DrawPurpleTriangle {
    public static void main(String[] args) {
        DrawingPanel panel = new DrawingPanel(300, 200);
        Color[][] pixels = panel.getPixels();
        for (int row = 50; row <= 150; row++) {
            for (int col = 50; col <= row; col++) {
                pixels[row][col] = Color.MAGENTA;
            }
        }
        panel.setPixels(pixels);
    }
}
```

You can use `getPixels` and `setPixels` to draw a shape like our purple triangle, but a more typical usage of these methods would be to grab the panel's existing state and alter it in some interesting way. The following `Mirror` program demonstrates the use of a 2D array of `Color` objects. The program's `mirror` method accepts a `DrawingPanel` parameter and flips the pixel contents horizontally, swapping each pixel's color with the one at the opposite horizontal location. The code uses the dimensions of the array to represent the size of the image; `pixels.length` is its height and `pixels[0].length` (the length of the first row of the 2D array) is its width. Figure 7.2 shows the program's graphical output before and after `mirror` is called.

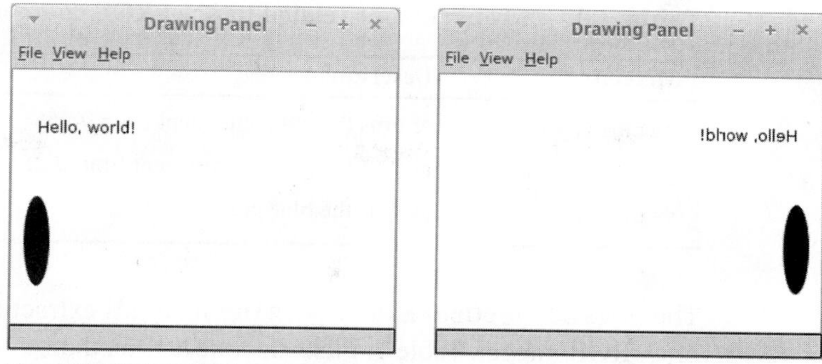

Figure 7.2 Output of `Mirror` before and after mirroring

```
// This program contains a mirror method that flips the appearance
// of a DrawingPanel horizontally pixel-by-pixel.

import java.awt.*;

public class Mirror {
    public static void main(String[] args) {
        DrawingPanel panel = new DrawingPanel(300, 200);
        Graphics g = panel.getGraphics();
        g.drawString("Hello, world!", 20, 50);
        g.fillOval(10, 100, 20, 70);
        mirror(panel);
    }

    // Flips the pixels of the given drawing panel horizontally.
    public static void mirror(DrawingPanel panel) {
        Color[][] pixels = panel.getPixels();
        for (int row = 0; row < pixels.length; row++) {
            for (int col = 0; col < pixels[0].length / 2; col++) {
                // swap with pixel at "mirrored" location
                int opposite = pixels[0].length - 1 - col;
                Color px = pixels[row][col];
                pixels[row][col] = pixels[row][opposite];
                pixels[row][opposite] = px;
            }
        }
        panel.setPixels(pixels);
    }
}
```

Often you'll want to extract the individual red, green, and blue components of a color to manipulate them. Each pixel's `Color` object has methods to help you do this.

Table 7.4 `Color` **methods related to pixel RGB components**

Method	Description
`getRed()`	returns the red component from 0-255
`getGreen()`	returns the green component from 0-255
`getBlue()`	returns the blue component from 0-255

The `getRed`, `getGreen`, and `getBlue` methods extract the relevant components out of an RGB integer. Table 7.4 lists the relevant methods.

The following code shows a method that computes the negative of an image, which is found by taking the opposite of each color's RGB values. For example, the opposite of (red = 255, green = 100, blue = 35) is (red = 0, green = 155, blue = 220). The simplest way to compute the negative is to subtract the pixel's RGB values from the maximum color value of 255. Figure 7.3 shows an example output.

```
// Produces the negative of the given image by inverting all color
// values in the panel.
public static void negative(DrawingPanel panel) {
    Color[][] pixels = panel.getPixels();
    for (int row = 0; row < pixels.length; row++) {
        for (int col = 0; col < pixels[0].length; col++) {
            // extract red/green/blue components from 0-255
            int r = 255 - pixels[row][col].getRed();
            int g = 255 - pixels[row][col].getGreen();
            int b = 255 - pixels[row][col].getBlue();

            // update the pixel array with the new color value
            pixels[row][col] = new Color(r, g, b);
        }
    }
    panel.setPixels(pixels);
}
```

All of the previous examples have involved making changes to a 2D pixel array in place. But sometimes you want to create an image with different dimensions, or want to set each pixel based on the values of pixels around it, and therefore you need to create a new pixel array. The following example shows a `stretch` method that widens the contents of a `DrawingPanel` to twice their current width. To do so, it creates an array `newPixels` that is twice as wide as the existing one. (Remember that the first index of the 2D array is y and the second is x, so to widen the array, the code must double the array's second dimension.) The `setPixels` method will resize the panel if necessary to accommodate our new larger array of pixels.

Figure 7.3 Negative of an image (before and after)

The loop to fill the new array sets the value at each index to the value at half as large an x-index in the original array. So, for example, the original array's pixel value at (52, 34) is used to fill the new array's pixels at (104, 68) and (105, 68). Figure 7.4 shows the graphical output of the stretched image.

```
// Stretches the given panel to be twice as wide.
// Any shapes and colors drawn on the panel are stretched to fit.
public static void stretch(DrawingPanel panel) {
    Color[][] pixels = panel.getPixels();
    Color[][] newPixels = new Color[pixels.length][2 * pixels[0].length];
    for (int row = 0; row < pixels.length; row++) {
        for (int col = 0; col < 2 * pixels[0].length; col++) {
            newPixels[row][col] = pixels[row][col / 2];
        }
    }
    panel.setPixels(newPixels);
}
```

Figure 7.4 Horizontally stretched image (before and after)

The pixel-based methods shown in this section are somewhat inefficient because they create large arrays of `Color` objects, which takes a lot of time and memory. These methods aren't efficient enough for an animation or a game. The `DrawingPanel` provides some additional methods like `getPixelsRGB` that use specially packed integers to represent red, green, and blue color information instead of `Color` objects to improve the speed and memory usage at the cost of a bit of code complexity. If you are interested, you can read about these additional methods in the online `DrawingPanel` documentation at buildingjavaprograms.com.

7.7 Case Study: Benford's Law

Let's look at a more complex program example that involves using arrays. When you study real-world data you will often come across a curious result that is known as *Benford's Law*, named after a physicist named Frank Benford who stated it in 1938.

Benford's Law involves looking at the first digit of a series of numbers. For example, suppose that you were to use a random number generator to generate integers in the range of 100 to 999 and you looked at how often the number begins with 1, how often it begins with 2, and so on. Any decent random number generator would spread the answers out evenly among the nine different regions, so we'd expect to see each digit about one-ninth of the time (11.1%). But with a lot of real-world data, we see a very different distribution.

When we examine data that matches the Benford distribution, we see a first digit of 1 over 30% of the time (almost one third) and, at the other extreme, a first digit of 9 only about 4.6% of the time (less than one in twenty cases). Table 7.5 shows the expected distribution for data that follows Benford's Law.

Why would the distribution turn out this way? Why so many 1s? Why so few 9s? The answer is that exponential sequences have different properties than simple linear sequences. In particular, exponential sequences have a lot more numbers that begin with 1.

Table 7.5 Expected Distribution Under Benford's Law

First Digit	Frequency
1	30.1%
2	17.6%
3	12.5%
4	9.7%
5	7.9%
6	6.7%
7	5.8%
8	5.1%
9	4.6%

To explore this phenomenon, let's look at two different sequences of numbers: one that grows linearly and one that grows exponentially. If you start with the number 1 and add 0.2 to it over and over, you get the following linear sequence:

1, 1.2, 1.4, 1.6, 1.8, 2, 2.2, 2.4, 2.6, 2.8, 3, 3.2, 3.4, 3.6, 3.8, 4, 4.2, 4.4, 4.6, 4.8, 5, 5.2, 5.4, 5.6, 5.8, 6, 6.2, 6.4, 6.6, 6.8, 7, 7.2, 7.4, 7.6, 7.8, 8, 8.2, 8.4, 8.6, 8.8, 9, 9.2, 9.4, 9.6, 9.8, 10

In this sequence there are five numbers that begin with 1, five numbers that begin with 2, five numbers that begin with 3, and so on. For each digit, there are five numbers that begin with that digit. That's what we expect to see with data that goes up by a constant amount each time.

But consider what happens when we make it an exponential sequence instead. Let's again start with 1 and continue until we get to 10, but this time let's multiply each successive number by 1.05 (we'll limit ourselves to displaying just two digits after the decimal, but the actual sequence takes into account all of the digits):

1.00, 1.05, 1.10, 1.16, 1.22, 1.28, 1.34, 1.41, 1.48, 1.55, 1.63, 1.71, 1.80, 1.89, 1.98, 2.08, 2.18, 2.29, 2.41, 2.53, 2.65, 2.79, 2.93, 3.07, 3.23, 3.39, 3.56, 3.73, 3.92, 4.12, 4.32, 4.54, 4.76, 5.00, 5.25, 5.52, 5.79, 6.08, 6.39, 6.70, 7.04, 7.39, 7.76, 8.15, 8.56, 8.99, 9.43, 9.91, 10.40

In this sequence there are 15 numbers that begin with 1 (31.25%), 8 numbers that begin with 2 (16.7%), and so on. There are only 2 numbers that begin with 9 (4.2%). In fact, the distribution of digits is almost exactly what you see in the table for Benford's Law.

There are many real-world phenomena that exhibit an exponential character. For example, population tends to grow exponentially in most regions. There are many other data sets that also seem to exhibit the Benford pattern, including sunspots, salaries, investments, heights of buildings, and so on. Benford's Law has been used to try to detect accounting fraud under the theory that when someone is making up data, he or she is likely to use a more random process that won't yield a Benford style distribution.

For our purposes, let's write a program that reads a file of integers and that shows the distribution of the leading digit. We'll read the data from a file and will run it on several sample inputs. First, though, let's consider the general problem of tallying.

Tallying Values

VideoNote

In programming we often find ourselves wanting to count the number of occurrences of some set of values. For example, we might want to know how many people got a 100 on an exam, how many got a 99, how many got a 98, and so on. Or we might want to know how many days the temperature in a city was above 100 degrees, how many days it was in the 90s, how many days it was in the 80s, and so on. The approach is very nearly the same for each of these tallying tasks. Let's look at a small tallying task in which there are only five values to tally.

Suppose that a teacher scores quizzes on a scale of 0 to 4 and wants to know the distribution of quiz scores. In other words, the teacher wants to know how many scores of 0 there are, how many scores of 1, how many scores of 2, how many scores of 3, and how many scores of 4. Suppose that the teacher has included all of the scores in a data file like the following:

```
1 4 1 0 3 2 1 4 2 0
3 0 2 3 0 4 3 3 4 1
2 4 1 3 1 4 3 3 2 4
2 3 0 4 1 4 4 1 4 1
```

The teacher could hand-count the scores, but it would be much easier to use a computer to do the counting. How can you solve the problem? First you have to recognize that you are doing five separate counting tasks: You are counting the occurrences of the number 0, the number 1, the number 2, the number 3, and the number 4. You will need five counters to solve this problem, which means that an array is a great way to store the data. In general, whenever you find yourself thinking that you need *n* of some kind of data, you should think about using an array of length *n*.

Each counter will be an `int`, so you want an array of five `int` values:

```
int[] count = new int[5];
```

This line of code will allocate the array of five integers and will auto-initialize each to `0`:

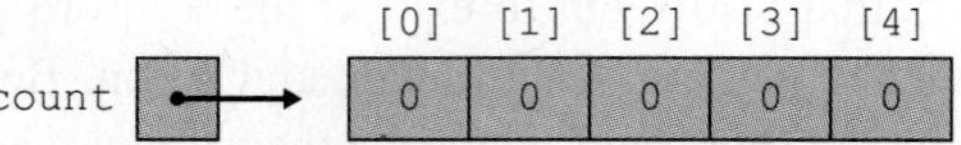

You're reading from a file, so you'll need a `Scanner` and a loop that reads scores until there are no more scores to read:

```
Scanner input = new Scanner(new File("tally.dat"));
while (input.hasNextInt()) {
    int next = input.nextInt();
    // process next
}
```

To complete this code, you need to figure out how to process each value. You know that `next` will be one of five different values: `0`, `1`, `2`, `3`, or `4`. If it is `0`, you want to increment the counter for `0`, which is `count[0]`; if it is `1`, you want to increment the counter for `1`, which is `count[1]`, and so on. We have been solving problems like this one with nested `if/else` statements:

```
if (next == 0) {
    count[0]++;
} else if (next == 1) {
    count[1]++;
} else if (next == 2) {
    count[2]++;
} else if (next == 3) {
    count[3]++;
} else { // next == 4
    count[4]++;
}
```

But with an array, you can solve this problem much more directly:

```
count[next]++;
```

This line of code is so short compared to the nested `if/else` construct that you might not realize at first that it does the same thing. Let's simulate exactly what happens as various values are read from the file.

When the array is constructed, all of the counters are initialized to `0`:

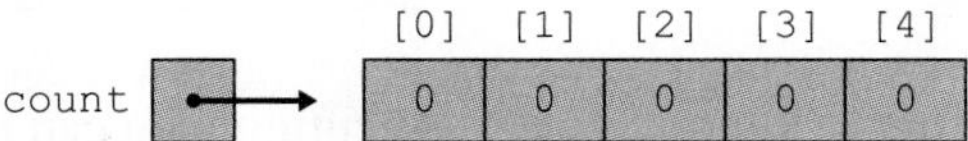

The first value in the input file is a `1`, so the program reads that into `next`. Then it executes this line of code:

```
count[next]++;
```

Because `next` is `1`, this line of code becomes

```
count[1]++;
```

So the counter at index `[1]` is incremented:

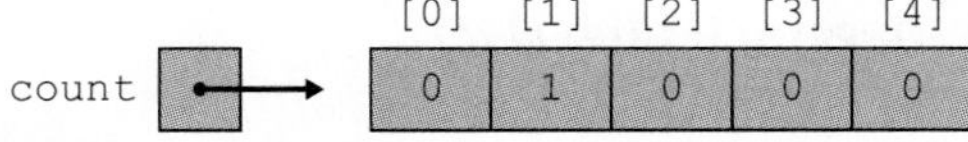

Then a `4` is read from the input file, which means `count[4]` is incremented:

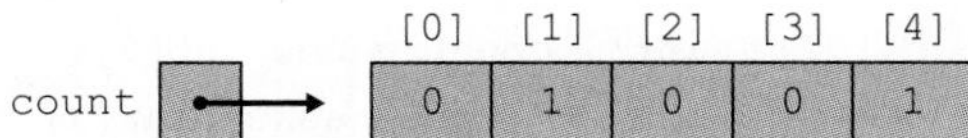

Next, another `1` is read from the input file, which increments `count[1]`:

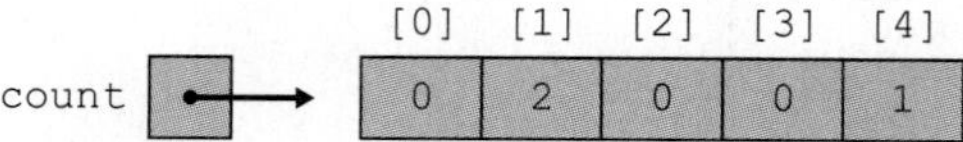

Then a `0` is read from the input file, which increments `count[0]`:

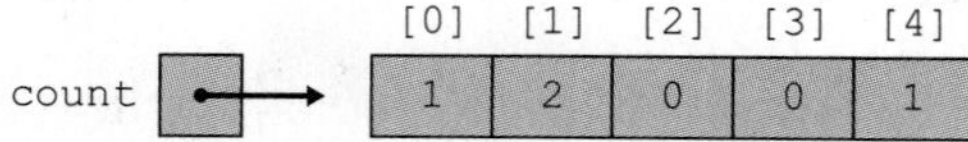

Notice that in just this short set of data you've jumped from index 1 to index 4, then back down to index 1, then to index 0. The program continues executing in this manner, jumping from counter to counter as it reads values from the file. This ability to jump around in the data structure is what's meant by random access.

After processing all of the data, the array ends up looking like this:

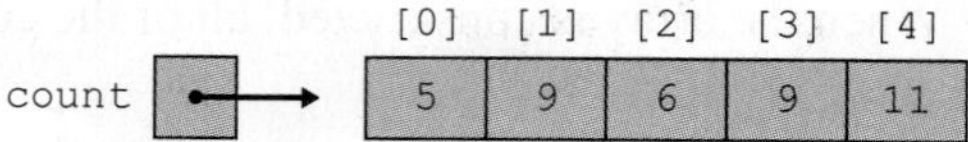

After this loop finishes executing, you can report the total for each score by using the standard traversing loop with a `println`:

```
for (int i = 0; i < count.length; i++) {
    System.out.println(i + "\t" + count[i]);
}
```

With the addition of a header for the output, the complete program is as follows:

```
// Reads a series of values and reports the frequency of
// occurrence of each value.

import java.io.*;
import java.util.*;

public class Tally {
    public static void main(String[] args)
            throws FileNotFoundException {
        Scanner input = new Scanner(new File("tally.dat"));
        int[] count = new int[5];
        while (input.hasNextInt()) {
```

```
                int next = input.nextInt();
                count[next]++;
            }
            System.out.println("Value\tOccurrences");
            for (int i = 0; i < count.length; i++) {
                System.out.println(i + "\t" + count[i]);
            }
        }
}
```

Given the sample input file shown earlier, this program produces the following output:

```
Value   Occurrences
0       5
1       9
2       6
3       9
4       11
```

It is important to realize that a program written with an array is much more flexible than programs written with simple variables and `if/else` statements. For example, suppose you wanted to adapt this program to process an input file with exam scores that range from 0 to 100. The only change you would have to make would be to allocate a larger array:

```
int[] count = new int[101];
```

If you had written the program with an `if/else` approach, you would have to add 96 new branches to account for the new range of values. When you use an array solution, you just have to modify the overall size of the array. Notice that the array size is one more than the highest score (101 rather than 100) because the array is zero-based and because you can actually get 101 different scores on the test, including 0 as a possibility.

Completing the Program

Now that we've explored the basic approach to tallying, we can fairly easily adapt it to the problem of analyzing a data file to find the distribution of leading digits. As we stated earlier, we're assuming that we have a file of integers. To count the leading digits, we will need to be able to get the leading digit of each. This task is specialized enough that it deserves to be in its own method.

So let's first write a method called `firstDigit` that returns the first digit of an integer. If the number is a one-digit number, then the number itself will be the answer. If the number is not a one-digit number, then we can chop off its last digit because we don't need it. If we do the chopping in a loop, then eventually we'll get down to a one-digit number (the first digit). This leads us to write the following loop:

```
while (result >= 10) {
    result = result / 10;
}
```

We don't expect to get any negative numbers, but it's not a bad idea to make sure we don't have any negatives. So putting this into a method that also handles negatives, we get the following code:

```
public static int firstDigit(int n) {
    int result = Math.abs(n);
    while (result >= 10) {
        result = result / 10;
    }
    return result;
}
```

In the previous section we explored the general approach to tallying. In this case we want to tally the digits 0 through 9, so we want an array of length 10. Otherwise the solution is nearly identical to what we did in the last section. We can put the tallying code into a method that constructs an array and returns the tally:

```
public static int[] countDigits(Scanner input) {
    int[] count = new int[10];
    while (input.hasNextInt()) {
        int n = input.nextInt();
        count[firstDigit(n)]++;
    }
    return count;
}
```

Notice that instead of tallying `n` in the body of the loop, we are instead tallying `firstDigit(n)` (just the first digit, not the entire number).

The value `0` presents a potential problem for us. Benford's Law is meant to apply to data that comes from an exponential sequence. But even if you are increasing exponentially, if you start with `0`, you never get beyond `0`. As a result, it is best to eliminate the `0` values from the calculation. Often they won't occur at all.

When reporting results, then, let's begin by reporting the excluded zeros if they exist:

```
if (count[0] > 0) {
    System.out.println("excluding " + count[0] + " zeros");
}
```

For the other digits, we want to report the number of occurrences of each and also the percentage of each. To figure the percentage, we'll need to know the sum of the values. This is a good place to introduce a method that finds the sum of an array of integers. It's a fairly straightforward array traversal problem that can be solved with a for-each loop:

```
public static int sum(int[] data) {
    int sum = 0;
    for (int n : data) {
        sum += n;
    }
    return sum;
}
```

Now we can compute the total number of digits by calling the method and subtracting the number of `0`s:

```
int total = sum(count) – count[0];
```

And once we have the total number of digits, we can write a loop to report each of the percentages. To compute the percentages, we multiply each count by 100 and divide by the total number of digits. We have to be careful to multiply by 100.0 rather than 100 to make sure that we are computing the result using `double` values. Otherwise we'll get truncated integer division and won't get any digits after the decimal point:

```
for (int i = 1; i < count.length; i++) {
    double pct = count[i] * 100.0 / total;
    System.out.println(i + "  " + count[i] + "  " + pct);
}
```

Notice that the loop starts at `1` instead of `0` because we have excluded the zeros from our reporting.

Here is a complete program that puts these pieces together. It also uses `printf` statements to format the output and includes a header for the table and a total afterward:

```
// This program finds the distribution of leading digits in a set
// of positive integers.  The program is useful for exploring the
// phenomenon known as Benford's Law.

import java.io.*;
import java.util.*;

public class Benford {
    public static void main(String[] args)
```

```
            throws FileNotFoundException {
        Scanner console = new Scanner(System.in);
        System.out.println("Let's count those leading digits...");
        System.out.print("input file name? ");
        String name = console.nextLine();
        Scanner input = new Scanner(new File(name));
        int[] count = countDigits(input);
        reportResults(count);
    }

    // Reads integers from input, computing an array of counts
    // for the occurrences of each leading digit (0-9).
    public static int[] countDigits(Scanner input) {
        int[] count = new int[10];
        while (input.hasNextInt()) {
            int n = input.nextInt();
            count[firstDigit(n)]++;
        }
        return count;
    }

    // Reports percentages for each leading digit, excluding zeros
    public static void reportResults(int[] count) {
        System.out.println();
        if (count[0] > 0) {
            System.out.println("excluding " + count[0] + " zeros");
        }
        int total = sum(count) - count[0];
        System.out.println("Digit Count Percent");
        for (int i = 1; i < count.length; i++) {
            double pct = count[i] * 100.0 / total;
            System.out.printf("%5d %5d %6.2f\n", i, count[i], pct);
        }
        System.out.printf("Total %5d %6.2f\n", total, 100.0);
    }

    // returns the sum of the integers in the given array
    public static int sum(int[] data) {
        int sum = 0;
        for (int n : data) {
            sum += n;
        }
```

```
        return sum;
    }

    // returns the first digit of the given number
    public static int firstDigit(int n) {
        int result = Math.abs(n);
        while (result >= 10) {
            result = result / 10;
        }
        return result;
    }
}
```

Now that we have a complete program, let's see what we get when we analyze various data sets. The Benford distribution shows up with population data because population tends to grow exponentially. Let's use data from the web page http://www.census.gov/popest/ which contains population estimates for various U.S. counties. The data set has information on 3000 different counties with populations varying from 100 individuals to over 9 million for the census year 2000. Here is a sample output of our program using these data:

```
Let's count those leading digits...
input file name? county.txt

Digit   Count  Percent
    1     970    30.90
    2     564    17.97
    3     399    12.71
    4     306     9.75
    5     206     6.56
    6     208     6.63
    7     170     5.24
    8     172     5.48
    9     144     4.59
Total    3139   100.00
```

These percentages are almost exactly the numbers predicted by Benford's Law.

Data that obey Benford's Law have an interesting property. It doesn't matter what scale you use for the data. So if you are measuring heights, for example, it doesn't matter whether you measure in feet, inches, meters, or furlongs. In our case, we counted the number of people in each U.S. county. If we instead count the number of human hands in each county, then we have to double each number. Look at the preceding output and see if you can predict the result when you double each number. Here is the actual result:

```
Let's count those leading digits...
input file name? county2.txt

Digit   Count  Percent
    1     900   28.67
    2     555   17.68
    3     415   13.22
    4     322   10.26
    5     242    7.71
    6     209    6.66
    7     190    6.05
    8     173    5.51
    9     133    4.24
Total    3139  100.00
```

Notice that there is very little change. Doubling the numbers has little effect because if the original data is exponential in nature, then the same will be true of the doubled numbers. Here is another sample run that triples the county population numbers:

```
Let's count those leading digits...
input file name? county3.txt

Digit   Count  Percent
    1     926   29.50
    2     549   17.49
    3     385   12.27
    4     327   10.42
    5     258    8.22
    6     228    7.26
    7     193    6.15
    8     143    4.56
    9     130    4.14
Total    3139  100.00
```

Another data set that shows Benford characteristics is the count of sunspots that occur on any given day. Robin McQuinn maintains a web page at http://sidc.oma.be/html/sunspot.html that has daily counts of sunspots going back to 1818. Here is a sample execution using these data:

```
Let's count those leading digits...
input file name? sunspot.txt

excluding 4144 zeros
Digit   Count  Percent
    1    5405   31.24
    2    1809   10.46
    3    2127   12.29
    4    1690    9.77
    5    1702    9.84
    6    1357    7.84
    7    1364    7.88
    8     966    5.58
    9     882    5.10
Total   17302  100.00
```

Notice that on this execution the program reports the exclusion of some `0` values.

Chapter Summary

An array is an object that groups multiple primitive values or objects of the same type under one name. Each individual value, called an element, is accessed with an integer index that ranges from 0 to one less than the array's length.

Attempting to access an array element with an index of less than 0 or one that is greater than or equal to the array's length will cause the program to crash with an `ArrayIndexOutOfBoundsException`.

Arrays are often traversed using `for` loops. The length of an array is found by accessing its length field, so the loop over an array can process indexes from 0 to `length - 1`. Array elements can also be accessed in order using a type of loop called a for-each loop.

Arrays have several limitations, such as fixed size and lack of support for common operations like == and `println`. To perform these operations, you must either use the `Arrays` class or write `for` loops that process each element of the array.

Several common array algorithms, such as printing an array or comparing two arrays to each other for equality, are implemented by traversing the elements and examining or modifying each one.

Java arrays are objects and use reference semantics, in which variables store references to values rather than to the actual values themselves. This means that two variables can refer to the same array or object. If the array is modified through one of its references, the modification will also be seen in the other.

Arrays of objects are actually arrays of references to objects. A newly declared and initialized array of objects actually stores `null` in all of its element indexes, so each element must be initialized individually or in a loop to store an actual object.

A multidimensional array is an array of arrays. These are often used to store two-dimensional data, such as data in rows and columns or *xy* data in a two-dimensional space.

Self-Check Problems

Section 7.1: Array Basics

1. Which of the following is the correct syntax to declare an array of ten integers?

   a. `int a[10] = new int[10];`
   b. `int[10] a = new int[10];`
   c. `[]int a = [10]int;`
   d. `int a[10];`
   e. `int[] a = new int[10];`

2. What expression should be used to access the first element of an array of integers called `numbers`? What expression should be used to access the last element of `numbers`, assuming it contains 10 elements? What expression can be used to access its last element, regardless of its length?

3. Write code that creates an array of integers named `data` of size 5 with the following contents:

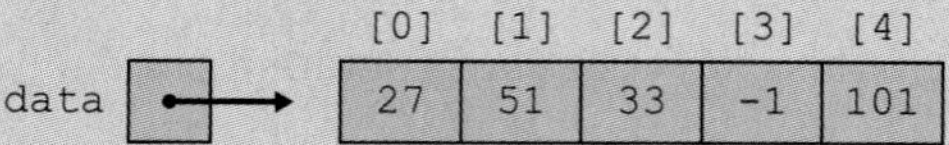

4. Write code that stores all odd numbers between −6 and 38 into an array using a loop. Make the array's size exactly large enough to store the numbers.

   Then, try generalizing your code so that it will work for any minimum and maximum values, not just –6 and 38.

5. What elements does the array `numbers` contain after the following code is executed?

```
int[] numbers = new int[8];
numbers[1] = 4;
numbers[4] = 99;
numbers[7] = 2;

int x = numbers[1];
numbers[x] = 44;
numbers[numbers[7]] = 11; // uses numbers[7] as index
```

6. What elements does the array `data` contain after the following code is executed?

```
int[] data = new int[8];
data[0] = 3;
data[7] = -18;
data[4] = 5;
data[1] = data[0];

int x = data[4];
data[4] = 6;
data[x] = data[0] * data[1];
```

7. What is wrong with the following code?

```
int[] first = new int[2];
first[0] = 3;
first[1] = 7;
int[] second = new int[2];
second[0] = 3;
second[1] = 7;

// print the array elements
System.out.println(first);
System.out.println(second);

// see if the elements are the same
if (first == second) {
    System.out.println("They contain the same elements.");
} else {
    System.out.println("The elements are different.");
}
```

8. Which of the following is the correct syntax to declare an array of the given six integer values?

   a. `int[] a = {17, -3, 42, 5, 9, 28};`
   b. `int a {17, -3, 42, 5, 9, 28};`
   c. `int[] a = new int[6] {17, -3, 42, 5, 9, 28};`
   d. `int[6] a = {17, -3, 42, 5, 9, 28};`
   e. `int[] a = int [17, -3, 42, 5, 9, 28] {6};`

9. Write a piece of code that declares an array called `data` with the elements `7`, `-1`, `13`, `24`, and `6`. Use only one statement to initialize the array.

10. Write a piece of code that examines an array of integers and reports the maximum value in the array. Consider putting your code into a method called `max` that accepts the array as a parameter and returns the maximum value. Assume that the array contains at least one element.

11. Write a method called `average` that computes the average (arithmetic mean) of all elements in an array of integers and returns the answer as a `double`. For example, if the array passed contains the values `[1, –2, 4, –4, 9, –6, 16, –8, 25, –10]`, the calculated average should be `2.5`. Your method accepts an array of integers as its parameter and returns the average.

Section 7.2: Array-Traversal Algorithms

12. What is an array traversal? Give an example of a problem that can be solved by traversing an array.

13. Write code that uses a `for` loop to print each element of an array named `data` that contains five integers:

```
element [0] is 14
element [1] is 5
element [2] is 27
element [3] is –3
element [4] is 2598
```

Consider generalizing your code so that it will work on an array of any size.

14. What elements does the array `list` contain after the following code is executed?

```
int[] list = {2, 18, 6, -4, 5, 1};
for (int i = 0; i < list.length; i++) {
    list[i] = list[i] + (list[i] / list[0]);
}
```

15. Write a piece of code that prints an array of integers in reverse order, in the same format as the `print` method from Section 7.2. Consider putting your code into a method called `printBackwards` that accepts the array as a parameter.

16. Describe the modifications that would be necessary to change the `count` and `equals` methods developed in Section 7.2 to process arrays of `Strings` instead of arrays of integers.

17. Write a method called `allLess` that accepts two arrays of integers and returns `true` if each element in the first array is less than the element at the same index in the second array. Your method should return `false` if the arrays are not the same length.

Section 7.3: Reference Semantics

18. Why does a method to swap two array elements work correctly when a method to swap two integer values does not?

19. What is the output of the following program?

```
public class ReferenceMystery1 {
    public static void main(String[] args) {
        int x = 0;
        int[] a = new int[4];
        x = x + 1;
        mystery(x, a);
        System.out.println(x + " " + Arrays.toString(a));
        x = x + 1;
        mystery(x, a);
        System.out.println(x + " " + Arrays.toString(a));
    }
    public static void mystery(int x, int[] a) {
        x = x + 1;
        a[x] = a[x] + 1;
        System.out.println(x + " " + Arrays.toString(a));
    }
}
```

20. What is the output of the following program?

```
public class ReferenceMystery2 {
    public static void main(String[] args) {
        int x = 1;
        int[] a = new int[2];
        mystery(x, a);
        System.out.println(x + " " + Arrays.toString(a));
        x--;
        a[1] = a.length;
        mystery(x, a);
```

```
        System.out.println(x + " " + Arrays.toString(a));
    }

    public static void mystery(int x, int[] list) {
        list[x]++;
        x++;
        System.out.println(x + " " + Arrays.toString(list));
    }
}
```

21. Write a method called `swapPairs` that accepts an array of integers and swaps the elements at adjacent indexes. That is, elements 0 and 1 are swapped, elements 2 and 3 are swapped, and so on. If the array has an odd length, the final element should be left unmodified. For example, the list `[10, 20, 30, 40, 50]` should become `[20, 10, 40, 30, 50]` after a call to your method.

Section 7.4: Advanced Array Techniques

22. What are the values of the elements in the array `numbers` after the following code is executed?

```
int[] numbers = {10, 20, 30, 40, 50, 60, 70, 80, 90, 100};
for (int i = 0; i < 9; i++) {
    numbers[i] = numbers[i + 1];
}
```

23. What are the values of the elements in the array `numbers` after the following code is executed?

```
int[] numbers = {10, 20, 30, 40, 50, 60, 70, 80, 90, 100};
for (int i = 1; i < 10; i++) {
    numbers[i] = numbers[i - 1];
}
```

24. Consider the following method, `mystery`:

```
public static void mystery(int[] a, int[] b) {
    for (int i = 0; i < a.length; i++) {
        a[i] += b[b.length - 1 - i];
    }
}
```

What are the values of the elements in array `a1` after the following code executes?

```
int[] a1 = {1, 3, 5, 7, 9};
int[] a2 = {1, 4, 9, 16, 25};
mystery(a1, a2);
```

25. Consider the following method, `mystery2`:

```
public static void mystery2(int[] a, int[] b) {
    for (int i = 0; i < a.length; i++) {
        a[i] = a[2 * i % a.length] - b[3 * i % b.length];
    }
}
```

What are the values of the elements in array `a1` after the following code executes?

```
int[] a1 = {2, 4, 6, 8, 10, 12, 14, 16};
int[] a2 = {1, 1, 2, 3, 5, 8, 13, 21};
mystery2(a1, a2);
```

26. Consider the following method, `mystery3`:

```
public static void mystery3(int[] data, int x, int y) {
    data[data[x]] = data[y];
    data[y] = x;
}
```

What are the values of the elements in the array `numbers` after the following code executes?

```
int[] numbers = {3, 7, 1, 0, 25, 4, 18, -1, 5};
mystery3(numbers, 3, 1);
mystery3(numbers, 5, 6);
mystery3(numbers, 8, 4);
```

27. Consider the following method:

```
public static int mystery4(int[] list) {
    int x = 0;
    for (int i = 1; i < list.length; i++) {
        int y = list[i] - list[0];
        if (y > x) {
            x = y;
        }
    }
    return x;
}
```

What value does the method return when passed each of the following arrays?

a. `{5}`

b. `{3, 12}`

c. `{4, 2, 10, 8}`

d. `{1, 9, 3, 5, 7}`

e. `{8, 2, 10, 4, 10, 9}`

28. Consider the following method:

```
public static void mystery5(int[] nums) {
    for (int i = 0; i < nums.length - 1; i++) {
        if (nums[i] > nums[i + 1]) {
            nums[i + 1]++;
        }
    }
}
```

What are the final contents of each of the following arrays if each is passed to the above method?

a. `{8}`

b. `{14, 7}`

c. `{7, 1, 3, 2, 0, 4}`

d. `{10, 8, 9, 5, 5}`

e. `{12, 11, 10, 10, 8, 7}`

29. Write a piece of code that computes the average `String` length of the elements of an array of `Strings`. For example, if the array contains `{"belt", "hat", "jelly", "bubble gum"}`, the average length is `5.5`.

30. Write code that accepts an array of `Strings` as its parameter and indicates whether that array is a palindrome—that is, whether it reads the same forward as backward. For example, the array `{"alpha", "beta", "gamma", "delta", "gamma", "beta", "alpha"}` is a palindrome.

Section 7.5: Multidimensional Arrays

31. What elements does the array `numbers` contain after the following code is executed?

```
int[][] numbers = new int[3][4];
for (int r = 0; r < numbers.length; r++) {
    for (int c = 0; c < numbers[0].length; c++) {
        numbers[r][c] = r + c;
    }
}
```

32. Assume that a two-dimensional rectangular array of integers called `data` has been declared with four rows and seven columns. Write a loop to initialize the third row of data to store the numbers 1 through 7.

33. Write a piece of code that constructs a two-dimensional array of integers with 5 rows and 10 columns. Fill the array with a multiplication table, so that array element `[i][j]` contains the value `i * j`. Use nested `for` loops to build the array.

34. Assume that a two-dimensional rectangular array of integers called `matrix` has been declared with six rows and eight columns. Write a loop to copy the contents of the second column into the fifth column.

35. Consider the following method:

```
public static void mystery2d(int[][] a) {
    for (int r = 0; r < a.length; r++) {
        for (int c = 0; c < a[0].length - 1; c++) {
            if (a[r][c + 1] > a[r][c]) {
                a[r][c] = a[r][c + 1];
            }
        }
    }
}
```

If a two-dimensional array `numbers` is initialized to store the following integers, what are its contents after the call shown?

```
int[][] numbers = {{3, 4, 5, 6},
                   {4, 5, 6, 7},
                   {5, 6, 7, 8}};
mystery2d(numbers);
```

36. Write a piece of code that constructs a jagged two-dimensional array of integers with five rows and an increasing number of columns in each row, such that the first row has one column, the second row has two, the third has three, and so on. The array elements should have increasing values in top-to-bottom, left-to-right order (also called row-major order). In other words, the array's contents should be the following:

```
1
2, 3
4, 5, 6
7, 8, 9, 10
11, 12, 13, 14, 15
```

Use nested `for` loops to build the array.

37. When examining a 2D array of pixels, how could you figure out the width and height of the image even if you don't have access to the `DrawingPanel` object?

38. Finish the following code for a method that converts an image into its red channel; that is, removing any green or blue from each pixel and keeping only the red component.

```
public static void toRedChannel(DrawingPanel panel) {
    Color[][] pixels = panel.getPixels();
    for (int row = 0; row < pixels.length; row++) {
        for (int col = 0; col < pixels[0].length; col++) {
            // your code goes here
        }
    }
    panel.setPixels(pixels);
}
```

39. What is the result of the following code? What will the image look like?

```
public static void pixelMystery(DrawingPanel panel) {
    Color[][] pixels = panel.getPixels();
    for (int row = 0; row < pixels.length; row++) {
        for (int col = 0; col < pixels[0].length; col++) {
            int n = Math.min(row + col, 255);
            pixels[row][col] = new Color(n, n, n);
        }
    }
    panel.setPixels(pixels);
}
```

Exercises

1. Write a method called `lastIndexOf` that accepts an array of integers and an integer value as its parameters and returns the last index at which the value occurs in the array. The method should return `-1` if the value is not found. For example, in the array `[74, 85, 102, 99, 101, 85, 56]`, the last index of the value `85` is 5.

2. Write a method called `range` that returns the range of values in an array of integers. The range is defined as 1 more than the difference between the maximum and minimum values in the array. For example, if an array called `list` contains the values [36, 12, 25, 19, 46, 31, 22], the call of `range(list)` should return 35 (46 − 12 + 1). You may assume that the array has at least one element.

3. Write a method called `countInRange` that accepts an array of integers, a minimum value, and a maximum value as parameters and returns the count of how many elements from the array fall between the minimum and maximum (inclusive). For example, in the array [14, 1, 22, 17, 36, 7, −43, 5], for minimum value 4 and maximum value 17, there are four elements whose values fall between 4 and 17.

4. Write a method called `isSorted` that accepts an array of real numbers as a parameter and returns `true` if the list is in sorted (nondecreasing) order and `false` otherwise. For example, if arrays named `list1` and `list2` store [16.1, 12.3, 22.2, 14.4] and [1.5, 4.3, 7.0, 19.5, 25.1, 46.2] respectively, the calls `isSorted(list1)` and `isSorted(list2)` should return `false` and `true` respectively. Assume the array has at least one element. A one-element array is considered to be sorted.

5. Write a method called `mode` that returns the most frequently occurring element of an array of integers. Assume that the array has at least one element and that every element in the array has a value between 0 and 100 inclusive. Break ties by choosing the lower value. For example, if the array passed contains the values [27, 15, 15, 11, 27], your method should return 15. (*Hint*: You may wish to look at the `Tally` program from this chapter to get an idea how to solve this problem.) Can you write a version of this method that does not rely on the values being between 0 and 100?

6. Write a method called `stdev` that returns the standard deviation of an array of integers. Standard deviation is computed by taking the square root of the sum of the squares of the differences between each element and the mean, divided by one less than the number of elements. (It's just that simple!) More concisely and mathematically, the standard deviation of an array *a* is written as follows:

$$stdev(a) = \sqrt{\frac{\sum_{i=0}^{a.length-1} (a[i] - average(a)^2)}{a.length - 1}}$$

For example, if the array passed contains the values [1, −2, 4, −4, 9, −6, 16, −8, 25, −10], your method should return approximately 11.237.

7. Write a method called `kthLargest` that accepts an integer *k* and an array *a* as its parameters and returns the element such that *k* elements have greater or equal value. If *k* = 0, return the largest element; if *k* = 1, return the second-largest element, and so on. For example, if the array passed contains the values [74, 85, 102, 99, 101, 56, 84] and the integer *k* passed is 2, your method should return 99 because there are two values at least as large as 99 (101 and 102). Assume that 0 ≤ *k* < `a.length`. (*Hint:* Consider sorting the array or a copy of the array first.)

8. Write a method called `median` that accepts an array of integers as its parameter and returns the median of the numbers in the array. The median is the number that appears in the middle of the list if you arrange the elements in order. Assume that the array is of odd size (so that one sole element constitutes the median) and that the numbers in the array are between 0 and 99 inclusive. For example, the median of [5, 2, 4, 17, 55, 4, 3, 26, 18, 2, 17] is 5 and the median of [42, 37, 1, 97, 1, 2, 7, 42, 3, 25, 89, 15, 10, 29, 27] is 25. (*Hint*: You may wish to look at the `Tally` program from earlier in this chapter for ideas.)

9. Write a method called `minGap` that accepts an integer array as a parameter and returns the minimum difference or gap between adjacent values in the array, where the gap is defined as the later value minus the earlier value. For example, in the array [1, 3, 6, 7, 12], the first gap is 2 (3 − 1), the second gap is 3 (6 − 3), the third gap is 1 (7 − 6), and the fourth gap is 5 (12 − 7). So your method should return 1 if passed this array. The minimum gap could be a negative number if the list is not in sorted order. If you are passed an array with fewer than two elements, return 0.

10. Write a method called `percentEven` that accepts an array of integers as a parameter and returns the percentage of even numbers in the array as a real number. For example, if the array stores the elements `[6, 2, 9, 11, 3]`, then your method should return `40.0`. If the array contains no even elements or no elements at all, return `0.0`.

11. Write a method called `isUnique` that accepts an array of integers as a parameter and returns a `boolean` value indicating whether or not the values in the array are unique (`true` for yes, `false` for no). The values in the list are considered unique if there is no pair of values that are equal. For example, if passed an array containing `[3, 8, 12, 2, 9, 17, 43, −8, 46]`, your method should return `true`, but if passed `[4, 7, 3, 9, 12, −47, 3, 74]`, your method should return `false` because the value `3` appears twice.

12. Write a method called `priceIsRight` that mimics the guessing rules from the game show *The Price Is Right*. The method accepts as parameters an array of integers representing the contestants' bids and an integer representing a correct price. The method returns the element in the bids array that is closest in value to the correct price without being larger than that price. For example, if an array called `bids` stores the values `[200, 300, 250, 1, 950, 40]`, the call of `priceIsRight(bids, 280)` should return `250`, since 250 is the bid closest to 280 without going over 280. If all bids are larger than the correct price, your method should return `−1`.

13. Write a method called `longestSortedSequence` that accepts an array of integers as a parameter and returns the length of the longest sorted (nondecreasing) sequence of integers in the array. For example, in the array `[3, 8, 10, 1, 9, 14, −3, 0, 14, 207, 56, 98, 12]`, the longest sorted sequence in the array has four values in it (the sequence −3, 0, 14, 207), so your method would return `4` if passed this array. Sorted means nondecreasing, so a sequence could contain duplicates. Your method should return `0` if passed an empty array.

14. Write a method called `contains` that accepts two arrays of integers *a1* and *a2* as parameters and that returns a `boolean` value indicating whether or not the sequence of elements in *a2* appears in *a1* (`true` for yes, `false` for no). The sequence must appear consecutively and in the same order. For example, consider the following arrays:

```
int[] list1 = {1, 6, 2, 1, 4, 1, 2, 1, 8};
int[] list2 = {1, 2, 1};
```

The call of `contains(list1, list2)` should return `true` because the sequence of values in `list2` `[1, 2, 1]` is contained in `list1` starting at index 5. If `list2` had stored the values `[2, 1, 2]`, the call of `contains(list1, list2)` would return `false`. Any two lists with identical elements are considered to contain each other. Every array contains the empty array, and the empty array does not contain any arrays other than the empty array itself.

15. Write a method called `collapse` that accepts an array of integers as a parameter and returns a new array containing the result of replacing each pair of integers with the sum of that pair. For example, if an array called `list` stores the values `[7, 2, 8, 9, 4, 13, 7, 1, 9, 10]`, then the call of `collapse(list)` should return a new array containing `[9, 17, 17, 8, 19]`. The first pair from the original list is collapsed into 9 (7 + 2), the second pair is collapsed into 17 (8 + 9), and so on. If the list stores an odd number of elements, the final element is not collapsed. For example, if the list had been `[1, 2, 3, 4, 5]`, then the call would return `[3, 7, 5]`. Your method should not change the array that is passed as a parameter.

16. Write a method called `append` that accepts two integer arrays as parameters and returns a new array that contains the result of appending the second array's values at the end of the first array. For example, if arrays `list1` and `list2` store `[2, 4, 6]` and `[1, 2, 3, 4, 5]` respectively, the call of `append(list1, list2)` should return a new array containing `[2, 4, 6, 1, 2, 3, 4, 5]`. If the call instead had been `append(list2, list1)`, the method would return an array containing `[1, 2, 3, 4, 5, 2, 4, 6]`.

17. Write a method called `vowelCount` that accepts a `String` as a parameter and produces and returns an array of integers representing the counts of each vowel in the string. The array returned by your method should hold five elements: the first is the count of As, the second is the count of Es, the third Is, the fourth Os, and the fifth Us. Assume that the string contains no uppercase letters. For example, the call `vowelCount("i think, therefore i am")` should return the array `[1, 3, 3, 1, 0]`.

18. Write a method called `wordLengths` that accepts a `Scanner` for an input file as its parameter. Your method should open the given file, count the number of letters in each token in the file, and output a result diagram of how many words contain each number of letters. For example, consider a file containing the following text:

```
Before sorting:
13 23 480 -18 75
hello how are you feeling today

After sorting:
-18 13 23 75 480
are feeling hello how today you
```

Your method should produce the following output to the console. Use tabs so that the stars line up:

```
1: 0
2: 6 ******
3: 10 **********
4: 0
5: 5 *****
6: 1 *
7: 2 **
8: 2 **
```

Assume that no token in the file is more than 80 characters in length.

19. Write a method called `matrixAdd` that accepts a pair of two-dimensional arrays of integers as parameters, treats the arrays as two-dimensional matrixes, and returns their sum. The sum of two matrixes `A` and `B` is a matrix `C`, where for every row `i` and column `j`, $C_{ij} = A_{ij} + B_{ij}$. You may assume that the arrays passed as parameters have the same dimensions.

20. Write a method called `isMagicSquare` that accepts a two-dimensional array of integers as a parameter and returns `true` if it is a magic square. A square matrix is a *magic square* if all of its row, column, and diagonal sums are equal. For example, `[[2, 7, 6], [9, 5, 1], [4, 3, 8]]` is a square matrix because all eight of the sums are exactly 15.

21. Write a method `grayscale` that converts a color image into a black-and-white image. This is done by averaging the red, green, and blue components of each pixel. For example, if a pixel has RGB values of (red = 100, green = 30, blue = 80), the average of the three components is (100 + 30 + 80)/3 = 70, so that pixel becomes (red = 70, green = 70, blue = 70).

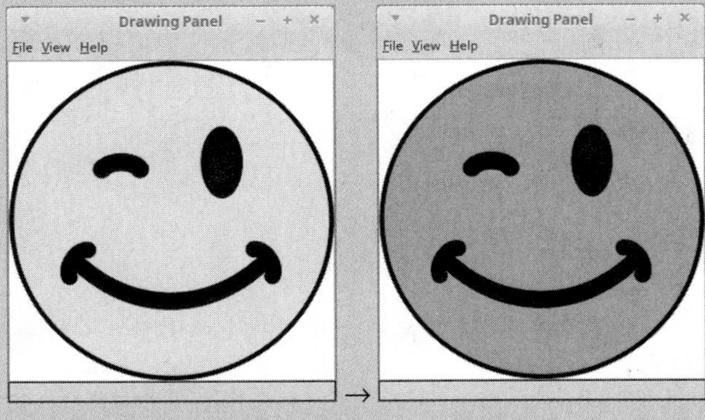

22. Write a method `transpose` that accepts a `DrawingPanel` as a parameter and inverts the image about both the *x* and *y* axes. You may assume that the image is square, that is, that its width and height are equal.

→

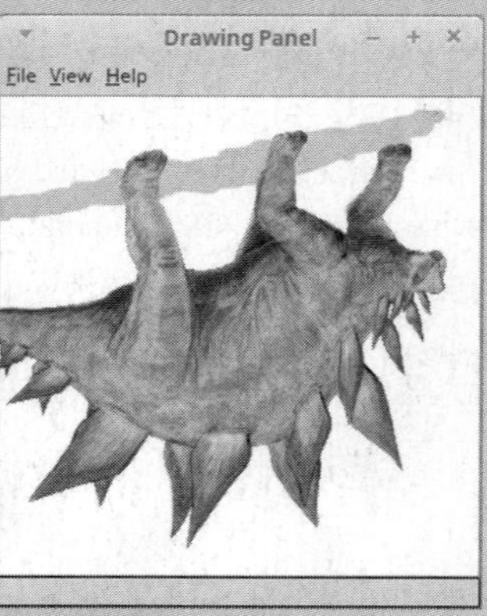

23. Write a method `zoomIn` that accepts a `DrawingPanel` as a parameter and converts it into an image twice as large in both dimensions. Each pixel from the original image becomes a cluster of 4 pixels (2 rows and 2 columns) in the new zoomed image.

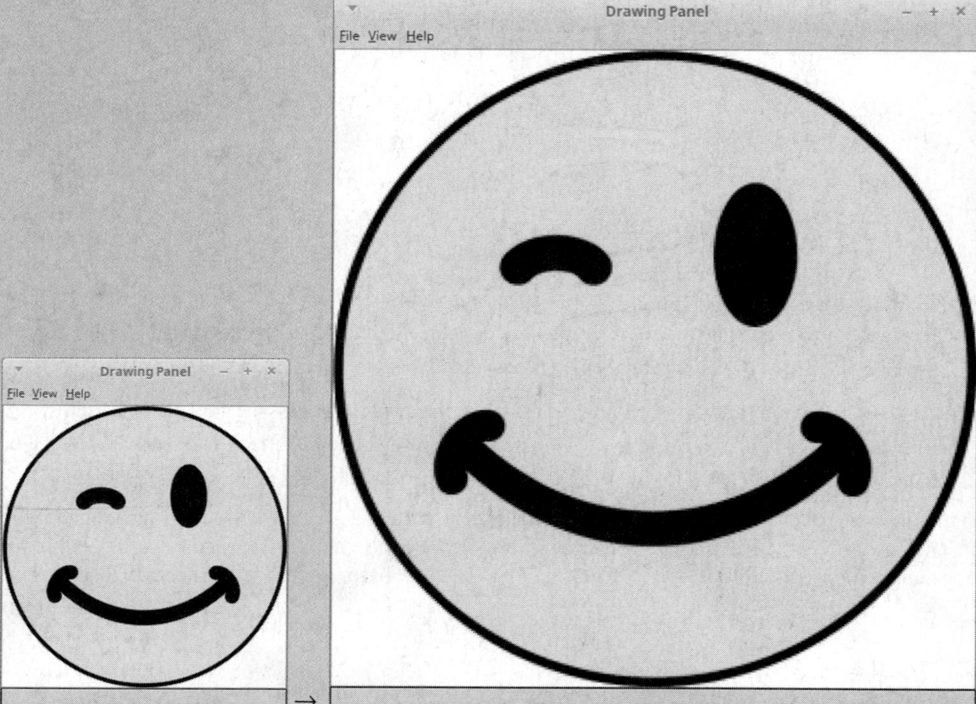

24. Write methods `rotateLeft` and `rotateRight` that rotate the pixels of an image counter-clockwise or clockwise by 90 degrees respectively. You should not assume that the image is square in shape; its width and height might be different.

→
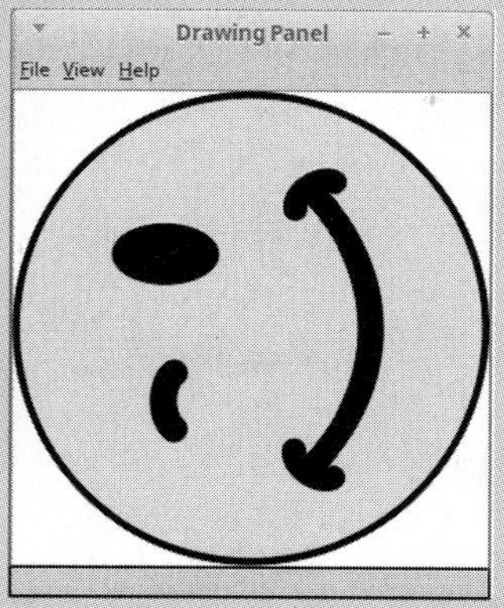

→

25. Write a method `blur` that makes an image look "blurry" using the following specific algorithm. Set each pixel to be the average of itself and the 8 pixels around it. That is, for the pixel at position (x, y), set its RGB value to be the average of the RGB values at positions $(x - 1, y - 1)$ through $(x + 1, y + 1)$. Be careful not to go out of bounds near the edge of the image; if a pixel lies along the edge of the image, average whatever neighbors it does have.

→

Programming Projects

1. Java's type `int` has a limit on how large an integer it can store. This limit can be circumvented by representing an integer as an array of digits. Write an interactive program that adds two integers of up to 50 digits each.

2. Write a game of Hangman using arrays. Allow the user to guess letters and represent which letters have been guessed in an array.

3. Write a program that plays a variation of the game of Mastermind with a user. For example, the program can use pseudorandom numbers to generate a four-digit number. The user should be allowed to make guesses until she gets the number correct. Clues should be given to the user indicating how many digits of the guess are correct and in the correct place and how many digits are correct but in the wrong place.

4. Write a program to score users' responses to the classic Myers–Briggs personality test. Assume that the test has 70 questions that determine a person's personality in four dimensions. Each question has two answer choices that we'll

call the “A” and “B” answers. Questions are organized into 10 groups of seven questions, with the following repeating pattern in each group:

- The first question in each group (questions 1, 8, 15, 22, etc.) tells whether the person is introverted or extroverted.
- The next two questions (questions 2 and 3, 9 and 10, 16 and 17, 23 and 24, etc.) test whether the person is guided by his or her senses or intuition.
- The next two questions (questions 4 and 5, 11 and 12, 18 and 19, 25 and 26, etc.) test whether the person focuses on thinking or feeling.
- The final two questions in each group (questions 6 and 7, 13 and 14, 20 and 21, 27 and 28, etc.) test whether the person prefers to judge or be guided by perception.

In other words, if we consider introversion/extraversion (I/E) to be dimension 1, sensing/intuition (S/N) to be dimension 2, thinking/feeling (T/F) to be dimension 3, and judging/perception (J/P) to be dimension 4, the map of questions to their respective dimensions would look like this:

```
1223344122334412233441223344122334412233441223344122334412233441223344
BABAAAABAAAAAAABAAAABBAAAAAABAAAABABAABAAABABABAABAAAAAABAAAAAABAAAAAA
```

The following is a partial sample input file of names and responses:

```
Betty Boop
BABAAAABAAAAAAABAAAABBAAAAAABAAAABABAABAAABABABAABAAAAAABAAAAAABAAAAAA
Snoopy
AABBAABBBBBABABAAAAABABBAABBAAAABBBAAABAABAABABAAAABAABBBBAAABBAABABBB
```

If less than 50% of a person’s responses are B for a given personality dimension, the person’s type for that dimension should be the first of its two choices. If the person has 50% or more B responses, the person’s type for that dimension is the second choice. Your program should output each person’s name, the number of A and B responses for each dimension, the percentage of Bs in each dimension, and the overall personality type. The following should be your program’s output for the preceding input data:

```
Betty Boop:
    1A–9B 17A–3B 18A–2B 18A–2B
    [90%, 15%, 10%, 10%] = ISTJ
Snoopy:
    7A–3B 11A–9B 14A–6B 6A–14B
    [30%, 45%, 30%, 70%] = ESTP
```

5. Use a two-dimensional array to write a game of Tic-Tac-Toe that represents the board.

6. Write a program that reads a file of DNA data and searches for protein sequences. DNA data consists of long `Strings` of the letters A, C, G, and T, corresponding to chemical nucleotides called adenine, cytosine, guanine, and thymine. Proteins can be identified by looking for special triplet sequences of nucleotides that indicate the start and stop of a protein range. Store relevant data in arrays as you make your computation. See our textbook’s web site for example DNA input files and more details about heuristics for identifying proteins.

7. Write a basic Photoshop or Instagram-inspired program with a menu of available image manipulation algorithms similar to those described in the exercises in this chapter. The user can load an image from a file and then select which manipulation to perform, such as grayscale, zoom, rotate, or blur.

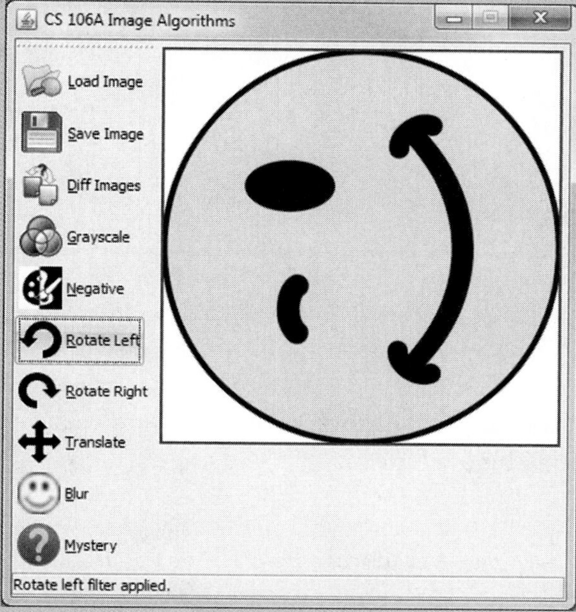

Chapter 8

Classes

Introduction

Now that you've mastered the basics of procedural-style programming in Java, you're finally ready to explore what Java was designed for: object-oriented programming. This chapter introduces the basic terminology that you should use to talk about objects and shows you how to declare your own classes to create your own objects.

Objects are entities that contain state and behavior and that can be used as parts of larger programs. We'll discuss the concepts of abstraction and encapsulation, which allow you to use objects at a high level without understanding their inner details. We'll also discuss ideas for designing new classes of objects and implementing the programs that utilize them.

8.1 Object-Oriented Programming

Most of our focus so far has been on procedural decomposition, the technique of breaking complex tasks into smaller subtasks. This is the oldest style of programming, and even in a language like Java we still use procedural techniques. But Java also provides a different approach to programming that we call *object-oriented programming.*

Object-Oriented Programming (OOP)

Reasoning about a program as a set of objects rather than as a set of actions.

Object-oriented programming involves a particular view of programming that has its own terminology. Let's explore that terminology with nonprogramming examples first. Recall the definition of *object* from Chapter 3.

Object

A programming entity that contains state (data) and behavior (methods).

To truly understand this definition, you have to understand the terms "state" and "behavior." These are some of the most fundamental concepts in object-oriented programming.

Let's consider the class of objects we call radios. A radio can be in different states. It can be turned on or turned off. It can be tuned to one of many different stations, and it can be set to one of many different volumes. Any given radio has to "know" what state it is in, which means that it has to keep track of this information internally. We call the collection of such internal values the *state* of an object.

State

A set of values (internal data) stored in an object.

What are the behaviors of a radio? The most obvious one is that it produces sound when it is turned on and the volume is turned up. But there are actions that you can perform on a radio that manipulate its internal state. We can turn a radio on or off, and we can change the station or volume. We can also check what station the radio is set to right now. We call the collection of these operations the *behavior* of an object.

Behavior

A set of actions an object can perform, often reporting or modifying its internal state.

Objects themselves are not complete programs; they are components that are given distinct roles and responsibilities. Objects can be used as part of larger programs to solve problems. The pieces of code that create and use objects are known as *clients.*

Client (or Client Code)

Code that interacts with a class or objects of that class.

Client programs interact with objects by sending messages to them and asking them to perform behaviors. A major benefit of objects is that they provide reusable pieces of code that can be used in many client programs. You've already used several interesting objects, such as those of type `String`, `Scanner`, `Random`, and `File`. In other words, you and your programs have been clients of these objects. Java's class libraries contain thousands of existing classes of objects.

As you write larger programs, however, you'll find that Java doesn't always have a pre-existing object for the problem you're solving. For example, if you were creating a calendar application, you might want to use objects to represent dates, contacts, and appointments. If you were creating a three-dimensional graphical simulation, you might want objects to represent three-dimensional points, vectors, and matrices. If you were writing a financial program, you might want classes to represent your various assets, transactions, and expenses. In this chapter you'll learn how to create your own classes of objects that can be used by client programs like these.

Our definition of object-oriented programming is somewhat simplified. A full exploration of this programming paradigm includes other advanced concepts called polymorphism and inheritance that will be discussed in the next chapter.

Classes and Objects

In the previous chapters, we've considered the words "class" and "program" to be roughly synonymous. We wrote programs by creating new classes and placing static `main` methods into them.

But classes have another use in Java: to serve as blueprints for new types of objects. To create a new type of object in Java, we must create a class and add code to it that specifies the following elements:

- The state stored in each object
- The behavior each object can perform
- How to construct objects of that type

Once we have written the appropriate code, we can use the class to create objects of its type. We can then use those objects in our client programs. We say that the created objects are *instances* of the class because one class can be used to construct many objects. This is similar to the way that a blueprint works: One blueprint can be used to create many similar houses, each of which is an instance of the original blueprint.

Did You Know?

Operating Systems History and Objects

In 1983 the IBM PC and its "clones" dominated the PC market, and most people ran an operating system called DOS. DOS uses what we call a "command-line interface," in which the user types commands at a prompt. The console window is a similar interface. To delete a file in DOS, for example, you would give the command "del" (short for "delete") followed by the file name:

```
del data.txt
```

This interface can be described in simple terms as "verb noun." In fact, if you look at a DOS manual, you will find that it is full of verbs. This structure closely parallels the procedural approach to programming. When we want to accomplish some task, we issue a command (the verb) and then mention the object of the action (the noun, the thing we want to affect).

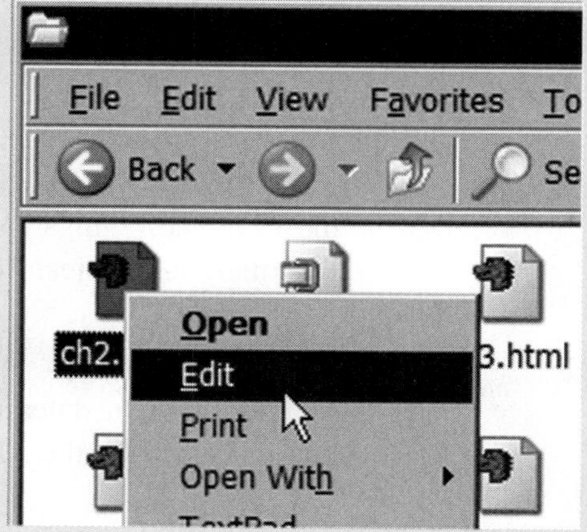

In 1984, Apple Computer released a new computer called a Macintosh that used what we call a graphical user interface, or GUI. The GUI interface uses a graphical "desktop" metaphor that has become so well known that people now tend to forget it is a metaphor. Later, Microsoft brought this functionality to IBM PCs with its Windows operating system.

To delete a file on a Macintosh or on a Windows machine, you locate the icon for the file and click on it. Then you have several options. You can drag it to the trash/recycling bin, or you can select a "delete" command from the menu. Either way, you start with the object you want to delete and then give the command you want to perform. This is a reversal of the fundamental paradigm: With a GUI it's "noun verb." This different method of interaction is the core of object-oriented programming.

Most modern programs use GUIs because we have learned that people find it more natural to work this way. We are used to pointing at things, picking up things, grabbing things. Starting with the object is very natural for us. This approach has also proved to be a helpful way to structure our programs, enabling us to divide our programs into different objects that each can do a certain task, rather than dividing up the central task into subtasks.

Point Objects

To learn about objects we will first examine an existing Java class, and then we will implement our own version of that class from scratch. The `java.awt` package has a class named `Point`. A `Point` object stores the (*x*, *y*) coordinates of a position in two-dimensional space. These coordinates are expressed as integers, although there are also variations for storing points using floating-point numbers. `Point` objects are useful for applications that store many two-dimensional locations, such as maps of cities, graphical animations, and games.

Like most objects, `Point` objects have to be explicitly constructed by calling a constructor. To construct a specific `Point` object, you have to pass the values you want for `x` and `y`:

```
Point p = new Point(3, 8);
```

After the program executes the previous line of code, you have the following situation:

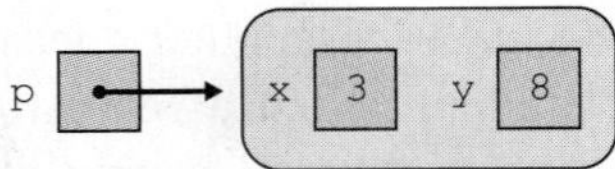

Once you have constructed a `Point` object, what can you do with it? One of the most common things you do with an object is print it to the console. A `Point` object, like many Java objects, can be printed with the `println` statement.

```
System.out.println(p);
```

The `println` statement produces the following output. The format is a little ugly, but it lets you see the `x` and `y` values inside a given `Point`.

```
java.awt.Point[x=3,y=8]
```

`Point` objects also have a method called `translate` that can be used to shift the coordinates by a specific delta-x and delta-y, which are passed as parameters. When you translate a `Point`, you shift its location by the specified amount. For example, you might say:

```
p.translate(-1, -2); // subtract 1 from x, subtract 2 from y
```

Given that the `Point` started out with coordinates (3, 8), this translation would leave the `Point` with coordinates (2, 6). Thus, after this line of code is executed, you'd end up with the following situation:

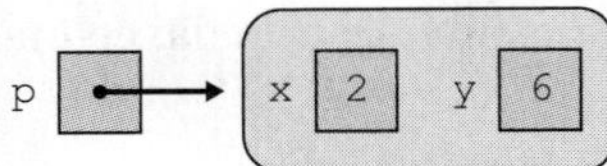

Table 8.1 Useful Methods of `Point` Objects

Method	Description
`translate(dx, dy)`	Translates the coordinates by the given amounts
`setLocation(x, y)`	Sets the coordinates to the given values
`distance(p2)`	Returns the distance from this point to `p2`

One of the other things you can do with a `Point` object is to refer to its `x` and `y` values using the dot notation:

```
int sum = p.x + p.y;
System.out.println("Sum of coordinates = " + sum);
```

You can even change these internal values directly:

```
p.x = 12;
p.y = 15;
```

Table 8.1 includes some useful methods of each `Point` object.

Here is a complete program that constructs a `Point` object and translates its coordinates, using `println` statements to examine the coordinates before and after the call:

```
import java.awt.*;

public class PointExample1 {
    public static void main(String[] args) {
        Point p = new Point(3, 8);
        System.out.println("initially p = " + p);
        p.translate(-1, -2);
        System.out.println("after translating p = " + p);
    }
}
```

This code produces the following output:

```
initially p = java.awt.Point[x=3,y=8]
after translating p = java.awt.Point[x=2,y=6]
```

8.2 Object State and Behavior

In the next few sections, we'll explore the structure of classes by writing a new class incrementally. We'll write our own version of the `Point` class that was just described.

Here are the main components of a class that we'll see in the sections that follow:

- Fields (the data stored in each object)
- Methods (the behavior each object can execute)
- Constructors (code that initializes an object as it is being constructed with the `new` keyword)
- Encapsulation (protects an object's data from outside access)

We'll focus on these concepts by creating several major versions of the `Point` class. The first version will give us `Point` objects that contain only data. The second version will add behavior to the objects. The third version will allow us to construct `Point`s at any initial position. The finished code will encapsulate each `Point` object's internal data to protect it from unwanted outside access. The early versions of the class will be incomplete and will be used to illustrate each feature of a class in isolation. Only the finished version of the `Point` class will be written in proper object-oriented style.

Object State: Fields

The first version of our `Point` class will contain state only. To specify each object's state, we declare special variables inside the class called *fields*. There are many synonyms for "field" that come from other programming languages and environments, such as "instance variable," "data member," and "attribute."

Field

A variable inside an object that makes up part of its internal state.

The syntax for declaring a field is the same as the syntax for declaring normal variables: a type followed by a name and a semicolon. But unlike normal variables, fields are declared directly inside the `{` and `}` braces of your class. When we declare a field, we're saying that we want every object of this class to have that variable inside it.

In previous chapters we've seen that every class should be placed into its own file. The following code, written in the file `Point.java`, defines the first version of our `Point` class:

```
// A Point object represents a pair of (x, y) coordinates.
// First version: state only.

public class Point {
    int x;
    int y;
}
```

This code specifies that each `Point` object will contain two fields (an integer called `x` and an integer called `y`). It may look as though the code declares a pair of int variables, x and y. But actually it indicates that *each* Point object will contain two int variables inside it, called x and y. If we create 100 Point objects, we'll have 100 pairs of x and y fields, one in each instance of the class.

The Point class isn't itself an executable Java program; it simply defines a new class of objects for client programs to use. The client code that uses Point will be a separate class that we will store in a separate file. Client programs can create Point objects using the new keyword and empty parentheses:

```
Point origin = new Point();
```

When a Point object is constructed, its fields are given default initial values of 0, so a new Point object always begins at the origin of (0, 0) unless you change its x or y value. This is another example of auto-initialization, similar to the way that array elements are automatically given default values.

The following lines of code form the first version of a client program that uses our Point class (the code is saved in a file called PointMain.java, which should be in the same folder or project as Point.java in order for the program to compile successfully):

```
// A program that deals with points.
// First version, to accompany Point class with state only.

public class PointMain {
    public static void main(String[] args) {
        // create two Point objects
        Point p1 = new Point();
        p1.x = 7;
        p1.y = 2;

        Point p2 = new Point();
        p2.x = 4;
        p2.y = 3;

        // print each point and its distance from the origin
        System.out.println("p1 is (" + p1.x + ", " + p1.y + ")");
        double dist1 = Math.sqrt(p1.x * p1.x + p1.y * p1.y);
        System.out.println("distance from origin = " + dist1);

        System.out.println("p2 is (" + p2.x + ", " + p2.y + ")");
        double dist2 = Math.sqrt(p2.x * p2.x + p2.y * p2.y);
        System.out.println("distance from origin = " + dist2);
        System.out.println();

```

```
        // translate each point to a new location
        p1.x += 11;
        p1.y += 6;
        p2.x += 1;
        p2.y += 7;

        // print the points again
        System.out.println("p1 is (" + p1.x + ", " + p1.y + ")");
        System.out.println("p2 is (" + p2.x + ", " + p2.y + ")");
    }
}
```

The code produces the following output:

```
p1 is (7, 2)
distance from origin = 7.280109889280518
p2 is (4, 3)
distance from origin = 5.0

p1 is (18, 8)
p2 is (5, 10)
```

The client program has some redundancy that we'll eliminate as we improve our `Point` class in the sections that follow.

Our initial `Point` class essentially serves as a way to group two `int` values into one object. This technique is somewhat useful for the client program, but the client could have been written using primitive `int`s instead. Using `Point` objects is not yet substantially better than using primitive `int` values, because our `Point` objects do not yet have any behavior. An object that contains state, but no behavior, is sometimes called a *record* or *struct.* In the sections that follow, we'll grow our `Point` class from a minimal implementation into a proper Java class.

Object Behavior: Methods

The second version of our `Point` class will contain both state and behavior. Behavior of objects is specified by writing *instance methods.* The instance methods of an object describe the messages to which that object can respond.

Instance Method

A method inside an object that operates on that object.

The objects introduced in previous chapters all contained instance methods that represented their behavior. For example, a `String` object has a `length` method and a `Scanner` object has a `nextInt` method. We think of these methods as being stored inside the object. As you recall, they use different call syntax than static methods: You write the object's name, then a dot, and then the method's name and parameters. Each object's methods are able to interact with the data stored inside that object.

The preceding client program translates the position of two `Point` objects. It does this by manually adjusting their `x` and `y` values:

```
p1.x += 11; // client code translating a Point
p1.y += 6;
```

Since translating points is a common operation, we should represent it as a method. One option would be to write a static `translate` method in the client code that accepts a `Point`, a delta-`x`, and a delta-`y` as parameters. Its code would look like the following:

```
// a static method to translate a Point;
// not a good choice in this case
public static void translate(Point p, int dx, int dy) {
    p.x += dx;
    p.y += dy;
}
```

A call to the static method would look like the following line of code:

```
translate(p1, 11, 6); // calling a translate static method
```

However, a static method isn't the best way to implement the behavior. The `Point` class is supposed to be reusable so that many client programs can use it. If the `translate` method is placed into our `PointMain` client, other clients won't be able to use it without copying and pasting its code redundantly. Also, one of the biggest benefits of programming with objects is that we can put related data and behavior together. The ability of a `Point` to translate data is closely related to that `Point` object's (x, y) data, so it is better to specify that each `Point` object will know how to translate itself. We'll do this by writing an instance method in the `Point` class.

We know from experience with objects that you can call an instance method called `translate` using "dot notation":

```
p1.translate(11, 6); // calling a translate instance method
```

Notice that the instance method needs just two parameters: `dx` and `dy`. The client doesn't pass the `Point` as a parameter, because the call begins by indicating which `Point` object it wants to translate (`p1`). In our example, the client is sending a `translate` message to the object to which `p1` refers.

Instance method headers do not have the `static` keyword found in static method headers, but they still include the public keyword, the method's return type, its name, and any parameters that the method accepts. Here's the start of a `Point` class with a `translate` method, with the header declared but the body blank:

```
public class Point {
    int x;
    int y;

    public void translate(int dx, int dy) {
        ...
    }
}
```

When we declare a `translate` method in the `Point` class, we are saying that *each* `Point` object has its own copy of that method. Each `Point` object also has its own `x` and `y` values. A `Point` object would look like the following:

```
x [7]  y [2]

public void translate(int dx, int dy) {
    ...
}
```

Whenever an instance method is called, it is called on a particular object. So, when we're writing the body of the `translate` method, we'll think of that code from the perspective of the particular `Point` object that receives the message: "The client has given me a `dx` and `dy` and wants me to change my `x` and `y` values by those amounts." Essentially, we need to write code to match the following pseudocode:

```
public void translate(int dx, int dy) {
    add dx to this Point object's x value.
    add dy to this Point object's y value.
}
```

It's helpful to know that an object's instance methods can refer to its fields. In previous chapters we've talked about *scope,* the range in which a variable can be seen and used. The scope of a variable is the set of braces in which it is declared. The same rule applies to fields: Since they are declared directly inside a class, their scope is the entire class.

This rule means that the `translate` method can directly refer to the fields `x` and `y`. For example, the statement `x += 3;` would increase the `Point` object's `x` value by `3`.

Here is a working `translate` method that adjusts the `Point` object's location:

```
public void translate(int dx, int dy) {
    x += dx;
    y += dy;
}
```

The `translate` method can refer to `x` and `y` directly without being more specific about which object it is affecting. It's as though you were riding inside a car and wanted the driver to turn left; you'd simply say, "Turn left." Though there are millions of cars in the world, you wouldn't feel a need to specify which car you meant. It is implied that you mean the car you're currently occupying. Similarly, in instance methods we don't need to specify which object's `x` or `y` we're using, because it is implied that we want to use the fields of the object that receives the message.

Here's the complete `Point` class that contains the `translate` method. The Java style guidelines suggest declaring fields at the top of the class, with methods below, but in general it is legal for a class's contents to appear in any order.

```
public class Point {
    int x;
    int y;

    // shifts this point's location by the given amount
    public void translate(int dx, int dy) {
        x += dx;
        y += dy;
    }
}
```

Here is the general syntax for instance methods:

```
public <type> <name>(<type> <name>, ..., <type> <name>) {
    <statement>;
    <statement>;
    ...
    <statement>;
}
```

Methods like `translate` are useful because they give our objects useful behavior that lets us write more expressive and concise client programs. Having the client code manually adjust the `x` and `y` values of `Point` objects to move them is tedious, especially in larger client programs that translate many times. By adding the `translate` method, we have provided a clean way to adjust the location of a `Point` object in a single statement.

The Implicit Parameter

The code for an instance method has an implied knowledge of the object on which it operates. This object is called the *implicit parameter*.

Implicit Parameter

The object that is referenced during an instance method call.

Let's walk through an example to demonstrate exactly how instance methods use the implicit parameter. The following client code constructs two `Point` objects and sets initial locations for them:

```
// construct two Point objects
Point p1 = new Point();
p1.x = 7;
p1.y = 2;
Point p2 = new Point();
p2.x = 4;
p2.y = 3;
```

After the preceding code has executed, the variables and objects in memory would appear as follows (remember that each object has its own copy of the `translate` method):

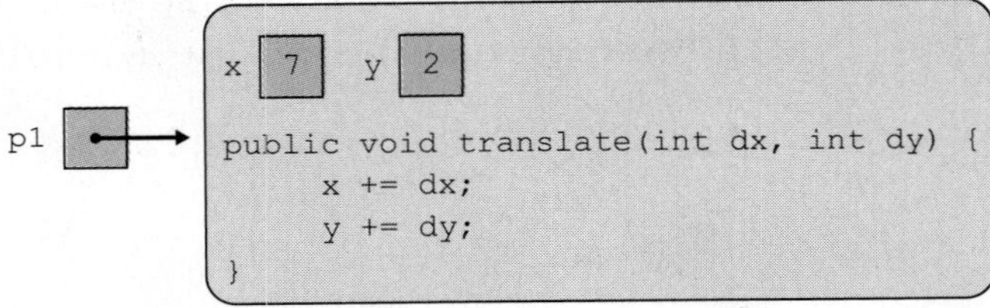

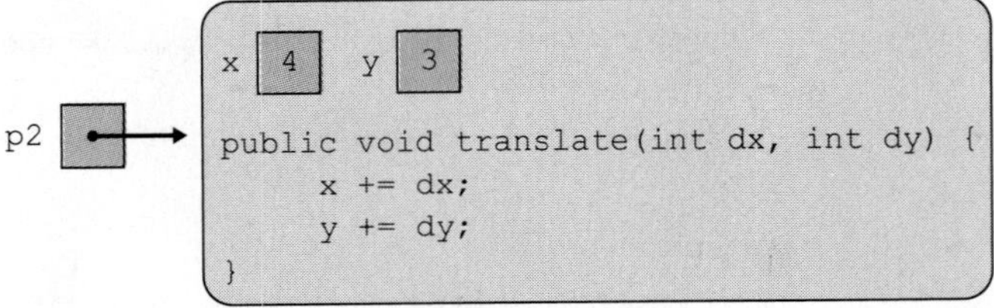

Now we'll call the `translate` method on each object. First, `p1` is translated. During this call, `p1`'s `translate` method is passed the parameters `11` and `6`. The implicit parameter here is `p1`'s object, so the statements `x += dx;` and `y += dy;` affect `p1.x` and `p1.y`:

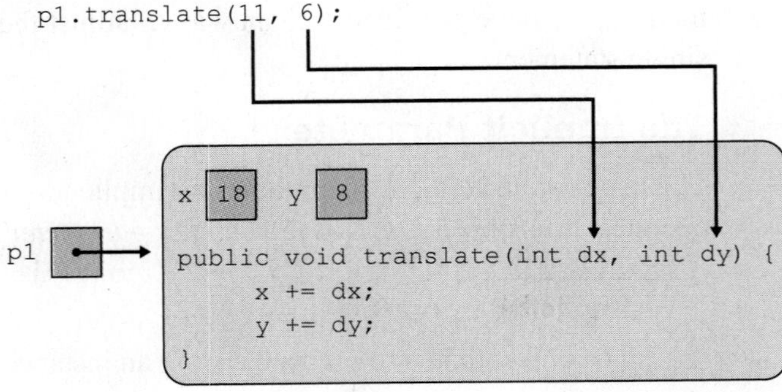

During the second method call p2's `translate` method is executed, so the lines in the body of the `translate` method change `p2.x` and `p2.y`:

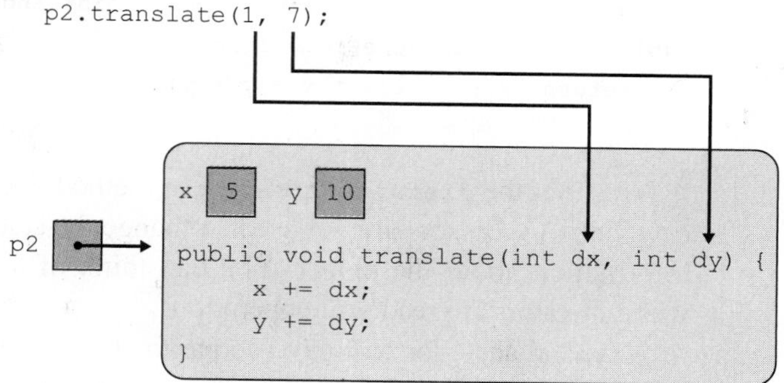

Mutators and Accessors

The `translate` method is an example of a *mutator.*

Mutator

An instance method that modifies the object's internal state.

Generally, a mutator assigns a new value to one of the object's fields. Going back to the radio example, the mutators would be the switches and knobs that turn the radio on and off or change the station or volume.

It is a common convention for a mutator method's name to begin with "set," as in `setID` or `setTitle`. Usually, a mutator method has a `void` return type. Mutators often accept parameters that specify the new state of the object or the amount by which to modify the object's current state.

Accessors form a second important category of instance methods.

Accessor

An instance method that provides information about the state of an object without modifying it.

Generally, an accessor returns the value of one of the object's fields. Using our radio analogy, an accessor might return the current station or volume. Examples of accessor methods you have seen in previous chapters include the `length` and `substring` methods of `String` objects and the `exists` method of `File` objects.

Our client program computes the distance of two `Point`s from the origin, (0, 0). Since this is a common operation related to the data in a `Point`, let's give each `Point` object an accessor called `distanceFromOrigin` that computes and returns that `Point` object's distance from the origin. The method accepts no parameters and returns the distance as a `double`.

The distance from the origin is computed using the Pythagorean Theorem, taking the square root of the sum of the squares of the `x` and `y` values. As we did when we used the `translate` method, we'll refer to the `Point` object's `x` and `y` fields directly in our computation:

```
// returns the distance between this point and (0, 0)
public double distanceFromOrigin() {
    return Math.sqrt(x * x + y * y);
}
```

Note that the `distanceFromOrigin` method doesn't change the `Point` object's `x` or `y` value. Accessors are not used to change the state of the object—they only report information about the object. You can think of accessors as read-only operations while mutators are read/write operations.

A typical accessor will have no parameters and will not have a `void` return type, because it must return a piece of information. An accessor returns a value that is part of the state of the object or is derived from it. The names of many accessors begin with "get" or "is," as in `getBalance` or `isEmpty`.

Here's the complete second version of our `Point` class that now contains both state and behavior:

```
// A Point object represents a pair of (x, y) coordinates.
// Second version: state and behavior.

public class Point {
    int x;
    int y;

    // returns the distance between this point and (0, 0)
    public double distanceFromOrigin() {
        return Math.sqrt(x * x + y * y);
    }

    // shifts this point's location by the given amount
    public void translate(int dx, int dy) {
        x += dx;
        y += dy;
    }
}
```

The client program can now use the new behavior of the `Point` class. The program produces the same output as before, but it is shorter and more readable than the original. The following lines show examples of the changes made to `PointMain`:

```
System.out.println("distance from origin = " + p1.distanceFromOrigin());
...
p1.translate(11, 6);
```

The toString Method

The designers of Java felt that it was important for all types of values to work well with Strings. You've seen that you can concatenate Strings with any other type of value, such as primitive ints or other objects. Consider the following code:

```
int i = 42;
String s = "hello";
Point p = new Point();

System.out.println("i is " + i);
System.out.println("s is " + s);
System.out.println("p is " + p);
```

Using the Point class that we've written so far, the preceding code produces output like the following:

```
i is 42
s is hello
p is Point@119c082
```

Notice that printing p generated a strange result. We'd rather have it print the object's state of (0, 0), but Java doesn't know how to do so unless we write a special method in our Point class.

When a Java program is printing an object or concatenating it with a String, the program calls a special method called toString on the object to convert it into a String. The toString method is an instance method that returns a String representation of the object. A toString method accepts no parameters and has a String return type:

```
public String toString() {
    <code to produce and return the desired string>;
}
```

If you don't write a toString method in your class, your class will use a default version that returns the class name followed by an @ sign and some letters and numbers related to the object's address in memory. If you define your own toString method, it replaces this default version.

The following code implements a toString method for our Point objects and returns a String such as "(0, 0)":

```
// returns a String representation of this point
public String toString() {
    return "(" + x + ", " + y + ")";
}
```

Now that our class has this method, the preceding client code produces the following output.

```
i is 42
s is hello
p is (0, 0)
```

Note that the client code didn't explicitly call the `toString` method; the compiler did it automatically because the `Point` object was being concatenated with a `String`. The `toString` method is also implicitly called when printing an object by itself, as in the following code:

```
System.out.println(p);
```

In order for this implicit calling behavior to work properly, your `toString` method's signature must exactly match the one shown in this section. Changing the name or signature even slightly (for example, naming the method `ToString` with a capital T, or `convertToString`) will cause the class to produce the old output (e.g., `"Point@119c082"`). The reason has to do with concepts called inheritance and overriding that we will explore in the next chapter.

It is also legal to call `toString` explicitly if you prefer. The following client code uses an explicit `toString` call and produces the same output as the original client code:

```
System.out.println("p is " + p.toString());
```

The Java guidelines recommend writing a `toString` method in every class you write.

Common Programming Error

`println` Statement in `toString` Method

Since the `toString` method is closely related to printing, some students mistakenly think that they should place `println` statements in their `toString` methods, as in the following method:

```
// this toString method is flawed;
// it should return the String rather than printing it
public String toString() {
    System.out.println("(" + x + ", " + y + ")");
    return "";
}
```

Continued on next page

Continued from previous page

A key idea to understand about `toString` is that it doesn't directly print anything: It simply returns a `String` that the client can use in a `println` statement.

In fact, many well-formed classes of objects do not contain any `println` statements at all. The inclusion of `println` statements in a class binds that class to a particular style of output. For example, the preceding code prints a `Point` object on its own line, making the class unsuitable for a client that doesn't want the output to appear exactly this way (say, a client that wants to print many `Point` objects on the same line).

You may wonder why the designers of Java chose to use a `toString` method rather than, say, a `print` method that would output the object to the console. The reason is that `toString` is more versatile. You can use `toString` to output the object to a file, display it on a graphical user interface, or even send the text over a network.

8.3 Object Initialization: Constructors

VideoNote

Our third version of the `Point` class will include the ability to create `Point` objects at any initial location. The initial state of objects is specified by writing *constructors*, which were introduced in Chapter 3. Recall that a constructor is a piece of code that initializes the state of new objects as they are created.

A clumsy aspect of our existing client code is that it takes three lines to create and initialize the state of one `Point` object:

```
// client needs 3 statements to initialize one Point object
Point p1 = new Point();
p1.x = 7;
p1.y = 2;
```

In general, when we have constructed objects, we have been able to declare and initialize them in a single statement. We might expect that we could initialize a `Point` by writing its initial (*x*, *y*) values in parentheses as we constructed it:

```
Point p1 = new Point(7, 2); // desired behavior
```

However, such a statement wouldn't be legal for our `Point` class, because we haven't written any code specifying how to create a `Point` with an initial (*x*, *y*) location. We can specify how to do this by writing a constructor in our `Point` class. The constructor executes when the client uses the `new` keyword to create a new object. When you write a constructor, you specify what parameters must be passed when clients use the `new` keyword with your type and how those parameters should be used to initialize the newly created object.

A constructor's header begins with the keyword `public`, followed by the class's name and any parameters. It looks like a method header with the same name as the class, except that you do not specify a return type. A constructor often has parameters that specify the object's initial state. Our constructor for the `Point` class will accept initial `x` and `y` values as parameters and store them into the new `Point` object's `x` and `y` fields:

```
// constructs a new point with the given (x, y) location
public Point(int initialX, int initialY) {
    x = initialX;
    y = initialY;
}
```

Like instance methods, constructors execute on a particular object (the one that's being created with the `new` keyword) and can refer to that object's fields and methods directly. In this case, we store `initialX` and `initialY` parameter values into the new `Point` object's `x` and `y` fields:

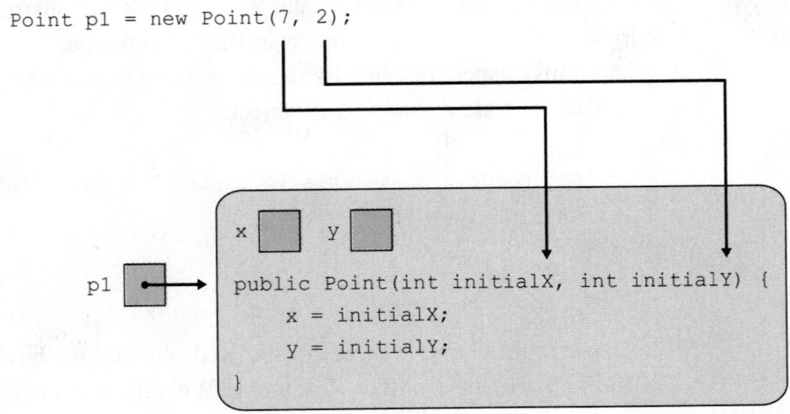

Now that we are exploring constructors, it makes sense to think about the process of creating objects in more detail. When an executing Java program reaches a statement that creates a new `Point` object, several operations occur:

1. A new `Point` object is created and allocated in memory.
2. The `Point` constructor is called on the newly created object, passing `7` and `2` as the `initialX` and `initialY` parameter values.
3. A `Point` reference variable named `p` is created and set to refer to the newly created object.

Here is the complete code for the third version of our `Point` class, which now contains a constructor:

```
// A Point object represents a pair of (x, y) coordinates.
// Third version: state and behavior with constructor.

public class Point {
    int x;
    int y;

    // constructs a new point with the given (x, y) location
    public Point(int initialX, int initialY) {
        x = initialX;
        y = initialY;
    }

    // returns the distance between this point and (0, 0)
    public double distanceFromOrigin() {
        return Math.sqrt(x * x + y * y);
    }

    // returns a String representation of this Point
    public String toString() {
        return "(" + x + ", " + y + ")";
    }

    // shifts this point's location by the given amount
    public void translate(int dx, int dy) {
        x += dx;
        y += dy;
    }
}
```

Calling a constructor with parameters is similar to ordering a car from a factory: "I'd like the yellow one with power windows and leather seats." You might not need to specify every detail about the car, such as the fact that it should have four wheels and headlights, but you do specify some initial attributes that are important to you.

The general syntax for constructors is the following:

```
public <class name>(<type> <name>, ..., <type> <name>) {
    <statement>;
    <statement>;
    ...
    <statement>;
}
```

When a class doesn't have a constructor, as in our previous versions of the `Point` class, Java automatically supplies a *default constructor* with no parameters. That is why it was previously legal to construct a `new Point()`. The default constructor auto-initializes all fields to zero-equivalent values. However, Java doesn't supply the default empty constructor when we supply a constructor of our own, so it is illegal to construct `Point` objects without passing in the initial `x` and `y` parameters:

```
Point p1 = new Point(); // will not compile for this version
```

In the next sections, we'll write additional code to restore this ability.

Common Programming Error

Using `void` with a Constructor

Many new programmers accidentally include the keyword `void` in the header of a constructor, since they've gotten used to writing a return type for every method:

```
// this code has a bug
public void Point(int initialX, int initialY) {
    x = initialX;
    y = initialY;
}
```

This is actually a very tricky and annoying bug. Constructors aren't supposed to have return types. When you write a return type such as `void`, what you've created is not a constructor, but rather a normal instance method called `Point` that accepts `x` and `y` parameters and has a `void` return type. This error is tough to catch, because the `Point.java` file still compiles successfully.

You will see an error when you try to call the constructor that you thought you just wrote, though, because it isn't actually a constructor. The client code that

Continued on next page

Continued from previous page

tries to construct the `Point` object will indicate that it can't find an `(int, int)` constructor for a `Point`:

```
PointMain.java:7: cannot find symbol
symbol : constructor Point(int, int)
location: class Point
        Point p1 = new Point(7, 2);
```

If you see "cannot find symbol" constructor errors and you were positive that you wrote a constructor, double-check its header to make sure there's no return type.

Common Programming Error

Redeclaring Fields in a Constructor

Another common bug associated with constructors occurs when you mistakenly redeclare fields by writing their types. Here's an example that shows this mistake:

```
// this constructor code has a bug
public Point(int initialX, int initialY) {
    int x = initialX;
    int y = initialY;
}
```

The preceding code behaves in an odd way. It compiles successfully, but when the client code constructs a `Point` object its initial coordinates are always (0, 0), regardless of the parameter values that are passed to the constructor:

```
// this client code will print that p1 is (0, 0)
Point p1 = new Point(7, 2);
System.out.println("p1 is " + p1);
```

The problem is that rather than storing `initialX` and `initialY` in the `Point` object's `x` and `y` fields, we've actually declared local variables called `x` and `y` inside the `Point` constructor. We store `initialX` and `initialY` in those local variables, which are thrown away when the constructor finishes running. No values are ever assigned to the `x` and `y` fields in the constructor, so they are automatically initialized to `0`. We say that these local `x` and `y` variables *shadow* our `x` and `y` fields because they obscure the fields we intended to set.

If you observe that your constructor doesn't seem to be setting your object's fields, check closely to make sure that you didn't accidentally declare local variables that shadow your fields. The key thing is not to include a type at the front of the statement when you assign a value to a field.

The Keyword this

When we discussed instance methods we mentioned that an object's instance methods can refer to its other methods and fields, because the instance method code knows which object it's operating on. We called this idea the "implicit parameter." Now we will explore the mechanics behind the implicit parameter and introduce a keyword that allows us to refer to it directly.

The implicit parameter is actually a special reference that is set each time an instance method is called. You can access this reference in your code using the keyword `this`.

> **this**
>
> A Java keyword that allows you to refer to the implicit parameter inside a class.

When you refer to a field such as `x` in your code, you are actually using shorthand. The compiler converts an expression such as `x` to `this.x`. You can use the longer form in your code if you want to be more explicit. For example, our `translate` method could be rewritten as follows:

```
public void translate(int dx, int dy) {
    this.x += dx;
    this.y += dy;
}
```

The code behaves the same way as the original version of the method. The explicit style is less common, but some programmers prefer it because it's clearer. It also more closely matches the style used in client code, where all messages to objects begin with a variable name and a dot.

The general syntax for using the keyword `this` to refer to fields is

```
this.<field name>
```

Similarly, when you call an instance method such as `translate`, you're actually using shorthand for a call of `this.translate`. You can use the longer form if you prefer. It has the following general syntax:

```
this.<method name>(<expression>, <expression>, ..., <expression>);
```

When the implicit parameter was introduced, we diagrammed the behavior of some method calls on two `Point` objects. Let's revisit the same example using the keyword `this`. Consider the following two `Point` objects:

```
Point p1 = new Point(7, 2);
Point p2 = new Point(4, 3);
```

After constructing the `Point` objects, we make the following method calls:

```
p1.translate(11, 6);
p2.translate(1, 7);
```

Essentially, the behavior of these two method calls is the following:

- Set `this` to refer to the same object as `p1`, and execute the `translate` method with parameters `(11, 6)`.
- Set `this` to refer to the same object as `p2`, and execute the `translate` method with parameters `(1, 7)`.

During the first call, `this` refers to the same object as `p1`. Therefore, the method call adjusts the `(x, y)` coordinates of `p1`'s object:

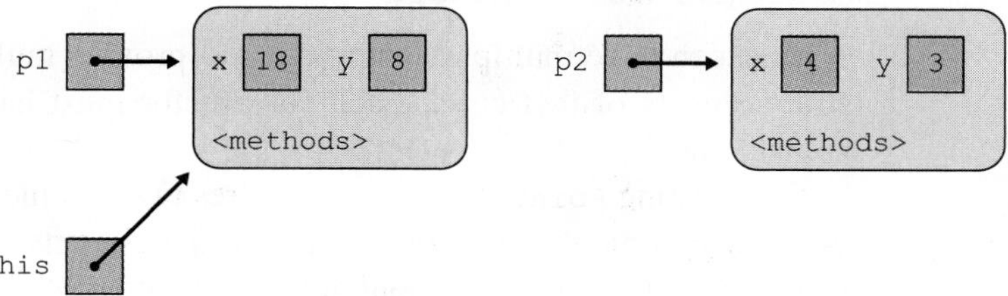

During the second method call `this` refers to the same object as `p2`, so the lines in the body of the `translate` method change the `x` and `y` fields of `p2`'s object:

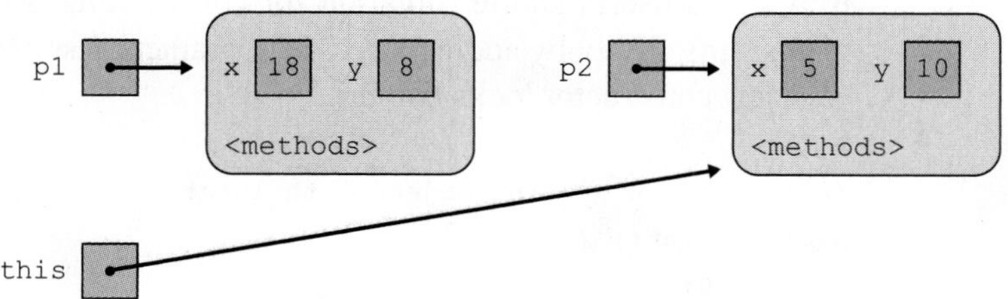

One common usage of the keyword `this` is to deal with shadowed variables. As described earlier, shadowing occurs when a field is obscured by another variable with the same name. Shadowing can happen when a field has the same name as a parameter or local variable in a class. For example, the following is a legal header for our `Point` method, even though our fields are also called `x` and `y`:

```
public Point(int x, int y) {
```

As explained at the beginning of this section, Java would normally interpret the expression `x` to mean `this.x`. However, if a parameter or local variable called `x` exists, the program will use that one instead if you just write `x`, because the field `x` is shadowed by the parameter/variable. If you write `this.x`, though, the program will always use the field `x`.

```
public Point(int x, int y) {
    this.x = x;
    this.y = y;
}
```

Of course, you can avoid this situation by naming parameters and local variables differently from fields. However, some programmers prefer the style in which a variable takes the same name as a closely related field, because it saves them from having to concoct separate parameter names like `initialX` or `newY`.

In most cases, the compiler will not allow two variables to have the same name at the same point in a program. Fields are a special case that present the risk of shadowing. Java's designers decided to allow this risk so that parameter names could match their related fields.

Multiple Constructors

A class can have multiple constructors to provide multiple ways for clients to construct objects of that class. Each constructor must have a different signature (i.e., number and type of parameters).

Our existing `Point` constructor requires two parameters (the `Point` object's initial *x*- and *y*-coordinates). Before we added the constructor, we were able to construct `Point` objects at (0, 0) without any parameters. When a class does not have a constructor, Java provides a parameterless default constructor that initializes all of the new object's fields to a zero-equivalent value. But when we added our two-parameter constructor, we lost the default constructor. This is unfortunate, because the default provided a useful shorter notation for constructing a `Point` at the origin. We can restore this ability by adding a second, parameterless constructor to our `Point` class. Our new constructor looks like this:

```
// constructs a Point object with location (0, 0)
public Point() {
    x = 0;
    y = 0;
}
```

Now it's possible to construct `Points` in two ways:

```
Point p1 = new Point(5, –2);    // (5, –2)
Point p2 = new Point();         // (0, 0)
```

Returning to the analogy of purchasing cars, you can imagine that some customers wish to specify many details about their new cars (e.g., "I'd like a yellow Civic with gold trim, upgraded stereo system, and a sun roof"), while other customers wish to specify fewer details and want the car to contain default options instead. Having multiple constructors gives clients similar flexibility when they ask for new objects of your class.

Notice that both constructors perform similar actions; the only difference is what initial values the x and y fields receive. Another way of saying this is that the new constructor can be expressed in terms of the old constructor. The following two lines construct equivalent objects:

```
Point p1 = new Point();        // construct Point at (0, 0)
Point p2 = new Point(0, 0);    // construct Point at (0, 0)
```

A common programming practice when writing classes with multiple constructors is for one constructor to contain the true initialization code and for all other constructors to call it. This means that every object created passes through a common code path. This system can be useful when you are testing and debugging your code later. The syntax for one constructor to call another is to write the keyword `this`, followed by the parameters to pass to the other constructor in parentheses:

```
this(<expression>, <expression>, ..., <expression>);
```

This is really just the normal syntax for a method call, except that we use the special keyword `this` where we would normally put the name of a method. In our case, we want to pass parameter values of `0` and `0` to initialize each field:

```
// constructs a new point at the origin, (0, 0)
public Point() {
    this(0, 0); // calls Point(int, int) constructor
}
```

8.4 Encapsulation

VideoNote

Our next version of the `Point` class will protect its data from unwanted access using a concept known as *encapsulation*.

Encapsulation
Hiding the implementation details of an object from the clients of the object.

To understand the notion of encapsulation, recall the analogy of radios as objects. Almost everyone knows how to use a radio, but few people know how to build a radio or understand how the circuitry inside a radio works. It is a benefit of the radio's design that we don't need to know those details in order to use it.

The radio analogy demonstrates an important dichotomy of external versus internal views of an object. From the outside, we just see behavior. From the inside, we see the internal state that is used to accomplish that behavior (Figure 8.1).

Focusing on the radio's external behavior enables us to use it easily while ignoring the details of its inner workings that are unimportant to us. This is an example of an important computer science concept known as *abstraction*.

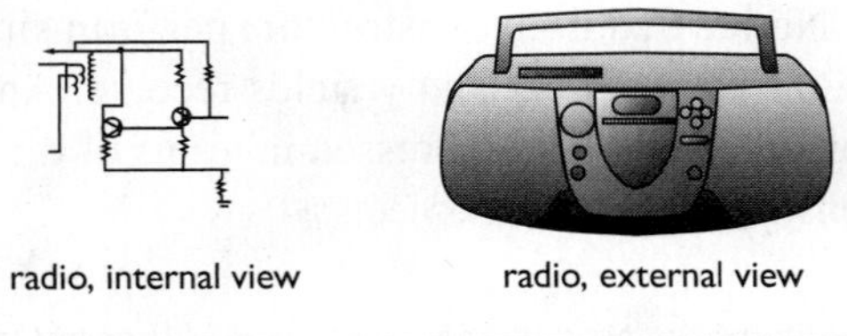

Figure 8.1 The internal and external views of a radio.

Abstraction
Focusing on essential properties rather than inner details.

In fact, a radio (like most other electronic devices) has a case or chassis that houses all of the electronics so that we don't see them from the outside. Dials, buttons, and displays on the case allow us to manipulate the radio without having to deal with all of the circuitry that makes it work. In fact, you wouldn't want someone to give you a fully functional radio that had wires and capacitors hanging out of it, because they would make the radio less pleasant to use.

In programming, the concept of hiding internal state from outside view is called encapsulation. When an object is properly encapsulated, its clients cannot directly access or modify its internal workings, nor do they need to do so. Only the implementer of the class needs to know about those details. Encapsulation leads to abstraction; an encapsulated object presents a more pure abstraction than one that has data which can be accessed directly.

In previous chapters you have already taken advantage of the abstraction provided by well-encapsulated objects. For example, you have used `Scanner` objects to read data from the console without knowing exactly how the `Scanner` stores and tokenizes the input data, and you have used `Random` objects to create random numbers without knowing exactly what algorithm the random number generator uses.

But so far, our `Point` class is not encapsulated. We've built a working radio, but its wires (its `x` and `y` fields) are still hanging out. Using encapsulation, we'll put a casing around our `Point` objects so that clients will only need to use the objects' methods and will not access the fields directly.

Private Fields

To encapsulate the fields of an object, we declare them to be private by writing the keyword `private` at the start of the declaration of each field. The fields of our `Point` class would be declared as follows:

```
// encapsulated fields of Point objects
private int x;
private int y;
```

We haven't yet shown a syntax template for fields because we wanted to show the preferred style with the fields private. The syntax for declaring encapsulated fields is

```
private <type> <name>;
```

Fields can also be declared with an initial value:

```
private <type> <name> = <value>;
```

Declaring fields `private` encapsulates the state of the object, in the same way that a radio's casing keeps the user from seeing the wires and circuitry inside it. Private fields are visible to all of the code inside the `Point` class (i.e., inside the `Point.java` file), but not anywhere else. This means that we can no longer directly refer to a `Point` object's `x` or `y` fields in our client code. The following client code will not compile successfully:

```
// this client code doesn't work with encapsulated points
System.out.println("p1 is (" + p1.x + ", " + p1.y + ")");
```

The compiler produces error messages such as the following:

```
PointMain.java:11: x has private access in Point
PointMain.java:11: y has private access in Point
```

To preserve the functionality of our client program, we need to provide a way for client code to access a `Point` object's field values. We will do this by adding some new accessor methods to the `Point` class. If the value of an object's field might be useful externally, it is common to write an accessor to return that value. Here are the methods that provide access to a `Point` object's `x` and `y` fields:

```
// returns the x-coordinate of this point
public int getX() {
    return x;
}
// returns the y-coordinate of this point
public int getY() {
    return y;
}
```

The client code to print a `Point` object's `x` and `y` values must be changed to the following:

```
// this code works with our encapsulated Points
System.out.println("p1 is (" + p1.getX() + ", " + p1.getY() + ")");
```

It probably seems odd to grant access to a `Point` object's `x` and `y` fields when we said our goal was to encapsulate those fields, but having accessors like `getX` and `getY` doesn't actually violate the encapsulation of the object. The accessor methods just return a copy of the fields' values to the client, so that the client can see the `x` or `y` values but doesn't have any way to change them. In other words, these accessor methods give the client read-only access to the state of the object.

One drawback of encapsulating the `Point` class is that it is no longer easy for the client code to set a `Point` to a new location. For convenience, we'll add a new mutator to our encapsulated `Point` class that sets both the `x` and `y` fields of the object to new values passed as parameters:

```
// sets this point's (x, y) location to the given values
public void setLocation(int newX, int newY) {
    x = newX;
    y = newY;
}
```

Another way to set a `Point` to a new location would be to write separate methods called `setX` and `setY`. We have chosen `setLocation` partly for brevity and partly because it matches Java's actual `Point` class.

Notice that the `Point` class now has some redundancy between its two-parameter constructor and its `setLocation` method. The two bodies are essentially the same, setting the `Point` to have new *x*- and *y*-coordinates. We can eliminate this redundancy by having the constructor call `setLocation` rather than setting the field values manually. It is legal for an object to call its own instance methods from a constructor or another instance method:

```
// constructs a new point with the given (x, y) location
public Point(int x, int y) {
    setLocation(x, y);
}
```

We can eliminate a bit more redundancy using this technique. Translating a `Point` can be thought of as setting its location to the old location plus the `dx` and `dy`, so we can modify the `translate` method to call the `setLocation` method:

```
// shifts this point's location by the given amount
public void translate(int dx, int dy) {
    setLocation(x + dx, y + dy);
}
```

Did You Know?

The Perils of Poor Encapsulation

Many novices (as well as many professional programmers) do not fully appreciate the concepts of abstraction and encapsulation. It is tempting to write classes that directly expose their data for clients to use, since private fields introduce some complexity and restrictions into a program. However, there have been some famous examples where a lack of proper encapsulation and abstraction caused a large problem.

One such example is the "Y2K" (year 2000) or "millennium bug" scare of late 1999. The issue arose because a large number of computer programs represented years by using only two digits, such as 72 for 1972. They followed this convention largely to save memory, since many of them were older programs written in a language called COBOL during a time when memory was more scarce. Once the year became 2000, the programs would incorrectly think that the year was 1900, and this might cause them to fail.

Making matters worse was the fact that many of these programs contained their own handwritten logic for representing dates, which sometimes appeared in many places in the code. In order for the program to represent a year with more than two digits, many places in the code needed to be changed. In total, over $300 billion was spent on repairing old programs and systems to correct the Y2K problem.

If the old programs had used an encapsulated `Date` class that included a field representing the year, far less work would have been needed to fix the Y2K bug. This `Date` class could have been updated once and all the client code would have received the benefits.

Surprisingly, Java's class libraries also contain examples of poorly encapsulated classes. In the `java.awt` package, for example, the `Point` and `Dimension` classes have public fields. (A `Dimension` object stores `width` and `height` fields to represent the size of an onscreen region.) Many client programs access the fields directly when they use these objects. Java's developers regret this decision:

> Several classes in the Java platform libraries violate the advice that public classes should not expose fields directly. Prominent examples include the `Point` and `Dimension` classes in the `java.awt` package. Rather than examples to be emulated, these classes should be regarded as cautionary tales. [. . .] The decision to expose the internals of the `Dimension` class resulted in a serious performance problem that could not be solved without affecting clients.
>
> —Joshua Bloch, *Effective Java*

Now that we've introduced all the major elements of a well-encapsulated class, it's time to look at a proper syntax template for an entire class. The Java style guidelines suggest putting fields at the top of the class, followed by constructors, followed by methods:

```
public class <class name> {
    // fields
    private <type> <name>;
    private <type> <name>;
    ...
    // constructors
    public <class name>(<type> <name>, ..., <type> <name>) {
        <statement>;
        <statement>;
        ...
        <statement>;
    }
    ...
    // methods
    public <type> <name>(<type> <name>, ..., <type> <name>) {
        <statement>;
        <statement>;
        ...
        <statement>;
    }
    ...
}
```

Here is the fourth complete version of our `Point` class, including encapsulated fields and accessor methods `getX` and `getY`:

```
// A Point object represents a pair of (x, y) coordinates.
// Fourth version: encapsulated.

public class Point {
    private int x;
    private int y;

    // constructs a new point at the origin, (0, 0)
    public Point() {
        this(0, 0); // calls Point(int, int) constructor
    }

    // constructs a new point with the given (x, y) location
    public Point(int x, int y) {
```

```
        setLocation(x, y);
    }

    // returns the distance between this Point and (0, 0)
    public double distanceFromOrigin() {
        return Math.sqrt(x * x + y * y);
    }

    // returns the x-coordinate of this point
    public int getX() {
        return x;
    }

    // returns the y-coordinate of this point
    public int getY() {
        return y;
    }

    // sets this point's (x, y) location to the given values
    public void setLocation(int x, int y) {
        this.x = x;
        this.y = y;
    }

    // returns a String representation of this point
    public String toString() {
        return "(" + x + ", " + y + ")";
    }

    // shifts this point's location by the given amount
    public void translate(int dx, int dy) {
        setLocation(x + dx, y + dy);
    }
}
```

Here's the corresponding final version of our client program, which now uses the `Point` constructors and methods appropriately:

```
// A program that deals with points.
// Fourth version, to accompany encapsulated Point class.

public class PointMain {
    public static void main(String[] args) {
        // create two Point objects
        Point p1 = new Point(7, 2);
```

```
        Point p2 = new Point(4, 3);

        // print each point and its distance from the origin
        System.out.println("p1 is " + p1);
        System.out.println("distance from origin = " +
                           p1.distanceFromOrigin());
        System.out.println("p2 is " + p2);
        System.out.println("distance from origin = " +
                           p2.distanceFromOrigin());

        // translate each point to a new location
        p1.translate(11, 6);
        p2.translate(1, 7);

        // print the points again
        System.out.println("p1 is " + p1);
        System.out.println("p2 is " + p2);
    }
}
```

Class Invariants

In this section we will develop another new class to illustrate a particular benefit of encapsulation. Consider a program that measures or deals with elapsed intervals of time, such as a program for a stopwatch, a scheduler, a TV recorder, or an airline flight system. A useful abstraction in such a program would be an object representing an elapsed span of time.

Let's write a class called `TimeSpan`, in which each `TimeSpan` object represents an interval of elapsed hours and minutes. For example, we could construct a `TimeSpan` representing an interval of 6 hours and 15 minutes. We'll represent only hours and minutes, ignoring larger or smaller units such as days or seconds.

Since we're representing intervals of hours and minutes, it seems natural to use these two quantities as fields in our class. We will encapsulate the class properly from the start by declaring the fields as `private`:

```
// represents a time span of elapsed hours and minutes
public class TimeSpan {
    private int hours;
    private int minutes;
    ...
}
```

The constructor for a `TimeSpan` object will accept `hours` and `minutes` as parameters and store the values into the object's fields. However, there is a potential problem: What should we do about values of `minutes` that are `60` or greater? Should the client program be allowed to construct a `TimeSpan` object representing 0 hours and 157 minutes? A more natural representation of this amount would be 2 hours and 37 minutes. And what about values for hours or minutes that are negative? It doesn't make sense to have a span of –2 hours or –35 minutes. Ideally we should not allow a `TimeSpan` object to store such a value.

Let's make a design decision that we will only allow `TimeSpan` objects to store a value for `minutes` that is between 0 and 59 inclusive. If the client tries to construct a `TimeSpan` object with a negative number of hours or minutes, we could resolve the problem by printing an error message or by setting the fields to 0. But in cases like this, the negative value often comes from a bug or a mistake in the client's understanding of our class. The best way to handle a violation like this is to throw an exception so that the client will know the parameter values passed were illegal.

If the user tries to construct a `TimeSpan` object with more than 60 minutes, we will convert the excess minutes into hours. You might be tempted to use an `if/else` statement or a loop to handle minutes above 60, but there is a simpler solution. For a large number of minutes such as 157, dividing by 60 will produce the hours (2) and using the `%` operator by 60 will produce the remaining minutes (37). The `hours` field should really store the `hours` parameter plus the `minutes` parameter divided by 60, and the `minutes` field should store the remaining minutes:

```
public TimeSpan(int hours, int minutes) {
    if (hours < 0 || minutes < 0) {
        throw new IllegalArgumentException();
    }

    this.hours = hours + minutes / 60;
    this.minutes = minutes % 60;
}
```

A useful behavior of a `TimeSpan` object would be the ability to add more hours and minutes to the span. An airline scheduling program might use this behavior to add the elapsed times for two back-to-back flights to determine the total travel time for a passenger's trip. Let's implement this behavior as a method called `add` that accepts `hours` and `minutes` as parameters. Here's an initial incorrect version of that method:

```
// an incorrect version of an add method
public void add(int hours, int minutes) {
    this.hours += hours;
    this.minutes += minutes;
}
```

The problem with the preceding code is that it allows the client to put the object into an invalid state. If the client passes a value of `minutes` that is large enough to make the total minutes greater than 60, the `minutes` field will have an invalid value.

For example, if the client adds 45 minutes to a time span of 1 hour and 30 minutes, the result will be 1 hour and 75 minutes.

We decided that we wanted every `TimeSpan` object to store only valid numbers of minutes between 0 and 59. We wrote code in our constructor to ensure that this would be true of each object's initial state, but really we want to ensure that the condition is true for every object throughout its entire lifespan, not just when it is initially created. Such a property that is true of every object of a class is called a *class invariant.*

Class Invariant

An assertion about an object's state that is true for the lifetime of that object.

Class invariants are related to preconditions, postconditions, and assertions, as presented in Chapters 4 and 5. We cannot allow any mutator method such as `add` to break the invariants we have decided upon; a class invariant should be treated as an implicit postcondition of every method in the class. Enforcing an invariant may cause you to add preconditions to the constructors and mutator methods of your class.

We can write code at the end of the `add` method to deal with invalid numbers of minutes and hours. First we want the program to throw an exception if the hours or minutes that are passed are negative. We will also make sure that we convert each group of 60 minutes into an hour. The following code implements the behavior:

```
public void add(int hours, int minutes) {
    if (hours < 0 || minutes < 0) {
        throw new IllegalArgumentException();
    }
    this.hours += hours;
    this.minutes += minutes;

    // converts each 60 minutes into one hour
    this.hours += this.minutes / 60;
    this.minutes = this.minutes % 60;
}
```

The code now enforces its invariant in two places: the constructor and `add`. It would be preferable to solve this problem in one place rather than redundantly checking for it throughout the class. A more elegant solution is to have the constructor initialize the fields to `0` and then call the `add` method, which performs the necessary invariant checks and stores the values of `hours` and `minutes`:

```
public TimeSpan(int hours, int minutes) {
    this.hours = 0;
    this.minutes = 0;
    add(hours, minutes);
}
```

The fields would have been auto-initialized to `0` anyway, but many programmers prefer to explicitly initialize field values for clarity.

Another useful operation for `TimeSpan` objects is the ability to print them on the console. We'll add this ability by including a `toString` method that returns a `String` such as `"2h 35m"` for 2 hours and 35 minutes.

Here is the code for the complete `TimeSpan` class that enforces its invariant:

```
// Represents a time span of hours and minutes elapsed.
// Class invariant: hours >= 0 && minutes >= 0 && minutes < 60

public class TimeSpan {
    private int hours;
    private int minutes;

    // Constructs a time span with the given interval.
    // pre: hours >= 0 && minutes >= 0
    public TimeSpan(int hours, int minutes) {
        this.hours = 0;
        this.minutes = 0;
        add(hours, minutes);
    }

    // Adds the given interval to this time span.
    // pre: hours >= 0 && minutes >= 0
    public void add(int hours, int minutes) {
        if (hours < 0 || minutes < 0) {
            throw new IllegalArgumentException();
        }

        this.hours += hours;
        this.minutes += minutes;

        // converts each 60 minutes into one hour
        this.hours += this.minutes / 60;
        this.minutes = this.minutes % 60;
    }

    // returns a String for this time span, such as "6h 15m"
    public String toString() {
        return hours + "h " + minutes + "m";
    }
}
```

Some additional features should be included in the class, such as accessors for the field values, but these are left as exercises.

Invariants bring to light the importance of proper encapsulation. If the `TimeSpan` class weren't encapsulated, we would not be able to properly enforce our invariant. A buggy or malicious client would be able to make a `TimeSpan` object's state invalid by setting its fields' values directly. When the class is encapsulated, it has much better control over how clients can use its objects, making it impossible for a misguided client program to violate the class invariant.

Changing Internal Implementations

Another important benefit of encapsulation is that it allows us to make internal design changes to a class without affecting its clients. A subtlety of classes is that the internal representation of a class does not necessarily have to match the external view that the client sees. A client of the `TimeSpan` class thinks of each time span as a number of hours and a number of minutes. But the `TimeSpan` object does not have to internally store its time using those two data fields. In fact, the code for `TimeSpan` becomes simpler if we simply store a single field for the total number of minutes. For example, we can represent 2 hours and 15 minutes as 135 total minutes by converting each hour into 60 minutes.

Let's rewrite the `TimeSpan` class to use only a single total minutes field:

```
// alternate implementation using only total minutes
public class TimeSpan {
    private int totalMinutes;
    ...
}
```

Because our class is encapsulated, as long as our methods still produce the same results from an external point of view, we can change the implementation of the object's internal state and the clients will not need to be modified. We can implement the same constructor, `add`, and `toString` behavior using total minutes. For example, the `add` method needs to combine the `hours` and `minutes` together and add both of them into the `totalMinutes`. We'll scale the hours by 60 as we add them to the total:

```
public void add(int hours, int minutes) {
    if (hours < 0 || minutes < 0) {
        throw new IllegalArgumentException();
    }
    totalMinutes += 60 * hours + minutes;
}
```

Notice that this new implementation makes it easier to enforce our class invariant about objects having valid state. We must still check for negative parameters, but we no longer need to worry about storing minutes of 60 or greater. All minutes added are properly grouped into the common total.

The constructor and `toString` method also require minor modifications to account for our new representation. Here is the complete class, implemented with total minutes instead of hours and minutes. This version is shorter and simpler than the original:

```
// Represents a time span of elapsed hours and minutes.
// Second implementation using a single field for total minutes.
// Class invariant: totalMinutes >= 0

public class TimeSpan {
    private int totalMinutes;

    // Constructs a time span with the given interval.
    // pre: hours >= 0 && minutes >= 0
    public TimeSpan(int hours, int minutes) {
        totalMinutes = 0;
        add(hours, minutes);
    }

    // Adds the given interval to this time span.
    // pre: hours >= 0 && minutes >= 0
    public void add(int hours, int minutes) {
        if (hours < 0 || minutes < 0) {
            throw new IllegalArgumentException();
        }
        totalMinutes += 60 * hours + minutes;
    }

    // returns a String for this time span, such as "6h 15m"
    public String toString() {
        return (totalMinutes / 60) + "h " +
               (totalMinutes % 60) + "m";
    }
}
```

As another example, we could revisit our encapsulated `Point` class and change its internal structure without having to modify the client code. For example, sometimes it is useful to express two-dimensional points in polar coordinates in terms of a radius *r* and an angle *theta*. In this representation, the (*x*, *y*) coordinates of a point are not stored directly but can be computed as (*r* cos(*theta*), *r* sin(*theta*)). When the `Point` class is encapsulated, we can modify it to use *r* and *theta* fields internally, then modify `getX`, `getY`, and other methods so that they still return appropriate values. The polar representation would not reap the same benefits we saw in our second implementation of `TimeSpan`, but it might make it easier for us to add certain functionality to the `Point` class later.

8.5 Case Study: Designing a `Stock` Class

VideoNote

So far we have written several classes, but we have not talked about how to design a class or how to break apart a programming problem into classes. In this section we'll examine a larger programming problem and design a class and client to solve it. We will create a class called `Stock` and a client program that compares the performance of stocks that the user has purchased.

Consider the task of writing a financial program to record purchases of shares of two stocks and report which has the greatest profit. The investor may have made several purchases of the same `Stock` at different times and prices. The interaction with the program might look like this:

```
First stock's symbol: AMZN
How many purchases did you make? 2
1: How many shares, at what price per share? 50 35.06
2: How many shares, at what price per share? 25 38.52
What is today's price per share? 37.29
Net profit/loss: $80.75

Second stock's symbol: INTC
How many purchases did you make? 3
1: How many shares, at what price per share? 15 16.55
2: How many shares, at what price per share? 10 18.09
3: How many shares, at what price per share? 20 17.15
What is today's price per share? 17.82
Net profit/loss: $29.75

AMZN was more profitable than INTC.
```

The program must perform several actions: prompting the user for input, calculating the amount spent on each purchase of stock, reporting profits, and so on. The client program could perform all of these actions and could keep track of the financial data using existing types such as `double`s and `String`s. However, recall that we began this chapter by talking about object-oriented reasoning. When you are studying complex programs, it is often useful to think about the problem in terms of the relevant objects that could solve it, rather than placing all behavior in the client program. In this particular program, we must perform several computations that involve keeping track of purchases of shares of a particular stock, so it would be useful to store the purchase information in an object.

One possible design would be to create a `Purchase` class that records information about a single purchase of shares of a particular stock. For example, if the user specified three purchases, the program should construct three `Purchase` objects. However, a more useful abstraction here would be to hold the overall information about all purchases of one stock in one place. The investor may make many purchases of the same stock, so you want to have an easy way to accumulate these shares and their total cost into a single object.

Therefore, instead of a `Purchase` class, we'll write a `Stock` class. Each `Stock` object will keep track of the investor's accumulated shares of one stock and can provide profit/loss information. Our `Stock` class will reside in a file called `Stock.java`, and the client program itself will reside in a separate file called `StockMain.java`.

Object-Oriented Design Heuristics

We now face the important task of deciding on the contents of our `Stock` class. It can be tricky to choose a good set of classes and objects to solve a complex programming problem. Chapter 4's case study introduced a set of procedural design *heuristics*, or guidelines for good design, for effectively dividing a problem into methods. There are similar guidelines for effectively breaking a large program into a set of classes and objects. The heuristics we'll discuss here are based on those listed in computer scientist Arthur Riel's influential book, *Object-Oriented Design Heuristics*.

First let's look at the overall set of responsibilities, the things that a class must know or do to solve the overall problem:

- Prompt the user for each stock's symbol and store the information somewhere.
- Prompt the user for the number of purchases of each stock.
- Read each purchase (number of shares and price per share) from the console and store the information somewhere.
- Compute the total profit/loss of each stock.
- Print the total profit/loss of each stock to the console.
- Compare the two total profits/losses and print a message to the console about which stock performed better.

It might be tempting to make most or all of these tasks responsibilities of our `Stock` class. We could make a `Stock` object store all the purchases of both stocks, prompt for information from the console, print the results, and so on. But a key guideline when writing classes is that they should have *cohesion*.

Cohesion

The extent to which the code for a class represents a single abstraction.

Placing all the responsibilities in the `Stock` class would not allow that class to represent a single clear abstraction. The abstraction we want to represent in the `Stock` class is the accumulated purchases of a single stock.

One set of responsibilities that `Stock` objects should not handle is producing the console input and output. We need to prompt the user for information and print messages, but these functions are specific to the current client program. Objects are meant to be reusable pieces of software, and other programs might wish to track stock purchases without using these exact messages or prompts. If the `Stock` class handles the prompts and printing, it will be heavily intertwined with this client program and will not be easily reusable by other clients.

In general, we want to reduce unnecessary dependencies among classes. Dependencies among classes in an object-oriented program contribute to *coupling*, the degree to which one part of a program depends on another.

Striving to avoid unnecessary coupling is a second design heuristic commonly used in object-oriented programming. A design that avoids this problem is sometimes said to have *loose coupling.*

Let's divide some of the responsibilities now, based on our heuristics. Since the `StockMain` client program will perform the console I/O, it should handle the following responsibilities:

`StockMain`

- Prompt for each stock's symbol.
- Prompt for the number of purchases of each stock.
- Read each purchase (number of shares and price per share) from the console.
- Print the total profit/loss of each stock.
- Compare the two total profits/losses and print a message about which stock generated higher profits.

Since the `StockMain` client program will be performing the console I/O, it might seem natural for it also to store the information about each stock purchase (that is, the number of shares and the price paid). But our `Stock` object should contain the functionality to compute a stock's total profit or loss, and it will need to have the data about all purchases to do so. This leads us to a third design heuristic: Related data and behavior should be in the same place. With that in mind, we can write out the responsibilities for the `Stock` class as follows:

`Stock`

- Store a stock's symbol.
- Store accumulated information about the investor's purchases of the stock.
- Record a purchase of the stock.
- Compute the total profit/loss for the stock.

When they are designing large object-oriented programs, many software engineers write information about classes as we've done here. A common technique to brainstorm ideas for classes is to write information on index cards. Each card is called a

CRC card and lists the Class, its Responsibilities, and its Collaborators (other classes to which it is coupled).

The following list summarizes the design heuristics discussed in this section:

- A class should be cohesive, representing only one abstraction.
- A class should avoid unnecessary coupling.
- Related data and behavior should be in the same class.

Note that we began our design by looking at responsibilities rather than by specifying fields as we did when we developed our `Point` class. We began writing the `Point` class by discussing fields because the data associated with a point is simple and more obvious than the data associated with stock purchases. But in many larger problems like this one, working backward from behavior and responsibilities is a better technique.

Stock Fields and Method Headers

In this section we'll decide on a design for the method names and signatures the `Stock` should use to implement its behavior. We'll use this design to determine which fields are required to implement the behavior.

We've decided that a `Stock` object should allow clients to record purchases and request the total profit or loss. Each of these tasks can be represented as a method. The recording of a purchase can be represented as a method called `purchase`. The retrieval of the total profit or loss can be represented as a method called `getProfit`.

The `purchase` method should record information about a single purchase. A purchase consists of a number of shares that the user bought (which we can assume is a whole number) and a price per share (which can include real numbers with both dollars and cents). Our `purchase` method should accept two parameters: an `int` for the number of shares bought and a `double` for the price per share. The method can use a `void` return type, since nothing needs to be returned after each purchase is recorded:

```
public void purchase(int shares, double pricePerShare)
```

The `getProfit` method will return the amount of money that the user made or lost on all accumulated purchases of this stock. Consider an investor who has made the following three purchases of a stock:

Purchase #1: 20 shares * $10 per share = $ 200 cost
Purchase #2: 20 shares * $30 per share = $ 600 cost
Purchase #3: 10 shares * $20 per share = $ 200 cost
50 total shares, $1000 total cost

If today's price per share is $22.00, the current market value of the investor's 50 shares is (50 * 22) or $1100. Since the investor paid $1000 total for the shares and they are now worth $1100, the investor has made ($1100 – $1000) = $100 of profit.

The general formula for the profit is the following:

profit = ([total shares] * [current share price]) − (total cost)

The total number of shares and total cost figure needed for this calculation are the accumulated information from all the purchases that have been made of this stock. This means that information will need to be stored during each call of the `purchase` method to be used later in the `getProfit` method. A key observation is that we do not need to store the number of shares, price per share, and cost for every purchase: We only need to store cumulative sums of the total shares purchased so far and the total dollars spent so far to acquire those values.

The third value we need in order to calculate the profit is the current share price. We could choose to make this a field in the `Stock` class as well, but the share price is a dynamic value that changes regularly. We use it during a single call to the `getProfit` method, but the next call may come at a later date when the price per share has changed.

This problem leads us to another design heuristic: Fields should represent values of core importance to the object and values that are used in multiple methods. Adding too many fields clutters a class and can make its code harder to read. If a value is used in only one method of the class, it's best to make it a parameter to that method rather than a field. Therefore, we'll make the share price a parameter to the `getProfit` method.

```
public double getProfit(double currentPrice)
```

One piece of state that we haven't discussed yet is that each stock has a symbol, such as `"AMZN"`. We'll store the symbol as a `String` field in each `Stock` object.

Here's a skeleton of our `Stock` class so far:

```
// incomplete Stock class
public class Stock {
    private String symbol;
    private int totalShares;
    private double totalCost;
    ...

    public double getProfit(double currentPrice) {
        ...
    }

    public void purchase(int shares, double pricePerShare) {
        ...
    }
}
```

Stock Method and Constructor Implementation

Now that we've decided on some of the Stock's state and behavior, let's think about how to construct Stock objects. The client program will need the ability to create two Stocks and record purchases of them.

It may be tempting to write a constructor that accepts three parameters: the symbol, the total number of shares purchased, and the total cost. But our Stock objects are accumulators of purchases, and we may want to be able to create new Stock objects before the program records initial purchases. Let's design our class to require only the symbol as a parameter and initialize the other fields to 0:

```
// initializes a new Stock with no shares purchased
public Stock(String theSymbol) {
    symbol = theSymbol;
    totalShares = 0;
    totalCost = 0.0;
}
```

When a constructor takes an object as a parameter (such as the String theSymbol), it might make sense to check that parameter's value to make sure it isn't null. One possible way to handle this case would be to throw an exception if a null symbol is passed when the program creates a Stock object. We could do this by inserting the following lines at the start of the Stock's constructor:

```
if (theSymbol == null) {
    throw new NullPointerException();
}
```

The Java convention is to throw a NullPointerException when a parameter's value is null but should not be. For other invalid parameter values, throw an IllegalArgumentException.

Now let's write the body of the purchase method. The task of recording the purchase consists of adding the new number of shares to the total number of shares and adding the new price paid for these shares to the total cost. The price paid is equal to the number of shares times the price per share. Here's the code for the purchase method to implement this behavior:

```
// records a purchase of the given number of shares of this stock
// at the given price per share
public void purchase(int shares, double pricePerShare) {
    totalShares += shares;
    totalCost += shares * pricePerShare;
}
```

It might make sense here to check the parameters passed in to make sure they are valid, as we did with the constructor. In this case, valid numbers of shares and prices per share must not be negative numbers. To perform this test, we can insert the following lines at the start of our `purchase` method:

```
if (shares < 0 || pricePerShare < 0) {
    throw new IllegalArgumentException();
}
```

Next, we'll write the body of the `getProfit` method. As we noted previously, the profit of a `Stock` is equal to its current market value minus the amount that was paid for it:

$$\text{profit} = ([\text{total shares}] * [\text{current share price}]) - (\text{total cost})$$

We can implement this formula in a straightforward manner using the `totalShares` and `totalCost` fields and the `currentPrice` parameter:

```
// Returns the total profit or loss earned on this stock,
// based on the given price per share.
public double getProfit(double currentPrice) {
    return totalShares * currentPrice – totalCost;
}
```

Note that parentheses are not needed in the code because multiplication has a higher precedence than subtraction.

As we did for the other methods, we should check for illegal parameter values. In this case, we shouldn't allow a negative current price per share. To ensure that this doesn't happen, we can place the following code at the start of the method:

```
if (currentPrice < 0.0) {
    throw new IllegalArgumentException();
}
```

After we've written all the fields, the constructor, and the methods of our `Stock`, the class will look like this:

```
// A Stock object represents purchases of shares of a stock.

public class Stock {
    private String symbol;        // stock symbol, e.g. "YHOO"
    private int totalShares;      // total shares purchased
    private double totalCost;     // total cost for all shares

    // initializes a new Stock with no shares purchased
    // pre: symbol != null
```

```
    public Stock(String theSymbol) {
        if (theSymbol == null) {
            throw new NullPointerException();
        }

        symbol = theSymbol;
        totalShares = 0;
        totalCost = 0.0;
    }

    // returns the total profit or loss earned on this stock,
    // based on the given price per share
    // pre: currentPrice >= 0.0
    public double getProfit(double currentPrice) {
        if (currentPrice < 0.0) {
            throw new IllegalArgumentException();
        }

        double marketValue = totalShares * currentPrice;
        return marketValue – totalCost;
    }

    // records purchase of the given shares at the given price
    // pre: shares >= 0 && pricePerShare >= 0.0
    public void purchase(int shares, double pricePerShare) {
        if (shares < 0 || pricePerShare < 0.0) {
            throw new IllegalArgumentException();
        }

        totalShares += shares;
        totalCost += shares * pricePerShare;
    }
}
```

Here's the client code to use the Stock class:

```
// This program tracks the user's purchases of two stocks,
// computing and reporting which stock was more profitable.

import java.util.*;

public class StockMain {
    public static void main(String[] args) {
        Scanner console = new Scanner(System.in);
```

```

        // first stock
        System.out.print("First stock's symbol: ");
        String symbol1 = console.next();
        Stock stock1 = new Stock(symbol1);
        double profit1 = makePurchases(stock1, console);

        // second stock
        System.out.print("Second stock's symbol: ");
        String symbol2 = console.next();
        Stock stock2 = new Stock(symbol2);
        double profit2 = makePurchases(stock2, console);

        // report which stock made more money
        if (profit1 > profit2) {
            System.out.println(symbol1 + " was more " +
                    "profitable than" + symbol2 + ".");
        } else if (profit2 > profit1) {
            System.out.println(symbol2 + " was more " +
                    "profitable than " + symbol1 + ".");
        } else {  // profit1 == profit2
            System.out.println(symbol1 + " and " + symbol2 +
                    " are equally profitable.");
        }
    }

    // make purchases of stock and return the profit
    public static double makePurchases(Stock currentStock,
                                       Scanner console) {
        System.out.print("How many purchases did you make? ");
        int numPurchases = console.nextInt();

        // ask about each purchase
        for (int i = 1; i <= numPurchases; i++) {
            System.out.print(i +
                ": How many shares, at what price per share? ");
            int numShares = console.nextInt();
            double pricePerShare = console.nextDouble();

            // ask the Stock object to record this purchase
            currentStock.purchase(numShares, pricePerShare);
        }

        // use the Stock object to compute profit
```

```
        System.out.print("What is today's price per share? ");
        double currentPrice = console.nextDouble();

        double profit = currentStock.getProfit(currentPrice);
        System.out.println("Net profit/loss: $" + profit);
        System.out.println();
        return profit;
    }
}
```

It would be useful to have a few other methods in our `Stock` objects. For example, it would be good to implement accessors for the `Stock`'s data (the symbol, number of shares, and so on), and a `toString` method to easily print `Stock` objects. We could even add a second constructor that would accept an initial number of shares and cost. These features are left for you to implement as exercises.

Chapter Summary

Object-oriented programming is a different philosophy of writing programs that focuses on nouns or entities in a program, rather than on verbs or actions of a program. In object-oriented programming, state and behavior are grouped into objects that communicate with each other.

A class serves as the blueprint for a new type of object, specifying the object's data and behavior. The class can be asked to construct many objects (also called "instances") of its type.

Java's `java.awt` package has a class named `Point`. Each object holds two `int` values, `x` and `y`. A `Point` can be constructed, translated to a new location, and printed on the console.

The data for each object are specified using special variables called fields.

The behavior of each object is specified by writing instance methods in the class. Instance methods exist inside an object and can access that object's internal state.

To make objects easily printable, write a `toString` method that returns the object's text representation.

A class can define special code called a constructor that initializes the state of new objects as they are created. The constructor will be called when external client code creates a new object of your type using the `new` keyword.

You can use the keyword `this` to have an object refer to itself. It is also used when a class has multiple constructors and one constructor wishes to call another.

Objects can protect their internal data from unwanted external modification by declaring them to be `private`, an action known as encapsulation. Encapsulation provides abstraction so that clients can use the objects without knowing about their internal implementation.

A class should represent only one key abstraction with related data and behavior, and it should be independent from its clients.

Self-Check Problems

Section 8.1: Object-Oriented Programming

1. Describe the difference between object-oriented programming and procedural programming.

2. What is an object? How is an object different from a class?

3. What is the state of a `String` object? What is its behavior?

4. What is the output of the following program?

```
public class ReferenceMystery3 {
    public static void main(String[] args) {
        int a = 7;
        int b = 9;
        Point p1 = new Point(2, 2);
        Point p2 = new Point(2, 2);
        addToXTwice(a, p1);
        System.out.println(a + " " + b + " " + p1.x + " " + p2.x);
        addToXTwice(b, p2);
        System.out.println(a + " " + b + " " + p1.x + " " + p2.x);
    }

    public static void addToXTwice(int a, Point p1) {
        a = a + a;
        p1.x = a;
        System.out.println(a + " " + p1.x);
    }
}
```

5. Imagine that you are creating a class called `Calculator`. A `Calculator` object could be used to program a simple mathematical calculator device like the ones you have used in math classes in school. What state might a `Calculator` object have? What might its behavior be?

Section 8.2: Object State and Behavior

6. Explain the differences between a field and a parameter. What is the difference in their syntax? What is the difference in their scope and the ways in which they may be used?

7. Create a class called `Name` that represents a person's name. The class should have fields representing the person's first name, last name, and middle initial. (Your class should contain only fields for now.)

8. What is the difference between an accessor and a mutator? What naming conventions are used with accessors and mutators?

9. Suppose we have written a class called `BankAccount` with a method inside it, defined as:

```
public double computeInterest(int rate)
```

If the client code has declared a `BankAccount` variable named `acct`, which of the following would be a valid call to the above method?

a. `double result = computeInterest(acct, 42);`

b. `acct.computeInterest(42.0, 15);`

c. `int result = BankAccount.computeInterest(42);`

d. `double result = acct.computeInterest(42);`

e. `new BankAccount(42).computeInterest();`

10. Add a new method to the `Point` class we developed in this chapter:

```
public double distance(Point other)
```

Returns the distance between the current `Point` object and the given other `Point` object. The distance between two points is equal to the square root of the sum of the squares of the differences of their *x*- and *y*-coordinates. In other words, the distance between two points (x_1, y_1) and (x_2, y_2) can be expressed as the square root of $(x_2 - x_1)^2 + (y_2 - y_1)^2$. Two points with the same (x, y) coordinates should return a distance of `0.0`.

11. (You must complete Self-Check Problem 7 before answering this question.)
Add two new methods to the `Name` class:

```
public String getNormalOrder()
```

Returns the person's name in normal order, with the first name followed by the middle initial and last name. For example, if the first name is `"John"`, the middle initial is `"Q"`, and the last name is `"Public"`, returns `"John Q. Public"`.

```
public String getReverseOrder()
```

Returns the person's name in reverse order, with the last name preceding the first name and middle initial. For example, if the first name is `"John"`, the middle initial is `"Q"`, and the last name is `"Public"`, returns `"Public, John Q."`.

12. How do you write a class whose objects can easily be printed on the console?

13. The following `println` statement (the entire line) is equivalent to what?

```
Point p1 = new Point();
...
System.out.println(p1);
```

a. `System.out.println(toString(p1));`

b. `p1.toString();`

c. `System.out.println(p1.toString());`

d. `System.out.println(p1.string());`

e. `System.out.println(Point.toString());`

14. The `Point` class in the `java.awt` package has a `toString` method that returns a `String` in the following format:

```
java.awt.Point[x=7,y=2]
```

Write a modified version of the `toString` method on our `Point` class that returns a result in this format.

15. (You must complete Self-Check Problem 7 before answering this question.)

Write a `toString` method for the `Name` class that returns a `String` such as `"John Q. Public"`.

16. Finish the following client code so that it constructs two `Point` objects, translates each, and then prints their coordinates.

```
// construct two Point objects, one at (8, 2) and one at (4, 3)

System.out.println("p1 is " ...);    // display the objects' state
System.out.println("p2 is " ...);

System.out.println("p1's distance from origin is " ...);

// translate p1 to (9, 4) and p2 to (3, 13)

System.out.println("p1 is now " ...);    // display state again
System.out.println("p2 is now " ...);
```

Section 8.3: Object Initialization: Constructors

17. What is a constructor? How is a constructor different from other methods?

18. What are two major problems with the following constructor?

```
public void Point(int initialX, int initialY) {
    int x = initialX;
    int y = initialY;
}
```

19. (You must complete Self-Check Problem 7 before answering this question.)

Add a constructor to the `Name` class that accepts a first name, middle initial, and last name as parameters and initializes the `Name` object's state with those values.

20. What is the meaning of the keyword `this`? Describe three ways that the keyword can be used.

21. Add a constructor to the `Point` class that accepts another `Point` as a parameter and initializes this new `Point` to have the same (*x*, *y*) values. Use the keyword `this` in your solution.

Section 8.4: Encapsulation

22. What is abstraction? How do objects provide abstraction?

23. What is the difference between the `public` and `private` keywords? What items should be declared `private`?

24. When fields are made private, client programs cannot see them directly. How do you allow classes access to read these fields' values, without letting the client break the object's encapsulation?

25. Add methods named `setX` and `setY` to the `Point` class that allow clients to change a `Point` object's *x*- and *y*-coordinates, respectively.

26. (You must complete Self-Check Problem 7 before answering this question.)

Encapsulate the `Name` class. Make its fields private and add appropriate accessor methods to the class.

27. (You must complete Self-Check Problem 26 before answering this question.)

Add methods called `setFirstName`, `setMiddleInitial`, and `setLastName` to your `Name` class. Give the parameters the same names as your fields, and use the `this` keyword in your solution.

28. How does encapsulation allow you to change the internal implementation of a class?

Section 8.5: Case Study: Designing a `Stock` Class

29. What is cohesion? How can you tell whether a class is cohesive?

30. Why didn't we choose to put the console I/O code into the `Stock` class?

31. Add accessor methods to the `Stock` class to return the stock's symbol, total shares, and total cost.

Exercises

1. Add the following accessor method to the `Point` class:

```
public int quadrant()
```

Returns which quadrant of the x/y plane the current `Point` object falls in. Quadrant 1 contains all points whose `x` and `y` values are both positive. Quadrant 2 contains all points with negative `x` but positive `y`. Quadrant 3 contains all points with negative `x` and `y` values. Quadrant 4 contains all points with positive `x` but negative `y`. If the point lies directly on the *x* and/or *y* axis, return `0`.

2. Add the following mutator method to the `Point` class:

```
public void flip()
```

Negates and swaps the *x*/*y* coordinates of the `Point` object. For example, if an object `pt` initially represents the point (5, −3), after a call of `pt.flip();` the object should represent (3, −5). If the same object initially represents the point (4, 17), after a call to `pt.flip();` the object should represent (−17, −4).

3. Add the following accessor method to the `Point` class:

```
public int manhattanDistance(Point other)
```

Returns the "Manhattan distance" between the current `Point` object and the given other `Point` object. The Manhattan distance refers to the distance between two places if one can travel between them only by moving horizontally or vertically, as though driving on the streets of Manhattan. In our case, the Manhattan distance is the sum of the absolute values of the differences in their coordinates; in other words, the difference in `x` plus the difference in `y` between the points.

4. Add the following accessor method to the `Point` class:

```
public boolean isVertical(Point other)
```

Returns `true` if the given `Point` lines up vertically with this `Point`, that is, if their *x*-coordinates are the same.

5. Add the following accessor method to the `Point` class:

```
public double slope(Point other)
```

Returns the slope of the line drawn between this `Point` and the given other `Point`. Use the formula $(y_2 - y_1) / (x_2 - x_1)$ to determine the slope between two points (x_1, y_1) and (x_2, y_2). Note that this formula fails for points with identical *x*-coordinates, so throw an `IllegalArgumentException` in this case.

6. Add the following accessor method to the `Point` class:

```
public boolean isCollinear(Point p1, Point p2)
```

Returns whether this `Point` is collinear with the given two other `Points`. `Points` are collinear if a straight line can be drawn that connects them. Two basic examples are three points that have the same *x*- or *y*-coordinate. The more general case can be determined by calculating the slope of the line between each pair of points and checking whether this slope is the same for all pairs of points. Use the formula $(y_2 - y_1) / (x_2 - x_1)$ to determine the slope between two points (x_1, y_1) and (x_2, y_2). (Note that this formula fails for points with identical *x*-coordinates so this will have to be a special case in your code.) Since Java's `double` type is imprecise, round all slope values to a reasonable accuracy such as four digits past the decimal point before you compare them.

7. Add the following mutator method to the `TimeSpan` class:

```
public void add(TimeSpan span)
```

Adds the given amount of time to this time span.

8. Add the following mutator method to the `TimeSpan` class:

```
public void subtract(TimeSpan span)
```

Subtracts the given amount of time from this time span.

9. Add the following mutator method to the `TimeSpan` class:

```
public void scale(int factor)
```

Scales this time span by the given factor. For example, 1 hour and 45 minutes scaled by 2 equals 3 hours and 30 minutes.

10. Add the following mutator method to the `Stock` class:

```
public void clear()
```

Resets this `Stock`'s number of shares purchased and total cost to `0`.

11. Suppose the following `BankAccount` class has been created:

```
// Each BankAccount object represents one user's account
// information including name and balance of money.
public class BankAccount {
    String name;
    double balance;

    public void deposit(double amount) {
        balance = balance + amount;
    }

    public void withdraw(double amount) {
        balance = balance - amount;
    }
}
```

Add a field to the `BankAccount` class named `transactionFee` for a real number representing an amount of money to deduct every time the user withdraws money. The default value is $0.00, but the client can change the value. Deduct the transaction fee money during every `withdraw` call (but not from deposits). Make sure that the balance cannot go negative during a withdrawal. If the withdrawal (amount plus transaction fee) would cause it to become negative, don't modify the balance at all.

12. Add a `toString` method to the `BankAccount` class from the previous exercise. Your method should return a string that contains the account's name and balance separated by a comma and space. For example, if an account object named `yana` has the name `"Yana"` and a balance of `3.03`, the call `yana.toString()` should return the string `"Yana, $3.03"`.

13. Add a `transfer` method to the `BankAccount` class from the previous exercises. Your method should move money from the current bank account to another account. The method accepts two parameters: a second `BankAccount` to accept the money, and a real number for the amount of money to transfer. There is a $5.00 fee for transferring money, so this much must be deducted from the current account's balance before any transfer. The method should modify the two `BankAccount` objects such that "this" current object has its balance decreased by the given amount plus the $5 fee, and the other account's balance is increased by the given amount. If this account object does not have enough money to make the full transfer, transfer whatever money is left after the $5 fee is deducted. If this account has under $5 or the amount is 0 or less, no transfer should occur and neither account's state should be modified. The following are some example calls to the method:

```
BankAccount ben = new BankAccount();
ben.deposit(80.00);
BankAccount hal = new BankAccount();
hal.deposit(20.00);
ben.transfer(hal, 20.00);    // ben $55, hal $40  (ben -$25, hal +$20)
ben.transfer(hal, 10.00);    // ben $40, hal $50  (ben -$15, hal +$10)
hal.transfer(ben, 60.00);    // ben $85, hal $ 0  (ben +$45, hal -$50)
```

14. Write a class called `Line` that represents a line segment between two `Points`. Your `Line` objects should have the following methods:

```
public Line(Point p1, Point p2)
```

Constructs a new `Line` that contains the given two `Points`.

```
public Point getP1()
```

Returns this `Line`'s first endpoint.

```
public Point getP2()
```

Returns this `Line`'s second endpoint.

```
public String toString()
```

Returns a `String` representation of this `Line`, such as `"[(22, 3), (4, 7)]"`.

15. Add the following accessor method to your `Line` class:

```
public double getSlope()
```

Returns the slope of this `Line`. The slope of a line between points (x_1, y_1) and (x_2, y_2) is equal to $(y_2 - y_1) / (x_2 - x_1)$. If x_2 equals x_1 the denominator is zero and the slope is undefined, so you may throw an exception in this case.

16. Add the following constructor to your `Line` class:

```
public Line(int x1, int y1, int x2, int y2)
```

Constructs a new `Line` that contains the given two `Points`.

17. Add the following accessor method to your `Line` class:

```
public boolean isCollinear(Point p)
```

Returns `true` if the given `Point` is collinear with the `Points` of this `Line`—that is, if, when this `Line` is stretched infinitely, it would eventually hit the given `Point`. `Points` are collinear if a straight line can be drawn that connects them. Two basic examples are three points that have the same *x*- or *y*-coordinate. The more general case can be determined by calculating the slope of the line between each pair of points and checking whether this slope is the same for all pairs of points. Use the formula $(y_2 - y_1) / (x_2 - x_1)$ to determine the slope between two points (x_1, y_1) and (x_2, y_2). (Note that this formula fails for points with identical *x*-coordinates, so this will have to be a special case in your code.) Since Java's `double` type is imprecise, round all slope values to a reasonable accuracy such as four digits past the decimal point before you compare them.

18. Write a class called `Rectangle` that represents a rectangular two-dimensional region. Your `Rectangle` objects should have the following methods:

```
public Rectangle(int x, int y, int width, int height)
```

Constructs a new `Rectangle` whose top-left corner is specified by the given coordinates and with the given `width` and `height`. Throw an `IllegalArgumentException` on a negative `width` or `height`.

```
public int getHeight()
```

Returns this `Rectangle`'s height.

```
public int getWidth()
```

Returns this `Rectangle`'s width.

```
public int getX()
```

Returns this `Rectangle`'s *x*-coordinate.

```
public int getY()
```

Returns this `Rectangle`'s *y*-coordinate.

```
public String toString()
```

Returns a `String` representation of this `Rectangle`, such as `"Rectangle[x=1,y=2,width=3, height=4]"`.

19. Add the following constructor to your `Rectangle` class:

```
public Rectangle(Point p, int width, int height)
```

Construct a new `Rectangle` whose top-left corner is specified by the given `Point` and with the given `width` and `height`.

20. Add the following accessor methods to your `Rectangle` class:

```
public boolean contains(int x, int y)
public boolean contains(Point p)
```

Returns whether the given `Point` or coordinates lie inside the bounds of this `Rectangle`.

21. Add the following method to your `Rectangle` class:

```
public Rectangle union(Rectangle rect)
```

Returns a new `Rectangle` that represents the area occupied by the tightest bounding box that contains both this `Rectangle` and the given other `Rectangle`.

22. Add the following method to your `Rectangle` class:

```
public Rectangle intersection(Rectangle rect)
```

Return a new `Rectangle` that represents the largest rectangular region completely contained within both this `Rectangle` and the given other `Rectangle`. If the `Rectangles` do not intersect at all, returns a `Rectangle` with `width` and `height` both equal to `0`.

Programming Projects

1. Write a class called `RationalNumber` that represents a fraction with an integer numerator and denominator. A `RationalNumber` object should have the following methods:

```
public RationalNumber(int numerator, int denominator)
```

Constructs a new rational number to represent the ratio (numerator/denominator). The denominator cannot be `0`, so throw an `IllegalArgumentException` if `0` is passed.

```
public RationalNumber()
```

Constructs a new rational number to represent the ratio (0/1).

```
public int getDenominator()
```

Returns this rational number's `denominator` value; for example, if the ratio is (3/5), returns `5`.

```
public int getNumerator()
```

Returns this rational number's `numerator` value; for example, if the ratio is (3/5), returns `3`.

```
public String toString()
```

Returns a `String` representation of this rational number, such as `"3/5"`. You may wish to omit denominators of `1`, returning `"4"` instead of `"4/1"`.

An extra challenge would be to maintain your `RationalNumber` objects in reduced form, avoiding rational numbers such as `3/6` in favor of `1/2`, or avoiding `2/-3` in favor of `-2/3`. Another possible extra feature would be methods to add, subtract, multiply, and divide two rational numbers.

2. Write a class called `Date` that represents a date consisting of a year, month, and day. A `Date` object should have the following methods:

`public Date(int year, int month, int day)`

Constructs a new `Date` object to represent the given date.

`public void addDays(int days)`

Moves this `Date` object forward in time by the given number of days.

`public void addWeeks(int weeks)`

Moves this `Date` object forward in time by the given number of seven-day weeks.

`public int daysTo(Date other)`

Returns the number of days that this `Date` must be adjusted to make it equal to the given other `Date`.

`public int getDay()`

Returns the day value of this date; for example, for the date 2006/07/22, returns `22`.

`public int getMonth()`

Returns the month value of this date; for example, for the date 2006/07/22, returns `7`.

`public int getYear()`

Returns the year value of this date; for example, for the date 2006/07/22, returns `2006`.

`public boolean isLeapYear()`

Returns `true` if the year of this date is a leap year. A leap year occurs every four years, except for multiples of 100 that are not multiples of 400. For example, 1956, 1844, 1600, and 2000 are leap years, but 1983, 2002, 1700, and 1900 are not.

`public String toString()`

Returns a `String` representation of this date in year/month/day order, such as `"2006/07/22"`.

3. Write a class named `GroceryList` that represents a list of items to buy from the market, and another class named `GroceryItemOrder` that represents a request to purchase a particular item in a given quantity (e.g., four boxes of cookies). The `GroceryList` class should use an array field to store the grocery items and to keep track of its size (number of items in the list so far). Assume that a grocery list will have no more than 10 items. A `GroceryList` object should have the following methods:

`public GroceryList()`

Constructs a new empty grocery list.

`public void add(GroceryItemOrder item)`

Adds the given item order to this list if the list has fewer than 10 items.

`public double getTotalCost()`

Returns the total sum cost of all grocery item orders in this list.

The `GroceryItemOrder` class should store an item quantity and a price per unit. A `GroceryItemOrder` object should have the following methods:

`public GroceryItemOrder(String name, int quantity, double pricePerUnit)`

Constructs an item order to purchase the item with the given name, in the given quantity, which costs the given price per unit.

`public double getCost()`

Returns the total cost of this item in its given quantity. For example, four boxes of cookies that cost 2.30 per unit have a total cost of 9.20.

`public void setQuantity(int quantity)`

Sets this grocery item's quantity to be the given value.

Chapter 9

Inheritance and Interfaces

Introduction

In this chapter, we will explore two of the most important techniques the Java language provides to help you write better structured solutions. Inheritance allows you to share code between classes to reduce redundancy and lets you treat different classes of objects in the same way. Interfaces allow you to treat several different classes of objects the same way without sharing code.

It is difficult to show the usefulness of inheritance and interfaces in simple examples, but in larger and more complex projects these techniques are invaluable. The Java class libraries make extensive use of these two features. Inheritance and interfaces make it possible to create well-structured code on a scale that is as large as the entire Java class libraries.

9.1 Inheritance Basics

We'll begin our discussion of inheritance by exploring how the concept originated and considering a nonprogramming example that will lead us toward programming with inheritance in Java.

Large programs demand that we write versatile and clear code on a large scale. In this textbook, we've examined several ways to express programs more concisely and elegantly on a small scale. Features like static methods, parameterization, loops, and classes help us organize our programs and extract common features that can be used in many places. This general practice is called *code reuse.*

Code Reuse

The practice of writing program code once and using it in many contexts.

Did You Know?

The Software Crisis

Software has been getting more and more complicated since the advent of programming. By the early 1970s, teams writing larger and more complex programs began to encounter some common problems. Despite much effort, software projects were running over budget and were not being completed on time; also, the software often had bugs, didn't do what it was supposed to do, or was otherwise of low quality. In his 1975 book *The Mythical Man-Month: Essays on Software Engineering*, software engineer Fred Brooks argued that adding manpower to a late software project often made it finish even later. Collectively, these problems came to be called the "software crisis."

A particularly sticky issue involved program maintenance. Companies found that they spent much of their time not writing new code but modifying and maintaining existing code (also called *legacy code*). This proved to be a difficult task, because it was easy to write disorganized and redundant code. Maintenance of such code was likely to take a long time and to introduce new bugs into the system.

The negative effects of the software crisis and maintenance programming were particularly noticeable when graphical user interfaces became prominent in the 1980s. User interfaces in graphical systems like Microsoft Windows and Apple's Mac OS X were much more sophisticated than the text interfaces that preceded them. The original graphical programs were prone to redundancy because they had to describe in detail how to implement buttons, text boxes, and other onscreen components. Also, the graphical components themselves contained a lot of common states and behavior, such as particular sizes, shapes, colors, positions, or scrollbars.

Object-oriented programming provides us with a feature called inheritance that increases our ability to reuse code by allowing one class to be an extension of another. Inheritance also allows us to write programs with hierarchies of related object types.

Nonprogramming Hierarchies

In order to use inheritance, you'll want to identify similarities between different objects and classes in your programs. Let's start by looking at a nonprogramming example: a hierarchy of employees at a company.

Imagine a large law firm that hires several classes of employees: lawyers, general secretaries, legal secretaries, and marketers. The company has a number of employee rules about vacation and sick days, medical benefits, harassment regulations, and so on. Each subdivision of the company also has a few of its own rules; for example, lawyers may use a different form to ask for vacation leave than do secretaries.

Suppose that all the employees attend a common orientation where they learn the general rules. Each employee receives a 20-page manual of these rules to read. A mixed group of employees could attend the orientation together: Lawyers, secretaries, and marketers all might sit in the same orientation group.

Afterward, the employees go to their subdivisions and receive secondary, smaller orientations covering any rules specific to those divisions. Each employee receives a smaller manual, two or three pages in length, covering that subdivision's specific rules. Some rules are added to those in the general 20-page manual, and a few are replaced. For example, one class of employees may get three weeks of vacation instead of two, and one class may use a pink form to apply for time off rather than the yellow form listed in the 20-page manual. Each class has its own submanual with unique contents as shown in Figure 9.1.

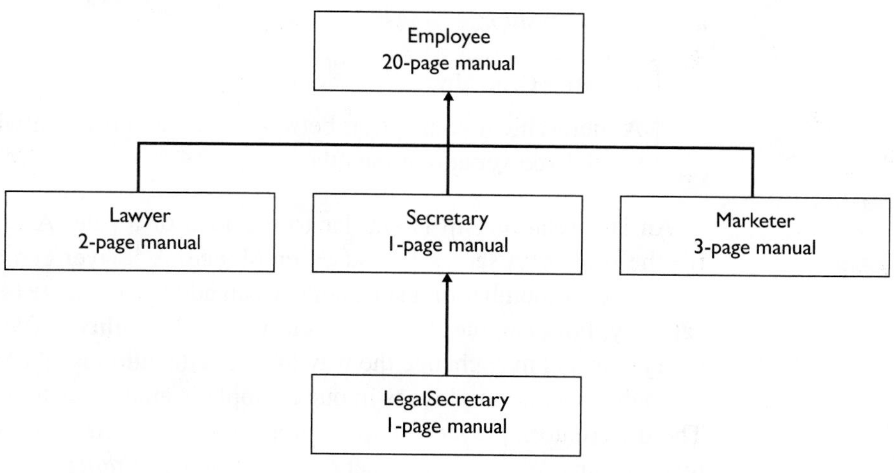

Figure 9.1 A hierarchy of employee manuals

An alternative solution would be to give every employee a large manual containing both the applicable general rules and the rules of their subdivisions. For example, there might be a 22-page manual for the lawyers, a 21-page manual for secretaries, and a 23-page manual for marketers. The consolidation might even save a few pages. So why does the company bother to generate two manuals for every employee?

The main reason has to do with redundancy and maintenance. The 22-page lawyer manual contains a lot of the same text as the 21-page secretary manual. If a common rule is changed under the one-manual scenario, all the manuals need to be updated individually, which is a tedious process. Making the same change to many manuals is also likely to introduce errors, because it is easy to make the change in one copy but forget to do it in another.

In addition, there's a certain practical appeal to using the shorter, more specific manuals. Someone who wants to know all the rules that are specific to lawyers can simply read the 2-page lawyer manual, rather than combing through a 22-page lawyer manual trying to spot differences.

There are two key ideas here:

1. It's useful to be able to specify a broad set of rules that will apply to many related groups (the 20-page manual).
2. It's also useful to be able to specify a smaller set of rules specific to a particular group, and to be able to replace some rules from the broad set (e.g., "use the pink form instead of the yellow form").

An important thing to notice about the categories is that they are hierarchical. For example, every legal secretary is also a secretary, and every marketer is also an employee. In a pinch, you could ask a legal secretary to work as a standard secretary for a short period, because a legal secretary is a secretary. We call such a connection an *is-a relationship.*

Is-a Relationship

A hierarchical connection between two categories in which one type is a specialized version of the other.

An is-a relationship is similar to the idea of a role. A legal secretary can also fill the roles of a secretary and an employee. A lawyer can also fill the role of an employee. A member of a subcategory can add to or change behavior from the larger category. For example, a legal secretary adds the ability to file legal briefs to the secretary role and may change the way in which dictation is taken.

Each group of employees in our example is analogous to a class in programming. The different employee groups represent a set of related classes connected by is-a relationships. We call such a set of classes an *inheritance hierarchy.*

Inheritance Hierarchy

A set of hierarchical relationships between classes of objects.

As you'll see, inheritance hierarchies are commonly used in Java to group related classes of objects and reuse code between them.

Extending a Class

The previous section presented a nonprogramming example of hierarchies. But as an exercise, we could write small Java classes to represent those categories of employees. The code will be a bit silly but will illustrate some important concepts.

Let's imagine that we have the following rules for our employees:

- Employees work 40 hours per week.
- All employees earn a salary of $40,000 per year, with the exception of marketers, who make $50,000 per year, and legal secretaries, who make $45,000 per year.
- Employees have two weeks of paid vacation leave per year, with the exception of lawyers, who have three weeks of vacation leave.
- Employees use a yellow form to apply for vacation leave, with the exception of lawyers, who use a special pink form.
- Each type of employee has unique behavior: Lawyers know how to handle lawsuits, marketers know how to advertise, secretaries know how to take dictation, and legal secretaries know how to file legal briefs.

Let's write a class to represent the common behavior of all employees. (Think of this as the 20-page employee manual.) We'll write methods called `getHours`, `getSalary`, `getVacationDays`, and `getVacationForm` to represent these behaviors. To keep things simple, each method will just return some value representing the default employee behavior, such as the $40,000 salary and the yellow form for vacation leave. We won't declare any fields for now. Here is the code for the basic `Employee` class:

```
// A class to represent employees in general.
public class Employee {
    public int getHours() {
        return 40;
    }

    public double getSalary() {
        return 40000.0;
    }

    public int getVacationDays() {
        return 10;
    }

```

```
    public String getVacationForm() {
        return "yellow";
    }
}
```

Now let's think about implementing the `Secretary` subcategory. As we mentioned in the previous section, every `Secretary` is also an `Employee` and, consequently, retains the abilities that `Employees` have. Secretaries also have one additional ability: the ability to take dictation. If we wrote `Secretary` as a standalone class, its code would not reflect this relationship very elegantly. We would be forced to repeat all of the same methods from `Employee` with identical behavior. Here is the redundant class:

```
// A redundant class to represent secretaries.
public class Secretary {
    public int getHours() {
        return 40;
    }

    public double getSalary() {
        return 40000.0;
    }

    public int getVacationDays() {
        return 10;
    }

    public String getVacationForm() {
        return "yellow";
    }

    // this is the only added behavior
    public void takeDictation(String text) {
        System.out.println("Dictating text: " + text);
    }
}
```

The only code unique to the `Secretary` class is its `takeDictation` method. What we'd really like to do is to be able to copy the behavior from class `Employee` without rewriting it in the `Secretary` class file.

```
public class Secretary {
    copy all the methods from the Employee class.

    // this is the only added behavior
    public void takeDictation() {
        System.out.println("I know how to take dictation.");
    }
}
```

Fortunately, Java provides a mechanism called *inheritance* that can help us remove this sort of redundancy between similar classes of objects. Inheritance allows the programmer to specify a relationship between two classes in which one class includes ("inherits") the state and behavior of another.

Inheritance (Inherit)

A programming technique that allows a derived class to extend the functionality of a base class, inheriting all of its state and behavior.

The derived class, more commonly called the *subclass,* inherits all of the state and behavior of its parent class, commonly called the *superclass.*

Superclass

The parent class in an inheritance relationship.

Subclass

The child, or derived, class in an inheritance relationship.

We say that the subclass *extends* the superclass because it not only receives the superclass's state and behavior but can also add new state and behavior of its own. The subclass can also replace inherited behavior with new behavior as needed, which we'll discuss in the next section.

A Java class can have only one superclass; it is not possible to extend more than one class. This is called *single inheritance.* On the other hand, one class may be extended by many subclasses.

To declare one class as the subclass of another, place the `extends` keyword followed by the superclass name at the end of the subclass header. The general syntax is the following:

```
public class <name> extends <superclass> {
    ...
}
```

We can rewrite the `Secretary` class to extend the `Employee` class. This will create an is-a relationship in which every `Secretary` also is an `Employee`. `Secretary` objects will inherit copies of the `getHours`, `getSalary`, `getVacationDays`, and `getVacationForm` methods, so we won't need to write these methods in the `Secretary` class. This will remove the redundancy between the classes.

It's legal and expected for a subclass to add new behavior that wasn't present in the superclass. We said previously that secretaries add an ability not seen in other employees: the ability to take dictation. We can add this to our otherwise empty `Secretary` class. The following is the complete `Secretary` class:

```
// A class to represent secretaries.
public class Secretary extends Employee {
    public void takeDictation(String text) {
        System.out.println("Dictating text: " + text);
    }
}
```

This concise new version of the `Secretary` class has the same behavior as the longer class shown before. Like the two-page specialized manual, this class shows only the features that are unique to the specific job class. In this case, it is very easy to see that the unique behavior of secretaries in our system is to take dictation.

The following client code would work with our new `Secretary` class:

```
public class EmployeeMain {
    public static void main(String[] args) {
        System.out.print("Employee: ");
        Employee edna = new Employee();
        System.out.print(edna.getHours() + ", ");
        System.out.printf("$%.2f, ", edna.getSalary());
        System.out.print(edna.getVacationDays() + ", ");
        System.out.println(edna.getVacationForm());

        System.out.print("Secretary: ");
        Secretary stan = new Secretary();
        System.out.print(stan.getHours() + ", ");
        System.out.printf("$%.2f, ", stan.getSalary());
        System.out.print(stan.getVacationDays() + ", ");
        System.out.println(stan.getVacationForm());
        stan.takeDictation("hello");
    }
}
```

The code would produce the following output:

```
Employee: 40, $40000.00, 10, yellow
Secretary: 40, $40000.00, 10, yellow
Dictating text: hello
```

Notice that the first four methods produce the same output for both objects, because Secretary inherits that behavior from Employee. The fifth line of Secretary output reflects the new extended behavior of the takeDictation method.

Overriding Methods

We can use inheritance in our other types of Employees, creating Lawyer, LegalSecretary, and Marketer classes that are subclasses of Employee. But while the Secretary class merely adds behavior to the standard Employee behavior, these other classes also need to replace some of the standard Employee behavior with their own. Lawyers receive three weeks of vacation and use a pink form to apply for vacation, and they know how to handle lawsuits. Legal secretaries receive $45,000 a year (a $5,000 raise over the standard amount), they know how to take dictation (like regular secretaries), and they can file legal briefs. Marketers receive $50,000 a year (a $10,000 raise over the standard amount), and they know how to advertise.

We'd like these new classes to inherit most of the behavior from the Employee class, but we need to change or replace certain parts of the behavior. It's legal to replace superclass behavior by writing new versions of the relevant method(s) in the subclasses. The new version in the subclass will replace the one inherited from Employee. This idea of replacing behavior from the superclass is called *overriding*.

Override

To implement a new version of a method to replace code that would otherwise have been inherited from a superclass.

To override a method, just write the method you want to replace in the subclass. No special syntax is required, but the method's name and signature must exactly match those of the method from the superclass.

Here is the Lawyer class that extends Employee and overrides the relevant methods:

```
// A class to represent lawyers.
public class Lawyer extends Employee {
    // overrides getVacationDays from Employee class
    public int getVacationDays() {
        return 15;
    }

    // overrides getVacationForm from Employee class
    public String getVacationForm() {
        return "pink";
    }

```

```
    // this is the Lawyer's added behavior
    public void sue() {
        System.out.println("I'll see you in court!");
    }
}
```

The `LegalSecretary` class could also be written to extend `Employee`, but it has more in common with `Secretary`. It is legal for a class to extend a class that itself extends a class, creating a multi-level hierarchy. So we will write the class for `LegalSecretary` as an extension of the class `Secretary` so it inherits the ability to take dictation:

```
// A class to represent legal secretaries.
public class LegalSecretary extends Secretary {
    // overrides getSalary from Employee class
    public double getSalary() {
        return 45000.0;
    }

    // new behavior of LegalSecretary objects
    public void fileLegalBriefs() {
        System.out.println("I could file all day!");
    }
}
```

The following client program uses our `Lawyer` and `LegalSecretary` classes. Notice that the legal secretary inherits not only the normal employee behavior, but also the behavior to take dictation from the standard secretary:

```
public class EmployeeMain2 {
    public static void main(String[] args) {
        System.out.print("Lawyer: ");
        Lawyer lucy = new Lawyer();
        System.out.print(lucy.getHours() + ", ");
        System.out.printf("$%.2f, ", lucy.getSalary());
        System.out.print(lucy.getVacationDays() + ", ");
        System.out.println(lucy.getVacationForm());
        lucy.sue();

        System.out.print("Legal Secretary: ");
        LegalSecretary leo = new LegalSecretary();
        System.out.print(leo.getHours() + ", ");
        System.out.printf("$%.2f, ", leo.getSalary());
        System.out.print(leo.getVacationDays() + ", ");
```

```
        System.out.println(leo.getVacationForm());
        leo.takeDictation("neato");
        leo.fileLegalBriefs();
    }
}
```

The program produces the following output:

```
Lawyer: 40, $40000.00, 15, pink
I'll see you in court!
Legal Secretary: 40, $45000.00, 10, yellow
Dictating text: neato
I could file all day!
```

Be careful not to confuse overriding with overloading. Overloading, introduced in Chapter 3, occurs when one class contains multiple methods that have the same name but different parameter signatures. Overriding occurs when a subclass substitutes its own version of an otherwise inherited method that uses exactly the same name and the same parameters.

9.2 Interacting with the Superclass

VideoNote

The classes in the previous sections demonstrated inheritance in classes containing only methods. But you'll want to write more meaningful classes that use inheritance with fields, methods, and constructors. These subclasses require more complex interaction with the state and behavior they inherit from their superclass. To show you how to perform this interaction properly, we'll need to introduce a new keyword called `super`.

Calling Overridden Methods

Suppose things are going well at our example legal firm, so the company decides to give every employee a $10,000 raise. What is the best way to enact this policy change in the code we've written? We can edit the `Employee` class and change its `getSalary` method to return 50000 instead of 40000. But some of the other types of employees have salaries higher than the original $40,000 rate (legal secretaries at $45,000 and marketers at $50,000), and these will need to be raised as well. We'll end up needing to change several files to enact this single overall raise.

The problem is that our existing code does not represent the relationship between the various salaries very well. For example, in the `LegalSecretary` class, instead of saying that we want to return 45000, we'd like to return the `Employee` class's salary plus $5000. You may want to write code like the following, but it does not work, because the `getSalary` method has overridden the one from the superclass, meaning that the code that follows calls itself infinitely:

```
// flawed implementation of LegalSecretary salary code
public double getSalary() {
    return getSalary() + 5000;
}
```

You also can't just call the `Employee` version of `getSalary` by writing `Employee.getSalary()`, because that is the syntax for executing static methods, not instance methods of objects. Instead, Java provides a keyword `super` that refers to a class's superclass. This keyword is used when calling a superclass method or constructor. Here is the general syntax for calling an overridden method using the `super` keyword:

```
super.<method name>(<expression>, <expression>, ..., <expression>)
```

The correct version of the legal secretary's salary code is the following. Writing the marketer's version is left as an exercise.

```
// working LegalSecretary salary code
public double getSalary() {
    return super.getSalary() + 5000; // $5k more than general employees
}
```

Accessing Inherited Fields

To examine the interactions of more complex classes in a hierarchy, let's shift to a more complex example than the employee classes we've been using so far. In Chapter 8's case study, we built a `Stock` class representing purchased shares of a given stock. Here's the code for that class, which has been shortened a bit for this section by removing tests for illegal arguments:

```
// A Stock object represents purchases of shares of a stock.
public class Stock {
    private String symbol;
    private int totalShares;
    private double totalCost;

    // initializes a new Stock with no shares purchased
    public Stock(String symbol) {
        this.symbol = symbol;
        totalShares = 0;
        totalCost = 0.0;
    }
```

```

    // returns the total profit or loss earned on this stock
    public double getProfit(double currentPrice) {
        double marketValue = totalShares * currentPrice;
        return marketValue – totalCost;
    }

    // records purchase of the given shares at the given price
    public void purchase(int shares, double pricePerShare) {
        totalShares += shares;
        totalCost += shares * pricePerShare;
    }
}
```

Now let's imagine that you want to create a type of object for stocks which pay dividends. Dividends are profit-sharing payments that a corporation pays its shareholders. The amount that each shareholder receives is proportional to the number of shares that person owns. Not every stock pays dividends, so you wouldn't want to add this functionality directly to the `Stock` class. Instead, you should create a new class called `DividendStock` that extends `Stock` and adds this new behavior.

Each `DividendStock` object will inherit the symbol, total shares, and total cost from the `Stock` superclass. You'll simply need to add a field to record the amount of the dividends paid:

```
public class DividendStock extends Stock {
    private double dividends; // amount of dividends paid
    ...
}
```

Using the `dividends` field, you can write a method in the `DividendStock` class that lets the shareholder receive a per-share dividend. Your first thought might be to write code like the following, but this won't compile:

```
// this code does not compile
public void payDividend(double amountPerShare) {
    dividends += amountPerShare * totalShares;
}
```

A `DividendStock` cannot access the `totalShares` field it has inherited, because `totalShares` is declared private in `Stock`. A subclass may not refer directly to any private fields that were declared in its superclass, so you'll get a compiler error like the following:

```
DividendStock.java:17: totalShares has private access in Stock
```

It may seem unnecessarily restrictive that a class isn't able to examine the fields it has inherited, since those fields are part of the object. The reason Java is built this way is to prevent a subclass from violating the encapsulation of the superclass. If a superclass object held sensitive data and subclasses were allowed to access that data directly, they could change it in malicious ways the superclass did not intend.

The solution here is to use accessor or mutator methods associated with our fields to access or change their values. The `Stock` class doesn't have a public accessor method for the `totalShares` field, but you can now add a `getTotalShares` method to the `Stock` class:

```
// returns the total shares purchased of this stock
public int getTotalShares() {
    return totalShares;
}
```

Here is a corrected version of the `payDividend` method that uses the `getTotalShares` method from `Stock`:

```
// records a dividend of the given amount per share
public void payDividend(double amountPerShare) {
    dividends += amountPerShare * getTotalShares();
}
```

The `DividendStock` subclass is allowed to call the public `getTotalShares` method, so the code now behaves properly. If we had a similar situation in which subclasses needed to modify total shares from a stock, the `Stock` class would need to provide a `setTotalShares` method or something similar.

Calling a Superclass's Constructor

Unlike other behaviors, constructors are not inherited. You'll have to write your own constructor for the `DividendStock` class, and when you do so the problem of the inability to access private fields will arise again.

The `DividendStock` constructor should accept the same parameter as the `Stock` constructor: the stock symbol. It should have the same behavior as the `Stock` constructor but should also initialize the `dividends` field to `0.0`. The following constructor implementation might seem like a good start, but it is redundant with `Stock`'s constructor and won't compile successfully:

```
// this constructor does not compile
public DividendStock(String symbol) {
    this.symbol = symbol;
    totalShares = 0;
    totalCost = 0.0;
    dividends = 0.0; // this line is the new code
}
```

The compiler produces four errors: one error for each line that tries to access an inherited private field, and a message about a missing `Stock()` constructor:

```
DividendStock.java:5: cannot find symbol
symbol : constructor Stock()
location: class Stock
public DividendStock(String symbol) {
                                    ^
DividendStock.java:6: symbol has private access in Stock
DividendStock.java:7: totalShares has private access in Stock
DividendStock.java:8: totalCost has private access in Stock
```

The first problem is that even though a `DividendStock` does contain the `symbol`, `totalShares`, and `totalCost` fields by inheritance, it cannot refer to them directly because they were declared private in the `Stock` class.

The second problem—the missing `Stock()` constructor—is a subtle and confusing detail of inheritance. A subclass's constructor must always begin by calling a constructor from the superclass. The reason is that a `DividendStock` object partially consists of a `Stock` object, and you must initialize the state of that `Stock` object first by calling a constructor for it. If you don't do so explicitly, the compiler assumes that `Stock` has a parameterless `Stock()` constructor and tries to initialize the `Stock` data by calling this constructor. Since the `Stock` class doesn't actually have a parameterless constructor, the compiler prints a bizarre error message about a missing `Stock()` constructor. (It's a shame that the error message isn't more informative.)

The solution to this problem is to explicitly call the `Stock` constructor that accepts a `String` symbol as its parameter. Java uses the keyword `super` for a subclass to refer to behavior from its superclass. To call a constructor of a superclass, write the keyword `super`, followed by the constructor's parameter values in parentheses:

```
super(<expression>, <expression>, ..., <expression>);
```

In the case of the `DividendStock` constructor, the following code does the trick. Use the `super` keyword to call the superclass constructor, passing it the same `symbol` value that was passed to the `DividendStock` constructor. This action will initialize the `symbol`, `totalShares`, and `totalCost` fields. Then set the initial dividends to `0.0`:

```
// constructs a new dividend stock with the given symbol
// and no shares purchased
public DividendStock(String symbol) {
    super(symbol); // call Stock constructor
    dividends = 0.0;
}
```

The call to the superclass's constructor using `super` must be the first statement in a subclass's constructor. If you reverse the order of the statements in `DividendStock`'s constructor and set the dividends before you call `super`, you'll get a compiler error like the following:

```
Call to super must be first statement in constructor
    super(symbol); // call Stock constructor
    ^
```

Here's the `DividendStock` class so far. The class isn't complete yet because you haven't yet implemented the behavior to make dividend payments:

```
// A DividendStock object represents a stock purchase that also pays
// dividends.
public class DividendStock extends Stock {
    private double dividends; // amount of dividends paid

    // constructs a new dividend stock with the given symbol
    // and no shares purchased
    public DividendStock(String symbol) {
        super(symbol); // call Stock constructor
        this.dividends = 0.0;
    }
    ...
}
```

DividendStock Behavior

To implement dividend payments, we'll begin by writing a method called `payDividend` that accepts a dividend amount per share and adds the proper amount to `DividendStock`'s `dividends` field. The amount per share should be multiplied by the number of shares the shareholder owns:

```
// records a dividend of the given amount per share
public void payDividend(double amountPerShare) {
    dividends += amountPerShare * getTotalShares();
}
```

The dividend payments that are being recorded should be considered to be profit for the stockholder. The overall profit of a `DividendStock` object is equal to the profit from the stock's price plus any dividends. This amount is computed as the market value (number of shares times current price) minus the total cost paid for the shares, plus the amount of dividends paid.

Notice that you don't need to use `super.getTotalShares` in the preceding code. You have to use the `super` keyword only when you are accessing overridden methods or constructors from the superclass. `DividendStock` doesn't override the `getTotalShares` method, so you can call it without the `super` keyword.

Because the profit of a `DividendStock` object is computed differently from that of a regular `Stock` object, you should override the `getProfit` method in the `DividendStock` class to implement this new behavior. An incorrect initial attempt might look like the following code:

```
// this code does not compile
public double getProfit(double currentPrice) {
    double marketValue = totalShares * currentPrice;
    return marketValue – totalCost + dividends;
}
```

The preceding code has two problems. First, you can't refer directly to the various fields that were declared in `Stock`. To get around this problem, you can add accessor methods for each field. The second problem is that the code is redundant: It duplicates much of the functionality from `Stock`'s `getProfit` method, which was shown earlier. The only new behavior is the adding of dividends into the total.

To remove this redundancy, you can have `DividendStock`'s `getProfit` method call `Stock`'s `getProfit` method as part of its computation. However, since the two methods share the same name, you must explicitly tell the compiler that you want to call `Stock`'s version. Again, you do this using the `super` keyword.

Here is the corrected code, which does compile and eliminates the previous redundancy:

```
// returns the total profit or loss earned on this stock,
// including profits made from dividends
public double getProfit(double currentPrice) {
    return super.getProfit(currentPrice) + dividends;
}
```

And here is the code for the completed `DividendStock` class:

```
// A DividendStock object represents a stock purchase that also pays
// dividends.
public class DividendStock extends Stock {
    private double dividends; // amount of dividends paid

    // constructs a new dividend stock with the given symbol
    // and no shares purchased
    public DividendStock(String symbol) {
        super(symbol); // call Stock constructor
        dividends = 0.0;
    }

    // returns the total profit or loss earned on this stock,
```

```
    // including profits made from dividends
    public double getProfit(double currentPrice) {
        return super.getProfit(currentPrice) + dividends;
    }

    // records a dividend of the given amount per share
    public void payDividend(double amountPerShare) {
        dividends += amountPerShare * getTotalShares();
    }
}
```

It's possible to have a deeper inheritance hierarchy with multiple layers of inheritance and overriding. However, the `super` keyword reaches just one level upward to the most recently overridden version of the method. It's not legal to use `super` more than once in a row; you cannot make calls like `super.super.getProfit`. If you need such a solution, you'll have to find a workaround such as using different method names.

The `Object` Class

A class called `Object` serves as the ultimate superclass for all other Java classes, even those that do not declare explicit superclasses in their headers. In fact, classes with headers that do not have `extends` clauses are treated as though their headers say `extends Object` when they are compiled. (You can explicitly write the `extends Object` in a class header, but this is unnecessary and not a common style.)

The `Object` class contains methods that are common to all objects. Table 9.1 summarizes the methods of the `Object` class. Note that some of the methods are not public and therefore cannot be called externally.

In Chapter 8, we mentioned that without a `toString` method in a class, the objects will not print properly. For example, our `Point` class printed `Point@119c082` by

Table 9.1 Methods of the `Object` Class

Method	Description
`clone()`	Creates and returns a copy of the object (not a public method)
`equals(obj)`	Indicates whether the other object is equal to this one
`finalize()`	Called automatically by Java when objects are destroyed (not public)
`getClass()`	Returns information about the type of the object
`hashCode()`	Returns a number associated with the object; used in some collections
`toString()`	Returns the state of the object as a `String`
`notify()`, `notifyAll()`, `wait()`	Advanced methods for multithreaded programming

default before we wrote its `toString` method. This default message was the behavior of the `Object` class's `toString` method, which we inherited in our `Point` class. The `Object` class provides a generic `toString` output that will work for every class: the class name followed by some internal numeric information about the object. When we wrote our own `toString` method, we overrode this default behavior.

It is sometimes useful to refer to the `Object` class in your programs. For example, if you wish to write a method that can accept any object as a parameter, you can declare a parameter of type `Object`:

```
// this method can accept any object as its parameter
public static void myMethod(Object o) {
    ...
}
```

Of course, since your parameter can be anything, you are only allowed to call the methods from the `Object` class on it, such as `toString` or `getClass`. It is also legal to have a method whose return type is `Object`.

The `Object` class is used extensively in the Java class libraries. For example, the `println` method of the `PrintStream` class (the class of which `System.out` is an instance) accepts a parameter of type `Object`, which allows you to print any object to the console.

The `equals` Method

For several chapters now, you have used the == operator to compare for equality. You have seen that this operator does not behave as expected when used on objects, because it is possible to have two distinct objects with equivalent states, such as two `Point` objects with the coordinates (5, 2). This observation is a reminder that an object has an *identity* and is distinct from other objects, even if another object happens to have the same state.

A nonprogramming analogy would be if you and your friend both purchased identical pairs of shoes. They are in some ways equivalent, but you still consider them distinct and separate items. You might not want to share them. And the items' states are not linked in any way. Over time, their state might become visibly unequal, such as if one of you wore your new shoes more often than the other.

The == operator does not behave as expected with objects because it tests whether two objects have the same identity. The == comparison actually tests whether two variables refer to the same object, not whether two distinct objects have the same state. Consider the following three variable declarations:

```
Point p1 = new Point(7, 2);
Point p2 = new Point(7, 2);
Point p3 = p2;
```

The following diagram represents the state of these objects and the variables that refer to them. Notice that `p3` is not a reference to a third object but a second reference to the object that was referred to by `p2`. This means that a change to `p2`, such as a call of its `translate` method, would also be reflected in `p3`:

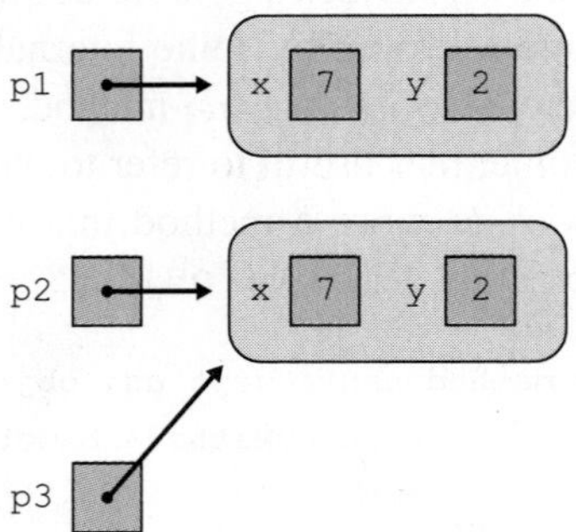

In the case of the preceding `Point` objects, the expression `p1 == p2` would evaluate to false because `p1` and `p2` do not refer to the same object. The object referred to by `p1` has the same state as `p2`'s object, but they have different identities. The expression `p2 == p3` would evaluate to `true`, though, because `p2` does refer to the same object as `p3`.

Often, when comparing two objects, we want to know whether the objects have the same state. To perform such a comparison, we use a special method called `equals`. Every Java object contains an `equals` method that it uses to compare itself to other objects.

The previous section mentioned that a class without a `toString` method receives a default version of the method. Similarly, a class without an `equals` method receives a default version that uses the most conservative definition of equality, considering two objects to be equal only if they have the same identity. This means that the default `equals` method behaves identically to the == operator. If you want a method that will behave differently, you must write your own `equals` method to replace the default behavior.

A proper `equals` method performs a comparison of two objects' states and returns `true` if the states are the same. With the preceding `Point` objects, we'd like the expressions `p1.equals(p2)`, `p1.equals(p3)`, and `p2.equals(p3)` to evaluate to `true` because the `Points` all have the same (*x*, *y*) coordinates.

You can imagine a piece of client code that examines two `Point` objects to see whether they have the same `x` and `y` field values:

```
if (p1.getX() == p2.getX() && p1.getY() == p2.getY()) {
    // the objects have equal state
    ...
}
```

But the `equals` functionality should actually be implemented in the `Point` class itself, not in the client code. Rather than having two `Points`, `p1` and `p2`, the `equals` method considers the first object to be the "implicit parameter" and accepts the second object as a parameter. It returns `true` if the two objects are equal.

The following code is an initial implementation of the `equals` method that has several flaws:

```
// a flawed implementation of an equals method
public boolean equals(Point p2) {
    if (x == p2.getX() && y == p2.getY()) {
        return true;
    } else {
        return false;
    }
}
```

An initial flaw we can correct is that the preceding code doesn't make good use of "Boolean Zen," described in Chapter 5. Recall that when your code uses an `if/else` statement to return a `boolean` value of `true` or `false`, often you can directly return the value of the `if` statement's condition:

```
return x == p2.getX() && y == p2.getY();
```

It's legal for the `equals` method to access `p2`'s fields directly, so we can optionally modify this further. Private fields are visible to their entire class, including other objects of that same class, so it is legal for one `Point` object to examine the fields of another:

```
return x == p2.x && y == p2.y;
```

Some programmers respect `p2`'s encapsulation even against other `Point` objects and therefore would not make the preceding change.

To keep our `equals` method consistent with other Java classes, we must also make a change to its header. The `equals` method's parameter should not be of type `Point`. The method must instead accept a parameter of type `Object`:

```
public boolean equals(Object o)
```

A variable or parameter of type `Object` can refer to any Java object, which means that any object may be passed as the parameter to the `equals` method. Thus, we can compare `Point` objects against any type of object, not just other `Points`. For example, an expression such as `p1.equals("hello")` would now be legal. The `equals` method should return `false` in such a case because the parameter isn't a `Point`.

You might think that the following code would correctly compare the two `Point` objects and return the proper result. Unfortunately, it does not even compile successfully:

```
return x == o.x && y == o.y; // does not compile
```

The Java compiler doesn't allow us to write an expression such as `o.x` because it doesn't know ahead of time whether `o`'s object will have a field called `x`. The preceding code produces errors such as the following for each of `o`'s fields that we try to access:

```
Point.java:36: cannot find symbol
symbol : variable x
location: class java.lang.Object
```

If we want to treat `o` as a `Point` object, we must cast it from type `Object` to type `Point`. We've already discussed typecasting to convert between primitive types, such as casting `double` to `int`. Casting between object types has a different meaning. A cast of an object is a promise to the compiler. The cast is your assurance that the reference actually refers to a different type and that the compiler can treat it as that type. In our method, we'll write a statement that casts `o` into a `Point` object so the compiler will trust that we can access its `x` and `y` fields:

```
// returns whether the two Points have the same (x, y) values
public boolean equals(Object o) {
    Point other = (Point) o;
    return x == other.x && y == other.y;
}
```

Don't forget that if your object has fields that are objects themselves, such as a string or `Point` as a field, then those fields should be compared for equality using their `equals` method and not using the == operator.

The instanceof Keyword

By changing our `equals` method's parameter to type `Object`, we have allowed objects that are not `Points` to be passed. However, our method still doesn't behave properly when clients pass these objects. An expression in client code such as `p.equals("hello")` will produce an exception like the following at runtime:

```
Exception in thread "main"
java.lang.ClassCastException: java.lang.String
        at Point.equals(Point.java:25)
        at PointMain.main(PointMain.java:25)
```

The exception occurs because it is illegal to cast a `String` into a `Point`; these are not compatible types of objects. To prevent the exception, our `equals` method will need to examine the type of the parameter and return `false` if it isn't a `Point`. The following pseudocode shows the pattern that the code should follow:

```
public boolean equals(Object o) {
    if (o is a Point object) {
        compare the x and y values.
```

```
    } else {
        return false, because o is not a Point object.
    }
}
```

An operator called `instanceof` tests whether a variable refers to an object of a given type. An `instanceof` test is a binary expression that takes the following form and produces a `boolean` result:

```
<expression> instanceof <type>
```

Table 9.2 lists some example expressions using `instanceof` and their results, given the following variables:

```
String s = "carrot";
Point p = new Point(8, 1);
```

Table 9.2 Sample `instanceof` Expressions

Expression	Result
`s instanceof String`	`true`
`s instanceof Point`	`false`
`p instanceof String`	`false`
`p instanceof Point`	`true`
`"hello" instanceof String`	`true`
`null instanceof Point`	`false`

The `instanceof` operator is unusual because it looks like the name of a method but is used more like a relational operator such as > or ==. It is separated from its operands by spaces but doesn't require parentheses, dots, or any other notation. The operand on the left side is generally a variable, and the operand on the right is the name of the class against which you wish to test.

We must examine the parameter `o` in our `equals` method to see whether it is a `Point` object. The following code uses the `instanceof` keyword to implement the `equals` method correctly:

```
// returns whether o refers to a Point with the same (x, y)
// coordinates as this Point
public boolean equals(Object o) {
    if (o instanceof Point) {
        Point other = (Point) o;
        return x == other.x && y == other.y;
    } else { // not a Point object
```

```
            return false;
        }
}
```

You might think that our `instanceof` test would allow us to remove the type cast below it. After all, the `instanceof` test ensures that the comparison occurs only when `o` refers to a `Point` object. However, the type cast cannot be removed because the compiler doesn't allow the code to compile without it.

A nice side benefit of the `instanceof` operator is that it produces a `false` result when `o` is `null`. Thus, if the client code contains an expression such as `p1.equals(null)`, it will correctly return `false` rather than throwing a `NullPointerException`.

Many classes implement an `equals` method like ours, so much of the preceding `equals` code can be reused as boilerplate code. The following is a template for a well-formed `equals` method. The `instanceof` test and type cast are likely the first two things you'll want to do in any `equals` method that you write:

```
public boolean equals(Object o) {
    if (o instanceof <type>) {
        <type> <name> = (<type>) o;
        <compare the data and return the result.>
    } else {
        return false;
    }
}
```

9.3 Polymorphism

VideoNote

One of the most powerful benefits of inheritance is that it allows client code to treat different kinds of objects in the same way. For example, with the employee class hierarchy described earlier, it's possible for client code to create an array or other data structure that contains both lawyers and legal secretaries, and then perform operations on each element of that array. The client code will behave differently depending on the type of object that is used, because each subclass overrides and changes some of the behavior from the superclass. This ability for the same code to be used with several different types of objects is called *polymorphism.*

> **Polymorphism**
>
> The ability for the same code to be used with several different types of objects and for the code to behave differently depending on the actual type of object used.

Polymorphism is made possible by the fact that the type of a reference variable (one that refers to an object) does not have to exactly match the type of the object it refers to. More specifically, it is legal for a superclass variable to refer to an object of its subclass. The following is a legal assignment statement:

```
Employee ed = new Lawyer();
```

When we were studying the primitive types, we saw cases in which a variable of one type could store a value of another type (for example, an `int` value can be stored in a `double` variable). In the case of primitive values, Java converts variables from one type to another: `int` values are automatically converted to `doubles` when they are assigned.

When a subclass object is stored in a superclass variable, no such conversion occurs. The object referred to by `ed` really is a `Lawyer` object, not an `Employee` object. If we call methods on it, it will behave like a `Lawyer` object. For example, the call of `ed.getVacationForm()` returns `"pink"`, which is the `Lawyer`'s behavior, not the `Employee`'s.

This ability for variables to refer to subclass objects allows us to write flexible code that can interact with many types of objects in the same way. For example, we can write a method that accepts an `Employee` as a parameter, returns an `Employee`, or creates an array of `Employee` objects. In any of these cases, we can substitute a `Secretary`, `Lawyer`, or other subclass object of `Employee`, and the code will still work. Even more importantly, code will actually behave differently depending on which type of object is used, because each subclass overrides and changes some of the behavior from the superclass. This is polymorphism at work.

Here is an example test file that uses `Employee` objects polymorphically as parameters to a static method:

```
// Demonstrates polymorphism by passing many types of employees
// as parameters to the same method.
public class EmployeeMain3 {
    public static void main(String[] args) {
        Employee edna = new Employee();
        Lawyer lucy = new Lawyer();
        Secretary stan = new Secretary();
        LegalSecretary leo = new LegalSecretary();

        printInfo(edna);
        printInfo(lucy);
        printInfo(stan);
        printInfo(leo);
    }

    // Prints information about any kind of employee.
    public static void printInfo(Employee e) {
        System.out.print(e.getHours() + ", ");
```

```
            System.out.printf("$%.2f, ", e.getSalary());
            System.out.print(e.getVacationDays() + ", ");
            System.out.print(e.getVacationForm() + ", ");
            System.out.println(e); // toString representation of employee
    }
}
```

Notice that the method lets us pass many different types of `Employees` as parameters, and it produces different behavior depending on the type that is passed. Polymorphism gives us this flexibility. The last token of output printed for each employee is the employee object itself, which calls the `toString` method on the object. Our classes don't have `toString` methods, so the program uses the default behavior, which prints the class name plus some extra hexadecimal characters. This allows us to distinguish the classes in the output. The program produces output such as the following:

```
40, $40000.00, 10, yellow, Employee@10b30a7
40, $40000.00, 15, pink, Lawyer@1a758cb
40, $40000.00, 10, yellow, Secretary@1b67f74
40, $45000.00, 10, yellow, LegalSecretary@69b332
```

The word "polymorphism" comes from the Greek words "poly" and "morph," which mean "many" and "forms," respectively. The lines of code in the `printInfo` method are polymorphic because their behavior will take many forms depending on what type of employee is passed as the parameter.

The program doesn't know which `getSalary` or `getVacationForm` method to call until it's actually running. When the program reaches a particular call to an object's method, it examines the actual object to see which method to call. This concept has taken many names over the years, such as *late binding*, *virtual binding*, and *dynamic dispatch.*

When you send messages to an object stored in a variable of a superclass type, it is legal only to call methods that are known to the superclass. For example, the following code will not compile because the `Employee` class does not have a `takeDictation` or `fileLegalBriefs` method:

```
Employee ed = new LegalSecretary();
ed.takeDictation("Hello!"); // compiler error
ed.fileLegalBriefs(); // compiler error
```

The compiler does not allow this code because the variable `ed` could theoretically refer to any kind of employee, including one that does not know how to take dictation or file legal briefs. Even though we know it must refer to a `LegalSecretary` because the code is so simple, the compiler enforces this rule strictly and returns an error message. The same thing happens if you write a method that accepts an `Employee` as a parameter; you cannot call subclass-only methods such as `takeDictation`, `sue`, or `fileLegalBriefs` on the object that is passed in, even if the actual object might have those methods.

The variable's type can be any type equal or higher in the inheritance hierarchy compared to the actual object. So we could store a legal secretary in a variable of type `Secretary`, which would allow us to execute any standard secretary behavior, including taking dictation:

```
Secretary steve = new LegalSecretary();
steve.takeDictation("Hello!"); // OK
steve.fileLegalBriefs(); // compiler error
```

It is legal to cast a variable into a different type of reference in order to make a call on it. This does not change the type of the object, but it promises the compiler that the variable really refers to an object of the other type. For example, the following code works successfully:

```
Employee ed = new Secretary();
((Secretary) ed).takeDictation("Hello!"); // OK
```

You can only cast a reference to a compatible type, one above or below it in its inheritance hierarchy. The preceding code will compile, but it would crash at runtime if the variable `ed` did not actually refer to an object of type `Secretary` or one of its subclasses.

Polymorphism Mechanics

Inheritance and polymorphism introduce some complex new mechanics and behavior into programs. One useful way to get the hang of these mechanics is to perform exercises to interpret the behavior of programs with inheritance. The main goal of these exercises is to help you understand in detail what happens when a Java program with inheritance executes.

The `EmployeeMain3` program developed in the previous section serves as a template for inheritance questions of the following form: Given a certain hierarchy of classes, what behavior would result if we created several objects of the different types and called their various methods on them?

In order to use polymorphism and keep our program compact, we'll store the objects in an array. In the case of the `Employee` hierarchy, it's legal for an object of class `Lawyer`, `Secretary`, or any other subclass of `Employee` to reside as an element of an `Employee[]`.

The following program produces the same output as the `EmployeeMain3` program from the previous section:

```
public class EmployeeMain4 {
    public static void main(String[] args) {
```

```
        Employee[] employees = {new Employee(), new Lawyer(),
            new Secretary(), new LegalSecretary()};

        // print information about each employee
        for (Employee e : employees) {
            System.out.print(e.getHours() + ", ");
            System.out.printf("$%.2f, ", e.getSalary());
            System.out.print(e.getVacationDays() + ", ");
            System.out.print(e.getVacationForm() + ", ");
            System.out.println(e); // calls toString
        }
    }
}
```

Even if you didn't understand inheritance, you might be able to deduce some things about the hierarchy from the classes' names and the relationships among employees in the real world. So let's take this exercise one step further. Instead of using descriptive names for the classes, we'll use letters so that you have to read the code in order to determine the class relationships and behavior.

Assume that the following classes have been defined:

```
public class A {
    public void method1() {
        System.out.println("A 1");
    }

    public void method2() {
        System.out.println("A 2");
    }

    public String toString() {
        return "A";
    }
}
```

```
public class B extends A {
    public void method2() {
        System.out.println("B 2");
    }
}
```

```
public class C extends A {
    public void method1() {
        System.out.println("C 1");
    }

```

```
    public String toString() {
        return "C";
    }
}
```

```
public class D extends C {
    public void method2() {
        System.out.println("D 2");
    }
}
```

Consider the following client code that uses these classes. It takes advantage of the fact that every other class extends class `A` (either directly or indirectly), so the array can be of type `A[]`. When you call methods on the elements of the array, polymorphic behavior will result:

```
// Client program to use the A, B, C, and D classes.
public class ABCDMain {
    public static void main(String[] args) {
        A[] elements = {new A(), new B(), new C(), new D()};

        for (int i = 0; i < elements.length; i++) {
            System.out.println(elements[i]);
            elements[i].method1();
            elements[i].method2();
            System.out.println();
        }
    }
}
```

It's difficult to interpret such code and correctly determine its output. In the next section we'll present techniques for doing so.

Interpreting Inheritance Code

To determine the output of a polymorphic program like the one in the previous section, you must determine what happens when each element is printed (i.e., when its `toString` method is called) and when its `method1` and `method2` methods are called. You can draw a diagram of the classes and their methods to see the hierarchy ordering and see which methods exist in each class. Draw each class as a box listing its methods, and connect subclasses to their superclasses with arrows, as shown in Figure 9.2. (This is a simplified version of a common design document called a UML class diagram.)

A good second step is to write a table that lists each class and its methods' output. Write the output not just for the methods defined in each class, but also for the ones that the class inherits. Since the `A` class is at the top of the hierarchy, we'll start there.

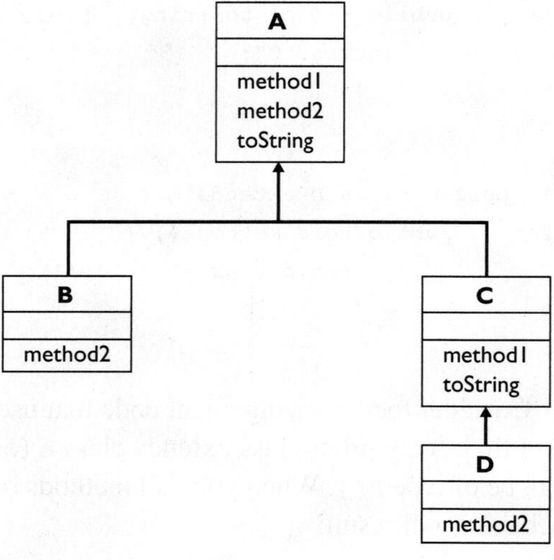

Figure 9.2 Hierarchy of classes A, B, C, and D

When someone calls `method1` on an `A` object, the resulting output is `"A 1"`. When someone calls `method2` on an `A` object, the resulting output is `"A 2"`. When someone prints an `A` object with `toString`, the resulting output is `"A"`. We can fill in the first column of our table as shown in Table 9.3.

Table 9.3 Method Output for Class `A`

	A
toString	A
method1	A 1
method2	A 2

The next layer in the hierarchy is the `B` class, which inherits all the behavior from `A`, except that it overrides the `method2` output to be `"B 2"`. That means you can fill in the `B` output on your table identically to the `A` output, except that you replace `"A 2"` with `"B 2"`. Table 9.4 shows the table so far.

Table 9.4 Method Output for Classes `A` and `B`

	A	**B**
toString	A	A
method1	A 1	A 1
method2	A 2	B 2

The `C` class also inherits all the behavior from `A`, but it overrides the `method1` output to be `"C 1"` and it overrides the `toString` method to return `"C"`. Thus, the `C` output in the table will have the same second line as the `A` output, but we replace `"A 1"` with `"C 1"` and `"A"` with `"C"`. Table 9.5 shows the updated table.

Table 9.5 Method Output for Classes `A`, `B`, and `C`

	A	B	C
toString	A	A	C
method1	A 1	A 1	C 1
method2	A 2	B 2	A 2

The `D` class inherits all the behavior from `C`, except that it overrides the `method2` output to say `"D 2"`. The final output data are shown in Table 9.6.

Table 9.6 Method Output for Classes `A`, `B`, `C`, and `D`

	A	B	C	D
toString	A	A	C	C
method1	A 1	A 1	C 1	C 1
method2	A 2	B 2	A 2	D 2

Once you've created your table, you can find the output of the client code. The array contains an `A` object, a `B` object, a `C` object, and a `D` object. For each of these it prints the `toString` output, then calls `method1`, then calls `method2`, then prints a blank line. When a method gets called on an object, you can look up the output of that method for that type in the table. The following is the complete output for the exercise:

```
A
A 1
A 2

A
A 1
B 2

C
C 1
A 2

C
C 1
D 2
```

Interpreting Complex Calls

In a more complicated version of the previous inheritance exercise, a class's methods might call each other or interact with the superclass. Consider the following classes.

Notice that they are listed in random order and that their methods' behavior is more complicated than the previous example:

```
public class E extends F {
    public void method2() {
        System.out.print("E 2 ");
        method1();
    }
}
```

```
public class F extends G {
    public String toString() {
        return "F";
    }

    public void method2() {
        System.out.print("F 2 ");
        super.method2();
    }
}
```

```
public class G {
    public String toString() {
        return "G";
    }

    public void method1() {
        System.out.print("G 1 ");
    }

    public void method2() {
        System.out.print("G 2 ");
    }
}
```

```
public class H extends E {
    public void method1() {
        System.out.print("H 1 ");
    }
}
```

In order to determine the best order in which to examine the classes, you could draw a diagram like the one in Figure 9.2. Then make a table and fill in each class's behavior from top to bottom in the hierarchy. First identify the top class in the hierarchy. Look for the one whose header has no `extends` clause. In this example, that is the `G` class. Its methods have simple behavior, so we can fill in that row of the table immediately, as shown in Table 9.7.

Table 9.7 Method Output for Class `G`

	G
toString	G
method1	G 1
method2	G 2

The next class in the hierarchy is `F`, which extends `G`. The `method1` is not overridden, so its output is `"G 1 "` as it was in the superclass. `F` does override `toString` to return `"F"`. It also overrides `method2` to print `"F 2 "` and then call the superclass's (`G`'s) version of `method2`. When there is a call to a superclass's method, we can evaluate its output immediately and put it into our table by looking at the superclass. This means that the `F` class's `method2` prints `"F 2 G 2"`. Table 9.8 shows this information.

Table 9.8 Method Output for Classes `F` and `G`

	F	G
toString	F	G
method1	G 1	G 1
method2	F 2 G 2	G 2

The next class to tackle is `E`, which extends `F`. It does not override `method1` or `toString`, so these methods produce the same output as they do in superclass `F`. Class `E` does override `method2` to print `"E 2 "` and then call `method1`. Since `method1` prints `"G 1 "`, calling `method2` on an `E` object prints `"E 2 G 1 "`.

But here's where things get tricky: You shouldn't write this output in your table. The reason will become clear when we look at the `H` class, which is a subclass of `E` that overrides `method1`. Because of polymorphism, if you call `method2` on an `H` object, when it makes the inner call to `method1`, it will use the version from the `H` class. What you should write into your table for `E`'s `method2` output is that it prints `"E 2 "` and then calls `method1`. Table 9.9 shows the information for class `E`.

Table 9.9 Method Output for Classes `E`, `F`, and `G`

	E	F	G
toString	F	F	G
method1	G 1	G 1	G 1
method2	E 2 method1()	F 2 G 2	G 2

Lastly we will examine class `H`, which extends `E`. It does not override `toString`, so it produces the same output as in superclass `E`. It overrides only `method1` to print `"H 1 "`. These methods are simple (they don't call any others), so we can write the `toString` and `method1` output into the table immediately.

Table 9.10 Method Output for Classes E, F, G, and H

	E	F	G	H
toString	F	F	G	F
method1	G 1	G 1	G 1	H 1
method2	E 2 method1()	F 2 G 2	G 2	E 2 method1()

Class `H` doesn't override `method2`, so you may think that you can copy over its output from superclass `E`. But remember that the inherited `method2` prints `"E 2 "` and then calls `method1`. In this case, we are thinking from the perspective of an `H` object. So that inner call to `method1` now prints `"H 1 "` instead of the old output. This means that calling `method2` on an `H` object actually prints `"E 2 H 1 "`. Table 9.10 shows the final output for all methods.

9.4 Inheritance and Design

Inheritance affects the thought processes you should use when designing object-oriented solutions to programming problems. You should be aware of similarities between classes and potentially capture those similarities with inheritance relationships and hierarchies. The designers of the Java class libraries have followed these principles, as we'll see when we examine a graphical subclass in this section.

However, there are also situations in which using inheritance seems like a good choice but turns out to produce poor results. Misuse of inheritance can introduce some pitfalls and problems that we'll now examine.

A Misuse of Inheritance

Imagine that you want to write a program that deals with points in three-dimensional space, such as a three-dimensional game, rendering program, or simulation. A `Point3D` class would be useful for storing the positions of objects in such a program.

This seems to be a case in which inheritance will be useful to extend the functionality of existing code. Many programmers would be tempted to have `Point3D` extend `Point` and simply add the new code for the *z*-coordinate. Here's a quick implementation of a minimal `Point3D` class that extends `Point`:

```
// A Point3D object represents an (x, y, z) location.
// This is not a good design to follow.

public class Point3D extends Point {
    private int z;

    // constructs a new 3D point with the given coordinates
    public Point3D(int x, int y, int z) {
```

```
        super(x, y);
        this.z = z;
    }

    // returns the z-coordinate of this Point3D
    public int getZ() {
        return z;
    }
}
```

On the surface, this seems to be a reasonable implementation. However, consider the `equals` method defined in the `Point` class. It compares the *x*- and *y*-coordinates of two `Point` objects and returns `true` if they are the same:

```
// returns whether o refers to a Point with the same
// (x, y) coordinates as this Point
public boolean equals(Object o) {
    if (o instanceof Point) {
        Point other = (Point) o;
        return x == other.x && y == other.y;
    } else { // not a Point object
        return false;
    }
}
```

You might also want to write an `equals` method for the `Point3D` class. Two `Point3D` objects are equal if they have the same *x*-, *y*-, and *z*-coordinates. The following is a working implementation of `equals` that is correct but stylistically unsatisfactory:

```
public boolean equals(Object o) {
    if (o instanceof Point3D) {
        Point3D p = (Point3D) o;
        return getX() == p.getX() && getY() == p.getY() && z == p.z;
    } else {
        return false;
    }
}
```

The preceding code compiles and runs correctly in many cases, but it has a subtle problem that occurs when you compare `Point` objects to `Point3D` objects. The `Point` class's `equals` method tests whether the parameter is an instance of `Point` and returns `false` if it is not. However, the `instanceof` operator will return `true` not only if the variable refers to that type, but also if it refers to any of its subclasses. Consider the following test in the `equals` method of the `Point` class:

```
if (o instanceof Point) {
    ...
}
```

The test will evaluate to `true` if `o` refers to a `Point` object or a `Point3D` object. The `instanceof` operator is like an is-a test, asking whether the variable refers to any type that can fill the role of a `Point`. By contrast, `Point3D`'s `equals` method tests whether the parameter is an instance of `Point3D` and rejects it if it is not. A `Point` cannot fill the role of a `Point3D` (not every `Point` is a `Point3D`), so the method will return `false` if the parameter is of type `Point`.

Consequently, the `equals` behavior is not symmetric when it is used with a mixture of `Point` and `Point3D` objects. The following client code demonstrates the problem:

```
Point p = new Point(12, 7);
Point3D p3d = new Point3D(12, 7, 11);
System.out.println("p.equals(p3d) is " + p.equals(p3d));
System.out.println("p3d.equals(p) is " + p3d.equals(p));
```

The code produces the output that follows. The first test returns `true` because a `Point` can accept a `Point3D` as the parameter to `equals`, but the second test returns `false` because a `Point3D` cannot accept a `Point` as its parameter to `equals`:

```
p.equals(p3d) is true
p3d.equals(p) is false
```

This is a problem, because the contract of the `equals` method requires it to be a symmetric operation. You'd encounter other problems if you added more behavior to `Point3D`, such as a `setLocation` or `distance` method.

Proper object-oriented design would not allow `Point3D` to extend `Point`, because any code that asks for a `Point` object should be able to work correctly with a `Point3D` object as well. We call this principle *substitutability*. (It is also sometimes called the Liskov substitution principle, in honor of the Turing Award–winning author of a 1993 paper describing the idea.)

Substitutability

The ability of an object of a subclass to be used successfully anywhere an object of the superclass is expected.

Fundamentally, a `Point3D` isn't the same thing as a `Point`, so an is-a relationship with inheritance is the wrong choice. In this case, you're better off writing `Point3D` from scratch and avoiding these thorny issues.

Is-a Versus Has-a Relationships

There are ways to connect related objects without using inheritance. Consider the task of writing a `Circle` class, in which each `Circle` object is specified by a center point and a radius. It might be tempting to have `Circle` extend `Point` and add the `radius` field. However, this approach is a poor choice because a class is only supposed to capture one abstraction, and a circle simply isn't a point.

A point does make up a fundamental part of the state of each `Circle` object, though. To capture this relationship in the code, you can have each `Circle` object hold a `Point` object in a field to represent its center. One object containing another as state is called a *has-a relationship.*

> **Has-a Relationship**
>
> A connection between two objects where one has a field that refers to the other. The contained object acts as part of the containing object's state.

Has-a relationships are preferred over is-a relationships in cases in which your class cannot or should not substitute for the other class. As a nonprogramming analogy, people occasionally need legal services in their lives, but most of them will choose to *have* a lawyer handle the situation rather than to *be* a lawyer themselves.

The following code presents a potential initial implementation of the `Circle` class:

```
// Represents circular shapes.
public class Circle {
    private Point center;
    private double radius;

    // constructs a new circle with the given radius
    public Circle(Point center, double radius) {
        this.center = center;
        this.radius = radius;
    }

    // returns the area of this circle
    public double getArea() {
        return Math.PI * radius * radius;
    }
}
```

This design presents a `Circle` object as a single clear abstraction and prevents awkward commingling of `Circle` and `Point` objects.

Graphics2D

Use of inheritance is prevalent in the Java class libraries. One notable example is in the drawing of two-dimensional graphics. In this section we'll discuss a class that uses inheritance to draw complex two-dimensional shapes and to assign colors to them.

In the Chapter 3 supplement on graphics, we introduced an object called `Graphics` which acts like a pen that you can use to draw shapes and lines onto a window. When Java's designers wanted additional graphical functionality, they extended the `Graphics` class into a more powerful class called `Graphics2D`. This is a good example of one of the more common uses of inheritance: to extend and reuse functionality from a powerful existing object.

Why didn't the designers of Java simply add the new methods into the existing `Graphics` class? The `Graphics` class already worked properly, so they decided it was best not to perform unnecessary surgery on it. John Vlissides, part of a famous foursome of software engineers affectionately called the "Gang of Four," once described the idea this way: "A hallmark—if not the hallmark—of good object-oriented design is that you can modify and extend a system by adding code rather than by hacking it. In short, change is additive, not invasive."

Making `Graphics2D` extend `Graphics` retains *backward compatibility*. Backward compatibility is the ability of new code to work correctly with old code without modifying the old code. Leaving `Graphics` untouched ensured that old programs would keep working properly and gave new programs the option to use the new `Graphics2D` functionality.

The documentation for `Graphics2D` describes the purpose of the class as follows. "This `Graphics2D` class extends the `Graphics` class to provide more sophisticated control over geometry, coordinate transformations, color management, and text layout. This is the fundamental class for rendering 2-dimensional shapes, text, and images on the Java™ platform." To be specific, `Graphics2D` adds the ability to perform transformations such as scaling and rotation when you're drawing. These capabilities can lead to some fun and interesting images on the screen.

If you used the `DrawingPanel` class from Chapter 3's graphical supplement, you previously wrote statements like the following to get access to the panel's `Graphics` object:

```
Graphics g = panel.getGraphics();
```

Actually, the `getGraphics` method doesn't return a `Graphics` object at all, but rather a `Graphics2D` object. Because of polymorphism, though, it is legal for your program to treat it as a `Graphics` object, because every `Graphics2D` object "is" a `Graphics` object. To use it as a `Graphics2D` object instead, simply write the following line of code:

```
Graphics2D g2 = panel.getGraphics();
```

Table 9.11 Useful Methods of `Graphics2D` Objects

Method	Description
`rotate(angle)`	Rotates subsequently drawn items by the given angle in radians with respect to the origin
`scale(sx, sy)`	Adjusts the size of any subsequently drawn items by the given factors (1.0 means equal size)
`shear(shx, shy)`	Gives a slant to any subsequently drawn items
`translate(dx, dy)`	Shifts the origin by (*dx*, *dy*) in the current coordinate system

Table 9.11 lists some of `Graphics2D`'s extra methods.

The following program demonstrates `Graphics2D`. The `rotate` method's parameter is an angle of rotation measured in radians instead of degrees. Rather than memorizing the conversion between degrees and radians, we can use a static method from the `Math` class called `toRadians` that converts a degree value into the equivalent radian value:

```
// Draws a picture of rotating squares using Graphics2D.

import java.awt.*;

public class FancyPicture {
    public static void main(String[] args) {
        DrawingPanel panel = new DrawingPanel(250, 220);
        Graphics2D g2 = panel.getGraphics();
        g2.translate(100, 120);
        g2.fillRect(–5, –5, 10, 10);

        for (int i = 0; i <= 12; i++) {
            g2.setColor(Color.BLUE);
            g2.fillRect(20, 20, 20, 20);

            g2.setColor(Color.BLACK);
            g2.drawString("" + i, 20, 20);

            g2.rotate(Math.toRadians(30));
            g2.scale(1.1, 1.1);
        }
    }
}
```

Figure 9.3 shows the program's output.

Figure 9.3 Output of `FancyPicture`

9.5 Interfaces

Inheritance is a very useful tool because it enables polymorphism and code sharing, but it does have several limitations. Because Java uses single inheritance, a class can extend only one superclass. This makes it impossible to use inheritance to set up multiple is-a relationships for classes that share multiple characteristics, such as an employee who is both part-time and a secretary. (Some languages, such as C++, do allow multiple inheritance, but this can be complicated and cause subtle problems, so the designers of Java left it out of the language.) There are also situations in which you want is-a relationships and polymorphism but you don't want to share code, in which case inheritance isn't the right tool for the job.

To this end, Java provides a feature called an *interface* that can represent a common supertype between several classes without code sharing.

Interface

A type that consists of a set of method declarations; when classes promise to implement an interface, you can treat those classes similarly in your code.

An interface is like a class, but it contains only method headers without bodies. A class can promise to *implement* an interface, meaning that the class promises to provide implementations of all the methods that are declared in the interface. Classes that implement an interface form an is-a relationship with that interface. In a system with an interface that is implemented by several classes, polymorphic code can handle objects from any of the classes that implement that interface.

A nonprogramming analogy for an interface is a professional certification. It's possible for a person to become certified as a teacher, nurse, accountant, or doctor. To do this, the person must demonstrate certain abilities required of members of those professions. When employers hire someone who has received the proper certification, they expect that the person will be able to perform certain job duties. An interface acts as a certification that classes can meet by implementing all the behavior described in the interface. Code that receives an object implementing an interface can rely on the object having certain behavior.

Interfaces are also used to define roles that objects can play; for example, a `Date` class might implement the `Comparable` interface to indicate that `Date` objects can be compared to each other, or a `Point` class might implement the `Cloneable` interface to indicate that a `Point` object can be replicated.

Interfaces are used in many other places in Java's class libraries. Here are just a few of Java's important interfaces:

- The `ActionListener` interface in the `java.awt` package is used to assign behavior to events when a user clicks on a button or other graphical control.
- The `Serializable` interface in the `java.io` package denotes classes whose objects may be saved to files and transferred over a network.
- The `Comparable` interface allows you to describe how to compare objects of your type to determine which are less than, greater than, or equal to each other. This technique can be used to search or sort a collection of objects.
- The `Formattable` interface lets objects describe different ways that they can be printed by the `System.out.printf` command.
- The `Runnable` interface is used for multithreading, which allows a program to execute two pieces of code at the same time.
- Interfaces such as `List`, `Set`, `Map`, and `Iterator` in the `java.util` package describe data structures that you can use to store collections of objects.

We will cover some of these interfaces in later chapters.

An Interface for Shapes

In this section, we'll use an interface to define a polymorphic hierarchy of shape classes without sharing code between them. Imagine that we are creating classes to represent many different types of shapes, such as rectangles, circles, and triangles. We might be tempted to use inheritance with these shape classes because they seem to share some common behavior (all shapes have an area and a perimeter, for example).

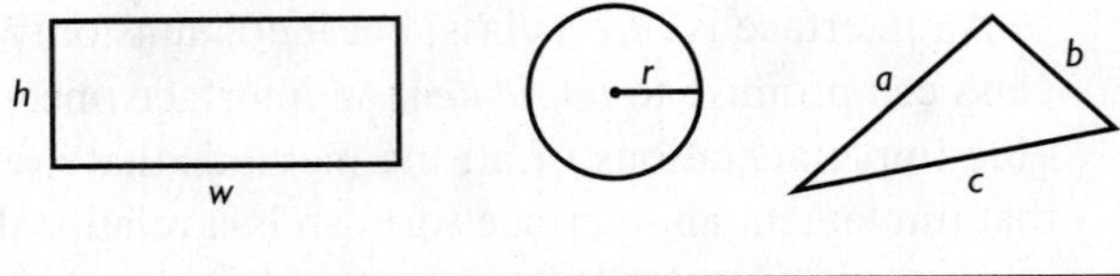

Figure 9.4 Three types of shapes

There is an is-a relationship here, because a rectangle, a circle, and a triangle are all shapes. But code sharing isn't useful in this case because each class implements its behavior differently. As depicted in Figure 9.4 and Table 9.12, each shape computes its area and perimeter in a totally different way. The w and h represent the rectangle's width and height; the r represents the circle's radius; and the a, b, and c represent the lengths of the triangle's three sides.

Since no code is shared among these classes, we should not create a common superclass to represent their is-a relationship. Java uses single inheritance, and we don't want to use up our only potential inheritance relationship here. A better solution would be to write an interface called `Shape` to represent the common functionality of all shapes: the ability to ask for an area and a perimeter. Our various shape classes will implement this interface.

To write an interface, we create a new file with the same name as the interface's name; our `Shape` interface, for example, would be stored in `Shape.java`. We give the interface a header with the keyword `interface` in place of the word `class`:

```
public interface Shape {
    ...
}
```

Inside the interface, we write headers for each method that we want a `Shape` to contain. But instead of writing method bodies with braces, we simply place a semicolon at the end of each header. We don't specify how the methods are implemented. Instead, we're requiring that any class that wants to be considered a shape must implement these methods. In fact, it isn't legal for an interface to contain method bodies; an interface can only contain method headers and class constants.

Table 9.12 Formulas for Area and Perimeter of Each Shape Type

	Rectangle	Circle	Triangle
Area	$w * h$	πr^2	$\sqrt{s(s-a)(s-b)(s-c)}$ where $s = \dfrac{a+b+c}{2}$
Perimeter	$2(w+h)$	$2\pi r$	$a+b+c$

The following is the complete code for our `Shape` interface. It declares that shapes have methods to compute their areas and perimeters as type `double`:

```
// A general interface for shape classes.
public interface Shape {
    public double getArea();
    public double getPerimeter();
}
```

The methods of an interface are sometimes called *abstract methods* because we only declare their names and signatures; we don't specify how they will be implemented.

Abstract Method

A method that is declared (as in an interface) but not implemented. Abstract methods represent the behavior that a class promises to implement when it implements an interface.

Writing the `public` keyword on an interface's method headers is optional. We chose to include the `public` keyword so that the declarations in the interface would match the headers of the method implementations in the classes. The general syntax we'll use for declaring an interface is the following:

```
public interface <name> {
    public <type> <name>(<type> <name>, ..., <type> <name>);
    public <type> <name>(<type> <name>, ..., <type> <name>);
    ...
    public <type> <name>(<type> <name>, ..., <type> <name>);
}
```

Although superficially, classes and interfaces look alike, an interface cannot be *instantiated;* that is, you cannot create objects of its type. In our case, any code trying to create a `new Shape()` would not compile. It is, however, legal to declare variables of type `Shape` that can refer to any object that implements the `Shape` interface, as we'll explore in a moment.

Implementing an Interface

Now that we've written a `Shape` interface, we want to connect the various classes of shapes to it. To connect a class to our interface with an is-a relationship, we must do two things:

1. Declare that the class "implements" the interface.

2. Implement each of the interface's methods in the class.

The general syntax for declaring that a class implements an interface is the following:

```
public class <name> implements <interface> {
    ...
}
```

We must modify the headers of our various shape classes to indicate that they implement all of the methods in the `Shape` interface. The file `Rectangle.java`, for example, should begin like this:

```
public class Rectangle implements Shape {
    ...
}
```

When we claim that our `Rectangle` class implements `Shape`, we are promising that the `Rectangle` class will contain implementations of the `getArea` and `getPerimeter` methods. If a class claims to implement `Shape` but does not have a suitable `getArea` or `getPerimeter` method, it will not compile. For example, if we leave the body of our `Rectangle` class empty and try to compile it, the compiler will give errors like the following:

```
Rectangle.java:2: Rectangle is not abstract and does not override abstract
    method getPerimeter()
public class Rectangle implements Shape {
       ^
1 error
```

In order for the code to compile, we must implement the `getArea` and `getPerimeter` methods in our `Rectangle` class. We'll define a `Rectangle` object by a width and a height. Since the area of a rectangle is equal to its width times its height, we'll implement the `getArea` method by multiplying its fields. We'll then use the perimeter formula `2 * (w + h)` to implement `getPerimeter`. Here is the complete `Rectangle` class that implements the `Shape` interface:

```
// Represents rectangular shapes.
public class Rectangle implements Shape {
    private double width;
    private double height;

    // constructs a new rectangle with the given dimensions
    public Rectangle(double width, double height) {
        this.width = width;
        this.height = height;
    }
```

```

    // returns the area of this rectangle
    public double getArea() {
        return width * height;
    }

    // returns the perimeter of this rectangle
    public double getPerimeter() {
        return 2.0 * (width + height);
    }
}
```

The other classes of shapes are implemented in a similar fashion. We'll define a `Circle` object to have a field called `radius`. (We'll abandon the center `Point` object used in the `Circle` class earlier in the chapter, since we don't need it here.) We can determine the area by multiplying π by the radius squared. To find the perimeter, we'll use the equation `2 * π * r`. Notice that there is no common code between `Circle` and `Rectangle`, so inheritance is unnecessary. Here is the complete `Circle` class:

```
// Represents circular shapes.
public class Circle implements Shape {
    private double radius;

    // constructs a new circle with the given radius
    public Circle(double radius) {
        this.radius = radius;
    }

    // returns the area of this circle
    public double getArea() {
        return Math.PI * radius * radius;
    }

    // returns the perimeter of this circle
    public double getPerimeter() {
        return 2.0 * Math.PI * radius;
    }
}
```

Finally, we'll specify a triangle's shape by its three side lengths, *a*, *b*, and *c*. The perimeter of the triangle is simply the sum of the three side lengths. The `getArea` method is a bit trickier, but there is a useful geometric formula called

Heron's formula which says that the area of a triangle with sides of lengths a, b, and c is related to a value s that is equal to half the triangle's perimeter:

$$\text{area} = \sqrt{s(s - a)(s - b)(s - c)} \text{ where } s = \frac{a + b + c}{2}$$

Here is a complete version of the `Triangle` class:

```
// Represents triangular shapes.
public class Triangle implements Shape {
    private double a;
    private double b;
    private double c;

    // constructs a new triangle with the given side lengths
    public Triangle(double a, double b, double c) {
        this.a = a;
        this.b = b;
        this.c = c;
    }

    // returns this triangle's area using Heron's formula
    public double getArea() {
        double s = (a + b + c) / 2.0;
        return Math.sqrt(s * (s - a) * (s - b) * (s - c));
    }

    // returns the perimeter of this triangle
    public double getPerimeter() {
        return a + b + c;
    }
}
```

Using these shape classes and their common interface, a client program can now construct an array of shapes, write a method that accepts a general shape as a parameter, and otherwise take advantage of polymorphism.

Benefits of Interfaces

Classes that implement a common interface form a type hierarchy similar to those created by inheritance. The interface serves as a parent type for the classes that implement it. The following diagram represents our type hierarchy after our modifications. The way we represent an interface is similar to the way we represent a class, but we use the word "interface" for clarity. The methods are italicized to emphasize that they are abstract. Figure 9.5 shows our use of dashed lines to connect the classes and the interface they implement.

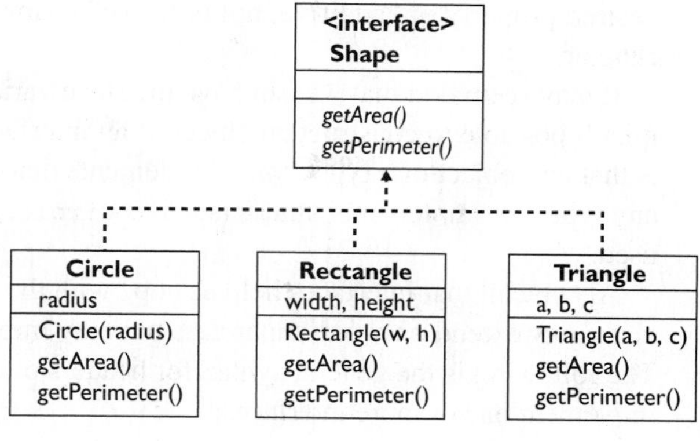

Figure 9.5 Hierarchy of shape classes

The major benefit of interfaces is that we can use them to achieve polymorphism. We can create an array of `Shapes`, pass a `Shape` as a parameter to a method, return a `Shape` from a method, and so on. The following program uses the shape classes in an example that is similar to the polymorphism exercises in Section 9.3:

```
// Demonstrates shape classes.
public class ShapesMain {
    public static void main(String[] args) {
        Shape[] shapes = new Shape[3];
        shapes[0] = new Rectangle(18, 18);
        shapes[1] = new Triangle(30, 30, 30);
        shapes[2] = new Circle(12);

        for (int i = 0; i < shapes.length; i++) {
            System.out.println("area = " + shapes[i].getArea() +
                               ", perimeter = " +
                               shapes[i].getPerimeter());
        }
    }
}
```

This program produces the following output:

```
area = 324.0, perimeter = 72.0
area = 389.7114317029974, perimeter = 90.0
area = 452.3893421169302, perimeter = 75.39822368615503
```

It would be fairly easy to modify our client program if another shape class, such as `Hexagon` or `Ellipse`, were added to the hierarchy. This is another example of the desired property of "additive, not invasive" change that we mentioned earlier in this chapter.

It may seem odd that we can have interface variables, arrays, and parameters when it isn't possible to construct an object of an interface type, but all this capacity means is that any object of a type which implements that interface may be used. In our case, any type that implements `Shape` (such as `Circle`, `Rectangle`, or `Triangle`) may be used.

Also recall that interfaces help us cope with the limitations of single inheritance. A class may extend only one superclass but may implement arbitrarily many interfaces. The following is the general syntax for headers of classes that extend a superclass and implement one or more interfaces:

```
public class <name> extends <superclass>
        implements <interface>, <interface>, ..., <interface> {
    ...
}
```

Many classes in the Java class libraries both extend a superclass and implement one or more interfaces. For example, the `PrintStream` class (of which `System.out` is an instance) has the following header:

```
public class PrintStream extends FilterOutputStream
        implements Appendable, Closeable
```

9.6 Case Study: Financial Class Hierarchy

As you write larger and more complex programs, you will end up with more classes and more opportunities to use inheritance and interfaces. It is important to practice devising sensible hierarchies of types, so that you will be able to solve large problems by breaking them down into good classes in the future.

When you are designing an object-oriented system, you should ask yourself the following questions:

- What classes of objects should I write?
- What behavior does the client want each of these objects to have?
- What data do the objects need to store in order to implement this behavior?
- Are the classes related? If so, what is the nature of the relationships?

Having good answers to these questions, along with a good knowledge of the necessary Java syntax, is a good start toward designing an object-oriented system. Such a process is called *object-oriented design*. We discussed some object-oriented design heuristics in the case study of Chapter 8.

> **Object-Oriented Design (OOD)**
>
> Modeling a program or system as a collection of cooperating objects, implemented as a set of classes using class hierarchies.

Let's consider the problem of gathering information about a person's financial investments. We've already explored a `Stock` example in this chapter and the previous chapter, as well as a `DividendStock` class to handle stocks that pay dividends. But stocks are not the only type of asset that investors might have in their financial portfolios. Other investments might include mutual funds, real estate, or cash.

How would you design a complete portfolio system? What new types of objects would you write? Take a moment to consider the problem. We'll discuss an example design next.

Designing the Classes

Each type of asset deserves its own class. We already have the `Stock` class from the last chapter and its `DividendStock` subclass from earlier in this chapter, and we can add classes like `MutualFund` and `Cash`. Each object of each of these types will represent a single investment of that type. For example, a `MutualFund` object will represent a purchase of a mutual fund, and a `Cash` object will represent a sum of money in the user's portfolio. The available types are shown in Figure 9.6. What data and behavior are necessary in each of these types of objects? Take a moment to consider it.

Though each type of asset is unique, the types do have some common behavior: Each asset should be able to compute its current market value and profit or loss, if any. These values are computed in different ways for different asset types, though. For instance, a stock's market value is the total number of shares that the shareholder owns, times the current price per share, while cash is always worth exactly its own amount.

In terms of data, we decided previously that a `Stock` object should store the stock's symbol, the number of shares purchased, the total cost paid for all shares, and the current price of the stock. Dividend stocks also need to store the amount of dividends paid. A `MutualFund` object should store the same data as a `Stock` object, but mutual funds can hold partial shares. Cash only needs to store its own amount. Figure 9.7 updates our diagram of types to reflect this data and behavior.

The asset types are clearly related. Perhaps we'd want to gather and store a person's portfolio of assets in an array. It would be convenient to be able to treat any asset the same way, insofar as they share similar functionality. For example, every asset

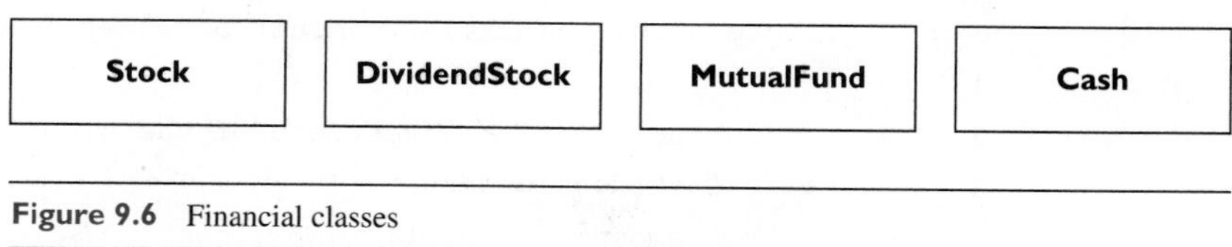

Figure 9.6 Financial classes

Stock
symbol total share: int total cost current price
getMarketValue() getProfit()

DividendStock
symbol total share: int total cost current price dividends
getMarketValue() getProfit()

MutualFund
symbol total share: double total cost current price
getMarketValue() getProfit()

Cash
amount
getMarketValue()

Figure 9.7 Financial classes with state and behavior

has a market value, so it would be nice to be able to compute the total market value of all assets in an investor's portfolio, without worrying about the different types of assets.

Because different assets compute their market values in different ways, we should consider using an interface to represent the notion of an asset and have every class implement the asset interface. Our interface will demand that all assets have methods to calculate the market value and profit. The interface is a way of saying, "Classes that want to consider themselves assets must have `getMarketValue` and `getProfit` methods." Our interface for financial assets would be saved in a file called `Asset.java` and would look like this:

```
// Represents financial assets that investors hold.
public interface Asset {
    // how much the asset is worth
    public double getMarketValue();

    // how much money has been made on this asset
    public double getProfit();
}
```

We'll have our various classes certify that they are assets by making them implement the `Asset` interface. For example, let's look at the `Cash` class. We didn't write a `getProfit` method in our previous diagram of `Cash`, because the value of cash doesn't change and therefore it doesn't have a profit. To indicate this quality, we can write a `getProfit` method for `Cash` that returns `0.0`. The `Cash` class should look like this:

```
// A Cash object represents an amount of money held by an investor.
public class Cash implements Asset {
    private double amount; // amount of money held

    // constructs a cash investment of the given amount
    public Cash(double amount) {
        this.amount = amount;
```

```
    }

    // returns this cash investment's market value, which
    // is equal to the amount of cash
    public double getMarketValue() {
        return amount;
    }

    // since cash is a fixed asset, it never has any profit
    public double getProfit() {
        return 0.0;
    }

    // sets the amount of cash invested to the given value
    public void setAmount(double amount) {
        this.amount = amount;
    }
}
```

As we discussed earlier in this chapter, a `DividendStock` is very similar to a normal `Stock`, but it has a small amount of behavior added. Let's display `DividendStock` as a subclass of `Stock` through inheritance, matching the design from earlier in the chapter. Figure 9.8 shows how our hierarchy should now look.

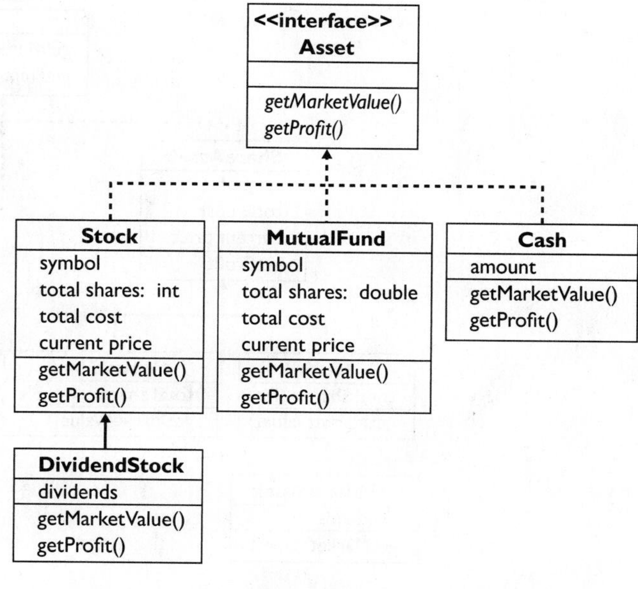

Figure 9.8 Financial class hierarchy

What about the similarity between mutual funds and stocks? They both store assets that are based on shares, with a symbol, total cost, and current price. It wouldn't work very well to make one of them a subclass of the other, though, because the type of shares (integer or real number) isn't the same, and also because it's not a sensible is-a relationship: stocks aren't really mutual funds, and vice versa. It might seem excessive to have a separate class for mutual funds when the only difference is the existence of partial shares. But conceptually, these are separate types of investments, and many investors want to keep them separate. Also, there are some aspects of mutual funds, such as tax ramifications and Morningstar ratings, that are unique and that we might want to add to the program later.

Let's modify our design by making a new superclass called `ShareAsset` which represents any asset that has shares and that contains the common behavior of `Stock` and `MutualFund`. Then we can have both `Stock` and `MutualFund` extend `ShareAsset`, to reduce redundancy.

Our previous versions of the `Stock` and `DividendStock` classes each had a `getProfit` method that required a parameter for the current price per share. In order to implement the `Asset` interface with its parameterless `getMarketValue` and `getProfit` methods, we'll change our design and create a field for the current price. We'll also add methods to get and set the value of the current price. The updated type hierarchy is shown in Figure 9.9.

This practice of redesigning code to meet new requirements is sometimes called *refactoring*.

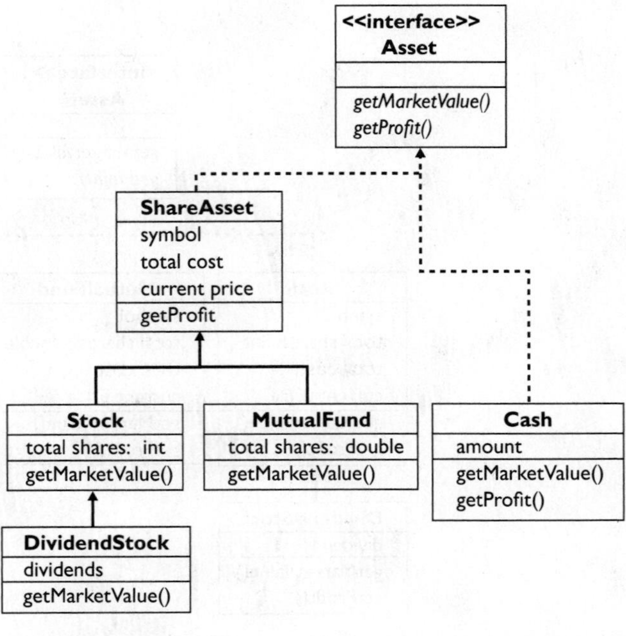

Figure 9.9 Updated financial class hierarchy

Refactoring

Changing a program's internal structure without modifying its external behavior to improve simplicity, readability, maintainability, extensibility, performance, etc.

Redundant Implementation

Here's some potential code for the `ShareAsset` class:

```
// A ShareAsset object represents a general asset that has a symbol
// and holds shares. Initial version.
public class ShareAsset {
    private String symbol;
    private double totalCost;
    private double currentPrice;

    // constructs a new share asset with the given symbol
    // and current price
    public ShareAsset(String symbol, double currentPrice) {
        this.symbol = symbol;
        this.currentPrice = currentPrice;
        totalCost = 0.0;
    }

    // adds a cost of the given amount to this asset
    public void addCost(double cost) {
        totalCost += cost;
    }

    // returns the price per share of this asset
    public double getCurrentPrice() {
        return currentPrice;
    }

    // returns this asset's total cost for all shares
    public double getTotalCost() {
        return totalCost;
    }

    // sets the current share price of this asset
    public void setCurrentPrice(double currentPrice) {
        this.currentPrice = currentPrice;
    }
}
```

We stole some code from the `Stock` class and then made a few changes so that the code would fit this interface. Our `Stock` code accepted the current share price as a parameter to its `getProfit` method. Since the `getProfit` method cannot accept any parameters if we wish to implement the interface, we'll instead store the current share price as a field in the `ShareAsset` class and supply a `setCurrentPrice` mutator method that can be called to set its proper value. We also include a constructor that can initialize a `Stock` object with any number of shares and a total cost.

One last modification we made in creating `ShareAsset` was to include an `addCost` method, which we'll use to add a given amount to the asset's total cost. We will need this because purchases of `Stocks` and `MutualFunds` need to update the `totalCost` field, but they cannot do so directly because it is private.

The `Stock` class can now extend `ShareAsset` to implement its remaining functionality. Notice that we both extend `ShareAsset` and implement the `Asset` interface in the class's header:

```
// A Stock object represents purchases of shares of a stock.
// Initial version.
public class Stock extends ShareAsset implements Asset {
    private int totalShares;

    // constructs a new Stock with the given symbol and
    // current price per share
    public Stock(String symbol, double currentPrice) {
        super(symbol, currentPrice);
        totalShares = 0;
    }

    // returns the market value of this stock, which is
    // the number of total shares times the share price
    public double getMarketValue() {
        return totalShares * getCurrentPrice();
    }

    // returns the total number of shares purchased
    public int getTotalShares() {
        return totalShares;
    }

    // returns the profit made on this stock
    public double getProfit() {
        return getMarketValue() - getTotalCost();
    }

    // records a purchase of the given number of shares of
```

```
    // the stock at the given price per share
    public void purchase(int shares, double pricePerShare) {
        totalShares += shares;
        addCost(shares * pricePerShare);
    }
}
```

The `MutualFund` class receives similar treatment, but with a `double` for its total shares (the two classes are highly redundant; we'll improve them in the next section):

```
// A MutualFund object represents a mutual fund asset.
// Initial version.
public class MutualFund extends ShareAsset implements Asset {
    private double totalShares;

    // constructs a new MutualFund investment with the given
    // symbol and price per share
    public MutualFund(String symbol, double currentPrice) {
        super(symbol, currentPrice);
        totalShares = 0.0;
    }

    // returns the market value of this mutual fund, which
    // is the number of shares times the price per share
    public double getMarketValue() {
        return totalShares * getCurrentPrice();
    }

    // returns the number of shares of this mutual fund
    public double getTotalShares() {
        return totalShares;
    }

    // returns the profit made on this mutual fund
    public double getProfit() {
        return getMarketValue() – getTotalCost();
    }

    // records purchase of the given shares at the given price
    public void purchase(double shares, double pricePerShare) {
        totalShares += shares;
        addCost(shares * pricePerShare);
    }
}
```

The `DividendStock` simply adds an amount of dividend payments to a normal `Stock`, which affects its market value. We don't need to override the `getProfit` method in `DividendStock`, because `DividendStock` already inherits a `getProfit` method with the following body:

```
return getMarketValue() – getTotalCost();
```

Notice that `getProfit`'s body calls `getMarketValue`. The `DividendStock` class overrides the `getMarketValue` method, with the convenient side effect that any other method that calls `getMarketValue` (such as `getProfit`) will also behave differently. This occurs because of polymorphism; since `getMarketValue` is overridden, `getProfit` calls the new version of the method. The profit will be correctly computed with dividends because the dividends are added to the market value.

The following code implements the `DividendStock` class:

```
// A DividendStock object represents a stock purchase that also pays
// dividends.
public class DividendStock extends Stock {
    private double dividends; // amount of dividends paid

    // constructs a new DividendStock with the given symbol
    // and no shares purchased
    public DividendStock(String symbol, double currentPrice) {
        super(symbol, currentPrice); // call Stock constructor
        dividends = 0.0;
    }

    // returns this DividendStock's market value, which is
    // a normal stock's market value plus any dividends
    public double getMarketValue() {
        return super.getMarketValue() + dividends;
    }

    // records a dividend of the given amount per share
    public void payDividend(double amountPerShare) {
        dividends += amountPerShare * getTotalShares();
    }
}
```

Abstract Classes

So far we have written classes, which are concrete implementations of state and behavior, and interfaces, which are completely abstract declarations of behavior. There is an entity that exists between these two extremes, allowing us to define some concrete state and behavior while leaving some abstract, without defined method bodies. Such an entity is called an *abstract class*.

> **Abstract Class**
>
> A Java class that cannot be instantiated, but that instead serves as a superclass to hold common code and declare abstract behavior.

You probably noticed a lot of redundancy between the `Stock` and `MutualFund` code in the last section. For example, although the `getMarketValue` and `getProfit` methods have identical code, they can't be moved up into the `ShareAsset` superclass because they depend on the number of shares, which is different in each child class. Ideally, we should get rid of this redundancy somehow.

There is also a problem with our current `ShareAsset` class. A `ShareAsset` isn't really a type of asset that a person can buy; it's just a concept that happens to be represented in our code. It would be undesirable for a person to actually try to construct a `ShareAsset` object—we wrote the class to eliminate redundancy, not for clients to instantiate it.

We can resolve these issues by designating the `ShareAsset` class as abstract. Writing abstract in a class's header will modify the class in two ways. First, the class becomes noninstantiable, so client code will not be allowed to construct an object of that type with the new keyword. Second, the class is enabled to declare abstract methods without bodies. Unlike an interface, though, an abstract class can also declare fields and implement methods with bodies, so the `ShareAsset` class can retain its existing code.

The general syntax for declaring an abstract class is

```
public abstract class <name> {
    ...
}
```

Thus, our new `ShareAsset` class header will be

```
public abstract class ShareAsset {
    ...
}
```

An attempt to create a `ShareAsset` object will now produce a compiler error such as the following:

```
ShareAsset is abstract; cannot be instantiated
    ShareAsset asset = new ShareAsset("MSFT", 27.46);
    ^
1 error
```

Really, the `Employee` class introduced earlier in this chapter should also have been an abstract class. We did not especially want client code to construct `Employee` objects. No one is *just* an employee; the `Employee` class merely represented a general category that we wanted the other classes to extend.

Abstract classes are allowed to implement interfaces. Rather than requiring all subclasses of `ShareAsset` to implement the `Asset` interface, we can specify that `ShareAsset` implements `Asset`:

```
public abstract class ShareAsset implements Asset {
    ...
}
```

This indication will save `ShareAsset` subclasses from having to write `implements Asset` in their class headers.

`ShareAsset` does not implement the `getMarketValue` method required by `Asset`; that functionality is left for its subclasses. We can instead declare `getMarketValue` as an abstract method in the `ShareAsset` class. Abstract methods declared in abstract classes need to have the keyword `abstract` in their headers in order to compile properly. Otherwise, the syntax is the same as when we declare an abstract method in an interface, with a semicolon replacing the method's body:

```
// returns the current market value of this asset
public abstract double getMarketValue();
```

The general syntax for an abstract method declaration in an abstract class is the following:

```
public abstract <type> <name> (<type> <name>, ..., <type> <name>);
```

Another benefit of this design is that code in the abstract class can actually call any of its abstract methods, even if they don't have implementations in that class. This is allowed because the abstract class can count on its subclasses to implement the abstract methods. Now that `ShareAsset` implements `Asset`, we can move the common redundant `getProfit` code up to `ShareAsset` and out of `Stock` and `MutualFund`:

```
// returns the profit earned on shares of this asset
public double getProfit() {
    // calls an abstract getMarketValue method
    // (the subclass will provide its implementation)
    return getMarketValue() – totalCost;
}
```

`ShareAsset` objects can call `getMarketValue` from their `getProfit` methods even though that method isn't present in `ShareAsset`. The code compiles because the compiler knows that whatever class extends ShareAsset will have to implement getMarketValue.

The following is the final version of the ShareAsset abstract class:

```
// A ShareAsset represents a general asset that has a symbol and
// holds shares.
public abstract class ShareAsset implements Asset {
    private String symbol;
    private double totalCost;
    private double currentPrice;

    // constructs a new share asset with the given symbol
    // and current price
    public ShareAsset(String symbol, double currentPrice) {
        this.symbol = symbol;
        this.currentPrice = currentPrice;
        totalCost = 0.0;
    }

    // adds a cost of the given amount to this asset
    public void addCost(double cost) {
        totalCost += cost;
    }

    // returns the price per share of this asset
    public double getCurrentPrice() {
        return currentPrice;
    }

    // returns the current market value of this asset
    public abstract double getMarketValue();

    // returns the profit earned on shares of this asset
    public double getProfit() {
        // calls an abstract getMarketValue method
        // (the subclass will provide its implementation)
        return getMarketValue() – totalCost;
    }

    // returns this asset's total cost for all shares
    public double getTotalCost() {
        return totalCost;
    }
```

```java

    // sets the current share price of this asset
    public void setCurrentPrice(double currentPrice) {
        this.currentPrice = currentPrice;
    }
}
```

An abstract class is a useful hybrid that can contain both abstract and nonabstract methods. All methods declared in an interface are implicitly abstract; they can be declared with the abstract keyword if you wish. Declaring them without the abstract keyword as we have done in this chapter is a commonly used shorthand for the longer explicit form. Unfortunately, abstract classes disallow this shorthand to avoid ambiguity.

Nonabstract classes like `Stock` and `MutualFund` are sometimes called *concrete classes* to differentiate them from abstract classes. We can modify the `Stock` and `MutualFund` classes to take advantage of `ShareAsset` and reduce redundancy. The following are the final versions of the `Stock` and `MutualFund` classes. (`DividendStock` is unmodified.) Notice that the subclasses of `ShareAsset` must implement `getMarketValue`, or we'll receive a compiler error:

```java
// A Stock object represents purchases of shares of a stock.
public class Stock extends ShareAsset {
    private int totalShares;

    // constructs a new Stock with the given symbol and
    // current price per share
    public Stock(String symbol, double currentPrice) {
        super(symbol, currentPrice);
        totalShares = 0;
    }

    // returns the market value of this stock, which is
    // the number of total shares times the share price
    public double getMarketValue() {
        return totalShares * getCurrentPrice();
    }

    // returns the total number of shares purchased
    public int getTotalShares() {
        return totalShares;
    }

    // records a purchase of the given number of shares of
    // the stock at the given price per share
```

```
    public void purchase(int shares, double pricePerShare) {
        totalShares += shares;
        addCost(shares * pricePerShare);
    }
}
```

```
// A MutualFund object represents a mutual fund asset.
public class MutualFund extends ShareAsset {
    private double totalShares;

    // constructs a new MutualFund investment with the given
    // symbol and price per share
    public MutualFund(String symbol, double currentPrice) {
        super(symbol, currentPrice);
        totalShares = 0.0;
    }

    // returns the market value of this mutual fund, which
    // is the number of shares times the price per share
    public double getMarketValue() {
        return totalShares * getCurrentPrice();
    }

    // returns the number of shares of this mutual fund
    public double getTotalShares() {
        return totalShares;
    }

    // records purchase of the given shares at the given price
    public void purchase(double shares, double pricePerShare) {
        totalShares += shares;
        addCost(shares * pricePerShare);
    }
}
```

Abstract classes can do everything interfaces can do and more, but this does not mean that it is always better to use them than interfaces. One important difference between interfaces and abstract classes is that a class may choose to implement arbitrarily many interfaces, but it can extend just one abstract class. That is why an interface often forms the top of an inheritance hierarchy, as our `Asset` interface did in this design. Such placement allows classes to become part of the hierarchy without having it consume their only inheritance relationships.

Chapter Summary

Inheritance is a feature of Java programs that allows the creation of a parent–child relationship between two types.

The child class of an inheritance relationship (commonly called a subclass) will receive a copy of ("inherit") every field and method from the parent class (superclass). The subclass "extends" the superclass, because it can add new fields and methods to the ones it inherits from the superclass.

A subclass can override a method from the superclass by writing its own version, which will replace the one that was inherited.

Treating objects of different types interchangeably is called polymorphism.

Subclasses can refer to the superclass's constructors or methods using the `super` keyword.

The `Object` class represents the common superclass of all objects and contains behavior that every object should have, such as the `equals` and `toString` methods.

Inheritance provides an "is-a" relationship between two classes. If the two classes are not closely related, inheritance may be a poor design choice and a "has-a" relationship between them (in which one object contains the other as a field) may be better.

An interface is a list of method declarations. An interface specifies method names, parameters, and return types but does not include the bodies of the methods. A class can implement (i.e., promise to implement all of the methods of) an interface.

Interfaces help us achieve polymorphism so that we can treat several different classes in the same way. If two or more classes both implement the same interface, we can use either of them interchangeably and can call any of the interface's methods on them.

An abstract class cannot be instantiated. No objects of the abstract type can be constructed. An abstract class is useful because it can be used as a superclass and can also define abstract behavior for its subclasses to implement.

An abstract class can contain abstract methods, which are declared but do not have bodies. All subclasses of an abstract class must implement the abstract superclass's abstract methods.

Self-Check Problems

Section 9.1: Inheritance Basics

1. What is code reuse? How does inheritance help achieve code reuse?
2. What is the difference between overloading and overriding a method?
3. Which of the following is the correct syntax to indicate that class `A` is a subclass of `B`?

    a. `public class B extends A {`
    b. `public class A : super B {`
    c. `public A(super B) {`
    d. `public class A extends B {`
    e. `public A implements B {`

Section 9.2: Interacting with the Superclass

4. Explain the difference between the `this` keyword and the `super` keyword. When should each be used?

5. For the next three problems, consider the following class:

```
// Represents a university student.
public class Student {
    private String name;
    private int age;

    public Student(String name, int age) {
        this.name = name;
        this.age = age;
    }

    public void setAge(int age) {
        this.age = age;
    }
}
```

Also consider the following partial implementation of a subclass of `Student` to represent undergraduate students at a university:

```
public class UndergraduateStudent extends Student {
    private int year;
    ...
}
```

Can the code in the `UndergraduateStudent` class access the `name` and `age` fields it inherits from `Student`? Can it call the `setAge` method?

6. Write a constructor for the `UndergraduateStudent` class that accepts a name as a parameter and initializes the `UnderGraduateStudent`'s state with that name, an `age` value of `18`, and a `year` value of `0`.

7. Write a version of the `setAge` method in the `UndergraduateStudent` class that not only sets the `age` but also increments the `year` field's value by one.

8. Consider the following two automobile classes:

```
public class Car {
    public void m1() {
        System.out.println("car 1");
    }

    public void m2() {
        System.out.println("car 2");
    }

    public String toString() {
        return "vroom";
    }
```

```
}
public class Truck extends Car {
    public void m1() {
        System.out.println("truck 1");
    }
}
```

Given the following declared variables, what is the output from the following statements?

```
Car mycar = new Car();
Truck mytruck = new Truck();

System.out.println(mycar);
mycar.m1();
mycar.m2();
System.out.println(mytruck);
mytruck.m1();
mytruck.m2();
```

9. Suppose the `Truck` code from the previous problem changes to the following:

```
public class Truck extends Car {
    public void m1() {
        System.out.println("truck 1");
    }

    public void m2() {
        super.m1();
    }

    public String toString() {
        return super.toString() + super.toString();
    }
}
```

Using the same variables from the previous problem, what is the output from the following statements?

```
System.out.println(mytruck);
mytruck.m1();
mytruck.m2();
```

Section 9.3: Polymorphism

10. Consider the following classes:

```
public class Vehicle {...}

public class Car extends Vehicle {...}

public class SUV extends Car {...}
```

Which of the following are legal statements?

a. `Vehicle v = new Car();`

b. `Vehicle v = new SUV();`

c. `Car c = new SUV();`

d. `SUV s = new SUV();`

e. `SUV s = new Car();`

f. `Car c = new Vehicle();`

11. Using the `A`, `B`, `C`, and `D` classes from this section, what is the output of the following code fragment?

```
public static void main(String[] args) {
    A[] elements = {new B(), new D(), new A(), new C()};
    for (int i = 0; i < elements.length; i++) {
        elements[i].method2();
        System.out.println(elements[i]);
        elements[i].method1();
        System.out.println();
    }
}
```

12. Assume that the following classes have been defined:

```
public class Flute extends Blue {
    public void method2() {
        System.out.println("flute 2");
    }

    public String toString() {
        return "flute";
    }
}
```

```
public class Blue extends Moo {
    public void method1() {
        System.out.println("blue 1");
    }
}
```

```
public class Shoe extends Flute {
    public void method1() {
        System.out.println("shoe 1");
    }
}
```

```
public class Moo {
    public void method1() {
        System.out.println("moo 1");
    }
```

```
    public void method2() {
        System.out.println("moo 2");
    }

    public String toString() {
        return "moo";
    }
}
```

What is the output produced by the following code fragment?

```
public static void main(String[] args) {
    Moo[] elements = {new Shoe(), new Flute(), new Moo(), new Blue()};
    for (int i = 0; i < elements.length; i++) {
        System.out.println(elements[i]);
        elements[i].method1();
        elements[i].method2();
        System.out.println();
    }
}
```

13. Using the classes from the previous problem, write the output that is produced by the following code fragment.

```
public static void main(String[] args) {
    Moo[] elements = {new Blue(), new Moo(), new Shoe(), new Flute()};
    for (int i = 0; i < elements.length; i++) {
        elements[i].method2();
        elements[i].method1();
        System.out.println(elements[i]);
        System.out.println();
    }
}
```

14. Assume that the following classes have been defined:

```
public class Mammal extends SeaCreature {
    public void method1() {
        System.out.println("warm-blooded");
    }
}
```

```
public class SeaCreature {
    public void method1() {
        System.out.println("creature 1");
    }
```

```
    public void method2() {
        System.out.println("creature 2");
    }

    public String toString() {
        return "ocean-dwelling";
    }
}
```

```
public class Whale extends Mammal {
    public void method1() {
        System.out.println("spout");
    }

    public String toString() {
        return "BIG!";
    }
}
```

```
public class Squid extends SeaCreature {
    public void method2() {
        System.out.println("tentacles");
    }

    public String toString() {
        return "squid";
    }
}
```

What output is produced by the following code fragment?

```
public static void main(String[] args) {
    SeaCreature[] elements = {new Squid(), new Whale(),
                              new SeaCreature(), new Mammal()};
    for (int i = 0; i < elements.length; i++) {
         System.out.println(elements[i]);
         elements[i].method1();
         elements[i].method2();
         System.out.println();
    }
}
```

15. Using the classes from the previous problem, write the output that is produced by the following code fragment:

```
public static void main(String[] args) {
    SeaCreature[] elements = {new SeaCreature(),
                              new Squid(), new Mammal(), new Whale()};
```

```
        for (int i = 0; i < elements.length; i++) {
            elements[i].method2();
            System.out.println(elements[i]);
            elements[i].method1();
            System.out.println();
        }
    }
```

16. Assume that the following classes have been defined:

```
public class Bay extends Lake {
    public void method1() {
        System.out.print("Bay 1 ");
        super.method2();
    }
    public void method2() {
        System.out.print("Bay 2 ");
    }
}
```

```
public class Pond {
    public void method1() {
        System.out.print("Pond 1 ");
    }
    public void method2() {
        System.out.print("Pond 2 ");
    }
    public void method3() {
        System.out.print("Pond 3 ");
    }
}
```

```
public class Ocean extends Bay {
    public void method2() {
        System.out.print("Ocean 2 ");
    }
}
```

```
public class Lake extends Pond {
    public void method3() {
        System.out.print("Lake 3 ");
        method2();
    }
}
```

What output is produced by the following code fragment?

```
Pond[] ponds = {new Ocean(), new Pond(), new Lake(), new Bay()};
for (Pond p : ponds) {
```

```
        p.method1();
        System.out.println();
        p.method2();
        System.out.println();
        p.method3();
        System.out.println("\n");
    }
```

17. Suppose that the following variables referring to the classes from the previous problem are declared:

```
Pond var1 = new Bay();
Object var2 = new Ocean();
```

Which of the following statements produce compiler errors? For the statements that do not produce errors, what is the output of each statement?

```
((Lake) var1).method1();
((Bay) var1).method1();
((Pond) var2).method2();
((Lake) var2).method2();
((Ocean) var2).method3();
```

Section 9.4: Inheritance and Design

18. What is the difference between an is-a and a has-a relationship? How do you create a has-a relationship in your code?

19. Imagine a `Rectangle` class with objects that represent two-dimensional rectangles. The `Rectangle` has `width` and `height` fields with appropriate accessors and mutators, as well as `getArea` and `getPerimeter` methods.

    You would like to add a `Square` class into your system. Is it a good design to make `Square` a subclass of `Rectangle`? Why or why not?

20. Imagine that you are going to write a program to play card games. Consider a design with a `Card` class and 52 subclasses, one for each of the unique playing cards (for example, `NineOfSpades` and `JackOfClubs`). Is this a good design? If so, why? If not, why not, and what might be a better design?

21. In Section 9.2 we discussed adding functionality for dividend payments to the `Stock` class. Why was it preferable to create a `DividendStock` class rather than editing the `Stock` class and adding this feature directly to it?

Section 9.5: Interfaces

22. What is the difference between implementing an interface and extending a class?

23. Consider the following interface and class:

```
public interface I {
    public void m1();
    public void m2();
}
public class C implements I {
    // code for class C
}
```

What must be true about the code for class `C` in order for that code to compile successfully?

24. What's wrong with the code for the following interface? What should be changed to make a valid interface for objects that have colors?

```
public interface Colored {
    private Color color;
    public Color getColor() {
        return color;
    }
}
```

25. Modify the `Point` class from Chapter 8 so that it implements the `Colored` interface and `Points` have colors. (You may wish to create a `ColoredPoint` class that extends `Point`.)

26. Declare a method called `getSideCount` in the `Shape` interface that returns the number of sides that the shape has. Implement the method in all shape classes. A circle is defined to have 0 sides.

Section 9.6: Case Study: Financial Class Hierarchy

27. What is an abstract class? How is an abstract class like a normal class, and how does it differ? How is it like an interface?

28. Consider the following abstract class and its subclass. What state and behavior do you know for sure will be present in the subclass? How do you know?

```
public abstract class Ordered {
    private String[] data;
    public void getElement(int i) {
        return data[i];
    }
    public abstract void arrange();
}

public class OrderedByLength extends Ordered {
    ...
}
```

29. Consider writing a program to be used to manage a collection of movies. There are three kinds of movies in the collection: dramas, comedies, and documentaries. The collector would like to keep track of each movie's title, the name of its director, and the year the movie was made. Some operations are to be implemented for all movies, and there will also be special operations for each of the three different kinds of movies. How would you design the class(es) to represent this system of movies?

Exercises

1. Write the class `Marketer` to accompany the other law firm classes described in this chapter. Marketers make $50,000 ($10,000 more than general employees) and have an additional method called `advertise` that prints `"Act now, while supplies last!"` Make sure to interact with the superclass as appropriate.

2. Write a class `Janitor` to accompany the other law firm classes described in this chapter. Janitors work twice as many hours per week as other employees (80 hours/week), they make $30,000 ($10,000 *less* than general employees), they get half as much vacation as other employees (only 5 days), and they have an additional method `clean` that prints `"Workin' for the man."` Make sure to interact with the superclass as appropriate.

3. Write a class `HarvardLawyer` to accompany the other law firm classes described in this chapter. Harvard lawyers are like normal lawyers, but they make 20% more money than a normal lawyer, they get 3 days more vacation, and they have to fill out four of the lawyer's forms to go on vacation. That is, the `getVacationForm` method should return `"pinkpinkpinkpink"`. Make sure to interact with the superclass as appropriate.

4. Write a class `MonsterTruck` that relates to the `Car` and `Truck` classes from Self-Check Problems 9 and 10 and whose methods have the following behavior. Whenever possible, use inheritance to reuse behavior from the superclasses.

Method	Output/Return
`m1`	`monster 1`
`m2`	`truck 1`
	`car 1`
`toString`	`"monster vroomvroom"`

5. For the next four problems, consider the task of representing types of tickets to campus events. Each ticket has a unique number and a price. There are three types of tickets: walk-up tickets, advance tickets, and student advance tickets. Figure 9.10 illustrates the types:

   - Walk-up tickets are purchased the day of the event and cost $50.
   - Advance tickets purchased 10 or more days before the event cost $30, and advance tickets purchased fewer than 10 days before the event cost $40.
   - Student advance tickets are sold at half the price of normal advance tickets: When they are purchased 10 or more days early they cost $15, and when they are purchased fewer than 10 days early they cost $20.

   Implement a class called `Ticket` that will serve as the superclass for all three types of tickets. Define all common operations in this class, and specify all differing operations in such a way that every subclass must implement them. No actual objects of type `Ticket` will be created: Each actual ticket will be an object of a subclass type. Define the following operations:

   - The ability to construct a ticket by number.
   - The ability to ask for a ticket's price.
   - The ability to `println` a ticket object as a `String`. An example `String` would be `"Number: 17, Price: 50.0"`.

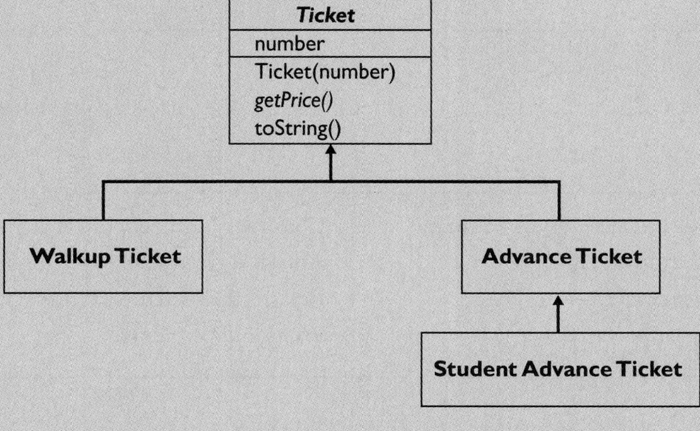

Figure 9.10 Classes of tickets that are available to campus events

6. Implement a class called `WalkupTicket` to represent a walk-up event ticket. Walk-up tickets are also constructed by number, and they have a price of $50.

7. Implement a class called `AdvanceTicket` to represent tickets purchased in advance. An advance ticket is constructed with a ticket number and with the number of days in advance that the ticket was purchased. Advance tickets purchased 10 or more days before the event cost $30, and advance tickets purchased fewer than 10 days before the event cost $40.

8. Implement a class called `StudentAdvanceTicket` to represent tickets purchased in advance by students. A student advance ticket is constructed with a ticket number and with the number of days in advance that the ticket was purchased. Student advance tickets purchased 10 or more days before the event cost $15, and student advance tickets purchased fewer than 10 days before the event cost $20 (half of a normal advance ticket). When a student advance ticket is printed, the `String` should mention that the student must show his or her student ID (for example, `"Number: 17, Price: 15.0 (ID required)"`).

9. `MinMaxAccount`. A company has written a large class `BankAccount` with many methods including:

`public BankAccount(Startup s)`	Constructs a `BankAccount` object using information in `s`
`public void debit(Debit d)`	Records the given debit
`public void credit(Credit c)`	Records the given credit
`public int getBalance()`	Returns the current balance in pennies

Design a new class `MinMaxAccount` whose instances can be used in place of a bank account but include new behavior of remembering the minimum and maximum balances ever recorded for the account. The class should have a constructor that accepts a `Startup` parameter. The bank account's constructor sets the initial balance on the basis of the startup information. Assume that only debits and credits change an account's balance. Include these new methods in your class:

`public int getMin()`	Returns the minimum balance in pennies
`public int getMax()`	Returns the maximum balance in pennies

10. `DiscountBill`. Suppose a class `GroceryBill` keeps track of a list of items being purchased at a market:

`public GroceryBill(Employee clerk)`	Constructs a grocery bill object for the given clerk
`public void add(Item i)`	Adds the given item to this bill
`public double getTotal()`	Returns the total cost of these items
`public void printReceipt()`	Prints a list of items

Grocery bills interact with `Item` objects, each of which has the public methods that follow. A candy bar item might cost 1.35 with a discount of 0.25 for preferred customers, meaning that preferred customers get it for 1.10. (Some items will have no discount, 0.0.) Currently the preceding classes do not consider discounts. Every item in a bill is charged full price, and item discounts are ignored.

`public double getPrice()`	Returns the price for this item
`public double getDiscount()`	Returns the discount for this item

Define a class `DiscountBill` that extends `GroceryBill` to compute discounts for preferred customers. Its constructor accepts a parameter for whether the customer should get the discount. Your class should also adjust the total reported for preferred customers. For example, if the total would have been $80 but a preferred customer is getting $20 in discounts, then `getTotal` should report the total as $60 for that customer. Also keep track of the number of items on which a customer is getting a nonzero discount and the sum of these discounts, both as a total amount and as a percentage of the original bill. Include the extra methods that follow, which allow a client to ask about the discount. Return 0.0 if the customer is not a preferred customer or if no items were discounted.

`public DiscountBill(Employee clerk, boolean preferred)`	Constructs bill for given clerk
`public int getDiscountCount()`	Returns the number of items that were discounted, if any
`public double getDiscountAmount()`	Returns the total discount for this list of items, if any
`public double getDiscountPercent()`	Returns the percent of the total discount as a percent of what the total would have been otherwise

11. `FilteredAccount`. A cash processing company has a class called `Account` used to process transactions:

`public Account(Client c)`	Constructs an account using client information
`public boolean process(Transaction t)`	Processes the next transaction, returning `true` if the transaction was approved and `false` otherwise

Account objects interact with `Transaction` objects, which have many methods including

`public int value()`	Returns the value of this transaction in pennies (could be negative, positive or zero)

Design a new class called `FilteredAccount` whose instances can be used in place of normal accounts but which include the extra behavior of not processing transactions with a value of 0. More specifically, the new class should indicate that a zero-valued transaction was approved but shouldn't call the `process` method for it. Your class should have a single constructor that accepts a parameter of type `Client`, and it should include the following method:

`public double percentFiltered()`	Returns the percent of transactions filtered out (between 0.0 and 100.0); returns 0.0 if no transactions are submitted

12. Add an `equals` method to the `TimeSpan` class introduced in Chapter 8. Two time spans are considered equal if they represent the same number of hours and minutes.

13. Add an `equals` method to the `Cash` class introduced in this chapter. Two cash objects are considered equal if they represent the same amount of money.

14. Add an `equals` method to each of the `Rectangle`, `Circle`, and `Triangle` classes introduced in this chapter. Two shapes are considered equal if their fields have equivalent values.

15. Write a class named `Octagon` whose objects represent regular octagons (eight-sided polygons). Your class should implement the `Shape` interface defined in this chapter, including methods for its area and perimeter. An `Octagon` object is defined by its side length. (You may need to search online to find formulas for the area and perimeter of a regular octagon.)

16. Write a class named `Hexagon` whose objects represent regular hexagons (6-sided polygons). Your class should implement the `Shape` interface defined in this chapter.

17. Declare an interface called `Incrementable` which represents items that store an integer that can be incremented in some way. The interface has a method called `increment` that increments the value and a method called `getValue` that returns the value. Once you have written the interface, write two classes called `SequentialIncrementer` and `RandomIncrementer` that implement the interface. The `SequentialIncrementer` begins its value at `0` and increases it by 1 each time it is incremented. The `RandomIncrementer` begins its value at a random integer and changes it to a new random integer each time it is incremented.

Programming Projects

1. Write an inheritance hierarchy of three-dimensional shapes. Make a top-level shape interface that has methods for getting information such as the volume and surface area of a three-dimensional shape. Then make classes and subclasses that implement various shapes such as cubes, rectangular prisms, spheres, triangular prisms, cones, and cylinders. Place common behavior in superclasses whenever possible, and use abstract classes as appropriate. Add methods to the subclasses to represent the unique behavior of each three-dimensional shape, such as a method to get a sphere's radius.

2. Write a set of classes that define the behavior of certain animals. They can be used in a simulation of a world with many animals moving around in it. Different kinds of animals will move in different ways (you are defining those differences). As the simulation runs, animals can "die" when two or more of them end up in the same location, in which case the simulator randomly selects one animal to survive the collision. See your course web site or www.buildingjavaprograms.com for supporting files to run such a simulation.

The following is an example set of animals and their respective behavior:

Class	`toString`	`getMove`
Bird	B	Moves randomly 1 step in one of the four directions each time
Frog	F	Moves randomly 3 steps in one of the four directions
Mouse	M	Moves west 1 step, north 1 step (zig-zag to the northwest)
Rabbit	V	Move north 2 steps, east 2 steps, south 2 steps ("hops" to the right)
Snake	S	Moves south 1 step, east 1 step, south 1 step, west 2 steps, south 1 step, east 3 steps, south 1 step, west 4 steps, ... ("slithers" left and right in increasing length)
Turtle	T	Moves south 5 steps, west 5 steps, north 5 steps, east 5 steps (clockwise box)
Wolf	W	Has custom behavior that you define

Your classes should be stored in files called Bird.java, Frog.java, Mouse.java, Rabbit.java, Snake.java, Turtle.java, and Wolf.java.

3. Write an inheritance hierarchy that stores data about sports players. Create a common superclass and/or interface to store information common to any player regardless of sport, such as name, number, and salary. Then create subclasses for players of your favorite sports, such as basketball, soccer, or tennis. Place sport-specific information and behavior (such as kicking or vertical jump height) into subclasses whenever possible.

4. Write an inheritance hierarchy to model items at a library. Include books, magazines, journal articles, videos, and electronic media such as CDs. Include in a superclass and/or interface common information that the library must have for every item, such as a unique identification number and title. Place behavior and information that is specific to items, such as a video's runtime length or a CD's musical genre, into the subclasses.

Chapter 10

ArrayLists

Introduction

One of the most fundamental data structures you will encounter in programming is a list. You'll want to store lists of words, lists of numbers, lists of names, and so on. Chapter 7 demonstrated using arrays to store sequences of values, but arrays are fixed-size structures that require you to declare in advance exactly how many elements you want to store. In this chapter we'll explore a new structure, known as an `ArrayList`, that provides more flexibility than an array. An `ArrayList` is a dynamic structure with a variable length, so it can grow and shrink as the program executes.

The `ArrayList` structure is the first example we have discussed of a generic structure that can be used to store values of different types. As a result, we will need to explore some issues related to generic structures in this chapter. We will also look at how to use primitive data with such structures, using what are known as the wrapper classes. Finally, we will demonstrate how to use the `Comparable` interface to put values of a particular type into sorted order and how to write classes that implement the `Comparable` interface.

10.1 ArrayLists

In our daily lives, we often manipulate lists of one kind or another. For example, on social networking sites like Facebook.com, people list the bands they like. Suppose someone listed the following bands:

```
Tool, U2, Phish, Pink Floyd, Radiohead
```

You saw in Chapter 7 that you can declare an array to store a sequence of values. For example, to store the preceding list, you could declare an array of `String`s of length 5. But what happens if you want to change the list later (say, to remove Tool and U2 from the list)? You would have to shift values over, and you'd be left with empty array slots at the end. And what if you wanted to add to the list, so that it ended up with more than five names? You wouldn't have room to store more than five values in the original array, so you would have to construct a new array with a larger size to store the list.

Most of us think of lists as being more flexible than that. We don't want to have to worry about the kind of low-level details that come up in the course of manipulating an array. We want to be able to just say, "Add something to the list" or "Remove this value from the list," and we want the lists to grow and shrink over time as we add or remove values. Computer scientists would say that we have in mind a *list abstraction* that enables us to specify certain operations to be performed (add, remove) without having to worry about the details of how those operations are performed (shifting, constructing new arrays).

Java provides this functionality in a class called `ArrayList`. Internally, each `ArrayList` object uses an array to store its values. As a result, an `ArrayList` provides the same fast random access as an array. But unlike with an array, with an `ArrayList` you can make simple requests to add or remove values, and the `ArrayList` takes care of all of the details for you: If you add values to the list it makes the array bigger, and if you remove values it handles any shifting that needs to be done.

Remember that you can declare arrays of different types. If you want an array of `int` values, you declare a variable of type `int[]`. For an array of `String` values, you use the type `String[]`. This is a special syntax that works just for arrays, but the `ArrayList` class has almost the same flexibility. If you read the API documentation for `ArrayList`, you'll see that it is actually listed as `ArrayList<E>`. This is an example of a *generic class* in Java.

> **Generic Class (Generic)**
> A class such as `ArrayList<E>` that takes a type parameter to indicate what kind of values it will use.

The "E" in `ArrayList<E>` is short for "Element," and it indicates the type of elements that will be included in the `ArrayList`. Generic classes are similar to parameterized methods. Remember from Chapter 3 that you can use a parameter to define a family of related tasks that differ just by a particular characteristic like height or width. In this case, the parameter is a type and it is used to declare another type. The type ArrayList<E> represents a family of types that differ just by the type of element they store. You would use ArrayList<String> to store a list of Strings, ArrayList<Point> to store a list of Points, ArrayList<Color> to store a list of Colors, and so on. Notice that you would never actually declare something to be of type ArrayList<E>. As with any parameter, you have to replace the E with a specific value to make it clear which of the many possible ArrayList types you are using.

Basic ArrayList Operations

The ArrayList class is part of the java.util package, so to include it in a program you must include an import declaration. The syntax for constructing an ArrayList is more complicated than what we've seen before because of the type parameter. For example, you would construct an ArrayList of Strings as follows:

```
ArrayList<String> list = new ArrayList<String>();
```

This code constructs an empty ArrayList<String>. This syntax is complicated, but it will be easier to remember if you keep in mind that the <String> notation is actually part of the type: This isn't simply an ArrayList, it is an ArrayList<String> (often read as "an ArrayList of String"). Notice how the type appears when you declare the variable and when you call the constructor:

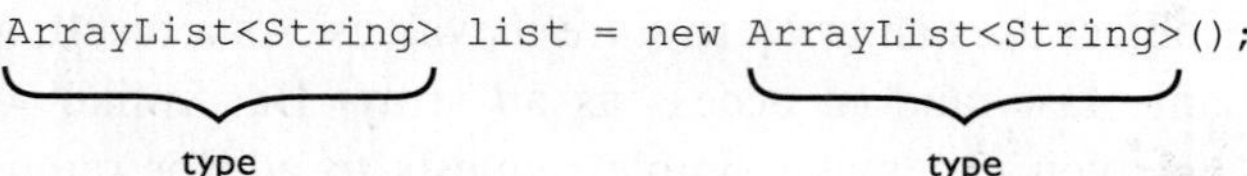

If you think in terms of the type being ArrayList<String>, you'll see that this line of code isn't all that different from the code used to construct an object like a Point:

```
Point p = new Point();
```

type type

It can be cumbersome to list the element type <String> twice, so Java version 7 has introduced a new shorter syntax for declaring collections called the "diamond operator" where by the element type may be omitted on the right side of the statement and replaced by <>. The shorter syntax can be convenient, but because it is incompatible with previous versions of Java, we choose to use the longer syntax in this textbook.

```
// Java 7's shorter "diamond operator" syntax
ArrayList<String> list = new ArrayList<>();
```

Once you've constructed an ArrayList, you can add values to it by calling the add method:

```
ArrayList<String> list = new ArrayList<String>();
list.add("Tool");
list.add("Phish");
list.add("Pink Floyd");
```

Java will make sure that you add values of an appropriate type. In this case, because you requested an ArrayList<String>, you can add Strings to the list. When you ask an ArrayList to add a new value to the list, it appends the new value to the end of the list.

Unlike with simple arrays, printing an ArrayList is straightforward because the ArrayList class overrides Java's toString method. The ArrayList version of toString constructs a String that includes the contents of the list inside square brackets, with the values separated by commas. Remember that the toString method is called when you print an object or concatenate an object to a String. As a result, you can print ArrayLists with a simple println:

```
System.out.println("list = " + list);
```

For example, you can add println statements as you add values to the list:

```
ArrayList<String> list = new ArrayList<String>();
System.out.println("list = " + list);
list.add("Tool");
System.out.println("list = " + list);
list.add("Phish");
System.out.println("list = " + list);
list.add("Pink Floyd");
System.out.println("list = " + list);
```

Executing this code produces the following output:

```
list = []
list = [Tool]
list = [Tool, Phish]
list = [Tool, Phish, Pink Floyd]
```

Notice that you can print the ArrayList even when it is empty and each time that new values are added to the end of the list. The ArrayList class also provides an overloaded version of the add method for adding a value at a particular index in the list. It preserves the order of the other list elements, shifting values to the right to make room for the new value. This version of add takes two parameters: an index and a value to insert. ArrayLists use zero-based indexing, just as arrays and

Strings do. For example, given the preceding list, consider the effect of inserting a value at index 1:

```
System.out.println("before list = " + list);
list.add(1, "U2");
System.out.println("after list  = " + list);
```

The call on add instructs the computer to insert the new String at index 1. Therefore, the old value at index 1 and everything that follows it gets shifted to the right. So, the code produces the following output:

```
before list = [Tool, Phish, Pink Floyd]
after list  = [Tool, U2, Phish, Pink Floyd]
```

ArrayList also has a method for removing a value at a particular index. The remove method also preserves the order of the list by shifting values to the left to fill in any gap. For example, consider what happens to the previous list if we remove the value at position 0 and then remove the value at position 1:

```
System.out.println("before remove list = " + list);
list.remove(0);
list.remove(1);
System.out.println("after remove list  = " + list);
```

This code produces the following output:

```
before remove list = [Tool, U2, Phish, Pink Floyd]
after remove list  = [U2, Pink Floyd]
```

This result is a little surprising. We asked the list to remove the value at position 0 and then to remove the value at position 1. You might imagine that this would get rid of the Strings "Tool" and "U2", since they were at positions 0 and 1, respectively, before this code was executed. However, an ArrayList is a dynamic structure whose values move around and shift into new positions in response to your commands. The order of events is demonstrated more clearly if we include a third println statement in the code:

```
System.out.println("before remove list     = " + list);
list.remove(0);
System.out.println("after 1st remove list = " + list);
list.remove(1);
System.out.println("after 2nd remove list = " + list);
```

This code produces the following output:

```
before remove list     = [Tool, U2, Phish, Pink Floyd]
after 1st remove list = [U2, Phish, Pink Floyd]
after 2nd remove list = [U2, Pink Floyd]
```

The first call on remove removes the String "Tool" because it's the value currently in position 0. But once that value has been removed, everything else shifts over: The String "U2" moves to the front (to position 0), the String "Phish" shifts into position 1, and the String "Pink Floyd" moves into position 2. So, when the second call on remove is performed, Java removes "Phish" from the list because it is the value that is in position 1 at that point in time.

If you want to find out the number of elements in an ArrayList, you can call its size method. If you want to obtain an individual item from the list, you can call its get method, passing it a specific index. For example, the following loop would add up the lengths of the Strings in an ArrayList<String>:

```
int sum = 0;
for (int i = 0; i < list.size(); i++) {
    String s = list.get(i);
    sum += s.length();
}
System.out.println("Total of lengths = " + sum);
```

This loop looks similar to the kind of loop you would use to access the various elements of an array, but instead of asking for list.length as you would for an array, you ask for list.size(), and instead of asking for list[i] as you would with an array, you ask for list.get(i).

Calling add and remove can be expensive in terms of time because the computer has to shift the values around. If all you want to do is to replace a value, you can use a method called set, which takes an index and a value and replaces the value at the given index with the given value, without doing any shifting. For example, you could replace the value at the front of the sample list by writing the following line of code:

```
list.set(0, "The Violent Femmes");
```

As noted earlier, when you construct an ArrayList it will initially be empty. After you have added values to a list, you can remove them one at a time. But what if you want to remove all of the values from the list? In that case, you can call the clear method of the ArrayList.

Table 10.1 summarizes the ArrayList operations introduced in this section. A more complete list can be found in the online Java documentation.

ArrayList Searching Methods

Once you have built up an ArrayList, you might be interested in searching for a specific value in the list. The ArrayList class provides several mechanisms for doing so. If you just want to know whether or not something is in the list, you can call the contains method, which returns a Boolean value. For example, suppose you have an input file of names that has some duplicates, and you want to get rid of the duplicates. The file might look like this:

```
Maria Derek Erica
Livia Jack Anita
Kendall Maria Livia Derek
Jamie Jack
Erica
```

Table 10.1 Basic `ArrayList` Methods

Method	Description	`ArrayList<String>` example
`add(value)`	adds the given value at the end of the list	`list.add("end");`
`add(index, value)`	adds the given value at the given index, shifting subsequent values right	`list.add(1, "middle");`
`clear()`	removes all elements from the list	`list.clear();`
`get(index)`	gets the value at the given index	`list.get(1)`
`remove(index)`	removes the value at the given index, shifting subsequent values left	`list.remove(1);`
`set(index, value)`	replaces the value at the given index with the given value	`list.set(2, "hello");`
`size()`	returns the current number of elements in the list	`list.size()`

You can construct an `ArrayList<String>` to hold these names and use the `contains` method to ensure that there are no duplicates:

```
// removes duplicates from a list
Scanner input = new Scanner(new File("names.txt"));
ArrayList<String> list = new ArrayList<String>();
while (input.hasNext()) {
    String name = input.next();
    if (!list.contains(name)) {
        list.add(name);
    }
}
System.out.println("list = " + list);
```

Given the sample input file, this code produces the following output:

```
list = [Maria, Derek, Erica, Livia, Jack, Anita, Kendall, Jamie]
```

Notice that only 8 of the original 13 names appear in this list, because the various duplicates have been eliminated.

Sometimes it is not enough to know that a value appears in the list. You may want to know exactly where it occurs. For example, suppose you want to write a method to replace the first occurrence of one word in an `ArrayList<String>` with another word. You can call the `set` method to replace the value, but you have to know where it appears in the list. You can find out the location of a value in the list by calling the `indexOf` method.

The `indexOf` method takes a particular value and returns the index of the first occurrence of the value in the list. If it doesn't find the value, it returns `-1`. So, you could write a `replace` method as follows:

```
public static void replace(ArrayList<String> list,
                           String target, String replacement) {
    int index = list.indexOf(target);
    if (index >= 0) {
        list.set(index, replacement);
    }
}
```

Notice that the return type of this method is `void`, even though it changes the contents of an `ArrayList` object. Some novices think that you have to return the changed `ArrayList`, but the method doesn't actually create a new `ArrayList`; it merely changes the contents of the list. As you've seen with arrays and other objects, a parameter is all you need to be able to change the current state of an object because objects involve reference semantics in which the method is passed a reference to the object.

You can test the method with the following code:

```
ArrayList<String> list = new ArrayList<String>();
list.add("to");
list.add("be");
list.add("or");
list.add("not");
list.add("to");
list.add("be");
System.out.println("initial list = " + list);
replace(list, "be", "beep");
System.out.println("final list   = " + list);
```

This code produces the following output:

```
initial list = [to, be, or, not, to, be]
final list   = [to, beep, or, not, to, be]
```

There is also a variation of `indexOf` known as `lastIndexOf`. As its name implies, this method returns the index of the last occurrence of a value. There are many situations where you might be more interested in the last occurrence rather than the first occurrence. For example, if a bank finds a broken automated teller machine, it might want to find out the name and account number of the last customer to use that machine. Table 10.2 summarizes the `ArrayList` searching methods.

Table 10.2 `ArrayList` Searching Methods

Method	Description	ArrayList<String> example
`contains(value)`	returns `true` if the given value appears in the list	`list.contains("hello")`
`indexOf(value)`	returns the index of the first occurrence of the given value in the list (−1 if not found)	`list.indexOf("world")`
`lastIndexOf(value)`	returns the index of the last occurrence of the given value in the list (−1 if not found)	`list.lastIndexOf("hello")`

All of the `ArrayList` searching methods call the `equals` method for comparing values. The method names are fairly standard and appear elsewhere in the Java class libraries. For example, the `String` class also has methods called `indexOf` and `lastIndexOf` that allow you to search for the position of a character or substring inside a string.

A Complete ArrayList Program

Before we go further, let's look at a complete `ArrayList` program. Search engines like Google ignore the *stop words* in users' queries. The idea is that certain words like "a" and "the" appear so often that they aren't worth indexing. Google won't disclose the exact list of words it uses, although a few examples are listed on the web site and people have speculated about what they think is on the list.

Google's full list of stop words is believed to have at least 35 entries, but we'll settle for 15 of the most obvious choices. To explore how removing stop words can affect a text, our program will read a file called `speech.txt` that contains the first part of Hamlet's famous speech:

```
To be or not to be – that is the question:
Whether 'tis nobler in the mind to suffer
The slings and arrows of outrageous fortune
Or to take arms against a sea of troubles,
And by opposing end them.
```

The program constructs a list of stop words and then reads the file word by word, printing every word that is not a stop word. To avoid issues of case, the stop words are all in lowercase and the call on `contains` is passed a lowercase version of each word from the input file. Here is the complete program:

```
// This program constructs a list of stop words and echoes
// Hamlet's famous speech with the stop words removed.

```

```
import java.util.*;
import java.io.*;

public class StopWords {
    public static void main(String[] args)
            throws FileNotFoundException {
        // build the list of stop words
        ArrayList<String> stopWords = new ArrayList<String>();
        stopWords.add("a");
        stopWords.add("be");
        stopWords.add("by");
        stopWords.add("how");
        stopWords.add("in");
        stopWords.add("is");
        stopWords.add("it");
        stopWords.add("of");
        stopWords.add("on");
        stopWords.add("or");
        stopWords.add("that");
        stopWords.add("the");
        stopWords.add("this");
        stopWords.add("to");
        stopWords.add("why");

        // process the file, printing all but stop words
        Scanner input = new Scanner(new File("speech.txt"));
        while (input.hasNext()) {
            String next = input.next();
            if (!stopWords.contains(next.toLowerCase())) {
                System.out.print(next + " ");
            }
        }
    }
}
```

The program produces the following output:

```
not — question: Whether 'tis nobler mind suffer slings and
arrows outrageous fortune take arms against sea troubles,
And opposing end them.
```

This output represents the search view of the original text (the core set of words that will be used by a search engine).

Adding to and Removing from an ArrayList

VideoNote

In this section, we will explore some of the issues that come up when you dynamically add values to or remove values from the middle of an `ArrayList`. The results are often surprising, so it is worth exploring the common pitfalls.

Consider the following code, which creates an `ArrayList` and stores several words in it:

```
ArrayList<String> words = new ArrayList<String>();
words.add("four");
words.add("score");
words.add("and");
words.add("seven");
words.add("years");
words.add("ago");
System.out.println("words = " + words);
```

This code produces the following output:

```
words = [four, score, and, seven, years, ago]
```

We'll explore the problem of inserting a tilde ("~") in front of each word, doubling the size of the list. Inserting tildes isn't the most exciting operation you can imagine doing with a list, but we want to keep things simple so we can focus on the programming issues, and you'll find that you often want to perform operations like this. For example, if you put a tilde in front of a search term, Google does a different search that includes synonyms of the word. Searching for "~four ~score" yields more than 10 times as many pages as searching for just "four score."

In our case, we want to keep the tildes separate from the words themselves, so we want to insert a new `String` containing just a tilde in front of each word in the list. Here is a first attempt that makes sense intuitively but doesn't work:

```
// doesn't work properly
for (int i = 0; i < words.size(); i++) {
    words.add(i, "~");
}
System.out.println("after loop words = " + words);
```

This `for` loop is a slight variation of the standard array-traversal loop. It has an index variable `i` whose value starts at `0` and goes up by one each time. In this case, the loop is inserting a tilde at position `i` each time it executes the loop. The problem is that the loop never terminates. (If you're patient enough, you will find that the program does eventually terminate with an "out of memory" error.)

The loop fails to terminate because the `ArrayList` structure is dynamic in nature. Let's think about this carefully to see what's happening. Initially we have the following list, with the `String "four"` in position 0:

```
[four, score, and, seven, years, ago]
```

The first time the program executes the loop, it inserts a tilde at position 0. To make room for the tilde at position 0, the `ArrayList` has to shift all the other values one place to the right. As a result, the `String "four"` ends up in position 1:

```
[~, four, score, and, seven, years, ago]
```

Then we come around the `for` loop, increment `i` to be `1`, and insert a tilde at position 1. But because the word `"four"` is currently at position 1, this second tilde also goes in front of the word `"four"`, shifting it into position 2:

```
[~, ~, four, score, and, seven, years, ago]
```

We then go around the loop again, incrementing `i` to be `2` and inserting a tilde at that position, which is once again in front of the word `"four"`:

```
[~, ~, ~, four, score, and, seven, years, ago]
```

This loop continues indefinitely, because we keep inserting tildes in front of the first word in the list. The `for` loop test compares `i` to the size of the list, but because the list is growing, the size keeps going up. So, this process continues until all the computer's available memory is exhausted.

To fix this loop, we have to take into account the fact that inserting a tilde at position `i` is going to shift everything one place to the right. So, on the next iteration of the loop, we will want to insert the tilde in the position that is two to the right, not one to the right. We can fix the code simply by changing the update part of the `for` loop to add 2 to `i` instead of adding 1 to `i`:

```
for (int i = 0; i < words.size(); i += 2) {
    words.add(i, "~");
}
System.out.println("after loop words = " + words);
```

When we execute this version of the code, we get the following output:

```
after loop words = [~, four, ~, score, ~, and, ~, seven, ~, years, ~, ago]
```

As another example, let's consider what code we would need to write to undo this operation. We want to write code that will remove every other value from the list, starting with the first value—in other words, the values that are currently at indexes 0, 2, 4, 6, 8, and 10. We might write code like the following:

```
// doesn't work properly
for (int i = 0; i < words.size(); i += 2) {
    words.remove(i);
}
System.out.println("after second loop words = " + words);
```

Looking at the loop, you can see that `i` starts at `0` and goes up by 2 each time, which means it produces a sequence of even values (`0`, `2`, `4`, and so on). That seems to be what we want, given that the values to be removed are at those indexes. But this code doesn't work. It produces the following output:

```
after second loop words = [four, ~, ~, and, seven, ~, ~, ago]
```

Again, the problem comes from the fact that in the `ArrayList` values are shifted dynamically from one location to another. The first tilde we want to remove is at index 0:

```
[~, four, ~, score, ~, and, ~, seven, ~, years, ~, ago]
```

But once we remove the tilde at position 0, everything is shifted one position to the left. The second tilde moves into index 1:

```
[four, ~, score, ~, and, ~, seven, ~, years, ~, ago]
```

So the second remove should be at index 1, not index 2. And once we perform that second remove, the third tilde will be in index 2:

```
[four, score, ~, and, ~, seven, ~, years, ~, ago]
```

In this case, we don't want to increment `i` by 2 each time through the loop. Here, the simple loop that increments by 1 is the right choice:

```
for (int i = 0; i < words.size(); i++) {
    words.remove(i);
}
System.out.println("after second loop words = " + words);
```

After the program executes this code, it produces the following output:

```
after second loop words = [four, score, and, seven, years, ago]
```

Putting all of these pieces together gives us the following complete program:

```
// Builds up a list of words, adds tildes, and removes them.

import java.util.*;

public class TildeFun {
    public static void main(String[] args) {
        // construct and fill up ArrayList
        ArrayList<String> words = new ArrayList<String>();
```

```
        words.add("four");
        words.add("score");
        words.add("and");
        words.add("seven");
        words.add("years");
        words.add("ago");
        System.out.println("words = " + words);

        // insert one tilde in front of each word
        for (int i = 0; i < words.size(); i += 2) {
            words.add(i, "~");
        }
        System.out.println("after loop words = " + words);

        // remove tildes
        for (int i = 0; i < words.size(); i++) {
            words.remove(i);
        }
        System.out.println("after second loop words = " + words);
    }
}
```

If we want to write the loops in a more intuitive manner, we can run them backwards. The loops we have written go from left to right, from the beginning of the list to the end of the list. We could instead go from right to left, from the end of the list to the beginning of the list. By going backward, we ensure that any changes we are making occur in parts of the list that we have already visited.

For example, we found that the following loop did not work properly even though it seemed like the intuitive approach:

```
// doesn't work properly
for (int i = 0; i < words.size(); i++) {
    words.add(i, "~");
}
```

But if we turn this loop around and have it iterate backward rather than going forward, it does work properly:

```
// works properly because loop goes backwards
for (int i = words.size() – 1; i >= 0; i––) {
    words.add(i, "~");
}
```

The problem with the original code was that we were inserting a value into the list and then moving our index variable onto that spot in the list. If instead we work backward, the changes that we make affect only those parts of the list that we have already processed.

Similarly, we tried to write the second loop as follows:

```
// doesn't work properly
for (int i = 0; i < words.size(); i += 2) {
    words.remove(i);
}
```

Again, the problem was that we were changing a part of the list that we were about to process. We can keep the overall structure intact by running the loop backward:

```
// works properly because loop goes backwards
for (int i = words.size() — 2; i >= 0; i —= 2) {
    words.remove(i);
}
```

Using the For-Each Loop with ArrayLists

You saw in Chapter 7 that you can use a for-each loop to iterate over the elements of an array. You can do the same with an `ArrayList`. For example, earlier we mentioned that the following code could be used to add up the lengths of the `Strings` stored in an `ArrayList<String>` called `list`:

```
int sum = 0;
for (int i = 0; i < list.size(); i++) {
    String s = list.get(i);
    sum += s.length();
}
System.out.println("Total of lengths = " + sum);
```

We can simplify this code with a for-each loop. Remember that the syntax of this kind of loop is as follows:

```
for (<type> <name> : <structure>) {
    <statement>;
    <statement>;
    ...
    <statement>;
}
```

Thus, the preceding loop to add up the lengths of the `Strings` can be rewritten as follows:

```
int sum = 0;
for (String s : list) {
```

```
    sum += s.length();
}
System.out.println("Total of lengths = " + sum);
```

This loop is another way of saying, "For each `String s` contained in `list` ...."

Because the for-each loop has such a simple syntax, you should use it whenever you want to process each value stored in a list sequentially. You will find, however, that the for-each loop is not appropriate for more complex list problems. For example, there is no simple way to skip around in a list using a for-each loop. You must process the values in sequence from first to last. Also, you cannot modify the list while you are iterating over it.

Consider, for example, the following sample code:

```
// this doesn't work
for (String s : words) {
    System.out.println(s);
    words.remove(0);
}
```

This code prints a `String` from the list and then attempts to remove the value at the front of the list. When you execute this code, the program halts with a `ConcurrentModificationException`. Java is letting you know that you are not allowed to iterate over the list and to modify the list at the same time (concurrently). Because of this limitation, neither of the problems discussed in the previous section could be solved using a for-each loop.

Chapter 7 also mentioned that starting with version 8 of Java, there is a different approach to manipulating structures like arrays and lists that allows you to write more concise code. The following two lines of code perform the same task as the two loop versions above.

```
int sum = list.stream().mapToInt(String::length).sum();
System.out.println("Total of lengths = " + sum);
```

You can read more about this approach in Chapter 19.

Wrapper Classes

VideoNote

So far, all of the `ArrayList` examples we have studied have involved `ArrayList`s of `String` objects. What if you wanted to form a list of integers? Given that `ArrayList<E>` is a generic class, you'd think that Java would allow you to define an `ArrayList<int>`, but that is not the case. The `E` in `ArrayList<E>` can be filled in with any object or reference type (i.e., the name of a class). The primitive types (e.g., `int`, `double`, `char`, and `boolean`), cannot be used as type parameters for an `ArrayList`.

Instead, Java defines a series of *wrapper classes* that allow you to store primitive data as objects.

Wrapper Class

A class that "wraps" (stores) primitive data as an object.

To understand the role of a wrapper class, think of a piece of candy packaged in a wrapper. Pieces of candy can be sticky and inconvenient to handle directly, so we put them inside wrappers that make handling them more convenient. When we want to eat the actual candy, we open up the wrapper to get the candy out. The Java wrapper classes fill a similar role.

For example, consider simple integers, which are of type `int`, a primitive type. Primitive types are not objects, so we can't use values of type `int` in an object context. To allow such use, we must wrap up each `int` into an object of type `Integer`. `Integer` objects are very simple. They have just one field: an `int` value. When we construct an `Integer`, we pass an `int` value to be wrapped; when we want to get the `int` back, we call a method called `intValue` that returns the `int`.

To understand the distinction between `int` and `Integer`, consider the following variable declarations:

```
int x = 38;
Integer y = new Integer(38);
```

This code leads to the following situation in memory:

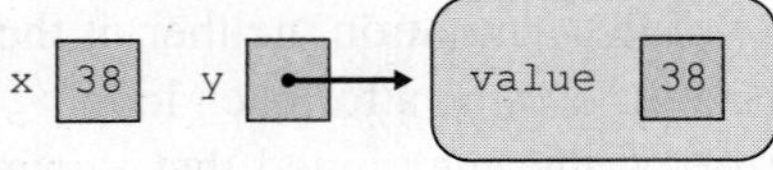

Primitive data is stored directly, so the variable `x` stores the actual value `38`. Objects, by contrast, are stored as references, so the variable `y` stores a reference to an object that contains `38`.

If we later want to get the `38` out of the object (to unwrap it and remove the candy inside), we call the method `intValue`:

```
int number = y.intValue();
```

The wrapper classes are of particular interest in this chapter because when you use an ArrayList<E>, the `E` needs to be a reference type. You can't form an ArrayList<int>, but you can form an ArrayList<Integer>. For example, you can write code like the following that enters several integer values into a list and adds them together:

```
ArrayList<Integer> list = new ArrayList<Integer>();
list.add(13);
list.add(47);
list.add(15);
list.add(9);
```

```
int sum = 0;
for (int n : list) {
    sum += n;
}
System.out.println("list = " + list);
System.out.println("sum = " + sum);
```

This code produces the following output:

```
list = [13, 47, 15, 9]
sum = 84
```

The code takes advantage of a mechanism that Java provides for simplifying code which involves the use of wrapper classes. For example, Java will convert between `Integer` values and `int` values for you when your intent seems clear. Given the declaration of the variable `list` as an `ArrayList<Integer>`, Java would normally expect you to add values of type `Integer` to the list. But in the preceding code you were adding simple `int` values, as in:

```
list.add(13);
```

When it reaches this line of code, Java sees that you are adding an `int` to a structure that is expecting an `Integer`. Because Java understands the relationship between `int` and `Integer` (each `Integer` is simply an `int` wrapped up as an object), it will automatically convert the `int` value into a corresponding `Integer` object. This process is known as *boxing*.

Boxing

An automatic conversion from primitive data to a wrapped object of the appropriate type (e.g., an `int` boxed to form an `Integer`).

Similarly, you don't have to do anything special to unwrap an `Integer` to get the `int` inside. You could write code like the following:

```
int product = list.get(0) * list.get(1);
```

This code multiplies two values from the `ArrayList<Integer>` and stores the result in a variable of type `int`. The calls on `get` will return an `Integer` object, so normally these values would be incompatible. However, because Java understands the relationship between `int` and `Integer` it will unwrap the `Integer` objects for you and give you the `int` values stored inside. This process is known as *unboxing*.

Unboxing

An automatic conversion from a wrapped object to its corresponding primitive data (e.g., an `Integer` unboxed to yield an `int`).

Table 10.3 Common Wrapper Classes

Primitive type	Wrapper class
int	Integer
double	Double
char	Character
boolean	Boolean

Notice that you can write a for-each loop to use a variable of type int even though the ArrayList stores values of type Integer. Java will unbox the objects and perform the appropriate conversions for you.

Because Java has boxing and unboxing, the only place you generally need to use the wrapper class is when you describe a type like ArrayList<Integer>. You can't actually declare it to be of type ArrayList<int>, but you can manipulate it as if it is of type ArrayList<int>.

Table 10.3 lists the major primitive types and their corresponding wrapper classes.

10.2 The Comparable Interface

The method Collections.sort can be used to sort an ArrayList. It is part of the java.util package. The following short program demonstrates how to use Collections.sort:

```
// Constructs an ArrayList of Strings and sorts it.

import java.util.*;

public class SortExample {
    public static void main(String[] args) {
        ArrayList<String> words = new ArrayList<String>();
        words.add("four");
        words.add("score");
        words.add("and");
        words.add("seven");
        words.add("years");
        words.add("ago");

        // show list before and after sorting
        System.out.println("before sort, words = " + words);
        Collections.sort(words);
        System.out.println("after sort, words  = " + words);
    }
}
```

This program produces the following output:

```
before sort, words = [four, score, and, seven, years, ago]
after sort, words  = [ago, and, four, score, seven, years]
```

In Chapter 13, we will explore how this sorting method actually works. For now we are simply going to be clients of the method without worrying about how it works.

If you try to make a similar call to an `ArrayList<Point>`, you will find that the program does not compile. Why is it possible to sort a list of `String` objects but not a list of `Point` objects? The answer is that the `String` class implements the `Comparable` interface, while the `Point` class does not. In this section we will explore the details of the `Comparable` interface and explain how to write classes that implement it.

Did You Know?

Controversy over Boxing and Unboxing

Not all software developers are happy with the decision to add boxing and unboxing to the Java language. The ability to manipulate an `ArrayList<Integer>` almost as if it were an `ArrayList<int>` can simplify code, and everyone agrees that simplification is good. The disagreement comes from the fact that it is *almost* like an `ArrayList<int>`. Some argue that "almost" isn't good enough. Because it comes close, programmers are likely to use it and eventually come to count on it. That can prove disastrous when "almost" isn't "always."

As an analogy, suppose someone told you that you could use a device that is almost like a potholder to pick up hot objects. In most cases, it will protect your hand from heat. So you start using it, and while you might be nervous at first, you soon find that it seems to work just fine. And then one day you pick up a new object and you get burned. You can think of similar analogies with aircraft landing gear that almost works or vests that are almost bulletproof.

For a programming example, consider the following code:

```
int n = 420;
ArrayList<Integer> list = new ArrayList<Integer>();
list.add(n);
list.add(n);
if (list.get(0) == list.get(1)) {
    System.out.println("equal");
} else {
    System.out.println("unequal");
}
```

Continued on next page

Continued from previous page

It's difficult to know exactly what this code will do. If you assume that `ArrayList<Integer>` is "almost" like an `ArrayList<int>`, you'd probably think that the code would print the message that the two values are equal. In fact, there is no guarantee as to what it will do. In the current version of Java, it prints the message "unequal."

Remember that testing for object equality is not as simple as testing for equality of primitive data. Two `Strings` might store the same text but might not be the same object, which is why we call the `equals` method to compare `Strings`. The same principle applies here: The two `list` elements might store the same `int` but might not be the same object. The code prints "unequal" in the current release of Java because the program creates two different `Integer` objects that each store the value `420`. However, to add to the confusion, if we change the value from `420` to `42`, the program will print that the two values are equal.

The Java Language Specification guarantees that this code will work for any value of `n` between `–128` and `127`, but it provides no guarantee as to how the code will behave for other values of `n`. For those other values, it could print either message, and this might change from one implementation of Java to another. It might be that in the next version of Java released, the code will print "equal" for `420` but not for a value like `420000`.

Some people have argued that because boxing and unboxing cover up what is happening underneath, it is better not to use them at all. Boxing and unboxing don't necessarily simplify anything if they work only "sometimes," because you have to be able to understand the cases in which they don't work.

Natural Ordering and compareTo

We are all familiar with many kinds of data that can be sorted. For example, we are used to putting numbers in order from lowest to highest or alphabetizing lists of names. We describe types that can be sorted as having a *natural ordering* of values. To have such an ordering of values, a type needs to have a well-defined *comparison function* that indicates the relationship between any pair of values.

Comparison Function

A well-defined procedure for deciding, given a pair of values, the relative order of the two values (less than, equal to, or greater than).

Natural Ordering

The order imposed on a type by its comparison function.

Not all types have natural orderings because not all types have comparison functions. For example, in this chapter we have been exploring how to construct a variety of `ArrayList` objects. How would you compare two `ArrayList` objects to determine whether one is less than another? What would it mean for one `ArrayList` to be less than another? You might decide to use the lengths of the lists to determine which one is less, but what would you do with two `ArrayList` objects of equal length that store different values? You wouldn't want to describe them as "equal." There is no agreed-upon way of ordering `ArrayLists`, and therefore there is no comparison function for this type. As a result, we say that the `ArrayList` type does not have a natural ordering.

Java has a convention for indicating the natural ordering of a type. Any type that has such an ordering should implement the `Comparable` interface:

```
public interface Comparable<T> {
    public int compareTo(T other);
}
```

This interface provides a second example of a generic type in Java. In the case of `ArrayList`, Java uses the letter "E," which is short for "Element." In the case of `Comparable`, Java uses the letter "T," which is short for "Type."

The `compareTo` method is the comparison function for the type. A `boolean` return type can't be used because there are three possible answers: less than, equal to, or greater than. The convention for `compareTo` is that an object should return one of the following results:

- A negative number to indicate a less-than relationship
- `0` to indicate equality
- A positive number to indicate a greater-than relationship

Let's look at a few examples to help you understand this concept. We have seen that Java has `Integer` objects that serve as wrappers for individual `int` values. We know how to compare `int` values to determine their relative order, so it is not surprising that the `Integer` class implements the `Comparable` interface. Consider the following code:

```
Integer x = 7;
Integer y = 42;
Integer z = 7;
System.out.println(x.compareTo(y));
System.out.println(x.compareTo(z));
System.out.println(y.compareTo(x));
```

This code begins by constructing three `Integer` objects:

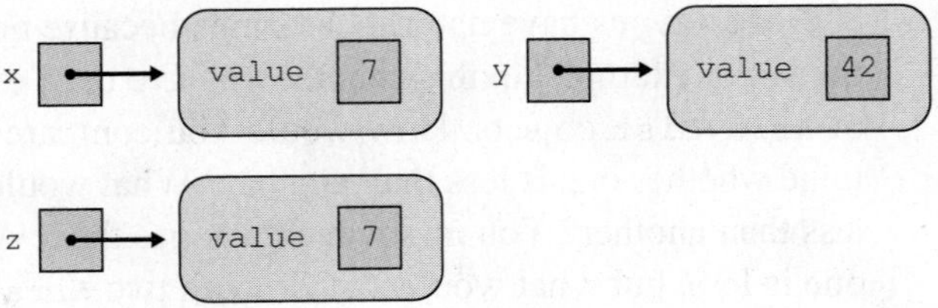

Then it includes a series of `println` statements that report the results of various pairwise comparisons. In the first `println` statement, we compare `x` to `y`, which involves comparing the `int` value `7` to the `int` value `42`. This pair has a less-than relationship because `x` is less than `y`, so the method call returns a negative integer. In the second `println` statement, we compare `x` to `z`, which involves comparing one occurrence of the `int` value `7` with another occurrence of the `int` value `7`. This second pair has an equality relationship because `x` equals `z`, so the method call returns `0`. In the final `println` statement, we compare `y` to `x`, which involves comparing the `int` value `42` to the `int` value `7`. This final pair has a greater-than relationship because `y` is greater than `x`, so the method call returns a positive integer.

Here is the actual output of the code:

```
-1
0
1
```

The values `-1`, `0`, and `1` are the standard values returned, but the `compareTo` method is not required to return these specific values. For example, consider a similar piece of code that compares `String` values:

```
String x = "hello";
String y = "world";
String z = "hello";
System.out.println(x.compareTo(y));
System.out.println(x.compareTo(z));
System.out.println(y.compareTo(x));
```

The `compareTo` method of the `String` class compares strings alphabetically, so there are similar relationships in this code: `x` is less than `y` because in an alphabetical list `"hello"` comes before `"world"`, `x` is equal to `z` because the two occurrences of `"hello"` are equal, and `y` is greater than `x` because in an alphabetical list `"world"` comes after `"hello"`. But the output produced is slightly different from that produced by the `Integer` example:

```
-15
0
15
```

Instead of -1 and 1, we get -15 and 15. You don't really need to know where these numbers come from—the only important fact is whether they are negative or positive—but for those of you who are curious, the -15 and 15 represent the distance between the positions of the characters 'h' and 'w' in type char. 'w' appears 15 positions later than 'h'.

So while the values -1 and 1 are often returned by a comparison function, that won't always be the case. The important thing to remember is that "less-than" relationships are indicated by a negative number and "greater-than" relationships are indicated by a positive number.

Also keep in mind that the relationship operators that we've been using since Chapter 4 have a different syntax. For example, you've seen that if two variables x and y are of type int or double, you can compare them by using operators like < and >:

```
int x = 7;
int y = 42;
if (x < y) {
    System.out.println("x less than y");
}
```

Even though the String class implements the Comparable interface, you can't use the relational operators to compare Strings. The following code will not compile:

```
// illegal--can't compare objects this way
String s1 = "hello";
String s2 = "world";
if (s1 < s2) {
    System.out.println("s1 less than s2");
}
```

Instead, call the compareTo method, as in:

```
String s1 = "hello";
String s2 = "world";
if (s1.compareTo(s2) < 0) {
    System.out.println("s1 less than s2");
}
```

You can use a relational operator in this context because the `compareTo` method returns an `int`. Notice that the specific value of `–1` isn't used for `compareTo` because you are only guaranteed to get a negative value for a less-than relationship. Table 10.4 summarizes the standard way to compare objects that implement the `Comparable` interface.

Implementing the Comparable Interface

VideoNote

Many of the standard Java classes, such as `String`, implement the `Comparable` interface. You can have your own classes implement the interface as well. Implementing the `Comparable` interface will open up a wealth of off-the-shelf programming solutions that are included in the Java class libraries. For example, there are built-in methods for sorting lists and for speeding up searches. Many of these features will be discussed in the next chapter.

As a fairly simple example, let's explore a class that can be used to keep track of a calendar date. The idea is to keep track of a particular month and day, but not the year. For example, the United States celebrates its independence on July 4 each year. Similarly, an organization might want a list of its employees' birthdays that doesn't indicate how old they are.

Table 10.4 Comparing Values Summary

Relationship	Primitive data (`int`, `double`, etc.)	Objects (`Integer`, `String`, etc.)
less than	`if (x < y) {` `...` `}`	`if (x.compareTo(y) < 0) {` `...` `}`
less than or equal to	`if (x <= y) {` `...` `}`	`if (x.compareTo(y) <= 0) {` `...` `}`
equal to	`if (x == y) {` `...` `}`	`if (x.compareTo(y) == 0) {` `...` `}`
not equal to	`if (x != y) {` `...` `}`	`if (x.compareTo(y) != 0) {` `...` `}`
greater than	`if (x > y) {` `...` `}`	`if (x.compareTo(y) > 0) {` `...` `}`
greater than or equal to	`if (x >= y) {` `...` `}`	`if (x.compareTo(y) >= 0) {` `...` `}`

Did You Know?

Why Not –1, 0, and 1 for compareTo?

As we discussed earlier, some types like `Integer` return the values `–1`, `0`, and `1` when you call `compareTo`. These are the *canonical* values for `compareTo` to return, because they correspond to a function in mathematics known as the *signum* function (sometimes abbreviated "sgn"). However, other types like `String` do not return the standard values. You might wonder why Java doesn't require that all classes return `–1`, `0`, and `1` when you call `compareTo`.

One answer to this question is that Java doesn't have a convenient ternary type. For any binary decision, we can use `boolean` as the return type. But what type do we use if we want to return exactly one of three different values? There is no predefined type that has just three values, so it's more honest in a sense to use the rule that any negative number will do and any positive number will do. Suppose that Java said that `compareTo` should return only `–1`, `0`, and `1`. What should happen when someone writes a `compareTo` that returns something else? Ideally, any code calling that particular `compareTo` would throw an exception when it gets an illegal return value, but that would require programmers to write a lot of error-checking code. By saying that all negatives will be interpreted one way, all positives will be interpreted a second way, and `0` will be interpreted a third way, Java provides a complete definition for all values of type `int`, which makes it easier for programmers to work with the `compareTo` method.

A second reason for having `compareTo` behave this way is that it then is easy to express many comparison tasks directly. It is often convenient to express the comparison as a difference between two values. This pattern occurs in many places. For example, the `String` class uses *lexicographic* order (also called "dictionary" or "alphabetic" order). To determine the relationship between two `Strings`, you scan through them until you find the first pair of letters that differ. For example, if you were comparing `"nattering"` and `"nabobs"`, you'd find that the first pair of characters that differ is the third pair (`"nat..."` versus `"nab..."`). You would then return the difference between the character values (`'t' – 'b'`). If you don't find such a pair, then you return the difference between the lengths. For example, `"nattering"` is considered greater than `"nat"` on the basis of length.

The `compareTo` behavior for the `String` class can be described with the following pseudocode:

```
search for a pair of characters in corresponding positions that differ.
if (such a pair exists) {
```

Continued on next page

Continued from previous page

```
    return the difference between the two characters.
} else {
    return the difference between the two lengths.
}
```

Notice that this approach returns `0` in just the right case, when there are no character pairs that differ and when the strings have the same length. Having the flexibility to return any negative integer for "less than" and any positive integer for "greater than" makes it easier to implement this approach.

The final reason not to specify the return values for `compareTo` is efficiency. By having a less strict rule, Java allows programmers to write faster `compareTo` methods. The `compareTo` method in the `String` class is one of the most frequently called methods. All sorts of data comparisons are built on `String` comparisons, and performing a task like sorting thousands of records will lead to thousands of calls on the `String` class's `compareTo` method. As a result, it's important for the method to run quickly. We wouldn't want to unnecessarily complicate the code by requiring that it always return `–1`, `0`, or `1`.

We can implement this class of dates with two fields to store the month and day:

```
public class CalendarDate {
    private int month;
    private int day;

    public CalendarDate(int month, int day) {
        this.month = month;
        this.day = day;
    }
    // other methods
}
```

Remember that to implement an interface, you include an extra notation in the class header. Implementing the `Comparable` interface is a little more challenging because it is a generic interface (`Comparable<T>`). We can't simply write code like the following:

```
// not correct
public class CalendarDate implements Comparable {
    ...
}
```

We have to replace the <T> in Comparable<T>. Whenever you implement Comparable, you compare pairs of values from the same class. So a class called CalendarDate should implement Comparable<CalendarDate>. If you look at the header for the Integer class, you will find that it implements Comparable<Integer>. Likewise, the String class implements Comparable<String>. So we need to change the header to the following one:

```
public class CalendarDate implements Comparable<CalendarDate> {
    ...
}
```

Of course, claiming to implement the interface is not enough. We also have to include appropriate methods. In this case, the Comparable interface includes just a single method:

```
public interface Comparable<T> {
    public int compareTo(T other);
}
```

Because we are using CalendarDate in place of T, we need to write a compareTo method that takes a parameter of type CalendarDate:

```
public int compareTo(CalendarDate other) {
    ...
}
```

Now we have to figure out how to compare two dates. Each CalendarDate object will contain fields that store the month and day. With calendars, the month takes precedence over the day. If we want to compare January 31 (1/31) with April 5 (4/5), we don't care that 5 comes before 31; we care instead that January comes before April. So, as a first attempt, consider the following method that compares only the months:

```
// compares only the months
public int compareTo(CalendarDate other) {
    if (month < other.month) {
        return -1;
    } else if (month == other.month) {
        return 0;
    } else { // month > other.month
        return 1;
    }
}
```

We need to consider more than just the month, but before we do that, we can improve on what we have here. This code uses a nested if/else construct to return the standard values of −1, 0, and 1, but a simpler option is available. We can simply return the difference between month and other.month, because it will be negative when month is less than other.month, it will be 0 when they are equal, and it will be positive when month is greater than other.month. So, we can simplify the code as follows:

```
// still uses only the month, but more compact
public int compareTo(CalendarDate other) {
    return month - other.month;
}
```

It is a good idea to keep things simple when you can, so this version is preferable to the original one. It returns slightly different values than the earlier version, but it satisfies the contract of the Comparable interface just as well. However, the code still has a problem.

Consider, for example, a comparison of April 1 (4/1) and April 5 (4/5). The current version of compareTo would subtract the months and return a value of 0, indicating that these two dates are equal. However, the dates aren't equal: April 1 comes before April 5.

The day of the month becomes important only when the months are equal. If the months differ, we can use the months to determine order. Otherwise (when the months are equal), we must use the day of the month to determine order. This common ordering principle is present in many tasks. We can implement it as follows:

```
public int compareTo(CalendarDate other) {
    if (month != other.month) {
        return month - other.month;
    } else {
        return day - other.day;
    }
}
```

It is still possible for this code to return 0. Suppose that we have two CalendarDate objects that both store the date April 5 (4/5). The months are equal, so the program returns the difference between the days. That difference is 0, so the program returns 0, which correctly indicates that the two dates are equal.

Here is a complete CalendarDate class with the compareTo method, two accessor methods, and a toString method:

```
// The CalendarDate class stores information about a single
// calendar date (month and day but no year).

public class CalendarDate implements Comparable<CalendarDate> {
    private int month;
    private int day;

    public CalendarDate(int month, int day) {
        this.month = month;
```

```
        this.day = day;
    }

    // Compares this calendar date to another date.
    // Dates are compared by month and then by day.
    public int compareTo(CalendarDate other) {
        if (month != other.month) {
            return month - other.month;
        } else {
            return day - other.day;
        }
    }

    public int getMonth() {
        return month;
    }

    public int getDay() {
        return day;
    }

    public String toString() {
        return month + "/" + day;
    }
}
```

One of the major benefits of implementing the `Comparable` interface is that it gives you access to built-in utilities like `Collections.sort`. As we mentioned previously, you can use `Collections.sort` to sort an `ArrayList<String>` but not to sort an `ArrayList<Point>`, because the `Point` class does not implement `Comparable`. The `CalendarDate` class implements the `Comparable` interface, so, as the following short program demonstrates, we can use `Collections.sort` for an `ArrayList<CalendarDate>`:

```
// Short program that creates a list of the birthdays of the
// first 5 U.S. Presidents and that puts them into sorted order.

import java.util.*;

public class CalendarDateTest {
    public static void main(String[] args) {
        ArrayList<CalendarDate> dates =
                new ArrayList<CalendarDate>();
        dates.add(new CalendarDate(2, 22));   // Washington
        dates.add(new CalendarDate(10, 30));  // Adams
```

```
        dates.add(new CalendarDate(4, 13));    // Jefferson
        dates.add(new CalendarDate(3, 16));    // Madison
        dates.add(new CalendarDate(4, 28));    // Monroe

        System.out.println("birthdays = " + dates);
        Collections.sort(dates);
        System.out.println("birthdays = " + dates);
    }
}
```

This program produces the following output:

```
birthdays = [2/22, 10/30, 4/13, 3/16, 4/28]
birthdays = [2/22, 3/16, 4/13, 4/28, 10/30]
```

Notice that the dates appear in increasing calendar order after the call on `Collections.sort`.

10.3 Case Study: Vocabulary Comparison

In this section, we will use `ArrayLists` to solve a complex problem. We will develop a program that will read two different text files and compare their vocabulary. In particular, we will determine the set of words used in each file and compute the overlap between them. Researchers in the humanities often perform such comparisons of vocabulary in selections of text to answer questions like, "Did Christopher Marlowe actually write Shakespeare's plays?"

As we have done with most of our case studies, we will develop the program in stages:

1. The first version will read the two files and report the unique words in each. We will use short testing files for this stage.
2. The second version will also compute the overlap between the two files (i.e., the set of words that appear in both files). We will continue to use short testing files for this stage.
3. The third version will read from large text files and will perform some analysis of the results.

Some Efficiency Considerations

Many of the early programs in this book involved fairly simple computations and fairly small data sets. As you start writing more complex programs, you'll find that you have to worry about programs running slowly because they are performing complex computations or handling large amounts of data. We are going to explore this in much more detail in Chapter 13, but we need to explore it at least briefly for this case study because otherwise we are likely to pursue an approach that won't work well.

For example, in the program we are about to write, we have to read in a file and come up with a list of the words from the file that doesn't have any duplicates. One approach would be to test each word as we read it in to see if it is in the list, as described in the following pseudocode:

```
list = new empty list.
while (more words to process) {
    word = next word from file.
    if (list does not contain word) {
        add word to list.
    }
}
```

The problem with this approach is that it would require us to call the `ArrayList` method called `contains` each time the program executes the loop. It turns out that the `contains` method can be fairly expensive to call in terms of time. To find out whether a particular value is in the list, the method has to go through each different value in the list. So as the list becomes larger and larger, it becomes more and more expensive to search through it to see if it contains a particular word.

We will run into a similar problem when we get to the second version of the program and have to compute the overlap between the two lists. The simplest way to compute the overlap would be to write a method like this:

```
overlap = new empty list.
for (each word in list1) {
    if (word is in list2) {
        add word to overlap.
    }
}
```

This approach will again require calling the `contains` method for a list that could potentially be very large. If both lists are large, then the approach will run particularly slowly.

Both of these potential bottlenecks can be addressed by dealing with sorted lists. In a sorted list of words, all of the duplicates are grouped together, which makes them easier to spot. And looking for the overlap between two sorted lists is easier than looking for overlap in two lists that are not ordered.

Of course, sorting isn't cheap either. It takes a nontrivial amount of time to sort a list. But if we can manage to sort the list just once, it will turn out to be cheaper than making all of those calls on the `contains` method.

Instead of trying to eliminate the duplicates as we read the words, we can just read all of the words directly into the list. That way we won't make any expensive calls on the `contains` method. After we have read everything in, we can put the list into sorted order. When we do that, all of the duplicates will appear right next to one another, so we can fairly easily get rid of them.

Reading all of the words into the list and then eliminating duplicates will require more memory than eliminating the duplicates as we go, but it will end up running faster because the only expensive operation we will have is the sorting step. This is a classic tradeoff between running time and memory that comes up often in computer science. We can make programs run faster if we're willing to use more memory or we can limit memory if we don't mind having the program take longer to run.

Our approach to building up the list of words, then, will be as follows:

```
list = new empty list.
while (there are more words to process) {
    add word to list.
}
sort list.
eliminate duplicates.
```

The task of eliminating duplicates also brings up an efficiency consideration. One obvious approach would be the following:

```
for (each word in list) {
    if (word is a duplicate) {
        remove word from list.
    }
}
```

It turns out that `remove` is another expensive operation. A better approach is to simply build up a new list that doesn't have duplicates:

```
result = new empty list.
for (each word in list) {
    if (word is not a duplicate) {
        add word to result.
    }
}
```

This code runs faster because the method that adds a word at the end of the list runs very fast compared with the method that removes a word from the middle of the list.

As we write the actual code, we will refine the pseudocode presented here, but at least we have an idea of the approach we're going to take. For each file, we'll read in all of the words into a list and sort it once. Then we'll use the sorted lists to build up lists that have no duplicates. Then we'll use those two sorted lists to look for the overlap between the two lists.

Version 1: Compute Vocabulary

The program we are writing will only be interesting when we compare large input files, but while we are developing the program it will be easier to use short input files so we can easily check whether we are getting the right answer. Using short input files also means that we don't have to worry about execution time. When you use a large input file and the program takes a long time to execute, it is difficult to know whether the program will ever finish executing. If we develop the program with the use of short input files, we'll know that it should never take a long time to execute. So if we accidentally introduce an infinite loop into our program, we'll know right away that the problem has to do with our code, not with the fact that we have a lot of data to process.

We'll use the first two stanzas of a popular children's song as our input files. We'll create a file called `test1.txt` that contains the following text:

```
The wheels on the bus go Round and round
Round and round
Round and round.
The wheels on the bus go Round and round
All through the town.
```

We'll also use a file called `test2.txt` that contains the following text:

```
The wipers on the bus go Swish, swish, swish,
Swish, swish, swish,
Swish, swish, swish.
The wipers on the bus go Swish, swish, swish,
All through the town.
```

We need to open each of these files with a `Scanner`, so our `main` method will begin with the following lines of code:

```
Scanner in1 = new Scanner(new File("test1.txt"));
Scanner in2 = new Scanner(new File("test2.txt"));
```

Then we want to compute the unique vocabulary contained in each file. We can store this list of words in an `ArrayList<String>`. The operation will be the same for each file, so it makes sense to write a single method that we call twice. The method should take the `Scanner` as a parameter and it should convert it into an `ArrayList<String>` that contains the vocabulary. So, after opening the files, we can execute the following code:

```
ArrayList<String> list1 = getWords(in1);
ArrayList<String> list2 = getWords(in2);
```

This initial version is meant to be fairly simple, so after we have computed the vocabulary for each file, we can simply report it:

```
System.out.println("list1 = " + list1);
System.out.println("list2 = " + list2);
```

The difficult work for this version of the program reduces to writing the `getWords` method. This method should read all of the words from the `Scanner`, building up an `ArrayList<String>` that contains those words and eliminating any duplicates. Remember that our first task is to read all of the words into a list and then to sort the list. For our purposes, we don't care about capitalization, so we can convert each word to lowercase before we add it to the list and then, because we are using an `ArrayList<String>`, we can call `Collections.sort` to put the list into sorted order. Thus, we can build up the list using the following code:

```
while (input.hasNext()) {
    String next = input.next().toLowerCase();
    words.add(next);
}
Collections.sort(words);
```

Once the list has been sorted, duplicates of any words will be grouped together. Remember that our plan is to build up a new list that has no duplicates. The simplest way to eliminate duplicates is to look for transitions between words. For example, if we have 5 occurrences of one word followed by 10 occurrences of another word, most of the pairs of adjacent words will be equal to each other. However, in the middle of those equal pairs, when we make the transition from the first word to the second word, there will be a pair of words that are not equal. Whenever we see such a transition, we know that we are seeing a new word that should be added to our new list.

Looking for transitions leads to a classic fencepost problem. For example, if there are 10 unique words, there will be 9 transitions. We can solve the fencepost problem by adding the first word before the loop begins. Then we can look for words that are not equal to the words that precede them and add them to the list. Expressed as pseudocode, our solution is as follows:

```
construct a new empty list.
add first word to new list.
for (each i) {
    if (value at i does not equal value at i-1) {
        add value at i.
    }
}
```

This outline can be converted into actual code fairly directly, but we have to be careful to start `i` at `1` rather than at `0` because in the loop we compare each word to the one that comes before it and the first word has nothing before it. We also have to be careful to call the `ArrayList get` method to obtain individual values and to use the `equals` method to compare `Strings` for equality:

```
ArrayList<String> result = new ArrayList<String>();
result.add(words.get(0));
```

```
for (int i = 1; i < words.size(); i++) {
    if (!words.get(i).equals(words.get(i - 1))) {
        result.add(words.get(i));
    }
}
```

There is still one minor problem with this code: If the input file is empty, there won't be a first word to add to the new list. So, we need an extra `if` to make sure that we don't try to add values to the new list if the input file is empty.

Our program now reads as follows:

```
// First version of vocabulary program that reads two files and
// determines the unique words in each.

import java.util.*;
import java.io.*;

public class Vocabulary1 {
    public static void main(String[] args)
            throws FileNotFoundException {
        Scanner in1 = new Scanner(new File("test1.txt"));
        Scanner in2 = new Scanner(new File("test2.txt"));

        ArrayList<String> list1 = getWords(in1);
        ArrayList<String> list2 = getWords(in2);

        System.out.println("list1 = " + list1);
        System.out.println("list2 = " + list2);
    }

    public static ArrayList<String> getWords(Scanner input) {
        // read all words and sort
        ArrayList<String> words = new ArrayList<String>();
        while (input.hasNext()) {
            String next = input.next().toLowerCase();
            words.add(next);
        }
        Collections.sort(words);

        // add unique words to new list and return
        ArrayList<String> result = new ArrayList<String>();
        if (words.size() > 0) {
            result.add(words.get(0));
```

```
            for (int i = 1; i < words.size(); i++) {
                if (!words.get(i).equals(words.get(i - 1))) {
                    result.add(words.get(i));
                }
            }
        }
        return result;
    }
}
```

The program produces the following output:

```
list1 = [all, and, bus, go, on, round, round., the, through, town., wheels]
list2 = [all, bus, go, on, swish,, swish., the, through, town., wipers]
```

The original input files each have 28 words in them. We have reduced the first file to 11 unique words and the second to 10 unique words. The program is correctly ignoring differences in case, but it isn't ignoring differences in punctuation. For example, it considers `"round"` and `"round."` to be different words (one with a period, one without). Similarly, it considers `"swish,"` (with a comma) and `"swish."` (with a period) to be different words. We will fix that problem in Version 3 of our program.

Version 2: Compute Overlap

The first version of the program produces two sorted `ArrayLists` containing sets of unique words. For the second version, we want to compute the overlap between the two lists of words and report it. This operation is complex enough that it deserves to be in its own method. So, we'll add the following line of code to the `main` method right after the two word lists are constructed:

```
ArrayList<String> common = getOverlap(list1, list2);
```

The primary task for the second version of our program is to implement the `getOverlap` method. Look closely at the two lists of words produced by the first version:

```
list1 = [all, and, bus, go, on, round, round., the, through, town., wheels]
list2 = [all, bus, go, on, swish,, swish., the, through, town., wipers]
```

People are pretty good at finding matches, so you can probably see exactly which words overlap. Both lists begin with `"all"`, so that is part of the overlap. Skipping past the word `"and"` in the first list, we find the next match is for the word `"bus"`. Then we have two more matches with the words `"go"` and `"on"`. Next there are a couple of words in a row in both lists that don't match, followed by matches with the words `"the"`, `"through"`, and `"town."`, and a final unique word in each list. The complete set of matches is as follows:

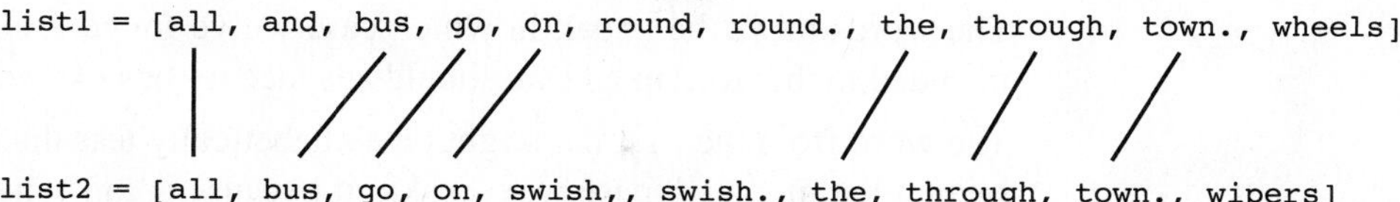
list1 = [all, and, bus, go, on, round, round., the, through, town., wheels]
list2 = [all, bus, go, on, swish,, swish., the, through, town., wipers]

We want to design an algorithm that parallels what people do when they look for matches. Imagine putting a finger from your left hand on the first list and putting a finger from your right hand on the second list to keep track of where you are in each list. We will compare the words at which you are pointing and, depending on how they compare, move one or both fingers forward.

We start with the left finger on the word `"all"` in the first list and the right finger on the word `"all"` in the second list.

```
list1 = [all, and, bus, go, on, round, round., the, through, town., wheels]
          ↑

list2 = [all, bus, go, on, swish,, swish., the, through, town., wipers]
          ↑
```

The words match, so we add that word to the overlap and move both fingers forward:

```
list1 = [all, and, bus, go, on, round, round., the, through, town., wheels]
               ↑

list2 = [all, bus, go, on, swish,, swish., the, through, town., wipers]
               ↑
```

Now we are pointing at the word `"and"` from the first list and the word `"bus"` from the second list. The words don't match. So what do you do? It turns out that the word `"bus"` in `list2` is going to match a word in `list1`. So how do you know to move the left finger forward? Because the lists are sorted and because the word `"and"` comes before the word `"bus"`, we know that there can't be a match for the word `"and"` in the second list. Every word that comes after `"bus"` in the second list will be alphabetically greater than `"bus"`, so the word `"and"` can't be there. Thus, we can move the left finger forward to skip the word `"and"`:

```
list1 = [all, and, bus, go, on, round, round., the, through, town., wheels]
                    ↑

list2 = [all, bus, go, on, swish,, swish., the, through, town., wipers]
               ↑
```

This gets us to the second match, for `"bus"`, and the algorithm proceeds. In general, we find ourselves in one of three situations when we compare the current word in `list1` with the current word in `list2`:

- The words might be equal, in which case we've found a match that should be included in the overlap and we should advance to the next word in each list.
- The word from the first list might be alphabetically less than the word from the second list, in which case we can skip it because it can't match anything in the second list.
- The word from the second list might be alphabetically less than the word from the first list, in which case we can skip it because it can't match anything in the first list.

Thus, the basic approach we want to use can be described with the following pseudocode:

```
if (word from list1 equals word from list2) {
    record match.
    skip word in each list.
} else if (word from list1 < word from list2) {
    skip word in list1.
} else {
    skip word in list2.
}
```

We can refine this pseudocode by introducing two index variables and putting this code inside a loop:

```
i1 = 0.
i2 = 0.
while (more values to compare) {
    if (list1.get(i1) equals list2.get(i2)) {
        record match.
        increment i1.
        increment i2.
    } else if (list.get(i1) less than list.get(i2)) {
        increment i1.
    } else {
        increment i2.
    }
}
```

This version of the pseudocode is now fairly close to actual code. First, we have to figure out an appropriate loop test. We start the two index variables at `0` and increment one or both each time through the loop. Eventually we'll run out of values in one or both lists, and when that happens there won't be any more matches to find. So, we want to continue in the `while` loop as long as the two index variables haven't reached the end of the list. We also have to figure out how to compare the two words. Because the `String` class implements the `Comparable` interface, we can use its `compareTo` method. Finally, we have to construct an `ArrayList` to store the overlap, and we have to return this list after the loop has completed executing.

Thus, we can turn our pseudocode into the following actual code:

```
ArrayList<String> result = new ArrayList<String>();
int i1 = 0;
int i2 = 0;
while (i1 < list1.size() && i2 < list2.size()) {
    int num = list1.get(i1).compareTo(list2.get(i2));
    if (num == 0) {
        result.add(list1.get(i1));
        i1++;
        i2++;
    } else if (num < 0) {
        i1++;
    } else {  // num > 0
        i2++;
    }
}
return result;
```

After we turn this code into a method and modify `main` to call the method and to report the overlap, we end up with the following new version of the program:

```
// Second version of vocabulary program which reads two files
// and reports the overlap between them.

import java.util.*;
import java.io.*;

public class Vocabulary2 {
    public static void main(String[] args)
            throws FileNotFoundException {
        Scanner in1 = new Scanner(new File("test1.txt"));
        Scanner in2 = new Scanner(new File("test2.txt"));

        ArrayList<String> list1 = getWords(in1);
        ArrayList<String> list2 = getWords(in2);
        ArrayList<String> common = getOverlap(list1, list2);

        System.out.println("list1 = " + list1);
        System.out.println("list2 = " + list2);
```

```
            System.out.println("overlap = " + common);
    }

    public static ArrayList<String> getWords(Scanner input) {
        // read all words and sort
        ArrayList<String> words = new ArrayList<String>();
        while (input.hasNext()) {
            String next = input.next().toLowerCase();
            words.add(next);
        }
        Collections.sort(words);

        // add unique words to new list and return
        ArrayList<String> result = new ArrayList<String>();
        if (words.size() > 0) {
            result.add(words.get(0));
            for (int i = 1; i < words.size(); i++) {
                if (!words.get(i).equals(words.get(i - 1))) {
                    result.add(words.get(i));
                }
            }
        }
        return result;
    }

    public static ArrayList<String> getOverlap(
            ArrayList<String> list1, ArrayList<String> list2) {
        ArrayList<String> result = new ArrayList<String>();
        int i1 = 0;
        int i2 = 0;
        while (i1 < list1.size() && i2 < list2.size()) {
            int num = list1.get(i1).compareTo(list2.get(i2));
            if (num == 0) {
                result.add(list1.get(i1));
                i1++;
                i2++;
            } else if (num < 0) {
                i1++;
            } else {  // num > 0
                i2++;
            }
        }
        return result;
    }
}
```

This version of the program produces the following output:

```
list1 = [all, and, bus, go, on, round, round., the, through, town., wheels]
list2 = [all, bus, go, on, swish,, swish., the, through, town., wipers]
overlap = [all, bus, go, on, the, through, town.]
```

Version 3: Complete Program

Our program now correctly builds a vocabulary list for each of two files and computes the overlap between them. The program printed the three lists of words, but that won't be very convenient for large text files containing thousands of different words. We would prefer to have the program report overall statistics, including the number of words in each list, the number of words of overlap, and the percentage of overlap.

The program also should contain at least a brief introduction to explain what it does, and we can write it so that it prompts for file names rather than using hard-coded file names.

This also seems like a good time to think about punctuation. The first two versions allowed words to contain punctuation characters such as commas, periods, and dashes that we wouldn't normally consider to be part of a word.

We can improve our solution by telling the `Scanner` what parts of the input file to ignore. `Scanner` objects have a method called `useDelimiter` that you can call to tell them what characters to use when they break the input file into tokens. When you call the method, you pass it what is known as a *regular expression.* Regular expressions are a highly flexible way to describe patterns of characters. There is some documentation about them in the API pages for the class called `Pattern`.

For our purposes, we want to form a regular expression that will instruct the `Scanner` to look just at characters that are part of what we consider words. That is, we want the `Scanner` to look at letters and apostrophes. The following regular expression is a good starting point:

```
[a–zA–Z']
```

This regular expression would be read as, "Any character in the range of a to z, the range of A to Z, or an apostrophe." This is a good description of the kind of characters we want the `Scanner` to include. But we actually need to tell the `Scanner` what characters to *ignore,* so we need to indicate that it should use the opposite set of characters. The easy way to do this is by including a caret (∧) in front of the list of legal characters:

```
[∧a-zA-Z']
```

This regular expression would be read as, "Any character other than the characters that are in the range of a to z, the range of A to Z, or an apostrophe." Even this expression isn't quite right, though, because there might be many such characters in a row. For example, there might be several spaces, dashes, or other punctuation characters separating two words. We can indicate that a sequence of illegal characters should be ignored by putting a plus after the square brackets to indicate "Any sequence of one or more of these characters":

```
[^a-zA-Z']+
```

We pass this regular expression as a `String` to a call on `useDelimiter`. We can add this at the beginning of the `getWords` method:

```
public static ArrayList<String> getWords(Scanner input) {
    input.useDelimiter("[^a-zA-Z']+");
    ...
}
```

The following is a complete program that incorporates all of these changes and includes more extensive commenting:

```
// This program reads two text files and compares the
// vocabulary used in each.

import java.util.*;
import java.io.*;

public class Vocabulary3 {
    public static void main(String[] args)
            throws FileNotFoundException {
        Scanner console = new Scanner(System.in);
        giveIntro();

        System.out.print("file #1 name? ");
        Scanner in1 = new Scanner(new File(console.nextLine()));
        System.out.print("file #2 name? ");
        Scanner in2 = new Scanner(new File(console.nextLine()));
        System.out.println();

        ArrayList<String> list1 = getWords(in1);
        ArrayList<String> list2 = getWords(in2);
        ArrayList<String> common = getOverlap(list1, list2);

        reportResults(list1, list2, common);
    }

```

```
    // post: reads words from the Scanner, converts them to
    //       lowercase, returns a sorted list of unique words
    public static ArrayList<String> getWords(Scanner input) {
        // ignore all but alphabetic characters and apostrophes
        input.useDelimiter("[^a-zA-Z']+");
        // read all words and sort
        ArrayList<String> words = new ArrayList<String>();
        while (input.hasNext()) {
            String next = input.next().toLowerCase();
            words.add(next);
        }
        Collections.sort(words);

        // add unique words to new list and return
        ArrayList<String> result = new ArrayList<String>();
        if (words.size() > 0) {
            result.add(words.get(0));
            for (int i = 1; i < words.size(); i++) {
                if (!words.get(i).equals(words.get(i - 1))) {
                    result.add(words.get(i));
                }
            }
        }
        return result;
    }

    // pre : list1 and list2 are sorted and have no duplicates
    // post: constructs and returns an ArrayList containing
    //       the words in common between list1 and list2
    public static ArrayList<String> getOverlap(
            ArrayList<String> list1, ArrayList<String> list2) {
        ArrayList<String> result = new ArrayList<String>();
        int i1 = 0;
        int i2 = 0;
        while (i1 < list1.size() && i2 < list2.size()) {
            int num = list1.get(i1).compareTo(list2.get(i2));
            if (num == 0) {
                result.add(list1.get(i1));
                i1++;
                i2++;
            } else if (num < 0) {
                i1++;
            } else {  // num > 0
```

```
                i2++;
            }
        }
        return result;
    }

    // post: explains program to user
    public static void giveIntro() {
        System.out.println("This program compares two text files");
        System.out.println("and reports the number of words in");
        System.out.println("common and the percent overlap.");
        System.out.println();
    }

    // pre : common contains overlap between list1 and list2
    // post: reports statistics about lists and their overlap
    public static void reportResults(ArrayList<String> list1,
            ArrayList<String> list2, ArrayList<String> common) {
        System.out.println("file #1 words = " + list1.size());
        System.out.println("file #2 words = " + list2.size());
        System.out.println("common words = " + common.size());

        double pct1 = 100.0 * common.size() / list1.size();
        double pct2 = 100.0 * common.size() / list2.size();
        System.out.println("% of file 1 in overlap = " + pct1);
        System.out.println("% of file 2 in overlap = " + pct2);
    }
}
```

The following program output is an execution of the program that compares the texts of Shakespeare's *Hamlet* and *King Lear:*

```
This program compares two text files
and reports the number of words in
common and the percent overlap.

file #1 name? hamlet.txt
file #2 name? lear.txt

file #1 words = 4874
file #2 words = 4281
common words = 2108
% of file 1 in overlap = 43.24989741485433
% of file 2 in overlap = 49.24083158140621
```

Notice that the two files have about the same number of unique words and that about half of the unique words appear in both files. Here is a second execution that compares the text of Herman Melville's *Moby-Dick* to the text of *Hamlet:*

```
This program compares two text files
and reports the number of words in
common and the percent overlap.

file #1 name? moby.txt
file #2 name? hamlet.txt

file #1 words = 17305
file #2 words = 4874
common words = 3079
% of file 1 in overlap = 17.792545507078877
% of file 2 in overlap = 63.17193270414444
```

In this case, it is obvious that *Moby-Dick* has a much larger vocabulary. As a result, only a small fraction of the words from *Moby-Dick* appear in *Hamlet* but a large proportion of the words from *Hamlet* appear in *Moby-Dick.* It is well known that Melville admired Shakespeare, so it is not surprising that his novel has a high overlap with one of Shakespeare's plays.

As we mentioned in Chapter 6, you can obtain classic texts like these from the Project Gutenberg web site at http://www.gutenberg.org.

Chapter Summary

The `ArrayList` class in Java's `java.util` package represents a growable list of objects implemented using an array. You can use an `ArrayList` to store objects in sequential order. Each element has a zero-based index.

`ArrayList` is a generic class. A generic class accepts a data type as a parameter when it is created, like `ArrayList<String>`.

An `ArrayList` maintains its own size for you; elements can be added to or removed from any position up to the size of the list. Other `ArrayList` operations include `get`, `set`, `clear`, and `toString`.

`ArrayLists` can be searched using methods named `contains`, `indexOf`, and `lastIndexOf`.

Java's for-each loop can be used to examine each element of an `ArrayList`. The list cannot be modified during the execution of the for-each loop.

When you are storing primitive values such as `int`s or `double`s into an `ArrayList`, you must declare the list with special wrapper types such as `Integer` and `Double`.

The `Comparable` interface defines a natural ordering for the objects of a class. Objects that implement `Comparable` can be placed into an `ArrayList` and sorted. Many common types (such as `String` and `Integer`) implement `Comparable`.

You can implement the `Comparable` interface in your own classes by writing a method `compareTo`.

Self-Check Problems

Section 10.1: ArrayLists

1. What is an `ArrayList`? In what cases should you use an `ArrayList` rather than an array?

2. Which of the following is the correct syntax to construct an `ArrayList` to store integers?

   a. `ArrayList list = new ArrayList();`

   b. `ArrayList[int] list = new ArrayList[int]();`

   c. `ArrayList list<integer> = new ArrayList<integer>();`

   d. `ArrayList<Integer> list = new ArrayList();`

   e. `ArrayList<Integer> list = new ArrayList<Integer>();`

3. The next five questions refer to the following `String` elements:

   `["It", "was", "a", "stormy", "night"]`

   Write the code to declare an `ArrayList` containing these elements. What is the size of the list? What is its type?

4. Write code to insert two additional elements, `"dark"` and `"and"`, at the proper places in the list to produce the following `ArrayList` as the result:

   `["It", "was", "a", "dark", "and", "stormy", "night"]`

5. Write code to change the second element's value to `"IS"`, producing the following `ArrayList` as the result:

   `["It", "IS", "a", "dark", "and", "stormy", "night"]`

6. Write code to remove from the list any `String`s that contain the letter `"a"`. The following should be the list's contents after your code has executed:

   `["It", "IS", "stormy", "night"]`

7. Write code to declare an `ArrayList` holding the first 10 multiples of 2: 0, 2, 4, . . . , 18. Use a loop to fill the list with the proper elements.

8. Write a method called `maxLength` that takes an `ArrayList` of `String`s as a parameter and that returns the length of the longest `String` in the list. If your method is passed an empty `ArrayList`, it should return `0`.

9. Write code to print out whether or not a list of `String`s contains the value `"IS"`. Do not use a loop.

10. Given the `ArrayList` from problem 4, write code to print out the index at which your list contains the value `"stormy"` and the index at which it contains `"dark"`. Do not use a loop.

11. Given the `ArrayList` from problem 4, write a for-each loop that prints the uppercase version of each `String` in the list on its own line.

12. When the code that follows runs on an `ArrayList` of `String`s, it throws an exception. Why?

```
for (String s : words) {
    System.out.println(s);
    if (s.equals("hello")) {
```

```
        words.add("goodbye");
    }
}
```

13. The code that follows does not compile. Why not? Explain how to fix it.

```
ArrayList<int> numbers = new ArrayList<int>();
numbers.add(7);
numbers.add(19);
System.out.println(numbers);
```

14. What is a wrapper class? Describe the difference between an `int` and an `Integer`.

15. Write the output produced when the following method is passed each of the following lists:

```
public static void mystery1(ArrayList<Integer> list) {
    for (int i = list.size() - 1; i > 0; i--) {
        if (list.get(i) < list.get(i - 1)) {
            int element = list.get(i);
            list.remove(i);
            list.add(0, element);
        }
    }
    System.out.println(list);
}
```

a. `[2, 6, 1, 8]`
b. `[30, 20, 10, 60, 50, 40]`
c. `[-4, 16, 9, 1, 64, 25, 36, 4, 49]`

16. Write the output produced when the following method is passed each of the following lists:

```
public static void mystery2(ArrayList<Integer> list) {
    for (int i = list.size() - 1; i >= 0; i--) {
        if (i % 2 == 0) {
            list.add(list.get(i));
        } else {
            list.add(0, list.get(i));
        }
    }
    System.out.println(list);
}
```

a. `[10, 20, 30]`
b. `[8, 2, 9, 7, 4]`
c. `[-1, 3, 28, 17, 9, 33]`

17. Write the output produced when the following method is passed each of the following lists:

```
public static void mystery3(ArrayList<Integer> list) {
    for (int i = list.size() - 2; i > 0; i--) {
        int a = list.get(i);
```

```
            int b = list.get(i + 1);
            list.set(i, a + b);
        }
        System.out.println(list);
    }
```

a. `[72, 20]`
b. `[1, 2, 3, 4, 5, 6]`
c. `[10, 20, 30, 40]`

18. Write the output produced when the following method is passed each of the following lists:

```
public static void mystery4(ArrayList<Integer> list) {
    for (int i = 0; i < list.size(); i++) {
        int element = list.get(i);
        list.remove(i);
        list.add(0, element + 1);
    }
    System.out.println(list);
}
```

a. `[10, 20, 30]`
b. `[8, 2, 9, 7, 4]`
c. `[-1, 3, 28, 17, 9, 33]`

Section 10.2: The `Comparable` Interface

19. Describe how to arrange an `ArrayList` into sorted order. What must be true about the type of elements in the list in order to sort it?

20. What is a natural ordering? How do you define a natural ordering for a class you've written?

21. Consider the following variable declarations:

```
Integer n1 = 15;
Integer n2 = 7;
Integer n3 = 15;
String s1 = "computer";
String s2 = "soda";
String s3 = "pencil";
```

Indicate whether the result of each of the following comparisons is positive, negative, or `0`:

a. `n1.compareTo(n2)`
b. `n3.compareTo(n1)`
c. `n2.compareTo(n1)`
d. `s1.compareTo(s2)`
e. `s3.compareTo(s1)`
f. `s2.compareTo(s2)`

22. Use the `compareTo` method to write code that reads two names from the console and prints the one that comes first in alphabetical order. For example, the program's output might look like the following:

```
Type a name: Tyler Durden
Type a name: Marla Singer
Marla Singer goes before Tyler Durden
```

23. Write code to read a line of input from the user and print the words of that line in sorted order, without removing duplicates. For example, the program output might look like the following:

```
Type a message to sort: to be or not to be that is the question
Your message sorted: be be is not or question that the to to
```

Exercises

1. Write a method called `averageVowels` that takes an `ArrayList` of strings as a parameter and returns the average number of vowel characters (a, e, i, o, u) in all Strings in the list. If your method is passed an empty `ArrayList`, it should return `0.0`.

2. Write a method called `swapPairs` that switches the order of values in an `ArrayList` of strings in a pairwise fashion. Your method should switch the order of the first two values, then switch the order of the next two, then the next two, and so on. If the number of values in the list is odd, the method should not move the final element. For example, if the list initially stores `["to", "be", "or", "not", "to", "be", "hamlet"]`, your method should change the list's contents to `["be", "to", "not", "or", "be", "to", "hamlet"]`.

3. Write a method called `removeEvenLength` that takes an `ArrayList` of strings as a parameter and removes all of the strings of even length from the list.

4. Write a method called `doubleList` that takes an `ArrayList` of strings as a parameter and replaces every string with two of that same string. For example, if the list stores the values `["how", "are", "you?"]` before the method is called, it should store the values `["how", "how", "are", "are", "you?", "you?"]` after the method finishes executing.

5. Write a method called `scaleByK` that takes an `ArrayList` of integers as a parameter and replaces every integer of value *k* with *k* copies of itself. For example, if the list stores the values `[4, 1, 2, 0, 3]` before the method is called, it should store the values `[4, 4, 4, 4, 1, 2, 2, 3, 3, 3]` after the method finishes executing. Zeroes and negative numbers should be removed from the list by this method.

6. Write a method called `minToFront` that takes an `ArrayList` of integers as a parameter and moves the minimum value in the list to the front, otherwise preserving the order of the elements. For example, if a variable called `list` stores `[3, 8, 92, 4, 2, 17, 9]`, the value `2` is the minimum, so your method should modify the list to store the values `[2, 3, 8, 92, 4, 17, 9]`.

7. Write a method called `removeDuplicates` that takes as a parameter a sorted `ArrayList` of strings and eliminates any duplicates from the list. For example, if the list stores the values `["be", "be", "is", "not", "or", "question", "that", "the", "to", "to"]` before the method is called, it should store the values `["be", "is", "not", "or", "question", "that", "the", "to"]` after the method finishes executing. Because the values will be sorted, all of the duplicates will be grouped together. Assume that the `ArrayList` contains only `String` values, but keep in mind that it might be empty.

8. Write a method called `removeZeroes` that takes as a parameter an `ArrayList` of integers and eliminates any occurrences of the number `0` from the list. For example, if the list stores the values `[0, 7, 2, 0, 0, 4, 0]` before the method is called, it should store the values `[7, 2, 4]` after the method finishes executing.

9. Write a method called `rangeBetweenZeroes` that takes as a parameter an `ArrayList` of integers and returns the number of indexes apart the two farthest occurrences of the number `0` are. For example, if the list stores the values `[7, 2, 0, 0, 4, 0, 9, 0, 6, 4, 8]` when the method is called, it should return `6`, because the occurrences of `0` that are farthest apart are at indexes 2 and 7, and the range 2 through 7 has six elements. If only one `0` occurs in the list, your method should return `1`. If no `0`s occur, your method should return `0`.

10. Write a method called `removeInRange` that accepts three parameters, an `ArrayList` of strings, a beginning string, and an ending string, and removes from the list any strings that fall alphabetically between the start and end strings. For example, if the method is passed a list containing the elements `["to", "be", "or", "not", "to", "be", "that", "is", "the", "question"]`, `"free"` as the start String, and `"rich"` as the end String, the list's elements should be changed to `["to", "be", "to", "be", "that", "the"]`. The `"or"`, `"not"`, `"is"`, and `"question"` should be removed because they occur alphabetically between `"free"` and `"rich"`. You may assume that the start string alphabetically precedes the ending string.

11. Write a method called `stutter` that accepts an `ArrayList` of strings and an integer *k* as parameters and that replaces every string with *k* copies of that string. For example, if the list stores the values `["how", "are", "you?"]` before the method is called and *k* is 4, it should store the values `["how", "how", "how", "how", "are", "are", "are", "are", "you?", "you?", "you?", "you?"]` after the method finishes executing. If *k* is 0 or negative, the list should be empty after the call.

12. Write a method called `markLength4` that accepts an `ArrayList` of strings as a parameter and that places a string of four asterisks `"****"` in front of every string of length 4. For example, suppose that a variable called `list` contains the values `["this", "is", "lots", "of", "fun", "for", "Java", "coders"]`. The call of `markLength4(list);` should change the list to store the values `["****", "this", "is", "****", "lots", "of", "fun", "for", "****", "Java", "coders"]`.

13. Write a method called `reverse3` that accepts an `ArrayList` of integer values as a parameter and reverses each successive sequence of three values in the list. If the list has extra values that are not part of a sequence of three, those values are unchanged. For example, if a list stores values `[3, 8, 19, 42, 7, 26, 19, -8]`, after the call the list should store the values `[19, 8, 3, 26, 7, 42, 19, -8]`. The first sequence of three `(3, 8, 19)` has been reversed to be `(19, 8, 3)`. The second sequence `(42, 7, 26)` has been reversed to be `(26, 7, 42)`, and so on. Notice that `19` and `–8` are unchanged because they were not part of a sequence of three values.

14. Write a method called `removeShorterStrings` that accepts an `ArrayList` of strings as a parameter and removes from each pair of values the shorter string in the pair. If the list is of odd length, the final element is unchanged. For example, suppose that a list contains `["four", "score", "and", "seven", "years", "ago", "our"]`. In the first pair (`"four"` and `"score"`) the shorter string is `"four"`. In the second pair (`"and"` and `"seven"`) the shorter string is `"and"`. In the third pair (`"years"` and `"ago"`) the shorter string is `"ago"`. Your method should remove these shorter strings, changing the list to store `["score", "seven", "years", "our"]`. If both strings in a pair have the same length, remove the first string in the pair.

15. Write a method called `filterRange` that accepts an `ArrayList` of integers and two integer values *min* and *max* as parameters and removes all elements whose values are in the range *min* through *max* (inclusive). For example, if a variable called `list` stores the values `[4, 7, 9, 2, 7, 7, 5, 3, 5, 1, 7, 8, 6, 7]`, the call of `filterRange(list, 5, 7);` should remove all values between `5` and `7`, changing the list to store

[4, 9, 2, 3, 1, 8]. If no elements in range *min-max* are found in the list, or if the list is initially empty, the list's contents are unchanged.

16. Write a method called `clump` that accepts an `ArrayList` of strings as a parameter and replaces each pair of strings with a single string that consists of the two original strings in parentheses separated by a space. If the list is of odd length, the final element is unchanged. For example, suppose that a list contains `["four", "score", "and", "seven", "years", "ago", "our"]`. Your method should change the list to store `["(four score)", ("and seven"), ("years ago"), "our"]`.

17. Write a method called `interleave` that accepts two `ArrayLists` of integers *a1* and *a2* as parameters and inserts the elements of *a2* into *a1* at alternating indexes. If the lists are of unequal length, the remaining elements of the longer list are left at the end of *a1*. For example, if *a1* stores `[10, 20, 30]` and *a2* stores `[4, 5, 6, 7, 8]`, the call of `interleave(a1, a2);` should change *a1* to store `[10, 4, 20, 5, 30, 6, 7, 8]`. If *a1* had stored `[10, 20, 30, 40, 50]` and *a2* had stored `[6, 7, 8]`, the call of `interleave(a1, a2);` would change *a1* to store `[10, 6, 20, 7, 30, 8, 40, 50]`.

18. Modify the `Point` class from Chapter 8 so that it defines a natural ordering by implementing the `Comparable` interface. Compare the `Points` by *y*-major order; that is, points with smaller *y*-coordinate values should come before those with higher *y*-coordinate values. Break ties by comparing *x*-coordinate values.

19. Modify the `TimeSpan` class from Chapter 8 to include a `compareTo` method that compares time spans by their length. A time span that represents a shorter amount of time is considered to be "less than" one that represents a longer amount of time. For example, a span of 3 hours and 15 minutes is greater than a span of 1 hour and 40 minutes.

20. Modify the `CalendarDate` class from this chapter to include a year field, and modify its `compareTo` method to take years into account when making comparisons. Years take precedence over months, which take precedence over days. For example, July 18, 1995, comes before March 2, 2001.

Programming Projects

1. Write classes to model a shopping list. Make an `Item` class that represents a grocery item's name and price, such as tissues for $3. Also implement an `ItemOrder` class that represents a shopper's desire to purchase a given item in a given quantity, such as five boxes of tissues. You might wish to implement bulk-discounted items, such as two boxes of tissues for $4, which would bring the cost of the given item order of 2 + 2 + 1 boxes of tissues to $4 + $4 + $3, or $11.00. Lastly, implement a `ShoppingCart` class that stores `ItemOrders` in an `ArrayList` and allows item orders to be added to, removed from, or searched for in the cart. The cart should be able to report the total price of all item orders it currently carries.

2. Write a program to reverse the lines of a file and also to reverse the order of the words in each line of the file. Use `ArrayLists` to help you.

3. Write a family database program. Create a class to represent a person and to store references to the person's mother, father, and any children the person has. Read a file of names to initialize the name and parent–child relationships of each `Person`. (You might wish to create a file representing your own family tree.) Store the overall list of `Persons` as an `ArrayList`. Write an overall main user interface that asks for a name and prints the maternal and paternal family line for that person.

Here's a hypothetical execution of the program, using as an input file the line of English Tudor monarchs:

```
Person's name? Henry VIII
Maternal line:
    Henry VIII
        Elizabeth of York
Paternal line:
    Henry VIII
        Henry VII
Children:
    Mary I
    Elizabeth I
    Edward VI
```

4. Write a class that models a list of possibly overlapping rectangular two-dimensional window regions, like the windows for the programs open on your computer. The order of the rectangles in the list implies the order in which they would display on the screen (sometimes called the "*z*-order"), from `0` on the bottom to `size() - 1` on the top.

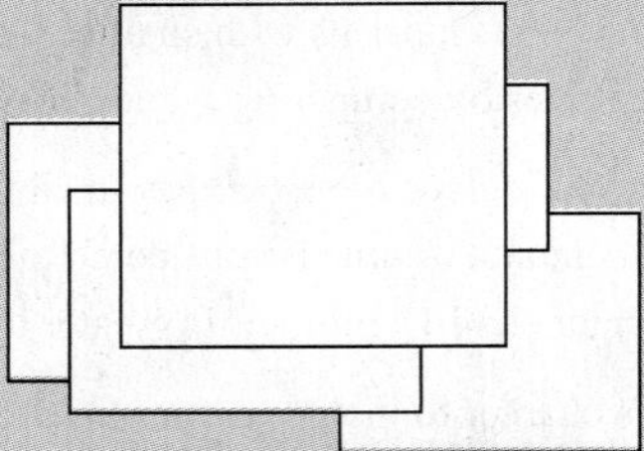

Each rectangle stores its (*x*, *y*) position, width, and height. Your rectangle list class should have a method that takes a `Point` as a parameter, treats it as though the user clicked that `Point` on the screen, and moves the topmost rectangle touching that `Point` to the front of the list.

Chapter 11

Java Collections Framework

Introduction

The previous chapter explored the `ArrayList` class. An `ArrayList` is one of many ways to store data in Java. In this chapter we'll explore Java's framework of collections, including lists, sets, and maps. We'll see how to use these structures together to manipulate and examine data in many ways to solve programming problems. This chapter will examine a trio of smaller interesting programs as case studies rather than presenting a unified case study at the end of the chapter.

We'll introduce a new type of list called a linked list that stores its data differently from an `ArrayList` but supports the same operations. We'll also discuss collections called sets that don't allow duplicate elements and that are easy to search. Another collection type we'll explore is the map, which creates associations between pairs of data values. We'll also delve into the notion of abstract data types as a way to separate the capabilities of a collection from the details of its implementation.

11.1 Lists

The `ArrayList` class from Chapter 10 has several advantages over an array: It keeps track of its own size for you, it allows you to insert and remove data at arbitrary places in the array, and it resizes itself for you if it gets full.

In this section we'll learn about an object called a `LinkedList`, which is similar to an `ArrayList`. We'll also look at generalizing collections and discuss a useful object called an iterator that lets you examine the elements of any collection.

Collections

In Chapters 7 and 8, we discussed ways to use arrays and classes to store data. The notion of organizing and structuring data is an important one that helps us solve complex problems. Entities that store and manage data are also called *data structures*. Data structures can be used to implement sophisticated data storage objects called *collections*.

Collection

An object that stores a group of other objects, called its *elements*.

An `ArrayList` is an example of a collection. A collection uses a data structure internally to store its elements, such as an array or a set of objects that refer to one another. For example, an `ArrayList` is implemented using an array as its data structure, and a `TreeSet` (a collection introduced later in this chapter) is implemented using a data structure called a binary search tree.

Collections are categorized by the types of elements they store, the operations they allow you to perform on those elements, and the speed or efficiency of those operations. Here are some examples of collections:

- *List:* An ordered collection of elements, often accessed by integer indexes or by iteration.
- *Stack:* A collection in which the last element added is the first one to be removed.
- *Queue:* A collection in which elements are removed in the same order in which they were added.
- *Set:* A collection of elements that is guaranteed to contain no duplicates.
- *Map:* A collection of key/value pairs in which each key is associated with a corresponding value.

Java provides a large group of useful collections that allow you to store, access, search, sort, and manipulate data in a variety of ways. Together, these collections and classes are known as the *Java Collections Framework*. This framework is largely contained in the package `java.util`.

Table 11.1 Useful Methods of the `Collection` Interface

Method	Description
`add(element)`	Adds the specified element to this collection
`addAll(collection)`	Adds all elements from the given collection to this collection
`clear()`	Removes all elements from this collection
`contains(element)`	Returns `true` if this collection contains the given element
`containsAll(collection)`	Returns `true` if this collection contains all elements of the given collection
`isEmpty()`	Returns `true` if this collection contains no elements
`iterator()`	Returns an object that can be used to traverse the elements of this collection
`remove(element)`	Removes one occurrence of the specified element, if it is contained in this collection
`removeAll(collection)`	Removes all elements of the given collection from this collection
`retainAll(collection)`	Removes all elements not found in the given collection from this collection
`size()`	Returns the number of elements in this collection
`toArray()`	Returns an array containing the elements of this collection

The `java.util` package contains an interface called `Collection` that is implemented by all collections except `Map`. This interface specifies the operations that most collections support. Table 11.1 lists those operations.

The `Collection` interface is extended and implemented by the other interfaces and classes in the Java Collections Framework. Figure 11.1 summarizes the various interfaces and the classes that implement them, all of which will be discussed in this chapter.

`LinkedList` versus `ArrayList`

Now we'll look at a collection called `LinkedList` and compare and contrast it with `ArrayList`.

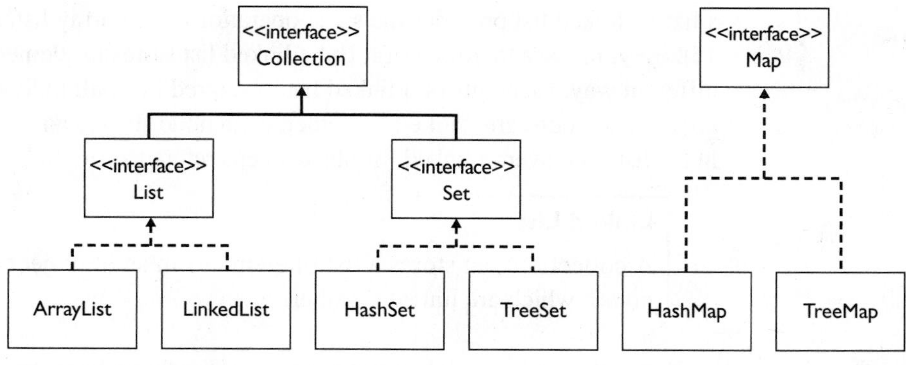

Figure 11.1 An abridged view of the Java Collections Framework

`ArrayList` is a powerful and useful collection, but there are some cases in which using an `ArrayList` isn't ideal. For example, suppose we want to write a program to remove each `String` of even length from an `ArrayList` of `Strings`. We can do this by using a loop that examines each element of the list and either removes it if its length is even or advances to the next string if its length is odd:

```
// Removes all strings of even length from the given list.
public static void removeEvenLength(ArrayList<String> list) {
    int i = 0;
    while (i < list.size()) {
        String element = list.get(i);
        if (element.length() % 2 == 0) {
            list.remove(i);
        } else {
            i++; // skip to next element
        }
    }
}
```

The preceding code is correct, but it doesn't perform well when the list has a lot of elements. On a relatively modern machine, it can take several minutes to process a list of a million elements. The reason it is so slow is that every time we remove an element from the list, we have to shift all subsequent elements to the left by one. This repeated shifting results in a slow program.

Another case in which an `ArrayList` behaves slowly is when it's used to model a waiting line or queue, where elements (customers) are always added to the end of the list (line) and always removed from the front. As customers arrive, they are added to the end of the list. Customers are removed from the front of the list and processed in turn. Removing an element from the front of a large `ArrayList` is a slow operation because all the other elements have to be shifted to the left.

Another type of collection, called a *linked list,* can give better performance in problems like these that involve a lot of additions to or removals from the front or middle of a list. A linked list provides the same operations as an array list, such as `add`, `remove`, `isEmpty`, `size`, and `contains`. But a linked list stores its elements in a fundamentally different way. Elements of a linked list are stored in small individual containers called *nodes.* The nodes are "linked" together, each node storing a reference to the next node in the list. The overall linked list object keeps references to the front and back nodes.

Linked List

A collection that stores a list of elements in small object containers called *nodes,* which are linked together.

You can envision a linked list as an array list that's been "broken apart," with each element then stored in a small box (a node) connected to its neighboring box by an arrow.

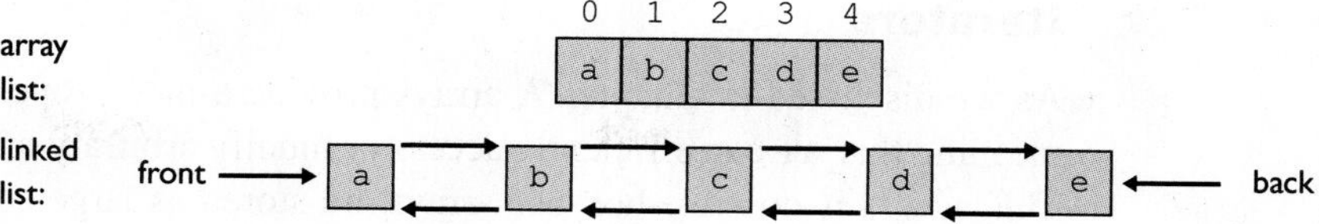

One major advantage of using a linked list is that elements can generally be added at the front of the list quickly, because rather than shifting all the elements in an array, the list just creates a new node object and links it with the others in the list. We don't have to do this ourselves; we simply call methods on the list, which takes care of it for us internally. Figure 11.2 shows what happens inside a linked list when an element is added at the front.

To use a linked list in Java, create an object of type `LinkedList` instead of type `ArrayList`. A `LinkedList` object has the same methods you've used when working with `ArrayList`:

```
LinkedList<String> words = new LinkedList<String>();
words.add("hello");
words.add("goodbye");
words.add("this");
words.add("that");
```

We could write a version of our `removeEvenLength` method that accepts a `LinkedList<String>` as its parameter rather than an `ArrayList<String>`. However, this change alone won't have much impact on performance. Since the `removeEvenLength` method examines each element of the list in sequential order, we can make the code more efficient by employing another type of object called an iterator.

1. Make a new node to hold the new element.

2. Connect the new node to the other nodes in the list.

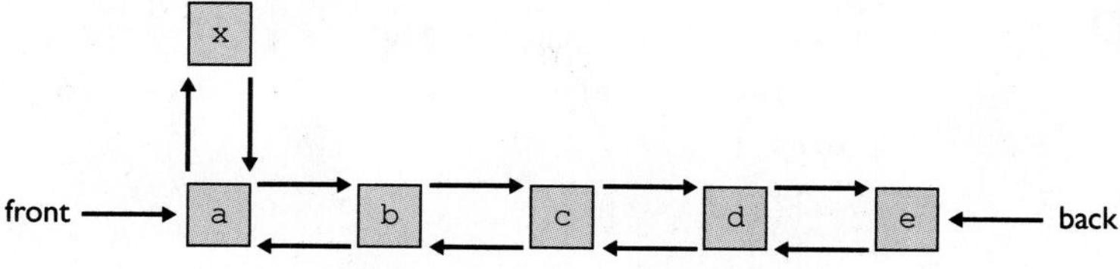

3. Change the front of the list to point to the new node.

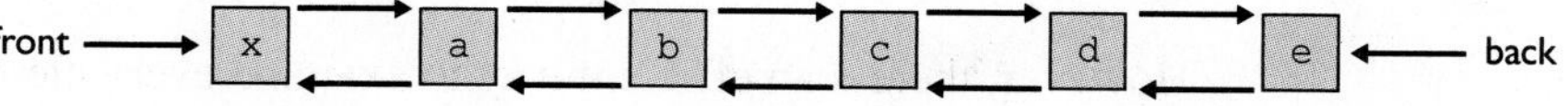

Figure 11.2 Adding an element to the front of a linked list

Iterators

As we discussed in Chapter 7, arrays provide a nice property called *random access,* meaning that we can efficiently access or modify arbitrary array elements in any order. This access is possible because arrays are stored as large contiguous blocks of memory, so the computer can quickly compute the memory location of any of the array's elements. Linked lists, unfortunately, do not provide fast random access. A linked list is made up of many small node objects and generally keeps a direct reference only to one or two particular elements, such as the front and back elements. Therefore it is not possible to quickly access arbitrary elements of the list. A linked list is somewhat like a VHS tape or audio cassette tape in this way; if we wish to access an element, we must "fast-forward" or "rewind" through the list to the proper position.

When you call a method like `get`, `set`, `add`, or `remove` on a linked list, the code internally creates a temporary reference that begins at the front of the list and traverses the links between nodes until it reaches the desired index. The amount of time that this takes depends on the index you chose: If you ask for the element at index 5 it will be returned quickly, but if you ask for the element at index 9,000 the loop inside the `get` method must advance through 9,000 nodes, which will take much longer.

These methods tend to be slow when you use them on a linked list, especially if you call them many times or call them on a list with many elements. Imagine that after the preceding example call of `get(9000)` you decided to call `get(9001)`. The linked list doesn't remember its previous position, so it starts from the front again and advances 9,001 times. The only case in which the methods run quickly is when you pass an index near the front or back of the list.

Earlier in this chapter, we wrote a method to remove strings of even length from an `ArrayList`. If we adapted this code to use a `LinkedList` and made no other modifications we would find that it still runs very slowly on large lists, because it calls the `get` and `remove` methods many times:

```
// performs poorly on a linked list
public static void removeEvenLength(LinkedList<String> list) {
    int i = 0;
    while (i < list.size()) {
        String element = list.get(i); // slow
        if (element.length() % 2 == 0) {
            list.remove(i);           // slow
        } else {
            i++;
        }
    }
}
```

However, there's an efficient way to examine every element of a linked list if we want sequential access (i.e., if we want to examine each element in order from the front to the back). To perform this task, we can use a special object called an *iterator* that keeps track of our current position in the list.

Iterator
An object that allows the efficient retrieval of the elements of a list in sequential order.

Using an iterator, when we move from one element to the next, we don't have to go back to the beginning of the list at each call and follow the links all the way from the front of the list to the desired index. As we'll see in this chapter, iterators are central to the Java Collections Framework. Every collection provides iterators to access its elements. In other words, there's a familiar interface for examining the elements of any collection.

An iterator object has the methods listed in Table 11.2. The methods `next` and `hasNext` should be familiar from the `Scanner` class that you have already studied, and their behavior is similar here.

To get an iterator from most collections, such as an `ArrayList` or a `LinkedList`, you call the method `iterator` on the list, which returns an object of type `Iterator` for examining that list's elements. (You don't use the `new` keyword.) Generally, a variable named `list` storing elements of type `E` uses an iterator in the following way:

```
Iterator<E> itr = list.iterator();
while (itr.hasNext()) {
    <do something with itr.next()>;
}
```

The example of removing strings that have even length from a collection can be implemented much more efficiently using an iterator:

```
// removes all strings of even length from the given linked list
public static void removeEvenLength(LinkedList<String> list) {
    Iterator<String> i = list.iterator();
    while (i.hasNext()) {
        String element = i.next();
        if (element.length() % 2 == 0) {
            i.remove();
        }
    }
}
```

Table 11.2 Methods of `Iterator` Objects

Method	Description
`hasNext()`	Returns `true` if there are more elements to be examined
`next()`	Returns the next element from the list and advances the position of the iterator by one
`remove()`	Removes the element most recently returned by `next()`

Whereas the original `ArrayList` version required up to several minutes to process a list of one million elements on a modern computer, this new code finishes a million-element list in under one-tenth of a second. It performs so quickly because the iterator retains the current position in the list between calls to get or remove elements.

Iterators are also used internally by Java's for-each loop. When you use a for-each loop like the following, Java is actually accessing the elements using an iterator under the hood:

```
for (String word : list) {
    System.out.println(word + " " + word.length());
}
```

Common Programming Error

Calling `next` on an Iterator Too Many Times

Iterators can be a bit confusing to new programmers, so you have to be careful to use them correctly. The following code attempts to use an iterator to find and return the longest string in a linked list, but it has a bug:

```
// returns the longest string in the list (does not work!)
public static String longest(LinkedList<String> list) {
    Iterator<String> itr = list.iterator();
    String longest = itr.next(); // initialize to first element
    while (itr.hasNext()) {
        if (itr.next().length() > longest.length()) {
            longest = itr.next();
        }
    }
    return longest;
}
```

The problem with the previous code is that its loop calls the `next` method on the iterator in two places: once when it tests the length of the string, and again when it tries to store the string as the longest. Each time you call `next`, the iterator advances by one position, so if it's called twice in the loop, you'll skip an element when you find a match. For example, if the list contains the elements (`"oh"`, `"hello"`, `"how"`, `"are"`, `"you"`), the program might see the `"hello"` and intend to store it, but the second call to `next` would actually cause it to store the element that follows `"hello"`, namely, `"how"`.

The solution is to save the result of the `itr.next()` call into a variable. The following code would replace the `while` loop in the previous code:

```
// this version of the code is correct
while (itr.hasNext()) {
```

Continued on next page

Continued from previous page

```
String current = itr.next();
    if (current.length() > longest.length()) {
        longest = current;
    }
} *
```

As the compiler processes the for-each loop, it essentially converts the loop into the following code:

```
Iterator<String> i = list.iterator();
while (i.hasNext()) {
    String word = i.next();
    System.out.println(word + " " + word.length());
}
```

There's a more advanced version of `Iterator` called `ListIterator` that works only on lists. A `ListIterator` provides operations like adding elements, setting element values, and reversing iteration from back to front. Because it is more complex, we won't discuss `ListIterator` in detail in this book. You can read more about it online in the Java API and Java Tutorial pages.

In summary, the following table compares the major benefits of `ArrayList` and `LinkedList`:

Collection	Strengths
`ArrayList`	• Random access: any element can be accessed quickly • Adding and removing at the end of the list is fast
`LinkedList`	• Adding and removing at either the beginning or end of the list is fast • Adding and removing during a sequential access with an iterator is fast • Unlike with arrays, there is no need to expand when full • Can be more easily used as a queue than arrays can

Java 8 has introduced some powerful new features for processing lists and other collections. The following Java 8 code would produce a new list that does not contain any even-length strings:

```
public static List<String> removeEvenLength(List<String> list) {
    return list.stream()
        .filter(s -> s.length() % 2 != 0)
        .collect(Collectors.toList());
}
```

You can read more about this approach in Chapter 19.

Abstract Data Types (ADTs)

It's no accident that the `LinkedList` collection provides the same methods as the `ArrayList`. They both implement the same kind of collection: a *list.* At a high level, the most important thing isn't the way the list is implemented internally, but the operations we can perform on it. This set of operations is an example of an *abstract data type,* or ADT.

> **Abstract Data Type (ADT)**
> A specification of a type of data and the operations that can be performed on it.

An ADT specifies operations that can be performed on data without specifying exactly how those operations are implemented. Linked lists and array lists are both examples of the list ADT because they both provide the same operations, such as storing data by index, adding and removing data at particular indexes, and so on.

In Java, ADTs are specified by interfaces. Each ADT's operations are specified by the methods of its interface. For example, both `LinkedList` and `ArrayList` implement an interface in the `java.util` package called `List`. The `List` interface declares all the common methods that both types of lists implement.

It's a good practice to declare any variables and parameters of a collection type using the appropriate interface type for that ADT rather than the actual class's type. For example, the following code constructs a `LinkedList` object but stores it in a variable of type `List`:

```
List<Integer> list = new LinkedList<Integer>();
```

Joshua Bloch, one of the authors of the Java Collections Framework, says that this programming practice is "strongly recommended" because "it gives you the flexibility to change implementations." Note that you cannot create an object of type `List`, but you can use `List` as the type of a variable.

You can also use the interface types for ADTs like `List` when you declare parameters, return types, or fields. Doing so is useful when you're writing a method that accepts a collection as a parameter, because it means that the method will be able to operate successfully on any collection that implements that ADT's interface. For example, the following method can accept a `LinkedList<String>` or an `ArrayList<String>` as its actual parameter:

```
// returns the longest string in the given list
// pre: list.size() > 0
public static String longest(List<String> list) {
    Iterator<String> i = list.iterator();
    String result = i.next();
    while (i.hasNext()) {
        String next = i.next();
        if (next.length() > result.length()) {
```

```
                result = next;
            }
        }
        return result;
    }
```

It works with either type of list and is efficient for both. This flexibility is another benefit of polymorphism (discussed in Chapter 9). In fact, you could make the method even more general by having it accept a parameter of type `Collection` rather than `List`, since every collection has an `iterator` method.

The `java.util` package has a class called `Collections` that contains several useful methods related to all collections. (Note that this class is not the same as the `Collection` interface that many collection classes implement.) The `Collections` class contains static methods that operate on lists. These methods' headers specify parameters of type `List` rather than `LinkedList` or `ArrayList`. The methods perform common tasks on lists, such as sorting, shuffling, and searching. Table 11.3 presents a short list of useful methods from the `Collections` class that operate on lists.

Notice that these methods are static, so they must be called by writing the word `Collections` followed by a dot and the method's name. For example, if you had

Table 11.3 Useful Static Methods of the `Collections` Class

Method	Description
`binarySearch(list, value)`	Searches a sorted list for a given element value and returns its index
`copy(destinationList, sourceList)`	Copies all elements from the source list to the destination list
`fill(list, value)`	Replaces every element in the given list with the given value
`max(list)`	Returns the element with the highest value
`min(list)`	Returns the element with the lowest value
`replaceAll(list, oldValue, newValue)`	Replaces all occurrences of the old value with the new value
`reverse(list)`	Reverses the order of the elements in the given list
`rotate(list, distance)`	Shifts each element to the right by the given number of indexes, moving the final element to the front
`shuffle(list)`	Rearranges the elements into random order
`sort(list)`	Rearranges the elements into sorted (nondecreasing) order
`swap(list, index1, index2)`	Switches the element values at the given two indexes

a `LinkedList` variable called `list` and you wanted to reverse the list's contents, you'd write

```
Collections.reverse(list);
```

In addition to `List`, there are several other interfaces, such as `Queue`, `Set`, and `Map`, representing ADTs in the Java Collections Framework. We'll explore several of them in this chapter.

LinkedList Case Study: Sieve

Consider the task of finding all prime numbers up to a given maximum. Prime numbers are integers that have no factors other than 1 and themselves. The number 2 is the smallest prime number.

To build a list of prime numbers, you could just write a brute-force solution using `for` loops:

```
for (each number from 2 to maximum) {
    if (number is prime) {
        add number to list of prime numbers.
    }
}
```

But you would need a way to figure out whether each number is prime. One option would be to write another `for` loop that tested all lower integers to see whether they were factors of that number. However, there's an easier way.

The *sieve of Eratosthenes,* named for the Ancient Greek mathematician who devised it, is a classic algorithm for finding prime numbers. The sieve algorithm starts by creating two lists of numbers: one list of numbers to process (some of which may be prime), and another list of numbers known to be prime. Initially, the list of numbers to process can contain every number from 2 to the maximum, while the list of primes will be empty. Here are the initial two lists for a maximum of 25:

```
numbers: [2, 3, 4, 5, 6, 7, 8, 9, 10, 11, 12, 13, 14, 15, 16, 17, 18, 19,
          20, 21, 22, 23, 24, 25]
primes:  []
```

The sieve algorithm begins by removing the first element from the `numbers` list and adding it to the `primes` list. This number is found to be prime because of the nature of the algorithm. Next, the algorithm filters out all the other elements from the `numbers` list that are multiples of this prime number. On the first pass of the algorithm, for example, the program selects 2 from the `numbers` list, places it into the `primes` list, and removes all multiples of 2 from the `numbers` list. Now the number at the front of the `numbers` list is 3. This number will be placed into the `primes` list during the next pass of the algorithm, and all the multiples of 3 that appear in the `numbers` list will be removed.

The numbers taken from the front of the `numbers` list are guaranteed to be prime. A nonprime number cannot reach the front of the `numbers` list because every nonprime number must be a multiple of some prime number, and any such multiples will have been removed by a previous pass of the algorithm.

Here are the two lists after the first three passes of the algorithm:

```
numbers: [3, 5, 7, 9, 11, 13, 15, 17, 19, 21, 23, 25]
primes:  [2]

numbers: [5, 7, 11, 13, 17, 19, 23, 25]
primes:  [2, 3]

numbers: [7, 11, 13, 17, 19, 23]
primes:  [2, 3, 5]
```

Now let's implement the sieve algorithm. We'll use `LinkedLists` to represent the lists of numbers and primes. This tool is preferable to `ArrayLists` because, as we discussed previously, removing elements from the front of an `ArrayList` is inefficient.

First we'll create an empty list of primes and a list of all the numbers up to the given maximum. Since we've discussed ADTs and the `List` interface, we'll declare our variables as the ADT interface type `List<Integer>`:

```
List<Integer> primes = new LinkedList<Integer>();
List<Integer> numbers = new LinkedList<Integer>();
for (int i = 2; i <= max; i++) {
    numbers.add(i);
}
```

Next, we'll process the list of numbers. We'll use an iterator to make passes over the `numbers` list and remove elements that are multiples of the `front` element:

```
while (!numbers.isEmpty()) {
    // remove a prime number from the front of the list
    int front = numbers.remove(0);
    primes.add(front);
    // remove all multiples of this prime number
    Iterator<Integer> itr = numbers.iterator();
    while (itr.hasNext()) {
        int current = itr.next();
        if (current % front == 0) {
            itr.remove();
        }
    }
}
```

The lines of code that follow are the complete program. The most significant addition is a `main` method that prompts the user for the maximum number:

```
// Uses a linked list to implement the sieve of
// Eratosthenes algorithm for finding prime numbers.

import java.util.*;

public class Sieve {
    public static void main(String[] args) {
        System.out.println("This program will tell you all prime");
        System.out.println("numbers up to a given maximum.");
        System.out.println();

        Scanner console = new Scanner(System.in);
        System.out.print("Maximum number? ");
        int max = console.nextInt();

        List<Integer> primes = sieve(max);
        System.out.println("Prime numbers up to " + max + ":");
        System.out.println(primes);
    }

    // Returns a list of all prime numbers up to given max
    // using the sieve of Eratosthenes algorithm.
    public static List<Integer> sieve(int max) {
        List<Integer> primes = new LinkedList<Integer>();

        // add all numbers from 2 to max to a list
        List<Integer> numbers = new LinkedList<Integer>();
        for (int i = 2; i <= max; i++) {
            numbers.add(i);
        }

        while (!numbers.isEmpty()) {
            // remove a prime number from the front of the list
            int front = numbers.remove(0);
            primes.add(front);

            // remove all multiples of this prime number
            Iterator<Integer> itr = numbers.iterator();
            while (itr.hasNext()) {
                int current = itr.next();
                if (current % front == 0) {
                    itr.remove();
```

```
                }
            }
        }

        return primes;
    }
}
```

The following is a sample log of execution of the program:

```
This program will tell you all prime
numbers up to a given maximum.

Maximum number? 50
Prime numbers up to 50:
[2, 3, 5, 7, 11, 13, 17, 19, 23, 29, 31, 37, 41, 43, 47]
```

Our version of the sieve algorithm has been simplified. The real algorithm stops when the first element of the `numbers` list is greater than the square root of the maximum, because any number this large that remains in the list cannot have any multiples remaining in the list. For example, when the maximum is 25, once the item at the front of the `numbers` list exceeds 5, all remaining numbers in the list are known to be prime and can be placed in the `primes` list.

The algorithm can be improved in other ways. For example, the initial list of numbers doesn't need to store every integer from 2 through the maximum. It can instead store 2 and each odd integer up to the maximum, because no other even numbers are prime. This modification makes the algorithm more efficient because fewer numbers need to be processed. These two improvements to the algorithm are left as an exercise.

11.2 Sets

A major limitation of both linked and array lists is that searching them takes a long time. Generally, if you want to search a list, you have to look at each element sequentially to see whether you've found the target. This can take a long time for a large list.

Another limitation of lists is that it's not easy to prevent a list from storing duplicate values. In many cases this isn't a problem, but if, for example, you are storing a collection to count the number of unique words in a book, you don't want any duplicates to exist. To prevent duplicates in a list, you have to sequentially search the list every time you add to it, in order to make sure you aren't adding a word that's already present.

When you want to maintain a collection of elements that can be searched quickly and that prevents duplicates, you're better off using another abstract data type called a *set*.

Set
A collection that cannot contain duplicates.

The `Set` collection is very much like the mathematical notion of a set. Sets do not support all the operations you can perform on lists (namely, any operation that requires an index), but they do offer the benefits of fast searching and effortless elimination of duplicates.

Set Concepts

The two primary implementations of the Java Collections Framework's `Set` interface are called `HashSet` and `TreeSet`. `HashSet` is the general-purpose set class, whereas `TreeSet` offers a few advantages that will be discussed later. If you wanted to store a set of `String` values, you could write code like the following:

```
Set<String> stooges = new HashSet<String>();
stooges.add("Larry");
stooges.add("Moe");
stooges.add("Curly");
stooges.add("Moe"); // duplicate, won't be added
stooges.add("Shemp");
stooges.add("Moe"); // duplicate, won't be added
```

After the code executes, the set will contain only four elements, because `"Moe"` will be placed into the set only once. Notice that, as with lists, you can declare your collection variable to be of the interface type rather than the class type (type `Set` rather than type `HashSet`).

A `Set` provides all of the operations from the `Collection` interface introduced earlier in this chapter, such as `add`, `contains`, and `remove`. It's generally assumed that the `Set` performs these operations efficiently, so you can add many elements to a `Set` and search it many times without experiencing poor performance. A `Set` also provides a `toString` method that lets you see its elements. Printing the preceding `stooges` set would produce the following output:

```
[Moe, Shemp, Larry, Curly]
```

One of the most important benefits of using a `Set` such as `HashSet` is that it can be searched incredibly quickly. Recall that the `contains` method of an `ArrayList` or `LinkedList` must examine every element of the list in order until it finds the target value. By contrast, the `contains` method of a `HashSet` is implemented in such a way that it often needs to examine just one element, making it a much more efficient operation.

A `HashSet` is implemented using a special internal array called a *hash table* that places elements into specific positions based upon integers called *hash codes.* (Every Java object has a hash code that can be accessed through its `hashCode` method.) You don't need to understand the details of `HashSet`'s implementation to use it—the bottom line is that it's implemented in such a way that you can add, remove, and search for elements very quickly. We will discuss hash set implementations in detail in Chapter 18.

One drawback of `HashSet` is that it stores its elements in an unpredictable order. The elements of the `stooges` set were not alphabetized, nor did they match the order in which they were inserted. This storage practice is a tradeoff for the `HashSet`'s fast performance. (Java now includes a variation called `LinkedHashSet` that is almost as fast as `HashSet` but stores its elements in the order they were inserted.)

Sets allow you to examine lots of data while ignoring duplicates. For example, if you wanted to see how many unique words appear in the book *Moby-Dick*, you could write code such as the following:

```
Set<String> words = new HashSet<String>();
Scanner in = new Scanner(new File("mobydick.txt"));
while (in.hasNext()) {
    String word = in.next();
    word = word.toLowerCase();
    words.add(word);
}
System.out.println("Number of unique words = " + words.size());
```

This code produces the following output when run on the text of *Moby-Dick* (available from http://www.gutenberg.org):

```
Number of unique words = 30368
```

The `HashSet` class has a convenient constructor that accepts another collection as a parameter and puts all the unique elements from that collection into the `Set`. One clever usage of this constructor is to find out whether a `List` contains any duplicates. To do so, simply construct a `HashSet` from the list and see whether the sizes differ:

```
// returns true if the given list contains any duplicate elements
public static boolean hasDuplicates(List<Integer> list) {
    Set<Integer> set = new HashSet<Integer>(list);
    return set.size() < list.size();
}
```

One drawback of a `Set` is that it doesn't store elements by indexes. The following loop doesn't compile on a `Set`, because it doesn't have a `get` method:

```
// this code does not compile
for (int i = 0; i < words.size(); i++) {
    String word = words.get(i); // error -- no get method
    System.out.println(word);
}
```

Instead, if you want to loop over the elements of a `Set`, you must use an iterator. Like other collections, a `Set` has an `iterator` method that creates an `Iterator` object to examine its elements. You can then use the familiar `hasNext`/`next` loop to examine each element:

```
// this code works correctly
Iterator<String> itr = words.iterator();
```

```
while (itr.hasNext()) {
    String word = itr.next();
    System.out.println(word);
}
```

A shorter alternative to the preceding code is to use a for-each loop over the elements of the set. As mentioned previously, the code behaves the same way but is easier to write and read than the version with the `while` loop:

```
for (String word : words) {
    System.out.println(word);
}
```

TreeSet versus HashSet

The examples in the preceding section used `HashSet`, but there's another class called `TreeSet` that also implements the `Set` interface. A `TreeSet` uses an internal linked data structure called a *binary search tree* to store its elements in sorted order. We will discuss binary tree implementations in detail in Chapter 17. A `TreeSet` is efficient for adding, removing, and searching, though it is a bit slower than a `HashSet`.

A `TreeSet` can be useful if you want to print the set and have the output ordered. For example, the following code displays the sorted set of all three-letter words in *Moby Dick* that start with "a":

```
Set<String> words = new TreeSet<String>();
Scanner in = new Scanner(new File("mobydick.txt"));
while (in.hasNext()) {
    String word = in.next();
    word = word.toLowerCase();
    if (word.startsWith("a") && word.length() == 3) {
        words.add(word);
    }
}
System.out.println("Three-letter 'a' words = " + words);
```

The code produces the following output:

```
Three-letter 'a' words = [act, add, ado, aft, age, ago, ah!,
ah,, aid, aim, air, alb, ale, ali, all, am,, am-, am:, and,
ant, any, apt, arc, are, ark, arm, art, as,, as-, as., ash,
ask, ass, at,, at., at;, at?, ate, awe, axe, aye]
```

A `TreeSet` can be used with data that has a natural ordering. This means that it will work if its elements are of any type that implements the `Comparable` interface, such as `Integer` or `String`. You can also provide your own object that specifies how to compare elements, called a *comparator*. Comparators will be discussed in Chapter 13 when we cover searching and sorting.

You should not try to construct a `TreeSet` of objects without a natural ordering, such as `Point` objects:

```
// this code compiles but will lead to a runtime error
Set<Point> points = new TreeSet<Point>();
```

The preceding code compiles (unfortunately), but it generates an exception when you run it because it doesn't know how to order the `Point` objects in the `TreeSet`:

```
Exception in thread "main"
    java.lang.ClassCastException: java.awt.Point
        at java.util.TreeMap.compare(Unknown Source)
        at java.util.TreeMap.put(Unknown Source)
        at java.util.TreeSet.add(Unknown Source)
```

You'd be better off using a `HashSet` in this case.

In summary, the following are some of the major differences between `HashSet` and `TreeSet`:

Collection	Strengths
`HashSet`	• Extremely fast performance for add, contains, and remove tasks • Can be used with any type of objects as its elements
`TreeSet`	• Elements are stored in sorted order • Must be used with elements that can be compared (such as `Integer`, `String`)

Set Operations

Consider the task of figuring out how many unique elements appear in two given sets. You cannot just add the sets' sizes, since they might have some elements in common that should not be counted twice in your total. Instead, you could count all elements from the first set and then count only the unique elements of the second, by checking to see whether each element from the second is also in the first:

```
// Returns the number of unique elements contained
// in either set1 or set2. Not a good model to follow.
public static int totalElements(Set<String> set1, Set<String> set2) {
    int count = set1.size();
    for (String element : set2) {
        if (!set1.contains(element)) {
            count++;
        }
    }
    return count;
}
```

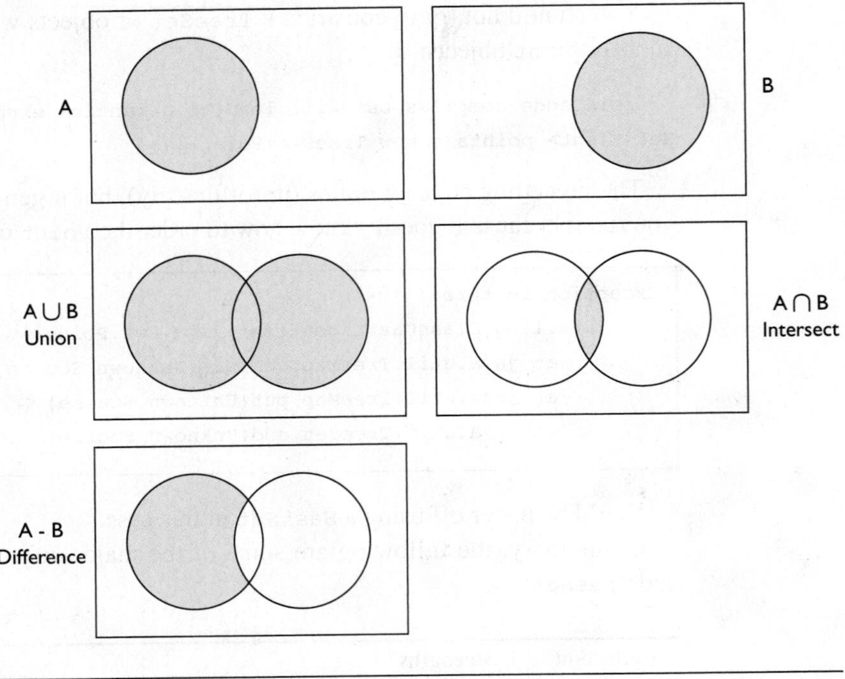

Figure 11.3 Set operation Venn diagrams

However, a more elegant way to perform this calculation is to compute a *union* between the sets. The union of two sets A and B is the set of all elements contained in either A, B, or both. Union is an example of a *set operation*. Other examples of set operations are *intersection* (the set of all elements that are in both A and B) and *difference* (the set of all elements that are in A but not in B). Many set operations combine two sets to produce a new set as their result.

Set operations are often depicted by drawings called Venn diagrams, which depict sets as circles and set operations as shaded overlapping between the circles. Figure 11.3 shows some examples.

You can write code to perform set operations by calling methods whose names end with "All" using the relevant pair of sets. Table 11.4 summarizes which methods correspond to which `set` operations.

Table 11.4 Common Set Operations, Given Two Sets A and B

Set operation	Method	Description
union	`addAll`	Set of all elements that are in A, B, or both
intersection	`retainAll`	Set of all elements that are in both A and B
difference	`removeAll`	Set of all elements that are in A but not in B
superset, subset	`containsAll`	Returns `true` if A is a superset of (contains all elements of) B

For example, we could rewrite the `totalElements` code to use a union with the `addAll` method:

```
// returns the number of elements contained in both set1 and set2
public static int totalElements(Set<String> set1, Set<String> set2) {
    Set<String> union = new HashSet<String>(set1);
    union.addAll(set2);
    return union.size();
}
```

It's important to note that the set operations in Java modify the existing sets on which you call them, rather than creating new sets for you. Notice that in the preceding code, we initialize a new `HashSet` that contains all the elements from `set1` and then add the contents of `set2` to the new set, rather than combining `set1` and `set2` directly. We do this because the caller might not want us to disturb the sets' original contents.

Set Case Study: `Lottery`

Consider the task of writing a lottery program. The program should randomly generate a winning lottery ticket, then prompt the player to enter lotto numbers. Depending on how many numbers match, the player wins various prizes.

Sets make excellent collections for storing the winning lotto numbers and the player's numbers. They prevent duplicates, and they allow us to efficiently test whether a number in one set exists in the other. These features will help us to count the number of winning numbers the player has entered.

The following code uses a `Random` object to initialize a set of six winning lottery numbers between 1 and 40. The code uses a `while` loop because the same number might be randomly generated more than once:

```
Set<Integer> winningNumbers = new TreeSet<Integer>();
Random r = new Random();
while (winningNumbers.size() < 6) {
    int number = r.nextInt(40) + 1;
    winningNumbers.add(number);
}
```

Once the program has generated the winning number set, we'll read the player's lottery numbers into a second set. To figure out how many numbers the player has chosen correctly, we could search the winning number set to see whether it contains each number from the ticket. However, a more elegant way to perform this test is to determine the intersection between the winning numbers set and the player's ticket set. The following code creates the intersection of the player's ticket and the winning numbers by copying the ticket and then removing any elements from it that aren't winning numbers:

```
// find the winning numbers from the user's ticket
Set<Integer> intersection = new TreeSet<Integer>(ticket);
intersection.retainAll(winningNumbers);
```

Once we have the intersection, we can ask for its size to see how many of the player's numbers were winning numbers; we can then calculate the appropriate cash prize amount for the player on the basis of that number. (Our version starts with a $100 prize and doubles that figure for each winning number.)

Here is a complete implementation of the lottery program. We've created a few static methods for structure and added a few constants to represent the number of numbers, maximum number, and lotto prize amounts:

```
// Plays a lottery game with the user, reading
// the user's numbers and printing how many matched.

import java.util.*;

public class Lottery {
    public static final int NUMBERS = 6;
    public static final int MAX_NUMBER = 40;
    public static final int PRIZE = 100;

    public static void main(String[] args) {
        // get winning number and ticket sets
        Set<Integer> winning = createWinningNumbers();
        Set<Integer> ticket = getTicket();
        System.out.println();

        // keep only winning numbers from user's ticket
        Set<Integer> matches = new TreeSet<Integer>(ticket);
        matches.retainAll(winning);

        // print results
        System.out.println("Your ticket was: " + ticket);
        System.out.println("Winning numbers: " + winning);
        if (matches.size() > 0) {
            double prize = PRIZE * Math.pow(2, matches.size());
            System.out.println("Matched numbers: " + matches);
            System.out.printf("Your prize is $%.2f\n", prize);
        }
    }

    // generates a set of the winning lotto numbers
    public static Set<Integer> createWinningNumbers() {
        Set<Integer> winning = new TreeSet<Integer>();
        Random r = new Random();
        while (winning.size() < NUMBERS) {
            int number = r.nextInt(MAX_NUMBER) + 1;
```

```
            winning.add(number);
        }
        return winning;
    }

    // reads the player's lottery ticket from the console
    public static Set<Integer> getTicket() {
        Set<Integer> ticket = new TreeSet<Integer>();
        Scanner console = new Scanner(System.in);
        System.out.print("Type " + NUMBERS + " lotto numbers: ");
        while (ticket.size() < NUMBERS) {
            int number = console.nextInt();
            ticket.add(number);
        }
        return ticket;
    }
}
```

Here's one example output from running the program:

```
Type 6 lotto numbers: 2 8 15 18 21 32
Your ticket was: [2, 8, 15, 18, 21, 32]
Winning numbers: [1, 3, 15, 16, 18, 39]
Matched numbers: [15, 18]
Your prize is $400.00
```

11.3 Maps

VideoNote

Consider the task of writing a telephone book program that allows users to type a person's name and search for that person's phone number. You could store the data in an array, a list, or a set. Perhaps you'd make a small class called `PhoneBookRecord` that stores a person's name and phone number and a list to contain the `PhoneBookRecord` objects. When you want to search for a phone number, you'd traverse the list, looking for the `PhoneBookRecord` that matches the name entered by the user, and return the associated phone number.

A solution such as the one just described isn't very practical. If the list of records is large, it would take the program a long time to look at each one to find the right record to retrieve the phone number.

In many data-processing tasks, it's useful to link pairs of objects (such as a name and a telephone number). We often find ourselves saying, "I'd like to associate every A with a B." Perhaps we'd like to associate names with addresses so that when the user types a name, we can quickly look up that person's address. Or perhaps we want to count the number of occurrences of every word in a book by associating each word with its count of occurrences.

The abstract data type *map* describes a collection that allows you to create one-way associations between pairs of objects to solve these kinds of problems.

> **Map**
> A collection that associates objects called keys with objects called values.

Maps can be used to solve a surprisingly large number of problems. A map can group all the words in a book by length and report how many words there are of each length. Maps can associate chat users with their set of friends and buddies. Maps can even represent a family tree associating each person with his or her mother and father.

A map associates *keys* with *values*. You can store a key/value pair into a map; later in your code, if you supply just the key to the map, it will give you back the value associated with that key. A key can map to only one value, but it's possible for multiple keys to map to the same value. The Java Collections Framework includes an interface called `Map` representing this ADT.

You can think of a map as a pair of connected collections: a set of keys and a collection of values associated with those keys. Figure 11.4 is an example of this idea that maps first names to last names.

Basic Map Operations

The two primary classes that implement the `Map` interface are called `HashMap` and `TreeMap`. These class names parallel the ones used in the set collections, because the maps and sets have similar internal implementations. `HashMap` is the more general-purpose map; a `TreeMap` stores comparable keys in sorted order.

A `Map` is constructed with not one but two generic type parameters, separated by a comma. The first type parameter represents the type of the keys, and the second represents the type of the values. The inclusion of two parameters makes the declaration line in your code lengthy. The line of code that follows is an example of constructing

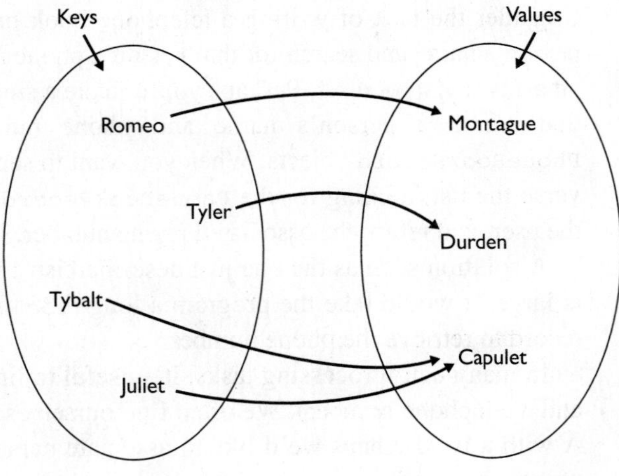

Figure 11.4 Mapping keys (first names) to values (last names)

a salary map that associates people's names with their salaries. Notice that we have to use the wrapper type `Double` rather than the primitive type `double`:

```
Map<String, Double> salaryMap = new HashMap<String, Double>();
```

Key/value pairings are added to a map using its `put` method, which is roughly similar to the `add` method of most other collections. The `put` method accepts a key and a value as parameters and stores a mapping between the key and value in the map. If the key was previously associated with some other value, the new association replaces the old one. We can add key/value pairs to our salary map using code like the following:

```
salaryMap.put("Stuart Reges", 10000.00);
salaryMap.put("Marty Stepp", 95500.00);
salaryMap.put("Jenny", 86753.09);
```

Once you've added key/value pairs to a map, you can look up a value later by calling the map's `get` method, which accepts a key as a parameter and returns the value associated with that key:

```
double jenSalary = salaryMap.get("Jenny");
System.out.printf("Jenny's salary is $%.2f\n", jenSalary);
```

To see whether a map contains a mapping for a given key, you can use the `containsKey` method, or you can call the `get` method and test for a `null` result:

```
Scanner console = new Scanner(System.in);
System.out.print("Type a person's name: ");
String name = console.nextLine();
// search the map for the given name
if (salaryMap.containsKey(name)) {
    double salary = salaryMap.get(name);
    System.out.printf("%s's salary is $%.2f\n", name, salary);
} else {
    System.out.println("I don't have a record for " + name);
}
```

Table 11.5 lists several useful `Map` methods.

A `Map`'s `toString` method displays a comma-separated list of its key/value pairs. The order in which the keys appear depends on the type of map used, which we'll discuss in a moment. Here's what the salary map declared previously would look like when the program prints it:

```
{Jenny=86753.09, Stuart Reges=10000.0, Marty Stepp=95500.0}
```

Table 11.5 Useful Methods of Maps

Method	Description
`clear()`	Removes all keys and values from a map
`containsKey(key)`	Returns `true` if the given key maps to some value in this map
`containsValue(value)`	Returns `true` if some key maps to the given value in this map
`get(key)`	Returns the value associated with this key, or `null` if not found
`isEmpty()`	Returns `true` if this collection contains no keys or values
`keySet()`	Returns a `Set` of all keys in this map
`put(key, value)`	Associates the given key with the given value
`putAll(map)`	Adds all key/value mappings from the given map to this map
`remove(key)`	Removes the given key and its associated value from this map
`size()`	Returns the number of key/value mappings in this map
`values()`	Returns a `Collection` of all values in this map

Map Views (keySet and values)

Unlike most collections, a map doesn't have an `iterator` method, because it wouldn't be clear what you wanted to examine. The keys? The values? Both? Instead, maps have a pair of methods called `keySet` and `values` that respectively return a `Set` of all keys in the map and a `Collection` of all values in the map. These are sometimes called *collection views* of a map because each is a collection that exists conceptually within the map.

For example, consider a map that associates people's social security numbers with their names. In other words, the map's keys are nine-digit social security numbers and its values are names. We could create the map with the following code:

```
Map<Integer, String> ssnMap = new HashMap<Integer, String>();
ssnMap.put(867530912, "Jenny");
ssnMap.put(239876305, "Stuart Reges");
ssnMap.put(504386382, "Marty Stepp");
```

If we wanted to write a loop that printed the social security numbers of every person in the map, we could then call the `keySet` method on the map. This method returns a `Set` containing every key from the hash table—in this case, every `int` for a person's number. If you store the `keySet` in a variable, you should declare that variable as type `Set`, with the type of the map's keys between the < and > brackets:

```
Set<Integer> ssnSet = ssnMap.keySet();
for (int ssn : ssnSet) {
    System.out.println("SSN: " + ssn);
}
```

The preceding code would produce the following output (the keys are in an unpredictable order since a `HashMap` is used):

```
SSN: 239876305
SSN: 867530912
SSN: 504386382
```

If we instead wanted to loop over every name (every value) stored in the map, we'd call the `values` method on the map. The `values` method returns a reference of type `Collection`, not of type `Set`, because the values may contain duplicates (it's legal for two keys to map to the same value). If you store the `values` result in a variable, you should declare that variable as type `Collection`, with the type of the map's values between the < and >:

```
Collection<String> names = ssnMap.values();
for (String name : names) {
    System.out.println("name: " + name);
}
```

The preceding code would produce output such as the following:

```
name: Stuart Reges
name: Jenny
name: Marty Stepp
```

You can combine the keys and the values by looping over the keys and then getting the value for each key:

```
for (int ssn : ssnMap.keySet()) {
    String name = ssnMap.get(ssn);
    System.out.println(name + "'s SSN is " + ssn);
}
```

Notice that this code doesn't declare a variable to store the key set, but instead calls `keySet` directly in the for-each loop. The code produces the following output:

```
Stuart Reges's SSN is 239876305
Jenny's SSN is 867530912
Marty Stepp's SSN is 504386382
```

A related method called `entrySet` returns objects of a type called `Map.Entry` that represents key/value pairs, but we won't explore this method here.

TreeMap versus HashMap

Just as there are two set implementations, `HashSet` and `TreeSet`, there are two flavors of `Map` collections in Java: `HashMap` and `TreeMap`. A `HashMap` performs a bit faster than a `TreeMap` and can store any type of data, but it keeps its keys in a somewhat haphazard order. A `TreeMap` can store only comparable data and performs a bit slower, but it keeps its keys in sorted order.

We could store the social security number information from the previous section in a `TreeMap` as follows:

```
Map<Integer, String> ssnMap = new TreeMap<Integer, String>();
ssnMap.put(867530912, "Jenny");
ssnMap.put(239876305, "Stuart Reges");
ssnMap.put(504386382, "Marty Stepp");
System.out.println(ssnMap);
```

The keys would be ordered differently, leading to the following output when printing the map:

```
{239876305=Stuart Reges, 504386382=Marty Stepp, 867530912=Jenny}
```

Notice that the social security numbers (the map's keys) are sorted in numeric order. This sorting can be useful for certain applications, but `HashMap` is still recommended for general use over `TreeMap`. Many applications don't care about the order of the keys and benefit from the better performance of `HashMap`. `HashMap` works even on data that does not have a natural ordering.

Map Case Study: WordCount

In an earlier example, we counted the number of unique words in the book *Moby Dick.* What if we wanted to find the words that occur most frequently in the book? To do this, we should count how many times each word in the book occurs, then examine all of those counts and print the ones with the largest values.

Maps are very useful for solving these kinds of problems. We can create a word-count map in which each key is a word and its associated value is the number of occurrences of that word in the book:

```
wordCountMap = empty.
for (each word from file) {
    if (I have never seen this word before) {
        set this word's count to 1.
    } else {
        increase this word's count by one.
    }
}
```

We'll need a `Scanner` to read the appropriate file and a `Map` to store the word counts. We'll use a `TreeMap` so that the frequently used words will be shown in alphabetical order:

```
Map<String, Integer> wordCountMap = new TreeMap<String, Integer>();
Scanner in = new Scanner(new File("mobydick.txt"));
```

We can now read the file's contents and store each word that the program encounters in the map. If we come across a word that we have already seen, we retrieve its old `count` value, increment it by 1, and put the new value back into the map. Recall that when you put a key/value mapping into a map that already contains that key, the old mapping is replaced. For example, if the word `"ocean"` was mapped to the number 25 and we put in a new mapping from `"ocean"` to 26, the old mapping from `"ocean"` to 25 would be replaced; we don't have to remove it manually. Here's the code to build up the map:

```
while (in.hasNext()) {
    String word = in.next().toLowerCase();
    if (wordCountMap.containsKey(word)) {  // seen before
        int count = wordCountMap.get(word);
        wordCountMap.put(word, count + 1);
    } else {  // never seen before
        wordCountMap.put(word, 1);
    }
}
```

Once we've built the word-count map, if we want to print all words that appear more than, say, 2,000 times in the book, we can write code like the following:

```
for (String word : wordCountMap.keySet()) {
    int count = wordCountMap.get(word);
    if (count > 2000) {
        System.out.println(word + " occurs " + count + " times.");
    }
}
```

Here's the complete program, with a method added for structure and a constant added for the number of occurrences that are needed for a word to be considered among the most frequent:

```
// Uses maps to implement a word count, so that the user
// can see which words occur the most in the book Moby-Dick.

import java.io.*;
import java.util.*;

public class WordCount {
    // minimum number of occurrences needed to be printed
```

```
    public static final int OCCURRENCES = 2000;

    public static void main(String[] args)
            throws FileNotFoundException {
        System.out.println("This program displays the most");
        System.out.println("frequently occurring words from");
        System.out.println("the book Moby Dick.");
        System.out.println();

        // read the book into a map
        Scanner in = new Scanner(new File("mobydick.txt"));
        Map<String, Integer> wordCountMap = getCountMap(in);

        for (String word: wordCountMap.keySet()) {
            int count = wordCountMap.get(word);
            if (count > OCCURRENCES) {
                System.out.println(word + " occurs " +
                                   count + " times.");
            }
        }
    }

    // Reads book text and returns a map from words to counts.
    public static Map<String, Integer> getCountMap(Scanner in) {
        Map<String, Integer> wordCountMap =
                new TreeMap<String, Integer>();

        while (in.hasNext()) {
            String word = in.next().toLowerCase();
            if (wordCountMap.containsKey(word)) {
                // seen this word before; increment count
                int count = wordCountMap.get(word);
                wordCountMap.put(word, count + 1);
            } else {
                // never seen this word before
                wordCountMap.put(word, 1);
            }
        }

        return wordCountMap;
    }
}
```

The program produces the following output for *Moby-Dick:*

```
This program displays the most
frequently occurring words from
the book Moby-Dick.

a occurs 4509 times.
and occurs 6138 times.
his occurs 2451 times.
in occurs 3975 times.
of occurs 6405 times.
that occurs 2705 times.
the occurs 13991 times.
to occurs 4433 times.
```

Collection Overview

We've discussed three major abstract data types in this chapter: lists, sets, and maps. It's important to understand the differences between them and to know when each should be used. Table 11.6 summarizes the different types of collections and their pros and cons.

When you approach a new programming problem involving data, you can ask yourself questions to decide what type of collection is most appropriate. Here are some examples:

- What are you going to do with the data? Do you intend to add and remove many elements, search the data many times, or connect this data to other data?

Table 11.6 Comparison of Lists, Sets, and Maps

ADT	Implementations	Description/Strengths	Weaknesses	Example Usages
`List`	`ArrayList`, `LinkedList`	A sequence of elements arranged in order of insertion	Slow to search, slow to add/remove arbitrary elements	List of accounts; prime numbers; the lines of a file
`Set`	`HashSet`, `TreeSet`	A set of unique elements that can be searched quickly	Does not have indexes; user cannot retrieve arbitrary elements	Unique words in a book; lottery ticket numbers
`Map`	`HashMap`, `TreeMap`	A group of associations between pairs of "key" and "value" objects	Not a general-purpose collection; cannot easily map backward from a value to its key	Word counting; phone book creation

- Do you plan to search the data? If so, how? If you want to examine elements in order of insertion, you want a list. If you intend to search for arbitrary elements, a set may be better. If you need to find an object, given partial information about it (for example, a PIN or ID number, to find a user's bank account object), a map may be best.
- In what order should the elements be stored? Lists hold their elements in order of insertion, whereas the tree collections (`TreeSet` and `TreeMap`) order elements by their natural ordering. If order doesn't matter, you may want a hash table collection such as a `HashSet`.

Chapter Summary

A collection is an object that stores a group of other objects. Examples of collections are `ArrayList`, `HashSet`, and `TreeMap`. Collections are used to structure, organize, and search data.

A linked list is a collection that's similar to an `ArrayList` but that is implemented internally by storing each element in a small container object called a node. Linked lists can perform certain operations faster than array lists, such as adding data to and removing data from the front or middle of the list.

An iterator is an object that keeps track of the current position in a list and expedites the examination of its elements in sequential order. Linked lists are often used with iterators for increased efficiency.

An abstract data type (ADT) is a specification of the operations that can be performed on data. Two examples of ADTs are `List` and `Set`. ADTs in the Java Collections Framework are represented as interfaces (e.g., the `List` interface, which is implemented both by `LinkedList` and by `ArrayList`).

A set is a collection that doesn't allow duplicates. Sets generally can be searched very quickly to see whether they contain a particular element value. The `Set` interface represents sets.

There are two major set classes in Java: `TreeSet` and `HashSet`. A `TreeSet` holds `Comparable` data in a sorted order; a `HashSet` can hold any data and can be searched faster, but its elements are stored in an unpredictable order.

A map is a collection that associates key objects with value objects. Maps are used to create relationships of association between pieces of data, such as a person's name and phone number.

There are two major map classes in Java: `TreeMap` and `HashMap`. A `TreeMap` holds `Comparable` keys in a sorted order; a `HashMap` can hold any data as its keys and performs value lookups faster, but its keys are stored in an unpredictable order.

Self-Check Problems

Section 11.1: Lists

1. When should you use a `LinkedList` instead of an `ArrayList`?
2. Would a `LinkedList` or an `ArrayList` perform better when run on the following code? Why?

```
public static int min(List<Integer> list) {
    int min = list.get(0);
    for (int i = 1; i < list.size(); i++) {
```

```
            if (list.get(i) < min) {
                min = list.get(i);
            }
        }
        return min;
    }
```

3. What is an iterator? Why are iterators often used with linked lists?

4. Write a piece of code that counts the number of duplicate elements in a linked list, that is, the number of elements whose values are repeated at an earlier index in the list. Assume that all duplicates in the list occur consecutively. For example, the list `[1, 1, 3, 5, 5, 5, 5, 7, 7, 11]` contains five duplicates: one duplicate of element value `1`, three duplicates of element value `5`, and one duplicate of element value `7`.

5. Write a piece of code that inserts a `String` into an ordered linked list of `Strings`, maintaining sorted order. For example, for the list `["Alpha", "Baker", "Foxtrot", "Tango", "Whiskey"]`, inserting `"Charlie"` in order would produce the list `["Alpha", "Baker", "Charlie", "Foxtrot", "Tango", "Whiskey"]`.

6. Write a method called `removeAll` that accepts a linked list of integers as a parameter and removes all occurrences of a particular value. You must preserve the original relative order of the remaining elements of the list. For example, the call `removeAll(list, 3)` would change the list `[3, 9, 4, 2, 3, 8, 17, 4, 3, 18, 2, 3]` to `[9, 4, 2, 8, 17, 4, 18, 2]`.

7. Write a method called `wrapHalf` that accepts a linked list of integers as a parameter and moves the first half of the list to the back of the list. If the list contains an odd number of elements, the smaller half is wrapped (in other words, for a list of size N, the middle element, N/2, becomes the first element in all cases). For example, calling `wrapHalf` on the list `[1, 2, 3, 4, 5, 6]`, would change that list into `[4, 5, 6, 1, 2, 3]`. For the list `[5, 6, 7, 8, 9]`, the result would be `[7, 8, 9, 5, 6]`.

8. What is an abstract data type (ADT)? What ADT does a linked list implement?

9. Self-Check Problem 4 asked you to write code that would count the duplicates in a linked list. Rewrite your code as a method called `countDuplicates` that will allow either an `ArrayList` or a `LinkedList` to be passed as the parameter.

Section 11.2: Sets

10. A `List` has every method that a `Set` has, and more. So why would you use a `Set` rather than a `List`?

11. When should you use a `TreeSet`, and when should you use a `HashSet`?

12. A `Set` doesn't have the `get` and `set` methods that an `ArrayList` has. How do you examine every element of a `Set`?

13. What elements are contained in the following set after this code executes?

```
Set<Integer> set = new HashSet<Integer>();
set.add(74);
set.add(12);
set.add(74);
set.add(74);
set.add(43);
set.remove(74);
set.remove(999);
set.remove(43);
```

```
set.add(32);
set.add(12);
set.add(9);
set.add(999);
```

14. How do you perform a union operation on two sets? An intersection? Try to give an answer that doesn't require any loops.

15. Write the output produced when the following method is passed each of the following lists:

```
public static void mystery(List<String> list) {
    Set<String> result = new TreeSet<String>();
    for (String element : list) {
        if (element.compareTo(list.get(0)) < 0) {
            result.add(element);
        } else {
            result.clear();
        }
    }
    System.out.println(result);
}
```

a. `[marty, stuart, helene, jessica, amanda]`
b. `[sara, caitlin, janette, zack, riley]`
c. `[zorah, alex, tyler, roy, roy, charlie, phil, charlie, tyler]`

Section 11.3: Maps

16. Write the code to declare a `Map` that associates people's names with their ages. Add mappings for your own name and age, as well as those of a few friends or relatives.

17. A `Map` doesn't have the `get` and `set` methods that an `ArrayList` has. It doesn't even have an iterator method like a `Set` does, nor can you use a for-each loop on it directly. How do you examine every key (or every value) of a `Map`?

18. What keys and values are contained in the following map after this code executes?

```
Map<Integer, String> map = new HashMap<Integer, String>();
map.put(8, "Eight");
map.put(41, "Forty-one");
map.put(8, "Ocho");
map.put(18, "Eighteen");
map.put(50, "Fifty");
map.put(132, "OneThreeTwo");
map.put(28, "Twenty-eight");
map.put(79, "Seventy-nine");
map.remove(41);
map.remove(28);
map.remove("Eight");
map.put(50, "Forty-one");
map.put(28, "18");
map.remove(18);
```

19. Write the output produced when the following method is passed each of the following maps:

```
public static void mystery(Map<String, String> map) {
    Map<String, String> result = new TreeMap<String, String>();
    for (String key : map.keySet()) {
        if (key.compareTo(map.get(key)) < 0) {
            result.put(key, map.get(key));
        } else {
            result.put(map.get(key), key);
        }
    }
    System.out.println(result);
}
```

a. `{two=deux, five=cinq, one=un, three=trois, four=quatre}`
b. `{skate=board, drive=car, program=computer, play=computer}`
c. `{siskel=ebert, girl=boy, H=T, ready=begin, first=last, begin=end}`
d. `{cotton=shirt, tree=violin, seed=tree, light=tree, rain=cotton}`

20. Write the output produced when the following method is passed each of the following maps:

```
public static void mystery(Map<String, String> m) {
    Set<String> s = new TreeSet<String>();
    for (String key : m.keySet()) {
        if (!m.get(key).equals(key)) {
            s.add(m.get(key));
        } else {
            s.remove(m.get(key));
        }
    }
    System.out.println(s);
}
```

a. `{sheep=wool, house=brick, cast=plaster, wool=wool}`
b. `{ball=blue, winkie=yellow, corn=yellow, grass=green, emerald=green}`
c. `{pumpkin=peach, corn=apple, apple=apple, pie=fruit, peach=peach}`
d. `{lab=ipl, lion=cat, corgi=dog, cat=cat, emu=animal, nyan=cat}`

21. Write the map returned when the following method is passed the following maps:

```
public Map<String, String> mystery(Map<String, Integer> map1,
                                   Map<Integer, String> map2) {
    Map<String, String> result = new TreeMap<String, String>();
    for (String s1 : map1.keySet()) {
        if (map2.containsKey(map1.get(s1))) {
            result.put(s1, map2.get(map1.get(s1)));
        }
    }
```

```
        return result;
    }
```

a. `map1: {bar=1, baz=2, foo=3, mumble=4},`
   `map2: {1=earth, 2=wind, 3=air, 4=fire}`

b. `map1: {five=105, four=104, one=101, six=106, three=103, two=102},`
   `map2: {99=uno, 101=dos, 103=tres, 105=quatro}`

c. `map1: {a=42, b=9, c=7, d=15, e=11, f=24, g=7},`
   `map2: {1=four, 3=score, 5=and, 7=seven, 9=years, 11=ago}`

22. Modify the `WordCount` program so that it prints the most frequently occurring words sorted by number of occurrences. To do this, write code at the end of the program to create a reverse map from counts to words that is based on the original map. Assume that no two words of interest occur the exact same number of times.

Exercises

1. Modify the `Sieve` program developed in Section 11.1 to make two optimizations. First, instead of storing all integers up to the maximum in the `numbers` list, store only 2 and all odd numbers from 3 upward. Second, write code to ensure that if the first number in the `numbers` list ever reaches the square root of the maximum, all remaining values from the `numbers` list are moved into the `primes` list. (Why is this a valid operation?)

2. Write a method called `alternate` that accepts two `Lists` as its parameters and returns a new `List` containing alternating elements from the two lists, in the following order:
   - First element from first list
   - First element from second list
   - Second element from first list
   - Second element from second list
   - Third element from first list
   - Third element from second list
   - . . .

   If the lists do not contain the same number of elements, the remaining elements from the longer list should be placed consecutively at the end. For example, for a first list of `[1, 2, 3, 4, 5]` and a second list of `[6, 7, 8, 9, 10, 11, 12]`, a call of `alternate(list1, list2)` should return a list containing `[1, 6, 2, 7, 3, 8, 4, 9, 5, 10, 11, 12]`.

3. Write a method called `removeInRange` that accepts four parameters: a `LinkedList`, an element value, a starting index, and an ending index. The method's behavior is to remove all occurrences of the given element that appear in the list between the starting index (inclusive) and the ending index (exclusive). Other values and occurrences of the given value that appear outside the given index range are not affected.

   For example, for the list `[0, 0, 2, 0, 4, 0, 6, 0, 8, 0, 10, 0, 12, 0, 14, 0, 16]`, a call of `removeInRange(list, 0, 5, 13)` should produce the list `[0, 0, 2, 0, 4, 6, 8, 10, 12, 0, 14, 0, 16]`. Notice that the zeros located at indexes between 5 inclusive and 13 exclusive in the original list (before any modifications were made) have been removed.

4. Write a method called `partition` that accepts a list of integers and an integer value `E` as its parameter, and rearranges (partitions) the list so that all the elements with values less than `E` occur before all elements with values greater than `E`. The exact order of the elements is unimportant, so long as all elements less than `E` appear before all elements greater than `E`. For example, for the linked list `[15, 1, 6, 12, -3, 4, 8, 21, 2, 30, -1, 9]`, one acceptable ordering of

the list after a call of `partition(list, 5)` would be `[-1, 1, 2, 4, -3, 12, 8, 21, 6, 30, 15, 9]`. You may assume that the list contains no duplicates and does not contain the element value `E`.

5. Write a method called `sortAndRemoveDuplicates` that accepts a list of integers as its parameter and rearranges the list's elements into sorted ascending order, as well as removing all duplicate values from the list. For example, the list `[7, 4, -9, 4, 15, 8, 27, 7, 11, -5, 32, -9, -9]` would become `[-9, -5, 4, 7, 8, 11, 15, 27, 32]` after a call to your method. Use a `Set` as part of your solution.

6. Write a method `countUnique` that accepts a list of integers as a parameter and returns the number of unique integer values in the list. Use a set as auxiliary storage to help you solve this problem. For example, if a list contains the values `[3, 7, 3, -1, 2, 3, 7, 2, 15, 15]`, your method should return `5`. The empty list contains `0` unique values.

7. Write a method `countCommon` that accepts two lists of integers as parameters and returns the number of unique integers that occur in both lists. Use one or more sets as storage to help you solve this problem. For example, if one list contains the values `[3, 7, 3, -1, 2, 3, 7, 2, 15, 15]` and the other list contains the values `[-5, 15, 2, -1, 7, 15, 36]`, your method should return `4` because the elements `-1, 2, 7,` and `15` occur in both lists.

8. Write a method `maxLength` that accepts a set of strings as a parameter and that returns the length of the longest string in the list. If your method is passed an empty set, it should return `0`.

9. Write a method `hasOdd` that accepts a set of integers as a parameter and returns `true` if the set contains at least one odd integer and `false` otherwise. If passed the empty set, your method should return `false`.

10. Write a method `removeEvenLength` that accepts a set of strings as a parameter and that removes all of the strings of even length from the set.

11. Write a method called `symmetricSetDifference` that accepts two `Set`s as parameters and returns a new `Set` containing their symmetric set difference (that is, the set of elements contained in either of the two sets but not in both). For example, the symmetric difference between the sets `[1, 4, 7, 9]` and `[2, 4, 5, 6, 7]` is `[1, 2, 5, 6, 9]`.

12. Write a method `contains3` that accepts a list of strings as a parameter and returns `true` if any single string occurs at least 3 times in the list, and `false` otherwise. Use a map as auxiliary storage.

13. Write a method `isUnique` that accepts a map whose keys and values are strings as a parameter and returns `true` if no two keys map to the same value (and `false` if any two or more keys do map to the same value). For example, if the map contains the following key/value pairs, your method would return `true`: `{Marty=Stepp, Stuart=Reges, Jessica=Miller, Amanda=Camp, Hal=Perkins}`. But calling it on the following map would return `false`, because of two mappings for `Perkins` and `Reges`: `{Kendrick=Perkins, Stuart=Reges, Jessica=Miller, Bruce=Reges, Hal=Perkins}`.

14. Write a method `intersect` that accepts two maps whose keys are strings and whose values are integers as parameters and returns a new map containing only the key/value pairs that exist in both of the parameter maps. In order for a key/value pair to be included in your result, not only do both maps need to contain a mapping for that key, but they need to map it to the same value. For example, if the two maps passed are `{Janet=87, Logan=62, Whitaker=46, Alyssa=100, Stefanie=80, Jeff=88, Kim=52, Sylvia=95}` and `{Logan=62, Kim=52, Whitaker=52, Jeff=88, Stefanie=80, Brian=60, Lisa=83, Sylvia=87}`, your method would return the following new map (the order of the key/value pairs does not matter): `{Logan=62, Stefanie=80, Jeff=88, Kim=52}`.

15. Write a method `maxOccurrences` that accepts a list of integers as a parameter and returns the number of times the most frequently occurring integer (the "mode") occurs in the list. Solve this problem using a map as auxiliary storage. If the list is empty, return `0`.

16. Write a method called `is1to1` that accepts a map whose keys and values are strings as its parameter and returns `true` if no two keys map to the same value. For example, `{Marty=206-9024, Hawking=123-4567, Smith=949-0504,`

`Newton=123–4567}` should return `false`, but `{Marty=206–9024, Hawking=555–1234, Smith=949–0504, Newton=123–4567}` should return `true`. The empty map is considered 1-to-1 and returns `true`.

17. Write a method called `subMap` that accepts two maps from strings to strings as its parameters and returns `true` if every key in the first map is also contained in the second map and maps to the same value in the second map. For example, `{Smith=949–0504, Marty=206–9024}` is a submap of `{Marty=206–9024, Hawking=123–4567, Smith=949–0504, Newton=123–4567}`. The empty map is a submap of every map.

18. Write a method called `reverse` that accepts a map from strings to strings as a parameter and returns a new map that is the reverse of the original. The reverse of a map is a new map that uses the values from the original as its keys and the keys from the original as its values. Since a map's values need not be unique but its keys must be, you should have each value map to a set of keys. In other words, if the original map maps keys of type *K* to values of type *V*, the new map should map keys of type *V* to values that are `Set`s containing elements of type *K*. For example, the map `{42=Marty, 81=Sue, 17=Ed, 31=Dave, 56=Ed, 3=Marty, 29=Ed}` has a reverse of `{Marty=[42, 3], Sue=[81], Ed=[17, 56, 29], Dave=[31]}`. (The order of the keys and values does not matter.)

19. Write a method called `rarest` that accepts a map whose keys are strings and whose values are integers as a parameter and returns the integer value that occurs the fewest times in the map. If there is a tie, return the smaller integer value. If the map is empty, throw an exception.

20. Write a modified version of the `Vocabulary` program developed in Chapter 10 that uses sets rather than `ArrayLists` to store its words. (The program will be noticeably shorter and will run faster!)

Programming Projects

1. Write a program that computes the edit distance (also called the Levenshtein distance, for its creator Vladimir Levenshtein) between two words. The edit distance between two strings is the minimum number of operations that are needed to transform one string into the other. For this program, an operation is a substitution of a single character, such as from "brisk" to "brick". The edit distance between the words "dog" and "cat" is 3, following the chain of "dot", "cot", and "cat" to transform "dog" into "cat". When you compute the edit distance between two words, each intermediate word must be an actual valid word. Edit distances are useful in applications that need to determine how similar two strings are, such as spelling checkers.

Read your input from a dictionary text file. From this file, compute a map from every word to its immediate neighbors, that is, the words that have an edit distance of 1 from it. Once this map is built, you can walk it to find paths from one word to another.

A good way to process paths to walk the neighbor map is to use a linked list of words to visit, starting with the beginning word, such as "dog". Your algorithm should repeatedly remove the front word of the list and add all of its neighbors to the end of the list, until the ending word (such as "cat") is found or until the list becomes empty, which indicates that no path exists between the two words.

2. Write a program that solves the classic "stable marriage" problem. This problem deals with a group of men and a group of women. The program tries to pair them up so as to generate as many stable marriages as possible. A set of marriages is unstable if you can find a man and a woman who would rather be married to each other than to their current spouses (in which case the two would be inclined to divorce their spouses and marry each other).

The input file for the program will list all of the men, one per line, followed by a blank line, followed by all of the women, one per line. The men and women are numbered according to their positions in the input file (the first man is #1, the second man is #2, and so on; the first woman is #1, the second woman is #2, and so on). Each input line (except for the blank line separating men from women) lists the person's name, followed by a colon, followed by a list of integers. These integers are the marriage partner preferences of this particular person. For example, see the following input line in the men's section:

```
Joe: 10 8 35 9 20 22 33 6 29 7 32 16 18 25
```

This line indicates that the person is named "Joe" and that his first choice for marriage is woman #10, his second choice is woman #8, and so on. Any women not listed are considered unacceptable to Joe.

The stable marriage problem is solved by the following algorithm:

```
assign each person to be free.
while (some man M with a nonempty preference list is free) {
    W = first woman on M's list.

    if (some man P is engaged to W) {
        assign P to be free.
    }
    assign M and W to be engaged to each other.

    for (each successor Q of M who is on W's list) {
        delete W from Q's preference list.
        delete Q from W's preference list.
    }
}
```

Consider the following input:

```
Man 1: 4 1 2 3
Man 2: 2 3 1 4
Man 3: 2 4 3 1
Man 4: 3 1 4 2
Woman 1: 4 1 3 2
Woman 2: 1 3 2 4
Woman 3: 1 2 3 4
Woman 4: 4 1 3 2
```

The following is a stable marriage solution for this input:

```
Man 1 and Woman 4
Man 3 and Woman 2
Man 2 and Woman 3
Man 4 and Woman 1
```

3. Write a program that solves the classic "random writer" problem. This problem deals with reading input files of text and examining the frequencies of characters. On the basis of those frequencies, you can generate randomized output that appears to match the writing style of the original document. The longer the chains you link together, the more accurate the random text will sound. For example, level 4 random text (text with chains of 4 letters long) generated from *Tom Sawyer* might look like this: "en themself, Mr. Welshman, but him awoke, the balmy shore. I'll give him that he couple overy because in the slated snufflindeed structure's kind was rath. She said that the wound the door a fever eyes that WITH him." Level 10 random text from the same source might look like this: "you understanding that they don't come around in the cave should get the word beauteous was over-fondled, and that together and decided that he might as we used to do—it's nobby fun. I'll learn you." Search the Internet for "Random Writer" to learn more about this problem, such as the specification posed by computer scientist Joseph Zachary.

Chapter 12
Recursion

Introduction

This chapter focuses on a programming technique known as *recursion* that allows us to solve certain complex problems in a highly elegant manner. The chapter begins by comparing recursion with the problem-solving techniques you already know. Then it discusses the low-level mechanics that make recursion work in Java. Finally, we examine a number of problems that are easily expressed using this technique.

Recursion turns out to have a surprising range of useful applications, including recursive graphics that are known as fractals. But programming recursively also requires some special techniques that we'll have to explore. Recursive programming also requires a different mind-set in general, so the chapter explores a large set of example problems to reinforce this new way of thinking.

12.1 Thinking Recursively

The problem-solving techniques we have employed so far fall under the heading of classical *iteration,* also known as the *iterative approach.*

> **Iteration (Iterative)**
>
> A programming technique in which you describe actions to be repeated using a loop.

In this chapter, we will explore a new technique known as *recursion.*

> **Recursion (Recursive)**
>
> A programming technique in which you describe actions to be repeated using a method that calls itself.

You have spent so much time writing solutions iteratively that it will take a while to get used to thinking about problems recursively. This chapter will help you get acclimated.

A Nonprogramming Example

If you're standing in line, you might wonder what position you're in. Are you number 10 in the line? Number 20? How would you find out?

Most people would solve this problem iteratively, by counting the people in the line: one, two, three, and so on. This approach is like a `while` loop that continues while there are more people left to count. The iterative approach is a natural one, but it has some limitations. For example, what if the person in front of you is taller than you? Will you be able to see past that person to count all the people in front of him? And what if the line goes around the block and you can't see around the corner to count the people there?

Can you think of another way to determine your position in the line? To think about the problem recursively, you have to imagine that all the people standing in line work together to solve the problem: Instead of having one person do all of the counting, each person is responsible for a little piece.

One cooperative approach would be to ask the person in front of you what your place in line is. That person might ask another person, who might ask another person. But that doesn't help much, because it just leads to a bunch of people saying, "This guy wants to know what place he is in line. Does anyone know?" Someone would probably eventually start counting and solve the problem iteratively.

You have to make the problem simpler. Instead of asking the person in front of you what place *you* are in line, ask that person what place *he* or *she* is in line:

The key difference is that the person in front of you is closer to the front of the line. Suppose, for example, that you're 4th in line. The person in front of you is 3rd in line, which is closer to the front. But notice that you're asking the person in front of you to think about the exact same *kind* of question you're considering: You're both trying to figure out your places in line. That's where recursion comes in—the problem *recurs* because each of you wants to answer the same question.

The idea is to set up a chain reaction of people, all asking the person in front the same question:

This process has to end eventually, when someone asks the person who is first in line:

At this point you've reached what is sometimes referred to as the *bottom* of the recursion. You've gotten a bunch of people involved in collectively solving the problem, and you've finally reached a point where you can start assembling the answer. The person at the front is in position 1. That means the person just before is at position 2, and the person just before that person is at position 3, and so on. Once you reach the bottom of the recursion, you *unwind* it to figure out the answer to your initial problem:

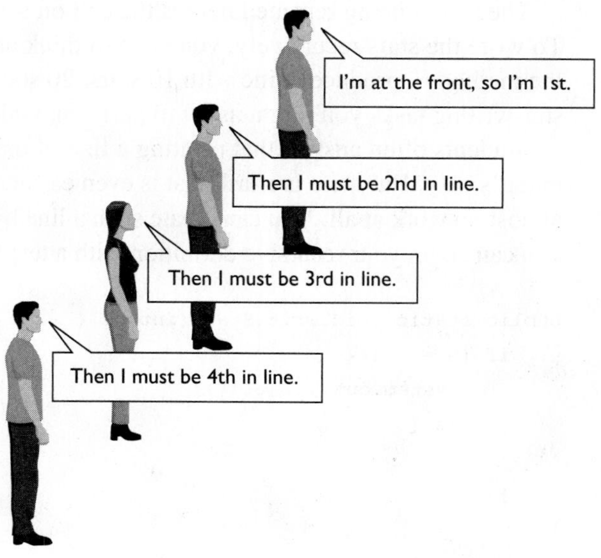

These diagrams included just 4 individuals for the sake of brevity, but this process would still work even if there were 30 or even 300 people in the line.

One of the key aspects to notice here is that recursion involves many cooperating entities, each of which solves a little bit of the problem. Instead of one person doing all of the counting, each individual asks one question as we go toward the front of the line and answers one question as we come back down the line.

In programming, the iterative solution of having one person do all the counting is like having a loop that repeats some action. The recursive solution of having many people each do a little bit of work translates into many different method calls, each of which performs a little bit of work. Let's look at an example of how a simple iterative solution can be turned into a recursive solution.

An Iterative Solution Converted to Recursion

As a first example, we will explore a problem that has a simple iterative solution. It won't be a very impressive use of recursion because the problem is easily solved with iteration. But exploring a problem that has a straightforward iterative solution allows us to compare the two solutions.

Suppose you want to create a method called `writeStars` that will take an integer parameter `n` and will produce a line of output with exactly `n` stars on it. You can solve this problem with a simple `for` loop:

```
public static void writeStars(int n) {
    for (int i = 1; i <= n; i++) {
        System.out.print("*");
    }
    System.out.println();
}
```

The action being repeated here is the call on `System.out.print` that prints a star. To write the stars recursively, you need to think about different cases. You might ask the method to produce a line with 10 stars, 20 stars, or 50 stars. Of all of the possible star-writing tasks you might ask it to perform, which is the simplest?

Students often answer that printing a line of one star is very easy and they're right that it's easy. But there is a task that is even easier. Printing a line of zero stars requires almost no work at all. You can create such a line by calling `System.out.println`, so you can begin your recursive definition with a test for this case:

```
public static void writeStars(int n) {
    if (n == 0) {
        System.out.println();
    } else {
        ...
    }
}
```

The code in the `else` part will deal with lines that have more than zero stars on them. Your instinct will probably be to fill in the `else` part with the `for` loop shown earlier, but you'll have to fight the instinct to solve the entire problem that way. To solve this second part of the problem, it is important to think about how you can do just a small amount of work that will get you closer to the solution. If the number of stars is greater than zero, you know you have to print at least one star, so you can add that action to the code:

```
public static void writeStars(int n) {
    if (n == 0) {
        System.out.println();
    } else {
        System.out.print("*");
        // what is left to do?
        ...
    }
}
```

At this point in the process you have to make a leap of faith: You have to believe that recursion actually works. Once you've printed a single star, what's left to do? The answer is that you want to write `(n – 1)` more stars, along with a `println`. In other words, after writing one star, the task that remains is to write a line of `(n – 1)` stars. You may think, "If only I had a method that would produce a line of `(n – 1)` stars, I could call that method." But you *do* have such a method—the method you're writing. So, after your method writes a single star, you can call the `writeStars` method itself to complete the line of output:

```
public static void writeStars(int n) {
    if (n == 0) {
        System.out.println();
    } else {
        System.out.print("*");
        writeStars(n – 1);
    }
}
```

Many novices complain that this seems like cheating. You're supposed to be writing the method called `writeStars`, so how can you call `writeStars` from inside `writeStars`? Welcome to the world of recursion.

In the earlier example, we talked about people standing in a line and solving a problem together. To understand a recursive method like `writeStars`, it is useful to imagine that each method invocation is like a person in the line. The key insight is that there isn't just one person who can do the `writeStars` task; there's an entire army of people, each of whom can do the task.

Let's think about what happens when you call the method and request a line of three stars:

```
writeStars(3);
```

Imagine that you're calling up the first person from the `writeStars` army and saying, "I want a line of three stars." That person looks at the code in the method and sees that the way to write a line of three stars is to execute the following lines:

```
System.out.print("*");
writeStars(2);
```

In other words, the first member of the army writes a star and calls up the next member of the army to write a line of two stars, and so on down the line. Just as in the earlier example you had a series of people figuring out their places in line, now you have a series of people each printing one star and then calling on someone else to write the rest of the line. In the line example, you eventually reached the person at the front of the line. In this case, you eventually reach a request to write a line of zero stars, which leads you into the `if` branch rather than the `else` branch. At this point, you complete the task with a simple `println`.

Here is a trace of the calls that would be made to print the line:

```
writeStars(3); // n > 0, execute else
    System.out.print("*");
    writeStars(2); // n > 0, execute else
        System.out.print("*");
        writeStars(1); // n > 0, execute else
            System.out.print("*");
            writeStars(0); // n == 0, execute if
                System.out.println();
```

A total of four different calls are made on the method. Continuing the analogy, you could say that four members of the army are called up to solve the task together. Each one solves a star-writing task, but the tasks are slightly different (three stars, two stars, one star, zero stars). This is similar to the example in which the various people standing in line were all answering the same question but were solving slightly different problems because their positions in line were different.

Structure of Recursive Solutions

Writing recursive solutions requires you to make a certain leap of faith, but there is nothing magical about recursion. Let's look a bit more closely at the structure of a recursive solution. The following method is not a solution to the task of writing a line of n stars:

```
// does not work
public static void writeStars(int n) {
    writeStars(n);
}
```

This version never finishes executing, a phenomenon called *infinite recursion.* For example, if you ask the method to write a line of 10 stars, it tries to accomplish that by asking the method to write a line of 10 stars, which asks the method to write a line of 10 stars, which asks the method to write a line of 10 stars, and so on. This solution is the recursive equivalent of an infinite loop.

Every recursive solution that you write will have two key ingredients: a *base case* and a *recursive case.*

Base Case

A case within a recursive solution that is so simple that it can be solved directly without a recursive call.

Recursive Case

A case within a recursive solution that involves reducing the overall problem to a simpler problem of the same kind that can be solved by a recursive call.

Here is the `writeStars` method again, with comments indicating the base case and recursive case:

```
public static void writeStars(int n) {
    if (n == 0) {
        // base case
        System.out.println();
    } else {
        // recursive case
        System.out.print("*");
        writeStars(n – 1);
    }
}
```

The base case is the task of writing a line of zero stars. This task is so simple that it can be done immediately. The recursive case is the task of writing lines with one or more stars. To solve the recursive case, you begin by writing a single star, which reduces the remaining task to that of writing a line of `(n – 1)` stars. This is the task that the `writeStars` method is designed to solve and it is simpler than the original task, so you can solve it by making a recursive call.

As an analogy, suppose you're at the top of a ladder with `n` rungs on it. If you have a way to get from one rung to the one below and if you can recognize when you've reached the ground, you can handle a ladder of any height. Stepping from one rung to the one below is like the recursive case in which you perform some small amount of work that reduces the problem to a simpler one of the same form (get down from rung `(n – 1)` versus get down from rung `n`). Recognizing when you reach the ground is like the base case that can be solved directly (stepping off the ladder).

Some problems involve multiple base cases and some problems involve multiple recursive cases, but there will always be at least one of each case in a correct recursive solution. If you are missing either, you run into trouble. Without the ability to step down from one rung to the one below, you'd be stuck at the top of the ladder. Without the ability to recognize when you reach the ground, you'd keep trying to step down onto another rung even when there were no rungs left in the ladder.

Keep in mind that your code can have infinite recursion even if it has a proper recursive case. Consider, for example, this version of `writeStars`:

```
// does not work
public static void writeStars(int n) {
    System.out.print("*");
    writeStars(n - 1);
}
```

This version correctly reduces from the case of `n` to the case of `n - 1`, but it has no base case. As a result, it goes on infinitely. Instead of stopping when it reaches the task of writing zero stars, it instead recursively tries to write −1 stars, then −2 stars, then −3 stars, and so on.

Because recursive solutions include some combination of base cases and recursive cases, you will find that they are often written with `if/else` statements, nested `if` statements, or some minor variation thereof. You will also find that recursive programming generally involves a case analysis, in which you categorize the possible forms the problem might take into different cases and write a solution for each case.

12.2 A Better Example of Recursion

Solving the `writeStars` task with recursion may have been an interesting exercise, but it isn't a very compelling example. Let's look in detail at a problem in which recursion simplifies the work to be done.

Suppose you have a `Scanner` that is tied to an external input file and you want to print the lines of the file in reverse order. For example, the file might contain the following four lines of text:

```
this
is
fun
no?
```

Printing these lines in reverse order would produce this output:

```
no?
fun
is
this
```

To perform this task iteratively, you'd need some kind of data structure for storing the lines of text, such as an `ArrayList<String>`. However, recursion allows you to solve the problem without using a data structure.

Remember that recursive programming involves thinking about cases. What would be the simplest file to reverse? A one-line file would be fairly easy to reverse, but it would be even easier to reverse an empty file. So, you can begin writing your method as follows:

```
public static void reverse(Scanner input) {
    if (!input.hasNextLine()) {
        // base case (empty file)
        ...
    } else {
        // recursive case (nonempty file)
        ...
    }
}
```

In this problem, the base case is so simple that there isn't anything to do. An empty file has no lines to reverse. Thus, in this case it makes more sense to turn around the `if/else` statement so that you test for the recursive case. That way you can write a simple `if` statement that has an implied "`else` there is nothing to do":

```
public static void reverse(Scanner input) {
    if (input.hasNextLine()) {
        // recursive case (nonempty file)
        ...
    }
}
```

Again, the challenge is to solve only a little bit of the problem. How do you take just one step that will get you closer to completing the task? You can read one line of text from the file:

```
public static void reverse(Scanner input) {
    if (input.hasNextLine()) {
        // recursive case (nonempty file)
        String line = input.nextLine();
        ...
    }
}
```

For the sample file, this code would read the line `"this"` into the variable `line` and leave you with the following three lines of text in the `Scanner`:

```
is
fun
no?
```

Recall that your aim is to produce the following overall output:

```
no?
fun
is
this
```

You might be asking yourself questions like, "Is there another line of input to process?" But that's not recursive thinking. If you're thinking recursively, you'll be thinking about what a call on the method will get you. Since the `Scanner` is positioned in front of the three lines `"is"`, `"fun"`, and `"no?"`, a call on `reverse` should read in those lines and produce the first three lines of output that you're looking for. If that works, you'll only have to write out the line `"this"` afterward to complete the output.

This is where the leap of faith comes in—you have to believe that the `reverse` method actually works. If it does, this code can be completed as follows:

```
public static void reverse(Scanner input) {
    if (input.hasNextLine()) {
        // recursive case (nonempty file)
        String line = input.nextLine();
        reverse(input);
        System.out.println(line);
    }
}
```

This code does work. To reverse a sequence of lines, simply read in the first one, reverse the others, and then write out the first one.

Mechanics of Recursion

Novices seem to understand recursion better when they know more about the underlying mechanics that make it work. Before we examine a recursive method in detail, let's review how nonrecursive methods work. Consider the following simple program:

```
// Simple program that draws three triangles.
public class DrawTriangles {
    public static void main(String[] args) {
        drawTriangle();
        drawTwoTriangles();
```

```
    }

    public static void drawTriangle() {
        System.out.println("  *");
        System.out.println(" ***");
        System.out.println("*****");
        System.out.println();
    }

    public static void drawTwoTriangles() {
        drawTriangle();
        drawTriangle();
    }
}
```

The program prints three triangles:

```
  *
 ***
*****

  *
 ***
*****

  *
 ***
*****
```

How do we describe the method calls that take place in this program? Imagine that each method call has been written on a different piece of paper. We begin program execution with the `main` method, so imagine that we're grabbing the sheet of paper with `main` on it:

```
public static void main(String[] args) {
    drawTriangle();
    drawTwoTriangles();
}
```

We then execute each of the statements in `main` in turn, from first to last. First we execute the call on `drawTriangle`:

```
public static void main(String[] args) {
➔   drawTriangle();
    drawTwoTriangles();
}
```

We know that at this point, the computer stops executing `main` and turns its attention to the `drawTriangle` method. This step is analogous to picking up the piece of paper with `drawTriangle` written on it and placing it over the piece of paper with `main` on it:

```
public static void main(String[] args) {
    public static void drawTriangle() {
        System.out.println("  *");
        System.out.println(" ***");
        System.out.println("*****");
        System.out.println();
    }
```

Now we execute each of the statements in `drawTriangle` from first to last, then go back to `main`, removing the `drawTriangle` sheet. When we go back to `main` we will have finished the call on `drawTriangle`, so the next step is the call on `drawTwoTriangles`:

```
public static void main(String[] args) {
    drawTriangle();
➔   drawTwoTriangles();
}
```

So we grab the piece of paper with `drawTwoTriangles` on it and place it over the paper with `main` on it:

```
public static void main(String[] args) {
    public static void drawTwoTriangles() {
        drawTriangle();
        drawTriangle();
    }
```

The first thing to do here is the first call on `drawTriangle`:

```
public static void main(String[] args) {
    public static void drawTwoTriangles() {
    ➔   drawTriangle();
        drawTriangle();
    }
```

To execute this method, we take out the sheet of paper with `drawTriangle` on it and place it on top of the `drawTwoTriangles` sheet:

```
public static void main(String[] args) {
  public static void drawTwoTriangles() {
    public static void drawTriangle() {
        System.out.println("  *");
        System.out.println(" ***");
        System.out.println("*****");
        System.out.println();
    }
```

This diagram makes it clear that we started with the method `main`, which called the method `drawTwoTriangles`, which called the method `drawTriangle`. So, at this moment in time, three different methods are active. The one on top is the one that we are actively executing. Once we complete it, we'll go back to the one underneath, and once we finish that one, we'll go back to `main`. We could continue with this example, but you probably get the idea by now.

The idea of representing each method call as a piece of paper and putting each one on top of the others as it is called is a metaphor for Java's *call stack*.

Call Stack

The internal structure that keeps track of the sequence of methods that have been called.

If you envision the call stack as a stack of papers with the most recently called method on top, you'll have a pretty good idea of how it works.

Let's use the idea of the call stack to understand how the recursive file-reversing method works. To visualize the call stack, we need to put the method definition on a piece of paper:

```
public static void reverse(Scanner input) {
    if (input.hasNextLine()) {
        String line = input.nextLine();
        reverse(input);
        System.out.println(line);
    }
}
line [          ]
```

Notice that the paper includes a place to store the value of the local variable `line`. This is an important detail.

Suppose that we call this method with the earlier sample input file, which contains the following four lines of text:

```
this
is
fun
no?
```

When we call the method, it reads the first line of text into its `line` variable, and then it reaches the recursive call on `reverse`:

```
public static void reverse(Scanner input) {
    if (input.hasNextLine()) {
        String line = input.nextLine();
→       reverse(input);
        System.out.println(line);
    }
}
line "this"
```

Then what happens? In the `DrawTriangles` program, we took the sheet of paper for the method being called and placed it on top of the current sheet of paper. But here we have the method `reverse` calling the method `reverse`. To understand what happens, you have to realize that each method invocation is independent of the others. We don't have only a single sheet of paper with the `reverse` method written on it; we have as many copies as we want. So, we can grab a second copy of the method definition and place it on top of the current one:

```
public static void reverse(Scanner input) {
  public static void reverse(Scanner input) {
      if (input.hasNextLine()) {
          String line = input.nextLine();
          reverse(input);
          System.out.println(line);
      }
  }
  line
```

This new version of the method has a variable of its own, called `line`, in which it can store a line of text. Even though the previous version (the one underneath this one) is in the middle of its execution, this new one is at the beginning of its execution. Think back to the analogy of being able to employ an entire army of people to write out a line of stars. Just as you could call on as many people as you needed to solve that problem, you can bring up as many copies of the `reverse` method as you need to solve this problem.

The second call on `reverse` reads another line of text (the second line, `"is"`). After the program reads the second line, it makes another recursive call on `reverse`:

```
public static void reverse(Scanner input) {
  public static void reverse(Scanner input) {
      if (input.hasNextLine()) {
          String line = input.nextLine();
  →       reverse(input);
          System.out.println(line);
      }
  }
  line "is"
```

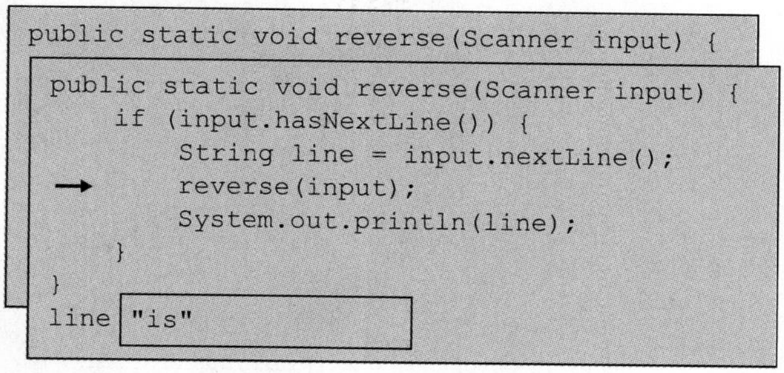

So Java sets aside this version of the method as well and brings up a third version:

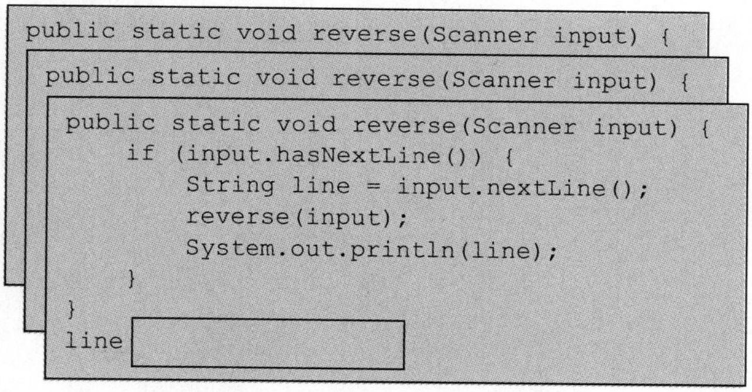

```
public static void reverse(Scanner input) {
  public static void reverse(Scanner input) {
    public static void reverse(Scanner input) {
        if (input.hasNextLine()) {
            String line = input.nextLine();
            reverse(input);
            System.out.println(line);
        }
    }
    line
```

Again, notice that this version has its own variable called `line` that is independent of the other variables called `line`. This version of the method also reads in a line (the third line, `"fun"`) and reaches a recursive call on `reverse`:

```
public static void reverse(Scanner input) {
  public static void reverse(Scanner input) {
    public static void reverse(Scanner input) {
        if (input.hasNextLine()) {
            String line = input.nextLine();
    →       reverse(input);
            System.out.println(line);
        }
    }
    line "fun"
```

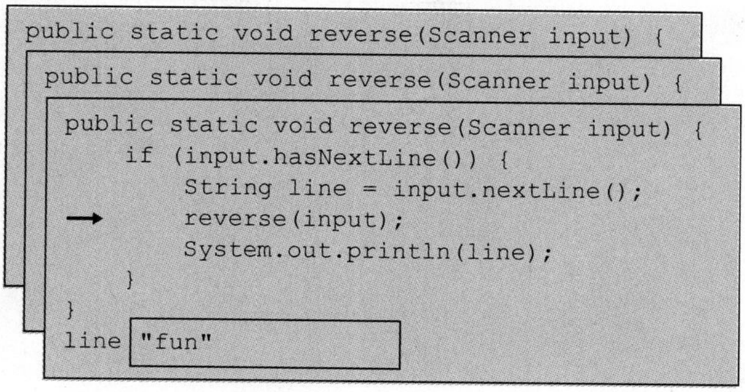

This brings up a fourth version of the method:

```
public static void reverse(Scanner input) {
  public static void reverse(Scanner input) {
    public static void reverse(Scanner input) {
      public static void reverse(Scanner input) {
          if (input.hasNextLine()) {
              String line = input.nextLine();
              reverse(input);
              System.out.println(line);
          }
      }
      line [          ]
```

This version finds a fourth line of input (`"no?"`), so it reads that in and reaches the recursive call:

```
public static void reverse(Scanner input) {
  public static void reverse(Scanner input) {
    public static void reverse(Scanner input) {
      public static void reverse(Scanner input) {
          if (input.hasNextLine()) {
              String line = input.nextLine();
   -->        reverse(input);
              System.out.println(line);
          }
      }
      line ["no?"     ]
```

This call brings up a fifth version of the method:

```
public static void reverse(Scanner input) {
  public static void reverse(Scanner input) {
    public static void reverse(Scanner input) {
      public static void reverse(Scanner input) {
        public static void reverse(Scanner input) {
            if (input.hasNextLine()) {
                String line = input.nextLine();
                reverse(input);
                System.out.println(line);
            }
        }
        line [          ]
```

This version turns out to have the easy task, like the final person who was asked to print a line of zero stars. This time around the `Scanner` is empty (`input.hasNextLine()` returns `false`). The program has reached the very important base case that stops this process from going on indefinitely. This version of the method recognizes that there are no lines to reverse, so it simply terminates.

Then what? Having completed this call, we throw it away and return to where we were just before executing the call:

```
public static void reverse(Scanner input) {
 public static void reverse(Scanner input) {
  public static void reverse(Scanner input) {
   public static void reverse(Scanner input) {
       if (input.hasNextLine()) {
           String line = input.nextLine();
           reverse(input);
   →       System.out.println(line);
       }
   }
   line "no?"
```

We've finished the call on `reverse` and are positioned at the `println` right after it, so we print the text in the `line` variable (`"no?"`) and terminate. Where does that leave us? This method has been executed and we return to where we were just before:

```
public static void reverse(Scanner input) {
 public static void reverse(Scanner input) {
  public static void reverse(Scanner input) {
      if (input.hasNextLine()) {
          String line = input.nextLine();
          reverse(input);
  →       System.out.println(line);
      }
  }
  line "fun"
```

We then print the current line of text, which is `"fun"`, and this version also goes away:

```
public static void reverse(Scanner input) {
 public static void reverse(Scanner input) {
     if (input.hasNextLine()) {
         String line = input.nextLine();
         reverse(input);
 →       System.out.println(line);
     }
 }
 line "is"
```

Now we execute this `println`, for the text `"is"`, and eliminate one more call:

```
public static void reverse(Scanner input) {
    if (input.hasNextLine()) {
        String line = input.nextLine();
        reverse(input);
-->     System.out.println(line);
    }
}
line "this"
```

Notice that we've written out three lines of text so far:

```
no?
fun
is
```

Our leap of faith was justified. The recursive call on `reverse` read in the three lines of text that followed the first line of input and printed them in reverse order. We complete the task by printing the first line of text, which leads to this overall output:

```
no?
fun
is
this
```

Then this version of the method terminates, and the program has finished executing.

12.3 Recursive Functions and Data

VideoNote

Both of the examples of recursion we have studied so far have been action-oriented methods with a return type of `void`. In this section we will examine some of the issues that arise when you want to write methods that compute values and return a result. Such methods are similar to mathematical functions in that they accept a set of input values and produce a set of possible results. We'll also explore an example that involves manipulating recursive data and an example that requires a helper method.

Integer Exponentiation

Java provides a method called `Math.pow` that allows you to compute an exponent. If you want to compute the value of x^y, you can call `Math.pow(x, y)`. Let's consider how we could implement the `pow` method. To keep things simple, we'll limit ourselves to the domain of integers. But because we are limiting ourselves to integers, we have to recognize an important precondition of our method: We won't be able to compute negative exponents because the results would not be integers.

The method we want to write will look like the following:

```
// pre : y >= 0
// post: returns x^y
public static int pow(int x, int y) {
    ...
}
```

We could obviously solve this problem by writing a loop, but we want to explore how to write the method recursively. Again, we should start by thinking about different cases. What would be the easiest exponent to compute? It's pretty easy to compute x^1, so that's a good candidate, but there is an even more basic case. The simplest possible exponent is 0. By definition, any integer to the 0 power is considered to be 1. So we can begin our solution with the following code:

```
public static int pow(int x, int y) {
    if (y == 0) {
        // base case with y == 0
        return 1;
    } else {
        // recursive case with y > 0
        ...
    }
}
```

In the recursive case, we know that `y` is greater than `0`. In other words, there will be at least one factor of `x` in the result. We know from mathematics that

$$x^y = x \cdot x^{y-1}$$

This equation expresses `x` to the `y` power in terms of `x` to a smaller power, `(y - 1)`. Therefore, it can serve as our recursive case. All we have to do is to translate it into its Java equivalent:

```
public static int pow(int x, int y) {
    if (y == 0) {
        // base case with y == 0
        return 1;
    } else {
        // recursive case with y > 0
        return x * pow(x, y - 1);
    }
}
```

This is a complete recursive solution. Tracing the execution of a recursive function is a little more difficult than using a `void` method, because we have to keep track of the values that are returned by each recursive call. The following is a trace of execution showing how we would compute 3^5:

```
pow(3, 5) = 3 * pow(3, 4)
|   pow(3, 4) = 3 * pow(3, 3)
|   |   pow(3, 3) = 3 * pow(3, 2)
|   |   |   pow(3, 2) = 3 * pow(3, 1)
|   |   |   |   pow(3, 1) = 3 * pow(3, 0)
|   |   |   |   |   pow(3, 0) = 1
|   |   |   |   pow(3, 1) = 3 * 1 = 3
|   |   |   pow(3, 2) = 3 * 3 = 9
|   |   pow(3, 3) = 3 * 9 = 27
|   pow(3, 4) = 3 * 27 = 81
pow(3, 5) = 3 * 81 = 243
```

Notice that we make a series of six recursive calls in a row until we reach the base case of computing 3 to the 0 power. That call returns the value `1` and then the recursion unwinds, computing the various answers as it returns from each method call.

It is useful to think about what will happen if someone violates the precondition by asking for a negative exponent. For example, what if someone asked for `pow(3, –1)`? The method would recursively ask for `pow(3, –2)`, which would ask for `pow(3, –3)`, which would ask for `pow(3, –4)`, and so on. In other words, it would lead to an infinite recursion. In a sense, it's okay for this to occur, because the person calling the method should pay attention to the precondition and should not enter a negative exponent. But it's not much work for us to handle this case in a more elegant manner. Our solution is structured as a series of cases, so we can simply add a new case for illegal exponents:

```
public static int pow(int x, int y) {
    if (y < 0) {
        throw new IllegalArgumentException("negative exponent: " + y);
    } else if (y == 0) {
        // base case with y == 0
        return 1;
    } else {
        // recursive case with y > 0
        return x * pow(x, y – 1);
    }
}
```

One of the advantages of writing functions recursively is that if we can identify other cases, we can potentially make the function more efficient. For example, suppose that you want to compute 2^{16}. In its current form, the method will multiply 2 by 2 by 2 a total of 16 times. But we can do better than that. If `y` is an even exponent, then

$$x^y = (x^2)^{\frac{y}{2}}$$

So instead of computing 2^{16}, we can compute 4^8, which is simpler. Adding this case to our method is relatively easy:

```
public static int pow(int x, int y) {
    if (y < 0) {
        throw new IllegalArgumentException("negative exponent: " + y);
    } else if (y == 0) {
        // base case with y == 0
        return 1;
    } else if (y % 2 == 0) {
        // recursive case with y > 0, y even
        return pow(x * x, y / 2);
    } else {
        // recursive case with y > 0, y odd
        return x * pow(x, y - 1);
    }
}
```

This version of the method is more efficient than the original. The following is a trace of execution for computing 2^{16}:

```
pow(2, 16) = pow(4, 8)
   |    pow(4, 8) = pow(16, 4)
   |       |    pow(16, 4) = pow(256, 2)
   |       |       |    pow(256, 2) = pow(65536, 1)
   |       |       |       |    pow(65536, 1) = 65536 * pow(65536, 0)
   |       |       |       |       |    pow(65536, 0) = 1
   |       |       |       |    pow(65536, 1) = 65536 * 1 = 65536
   |       |       |    pow(256, 2) = 65536
   |       |    pow(16, 4) = 65536
   |    pow(4, 8) = 65536
pow(2, 16) = 65536
```

Without the special case for even exponents, this call would have required 17 different calls on pow (16 recursive cases and one base case).

Greatest Common Divisor

In mathematics, we often want to know the largest integer that goes evenly into two different integers, which is known as the *greatest common divisor* (or GCD) of the two integers. Let's explore how to write a GCD method recursively.

For now, let's not worry about negative values of x and y. We want to write the following method:

```
// pre: x >= 0, y >= 0
// post: returns the greatest common divisor of x and y
public static int gcd(int x, int y) {
    ...
}
```

To introduce some variety, let's try to figure out the recursive case first and then figure out the base case. Suppose, for example, that we are asked to compute the GCD of 20 and 132. The GCD is 4, because 4 is the largest integer that goes evenly into both numbers.

There are many ways to compute the GCD of two numbers. One of the most efficient algorithms dates back at least to the time of Euclid and perhaps even farther. This algorithm eliminates any multiples of the smaller integer from the larger integer. In the case of 20 and 132, we know that

$$132 = 20 \cdot 6 + 12$$

There are six multiples of 20 in 132, with a remainder of 12. Euclid's algorithm says that we can ignore the six multiples of 20 and just focus on the value 12. In other words, we can replace 132 with 12:

```
gcd(132, 20) = gcd(12, 20)
```

We haven't figured out the base case yet, but no matter what the base case ends up being, we're making progress if we can reduce the numbers using Euclid's algorithm. When you're dealing with nonnegative integers, you can't reduce them forever.

The proof of this principle is beyond the scope of this book, but that is the basic idea. This algorithm is easy to express in Java terms because the mod operator gives us the remainder when one number is divided by another. Expressing this principle in general terms, we know that

`gcd(x, y) = gcd(x % y, y)` when `y > 0`

Again, the proof is beyond the scope of this book, but given this basic principle we can produce a recursive solution to the problem. We might try to write the method as follows:

```
public static int gcd(int x, int y) {
    if (...) {
        // base case
        ...
    } else {
        // recursive case
        return gcd(x % y, y);
    }
}
```

This isn't a bad first attempt, but it has a problem: It's not enough for the solution to be mathematically correct; we also need our recursive solution to keep reducing the overall problem to a simpler problem. If we start with the numbers 132 and 20, the method makes progress on the first call, but then it starts repeating itself:

```
gcd(132, 20) = gcd(12, 20)
       gcd(12, 20) = gcd(12, 20)
```

```
            gcd(12, 20) = gcd(12, 20)
                      gcd(12, 20) = gcd(12, 20)
                                   ...
```

This pattern will lead to infinite recursion. The Euclidean trick helped the first time around, because for the first call x was greater than y (132 is greater than 20). But the algorithm makes progress only if the first number is larger than the second number.

Here is the line of code that is causing the problem:

```
return gcd(x % y, y);
```

When we compute (x % y), we are guaranteed to get a result that is smaller than y. That means that on the recursive call, the first value will always be smaller than the second value. To make the algorithm work, we need the opposite to be true. We can achieve this goal simply by reversing the order of the arguments:

```
return gcd(y, x % y);
```

On this call, we are guaranteed to have a first value that is larger than the second value. If we trace this version of the method for computing the GCD of 132 and 20, we get the following sequence of calls:

```
gcd(132, 20) = gcd(20, 12)
           gcd(20, 12) = gcd(12, 8)
                      gcd(12, 8) = gcd(8, 4)
                                gcd(8, 4) = gcd(4, 0)
                                           ...
```

At this point we have to decide what the GCD of 4 and 0 is. It may seem strange, but the answer is 4. In general, gcd(n, 0) is n. Obviously, the GCD can't be any larger than n, and n goes evenly into n. But n also goes evenly into 0, because 0 can be written as an even multiple of n: (0 * n) = 0.

This observation leads us to the base case. If y is 0, the GCD is x:

```
public static int gcd(int x, int y) {
    if (y == 0) {
        // base case with y == 0
        return x;
    } else {
        // recursive case with y > 0
        return gcd(y, x % y);
    }
}
```

This base case also solves the potential problem that the Euclidean formula depends on y not being 0. However, we still have to think about the case in which either or both of x and y are negative. We could keep the precondition and throw an exception when this occurs, but it is more common in mathematics to return the GCD of the absolute value of the two values. We can accomplish this by including one extra case for negatives:

```
public static int gcd(int x, int y) {
    if (x < 0 || y < 0) {
        // recursive case with negative value(s)
        return gcd(Math.abs(x), Math.abs(y));
    } else if (y == 0) {
        // base case with y == 0
        return x;
    } else {
        // recursive case with y > 0
        return gcd(y, x % y);
    }
}
```

Common Programming Error

Infinite Recursion

Everyone who uses recursion to write programs eventually accidentally writes a solution that leads to infinite recursion. For example, the following is a slight variation of the gcd method that doesn't work:

```
// flawed definition
public static int gcd(int x, int y) {
    if (x <= 0 || y <= 0) {
        // recursive case with negative value(s)
        return gcd(Math.abs(x), Math.abs(y));
    } else if (y == 0) {
        // base case with y == 0
        return x;
    } else {
        // recursive case with y > 0
        return gcd(y, x % y);
    }
}
```

This solution is just slightly different than the one we wrote previously. In the test for negative values, this code tests whether x and y are less than or equal to 0.

Continued on next page

Continued from previous page

The original code tests whether they are strictly less than `0`. It doesn't seem like this variation should make much difference, but it does. If we execute this version of the code to solve our original problem of finding the GCD of 132 and 20, the program produces many lines of output that look like the following:

```
at Bug.gcd(Bug.java:9)
at Bug.gcd(Bug.java:9)
at Bug.gcd(Bug.java:9)
at Bug.gcd(Bug.java:9)
at Bug.gcd(Bug.java:9)
at Bug.gcd(Bug.java:9)
at Bug.gcd(Bug.java:9)
```

The first time you see this, you are likely to think that something has broken on your computer because you will get so many lines of output. The number of lines of output will vary from one system to another, but it's likely to be hundreds, if not thousands. If you scroll all the way back up, you'll see that the output begins with this message:

```
Exception in thread "main" java.lang.StackOverflowError
        at Bug.gcd(Bug.java:9)
        at Bug.gcd(Bug.java:9)
        at Bug.gcd(Bug.java:9)
        ...
```

Java is letting you know that the call stack has gotten too big. Why did this happen? Remember the trace of execution for this case:

```
gcd(132, 20) = gcd(20, 12)
        gcd(20, 12) = gcd(12, 8)
                gcd(12, 8) = gcd(8, 4)
                        gcd(8, 4) = gcd(4, 0)
                              ...
```

Consider what happens at this point, when we call `gcd(4, 0)`. The value of `y` is `0`, which is our base case, so normally we would expect the method to return the value `4` and terminate. But the method begins by checking whether either `x` or `y` is less than or equal to `0`. Since `y` is `0`, this test evaluates to `true`, so the method makes a recursive call with the absolute values of `x` and `y`. But the absolute values of 4 and 0 are 4 and 0. So the method decides that `gcd(4, 0)` must be equal to `gcd(4, 0)`, which must be equal to `gcd(4, 0)`:

Continued on next page

Continued from previous page

```
gcd(132, 20) = gcd(20, 12)
           gcd(20, 12) = gcd(12, 8)
                     gcd(12, 8) = gcd(8, 4)
                               gcd(8, 4) = gcd(4, 0)
                                        gcd(4, 0) = gcd(4, 0)
                                                  gcd(4, 0) = gcd(4, 0)
                                                           gcd(4, 0) = gcd(4, 0)
                                                                    gcd(4, 0) = gcd(4, 0)
                                                                    ...
```

In other words, this version generates infinitely many recursive calls. Java allows you to make a lot of recursive calls, but eventually it runs out of space. When it does, it gives you a back trace to let you know how you got to the error. In this case, the back trace is not nearly as helpful as usual because almost all of the calls will involve the infinite recursion.

Again, think in terms of stacking pieces of paper on top of each other as methods are called. You'd wind up with a stack containing hundreds or even thousands of sheets, and you would have to look back through all of these to find the problem.

To handle these situations, you have to look closely at the line number to see which line of your program generated the infinite recursion. In this simple case, we know that it is the recursive call for negative `x` and `y` values. That alone might be enough to allow us to pinpoint the error. If the problem isn't obvious, though, you might need to include `println` statements to figure out what is going on. For example, in this code, we could add a `println` just before the recursive call:

```
public static int gcd(int x, int y) {
    if (x <= 0 || y <= 0) {
        // recursive case with negative value(s)
        System.out.println("x = " + x + " and y = " + y);
        return gcd(Math.abs(x), Math.abs(y));
    } else if (y == 0) {
    ...
}
```

When we run the program with that `println` in place, the code produces hundreds of lines of output of the form:

```
x = 4 and y = 0
```

If we examine that case closely, we'll see that we don't have negative values and will realize that we have to fix the test we are using.

Directory Crawler

Recursion is particularly useful when you're working with data that is itself recursive. For example, consider how files are stored on a computer. Each file is kept in a folder or directory. But directories can contain more than just files: Directories can contain other directories, those inner directories can contain directories, and even those directories can contain directories. Directories can be nested to an arbitrary depth. This storage system is an example of recursive data.

In Chapter 6, you learned to use `File` objects to keep track of files stored on your computer. For example, if you have a file called `data.txt`, you can construct a `File` object that can be used to get information about that file:

```
File f = new File("data.txt");
```

Several useful methods for the `File` class were introduced in Chapter 6. For example, the `exists` method indicates whether or not a certain file exists, and the `isDirectory` method indicates whether or not the name supplied corresponds to a file or a directory.

Let's write a program that will prompt the user for the name of a file or directory and recursively explore all the files that can be reached from that starting point. If the user provides the name of a file, the program should simply print the name. But if the user gives the name of a directory, the program should print the directory name and list all the directories and files inside that directory.

We can write a fairly simple `main` method that prompts for a file or directory name and checks to make sure it exists. If it does not, the program tells the user that there is no such file or directory. If it does exist, the program calls a method to print the information for that `File` object:

```
public static void main(String[] args) {
    Scanner console = new Scanner(System.in);
    System.out.print("directory or file name?");
    String name = console.nextLine();
    File f = new File(name);
    if (!f.exists()) {
        System.out.println("No such file/directory");
    } else {
        print(f);
    }
}
```

Our job will be to write the `print` method. The method should begin by printing the name of the file or directory:

```
public static void print(File f) {
    System.out.println(f.getName());
    ...
}
```

If the `File` object `f` represents a simple file, we have completed the task. But if `f` represents a directory, we also want to print the names of all the files contained in the directory:

```
public static void print(File f) {
    System.out.println(f.getName());
    if (f.isDirectory()) {
        // print contents of directory
    }
}
```

We can accomplish this task with the `listFiles` method, which returns an array of `File` objects that represent the contents of the directory. We can use a for-each loop to process each object:

```
public static void print(File f) {
    System.out.println(f.getName());
    if (f.isDirectory()) {
        for (File subF : f.listFiles()) {
            // print information for subF
        }
    }
}
```

To complete the method, we have to figure out how to print information about each of the individual `subF` objects in the directory. An obvious approach is to simply print the names of the subfiles:

```
// not quite right
public static void print(File f) {
    System.out.println(f.getName());
    if (f.isDirectory()) {
        for (File subF : f.listFiles()) {
            System.out.println(subF.getName());
        }
    }
}
```

This method works in that it prints the names of the subfiles inside the directory. But remember that there can be directories inside this directory, so some of those subfiles might actually be directories whose contents also need to be printed. We could try to fix our code by adding a test:

```
// getting worse, not better
public static void print(File f) {
    System.out.println(f.getName());
```

```
        if (f.isDirectory()) {
            for (File subF : f.listFiles()) {
                System.out.println(subF.getName());
                if (subF.isDirectory()) {
                    // print contents of subdirectory
                }
            }
        }
    }
```

But even this won't work, because there might be directories within those inner directories, and those directories might have subdirectories. There is no simple way to solve this problem with standard iterative techniques.

The solution is to think recursively. You might be tempted to envision many different cases: a file, a directory with files, a directory with subdirectories, a directory with subdirectories that have subdirectories, and so on. However, there are really only two cases to consider: Each object is either a file or a directory. If it's a file, we simply print its name. If it's a directory, we print its name and then print information about every file and directory inside of it. How do we get the code to recursively explore all of the possibilities? We call our own `print` method to process whatever appears inside a directory:

```
public static void print(File f) {
    System.out.println(f.getName());
    if (f.isDirectory()) {
        for (File subF : f.listFiles()) {
            print(subF);
        }
    }
}
```

This version of the code recursively explores the structure. Each time the method finds something inside a directory, it makes a recursive call that can handle either a file or a directory; that recursive call might make yet another recursive call to handle either a file or directory, and so on.

If we run this version of the method, we'll get output like the following:

```
homework
assignments.doc
hw1
Song.java
Song.class
hw2
DrawRocket.java
DrawRocket.class
```

The problem with this output is that it doesn't indicate the structure to us. We know that the first line of output is the name of the starting directory (`homework`) and that everything that follows is inside that directory, but we can't easily see the substructure. It would be more convenient if the output used indentation to indicate the inner structure, as in the following lines of output:

```
homework
    assignments.doc
    hw1
        Song.java
        Song.class
    hw2
        DrawRocket.java
        DrawRocket.class
```

In this output, we can more clearly see that the directory called `homework` contains three elements, two of which are directories that have their own files (`hw1` and `hw2`). We can get this output by including an extra parameter in the `print` method that indicates the desired level of indentation. On the initial call in `main`, we can pass the method an indentation of 0. On each recursive call, we can pass it a value one higher than the current level. We can then use that parameter to print some extra spacing at the beginning of the line to generate the indentation.

Here is our program, including the new version of the method with indentation:

```
// This program prompts the user for a file or directory name
// and shows a listing of all files and directories that can be
// reached from it (including subdirectories).

import java.io.*;
import java.util.*;

public class DirectoryCrawler {
    public static void main(String[] args) {
        Scanner console = new Scanner(System.in);
        System.out.print("directory or file name?");
        String name = console.nextLine();
        File f = new File(name);
        if (!f.exists()) {
            System.out.println("No such file/directory");
        } else {
            print(f, 0);
        }
    }

```

```
    // Prints information for the given file/directory using the
    // given level of indentation
    public static void print(File f, int level) {
        for (int i = 0; i < level; i++) {
            System.out.print("    ");
        }
        System.out.println(f.getName());
        if (f.isDirectory()) {
            for (File subF : f.listFiles()) {
                print(subF, level + 1);
            }
        }
    }
}
```

Helper Methods

Sometimes when you solve a problem recursively, you need to introduce an extra method to solve the problem. We call such methods *helper* methods.

For example, consider the task of writing a method called `sum` that takes an array of integers as a parameter and that returns the sum of the numbers in the array. Even though this is a fairly simple task, it turns out to be challenging to implement it using recursion. We could make a base case for an empty array (an array of length `0`):

```
public int sum(int[] list) {
    if (list.length == 0) {
        return 0;
    } else {
        ...
    }
}
```

If we write the code this way, what would we use for a recursive case? Suppose, for example, that we are asked to work with an array of length 10. How do we simplify an array of length 10 to bring it closer to being an empty array? The only way to do that would be to construct a new array with a shorter length, but that would be wasteful.

It is useful to consider how you would solve this iteratively. Here is an iterative version that follows a classic cumulative sum approach:

```
int sum = 0;
for (int i = 0; i < list.length; i++) {
    sum += list[i];
}
```

The key to the iterative approach is to work with an index variable that starts at 0 and continues iterating until it equals the length of the array. We can apply this same idea to a recursive solution. Remember that you want to think about how to pick off some small piece of the problem. Consider the following line of pseudocode:

```
sum(entire list) = list[0] + sum(list starting at 1)
```

This code states that we have to add in `list[0]`. That leaves us with the task of adding up the remaining values of the list (the values starting at index 1). And how would we do that? We can similarly say that:

```
sum(list starting at 1) = list[1] + sum(list starting at 2)
```

This approach leads to a series of recursive calls, each of which handles one element of the array:

```
sum(entire list) = list[0] + sum(list starting at 1)
    sum(list starting at 1) = list[1] + sum(list starting at 2)
        sum(list starting at 2) = list[2] + sum(list starting at 3)
            ...
```

When does this process end? We could end when we get to the last element of the array:

```
sum(list starting at list.length - 1) = list[list.length - 1]
```

Unfortunately, this choice of ending point assumes that a last element exists. That won't be true of an array of length 0. An easier approach is to end when we reach an index beyond the last element of the array. The `for` loop version of this method executes for as long as the index is less than the length of the array. Once the index becomes equal to the length of the array, it stops. Our recursion can similarly stop when the index becomes equal to the length of the array. And what does that add up to? It adds up to 0:

```
sum(list starting at list.length) = 0
```

Returning 0 in this case is the recursive equivalent of initializing the cumulative sum to 0.

We are almost ready to write the recursive method, but to express this idea as a method, we have to pass the method both the array and the starting index. So we want our method to look like the following:

```
// computes the sum of the list starting at the given index
public int sum(int[] list, int index) {
    ...
}
```

Using those two parameters, you'll find that the code is fairly simple to write using the approach described before:

```
// computes the sum of the list starting at the given index
public int sum(int[] list, int index) {
    if (index == list.length) {
        return 0;
    } else {
        return list[index] + sum(list, index + 1);
    }
}
```

Of course, there's the issue of that extra parameter. We were asked to write a method that is passed just the array. We could complain that we were asked to solve the wrong problem, but that's a bad attitude to have. We should allow a client to call methods using parameters that are convenient. We need the second parameter to write our recursive solution, but we shouldn't burden the client with the need to understand that detail.

This is a common situation. We often find ourselves wanting to write a recursive method that has extra parameters relative to the public method we are being asked to implement. The solution is to introduce a private method that has the parameter passing we want. So the client gets the convenient public method with the kind of parameter passing that the client wants, and we get our convenient private method with the kind of parameter passing that we want. We call the private method a helper method because it helps us to write the public method we've been asked to implement.

Here is the code that includes the private method:

```
// returns the sum of the numbers in the given array
public int sum(int[] list) {
    return sum(list, 0);
}

// computes the sum of the list starting at the given index
private int sum(int[] list, int index) {
    if (index == list.length) {
        return 0;
    } else {
        return list[index] + sum(list, index + 1);
    }
}
```

The public method simply calls the private method, passing it an appropriate value for the second parameter. Both methods can be called `sum` because they have different signatures (one parameter versus two). We make the second method a private method because we don't want to clutter up the public interface seen by the client.

There is a final benefit to this two-method approach. Sometimes you want to perform an action once, either before or after the recursive method executes. By dividing the recursive method into a public and a private method, you can include this one-time code in the public method either just before or just after the call on the private method.

12.4 Recursive Graphics

There has been a great deal of interest in the past 30 years about an emerging field of mathematics called *fractal geometry.* A fractal is a geometric object that is recursively constructed or self-similar. A fractal shape contains smaller versions of itself, so that it looks similar at all magnifications.

Benoit Mandelbrot founded the field of fractals in 1975 with his first publication about these intriguing objects, particularly a specific fractal that has come to be known as the Mandelbrot set. The most impressive aspect of fractal geometry is that extremely intricate and complex phenomena can be described with a simple set of rules. When Mandelbrot and others began drawing pictures of their fractals, they were an instant hit.

Many fractals can be described easily with recursion. As an example, we will explore a recursive method for drawing what is known as the Sierpinski triangle. We can't draw the actual fractal, because it is composed of infinitely many subtriangles. Instead, we will write a method that produces various levels that approximate the actual fractal.

At level 1, we draw an equilateral triangle as shown in Figure 12.1:

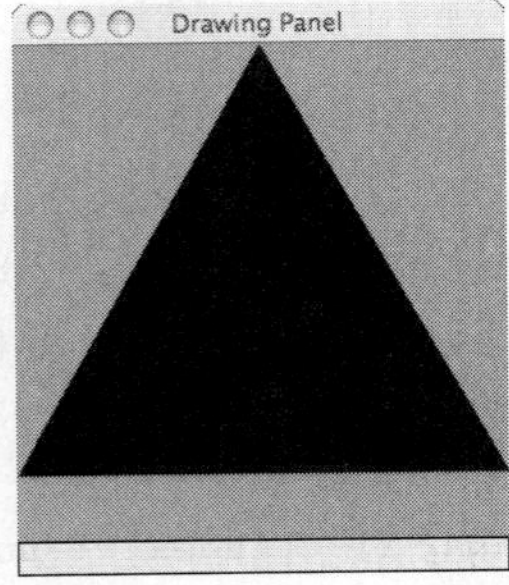

Figure 12.1 Sierpinski triangle, level 1

Proceeding to level 2, we draw three smaller triangles that are contained within the original triangle (see Figure 12.2):

Figure 12.2 Sierpinski triangle, level 2

We apply this principle in a recursive manner. Just as we replaced the original triangle with three inner triangles, we replace each of these three triangles with three inner triangles to obtain Figure 12.3 with nine triangles in level 3:

Figure 12.3 Sierpinski triangle, level 3

This process continues indefinitely, making a more intricate pattern at each new level. Figure 12.4 shows the result at level 7:

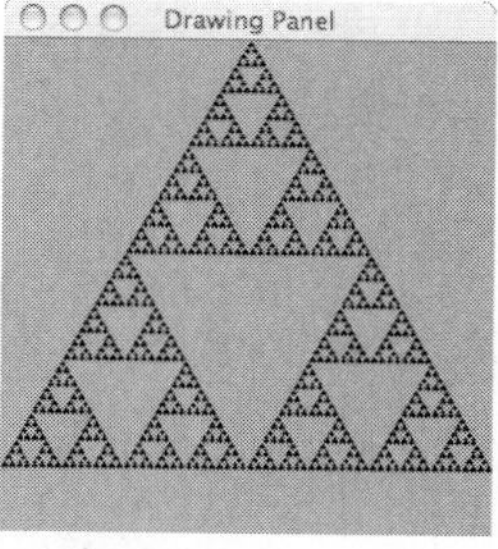

Figure 12.4 Sierpinski triangle, level 7

We can solve this problem using the `DrawingPanel` class from Supplement 3G. We'll pass the `Graphics` object for the panel to the method that is to draw the triangles. The method will also need to know the level to use and the three vertices of the triangle, which we can pass as `Point` objects. Our method will look like this:

```
public static void drawFigure(int level, Graphics g,
                              Point p1, Point p2, Point p3) {
    ...
}
```

Our base case will be to draw the basic triangle for level 1. The `Graphics` class has methods for filling rectangles and ovals, but not for filling triangles. Fortunately, there is a `Polygon` class in the `java.awt` package. We can construct a `Polygon` and then add a series of points to it. Once we've specified the three vertices, we can use the `fillPolygon` method of the `Graphics` class to fill the polygon. Our base case will look like this:

```
public static void drawFigure(int level, Graphics g,
                              Point p1, Point p2, Point p3) {
    if (level == 1) {
        // base case: simple triangle
        Polygon p = new Polygon();
        p.addPoint(p1.x, p1.y);
        p.addPoint(p2.x, p2.y);
        p.addPoint(p3.x, p3.y);
        g.fillPolygon(p);
    } else {
        // recursive case, split into 3 triangles
        ...
    }
}
```

Most of the work happens in the recursive case. We have to split the triangle into three smaller triangles. We'll label the vertices of the overall triangle (see Figure 12.5).

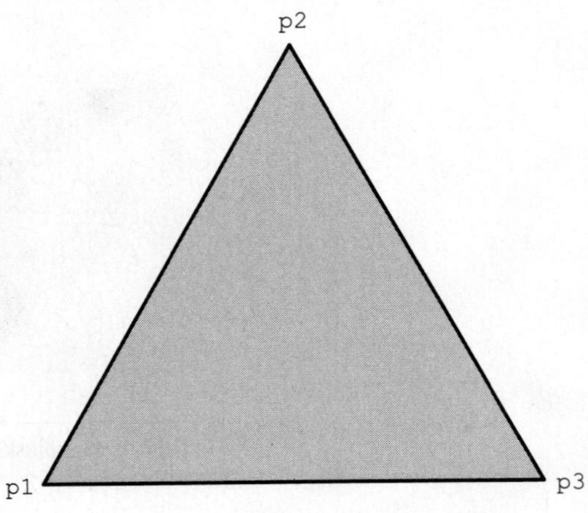

Figure 12.5 Triangle before splitting

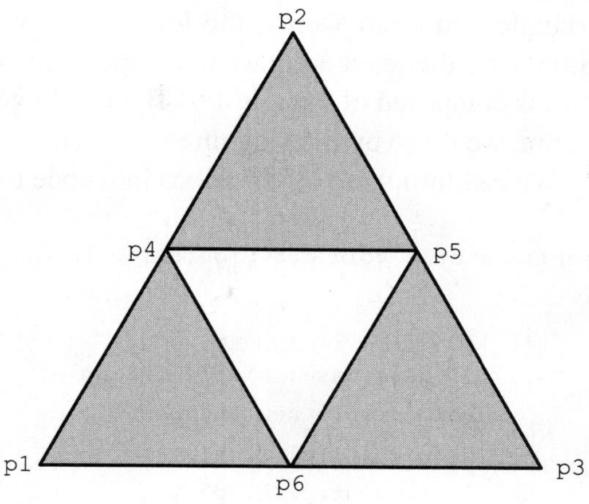

Figure 12.6 Triangle split into subtriangles

We then need to compute three new points that are the midpoints of the three sides of this triangle as shown in Figure 12.6.

From Figure 12.6, we see that

- p4 is the midpoint of p1 and p2
- p5 is the midpoint of p2 and p3
- p6 is the midpoint of p1 and p3

Once we have computed those points, we can describe the smaller triangles as follows:

- In the lower-left corner is the triangle formed by p1, p4, and p6.
- On top is the triangle formed by p4, p2, and p5.
- In the lower-right corner is the triangle formed by p6, p5, and p3.

There are three different midpoint computations involved here, so clearly it will be helpful to first write a method that will compute the midpoint of a segment given two endpoints. Computing the midpoints involves finding the arithmetic average (halfway point) of the x values and the y values:

```
public static Point midpoint(Point p1, Point p2) {
    return new Point((p1.x + p2.x) / 2, (p1.y + p2.y) / 2);
}
```

Given this method, we can easily compute the three midpoints.

The final detail we have to think about is the level. If you look again at the level 2 version of the figure (Figure 12.2), you will notice that it is composed of three simple triangles. In other words, the level 2 figure is composed of three level 1 figures. Similarly, the level 3 figure is composed of three level 2 figures, each of which in turn is composed of three level 1 figures. In general, if we are asked to draw a level `n` figure, we do so by drawing three level `(n – 1)` figures.

We can turn these observations into code to complete the recursive method:

```
public static void drawFigure(int level, Graphics g,
                              Point p1, Point p2, Point p3) {
    if (level == 1) {
        // base case: simple triangle
        Polygon p = new Polygon();
        p.addPoint(p1.x, p1.y);
        p.addPoint(p2.x, p2.y);
        p.addPoint(p3.x, p3.y);
        g.fillPolygon(p);
    } else {
        // recursive case, split into 3 triangles
        Point p4 = midpoint(p1, p2);
        Point p5 = midpoint(p2, p3);
        Point p6 = midpoint(p1, p3);

        // recurse on 3 triangular areas
        drawFigure(level – 1, g, p1, p4, p6);
        drawFigure(level – 1, g, p4, p2, p5);
        drawFigure(level – 1, g, p6, p5, p3);
    }
}
```

There is a limit to the number of levels down that we can go. The `DrawingPanel` has a finite resolution, so at some point we won't be able to subdivide our triangles any further. Also bear in mind that at each new level the number of triangles that we draw triples, which means that the number of triangles increases exponentially with the level.

The complete program is available from http://www.buildingjavaprograms.com. Remember that you need to also download `DrawingPanel.java` to execute the program.

12.5 Recursive Backtracking

Many programming problems can be solved by systematically searching a set of possibilities. For example, if you want to find a path through a maze from a starting point to an exit point, you can explore all possible paths through the maze until you find one that works. For many games like tic-tac-toe, you can explore all possible moves and countermoves to see if there is some move that guarantees that you win.

Many of these exhaustive search problems can be solved with an approach called *backtracking*. It is a particular approach to problem solving that is nicely expressed using recursion. As a result, it is sometimes referred to as *recursive backtracking*.

(Recursive) Backtracking

A general algorithm for finding solutions to a problem by exploring possible candidate solutions and abandoning ("backtracking") once a given candidate is deemed unsuitable.

Backtracking involves searching all possibilities, so it can be an expensive technique to use. But many problems are small enough in scope that they are nicely solved with a backtracking approach.

A Simple Example: Traveling North/East

To introduce the basic concepts and terminology of backtracking, let's explore a simple example. Consider a standard Cartesian plane with (x, y) coordinates. Suppose that you start at the origin, (0, 0), and you are allowed to repeatedly make one of these three moves:

- You can move North (abbreviated "N"), which will increase your y-coordinate by 1.
- You can move East (abbreviated "E"), which will increase your x-coordinate by 1.
- You can move Northeast (abbreviated "NE"), which will increase both your x-coordinate and y-coordinate by 1.

Starting from the origin, these three different moves would leave you in the locations shown in Figure 12.7. We can think of this as a traveling problem where we can make a series of moves that take us from the origin to some other (x, y) point. For example, the sequence of moves N, NE, N would leave us at (1, 3).

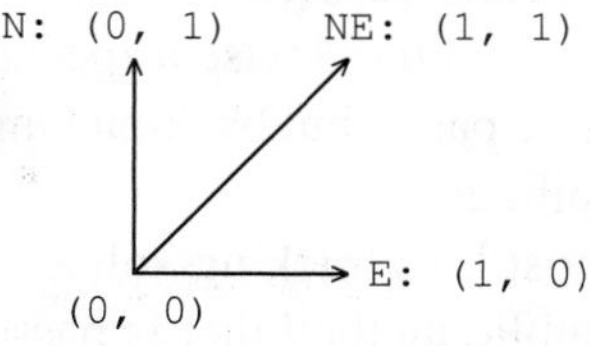

Figure 12.7 Traveling north, east, or northeast from the origin

Every backtracking problem involves a *solution space* of possible answers that you want to explore. We try to view the problem as a sequence of *choices*, which allows us to think of the solution space as a *decision tree*. For our traveling problem the choices are the sequence of moves that we make. Figure 12.8 shows a decision tree showing all of the possible ways to make two moves and where each sequence leaves us. These decision trees can be quite large even for a small problem like this.

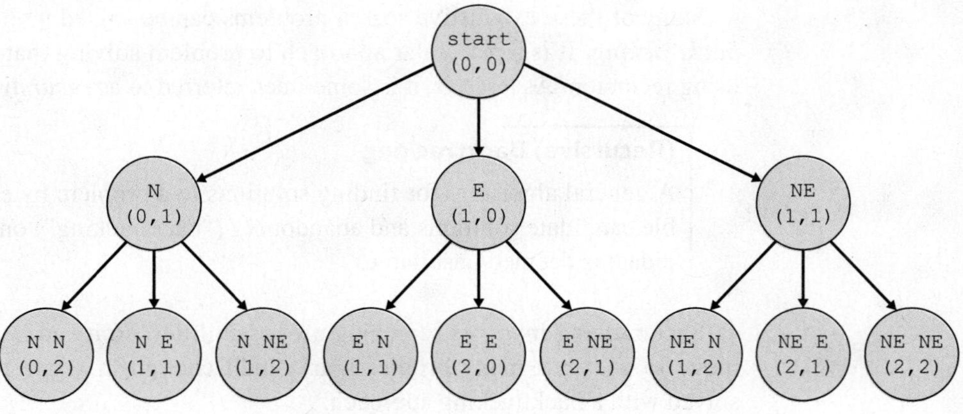

Figure 12.8 Decision tree for two moves

Consider the problem of traveling from the origin to the point (1, 2). What are the possible sequences of moves that would get you there? People are fairly good at solving problems like these, so you can probably pretty easily come up with all five of the possibilities:

- N, N, E
- N, E, N
- N, NE
- E, N, N
- NE, N

How would we write a computer program to find these solutions? For this simple problem, we could devise a specialized algorithm that takes into account the properties of these paths, but backtracking provides a convenient way to exhaustively search all possibilities.

For most backtracking solutions we end up writing two methods. We generally want a public method that is passed the details of the problem to be solved. But we almost always need extra parameters for the backtracking, so we almost always have an extra private method that does the actual backtracking.

The basic form that our backtracking solution will take is a method to explore all possible choices recursively:

```
private static void explore(a scenario) {
    ...
}
```

Because we are using recursion, we need to identify base cases and recursive cases. Backtracking solutions generally involve two different base cases. You tend to stop the backtracking when you find a solution, so that becomes one of our base cases. Often what you want to do when you find a solution is to report it:

```
private static void explore(a scenario) {
    if (this is a solution) {
        report it.
    } else {
        ...
    }
}
```

We don't want to search forever, so we also have to be on the lookout for what is called a *dead-end*. We might make a set of choices that lead us to a scenario where it is clear that no solution is possible with this set of choices. We make this a base case in our recursion so that we stop exploring when we reach a dead-end:

```
private static void explore(a scenario) {
    if (this is a solution) {
        report it.
    } else if (this is not a dead-end) {
        ...
    }
}
```

If our backtracking search has led us to a scenario where we haven't yet solved the problem and haven't yet reached a dead-end, then we want to explore each possible choice available to us. For each possible choice, we recursively explore the scenario of making that choice:

```
private static void explore(a scenario) {
    if (this is a solution) {
        report it.
    } else if (this is not a dead-end) {
        use recursive calls to explore each available choice.
    }
}
```

This pseudocode captures the essence of the backtracking approach. Not all backtracking solutions will take exactly this form, but they will all have some variation of each of these elements.

We can flesh out the pseudocode a bit by filling in some details for this particular problem. We are considering the problem of moving from a current position to a target position, both specified with (x, y) coordinates. And we have three available moves from any given position: N, E, and NE:

```
private static void explore(current (x, y) and target (x, y)) {
    if (this is a solution) {
        report it.
    } else if (this is not a dead-end) {
        explore(moving N).
        explore(moving E).
        explore(moving NE).
    }
}
```

Often it can be challenging to figure out what parameters to pass to the exploration method. In this case, we need a current x and y and a target x and y. We also need some way of keeping track of the choices that we have made so that we can report the path that we have taken. There are many ways to do this, but for simplicity, let's build up a string that stores the sequence of moves.

We can test whether we have a solution by testing whether the current and target coordinates match. But how do we test for a dead-end? In this problem, our x-coordinates and y-coordinates never go down. If we reach a point where the current x is greater than the target x or the current y is greater than the target y, then we know that we have traveled too far in that direction and we will never reach the target.

Putting these details together, we end up with the following exploration method:

```
private static void explore(int targetX, int targetY,
                            int currX, int currY, String path) {
    if (currX == targetX && currY == targetY) {
        System.out.println(path);
    } else if (currX <= targetX && currY <= targetY) {
        explore(targetX, targetY, currX, currY + 1, path + " N");
        explore(targetX, targetY, currX + 1, currY, path + " E");
        explore(targetX, targetY, currX + 1, currY + 1, path + " NE");
    }
}
```

We can complete the solution by providing a public method that starts the recursive search by passing the initial coordinates (0, 0) and an appropriate value to appear at the front of the string that stores the path:

```
public static void travel(int targetX, int targetY) {
    explore(targetX, targetY, 0, 0, "moves:");
}
```

If we ask the method to find all ways of traveling to (1, 2), it produces the following output:

```
moves: N N E
moves: N E N
moves: N NE
moves: E N N
moves: NE N
```

Figure 12.9 shows the complete decision tree that is explored by this particular call with the five solutions shaded.

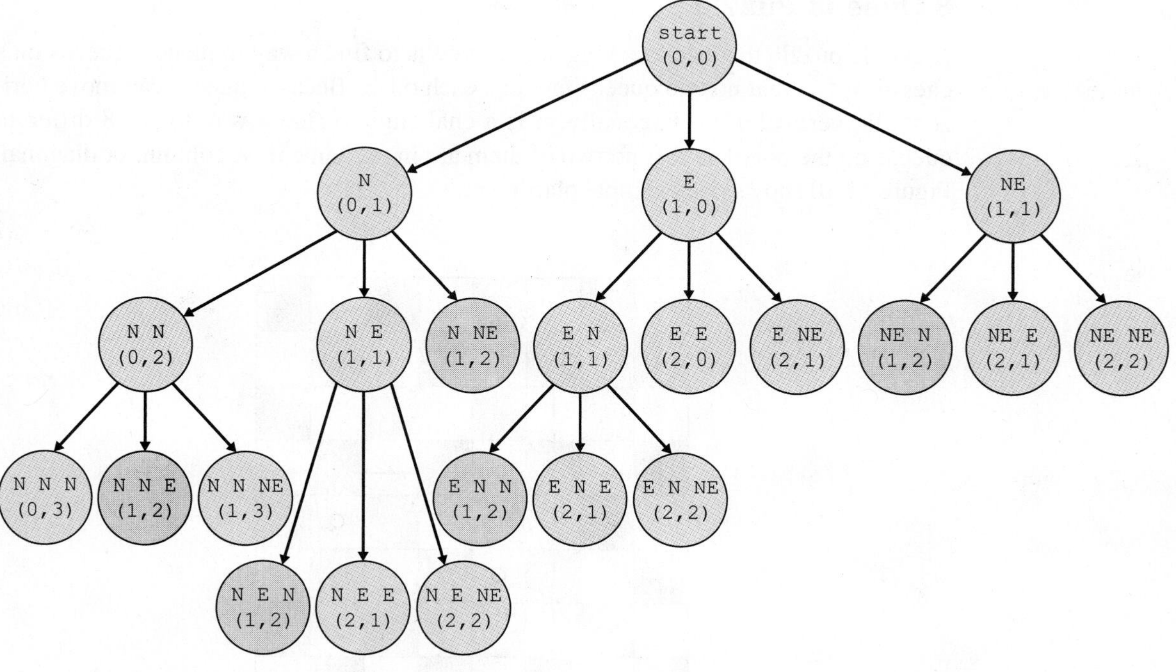

Figure 12.9 Complete decision tree for paths to (1, 2)

Notice that the tree does not contain all of the possible combinations of three moves. That is because we don't explore past a solution and we don't explore past a dead-end (such as (2, 1)).

It is useful to consider the order in which the recursive method searches these possibilities. In general, as with most recursive solutions, the recursive calls lead to a depth-first traversal. From the starting point at the top of the tree it first considers moving North to (0, 1). That entire branch of the tree is explored before any other branches are explored. The next call considers moving North again to (0, 2). Then it considers another move North to (0, 3). So the initial sequence of calls leads it down to the leftmost node of the three. This is a dead-end, so it stops exploring. At that point, it returns to where it last had another choice to consider. It backs up to where it had chosen two North moves in a row (N N) and it considers moving East instead of moving North. That turns out to be a solution (N N E), so it reports a success. Then it backs up again to where it last had another choice to make and it considers the remaining possibilities.

This property of going back to where it still has other choices to explore is the source of the term "backtracking." As it finds solutions and dead-ends, it goes back (backtracks) to where it last had some other move to consider. It continues to search until it has exhausted all possible sequences of choices.

8 Queens Puzzle

A classic puzzle that backtracking solves well is to find a way to place 8 queens on a chessboard so that no two queens threaten each other. Because queens can move horizontally, vertically, or diagonally, it is a challenge to find a way to put 8 different queens on the board so that no two of them are in the same row, column, or diagonal. Figure 12.10 shows one example placement.

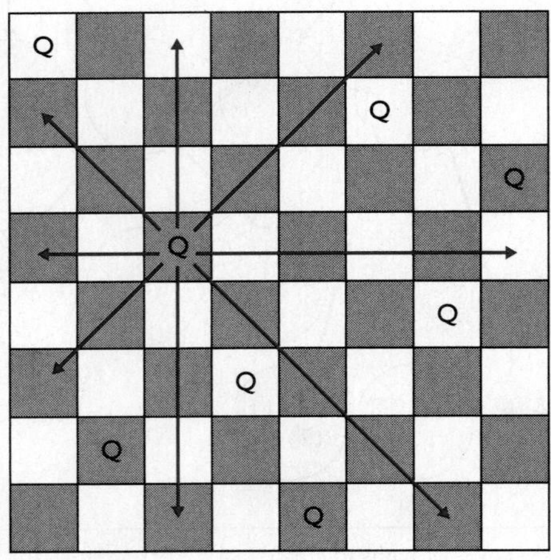

Figure 12.10 The 8 queens problem

To solve this problem with backtracking, we have to think of it in terms of a sequence of choices. The simplest way to do this is to think in terms of choosing where the first queen goes, then choosing where the second queen goes, and so on. There are 64 places to put the first queen because the chessboard is an 8-by-8 board. At the top of the tree, there are 64 different choices you could make for placing the first queen. Then once you've placed one queen, there are 63 squares left to choose from for the second queen, then 62 squares for the third queen, and so on.

Because backtracking searches all possibilities, it can take a long time to execute as there are many possibilities to explore. If we explore them all, we'll need to look at 64 * 63 * 62 * . . . * 57 states, which is too many even for a fast computer. We need to be as smart as we can about the choices we explore. In the case of 8 queens, we can do better than to consider 64 choices followed by 63 choices followed by 62 choices, and so on. We know that most of these aren't worth exploring.

One approach is to observe that if there is any solution at all to this problem, then the solution will have exactly one queen in each row and exactly one queen in each column. That's because you can't have two in the same row or two in the same column and there are 8 of them on an 8-by-8 board. We can search more efficiently if we go row-by-row or column-by-column. It doesn't matter which choice we make, so let's explore column by column. Eliminating undesirable candidates from being explored is also called *pruning* the decision tree.

In this new way of looking at the search space, the first choice is for column 1. We have 8 different rows where we could put a queen in column 1. At the next level we consider all of the places to put a queen in column 2, and so on. Figure 12.11 shows the top of our decision tree.

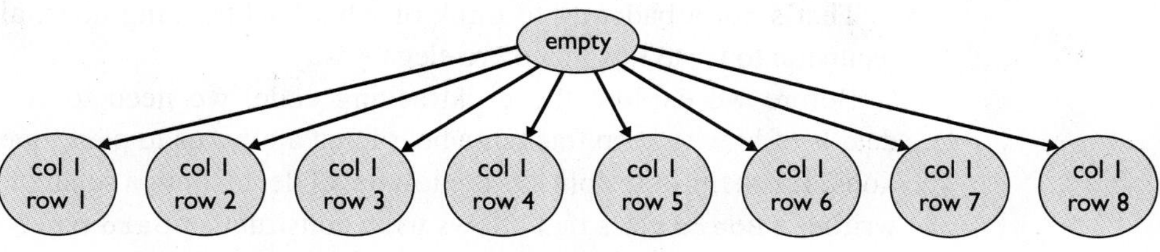

Figure 12.11 Decision tree for first column

There are eight different branches for each column. Under each of these branches, we have eight branches for each of the possible rows where we might place a queen in column 2. For example, if we think just about the possibility of placing the first queen in column 1 and row 5 and then think about all of the ways to place a second queen, we end up with an extra level of the tree as shown in Figure 12.12.

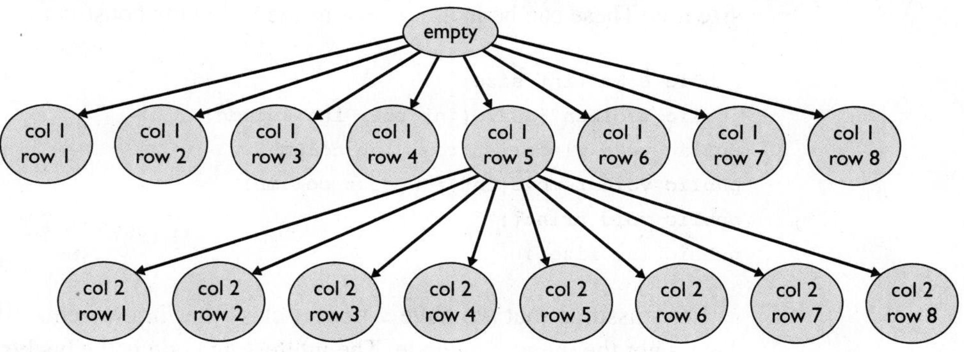

Figure 12.12 A decision tree for second column

These pictures don't capture the whole story because the tree is so large. There are eight branches at the top. From each of these eight branches there are eight branches. And from each of those branches there are eight branches. This continues eight levels deep (one level for each column of the board).

It's clear that the eight choices could be coded fairly nicely in a `for` loop, something along the lines of:

```
for (int row = 1; row <= 8; row++) {
```

But what we need for backtracking is something more like a deeply nested `for` loop:

```
for (int row = 1; row <= 8; row++) {  // explore column 1
    for (int row = 1; row <= 8; row++) {   // explore column 2
        for (int row = 1; row <= 8; row++) {  // explore column 3
            for (int row = 1; row <= 8; row++) {  // explore column 4
                ....
```

That's not a bad way to think of what backtracking does, although we will use recursion to write this in a more elegant way.

Before we explore the backtracking code, we need to consider the low-level details of how to keep track of a board that allows us to place queens in specific locations. It is helpful to split off the low-level details into a separate class. Let's plan on writing a `Board` class that allows us to construct a `Board` object to keep track of the state of the chessboard.

What kind of methods would we want to have for a `Board` object? Obviously it would need some kind of constructor. We want to pass it an integer *n* so we could solve the more general "*n* queens" problem with an *n*-by-*n* board. We need to be able to test whether it's safe to place a queen at a particular location. We need a way to place a queen on the board. We need a way to remove a queen because the backtracking involves trying different possibilities. We need a way to display output showing where the queens have been placed. Lastly, we'd like to be able to ask the board what size it is. These can be implemented as the following constructor and methods:

```
public Board(int size)
public boolean isSafe(int row, int column)
public void place(int row, int column)
public void remove(int row, int column)
public void print()
public int size()
```

Let's assume that we have a `Board` class that implements all of these methods. That's not the interesting code. The interesting code is the backtracking code which, given this class, we can now write in a very straightforward manner.

Once again we will introduce a public/private pair of methods to perform the backtracking. The public method can be passed a `Board` object and it will call the private recursive method that performs the backtracking:

```
public static void solve(Board b) {
    ...
}
```

Recall that we had this general pseudocode for backtracking solutions:

```
private static void explore(a scenario) {
    if (this is a solution) {
        report it.
    } else if (this is not a dead-end) {
        use recursive calls to explore each available choice.
    }
}
```

The 8-queens backtracking problem differs in several important ways from the simple backtracking we saw before. Let's consider each of the differences and see how to adapt our pseudocode for each of them.

In the traveling problem we had just three possibilities to consider, so it made sense to write three recursive calls to explore each possibility. Here we have eight possibilities for the 8-queens problem and potentially a different number of possibilities if the board size is something other than 8. In this case, we want to use a loop to consider the different possibilities. Many backtracking problems will require using a loop instead of individual calls; it is useful to adapt our pseudocode to fit that approach.

```
private static void explore(a scenario) {
    if (this is a solution) {
        report it.
    } else {
        for (each available choice) {
            if (this is not a dead-end) {
                use a recursive call to explore that choice.
            }
        }
    }
}
```

We can also be more specific about what it means to explore a choice. In our simple example, we were building up a string that stored the path. That meant that we didn't have to undo a choice to move on to the next choice. More complex backtracking problems require a cleanup step where you undo a choice. That will be true of 8-queens. We will place a queen on the board to explore that branch and when we come back from the recursive exploration, we will need to remove the queen to get ready to explore the next possible choice. So the pseudocode can be expanded to include the pattern of making a choice, recursively exploring, and then undoing the choice:

```
private static void explore(a scenario) {
    if (this is a solution) {
        report it.
    } else {
        for (each available choice) {
            if (this is not a dead-end) {
                make the choice.
                recursively explore subsequent choices.
                undo the choice.
            }
        }
    }
}
```

This pseudocode is general enough that it can be used for many backtracking problems. Some programmers refer to this as the "choose, explore, un-choose" pattern for backtracking.

This is appropriate code to use if you want to search all possibilities. In the case of 8-queens, there are many solutions (over 90 different solutions). We don't really want to see all of these solutions. We're happy to have just one. For this backtracking problem, we will consider a variation that stops when it finds a solution. That means that our recursive method will need to have a way to let us know whether a certain path worked out or whether it turned out to be a dead-end. A good way to do this is to have a `boolean` return type and to have the method return `true` if it succeeds, `false` if it is a dead-end.

```
private static boolean explore(a scenario) {
    if (this is a solution) {
        report it.
        return true;
    } else {
        for (each available choice) {
            if (this is not a dead-end) {
                make the choice.
                if (recursive call to explore subsequent choices) {
                    return true;
                }
```

```
            undo the choice.
        }
    }
    return false;
}
```

This pseudocode is also general enough that it can be used for many backtracking problems when you want to stop the process after finding a solution.

We can adapt this to the 8-queens problem by filling in the details. What parameters will it need to specify a scenario? It certainly needs the `Board` object. Recall that each level of the decision tree involves a different column of the board. The first invocation will handle column 1, the second will handle column 2, and so on. Therefore, in addition to the board, the method also needs to know the column to work on. That leaves us with this header:

```
private static boolean explore(Board b, int col) {
    ...
}
```

How do we know if we've found a solution? This backtracking code doesn't explore dead-ends. As a result, it has the following precondition:

```
// pre: queens have been safely placed in previous columns
```

What would be a nice column to get to? A tempting answer is 8. It would be nice to get to column 8 because it would mean that 7 of the 8 queens have been placed properly. But an even better answer is 9, because the precondition tells us that if we ever reach column 9, then queens have been safely placed in each of the first 8 columns.

This turns out to be our test for whether we have found a solution:

```
private static boolean explore(Board b, int col) {
    if (col > b.size()) {
        return true;
    } else {
        ...
    }
}
```

The pseudocode indicates that we should print the answer before returning `true`. We could do that, but because the solution is stored in the `Board` object, we can simply return and allow the calling method to print out the solution.

Now we have to fill in the details of the `for` loop that explores the various possibilities. We have eight possibilities to explore (the eight rows of this column where we might place a queen). A `for` loop works nicely to explore the different row numbers.

The pseudocode indicates that we should test to make sure it is not a dead-end. We can do that by making sure that it is safe to place a queen in that row and column:

```
for (int row = 1; row <= b.size(); row++) {
    if (b.isSafe(row, col)) {
        ...
    }
}
```

We now need to fill in the three steps that are involved in exploring a choice: making the choice, recursively exploring subsequent choices, and undoing the choice. We make the choice by telling the board to place a queen in that row and column:

```
for (int row = 1; row <= b.size(); row++) {
    if (b.isSafe(row, col)) {
        b.place(row, col);
        ...
    }
}
```

Then we recursively explore subsequent choices (later columns) and return `true` to stop the process if it finds a solution:

```
for (int row = 1; row <= b.size(); row++) {
    if (b.isSafe(row, col)) {
        b.place(row, col);
        if (explore(b, col + 1)) {
            return true;
        }
        ...
    }
}
```

Finally we have to undo our choice in case that turns out to be a dead-end:

```
for (int row = 1; row <= b.size(); row++) {
    if (b.isSafe(row, col)) {
        b.place(row, col);
        if (explore(b, col + 1)) {
            return true;
        }
        b.remove(row, col);
    }
}
```

Putting it all together we get:

```
private static boolean explore(Board b, int col) {
    if (col > b.size()) {
        return true;
    } else {
        for (int row = 1; row <= b.size(); row++) {
            if (b.isSafe(row, col)) {
                b.place(row, col);
                if (explore(b, col + 1)) {
                    return true;
                }
                b.remove(row, col);
            }
        }
        return false;
    }
}
```

We need some code in the `solve` method that starts the recursion in column 1 and that either prints the solution or a message about there not being solutions:

```
public static void solve(Board solution) {
    if (explore(solution, 1)) {
        System.out.println("One solution is as follows:");
        solution.print();
    } else {
        System.out.println("No solution.");
    }
}
```

On our web site http://www.buildingjavaprograms.com/ you will find the `Board` class and a full runnable version of the program that you can run to see that it finds a solution to 8 queens, 4 queens, and so on. In the case of 2 queens, there are no solutions. Our graphical variation of the program includes an animation generated by the backtracking itself.

Solving Sudoku Puzzles

Let's look at one more example of backtracking. Sudoku puzzles have become very popular. The puzzle involves a 9-by-9 grid that is to be filled in with the digits 1 through 9. Each row and column is required to have exactly one occurrence of each of the nine digits. The grid is further divided into nine 3-by-3 grids, and each grid is also required to have exactly one occurrence of each of the nine digits. A specific Sudoku puzzle will fill in some of the cells of the grid with specific digits, such as the puzzle shown in Figure 12.13.

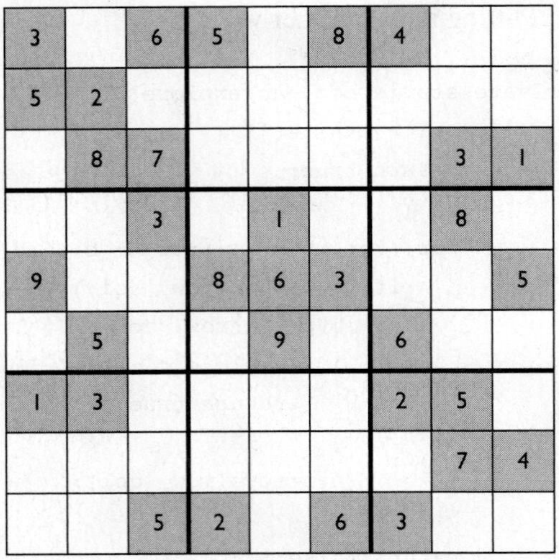

Figure 12.13 A Sudoku board

When people play Sudoku, they use all sorts of heuristics and intuitions to find a way to fill in the empty cells of the grid while still meeting the constraints. With a backtracking approach, we just use brute force to try all possibilities.

The choices involved are what digit to put in each of the unoccupied cells of the grid. There are nine possibilities to explore for each empty cell (the digits 1 through 9). This approach to Sudoku is not necessarily going to run quickly, but backtracking provides a framework for quickly writing a complete solution.

As with many backtracking tasks, the real work involves keeping track of the details of this particular scenario. With the 8-queens problem we introduced a `Board` class to keep track of the chessboard. In this case we should develop a `Grid` class that keeps track of the state of the Sudoku grid.

In the case of the Sudoku grid, we have to start with some of the cells filled in. That will mean that our `Grid` class will need to read the initial configuration. Let's assume that each puzzle is stored in a text file with a 9-by-9 grid of numbers and dashes, as in:

```
3 - 6 5 - 8 4 - -
5 2 - - - - - - -
- 8 7 - - - - 3 1
- - 3 - 1 - - 8 -
9 - - 8 6 3 - - 5
- 5 - - 9 - 6 - -
1 3 - - - - 2 5 -
- - - - - - - 7 4
- - 5 2 - 6 3 - -
```

That means that our `Grid` class constructor will need to read the initial configuration:

```
public Grid(Scanner input)
```

We immediately run into another problem. If some of the cells are filled in, then it's not as simple as the 8-queens case where we could just systematically explore each different cell of an empty board. In the Sudoku case, we have to figure out which cell to explore first, which cell to go to after that, and so on. There are many ways we could approach this, but the simplest is to give this responsibility to the `Grid` class. We can introduce a method that allows us to ask the grid to give us the next unassigned location in the grid.

Then we are faced with the question of how to specify a grid location. An obvious approach would be to give row and column numbers, but a method can return only one value. If the grid is going to identify the unassigned locations, then we don't really need to keep track of rows and columns ourselves. To keep thing simple, let's assume that the grid returns a cell number as a simple `int`:

```
public int getUnassignedLocation()
```

Eventually the grid will fill up, so we have to adopt a convention for what happens when there is no unassigned location left. Let's assume that the method returns `-1` in that case to indicate that the grid is full.

In addition to these methods, we will want similar methods to the ones we had in 8-queens. We want to be able to test whether it's safe to set a particular cell to a particular digit. This is the method that will make sure that the grid we are building up is legal. So it will have to check to see if this new digit doesn't already appear in the given row, column, or subgrid. We'll need a method to set a cell to a specific digit. An "undo" method to remove a digit from a cell will be necessary. We will also want a method to print our solution. These are implemented as the following methods, respectively:

```
public boolean noConflicts(int cellNumber, int n)
public void place(int cellNumber, int n)
public void remove(int cellNumber)
public void print()
```

As with 8-queens, we'll want to stop searching once we find a solution, so we start with the standard pseudocode for the single-solution backtracking:

```
private static boolean explore(a scenario) {
    if (this is a solution) {
        report it.
        return true;
    } else {
        for (each available choice) {
            if (this is not a dead-end) {
```

```
                make the choice.
                if (recursive call to explore subsequent choices) {
                    return true;
                }
                undo the choice.
            }
        }
        return false;
    }
}
```

In this case, the information about a scenario is stored in the grid object. We know that we have a solution if we manage to fill every cell of the grid. To test whether we have a solution we can ask the grid to give us the next unassigned location and see if the method returns `-1` (the value that signals that the grid is full):

```
private static boolean explore(Grid g) {
    int cellNumber = g.getUnassignedLocation();
    if (cellNumber == -1) {
        return true;
    } else {
        ...
    }
}
```

The available choices are the digits 1 through 9 and we have methods for performing each of the operations described in the pseudocode, so we can fill in the blanks to complete the method as follows:

```
private static boolean explore(Grid g) {
    int cellNumber = g.getUnassignedLocation();
    if (cellNumber == -1) {
        return true;
    } else {
        for (int n = 1; n <= 9; n++) {
            if (g.noConflicts(cellNumber, n)) {
                g.place(cellNumber, n);
                if (explore(g)) {
                    return true;
                }
                g.remove(cellNumber);
            }
        }
        return false;
    }
}
```

You will find the `Grid` class and a full runnable version of this program on our web site http://www.buildingjavaprograms.com/ along with a graphical version that shows the choices as they are being considered by the backtracking.

12.6 Case Study: Prefix Evaluator

VideoNote

In this section, we will explore the use of recursion to evaluate complex numeric expressions. First we will examine the different conventions for specifying numeric expressions and then we will see how recursion makes it relatively easy to implement one of the standard conventions.

Infix, Prefix, and Postfix Notation

When we write numeric expressions in a Java program, we typically put numeric operators like + and * between the two operands, as in the following:

```
3.5 + 8.2
9.1 * 12.7
7.8 * (2.3 + 2.5)
```

Putting the operator between the operands is a convention known as *infix notation.* A second convention is to put the operator in front of the two operands, as in the following examples:

```
+ 3.5 8.2
* 9.1 12.7
* 7.8 + 2.3 2.5
```

Putting the operator in front of the operands is a convention known as *prefix notation.* Prefix notation looks odd for symbols like + and *, but it resembles mathematical function notation, in which the name of the function goes first. For example, if we were calling methods instead of using operators, we would write

```
plus(3.5, 8.2)
times(9.1, 12.7)
times(7.8, plus(2.3, 2.5))
```

There is also a third convention, in which the operator appears after the two operands, as in the following examples:

```
3.5 8.2 +
9.1 12.7 *
7.8 2.3 2.5 + *
```

This convention is known as *postfix notation.* It is also sometimes referred to as reverse Polish notation, or RPN. For many years Hewlett–Packard has sold scientific calculators that use RPN rather than normal infix notation.

We are so used to infix notation that it takes a while to get used to the other two conventions. One of the interesting facts you will discover if you take the time to learn the prefix and postfix conventions is that infix is the only notation that requires parentheses. The other two notations are unambiguous.

Table 12.1 summarizes the three notations.

Table 12.1 Arithmetic Notations

Notation	Description	Examples

infix	operator between operands	`2.3 + 4.7`
		`2.6 * 3.7`
		`(3.4 + 7.9) * 18.6 + 2.3 / 4.7`

prefix	operator before operands
	(functional notation)
		`+ 2.3 4.7`
		`* 2.6 3.7`
		`+ * + 3.4 7.9 18.6 / 2.3 4.7`

postfix	operator after operands
	(reverse Polish notation)
		`2.3 4.7 +`
		`2.6 3.7 *`
		`3.4 7.9 + 18.6 * 2.3 4.7 / +`

Evaluating Prefix Expressions

Of the three standard notations, prefix notation is most easily implemented with recursion. In this section we will write a method that reads a prefix expression from a `Scanner` and computes its value. Our method will look like this:

```
// pre : input contains a legal prefix expression
// post: expression is consumed and the result is returned
public static double evaluate(Scanner input) {
    ...
}
```

Before we can begin writing the method, we have to consider the kind of input that we are going to get. As the precondition indicates, we will assume that the `Scanner` contains a legal prefix expression. The simplest possible expression would be a number like

```
38.9
```

There isn't much to evaluate in this case—we can simply read and return the number. More complex prefix expressions will involve one or more operators. Remember that the operator goes in front of the operands in a prefix expression. A slightly more complex expression would be two numbers as operands with an operator in front:

```
+ 2.6 3.7
```

This expression could itself be an operand in a larger expression. For example, we might ask for

```
* + 2.6 3.7 + 5.2 18.7
```

At the outermost level, we have a multiplication operator with two operands:

```
 *        + 2.6 3.7     + 5.2 18.7
 ↑        └───┬───┘     └───┬────┘
operator   operand #1     operand #2
```

In other words, this expression is computing the product of two sums. Here is the same expression written in the more familiar infix notation:

```
(2.6 + 3.7) * (5.2 + 18.7)
```

These expressions can become arbitrarily complex. The key observation to make about them is that they all begin with an operator. In other words, every prefix expression is of one of two forms:

- A simple number
- An operator followed by two operands

This observation will become a road map for our recursive solution. The simplest prefix expression will be a number, and we can distinguish it from the other case because any other expression will begin with an operator. So we can begin our recursive solution by checking whether the next token in the `Scanner` is a number. If it is, we have a simple case and we can simply read and return the number:

```
public static double evaluate(Scanner input) {
    if (input.hasNextDouble()) {
        // base case with a simple number
        return input.nextDouble();
    } else {
        // recursive case with an operator and two operands
        ...
    }
}
```

Turning our attention to the recursive case, we know that the input must be an operator followed by two operands. We can begin by reading the operator:

```
public static double evaluate(Scanner input) {
    if (input.hasNextDouble()) {
        // base case with a simple number
        return input.nextDouble();
    } else {
        // recursive case with an operator and two operands
        String operator = input.next();
        ...
    }
}
```

At this point, we reach a critical decision. We have read in the operator, and now we need to read in the first operand and then the second operand. If we knew that the operands were simple numbers, we could write code like the following:

```
// not the right approach
public static double evaluate(Scanner input) {
    if (input.hasNextDouble()) {
        // base case with a simple number
        return input.nextDouble();
    } else {
        // recursive case with an operator and two operands
        String operator = input.next();
        double operand1 = input.nextDouble();
        double operand2 = input.nextDouble();
        ...
    }
}
```

But we have no guarantee that the operands are simple numbers. They might be complex expressions that begin with operators. Your instinct might be to test whether or not the original operator is followed by another operator (in other words, whether the first operand begins with an operator), but that reasoning won't lead you to a satisfactory outcome. Remember that the expressions can be arbitrarily complex, so either of the operands might contain dozens of operators to be processed.

The solution to this puzzle involves recursion. We need to read two operands from the `Scanner`, and they might be very complex. But we know that they are in prefix form and we know that they aren't as complex as the original expression we were asked to evaluate. The key is to recursively evaluate each of the two operands:

```
public static double evaluate(Scanner input) {
    if (input.hasNextDouble()) {
        // base case with a simple number
        return input.nextDouble();
    } else {
        // recursive case with an operator and two operands
        String operator = input.next();
        double operand1 = evaluate(input);
        double operand2 = evaluate(input);
        ...
    }
}
```

This simple solution works. Of course, we still have the task of evaluating the operator. After the two recursive calls have executed, we will have an operator and two numbers (say, +, `3.4`, and `2.6`). It would be nice if we could just write a statement like the following:

```
return operand1 operator operand2; // does not work
```

Unfortunately, Java doesn't work that way. We have to use a nested `if/else` statement to test what kind of operator we have and to return an appropriate value:

```
if (operator.equals("+")) {
    return operand1 + operand2;
} else if (operator.equals("-")) {
    return operand1 - operand2;
} else if (operator.equals("*")) {
    ...
```

We can include this code in its own method so that our recursive method stays fairly short:

```
public static double evaluate(Scanner input) {
    if (input.hasNextDouble()) {
        // base case with a simple number
        return input.nextDouble();
    } else {
        // recursive case with an operator and two operands
        String operator = input.next();
        double operand1 = evaluate(input);
        double operand2 = evaluate(input);
        return apply(operator, operand1, operand2);
    }
}
```

Complete Program

When you program with recursion, you'll notice two things. First, the recursive code that you write will tend to be fairly short, even though it might be solving a very complex task. Second, most of your program will generally end up being supporting code for the recursion that does low-level tasks. For our current task of evaluating a prefix expression, we have a short and powerful prefix evaluator, but we need to include some supporting code that explains the program to the user, prompts for a prefix expression, and reports the result. We also found that we needed a method that would apply an operator to two operands. The nonrecursive parts of the program are fairly straightforward, so they are included in the following code without detailed discussion:

```
// This program prompts for and evaluates a prefix expression.

```

```
import java.util.*;

public class PrefixEvaluator {
    public static void main(String[] args) {
        Scanner console = new Scanner(System.in);
        System.out.println("This program evaluates prefix");
        System.out.println("expressions that include the");
        System.out.println("operators +, -, *, / and %");
        System.out.print("expression? ");
        double value = evaluate(console);
        System.out.println("value = " + value);
    }

    // pre : input contains a legal prefix expression
    // post: expression is consumed and the result is returned
    public static double evaluate(Scanner input) {
        if (input.hasNextDouble()) {
            return input.nextDouble();
        } else {
            String operator = input.next();
            double operand1 = evaluate(input);
            double operand2 = evaluate(input);
            return apply(operator, operand1, operand2);
        }
    }

    // pre : operator is one of +, -, *, / or %
    // post: returns the result of applying the given operator
    //       to the given operands
    public static double apply(String operator, double operand1,
                               double operand2) {
        if (operator.equals("+")) {
            return operand1 + operand2;
        } else if (operator.equals("-")) {
            return operand1 - operand2;
        } else if (operator.equals("*")) {
            return operand1 * operand2;
        } else if (operator.equals("/")) {
            return operand1 / operand2;
        } else if (operator.equals("%")) {
            return operand1 % operand2;
        } else {
            throw new IllegalArgumentException("bad operator: "
                                               + operator);
```

```
            }
        }
}
```

The program can handle simple numbers, as in the following sample execution:

```
This program evaluates prefix
expressions that include the
operators +, -, *, / and %
expression? 38.9
value = 38.9
```

It can also handle expressions with a single operator, as in the following execution:

```
This program evaluates prefix
expressions that include the
operators +, -, *, / and %
expression? + 2.6 3.7
value = 6.300000000000001
```

And it handles the case we considered that involved a product of two sums:

```
This program evaluates prefix
expressions that include the
operators +, -, *, / and %
expression? * + 2.6 3.7 + 5.2 18.7
value = 150.57000000000002
```

In fact, it can handle arbitrarily complex expressions, as in the following sample execution:

```
This program evaluates prefix
expressions that include the
operators +, -, *, / and %
expression? / + * - 17.4 8.9 - 3.9 4.7 18.4 - 3.8 * 7.9 2.3
value = -0.8072372999304106
```

The expression being computed in the previous example is the prefix equivalent of the following infix expression:

```
((17.4 - 8.9) * (3.9 - 4.7) + 18.4) / (3.8 - 7.9 * 2.3)
```

Chapter Summary

Recursion is an algorithmic technique in which a method calls itself. A method that uses recursion is called a recursive method.

Recursive methods include two cases: a base case that the method can solve directly without recursion, and a recursive case in which the method reduces a problem into a simpler problem of the same kind using a recursive call.

Recursive method calls work internally by storing information about each call into a structure called a call stack. When the method calls itself, information about the call is placed on top of the stack. When a method call finishes executing, its information is removed from the stack and the program returns to the call underneath.

A recursive method without a base case, or one in which the recursive case doesn't properly transition into the base case, can lead to infinite recursion.

A helper method is written to help solve a subtask of an overall problem. Recursive helper methods often have parameters in addition to the ones passed to the overall recursive method that calls them, to allow them to more easily implement the overall recursive solution.

Recursion can be used to draw graphical figures in complex patterns, including fractal images. Fractals are images that are recursively self-similar, and they are often referred to as "infinitely complex."

Self-Check Problems

Section 12.1: Thinking Recursively

1. What is recursion? How does a recursive method differ from a standard iterative method?
2. What are base cases and recursive cases? Why does a recursive method need to have both?
3. Consider the following method:

```
public static void mystery1(int n) {
    if (n <= 1) {
        System.out.print(n);
    } else {
        mystery1(n / 2);
        System.out.print(", " + n);
    }
}
```

For each of the following calls, indicate the output that is produced by the method:

a. `mystery1(1);`
b. `mystery1(2);`
c. `mystery1(3);`

d. `mystery1(4);`

e. `mystery1(16);`

f. `mystery1(30);`

g. `mystery1(100);`

4. Consider the following method:

```
public static void mystery2(int n) {
    if (n > 100) {
        System.out.print(n);
    } else {
        mystery2(2 * n);
        System.out.print(", " + n);
    }
}
```

For each of the following calls, indicate the output that is produced by the method:

a. `mystery2(113);`

b. `mystery2(70);`

c. `mystery2(42);`

d. `mystery2(30);`

e. `mystery2(10);`

5. Consider the following method:

```
public static void mystery3(int n) {
    if (n <= 0) {
        System.out.print("*");
    } else if (n % 2 == 0) {
        System.out.print("(");
        mystery3(n - 1);
        System.out.print(")");
    } else {
        System.out.print("[");
        mystery3(n - 1);
        System.out.print("]");
    }
}
```

For each of the following calls, indicate the output that is produced by the method:

a. `mystery3(0);`

b. `mystery3(1);`

c. `mystery3(2);`

d. `mystery3(4);`

e. `mystery3(5);`

6. Consider the following method:

```
public void mysteryXY(int x, int y) {
    if (y == 1) {
        System.out.print(x);
    } else {
        System.out.print(x * y + ", ");
        mysteryXY(x, y - 1);
        System.out.print(", " + x * y);
    }
}
```

For each of the following calls, indicate the output that is produced by the method:

a. `mysteryXY(4, 1);`

b. `mysteryXY(4, 2);`

c. `mysteryXY(8, 2);`

d. `mysteryXY(4, 3);`

e. `mysteryXY(3, 4);`

7. Convert the following iterative method into a recursive method:

```
// Prints each character of the string reversed twice.
// doubleReverse("hello") prints oollllleehh
public static void doubleReverse(String s) {
    for (int i = s.length() – 1; i >= 0; i--) {
        System.out.print(s.charAt(i));
        System.out.print(s.charAt(i));
    }
}
```

Section 12.2: A Better Example of Recursion

8. What is a call stack, and how does it relate to recursion?

9. What would be the effect if the code for the `reverse` method were changed to the following?

```
public static void reverse(Scanner input) {
    if (input.hasNextLine()) {
        // recursive case (nonempty file)
        String line = input.nextLine();
        System.out.println(line);      // swapped order
        reverse(input);                // swapped order
    }
}
```

10. What would be the effect if the code for the `reverse` method were changed to the following?

```
public static void reverse(Scanner input) {
    if (input.hasNextLine()) {
```

```
        // recursive case (nonempty file)
        reverse(input);                    // moved this line
        String line = input.nextLine();
        System.out.println(line);
    }
}
```

Section 12.3: Recursive Functions and Data

11. The following method is an attempt to write a recursive pow method to compute exponents. What is wrong with the code? How can it be fixed?

```
public static int pow(int x, int y) {
    return x * pow(x, y - 1);
}
```

12. What are the differences between the two versions of the pow method shown in Section 12.3? What advantage does the second version have over the first version? Are both versions recursive?

13. Consider the following method:

```
public static int mystery4(int x, int y) {
    if (x < y) {
        return x;
    } else {
        return mystery4(x – y, y);
    }
}
```

For each of the following calls, indicate the value that is returned:

a. `mystery4(6, 13)`
b. `mystery4(14, 10)`
c. `mystery4(37, 10)`
d. `mystery4(8, 2)`
e. `mystery4(50, 7)`

14. Consider the following method:

```
public static int mystery5(int x, int y) {
    if (x < 0) {
        return –mystery5(–x, y);
    } else if (y < 0) {
        return –mystery5(x, –y);
    } else if (x == 0 && y == 0) {
        return 0;
    } else {
        return 100 * mystery5(x / 10, y / 10) + 10 * (x % 10) + y % 10;
    }
}
```

For each of the following calls, indicate the value that is returned:

a. `mystery5(5, 7)`
b. `mystery5(12, 9)`
c. `mystery5(-7, 4)`
d. `mystery5(–23, –48)`
e. `mystery5(128, 343)`

15. Consider the following method:

```
public static int mystery6(int n, int k) {
    if (k == 0 || k == n) {
        return 1;
    } else if (k > n) {
        return 0;
    } else {
        return mystery6(n - 1, k - 1) + mystery6(n - 1, k);
    }
}
```

For each of the following calls, indicate the value that is returned:

a. `mystery6(7, 1)`
b. `mystery6(4, 2)`
c. `mystery6(4, 3)`
d. `mystery6(5, 3)`
e. `mystery6(5, 4)`

16. Convert the following iterative method into a recursive method:

```
// Returns n!, such as 5! = 1*2*3*4*5
public static int factorial(int n) {
    int product = 1;
    for (int i = 1; i <= n; i++) {
        product *= i;
    }
    return product;
}
```

17. The following method has a bug that leads to infinite recursion. What correction fixes the code?

```
// Adds the digits of the given number.
// Example: digitSum(3456) returns 3+4+5+6 = 18
public static int digitSum(int n) {
    if (n > 10) {
        // base case (small number)
        return n;
    } else {
```

```
        // recursive case (large number)
        return n % 10 + digitSum(n / 10);
    }
}
```

18. Sometimes the parameters that a client would like to pass to a method don't match the parameters that are best for writing a recursive solution to the problem. What should a programmer do to resolve this issue?

19. The Fibonacci sequence is a sequence of numbers in which the first two numbers are 1 and each subsequent number is the sum of the previous two Fibonacci numbers. The sequence is 1, 1, 2, 3, 5, 8, 13, 21, 34, and so on. The following is a correct, but inefficient, method to compute the *n*th Fibonacci number:

```
public static int fibonacci(int n) {
    if (n <= 2) {
        return 1;
    } else {
        return fib(n – 1) + fib(n - 2);
    }
}
```

The code shown runs very slowly for even relatively small values of `n`; it can take minutes or hours to compute even the 40th or 50th Fibonacci number. The code is inefficient because it makes too many recursive calls. It ends up recomputing each Fibonacci number many times. Write a new version of this method that is still recursive and has the same header but is more efficient. Do this by creating a helper method that accepts additional parameters, such as previous Fibonacci numbers, that you can carry through and modify during each recursive call.

Section 12.4: Recursive Graphics

20. What is a fractal image? How does recursive programming help to draw fractals?

21. Write Java code to create and draw a regular hexagon (a type of polygon).

Section 12.5: Recursive Backtracking

22. Why is recursion an effective way to implement a backtracking algorithm?

23. What is a decision tree? How are decision trees important for backtracking?

24. Draw the decision tree that would have resulted for Figure 12.9 if the backtracking solution had explored NE first instead of last in the recursive explore method. (Hint: the tree changes at every level.)

25. The original North/East backtracking solution printed the following ways of traveling to (1, 2) in this order. In what order would they be printed if the solution had explored NE first instead of last?

```
moves: N N E
moves: N E N
moves: N NE
moves: E N N
moves: NE N
```

26. Figure 12.12 shows only part of the decision tree for the first two levels. How many entries are there at the second level of the full tree? How many are at level 3 of the full tree?

27. If our 8 Queens algorithm tried every possible square on the board for placing each queen, how many entries are there at the 8th and final level of the full tree? What does our algorithm do to avoid having to explore so many possibilities?

28. The 8 Queens `explore` method stops once it finds one solution to the problem. What part of the code causes the algorithm to stop once it finds a solution? How could the code be modified so that it would find and output every solution to the problem?

Exercises

1. Write a recursive method called `starString` that accepts an integer as a parameter and prints to the console a string of stars (asterisks) that is 2^n (i.e., 2 to the nth power) long. For example,

- `starString(0)` should print `*` (because $2^0 == 1$)
- `starString(1)` should print `**` (because $2^1 == 2$)
- `starString(2)` should print `****` (because $2^2 == 4$)
- `starString(3)` should print `********` (because $2^3 == 8$)
- `starString(4)` should print `****************` (because $2^4 == 16$)

The method should throw an `IllegalArgumentException` if passed a value less than `0`.

2. Write a method called `writeNums` that takes an integer `n` as a parameter and prints to the console the first n integers starting with 1 in sequential order, separated by commas. For example, consider the following calls:

```
writeNums(5);
System.out.println(); // to complete the line of output
writeNums(12);
System.out.println(); // to complete the line of output
```

These calls should produce the following output:

```
1, 2, 3, 4, 5
1, 2, 3, 4, 5, 6, 7, 8, 9, 10, 11, 12
```

Your method should throw an `IllegalArgumentException` if passed a value less than `1`.

3. Write a method called `writeSequence` that accepts an integer n as a parameter and prints to the console a symmetric sequence of n numbers composed of descending integers that ends in 1, followed by a sequence of ascending integers that begins with 1. The following table indicates the output that should be produced for various values of n:

```
Method call                 Output produced
-------------------------------------------
writeSequence(1);           1
writeSequence(2);           1 1
writeSequence(3);           2 1 2
writeSequence(4);           2 1 1 2
writeSequence(5);           3 2 1 2 3
writeSequence(6);           3 2 1 1 2 3
writeSequence(7);           4 3 2 1 2 3 4
writeSequence(8);           4 3 2 1 1 2 3 4
writeSequence(9);           5 4 3 2 1 2 3 4 5
writeSequence(10);          5 4 3 2 1 1 2 3 4 5
```

Notice that when n is odd the sequence has a single 1 in the middle, whereas for even values it has two 1s in the middle. Your method should throw an `IllegalArgumentException` if it is passed a value less than `1`.

4. Write a recursive method called `doubleDigits` that accepts an integer n as a parameter and returns the integer obtained by replacing every digit of n with two of that digit. For example, `doubleDigits(348)` should return `334488`. The call `doubleDigits(0)` should return `0`. Calling `doubleDigits` on a negative number should return the negation of calling `doubleDigits` on the corresponding positive number; for example, `doubleDigits(–789)` should return `–778899`.

5. Write a recursive method called `writeBinary` that accepts an integer as a parameter and writes its binary representation to the console. For example, `writeBinary(44)` should print `101100`.

6. Write a recursive method called `writeSquares` that accepts an integer parameter n and prints the first n squares separated by commas, with the odd squares in descending order followed by the even squares in ascending order. For example, `writeSquares(8);` prints the following output:

```
49, 25, 9, 1, 4, 16, 36, 64
```

A call of `writeSquares(1);` prints `1`. The method should throw an `IllegalArgumentException` if it is passed a value less than 1.

7. Write a recursive method called `writeChars` that accepts an integer parameter n and that prints out a total of n characters. The middle character of the output should always be an asterisk (`"*"`). If you are asked to write out an even number of characters, then there will be two asterisks in the middle (`"**"`). Before the asterisk(s) you should write out less-than characters (`"<"`). After the asterisk(s) you should write out greater-than characters (`">"`). Your method should throw an `IllegalArgumentException` if it is passed a value less than 1. For example, the following calls produce the following output:

```
Method call              Output produced
----------------------------------------
writeChars(1);           *
writeChars(2);           **
writeChars(3);           <*>
writeChars(4);           <**>
writeChars(5);           <<*>>
writeChars(6);           <<**>>
writeChars(7);           <<<*>>>
writeChars(8);           <<<**>>>
```

8. Write a recursive method called `multiplyEvens` that returns the product of the first n even integers. For example, `multiplyEvens(1)` returns `2` and `multiplyEvens(4)` returns `384` (because $2 * 4 * 6 * 8 = 384$). The method should throw an `IllegalArgumentException` if it is passed a value less than or equal to 0.

9. Write a recursive method called `sumTo` that accepts an integer parameter n and returns a real number representing the sum of the first n reciprocals. In other words, `sumTo(n)` returns $(1 + 1/2 + 1/3 + 1/4 + \cdots + 1/n)$. For example, `sumTo(2)` should return `1.5`. The method should return `0.0` if it is passed the value 0 and throw an `IllegalArgumentException` if it is passed a value less than 0.

10. Write a recursive method called `digitMatch` that accepts two nonnegative integers as parameters and that returns the number of digits that match between them. Two digits match if they are equal and have the same position relative to the end of the number (i.e., starting with the ones digit). In other words, the method should compare the last digits of each number, the second-to-last digits of each number, the third-to-last digits of each number, and so forth, counting how many pairs match. For example, for the call of `digitMatch(1072503891, 62530841)`, the method would compare as follows, and return `4` because four of the pairs match (2-2, 5-5, 8-8, and 1-1).

```
1 0 7 2 5 0 3 8 9 1
    | | | | | | | |
    6 2 5 3 0 8 4 1
```

11. Write a recursive method called `repeat` that accepts a string *s* and an integer *n* as parameters and that returns *s* concatenated together *n* times. For example, `repeat("hello", 3)` returns `"hellohellohello"`, and `repeat("ok", 1)` returns `"ok"`, and `repeat("bye", 0)` returns `""`. String concatenation is an expensive operation, so for an added challenge try to solve this problem while performing fewer than *n* concatenations.

12. Write a recursive method called `isReverse` that accepts two strings as parameters and returns `true` if the two strings contain the same sequence of characters as each other but in the opposite order (ignoring capitalization), and `false` otherwise. For example, the call of `isReverse("hello", "eLLoH")` would return `true`. The empty string, as well as any one-letter string, is considered to be its own reverse.

13. Write a recursive method called `indexOf` that accepts two strings as parameters and that returns the starting index of the first occurrence of the second string inside the first string (or -1 if not found). For example, the call of `indexOf("Barack Obama", "bam")`would return `8`. (Strings already have an `indexOf` method, but you may not call it in your solution.)

14. Write a recursive method called `evenDigits` that accepts an integer parameter and that returns the integer formed by removing the odd digits from it. For example, `evenDigits(8342116)` returns `8426` and `evenDigits(-34512)` returns `-42`. If the number is 0 or has no even digits, such as 35159 or 7, return `0`. Leading zeros in the result should be ignored.

15. Write a recursive method called `permut` that accepts two integers *n* and *r* as parameters and returns the number of unique permutations of *r* items from a group of *n* items. For given values of *n* and *r*, this value *P*(*n*, *r*) can be computed as follows:

$$P(n,r) = \frac{n!}{(n - r)!}$$

For example, `permut(7, 4)` should return `840`. It may be helpful to note that `permut(6, 3)` returns `120`, or 840 / 7.

16. The Sierpinski carpet is a fractal that is defined as follows: The construction of the Sierpinski carpet begins with a square. The square is cut into nine congruent subsquares in a 3-by-3 grid, with the central subsquare removed. The same process is then applied recursively to the eight other subsquares. Figure 12.14 shows the first few iterations of the carpet.

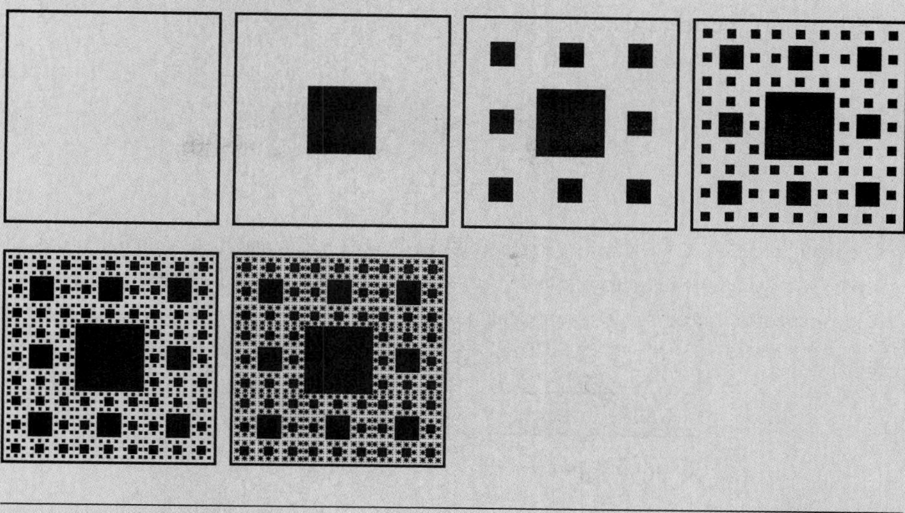

Figure 12.14 Sierpinski carpet

Write a program to draw the carpet on a `DrawingPanel` recursively.

17. The Cantor set is a fractal that is defined by repeatedly removing the middle thirds of line segments as shown in Figure 12.15.

Figure 12.15 Cantor set

Write a program to draw the Cantor set on a `DrawingPanel` recursively.

18. Write a recursive method called `waysToClimb` that takes a positive integer value representing a number of stairs and prints each unique way to climb a staircase of that height, taking strides of one or two stairs at a time. Do not use any loops. Output each way to climb the stairs on its own line, using a `1` to indicate a small stride of 1 stair, and a `2` to indicate a large stride of 2 stairs. The order in which you output the possible ways to climb the stairs is not important, so long as you list the right overall set of ways. For example, the call `waysToClimb(3);` should produce the following output:

```
[1, 1, 1]
[1, 2]
[2, 1]
```

The call `waysToClimb(4);` should produce the following output:

```
[1, 1, 1, 1]
[1, 1, 2]
[1, 2, 1]
[2, 1, 1]
[2, 2]
```

19. Write a recursive method called `countBinary` that accepts an integer *n* as a parameter and that prints all binary numbers that have exactly *n* digits in ascending order, each on its own line. All *n* digits should be shown for all numbers, including leading zeros if necessary. Assume that *n* is nonnegative. If *n* is 0, a blank line should be produced.

Call	Output
`countBinary(1);`	0 1
`countBinary(2);`	00 01 10 11
`countBinary(3);`	000 001 010 011 100 101 110 111

20. Write a recursive method called `subsets` to find every possible sub-list of a given list. A sub-list of a list *L* contains 0 or more of *L*'s elements. Your method should accept a list of strings as its parameter and print every sub-list that could be created from elements of that list, one per line. For example, if the list stores `[Janet, Robert, Morgan, Char]`, the output from your method would be:

```
[Janet, Robert, Morgan, Char]
[Janet, Robert, Morgan]
[Janet, Robert, Char]
[Janet, Robert]
[Janet, Morgan, Char]
[Janet, Morgan]
[Janet, Char]
[Janet]
[Robert, Morgan, Char]
[Robert, Morgan]
```

```
[Robert, Char]
[Robert]
[Morgan, Char]
[Morgan]
[Char]
[]
```

The order in which you show the sub-lists does not matter, and the order of the elements of each sub-list also does not matter. The key thing is that your method should produce the correct overall set of sub-lists as its output. Notice that the empty list is considered one of these sub-lists. You may assume that the list passed to your method is not null and that the list contains no duplicates. Do not use any loops.

21. Write a recursive method called `maxSum` that accepts a list of integers, *L*, and an integer limit *n* as parameters and uses backtracking to find the maximum sum that can be generated by adding elements of *L* that do not exceed *n*. For example, if you are given the list `[7, 30, 8, 22, 6, 1, 14]` and the limit of 19, the maximum sum that can be generated that does not exceed is 16, achieved by adding 7, 8, and 1. If the list *L* is empty, or if the limit is not a positive integer, or all of *L*'s values exceed the limit, return `0`.

Each index's element in the list can be added to the sum only once, but the same number value might occur more than once in a list, in which case each occurrence might be added to the sum. For example, if the list is `[6, 2, 1]` you may use up to one 6 in the sum, but if the list is `[6, 2, 6, 1]` you may use up to two sixes.

List *L*	Limit *n*	Return Value
`[7, 30, 8, 22, 6, 1, 14]`	`19`	`16`
`[5, 30, 15, 13, 8]`	`42`	`41`
`[30, 15, 20]`	`40`	`35`
`[10, 20, 30]`	`7`	`0`
`[10, 20, 30]`	`20`	`20`
`[]`	`10`	`0`

You may assume that all values in the list are nonnegative. Your method may alter the contents of the list *L* as it executes, but *L* should be restored to its original state before your method returns. Do not use any loops.

22. Write a recursive method called `printSquares` to find all ways to express an integer as a sum of squares of unique positive integers. For example, the call `printSquares(200);` should produce the following output:

```
1^2 + 2^2 + 3^2 + 4^2 + 5^2 + 8^2 + 9^2
1^2 + 2^2 + 3^2 + 4^2 + 7^2 + 11^2
1^2 + 2^2 + 5^2 + 7^2 + 11^2
1^2 + 3^2 + 4^2 + 5^2 + 6^2 + 7^2 + 8^2
1^2 + 3^2 + 4^2 + 5^2 + 7^2 + 10^2
```

```
2^2 + 4^2 + 6^2 + 12^2
2^2 + 14^2
3^2 + 5^2 + 6^2 + 7^2 + 9^2
6^2 + 8^2 + 10^2
```

Some numbers (such as 128 or 0) cannot be represented as a sum of squares, in which case your method should produce no output. Keep in mind that the sum has to be formed with unique integers. Otherwise you could always find a solution by adding 1^2 together until you got to whatever number you are working with.

As with any backtracking problem, this one amounts to a set of choices, one for each integer whose square might or might not be part of your sum. You may generate the choices by doing a `for` loop over an appropriate range of numbers. Note that the maximum possible integer that can be part of a sum of squares for an integer *n* is the square root of *n*.

Programming Projects

1. Write a recursive program to solve the "Missionaries and Cannibals" problem. Three missionaries and three cannibals come to a river and find a boat that holds two. If the cannibals ever outnumber the missionaries on either bank, the missionaries will be eaten. How might they cross safely?

   Your output should include the initial problem, the moves you make, and a "picture" of the current state of the puzzle after each move. Your final output should produce only the moves and the picture for the states that are on the solution path.

2. Write a recursive program to solve the Towers of Hanoi puzzle. The puzzle involves manipulating disks that you can move between three different towers. You are given a certain number of disks (four in this example) stacked on one of the three towers. The disks have decreasing diameters, with the smallest disk on the top (see Figure 12.16).

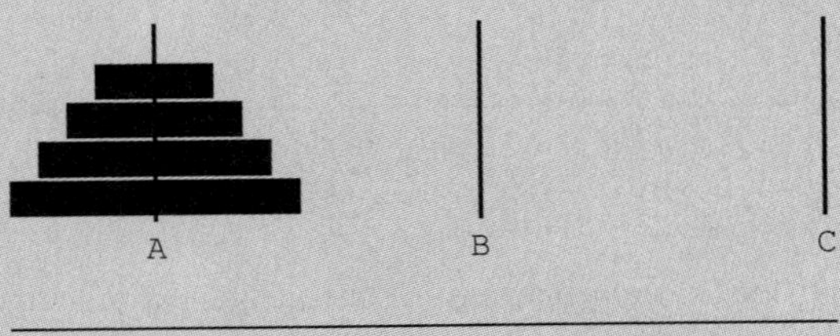

Figure 12.16 Towers of Hanoi

   The object of the puzzle is to move all of the disks from one tower to another (say, from A to B). The third tower is provided as a temporary storage space as you move disks around. You are allowed to move only one disk at a time, and you are not allowed to place a disk on top of a smaller one (i.e., one with a smaller diameter).

   Examine the rather simple solutions for one, two, and three disks, and see if you can discern a pattern. Then write a program that will solve the Towers of Hanoi puzzle for any number of disks. (*Hint:* Moving four disks is a lot like moving three disks, except that one additional disk is on the bottom.)

3. Write a recursive program to generate random sentences from a given BNF grammar. A BNF grammar is a recursively defined file that defines rules for creating sentences from tokens of text. Rules can be recursively self-similar. The following grammar can generate sentences such as "Fred honored the green wonderful child":

```
<s>::=<np> <vp>
<np>::=<dp> <adjp> <n>|<pn>
<dp>::=the|a
<adjp>::=<adj>|<adj> <adjp>
<adj>::=big|fat|green|wonderful|faulty|subliminal|pretentious
<n>::=dog|cat|man|university|father|mother|child|television
<pn>::=John|Jane|Sally|Spot|Fred|Elmo
<vp>::=<tv> <np>|<iv>
<tv>::=hit|honored|kissed|helped
<iv>::=died|collapsed|laughed|wept
```

4. The Koch snowflake is a fractal that is created by starting with a line segment, then recursively altering it as follows:

   1. Divide the line segment into three segments of equal length.
   2. Draw an equilateral triangle that has the middle segment from step 1 as its base.
   3. Remove the line segment that is the base of the triangle from step 2.

   Figure 12.17 shows the first several iterations of the snowflake.

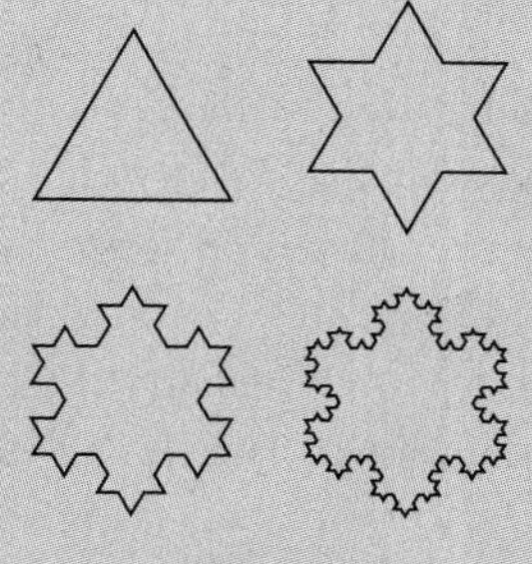

Figure 12.17 Koch snowflake

   Write a program to draw the Koch snowflake on a `DrawingPanel` recursively.

5. Write a program that uses recursive backtracking to generate all anagrams from a phrase typed by the user. An anagram is a word or phrase made by rearranging the letters of another word or phrase. For example, the words "midterm" and "trimmed" are anagrams. If you ignore spaces and capitalization and allow multiple words, a multi-word phrase can be an anagram of some other word or phrase. For example, the phrases

"Clint Eastwood" and "old west action" are anagrams. Your program will read a dictionary file of words and search for all words that can be formed using the letters in the user's phrase. Use backtracking to choose each word, explore what can be made out of the remaining letters, then un-choose the word afterward. Here is a possible example dialogue:

```
Phrase to search? barbara bush
Max words to use? 3
[abash, bar, rub]
[abash, rub, bar]
[bar, abash, rub]
[bar, rub, abash]
[rub, abash, bar]
[rub, bar, abash]
```

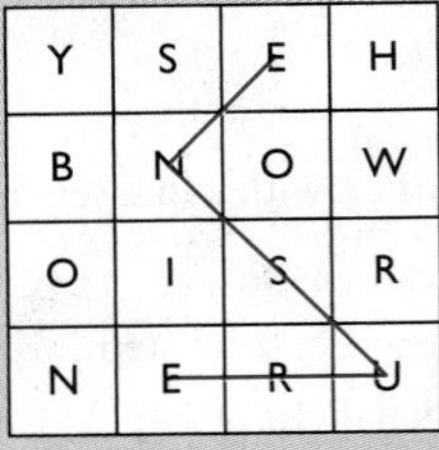

Figure 12.18 An example Boggle board

6. Write a program that uses recursive backtracking to play the game of Boggle. Boggle is a word game played on a 4 × 4 grid where the player tries to find all valid dictionary words that can be made by tracing a path between adjacent letters from the board. Each link in the path can be horizontal, vertical, or diagonal. Figure 12.18 shows an example path to form the word "ensure". Use recursive backtracking to explore each possible word that can be made using the letters on the board. Your algorithm should choose a starting square, explore what can be made from there, and un-choose the square afterward. (Hint: You will need a way to "mark" squares as being chosen or not chosen.)

7. Write a program that uses recursive backtracking to find all ancestors and descendants of a person given a file of familial relationships. For ancestors it must show all parents, all grandparents, all great grandparents, etc. For descendants it must show all children, all grandchildren, all great grandchildren, etc. The program also must use indentation to make it clear who is a parent of whom and who is a child of whom. Write two recursive

methods that use backtracking to explore for ancestors and descendants respectively. Here is a possible example dialogue:

```
Input file? tudor.dat
Whose info? Margaret

Ancestors:
    Margaret
        Elizabeth of York
        Henry VII

Descendants:
    Margaret
        James V
            Mary, Queen of Scots
                James VI & I
        Margaret Stuart
            Henry, Lord Darnley
                James VI & I
```

Chapter 13

Searching and Sorting

Introduction

When you are dealing with large amounts of data, you'll often want to search the data for particular values. For example, you might want to search the Internet for a web page that contains a certain keyword, or you might want to search a phone book for a person's phone number.

It's also useful to be able to rearrange a collection of data into sorted order. For example, you might want to sort a list of students' course grade data by name, student ID, or grade.

In this chapter we'll look at ways to use Java's class libraries to search and sort data. We'll practice implementing some searching and sorting algorithms and talk more generally about how to observe and analyze the runtimes of algorithms.

13.1 Searching and Sorting in the Java Class Libraries

To search an `ArrayList` or `LinkedList`, you can call its `indexOf` method. This method examines each element of the list, looking for a target value. It returns the first index at which the target value occurs in the list, or `–1` if the target doesn't occur.

Imagine a large `List` containing all the words in a book. The following code could read a large text file into such a list:

```
// reads the text of the given file into a list
public static List<String> readBook(String filename)
        throws FileNotFoundException {
    List<String> words = new ArrayList<String>();
    Scanner in = new Scanner(new File(filename));
    while (in.hasNext()) {
        words.add(in.next());
    }
    return words;
}
```

You could use the `indexOf` method to see whether a given word appears in the book and, if so, at what index the word appears:

```
System.out.print("Your word? ");
Scanner console = new Scanner(System.in);
String word = console.nextLine();
// search list for a word using indexOf
List<String> words = readBook("mobydick.txt");
int index = words.indexOf(word);
if (index >= 0) {
    System.out.println(word + " is word #" + index);
} else {
    System.out.println(word + " is not found.");
}
```

The `indexOf` method performs a *sequential search,* examining each element of the list in sequence until it finds the one that the user is looking for. If it reaches the end of the list without finding the requested word, it returns `–1`. When it searches a 1,000,000-element list for an element at index 675,000, a sequential search would have to examine all 675,000 elements that came before the desired element.

If you have an array of data instead of a list, there's no prewritten method to sequentially search the array. You'll have to write the code yourself (as we'll do later in this chapter) or put the array's elements into a `List` first and search the `List` with `indexOf`.

Binary Search

VideoNote

Sometimes you'll want to search through elements of an array or list that you know is in sorted order. For example, if you wanted to know whether "queasy" was a real English word, you could search the contents of an alphabetized dictionary text file. Likewise, you might find yourself looking for a book written by Robert Louis Stevenson in a list of books sorted by the author's last name. If the dictionary is large or the list of books is long, you probably won't want to sequentially examine all the items it contains.

There's a better algorithm called *binary search* that searches sorted data much faster than a sequential search. A normal sequential search of a million-element array may have to examine all the elements, but a binary search will need to look at only around 20 of them. Java's class libraries contain methods that implement the binary search algorithm for arrays and lists.

> **Binary Search**
>
> An algorithm that searches for a value in a sorted list by repeatedly dividing the search space in half.

The binary search algorithm begins by examining the center element of the array or list. If the center element is smaller than the target you're searching for, there's no reason to examine any elements to the left of the center (at lower indexes). If the center element is larger than the target you're searching for, there's no reason to examine any elements to the right of the center (at greater indexes). Each pass of the algorithm eliminates half the search space from consideration, so in most cases the algorithm finds the target value much faster than a sequential search would have found it.

The logic of the binary search algorithm is similar to the strategy that people use in a high/low guessing game in which the computer generates a random number between 1 and 100 and the user tries to guess it. After each incorrect guess, the program gives a hint about whether the user's guess was too high or too low. A poor algorithm for this game is to guess 1, 2, 3, and so on. A smarter algorithm is to guess the middle number and cut the range in half each time on the basis of whether the guess was too high or too low. Figure 13.1 shows how this works.

A binary search uses this same approach when it searches a sorted array for a target value. The algorithm scales extremely well to large input data. The `Arrays` class in the `java.util` package contains a static method called `binarySearch` that implements the binary search algorithm. It accepts an array of any suitable type and a target value as its parameters and returns the index where you can find the target element. If the element isn't found, the method returns a negative index.

The following code uses the `Arrays.binarySearch` method to find a number in an array of integers. It needs to examine only indexes 4, 6, and then 5 in order to find the target value at index 5:

```
// binary search on an array
int[] numbers = {-3, 2, 8, 12, 17, 29, 44, 58, 79};
```

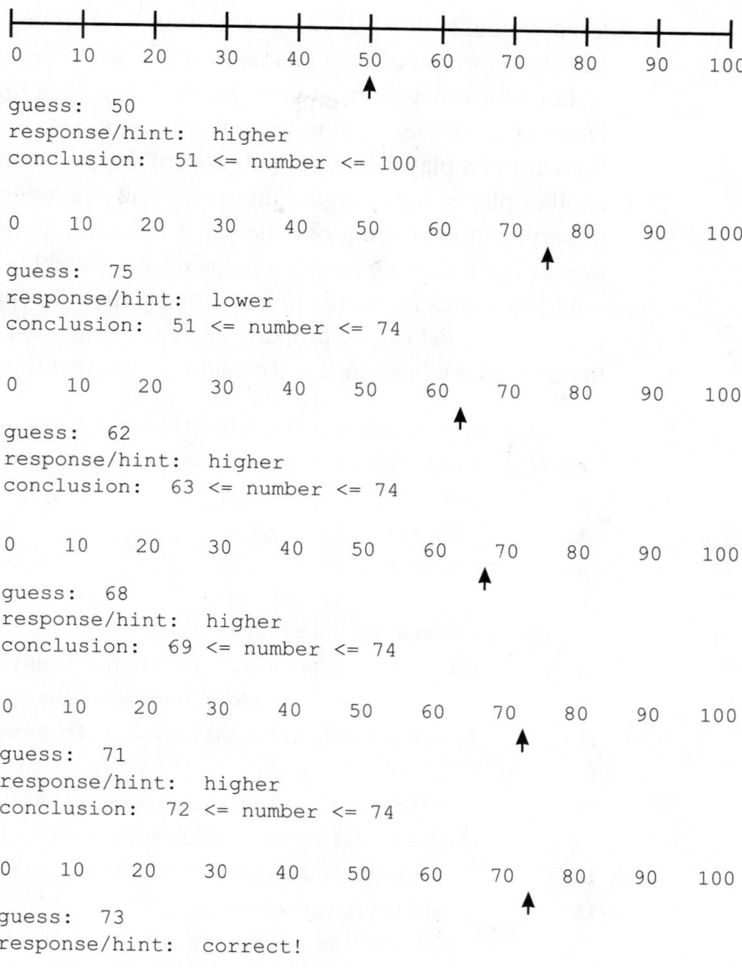

Figure 13.1 Passes of a binary search for a number between 1 and 100

```
int index = Arrays.binarySearch(numbers, 29);
System.out.println("29 is found at index " + index);
```

If you're using a list such as an `ArrayList` instead, you can call the static method `Collections.binarySearch` to search the list of elements. If you had an `ArrayList` called `list` containing the same elements as the array in the previous example, the following code would similarly search the elements at indexes 4, 6, and then 5 before assigning the value `5` to the variable `index`:

```
// binary search on an ArrayList
int index = Collections.binarySearch(list, 29);
System.out.println("29 is found at index " + index);
```

If you want to use the `binarySearch` method on either an array or a list, the data must be in sorted order, because the method relies on the ordering to quickly find the target value. If you call `binarySearch` on unsorted data, the results are undefined and the algorithm doesn't guarantee that it will return the right answer.

Let's look at a short program that benefits from the speed of binary search. In the game of Scrabble, players form words on a board using letter tiles to earn points. Sometimes a player tries to spell a word that is not a legal word in the dictionary, so another player "challenges" the word. The challenger looks up the word in the dictionary, and depending on whether it is found, the move may be revoked from the board. The following program helps resolve Scrabble word challenges by performing binary searches for words in a dictionary file. The input file's words occur in sorted order, so the list can be properly searched using `Collections.binarySearch`. (If the file had not been sorted, we could have sorted it with `Collections.sort`).

```
// Searches for words in a dictionary text file
// and reports each word's position in the file.

import java.io.*;
import java.util.*;

public class WordChallenge {
    public static void main(String[] args)
            throws FileNotFoundException {
        System.out.println("Welcome to Scrabble word challenge!");

        // read a sorted dictionary file into a List
        Scanner in = new Scanner(new File("words.txt"));
        List<String> words = new ArrayList<String>();
        while (in.hasNext()) {
            String word = in.next();
            words.add(word);
        }

        // binary search the list for words
        Scanner console = new Scanner(System.in);
        System.out.print("Word to challenge (Enter to quit)? ");
        String target = console.nextLine();
        while (target.length() > 0) {
            int index = Collections.binarySearch(words, target);
            if (index >= 0) {
                System.out.println("\"" + target + "\" is word #"
                        + index + " of " + words.size());
            } else {
                System.out.println("\"" + target + "\" is not found");
            }

            System.out.print("Word to challenge (Enter to quit)? ");
```

```
                target = console.nextLine();
            }
        }
}
```

Here is a sample execution of the program and its resulting output, using a Scrabble players' dictionary that contains 172,823 words:

```
Welcome to Scrabble word challenge!
Word to challenge (Enter to quit)? queazy
"queazy" is word #121788 of 172823
Word to challenge (Enter to quit)? kwyjibo
"kwyjibo" is not found
Word to challenge (Enter to quit)? building
"building" is word #18823 of 172823
Word to challenge (Enter to quit)? java
"java" is word #79156 of 172823
Word to challenge (Enter to quit)? programs
"programs" is word #118860 of 172823
Word to challenge (Enter to quit)?
```

Sorting

VideoNote

When you use a computer, you often need to sort data. When you browse your hard drive, for example, you might sort your files by file name, extension, and date. When you play music, you might sort your song collection by artist, year, or genre. You might also want to sort arrays and lists so that they can be searched efficiently with the binary search algorithm.

The Java class libraries provide sorting methods for arrays and lists. You can sort an array with the `Arrays.sort` method:

```
// demonstrate the Arrays.sort method
String[] strings = {"c", "b", "g", "h", "d", "f", "e", "a"};
Arrays.sort(strings);
System.out.println(Arrays.toString(strings));
```

The preceding code produces the following output:

```
[a, b, c, d, e, f, g, h]
```

Java 8 introduced a new sorting method called `Arrays.parallelSort` that generally runs faster than `Arrays.sort`. It takes advantage of computers with multiple processors or multi-core processors to sort multiple portions of the array at the same time, leading to faster performance. To use it, just write `parallelSort` instead of `sort` in your code. Other new features of Java 8 are discussed in more detail in Chapter 19.

```
Arrays.parallelSort(strings);
```

The array must be of a type that can be compared—that is, a type that stores either primitives or objects that implement the `Comparable` interface discussed in Chapter 10. For example, you can sort an array of integers or `Strings`, but you can't easily sort an array of `Point` objects or `Color` objects because those classes don't implement the `Comparable` interface.

To sort a list you can use the `Collections.sort` method, discussed briefly in Chapter 10, which accepts a list such as an `ArrayList` as a parameter and puts its elements into sorted order. The following code produces the same output as the preceding array code:

```
// demonstrate the Collections.sort method
List<String> list = new ArrayList<String>();
list.add("c");
list.add("b");
list.add("g");
list.add("h");
list.add("d");
list.add("f");
list.add("e");
list.add("a");
Collections.sort(list);
System.out.println(list);
```

When the `Arrays.sort` method is used with primitive data, it uses an algorithm called quicksort. `Collections.sort` and `Arrays.sort` use a different algorithm, called merge sort, when they deal with object data. We'll discuss the implementation of merge sort in detail later in this chapter.

Shuffling

The task of shuffling data, or rearranging the elements into a random order, is perhaps the opposite of sorting. Why would one want to do this?

One application for shuffling is a card game program. You might have a card deck stored as a list of `Card` objects. If the cards are in a predictable order, the game will be boring. You'd like to shuffle the deck of cards, rearranging them into a random ordering each time. This is a case in which chaos is preferable to order.

Another application is a situation in which you want a random permutation of a list of numbers. You can acquire a random permutation of the numbers from 1 through 5, for example, by storing those numbers into a list and shuffling the list.

The `Collections` class has a method called `shuffle` that accepts a list as its parameter and rearranges its elements randomly. The following example creates a deck of card strings, shuffles it, and examines the card at the top of the deck:

```
String[] ranks = {"2", "3", "4", "5", "6", "7", "8", "9",
                  "10", "Jack", "Queen", "King", "Ace"};
String[] suits = {"Clubs", "Diamonds", "Hearts", "Spades"};
```

```
List<String> deck = new ArrayList<String>();
for (String rank : ranks) {                    // build sorted deck
    for (String suit : suits) {
        deck.add(rank + " of " + suit);
    }
}
Collections.shuffle(deck);
System.out.println("Top card = " + deck.get(0));
```

The code randomly produces output such as the following, with different outputs on different runs:

```
Top card = 10 of Spades
```

Table 13.1 briefly summarizes the useful static methods in Java's class libraries for searching, sorting, and shuffling.

Table 13.1 Searching and Sorting in Java's Class Libraries

Method	Description
`Arrays.binarySearch(array, value)`	Returns the index of the given value in the given array, assuming that the array's elements are currently in sorted order, or returns a negative number if the given value is not found.
`Arrays.sort(array)`	Arranges the given array's elements into sorted order.
`Collections.binarySearch(list, value)`	Returns the index of the given value in the given list, assuming that the list's elements are currently in sorted order, or returns a negative number if the given value is not found.
`Collections.shuffle(list)`	Arranges the given list's elements into a random order.
`Collections.sort(list)`	Arranges the given list's elements into sorted order.

Custom Ordering with Comparators

Sometimes you'll want to search or sort a collection of objects in an ordering that is different from that of its `Comparable` implementation. For example, consider the following code, which sorts an array of `String`s and prints the result:

```
String[] strings = {"Foxtrot", "alpha", "echo", "golf",
                    "bravo", "hotel", "Charlie", "DELTA"};
```

```
Arrays.sort(strings);
System.out.println(Arrays.toString(strings));
```

This code produces the following output, which may not be what you expected:

```
[Charlie, DELTA, Foxtrot, alpha, bravo, echo, golf, hotel]
```

Notice that the elements are in case-sensitive alphabetical ordering, with all the uppercase strings placed before the lowercase ones.

Recall from Chapter 10 that many types (including `String`) have natural orderings that are defined by comparison functions, implemented as the `compareTo` method from the `Comparable` interface. The `compareTo` method of `String` objects uses a case-sensitive ordering, but in this case we would prefer a case-insensitive comparison. We might also want an option to sort in other orders, such as by length or in reverse alphabetical order.

In situations such as these, you can define your own external comparison functions with an object called a *comparator*. Comparators perform comparisons between pairs of objects. While a class can have only one natural ordering, arbitrarily many comparators can be written to describe other ways to order the class's objects. A comparator can also supply an external ordering on a class that does not implement a natural ordering of its own. The `Arrays.sort`, `Collections.sort`, and `Arrays.binarySearch` methods all have variations that accept a comparator as an additional parameter and use the comparator to guide the searching or sorting process.

Comparators are implemented as classes that implement the interface `Comparator` in the `java.util` package. This interface has a method called `compare` that accepts a pair of objects as parameters and compares them. Like `compareTo`, the `compare` method returns a negative number, zero, or a positive number to indicate a less-than, equal-to, or greater-than relationship, respectively:

```
public interface Comparator<T> {
    public int compare(T o1, T o2);
}
```

Implementing `Comparator` is like implementing the `Comparable` interface, except that instead of placing the code inside the class to be compared, you write a separate comparator class. The `compare` method is similar to the `compareTo` method from the `Comparable` interface, except that it accepts both of the objects to compare as parameters. (The `compareTo` method accepts only one object as a parameter because the other object compared is the implicit parameter.)

Like `Comparable`, `Comparator` is actually a generic interface `Comparator<T>` that requires you to specify the type of objects you'll be comparing. For example, if you wish to write a comparison function for `Strings`, you must write a class that implements `Comparator<String>`.

Before we implement a comparator of our own, let's use one that is part of Java's class libraries. If you want to sort `Strings` in case-insensitive alphabetical order, you can use a constant `Comparator` in the `String` class called `CASE_INSENSITIVE_ORDER`. The following code uses it to sort an array of mixed-case strings:

```
// sort Strings using case-insensitive Comparator
String[] strings = {"Foxtrot", "alpha", "echo", "golf",
                    "bravo", "hotel", "Charlie", "DELTA"};
Arrays.sort(strings, String.CASE_INSENSITIVE_ORDER);
System.out.println(Arrays.toString(strings));
```

This code produces the following output:

```
[alpha, bravo, Charlie, DELTA, echo, Foxtrot, golf, hotel]
```

Now let's write a `Comparator` that orders strings by their lengths. Our `compare` method should return a negative number if the first string is shorter than the second, `0` if they are equal in length, and a positive number if the first string is longer than the second. Recall from Chapter 10 that a `compareTo` method examining integer data can often simply subtract one number from the other and return the result. The following `compare` method is also based on this idea:

```
import java.util.*;

// compares String objects by length
public class LengthComparator implements Comparator<String> {
    public int compare(String s1, String s2) {
        return s1.length() - s2.length();
    }
}
```

Now that we've written a length comparator, we can pass one when we sort an array or list of `String` objects:

```
// sort array of strings by length using Comparator
Arrays.sort(strings, new LengthComparator());
System.out.println(Arrays.toString(strings));
```

Here's the output when we run this code on the `String` array from earlier in this section:

```
[echo, golf, alpha, bravo, hotel, DELTA, Foxtrot, Charlie]
```

Notice that the strings appear in order of increasing length.

Sometimes you'll want to search or sort a collection of objects that don't implement the `Comparable` interface. For example, the `Point` class doesn't implement `Comparable`, but you might want to sort an array of `Point` objects by *x*-coordinate, using the *y*-coordinate to break ties. The following code is an example `Comparator` that compares `Point` objects in this way:

```
import java.awt.*;
import java.util.*;

// compares Point objects by x-coordinate and then by y-coordinate
public class PointComparator implements Comparator<Point> {
    public int compare(Point p1, Point p2) {
        int dx = p1.x - p2.x;
        if (dx == 0) {
            int dy = p1.y - p2.y;
            return dy;
        } else {
            return dx;
        }
    }
}
```

It's important to understand that we are creating a separate class as our comparator; we are not modifying the `Point` class itself. This is one of the main benefits of comparators: you don't need to modify the class being ordered. The following code uses the `PointComparator` to sort an array of four `Point` objects:

```
Point[] points = {
    new Point(4, -2),
    new Point(3, 9),
    new Point(-1, 15),
    new Point(3, 7)
};
Arrays.sort(points, new PointComparator());
```

This code sorts the points into the following order: (–1, 15), (3, 7), (3, 9), (4, –2). This comparator also allows you to use `Point` objects in the "tree" collections that depend on ordering, `TreeSet` and `TreeMap`. Both of these collections have constructors that accept a comparator as a parameter and use it to order their elements internally.

If you have a group of objects with a natural ordering and you want to sort them in reverse order, you can call the method `Collections.reverseOrder` to receive a `Comparator` that inverts the objects' natural ordering. For example, the following code would sort the array of `Strings` that was used earlier in reverse alphabetical order:

```
Arrays.sort(strings, Collections.reverseOrder());
```

For types that do not have a natural ordering, you can ask for the reverse of a `Comparator`'s order by calling `Collections.reverseOrder` and passing the

Table 13.2 Useful Comparators and Methods

Comparator/Method	Description
`Arrays.binarySearch(array, value, comparator)`	Returns the index of the given value in the given array, assuming that the array is currently sorted in the ordering of the given comparator, or returns a negative number if the given value is not found.
`Arrays.sort(array, comparator)`	Sorts the given array in the ordering of the given comparator.
`Collections.binarySearch(list, value, comparator)`	Returns the index of the given value in the given list, assuming that the list is currently sorted in the ordering of the given comparator, or returns a negative number if the given value is not found.
`Collections.max(collection, comparator)`	Returns the largest value in the collection according to the ordering of the given comparator.
`Collections.min(collection, comparator)`	Returns the smallest value in the collection according to the ordering of the given comparator.
`Collections.reverseOrder()`	Returns a comparator that compares objects in the opposite of their natural order.
`Collections.reverseOrder(comparator)`	Returns a comparator that compares objects in the opposite of the ordering of the given comparator.
`Collections.sort(list, comparator)`	Sorts the given list in the ordering of the given comparator.
`String.CASE_INSENSITIVE_ORDER`	Sorts strings alphabetically, ignoring capitalization.

`Comparator` to be reversed. For example, the following code would sort the array of `Point` objects by decreasing *x*-coordinate:

```
Arrays.sort(points, Collections.reverseOrder(new PointComparator()));
```

The resulting order would be as follows: (4, –2), (3, 9), (3, 7), (–1, 15).

Table 13.2 summarizes several useful places that comparators appear in the Java class libraries.

13.2 Program Complexity

VideoNote

In Chapter 8, we talked about client code, the code that interacts with a class or object. In this chapter, we've studied how to be a client of Java's methods for searching and sorting data. Since searching and sorting are important programming ideas, it's worthwhile to understand how they are implemented. But before we dive into this, let's discuss some background ideas about how to analyze the efficiency of code.

As you progress in this textbook, you're writing increasingly complex programs. You're also seeing that there are often many ways to solve the same problem. How do you compare different solutions to the same problem to see which is better?

We desire algorithms that solve problems quickly or with high efficiency. The technical term that refers to algorithms' runtime is *complexity*. An algorithm with higher complexity uses more time or resources to solve a problem.

Complexity

A measure of the computing resources that are used by a piece of code, such as time, memory, or disk space.

Usually when we talk about the efficiency of a program we are talking about how long the program takes to run, or its *time complexity.* The time complexity for a program to be "fast enough" depends on the task. A program running on a modern computer that requires five minutes to look up a dictionary word is probably too slow. An algorithm that renders a complex three-dimensional movie scene in five minutes is probably very fast.

One way to determine an algorithm's approximate time complexity is to program it, run the program, and measure how long it takes to run. This is sometimes called an *empirical analysis* of the algorithm. For example, consider two algorithms to search an array: one that sequentially searches for the desired target element, and one that first sorts the array and then performs a binary search on the sorted array. You could empirically analyze the algorithms by writing both as programs, running them on the same input, and timing them.

But empirically analyzing an algorithm isn't a very reliable measure, because on a different computer with a different processor speed and more or less memory the program might not take the same amount of time. Also, in order to empirically test an algorithm, you must write it and time it, which can be a chore.

A more neutral way to measure a program's performance is to examine its code or pseudocode and roughly count the number of statements that are executed. This is a form of *algorithm analysis,* the practice of applying techniques to mathematically approximate the performance of various computing algorithms. Algorithm analysis is an important tool in computer science. One of the fundamental principles of science in general is that we can make predictions and hypotheses using formal models, which we can then test by experimentation.

Not all statements require the same amount of time to execute. For example, a CPU can handle addition faster than multiplication, and a method call generally takes more time than a statement that evaluates the Boolean test of an `if/else` statement. But for the purposes of simplification, let's assume that the following actions require an equal and fixed amount of time to execute:

- Variable declarations and assignments
- Evaluating mathematical and logical expressions

- Accessing or modifying an individual element of an array
- Simple method calls (where the method does not perform a loop)

One kind of variable that does not require a fixed amount of time to initialize is an array. When an array is constructed, Java zeroes each array element, which takes more time for longer arrays. Some types of objects also have lengthy code in their constructors that makes them take longer to construct.

From the preceding simple rules, we can extrapolate the runtimes of larger and more complex pieces of code. For example, the runtime of a group of statements in sequential order is the sum of the individual runtimes of the statements:

```
statement1.  ┐
statement2.  ├ 3
statement3.  ┘
```

The runtime of a loop is roughly equal to the runtime of its body times the number of iterations of the loop. For example, a loop with a body that contains *K* simple statements and that repeats *N* times will have a runtime of roughly (*K* * *N*):

```
for (N times) {   ┐
    statement1.   │
    statement2.   ├ 3N
    statement3.   │
}                 ┘
```

The runtime of multiple loops placed sequentially (not nested) with other statements is the sum of the loops' runtimes and the other statements' runtimes:

```
statement1.          ┐
for (N times) {  ┐   │
    statement2.  ├ N │
}                ┘   │
                     ├ M + N + 3
for (M times) {  ┐   │
    statement3.  ├ M │
}                ┘   │
statement4.          │
statement5.          ┘
```

The runtime of a loop containing a nested loop is roughly equal to the runtime of the inner loop multiplied by the number of repetitions of the outer loop:

```
for (M times) {                ┐
    for (N times) {        ┐   │
        statement1.  ┐     │   │
        statement2.  ├ 3   ├ 3N├ 3MN
        statement3.  ┘     │   │
    }                      ┘   │
}                              ┘
```

Normally, the loops in long-running algorithms are processing some kind of data. Many algorithms run very quickly if the input dataset is small, so we generally worry about the performance only for large datasets. For example, consider the following set of loops that process an array of N elements:

```
for (N times) {                    ┐  ┐
    for (N times) {                │  │
        statement1.                ├ N^2
    }                              │  │
}                                  ┘  │
                                      ├ N^2 + 2N
for (N times) {                    ┐  │
    statement2.                    ├ 2N
    statement3.                    │  │
}                                  ┘  ┘
```

When we analyze code like this, we often think about which line is most frequently executed in the code. In programs with several sequential blocks of code that all relate to some common value N (such as the size of an input dataset), the block raised to the highest power of N usually dominates the overall runtime. In the preceding code, the first N^2 loop executes its statement far more times than the second N loop executes its two statements. For example, if N is 1000, `statement1` executes (1000 * 1000) or 1,000,000 times, while `statement2` and `statement3` each execute only 1000 times.

When we perform algorithm analysis, we often ignore all but the most frequently executed part of the code, because the runtime of this statement will outweigh the combined runtimes of the other parts of the code. For example, we might refer to the preceding code as being "on the order of" N^2, ignoring the extra $2N$ statements altogether. We'll revisit this idea later in the chapter.

One key concept to take away from this brief discussion of algorithm analysis is how expensive it is to perform nested loops over large sets of input data. Algorithms that make many nested passes over a very large dataset tend to perform poorly, so it's important to come up with efficient algorithms that don't loop over data needlessly.

Now let's take a look at algorithm complexity in action, observing the runtimes of some actual algorithms that can be used to solve a programming problem on a large dataset.

Empirical Analysis

Consider the task of computing the range of numbers in an array. The range is the difference between the lowest and highest numbers in the array. An initial solution might use nested loops to examine every pair of elements in the array, computing their difference and remembering the largest difference found:

```
max = 0.
for (each index i) {
```

```
    for (each index j) {
        update max, if elements i and j differ by more than max.
    }
}
```

The following code implements the `range` method as described:

```
// returns the range of numbers in the given array
public static int range(int[] numbers) {
    int maxDiff = 0;
    for (int i = 0; i < numbers.length; i++) {
        for (int j = 0; j < numbers.length; j++) {
            int diff = Math.abs(numbers[j] - numbers[i]);
            maxDiff = Math.max(maxDiff, diff);
        }
    }
    return maxDiff;
}
```

Since the code has two nested `for` loops, each of which processes the entire array, we can hypothesize that the algorithm executes roughly N^2 statements, or some multiple thereof.

We can measure the speed of this range algorithm in milliseconds by calling `range` on various arrays and measuring the time elapsed. We measure the time by acquiring the current time before and after calling `range` on a large array and subtracting the start time from the end time.

As you can see in Figure 13.2, as the input size N doubles, the runtime of the `range` method approximately quadruples. This is consistent with our hypothesis. If the algorithm takes N^2 statements to run and we increase the input size to $2N$, the new runtime is roughly $(2N)^2$ or $4N^2$, which is four times as long as the original runtime.

Our code isn't very efficient for a large array. It requires over 12 seconds to examine 32,000 integers on a modern computer. In real-world data-processing situations,

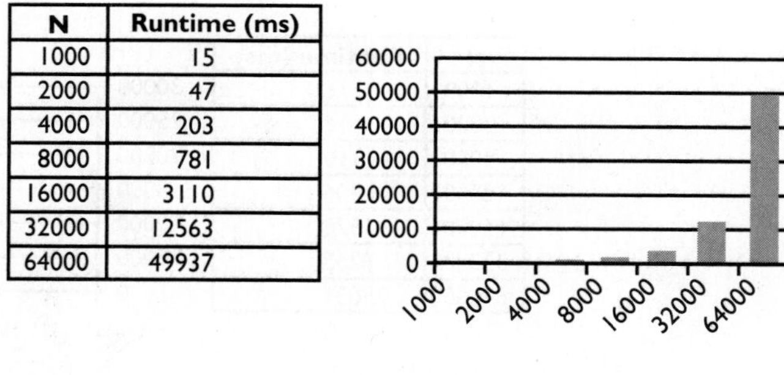

N	Runtime (ms)
1000	15
2000	47
4000	203
8000	781
16000	3110
32000	12563
64000	49937

Figure 13.2 Runtimes for first version of range algorithm

we would expect to see far larger input datasets than this, so this runtime isn't acceptable for general use.

Studying a piece of code and trying to figure out how to speed it up can be deceptively difficult. It's tempting to approach the problem by looking at each line of code and trying to reduce the amount of computation it performs. For example, you may have noticed that our `range` method actually examines every pair of elements in the array twice: For unique integers `i` and `j`, we examine the pair of elements at indexes (`i`, `j`) as well as the pair at (`j`, `i`).

We can perform a minor modification to our `range` method's code by starting each inner `j` loop ahead of `i`, so that we won't examine any pair (`i`, `j`) where `i` ≥ `j`. Performing minor modifications like this is sometimes called tweaking an algorithm. The following code implements our tweaked version of the range algorithm:

```
public static int range2(int[] numbers) {
    int maxDiff = 0;
    for (int i = 0; i < numbers.length; i++) {
        for (int j = i + 1; j < numbers.length; j++) {
            int diff = Math.abs(numbers[j] - numbers[i]);
            maxDiff = Math.max(maxDiff, diff);
        }
    }
    return maxDiff;
}
```

Since about half of the possible pairs of `i`/`j` values are eliminated by this tweak, we'd hope that the code would run about twice as fast. Figure 13.3 shows its actual measured runtime. As we estimated, the second version is about twice as fast as the first. We could implement other minor tweaks, such as replacing the `Math.max` call with a simple `if` test (which would speed up the algorithm by around 10% more), but there's a more important point to be made. When the input size doubles, the runtime of either version of the algorithm roughly quadruples. Consequently, regardless of which version we use, if the input array is very large the method will be too slow.

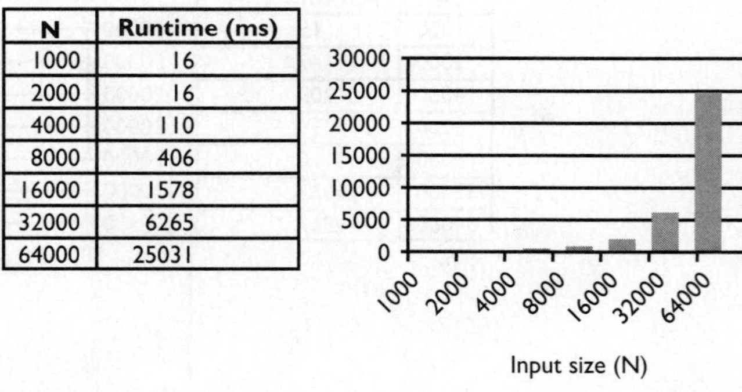

N	Runtime (ms)
1000	16
2000	16
4000	110
8000	406
16000	1578
32000	6265
64000	25031

Figure 13.3 Runtimes for second version of range algorithm

Rather than trying to further tweak our nested loop solution, let's try to think of a more efficient algorithm. As we noted earlier, the range of values in an array is the difference between the array's largest and smallest elements. We don't really need to examine all pairs of values to find this range; we just need to discover the pair representing the largest and smallest values. We can discover both of these values in a single loop over the array by using a min/max loop, discussed in Chapter 4. The following new algorithm demonstrates this idea:

```
public static int range3(int[] numbers) {
    int max = numbers[0];
    int min = max;
    for (int i = 1; i < numbers.length; i++) {
        if (numbers[i] > max) {
            max = numbers[i];
        } else if (numbers[i] < min) {
            min = numbers[i];
        }
    }
    return max – min;
}
```

Since this algorithm passes over the array only once, we'd hope that its runtime would be proportional to the array's length. If the array length doubles, the runtime should double, not quadruple. Figure 13.4 shows its runtime.

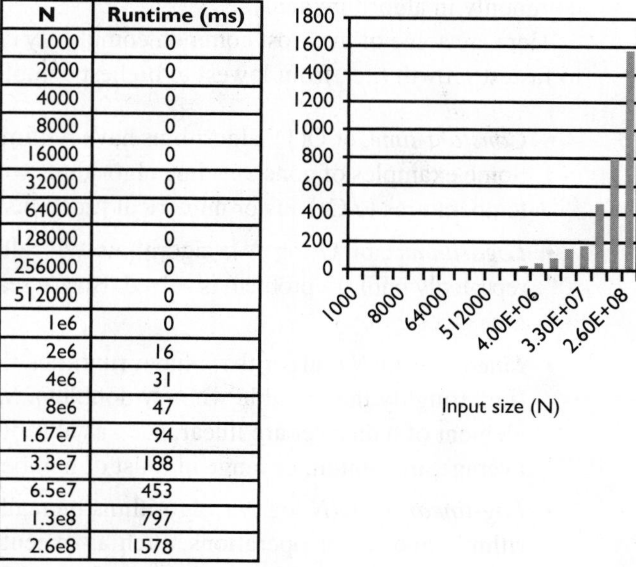

N	Runtime (ms)
1000	0
2000	0
4000	0
8000	0
16000	0
32000	0
64000	0
128000	0
256000	0
512000	0
1e6	0
2e6	16
4e6	31
8e6	47
1.67e7	94
3.3e7	188
6.5e7	453
1.3e8	797
2.6e8	1578

Figure 13.4 Runtimes for third version of range algorithm

Our runtime predictions were roughly correct. As the size of the array doubles, the runtime of this new range algorithm approximately doubles as well. The overall runtime of this algorithm is much better; we can examine over a hundred million integers in less than a second.

There are some important observations to take away from this exercise:

- Tweaking an algorithm's code often isn't as powerful an optimization as finding a better algorithm.
- An algorithm's rate of growth, or the amount by which its runtime increases as the input dataset grows, is the standard measure of the complexity of the algorithm.

Complexity Classes

We categorize rates of growth on the basis of their proportion to the input data size *N*. We call these categories *complexity classes* or *growth rates.*

> **Complexity Class**
>
> A set of algorithms that have a similar relationship between input data size and resource consumption.

The complexity class of a piece of code is determined by looking at the most frequently executed line of code, determining the number of times it is executed, and extracting the highest power of *N*. For example, if the most frequent line executes $(2N^3 + 4N)$ times, the algorithm is in the "order N^3" complexity class, or $O(N^3)$ for short. The shorthand notation with the capital O is called *big-Oh notation* and is used commonly in algorithm analysis.

Here are some of the most common complexity classes, listed in order from slowest to fastest growth (i.e., from lowest to highest complexity):

- *Constant-time,* or O(1), algorithms have runtimes that don't depend on input size. Some examples of constant-time algorithms would be code to convert Fahrenheit temperatures to Celsius or numerical functions such as `Math.abs`.
- *Logarithmic*, or O(log *N*), algorithms typically divide a problem space in half repeatedly until the problem is solved. Binary search is an example of a logarithmic-time algorithm.
- *Linear,* or O(*N*), algorithms have runtimes that are directly proportional to *N* (i.e., roughly they double when *N* doubles). Many algorithms that process each element of a data set are linear, such as algorithms that compute the count, sum, average, maximum, or range of a list of numbers.
- *Log-linear,* or O(*N* log *N*), algorithms typically perform a combination of logarithmic and linear operations, such as executing a logarithmic algorithm over every element of a dataset of size *N*. Many efficient sorting algorithms, such as merge sort (discussed later in this chapter), are log-linear.

Did You Know?

Timing Code and the Epoch

Java's method `System.currentTimeMillis` returns the number of milliseconds that have passed since 12:00 AM on January 1, 1970. This method can be used to measure the runtime of an algorithm. Over one trillion milliseconds have passed since the indicated time, so the value is too large to store in a simple `int` value. The milliseconds are instead returned as a value of type `long`, which is a primitive type that's similar to `int` but that is capable of holding much larger values. A `long` can store any number up to 9,223,372,036,854,775,807, or roughly 2^{63}.

The following lines of code show how a piece of code can be timed:

```
long startTime = System.currentTimeMillis();
<code to be timed>
long endTime = System.currentTimeMillis();
System.out.println("Elapsed time (ms): " + (endTime - startTime));
```

The choice of January 1, 1970, as the point of reference for system times is an example of an *epoch,* or an instant chosen as the origin of a particular time scale. This particular epoch was chosen because it matches the epochs of many popular operating systems, including Unix.

For historical reasons, many older Unix operating systems store the time that has passed since the epoch as a 32-bit integer value. However, unspecified problems may occur when this number exceeds its capacity, which is not necessarily a rare event. The clocks of some Unix systems will overflow on January 19, 2038, creating a Year 2038 problem similar to the famous Year 2000 (Y2K) problem.

- *Quadratic,* or $O(N^2)$, algorithms have runtimes that are proportional to the square of the input size. This means that quadratic algorithms' runtimes roughly quadruple when N doubles. The initial versions of the range algorithm developed in the previous section were quadratic algorithms.
- *Cubic,* or $O(N^3)$, algorithms have runtimes that are proportional to the cube of the input size. Such algorithms often make triply nested passes over the input data. Code to multiply two $N \times N$ matrices or to count the number of colinear trios of points in a large `Point` array would be examples of cubic algorithms.
- *Exponential,* or $O(2^N)$, algorithms have runtimes that are proportional to 2 raised to the power of the input size. This means that if the input size increases by just one, the algorithm will take roughly twice as long to execute. One example would be code to print the "power set" of a dataset, which is the set of all possible subsets of the data. Exponential algorithms are so slow that they should be executed only on very small input datasets.

Table 13.3 Algorithm Runtime Comparison Chart

Input size (N)	O(1)	O(log N)	O(N)	O(N log N)	O(N^2)	O(N^3)	O(2^N)
100	100 ms	100 ms	100 ms	100 ms	100 ms	100 ms	100 ms
200	100 ms	115 ms	200 ms	240 ms	400 ms	800 ms	32.7 sec
400	100 ms	130 ms	400 ms	550 ms	1.6 sec	6.4 sec	12.4 days
800	100 ms	145 ms	800 ms	1.2 sec	6.4 sec	51.2 sec	36.5 million years
1600	100 ms	160 ms	1.6 sec	2.7 sec	25.6 sec	6 min 49.6 sec	$4.21 * 10^{24}$ years
3200	100 ms	175 ms	3.2 sec	6 sec	1 min 42.4 sec	54 min 36 sec	$5.6 * 10^{61}$ years

Table 13.3 presents several hypothetical algorithm runtimes as the input size N grows, assuming that each algorithm requires 100 ms to process 100 elements. Notice that even though they all start at the same runtime for a small input size, as N grows the algorithms in higher complexity classes become so slow that they would be impractical.

When you look at the numbers in Table 13.3, you might wonder why anyone bothers to use O(N^3) or O(2^N), algorithms when O(1) and O(N) algorithms are so much faster. The answer is that not all problems can be solved in O(1) or even O(N) time. Computer scientists have been studying classic problems such as searching and sorting for many years, trying to find the most efficient algorithms possible. However, there will likely never be a constant-time algorithm that can sort 1,000,000 elements as quickly as it can sort 10 elements.

For large datasets it's very important to choose the most efficient algorithms possible (i.e., those with the lowest complexity classes). Algorithms with complexity classes of O(N^2) or worse will take a long time to run on extremely large datasets. Keeping this in mind, we'll now examine algorithms to search and sort data.

13.3 Implementing Searching and Sorting Algorithms

In this section, we'll implement methods that search and sort data. We'll start by writing code to search for an integer in an array of integers and return the index where it is found. If the integer doesn't appear in the array, we'll return a negative number. We'll examine two major searching algorithms, sequential and binary search, and discuss the tradeoffs between them.

There are literally hundreds of algorithms to sort data; we'll cover two in detail in this chapter. The first, seen later in this section, is one of the more intuitive algorithms, although it performs poorly on large datasets. The second, examined as a case study in the next section, is one of the fastest general-purpose sorting algorithms that is used in practice today.

Sequential Search

Perhaps the simplest way to search an array is to loop over the elements of the array and check each one to see if it is the target number. As we mentioned earlier, this is called a sequential search because it examines every element in sequence.

We implemented a sequential search of an array of integers in Chapter 7. The code uses a `for` loop and is relatively straightforward. The algorithm returns `-1` if the loop completes without finding the target number:

```
// Sequential search algorithm.
// Returns the index at which the given target number first
// appears in the given input array, or -1 if it is not found.
public static int indexOf(int[] list, int target) {
    for (int i = 0; i < list.length; i++) {
        if (list[i] == target) {
            return i;
        }
    }
    return -1; // not found
}
```

Using the rules stated in the previous section, we predict that the sequential search algorithm is a linear O(*N*) algorithm because it contains one loop that traverses at most *N* elements in an array. (We say "at most" because if the algorithm finds the target element, it stops and immediately returns the index.) Next, we'll time it to verify our prediction.

Figure 13.5 shows actual results of running the sequential search algorithm on randomly generated arrays of integers. Searches were conducted for a value known to be in the array and for a value not in the array.

N	Runtime when element is found (ms)	Runtime when element is not found (ms)
100000	0	0
200000	0	0
400000	0	0
800000	0	0
1.6e6	0	16
3.2e6	15	16
6.4e6	16	31
1.3e7	32	47
2.6e7	37	93
5.1e7	45	203
1.0e8	72	402
2.0e8	125	875

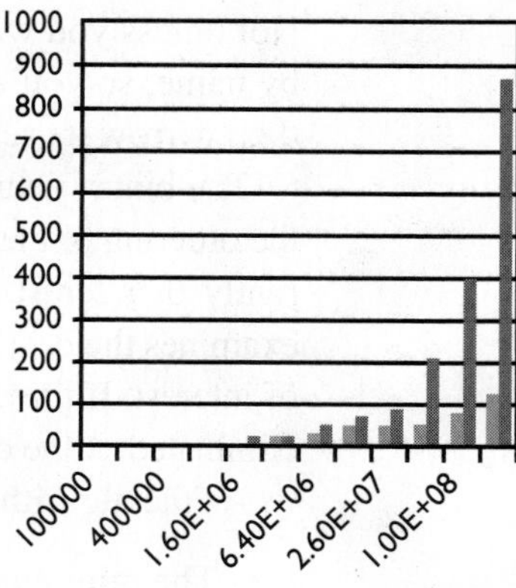

Figure 13.5 Runtimes for sequential search algorithm

When the algorithm searches for an integer that isn't in the array, it runs somewhat slower, because it can't exit its loop early by finding the target. This scenario raises the question of whether we should judge the algorithm by its fastest or slowest runtime. Often what's most important is the expected behavior for a typical input, or the average of its runtime over all possible inputs. This is called an *average case analysis.* But under certain conditions, we also care about the fastest possible outcome, the *best case analysis,* and/or the slowest possible outcome, the *worst case analysis.* In this algorithm, the average search looks at approximately half of the array, which is linear or O(N).

Binary Search

Consider a modified version of the searching problem, in which we can assume that the elements of the input array are in sorted order. Does this ordering affect our algorithm? Our existing algorithm will still work correctly, but now we know that we can stop the search if we ever get to a number larger than our target without finding the target. For example, if we're searching an array containing the elements `[1, 4, 5, 7, 7, 9, 10, 12, 56]` for the target value `8`, we can stop searching once we see the `9`.

We might think that such a modification to our sequential search algorithm would significantly speed up the algorithm, but in actuality it doesn't make much difference. The only case in which it speeds up the algorithm noticeably is when it is searching for a relatively small value that isn't found in the array. In fact, when the modified algorithm is searching for a large value that requires the code to examine most or all of the array elements, the algorithm actually performs slower than the original because it has to perform a few more Boolean tests. Most importantly, the algorithm is still O(N), which isn't the optimal solution.

Once again, tweaking the algorithm won't make as much difference as finding another, more efficient algorithm. If the input array is in sorted order, a sequential search isn't the best choice. If you had to instruct a robot how to look up a person's phone number in a phone book, would you tell the robot to read through all the entries on the first page, then the second, and so on until it found the person's name? Not unless you wanted to torture the poor robot. You know that the entries are sorted by name, so you'd tell the robot to flip open the book to somewhere near the middle, then narrow its search toward the first letter of the person's name.

The binary search algorithm discussed previously in this chapter takes advantage of the ordering of the array. A binary search keeps track of the range of the array that is currently of interest. (Initially, this range is the whole array.) The algorithm repeatedly examines the center element of the array and uses its value to eliminate half of the range of interest. If the center element is smaller than the target, the lower half of the range is eliminated; if the center element is larger than the target, the upper half is eliminated.

As the algorithm runs, we must keep track of three indexes:

- The minimum index of interest (`min`)
- The maximum index of interest (`max`)
- The middle index, halfway between the minimum and maximum, which will be examined during each pass of the algorithm (`mid`)

The algorithm repeatedly examines the element at the middle index and uses it to trim the range of indexes of interest in half. If we examine the middle element and find it's too small, we will eliminate all elements between `min` and `mid` from consideration. If the middle element is too large, we will eliminate all elements between `mid` and `max` from consideration.

Consider the following array:

```
int[] numbers = {11, 18, 29, 37, 42, 49, 51, 63,
                 69, 72, 77, 82, 88, 91, 98};
```

0	1	2	3	4	5	6	7	8	9	10	11	12	13	14
11	18	29	37	42	49	51	63	69	72	77	82	88	91	98

Let's run a binary search on the array for a target value of `77`. We'll start at the middle element, which is at index (14 / 2), or 7. The following diagrams show the `min`, `mid`, and `max` at each step of the algorithm:

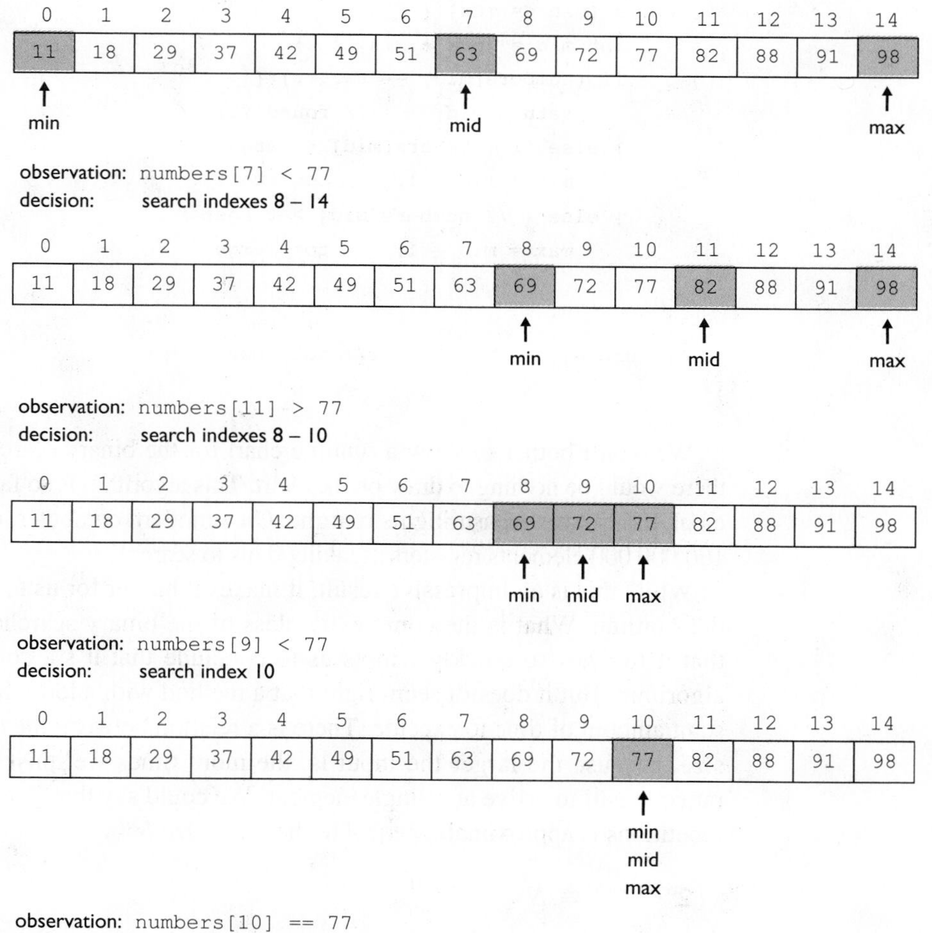

What about when we're searching for an element that isn't found in the array? Let's say we're searching for the value `78` instead of `77`. The steps of the algorithm will be the same, except that on the fourth pass the algorithm will reach `77` instead of the desired value, `78`. The algorithm will have eliminated the entire range without finding the target and will know that it should stop. Another way to describe the process is that the algorithm loops until the `min` and `max` have crossed each other.

The following code implements the binary search algorithm. Its loop repeats until the target is found or until the `min` and `max` have crossed:

```
// Binary search algorithm.
// Returns an index at which the target
// appears in the given input array, or -1 if not found.
// pre: array is sorted.
public static int binarySearch(int[] numbers, int target) {
    int min = 0;
    int max = numbers.length - 1;
    while (min <= max) {
        int mid = (max + min) / 2;
        if (numbers[mid] == target) {
            return mid;       // found it!
        } else if (numbers[mid] < target) {
            min = mid + 1;    // too small
        } else { // numbers[mid] > target
            max = mid - 1;    // too large
        }
    }
    return -1;                // not found
}
```

We won't bother to show a runtime chart for the binary search algorithm, because there would be nothing to draw on the chart. This algorithm is so fast that the computer's clock has trouble measuring its runtime. On a modern computer, even an array of over 100,000,000 elements registers as taking 0 ms to search!

While this is an impressive result, it makes it harder for us to empirically examine the runtime. What is the complexity class of the binary search algorithm? The fact that it finishes so quickly tempts us to conclude that it's a constant-time, or O(1), algorithm. But it doesn't seem right that a method with a loop in it would take a constant amount of time to execute. There is a relation between the runtime and the input size, because the larger the input is, the more times we must divide our `min–max` range in half to arrive at a single element. We could say that 2 raised to the number of repetitions is approximately equal to the input size *N*:

$$2^{\text{repetitions}} \cong N$$

Using some algebra and taking a logarithm base-2 of both sides of the equation, we find that

$$\text{repetitions} \cong \log_2 N$$

We conclude that the binary search algorithm is in the logarithmic complexity class, or $O(\log N)$.

The runtime of the binary search algorithm doesn't differ much between the best and worst cases. In the best case, the algorithm finds its target value in the middle on the first check. In the worst case, the code must perform the full ($\log N$) comparisons. But since logarithms are small numbers ($\log_2$ 1,000,000 is roughly 20), the performance is still excellent in the worst case.

Recursive Binary Search

In the previous section, binary search was implemented using an iterative algorithm with a `while` loop. But the algorithm can also be implemented elegantly using the concept of recursion introduced in Chapter 12. The recursive version of the method should accept the same parameters as the standard binary search:

```
public static int binarySearchR(int[] numbers, int target) {
    ...
}
```

But this header will not make it easy to write a recursive solution to the problem. Recall that the essence of a recursive solution is to break down the problem into smaller pieces and then solve the sub-problem(s). In this algorithm, the way to shrink the problem is to examine a smaller and smaller portion of the array until we find the right index. To do this, we can change our method to accept additional parameters for the range of indexes (min and max) that currently are being examined. Rather than changing the header just shown, we can add a private recursive helper with the additional parameters as described in Chapter 12. The public method can start the recursive process by calling the helper with `0` and `length – 1` as its minimum and maximum indexes to examine, respectively:

```
// Recursive binary search algorithm.
// Returns an index at which the target
// appears in the given input array, or –1 if not found.
// pre: array is sorted.
public static int binarySearchR(int[] numbers, int target) {
    return binarySearchR(numbers, target, 0, numbers.length – 1);
}

// private recursive helper to implement binary search
private static int binarySearchR(int[] numbers, int target,
                                 int min, int max) {
    ...
}
```

Our recursive binary search method accepts the minimum and maximum indexes of interest as parameters. On each pass of the recursive algorithm, the code examines the middle element. If this element is too small, the code recursively examines only the right half of the array. If the middle element is too large, the code recursively examines only the left half. This process repeats, recursively calling itself with different values of `min` and `max`, until it finds the target or until the entire array has been eliminated from consideration. The following code implements the algorithm:

```
// Recursive binary search algorithm.
// Returns an index at which the target
// appears in the given input array, or -1 if not found.
// pre: array is sorted.
private static int binarySearchR(int[] numbers, int target,
                                 int min, int max) {
    // base case
    if (min > max) {
        return -1; // not found
    } else {
        // recursive case
        int mid = (max + min) / 2;
        if (numbers[mid] == target) {
            return mid;
        } else if (numbers[mid] < target) {
            return binarySearchR(numbers, target, mid + 1, max);
        } else {
            return binarySearchR(numbers, target, min, mid - 1);
        }
    }
}
```

Some instructors don't like recursive versions of methods like binary search because there is a nonrecursive solution that's fairly easy to write and because recursion tends to have poor runtime performance because of the extra method calls it generates. However, that doesn't pose a problem here. The runtime of the recursive version of our binary search method is still O(log N), because it's essentially performing the same computation; it's still cutting the input in half at each step. In fact, the recursive version is fast enough that the computer still can't time it accurately. It produces a runtime of 0 ms even on arrays of tens of millions of integers.

In general, analyzing the runtimes of recursive algorithms is tricky. Recursive runtime analysis often requires a technique called *recurrence relations*, which are mathematical relations that describe an algorithm's runtime in terms of itself. That's a complex topic for a later course that won't be covered in this textbook.

Did You Know?

Binary Search Details

There are a few interesting things about Java's implementation of binary search in `Arrays.binarySearch` and `Collections.binarySearch` that we haven't mentioned yet. Take a look at this text from the Javadoc documentation of the `binarySearch` method:

> The array **must** be sorted (as by the `sort` method, above) prior to making this call. If it is not sorted, the results are undefined. If the array contains multiple elements with the specified value, there is no guarantee which one will be found.

Binary search depends on the array being sorted. If it isn't sorted, the documentation says the results are undefined. What does that mean? Why doesn't the algorithm just sort the array for you if it's unsorted?

There are two problems with that idea, both essentially related to runtime performance. For one, sorting takes much longer (O(N log N) time) than a binary search (O(log N) time). Second, to even discover that you need to sort the array, you'd need to look at each element to determine whether they're in order, which takes O(N) time. Essentially, the cost of examining the array and sorting it if necessary would be too great.

Even if the cost of sorting the array weren't so large, the client of the `binarySearch` method probably won't want its array modified by the `binarySearch` method. Searching is supposed to be a read-only operation, not one that rearranges the array.

Let's look at the other part of the previous quote: "If the array contains multiple elements with the specified value, there is no guarantee which one will be found." We didn't mention this earlier when we were discussing the algorithm, but in the case of duplicates, binary search isn't guaranteed to find the first occurrence of the element, because the moment it finds an occurrence it stops.

Here's another interesting blurb from the `binarySearch` documentation:

> Returns: index of the search key, if it is contained in the list; otherwise, `(-(insertion point) - 1)`. The insertion point is defined as the point at which the key would be inserted into the list: the index of the first element greater than the key, or `list.size()`, if all elements in the list are less than the specified key. Note that this guarantees that the return value will be >= `0` if and only if the key is found.

Continued on next page

Continued from previous page

Rather than returning `-1` for an unsuccessful search, the `Arrays.binarySearch` and `Collections.binarySearch` methods return (`-index - 1`), where `index` is the last index the algorithm examined before giving up, which is also the index of the first element whose value is greater than the target. The documentation for these methods calls this value the *insertion point* because if you wanted to add the target to the array in sorted position, you'd place it at that index. For example, because a binary search of the following array for the value `45` would finish at index 5, the algorithm would return `-6`:

0	1	2	3	4	5	6	7	8	9	10	11	12	13	14
11	18	29	37	42	49	51	63	69	72	77	82	88	91	98

If you were maintaining this sorted array and wanted to add `45` to it at the proper index to retain the sorted order, you could call `Arrays.binarySearch`, get the result of `-6`, negate it, and subtract 1 from it to get the index at which you should insert the value. This is much faster than linearly searching for the place to add the value or adding the value at the end and resorting the array.

We could modify our own binary search code to match this behavior by changing the last line of the method's body to the following line:

```
return -min - 1; // not found
```

Searching Objects

Searching for a particular object in an array of objects requires a few modifications to our searching code from the previous sections. Let's look at a sequential object search first, because it will work with any type of object. The most important modification to make to the code is to ensure that it uses the `equals` method to compare objects for equality:

```
// Sequential search algorithm.
// Returns the index at which the target first
// appears in the given input array, or -1 if not found.
public static int indexOf(Object[] objects, Object target) {
    for (int i = 0; i < objects.length; i++) {
        if (objects[i].equals(target)) {
            return i; // found it!
        }
    }
    return -1; // not found
}
```

If we want to do a binary search on objects, the objects must have an ordering (in other words, must be of a type that implements the `Comparable` interface or must be provided with a comparator) and the elements in the array or collection must be in sorted order. One common example would be an array of `String`s. Since we can't use relational operators like < and >= on objects, we must call the `compareTo` method on pairs of `String` objects and examine the value it returns. The following code implements a binary search on an array of `String`s:

```
// Binary search algorithm that works with Strings.
// Returns an index at which the given target String
// appears in the given input array, or -1 if not found.
// pre: array is sorted
public static int binarySearch(String[] strings, String target) {
    int min = 0;
    int max = strings.length - 1;
    while (min <= max) {
        int mid = (max + min) / 2;
        int compare = strings[mid].compareTo(target);
        if (compare == 0) {
            return mid;     // found it!
        } else if (compare < 0) {
            min = mid + 1; // too small
        } else {  // compare > 0
            max = mid - 1; // too large
        }
    }
    return -1;              // not found
}
```

Selection Sort

Selection sort is a well-known sorting algorithm that makes many passes over an input array to put its elements into sorted order. Each time it runs through a loop, it selects the smallest value and puts it in the proper place near the front of the array. Consider the following array:

```
int[] nums = {12, 123, 1, 28, 183, 16};
```

0	1	2	3	4	5
12	123	1	28	183	16

How would you put its elements into order from smallest to largest? The selection sort algorithm conceptually divides the array into two pieces: sorted elements at the front and unsorted elements at the end. The first step of the selection sort makes a pass over the array and finds the smallest number. In the sample array, the smallest is `nums[2]`, which equals `1`. The algorithm then swaps the smallest value with the value in the first position in the array, so that the smallest value will be at the front of the array. In this case, `nums[0]` and `nums[2]` are swapped:

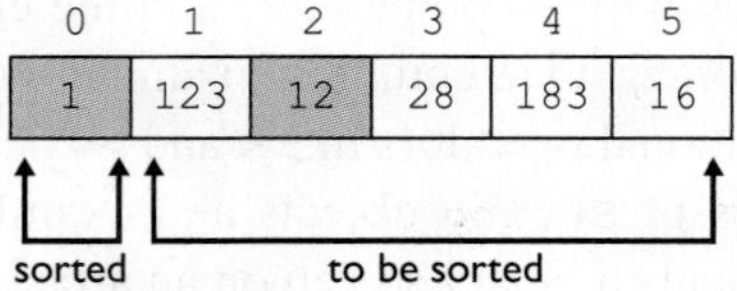

The element at index 0 now has the right value, and only the elements at indexes 1 through 5 remain to be ordered. The algorithm repeats the process of scanning the unsorted portion of the array and looking for the smallest element. On the second pass, it scans the remaining five elements and finds that `nums[2]`, which equals `12`, is the smallest element. The program swaps this value with `nums[1]`. After this swap, the sorted area of the array consists of its first two indexes:

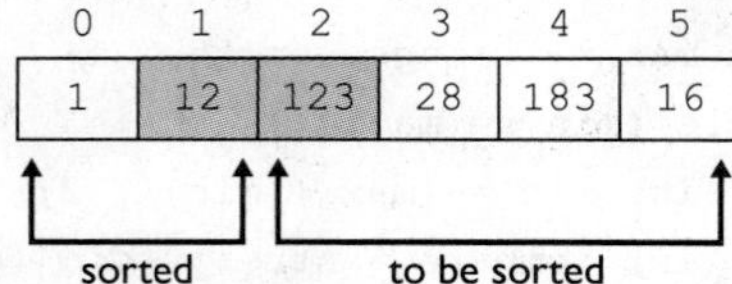

Now `nums[0]` and `nums[1]` have the correct values. The third pass of the algorithm scans the remaining four unsorted elements and finds that the smallest one is `nums[5]`, which equals `16`. It swaps this element with `nums[2]`.

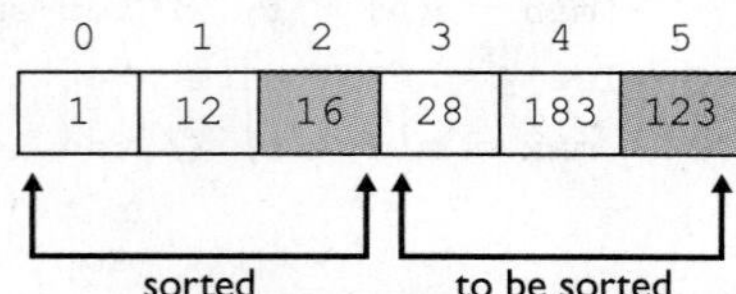

The algorithm continues this process until all the elements have the proper values. Each pass involves a scan followed by a swap. The scan/swap occurs five times to process six elements. You don't need to perform a sixth scan/swap because, if the first five elements have the correct values, the sixth element will be correct as well.

Here is a pseudocode description of the execution of the selection sort algorithm over an array `nums` that has six elements:

```
for (each i from 0 to 4) {
    scan nums[i] through nums[5] for the smallest value.
    swap nums[i] with the smallest element found in the scan.
}
```

You can write pseudocode like the following for the scan:

```
smallest = lowest array index of interest.
for (all other index values of interest) {
    if (nums[index] < nums[smallest]) {
        smallest = index.
    }
}
```

You can then incorporate this pseudocode into your larger pseudocode as follows:

```
for (each i from 0 to 4) {
    smallest = i.
    for (each index between (i + 1) and 5) {
        if (nums[index] < nums[smallest]) {
            smallest = index.
        }
    }
    swap nums[i] with nums[smallest].
}
```

You can translate this pseudocode almost directly into Java, except for the swap process. In Chapter 7, we wrote a `swap` method to swap two elements of an array. We can reuse it here:

```
public static void swap(int[] list, int i, int j) {
    int temp = list[i];
    list[i] = list[j];
    list[j] = temp;
}
```

We can also modify the code to work with arrays of any size. The following code implements the overall selection sort algorithm:

```
// places the elements of the given array into sorted order
// using the selection sort algorithm
// post: array is in sorted (nondecreasing) order
public static void selectionSort(int[] a) {
    for (int i = 0; i < a.length - 1; i++) {
        // find index of smallest element
        int smallest = i;
        for (int j = i + 1; j < a.length; j++) {
            if (a[j] < a[smallest]) {
                smallest = j;
            }
        }
        swap(a, i, smallest); // swap smallest to front
    }
}
```

Since selection sort makes roughly N passes over an array of N elements, its performance is $O(N^2)$. Technically, it examines $N + (N - 1) + (N - 2) + \cdots + 3 + 2 + 1$ elements, because each pass starts one index ahead of where the last one started. Chapter 3 mentioned a mathematical identity which states that the sum of all integers

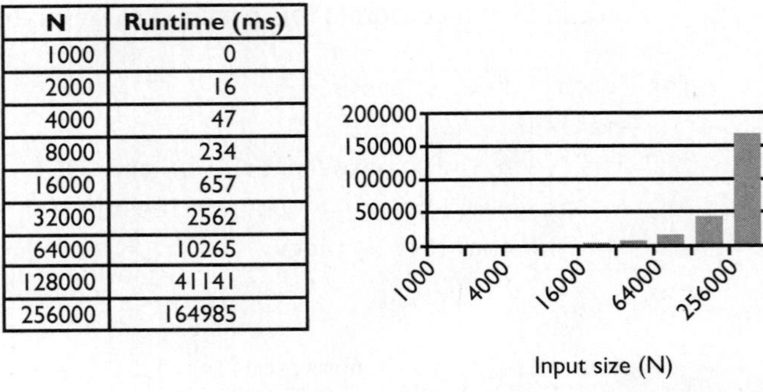

N	Runtime (ms)
1000	0
2000	16
4000	47
8000	234
16000	657
32000	2562
64000	10265
128000	41141
256000	164985

Figure 13.6 Runtimes for selection sort algorithm

from 1 to any maximum value N equals $(N)(N + 1)/2$, which is just over ½ N^2. Figure 13.6 supports this analysis, because the runtime quadruples every time the input size N is doubled, which is characteristic of an N^2 algorithm. The algorithm becomes impractically slow once the number of elements reaches tens of thousands.

The current `selectionSort` code will sort arrays of integer values, but you could adapt it to sort `Comparable` objects such as `Strings` using the techniques covered in the previous section on searching objects. For example, you could use the `compareTo` and `equals` methods to compare objects rather than relational operators like < and >=.

13.4 Case Study: Implementing Merge Sort

There are other algorithms similar to selection sort that make many passes over the array and swap various elements on each pass. An algorithm that searches for inverted pairs of elements and swaps them into order in this way cannot run faster than $O(N^2)$, on average. However, there is a better algorithm that breaks this barrier.

The *merge sort* algorithm is named for the observation that if you have two sorted subarrays, you can easily merge them into a single sorted array. For example, consider the following array:

```
int[] list = {14, 32, 67, 76, 23, 41, 58, 85};
```

You can think of it as two subarray halves, each of which (because of the element values we chose) happens to be sorted:

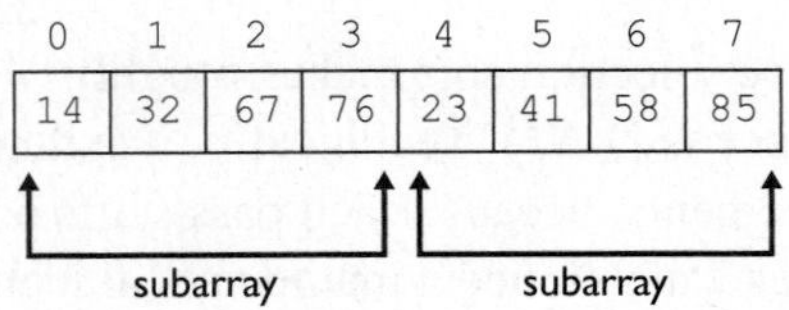

The following pseudocode provides the basic idea of the merge sort algorithm:

```
split the array into two halves.
sort the left half.
sort the right half.
merge the two halves.
```

Let's look at splitting the array and merging halves first; then we'll talk about the sorting.

Splitting and Merging Arrays

Splitting one array into its two halves is relatively straightforward. We'll set a midpoint at one half of the length of the array and consider everything before this midpoint to be part of the "left" half and everything that follows it to be in the "right" half. We can use the method `Arrays.copyOfRange` to extract the halves of an array as new arrays. The "left" half is from range 0 to half the length, and the "right" half is from half the length to the full length:

```
// split array into two halves
int[] left = Arrays.copyOfRange(a, 0, a.length / 2);
int[] right = Arrays.copyOfRange(a, a.length / 2, a.length);
```

We will need to sort these left/right halves, then merge them into a sorted whole. For now, let's think about how we would merge two sorted subarrays. (We'll come back to sorting them later.) Suppose that you have two stacks of exam papers, each sorted alphabetically by name, and you need to combine them into a single stack sorted by name. The simplest algorithm is to place both stacks in front of you, look at the top paper of each stack, pick up the paper that comes first in alphabetical order, and put it face down into a third pile. You then repeat this process, comparing the papers on the top of each stack and placing the one that comes first face down on the merged stack, until one of your two original stacks is empty. Once one is empty, you just grab the entire remaining stack and place it on your merged pile.

The idea behind merging two sorted arrays is similar, except that instead of physically removing papers (integers) from the piles (subarrays), we'll keep an index for each subarray and increment that index as we process a given element. Here is a pseudocode description of the merging algorithm:

```
i1 = 0.     // left index
i2 = 0.     // right index
for (number of elements in entire array) {
    if (left value at i1 <= right value at i2) {
        include value from left array in new array.
        i1++;
    } else {
        include value from right array in new array.
```

```
            i2++;
        }
    }
```

Here is a trace of the eight steps to merge the two subarrays into a sorted array:

Subarrays (left: i1)	Subarrays (right: i2)	Next include	Merged array	i
[**14**] 32 67 76 (i1 = 0)	[**23**] 41 58 85 (i2 = 0)	14 from left	14	0
14 [**32**] 67 76 (i1 = 1)	[**23**] 41 58 85 (i2 = 0)	23 from right	14 23	1
14 [**32**] 67 76 (i1 = 1)	23 [**41**] 58 85 (i2 = 1)	32 from left	14 23 32	2
14 32 [**67**] 76 (i1 = 2)	23 [**41**] 58 85 (i2 = 1)	41 from right	14 23 32 41	3
14 32 [**67**] 76 (i1 = 2)	23 41 [**58**] 85 (i2 = 2)	58 from right	14 23 32 41 58	4
14 32 [**67**] 76 (i1 = 2)	23 41 58 [**85**] (i2 = 3)	67 from left	14 23 32 41 58 67	5
14 32 67 [**76**] (i1 = 3)	23 41 58 [**85**] (i2 = 3)	76 from left	14 23 32 41 58 67 76	6
14 32 67 76	23 41 58 [**85**] (i2 = 3)	85 from right	14 23 32 41 58 67 76 85	7

The following code is an initial attempt to implement the merge algorithm that was just described:

```
// initial incorrect attempt
public static void merge(int[] result, int[] left, int[] right) {
    int i1 = 0;   // index into left array
    int i2 = 0;   // index into right array
    for (int i = 0; i < result.length; i++) {
        if (left[i1] <= right[i2]) {
            result[i] = left[i1];   // take from left
            i1++;
        } else {
            result[i] = right[i2];   // take from right
            i2++;
        }
    }
}
```

The preceding code is incorrect and will cause an out-of-bounds exception. After the program completes the seventh step of the preceding diagram, all of the elements in the left subarray will have been consumed and the left index `i1` will run off the end of the subarray. Then, when the code tries to access element `left[i1]`, it will crash. A similar problem would occur if the right index `i2` exceeded the bounds of the right array.

We need to modify our code to remain within the bounds of the arrays. The `if/else` logic needs to ensure that the index `i1` or `i2` is within the array bounds before the program attempts to access the appropriate element. The simple test in the pseudocode needs to be expanded:

```
if (i2 has passed the end of the right array, or
    left element at i1 <= right element at i2) {
    take from left.
} else {
    take from right.
}
```

The following second version of the code correctly implements the merging behavior. The preconditions and postconditions of the method are documented in comments:

```
// Merges the given left and right arrays into the given
// result array. Second, working version.
// pre : result is empty; left/right are sorted
// post: result contains result of merging sorted lists.
public static void merge(int[] result, int[] left, int[] right) {
    int i1 = 0;   // index into left array
    int i2 = 0;   // index into right array
```

```
    for (int i = 0; i < result.length; i++) {
        if (i2 >= right.length || (i1 < left.length &&
                                   left[i1] <= right[i2])) {
            result[i] = left[i1];     // take from left
            i1++;
        } else {
            result[i] = right[i2];    // take from right
            i2++;
        }
    }
}
```

Recursive Merge Sort

We've written the code to split an array into halves and to merge the sorted halves into a sorted whole. The overall merge sort method now looks like this:

```
public static void mergeSort(int[] a) {
    // split array into two halves
    int[] left = Arrays.copyOfRange(a, 0, a.length / 2);
    int[] right = Arrays.copyOfRange(a, a.length / 2, a.length);

    // sort the two halves
    ...

    // merge the sorted halves into a sorted whole
    merge(a, left, right);
}
```

The last piece of our program is the code to sort each half of the array. How can we sort the halves? We could call the `selectionSort` method created earlier in this chapter on the two halves. But in the previous chapter we discussed the recursive "leap of faith," the belief that our own method will work properly to solve a smaller version of the same problem. In this case, a better approach is to merge sort the two smaller halves. We can recursively call our own `mergeSort` method on the array halves, and if it's written correctly, it'll put each of them into sorted order. Our original pseudocode can now be rewritten as the following pseudocode:

```
split the array into two halves.
merge sort the left half.
merge sort the right half.
merge the two halves.
```

If we're making our merge sort algorithm recursive, it needs to have a base case and a recursive case. The preceding pseudocode specifies the recursive case, but for the base case, what are the simplest arrays to sort? An array with either no elements or just one element doesn't need to be sorted at all. At least two elements must be present in order for them to appear in the wrong order, so the simple case would be an array with a length less than 2. This means that our final pseudocode for the merge sort method is the following:

```
if (array length is more than 1) {
    split the array into two halves.
    merge sort the left half.
    merge sort the right half.
    merge the two halves.
}
```

No `else` case is needed because if the array size is 0 or 1, we don't need to do anything to the array. This recursive algorithm has an empty base case.

The following method implements the complete merge sort algorithm:

```
// Places the elements of the given array into sorted order
// using the merge sort algorithm.
// post: array is in sorted (nondecreasing) order
public static void mergeSort(int[] a) {
    if (a.length > 1) {
        // split array into two halves
        int[] left = Arrays.copyOfRange(a, 0, a.length / 2);
        int[] right = Arrays.copyOfRange(a, a.length / 2, a.length);

        // recursively sort the two halves
        mergeSort(left);
        mergeSort(right);

        // merge the sorted halves into a sorted whole
        merge(a, left, right);
    }
}
```

To get a better idea of the algorithm in action, we'll temporarily insert a few `println` statements into its code and run the method on the eight-element sample array shown previously in this section. We'll insert the following `println` statement at the start of the `mergeSort` method:

```
// at start of mergeSort method
System.out.println("sorting " + Arrays.toString(a));
```

We'll also put the following `println` statement at the start of the `merge` method:

```
// at start of merge method
System.out.println("merging " + Arrays.toString(left) +
                   " and " + Arrays.toString(right));
```

Here is the output from running `mergeSort` on the example array:

```
sorting [14, 32, 67, 76, 23, 41, 58, 85]
sorting [14, 32, 67, 76]
sorting [14, 32]
sorting [14]
sorting [32]
merging [14] and [32]
sorting [67, 76]
sorting [67]
sorting [76]
merging [67] and [76]
merging [14, 32] and [67, 76]
sorting [23, 41, 58, 85]
sorting [23, 41]
sorting [23]
sorting [41]
merging [23] and [41]
sorting [58, 85]
sorting [58]
sorting [85]
merging [58] and [85]
merging [23, 41] and [58, 85]
merging [14, 32, 67, 76] and [23, 41, 58, 85]
```

It's also important to test the code on an array that doesn't divide into subarrays of exactly equal size (i.e., one whose overall length is not a power of 2). Because it employs integer division, our code makes the left subarray one element smaller than the right subarray when the size is odd. Given an initial five-element list of `[14, 32, 67, 76, 23]` the algorithm prints the following output:

```
sorting [14, 32, 67, 76, 23]
sorting [14, 32]
sorting [14]
sorting [32]
merging [14] and [32]
sorting [67, 76, 23]
sorting [67]
sorting [76, 23]
sorting [76]
sorting [23]
merging [76] and [23]
merging [67] and [23, 76]
merging [14, 32] and [23, 67, 76]
```

Complete Program

The complete program containing the merge sort code follows. Its `main` method constructs a sample array and sorts it using the algorithm:

```
// This program implements merge sort for arrays of integers.
import java.util.*;

public class MergeSort {
    public static void main(String[] args) {
        int[] list = {14, 32, 67, 76, 23, 41, 58, 85};
        System.out.println("before: " + Arrays.toString(list));
        mergeSort(list);
        System.out.println("after : " + Arrays.toString(list));
    }

    // Places the elements of the given array into sorted order
    // using the merge sort algorithm.
    // post: array is in sorted (nondecreasing) order
    public static void mergeSort(int[] a) {
        if (a.length > 1) {
            // split array into two halves
            int[] left = Arrays.copyOfRange(a, 0, a.length / 2);
            int[] right = Arrays.copyOfRange(a, a.length / 2,
                                             a.length);

            // recursively sort the two halves
            mergeSort(left);
            mergeSort(right);

            // merge the sorted halves into a sorted whole
            merge(a, left, right);
        }
    }

    // Merges the given left and right arrays into the given
    // result array.
    // pre : result is empty; left/right are sorted
    // post: result contains result of merging sorted lists;
    public static void merge(int[] result, int[] left, int[] right) {
        int i1 = 0;    // index into left array
        int i2 = 0;    // index into right array
        for (int i = 0; i < result.length; i++) {
            if (i2 >= right.length || (i1 < left.length &&
                                       left[i1] <= right[i2])) {
```

```
                    result[i] = left[i1];       // take from left
                    i1++;
                } else {
                    result[i] = right[i2];      // take from right
                    i2++;
                }
            }
        }
    }
```

The program produces the following output:

```
before: [14, 32, 67, 76, 23, 41, 58, 85]
after:  [14, 23, 32, 41, 58, 67, 76, 85]
```

Figure 13.7 demonstrates the performance of our merge sort algorithm on a modern computer. The merge sort algorithm's performance is much better than that of the selection sort algorithm. For example, whereas our selection sort test run needed over 41 seconds to sort 128,000 elements, the merge sort algorithm handled the same job in a blistering 47 milliseconds. But what is merge sort's complexity class? It looks almost like an O(*N*) algorithm, because the runtime only slightly more than doubles when we double the array size.

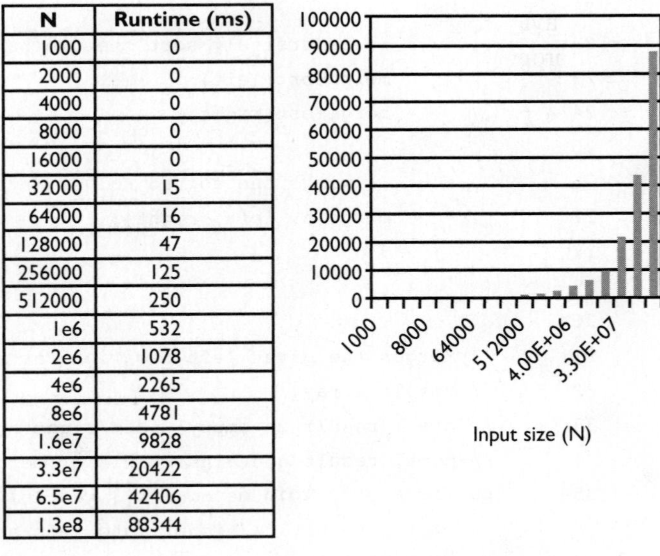

N	Runtime (ms)
1000	0
2000	0
4000	0
8000	0
16000	0
32000	15
64000	16
128000	47
256000	125
512000	250
1e6	532
2e6	1078
4e6	2265
8e6	4781
1.6e7	9828
3.3e7	20422
6.5e7	42406
1.3e8	88344

Figure 13.7 Runtimes for merge sort algorithm

However, merge sort is actually an O(N log N) algorithm. A formal proof of this statement is beyond the scope of this book, but a common-sense chain of reasoning is as follows: We have to split the array in half repeatedly until we hit the algorithm's base case, in which the subarrays each contain 1 element. For an array of size N, we must split the array $\log_2 N$ times. At each of those log N steps, we have to do a linear operation of order N (merging the halves after they're sorted). Multiplying these operations' runtimes together produces a O(N log N) overall runtime.

The preceding algorithm runtime analysis is informal and not rigorous. As with other recursive algorithms, a precise analysis of merge sort's performance is complicated and requires mathematical techniques such as recurrence relations, which are not discussed in this book.

Did You Know?

Cost of Java Array Allocation

Earlier in the chapter, we mentioned that variable declaration and assignment can be thought of as taking some constant amount of time. That is usually true, but there is one important exception: initializing arrays. Suppose you were to execute this line of code:

```
int[] list = new int[n];
```

Executing this line of code requires the computer to allocate a block of memory for the array. That can generally be done in a constant amount of time. But Java also insists on auto-initializing all array elements to `0` and that takes time proportional to `n`.

This subtlety of Java has stung several textbook authors who were translating textbooks from C and C++ into Java. When they were writing a solution to the merge sort algorithm, they included code that would allocate a temporary array as large as the entire array every time they did a merging operation.

For an array of size `n`, there are `n` different merging operations. If each one requires the computer to auto-initialize an array of length `n`, then the overall sorting algorithm becomes an O(N^2) algorithm. That is considerably slower than the O(N log N) behavior that we expect for a merge sort algorithm.

The authors made this mistake because C and C++ don't auto-initialize arrays. That means that their code ran fast in those languages, and when they tested their code they found that it behaved as expected. They apparently translated their code into Java without retesting whether it was fast. More than one textbook author has made this mistake, but out of respect for our fellow authors (and recognizing that we make mistakes ourselves), we won't name any names!

Chapter Summary

Searching is the task of attempting to find a particular target value in a collection or array.

Sorting is the task of arranging the elements of a list or array into a natural ordering.

Java's class libraries contain several methods for searching and sorting arrays and lists, such as `Arrays.binarySearch` and `Collections.sort`.

A `Comparator` object describes a customized way to compare objects, enabling arrays or lists of these objects to be searched and sorted in many orders.

Empirical analysis is the technique of running a program or algorithm to determine its runtime. Algorithm analysis is the technique of examining an algorithm's code or pseudocode to make inferences about its complexity.

Algorithms are grouped into complexity classes, which are often described using big-Oh notation such as $O(N)$ for a linear algorithm.

Sequential search is an $O(N)$ searching algorithm that looks at every element of a list until it finds the target value.

Binary search is an $O(\log N)$ searching algorithm that operates on a sorted dataset and successively eliminates half of the data until it finds the target element.

Selection sort is an $O(N^2)$ sorting algorithm that repeatedly finds the smallest unprocessed element of the array and moves it to the frontmost remaining slot of the array.

Merge sort is an $O(N \log N)$ sorting algorithm, often implemented recursively, that successively divides the input dataset into two halves, recursively sorts the halves, and then merges the sorted halves into a sorted whole.

Self-Check Problems

Section 13.1: Searching and Sorting in the Java Class Libraries

1. Describe two ways to search an unsorted array of `String` objects using the Java class libraries.
2. If you perform a binary search on an array of one million integers, which of the following is closest to the number of elements that the search algorithm will need to examine?
   a. all 1,000,000 of the integers
   b. roughly 3/4 (750,000) of the integers
   c. roughly half (500,000) of the integers
   d. roughly 1/10 (100,000)
   e. less than 1% (10,000 or fewer)
3. Should you use a sequential or binary search on an array of `Point` objects, and why?
4. Under what circumstances can the `Arrays.binarySearch` and `Collections.binarySearch` methods be used successfully?
5. In what order does the `Collections.sort` method arrange a list of strings? How could you arrange them into a different order?

6. Why wouldn't the `Collections.sort` method work when used on a list of `Point` objects? How can you make it so that the sort method can be used on `Points` or any other type of objects?

7. The following `Comparator` class is attempting to arrange `BankAccount` objects by account name, breaking ties by account balance. But the code has some syntax errors and some logic errors. What is wrong with the code? How would you correct it?

```
import java.util.*;
public class AccountComparator extends Comparator {
    public int compareTo(BankAccount account2) {
        if (!this.getName().equals(account2.getName())) {
            return this.getName().compareTo(account2.getName());
        } else {
            return this.getBalance() - account2.getBalance();
        }
    }
}
```

8. In this section, we wrote a `LengthComparator` that would allow a list or array of strings to be sorted in ascending order by length. How could we easily sort the collection in descending order by length, from longest to shortest, without modifying the code of `LengthComparator`?

Section 13.2: Program Complexity

9. Approximate the runtime of the following code fragment, in terms of *n*:

```
int sum = 0;
int j = 1;
while (j <= n) {
    sum++;
    j = j * 2;
}
```

10. Approximate the runtime of the following code fragment, in terms of *n*:

```
int sum = 0;
for (int j = 1; j < n; j++) {
    sum++;
    if (j % 2 == 0) {
        sum++;
    }
}
```

11. Approximate the runtime of the following code fragment, in terms of *n*:

```
int sum = 0;
for (int i = 1; i <= n * 2; i++) {
    for (int j = 1; j <= n; j++) {
        sum++;
    }
}
```

```
for (int j = 1; j < 100; j++) {
    sum++;
    sum++;
}
```

12. Approximate the runtime of the following code fragment, in terms of n:

```
int sum = 0;
for (int i = 1; i <= n; i++) {
    for (int j = 1; j <= i; j += 2) {
        sum += 4;
    }
}
for (int k = -50; k <= -1; k++) {
    sum--;
}
```

13. Approximate the runtime of the following code fragment, in terms of n:

```
int sum = 0;
for (int i = 1; i <= n; i++) {
    for (int j = 1; j <= 1000000; j++) {
        sum += 10;
    }
}
sum += 9999;
```

14. Determine the complexity classes of the algorithms that could be used to perform the following tasks:

   a. Finding the average of the numbers in an array of integers
   b. Finding the closest distance between any pair of points in an array of `Points`
   c. Finding the maximum value in an array of real numbers
   d. Counting the median length of the `Strings` in an array
   e. Raising an integer to a power—for example, A^B
   f. Examining an array of `Points` to see how many trios of points are colinear—that is, how many groups of three points could be connected by a straight line
   g. Counting the number of lines in a file
   h. Determining whether a given integer representing a year stores a leap year (a year divisible by 4, but not divisible by 100 unless also divisible by 400)

15. Suppose an algorithm takes exactly the given number of statements for each value below, in terms of an input size N. Give a tight big-Oh bound for each algorithm, representing the closest complexity class for that algorithm based on that runtime.

   a. $\frac{1}{2} N \log N + \log N$
   b. $N^2 - (N + N \log N + 1000)$
   c. $N^2 \log N + 2N$
   d. $\frac{1}{2} (3N + 5 + N)$
   e. $(2N + 5 + N^4) / N$

f. $\log(2^N)$

g. $N! + 2N$

Section 13.3: Implementing Searching and Sorting Algorithms

16. What is the runtime complexity class of a sequential search on an unsorted array? What is the runtime complexity class of the modified sequential search on a sorted array?

17. Why does the binary search algorithm require the input to be sorted?

18. How many elements (at most) does a binary search examine if the array contains 60 elements?

19. What indexes will be examined as the middle element by a binary search for the target value `8` when the search is run on the following input arrays? What value will the binary search algorithm return?

a. `int[] numbers = {1, 3, 6, 7, 8, 10, 15, 20, 30};`

b. `int[] numbers = {1, 2, 3, 4, 5, 7, 8, 9, 10};`

c. `int[] numbers = {1, 2, 3, 4, 5, 6, 7, 8, 9};`

d. `int[] numbers = {8, 9, 12, 14, 15, 17, 19, 25, 31};`

20. What indexes will be examined as the middle element by a binary search for the target value `8` when the search is run on the following input array? Notice that the input array isn't in sorted order. What can you say about the binary search algorithm's result?

```
int[] numbers = {6, 5, 8, 19, 7, 35, 22, 11, 9};
```

21. Consider the following sorted array of integers. When a binary search is performed on this array for each of the following integer values, what indexes are examined in order? What result value is returned?

```
// index             0   1   2   3   4   5   6   7   8   9  10  11  12  13  14
int[] numbers = {-1,  3,  5,  8, 15, 18, 22, 39, 40, 42, 50, 57, 71, 73, 74};
```

a. `42`

b. `11`

c. `74`

d. `30`

22. Consider the following sorted array of integers. When a binary search is performed on this array for each of the following integer values, what indexes are examined in order? What result value is returned?

```
// index              0   1   2   3   4   5   6   7   8   9  10  11  12  13
int[] numbers = {-30, -9, -6, -4, -2, -1,  0,  2,  4, 10, 12, 17, 22, 30};
```

a. `-5`

b. `0`

c. `11`

d. `-100`

23. What modifications would you have to make to the `selectionSort` method to cause it to sort an array of `double` values rather than one of integer values?

24. Consider the following array:

```
int[] numbers = {29, 17, 3, 94, 46, 8, -4, 12};
```

After a single pass of the selection sort algorithm (a single swap), what would be the state of the array?

a. `{-4, 29, 17, 3, 94, 46, 8, 12}`
b. `{29, 17, 3, 94, 46, 8, 12}`
c. `{-4, 29, 17, 3, 94, 46, 8, -4, 12}`
d. `{-4, 17, 3, 94, 46, 8, 29, 12}`
e. `{3, 17, 29, 94, -4, 8, 46, 12}`

25. Trace the execution of the selection sort algorithm as shown in this section when run on the following input arrays. Show each element that will be selected by the algorithm and where it will be moved, until the array is fully sorted.

a. `{29, 17, 3, 94, 46, 8, -4, 12}`
b. `{33, 14, 3, 95, 47, 9, -42, 13}`
c. `{7, 1, 6, 12, -3, 8, 4, 21, 2, 30, -1, 9}`
d. `{6, 7, 4, 8, 11, 1, 10, 3, 5, 9}`

Section 13.4: Case Study: Implementing Merge Sort

26. How many calls on the `mergeSort` method are generated by a call to sort a list of length 32?

27. Consider the following array of `int` elements:

```
int[] numbers = {7, 2, 8, 4, 1, 11, 9, 5, 3, 10};
```

a. Show the state of the elements after five passes of the outermost loop of selection sort have occurred.
b. Show a trace that is two levels deep of the merge sort algorithm. Show the splitting of the overall array, plus one level of the recursive calls.

28. Consider the following array of `int` elements:

```
int[] numbers = {7, 1, 6, 12, -3, 8, 4, 21, 2, 30, -1, 9};
```

a. Show the state of the elements after five passes of the outermost loop of selection sort have occurred.
b. Show a trace that is two levels deep of the merge sort algorithm. Show the splitting of the overall array, plus one level of the recursive calls.

29. Which one of the following statements about sorting and big-Oh is true?

a. Selection sort can sort an array of integers in $O(N)$ time.
b. Merge sort achieves an $O(N \log N)$ runtime by dividing the array in half at each step and then recursively sorting and merging the halves back together.
c. Merge sort runs faster than selection sort because it is recursive, and recursion is faster than loops.
d. Selection sort runs in $O(N)$ time if the array is already sorted to begin with, or $O(N^2)$ if it is not.
e. Sorting algorithms that rely on comparing elements can only be used with type `int`, because values from other types of data cannot be compared to each other.

30. Trace the complete execution of the merge sort algorithm when called on each array below. Show the sub-arrays that are created by the algorithm and show the merging of sub-arrays into larger sorted arrays.

a. `{29, 17, 3, 94, 46, 8, -4, 12}`
b. `{6, 5, 3, 7, 1, 8, 4, 2}`
c. `{33, 14, 3, 95, 47, 9, -42, 13}`

Exercises

1. Suppose the following array has been declared:

```
// index          0  1   2   3   4   5   6   7   8    9
int[] list = {-2, 8, 13, 22, 25, 25, 38, 42, 51, 103};
```

What indexes will be examined as the middle element by a binary search for each of the following target values? What value will be returned?

a. `103`
b. `30`
c. `8`
d. `-1`

2. Suppose the following array has been declared:

```
// index             0   1   2   3   4   5   6   7   8   9  10  11
int[] numbers = {-1,  3,  5,  8, 15, 18, 22, 39, 40, 42, 50, 57};
```

What indexes will be examined as the middle element by a binary search for each of the following target values? What value will be returned?

a. `13`
b. `39`
c. `50`
d. `2`

3. Suppose the following array has been declared:

```
// index             0   1   2   3   4   5   6   7   8   9  10  11  12  13   14
int[] numbers = {0,  0,  5, 10, 15, 40, 55, 60, 65, 70, 80, 85, 90, 95, 300};
```

What indexes will be examined as the middle element by a binary search for each of the following target values? What value will be returned?

a. `65`
b. `9`
c. `90`
d. `147`

4. To which complexity class does the following algorithm belong? Consider N to be the length or size of the array or collection passed to the method. Explain your reasoning.

```
public static int[] mystery1(int[] list) {
    int[] result = new int[2 * list.length];
    for (int i = 0; i < list.length; i++) {
        result[2 * i] = list[i] / 2 + list[i] % 2;
        result[2 * i + 1] = list[i] / 2;
    }
```

```
    return result;
}
```

5. To which complexity class does the following algorithm belong?

```
public static void mystery2(int[] list) {
    for (int i = 0; i < list.length / 2; i++) {
        int j = list.length - 1 - i;
        int temp = list[i];
        list[i] = list[j];
        list[j] = temp;
    }
}
```

6. To which complexity class does the following algorithm belong?

```
public static void mystery3(List<String> list) {
    for (int i = 0; i < list.size() - 1; i += 2) {
        String first = list.remove(i);
        list.add(i + 1, first);
    }
}
```

7. To which complexity class does the following algorithm belong?

```
public static void mystery4(List<String> list) {
    for (int i = 0; i < list.size() - 1; i += 2) {
        String first = list.get(i);
        list.set(i, list.get(i + 1));
        list.set(i + 1, first);
    }
}
```

8. Write the state of the elements of each of the following arrays after each pass of the outermost loop of the selection sort algorithm has occurred (after each element is selected and moved into place).

```
int[] numbers1 = {63, 9, 45, 72, 27, 18, 54, 36};
int[] numbers2 = {37, 29, 19, 48, 23, 55, 74, 12};
```

9. Using the same arrays from the previous problem, trace the complete execution of the merge sort algorithm when called on each array. Show the subarrays that are created by the algorithm and show the merging of subarrays into larger sorted arrays.

10. Write the state of the elements of each of the following arrays after each pass of the outermost loop of the selection sort algorithm has occurred (after each element is selected and moved into place).

```
int[] numbers3 = {8, 5, -9, 14, 0, -1, -7, 3};
int[] numbers4 = {15, 56, 24, 5, 39, -4, 27, 10};
```

11. Using the same arrays from the previous problem, trace the complete execution of the merge sort algorithm when called on each array. Show the subarrays that are created by the algorithm and show the merging of subarrays into larger sorted arrays.

12. Write the state of the elements of each of the following arrays after each pass of the outermost loop of the selection sort algorithm has occurred (after each element is selected and moved into place).

```
int[] numbers5 = {22, 44, 11, 88, 66, 33, 55, 77};
int[] numbers6 = {-3, -6, -1, -5, 0, -2, -4, -7};
```

13. Using the same arrays from the previous problem, trace the complete execution of the merge sort algorithm when called on each array. Show the subarrays that are created by the algorithm and show the merging of subarrays into larger sorted arrays.

14. Write code to read a dictionary from a file, then prompt the user for two words and tell the user how many words in the dictionary fall between those two words. Here is a sample run of the program:

```
Type two words: goodbye hello
There are 4418 words between goodbye and hello
```

Use the binary search algorithm in your solution.

15. Write a `Comparator` that compares `Point` objects by their distance from the origin of (0, 0). Points that are closer to the origin are considered to come before those which are further from the origin.

16. Write a `Comparator` that compares `String` objects by the number of words they contain. Consider any nonwhitespace string of characters to be a word. For example, "hello" comes before "I see", which comes before "You can do it".

17. Write a `Comparator` that compares `String` objects of a particular format. Each string is of a form such as `"123456 Seattle, WA"`, beginning with a numeric token that is followed by additional text tokens. Your job is to treat the first tokens as integers and compare them in numerical order. You cannot simply compare them by using the strings' `compareTo` method, since it would treat the numbers as text and not as integers. For example, `"276453 Helena, MT"` is greater than `"9847 New York, NY"`. Use a `Scanner` to tokenize the strings while comparing them.

18. Write a modified version of the selection sort algorithm that selects the largest element each time and moves it to the end of the array, rather than selecting the smallest element and moving it to the beginning. Will this algorithm be faster than the standard selection sort? What will its complexity class (big-Oh) be?

19. Write a modified "dual" version of the selection sort algorithm that selects both the largest and smallest elements on each pass and moves each of them to the appropriate end of the array. Will this algorithm be faster than the standard selection sort? What predictions would you make about its performance relative to the merge sort algorithm? What will its complexity class (big-Oh) be?

20. Implement an algorithm to shuffle an array of numbers or objects. The algorithm for shuffling should be the following:

```
for (each index i) {
    choose a random index j where j >= i.
    swap the elements at indexes i and j.
}
```

(The constraint about `j` being greater than or equal to `i` is actually quite important, if you want your shuffling algorithm to shuffle fairly. Why?)

21. Implement a "bogus" sorting algorithm called *bogo sort* that uses your shuffling algorithm from the previous exercise to sort an array of numbers. The bogo sort algorithm is the following:

```
while (array is not sorted) {
    shuffle array.
}
```

Obviously, this is not a very efficient sorting algorithm, but it eventually does shuffle the array into order if you let it run long enough. Try running it on a very small array, such as 8 or 10 elements, to examine its runtime. What is your best guess about the complexity class (big-Oh) of this silly algorithm?

Programming Projects

1. Write a program that reads a series of input lines and sorts them into alphabetical order, ignoring the case of words. The program should use the merge sort algorithm so that it efficiently sorts even a large file.

2. Perform a "Sort Detective" challenge to run several sorting algorithms without knowing which is which. Try to figure out which sorting algorithm is which on the basis of the runtime and characteristics of each algorithm. Search the web for "sort detective" for more ideas on such a project.

3. Write a program that processes a data file of students' course grade data. The data arrive in random order; each line stores information about a student's last name, first name, student ID number, grade as a percentage, and letter grade. For example, here are a few lines of data:

```
Smith      Kelly    438975    98.6    A
Johnson    Gus      210498    72.4    C
Reges      Stu      098736    88.2    B
Smith      Marty    346282    84.1    B
Reges      Abe      298575    78.3    C
```

Your program should be able to sort the data by any of the columns. Use `Comparators` to achieve the sort orderings. Make the data sortable by last name, student ID, and grade percentage in ascending and descending order. For example, here are the lines of student data sorted a few different ways:

```
Student data, by last name:
Johnson    Gus      210498    72.4    C
Reges      Stu      098736    88.2    B
Reges      Abe      298575    78.3    C
Smith      Kelly    438975    98.6    A
Smith      Marty    346282    84.1    B

Student data, by student ID:
Reges      Stu      098736    88.2    B
Johnson    Gus      210498    72.4    C
Reges      Abe      298575    78.3    C
Smith      Marty    346282    84.1    B
Smith      Kelly    438975    98.6    A
```

4. Write a program that discovers all anagrams of all words listed in an input file that stores the entries in a large dictionary. An anagram of a word is a rearrangement of its letters into a new legal word. For example, the anagrams of "share" include "shear", "hears", and "hares". Assume that you have a file available to you that lists many words, one per line. Your program should first read in the dictionary file and sort it, but instead of sorting in alphabetical order it should sort according to each word's canonical form. The canonical form of a word contains the same letters as the original, but in sorted order. Thus, the canonical form of "computer" is "cemoprtu", and the canonical form of "program" is "agmoprr". When your dictionary file is sorted, the word "program" would be placed before the word "computer", because its canonical form comes first in alphabetical order. Write code to retrieve a word's canonical form and a `Comparator` that compares words by using their canonical forms.

Chapter 14

Stacks and Queues

Introduction

In Chapter 11, we saw that the Java Collections Framework incorporates the idea of an abstract data type (ADT) with interfaces defined for the most fundamental ADTs and a variety of implementations for each. In this chapter we are going to explore two of the most fundamental ADTs in computer science, called *stacks* and *queues*. They are so simple that they almost seem not worth studying. They are like the programming equivalent of drawers and shelves. Drawers and shelves are very simple and, therefore, sort of boring, and yet we find uses for them everywhere we turn.

It is useful to study stacks and queues as a way to understand a minimal kind of data structure. We'll find, for example, that they are less powerful than the list structures we have been looking at. But we often find ourselves wanting to think in terms of the simplest possible solution to a problem, as in "Could you solve that with just a stack?" They are also part of the basic culture of computer science, so you will find it helpful to practice using these primitive structures and learning the terminology associated with each.

14.1 Stack/Queue Basics

Like a list, a stack or queue stores an ordered sequence of values. A minimal set of operations for such a structure would require at least:

- some way to put values into the structure (an "add" operation)
- a way to take values out (a "remove" operation)
- a way to test whether there is anything left in the structure (is the structure empty?)

These three operations are the bare bones that you'd need for such a structure and in their purest form, stacks and queues have just these three operations. Java's version of these also includes a `size` method that lets you ask for the number of elements in the structure and a `peek` method that lets you examine the next value to be removed without actually removing the value.

Stacks and queues are similar in that they each store a sequence of values in a particular order. Stacks are LIFO structures (Last-In, First-Out), meaning that the most recently inserted element is the one that can be accessed first. Queues are FIFO structures (First-In, First-Out), meaning that the first inserted element is the one that can be accessed first.

Stack	Queue
Last	First
In	In
First	First
Out	Out

Stack Concepts

With a stack, all of the action occurs at one end of the structure that we refer to as the top of the stack, as shown in Figure 14.1. The adding operation is called a *push* and the removing operation is called a *pop*. We push values onto the top and we pop them off the top. A good analogy for stacks is to think of a cafeteria and how trays are stacked up for the customers. When you go to get a tray, you take the one on the top of the stack. You don't bother to try to get the one on the bottom, because you'd have to move a lot of trays to get to it. Similarly, if someone brings clean trays to add to the stack, they are added on the top rather than on the bottom. The result is that stacks tend to reverse things. Each new value goes to the top of the stack, and when we take them values back out, we draw from the top, so they come back out in reverse order.

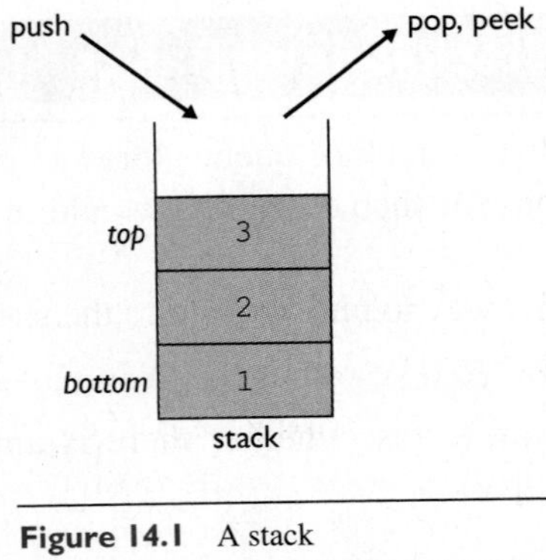

Figure 14.1 A stack

There are also methods for testing whether the stack is empty, requesting the current size of the stack, and peeking at the next value to be removed. The basic operations for the `Stack` class are listed in Table 14.1.

Table 14.1 Useful Methods of the `Stack` Class

Method	Description
`push(value)`	Pushes the given value onto the top of the stack
`pop()`	Removes and returns the value at the top of the stack
`isEmpty()`	Returns `true` if this stack contains no values
`peek()`	Returns the value at the top of the stack without removing it
`size()`	Returns the number of values in the stack

Stacks are generic structures like the other collections we have seen, so it is really `Stack<E>`, where `E` is filled in with some type. The `Stack` class is one of the oldest classes in the Java Collections Framework. It was included with the original release of Java. As a result, it was not designed as well as the later ADTs in the framework. In particular, there is no separate interface that specifies the ADT. Instead, it extends a class called `Vector`, which is an early version of the `ArrayList` class. Because of this inheritance relationship, you can treat the stack like a list. For example, you can add and remove values in the middle.

> **Stack**
>
> An ordered collection that allows adding and removing the "top" element, providing Last-In, First-Out (LIFO) access.

Even though it is badly designed, we think it is important to use the built-in version of this class. We highly recommend that you restrict yourself to the stack-like methods of Table 14.1 and not use other methods that would allow you to treat the stack like a list. The following `StackExample` is a complete program that shows basic manipulations of a stack.

```
// A program that demonstrates basic stack operations.

import java.util.*;

public class StackExample {
    public static void main(String[] args) {
        String[] data = {"to", "be", "or", "not", "to", "be"};
        Stack<String> s = new Stack<String>();

        for (String str : data) {
            s.push(str);
        }

        System.out.println("stack = " + s);
        System.out.println("size  = " + s.size());
        System.out.println("peek  = " + s.peek());
        while (!s.isEmpty()) {
            System.out.print(s.pop() + " ");
        }
        System.out.println();
    }
}
```

It produces the following output:

```
stack = [to, be, or, not, to, be]
size = 6
peek = be
be to not or be to
```

You can see from the first line of output that the `Stack` class has a `toString` method that formats the contents the same way a list is formatted. The first value listed inside brackets is the value at the bottom of the stack.

The second line of output uses the `size` method to report that there are 6 values in the stack. The third line of output uses the `peek` method to report that the top of the stack is `"be"`. Keep in mind that this peeking operation does not change the stack. The final line of output shows the sequence of values obtained by popping the stack until it becomes empty. Notice that the values come out in reverse order relative to the order in which they were added.

Queue Concepts

For a queue we manipulate both ends of the structure, adding new values at the back of the queue and removing values from the front, as shown in Figure 14.2. Queues have the same basic operations that stacks have, but they have different names. The adding and removing operations are simply called add and remove, although sometimes we use the more formal terms *enqueueing* and *dequeueing* to describe these.

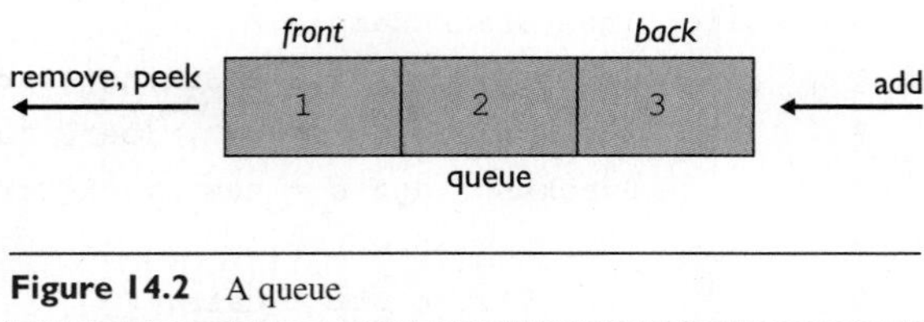

Figure 14.2 A queue

A good analogy for queues is to think about standing in line at the grocery store. As new people arrive, they are told to go to the back of the line. When the store is ready to help another customer, the person at the front of the line is helped. In fact, the British use the word "queue" the way Americans use the word "line," telling people to "queue up" or to "go to the back of the queue." Table 14.2 includes the five fundamental operations we will use for manipulating queues.

Table 14.2 Useful Methods of the `Queue` Interface

Method	Description
`add(value)`	Adds the given value at the back of the queue
`remove()`	Removes and returns the value at the front of the queue
`isEmpty()`	Returns `true` if this queue contains no values
`peek()`	Returns the value at the front of the queue without removing it
`size()`	Returns the number of values in the queue

Queues were added to the Java Collections Framework later and they were properly designed. There is a separate `Queue<E>` interface that describes the ADT and various implementations. We will use the `LinkedList<E>` implementation for all of the queues that we construct.

> **Queue**
>
> An ordered collection that allows adding the "back" element and removing the "front" element, providing First-In, First-Out (FIFO) access.

The following `QueueExample` is a simple client program that uses an array of `String` data to initialize and manipulate a queue. The program's output is similar to the earlier `StackExample` program, except for the order in which the elements are printed.

```
// A program that demonstrates basic queue operations.

import java.util.*;

public class QueueExample {
    public static void main(String[] args) {
        String[] data = {"to", "be", "or", "not", "to", "be"};
        Queue<String> q = new LinkedList<String>();

        for (String str : data) {
            q.add(str);
        }

        System.out.println("queue = " + q);
        System.out.println("size  = " + q.size());
        System.out.println("peek  = " + q.peek());
        while (!q.isEmpty()) {
            System.out.print(q.remove() + " ");
        }
        System.out.println();
    }
}
```

The queue example produces the following output:

```
queue = [to, be, or, not, to, be]
size = 6
peek = to
to be or not to be
```

In the first line of output you can see that the first value inside brackets is the value at the front of the queue. That is why the `peek` method returns `"to"`. And notice that the final line of output lists the values in the same order in which they were added to the structure.

14.2 Common Stack/Queue Operations

VideoNote

In this section we will become more familiar with stacks and queues by writing some client code for manipulating stacks and queues of `int` values. Recall that we have to use the `Integer` wrapper class to do so by constructing values of type

`Stack<Integer>` and `Queue<Integer>`. Let's write some code that would add 10 random values between 0 and 99 to a queue using a `Random` object:

```
Queue<Integer> q = new LinkedList<Integer>();
Random r = new Random();
for (int i = 0; i < 10; i++) {
    q.add(r.nextInt(100));
}
System.out.println("q = " + q);
```

Notice that our variable is of type `Queue<Integer>` (using the interface). We only use the name of the implementation (`LinkedList`) when we are constructing a new object with the `new` keyword. All variables, parameters, and return types should be defined using the interface.

This produces output like the following:

```
q = [25, 19, 83, 0, 70, 52, 76, 33, 81, 54]
```

We can put this code for generating a queue with random values into a method. It's helpful to have a `size` parameter indicating how many values to add to the queue. The return type for the method should be `Queue<Integer>`:

```
public static Queue<Integer> makeRandomQueue(int size) {
    Queue<Integer> q = new LinkedList<Integer>();
    Random r = new Random();
    for (int i = 0; i < size; i++) {
        q.add(r.nextInt(100));
    }
    return q;
}
```

We can change our client code to call this method and print the result:

```
Queue<Integer> q = makeRandomQueue(10);
System.out.println("q = " + q);
```

We can create a variation of `makeRandomQueue` called `makeRandomStack` for making a stack of random values. This is a fairly straightforward modification where we simply switch queue operations with stack operations:

```
public static Stack<Integer> makeRandomStack(int size) {
    Random r = new Random();
    Stack<Integer> s = new Stack<Integer>();
    for (int i = 0; i < size; i++) {
        s.push(r.nextInt(100));
    }
    return s;
}
```

Transferring Between Stacks and Queues

Consider the task of writing a method to transfer all values from a queue to a stack. We would need a loop that will remove values from the queue as long as there are more values left to remove. We can accomplish this with a `while` loop and the `isEmpty` and `remove` methods:

```
public static void queueToStack(Queue<Integer> q, Stack<Integer> s) {
    while (!q.isEmpty()) {
        int n = q.remove();
        ...
    }
}
```

Notice that the parameters are of type `Queue<Integer>` and `Stack<Integer>`.

This code removes values from the queue, but to add them to the stack, we have to include a call on `push` inside the loop. The following is an incorrect attempt:

```
public static void queueToStack(Queue<Integer> q, Stack<Integer> s) {
    while (!q.isEmpty()) {
        int n = q.remove();
        s.push(q.remove());
    }
}
```

The problem with this version is that it calls `remove` twice each time through the loop. It should be calling `push` with the value of `n`:

```
public static void queueToStack(Queue<Integer> q, Stack<Integer> s) {
    while (!q.isEmpty()) {
        int n = q.remove();
        s.push(n);
    }
}
```

We could eliminate the line that involves `n` altogether and have just the second line of code:

```
s.push(q.remove());
```

The following client code reports what was in the stack and queue after calling `queueToStack`:

```
Queue<Integer> q = makeRandomQueue(10);
Stack<Integer> s = new Stack<Integer>();
System.out.println("queue = " + q);
```

```
System.out.println("stack = " + s);
queueToStack(q, s);
System.out.println("after queueToStack:");
System.out.println("queue = " + q);
System.out.println("stack = " + s);
```

It produces output like the following:

```
queue = [75, 76, 53, 82, 88, 77, 63, 28, 86, 7]
stack = []
after queueToStack:
queue = []
stack = [75, 76, 53, 82, 88, 77, 63, 28, 86, 7]
```

We can write a similar method stackToQueue:

```
public static void stackToQueue(Stack<Integer> s, Queue<Integer> q) {
    while (!s.isEmpty()) {
        int n = s.pop();
        q.add(n);
    }
}
```

Sum of a Queue

How would we write a method to find the sum of the values in a queue? It is a cumulative sum task, which involves initializing a sum variable to 0 outside the loop and then adding each value to the sum as we progress through the loop. A first attempt might look like this:

```
public static int sum(Queue<Integer> q) {
    int sum = 0;
    while (!q.isEmpty()) {
        int n = q.remove();
        sum += n;
    }
    return sum;
}
```

If you call this version of the method and print the queue afterward, you'll find that the queue is empty. As a side effect of calculating the sum, we are destroying the contents of the queue. This is generally not acceptable behavior.

So how do we examine each of the queue elements while preserving the state of the structure? You could ask the queue for an iterator or use a for-each loop to get each value from the structure, but we are interested in understanding the queue in its most basic form, so we aren't going to use either iterators or for-each loops when working with stacks and queues.

The only other way to find out what is in a queue is to remove each of the values. We just need to find a way to do that while restoring the queue to its original form when we are done. One solution is to use a second queue as auxiliary storage:

```
// Improved version that uses auxiliary queue for storage
// so that it does not destroy the queue passed in.
public static int sum(Queue<Integer> q) {
    int sum = 0;
    Queue<Integer> temp = new LinkedList<Integer>();
    while (!q.isEmpty()) {
        int n = q.remove();
        sum += n;
        temp.add(n);
    }

    while (!temp.isEmpty()) {     // restore the queue
        q.add(temp.remove());
    }

    return sum;
}
```

This approach works, but there is an easier way. Why not use the original queue itself? As we remove values to be processed, we can add them back into the queue at the end. Think of it as cycling through values where the value at the front goes to the back.

Of course, then the queue never becomes empty. So instead of a `while` loop looking for an empty queue, we would write a `for` loop using the size of the queue:

```
// Best version that re-adds elements to the queue passed in
// so that it does not destroy the contents of the queue.
public static int sum(Queue<Integer> q) {
    int sum = 0;
    for (int i = 0; i < q.size(); i++) {
        int n = q.remove();
        sum += n;
        q.add(n);
    }
    return sum;
}
```

Sum of a Stack

Now let's write a `sum` method for stacks:

```
public static int sum(Stack<Integer> s) {
    ...
}
```

This method can also be called `sum` because the two methods have different signatures. Remember that a signature of a method is its name plus its parameters. These are both called `sum` and they both have just a single parameter, but the parameter types are different, so this is okay.

So how do we write the `sum` method for stacks? We can start out by trying to simply substitute stack operations for queue operations:

```
public static int sum(Stack<Integer> s) {
    int sum = 0;
    for (int i = 0; i < s.size(); i++) {
        int n = s.pop();
        sum += n;
        s.push(n);
    }
    return sum;
}
```

Unfortunately, this code doesn't work. We'd see output like this when we test it:

```
stack = [42, 19, 78, 87, 14, 41, 57, 25, 96, 85]
sum = 850
```

The sum of these numbers is not 850. We're getting that sum because the loop pops the value `85` off the stack 10 different times and then pushes it back onto the top of the stack. With a queue, values go in at one end and come out the other end. But with a stack, all the action is at one end of the structure (the top). So this approach isn't going to work.

In fact, you can't solve this in a simple way with just a stack. You'd need something extra like an auxiliary structure. Consider how we could solve it if we were allowed to use one queue available (and only one queue; no other auxiliary structures) as temporary storage. Then we can put things into the queue as we take them out of the stack and after we have computed the sum, we can transfer things from the queue back to the stack using our `queueToStack` method. Here is a second attempt:

```
public static int sum(Stack<Integer> s) {
    int sum = 0;
    Queue<Integer> q = new LinkedList<Integer>();
    for (int i = 0; i < s.size(); i++) {
        int n = s.pop();
        sum += n;
        q.add(n);
    }
    queueToStack(q, s);
    return sum;
}
```

This also doesn't work. Here is a sample execution:

```
initial stack = [32, 15, 54, 91, 47, 45, 88, 89, 13, 0]
sum = 235
after sum stack = [32, 15, 54, 91, 47, 0, 13, 89, 88, 45]
```

There are two problems here. Only half of the values were removed from the stack and those values now appear in reverse order. Why only half? We are using a `for` loop that compares a variable `i` against the size of the stack. The variable `i` is going up by 1 while the size is going down by 1 every time. The result is that halfway through the process, `i` is large enough relative to size to stop the loop. This is a case where we want a `while` loop instead of a `for` loop:

```
public static int sum(Stack<Integer> s) {
    int sum = 0;
    Queue<Integer> q = new LinkedList<Integer>();
    while (!s.isEmpty()) {
        int n = s.pop();
        sum += n;
        q.add(n);
    }
    queueToStack(q, s);
    return sum;
}
```

Even this is not correct. It finds the right sum, but it ends up reversing the values in the stack. If we could use a stack instead of a queue as auxiliary storage, then this problem would go away. In many of our sample problems, we purposely restrict you to a particular kind of structure so that you can practice working within constraints. It becomes almost a brain teaser to think of how to solve the problem with a given structure. A stack would be more convenient, but that doesn't mean that you have to use a stack to solve the problem.

The problem is that by transferring the data from the stack into the queue and then back into the stack, we have reversed the order. The fix is to do it again so that it goes back to the original order. So we add two extra calls at the end of the method that move values from the stack back into the queue and then from the queue back into the stack:

```
public static int sum(Stack<Integer> s) {
    int sum = 0;
    Queue<Integer> q = new LinkedList<Integer>();
    while (!s.isEmpty()) {
        int n = s.pop();
        sum += n;
        q.add(n);
    }
```

```
    queueToStack(q, s);
    stackToQueue(s, q);
    queueToStack(q, s);
    return sum;
}
```

This is not the most efficient way to solve the problem, but it demonstrates that it can be done with a queue.

14.3 Complex Stack/Queue Operations

VideoNote

In this section, we will examine two harder stack/queue problems that allow us to explore some of the issues and common bugs that come up when manipulating these structures.

Removing Values from a Queue

Consider the task of removing all occurrences of a certain value from a queue of integers. For example, suppose that a variable called `q` stores a reference to the following queue:

```
[18, 4, 7, 42, 9, 33, -8, 0, 14, 42, 7, 42, 42, 19]
```

and we make the following call:

```
removeAll(q, 42);
```

We would want the queue to store the following values after the call:

```
[18, 4, 7, 9, 33, -8, 0, 14, 7, 19]
```

This seems like a fairly straightforward task, but it leads to a subtle bug if we aren't careful. This task would be easier to solve if we could use a second queue. Then we could copy the values we want to keep from the first queue to the second and then copy them back when we are done. But this problem can be solved without an auxiliary data structure.

We saw that we can cycle through the elements of a queue by repeatedly removing the front value and then adding it back at the end of the queue. For example, the following loop cycles through the values in the queue exactly once:

```
for (int i = 0; i < q.size(); i++) {
    int n = q.remove();
    q.add(n);
}
```

As a first attempt, we could modify this loop so that it doesn't add the value back if it is the value we want to remove:

```
public static void removeAll(Queue<Integer> q, int value) {
    for (int i = 0; i < q.size(); i++) {
        int n = q.remove();
        if (n != value) {
            q.add(n);
        }
    }
}
```

This version doesn't work. For the sample queue, if we remove `42`, we end up with these values in the queue after the method finishes executing:

```
[42, 19, 18, 4, 7, 9, 33, −8, 0, 14, 7]
```

It's obvious that it didn't work because the queue now starts with a `42`. Even worse, the order of the elements has been damaged. The original queue started with the value `18`, which is now the third value in the queue. So it didn't finish the task and it has changed the order of the elements in the queue.

The problem is that our loop is using a counter to keep track of how many times to execute and it is comparing the counter against the size of the queue. But the size is changing. As we come across values to be removed, we skip them rather than adding them back into the queue, which makes the queue size go down by 1.

What happened in this specific case is that we came across two values of `42` that weren't added back in. That reduced the queue size by 2. As a result, the final two values from the original queue were never processed. That allowed a `42` to get past our filtering process, and it changed the order of the values in the queue because we didn't make a full pass through the data.

This is a subtle bug that can come up often when working with queues. You may think that you are making a complete cycle through the values when you are actually off by some amount that causes you to cycle either too little or too much.

In case the bug still isn't clear, let's look at a more extreme case. Suppose the queue consists entirely of six occurrences of the value `21`:

```
[21, 21, 21, 21, 21, 21]
```

If we call `removeAll` and pass this queue and the value `21`, the code should completely empty the queue. But the loop continues until the counter `i` reaches the queue's `size`. The algorithm goes through the following iterations:

```
[21, 21, 21, 21, 21, 21],  i = 0,  size() = 6
[21, 21, 21, 21, 21],      i = 1,  size() = 5
[21, 21, 21, 21],          i = 2,  size() = 4
[21, 21, 21],              i = 3,  size() = 3
```

After three loop iterations and elements removed, the value of `i` has reached the `size` value of `3`, so the loop stops executing. The problem is that the queue is shrinking, so the `size` method will return different values on different iterations of the loop. Regardless of how many elements are removed, we always want the loop to repeat once for each element in the original queue. So we need to store the initial size of the queue in a variable and use that to control the loop:

```
public static void removeAll(Queue<Integer> q, int value) {
    int oldSize = q.size();
    for (int i = 0; i < oldSize; i++) {
        int n = q.remove();
        if (n != value) {
            q.add(n);
        }
    }
}
```

This version works properly.

Comparing Two Stacks for Similarity

Consider the task of comparing two stacks of integers to see if they have the same pattern of parity (odd versus even). In other words, we want to test whether two stacks have even numbers and odd numbers in the same positions. To be considered equivalent, we will also require that the stacks have the same size. For example, suppose variables called `s1` and `s2` store these values:

```
[1, 2, 3, 4, 5, 7, 9, 11]
[13, 4, 17, 8, 1, 91, 81, 71]
```

We expect the call of `sameParityPattern(s1, s2)` to return `true` because both stacks store values with an (odd, even, odd, even, ...) parity pattern. To solve this problem, we will need an auxiliary data structure. It would be most convenient to have two auxiliary stacks, but suppose that we have been restricted to one auxiliary stack. The basic form of our method will be to set up our auxiliary stack and examine values until we find a solution. We can also add some code to make sure that the two stacks are of the same size. We can begin our solution with this code:

```
public static boolean sameParityPattern(Stack<Integer> s1,
                                        Stack<Integer> s2) {
    if (s1.size() != s2.size()) {
        return false;
    } else {
        Stack<Integer> s3 = new Stack<Integer>();
        ...
    }
}
```

Our task is to remove values from the two stacks and make sure they have the same parity. But we also have to be able to restore the two stacks to their original state. We have to use the third stack to store the values that we remove from the other two. If we find a pair of values that have different parity, then we would want to stop examining values. You might imagine writing code like the following:

```
while (!s1.isEmpty()) {
    int num1 = s1.pop();
    int num2 = s2.pop();
    if (num1 % 2 != num2 % 2) {
        return false;
    }
    s3.push(num1);
    s3.push(num2);
}
```

The preceding approach won't work. The code properly removes one value from each stack and stores the values into the third stack. But it returns from the method when it finds a difference. You have to be careful that you don't exit the method prematurely. Remember that we have to restore the stacks to their original state. So even though we know that we want to return `false`, we have to be careful to restore the stacks before we exit. We can accomplish this by introducing a `boolean` flag to keep track of whether we have seen a difference and stopping the loop when a difference has been encountered:

```
boolean same = true;
while (same && !s1.isEmpty()) {
    int num1 = s1.pop();
    int num2 = s2.pop();
    if (num1 % 2 != num2 % 2) {
        same = false;
    }
    s3.push(num1);
    s3.push(num2);
}
```

Now we need a loop that will restore the stacks to their original state. Our third stack has pairs of values that were originally in the other two stacks. We can repeatedly put each pair of values back to the appropriate stacks. In each pair, we first pushed a value from `s1` and then pushed a value from `s2`, so you might think that the correct loop to write is:

```
while (!s3.isEmpty()) {
    s1.push(s3.pop());
    s2.push(s3.pop());
}
```

The problem with this is that even though we pushed a value from `s1` and then a value from `s2`, they will come back out of the stack in the opposite order. So we need to reverse the order of the two lines inside our loop:

```
while (!s3.isEmpty()) {
    s2.push(s3.pop());
    s1.push(s3.pop());
}
```

This completes our method other than the return statement. Once we have restored the stacks, we can use our `boolean` flag to report whether or not the stacks had the same pattern. The following is a complete solution to the method:

```
public static boolean sameParityPattern(Stack<Integer> s1,
                                        Stack<Integer> s2) {
    if (s1.size() != s2.size()) {
        return false;
    } else {
        Stack<Integer> s3 = new Stack<Integer>();
        boolean same = true;
        while (same && !s1.isEmpty()) {
            int num1 = s1.pop();
            int num2 = s2.pop();
            if (num1 % 2 != num2 % 2) {
                same = false;
            }
            s3.push(num1);
            s3.push(num2);
        }
        while (!s3.isEmpty()) {
            s2.push(s3.pop());
            s1.push(s3.pop());
        }
        return same;
    }
}
```

14.4 Case Study: Expression Evaluator

In Chapter 12, we saw how to write a program that uses recursion to evaluate prefix expressions. We also saw that recursive solutions take advantage of the method call stack. But what if you didn't have recursion available to you? It turns out that many problems that are easily solved with recursion are also easily solved with a stack.

We are going to write a program that evaluates fully parenthesized arithmetic expressions using the standard operators for addition, subtraction, multiplication, and division, and a special operator for exponentiation ("^").

For example, if we wanted to evaluate this expression:

$$18.4 - \frac{2.3 \times 8.5}{19.5 + 2.7^{4.9}}$$

We would write it as a fully parenthesized expression as:

```
(18.4-((2.3*8.5)/(19.5+(2.7^4.9))))
```

We have conventions that allow us to leave out many of the parentheses in this expression, but it is very challenging to process such expressions because then we have to handle precedence issues. We will keep it simple by always requiring parentheses for every operator.

In the Chapter 12 case study, we assumed that spaces would be used to separate all of the individual tokens. That allowed us to use a `Scanner` for reading the tokens, but it can be very annoying to have to include spaces for each individual element. For example, the expression above would have to be rewritten as:

```
( 18.4 - ( ( 2.3 * 8.5 ) / ( 19.5 + ( 2.7 ^ 4.9 ) ) ) )
```

It turns out that separating a string like this into tokens leads to an interesting application for a queue. So we will write a more sophisticated version this time that allows you to have as little or as much spacing as you'd like.

We also should be careful to report most errors if the user leaves off parentheses or doesn't have them matched properly. This error checking is a nice complement to the other operations we will be performing to evaluate these expressions.

But we will avoid one thorny issue. We won't allow numbers to have a minus sign in front of them. So even though it makes sense to form an expression like this:

```
(-2.5/4.5)
```

We won't allow that minus sign in front of the `2.5`. Instead you'd have to form an expression like:

```
((0-2.5)/4.5)
```

Splitting into Tokens

We have seen that the `Scanner` class can be used to tokenize a string using whitespace, but we want to allow a user to leave out the whitespace and still have his or her input properly tokenized. We are going to build a supporting class called `StringSplitter` that will solve this fairly specialized task. It will behave somewhat like a `Scanner`, but it won't require whitespace to break apart the string.

We can use the standard method names from the `Scanner` class for getting a next token and asking if there is another token. We should also introduce a `peek` method that allows the client to ask about the next token without actually reading it. And we will need a constructor that takes the string to split as a parameter. So the public methods will be:

```
public StringSplitter(String line)
public boolean hasNext()
public String next()
public String peek()
```

This task is going to involve scanning through the letters of a string from beginning to end and returning to the client of the class the individual tokens that we find. Our class has to keep track of what has been read already and what it has left to read. It will also require a lot of peeking ahead to figure out how to separate the individual characters into tokens. For example, if the string is `"(2.3*4.8)"`, we will want to produce this sequence of tokens:

```
"(", "2.3", "*", "4.8", ")"
```

As we are reading a number like `2.3`, we will need to peek ahead to see what comes next so that we can recognize the end of the number.

It turns out that a queue is a great structure for solving this problem. It allows us to examine all of the characters from beginning to end and it keeps track of what we have already looked at and what we have left to look at. It also allows us to peek ahead.

The big difference between our splitter and a simple `Scanner` is that we need to recognize certain special characters as being tokens. If we encounter a parenthesis or one of the arithmetic operators, we have to make that a token whether or not it is surrounded by whitespace. It is best to include these special characters in a string constant for the class.

In terms of fields, since we are reading a character at a time, we will want a `Queue<Character>` to store the individual characters of the string and a field for storing the next token. Because we want to allow the client to peek ahead, we should have the field for the token always store the next token to be processed (that way we can allow the client to peek at it as much as he or she wants without actually reading anything).

We have to provide the client with a way to ask whether there is a next token to be processed. We could use an extra field for this, but we could also just set the token field to `null` when there are no tokens left to process.

Here is a basic outline of our class including our two fields, our special constant, and a constructor that adds the letters of the string to our queue of characters:

```
public class StringSplitter {
    private Queue<Character> characters;
    private String token;
```

```
    public static final String SPECIAL_CHARACTERS = "()+-*/^";

    public StringSplitter(String line) {
        characters = new LinkedList<Character>();
        for (int i = 0; i < line.length(); i++) {
            characters.add(line.charAt(i));
        }
        findNextToken();
    }

    ...
}
```

Notice that the constructor ends with a call on a method called `findNextToken`. The idea is that we want a private method that will process the queue and give an appropriate value to the field called `token`. Most of the work of writing this class is to write that method.

To write the `findNextToken` method, we have to consider all of the possible cases and make sure that we handle each one. We want to skip whitespace just as the `Scanner` does, so we will have to include code to do that. After skipping any leading whitespace, we would normally be ready to build up the next token. But we have to consider the case where we run out of characters, in which case there are no more tokens to produce. If we do have a token to produce, we'll have to remove characters one at a time from the queue and add them to the token that we are building up. The basic approach can be described with the following pseudocode:

```
skip whitespace.
if (nothing left) {
    token = null;
} else {
    initialize token to the next queue character.
    while (next queue character is part of this token) {
        token = token + (next character from the queue).
    }
}
```

To skip the leading whitespace, we can peek ahead in the queue to see if the next character is a whitespace character. We'll utilize a helpful static method from the `Character` wrapper class called `isWhitespace` that returns `true` if a given character is whitespace such as a space, tab, or line break. But we have to keep in mind we can't peek ahead when the queue is empty, so we have to include a special test for that as well:

```
while (!characters.isEmpty() &&
       Character.isWhitespace(characters.peek())) {
    characters.remove();
}
```

```
if (characters.isEmpty()) {
    token = null;
} else {
    ...
}
```

Now we need to write the code for building up a token character by character. We can initialize the token to the next character in the queue by saying:

```
token = "" + characters.remove();
```

Then we run into the problem of knowing how many more characters to include in this token. We have a set of special characters that are supposed to be one-character tokens, so if the token is any of those, then we need to stop adding characters to the token. We can use our string constant and a call on `contains` to handle that special case:

```
if (!SPECIAL_CHARACTERS.contains(token)) {
    ...
}
```

Now we need a loop that will append characters to the current token until it finds something that isn't part of the token. We would want to stop if we came across a whitespace character. But we would also want to stop if we came across any of the special characters. And we have an extra problem in that we might run out of characters completely if this is the last token to be processed.

The logic gets fairly complicated in this case, so it is helpful to introduce a `boolean` variable that keeps track of whether or not we are done:

```
boolean done = false;
while (!characters.isEmpty() && !done) {
    char ch = characters.peek();
    if (Character.isWhitespace(ch) ||
            SPECIAL_CHARACTERS.indexOf(ch) >= 0) {
        done = true;
    } else {
        token = token + characters.remove();
    }
}
```

This completes the private method for finding the next token. As mentioned earlier, the other parts of the class are fairly straightforward. The following is the complete class definition. Notice that the class has an extra private method called `checkToken` that throws a `NoSuchElementException` if the client calls the `peek` or `next` methods when there are no more tokens left.

```
// This class breaks up a string into a sequence of tokens using
// both whitespace and a list of special characters that are each
// considered tokens.  The special characters in this case are
// used to tokenize an arithmetic expression.  For example, the
// expression:
//      2*3.8/(4.95-7.8)
// would be tokenized as 2 * 3.8 / ( 4.95 - 7.8 ) even though it
// has no whitespace to separate these tokens.

import java.util.*;

public class StringSplitter {
    private Queue<Character> characters;
    private String token;

    public static final String SPECIAL_CHARACTERS = "()+-*/^";

    public StringSplitter(String line) {
        characters = new LinkedList<Character>();
        for (int i = 0; i < line.length(); i++) {
            characters.add(line.charAt(i));
        }
        findNextToken();
    }

    // post: Returns true if there is another token
    public boolean hasNext() {
        return token != null;
    }

    // pre : there is another token to return (throws
    //       NoSuchElementException if not)
    // post: returns and consumes the next token
    public String next() {
        checkToken();
        String result = token;
        findNextToken();
        return result;
    }

    // pre : there is another token to return (throws
    //       NoSuchElementException if not)
    // post: returns the next token without consuming it
    public String peek() {
```

```
        checkToken();
        return token;
    }

    // post: finds the next token, if any
    private void findNextToken() {
        while (!characters.isEmpty() &&
               Character.isWhitespace(characters.peek())) {
            characters.remove();
        }
        if (characters.isEmpty()) {
            token = null;
        } else {
            token = "" + characters.remove();
            if (!SPECIAL_CHARACTERS.contains(token)) {
                boolean done = false;
                while (!characters.isEmpty() && !done) {
                    char ch = characters.peek();
                    if (Character.isWhitespace(ch) ||
                        SPECIAL_CHARACTERS.indexOf(ch) >= 0) {
                        done = true;
                    } else {
                        token = token + characters.remove();
                    }
                }
            }
        }
    }

    // post: throws an exception if there is no token left
    private void checkToken() {
        if (!hasNext()) {
            throw new NoSuchElementException();
        }
    }
}
```

The Evaluator

Now that we have a support class that will allow us to read the tokens of a string, we can work on the code that will evaluate the tokens that we find in a fully parenthesized expression. We are going to implement a variation of a famous algorithm known as the shunting-yard algorithm that was invented by Edsger Dijkstra. It uses two stacks to save intermediate results. One stack stores numbers and the other stack stores symbols.

The basic idea is that we store values in the two stacks until we are ready to process them. As we see left parentheses and operators, we push them onto the symbol stack. As we see numbers, we push them onto the number stack. And when we see a right parenthesis, we know we have all of the information for a given sub-expression and we go ahead and evaluate it. We then push the result back onto the number stack.

Consider a simple case of evaluating `"(2+3)"`. Table 14.3 shows how the initially empty stacks have elements added to them until we encounter the right parenthesis, at which point we evaluate the sum and push the result onto the number stack.

Table 14.3 Evaluation of `"(2+3)"`

Token	Action	Symbol Stack	Number Stack
		`[]`	`[]`
`(`	Push onto symbol stack	`[(]`	`[]`
`2`	Push onto number stack	`[(]`	`[2.0]`
`+`	Push onto symbol stack	`[(, +]`	`[2.0]`
`3`	Push onto number stack	`[(, +]`	`[2.0, 3.0]`
`)`	Evaluate expression and push result onto number stack	`[]`	`[5.0]`

Notice that the overall value is the one and only value stored in the number stack when we are done and the symbol stack is empty when we are done. If there are other values left in either stack, then we know that we had an illegal expression.

This seems like a lot of work to do for a fairly simple computation. But remember that we can form complex sub-expressions that need to be evaluated as well. For example, what if the expression to evaluate had been `"((4/2)+(7−4))"`? This expression will have the same value because `(4/2)` evaluates to `2` and `(7−4)` evaluates to `3`. With the two stack approach, we can keep track of each part of this expression until we are ready to process it. Table 14.4 shows the evaluation of the more complex expression.

To write the code, we just have to implement the algorithm. It is easiest if we assume the input has no errors, but it's better to recognize errors when we can. We can't really recover from an error and it can get complex to report the nature of each error. So let's strike a middle ground of recognizing as many errors as we can, but giving just a simple error message if we encounter a mistake.

We know that we want to process tokens until we either encounter an error or run out of tokens. It is helpful to introduce a `boolean` flag that keeps track of whether an error has been seen. We expect to reach a point where the symbol stack is empty and the number stack has exactly one value in it. In that case, we could report that one number as the overall result. The basic structure of our solution is:

```
StringSplitter data = new StringSplitter(line);
Stack<String> symbols = new Stack<String>();
```

Table 14.4 Evaluation of "((4/2)+(7-4))"

Token	Action	Symbol Stack	Number Stack
		[]	[]
(	Push onto symbol stack	[(]	[]
(	Push onto symbol stack	[(, (]	[]
4	Push onto number stack	[(, (]	[4.0]
/	Push onto symbol stack	[(, (, /]	[4.0]
2	Push onto number stack	[(, (, /]	[4.0, 2.0]
)	Evaluate expression and push result onto number stack	[(]	[2.0]
+	Push onto symbol stack	[(, +]	[2.0]
(	Push onto symbol stack	[(, +, (]	[2.0]
7	Push onto number stack	[(, +, (]	[2.0, 7.0]
−	Push onto symbol stack	[(, +, (, −]	[2.0, 7.0]
4	Push onto number stack	[(, +, (, −]	[2.0, 7.0, 4.0]
)	Evaluate expression and push result onto number stack	[(, +]	[2.0, 3.0]
)	Evaluate expression and push result onto number stack	[]	[5.0]

```
Stack<Double> values = new Stack<Double>();
boolean error = false;
while (!error && data.hasNext()) {
    ...
}
if (error || values.size() != 1 || !symbols.isEmpty()) {
    System.out.println("illegal expression");
} else {
    System.out.println(values.pop());
}
```

Our remaining task is to fill in the body of the `while` loop for processing tokens. Two of the cases are relatively simple. When we see a left parenthesis or operator, we push it on the symbol stack. When we see a number, we push it on the number stack. The hard part is when we see a right parenthesis. The body of our `while` loop will look like this:

```
String next = data.next();
if (next.equals(")")) {
    // process )
} else if ("(+-*/^".contains(next)) {
    symbols.push(next);
```

```
} else {  // it should be a number
    values.push(Double.parseDouble(next));
}
```

Notice that in the final case we call the method `Double.parseDouble` to convert the token from a string into a `double`. As noted above, two out of three of these cases are simple. The third case is the hard one. How do we process a right parenthesis?

If an expression is legal, then we should have encountered a left parenthesis at the beginning of it and two numbers to work with and an operator to evaluate. So we expect that the symbol stack will have an operator on the top of the stack and a left parenthesis just below it. The two values should be on the number stack. In general we will remove the operator and left parenthesis, remove the two numbers, and then apply the operator. What makes this complicated is that there might be all sorts of errors. We have to be careful to check at every step that we have what we are supposed to have.

One thing we know is that the only values that are pushed onto the symbol stack are legal operators and left parentheses. We can use the stack sizes for several of our tests, but we have to make sure that we have an operator and not a left parenthesis and that below it on the stack is a left parenthesis. The following code checks for these errors and evaluates one operator, pushing the result back onto the numbers stack:

```
if (symbols.size() < 2 || symbols.peek().equals("(")) {
    error = true;
} else {
    String operator = symbols.pop();
    if (!symbols.peek().equals("(")) {
        error = true;
    } else {
        symbols.pop(); // to remove the "("
        double op2 = values.pop();
        double op1 = values.pop();
        double value = evaluate(operator, op1, op2);
        values.push(value);
    }
}
```

The code above involves a call on a method called `evaluate`. We wrote this method for the Chapter 12 case study. It takes an operator and two operands and returns the result of applying that operator to the two operands. Putting all of this together, we end up with the following complete program:

```
// This program prompts for fully parenthesized arithmetic
// expressions and it evalues each expression.  It uses two
// stacks to evaluate the expressions.

```

```
import java.util.*;

public class Evaluator {
    public static void main(String[] args) {
        System.out.println("This program evaluates fully");
        System.out.println("parenthesized expressions with the");
        System.out.println("operators +, -, *, /, and ^");
        System.out.println();
        Scanner console = new Scanner(System.in);
        System.out.print("expression (return to quit)? ");
        String line = console.nextLine().trim();
        while (line.length() > 0) {
            evaluate(line);
            System.out.print("expression (return to quit)? ");
            line = console.nextLine().trim();
        }
    }

    // pre : line contains a fully parenthesized expression
    // post: prints the value of the expression or an error
    //       message if the expression is not legal
    public static void evaluate(String line) {
        StringSplitter data = new StringSplitter(line);
        Stack<String> symbols = new Stack<String>();
        Stack<Double> values = new Stack<Double>();
        boolean error = false;
        while (!error && data.hasNext()) {
            String next = data.next();
            if (next.equals(")")) {
                if (symbols.size() < 2 ||
                    symbols.peek().equals("(")) {
                    error = true;
                } else {
                    String operator = symbols.pop();
                    if (!symbols.peek().equals("(")) {
                        error = true;
                    } else {
                        symbols.pop(); // to remove the "("
                        double op2 = values.pop();
                        double op1 = values.pop();
                        double value = evaluate(operator, op1, op2);
                        values.push(value);
                    }
                }
```

```
            } else if ("(+-*/^".contains(next)) {
                symbols.push(next);
            } else {  // it should be a number
                values.push(Double.parseDouble(next));
            }
        }
        if (error || values.size() != 1 || !symbols.isEmpty()) {
            System.out.println("illegal expression");
        } else {
            System.out.println(values.pop());
        }
    }

    // pre : operator is one of +, -, *, /, or ^
    // post: returns the result of applying the given operator to
    //       the given operands
    public static double evaluate(String operator, double operand1,
                                  double operand2) {
        if (operator.equals("+")) {
            return operand1 + operand2;
        } else if (operator.equals("-")) {
            return operand1 - operand2;
        } else if (operator.equals("*")) {
            return operand1 * operand2;
        } else if (operator.equals("/")) {
            return operand1 / operand2;
        } else if (operator.equals("^")) {
            return Math.pow(operand1, operand2);
        } else {
            throw new RuntimeException(
                "illegal operator " + operator);
        }
    }
}
```

Below is a sample log of execution:

```
This program evaluates fully
parenthesized expressions with the
operators +, -, *, /, and ^
expression (return to quit)? (2+3)
5.0
expression (return to quit)? ((4-2)+(7-4))
5.0
```

```
expression (return to quit)? (2+3–4)
illegal expression
expression (return to quit)? (19.4–3.8))
illegal expression
expression (return to quit)? ((7.5/(2.3^7.2))–(9.4–3.8))
–5.581352490199907
expression (return to quit)?
```

This program is fairly robust. The one bit of error checking it doesn't do is to handle illegal tokens. Any illegal tokens will be assumed to be numbers. The main token-processing loop includes a call on `Double.parseDouble` that will throw a `NumberFormatException` if it encounters such a token. This could be fixed by adding a `try/catch` block that sets the error flag to true if the `NumberFormatException` is thrown.

Chapter Summary

A stack is a collection that allows you to add and remove elements from its top, providing "Last-In, First-Out" (LIFO) access.

The common operations of a stack include adding ("push"), removing ("pop"), testing whether the stack is empty, asking for the stack's size, and "peeking" at the top element without removing it.

A queue is a collection that allows you to add elements to the back and remove elements from the front, providing "First-In, First-Out" (FIFO) access.

The common operations of a queue include adding ("enqueue"), removing ("dequeue"), testing whether the queue is empty, asking for the queue's size, and "peeking" at the front element without removing it.

To process all elements of a stack, the collection must be emptied. If you want to examine the contents without damaging the collection, you must keep a backup and restore the data afterward.

To process all elements of a queue, you must either backup and restore the data or cycle values to the end of the queue as you process them.

The size of a stack or queue changes as its elements are processed and removed, so many algorithms to process these collections need to keep track of the collection's size separately to avoid common bugs and pitfalls.

Self-Check Problems

Section 14.1: Stack/Queue Basics

1. Which of the following statements about stacks and queues is true?

    a. Stacks and queues can store only integers as their data.
    b. A stack returns elements in the same order as they were added (first-in, first-out).
    c. A queue's `remove` method removes and returns the element at the front of the queue.

d. Stacks and queues are similar to lists, but less efficient.
e. The `peek` method allows access to the element at the bottom of a stack.

2. What is a real-world example of data that could be modeled using a stack? Using a queue?

3. When you call `push` on a stack, where is the new element placed relative to the other elements in the stack? When you call `pop`, which element from the stack is returned?

4. When you call `add` on a queue, where is the new element placed relative to the other elements in the queue? When you call `remove`, which element from the queue is returned?

5. If you create a new empty stack and push the values 1, 2, and 3 in that order, and call `pop` on the stack once, what value will be returned?

6. If you create a new empty queue and add the values 1, 2, and 3 in that order, and call `remove` on the queue once, what value will be returned?

7. The following piece of code incorrectly attempts to declare a queue of integers. What is wrong with the code, and how would you fix it?

```
Queue<Integer> q = new Queue<Integer>();
```

8. Write a piece of code that declares a stack of strings and fills it with the following contents, such that `"howdy"` is at the top of the stack and `"hello"` is at the bottom: `[hello, hi, goodbye, howdy]`. You can print the stack to verify its state.

9. Write a piece of code that declares a stack of integers and uses a loop to fill it with the multiples of 2 from 0 through 100 inclusive, such that `0` is at the top of the stack and `100` is at the bottom: `[100, 98, 96, ..., 4, 2, 0]`. You can print the stack to verify its state.

10. Write a piece of code that declares a queue of strings and fills it with the following contents, such that `"alpha"` is at the front of the queue and `"delta"` is at the back: `[alpha, beta, gamma, delta]`. You can print the queue to verify its state.

Section 14.2: Common Stack/Queue Operations

11. Stacks and queues do not have index-based methods such as `get` from `ArrayList`. How can you access elements in the middle of a stack or queue?

12. Stacks and queues have less functionality than other similar collections like lists and maps. Why are they still useful despite lacking functionality? What possible advantages are there of using a less powerful collection?

13. What is the output of the following code?

```
Stack<String> s = new Stack<String>();
Queue<String> q = new LinkedList<String>();
s.push("how");
s.push("are");
s.push("you");
while (!s.isEmpty()) {
    q.add(s.pop());
}
System.out.println(q);
```

14. What is the output of the following code?

```
Stack s = new Stack<Integer>();
s.push(7);
s.push(10);
System.out.println(s.pop());
System.out.println(s.peek());
s.push(3);
s.push(5);
System.out.println(s.pop());
System.out.println(s.isEmpty());
System.out.println(s.size());
System.out.println(s.peek());
s.push(8);
System.out.println(s.pop());
System.out.println(s.pop());
```

15. What is the output of the following code?

```
Queue<Integer> q = new LinkedList<Integer>();
q.add(10);
q.add(4);
System.out.println(q.size());
System.out.println(q.peek());
q.add(6);
System.out.println(q.remove());
q.add(3);
System.out.println(q.remove());
System.out.println(q.peek());
System.out.println(q.remove());
q.add(7);
System.out.println(q.peek());
```

16. Write the output produced when the following method is passed each of the following stacks:

```
public static void mystery1(Stack<Integer> s) {
    Queue<Integer> q = new LinkedList<Integer>();
    while (!s.isEmpty()) {
        int n = s.pop();
        q.add(n);
        q.add(n);
    }
    while (!q.isEmpty()) {
        s.push(q.remove());
    }
    System.out.println(s);
}
```

a. `[2, 6, 1]`

b. `[42, -3, 4, 15, 9]`

c. `[30, 20, 10, 60, 50, 40]`

Section 14.3: Complex Stack/Queue Operations

17. Write the output produced when the following method is passed each of the following queues:

```
public static void mystery2(Queue<Integer> q) {
    Stack<Integer> s = new Stack<Integer>();
    int size = q.size();
    for (int i = 0; i < size; i++) {
        int n = q.remove();
        if (n % 2 == 0) {
            s.push(n);
        } else {
            q.add(n);
        }
    }
    System.out.println(q + " " + s);
}
```

a. `[1, 2, 3, 4, 5, 6]`

b. `[42, -3, 4, 15, 9, 71]`

c. `[30, 20, 10, 60, 50, 40, 3, 0]`

18. Write the output produced when the following method is passed each of the following queues:

```
public static void mystery3(Queue<Integer> q) {
    int size = q.size();
    for (int i = 0; i < size; i++) {
        int n = q.remove();
        if (n > 0) {
            q.add(-n);
        }
    }
    System.out.println(q);
}
```

a. `[1, -2, 3, -4, 5, -6]`

b. `[42, -3, 4, -15, -9, 71]`

c. `[-30, -20, 10, 60, 50, -40, -3, 0]`

19. The following piece of code incorrectly attempts to find the largest value in a queue of integers. What is wrong with the code, and how would you fix it?

```
int largest = q.remove();
for (int i = 0; i < q.size(); i++) {
    largest = Math.max(largest, q.remove());
}
```

20. The following piece of code incorrectly attempts to compute the sum of all positive values in a queue of integers. What is wrong with the code, and how would you fix it?

```
int sum = 0;
while (!q.isEmpty()) {
    if (q.remove() > 0) {
        sum += q.remove();
    }
}
```

21. The following piece of code incorrectly attempts to remove all even values from a stack of integers. What is wrong with the code, and how would you fix it?

```
while (!s.isEmpty()) {
    int n = s.pop();
    if (n % 2 != 0) {
        s.push(n);    // put back in stack if odd
    }
}
```

22. Write a piece of code that prints the elements of a queue of integers, one per line. When your code is done running, the queue should still contain the same contents as it had at the start. In other words, don't destroy the queue as you print it. If you like, put your code into a method called `print` that accepts the queue as a parameter.

23. Write a piece of code that finds and prints the longest string in a stack of strings. For example, in the stack `[hello, hi, goodbye, howdy]`, the longest string is `"goodbye"`. When your code is done running, the stack should still contain the same contents as it had at the start. In other words, if you destroy the stack as you examine it, restore its state afterward. If you like, put your code into a method called `printLongest` that accepts the stack as a parameter.

Exercises

Each problem will indicate what kind of structure to use as auxiliary storage. You should not use any other auxiliary data structures to solve the problems, although you can create as many simple variables as you'd like.

It is the authors' intent that you use stacks/queues in stack/queue-like ways only when solving these problems. For example, you should not call index-based methods such as `get`, `search`, or `set` (or use a for-each loop) on a stack/queue. You may call only `add`, `remove`, `push`, `pop`, `peek`, `isEmpty`, and `size`. It is also possible to solve all of the exercises without using `peek` if you want an extra challenge.

For problems that accept a stack or queue as a parameter, unless otherwise specified, you should make sure that your method does not damage the state of the parameter. That is, if you modify the parameter stack or queue's elements in your method, you should restore the parameter collection to its original state before your method returns.

Some of these problems have elegant recursive solutions, but the authors' intent is generally that you should not solve these problems recursively, because recursion can circumvent some of the tricky stack/queue manipulation that you are supposed to practice.

1. Write a method called `splitStack` that accepts a stack of integers as a parameter and rearranges its elements so that all the negatives appear on the bottom of the stack and all the nonnegatives appear on the top. If after this

method is called you were to pop numbers off the stack, you would first get all the nonnegative numbers and then get all the negative numbers. It does not matter what order the numbers appear in as long as all the negatives appear lower in the stack than all the nonnegatives. For example, if the stack stores `[3, -5, 1, 2, -4]`, an acceptable result from your method would be `[-5, -4, 3, 1, 2]`. Use a single queue as auxiliary storage.

2. Write a method called `stutter` that accepts a stack of integers as a parameter and replaces every value in the stack with two occurrences of that value. Preserve the original relative order. For example, if the stack stores `[3, 7, 1, 14, 9]`, your method should change it to store `[3, 3, 7, 7, 1, 1, 14, 14, 9, 9]`. Use a single queue as auxiliary storage.

3. Write a method called `copyStack` that accepts a stack of integers as a parameter and returns a copy of the original stack (i.e., a new stack with the same values as the original, stored in the same order as the original). Your method should create the new stack and fill it up with the same values that are stored in the original stack. When your method is done executing, the original stack must be restored to its original state. Use one queue as auxiliary storage.

4. Write a method called `collapse` that accepts a stack of integers as a parameter and that collapses it by replacing each successive pair of integers with the sum of the pair. For example, if the stack stores `[7, 2, 8, 9, 4, 11, 7, 1, 42]`, the first pair should be collapsed into 9 (7 + 2), the second pair should be collapsed into 17 (8 + 9), and so on. If the stack stores an odd number of elements, such as the `42` at the end of our example stack, the final element is not collapsed. So for this stack your method would yield `[9, 17, 15, 8, 42]`. Use one queue as auxiliary storage.

5. Write a method called `equals` that accepts two stacks of integers as parameters and returns `true` if the two stacks store exactly the same sequence of integer values in the same order. Your method must restore the two stacks to their original state before returning. Use one stack as auxiliary storage.

6. Write a method called `rearrange` that accepts a queue of integers as a parameter and rearranges the order of the values so that all of the even values appear before the odd values and that otherwise preserves the original order of the queue. For example, if the queue stores `[3, 5, 4, 17, 6, 83, 1, 84, 16, 37]`, your method should rearrange it to store `[4, 6, 84, 16, 3, 5, 17, 83, 1, 37]`. Notice that all of the evens appear at the front followed by the odds and that the relative order of the evens and odds is the same as in the original. Use one stack as auxiliary storage.

7. Write a method called `reverseHalf` that accepts a queue of integers as a parameter and reverses the order of all the elements in odd-numbered positions (position 1, 3, 5, etc.), assuming that the first value in the queue has position 0. For example, if the queue stores `[1, 8, 7, 2, 9, 18, 12, 0]`, your method should change it to store `[1, 0, 7, 18, 9, 2, 12, 8]`. Notice that numbers in even positions (positions 0, 2, 4, 6) have not moved. That subsequence of integers is still (1, 7, 9, 12). But notice that the numbers in odd positions (positions 1, 3, 5, 7) are now in reverse order relative to the original. In other words, the original subsequence (8, 2, 18, 0) has become (0, 18, 2, 8). Use a single stack as auxiliary storage.

8. Write a method called `isPalindrome` that accepts a queue of integers as a parameter and returns `true` if the numbers in the queue are the same in reverse order. For example, if the queue stores `[3, 8, 17, 9, 17, 8, 3]`, your method should return `true` because this sequence is the same in reverse order. If the queue stores `[3, 17, 9, 4, 17, 3]`, your method would return `false` because this sequence is not the same in reverse order (the `9` and `4` in the middle don't match). The empty queue should be considered a palindrome. Your method must restore the parameter queue to its original state before returning. Use one stack as auxiliary storage.

9. Write a method called `switchPairs` that accepts a stack of integers as a parameter and swaps neighboring pairs of numbers starting at the bottom of the stack. For example, if the stack initially stores `[1, 2, 8, 6, -1, 15, 7]`, your method should swap the first pair (1, 2), the second pair (8, 6), the third pair (−1, 15), and so on. If the stack

contains an odd number of elements, the element at the top should remain unmodified. So the final state of the stack would be `[2, 1, 6, 8, 15, −1, 7]`. Use one queue as auxiliary storage.

10. Write a method called `isConsecutive` that accepts a stack of integers as a parameter and that returns `true` if the stack contains a sequence of consecutive integers starting from the bottom of the stack. Consecutive integers are integers that come one after the other, as in 3, 4, 5, etc. If the stack stores `[5, 6, 7, 8, 9, 10]`, your method should return `true`. If the stack had instead contained `[7, 8, 9, 10, 12]`, your method should return `false` because the numbers `10` and `12` are not consecutive. Notice that we look at the numbers starting at the bottom of the stack. Any stack with fewer than two values should be considered to be a list of consecutive integers. Your method must restore the parameter stack to its original state before returning. Use one queue as auxiliary storage.

11. Write a method called `reorder` that accepts a queue of integers as a parameter and that puts the integers into sorted (nondecreasing) order, assuming that the queue is already sorted by absolute value. For example, if the queue stores `[1, 2, −2, 4, −5, 8, −8, 12, −15]`, notice that the values appear in sorted order if you ignore the sign of the numbers. Your method should reorder the values so that the queue stores `[−15, −8, −5, −2, 1, 2, 4, 8, 12]`. Use one stack as auxiliary storage.

12. Write a method called `shift` that accepts a stack of integers and an integer *n* as parameters and that shifts *n* values from the bottom of the stack to the top of the stack. For example, if the stack named `s` stores `[1, 2, 3, 4, 5, 6, 7, 8]`, and we make the call `shift(s, 3);` your method should shift the three values at the bottom of the stack to the top of the stack and leave the other values in the same order, producing `[4, 5, 6, 7, 8, 3, 2, 1]`. Notice that the value that was at the bottom of the stack is now at the top, the value that was second from the bottom is now second from the top, the value that was third from the bottom is now third from the top, and that the five values not involved in the shift are now at the bottom of the stack in their original order. Use one queue as auxiliary storage. You may assume that the parameter *n* is ≥ 0 and not larger than the number of elements in the stack.

13. Write a method called `expunge` that accepts a stack of integers as a parameter and makes sure that the stack's elements are in nondecreasing order from top to bottom, by removing from the stack any element that is smaller than any element(s) on top of it. For example, if the stack stores `[4, 20, 15, 15, 8, 5, 7, 12, 3, 10, 5, 1]`, the element values `3, 7, 5, 8,` and `4` should be removed because each has an element above it with a larger value. So your method should change the stack to store `[20, 15, 15, 12, 10, 5, 1]`. Notice that now the elements are in nondecreasing order from top to bottom. If the stack is empty or has just one element, nothing changes. Use one queue or stack (but not both) as auxiliary storage.

14. Write a method called `reverseFirstK` that accepts an integer *k* and a queue of integers as parameters and reverses the order of the first *k* elements of the queue, leaving the other elements in the same relative order. For example, if a queue named `q` stores `[10, 20, 30, 40, 50, 60, 70, 80, 90]`, the call of `reverseFirstK(4, q);` should change the queue to store `[40, 30, 20, 10, 50, 60, 70, 80, 90]`. If *k* is 0 or negative, no change should be made. If the queue does not contain at least *k* elements, your method should throw an `IllegalArgumentException`. Use one queue or stack (but not both) as auxiliary storage.

15. Write a method called `isSorted` that accepts a stack of integers as a parameter and returns `true` if the elements in the stack occur in ascending (nondecreasing) order from top to bottom. That is, the smallest element should be on top, growing larger toward the bottom. For example, if the stack stores `[20, 20, 17, 11, 8, 8, 3, 2]`, your method should return `true`. An empty or one-element stack is considered to be sorted. Your method must restore the parameter stack to its original state before returning. Use one queue or stack (but not both) as auxiliary storage.

16. Write a method called `mirror` that accepts a stack of integers as a parameter and replaces the stack contents with itself plus a mirrored version of itself (the same elements in the opposite order). For example, if the stack stores

[10, 53, 19, 24], your method should change it to store [10, 53, 19, 24, 24, 19, 53, 10]. If passed an empty stack, your result should be an empty stack. Use one stack or one queue (but not both) as auxiliary storage to solve this problem.

17. Write a method called `compressDuplicates` that accepts a stack of integers as a parameter and that replaces each sequence of duplicates with a pair of values: a count of the number of duplicates, followed by the actual duplicated number. For example, if the stack stores [2, 2, 2, 2, 2, −4, −4, −4, 82, 6, 6, 6, 6, 17, 17], your method should change it to store [5, 2, 3, −4, 1, 82, 4, 6, 2, 17]. This new stack indicates that the original had 5 occurrences of 2 at the bottom of the stack followed by 3 occurrences of −4 followed by 1 occurrence of 82, and so on. If the stack is empty, your method should not change it. Use one queue as auxiliary storage.

18. Write a method called `mirrorHalves` that accepts a queue of integers as a parameter and replaces each half of that queue with itself plus a mirrored version of itself (the same elements in the opposite order). For example, if the queue stores [10, 50, 19, 54, 30, 67], your method should change it to store [10, 50, 19, 19, 50, 10, 54, 30, 67, 67, 30, 54]. If your method is passed an empty queue, the result should be an empty queue. If your method is passed a queue whose size is not even, throw an `IllegalArgumentException`. Use one stack or one queue (but not both) as auxiliary storage.

19. Write a method called `removeMin` that accepts a stack of integers as a parameter and removes and returns the smallest value from the stack. For example, if the stack stores [2, 8, 3, 19, 2, 3, 2, 7, 12, −8, 4], your method should remove and return −8, leaving the stack storing [2, 8, 3, 19, 2, 3, 2, 7, 12, 4]. If the minimum value appears more than once, all occurrences of it should be removed. For example, given the same stack, if we again call `removeMin` on it, the method would return 2 and leave the stack storing [8, 3, 19, 3, 7, 12, 4]. Use one queue as auxiliary storage.

20. Write a method called `interleave` that accepts a queue of integers as a parameter and rearranges the elements by alternating the elements from the first half of the queue with those from the second half of the queue. For example, if the queue stores [2, 8, −5, 19, 7, 3, 24, 42], your method should change it to store [2, 7, 8, 3, −5, 24, 19, 42]. To understand the result, consider the two halves of this queue. The first half is [2, 8, −5, 19] and the second half is [7, 3, 24, 42]. These are combined in an alternating fashion to form a sequence of pairs: the first values from each half (2 and 7), then the second values from each half (8 and 3), and so on. Your method should throw an `IllegalArgumentException` if the queue does not have an even size. Use one stack as auxiliary storage.

Programming Projects

1. Write a Primes program that finds prime numbers using the Sieve of Eratosthenes, an algorithm devised by a Greek mathematician of the same name who lived in the third century BC. The algorithm finds all prime numbers up to some maximum value *n*, as described by the following pseudocode:

```
create a queue of numbers to process.
fill the queue with the integers 2 through n inclusive.
create an empty result queue to store primes.

repeat the following steps:
    obtain the next prime p by removing the first value
        from the queue of numbers.
    put p into the result queue of primes.
```

```
    loop through the queue of numbers,
        eliminating all numbers that are divisible by p.
while (p is less than the square root of n).

all remaining values in the numbers queue are prime,
    so transfer them to the result primes queue.
```

Several web sites have nice descriptions and animations of this algorithm in action; consider searching for "Sieve of Eratosthenes" in your web browser.

2. Write an HTML Validator program that reads files of HTML data and uses stacks and queues to verify whether the tags in the file are properly matched. A tag consists of a named element between less-than, <, and greater-than, >, symbols. Many tags apply to a range of text, in which case a pair of tags is used: an opening tag indicating the start of the range and a closing tag with a slash indicating the end of the range. For example, you can make some text bold `<b>`like this`</b>`. Tags can be nested to combine effects, `<b><i>`bold italic`</i></b>`. Some tags, such as the `br` tag for inserting a line break or `img` for inserting an image, do not cover a range of text and are considered to be "self-closing." Self-closing tags do not need a closing tag; for a line break, only a tag of `<br>` is needed. Some web developers write self-closing tags with an optional `/` before the >, such as `<br/>`.

   The following HTML file has some errors: the `<title>` tag is not closed; the `</head>` tag appears twice; an extraneous `</br>` tag appears; and the `<body>` tag is not properly closed.

```
<!DOCTYPE html>
<html>
  <!-- This is a comment -->
  <head>
    <title>Turtles are cool
  </head>
  </head>

  <body>
    <p>Turtles swim in the <a href="ocean.com">ocean</a>.</p>
    </br>
    <p>Some turtles are over 100 years old.
      Here is a picture of a turtle:
      <img src="turtle.jpg" /> </p>
</html>
```

3. Modify the expression evaluator case study program from this chapter to make a new program that accepts as input a fully parenthesized infix expression and returns a string representing an equivalent postfix expression. Postfix expressions are ones where each operator follows its two operands, such as `1 2 +` rather than `1 + 2`. Postfix expressions are elegant in that they do not need parentheses. For example, the given infix expression:

```
(9 + (8 * 7 - (6 / 5 ^ 4) * 3) * 2))
```

   is equivalent to the following postfix expression:

```
9 8 7 * 6 5 4 ^ / 3 * - 2 * +
```

   Your algorithm should read the expression token by token, using a stack to store operators. (You don't need the values stack from the original case study anymore.) Instead, each time a number is encountered, append it to a string that you are building up. Each time a right parenthesis is encountered, pop the stack to get an operator and append it to the string you are building up. Leave in place the rest of the code to preserve the error checking. Return the string `"illegal expression"` if an error is encountered.

4. Write a Maze Explorer program that uses stacks and queues to implement an algorithm to escape from a maze. The overall pseudocode of the algorithm is the following. The algorithm can be implemented using a stack or a queue. What are the pros and cons of each?

```
create an empty stack of locations to explore.
push the start location onto the stack.

while (stack is not empty) {
    pop a location L from the stack.
    if we have we pulled L from the stack before:
        no need to explore it again, so skip L.
    if L is the end location:
        the end was reachable!
    else, L is a new reachable non-finish location, so explore it:
        add all non-wall adjacent maze locations to the stack.
        record the fact that we have explored L.
}
if the stack is empty, the finish is unreachable.
```

5. Write a Guitar Hero program that uses a queue to simulate the creation of guitar notes. When a guitar string is plucked, it vibrates to generate sound. The sound starts from the note's initial note pitch or frequency, then it undergoes a wave-like oscillation and gradually fades in volume over time.

The oscillation and fading of notes can be computed using an algorithm called Karplus-Strong. The algorithm represents sound as time slices called samples (44,100 samples per second, in this case). You can compute samples that sound similar to the vibrations of a real guitar as displacements from the guitar string's original frequency. First create a queue of random displacements between −½ and ½. The length of the queue should be the sampling rate, 44,100, divided by the note's frequency. Then repeatedly remove the first queue element, average it with the next front element, slightly fade the volume by multiplying it by 0.996, then add the result back into the queue as shown in Figure 14.3.

This program requires support code to send output to your computer's sound card. The code is provided on our web site at http://buildingjavaprograms.com/.

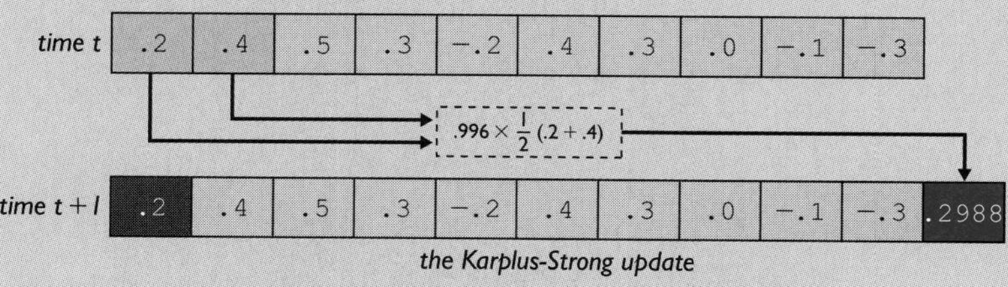

Figure 14.3 Karplus-Strong algorithm samples

Chapter 15

Implementing a Collection Class

Introduction

In Chapters 10, 11, and 14 we saw how to use various data structures that are part of the collections framework. As a Java programmer, you will find it useful to have these off-the-shelf solutions available to you, but you can learn a lot from examining how these structures are implemented. In this chapter we will explore in detail how to implement one such structure.

Our goal is to understand the `ArrayList` class that was described in detail in Chapter 10. Recall that `ArrayList` is a generic class that is best described as `ArrayList<E>`, where `E` is filled in with a specific element type. Because generic classes are not easy to implement, we will first explore the implementation of a class called `ArrayIntList` that can be used to store a list of simple integer values. There aren't a lot of applications for a simple `ArrayIntList` object, but the code we write for it will be similar to the code we need for the generic version. The chapter ends with a section that explores how to turn the more specific `ArrayIntList` into a generic `ArrayList<E>`.

15.1 Simple `ArrayIntList`

In this section, we will develop an initial version of the `ArrayIntList` class that contains appropriate fields for storing a list and a minimal set of operations for manipulating it.

Recall from Chapter 8 that there are two important perspectives of any class. The first is the external view that a client of the class will have. Clients in general don't want to understand all of the internal details of the class. They just want to know what it does. As a result, we want to have a clear specification for the client of what the `ArrayIntList` class is supposed to do. We think of this as a *contract* that we have with the client.

Contract

A clear specification that tells a client how an object behaves without describing the details of how it is implemented.

The second view is the internal view of the implementer. We have to figure out how to make the object work—how to satisfy the contract. When we are thinking as an implementer, we will consider the nitty-gritty details of the innards of an object.

It is sometimes confusing to switch between these two different perspectives, but you will get better at it as you practice.

Adding and Printing

Let's start by developing a version of the class which has a single mutator method that will append values to the end of the list and a single accessor method that will display the contents of the list. Assume that the client code will look something like the following:

```
public class Client1 {
    public static void main(String[] args) {
        // construct two lists
        ArrayIntList list1 = new ArrayIntList();
        ArrayIntList list2 = new ArrayIntList();

        // add 1, 82, 97 to list1
        list1.add(1);
        list1.add(82);
        list1.add(97);

        // add 7, -8 to list2
        list2.add(7);
        list2.add(-8);

        // report results
```

```
        System.out.println("list1 = " + list1);
        System.out.println("list2 = " + list2);
    }
}
```

The preceding code will produce the following output:

```
list1 = [1, 82, 97]
list2 = [7, −8]
```

You must implement three methods in this program: the constructor, the `add` method, and the `toString` method that `println` will call. First you have to figure out what kind of fields you need. We are trying to emulate the `ArrayList` class, which is built on top of a simple array, so you should do the same thing for your `ArrayIntList` class. All of the examples of arrays in Chapter 7 involved what could be called *filled arrays* in which each element of the array is in use. A filled array works fine in many applications, but this is not one of them. You are implementing a dynamic structure that will grow and shrink as the client adds and removes values, so you don't want to be forced to use an array that is exactly the same size as your list.

Instead, you should use an *unfilled array* in which some of the array elements are in use and some are not. This approach is similar to the way that a hotel is run. A hotel might have 100 guest rooms, but they don't all have to be occupied at once. There might be 90 rooms currently in use by customers and 10 vacant rooms that are available for later use.

This concept raises the question of how to distinguish between occupied cells and vacant cells in the array. One simple approach is to maintain a `size` variable that keeps track of the number of occupied cells and use the front of the array for cells that are currently in use and the back of the array for cells that are vacant. Unlike a hotel that has vacant occupied rooms interspersed, this kind of unfilled array groups all of the occupied cells together at the front of the array and all of the vacant cells at the end of the array.

For example, the sample client code at the beginning of this section constructs a list and adds the values `1`, `82`, and `97` to the list. That would mean that three of the array cells are occupied and any other cells are vacant. Suppose that you construct an array variable called `elementData` and you add these three values as the first three entries in the array:

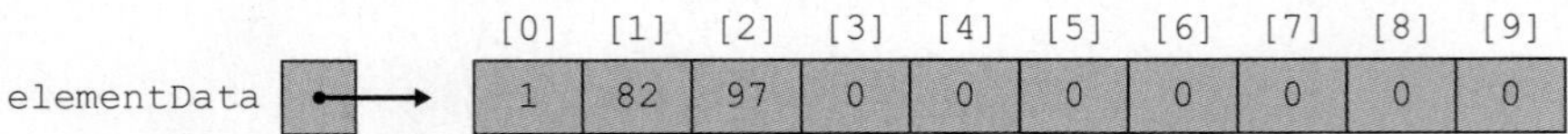

While it's true that the first vacant cell has the value `0` stored in it, you wouldn't want to count on this being the case because the client might want to store the value `0` in the list. Without a `size` variable, you wouldn't know for sure whether this list ends with `97` or whether it ends with one of the zeros. With the `size` variable, you can keep track of exactly how many cells are occupied and you know that all others are vacant:

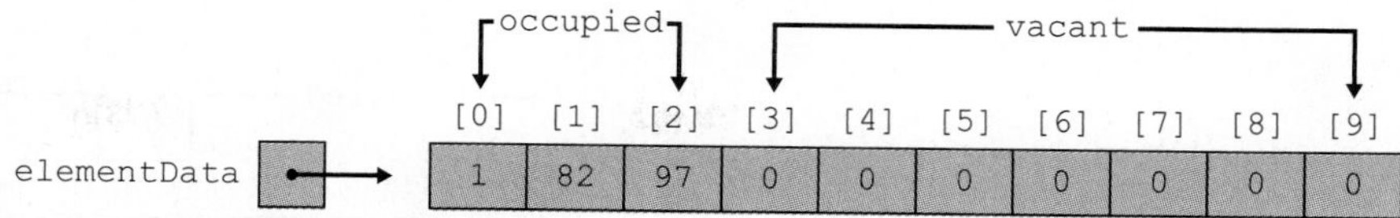

In the preceding example, the array has a length of 10. We refer to this length as the *capacity* of the list. In our hotel analogy, the hotel has 100 rooms, which means that it has the capacity to rent up to 100 rooms. But often the hotel is not filled to capacity. The same will be true for your list. The `size` variable keeps track of how much of the list is currently occupied whereas the capacity tells you how large the list can grow.

The fields you want to declare for your class are an array and a `size` variable:

```
public class ArrayIntList {
    private int[] elementData;
    private int size;
    ...
}
```

Your constructor should initialize these fields. The array in the preceding example had a capacity of 10, but let's increase it to 100:

```
public class ArrayIntList {
    private int[] elementData;
    private int size;

    public ArrayIntList() {
        elementData = new int[100];
        size = 0;
    }
    ...
}
```

Recall from Chapter 8 that fields are initialized to the zero-equivalent for the type, which means that the `size` field will be initialized to `0` with or without the line of code in the constructor. Some Java programmers prefer to leave out the line of code because they are familiar with the default initialization. Others prefer to be more explicit about the initialization. This is somewhat a matter of personal taste.

Now that you have the fields and constructor defined, you can turn your attention to the `add` method. It takes an integer as a parameter. The idea is that you should append the given value to the end of the list. The method will look like this:

```
public void add(int value) {
    ...
}
```

This turns out to be a fairly simple method to implement. Suppose, for example, that the list stores the values `[3, 6, 9, 12, 15]`:

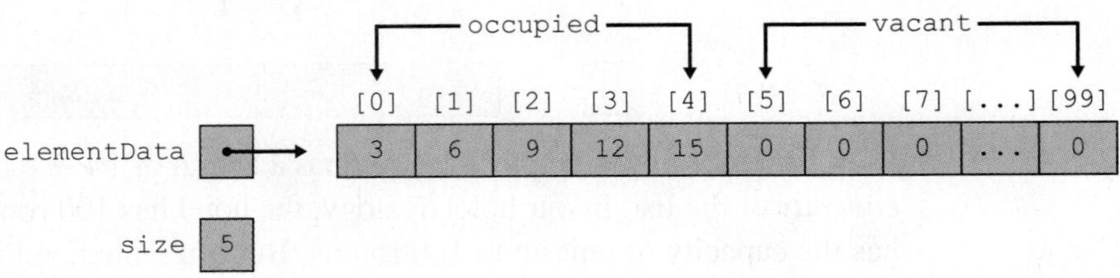

As indicated in the preceding figure, the current size of the list is 5. If you wanted to add the value `18` to the end of this list, you'd store it in the first vacant array element, which has index 5. In other words, when the list has a size of 5, you append the next value into index 5. And once you've added that value into index 5, then the list will have a size of 6 and the next vacant element will be at index 6.

Generally speaking, the size of the list will always match the index of the first vacant cell. This seems a bit odd, but it is a result of zero-based indexing. Because the first value is stored in index 0, the last value of a sequence of length n will be stored in index $n - 1$.

Therefore you should begin the `add` method by appending the given value at index `size`:

```
public void add(int value) {
    elementData[size] = value;
    ...
}
```

Storing the value into the array isn't enough. You have to increment the `size` to keep track of the fact that one more cell is now occupied:

```
public void add(int value) {
    elementData[size] = value;
    size++;
}
```

If your program did not increment `size`, it would keep adding values in the same index of the array. This would be like our hypothetical hotel checking every customer into the same hotel room because the hotel didn't keep track of which rooms are occupied.

It seems likely that this method will work, but so far the program doesn't have a good way of verifying it. You need some kind of method for displaying the contents of the list.

Chapter 7 explored the following code for printing the contents of an array of integers:

```
public static void print(int[] list) {
    if (list.length == 0) {
        System.out.println("[]");
    } else {
        System.out.print("[" + list[0]);
        for (int i = 1; i < list.length; i++) {
            System.out.print(", " + list[i]);
        }
        System.out.println("]");
    }
}
```

The code involves a fencepost loop because we use commas to separate values. If there are n numbers, they will be separated by $n - 1$ commas. The code uses the classic fencepost solution of printing the first value before the loop. The `if/else` is used because there is a special case if the array is empty. This code can be fairly easily adapted to your `ArrayIntList` class. You have to convert the static method into an instance method. As a result, instead of having a parameter called `list`, you refer to the field called `elementData`. You also want to modify the code so that it uses the size of the list rather than the length of the array:

```
public void print() {
    if (size == 0) {
        System.out.println("[]");
    } else {
        System.out.print("[" + elementData[0]);
        for (int i = 1; i < size; i++) {
            System.out.print(", " + elementData[i]);
        }
        System.out.println("]");
    }
}
```

But you don't want a method to print the list. If you want to make a truly useful class, you should provide flexible mechanisms that will work in a wide variety of situations. A better solution is to return a string representation of the list rather than printing it. As we saw in Chapter 8, Java has a standard name for such a method: `toString`. So you should rewrite the preceding method to construct and return a string representation of the list:

```
public String toString() {
    if (size == 0) {
```

```
            return "[]";
        } else {
            String result = "[" + elementData[0];
            for (int i = 1; i < size; i++) {
                result += ", " + elementData[i];
            }
            result += "]";
            return result;
        }
    }
```

Here is the complete class:

```
public class ArrayIntList {
    private int[] elementData;
    private int size;

    public ArrayIntList() {
        elementData = new int[100];
        size = 0;
    }

    public void add(int value) {
        elementData[size] = value;
        size++;
    }

    public String toString() {
        if (size == 0) {
            return "[]";
        } else {
            String result = "[" + elementData[0];
            for (int i = 1; i < size; i++) {
                result += ", " + elementData[i];
            }
            result += "]";
            return result;
        }
    }
}
```

This version of the class correctly executes the sample client program, producing the correct output.

Thinking about Encapsulation

When we declared the fields for `ArrayIntList`, we followed the usual convention of declaring them to be private. This can cause a problem for a client of the class. Suppose that the client has made a series of calls on the `add` method and wants to know how many elements are in the list. For example, the client might want to write code like the following:

```
Scanner input = new Scanner(new File("data.txt"));
ArrayIntList list = new ArrayIntList();
while (input.hasNextInt()) {
    list.add(input.nextInt());
}
System.out.println(list);
// report the size of the list, but how?
```

The information the client wants is stored internally in the field called `size`. But because the field is declared to be private, the client can't access the value.

There are several clumsy ways to solve this problem. One solution would be to change the field from private to public, but as we saw in Chapter 8, making the field public breaks encapsulation and leaves the list object open to unwanted modifications. It's not a problem to allow the client to examine the value of the field, but suppose the client tried to set it to an illegal value, as in the following two examples:

```
list.size = –38;
list.size = 5000;
```

Allowing the client to reach into the object opens the door for the client to put the object into a bad state.

Another solution would be to force the client to keep track of the size, but that is a rather silly solution. Why should both the object and the client keep track of this information? It puts an undue burden on the client and it leads to unnecessary duplication of effort.

The right solution is to keep the field private, but to introduce an accessor method that allows the client to examine the value of the `size` field:

```
public int size() {
    return size;
}
```

Then the client can write code like the following:

```
System.out.println("size = " + list.size());
```

This line of code looks fairly similar to code that accesses the field directly. The difference here is that we are calling a method called `size`. The method allows the client to examine the field without giving the client the ability to change the value of the field.

A client will also want the ability to access individual elements of the list. Internally, you access the list elements by referring to the array called elementData. Again, you don't want to break encapsulation by giving a client direct access to this field. Instead you can introduce another accessor method for examining the value stored at a given index:

```
public int get(int index) {
    return elementData[index];
}
```

Eventually, we want to make sure that this method can't be used by a client to access any of the vacant array elements (elements beyond the size of the list), but this simple version will do for now.

Dealing with the Middle of the List

VideoNote

So far we have explored how to add a value at the end of a list, but often a client is interested in dealing with values in the middle of the list. The client might want to search for the location of values or add them to or remove them from the middle of the list.

Let's begin with the task of searching for the location of a value in a list. The client could use the size and get methods to locate a value. But if it seems likely that a client will want to perform frequent searches for the locations of values, then it makes more sense to include the ability to do this as a method inside the class. That way, it will be readily available to all clients of the class.

In Chapter 7, we wrote the following code to find the index of the first occurrence of a value in an array of integers:

```
public static int indexOf(int[] list, int target) {
    for (int i = 0; i < list.length; i++) {
        if (list[i] == target) {
            return i;
        }
    }
    return -1;
}
```

This method is fairly easily converted from a static method to an instance method, as you did with print. To achieve the conversion, replace the array parameter with references to the elementData field and, instead of using the length of the array as a loop bound, use the size field so that the method searches only elements of the array that are currently in use:

```
public int indexOf(int value) {
    for (int i = 0; i < size; i++) {
        if (elementData[i] == value) {
```

```
            return i;
        }
    }
    return -1;
}
```

You haven't yet given the client the ability to remove a value from the list. Let's call the method `remove`. It should take as a parameter the index of the value to be removed:

```
public void remove(int index) {
    ...
}
```

Suppose, for example, that a list contains the five values `[12, 19, 8, 73, 14]`:

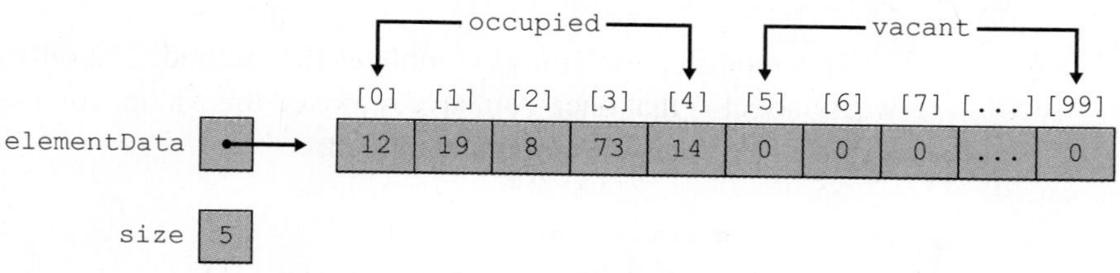

Suppose that you want to remove the value `19`, which is stored at index 1. This action will create a gap in the list unless you shift values over to fill in the gap. The three values that come after the value `19` each have to be shifted down by one position:

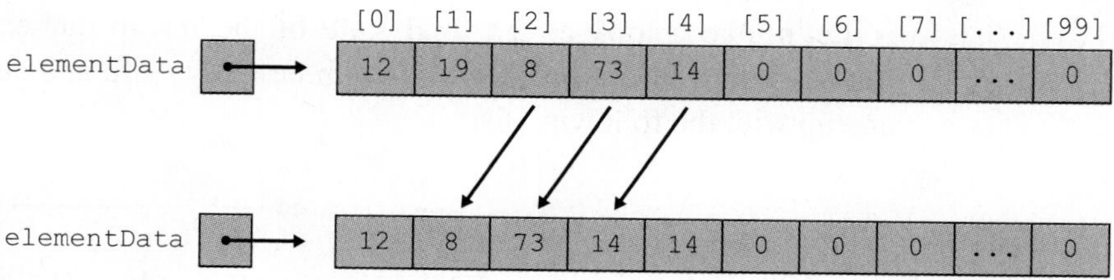

In order to shift the values over, you obviously need some kind of loop. You want to shift a value into index 1, another value into index 2, and another value into index 3. Why start at index 1? Because that's the target index, the index of the value you've been asked to remove. And why stop at index 3? Because that's when you run out of occupied cells to shift. The following code is a good first guess at the loop bounds:

```
for (int i = index; i < size; i++) {
    ...
}
```

We saw in Chapter 7 that we can use code like the following to accomplish the shifting task:

```
for (int i = index; i < size; i++) {
    elementData[i] = elementData[i + 1];
}
```

This code is almost correct. The problem is that the loop executes once too often. As we have noted, you want to shift values into indexes 1, 2, and 3. But when the `size` is `5`, as in our example, the loop will do one extra shift, shifting a value into index 4. You want to stop the loop one step earlier so that it won't perform this final shift. You can accomplish that by subtracting one from the final loop bound:

```
for (int i = index; i < size - 1; i++) {
    elementData[i] = elementData[i + 1];
}
```

This modification almost completes the method. The only other detail you need to worry about is that once you have removed this value, you need to decrement the size of the list. Here is the complete method:

```
public void remove(int index) {
    for (int i = index; i < size - 1; i++) {
        elementData[i] = elementData[i + 1];
    }
    size--;
}
```

Let's take a look at the final state of the list in our example. After we have removed the value at index 1, shifted three values left, and decremented the size, we end up with the following list:

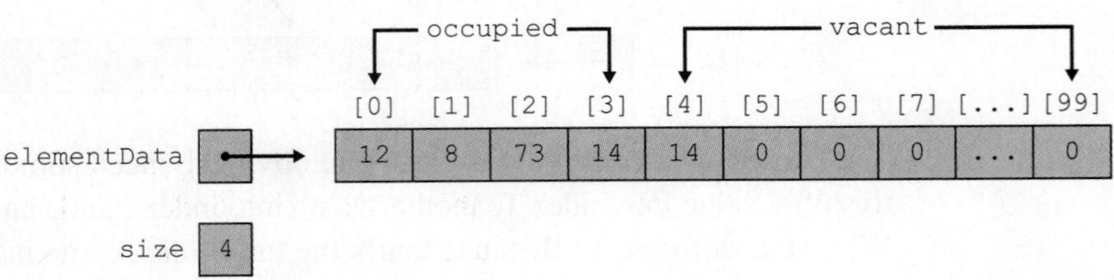

Notice that the first cell among the vacant cells has the value `14` in it. You might imagine that you have to set it back to `0`. In general, this isn't necessary for your `ArrayIntList`. Because the value is among the vacant cells, you know that it isn't a *real* value of the list. And if you ever need to use that cell again, you'll overwrite the `14` with some new value. It doesn't matter whether you overwrite a `14` or overwrite a `0`. In fact, in the final version of our program, we'll make sure that a client can't ever see that extra value of `14`. The situation is slightly different when you deal with the generic `ArrayList`, but we'll save that discussion for the end of the chapter.

Another operation that a client is likely to want to perform is to add a value in the middle of a list. You already wrote a simple `add` method that appends at the end of the list:

```
public void add(int value) {
    ...
}
```

You can call the new method `add` as well, but it will have different parameters. You will still need to know the value to add, as with the appending method. But this new method will also need to know the index where the new value is to be added. Thus, it will look like the following:

```
public void add(int index, int value) {
    ...
}
```

Implementing this method is more complicated than appending a value at the end of the list because you have to shift values over to make room for the value to be inserted. Suppose, for example, that your list contains the five values `[3, 6, 9, 12, 15]`:

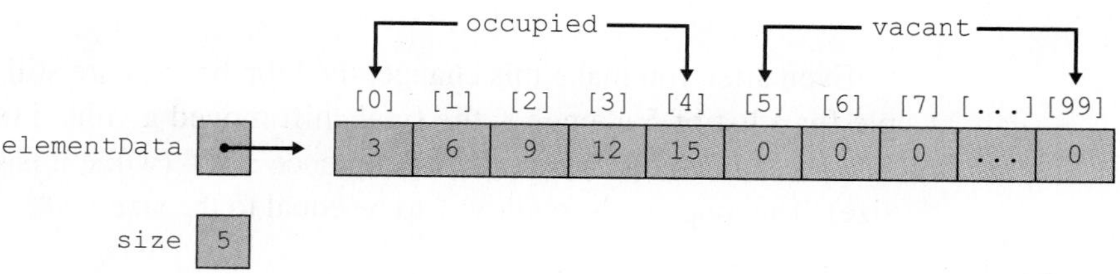

Suppose that you want to insert the value `7` at index 2. That insertion will require you to shift each of the values that are currently in indexes 2 through 4 to the right by one:

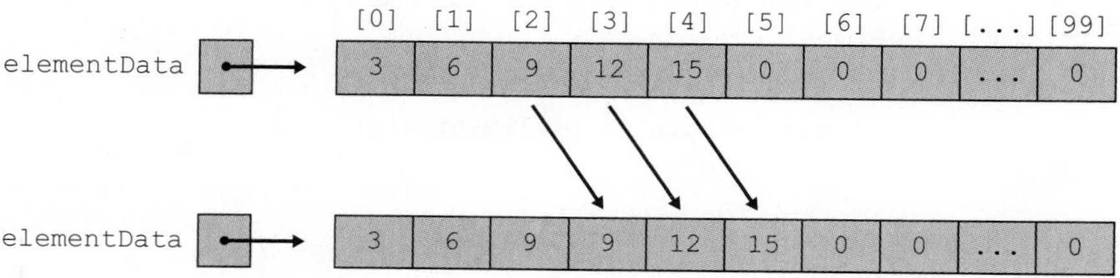

This insertion is similar to the remove operation. You want to deal with cells between the target index (where the new value is to be added) and the end of the sequence of occupied cells. Therefore, you know that the loop bounds will be something like the following:

```
for (int i = index; i < size; i++) {
    ...
}
```

We saw in Chapter 7 that you can shift values to the right by writing code like the following:

```
for (int i = index; i < size; i++) {
    elementData[i] = elementData[i – 1];
}
```

There are several problems with this code. First, it starts too early. In the example, you are trying to shift values so that you can add a new value at index 2. The first shift you want to do is to shift the value that is currently at index 2 into index 3. But the preceding loop will first shift the value at index 1 into index 2. The loop needs to start one index later:

```
for (int i = index + 1; i < size; i++) {
    elementData[i] = elementData[i – 1];
}
```

Even after you make this change, the loop bounds are still not correct. In the sample for a list of 5 elements, the final shift moved a value into the cell with index 5. The preceding code will stop the loop once `i` is 4 (while it is still strictly less than the size). The loop needs to allow `i` to be equal to the size:

```
for (int i = index + 1; i <= size; i++) {
    elementData[i] = elementData[i – 1];
}
```

The final problem, as described in detail in Chapter 7, is that this loop has to be run backward rather than forward. Otherwise you overwrite your list values with the value that is stored at the target index:

```
for (int i = size; i >= index + 1; i––) {
    elementData[i] = elementData[i – 1];
}
```

This modification completes the shifting, but you also have to store the new value at the target index now that there is room for it, and you have to increment the size of the list:

```
public void add(int index, int value) {
    for (int i = size; i >= index + 1; i--) {
        elementData[i] = elementData[i - 1];
    }
    elementData[index] = value;
    size++;
}
```

Another Constructor and a Constant

The `ArrayIntList` class is shaping up nicely, but so far you have just a single constructor that constructs a list with a capacity of 100:

```
public ArrayIntList() {
    elementData = new int[100];
    size = 0;
}
```

This constructor isn't very flexible. What if clients want to manipulate a list of 200 values? What are they supposed to do? You don't want to force them to rewrite the code just to use your class. That would be like having to open up a radio and rewire the insides just to change the volume or the station. If there is some value like the capacity that the client is likely to want to change, then you want to be sure to build in the flexibility to allow the client to do so.

You can accomplish this flexibility by changing the constructor to take a parameter that specifies the capacity of the list. You can then use that value when you construct the array:

```
public ArrayIntList(int capacity) {
    elementData = new int[capacity];
    size = 0;
}
```

This modification allows a client to write lines of code like the following:

```
ArrayIntList list1 = new ArrayIntList(200);
```

Unfortunately, if this is your only constructor, then the client loses the ability to write lines of code like the following:

```
ArrayIntList list2 = new ArrayIntList();
```

You could include both constructors, but then you have redundant code. As we saw in Chapter 8, you can avoid the duplication by having one constructor call the other. The constructor that takes the capacity is the more general constructor, so you can have the constructor that takes no arguments call it using the `this(...)` notation:

```
public ArrayIntList() {
    this(100);
}

public ArrayIntList(int capacity) {
    elementData = new int[capacity];
    size = 0;
}
```

You might wonder how Java can tell the two constructors apart. The answer is that they have different signatures. One constructor takes no arguments, whereas the second constructor takes an integer as an argument. When Java sees the call on `this(100)` in the first constructor, it knows that it is calling the second constructor because the call includes an integer value as a parameter.

Another improvement we can make is to introduce a constant for the rather arbitrary value of `100`:

```
public static final int DEFAULT_CAPACITY = 100;
```

It is a good idea to make this constant public because the client might want to be able to refer to the value to know what capacity a list has if the client doesn't specify a specific value to use. You would then rewrite the first constructor to use the constant instead of the specific value:

```
public ArrayIntList() {
    this(DEFAULT_CAPACITY);
}
```

Preconditions and Postconditions

VideoNote

We are almost ready to put all of these pieces together into a complete class. But before we do so, we should consider the issue of documentation. When you document the class, you want to think in terms of important information that should be conveyed to the client of the class. You want to describe what each method does and you want to describe any limitations of each method. This is a great place to use preconditions and postconditions, as described in Chapter 4.

Recall from Chapter 4 that preconditions are assumptions the method makes. They are a way of describing any dependencies that the method has ("this has to be true in order for me to do my work"). Also, recall that postconditions describe what the method accomplishes, assuming that the preconditions are met ("I'll do this as long as the preconditions are met"). The combination of preconditions and postconditions is a way of describing the contract that a method has with the client.

Consider, for example, the `get` method. It is a fairly simple method that allows the client to access individual elements of the list:

```
public int get(int index) {
    return elementData[index];
}
```

This method makes sense only if the value of `index` is in the range of occupied cells. In other words, it has to be greater than or equal to `0` and it has to be less than the size of the list. We can describe these constraints in a precondition comment:

```
// pre : 0 <= index < size()
public int get(int index) {
    return elementData[index];
}
```

The postcondition should describe what the method accomplishes, assuming that the precondition is met. You can do that with a short description of the method's behavior:

```
// pre : 0 <= index < size()
// post: returns the integer at the given index in the list
public int get(int index) {
    return elementData[index];
}
```

There are quite a few preconditions for the methods you have written. All of the methods that take an index as a parameter assume that it is a legal index. The constructor that takes a capacity can't work with a negative value. And there is another important precondition lurking out there. Remember that your list has a fixed capacity. What happens if the client calls the `add` method so many times that the capacity is exceeded? You should warn the client about that scenario to make the contract clear.

In the next section we'll examine how to handle bad values more directly, but for now we'll settle for documenting the various preconditions.

It is worth noting that the method comments for this class do not contain comments about implementation. For example, we wouldn't mention that the `remove` method shifts values in the array. That's a detail of the implementation that won't generally interest the client. If you think that the implementation is complicated enough to deserve comments, then include those comments with the code itself inside the method. The comment on the method itself should be written from the client perspective, not from the perspective of the implementer.

Professional Java programmers write their comments in Javadoc format so that they can be extracted from the actual program files and published as html files. If you've been referring to the Java API documentation, then you've been reading such comments. We don't use Javadoc format for our comments, but you can read about it in Appendix B.

Here is a complete version of the ArrayIntList class incorporating all of the pieces discussed in this section:

```
// Class ArrayIntList can be used to store a list of integers.

public class ArrayIntList {
    private int[] elementData;  // list of integers
    private int size;           // number of elements in the list

    public static final int DEFAULT_CAPACITY = 100;

    // post: constructs an empty list of default capacity
    public ArrayIntList() {
        this(DEFAULT_CAPACITY);
    }

    // pre : capacity >= 0
    // post: constructs an empty list with the given capacity
    public ArrayIntList(int capacity) {
        elementData = new int[capacity];
        size = 0;
    }

    // post: returns the current number of elements in the list
    public int size() {
        return size;
    }

    // pre : 0 <= index < size()
    // post: returns the integer at the given index in the list
    public int get(int index) {
        return elementData[index];
    }

    // post: returns comma-separated, bracketed version of list
    public String toString() {
        if (size == 0) {
            return "[]";
        } else {
            String result = "[" + elementData[0];
            for (int i = 1; i < size; i++) {
                result += ", " + elementData[i];
            }
```

```
            result += "]";
            return result;
        }
    }

    // post : returns the position of the first occurrence of the
    //        given value (-1 if not found)
    public int indexOf(int value) {
        for (int i = 0; i < size; i++) {
            if (elementData[i] == value) {
                return i;
            }
        }
        return -1;
    }

    // pre : size() < capacity
    // post: appends the given value to the end of the list
    public void add(int value) {
        elementData[size] = value;
        size++;
    }

    // pre : size() < capacity && 0 <= index <= size()
    // post: inserts the given value at the given index, shifting
    //       subsequent values right
    public void add(int index, int value) {
        for (int i = size; i >= index + 1; i--) {
            elementData[i] = elementData[i - 1];
        }
        elementData[index] = value;
        size++;
    }

    // pre : 0 <= index < size()
    // post: removes value at the given index, shifting
    //       subsequent values left
    public void remove(int index) {
        for (int i = index; i < size - 1; i++) {
            elementData[i] = elementData[i + 1];
        }
        size--;
    }
}
```

15.2 A More Complete ArrayIntList

In this section, we will extend the ArrayIntList class to throw exceptions when preconditions are violated and to include a more inclusive set of methods that parallel the methods available for the built-in ArrayList<E>.

Throwing Exceptions

VideoNote

In the previous version of ArrayIntList, we documented the various preconditions of the methods. It is a good practice to clearly specify the contract with potential clients, but you shouldn't assume that clients will always obey the preconditions. As we saw in Chapter 4, the convention in Java is to throw an exception when a precondition is violated.

For example, consider the constructor that takes a capacity as a parameter:

```
// pre : capacity >= 0
// post: constructs an empty list with the given capacity
public ArrayIntList(int capacity) {
    elementData = new int[capacity];
    size = 0;
}
```

The precondition indicates that the capacity is not supposed to be negative. You can go further than just documenting it by adding code to throw an exception. In this case, it is appropriate to throw an IllegalArgumentException:

```
if (capacity < 0) {
    throw new IllegalArgumentException();
}
```

You have the option to include a string that will be displayed with the exception. In this case, it would be useful to tell the client the value that was being passed for capacity:

```
if (capacity < 0) {
    throw new IllegalArgumentException("capacity: " + capacity);
}
```

You should also mention the exception in the comments for the method. It is important to mention exactly which type of exception will be thrown and under what circumstances. Here, then, is the final version of the method with the extra code to throw an exception when the precondition is violated:

```
// pre : capacity >= 0 (throws IllegalArgumentException if not)
// post: constructs an empty list with the given capacity
public ArrayIntList(int capacity) {
```

```
        if (capacity < 0) {
            throw new IllegalArgumentException("capacity: " + capacity);
        }
        elementData = new int[capacity];
        size = 0;
    }
```

In order to construct an exception object to be thrown, you have to decide what type of exception to use. All of the examples we have seen so far have constructed exceptions of type `IllegalArgumentException`. This is a kind of generic exception that is used to indicate that some value passed as an argument was not legal. But there are other exception types that you can use. The convention in Java is to pick the most specific exception that you can. Table 15.1 lists of some of the most common exception types.

`NullPointerException` and `ArrayIndexOutOfBoundsException` are thrown by Java automatically, so you don't generally write code to specify those exceptions. Java programmers often use the other four exceptions, however.

Both of the `add` methods in your `ArrayIntList` class have a precondition that the size of the list must be strictly less than the capacity. Otherwise you will attempt to store a value in an array index that doesn't exist. This is an appropriate situation for an `IllegalStateException`. It is not appropriate to add values to the list once it has reached its capacity. In this case, you want to let the client know that the problem doesn't come from the values passed as arguments, but rather, that the `add` method was called at an inappropriate time.

You could add code to each of the `add` methods to check for this exception, but to avoid redundancy, it is better to introduce a private method that each of the methods calls. You'll be introducing some other methods that add more than one value at a time, so it will be useful to write the private method in a fairly flexible way. You can write a method that takes a required capacity as a parameter and that checks to make

Table 15.1 Common Exception Types

Exception Type	Description
`NullPointerException`	A `null` value has been used in a case that requires an object.
`ArrayIndexOutOfBoundsException`	A value passed as an index to an array is illegal.
`IndexOutOfBoundsException`	A value passed as an index to some nonarray structure is illegal.
`IllegalStateException`	A method has been called at an illegal or inappropriate time.
`IllegalArgumentException`	A value passed as an argument to a method is illegal.
`NoSuchElementException`	A call was made on an iterator's `next` method when there are no values left to iterate over.

sure that the array has that capacity. In other words, you'll tell the method, "I need room for this many elements," and it will test whether the array has that much room. If it does not, the method throws an `IllegalStateException`:

```
// post: checks that the underlying array has the given capacity,
//       throwing an IllegalStateException if it does not
private void checkCapacity(int capacity) {
    if (capacity > elementData.length) {
        throw new IllegalStateException("exceeds list capacity");
    }
}
```

You can add the following line of code to each of the `add` methods to check that the array has the capacity to add one more value to the list:

```
checkCapacity(size + 1);
```

You also need to modify the comments to indicate that this exception is thrown. For example, here is the rewritten appending `add` method:

```
// pre : size() < capacity (throws IllegalStateException if not)
// post: appends the given value to the end of the list
public void add(int value) {
    checkCapacity(size + 1);
    elementData[size] = value;
    size++;
}
```

Several methods specify the index of a value. The `get` method, for example, is supposed to return the value at a particular index. If you provide a value that is outside the bounds of the underlying array, then the method will throw an `ArrayIndexOutOfBoundsException`. This exception is better than nothing, but it doesn't cover all cases. For example, your list might have a capacity of 100 but have only 10 values stored in it. The client might try to access a value at index 10 or 11 or 50, and your method will return a result when you'd prefer it to throw an exception to let the client know that the index is not legal for a list of 10 elements.

In this case, it is better to throw an `IndexOutOfBoundsException` and to include the illegal index to let the client see exactly what bad value was passed as a parameter. There are multiple methods that refer to index values, so it is again useful to introduce a private method that can be called by each method:

```
// post: throws an IndexOutOfBoundsException if the given index is
//       not a legal index of the current list
private void checkIndex(int index) {
    if (index < 0 || index >= size) {
```

```
        throw new IndexOutOfBoundsException("index: " + index);
    }
}
```

This private method will properly throw an exception for `get` and `remove`. It isn't quite the right test to use for the `add` method that takes an index as a parameter, because `add` has a slightly different precondition than the other methods. Normally, it doesn't make sense to refer to a value at index `size` because that index is beyond the last value stored in the list. For example, if the list stores 10 values, then you don't want to call `get` or `remove` for a nonexistent value at index 10. But for `add`, it makes sense to refer to this index. If there are currently 10 values in the list, then you would be allowed to add a new value at index 10 because it is a new value not currently in the list. Instead of calling the private method, the `add` method will have its own code for checking the index and throwing an `IndexOutOfBoundsException`.

There is a further benefit to adding all of this code to throw exceptions: Adding the code will ensure that your object is never in a corrupt state. It will always satisfy certain data invariants. (Data invariants were described in Chapter 8.) In particular, you know that

- `size <= elementData.length` always (your calls on `checkCapacity` make sure of that)
- the array elements that you examine are always in the range of 0 to `size - 1` (your calls on `checkIndex` make sure of that)
- your code will never generate an `ArrayIndexOutOfBoundsException`

It is extremely useful to know that your class will always satisfy these constraints. This knowledge is an added benefit of encapsulation. If a client could reach in and change the `size` or `elementData` fields, then you couldn't make these kind of guarantees.

Convenience Methods

The built-in `ArrayList<E>` class has many other methods besides the ones we have implemented so far, so it makes sense to go ahead and add some of those methods to your `ArrayIntList` class. These methods are largely for the convenience of the client, since you could achieve the same functionality by calling existing methods on the list.

Your class has a method called `indexOf` that can be used to search for the location of a value in the list. Sometimes, though, a client just wants to ask the simpler question of whether a particular value appears in the list somewhere. The convention in Java is to use a method called `contains` for this purpose. It has a `boolean` return type:

```
public boolean contains(int value) {
    ...
}
```

How do you write this method? You don't want to duplicate the code that you included in `indexOf`, so instead you'll call `indexOf`. Remember that it returns a value of –1 if the value is not found, so you can test whether or not `indexOf` returned an index that is greater than or equal to `0`:

```
public boolean contains(int value) {
    if (indexOf(value) >= 0) {
        return true;
    } else {
        return false;
    }
}
```

This version violates Boolean Zen, which was covered in Chapter 5. You can simply return the value of the expression, rather than including it in an `if/else` statement:

```
return indexOf(value) >= 0;
```

Thus, the method ends up being a single line of code:

```
public boolean contains(int value) {
    return indexOf(value) >= 0;
}
```

Another common method in the Java Collections Framework is called `isEmpty`. It returns a `boolean` value indicating whether or not the list is empty. This is another method that can be written concisely as a one-line method using the value of the `size` field:

```
public boolean isEmpty() {
    return size == 0;
}
```

Again, you don't need an `if/else` statement; you can simply return the value of the Boolean expression.

So far you have included methods to add values to and remove values from the list, but sometimes you simply want to replace the value at a certain location with some new value. This operation is referred to as the `set` method and is easy to implement. You have to remember to include a call on `checkIndex` because the method has a precondition that is similar to that of `get` and `remove`:

```
public void set(int index, int value) {
    checkIndex(index);
    elementData[index] = value;
}
```

Providing this method is important because it allows a client to avoid unnecessary inefficiency. For example, suppose that the list has 10,000 values stored in it and the client wants to replace the first value with something new. The `set` method does it very quickly. The alternative would be to call `remove`, which would shift over the other 9999 values, and then to call `add`, which would shift the other 9999 values back to where they were earlier. Using `set` is much more efficient.

You might think that the introduction of the `set` method breaks encapsulation, because it allows a client to change a value in the array. But it doesn't really break encapsulation because you force the client to get this access by calling a method. This fact allows your method to be in control of the client request. So, for example, you can call the `checkIndex` method to ensure that the array index is legal.

Another common operation that a client might wish to perform is to empty the structure of all values. This is referred to as the `clear` operation and can be accomplished quickly by resetting the `size` field back to its original value of `0`:

```
public void clear() {
    size = 0;
}
```

You might imagine that you have to reset all of the array elements back to `0`, but that's not necessary. You have written the code in such a way that a client can only get access to array elements 0 through `size – 1`. When `size` is reset to `0`, the client can't access any of the array elements. The only way those array elements will be used again is if the client makes calls on the `add` method, in which case the old values will be overwritten with new values supplied by the client. But just as with the `remove` method, you will find at the end of the chapter that you solve this problem slightly differently for the generic `ArrayList` class.

The last method we will add is a "bulk add" method called `addAll` that adds all of the values from a second `ArrayIntList`. It may seem a little odd to have one `ArrayIntList` deal with another `ArrayIntList`, but this actually happens fairly often. The idea is that the first `ArrayIntList` is supposed to add all of the values from the second `ArrayIntList`, which means that the header for the method looks like the following:

```
public void addAll(ArrayIntList other) {
    ...
}
```

You can call the appending `add` method to add values to the list. You just need a loop that iterates over the values in the second list. You also need to call your `checkCapacity` method to make sure that the array has sufficient capacity to store these new values:

```
public void addAll(ArrayIntList other) {
    checkCapacity(size + other.size);
```

```
    for (int i = 0; i < other.size; i++) {
        add(other.elementData[i]);
    }
}
```

This code refers to other.size and other.elementData, which you might imagine would generate an error because they are private fields. In fact, the code does not generate an error. Recall from the Chapter 8 examples that the word "private" means that it is "private to the class." This is not the way that we as humans understand the meaning of private. (If something is private to me, then it shouldn't be available to other humans.) But in Java, one ArrayIntList object can access private elements of another ArrayIntList object because they both belong to the same class.

You can find the complete third version of the ArrayIntList class on the web page http://buildingjavaprograms.com.

15.3 Advanced Features

In this section, we explore adding some extra advanced functionality to the ArrayIntList class. First we will see how to implement the class so that it has no fixed capacity and will grow larger if necessary. Then we will learn how to provide an iterator over the list.

Resizing When Necessary

The built-in ArrayList<E> class has a notion of capacity, as does our ArrayIntList class. But instead of throwing an exception when the capacity is exceeded, the class creates a larger array. In other words, its capacity grows as needed to accommodate the addition of new values to the list.

It isn't generally easy to make an array bigger. Java doesn't allow you to stretch an array that was constructed previously. Instead, you have to allocate a brand-new array and copy values from the old array to the new array. An analogy would be the way shops and other businesses work in the real world. If you need some extra space for your store, you can't generally break down the wall and grab some of the space from the store next door. More often, you have to relocate your store to a larger space.

Obviously you don't want to construct a new array too often. For example, suppose you had space for 1000 values and found you needed space for one more. A poor solution would be to allocate a new array of length 1001 and copy the 1000 values over. Then, if you find you need space for one more, you could make an array that is 1002 in length and copy the 1001 old values over. This kind of growth policy would be very expensive.

A better idea would be to double the size of the array when you run out of space. If you have filled up an array of length 1000, you double its size to 2000 when the client adds something more. That particular call on add is expensive because it has to copy 1000 values from the old array to the new array. But you won't need to copy again for a while. You can add another 999 values before you'd need extra space. As a result, we think of the expense as being spread out or *amortized* over all 1000 calls on `add`. When the cost is spread out over 1000 adds, it is fairly low (a constant).

The built-in `ArrayList` class does something similar. The documentation is a little coy about this: "The details of the growth policy are not specified beyond the fact that adding an element has constant amortized time cost." If you look at the actual code, you'll find that it increases the capacity by 50% each time (a multiplier of 1.5).

So how do you add this functionality to your `ArrayIntList` class? You included a method called `checkCapacity` that throws an exception if the array isn't big enough. You can simply replace this method with a new method that makes the array larger if necessary:

```
public void ensureCapacity(int capacity) {
    if (capacity > elementData.length) {
        int newCapacity = elementData.length * 2 + 1;
        if (capacity > newCapacity) {
            newCapacity = capacity;
        }
        int[] newList = new int[newCapacity];
        for (int i = 0; i < size; i++) {
            newList[i] = elementData[i];
        }
        elementData = newList;
    }
}
```

This version of the method works, but you can get a slight improvement by calling a built-in method called `Arrays.copyOf` that returns a copy of an array. It has the same functionality as the preceding code, but it is likely to run faster because this operation is what is known as a *block copy* operation that can be optimized to run faster. Thus, the method can be rewritten as follows:

```
public void ensureCapacity(int capacity) {
    if (capacity > elementData.length) {
        int newCapacity = elementData.length * 2 + 1;
        if (capacity > newCapacity) {
            newCapacity = capacity;
        }
        elementData = Arrays.copyOf(elementData, newCapacity);
    }
}
```

The `checkCapacity` method was declared to be private, but the preceding method has been declared to be public, because a client might also want to make use of that method. For example, if the client recognizes that the capacity needs to be significantly increased, then it is useful to be able to call this method to resize it once rather than resizing several times. The `ArrayList<E>` class has this method available as a public method.

Adding an Iterator

In Chapter 11, we saw that it is common in the collections framework to use an iterator object to traverse a collection. Recall that an iterator should provide three basic operations:

- `hasNext()`, which returns true if there are more elements to be examined
- `next()`, which returns the next element from the list and advances the position of the iterator by one
- `remove()`, which removes the element most recently returned by `next()`

We will develop a class called `ArrayIntListIterator` that implements this functionality for an `ArrayIntList`. The usual convention in Java is to ask the collection to construct the iterator by calling the method `iterator`:

```
ArrayIntList list = new ArrayIntList();
// code to fill up list ...
ArrayIntListIterator i = list.iterator();
```

Once we have obtained an iterator from the list, we can use its three methods to traverse the list. For example, the following program constructs an `ArrayIntList` and then computes the product of the list:

```
public class Client2 {
    public static void main(String[] args) {
        // construct and print list
        int[] data = {13, 4, 85, 13, 40, -8, 17, -5};
        ArrayIntList list = new ArrayIntList();
        for (int n : data) {
            list.add(n);
        }
        System.out.println("list = " + list);

        // obtain an iterator to find the product of the list
        ArrayIntListIterator i = list.iterator();
        int product = 1;
        while (i.hasNext()) {
            int n = i.next();
```

```
            product *= n;
        }
        System.out.println("product = " + product);
    }
}
```

The program produces the following output:

```
list = [13, 4, 85, 13, 40, –8, 17, –5]
product = 1562912000
```

Here is a variation that removes any `0` values from the list, computing the product of the nonzero values:

```
public class Client3 {
    public static void main(String[] args) {
        // construct and print list
        int[] data = {5, 19, 0, 2, 4, 0, 13, 85, –8, 0, 23};
        ArrayIntList list = new ArrayIntList();
        for (int n : data) {
            list.add(n);
        }
        System.out.println("list = " + list);

        // use an iterator to find the product, removing zeros
        ArrayIntListIterator i = list.iterator();
        int product = 1;
        while (i.hasNext()) {
            int n = i.next();
            if (n == 0) {
                i.remove();
            } else {
                product *= n;
            }
        }
        System.out.println("list now = " + list);
        System.out.println("product = " + product);
    }
}
```

The program produces the following output:

```
list = [5, 19, 0, 2, 4, 0, 13, 85, –8, 0, 23]
list now = [5, 19, 2, 4, 13, 85, –8, 23]
product = –154523200
```

So how do you implement the `ArrayIntListIterator` class? The main function that the iterator performs is to keep track of a particular position in a list, so the primary field will be an integer variable for storing this position:

```
public class ArrayIntListIterator {
    private int position;

    public ArrayIntListIterator(...) {
        position = 0;
        ...
    }
    ...
}
```

Initially you start `position` at `0` so that it will refer to the first value in the list. The `hasNext` method is supposed to determine whether any values remain to iterate over. To do so, it will have to compare this position to the size of the list:

```
public boolean hasNext() {
    // check position against size of the list
}
```

To perform this comparison, the iterator needs to be able to find out the size of the list. To do so, the iterator will need to keep track of the list over which it is iterating. That means that you will need a second field and the constructor will have to be passed a reference to the list to iterate over:

```
public class ArrayIntListIterator {
    private ArrayIntList list;
    private int position;

    public ArrayIntListIterator(ArrayIntList list) {
        this.list = list;
        position = 0;
        ...
    }

    ...
}
```

Using this field, you can now easily write the `hasNext` method:

```
public boolean hasNext() {
    return position < list.size();
}
```

What about the `next` method? It is supposed to return the next value from the list and then reset the position to be one later in the sequence, which you can accomplish by simply incrementing the value:

```
public int next() {
    int result = list.get(position);
    position++;
    return result;
}
```

But the method has an important precondition that you must consider. What if a client calls `next` when the iterator has run out of values to return? The method should throw an exception in that case. The convention in Java is to throw a `NoSuchElementException`:

```
public int next() {
    if (!hasNext()) {
        throw new NoSuchElementException();
    }
    int result = list.get(position);
    position++;
    return result;
}
```

The final operation performed by an iterator is the `remove` method. The method is supposed to remove the most recent value that was returned by `next`. The `position` field keeps track of the next value to be returned by the iterator, so the value to be removed is at index `position – 1`:

```
public void remove() {
    list.remove(position – 1);
    ...
}
```

Keep in mind what happens when you ask the `ArrayIntList` to remove that value. All of the other values will be shifted one to the left in the list. That means that `position` will no longer be positioned at the next value in the list. That value has been shifted one to the left, so you have to decrement `position` to account for the shift that has taken place:

```
public void remove() {
    list.remove(position – 1);
    position––;
}
```

This method also has an important precondition to consider. A client is supposed to call `next` before calling `remove`. One possibility is that the client will call `remove` before making any call on `next`. If that happens, it will be obvious from the fact that `position` will be zero. Another possibility is that the client will call `remove` twice in a row without calling `next` in between. That is not a legal operation either. You won't know just from looking at the value of `position` whether the client has violated this precondition.

In this case, you need an extra bit of state for the object. You need to keep track of whether it is currently legal to remove a value, so this is a good time to add a field. It will be of type `boolean` and you can call it `removeOK`. You can use this field to throw an exception if the precondition is violated. And once a call on `remove` has been performed, you have to remember that it is no longer legal to remove a value until `next` is called again:

```
public void remove() {
    if (!removeOK) {
        throw new IllegalStateException();
    }
    list.remove(position - 1);
    position--;
    removeOK = false;
}
```

Notice that you throw an `IllegalStateException` because a call on the method is not appropriate if it is not okay to remove a value. You can then add code to the constructor to initialize this field to `false`, and you can reset it to `true` whenever `next` is called.

Here is the final class definition:

```
// Objects of this class can be used to iterate over an
// ArrayIntList and remove values from the list.

import java.util.*;

public class ArrayIntListIterator {
    private ArrayIntList list;         // list to iterate over
    private int position;              // current list position
    private boolean removeOK;          // okay to remove now?

    // post: constructs an iterator for the given list
    public ArrayIntListIterator(ArrayIntList list) {
        this.list = list;
        position = 0;
        removeOK = false;
```

```
    }

    // post: returns true if there are more elements left
    public boolean hasNext() {
        return position < list.size();
    }

    // pre : hasNext() (throws NoSuchElementException if not)
    // post: returns the next element in the iteration
    public int next() {
        if (!hasNext()) {
            throw new NoSuchElementException();
        }
        int result = list.get(position);
        position++;
        removeOK = true;
        return result;
    }

    // pre : next() has been called without a call on remove
    //       (throws IllegalStateException if not)
    // post: removes the last element returned by the iterator
    public void remove() {
        if (!removeOK) {
            throw new IllegalStateException();
        }
        list.remove(position - 1);
        position--;
        removeOK = false;
    }
}
```

The program imports the `java.util` package because the class for one of the exceptions we want to throw, `NoSuchElementException`, comes from that package.

You also have to modify the `ArrayIntList` class. Remember that it needs to have a method called `iterator` that constructs an iterator, which means it will look like this:

```
public ArrayIntListIterator iterator() {
    return new ArrayIntListIterator(...);
}
```

So which list should you mention in the call on the `ArrayIntListIterator` constructor? The `ArrayIntList` is supposed to construct an iterator that is looking at itself. You can use the `this` keyword to say, "Construct an iterator that is iterating over me":

```
public ArrayIntListIterator iterator() {
    return new ArrayIntListIterator(this);
}
```

You can find a complete listing of this fourth version of the `ArrayIntList` class along with the `ArrayIntListIterator` class on the web page for this textbook at http://buildingjavaprograms.com.

15.4 ArrayList<E>

In this section, we will explore how to convert the version of `ArrayIntList` from the previous section into a generic `ArrayList<E>`. To start, you can simply replace all occurrences of `ArrayIntList` with `ArrayList<E>` and change references to `int` that refer to values to `E`. Of course, there are other uses of `int` that specify capacity, size, and indexes, and these don't change.

This approach almost works, but there are a few places where you have to be careful. For example, when you define constructors, you don't use the generic `E` when you're naming the constructor. So the zero-argument constructor becomes:

```
public ArrayList() {
    this(DEFAULT_CAPACITY);
}
```

You also run into trouble in the second constructor. After you perform the simple substitution, you end up with the following method:

```
public ArrayList(int capacity) {
    if (capacity < 0) {
        throw new IllegalArgumentException("capacity: " + capacity);
    }
    elementData = new E[capacity]; // illegal
    size = 0;
}
```

When you try to compile this version, you get an error indicating that you are not allowed to construct a generic array. This is a limitation of generic types. You can construct an array of type `Object[]`, but not an array of type `E[]`. You can solve this problem by introducing a cast. Replace the following line of code:

```
elementData = new E[capacity];
```

In its place, include this line of code:

```
elementData = (E[]) new Object[capacity];
```

This new version compiles, but it generates a warning about using unsafe or unchecked types. There's no real way to get around this because Java won't let you construct a generic array. That means you can ignore this warning. In this case, it is good to include an *annotation* for the method to indicate that you don't want it to generate the warning for this method:

```
@SuppressWarnings("unchecked")
public ArrayList(int capacity) {
    ...
}
```

Annotations are special Java syntax that mark metadata on a class or method. They give instructions to the compiler. This particular annotation is a way of telling the compiler, "Don't generate the warning for this method because I'm aware of the problem already." There are many different kinds of annotations that you can include in your Java programs, but we won't take time to explore them in this book.

There is also a problem with the `indexOf` method. After you perform the substitution of `E` for `int`, here is the result:

```
public int indexOf(E value) {
    for (int i = 0; i < size; i++) {
        if (elementData[i] == value) {
            return i;
        }
    }
    return -1;
}
```

This version compiles and would work, but it has a very strict definition of equality. It would require that the actual object you are searching for appears in the list. More often, you want to use an `equals` comparison to see whether the value for which you are searching is equal to some value in the list. You'll want to replace the following bit of code from your method:

```
if (elementData[i] == value) {
    ...
}
```

You can replace it with the following:

```
if (elementData[i].equals(value)) {
    ...
}
```

One final issue has to do with memory allocation. Consider what happens when a value is removed from the simple `ArrayIntList`. An array element that used to correspond to a list element is no longer being used. In general, this isn't a problem, and we haven't bothered to do any cleaning up afterward. For example, suppose that you have a list with a capacity of 10 and you store the values `[10, 20, 30, 40]` in the list. The array looks like this:

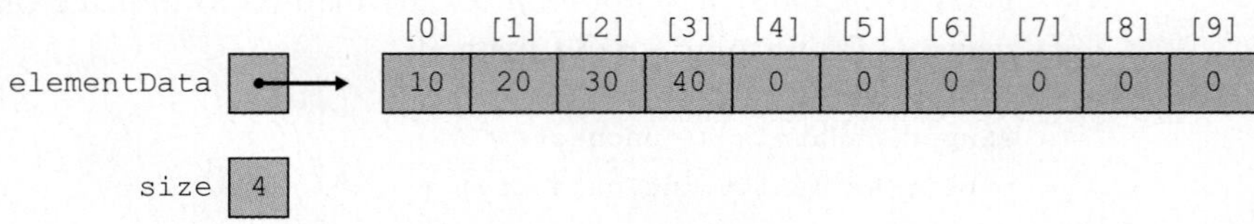

If you then remove the value at index `0`, you shift the other three values left and decrement `size`:

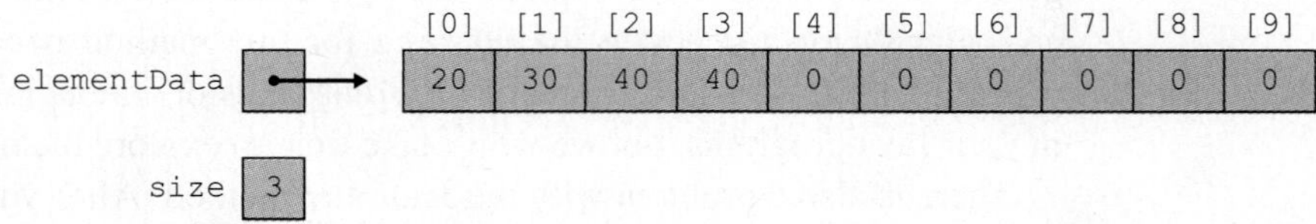

Notice that you now have two occurrences of `40` in the list. That isn't generally a problem because you know from the value of your `size` field that the `40` stored in index `3` isn't being used.

You can't be so cavalier when it comes to objects. We have to think about what is known as the *garbage collector*:

Garbage Collector

A process that is part of the Java Runtime Environment that periodically frees the memory used by objects that are no longer referenced.

In some programming languages, you have to explicitly destroy objects when you don't need to use them any longer. Java saves you the trouble of doing this. Instead, its garbage collector looks for objects that are no longer being used (i.e., objects that are no longer referenced). You want to make sure that your `ArrayList` doesn't interfere with what the garbage collector is trying to accomplish.

If your `ArrayList` is keeping a reference to some object that is no longer being used, then the garbage collector might not recognize that it can reclaim that space. So you have to explicitly set that array element back to `null`.

A direct translation of the code produces the following `remove` method:

```
public void remove(int index) {
    checkIndex(index);
    for (int i = index; i < size - 1; i++) {
```

```
        elementData[i] = elementData[i + 1];
    }
    size--;
}
```

You need to add an extra line of code after the shifting code that sets the unused array element back to `null`:

```
public void remove(int index) {
    checkIndex(index);
    for (int i = index; i < size - 1; i++) {
        elementData[i] = elementData[i + 1];
    }
    elementData[size - 1] = null;
    size--;
}
```

Similarly, the `clear` method needs to set all values to `null` before resetting the `size` field to `0`:

```
public void clear() {
    for (int i = 0; i < size; i++) {
        elementData[i] = null;
    }
    size = 0;
}
```

One final change that you will see in this class is that the iterator class has been converted to what is known as an *inner class*:

Inner Class

A class declared inside another class. Objects of the inner class have access to the methods and fields of the outer class.

In other words, the structure becomes

```
public class ArrayList<E> {
    ...
    private class ArrayListIterator implements Iterator<E> {
        ...
    }
}
```

The generic syntax can be a bit confusing with inner classes. We declare our inner `ArrayListIterator` class without an `<E>` type parameter, because the type `E` is already declared as part of the outer list class. But we do have to say that it implements `Iterator<E>` to match the interface from `java.util`. Accidentally declaring the inner class as `ArrayListIterator<E>` actually creates a second generic type `E` and leads to confusing compiler errors.

Inner classes are normally declared to be private. Using an inner class for the iterator is the more usual approach. It allows you to eliminate the field that keeps track of the list. As we indicated in the definition box, when you declare an inner class, the instances of the inner class have access to the methods and fields of the instance of the outer class that constructed it. For example, the old version of the `hasNext` method refers to a field called `list` that was used to keep track of the list over which the iterator was iterating:

```
public boolean hasNext() {
    return position < list.size();
}
```

This code can be simplified. Because the iterator class is now an inner class, you can write the `hasNext` method in a simple way:

```
public boolean hasNext() {
    return position < size();
}
```

This method is calling the `size` method even though the iterator has no such method. Because it has no such method, it calls the `ArrayList` method of the outer class.

This can cause problems in one part of the code. When you write the `remove` method for the iterator, you need to call the `remove` method of the list:

```
public void remove() {
    if (!removeOK) {
        throw new IllegalStateException();
    }
    remove(position − 1); // illegal
    position−−;
    removeOK = false;
}
```

Unfortunately, this version does not compile, because both the iterator and the list have a method called `remove`. One has no parameters and the other has one parameter, so you'd think that Java could tell the difference, but it can't. You have to use a special notation to make it clear that you want to refer to the outer object. You do that by referring to the `this` value of the outer class, which you refer to as `ArrayList.this`. Thus, you can rewrite the following line of code:

```
remove(position − 1);
```

Here is the new version of the code:

```
ArrayList.this.remove(position - 1);
```

Before we finish this exploration, we should consider at least briefly the issue of interfaces. As we saw in Chapters 9 and 11, interfaces allow clients to describe variables in a more generic way. For example, suppose that you want to iterate over an `ArrayList` of `String` values. You'll replace the following line of code:

```
ArrayListIterator i = list.iterator();
```

Instead, you'll use the `Iterator<E>` interface:

```
Iterator<String> i = list.iterator();
```

In order for this code to compile, it is important for the `ArrayListIterator` class to implement the `Iterator` interface and for the return type for the `iterator()` method to use the interface rather than the class name. These changes have been incorporated into the final version of the class. It turns out that there are other interfaces to consider as well, but we will save that discussion until the end of the next chapter. At that time we will see a final version of the `ArrayList` class that is even closer to the built-in version.

You will find the complete code for the `ArrayList` class on our web page at http://buildingjavaprograms.com.

Chapter Summary

In this chapter, we implemented an array list class to store lists of integers.

Collection classes have two views: the external view seen by client code and the internal view seen by the implementer.

An array list uses an unfilled array and a `size` field in which the first *size* elements are meaningful and the rest are empty zeroes that are not considered to be part of the list. The entire array length represents its capacity for storing values.

When we add values to or remove values from the front or middle of an array list, we must shift the values right or left respectively to account for the newly added or removed element.

Our array list has preconditions that the client will not pass an illegal capacity on construction or illegal indexes when accessing elements. If the client does try to do so, Java will throw an exception.

Our subsequent versions of the list class resize to a larger capacity when the array becomes full.

The array list has an iterator for examining its elements in sequence.

Our array list of integers can be converted into a generic class that can store a list of any type of objects. The code is similar, but we must make a few changes—for example, when we construct arrays of type `E[]` or compare objects for equality.

An inner class is declared inside the braces of another (outer) class and has access to the state of an object of that outer class. Our final list iterator is an inner class.

Self-Check Problems

Section 15.1: Simple `ArrayIntList`

1. What is the difference between an array list's size and its capacity? What is the relationship between the two values? (Is one always larger or smaller than the other, for instance?)
2. What fields must be included in the `ArrayIntList` class, and why is each field important? Would the class still work correctly if we removed any of these fields?
3. How would the output of the `Client1` program shown in this section change if each field from `ArrayIntList` were declared `static`?
4. In this version of the list class, what happens if the client adds too many values to fit in the array?
5. Why does the list class use a `toString` method rather than a `print` method?
6. We wrote the class to have public methods called `size` (to read the number of elements of the list) and `get` (to access the element value at a specific index). Why is this approach better than declaring the fields (such as `size`) `public`?
7. An element can be inserted at the beginning, middle, or end of an array list. Which of the three insertion points is the most computationally expensive, and why? Which is the most expensive location to remove an element from the list?
8. Write methods called `min` and `max` that return the smallest and largest values in the list respectively. For example, if a variable called `list` stores `[11, -7, 3, 42, 0, 14]`, the call of `list.min()` should return `-7` and the call of `list.max()` should return `42`. If the list is empty, the methods should throw an `IllegalStateException`.

Section 15.2: A More Complete `ArrayIntList`

9. Describe the overall preconditions placed on the list class in this section. What assumptions do we make about how clients will use the list?
10. What is the purpose of the `checkIndex` method? Where is it called in the list class? Describe a way that the client can utilize an `ArrayIntList` that will be caught by `checkIndex`.
11. What is the purpose of the `checkCapacity` method? Where is it called in the list class? Describe a way that the client can utilize an `ArrayIntList` that will be caught by `checkCapacity`.
12. Once we check thoroughly for preconditions in the code, what data invariants can we now assume about the list?
13. Why do we bother to add the `contains`, `isEmpty`, and `remove` methods to the list class, when the client can already perform this same functionality with the `indexOf`, `size`, and `remove` methods, respectively?

Section 15.3: Advanced Features

14. When this new version of the class fills to its capacity, it resizes. How much does it grow? Why choose this growth rate, rather than increasing the capacity by a single element or other constant amount?
15. What is the benefit of adding an iterator to the list class?

16. What state does the array list iterator store?

17. How does the array list iterator know if there are more elements left to examine? What does it do if the client tries to examine a next element but there are none left to examine?

18. What is a precondition of the iterator's `remove` method? How does the iterator enforce this precondition, and what does it do if the precondition is violated?

19. Write a method called `sum` that returns the sum of all values in the list. For example, if a variable called `list` stores `[11, -7, 3, 42, 0, 14]`, the call of `list.sum()` should return `63`. If the list is empty, `sum` should return `0`.

20. Write a method called `average` that returns the average of the values in the list as a real number. For example, if a variable called `list` stores `[11, -7, 3, 42, 0, 14]`, the call of `list.average()` should return `10.5`. If the list is empty, `average` should return `0.0`.

Section 15.4: `ArrayList<E>`

21. What problem do we encounter when we try to construct an array of type `E`? How do we resolve this problem?

22. Since our list stores an unfilled array, the empty elements were filled with the value `0` when our array was full of integers. What value occupies the empty cells when our list stores values of type `E`?

23. What changes need to be made to the `indexOf` method to search for objects of type `E` in the new list class, and why are these changes necessary?

24. What is an annotation? How are annotations useful in writing our `ArrayList<E>` class?

25. Why is it important to set empty elements to `null` when we are clearing or removing from the list of type `E`, when we didn't need to clear out these elements in the previous `ArrayIntList`?

26. What is one benefit of making the list iterator into an inner class?

Exercises

Each of the following exercises is a method to be added to the `ArrayIntList` class from this chapter.

1. Write a method called `lastIndexOf` that accepts an integer as a parameter and returns the index in the list of the last occurrence of that value, or −1 if the value is not found in the list. For example, if the list stores `[1, 18, 2, 7, 18, 39, 18, 40]`, then the last index of 18 is 6 and the last index of 3 is −1.

2. Write a method called `indexOfSubList` that accepts another list *L* as a parameter and returns the starting index of where *L* first appears in this list, or −1 if it is not found. All elements of *L* must appear in sequence and in the same order. For example, if variables called `list1` and `list2` store `[11, -7, 3, 42, 0, 14]` and `[3, 42, 0]`, respectively, the call of `list1.indexOfSubList(list2)` should return `2`.

3. Write a method called `replaceAll` that accepts two integer values as parameters and replaces all occurrences of the first value in the list with the second value. For example, if a variable called `list` stores `[11, -7, 3, 42, 3, 0, 14, 3]`, the call of `list.replaceAll(3, 999);` should change the list to store `[11, -7, 999, 42, 999, 0, 14, 999]`.

4. Write a method called `reverse` that reverses the order of the elements in the array list. For example, if a variable called `list` stores `[11, -7, 3, 42, 0, 14, 56]`, the call of `list.reverse();` should change the list to store `[56, 14, 0, 42, 3, -7, 11]`. An empty or one-element list is not changed by a call to this method.

5. Write a method called `runningTotal` that returns a new `ArrayIntList` that contains a running total of the original list. In other words, the *i*th value in the new list should store the sum of elements 0 through *i* of the original list.

For example, given a variable `list` that stores `[2, 3, 5, 4, 7, 15, 20, 7]`, consider what happens when the following call is made:

```
ArrayIntList list2 = list.runningTotal();
```

The variable `list2` should store `[2, 5, 10, 14, 21, 36, 56, 63]`. The original list should not be changed by the method. If the original list is empty, the result should be an empty list. The new list should have the same capacity as the original. Remember that there is a list constructor that accepts a capacity as a parameter.

6. Write a method called `fill` that accepts an integer value as a parameter and replaces every value in the list with that value. For example, if a variable called `list` initially stores `[42, –7, 3, 0, 15]` and the call of `list.fill(2);` is made, the list will be changed to store `[2, 2, 2, 2, 2]`.

7. Write a method called `isPairwiseSorted` that returns whether or not a list of integers is pairwise sorted. A list is considered pairwise sorted if each successive pair of numbers is in nondecreasing order. For example, if a variable called `list` stores `[3, 8, 2, 5, 19, 24, –3, 0, 4, 4, 8, 205, 42]`, then the call of `list.isPairwiseSorted()` should return `true` because the successive pairs of this list are all sorted: `(3, 8), (2, 5), (19, 24), (–3, 0), (4, 4), (8, 205)`. The extra value `42` at the end had no effect on the result because it is not part of a pair. If the list had instead stored `[7, 42, 308, 409, 19, 17, 2]`, then the method should return `false` because the pair `(19, 17)` is not in sorted order. If a list is so short that it has no pairs, then it is considered to be pairwise sorted.

8. Write a method called `count` that accepts an element value as a parameter and returns the number of occurrences of that value in the list. For example, suppose a variable named `list` stores `[2, -3, 2, 0, 5, 2, 2, 6]`. A call of `list.count(2)` should return `4` because there are four occurrences of that value in the list.

9. Write a method called `maxCount` that returns the number of occurrences of the most frequently occurring value in a sorted list of integers. Because the list will be sorted, all duplicates will be grouped together, which will make it easier to count duplicates. For example, if a variable called `list` stores `[1, 3, 4, 7, 7, 7, 7, 9, 9, 11, 13, 14, 14, 14, 16, 16, 18, 19, 19, 19]`, the call of `list.maxCount()` should return `4` because the most frequently occurring value (`7`) occurs four times. It is possible that there will be a tie for the most frequently occurring value, but that doesn't affect the outcome because you are just returning the count, not the value. If there are no duplicates in the list, then every value will occur exactly once and the max count is `1`. If the list is empty, the method should return `0`.

10. Write a method called `longestSortedSequence` that returns the length of the longest sorted sequence within a list of integers. For example, if a variable called `list` stores `[1, 3, 5, 2, 9, 7, –3, 0, 42, 308, 17]`, then the call of `list.longestSortedSequence()` would return `4` because it is the length of the longest sorted sequence within this list (the sequence `–3, 0, 42, 308`). If the list is empty, your method should return `0`. Notice that for a nonempty list the method will always return a value of at least `1` because any individual element constitutes a sorted sequence.

11. Write a method called `removeLast` that removes and returns the last value from a list of integers. For example, if a variable called list stores `[8, 17, 42, 3, 8]`, a call of `list.removeLast();` should return `8` and change the list's state to `[8, 17, 42, 3]`. The next call would return `3` and remove `3` from the list, and so on. If the list is empty, throw a `NoSuchElementException`.

12. Write a method called `removeFront` that takes an integer *n* as a parameter and that removes the first *n* values from a list of integers. For example, if a variable called `list` stores `[8, 17, 9, 24, 42, 3, 8]` and a call of `list.removeFront(4);` is made, the list's contents should become `[42, 3, 8]`. You may assume that the parameter value passed is between `0` and the size of the list inclusive.

13. Write a method `removeAll` that accepts an integer value as a parameter and that removes all occurrences of the given value from the list.

14. Write a method called `printInversions` that lists all inversions in a list of integers. An inversion is a pair of numbers in which the first appears before the second in the list, but the first is greater than the second. Thus, for a sorted list such as `[1, 2, 3, 4]` there are no inversions at all, and the method would produce no output. Suppose that a variable called `list` stores the values `[4, 3, 2, 1]`. The call of `list.printInversions();` would print many inversions:

```
(4, 3)
(4, 2)
(4, 1)
(3, 2)
(3, 1)
(2, 1)
```

The inversions can appear in any order, so this is just one possible correct output. You must reproduce this format exactly, but the inversions can appear in any order. You may assume that the list has no duplicates.

15. Write a method called `mirror` that doubles the size of a list by appending the mirror image of the original sequence to the end of the list. The mirror image is the same sequence of values in reverse order. For example, if a variable called `list` stores `[1, 3, 2, 7]` and the client calls `list.mirror();` then the list should be changed to store `[1, 3, 2, 7, 7, 2, 3, 1]`. Notice that it has doubled in size because the original sequence now appears in reverse order at the end of the list.

16. Write a method called `stutter` that replaces every value with two of that value. For example, if the list initially stores `[42, 7, 0, –3, 15]`, after the call it should store `[42, 42, 7, 7, 0, 0, –3, –3, 15, 15]`.

17. Write a method called `stretch` that takes an integer *n* as a parameter and that increases a list of integers by a factor of *n* by replacing each integer in the original list with *n* copies of that integer. For example, if a variable called `list` stores `[18, 7, 4, 24, 11]` and we make the call of `list.stretch(3);` the list should be changed to store `[18, 18, 18, 7, 7, 7, 4, 4, 4, 24, 24, 24, 11, 11, 11]`. If *n* is zero or negative, the list should become empty.

18. Write a method called `doubleList` that doubles the size of a list by appending a copy of the original sequence to the end of the list. For example, if the list stores `[1, 8, 2, 7]`, your method should change it to store `[1, 8, 2, 7, 1, 8, 2, 7]`.

19. Write a method called `compress` that replaces every pair of elements in the list with a single element equal to the sum of the pair. If the list is of odd size, leave the last element unchanged. For example, if the list stores `[1, 7, 3, 9, 4, 6, 5]`, your method should change it to store `[8, 12, 10, 5]` (1+7, then 3+9, then 4+6, then 5).

20. Write a method called `rotate` that moves the value at the front of a list of integers to the end of the list. For example, if a variable called `list` stores `[8, 23, 19, 7, 12, 4]`, the call of `list.rotate();` should move the value `8` from the front of the list to the back of the list, producing `[23, 19, 7, 12, 4, 8]`.

21. Write a method called `switchPairs` that switches the order of values in the list in a pairwise fashion. Your method should switch the order of the first two values, then switch the order of the next two, switch the order of the next two, and so on. If the list contains an odd number of values, the final element is not moved. For example, if the list initially stores `[10, 25, 31, 47, 52, 68, 77]`, your method should switch the first pair (`10` and `25`), the second pair (`31` and `47`), and the third pair (`52` and `68`) to yield `[25, 10, 47, 31, 68, 52, 77]`.

Programming Projects

1. The actual `List` interface in the `java.util` package has several methods beyond the ones implemented in this chapter. Write a version of `ArrayList<E>` that adds some or all of these methods. The methods to add are as follows (some headers are slightly modified; see the Java API Specification for descriptions of each method):

- public void addAll(int index, ArrayList<E> list)
- public boolean containsAll(ArrayList<E> list)
- public boolean equals(Object o)
- public int lastIndexOf(Object o)
- public boolean remove(Object o)
- public void removeAll(ArrayList<E> list)
- public void retainAll(ArrayList<E> list)
- public Object[] toArray()

2. The java.util package has an interface called ListIterator that extends the Iterator interface and includes additional methods specific to iterating through the elements of lists forward or backward. Write a class called ArrayListIterator2 that adds some or all of these methods. The methods to add are as follows (see the Java API Specification for descriptions of each method):

- public void add(E value)
- public boolean hasPrevious()
- public int nextIndex()
- public E previous()
- public int previousIndex()
- public void set(E value)

3. The actual ArrayList class in the java.util package has a method called subList that returns a view of a subportion of a list through a given range of indexes. It can be useful to think of part of a list as if it were its own list, complete with its own set of indexes and values. The sublist is "backed" by the original list, meaning that it is not a copy; if any change is made to the sublist, the original list is also affected.

   In order to implement this method, you will need to write an inner class inside ArrayList<E> that extends ArrayList and implements the behavior of the sublist. Override the methods for getting and setting values at particular indexes, as well as the size method, so that they reflect the sublist's index range and size. Also, modify the outer ArrayList<E> class so that it always refers to its own elements through the use of these methods. The outer class should be given the following new method that returns an object of your new inner sublist class:

   ```
   public ArrayList<E> subList(int fromIndex, int toIndex)
   ```

4. Based on the implementation of ArrayIntList or ArrayList, write a class SortedIntList or SortedList that provides most of the same operations but maintains its elements in sorted order. When a new value is added to the sorted list, rather than appending it to the end of the list, it is placed in the appropriate index to maintain sorted order of the overall list.

   For efficiency, you should discover the appropriate place to add new values to the list by using a binary search. Shift elements as needed and add the element in the proper index to maintain sorted order. (Do not manually re-sort the elements such as by calling Arrays.sort.). You should also modify the class's indexOf method to use a binary search to locate elements.

   Since the list must remain sorted, your sorted list should not retain the following operations from ArrayIntList or ArrayList:

   ```
   public void add(int index, int value)
   public void set(int index, int value)
   ```

Chapter 16

Linked Lists

Introduction

In the previous chapter, we explored how to build a list structure using an array as the underlying storage mechanism. In this chapter we will explore a different structure known as a *linked list*. Linked lists serve as a useful contrast to arrays because their strengths and weaknesses are completely opposite. And just as Java has an `ArrayList<E>` class as part of the collections framework, it also has a `LinkedList<E>` class.

Even though Java provides an off-the-shelf implementation of a linked list, it is useful to study how it is implemented because it will give you good insights into the properties of linked lists. It is also important for you to understand the concept of a linked structure. Almost all data structures are implemented using some combination of arrays or linking or both, which means that it is important to understand each approach.

We will once again develop a structure for storing simple `int` values, as we did with the development of `ArrayIntList` in the last chapter. Our new structure will be called `LinkedIntList`. Keeping the data simple will allow us to focus on the data structure issues and to learn how to manipulate linked lists in general. Then we will explore some issues related to interfaces. Finally, at the end of the chapter we will explore how to turn the fairly simple `LinkedIntList` into a more general `LinkedList<E>` class.

16.1 Working with Nodes

Because arrays are stored in one large contiguous block of memory, we can quickly locate any particular element of the array. Recall that this ability to quickly jump around in the array is called random access. The weaknesses of the array approach are that we can't easily insert values in or remove values from the middle without shifting other values, and we can't easily enlarge the size of the structure without constructing a brand-new array with a larger capacity.

The linked list structure has the opposite properties. It is not a random access structure, so it is not easy to jump around in the structure. It has the kind of sequential access we associate with a cassette tape. If you are playing a tape and want to skip forward 10 songs, you have to fast forward through the songs. You can't quickly skip to the position where you want to be on the tape. Linked lists have this property as well.

But where arrays are weak, linked lists are strong. We can quickly insert values in or delete values from the middle of a linked list without any shifting. It is also easy to make the list larger or smaller.

Linked lists are composed of individual elements called *nodes*.

Node

A single element of a structure such as a linked list; each node contains one data value.

A node is like a Lego building block. It looks unimpressive by itself, but once you put a bunch of them together, it can form an interesting structure.

A basic list node looks like this:

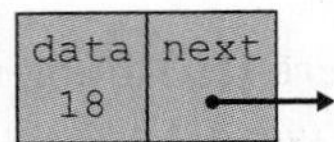

It's an object with two fields: one for storing a single item of data and one for storing a reference to the next node in the list. To store a list of integer values we'd declare the node class as follows:

```
public class ListNode {
    public int data;
    public ListNode next;
}
```

This class does not produce a nicely encapsulated object with private fields, but the technique of using public fields is the usual approach to defining nodes. In the next section we'll discuss why it is acceptable to avoid encapsulation in this case.

This is a recursive data structure. The `ListNode` class is defined in terms of itself because it has a field of type `ListNode`. As a result, it is often possible to solve linked list programming problems more effectively by writing recursive methods, as described in Chapter 12.

Constructing a List

Let's begin by constructing a series of nodes that store the sequence of values `[3, 7, 12]`. There are three values, which means you'll need three nodes that are linked together. When you're creating linked lists, if you keep a reference to the front of the list, then you can get to anything in the list. You'll usually use a single variable of type `ListNode` that refers to (or points to) the front of the list. You begin with this declaration:

```
ListNode list;
```

The variable `list` is not itself a node. It's a variable that is capable of referring to a node. You haven't yet given it a value, so you would draw the following picture for memory at this point in the program:

list ?

The "?" will be replaced with a reference to a node, which means that this box does not have a `data` field or a `next` field. It's a box where you can store a reference to such an object. You don't have an actual node yet. To understand this distinction between an object and a variable that stores a reference to an object, you might want to review the section on reference semantics in Chapter 7.

The way to get an actual node is to call `new`:

```
list = new ListNode();
```

This call constructs a new node and tells Java to have the variable `list` refer to it:

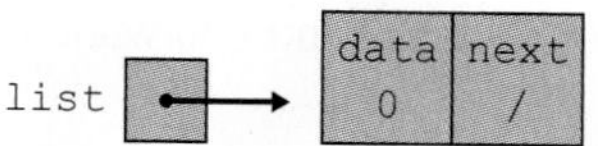

Recall that when objects are constructed, Java initializes the fields to the zero-equivalent for the type. That is why in the node above the `data` field has the value `0` and the `next` field has the value `null`. Notice that we use a slash through the box to indicate a `null` value.

What do you want to do with the node you have constructed? You want to store `3` in its `data` field (`list.data`) and you want its `next` field to point to a new node:

```
list.data = 3;
list.next = new ListNode();
```

The addition of these lines of code makes our linked list appear as follows:

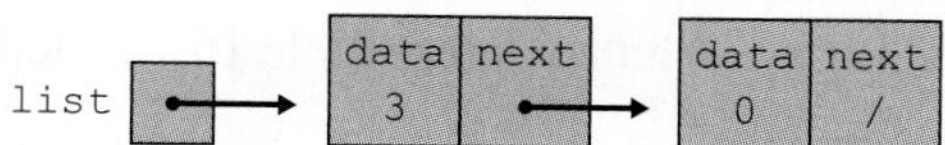

When you program linked lists, you have to understand how to access the different elements of the structure. The variable `list` stores a reference to the first node. You can get inside that node with the dot notation (`list.data` and `list.next`). So `list.next` is the way to refer to the `next` box of the first node. You wrote code to assign it to refer to a new node, which is why `list.next` is pointing at this second node.

Now you want to assign the second node's data field (`list.next.data`) to the value `7` and assign the second node's `next` field to refer to a third node:

```
list.next.data = 7;
list.next.next = new ListNode();
```

Now the linked list looks like this:

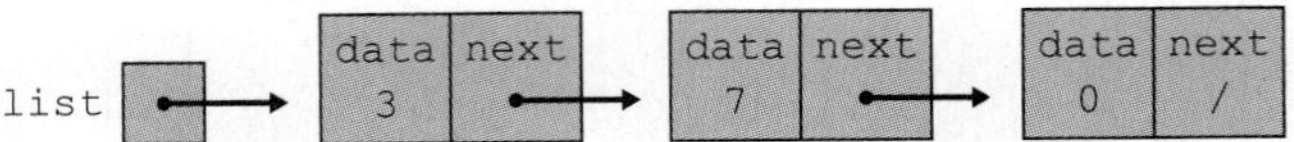

Again, pay close attention to the difference between `list`, `list.next`, and `list.next.next`, and remember which box is associated with each of these:

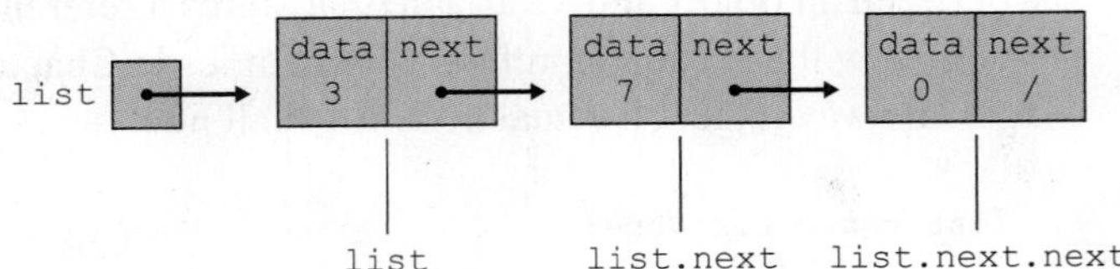

Finally, you want to set the `data` field of this third node to `12` (stored in `list.next.next.data`) and you want to set its `next` field to `null`:

```
list.next.next.data = 12;
list.next.next.next = null;
```

Our linked list now looks like this:

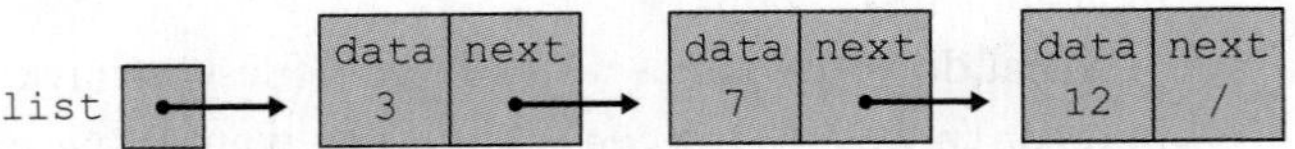

The assignment of the `next` field to `null` is actually unnecessary because Java initializes it to that value, but it's not a bad idea to be explicit about the value that you want to store in the field.

The dot notation is often very confusing for novices, so it is worth pausing for a moment to make sure that you understand the different combinations and the elements to which they refer. Table 16.1 includes each of the possibilities for the preceding diagram.

Table 16.1 Referring to Elements of a Sample List

Expression	Type	Description
`list`	`ListNode`	Our variable that refers to the first node in the list
`list.data`	`int`	`data` field of the first node (`3`)
`list.next`	`ListNode`	`next` field of the first node
`list.next.data`	`int`	`data` field of the second node (`7`)
`list.next.next`	`ListNode`	`next` field of the second node
`list.next.next.data`	`int`	`data` field of the third node (`12`)
`list.next.next.next`	`ListNode`	`next` field of the third node

Here is a complete program that includes all this code for constructing a three-element list along with code that prints the list:

```
// Constructs and prints the list [3, 7, 12] by setting each
// field of each node.

public class Construct1 {
    public static void main(String[] args) {
        ListNode list = new ListNode();
        list.data = 3;
        list.next = new ListNode();
        list.next.data = 7;
        list.next.next = new ListNode();
        list.next.next.data = 12;
        list.next.next.next = null;
        System.out.println(list.data + " " + list.next.data + " "
                           + list.next.next.data);
    }
}
```

The program produces the following output:

```
3 7 12
```

Obviously, this program represents a very tedious way to manipulate a list. It's much better to write code that involves loops to manipulate lists. But it takes a while to get used to this idea, so we're first going to practice doing some raw list operations without a loop.

List Basics

Our previous version of the node class has just two fields:

```
public class ListNode {
    public int data;
    public ListNode next;
}
```

In general, we like to keep the node class simple, so we don't want to add much to this. But it is a good idea to include some constructors:

```
// ListNode is a class for storing a single node of a linked
// list. This node class is for a list of integer values.

public class ListNode {
    public int data;          // data stored in this node
    public ListNode next;     // link to next node in the list

    // post: constructs a node with data 0 and null link
    public ListNode() {
        this(0, null);
    }

    // post: constructs a node with given data and null link
    public ListNode(int data) {
        this(data, null);
    }

    // post: constructs a node with given data and given link
    public ListNode(int data, ListNode next) {
        this.data = data;
        this.next = next;
    }
}
```

Like the other classes we've seen, this class has one "real" constructor (the one that takes two arguments). The other two constructors use the `this(...)` notation to call the third constructor with default values (`0` for the data, `null` for `next`). In the new version of the class, it is possible to write a single statement to construct the three-element list we have been studying:

```
// Constructs and prints the list [3, 7, 12]. This version uses
// node constructors rather than setting fields of each node.

public class Construct2 {
    public static void main(String[] args) {
        ListNode list = new ListNode(3,
                new ListNode(7, new ListNode(12)));
        System.out.println(list.data + " " + list.next.data + " "
                           + list.next.next.data);
    }
}
```

In some programming languages you have to explicitly free up memory when you are no longer using it. That is not the case in Java. In Java you can simply stop referring to a node when you no longer want to use it. For example, consider the following three-element list that we have constructed:

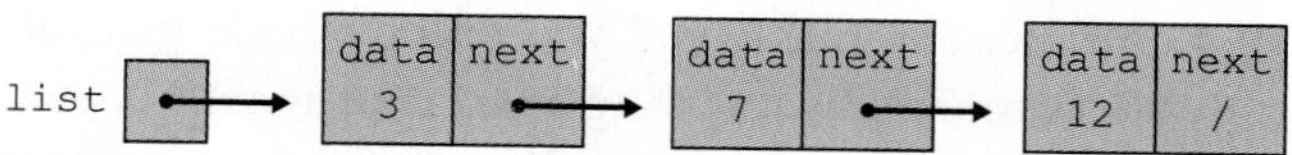

How would you get rid of the first node? You can reassign the variable `list` to point to the node that comes after it. In effect, you leapfrog over the node that stores `3` and instead have `list` point to the node that stores `7` by writing the following line of code:

```
list = list.next;
```

Now the linked list contains the following:

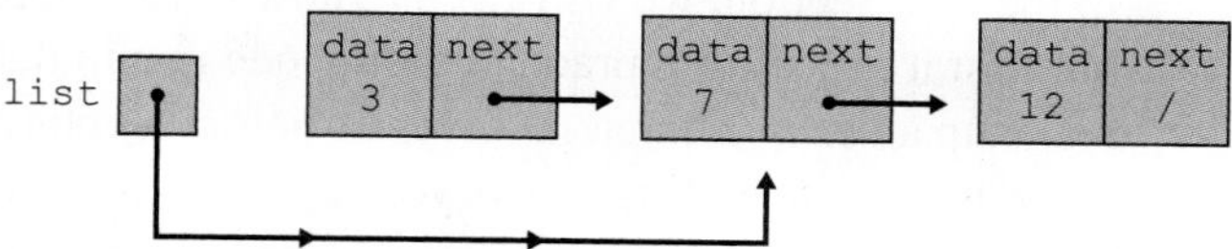

Now the variable `list` is pointing at a two-element list because it points at the node storing `7`, which in turn points to the node that stores `12`. The node that stores `3` is no longer pointed to by any variable.

What happens to a node when no variable points to it? As we mentioned at the end of the previous chapter, the Java runtime system periodically invokes the garbage collector to look for objects like this node and to reclaim the space so that it can be used again. Java programmers enjoy the convenience of relying on this process, which is sometimes called *automatic garbage collection.*

A good analogy is to think of each node as a helium balloon and the arrows as the strings that we use to hold on to the balloons. If you let go of a string, then the balloon floats away. But the garbage collector will find all of those stray balloons and reclaim the space.

As one final example, consider what happens if you were to reset the `list` variable to `null`:

```
list = null;
```

Our linked list would look like this:

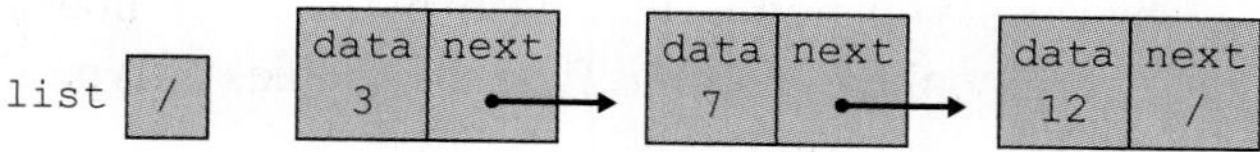

The value `null` is used to represent the empty list. There are three nodes floating around from the work we did earlier, but those are like helium balloons that have floated away because their strings were let go. They will eventually be recycled by the garbage collector.

You have to be careful about manipulating an empty list. For example, if the variable `list` is `null`, and you execute code that refers to `list.data`, Java will halt your program by throwing a `NullPointerException`. You will quickly discover that `NullPointerException` is one of the most common problems that you run into as you try to debug your linked list code. Just keep in mind that Java throws that exception when you attempt to dereference a `null` value. In other words, it occurs when you ask for `ptr.fieldName` where `ptr` has the value `null`. When Java throws the exception, it will show you the exact line number where it occurred. Look at that line of code carefully to find all occurrences of the dot notation, because one of them involves a `null` value.

Manipulating Nodes

VideoNote

In the next section, we will explore how to use loops to write more generalized code, but first it is useful to practice basic node manipulation. A good way to practice is to make up an exercise that involves a "before" picture and an "after" picture. The challenge is to write code that gets you from the first state to the second state.

As an example, suppose that you have two variables of type `ListNode` called `p` and `q` and that the following is the "before" situation:

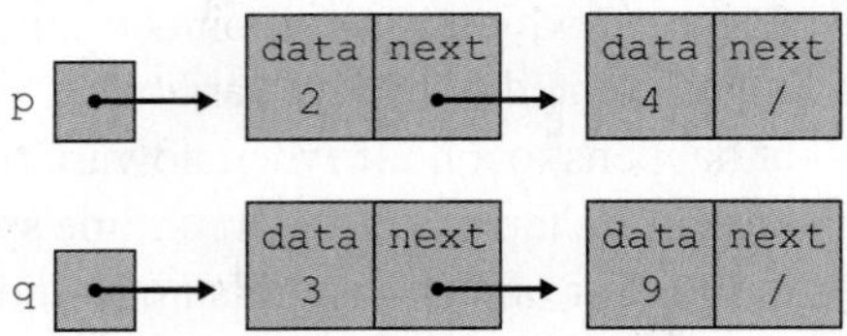

Suppose that you want to get to the following "after" situation:

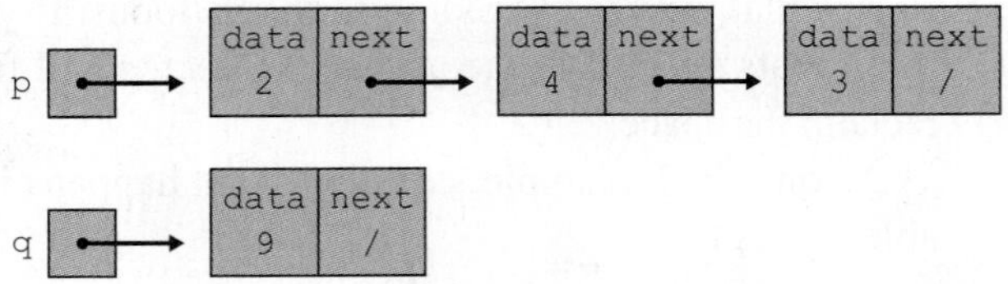

In order to accomplish this, you will have to rearrange the links of these two lists. As a starting point, think about how many variables of type `ListNode` there are. You might say two because there are two named variables, `p` and `q`. Or you might say four because you notice that each of the four nodes has a field of type `ListNode`. Actually, there are six different variables of type `ListNode`. The following diagram numbers each of the six variables:

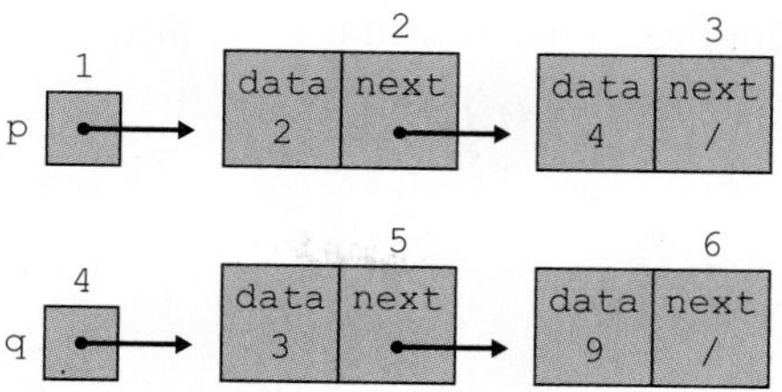

Having the variables numbered makes it easier to discuss the task at hand. Which of these variables has to change in value to get from the before picture to the after picture? The boxes numbered 3, 4, and 5 have to change. If we change them appropriately, we'll be done.

We have to be careful about how we change the links. The order can be important. For example, suppose we start by changing box 4 (the variable `q`). In the final situation, it's supposed to point at the node with `9` in it. We can accomplish this by leapfrogging over the current node to which it is pointing:

```
q = q.next;
```

But if we start with this change, what happens to the node that contains `3`? We lose track of it, as the following picture indicates:

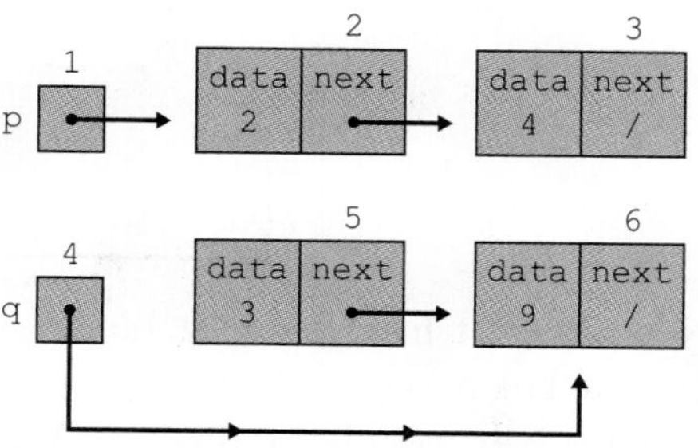

Once we have lost track of the node containing `3`, we have no way to get back to it. It's like a helium balloon that has floated away because we let go of the string.

This is a common problem in linked list programming that you have to consider carefully. One solution is to introduce a temporary variable that would keep track of the node to which the variable `q` used to point (the node containing `3`). Often, though, we can instead solve the problem by carefully choosing the order of the changes that we make.

Of the three values we have to change to solve this problem, the one that is safe to change is box 3 because it's currently `null`. We begin by setting it to point to the node containing `3`:

```
p.next.next = q;
```

Our linked list now looks like this:

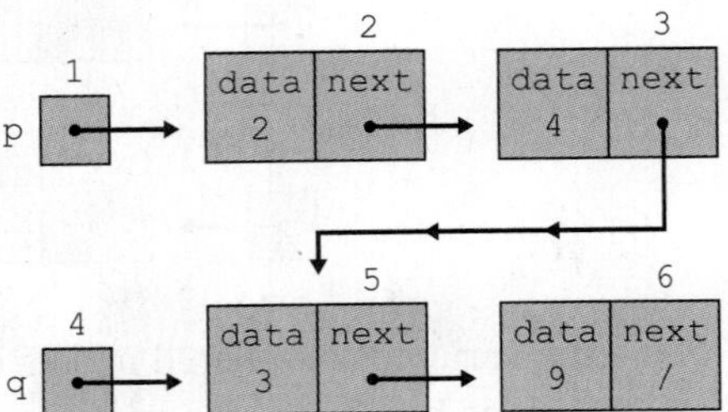

Now that we've used the value of box 4 to reset box 3, we can reset box 4. It's supposed to point to the node that has `9` in it. Now we can leapfrog over the current node to which it is pointing:

```
q = q.next;
```

Our linked list now looks like this:

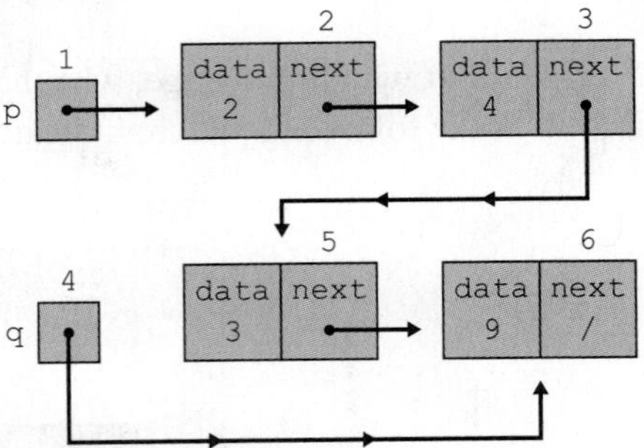

Now we just have to reset box 5. In the original picture, we would have referred to box 5 as `q.next`, but now that we've changed the value of `q`, we have to change the way we refer to this box. We can still get to box 5 by starting with the variable `p`:

```
p.next.next.next = null;
```

Our linked list now looks like this:

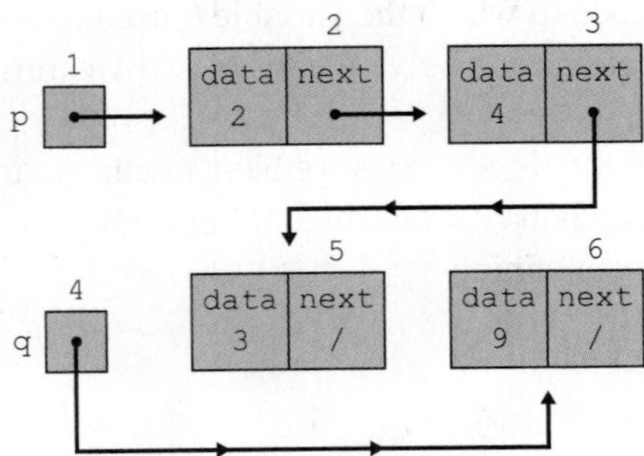

We can simplify this diagram by redrawing the three nodes that are now part of the first list all in a row. Keep in mind, though, that the nodes themselves haven't moved around in memory. We have only rearranged various links. But we can more easily understand the structure if we draw the picture in this way:

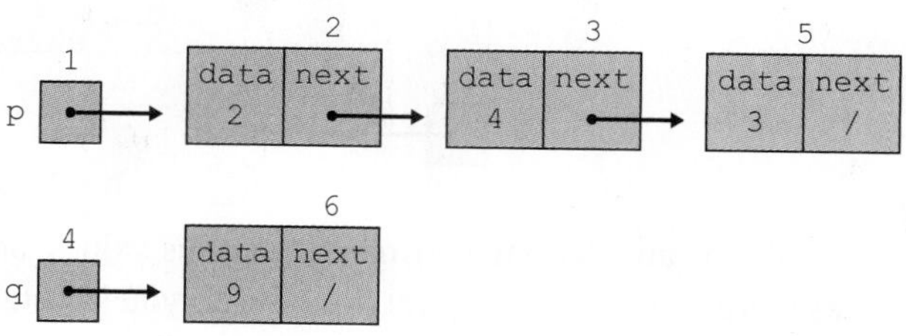

And now we can see that this diagram matches the "after" picture we were given. The three lines of code that are needed to get from the initial state to the final state are as follows:

```
p.next.next = q;
q = q.next;
p.next.next.next = null;
```

Obviously, this process can be very confusing. It is essential to draw pictures to keep track of what is pointing where and what is going on when this code executes. It's the only way to master linked list code.

Traversing a List

Consider the problem of printing each value in a list on a different line. For example, suppose we have a variable called `list` that stores a reference to the list `[3, 5, 2]`:

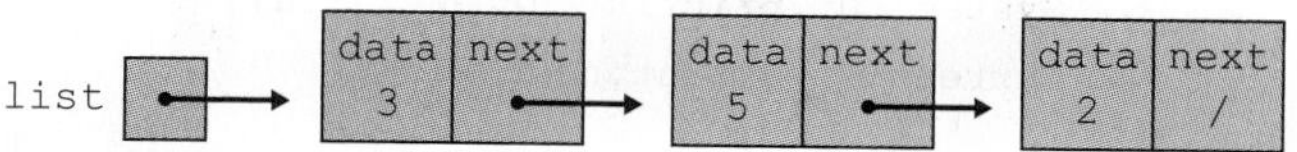

Using the techniques from the previous section you could refer to each of the three data fields: `list.data (3)`, `list.next.data (5)`, and `list.next.next.data (2)`. This approach can work for very short lists, but obviously won't work when you have hundreds or thousands of nodes to process. In that case, you'd want to write a loop.

You have just one variable to work with, the variable `list`, so that's clearly where you have to start. You could use it to move along the list and print things out, but then you would lose the original value of the variable, which would mean that you would have lost the list. Instead, it's better to declare a local variable of type `ListNode` that you use to access the different nodes of the list:

```
ListNode current = list;
```

You can use any variable name you like, although it is common in linked list programming to use a name like `current` or `curr`. The preceding line of code initializes `current` to point to the same value as `list` (the first node in the list):

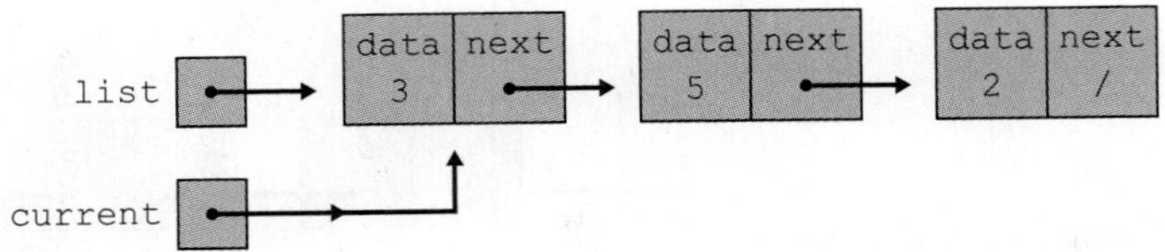

You want a loop that prints the various values, and you want it to keep going as long as there is more data to print. So how do you structure your loop? The variable `current` will refer to each different node in turn. The final node has the value `null` in its `next` field, so eventually the variable `current` will become equal to `null` and that's when you know your loop is finished. Thus, your basic loop structure will be as follows:

```
ListNode current = list;
while (current != null) {
    process next value.
    move current forward.
}
```

To process a node, you need to print out its value, which you can get from `current.data`, and you need to move `current` to the next node over. The position of the next node is stored in `current.next`, so moving to that next node involves resetting `current` to `current.next`:

```
ListNode current = list;
while (current != null) {
    System.out.println(current.data);
    current = current.next;
}
```

The first time through this loop, `current` is referring to the node with the `3` in it. It prints this value and then resets `current`, which causes `current` to refer to (or point to) the second node in the list:

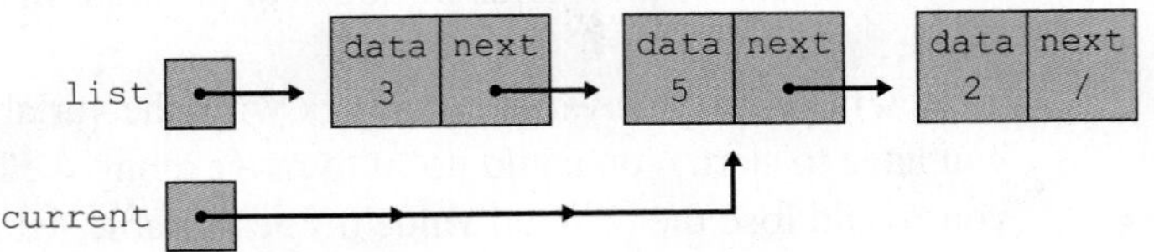

Some people prefer to visualize this differently. Instead of envisioning the variable `current` sitting still while its arrow moves, some people prefer to envision the variable itself moving. So, for the initial situation, you draw the following picture:

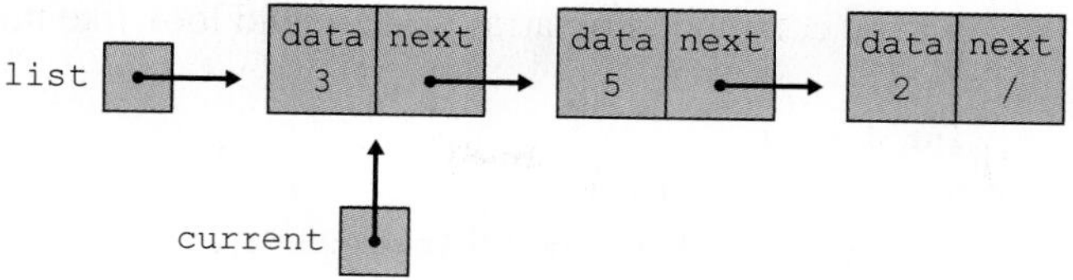

After execution of the statement `current = current.next`, the linked list would look like this:

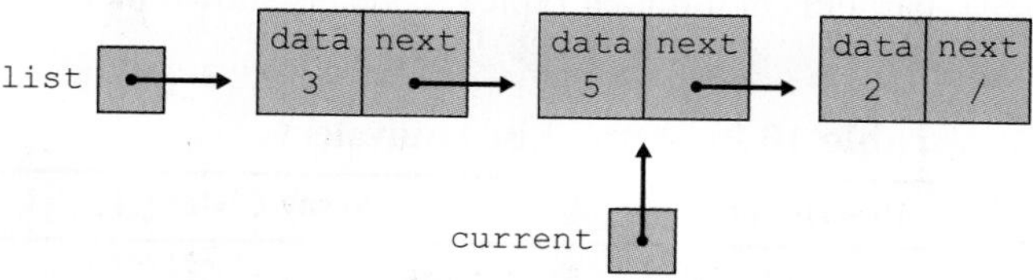

Either way of thinking about this scenario works. Because in this new situation the variable `current` is not `null`, you once again enter the loop, print out `current.data` (which is now `5`), and move `current` along again:

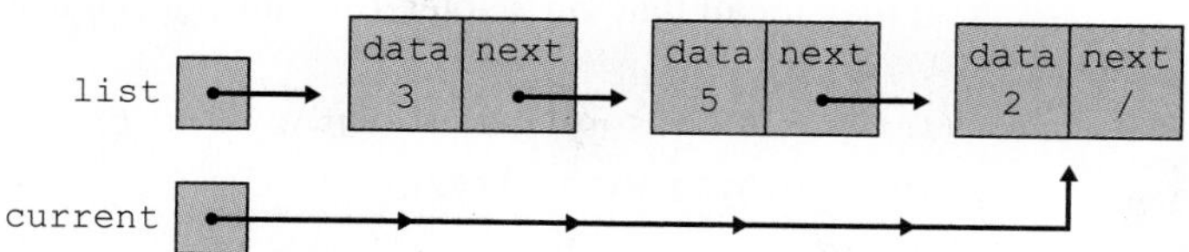

Once again `current` is not `null`, so you enter the loop a third time, print the value of `current.data` (`2`), and reset `current`. But this time `current.next` has the value `null`, so when you reset `current`, the computer's memory will look like this:

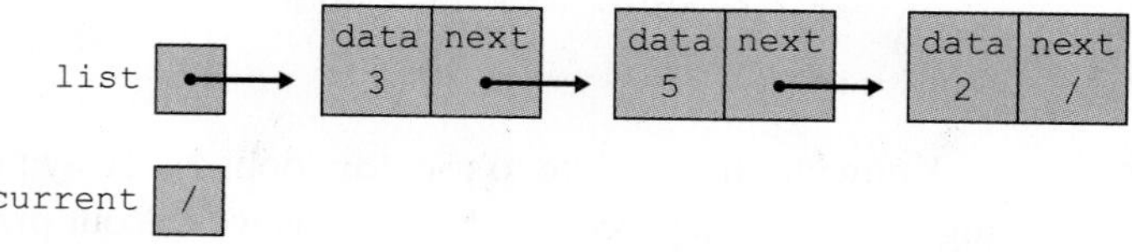

Because `current` has become `null`, when you break out of the loop the program has produced the following output:

```
3
5
2
```

The corresponding array code would look like this:

```
int i = 0;
while (i < size) {
    System.out.println(elementData[i]);
    i++;
}
```

Assuming that you have some comfort with array-style programming, this example might give you some useful insight into linked list programming. There are direct parallels in terms of typical code, as shown in Table 16.2.

Table 16.2 Array/List Equivalents

Description	Array Code	Linked List Code
Go to front of the list	`int i = 0;`	`ListNode current = list;`
Test for more elements	`i < size`	`current != null`
Current value	`elementData[i]`	`current.data`
Go to next element	`i++;`	`current = current.next;`

You may recall that in Chapter 7 we introduced a standard array traversal approach:

```
for (int i = 0; i < <array>.length; i++) {
    <do something with array[i]>;
}
```

You can write a similar standard linked list traversal pattern:

```
<temp variable> = <front of list>;
while (<temp variable> != null) {
    <do something with <temp variable>.data>;
    <temp variable> = <temp variable>.next;
}
```

Knowing that we like to use `for` loops for array processing, you can imagine writing `for` loops to process linked lists as well. Your previous code could be rewritten as the following code:

```
for (ListNode current = list; current != null; current = current.next) {
    System.out.println(current.data);
}
```

Some people like to write their list code this way, but most tend to use `while` loops. It's an issue of personal taste.

16.2 A Linked List Class

VideoNote

In this section, we will explore how to write a class called `LinkedIntList` that will be a parallel of the `ArrayIntList` class of Chapter 15.

Simple `LinkedIntList`

So far we have been discussing the low-level details of how to manipulate the nodes of a class. In general, we want to provide a potential client with a simple interface that doesn't require the client to understand these low-level details. For example, the `ArrayIntList` class that we examined in Chapter 15 uses an array as its underlying structure, but a client of the class never has to know that. In a similar way, we'd like to define a `LinkedIntList` class that a client can access without having to understand that it is implemented by means of a linked list of nodes.

First we have to consider the set of fields that we need. As we've seen, we can get to any element in the list as long as we have a reference to the front of the list. So at a minimum we need a reference to the front of the list:

```
public class LinkedIntList {
    private ListNode front;
    ...
}
```

There are several other fields we could add to improve efficiency. Two of the most commonly added fields keep track of the length of the list and keep a reference to the back of the list. But for this first version, we will keep it simple and store just a reference to the front of the list.

Notice that for this class, the field `front` is declared to be private. We do that to guarantee that the class is well encapsulated. But what about those public fields in the node class? In general public fields are a bad idea. But they're not of great concern in this case because we're going to make sure that only our `LinkedIntList` object will ever manipulate individual nodes. By the time we complete this program, we will have two classes: one for individual nodes of a list and one for the list itself. We'll be careful to have a clean, well-encapsulated list object, but we don't have to worry about doing the same thing for the node class.

Some people prefer to encapsulate even node objects to keep things simple, but if you want to learn how complex classes are written, it is important to understand this convention. When we are writing code to interact with a client, we want everything to be completely encapsulated. But when we are writing code that is seen only by the implementation, we can be more relaxed. As an analogy, think of how you behave in public versus in your own home. In your own home you might walk around in a bathrobe and slippers because you know that only you and your family have access to your home. You wouldn't tend to wear a bathrobe and slippers out in public. As another example, think of the post office boxes you find at a post office. Those post office boxes are locked for security, just like an encapsulated object, because anyone has access to the public post office. But in a corporate office setting, mailboxes often are not locked because only a limited number of people have access to them and, therefore, people are willing to be more informal.

Later in the chapter, we will see an even better way of handling this case by including the node class as a static inner class. But for now we'll work with the two classes to keep things simple.

As a first exercise, let's add a method to our class that will allow us to examine the contents of the list. We saw that code like the following could be used to print a list:

```
ListNode current = list;
while (current != null) {
    System.out.println(current.data);
    current = current.next;
}
```

We could turn that into a method of the class by initializing the local variable to the value of our field `front`:

```
public void print() {
    ListNode current = front;
    while (current != null) {
        System.out.println(current.data);
        current = current.next;
    }
}
```

But as we saw in Chapter 15, it is a better idea to make this a `toString` method that returns a `String` representation of the list. For the `ArrayIntList` class we wrote the following method:

```
public String toString() {
    if (size == 0) {
        return "[]";
    } else {
        String result = "[" + elementData[0];
        for (int i = 1; i < size; i++) {
            result += ", " + elementData[i];
        }
        result += "]";
        return result;
    }
}
```

The code is very similar for the `LinkedIntList` class because we will have the same special case for an empty list and the same fencepost loop to make sure that values are separated by commas. If we translate each array operation into its linked list equivalent, we end up with the following code:

```
public String toString() {
    if (front == null) {
        return "[]";
    } else {
        String result = "[" + front.data;
        ListNode current = front.next;
        while (current != null) {
            result += ", " + current.data;
            current = current.next;
        }
        result += "]";
        return result;
    }
}
```

Notice that in this code we initialize `current` to `front.next` because we handle the data for the first node outside the loop.

Appending add

Next let's consider how to write a method that will append a value to the end of the list. To do so, we have to locate the end of the list. Let's think about the general case in which we are appending a value to the end of a list that already contains a few values. For example, suppose the list stores `[3, 5, 2]`:

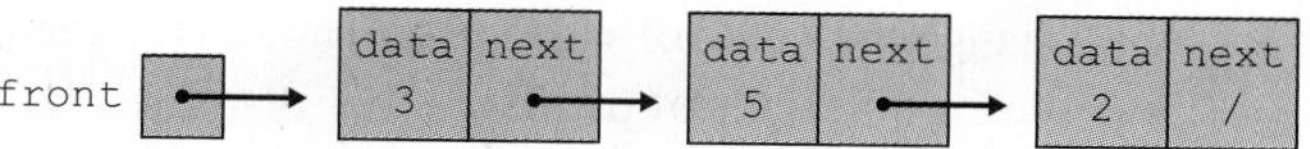

Suppose that you want to add the value `17` at the end of the list. First you have to get to the correct location. So here's a start:

```
ListNode current = front;
while (current != null) {
    current = current.next;
}
```

What happens when this code executes is that the variable `current` moves along the list from the first to the last node until the loop test fails—that is, until `current` becomes `null`. The computer's memory then looks like this:

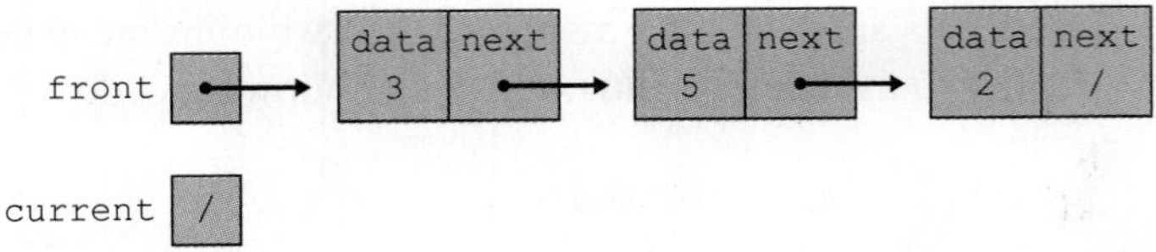

It's tempting to think that you could then execute the following line of code to complete the task:

```
current = new ListNode(17);
```

But that won't work. It leaves the computer's memory looking like this:

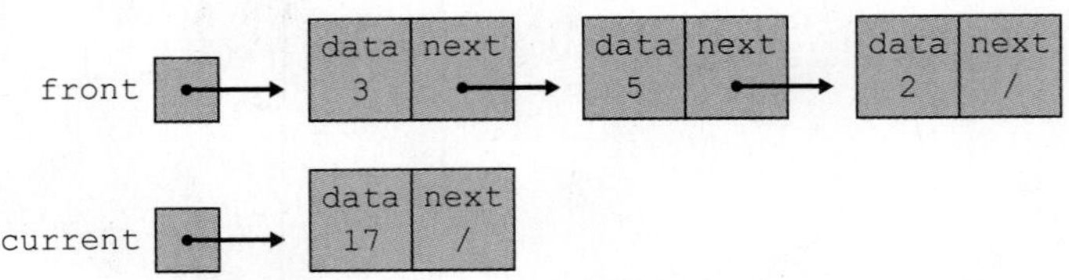

The preceding code allocates a new node, but this new node has no connection to the original list. The list is still composed of three nodes linked together. This fourth node has been constructed, but it hasn't been properly linked into the list.

As you learn about linked list programming, you'll find that there are only two ways to change the contents of a list:

- change the value of `front`, in which case you are changing the starting point for the list, or
- change the value of `<variable>.next` (for some variable), which changes one of the current links of the list.

To solve this problem, you have to stop one position early. You don't want to run off the end of the list as you did with the `print` and `toString` code. Instead, you want to position `current` to the final element. You can do this by changing your test. Instead of running the loop until `current` becomes `null`, you want to run it until `current.next` is `null`, because only the last node of the list will have a `next` field that is `null`:

```
ListNode current = front;
while (current.next != null) {
    current = current.next;
}
```

After the loop executes, `current` will be pointing at the last node in the list:

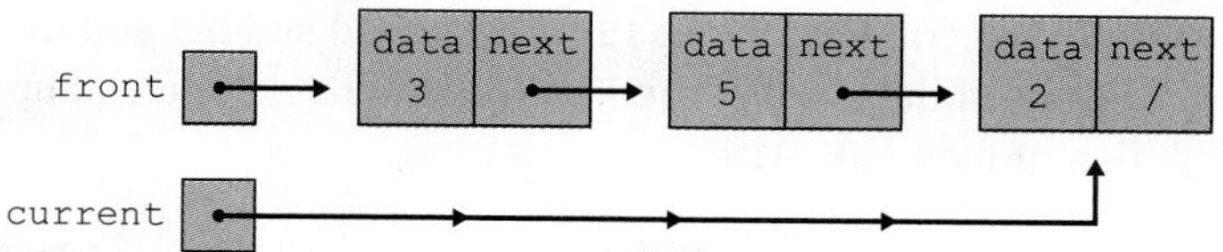

At that point, you can assign `current.next` to be a new node with `17` in it:

```
current.next = new ListNode(17);
```

In this case, you are changing the currently `null` value in that last node to instead link to a new node with `17` in it:

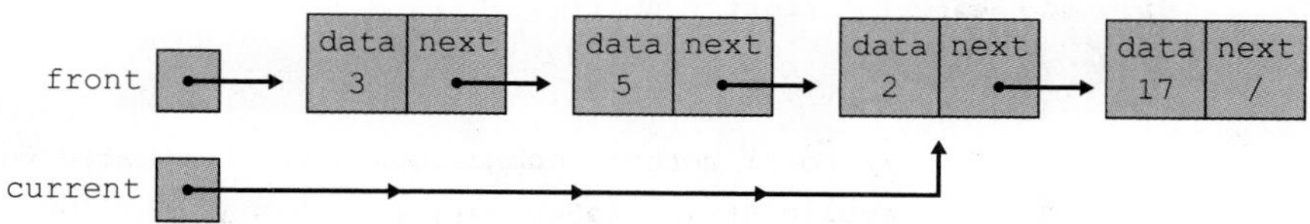

You have been preparing to write code for the appending `add`. So this code would be included inside a method, and you would have to alter it to use the name of the parameter:

```
public void add(int value) {
    ListNode current = front;
    while (current.next != null) {
        current = current.next;
    }
    current.next = new ListNode(value);
}
```

Even this code isn't quite correct, because you have to deal with the special case in which the list is empty:

```
public void add(int value) {
    if (front == null) {
        front = new ListNode(value);
    } else {
        ListNode current = front;
        while (current.next != null) {
            current = current.next;
        }
        current.next = new ListNode(value);
    }
}
```

If you combine the `toString` method and the `add` method, along with a constructor that initializes the front of the list to `null`, you end up with the following first version of the `LinkedIntList` class:

```
// Simple first version of LinkedIntList with just a constructor
// and methods for add and toString.

public class LinkedIntList {
    private ListNode front; // first value in the list

    // post: constructs an empty list
    public LinkedIntList() {
        front = null;
    }

    // post: returns comma-separated, bracketed version of list
    public String toString() {
        if (front == null) {
            return "[]";
        } else {
            String result = "[" + front.data;
            ListNode current = front.next;
            while (current != null) {
                result += ", " + current.data;
                current = current.next;
            }
            result += "]";
            return result;
        }
    }

    // post: appends the given value to the end of the list
    public void add(int value) {
        if (front == null) {
            front = new ListNode(value);
        } else {
            ListNode current = front;
            while (current.next != null) {
                current = current.next;
            }
            current.next = new ListNode(value);
        }
    }
}
```

The idea of stopping one step early in processing a list isn't limited to this appending operation. It is a fundamental pattern that comes up over and over in linked list programming, as you'll see with the other examples in the chapter.

The Middle of the List

If you want your `LinkedIntList` to have the same capabilities as the `ArrayIntList` that we developed in Chapter 15, you have to add several new methods. For example, you will want to have a method called `get` that returns a value at a given index. When the underlying structure was an array, you could simply ask for the array element at that index. But for a linked list, you have access only to the front of the list. So, to find a value at a particular index, you have no choice but to start at the front and examine each value until you get to the desired location:

```
public int get(int index) {
    ListNode current = front;
    for (int i = 0; i < index; i++) {
        current = current.next;
    }
    return current.data;
}
```

As we noted earlier, this means that your linked list does not have the fast random access property that arrays and our `ArrayIntList` have. Instead, we say that the linked list has sequential access, meaning that you have to go through the values in sequence until you get to the value of interest.

Let's now consider the task of adding a value at a particular index. There is a special case when you add at index 0, at the front of the list. For example, suppose a list contains the values `[19, 8, 42]`:

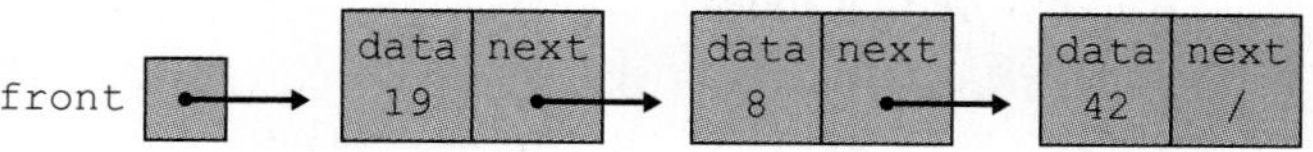

Suppose you want to add the value `5` at the front of this list. Then you will need to construct a new node that has the value `5` and that points to the current front of the list:

```
new ListNode(5, front)
```

Constructing this node generates the following situation:

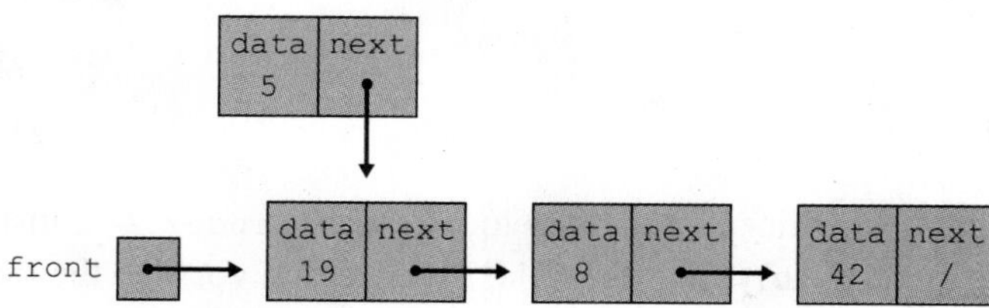

But that's only part of what you need to do. To link this node into the list, you have to reset `front` to point to this new node:

```
front = new ListNode(5, front);
```

Executing this line of code generates the following list:

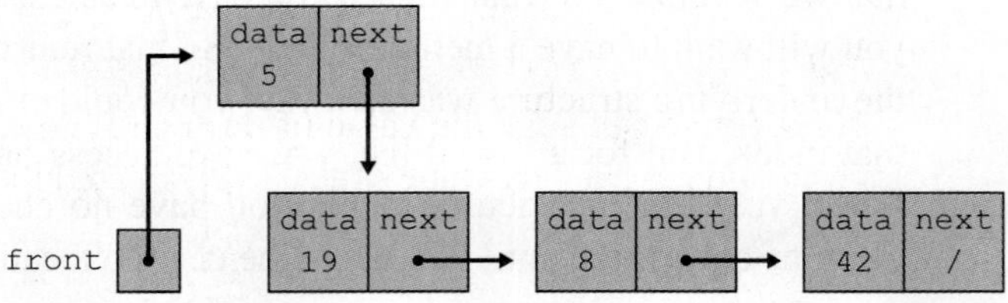

This is a special case for your `add` method that applies only when the index is `0`. So your method to add at an index should begin like this:

```
public void add(int index, int value) {
    if (index == 0) {
        front = new ListNode(value, front);
    } else {
        ...
    }
}
```

If you aren't adding at the front of the list, then you have to use a temporary variable to position yourself to the appropriate spot in the list. This is another case in which you have to stop one step early. In the case of the `get` method, you wanted to position a local variable to the node with the given index. Here you want to stop one step before that index:

```
public void add(int index, int value) {
    if (index == 0) {
        front = new ListNode(value, front);
    } else {
        ListNode current = front;
        for (int i = 0; i < index – 1; i++) {
            current = current.next;
        }
        ...
    }
}
```

Notice that the `for` loop test uses `index – 1` instead of `index` so that it stops one step early. For example, suppose that you had the same starting list of `[19, 8, 42]` and that you want to insert the value `5` at index 2. You'd want to position the variable `current` to point at the value with index 1 (the node storing `8`):

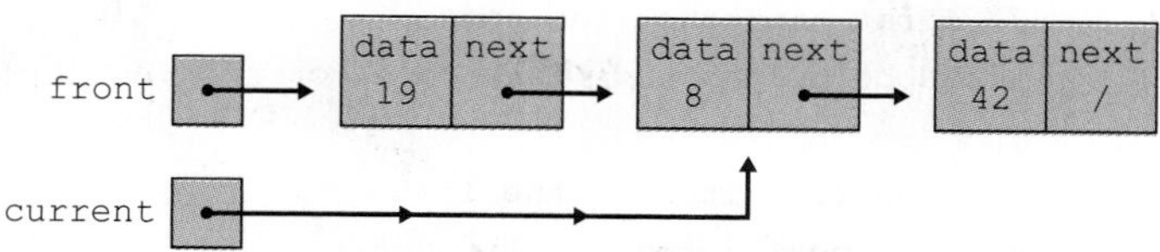

Now you can change the value of `current.next` to add the new node. This new node should have a data value of `5`. To what should its `next` link refer? It should refer to the node that has `42` in it, which is stored in `current.next`. So you'll want to construct the node as follows:

```
new ListNode(5, current.next)
```

Just calling the constructor leaves the computer's memory looking like this:

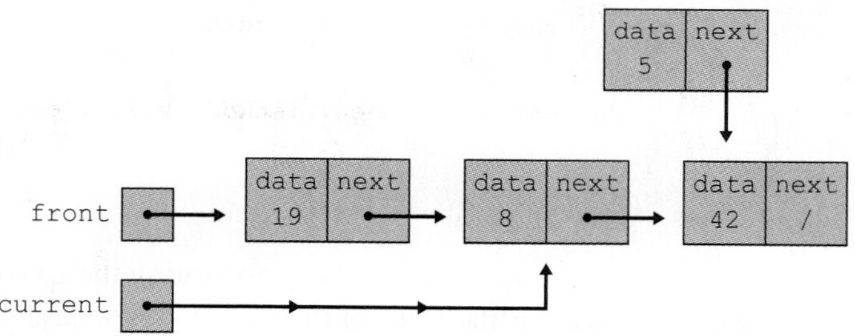

Your code is not complete. You've constructed a node that points at the list, but nothing in the list points at the node. Thus, you've taken care of half of what you need to do. The other half of the task is to change a link of the list to point to the new node. The link to change is `current.next`:

```
current.next = new ListNode(5, current.next);
```

After this modification has been made, the list will look like this:

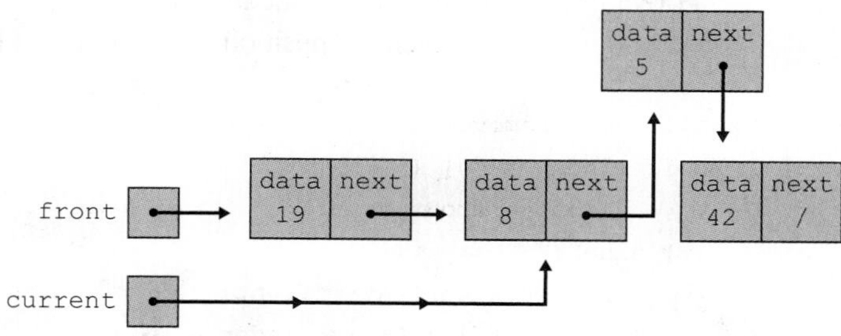

Some people prefer to write the code for creating the new node in two steps with a temporary variable, as in the following lines of code:

```
// first construct the node
ListNode temp = new ListNode(5, current.next);

// then link it into the list
current.next = temp;
```

Both approaches work. After you have incorporated this code into your method, the code looks like this:

```
public void add(int index, int value) {
    if (index == 0) {
        front = new ListNode(value, front);
    } else {
        ListNode current = front;
        for (int i = 0; i < index – 1; i++) {
            current = current.next;
        }
        current.next = new ListNode(value, current.next);
    }
}
```

You can use a similar approach to writing the `remove` method. You need to include a special case for the front of the list, in which case you can simply leapfrog over the first element:

```
public void remove(int index) {
    if (index == 0) {
        front = front.next;
    } else {
        ...
    }
}
```

For values that appear later in the list, you need a loop similar to the one that you used in the `add` method to reach the position at the node just before the one to be removed:

```
public void remove(int index) {
    if (index == 0) {
        front = front.next;
    } else {
        ListNode current = front;
        for (int i = 0; i < index – 1; i++) {
```

```
            current = current.next;
        }
        ...
    }
}
```

If you are working with the list `[19, 8, 42, 13]` and you are removing the value from index 2, your list will look like the following:

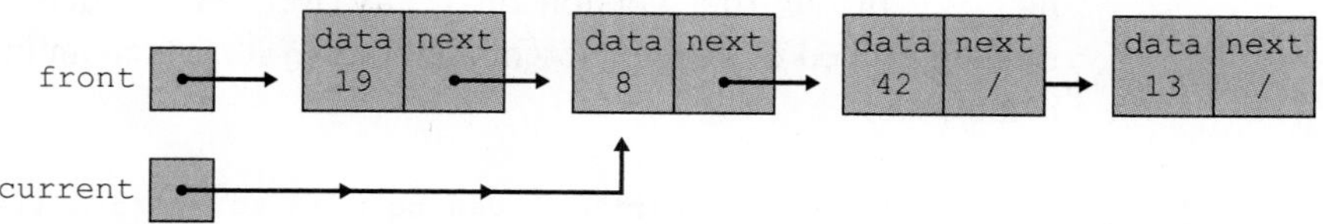

To remove the value from index 2, you need to change `current.next` to point to the value that comes next, which is stored in `current.next.next`:

```
public void remove(int index) {
    if (index == 0) {
        front = front.next;
    } else {
        ListNode current = front;
        for (int i = 0; i < index – 1; i++) {
            current = current.next;
        }
        current.next = current.next.next;
    }
}
```

Now the linked list looks like this:

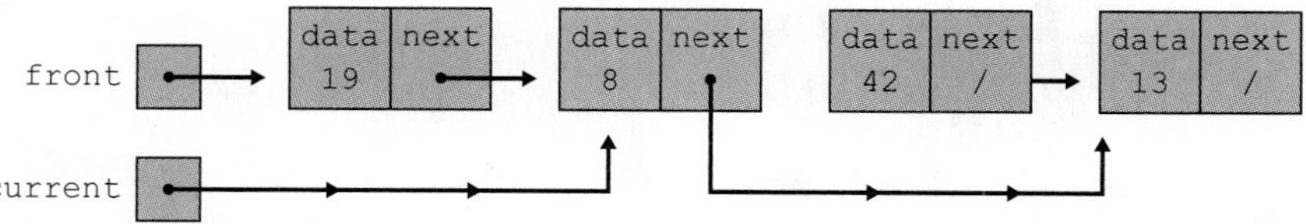

The code has properly linked around the node that stores the value `42` (which is the value that was stored at index 2), so the list now stores the sequence of values `[19, 8, 13]`.

As you write methods that involve manipulating values in the middle of the list, it becomes clear that you often end up writing the same kind of loop to position to a particular node in the list. This is a great place to introduce a private method:

```
private ListNode nodeAt(int index) {
    ListNode current = front;
```

```
    for (int i = 0; i < index; i++) {
        current = current.next;
    }
    return current;
}
```

The following is a complete implementation of the `LinkedIntList` that includes the methods we have just developed, along with the other basic operations that we included in our first version of `ArrayIntList`. Notice that the private `nodeAt` method is used in three different methods (`get`, `add` at an index, and `remove`). Here is the code:

```
// Class LinkedIntList can be used to store a list of integers.

public class LinkedIntList {
    private ListNode front; // first value in the list

    // post: constructs an empty list
    public LinkedIntList() {
        front = null;
    }

    // post: returns the current number of elements in the list
    public int size() {
        int count = 0;
        ListNode current = front;
        while (current != null) {
            current = current.next;
            count++;
        }
        return count;
    }

    // pre : 0 <= index < size()
    // post: returns the integer at the given index in the list
    public int get(int index) {
        return nodeAt(index).data;
    }

    // post: returns comma-separated, bracketed version of list
    public String toString() {
        if (front == null) {
            return "[]";
        } else {
```

```
            String result = "[" + front.data;
            ListNode current = front.next;
            while (current != null) {
                result += ", " + current.data;
                current = current.next;
            }
            result += "]";
            return result;
        }
    }

    // post: returns the position of the first occurrence of the
    //       given value (-1 if not found)
    public int indexOf(int value) {
        int index = 0;
        ListNode current = front;
        while (current != null) {
            if (current.data == value) {
                return index;
            }
            index++;
            current = current.next;
        }
        return -1;
    }

    // post: appends the given value to the end of the list
    public void add(int value) {
        if (front == null) {
            front = new ListNode(value);
        } else {
            ListNode current = front;
            while (current.next != null) {
                current = current.next;
            }
            current.next = new ListNode(value);
        }
    }

    // pre: 0 <= index <= size()
    // post: inserts the given value at the given index
    public void add(int index, int value) {
        if (index == 0) {
            front = new ListNode(value, front);
```

```
        } else {
            ListNode current = nodeAt(index - 1);
            current.next = new ListNode(value, current.next);
        }
    }

    // pre : 0 <= index < size()
    // post: removes value at the given index
    public void remove(int index) {
        if (index == 0) {
            front = front.next;
        } else {
            ListNode current = nodeAt(index - 1);
            current.next = current.next.next;
        }
    }

    // pre : 0 <= i < size()
    // post: returns a reference to the node at the given index
    private ListNode nodeAt(int index) {
        ListNode current = front;
        for (int i = 0; i < index; i++) {
            current = current.next;
        }
        return current;
    }
}
```

16.3 A Complex List Operation

VideoNote

Suppose that you want to write a new method for your `LinkedIntList` class called `addSorted` that would add values to the list in a way which preserves sorted order. In other words, the method would be specified as follows:

```
// pre : list is in sorted (nondecreasing) order
// post: given value is added to the list so as to preserve sorted
//       (nondecreasing) order, duplicates allowed
public void addSorted(int value) {
    ...
}
```

Our exploration of this task will point out important cases to consider and significant pitfalls that you must be careful to avoid when you program with linked lists.

Let's first look at the general case of adding a value to the middle of a list. Suppose that the list currently stores the values `[2, 5, 12]`:

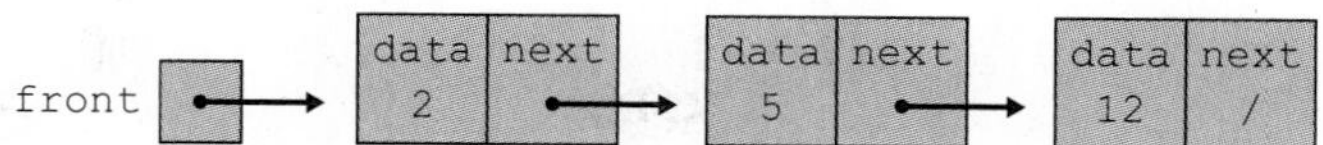

Now suppose that you call the `addSorted` method and pass it the value `10`. How do you add the value `10` to this list to preserve sorted order? First you need to find the right spot to insert it. It belongs between the `5` and `12`, because it is larger than `5` and smaller than `12`. And how do you write that as a loop? You have to compare the value against the various data values stored in the list, starting with the first value. The new node doesn't belong in front of the node with `2` in it because `2` is less than `10`. Likewise, it doesn't belong in front of the node with `5` in it because `5` is less than `10`. But it does belong in front of the node with `12` in it, because `12` is not less than `10`. Your first attempt at writing the code might look like the following:

```
ListNode current = front;
while (current.data < value) {
    current = current.next;
}
```

This code has the core of the right idea, but it has many problems. First of all, it ends up positioning you in the wrong spot. You want to stop one position early in order to add something to the list, just as you did with the two `add` methods. Remember that there are only two ways to change the structure of a linked list: Either change `front`, or change one of the `next` fields of one of the nodes.

In this case, you want to change the `next` field of the node that has `5` in it. So you don't want your variable `current` to end up referring to the node that has `12` in it. You want `current` to point to the node that has `5` in it. You have to modify the code to stop one position early. You can do this by changing the test to use `current.next` instead of `current`:

```
ListNode current = front;
while (current.next.data < value) {
    current = current.next;
}
```

In effect, your test now says, "While the value of the data one position to the right of my current position is less than `value`, keep advancing `current`." This loop stops when `current` refers to the node with `5` in it, which means that you can link in the new node by changing `current.next`. This new node should have a data value of `value` (`10` in our example). To what should its next link refer? It should refer to the node that has `12` in it, which is stored in `current.next`. So you'll want to construct the node in the following way:

```
new ListNode(value, current.next)
```

Just calling the constructor leaves the computer's memory looking like this:

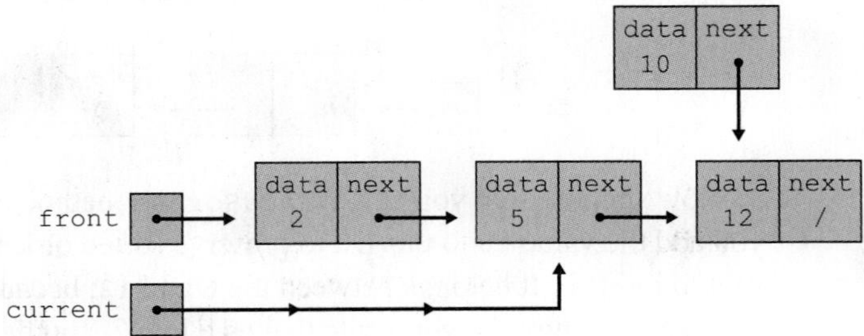

But now you have to link this into the list by changing `current.next`:

```
current.next = new ListNode(value, current.next);
```

Now the computer's memory looks like this:

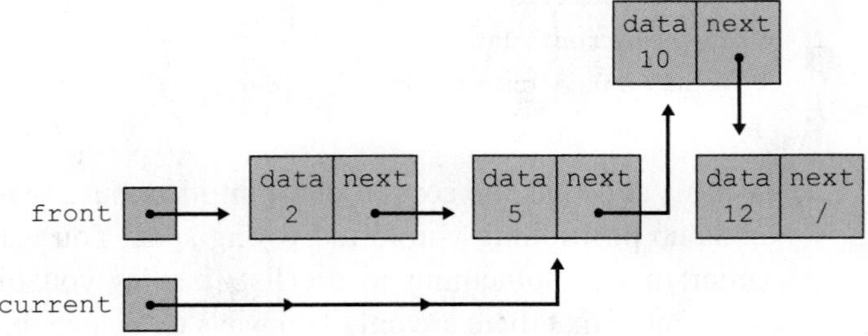

This diagram isn't the easiest picture to read, but if you follow the links carefully, you'll see that, starting at the front, the sequence of values is `2, 5, 10, 12,` which is what you want.

The code works for most cases, but it is incomplete. What if you want to insert the value `42`? Remember your loop test:

```
while (current.next.data < value)
```

This code depends on finding a value in the list that is less than the value you are trying to insert. What if there is no such value, as in the case of `42`? This code keeps moving `current` forward until `current.next` is `null`. At that point, when you try to ask for the value of `current.next.data`, you are asking for `null.data`, which throws a `NullPointerException` because Java is looking for the `data` field of a nonexistent object.

If the value that you wish to insert is greater than everything else in the list, then it belongs after the last node in the list. So you want to stop when `current` gets to the last node in the list. Thus, a second (still incorrect) attempt at writing the code for the test would be

```
while (current.next.data < value && current.next != null)
```

This code still doesn't work. The test for current.next being null should stop changing current at the right place, but when current.next is null, it is not legal to ask for the value of current.next.data. That test will throw a NullPointerException. This test is an example of a combination of a sensitive and robust test:

```
while (current.next.data < value && current.next != null)
```

sensitive test   robust test

You need to switch the order of these tests to make them work properly.

```
while (current.next != null && current.next.data < value)
```

Recall from Chapter 5 that Java uses what is known as short-circuited evaluation, which means that if the first test evaluates to false, Java doesn't bother to perform the second test. So the first test, in effect, protects you from the potential problem generated by the second test (the NullPointerException).

Incorporating these changes, you end up with the following code:

```
ListNode current = front;
while (current.next != null && current.next.data < value) {
    current = current.next;
}
current.next = new ListNode(value, current.next);
```

But even this code is not enough. The first test in this loop is the robust test, but it isn't very robust. If current is null, then it throws a NullPointerException. So you want to execute this code only in the case in which front isn't null.

There is another special case. If the value to be inserted belongs at the very front of the list, then this code will place it in the wrong spot. It always inserts after a node currently in the list, never in front of all nodes.

For example, suppose that you want to insert the value 1 in the previous list that begins with the value 2. The code that you have written starts current at the front of the list and inserts the value *after* that node by changing the value of current.next. So the value 1 would be inserted after the value 2, which is clearly wrong.

For the "front of the list" case, you have to write code that changes front rather than changing current.next. In what case would you want to do that? When the value is less than front.data. And what exactly do you want to do? You want to set front to a new list node that points at the old front of the list:

```
if (value < front.data) {
    front = new ListNode(value, front);
}
```

There is yet another special case. If you ran this program, you'd find that, after all of your hard work, the program throws a `NullPointerException` on the very first call to `addSorted`. Java throws an exception if the list is empty because a line in the code asks for `front.data` and `front` is `null`.

So you need to include yet another test in the code:

```
if (value <= front.data || front == null) {
    front = new ListNode(value, front);
}
```

Of course, we have purposely written this addition in the wrong way as well. This is another example of a sensitive test (referring to `front.data`) and a robust test (testing `front` for `null`). So you have to reverse the order of these two tests to make the modification to the code work properly.

The final version of the method is as follows:

```
public void addSorted(int value) {
    if (front == null || front.data >= value) {
        front = new ListNode(value, front);
    } else {
        ListNode current = front;
        while (current.next != null && current.next.data < value) {
            current = current.next;
        }
        current.next = new ListNode(value, current.next);
    }
}
```

The `if` statement in this code deals with the two special cases we just mentioned. If the list is currently empty (`front == null`) or if the value belongs at the front of the list (`front.data >= value`), then you insert the value at the front of the list rather than using the other code that you developed. The order in which this test appears is important because the test involving `front.data` will throw a `NullPointerException` if `front` is `null`.

This code is a good example to study because it has so many special cases. In the course of writing the code, you had to deal with the following cases:

- **middle:** the "typical" case in which a value is inserted in the middle of the list
- **back:** the special case in which we had to insert at the back of the list
- **front:** the special case in which we had to insert at the front of the list
- **empty:** the special case in which we had to insert into an empty list

The first two cases are handled by the `if` branch of the code:

```
if (front == null || front.data >= value)
```

empty list — front of list

The second two cases are handled inside the `else` branch of the code:

```
while (current.next != null && current.next.data < value)
```

back of list — middle of list

Inchworm Approach

Some people find it confusing to write code that involves expressions like `current.next.data`. Another approach is to use a pair of pointers that keep track of a current and a previous position in the list. In effect, the pointers keep track of a two-element window on the list, as in the following diagram:

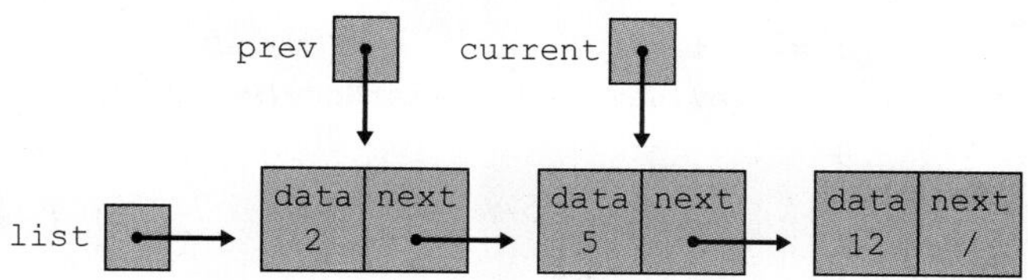

As an analogy, consider an inchworm that is two nodes in length. When the inchworm stretches out, its back half is on one node and the front half is on another node. To move forward, it scoots its back half up to where the front half is, then scoots the front half onto the next node. This is exactly analogous to the code you'd use to move this pair of variables forward one spot:

```
prev = current;
current = current.next;
```

Here is a solution to the `addSorted` problem using this approach:

```
public void addSorted(int value) {
    if (front == null || front.data >= value) {
        front = new ListNode(value, front);
    } else {
        ListNode prev = front;
        ListNode current = front.next;
        while (current != null && current.data < value) {
            prev = current;
```

```
            current = current.next;
        }
        prev.next = new ListNode(value, prev.next);
    }
}
```

Yet another variation is to set `prev` equal to `null` initially in order to eliminate the special case for the front of the list. Then you have to test after the loop to see whether `prev` is still `null`:

```
public void addSorted(int value) {
    ListNode prev = null;
    ListNode current = front;
    while (current != null && current.data < value) {
        prev = current;
        current = current.next;
    }
    if (prev == null) {
        front = new ListNode(value, front);
    } else {
        prev.next = new ListNode(value, prev.next);
    }
}
```

16.4 An `IntList` Interface

The `ArrayIntList` class from Chapter 15 and the `LinkedIntList` class we have explored in this chapter have very similar methods. They each have the following methods:

- a `size` method
- a `get` method
- a `toString` method
- an `indexOf` method
- a one-argument `add` method (the appending `add`)
- a two-argument `add` method (add at an index)
- a `remove` method (remove at an index)

This similarity isn't an accident. When we began studying linked lists, we purposely implemented new versions of these methods that worked for linked lists. The point is that these classes are similar in terms of what they can do, but they are very different in the ways that they do it.

Consider the following client code, which performs parallel operations on two different lists, adding three values, removing one, and printing the list before and after the `remove`:

```
public class ListClient1 {
    public static void main(String[] args) {
        ArrayIntList list1 = new ArrayIntList();
        list1.add(18);
        list1.add(27);
        list1.add(93);
        System.out.println(list1);
        list1.remove(1);
        System.out.println(list1);

        LinkedIntList list2 = new LinkedIntList();
        list2.add(18);
        list2.add(27);
        list2.add(93);
        System.out.println(list2);
        list2.remove(1);
        System.out.println(list2);
    }
}
```

The program produces the following output:

```
[18, 27, 93]
[18, 93]
[18, 27, 93]
[18, 93]
```

As we expected, the two kinds of list behave the same way. So what if you wanted to introduce a static method to eliminate this redundancy? What type would you use for the parameter? You can't use `ArrayIntList` because then you wouldn't be able to pass the `LinkedIntList` as a parameter, and vice versa.

As we saw in Chapters 9 and 11, the right way to approach this task is to introduce an interface. You want to think of these lists as being the same kind of thing. Even though you recognize that there are significant differences between the two, you can imagine an "integer list" abstraction of which these are two possible implementations. They're the same in the sense that they provide basic "integer list" functionality like an appending `add`. But they are different in the sense that they are implemented quite differently (one using an array and the other using a linked list).

You can introduce an interface with just the method headers to capture this notion of the integer list:

```
public interface IntList {
    public int size();
    public int get(int index);
    public String toString();
    public int indexOf(int value);
    public void add(int value);
    public void add(int index, int value);
    public void remove(int index);
}
```

Using the interface, you can write a `processList` method to use in the client program:

```
public class ListClient2 {
    public static void main(String[] args) {
        ArrayIntList list1 = new ArrayIntList();
        processList(list1);

        LinkedIntList list2 = new LinkedIntList();
        processList(list2);
    }

    public static void processList(IntList list) {
        list.add(18);
        list.add(27);
        list.add(93);
        System.out.println(list);
        list.remove(1);
        System.out.println(list);
    }
}
```

If this is the only change you make, then your program will include two errors instead of one. Now both calls on the method cause an error. That seems a bit odd, because both `ArrayIntList` and `LinkedIntList` have the methods mentioned in the `IntList` interface. But recall that Java requires classes to explicitly state which interfaces they implement. So you have to modify the two classes to include this notation:

```
public class ArrayIntList implements IntList {
    ...
}
```

```
public class LinkedIntList implements IntList {
    ...
}
```

After you make this change, the code compiles and executes properly.

It is important to keep in mind that you can't create instances of the interface type. The following line of code is an error:

```
IntList list = new IntList(); // error—can't instantiate the interface
```

Interfaces cannot be instantiated because they are incomplete. They specify behaviors, but they don't say how those behaviors are implemented. So when you create an instance, you have to pick one of the actual implementations.

Even though you can't create an instance of an interface, it is a good idea to use interfaces when you define the types of variables. Therefore, method `main` in the client code should be rewritten as follows:

```
public static void main(String[] args) {
    IntList list1 = new ArrayIntList();
    processList(list1);

    IntList list2 = new LinkedIntList();
    processList(list2);
}
```

These variables are more flexible than the old variables. The variable `list1`, for example, can now refer to any `IntList` object, not just one of type `ArrayIntList`.

16.5 LinkedList<E>

In this section, we will use the `LinkedIntList` that we have developed to produce a class that is similar to Java's `LinkedList<E>` class. In the collections framework, there is a close relationship between the `LinkedList<E>` class and the `ArrayList<E>` class. We'll mirror that relationship in the version that we create. The task will require making a few changes to the `ArrayList<E>` that we developed at the end of the previous chapter.

In particular, we'll introduce an interface `List<E>` that both classes will implement. We can include all of the methods that we implemented for the `ArrayList<E>`.

We can also introduce a slight improvement. Various structures can use the for-each loop that was introduced in Chapter 7. If you want to be able to use a for-each loop for your own class, you have to implement a special interface known as `Iterable<E>`. It has one and only one method:

```
public interface Iterable<E> {
    public Iterator<E> iterator();
}
```

In other words, we need to have a method that constructs an iterator for our collection. We'll discuss later in this section how to do that for a linked list. Under the hood, the for-each loop actually calls the iterator method on the collection and yields each next element to the loop's body.

In this case, we want our two classes to implement both the List<E> interface and the Iterable<E> interface. The usual way to accomplish that in Java is to have one interface extend another. This is similar to inheritance for classes and you use the same extends keyword. Here is the complete List<E> specification:

```
// Generic interface for a List of objects of type E.

public interface List<E> extends Iterable<E> {
    public int size();
    public E get(int index);
    public int indexOf(E value);
    public boolean isEmpty();
    public boolean contains(E value);
    public void add(E value);
    public void add(int index, E value);
    public void addAll(List<E> other);
    public void remove(int index);
    public void set(int index, E value);
    public void clear();
}
```

Notice that the header mentions that it extends the Iterable<E> interface. That means that any class implementing the interface must provide a method for constructing an iterator, which will allow the class to be used in for-each loops.

Before we write the actual code for LinkedList<E>, we'll explore some variations on linked lists and discuss the issue of iterators.

Linked List Variations

So far in this chapter, we have discussed the simplest possible linked list. Each node in this list has had a single link to the next value in the list, and we have terminated each list with the value null. We have used the value null to represent an empty list.

However, there are many variations on linked lists. Several of these ideas are used in Java's implementation of LinkedList, and we will use several for our own implementation. There are three primary variations: circular lists, lists with dummy nodes, and doubly linked lists. Let's consider each variation in turn.

Instead of making the final element of the list store the value null, we can have the final element of the list point back to the first value in the list. We refer to such a list as *circular*. For example, here is a circular list that stores the values [3, 7, 12]:

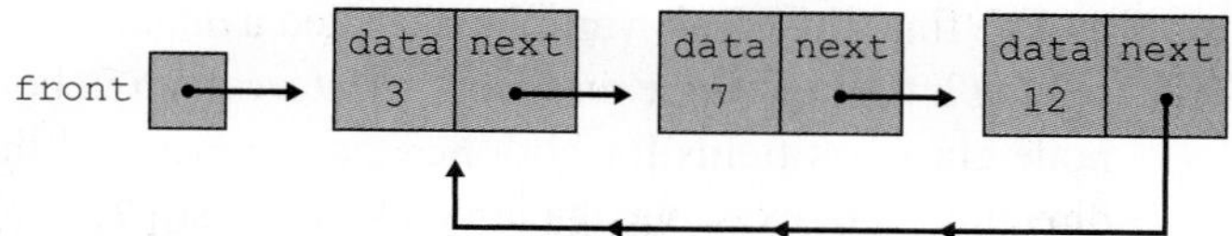

There are many applications in which it can be helpful to have the list point back to the front in this manner. To manipulate such a list, you use very different code. You can't test for `null` because there are no `null` links in the list. Instead, you test whether you have returned to the point at which you started. It is often helpful to use a `do/while` loop for processing a circular list. For example, the following code prints the values of the list, one per line:

```
ListNode current = front;
do {
    System.out.println(current.data);
    current = current.next;
} while (current != front);
```

One of the tricky aspects of working with a circular list is dealing with an empty list. The preceding code, for example, generates a `NullPointerException` if the variable `list` has the value `null`.

This brings us to our second variation. It is often helpful to have extra nodes in the list that do not store meaningful elements and that are not considered part of the list. We refer to such a node as a *dummy node*. For example, in a circular list it is often convenient to represent the empty list as a single dummy node that points back to itself. Dummy nodes are useful even with the kind of null-terminated lists we have been writing. By using a dummy header node, we represent the empty list as having just the dummy node:

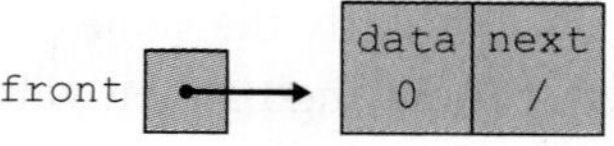

The `data` field in the preceding list stores `0`, but it doesn't matter what value we store in the dummy node. The advantage of using a dummy header node is that we no longer have to write special code to insert a value at the front of the list. Now the front of the list will always be this dummy header node. For example, if we were to insert the values `3`, `7`, and `12`, they would be inserted after the dummy node:

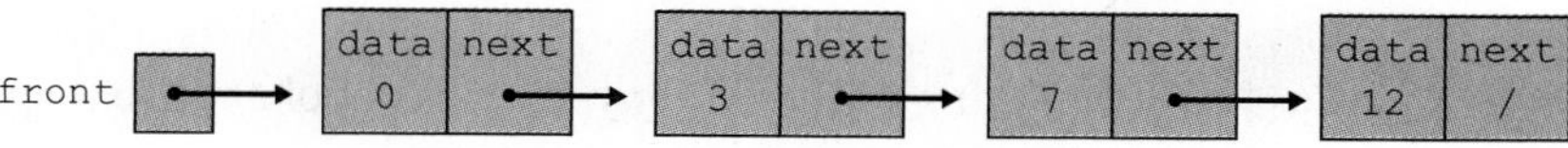

The final linked list variation is called a *doubly linked list*. The idea is that instead of storing links in a single direction, we store them in both directions. That means that our node class has fields for both `next` and `prev` and that we maintain the links in both directions. For example, the three-element list `[3, 7, 12]` would be stored as follows:

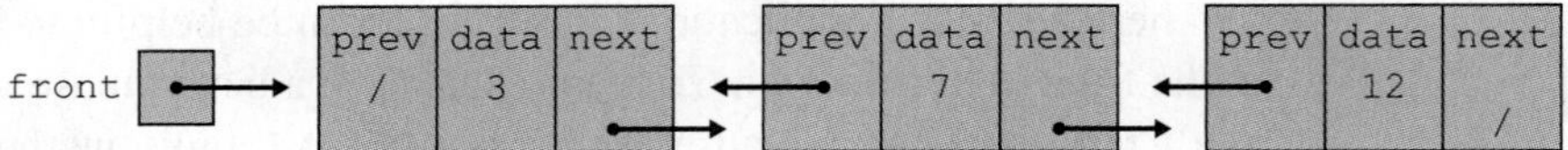

Notice that each node now has two different links pointing in different directions. The list also has two `null` links. The final node has a `next` field that is `null` and the first node has a `prev` field that is `null` to indicate in each case that there are no other nodes in that direction.

In practice, programmers use some combination of these techniques. For example, Java's `LinkedList<E>` is implemented as a doubly linked, circular list.

In our implementation, we will use two of these techniques. Our list will be doubly linked and will have two dummy nodes, one for the front of the list and one for the back of the list. We will also introduce an extra field to keep track of the back of the list. Thus, in our version, an empty list will look like this:

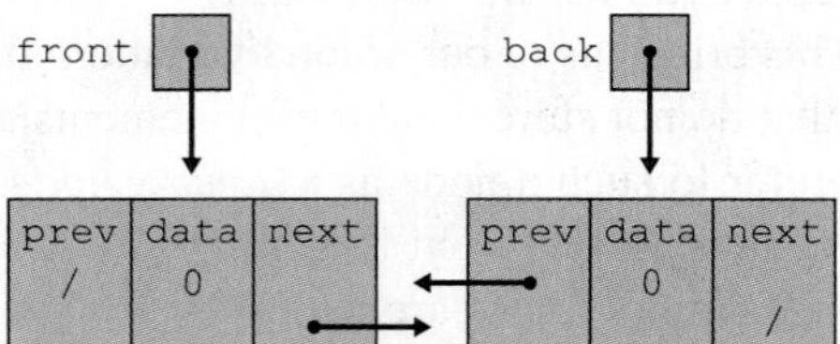

This list doesn't look very empty, but that's the idea. Even when it is empty, our list will have two dummy header nodes. That way, the fields `front` and `back` will always point to exactly the same dummy node and we won't have to write any special case code for changing their values. Instead, all insertions will occur between the two dummy nodes. For example, if we insert the values `18` and `73`, our list will look like this:

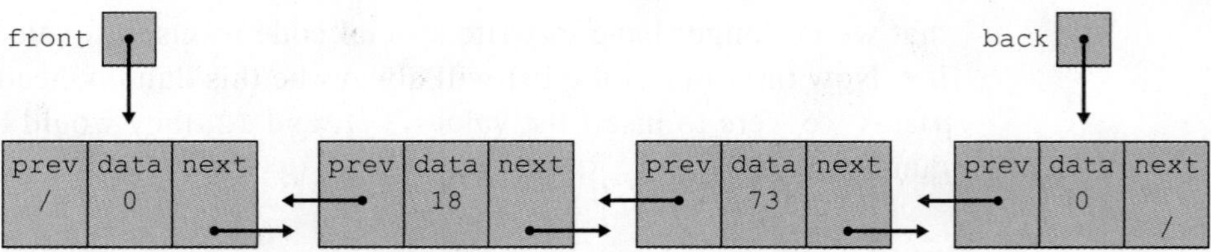

You can think of the dummy nodes as bookends that appear on either side of the actual nodes.

Linked List Iterators

To match our ArrayList class and to be able to implement the Iterable interface that allows us to use for-each loops, we need to implement an iterator for our LinkedList class. Just as we did with ArrayList, we can make the iterator class an inner class that has access to the fields of the outer object. In the case of the ArrayList, the primary field for our iterator was an integer index. For a linked list, we want to keep track of a current list node. We still need the removeOK field that we used for ArrayList. So our iterator class begins as follows:

```
private class LinkedIterator implements Iterator<E> {
    private ListNode<E> current; // location of next value to return
    private boolean removeOK; // whether it's okay to remove now
    ...
}
```

Notice that our node class is now also generic (ListNode<E>). As in the last chapter, we do not declare our class as LinkedIterator<E>, because the type E is already declared as part of the outer linked list class. But we do place an <E> type parameter after the Iterator and ListNode declarations.

To implement the iterator class, you have to take into consideration the fact that you will have two dummy nodes, one at the front of the list and one at the back. The first node you will want to process will come after that dummy node at the front, so the proper initialization for your iterator is as follows:

```
public LinkedIterator() {
    current = front.next;
    removeOK = false;
}
```

To test whether you have a next value to examine, you will use the dummy nodes again. You'll want to continue to move current forward until it reaches the dummy node at the end of the list. That means that you'll implement hasNext as follows:

```
public boolean hasNext() {
    return current != back;
}
```

For the other two operations, you can simply translate what you did with the array implementation into appropriate code for your linked list implementation. For the next method, your code will look like the following:

```
public E next() {
    if (!hasNext()) {
        throw new NoSuchElementException();
    }
```

```
    E result = current.data;
    current = current.next;
    removeOK = true;
    return result;
}
```

For the remove method, your code will look like this:

```
public void remove() {
    if (!removeOK) {
        throw new IllegalStateException();
    }
    ListNode<E> prev2 = current.prev.prev;
    prev2.next = current;
    current.prev = prev2;
    size--;
    removeOK = false;
}
```

Notice that, to remove a node, you have to reset both a `next` and a `prev` pointer in the list because now you are working with a doubly linked list.

Before we leave the subject of iterators, you should consider briefly how to implement the `addAll` method for your `LinkedList` class. Keep in mind that its header will refer to your `List` interface:

```
public void addAll(List<E> other) {
    ...
}
```

You have to write this code in such a way that it can take either a `LinkedList` or an `ArrayList` as a parameter. That means that you have to use methods mentioned in the interface. One misguided approach would be to use a `for` loop and repeatedly call `get` to retrieve each element:

```
// inefficient implementation of addAll method
public void addAll(List<E> other) {
    for (int i = 0; i < other.size(); i++) {
        add(other.get(i));
    }
}
```

This code will work, but it will be extremely inefficient when `other` is a `LinkedList`. Each time you call the `get` method, you have to start at the front of the list and skip nodes until you get to the right spot. It is much better to use an iterator to solve this problem. You can make it particularly simple by using a for-each loop and letting Java manage the iterator for you. This technique greatly simplifies the code:

```
public void addAll(List<E> other) {
    for (E value : other) {
        add(value);
    }
}
```

You should use this same implementation for the method in the `ArrayList` class to make sure that it also runs efficiently for all types of lists. It turns out that several of the methods can be implemented using the same code for both the array list and linked list. A better implementation would introduce an abstract list superclass to represent this similarity. This is left as a programming project idea.

Other Code Details

We are almost ready to put the pieces together. But first, let's consider the fields for our `LinkedList` class. We have already discussed keeping track of both the front and the back of the list. It is also useful to keep track of the current size in a field so that you don't have to traverse the list to find out its size. So there will be three fields:

```
public class LinkedList<E> implements List<E> {
    private ListNode<E> front;    // first value in the list
    private ListNode<E> back;     // last value in the list
    private int size;             // current number of elements

    ...
}
```

To initialize the list, you want to construct the two dummy nodes and then set up everything to refer to an empty list. You also have to implement the `clear` method that is supposed to return to an empty list, so this is a good opportunity to write the code once in the `clear` method and to have the constructor call it. The constructor will look like this:

```
public LinkedList() {
    front = new ListNode<E>(null);
    back = new ListNode<E>(null);
    clear();
}
```

Notice that you need to include the type parameter `<E>` when you construct the nodes. For the `clear` method, you simply make these two dummy nodes point to each other and reset the size:

```
public void clear() {
    front.next = back;
```

```
        back.prev = front;
        size = 0;
    }
```

When you implement the get method, you can introduce an optimization. In the case of a singly linked list, you always start at the beginning of the list and move forward until you find the appropriate spot in the list. This works well when the value appears toward the beginning of the list. What if the value appears near the end? Because your list is doubly linked, you can start at the end and work backward, following the prev links until you get to the appropriate spot. The best thing to do is to start from the front when the index is in the first half of the list and to start from the back when it is in the second half of the list. This optimization applies to any of the methods that involve going to a specific index (remove, set, add). All of these methods call the private nodeAt method, so the optimization appears in just one place in the code:

```
private ListNode<E> nodeAt(int index) {
    ListNode<E> current;
    if (index < size / 2) { // start from the front
        current = front;
        for (int i = 0; i < index + 1; i++) {
            current = current.next;
        }
    } else {  // start from the back
        current = back;
        for (int i = size; i >= index + 1; i--) {
            current = current.prev;
        }
    }
    return current;
}
```

In our final implementation of LinkedIntList, we didn't include methods for isEmpty, indexOf, or contains. The isEmpty method can simply check whether the size is 0, as you did for the ArrayList, and the contains method can check the result of calling indexOf.

To write indexOf, you loop over the list, looking for the value and returning its index if you find it. Because of your dummy nodes, the loop ends up looking slightly different than the other loops you have written:

```
ListNode<E> current = front.next;
while (current != back) {
    ...
}
```

You also have to be careful to call the `equals` method for comparisons.

The code involves ordinary list operations that you've seen throughout this chapter:

```
public int indexOf(E value) {
    int index = 0;
    ListNode<E> current = front.next;
    while (current != back) {
        if (current.data.equals(value)) {
            return index;
        }
        index++;
        current = current.next;
    }
    return -1;
}
```

Many of the methods that you wrote for `LinkedIntList` can be used with only slight modifications for the `LinkedList`. Let's look at `remove` as an example. Because of the dummy nodes, you don't have to make a special case for an empty list. But because of the doubly linking, you have to reset two links (a `next` and a `prev`) when you remove the node:

```
public void remove(int index) {
    checkIndex(index);
    ListNode<E> current = gotoIndex(index – 1);
    current.next = current.next.next;
    current.next.prev = current;
    size--;
}
```

You'll want to make similar changes to the `add` method.

The `LinkedList` class includes one final improvement. Instead of keeping the node class as a separate class, the `LinkedList` class includes it as a nested class. In this case, the individual node objects don't need access to the outer object, so it is best to declare the class to be a static inner class. The details of this code are beyond the scope of this book, but the quick explanation is that providing access to the outer class takes some extra storage and because we're likely to construct thousands and perhaps even millions of node objects, we want to be more efficient about the space that they take up. Declaring the class to be static accomplishes that goal.

The complete code for the `LinkedList` class can be found at http://buildingjavaprograms.com. You will also find the `List` interface and an updated version of `ArrayList` there.

Chapter Summary

A linked list is a data structure that stores an ordered sequence of elements using a chain of objects called nodes. Each node refers to at least one other node in the list. The overall list object keeps references to a small number of these nodes, such as the front or back node.

A node has a `data` and `next` field. You can connect one node to another by assigning its `next` field to refer to the other node. It is possible to make chains of nodes of arbitrary length in this way.

The end of a chain of nodes, the `next` reference of the last node, is `null`.

When you are trying to rearrange one ordering of nodes into another, you must be careful about the order in which you change the references. If you change the ordering so that no variable or field refers to a given node, the node is lost and cannot be recovered.

You can traverse a linked list by creating a temporary node reference (called `current` in our examples) and looping through the overall list of nodes. Such a loop can stop when the program finds a particular value or encounters a `null` next node (the end of the list).

It is often desirable to stop one node before the relevant part of the list that you are searching for, because, in order to change the list, you often must change the `next` field of the prior node.

When you are performing complex list operations such as adding to a sorted list, it is important to think about all of the possible cases in which the method might be called. Is the list empty, does it have a single element, or does it have many elements? Will our element of interest be added at or removed from the beginning, middle, or end of the list?

When you create two tests separated by an `&&` or `||`, be sure to place the more "robust" test before the more "sensitive" test, especially if the robust test's failure would cause the sensitive test to throw an exception.

One way to traverse a list is with two current references that are one node apart, also called the inchworm approach.

A list interface can be created to represent an abstract data type that is implemented by both array lists and linked lists. The list interface allows client code to treat both types of lists the same way.

A linked list iterator keeps a reference to its current position in the list. This class is often written as an inner class inside the overall list class so that the iterator has direct access to the list's nodes.

A generic linked list class can store objects of any type `E` rather than just integers.

Self-Check Problems

Section 16.1: Working with Nodes

1. What is the difference between a linked list and an array list? How are they similar?
2. What is the difference between a linked node and a linked list? How are they related and connected?

3. What value is stored as the `next` field of the last node of a list? What value will a node's `next` field have if none is specified?

4. What happens if you or the client try to go past the last element in a linked list? Be specific.

For each of the next four problems, draw a picture of what the given linked nodes would look like after the given code executes.

5. 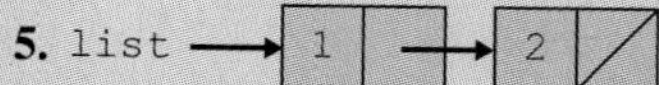


```
list.next = new LinkNode(3);
```

6. list → [1] → [2 /]

```
list.next = new LinkNode(3, list.next);
```

7. list → [1] → [2] → [3 /]

```
list = new LinkNode(4, list.next.next);
```

8. list → [1] → [2] → [3 /]

```
list.next.next = null;
```

For each of the next nine problems, you'll see pictures of linked nodes before and after changes. Write the code that will produce the given result by modifying links between the nodes shown and/or creating new nodes as needed. There may be more than one way to write the code, but you may not change any existing node's `data` field value. If a variable does not appear in the "after" picture, it doesn't matter what value it has after the changes are made.

Before **After**

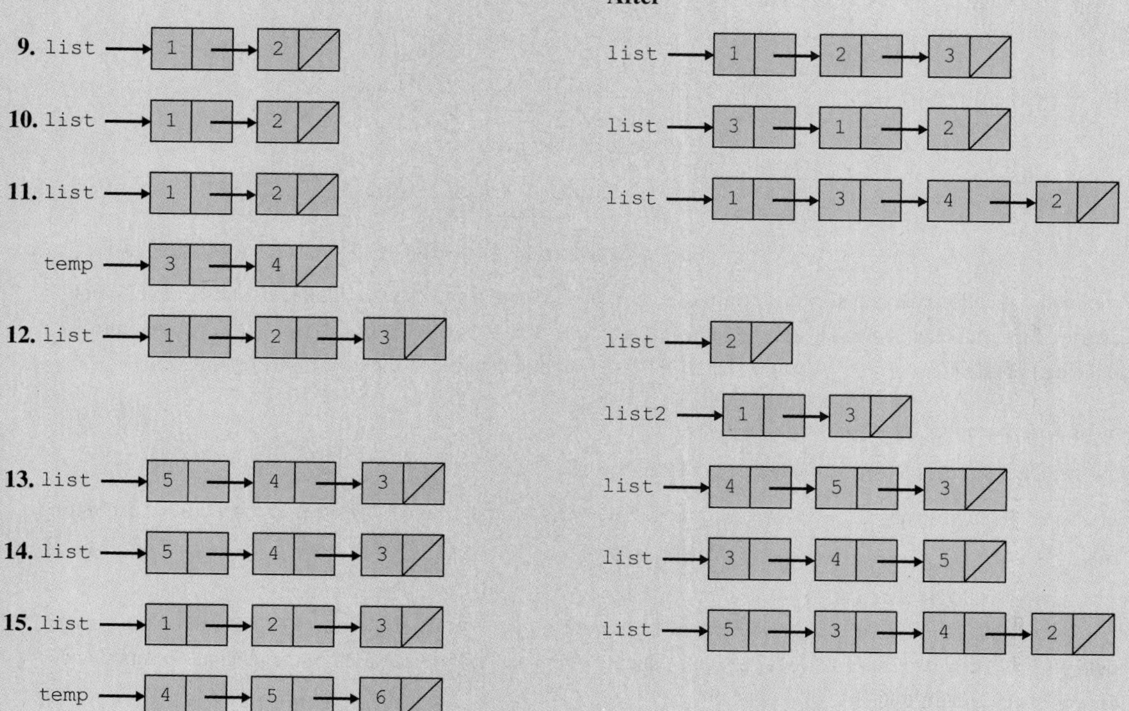

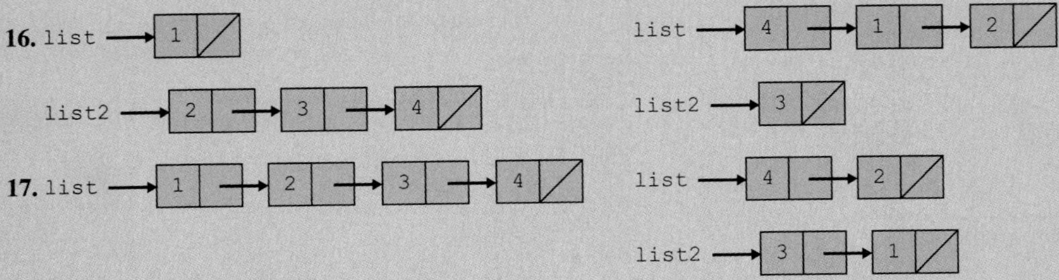

Section 16.2: A Linked List Class

18. What are the two ways to change the contents of a linked list?

19. An element can be inserted at or removed from the beginning, middle, or end of a linked list. Which of the three locations is the most computationally expensive, and why? How does this compare against the result for an array list?

20. When you add or remove the element found at index *i* of a list, you must create a temporary `current` node reference and advance it through the list. At which index's node should the loop stop, relative to *i*?

21. In an array list, it is possible to overrun the capacity of the array, at which point the list must be resized to fit. Is resizing necessary on a linked list? What limits the number of elements that a linked list can have?

For each of the next three problems, you'll see pictures of long chains of linked nodes before and after changes. (The . . . in the middle of the chain signifies an indeterminate large number of nodes.) Write the code that will produce the given result by modifying links between the nodes shown and/or creating new nodes as needed. You will need to write loops to advance to the end of the list in order to reach the node(s) to modify.

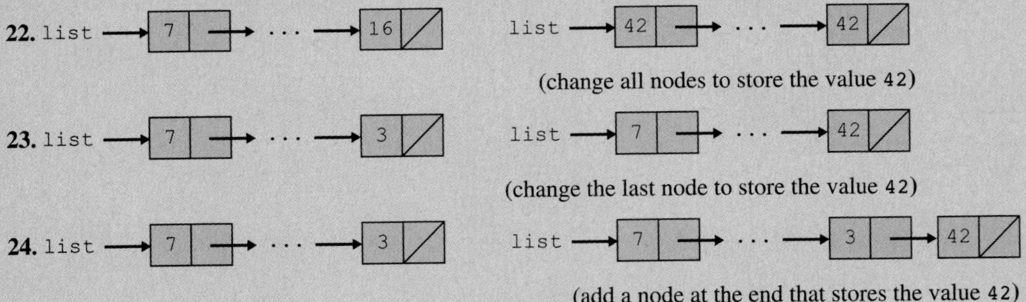

25. Write methods called `min` and `max` that return the smallest and largest values in the linked list, respectively. For example, if a variable called `list` stores `[11, -7, 3, 42, 0, 14]`, the call of `list.min()` should return –7 and the call of `list.max()` should return `42`. If the list is empty, throw an `IllegalStateException`.

Section 16.3: A Complex List Operation

26. What are the four cases examined in the `addSorted` method?

27. What is the "inchworm approach"? What advantages does this approach have over other approaches for examining a linked list?

28. Write methods called `sum` and `average` that return the sum of all values in the list and the average value as a real number, respectively. For example, if a variable called `list` stores `[11, -7, 3, 42, 0, 14]`, the call of `list.sum()` should return `63` and the call of `list.average()` should return `10.5`. If the list is empty, `sum` should return `0` and `average` should return `0.0`.

Section 16.4: An `IntList` Interface

29. What are some advantages of creating an `IntList` interface and having both types of lists implement it?

30. Write a method called `firstLast` that can accept either type of integer list as a parameter and that moves the first element of the list to the end. For example, if a variable called `list` contains the values `[12, 45, 78, 20, 36]`, the call of `firstLast(list);` will change the list to store `[45, 78, 20, 36, 12]`.

Section 16.5: `LinkedList<E>`

31. What are some changes that need to be made to the linked list class to convert it from storing integers to storing objects of type `E`?

32. Why is an iterator especially useful with linked lists?

33. What state does the linked list iterator store? How does the iterator know if there are more elements left to examine?

Exercises

Each of the following exercises is a method to be added to the `LinkedIntList` class from this chapter.

1. Write a method called `set` that accepts an index and a value and sets the list's element at that index to have the given value. You may assume that the index is between 0 (inclusive) and the size of the list (exclusive).

2. Write a method called `min` that returns the minimum value in a list of integers. If the list is empty, it should throw a `NoSuchElementException`.

3. Write a method called `isSorted` that returns `true` if the list is in sorted (nondecreasing) order and returns `false` otherwise. An empty list is considered to be sorted.

4. Write a method called `lastIndexOf` that accepts an integer value as a parameter and that returns the index in the list of the last occurrence of that value, or -1 if the value is not found in the list. For example, if a variable `list` stores the values `[1, 18, 2, 7, 18, 39, 18, 40]`, then the call of `list.lastIndexOf(18)` should return `6`. If the call had instead been `list.lastIndexOf(3)`, the method would return `–1`.

5. Write a method called `countDuplicates` that returns the number of duplicates in a sorted list. The list will be in sorted order, so all of the duplicates will be grouped together. For example, if a variable `list` stores the values `[1, 1, 1, 3, 3, 6, 9, 15, 15, 23, 23, 23, 40, 40]`, the call of `list.countDuplicates()` should return `7` because there are 2 duplicates of `1`, 1 duplicate of `3`, 1 duplicate of `15`, 2 duplicates of `23`, and 1 duplicate of `40`.

6. Write a method called `hasTwoConsecutive` that returns whether or not a list of integers has two adjacent numbers that are consecutive integers (`true` if such a pair exists and `false` otherwise). For example, if a variable `list` stores the values `[1, 18, 2, 7, 8, 39, 18, 40]`, then the call `list.hasTwoConsecutive()` should return `true` because the list contains the adjacent numbers `(7, 8)`, which are a pair of consecutive numbers.

7. Write a method called `deleteBack` that deletes the last value (the value at the back of the list) and returns the deleted value. If the list is empty, throw a `NoSuchElementException`.

8. Write a method called `switchPairs` that switches the order of values in the list in a pairwise fashion. Your method should switch the order of the first two values, then switch the order of the next two, switch the order of the next two, and so on. If the list contains an odd number of values, the final element is not moved. For example, if the list initially stores `[10, 25, 31, 47, 52, 68, 77]`, your method should switch the first pair (`10` and `25`), the second pair (`31` and `47`), and the third pair (`52` and `68`) to yield `[25, 10, 47, 31, 68, 52, 77]`.

9. Write a method called `stutter` that doubles the size of a list by replacing every integer in the list with two of that integer. For example, suppose a variable `list` stores the values `[1, 8, 19, 4, 17]`, after a call of `list.stutter()`, it should store `[1, 1, 8, 8, 19, 19, 4, 4, 17, 17]`.

10. Write a method called `stretch` that takes an integer *n* as a parameter and that increases a list of integers by a factor of *n* by replacing each integer in the original list with *n* copies of that integer. For example, if a variable called `list` stores `[18, 7, 4, 24, 11]` and we make the call of `list.stretch(3);` the list should be changed to store `[18, 18, 18, 7, 7, 7, 4, 4, 4, 24, 24, 24, 11, 11, 11]`. If *n* is zero or negative, the list should become empty.

11. Write a method called `compress` that replaces every pair of elements in the list with a single element equal to the sum of the pair. If the list is of odd size, leave the last element unchanged. For example, if the list stores `[1, 7, 3, 9, 4, 6, 5]`, your method should change it to store `[8, 12, 10, 5]` (1+7, then 3+9, then 4+6, then 5).

12. Write a method called `split` that rearranges the elements of a list so that all of the negative values appear before all of the nonnegatives. For example, suppose a variable `list` stores the values `[8, 7, -4, 19, 0, 43, -8, -7, 2]`. The call of `list.split();` should rearrange the list to put the negatives first: `[-4, -8, -7, 8, 7, 19, 0, 43, 2]`. It doesn't matter what order the numbers are in, only that the negatives appear before the nonnegatives, so this is only one possible solution. You must solve the problem by rearranging the links of the list, not by swapping `data` values or creating new nodes. You also may not use auxiliary structures like arrays or `ArrayLists` to solve this problem.

13. Write a method called `transferFrom` that accepts a second linked list as a parameter and that moves values from the second list to this list. You are to attach the second list's elements to the end of this list. You are also to empty the second list. For example, suppose two lists called `list1` and `list2` store `[8, 17, 2, 4]` and `[1, 2, 3]`, respectively. The call of `list1.transferFrom(list2);` should change `list1` to `[8, 17, 2, 4, 1, 2, 3]` and `list2` to an empty list, `[]`. The order of the arguments matters; `list2.transferFrom(list1);` should change `list1` to an empty list, `[]`, and `list2` to `[1, 2, 3, 8, 17, 2, 4]`. Either of the two lists could be empty, but you can assume that neither list is `null`. You are not to create any new nodes. Your method should simply change links of the lists to join them together.

14. Write a method called `removeAll` that removes all occurrences of a particular value. For example, if a variable `list` stores the values `[3, 9, 4, 2, 3, 8, 17, 4, 3, 18]`, the call of `list.removeAll(3);` would change the list to store `[9, 4, 2, 8, 17, 4, 18]`.

15. Write a method called `equals` that accepts a second list as a parameter, returns `true` if the two lists are equal, and returns `false` otherwise. Two lists are considered equal if they store exactly the same values in exactly the same order and have exactly the same length.

16. Write a method called `removeEvens` that removes the values in even-numbered indexes from a list, returning a new list that contains those values in their original order. For example, consider a variable `list1` that stores the values `[8, 13, 17, 4, 9, 12, 98, 41, 7, 23, 0, 92]` and imagine that the following call is made:

    ```
    LinkedIntList list2 = list1.removeEvens();
    ```

    After the call, `list1` should store `[13, 4, 12, 41, 23, 92]` and `list2` should store `[8, 17, 9, 98, 7, 0]`. You may not call any methods of the class other than the constructor to solve this problem. You may not create any new nodes nor change the values stored in `data` fields to solve this problem. You must solve it by rearranging the links of the list.

17. Write a method called `removeRange` that accepts a starting and ending index as parameters and removes the elements at those indexes (inclusive) from the list. For example, if a variable `list` stores the values `[8, 13, 17, 4, 9, 12, 98, 41, 7, 23, 0, 92]`, the call of `listRange.removeRange(3, 8);` should remove values between index 3 and index 8 (the values `4` and `7`), leaving the list of `[8, 13, 17, 23, 0, 92]`. The method

should throw an `IllegalArgumentException` if either of the positions is negative. Otherwise you may assume that the positions represent a legal range of the list ($0 \leq \text{start} \leq \text{end} < \text{size}$).

18. Write a method called `doubleList` that doubles the size of a list by appending a copy of the original sequence to the end of the list. For example, if a variable `list` stores the values `[1, 3, 2, 7]` and we make the call of `list.doubleList();` then after the call it should store `[1, 3, 2, 7, 1, 3, 2, 7]`. Notice that the list has been doubled in size by having the original sequence appear twice in a row. You may not make assumptions about how many elements are in the list. You may not call any methods of the class to solve this problem. If the original list contains *N* nodes, then you should construct exactly *N* nodes to be added. You may not use any auxiliary data structures such as arrays or `ArrayLists` to solve this problem. Your method should run in O(*N*) time where *N* is the number of nodes in the list.

19. Write a method called `rotate` that moves the value at the front of a list of integers to the end of the list. For example, if a variable called `list` stores the values `[8, 23, 19, 7, 45, 98, 102, 4]`, then the call of `list.rotate();` should move the value `8` from the front of the list to the back of the list, changing the list to store `[23, 19, 7, 45, 98, 102, 4, 8]`. If the method is called for a list of 0 elements or 1 element, it should have no effect on the list. You may neither construct any new nodes to solve this problem nor change any of the `data` values stored in the nodes. You must solve the problem by rearranging the links of the list.

20. Write a method called `shift` that rearranges the elements of a list of integers by moving to the end of the list all values that are in odd-numbered positions and otherwise preserving list order. For example, suppose that a variable `list` stores the values `[10, 31, 42, 23, 44, 75, 86]`. The call of `list.shift();` should rearrange the list to store `[10, 42, 44, 86, 31, 23, 75]`. It doesn't matter whether the value itself is odd or even; what matters is whether the value appears in an odd index (index 1, 3, 5, etc.). Also notice that the original order of the list is otherwise preserved. You may not construct any new nodes nor use any auxiliary data structures to solve this problem. You also may not change any `data` fields of the nodes; you must solve this problem by rearranging the links of the list.

21. Write a method called `reverse` that reverses the order of the elements in the list. (This is very challenging!) For example, if the variable `list` initially stores the values `[1, 8, 19, 4, 17]`, the call of `list.reverse();` should change the list to store `[17, 4, 19, 8, 1]`.

Programming Projects

1. The actual `List` interface in the `java.util` package has several methods beyond the ones implemented in this chapter. Write a version of `LinkedList<E>` that adds some or all of these methods. The methods to add are the following (some headers are slightly modified; see the Java API Specification for descriptions of each method):

- `public void addAll(int index, List<E> list)`
- `public boolean containsAll(List<E> list)`
- `public boolean equals(Object o)`
- `public int lastIndexOf(Object o)`
- `public boolean remove(Object o)`
- `public void removeAll(List<E> list)`
- `public void retainAll(List<E> list)`
- `public Object[] toArray()`

2. The `java.util` package has an interface called `ListIterator` that extends the `Iterator` interface and includes additional methods that are specific to iterating through the elements of lists forward or backward. Write a class called `LinkedListIterator2` that adds some or all of these methods for iterating over a doubly linked list. The methods to add are the following (see the Java API Specification for descriptions of each method):

- `public void add(E value)`
- `public boolean hasPrevious()`
- `public int nextIndex()`
- `public E previous()`
- `public int previousIndex()`
- `public void set(E value)`

3. The implementation of several methods is (or can be) the same between our `ArrayList` and `LinkedList`. Write a common abstract superclass called `AbstractList` that implements the common behavior and is extended by both `ArrayList` and `LinkedList`. Factor out the common code from the two list classes into this abstract superclass so that no code duplication occurs between the two. Use iterators wherever possible in the abstract code to ensure that the implementation is efficient for both types of lists.

4. "Assassin" is a real-life game in which a group of players all try individually to find and touch (or "kill") one other player. You can use a linked list to represent this "kill ring" of players in the game:

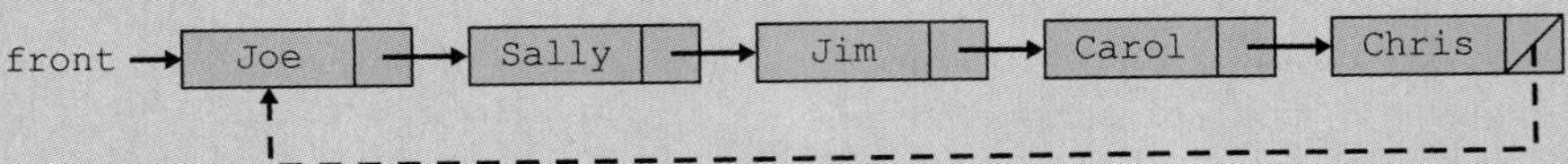

If a "kill" is made, the ring adjusts by removing that person from the list. For example, the following occurs if Sally kills Jim:

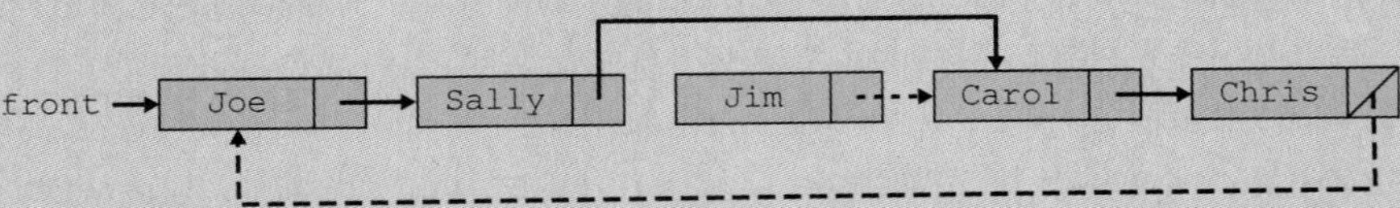

Write a program that models a game of Assassin. The game reads the names of the initial kill ring from a file and puts them into a linked list in random order. Then the game repeatedly prompts for the name of a person that has been killed. The game continues until only one player remains and is declared the winner. The program should also have methods for printing the current contents of the kill ring and printing a "graveyard" of all players who have been killed.

5. Write a graphical program that shows a set of overlapping rectangular regions, each in a different random color. The regions are represented internally as a linked list. The regions have a "*z*-ordering" in which rectangles closer to the end of the list are closer to the top, closer to the user's field of view. When the user clicks the mouse, the topmost region that touches the mouse pointer moves to the very top (end) of the linked list. For example, the following diagrams show the top-left rectangle before and after the mouse is clicked:

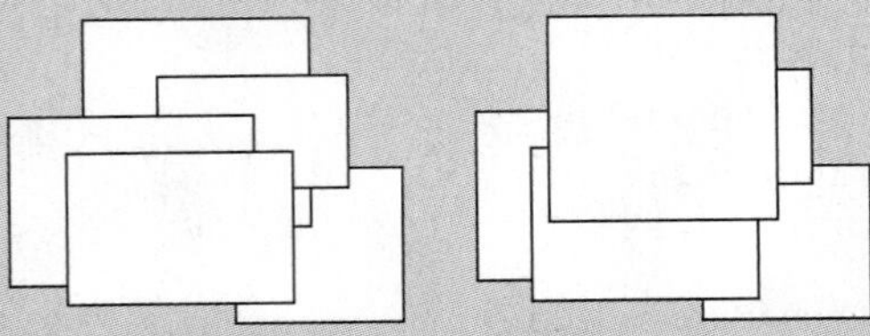

(See the Nifty Assignments page at http://nifty.stanford.edu for a more detailed description of this project, as written by its original author, Prof. Michael Clancy of the University of California, Berkeley.)

Chapter 17
Binary Trees

Introduction

In this chapter, we will explore a new data structure known as a *binary tree*. Like linked lists, binary trees are composed of interconnected nodes. But unlike linked lists, which involve a one-dimensional (straight line) sequence, binary trees can branch in two directions, which gives them a two-dimensional structure.

A surprising number of data relationships can be represented using binary trees. Any relationship that involves a division into two paths can be represented with a binary tree. Thus, binary trees can store information that involves a yes/no relationship, a high/low relationship, or a first and second relationship. For example, arithmetic expressions have operators like + and * that have a first operand and a second operand. Binary trees are a natural structure for storing such relationships. Such trees are often referred to as expression trees because they capture the structure of the arithmetic expressions they represent.

Because binary trees are linked structures, they share many of the useful properties of linked lists. It is fairly easy to grow or shrink a binary tree by rearranging the links of the nodes.

After looking at basic binary tree terminology and basic binary tree operations, we will explore a particular kind of binary tree known as a binary search tree. Binary search trees are used to capture high/low relationships and provide an efficient structure for keeping track of data that have a natural ordering. The `TreeSet` and `TreeMap` structures that are part of the collections framework are implemented as binary search trees.

As we study binary trees, we will find that recursion comes into play quite often. Many binary tree operations are best written recursively.

17.1 Binary Tree Basics

Here is a diagram of a simple binary tree of integer values.

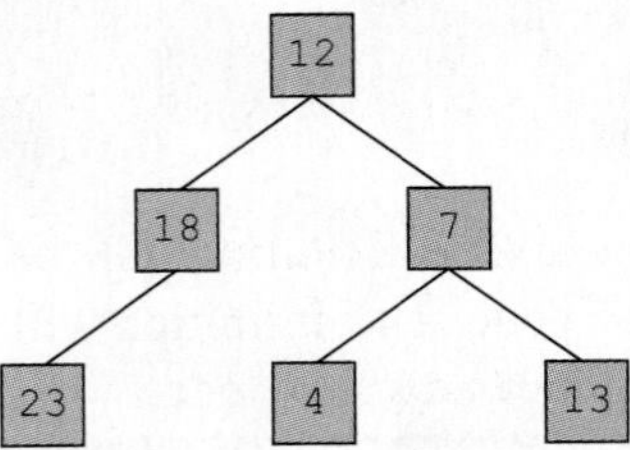

As we did with linked lists, we refer to each different data value as a node. This tree has a total of six nodes. Some people joke that computer scientists view the world upside down, so imagine turning the diagram around the other way:

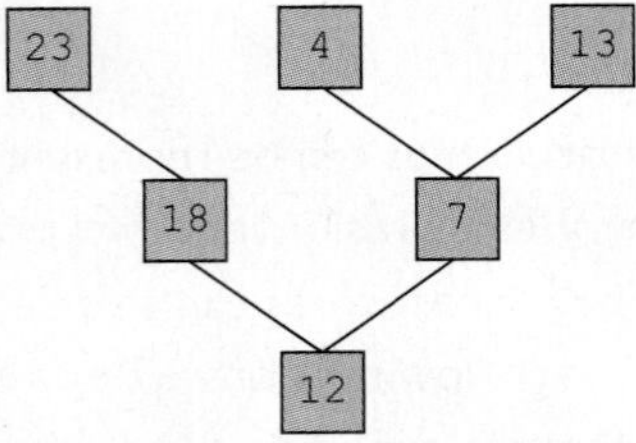

Viewed upside down, the diagram looks more like a tree. At the bottom of this structure is a node storing the value `12`. We refer to this value as the *root* of the tree. All nodes are connected either directly or indirectly to the root node. In this diagram, the nodes that store the values `12`, `18`, and `7` have connections branching out and up. These nodes are referred to as *branch nodes*. The nodes storing the values `23`, `4`, and `13` are at the top of this tree and have nothing above them. They are referred to as leaf *nodes* or *leaves* of the tree.

Before we try to formally define these terms, let's begin with a formal definition of a binary tree.

> **Binary Tree**
>
> A binary tree is either
>
> - an empty tree or
> - a root node (typically storing some data) that refers to two other trees known as the left subtree and the right subtree.

The key phrase in this definition is "subtree." The tree is composed of smaller trees. This definition is recursive. The base case or simple case is an empty tree that has no nodes at all. The recursive case describes a tree of the following form:

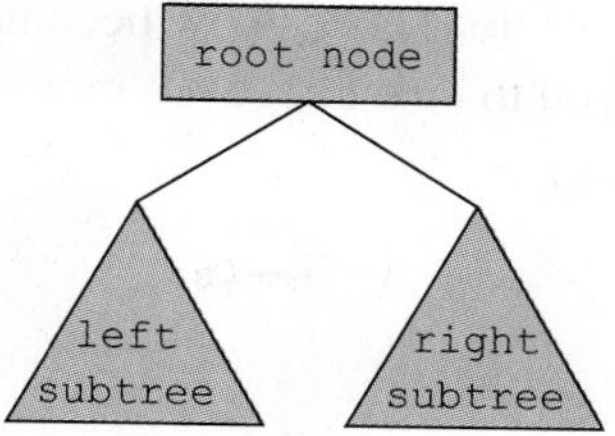

This recursive definition will be a useful way to think about trees as we write binary tree code. The definition will help us to more precisely define the concepts of a branch node and a leaf node.

Branch (Branch Node)

A node that has one or more nonempty subtrees.

Leaf (Leaf Node)

A node that has two empty subtrees.

Using our recursive definition, let's explore how we can form various kinds of trees. The simplest kind of tree is an empty tree, which can't really be drawn because it contains no values.

Once you understand the concept of an empty tree, you can use the second part of the definition to create a new kind of tree that is composed of a root node with left and right subtrees that are both empty. In other words, that tree would be a single leaf node, which you could represent with a star:

```
*
```

Now you can use the recursive rule to say that a tree can be a root node with a left tree that is empty and a right tree that is a leaf:

```
*
 \
  *
```

Or a tree can have an empty right and a leaf to the left:

```
  *
 /
*
```

Or a tree can have a leaf on either side:

```
  *
 / \
*   *
```

These different forms now become possibilities to use for the recursive definition, allowing you to construct even more kinds of trees:

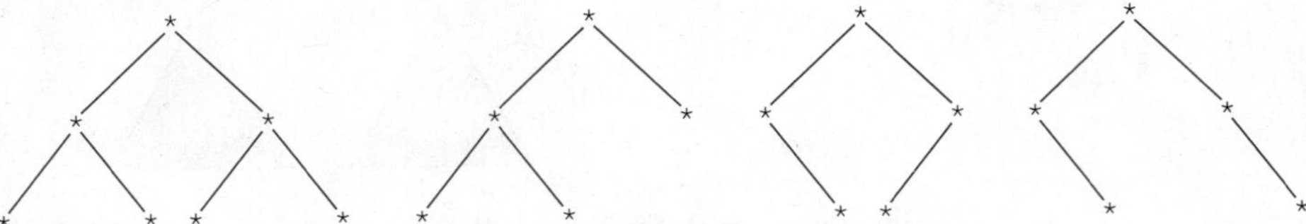

Using the recursive definition of a tree, we can define the concept of parent/child relationships in the tree:

Parent/Child/Sibling/Ancestor/Descendant

For every node p that has a nonempty subtree with root node q, we say that p is the parent of q and q is the child of p, which leads logically to ancestor relationships (parent of parent of . . .), descendant relationships (child of child of . . .), and sibling relationships (two nodes with the same parent).

Let us return to our original tree:

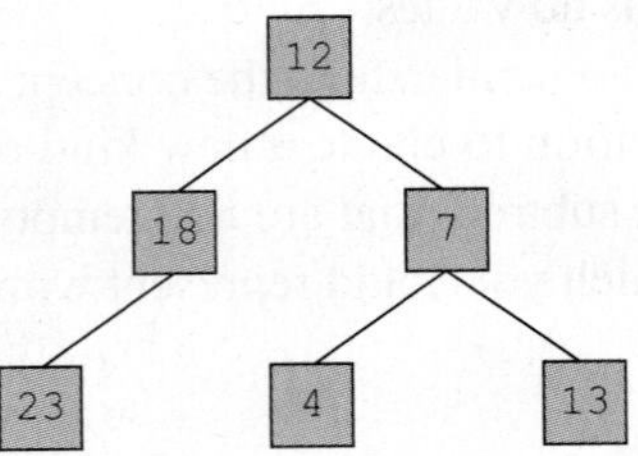

Let's start at the overall root node, which stores the value `12`. It has two nonempty subtrees. The left subtree stores the value `18` at its root and the right subtree stores the value `7` at its root. The nodes storing `18` and `7` are children of the node storing `12` and they are siblings of each other. Similarly, the node storing `23` is a child of the node storing `18`, and the nodes storing `4` and `13` are children of the node storing `7`, which makes them descendants of the overall root. The overall root is the ancestor of each of the other nodes.

Using this parent/child terminology, we can more precisely define our notion of the overall root of the tree.

Root of a Tree (Overall Root)

The node at the top of a binary tree, the only node in the tree that has no parent.

Another important aspect of binary trees is the distribution of nodes into different levels of the tree. Our sample tree has three different levels: the overall root, the children of the overall root, and the grandchildren of the overall root. This notion of levels leads us to the concept of the *depth* of an individual node (how many levels away from the root it is) and the overall *height* of the tree (how many levels it has).

Node and Tree Classes

When we studied linked lists, we found that each was built from a fairly simple building block that looks like this:

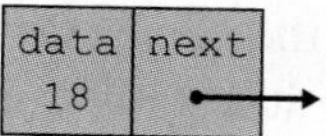

Our basic building block for a binary tree will be similar, but instead of one link, it will have two:

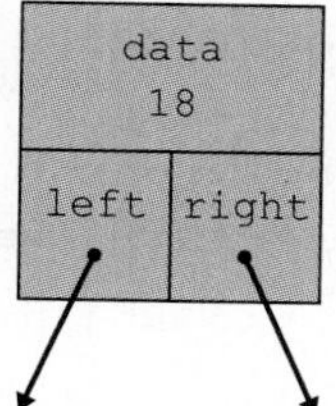

As we did with linked lists, we will first study how to manipulate a binary tree of simple `int` values. Here is a class definition for our binary tree nodes.

```
// Class for storing a single node of a binary tree of ints

public class IntTreeNode {
    public int data;
    public IntTreeNode left;
    public IntTreeNode right;

    // constructs a leaf node with given data
    public IntTreeNode(int data) {
        this(data, null, null);
    }

    // constructs a branch node with given data, left subtree,
    // right subtree
    public IntTreeNode(int data, IntTreeNode left,
                       IntTreeNode right) {
        this.data = data;
        this.left = left;
        this.right = right;
    }
}
```

Like our linked list node, this node is very simple; it has some public fields and a few constructors. The node has a field of type `int` for storing the data contained in this node and two links of type `IntTreeNode` for the left and right subtrees. The first constructor constructs a leaf node (using `null` for left and right). The second constructor is appropriate for a branch node where you want to specify the left and right subtrees.

The node class is not well encapsulated, but as we saw with linked lists, this is common practice in Java programming. In this chapter, we'll define a tree class that is well encapsulated and we will make sure that a client of the tree class never sees these nodes. In the final example of the chapter we will completely hide this node class by making it a static inner class, as we did with the final version of the linked list class.

Just as we could reach every node of a linked list by starting at the front and moving forward, we can reach every node of a binary tree by starting at the overall root and moving down in the tree. As a result, we need only one field in the tree class: a reference to the root of the tree:

```
public class IntTree {
    private IntTreeNode overallRoot;
    ...
}
```

We purposely use the name `overallRoot` to distinguish this root from all of the other roots. There is only one overall root. But each subtree is itself the root of a tree, and in our recursive methods we'll often use the parameter name `root` to indicate any of the roots.

As we did with our linked lists, we'll represent the empty tree by storing the value `null` in the `overallRoot` field:

17.2 Tree Traversals

We can't do much with our tree class unless we have some way of seeing what's inside. We want to traverse the tree in such a way that we visit each node exactly once. There are many different ways to do this. Because the tree is defined recursively, it is easiest to use a recursive approach to this problem. As a result, we want to traverse the entire left subtree without dealing with any of the elements from the right and, in a separate operation, traverse the entire right subtree without dealing with any of the elements from the left. Given this decision, there are three classic binary tree traversals. Because we read from left to right, we traverse the left subtree before the right subtree. The question becomes, at what point do you deal with the root of the tree?

There are three possible answers you might give. You can process the root before you traverse either subtree, after you traverse both subtrees, or in between traversing the two subtrees. These three approaches are known as *preorder, postorder,* and *inorder* traversals respectively.

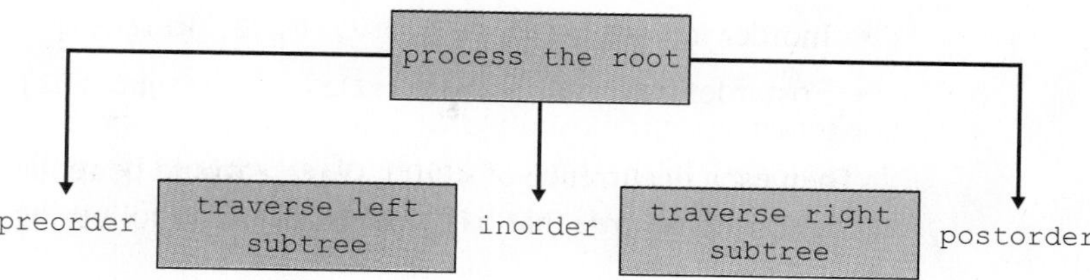

For example, consider the following simple tree:

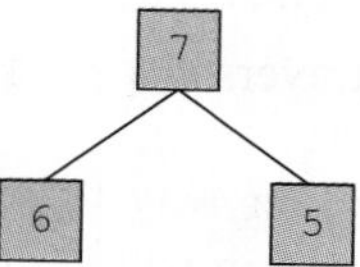

A preorder traversal visits the root, then the left subtree, then the right subtree, yielding the sequence `[7, 6, 5]`. An inorder traversal visits the left subtree, then the root, then the right subtree, yielding the sequence `[6, 7, 5]`. A postorder traversal visits the left subtree, then the right subtree, then the root, which yields `[6, 5, 7]`. Notice in this example that we always list `6` before `5` (left before right) and that the only value which changes position is the root value `7`.

When we traverse a more complex tree, we simply use the recursive nature of this definition to carry out the traversal. For example, consider the following tree.

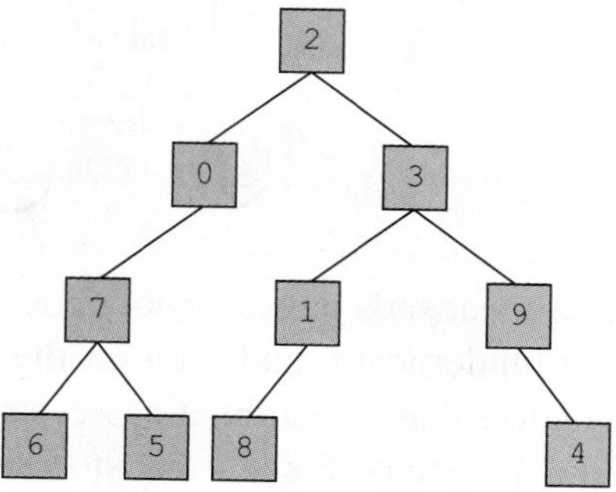

The overall root stores the value `2`, so we know that the different traversals will look like this:

- Preorder traversal: `[2, <left>, <right>]`
- Inorder traversal: `[<left>, 2, <right>]`
- Postorder traversal: `[<left>, <right>, 2]`

The left subtree of this tree stores the value `0` and has an empty right subtree. We know that each of the occurrences of `<left>` is going to be replaced by an appropriate traversal:

- Preorder traversal: `[2, 0, <left-left>, <right>]`
- Inorder traversal: `[<left-left>, 0, 2, <right>]`
- Postorder traversal: `[<left-left>, 0, <right>, 2]`

Then each occurrence of `<left-left>` would be replaced with an appropriate traversal for the subtree that has `7` as its root. The following are the complete traversal results:

- Preorder traversal: `[2, 0, 7, 6, 5, 3, 1, 8, 9, 4]`
- Inorder traversal: `[6, 7, 5, 0, 2, 8, 1, 3, 9, 4]`
- Postorder traversal: `[6, 5, 7, 0, 8, 1, 4, 9, 3, 2]`

There is another way to find the three different traversals. Imagine that each node in the tree is an island and that each link is a solid wall. Then imagine a sailboat sailing in from the upper left part of the tree and sailing around the tree, always hugging the coastline, and continuing around until it sails past the root on the right-hand side:

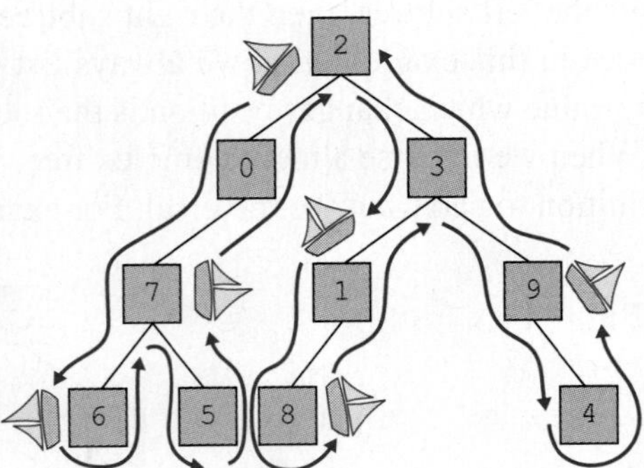

The sailboat sails past the root node three different times. It passes it first on the left, then underneath, and then on the right. If you think about it the right way, you'll realize that the sailboat passes each of the nodes three times. Even for a leaf node like the one on the left that stores `6`, it has to pass on the left, underneath, and on the right. It does them all in a row for a leaf node, but it still passes by in all three directions.

If you print the values as the sailboat passes them on the left, you get a preorder traversal. If you print the values as the sailboat passes underneath, you get an inorder traversal. And if you print the values as the sailboat passes them on the right, you get a postorder traversal. This technique is useful for double-checking your understanding of the different traversals.

Let's now see how we can write public methods for the `IntTree` class that will perform these traversals. Let's begin by writing a public method that will print the preorder traversal of a tree. Your public method will look like this:

```
public void printPreorder() {
    ...
}
```

At this point we run into a problem that we discussed in Chapter 12. Often when you write a recursive solution, you have to introduce a second method that we call a helper method. When you do so, it is best to write the second method as a private method. For these binary tree methods, it will almost always be the case that you actually have to write a pair of methods to solve any of these problems.

The issue is that the client makes a request to print the entire tree. But to solve this problem recursively, you need a method that works on every subtree, not just the overall tree. In other words, you need a method that takes an `IntTreeNode` as a parameter so that the recursive method will match the recursive structure of the tree. That way each recursive call will be able to pass on smaller and smaller subtrees, which allows you to get closer to reaching a base case. As a result, you will see a common pattern in binary tree code that looks like this:

```
public void doSomething(<parameters>) {
    doSomething(overallRoot, <parameters>);
}

private void doSomething(IntTreeNode root, <parameters>) {
    ...
}
```

Binary tree code won't always follow this pattern exactly because there might be other actions to perform in the public method, the return type might not be `void`, or there might be other parameters. But this general pattern will be there even with all of these variations.

To solve the problem of printing in preorder, you need a private method that has an `IntTreeNode` parameter:

```
private void printPreorder(IntTreeNode root) {
    ...
}
```

You start the recursive process by passing it the overall root. You can also include code to print text at the beginning and end of the line of output that you want to produce:

```
public void printPreorder() {
    System.out.print("preorder:");
```

```
    printPreorder(overallRoot);
    System.out.println();
}
```

How do you write the private method? It's good to go back to the basic definition of a binary tree. Remember that it is either an empty tree or a root node with left and right subtrees. If it's an empty tree, then there isn't anything to print. That means you could begin your private method this way:

```
private void printPreorder(IntTreeNode root) {
    if (root == null) {
        // do nothing
    }
    ...
}
```

But since this case leaves the method with nothing to do, it's better to test the negation of this statement:

```
private void printPreorder(IntTreeNode root) {
    if (root != null) {
        ...
    }
}
```

And what do you do if `root` is not `null`? In that case, you have a root node with some data in it and you have left and right subtrees that need to be printed. In a preorder traversal you handle the root node first, which means you'd print out the data for the root. You can include a space to separate it from other values on the line of output:

```
private void printPreorder(IntTreeNode root) {
    if (root != null) {
        System.out.print(" " + root.data);
        ...
    }
}
```

What do you do after you print the data for this node? You want to print the left subtree in a preorder manner and then print the right subtree in a preorder manner:

```
private void printPreorder(IntTreeNode root) {
    if (root != null) {
        System.out.print(" " + root.data);
        // then print left subtree in a preorder manner
```

```
            // then print right subtree in a preorder manner
        }
}
```

This is a time to make the leap of faith that is so essential in writing recursive methods. Thinking recursively, you'll think, "If only I had a method to print a subtree in a preorder manner . . . but I do have such a method . . . the one I'm writing." Therefore, this method becomes:

```
private void printPreorder(IntTreeNode root) {
    if (root != null) {
        System.out.print(" " + root.data);
        printPreorder(root.left);
        printPreorder(root.right);
    }
}
```

That modification completes the method. It may seem odd that it takes so little code to perform this task, but as we saw in Chapter 12, recursive code often ends up being very short.

Now let's consider how to modify the code to print the tree in an inorder manner. The new code will have a similar public/private pair of methods:

```
public void printInorder() {
    System.out.print("inorder:");
    printInorder(overallRoot);
    System.out.println();
}

private void printInorder(IntTreeNode root) {
    ...
}
```

The code will also have a similar test for an empty tree. But how do you change the body of the private printing method to make it print using an inorder traversal rather than a preorder traversal? You put the `print` in between the two recursive calls:

```
private void printInorder(IntTreeNode root) {
    if (root != null) {
        printInorder(root.left);
        System.out.print(" " + root.data);
        printInorder(root.right);
    }
}
```

This simple rearrangement of the three calls causes the code to print in an inorder manner rather than a preorder manner.

You can create another set of methods for printing in postorder by again rearranging the three operations so that the two recursive calls are made before the `print`.

It is important to understand why this seemingly small change of moving the `print` statement relative to the recursive calls generates such different behavior. It's because each recursive call potentially processes a large amount of data (an entire subtree). You'll find that this is a common property of binary tree code. A minor change to the code can produce very different results.

Constructing and Viewing a Tree

It's difficult to know whether our traversal methods work unless we can construct a tree and examine its structure. Most often we develop binary tree code with a specific application in mind. We're trying to keep things simple initially, so for now, let's construct a very specific tree that will allow us to test our code.

Using recursion, we can fairly easily construct a tree that has nodes numbered in a sequential manner level by level, as in this tree of nine nodes:

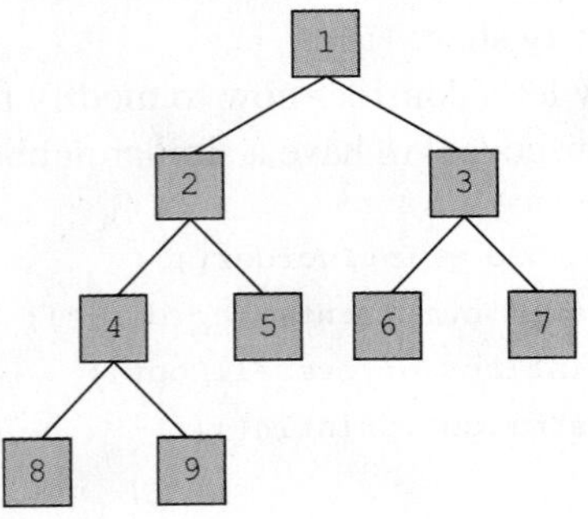

Notice how the number 1 is on the first level, then 2 and 3 on the next level, then 4, 5, 6, and 7, and so on. In this structure, we will fill in every possible node up to some maximum node number. Let's refer to this as a *sequential tree* to simplify our discussion.

Assume that the constructor for the class will be passed the maximum node number to include in the tree:

```
public IntTree(int max) {
    ...
}
```

This is another case in which you need to introduce a private method to do most of the work for you. In our previous pattern, we wrote methods that take a parameter of type `IntTreeNode` and our initial call passed the value of the field `overallRoot` to start the ball rolling. In this case, there is no tree to traverse. The whole point of the method is to construct the tree. Instead of passing `overallRoot` as a parameter, we want to use the method to give a value to overallRoot. And instead of passing a parameter of type IntTreeNode, we want the method to return a value of type IntTreeNode (a reference to the tree it has built). Thus, the pair of methods will look something like this:

```
public IntTree(int max) {
    overallRoot = buildTree();
}

private IntTreeNode buildTree() {
    ...
}
```

This is a good first approximation, but it isn't right. As you learn to write code for binary trees, you will discover that one of the most difficult tasks is figuring out the appropriate parameters to pass. As you practice more, you will see various patterns emerge.

One obvious parameter to include here is the value max that is passed to the public method. How can the private method do its job properly if it doesn't know when to stop? You can modify your pair to include that parameter:

```
public IntTree(int max) {
    overallRoot = buildTree(max);
}

private IntTreeNode buildTree(int max) {
    ...
}
```

This still isn't enough information for the private method to do its job. Think of it this way: The private method has to construct each of the different subtrees that are involved. One call on the method will construct the overall tree. Another will construct the left subtree of the overall root. Another will construct the right subtree of the overall root. How is the method supposed to know which of these tasks to solve?

We must include an extra parameter telling the method the node number to use for the root of the tree that it is constructing. When the method is passed the value 1, it will construct the overall root. When it is passed the value 2, it will construct the left subtree of the overall root, and so on. Including this second parameter, we end up with the following code:

```
public IntTree(int max) {
    overallRoot = buildTree(1, max);
}

// returns a sequential tree with n as its root unless n is
// greater than max, in which case it returns an empty tree
private IntTreeNode buildTree(int n, int max) {
    ...
}
```

Notice that in the public method you need to pass the value `1` to indicate that the first call should be generating a tree with `1` as its root value. And as the comments indicate, you only want to construct the tree if the value of `n` is less than or equal to the value of `max`.

The requirement that you want to stop building the tree for values of `n` that are greater than `max` gives you an appropriate base case for the private method:

```
private IntTreeNode buildTree(int n, int max) {
    if (n > max) {
        return null;
    } else {
        ...
    }
}
```

Now you just have to fill in the recursive case. You know that you need to construct a node that stores the value `n`. The less obvious part is how to construct the left and right subtrees. For the moment, you can introduce some local variables for the two subtrees; later, you will fill in the details about how to construct them. The method so far looks like this:

```
private IntTreeNode buildTree(int n, int max) {
    if (n > max) {
        return null;
    } else {
        IntTreeNode left = ...
        IntTreeNode right = ...
        return new IntTreeNode(n, left, right);
    }
}
```

We suggested building this particular tree because there is a simple mathematical relationship between each node in this tree and its children. If a node is numbered n, then its left child is numbered $2n$ and its right child is numbered $2n + 1$. For example, the overall root is numbered `1` and its children are numbered `2` and `3`. The left subtree is numbered `2` and its children are numbered `4` and `5`, and so on.

Getting back to our code, now that we know what value to store in each of the two children, we can use recursive calls to construct the left and right subtrees:

```
private IntTreeNode buildTree(int n, int max) {
    if (n > max) {
        return null;
    } else {
```

```
            IntTreeNode left = buildTree(2 * n, max);
            IntTreeNode right = buildTree(2 * n + 1, max);
            return new IntTreeNode(n, left, right);
        }
    }
```

The preceding code works and is very clear in terms of the steps performed. In the recursive case (the `else` branch), you can see that you construct a left subtree, then construct a right subtree, and finally put these pieces together into a new `IntTreeNode` that is returned by the method. Although this code is clear, many people prefer to write it even more concisely to eliminate the local variables. You can rewrite the method above as follows:

```
private IntTreeNode buildTree(int n, int max) {
    if (n > max) {
        return null;
    } else {
        return new IntTreeNode(n, buildTree(2 * n, max),
                                  buildTree(2 * n + 1, max));
    }
}
```

Even though this tree ends up having a very predictable structure, it is helpful to develop a method that shows the structure more clearly. Some programming environments like jGRASP have "structure viewers" that allow you to see a visual representation of a binary tree. If you don't have access to such a program, you might want to take a simplified approach to viewing the structure of the tree.

You can accomplish this by writing a simple variation of your inorder traversal. Instead of printing values all on a line, you will print them one per line and use indentation to indicate the level of the tree. For example, consider the following simple tree:

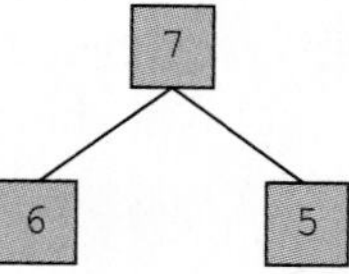

You'd want your program to produce output like this:

```
    5
7
    6
```

To read this output, you have to imagine rotating the page 90 degrees in a clockwise fashion or tilting your head slightly to the left. The output is a little easier to see if we throw in some lines:

The lines are a little tricky to produce, so let's settle for producing the simple output and you'll have to mentally add the lines. For example, you might get output like the following for a tree with four levels:

```
            15
        7
            14
    3
            13
        6
            12
1
            11
        5
            10
    2
            9
        4
            8
```

Again, imagine rotating this output 90 degrees (or rotating the page on which it is printed). The result looks like this:

```
                    1

          2                   3

     4         5         6         7

  8    9   10   11   12   13   14   15
```

If you add lines to this diagram, you'll see the tree:

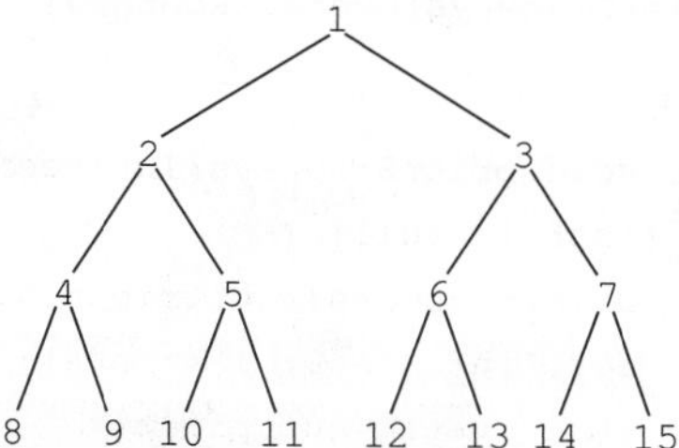

The output has the root node between its two subtrees, so this traversal is a variation of the inorder traversal. Oddly enough, you want to print the right subtree before the left subtree. For example, consider the following tree:

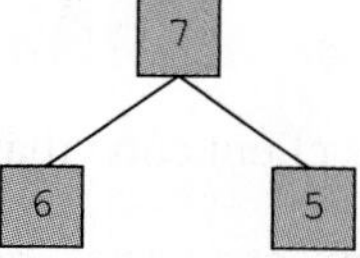

Your method would produce the following output:

```
    5
7
    6
```

Notice that the right subtree value of `5` is printed first, then the root, then the left subtree value of `6`. This happens because you are rotating the image.

You can fairly easily modify your inorder traversal code to produce this new set of methods:

```
public void printSideways() {
    printSideways(overallRoot);
}

private void printSideways(IntTreeNode root) {
    if (root != null) {
        printSideways(root.right);
        System.out.println(root.data);
        printSideways(root.left);
    }
}
```

But this version of the code does not indent the various levels of the tree. To obtain the proper indentation, you need to introduce an extra parameter to let the private method know the level at which each node appears. The initial call on the private method should pass the value `0` because the overall root should be indented `0` spaces. Each recursive call should pass an indentation level that is one higher for its children. The following code produces the indentation of the tree:

```
public void printSideways() {
    printSideways(overallRoot, 0);
}

private void printSideways(IntTreeNode root, int level) {
    if (root != null) {
        printSideways(root.right, level + 1);
        for (int i = 0; i < level; i++) {
            System.out.print("    ");
        }
        System.out.println(root.data);
        printSideways(root.left, level + 1);
    }
}
```

Here is some client code that calls the various methods we have developed:

```
// Short program that demonstrates the use of the IntTree class.

public class IntTreeClient {
    public static void main(String[] args) {
        IntTree t = new IntTree(12);
        System.out.println("Tree structure:");
        t.printSideways();
        System.out.println();
        t.printPreorder();
        t.printInorder();
        t.printPostorder();
    }
}
```

This method produces the following output:

```
Tree structure:
        7
    3
        6
            12
1
            11
        5
            10
    2
            9
        4
            8

preorder: 1 2 4 8 9 5 10 11 3 6 12 7
inorder: 8 4 9 2 10 5 11 1 12 6 3 7
postorder: 8 9 4 10 11 5 2 12 6 7 3 1
```

Here is the complete `IntTree` class:

```
// Simple binary tree class that includes methods to construct a
// tree of ints, to print the structure, and to print the data
// using a preorder, inorder, or postorder traversal. The trees
// built have nodes numbered starting with 1 and numbered
// sequentially level by level with no gaps in the tree. The
// documentation refers to these as "sequential trees."

public class IntTree {
    private IntTreeNode overallRoot;

    // pre : max >= 0 (throws IllegalArgumentException if not)
    // post: constructs a sequential tree with given number of
    //       nodes
    public IntTree(int max) {
        if (max < 0) {
            throw new IllegalArgumentException("max: " + max);
        }
        overallRoot = buildTree(1, max);
    }

    // post: returns a sequential tree with n as its root unless
    //       n is greater than max, in which case it returns an
    //       empty tree
    private IntTreeNode buildTree(int n, int max) {
        if (n > max) {
            return null;
        } else {
            return new IntTreeNode(n, buildTree(2 * n, max),
                                   buildTree(2 * n + 1, max));
        }
    }

    // post: prints the tree contents using a preorder traversal
    public void printPreorder() {
        System.out.print("preorder:");
        printPreorder(overallRoot);
        System.out.println();
    }

```

```
    // post: prints in preorder the tree with given root
    private void printPreorder(IntTreeNode root) {
        if (root != null) {
            System.out.print(" " + root.data);
            printPreorder(root.left);
            printPreorder(root.right);
        }
    }

    // post: prints the tree contents using an inorder traversal
    public void printInorder() {
        System.out.print("inorder:");
        printInorder(overallRoot);
        System.out.println();
    }

    // post: prints in inorder the tree with given root
    private void printInorder(IntTreeNode root) {
        if (root != null) {
            printInorder(root.left);
            System.out.print(" " + root.data);
            printInorder(root.right);
        }
    }

    // post: prints the tree contents using a postorder traversal
    public void printPostorder() {
        System.out.print("postorder:");
        printPostorder(overallRoot);
        System.out.println();
    }

    // post: prints in postorder the tree with given root
    private void printPostorder(IntTreeNode root) {
        if (root != null) {
            printPostorder(root.left);
            printPostorder(root.right);
            System.out.print(" " + root.data);
        }
    }

    // post: prints the tree contents, one per line, following an
    //       inorder traversal and using indentation to indicate
```

```
    //        node depth; prints right to left so that it looks
    //        correct when the output is rotated.
    public void printSideways() {
        printSideways(overallRoot, 0);
    }

    // post: prints in reversed preorder the tree with given
    //        root, indenting each line to the given level
    private void printSideways(IntTreeNode root, int level) {
        if (root != null) {
            printSideways(root.right, level + 1);
            for (int i = 0; i < level; i++) {
                System.out.print("    ");
            }
            System.out.println(root.data);
            printSideways(root.left, level + 1);
        }
    }
}
```

17.3 Common Tree Operations

VideoNote

This section discusses several common binary tree operations. All of these operations are built on top of a standard tree traversal and involve reasoning recursively about the subtrees.

Sum of a Tree

First let's write a method to find the sum of the values stored in a binary tree of `ints`. The method header will look like this:

```
public int sum() {
    ...
}
```

As usual, you will need to introduce a private method that allows you to pass a node as a parameter so that you can specify which subtree of the overall tree to work with. The public method should call the private method, pass it the overall root, and return the result:

```
public int sum() {
    return sum(overallRoot);
}
```

```
private int sum(IntTreeNode root) {
    ...
}
```

The recursive definition tells us that a tree is either empty or a root node with left and right subtrees. This definition provides an excellent basis for recursive code. You know that the empty tree has a sum of 0, so you can begin with that case:

```
private int sum(IntTreeNode root) {
    if (root == null) {
        return 0;
    } else {
        ...
    }
}
```

If the tree is not empty, then it is a root node that has left and right subtrees. To find the sum of the values, you have to combine all three parts: the data stored in the root node and the sums of the left and right subtrees. This task translates very easily into recursive code:

```
private int sum(IntTreeNode root) {
    if (root == null) {
        return 0;
    } else {
        return root.data + sum(root.left) + sum(root.right);
    }
}
```

Counting Levels

VideoNote

As a second example, let's write a method called `countLevels` that returns the number of levels in a tree. For our purposes, we consider the root node to be at level `1`, its children to be at level `2`, its grandchildren to be at level `3`, and so on. The `countLevels` method should return the level of the node that is furthest from the root.

You can again solve this task by writing a public/private pair of methods. The public method returns the result of invoking the private method with the overall root:

```
public int countLevels() {
    return countLevels(overallRoot);
}
```

```
private int countLevels(IntTreeNode root) {
    ...
}
```

You can again use the definition that a tree is either empty or a root node with left and right subtrees. If it is empty, then it has no levels at all (0 levels):

```
private int countLevels(IntTreeNode root) {
    if (root == null) {
        return 0;
    } else {
        ...
    }
}
```

If the tree is not empty, then it is a root node with left and right subtrees. In this case, the data stored in the tree don't matter. We are asking a question about the structure of the tree. To solve this problem, you should think about what a recursive call on the subtrees would return. It would tell you the number of levels in the left subtree and the number of levels in the right subtree. Those answers might match (they might have the same number of levels), but often you'll find that one subtree has more levels than the other. In that case, what matters more is the subtree that has more levels, because that determines the number of levels in the overall tree. Here's a first attempt at writing the method:

```
private int countLevels(IntTreeNode root) {
    if (root == null) {
        return 0;
    } else {
        return Math.max(countLevels(root.left), countLevels(root.right));
    }
}
```

Let's think about a specific case. Consider the following tree:

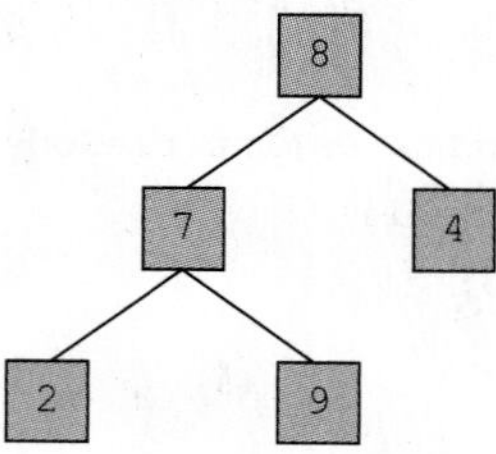

If the method has been called with the overall root of the tree as a parameter, then you expect the recursive calls to return `2` as the number of levels for the left subtree and `1` as the number of levels for the right subtree. The call on `Math.max` will correctly choose the `2` over the `1` for the overall answer, but the overall tree doesn't have two levels. It has three levels. You have to account for the root node, which is an extra level, by adding `1` to the previous expression:

```
private int countLevels(IntTreeNode root) {
    if (root == null) {
        return 0;
    } else {
        return 1 + Math.max(countLevels(root.left), countLevels(root.right));
    }
}
```

Without the "`1 +`" in this expression, the method would always return an answer of `0`. This is another example of a case in which a minor change in a recursive definition makes a big difference in how the method behaves.

The *height* of a binary tree is 1 less than its number of levels. When we count levels, we say that the empty tree has `0` levels and a tree composed of a single node has `1` level. According to the standard definition of binary tree height, a tree of one node is considered to have a height of `0` and the empty tree is considered either to have no height (undefined height) or a height of `–1`.

Counting Leaves

As a final example, let's write a method that returns a count of the number of leaf nodes in a tree. It will have the familiar public/private pair of methods that includes an initial call with the overall root. You can once again use the recursive definition of a tree to help you write this code. If a tree is empty, then it has no nodes at all, let alone any leaf nodes. Thus, you can begin your method with the following lines of code:

```
public int countLeaves() {
    return countLeaves(overallRoot);
}

private int countLeaves(IntTreeNode root) {
    if (root == null) {
        return 0;
    } else {
        ...
    }
}
```

The `else` case involves a root node with left and right subtrees. How many leaf nodes are in such a tree? Think about what recursive calls on the left and right subtrees will return. They will tell you how many leaves are in the subtrees. Each of those leaves is a leaf of the overall tree, so you might think that the answer is as simple as returning the sum of the subtree leaves:

```
private int countLeaves(IntTreeNode root) {
    if (root == null) {
        return 0;
    } else {
        return countLeaves(root.left) + countLeaves(root.right);
    }
}
```

If you were to test this version of the code, you'd find that it always returns `0` as the number of leaves in a tree. That's because you forgot one important case. When you have a root node that has left and right subtrees, the number of leaves in that tree is generally the sum of the number of leaves in the two subtrees, except in one important case. What if the subtrees are both empty? That would mean that the node you are looking at is itself a leaf node. That particular tree has exactly one leaf node (the root). You have to introduce a special case that handles that particular situation:

```
private int countLeaves(IntTreeNode root) {
    if (root == null) {
        return 0;
    } else if (root.left == null && root.right == null) {
        return 1;
    } else {
        return countLeaves(root.left) + countLeaves(root.right);
    }
}
```

It may seem odd, but that simple change makes this code work. Each leaf node returns an answer of `1`, and those answers are added together by the other calls to produce a count of the various leaf nodes in the tree.

17.4 Binary Search Trees

In this section, we will study a particularly useful kind of binary tree known as a *binary search tree*. Recall from Chapter 13 that we can efficiently search through a sorted array using the binary search algorithm. That algorithm is highly efficient because on each iteration it divides a range of sorted values in half, which allows you to eliminate half of the possibilities.

A binary search tree is a structural parallel to the binary search algorithm. At each level of the tree we divide the data in half, storing approximately half the values in the left subtree and approximately half the values in the right subtree. The result is a highly efficient structure for storing a sorted sequence of values that can be quickly searched for particular values. As we noted in the introduction, both the `TreeMap` and `TreeSet` classes in the Java Collections Framework are binary search trees. In this section we will explore how to add values to a binary search tree and how to search the tree. We will then explore some of the complexity issues related to binary search trees. We'll see that binary search trees can be very efficient, although they also can lose their efficiency if they become unbalanced. If you continue to study computer science, you will learn various techniques which guarantee that the tree stays balanced.

The Binary Search Tree Property

The values in a binary search tree are guaranteed to be arranged in such a way that the values in the left subtree are all less than the root data and the values in the right subtree are all greater than the root data. Sometimes we want to allow duplicates, in which case we have to adopt a convention about which subtree they appear in. It doesn't matter what convention we adopt, as long as we are consistent. For example, we can decide that if duplicates are allowed, then they should appear in the left subtree, which would lead to the following property:

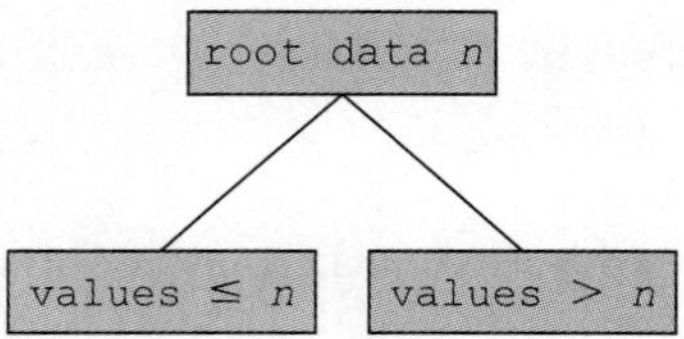

This property of nodes is known as the *binary search tree property*.

Binary Search Tree Property

Property of a node which stores data *n* if all values stored in the left subtree are less than *n* and all values in the right subtree are greater than *n*. If duplicates are allowed, then all values in the left subtree must be less than or equal to *n*.

For a tree to qualify as a binary search tree, each node of the tree must have this property. This is not just a property of the overall root.

Binary Search Tree

A binary tree in which every node has the binary search tree property.

Here is a binary search tree of names:

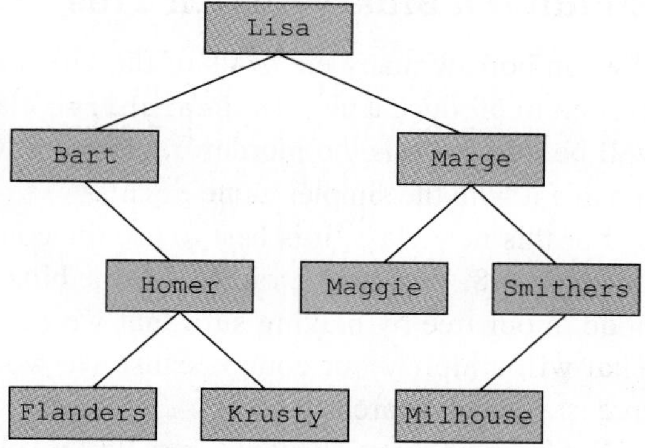

The names appear in the tree using alphabetical ordering (also known as *lexicographic ordering*). For example, the overall root stores `"Lisa"`, which means that all of the names in the left subtree are alphabetically less than or equal to `"Lisa"` and all names in the right subtree are alphabetically greater than `"Lisa"`.

Consider the result you obtain when you perform an inorder traversal of the tree:

```
Bart, Flanders, Homer, Krusty, Lisa, Maggie, Marge, Milhouse, Smithers
```

This list of names is in alphabetical order. This result isn't terribly surprising when you think about the binary search tree property. In a binary search tree, you know that values which are alphabetically less than or equal to the root appear in the left subtree and that values which are alphabetically greater appear in the right subtree. For any given subtree, an inorder traversal traverses the left subtree first, then the root, then the right subtree, which means you visit the nodes in this order:

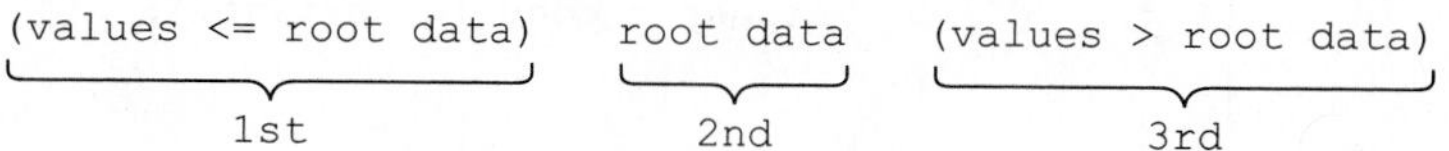

Therefore, the root value is printed at just the right point in time (after the values that are alphabetically less than or equal to it and before the values that are alphabetically greater than it). And because every node in the tree has the binary search tree property, you know that the value stored in each node is printed in the correct position relative to the values that appear below it in the tree. The overall result is that each data value is printed at just the right point in time relative to the rest of the data.

This observation highlights one of the useful properties of a binary search tree. Once it is constructed, we can traverse the values in sorted order by performing an inorder traversal of the tree.

Building a Binary Search Tree

We can borrow many elements of the `IntTree` class that we wrote in the previous section to produce a new `IntSearchTree` class. The primary traversal in which we will be interested is the inorder traversal, so we can include it in our new class and rename it with the simpler name `print`.

For this new class, it is best to use the concept of a data invariant, as introduced in Chapter 8. We can guarantee that the binary search tree property is true for every node in our tree by making sure that we never violate this invariant relationship. That will simplify our code because we won't have to test to make sure that our tree is a binary search tree.

We imagine that a client program will involve code like the following:

```
// This program tests the IntSearchTree class by constructing a
// binary search tree of integers and printing its contents as
// well as its structure.

import java.util.*;

public class IntSearchTreeClient {
    public static void main(String[] args) {
        Scanner console = new Scanner(System.in);
        IntSearchTree numbers = new IntSearchTree();
        System.out.print("Next int (0 to quit)? ");
        int number = console.nextInt();
        while (number != 0) {
            numbers.add(number);
            System.out.print("Next int (0 to quit)? ");
            number = console.nextInt();
        }
        System.out.println();

        System.out.println("Tree Structure:");
        numbers.printSideways();
        System.out.println("Sorted list:");
        numbers.print();
    }
}
```

This program prompts for a series of integers that are added one at a time into the tree until the user enters the sentinel value `0`. The program then prints the structure of the tree and the contents of the tree. The following is a sample execution. Notice that the numbers are printed in increasing order:

```
Next int (0 to quit)? 42
Next int (0 to quit)? 9
Next int (0 to quit)? 18
Next int (0 to quit)? 55
Next int (0 to quit)? 7
Next int (0 to quit)? 108
Next int (0 to quit)? 4
Next int (0 to quit)? 70
Next int (0 to quit)? 203
Next int (0 to quit)? 15
Next int (0 to quit)? 0

Tree Structure:
                203
            108
                70
        55
    42
            18
                15
        9
            7
                4

Sorted list:
4 7 9 15 18 42 55 70 108 203
```

To begin with, you will need a constructor that constructs an empty tree. Remember that the empty tree is represented by the value `null`. In fact you could simply not have a constructor and Java would provide you with a zero-argument constructor that initializes the field `overallRoot` to `null`. But it's not a bad idea to include the constructor anyway for clarity:

```
public IntSearchTree() {
    overallRoot = null;
}
```

Then you have to write the `add` method. Because of our data invariant, you can assume that, each time the method is called, the existing tree is a binary search tree. You have to make sure that you add the value in an appropriate place so as to preserve the binary search tree property.

The `add` method will have the usual structure of a public method that the client calls with no mention of tree nodes and a private recursive method that takes a node as a parameter and that does the actual work. Thus, your pair of methods will look like this:

```
public void add(int value) {
    add(overallRoot, value);
}

private void add(IntTreeNode root, int value) {
    ...
}
```

Recall that a binary tree is either empty or a root node with left and right subtrees. If it is empty, then you want to insert the value here. For example, initially the overall tree is empty and you insert the first value at the top of the tree (replacing the `null` value with a reference to a new leaf node that contains the given value). So the private `add` method would start like this:

```
private void add(IntTreeNode root, int value) {
    if (root == null) {
        root = new IntTreeNode(value);
    }
    ...
}
```

But what if it's not an empty tree? Then it must have a root node with some data. Let's assume that duplicates are allowed, so that you want to insert this value no matter what. In the case in which `root` is not `null`, you know that the new value has to be added to one of the subtrees. Which one? You can compare the value you are inserting to the data in the root to figure that out. If the value is less than or equal to the root's data, then you insert the value into the left subtree; otherwise, you insert into the right subtree. Your method will look something like this:

```
private void add(IntTreeNode root, int value) {
    if (root == null) {
        root = new IntTreeNode(value);
    } else if (value <= root.data) {
        // add to left
    } else {
        // add to right
    }
}
```

This is the general structure that you want, but exactly how do you add to the left or right subtree? Some novices try to test things about the left or right subtree, as in the following example:

```
// overly complex version
private void add(IntTreeNode root, int value) {
    if (root == null) {
        root = new IntTreeNode(value);
    } else if (value <= root.data) {
        if (root.left == null) {
            root.left = new IntTreeNode(value);
        } else {
            // even more stuff
        }
    } else {
        // add to right
    }
}
```

This is not a good way to approach the problem. If you're thinking recursively, you'll realize that it's another insertion task into either the left or the right subtree. You can call the add method itself:

```
// simpler, but does not quite work
private void add(IntTreeNode root, int value) {
    if (root == null) {
        root = new IntTreeNode(value);
    } else if (value <= root.data) {
        add(root.left, value);
    } else {
        add(root.right, value);
    }
}
```

The logic of this code is almost correct. Unfortunately, in this form the tree always remains empty. The `add` method never inserts a value. The problem has to do with the parameter called `root`. The parameter `root` will store a copy of whatever value is passed into it. As a result, when you reassign `root`, it has no effect on the value that is passed into it.

There is a particular approach to solving this problem that is very helpful in writing binary tree code. Let's explore this issue and the technique in some detail before we try to fix this code.

The Pattern `x = change(x)`

Consider the following short program:

```
import java.awt.*;

public class PointTest {
    public static void main(String[] args) {
        Point p = new Point(2, 8);
        System.out.println("p = " + p);
        change(p);
        System.out.println("now p = " + p);
    }

    public static void change(Point q) {
        q.translate(3, 5);
        q = new Point(-7, -14);
        System.out.println("q = " + q);
    }
}
```

The code in `main` constructs a `Point` object and passes it as a parameter. Inside the method we translate the coordinates of the `Point` object. This change is reflected in the original `Point` object because when we pass an object as a parameter, the parameter gets a copy of the reference to the object.

But what about the final line of the method that constructs a new `Point`? Does that change the `main` method's variable `p`? The answer is no. The overall output for this version of the program is as follows:

```
p = java.awt.Point[x=2,y=8]
q = java.awt.Point[x=-7,y=-14]
now p = java.awt.Point[x=5,y=13]
```

One of the changes (translating the coordinates) has an effect, but the other (constructing a new `Point`) does not. This happens because when we pass an object as a parameter, the parameter gets a copy of the reference to the object. When we call the `change` method, the variable `q` is set up as a copy of the variable `p`:

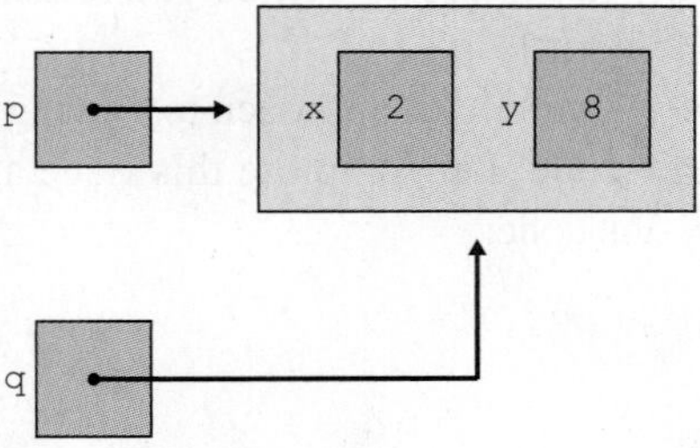

This is a situation we have seen before. There are two references to the same object. We discussed this scenario in detail in the section on reference semantics in Chapter 7. There is only one `Point` object here and we have two different ways of referring to it: using the variable `p` or using the variable `q`. That's why the method is able to change the object to which `p` refers when it executes this line of code:

```
q.translate(3, 5);
```

There are two different variables referring to the same object, so either variable is capable of changing the object:

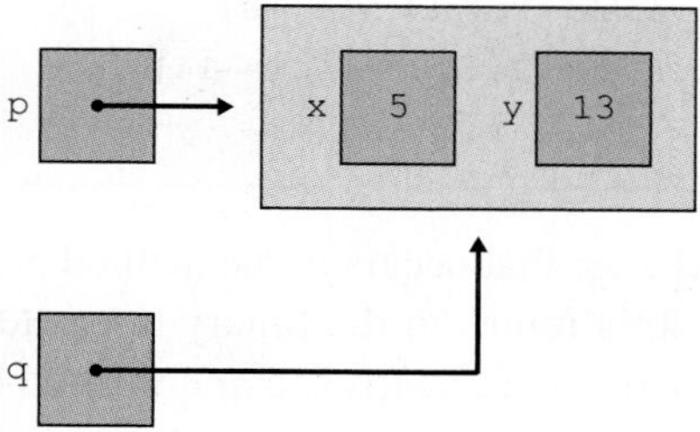

But that doesn't mean that `q` has the power to change `p` itself. It can change the object to which `p` refers (the `Point`), but it can't change the value that is stored in `p` (the reference, or pointer; or the arrow, or cell phone number). When we change `q` with the following line of code, it has no effect on `p`:

```
q = new Point(–7, –14);
```

This code gives a new value to `q`, but not to `p`, as you can see in the following diagram:

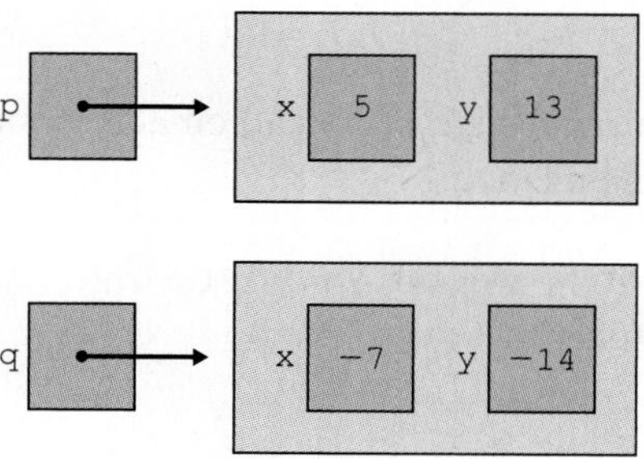

There are many ways to try to fix this, but there is a particular approach called the `x = change(x)` idiom that solves the problem rather nicely. We change the method so that it returns the value of the parameter just before it exits. This modification also requires us to change the return type for the method:

```
public static Point change(Point q) {
    q.translate(3, 5);
```

```
    q = new Point(-7, -14);
    System.out.println("q = " + q);
    return q;
}
```

Then we change the call on the method to the `x = change(x)` form:

```
p = change(p);
```

With these changes, the program produces the following output:

```
p = java.awt.Point[x=2,y=8]
q = java.awt.Point[x=-7,y=-14]
now p = java.awt.Point[x=-7,y=-14]
```

The change that occurs in the method propagates back to the `main` method.

Now let's return to the binary tree `add` method to see how we could apply this technique there. Currently the `add` method has a return type of `void`:

```
private void add(IntTreeNode root, int value) {
    ...
}
```

We can change it so that the last thing we do in the method is to return the value of `root`, which means we have to change the return type to `IntTreeNode`:

```
private IntTreeNode add(IntTreeNode root, int value) {
    ...
    return root;
}
```

Then we change every call on `add` to match the `x = change(x)` form. Recall our old public method:

```
public void add(int value) {
    add(overallRoot, value);
}
```

The code now becomes:

```
public void add(int value) {
    overallRoot = add(overallRoot, value);
}
```

The idea is that we pass the value of `overallRoot` to the `add` method and it passes back the value of the parameter, which might be the old value or might be a new value. We reassign `overallRoot` to this value passed back by `add`. That way, if the method changes the value of the parameter, `overallRoot` gets updated to that new value. If it doesn't change the value of `overallRoot`, then we are simply assigning a variable to the value that it already has (effectively saying `"x = x"`), which has no effect.

Two other calls on `add` inside the method itself need to be updated in a similar manner:

```
private IntTreeNode add(IntTreeNode root, int value) {
    if (root == null) {
        root = new IntTreeNode(value);
    } else if (value <= root.data) {
        root.left = add(root.left, value);
    } else {
        root.right = add(root.right, value);
    }
    return root;
}
```

After we make these changes, the `add` method works properly.

This `x = change(x)` idiom is very powerful and simplifies a lot of binary tree code, so it is important to learn how to use it well.

Searching the Tree

Once we have built a binary search tree, we will want to do more than just printing its contents or structure. One of the most common operations we might want to perform is to search the tree to see whether it contains a particular value.

The method to perform this search should return a `boolean` result and you will once again want to have a public/private pair of methods, so the basic form of your solution will be as follows:

```
public boolean contains(int value) {
    return contains(overallRoot, value);
}

private boolean contains(IntTreeNode root, int value) {
    ...
}
```

Now you just have to write the body of the private method. An empty tree again serves as the easy case. If you're asked whether the empty tree contains a value, the answer is no (`false`):

```
private boolean contains(IntTreeNode root, int value) {
    if (root == null) {
```

```
        return false;
    }
    ...
}
```

For the add method, you had two other cases. You either added to the left subtree or added to the right subtree. For this method, there are three cases, cases for searching the left and right subtree and the root:

```
private boolean contains(IntTreeNode root, int value) {
    if (root == null) {
        return false;
    } else if (value == root.data) {
        ...
    } else if (value < root.data) {
        ...
    } else { // value > root.data
        ...
    }
}
```

Now you just need to fill in the three different cases. If the value is less than `root.data`, then it is either in the left subtree or not in the tree at all. In other words, you want to search the left subtree to see whether it contains the value. You can accomplish this with a recursive call on `contains`. You can make a similar recursive call on `contains` to search the right subtree when the value is greater than `root.data`. In the final case in which the value is equal to `root.data`, you should simply report that you found the value. In other words, the answer is `true`. Putting these pieces together, you end up with the following code:

```
private boolean contains(IntTreeNode root, int value) {
    if (root == null) {
        return false;
    } else if (value == root.data) {
        return true;
    } else if (value < root.data) {
        return contains(root.left, value);
    } else { // value > root.data
        return contains(root.right, value);
    }
}
```

A clever reader might notice that this method violates the principle of Boolean Zen that we introduced in Chapter 5. This method can be written more concisely as a Boolean expression. For example, it can be written as a single expression as follows:

```
private boolean contains(IntTreeNode root, int value) {
    return root != null && (root.data == value ||
            (value < root.data && contains(root.left, value)) ||
             (value >= root.data && contains(root.left, value)));
}
```

In this case, it is debatable whether the single expression is more readable than the `if/else` version of the code. This is somewhat a matter of personal taste, so different programmers will prefer one version over the other, but our conclusion was that the longer version is actually easier to read in this case.

Here is the complete implementation of the `IntSearchTree` class:

```
// This class stores int values in a binary search tree.
// Duplicates are allowed. Each node of the tree has the binary
// search tree property.

public class IntSearchTree {
    private IntTreeNode overallRoot;

    // post: constructs an empty tree
    public IntSearchTree() {
        overallRoot = null;
    }

    // post: value is added to overall tree so as to preserve the
    //       binary search tree property
    public void add(int value) {
        overallRoot = add(overallRoot, value);
    }

    // post: value is added to given tree so as to preserve the
    //       binary search tree property
    private IntTreeNode add(IntTreeNode root, int value) {
        if (root == null) {
            root = new IntTreeNode(value);
        } else if (value <= root.data) {
            root.left = add(root.left, value);
        } else {
            root.right = add(root.right, value);
        }
```

```
        return root;
    }

    // post: returns true if overall tree contains value
    public boolean contains(int value) {
        return contains(overallRoot, value);
    }

    // post: returns true if given tree contains value
    private boolean contains(IntTreeNode root, int value) {
        if (root == null) {
            return false;
        } else if (value == root.data) {
            return true;
        } else if (value < root.data) {
            return contains(root.left, value);
        } else { // value > root.data
            return contains(root.right, value);
        }
    }


    // post: prints the tree contents using an inorder traversal
    public void print() {
        printInorder(overallRoot);
        System.out.println();
    }

    // post: prints contents of the tree with given root using an
    //       inorder traversal
    private void printInorder(IntTreeNode root) {
        if (root != null) {
            printInorder(root.left);
            System.out.print(root.data + " ");
            printInorder(root.right);
        }
    }

    // post: prints the tree contents, one per line, following an
    //       inorder traversal and using indentation to indicate
    //       node depth; prints right to left so that it looks
    //       correct when the output is rotated.
    public void printSideways() {
        printSideways(overallRoot, 0);
```

```
    }

    // post: prints in reversed preorder the tree with given
    //       root, indenting each line to the given level
    private void printSideways(IntTreeNode root, int level) {
        if (root != null) {
            printSideways(root.right, level + 1);
            for (int i = 0; i < level; i++) {
                System.out.print("    ");
            }
            System.out.println(root.data);
            printSideways(root.left, level + 1);
        }
    }
}
```

Binary Search Tree Complexity

Each level of a binary search tree can hold twice as many nodes as the level above it. The one root node can have two children, four grandchildren, eight great-grandchildren, and so on. As a result, we can store a lot of values in a tree that has a relatively small number of levels.

The number of nodes and the number of levels have an important relationship. If you have k levels in a tree, then you can store approximately 2^k values in the tree. Going in the other direction, if you want to include N nodes in a tree, you will need approximately $\log N$ levels for the tree. We normally use this second way of thinking about the relationship.

It may not seem immediately obvious how powerful this is because you may not realize how much smaller $\log N$ is than N. Consider some examples. To store a thousand values, you would need around 10 levels. Increase the number of values to a million, and you need 20 levels. Increase the number to a billion, and you need 30 levels. To store a trillion values, you need only 40 levels for the tree. As a result, binary search trees tend to be relatively short in height, even when they store vast amounts of data.

It is also important to realize that the insertion algorithm we have developed in this chapter does not guarantee that the tree will store data efficiently in the minimum number of levels. While it's true that you can store a trillion values with just 40 levels, you might end up with considerably more levels than that. Consider, for example, what happens if the data are inserted in sorted order. If you build a binary search tree by inserting the sequential numbers 1 through 1000, you end up with a tree that looks like this one:

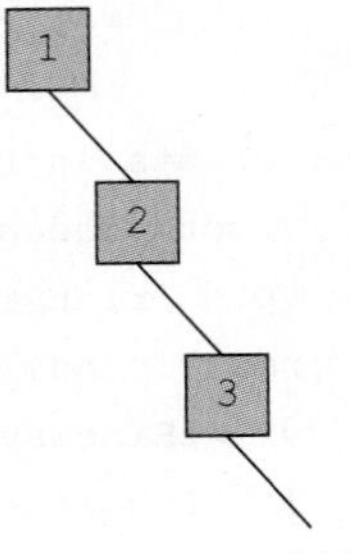

We refer to this as a *degenerate tree*. It's technically still a tree, but it's not a very good tree because it makes no use of the two branching possibilities. This is really a linked list turned on its side. You can get similar degenerate trees if the values are inserted in decreasing order, which produces a tree that expands indefinitely in the left direction.

If the values are inserted into a binary search tree in a random order, then the odds of getting a degenerate tree are fairly low. If you take a more advanced course in data structures, you will study techniques for ensuring that the tree is balanced. For example, the `TreeMap` and `TreeSet` structures in the Java class libraries are implemented as what are called red/black trees to guarantee that the resulting binary search tree is balanced.

Let's set aside the issue of degenerate trees and think about the case for randomized data or for binary search trees that guarantee balance. One important property of the binary search tree is that each insertion into the tree requires you to descend from level to level until you find an open spot to insert the value. Thus, insertion into a balanced binary search tree is an O(log N) operation. Similarly, finding a value in a balanced binary search tree involves descending from level to level, so it also is an O(log N) operation. To search for a value in a normal binary tree, you would have to search the entire tree. Although we haven't shown the solution here, we'll mention that removing a value from a balanced binary search tree can also be accomplished as an O(log N) operation.

The binary search tree, then, offers insertion, search, and removal all in O(log N) time. That means that if you are working with a trillion values, for example, you can add a new value, search for a value, or remove a value, all within around 40 steps. That makes the binary search tree a very efficient structure to use for these operations.

17.5 SearchTree<E>

In the previous section, we developed code for a binary search tree of integers. You might want to build other kinds of binary search trees with different kinds of data and you wouldn't want to make many copies of essentially the same code (one for integers, one for strings, etc.). Instead, you want to write the code in a more generic way.

We want to be able to build a search tree for any class that implements the `Comparable` interface. We want a class that we could call `SearchTree<E>` (for some element type `E`). Here is a client program which constructs a `SearchTree<String>` that puts words into alphabetical order and a `SearchTree<Integer>` that puts numbers into numerical order.

```
// This program uses the SearchTree class to construct a binary
// search tree of strings and a binary search tree of integers
// and print out each.

import java.util.*;

public class SearchTreeClient {
    public static void main(String[] args) {
        Scanner console = new Scanner(System.in);
        SearchTree<String> names = new SearchTree<String>();
        System.out.print("Name (blank to quit)? ");
        String name = console.nextLine();
        while (name.length() > 0) {
            names.add(name);
            System.out.print("Name (blank to quit)? ");
            name = console.nextLine();
        }
        System.out.println();
        System.out.println("Alphabetized list:");
        names.print();
        System.out.println();

        SearchTree<Integer> numbers = new SearchTree<Integer>();
        System.out.print("Next int (0 to quit)? ");
        int number = console.nextInt();
        while (number != 0) {
            numbers.add(number);
            System.out.print("Next int (0 to quit)? ");
            number = console.nextInt();
        }
        System.out.println();
        System.out.println("Sorted list:");
        numbers.print();
    }
}
```

Here is a sample log of execution:

```
Name (blank to quit)? Leonard
Name (blank to quit)? Sheldon
```

```
Name (blank to quit)? Howard
Name (blank to quit)? Penny
Name (blank to quit)? Raj
Name (blank to quit)? Leslie
Name (blank to quit)? Ma
Name (blank to quit)?

Alphabetized list:
Howard
Leonard
Leslie
Ma
Penny
Raj
Sheldon

Next int (0 to quit)? 38
Next int (0 to quit)? 19
Next int (0 to quit)? -47
Next int (0 to quit)? 2
Next int (0 to quit)? 42
Next int (0 to quit)? 13
Next int (0 to quit)? 9
Next int (0 to quit)? 0

Sorted list:
-47
2
9
13
19
38
42
```

To generate the `SearchTree` class, we can start with the `IntSearchTree` class and convert it into generic form.

First we need a node class for the tree. Our node class is almost the same as the `IntTreeNode` class, but instead of having data of type `int`, we have data of type `E`, and instead of saying `IntTreeNode`, we have to say `SearchTreeNode<E>` in most places other than the constructor headers:

```
public class SearchTreeNode<E> {
    public E data;                     // data stored in this node
    public SearchTreeNode<E> left;  // left subtree
    public SearchTreeNode<E> right; // right subtree
```

```java

    // post: constructs a leaf node with given data
    public SearchTreeNode(E data) {
        this(data, null, null);
    }

    // post: constructs a node with the given data and links
    public SearchTreeNode(E data, SearchTreeNode<E> left,
                          SearchTreeNode<E> right) {
        this.data = data;
        this.left = left;
        this.right = right;
    }
}
```

So what about the `SearchTree` class? You can get a pretty close approximation of the code for this class by replacing all occurrences of `int` with `E` and replacing all occurrences of `IntTreeNode` with `SearchTreeNode<E>`. But you have to make a few adjustments. First, the private `add` method looks like this after the substitution:

```java
private SearchTreeNode<E> add(SearchTreeNode<E> root, E value) {
    if (root == null) {
        root = new SearchTreeNode<E>(value);
    } else if (value <= root.data) {
        root.left = add(root.left, value);
    } else {
        root.right = add(root.right, value);
    }
    return root;
}
```

The problem here is that you have to call the `compareTo` method rather than using the <= operator. You'll replace the line of code:

```java
} else if (value <= root.data) {
```

with:

```java
} else if (value.compareTo(root.data) <= 0) {
```

You have to make a similar change in the private `contains` method. You have to use calls on the `compareTo` method rather than simple comparisons. Because the method has more than one comparison, in this case it makes sense to call `compareTo` once and store it in a local variable:

```java
private boolean contains(SearchTreeNode<E> root, E value) {
    if (root == null) {
```

```
            return false;
        } else {
            int compare = value.compareTo(root.data);
            if (compare == 0) {
                return true;
            } else if (compare < 0) {
                return contains(root.left, value);
            } else {
                return contains(root.right, value);
            }
        }
    }
```

You have to make one final change. Java knows only that these data values are of some generic type `E`. As a result, the calls on `compareTo` in your `add` and `contains` methods generate compiler errors. You could fix this problem with a cast. For example, you could replace the line:

```
int compare = value.compareTo(root.data);
```

with:

```
int compare = ((Comparable<E>) value).compareTo(root.data);
```

A better approach is to modify the class header to include this information. You want to add the constraint that the class `E` implements the `Comparable` interface. You specify that constraint by modifying the header as follows:

```
public class SearchTree<E extends Comparable<E>> {
    ...
}
```

It's odd that Java has you use the keyword `extends` because you want it to implement the interface, but that's how generics work in Java. If you are defining a class, you make a distinction between the cases in which the new class extends another class and those in which it implements an interface. But in generic declarations, you use the word `extends` for both kinds of extension.

This is a fairly quick explanation of a complex topic. We don't have time to explain the details of programming with generics in detail in this book, although there are many excellent online tutorials that you can find by entering "Java generics" into your favorite web browser.

The complete code for the `SearchTree` class can be found at http://www.buildingjavaprograms.com.

Chapter Summary

A binary tree is a linked structure in which each node refers to two other nodes. A tree is either empty (`null`) or a node with references to two other trees, called its subtrees.

The root is the top node of a tree. A leaf node is a node that has no children. A branch node is a node that has at least one child. Each node has a level related to the number of links that are between it and the root of the tree.

A tree node object stores a data value and left/right references to other nodes. An overall tree object stores a reference to a single tree node as its overall root.

A traversal is an examination of all elements in a binary tree. Traversals are commonly done in three orders: preorder, inorder, and postorder. The difference between the orders relates to when a given node is examined relative to its left/right subtrees.

Tree methods are often recursive and are often implemented with the use of a public/private pair, in which the private method accepts a reference to a tree node as a parameter. This technique allows the method to recursively operate on a given portion of the overall tree.

The elements of a binary search tree are arranged in order, with smaller elements on the left and larger elements on the right. Search trees are useful for implementing collections that can be searched quickly, such as sets and maps.

To add a node to a binary tree, traverse the tree to the left if the new element is smaller than the current node or to the right if it is larger. The end of this traversal will reveal the proper place to add the new node.

To search for a value in a binary tree, traverse the tree going left if the target value is smaller than the current node or right if it is larger. Because of the way in which the tree is ordered, the end of this traversal will either find the target's node or find a `null` dead end, in which case the value is not in the tree.

The `x = change(x)` is a pattern in which a recursive method is passed an object or value in its initial state (called `x` here) and returns the new state of `x`. This technique is often used in recursive tree methods; the recursive call accepts a node parameter and later returns the potentially changed node.

A tree can be made to store elements of any object type `E` rather than just integers. To do this, the tree class must be made into a generic class, and the generic type parameter `E` must be constrained so that it is a class which implements the `Comparable<E>` interface.

Self-Check Problems

Section 17.1: Binary Tree Basics

1. How many roots can a tree have? Does a tree have more branches or leaves?

2. Draw a tree that has twice as many leaves as branches and one that has the same number of leaves as branches.

3. a. How many levels does the given tree have?
   b. How many branches does it have, and which nodes are they?
   c. How many leaves does it have, and which nodes are they?

d. Which node is the root of the tree?

e. Which node(s) are the sibling(s) of the node storing the value 2? Which nodes are its children?

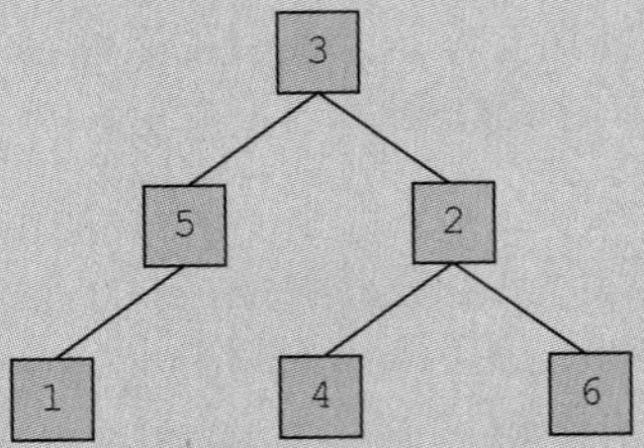

Section 17.2: Tree Traversals

For each of the next three problems, write the elements of the given tree in the order in which they would be seen by a preorder, inorder, and postorder traversal.

4.

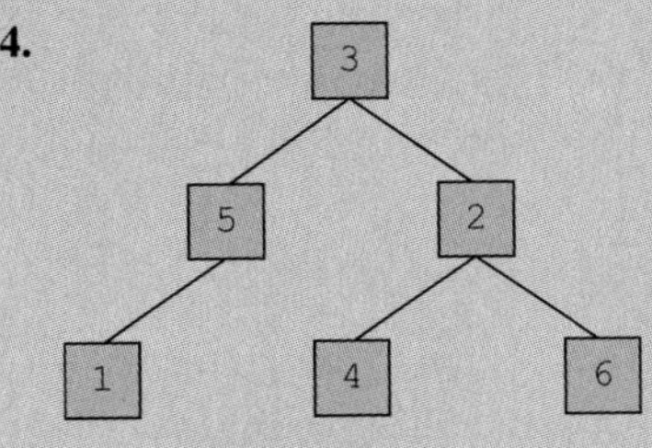

5.

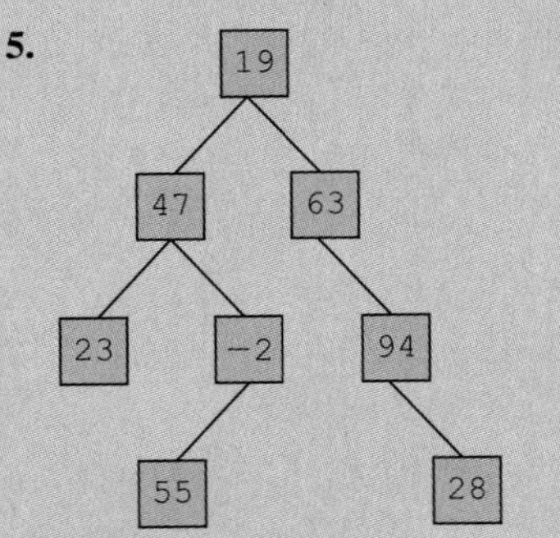

6.

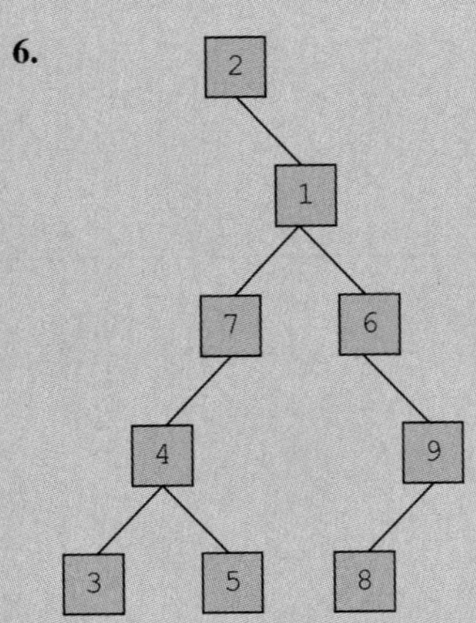

7. What would happen if we removed the `root != null` test from the `printPreorder` method?

8. Write a method called `printPostorder` that could be added to the `IntTree` class and that prints a postorder traversal of the tree.

9. Write a method called `printMirror` that could be added to the `IntTree` class and that prints a backward inorder traversal of the tree. That is, for a given node, it examines the right subtree, then the node itself, then the left subtree.

Section 17.3: Common Tree Operations

10. Why do many recursive tree methods use a public/private pair? What is the difference between the header of the public method and that of the private method?

11. Write a method called `size` that could be added to the `IntTree` class and that returns the total number of nodes in the tree.

12. Write methods called `min` and `max` that could be added to the `IntTree` class and that return the smallest and largest values in the tree, respectively. For example, if a variable called `tree` stores the values shown in Self-Check Problem 5, the call of `tree.min()` should return `-2` and the call of `tree.max()` should return `94`. If the tree is empty, the methods should throw an `IllegalStateException`.

13. Write a method called `countBranches` that could be added to the `IntTree` class and that returns the total number of branch nodes in the tree. A branch node is any node that is not a leaf node. (Hint: Look at the code for `countLeaves` written in Section 17.3.)

Section 17.4: Binary Search Trees

14. What is the difference between a regular binary tree and a binary search tree?

15. Which of the following trees are valid binary search trees?

a.

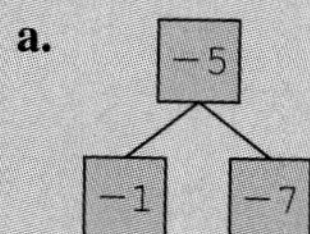

b.

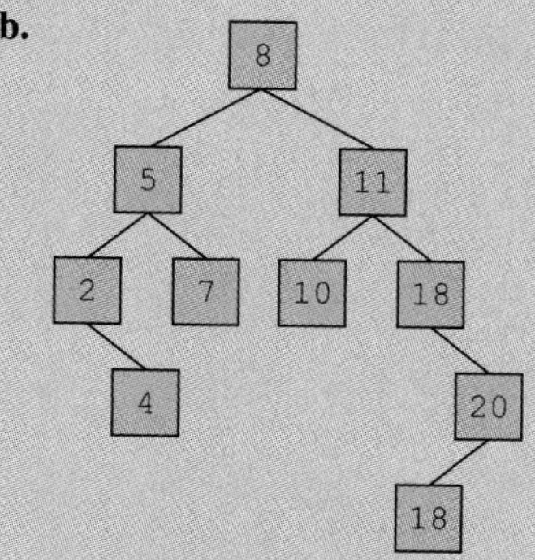

c. 42

d.

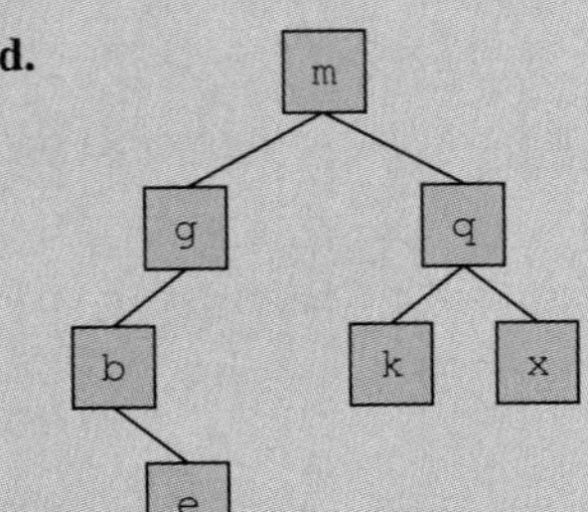

e.

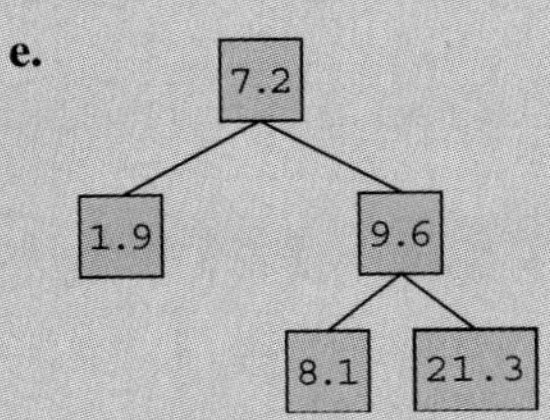

16. What will be true about the results of an inorder traversal of a binary search tree?

For each of the next four problems, draw the binary search tree that would result if the given elements were added to an empty binary search tree in the given order. Then write the elements of the tree in the order that they would be visited by each kind of traversal (preorder, inorder, and postorder).

17. Leia, Boba, Darth, R2D2, Han, Luke, Chewy, Jabba

18. Meg, Stewie, Peter, Joe, Lois, Brian, Quagmire, Cleveland

19. Kirk, Spock, Scotty, McCoy, Chekov, Uhuru, Sulu, Khaaaan!

20. Lisa, Bart, Marge, Homer, Maggie, Flanders, Smithers, Milhouse

21. Why does the `add` method of a binary search tree need to return the newly added/created node?

22. What is the `x = change(x)` pattern, and how is it used with binary trees?

23. How many nodes at most would be examined in a call to `contains` on a perfect binary search tree of height *N*?

24. Consider the following implementation of the `contains` method. How does it differ from the one we showed in Section 17.4? Is it better or worse, and why?

```
private boolean contains(IntTreeNode root, int value) {
    if (root == null) {
        return false;
    } else if (value == root.data) {
        return true;
    } else {
        return contains(root.left, value) || contains(root.right, value);
    }
}
```

25. Rewrite the `min` and `max` methods from Self-Check Problem 12 so that they will work on a binary search tree. The methods should take advantage of the fact that the tree is sorted and should not examine nodes unless necessary.

Section 17.5: `SearchTree<E>`

26. What are some changes that need to be made to the tree class to convert it from storing integers to storing objects of type `E`?

27. What kind of changes would you make to add an iterator to our binary tree class?

Exercises

Each of the following exercises is a method to be added to the `IntTree` class from this chapter. You may define additional private methods to implement your public method if necessary. Several problem descriptions refer to the following reference binary trees:

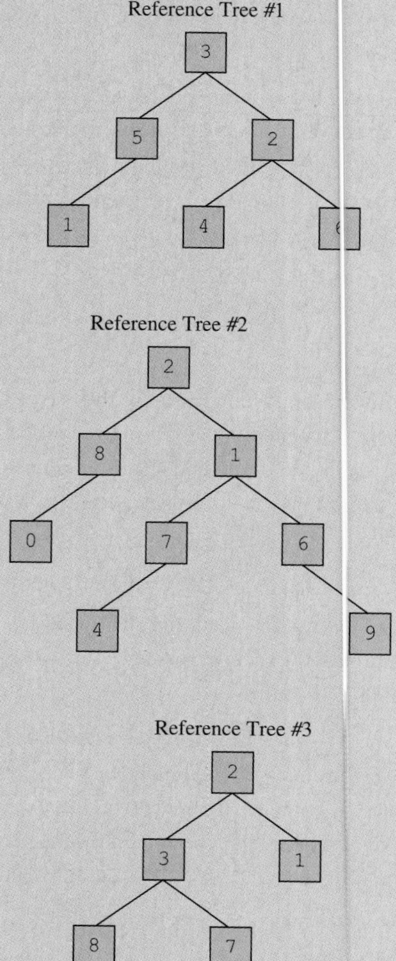

1. Write a method called `countLeftNodes` that returns the number of left children in the tree. A left child is a node that appears as the root of the left-hand subtree of another node. For example, reference tree #1 has 3 left children (the nodes storing the values `5`, `1`, and `4`).

2. Write a method called `countEmpty` that returns the number of empty branches in a tree. An empty tree is considered to have one empty branch (the tree itself). For nonempty trees, your methods should count the total number of empty branches among the nodes of the tree. A leaf node has two empty branches, a node with one nonempty child has one empty branch, and a node with two nonempty children has no empty branches. For example, reference tree #1 has 7 empty branches (two under the value `1`, one under `5`, and two under each of `4` and `6`).

3. Write a method called `depthSum` that returns the sum of the values stored in a binary tree of integers weighted by the depth of each value. The method should return the value at the root, plus 2 times the values stored at the next level of the tree, plus 3 times the values stored at the next level of the tree, and so on. For example, the depth sum of reference tree #1 would be computed as `(1 * 3) + (2 * (5 + 2)) + (3 * (1 + 4 + 6)) = 50`.

4. Write a method called `countEvenBranches` that returns the number of branch nodes in a binary tree that contain even numbers. A branch node has one or two children (i.e., it is not a leaf). For example, if a variable `t` refers to reference tree #2, then the call `t.countEvenBranches()` should return `3` because there are three branch nodes with even values (`2`, `8`, and `6`). Notice that leaf nodes with even values are not included (the nodes storing `0` and `4`).

5. Write a method called `printLevel` that accepts an integer parameter `n` and prints the values at level `n` from left to right, one per line. We will use the convention that the overall root is at level `1`, its children are at level `2`, and so on. If there are no values at the level, your method should produce no output. Your method should throw an `IllegalArgumentException` if it is passed a value for a level that is less than 1. For example, if a variable `t` refers to reference tree #2, then the call of `t.printLevel(3);` would produce the following output:

```
0
7
6
```

6. Write a method called `printLeaves` that prints to `System.out` the leaves of a binary tree from right to left. More specifically, the leaves should be printed in the *reverse* order that they would be printed using any of the standard traversals. If the tree is empty, your method should produce the output `"no leaves"`. For example, if a variable `t` refers to reference tree #2, the call of `t.printLeaves();` should produce the following output:

```
leaves: 9 4 0
```

7. Write a method called `isFull` that returns `true` if a binary tree is full and `false` if it is not. A full binary tree is one in which every node has 0 or 2 children. For example, reference trees #1 and #2 are not full, but #3 is full. By definition, the empty tree is considered full.

8. Write a `toString` method for a binary tree of integers. The method should return `"empty"` for an empty tree. For a leaf node, it should return the data in the node as a string. For a branch node, it should return a parenthesized `String` that has three elements separated by commas: the data at the root, a string representation of the left subtree, and then a string representation of the right subtree. For example, if a variable `t` refers to reference tree #2, then the call `t.toString()` should return the following `String` (without the surrounding quotes):

```
"(2, (8, 0, empty), (1, (7, 4, empty), (6, empty, 9)))"
```

9. Write a method called `equals` that accepts another binary tree of integers as a parameter and compares the two trees to see whether they are equal to each other. For example, if variables of type `IntTree` called `t1` and `t2` have been initialized, then `t1.equals(t2)` will return `true` if the trees are equal and `false` otherwise. Two empty trees are considered to be equal to each other.

10. Write a method called `doublePositives` that doubles all data values greater than 0 in a binary tree of integers.

11. Write a method called `numberNodes` that changes the data stored in a binary tree, assigning sequential integers starting with `1` to each node so that a preorder traversal will produce the numbers in order (`1, 2, 3,` etc.). For example, if a variable `t` refers to reference tree #1, the call of `t.numberNodes();` would overwrite the existing data, assigning values from `1` to `6` to the nodes so that a preorder traversal of the tree would produce `1, 2, 3, 4, 5, 6` as shown in the following diagram. Do not change the structure of the tree, only the values stored in the data fields. Your method should return the number of nodes in the tree.

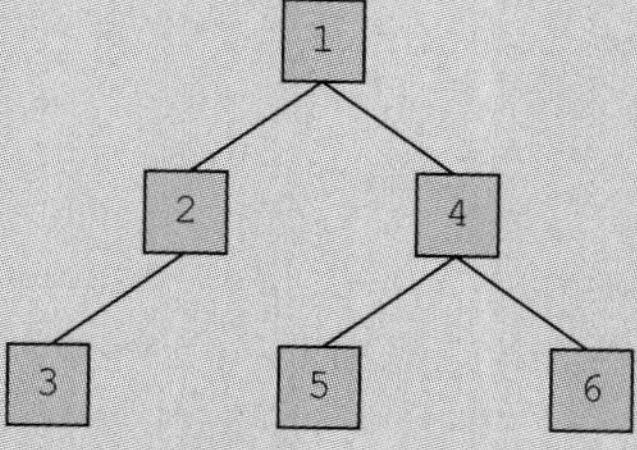

12. Write a method called `removeLeaves` that removes the leaves from a tree. A leaf is a node that has empty left and right subtrees. If your method is called on an empty tree, the method does not change the tree because there are no nodes of any kind (leaf or not).

13. Write a method called `copy` that returns a reference to a new `IntTree` that is an independent copy of the original tree. Do not change the original tree.

14. Write a method called `completeToLevel` that accepts an integer n as a parameter and that adds nodes to a tree to complete the first n levels. A level is complete if every possible node at that level is not `null`. We will use the convention that the overall root is at level `1`, its children are at level `2`, and so on. You should preserve any existing nodes in the tree. Any new nodes added to the tree should contain the value `-1`. Your method should throw an `IllegalArgumentException` if it is passed a value for a level that is less than `1`.

For example, if a variable called `t` refers to reference tree #2 and you make the call of `t.completeToLevel(4);`, the tree should change to the following tree:

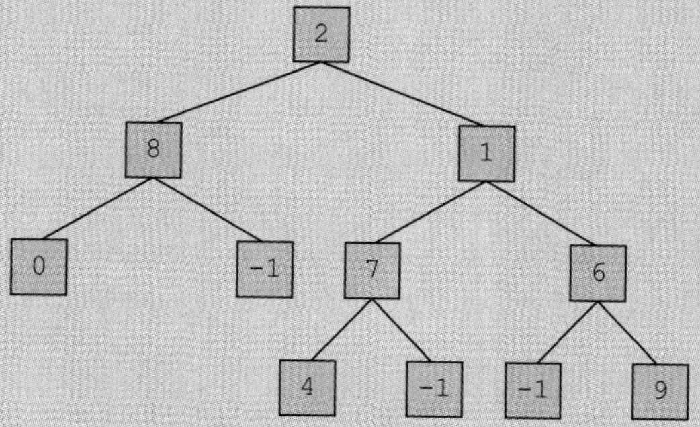

15. Write a method called `trim` that accepts minimum and maximum integers as parameters and removes from the tree any elements that are not within that range inclusive. For this method you should assume that your tree is a binary search tree and that its elements are in valid binary search tree order. Your method should maintain the binary search tree ordering property of the tree. This property is important for solving this problem.

16. Write a method called `tighten` that eliminates branch nodes that have only one child. Each such node should be replaced by its only child. (This can lead to multiple replacements because the child might itself be replaced.) For example, if a variable called `t` refers to reference tree #2, the call of `t.tighten();` should leave `t` storing the following tree.

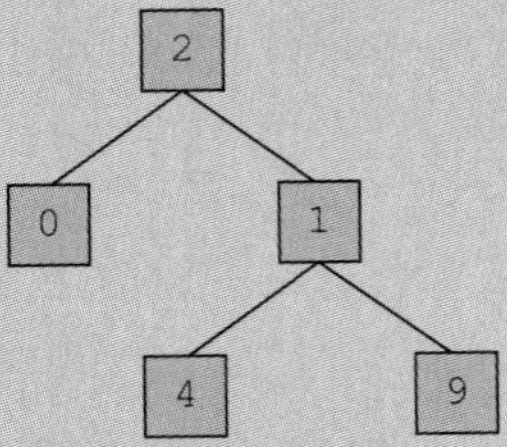

17. Write a method called `combineWith` that accepts another binary tree of integers as a parameter and combines the two trees into a new third tree that is returned. The new tree's structure should be a union of the structures of the two original trees; it should have a node in any location where there was a node in either of the original trees (or both). The nodes of the new tree should store an integer indicating which of the original trees had a node at that position (`1` if just the first tree had the node, `2` if just the second tree had the node, and `3` if both trees had the node). Your method should not change the structure or contents of either of the two original trees that are being combined.

For example, suppose `IntTree` variables `t2` and `t3` refer to reference trees #2 and #3, respectively. The call of `t2.combineWith(t3)` will return a reference to the following new tree. Keep in mind that nodes numbered `1` are those that appear only in `t2`, nodes numbered `2` appear only in `t3`, and nodes numbered `3` appear in both.

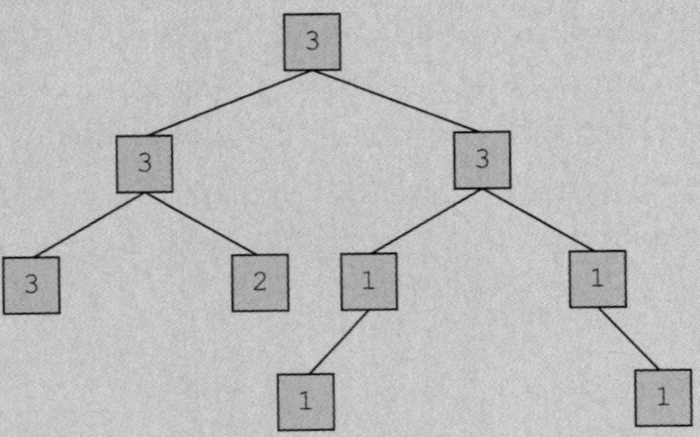

18. Write a method called `inOrderList` that returns a list containing the sequence of values obtained from an inorder traversal of your binary tree of integers. For example, if a variable `t` refers to reference tree #3, then the call `t.inOrderList()` should return the list `[8, 3, 7, 2, 1]`. If the tree is empty, your method should return an empty list.

19. Write a method called `evenLevels` that makes sure that all branches end on an even level. If a leaf node is on an odd level it should be removed from the tree. We will define the root as being on level `1`. For example, if a variable `t`

refers to reference tree #2, then the call `t.evenLevels();` should change the tree's state to the following, removing the leaf value `0` because it is on an odd level:

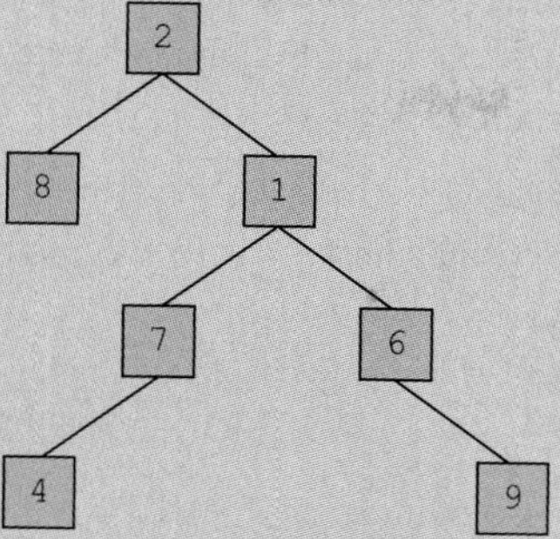

20. Write a method called `makePerfect` that adds nodes until the binary tree is a *perfect* tree. A perfect binary tree is one where all leaves are at the same level. Another way of thinking of it is that you are adding dummy nodes to the tree until every path from the root to a leaf is the same length. A perfect tree's shape is exactly triangular and every branch node has exactly two children, and all of the leaves are at the same level. Each new node you add to the tree should store the value `0`. For example, if a variable `t` refers to reference tree #2, then the call `t.makePerfect();` should change the tree's state to the following:

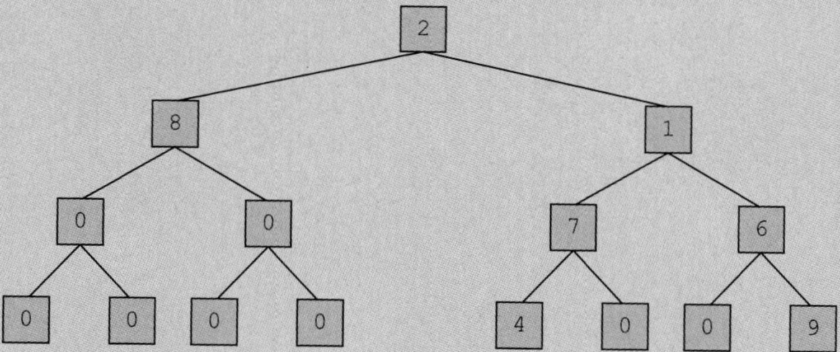

Programming Projects

1. Implement a yes/no guessing game called 20 Questions using a binary tree. At the beginning of each round of the game, the human player thinks of an object. The computer tries to guess the object by asking a series of no more than 20 yes-or-no questions. Eventually the computer guesses what the object is. If this guess is correct, the computer wins; if not, the human player wins.

   The computer keeps track of a binary tree with nodes representing questions and answers. A "question" node contains a left "yes" subtree and a right "no" subtree. An "answer" node is a leaf. This tree can be traversed to ask the human player questions until it reaches a leaf node, at which point the computer asks whether that answer is the correct one.

   Initially the computer is not very intelligent, but it grows more intelligent with each game. If the computer's answer guess is incorrect, the player must give it a new question to help it in future games. This is similar to the game found at the web site http://animalgame.com/. You should write methods to construct a tree, play a game, and save/load the tree's state from a file.

2. Write a program that encodes and decodes Morse code files using a binary tree. Morse code is a system that encodes the 26 English letters and 10 numeric digits into sequences of dots, dashes, and spaces. Your tree can store the encodings of each letter and number, going left for a dot and right for a dash. When your program reads a sequence of Morse code characters, it should traverse the tree in the appropriate direction for each character and output the letter or number it reaches at the end of each sequence.

3. Write a program that performs Huffman encoding and compression using a binary tree. Huffman coding is an algorithm devised by David A. Huffman of MIT in 1952 for compressing text data to make a file occupy a smaller number of bytes. The idea of Huffman coding is to abandon the rigid 8-bits-per-character requirement of ASCII encoding and use different-length binary encodings for different characters. The advantage of doing this is that if a character occurs frequently in the file, such as the letter *e*, it could be given a shorter encoding (fewer bits), making the file smaller.

   Your program should contain methods to read an input text file, count its characters, and use these counts to build a Huffman tree for the characters by frequency. Use this Huffman tree to output an encoded and compressed version of the file. Also write a method to read and decompress this file later. You may want to use helper classes for reading and writing a file one bit at a time. You can find classes called `BitInputStream` and `BitOutputStream` at our web site, http://buildingjavaprograms.com.

4. The actual `Set` interface in the `java.util` package has several methods that are beyond those implemented by our search tree in this chapter. Write a version of `SearchTree<E>` that adds some or all of these methods. The methods to add are the following (some headers are slightly modified; see the Java API Specification for descriptions of each method):

   - `public void addAll(SearchTree<E> tree)`
   - `public void clear()`
   - `public boolean containsAll(SearchTree<E> tree)`
   - `public boolean equals(Object o)`
   - `public boolean isEmpty()`
   - `public boolean remove(Object o)`
   - `public void removeAll(SearchTree<E> tree)`
   - `public void retainAll(SearchTree<E> tree)`
   - `public Object[] toArray()`

5. Add an iterator to the search tree. Write a class called `SearchTreeIterator` that has the methods that follow for iterating over a binary tree. You will also need to modify the tree nodes to store parent references so that the iterator can properly walk "up" the tree as necessary. (See the Java API Specification for descriptions of each method.) Here are the methods:

   - `public boolean hasNext()`
   - `public E next()`
   - `public void remove()`

6. Write a program that evaluates numeric expressions using a binary expression tree. A leaf node represents an operand (a number). A branch node represents an operator; its two subtrees represent its operands.

Chapter 18

Advanced Data Structures

Introduction

In this chapter, we will explore the implementation of two powerful data structures called hash tables and heaps. Both of these structures are used in Java's Collections Framework to implement collections such as `HashSet`, `HashMap`, and `PriorityQueue`. These clever data structures allow for efficient operations such as adding, removing, searching, and ordering elements.

Upon completion of this chapter you will have seen all of the major implementation strategies used in the primary collections in the Java Collections Framework: arrays (`ArrayList`, `Stack`), linked lists (`LinkedList`), binary trees (`TreeSet`, `TreeMap`), hash tables (`HashSet`, `HashMap`), and heaps (`PriorityQueue`).

18.1 Hashing

Hashing is a technique for efficiently mapping data elements to indexes in an array so that they can be added, removed, and searched very quickly. Hashing is the underlying technique used to implement the `HashSet` and `HashMap` classes. Hashing makes it possible to have a collection that can add, remove, and search for data elements in a constant amount of time (also called O(1), as discussed in Chapter 13), making it extremely fast for many common use cases.

Array Set Implementations

Suppose we want to store a set of integers using an array as the underlying data structure and that the most common operations we want to enable are insertion (`add`), deletion (`remove`), and testing for membership (`contains`). Further suppose that the order in which the elements are stored does not matter, so long as we can implement all of these operations efficiently. The key concern is that the structure should be fast for these three operations.

We could follow the same general idea as `ArrayIntList`, using an unfilled array and a `size` field to represent the data in the set:

```
public class ArrayIntSet {
    private int[] elementData;
    private int size;

    // Constructs an empty set.
    public ArrayIntSet() {
        elementData = new int[10];
        size = 0;
    }
    ...
```

As each element is inserted, it is stored at the next available index and the `size` field is incremented. So if the array's length is 10 and the client adds the values `7`, `5`, `1`, and `9`, the set would have the internal state shown in Figure 18.1. The blank array cells actually contain 0s, but they are unimportant because they are past the size.

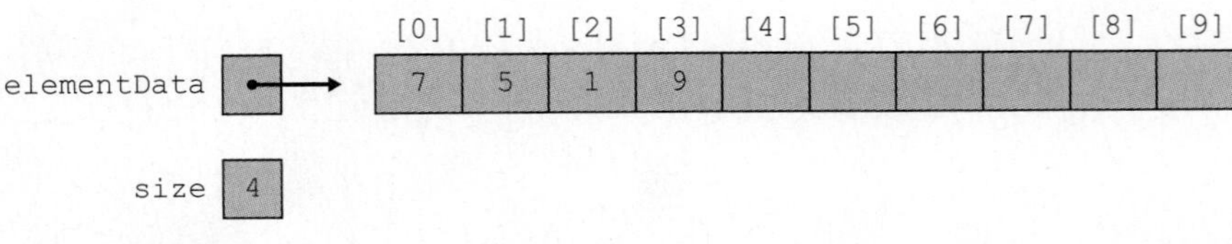

Figure 18.1 Representing a set as an unfilled, unsorted array

Is this a good way to implement a set? Think about how the common operations would be written. Adding an element is efficient (O(1)); simply place it in the next free slot and increment the `size` field. Removal is an inefficient linear search through the array for the value to remove. Once the value is found, since order is unimportant, you can quickly remove it by replacing it by the last element in the array, rather than having to shift any following elements left by one index; but the search to find it is still slow. We might have to examine all of the elements (on average, about half of them), so removal is O(*N*). Testing for membership is also slow, a linear search over all elements to try to find the value of interest. To figure out whether the set contains the value `9`, we must look at the `7`, `5`, `1`, and `9` before it is found.

Removal and searching from the unsorted array are slow because there's no particular way to guess where the element value will be found, if it is in the array at all. But with some creativity we can improve upon this situation. We've seen some strategies that take advantage of sorted data, such as the binary search algorithm. Binary search does not need to examine every index of the array to find an element; at each step the algorithm eliminates half of the remaining search space, resulting in a O(log *N*) runtime.

We could base our set on a sorted array, as shown in Figure 18.2. As elements are added to this sorted array, they must be placed into the proper indexes to maintain sorted order. The implementation of insertion or removal requires two steps: binary searching for the right index for the element, then shifting any following elements left or right. For example, if the value `2` is added, the `5`, `7`, and `9` must be shifted right by one index to make room for it.

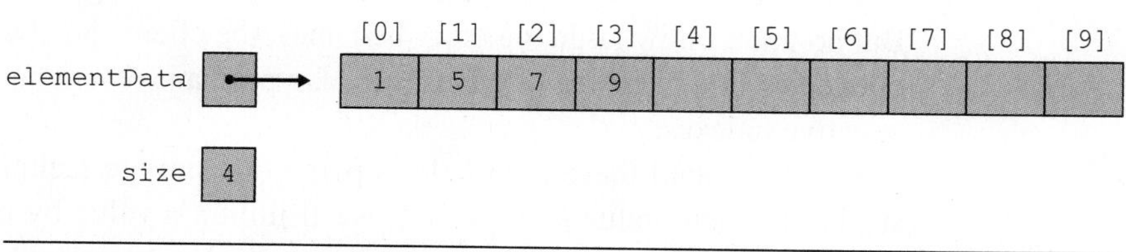

Figure 18.2 Representing a set as an unfilled, sorted array

The sorted array structure would be faster to search because we could implement our `contains` method as a binary search. Adding and removing would be O(*N*) in the worst case because of the shifting. Still, this is arguably a better implementation than the unsorted array if the primary concern is the speed of the `contains` operation.

Hash Functions and Hash Tables

Implementing a set using a sorted array is a step up from an unsorted one, but it's possible to do better. Let's explore how to use a special mapping strategy called a hash function to organize the elements of our set and search it quickly.

Recall that the order of the elements doesn't matter, as long as the set can add, remove, and find elements. The elements can be placed anywhere, as long as they can be found later. Here's an odd but powerful idea: What if we stored element value *k* at index *k*? For example, if you tell the set to add the value `5`, store it at index 5. If we used this technique, the set storing `7`, `5`, `1`, and `9` would have the structure shown in Figure 18.3.

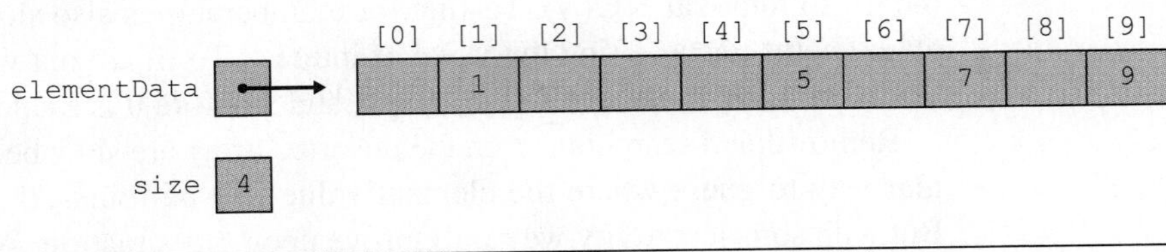

Figure 18.3 Storing set elements at corresponding indexes

If we stored our set data using this technique, the three basic set operations become extremely efficient to implement. Inserting a value *k* simply involves going to index *k* and storing *k* there; no searching or shifting is needed. Removing the value *k* requires going to index *k* and changing the value back to `0`. Testing for membership of a value *k* (`contains`) requires looking at index *k* to see whether *k* is stored there; if so, the value is part of the set, and if not, it isn't.

You may already be thinking of some problems with this implementation strategy. What if the client tries to add a value that is outside the range 0 to 9, such as `23`? We could start with a larger array; if `elementData` has length 100, our `23` will fit nicely. But no matter how large the array becomes, the client can always add a larger integer outside its bounds. Negative numbers also pose a problem because arrays never have negative indexes.

To get around these issues, let's patch our storage technique. Instead of always storing element value *k* at index *k*, we'll limit *k*'s value by modding it by the array capacity. So if the array length is 10, the value `23` would be inserted at index 3 because `23 % 10` equals `3`. To fix negative numbers, we'll take the absolute value of *k* and apply the same technique. So the value `-58` would be inserted at index 8.

Figure 18.4 shows what the array would look like after the insertion of `23` and `-58` using our new mod technique. The set still has the same speedy runtime for the common operations because each element still has a single index into which it will be placed.

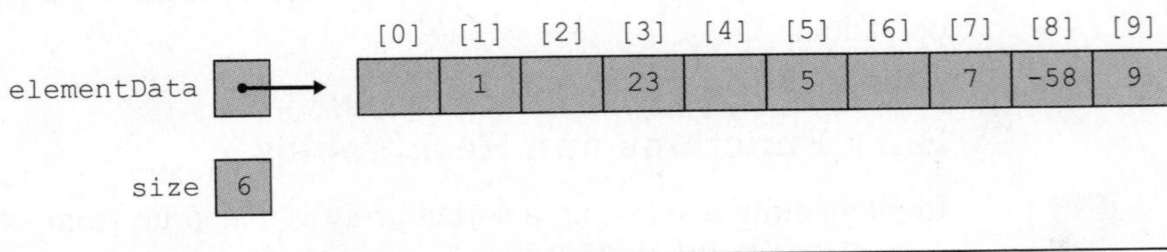

Figure 18.4 Use of hash function with wrap-around

Since our mapping from element value to preferred index now has a bit of complexity to it, we might turn it into a method that accepts the element value as a parameter and returns the right index for that value. Such a method is referred to as a *hash function*, and an array that uses such a function to govern insertion and deletion of its elements is called a *hash table*. The individual indexes in the hash table are also sometimes informally called *buckets*.

Our hash function so far is the following:

```
private int hashFunction(int value) {
    return Math.abs(value) % elementData.length;
}
```

Hash Function

A method for rapidly mapping between element values and preferred array indexes at which to store those values.

Hash Table

An array that stores its elements in indexes produced by a hash function.

Collisions

There is still a problem with our current hash table. Because our hash function wraps values to fit in the array bounds, it is now possible that two values could have the same preferred index. For example, if we try to insert `45` into the hash table, it maps to index 5, conflicting with the existing value `5`. This is called a *collision*. Our implementation is incomplete until we have a way of dealing with collisions. If the client tells the set to insert `45`, the value `45` must be added to the set somewhere; it's up to us to decide where to put it.

Collision

When two or more element values in a hash table produce the same result from its hash function, indicating that they both prefer to be stored in the same index of the table.

One common way of resolving collisions is called *probing*, which involves looking for another index to use if the preferred index is taken. For example, if the client wants to add `45` and index 5 is in use, we could just put `45` at the next available index, which is 6 in our example. (Looking forward one index at a time for the next free index is called *linear probing*, but there are other kinds of probing such as *quadratic probing*, which involves jumping around to various places in the hash table.)

Figure 18.5 shows the hash table's state if the values `45`, `91`, and `71` are added and linear probing is used to resolve the collisions. The `45` conflicts with `5` and is put into index 6. The `91` conflicts with existing value `1` and is put into index 2. The `71` conflicts with `1` and `91` and must be put into index 3.

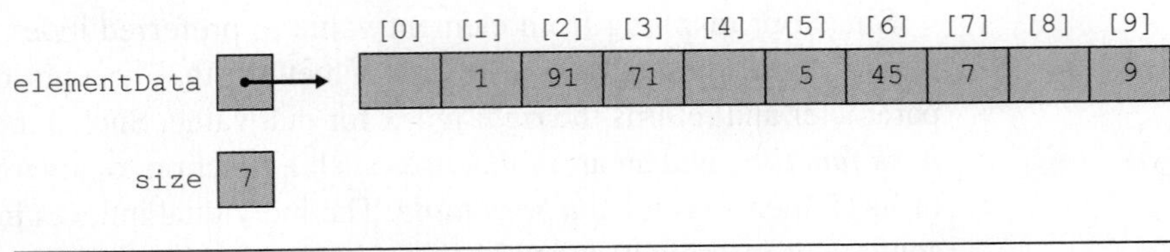

Figure 18.5 Hash collisions resolved by linear probing

Probing gets around the collision problem, but it introduces new problems of its own. For one, it is no longer as simple to find an element's value. A value whose hash function evaluates to *k* might be stored at index *k*, but if something other than *k* is there, it might be at index *k*+1, *k*+2, etc. So we would need to patch our other methods such as `contains` accordingly. We can make the appropriate modifications, but we also have to think about the original goals of this implementation. Searching for elements is supposed to be fast, and if we have to probe through a lot of elements to find anything, we're losing the efficiency we sought after in the first place.

Probing

Resolving hash collisions by placing elements at other indexes in the table rather than their preferred indexes.

Another problem is that the hash table can get full, resulting in no free slots to store a value. The example array of size 10 can hold only 10 elements. If the client tries to add an eleventh element, the array must be resized. Resizing a hash table is a nontrivial operation that we'll discuss in the next section.

Even if the array is not entirely full, if many elements are next to each other it can slow down the runtime for later operations. For example, to add the value `25` to the hash table in Figure 18.5 requires looking at four buckets: indexes 5, 6, 7, and 8 (where the value is finally placed). After doing so, a search for the value `95` (which is not found in the table) would need to examine indexes 5, 6, 7, 8, 9, and 0 before finally giving up. When elements clump up near each other like this, it is called *clustering*, and it is desirable to have as little clustering as possible in a hash table for it to perform efficiently.

Another way of dealing with the collision problem is to change our internal data structure. Collisions would not be a problem if each array index could store more than one value. This is possible if we change the array to be an array of lists rather than an array of integers. The list at index *k* will store all elements that the hash function maps to *k*. Figure 18.6 demonstrates this idea. To add an element to the hash table, we go to its preferred index and add the element value to the list stored at that index. Resolving collisions by storing hash elements in lists is called *separate chaining*. The real `HashSet` and `HashMap` provided in `java.util` use separate chaining internally to resolve collisions.

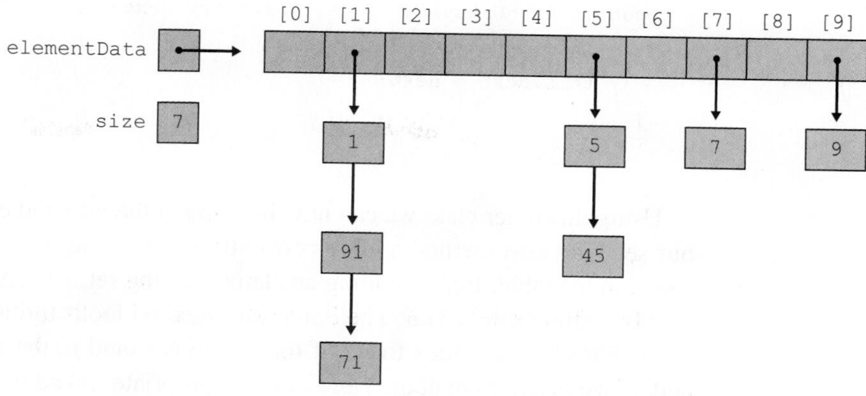

Figure 18.6 Hash collisions resolved by separate chaining

> **Separate Chaining**
>
> Resolving hash collisions by having each index of the table store a list of values rather than a single value.

As with probing, separate chaining faces an efficiency issue if the size of the set becomes large enough, especially if the numbers happen to have a lot of collisions with each other. For example, if the client adds a lot of numbers to the set that end with 1, there will be a long list of elements at index 1 in the hash table, and we'll have to perform a long search through the list to find values. One way to mitigate this issue is to use a larger array to store the element data, which will result in fewer collisions and shorter lists at each index. Another good idea is to use an array size that is not a multiple of 10 or any other round number, to avoid number patterns that are likely to collide. Many hash table implementations use a prime number for the table capacity.

We'll implement the lists of elements as lists of node objects, similar to the implementation of linked lists in Chapter 16. An inner class `HashEntry` represents a single node in such a list:

```
// Represents a single value in a chain stored in one hash bucket.
private class HashEntry {
    private int data;
    private HashEntry next;

    public HashEntry(int data) {
        this(data, null);
    }
```

```
    public HashEntry(int data, HashEntry next) {
        this.data = data;
        this.next = next;
    }
}
```

Using this inner class we can now implement the add and contains operations on our set. The add method adds a new entry to the table if the element is not already found in the table. Before adding an element to the set, we make sure it is not a duplicate by calling contains. The contains method looks through the list at the appropriate hash bucket index to see if that value is found in the list. When elements are added, we insert them at the front of the appropriate linked list. This is faster than traversing the links all the way to the end of the list to insert the element.

```
// Adds the given element to this set, if it was not
// already contained in the set.
public void add(int value) {
    if (!contains(value)) {
        // insert new value at front of list
        int bucket = hashFunction(value);
        elementData[bucket] = new HashEntry(value, elementData[bucket]);
        size++;
    }
}

// Returns true if the given value is found in this set.
public boolean contains(int value) {
    int bucket = hashFunction(value);
    HashEntry current = elementData[bucket];
    while (current != null) {
        if (current.data == value) {
            return true;
        }
        current = current.next;
    }
    return false;
}
```

We can also implement the remove method now. Removal is a bit trickier than adding, because we have to make sure to handle all of the possible cases. If the element to be removed is at the front of its linked list, we must adjust the front reference; otherwise we must change the next reference of some existing node in the list. As always with linked lists, we must be careful to check for null and not try to traverse past the end of a list.

```
// Removes the given value if it is contained in the set.
public void remove(int value) {
    int bucket = hashFunction(value);
    if (elementData[bucket] != null) {
        // check front of list
        if (elementData[bucket].data == value) {
            elementData[bucket] = elementData[bucket].next;
            size--;
        } else {
            // check rest of list
            HashEntry current = elementData[bucket];
            while (current.next != null && current.next.data != value) {
                current = current.next;
            }

            // if the element is found, remove it
            if (current.next != null) {
                current.next = current.next.next;
                size--;
            }
        }
    }
}
```

Removing from a hash table that uses probing has different complications. If we start with the hash table from Figure 18.5 and decide to remove the value `1`, we can't just replace it with a blank value, because there is a chain of other elements (`91` and `71`) that probed to the following indexes 2 and 3. If a later `contains(71)` call is made on the set, the code might mistakenly think that bucket 1 is empty and therefore incorrectly decide that `71` is not contained in the set. What is often done instead is to replace the removed value with a special marker value to indicate that a removal occurred. That way when `contains` or `add` is called later, it can recognize that value and realize that other values might follow the removed bucket. Flagging buckets with this special marker is more efficient than trying to shift values back in the hash table. Figure 18.7 shows an example removal of the value `1`.

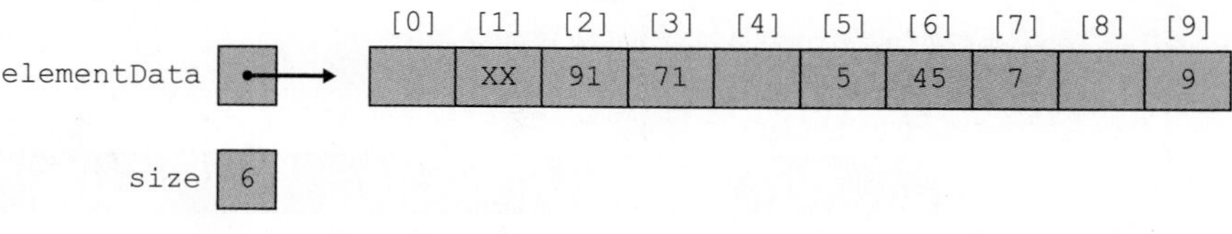

Figure 18.7 Removal of an element when probing is used

We will focus on our implementation that uses separate chaining rather than showing the code for the probing version. You can find both versions on our web site at http://buildingjavaprograms.com.

There are other ways of resolving collisions. For example, if the hash function results in a conflict, a secondary hash function can be used to find a new hash bucket. This is sometimes called *double hashing*. Double hashing and other methods of collision resolution are outside the scope of this chapter.

Rehashing

When a hash table becomes too full, it can be enlarged to give it additional capacity for storing elements. Consider the full hash table in Figure 18.8 that uses linear probing to resolve collisions. In addition to the elements previously added, the client has inserted `80`, `63`, and `57`, causing a completely full hash table. When the client tries to add an eleventh value, the hash table must be enlarged to make room for it.

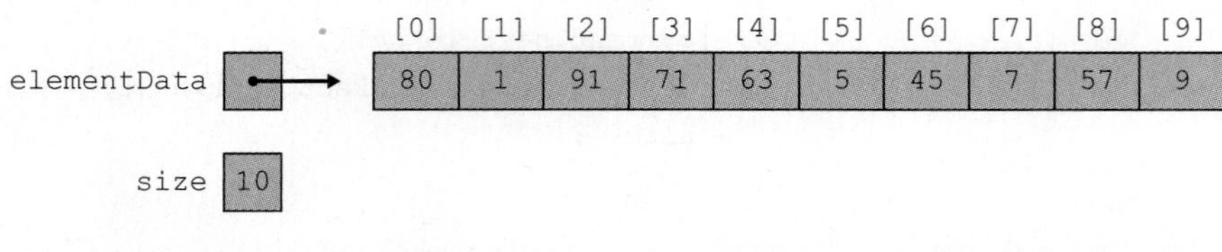

Figure 18.8 Full hash table with linear probing

Resizing a hash table is not as simple as creating a larger array and copying each element over into it. The reason is because the element values may not have the same hash function result in the new larger array. For example, the value `91` maps to index 1 in the array of length 10 because `91 % 10` equals `1`. But the same value `91` maps to index 11 in an array of length 20 because `91 % 20` equals 11. Therefore, when resizing a hash table array, it is important to reprocess each element using the hash function and place it into the new appropriate index. This process is called *rehashing*.

Suppose the client tries to add the value `35` to the full hash table. Figure 18.9 shows a properly resized and rehashed table. Notice that `91`, `71`, `35`, and `57` now sit in the second half of the array because their hash function results fall in that range. The value `63` also gets to sit in its preferred index of 3 because the element `71` that previously collided with it has moved to index 12. The rehashing also helps to decrease clustering; now the longest chain of consecutively occupied buckets is three.

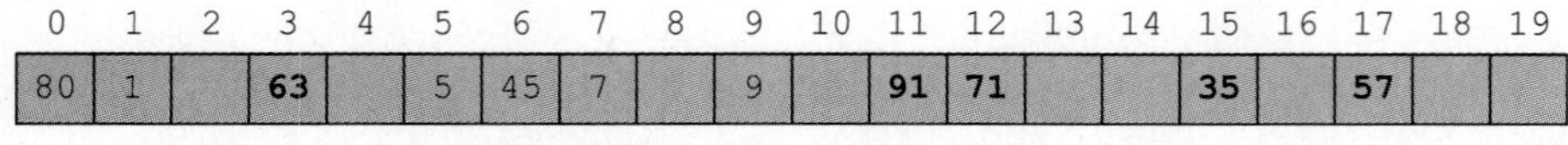

Figure 18.9 Enlarged hash table after rehashing

> **Rehashing**
> Resizing a hash table to increase its capacity and enabling it to store more elements, or store them more efficiently.

Hash tables that use separate chaining can also be rehashed, but the issues are slightly different. Technically a chained hash table never becomes completely "full" in the sense of becoming unable to add any more elements, because a new element can always be added to the list at a given index. But if the lists at each index become too long, the set operations become too slow. So it is still important to enlarge the hash table as its size grows. Figure 18.10 shows a chained table with the same elements as in Figure 18.8.

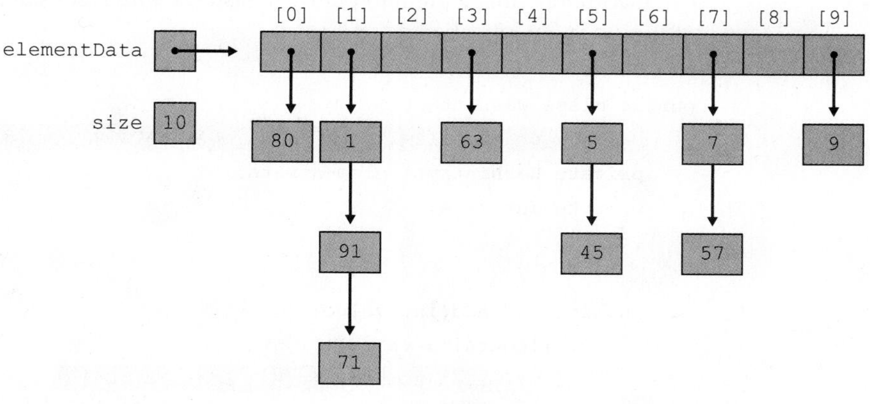

Figure 18.10 "Full" hash table with separate chaining

Figure 18.11 shows the same hash table after a rehashing to length 20 and the insertion of value `35`. The values `91`, `71`, `35`, and `57` are now stored in lists in the second half of the table.

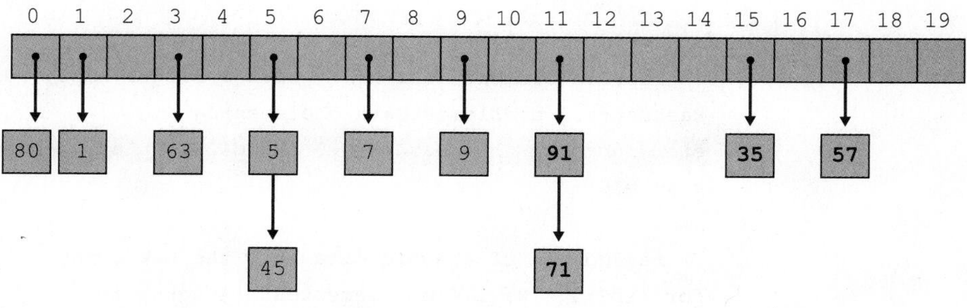

Figure 18.11 Enlarged chained hash table after rehashing

In our examples we chose to resize the hash table once its size exceeded its capacity. But most hash tables do not wait so long to rehash, because a nearly or entirely full table starts to exhibit poor performance. A better alternative is to monitor the table's size relative to the array capacity, also called the *load factor* of the table, and resize once this ratio exceeds some threshold. The load factor is fairly easy to compute:

```
private double loadFactor() {
    return (double) size / elementData.length;
}
```

The real Java `HashSet` uses a default load factor of 0.75; in other words, once the number of elements is three fourths as large as the capacity, the table is enlarged. We can incorporate this logic into our own hash set with a constant and a check at the start of the `add` method:

```
public class HashIntSet {
    private static final double MAX_LOAD_FACTOR = 0.75;
    private HashEntry[] elementData;
    private int size;
    ...

    public void add(int value) {
        if (!contains(value)) {
            if (loadFactor() >= MAX_LOAD_FACTOR) {
                rehash();
            }
        ...
```

The simplest way to implement the actual rehashing operation is to replace the set's internal hash table with a new larger one, then loop over the old table and read all of its contents back into the new hash table. We can call the set's own `add` method to reinsert all of the data to avoid duplicating code:

```
private void rehash() {
    // replace element data array with a larger empty version
    HashEntry[] oldElementData = elementData;
    elementData = new HashEntry[2 * oldElementData.length];
    size = 0;

    // re-add all of the old data into the new array
    for (int i = 0; i < oldElementData.length; i++) {
        HashEntry current = oldElementData[i];
```

```
        while (current != null) {
            add(current.data);
            current = current.next;
        }
    }
}
```

Hashing Non-Integer Data

Our hash set works well for storing integer data, but we have not yet discussed how to apply hashing techniques to non-integer data. The key idea is still the same: We need a way of mapping from values to preferred indexes at which to store them. It is possible to come up with hash functions for other kinds of data that convert them into integers. For example, we could convert a string into an integer by adding the integer ASCII values of its characters in some way.

The idea of hashing, and the importance of all kinds of data being able to be stored in a hash table, was close to the hearts of the original designers of Java. Recall that every Java class has an ancestor named `Object` that contains various basic behaviors that are common to every object. One of the methods of the `Object` class is named `hashCode`. You can call `hashCode` on any object to convert the object into an integer for use in a hash table. A modified version of our hash function that works for any type of objects is the following:

```
public int hashFunction(Object value) {
    return Math.abs(value.hashCode()) % elementData.length;
}
```

According to the official Java documentation for the `hashCode` method, a proper hash function must be consistent. That is, when called multiple times on an object whose state is not changing, it should return the same value each time. Similarly, when `hashCode` is called on two objects with equivalent states (such that `equals` would return `true` for the two objects), it should return the same value.

In general it is also desirable for `hashCode` to return unequal values when two objects have different states. But it is not mandatory for unequal objects to always have different hash codes. In fact, it is impossible to guarantee such a thing; for example, there are only four billion unique integer values, but there are infinitely many unique strings, so some strings must naturally have the same hash code as others. Unequal objects having equal hash codes does not break the hash table, but it does mean that those objects will hash to the same index and will collide, so they will be placed into the same list if separate chaining is used on the hash table.

The default version of `hashCode` from the `Object` class computes an integer based on the memory address of the object. This function satisfies the consistency requirement, but it is not ideal because it does not take into account the state of each object. For this reason many classes override `hashCode` with their own versions that compute an integer by somehow combining the object's state. Good hash functions try to do their best about spreading the hash values over a wide range of numbers to minimize conflicts.

When writing your own class, if your class has an `equals` method, you are expected to also provide a `hashCode` method to override the one provided by the `Object` superclass. The reason is that objects with "equal" state are supposed to have equal hash codes, and this would not be guaranteed by the version of `hashCode` inherited from class `Object`. Your `hashCode` method should combine the object's state in some way into a single integer and return it. The state can be combined in any way as long as it consistently produces the same integer for the same state.

The following is a possible `hashCode` method for the `Point` class implemented in Chapter 8. The code adds the `x` and `y` values but scales the `y` value up by a large number to spread out the space of integers returned. This is to avoid collisions between points like (4, 7) and (7, 4). Simply adding `x + y` and returning the result would also be correct but would not distribute the integer codes as much.

```
// a possible hashCode method for Ch. 8's Point class
public class Point {
    private int x;
    private int y;
    ...
    public int hashCode() {
        return 31337 * y + x;
    }
```

Many classes in the Java class libraries have their own `hashCode` methods. For example, the `String` class code has a `hashCode` method whose code is roughly the following. The code seems odd in that it multiplies by 31 at each pass through the loop. If the characters were simply added, there would be conflicts between various kinds of strings. For example, strings of similar length would all be clustered within a small range of hash codes, and strings that are anagrams, such as "file" and "life", would always collide. Multiplying the result by some number at each pass spreads out the space of codes and reduces these potential collisions.

```
// the hashCode method inside Java's String class
public int hashCode() {
    int hash = 0;
    for (int i = 0; i < this.length(); i++) {
        hash = 31 * hash + this.charAt(i);
```

```
    }
    return hash;
}
```

If you are writing a hashCode method for a class that has fields that are not integers, it is less clear how to combine the fields' state into a single hash code integer. Remember that if the fields are objects, they have their own hashCode methods that you can call. And primitives like double can be converted into their object wrapper equivalents, such as Double, and you can call hashCode on those. Here is an example class BankAccount with non-integer fields and a possible hashCode method based on its state. Notice that we again multiply the various fields by large integer constants to spread out the results of the function.

```
// a possible hashCode method for a BankAccount class
public class BankAccount {
    private int id;
    private String name;
    private double balance;
    ...
    public int hashCode() {
        return id +
               31 * name.hashCode() +
               16581 * new Double(balance).hashCode();
    }
}
```

If we want our set to be able to store any kind of object as its data, we can convert our HashIntSet into a generic HashSet, giving it a type parameter E for its elements. This requires small changes throughout the code, such as changing methods to accept parameters of type E rather than int, and comparing values using equals rather than ==. The process is very similar to our conversions of ArrayIntList and LinkedIntList to generic collections in previous chapters. The complete generic version of the class is not shown, but a few of the relevant lines to change are found in the following abbreviated code:

```
public class HashSet<E> {
    ...
    public void add(E value) { ... }
    public boolean contains(E value) {
        ...
        while (current != null) {
            if (current.data.equals(value)) { ...
    }
    public void remove(E value) { ... }
```

```
    ...
    private class HashEntry {
        private E data;
        private HashEntry next;
        ...
    }
}
```

Hash Map Implementation

The ideas shown so far form the core of the implementation of the `HashSet` class. The `HashMap` has a very similar internal structure. Recall that a map stores key/value pairs rather than simple element values. A `HashMap` is still implemented using a hash table, but the hash entry objects in each linked list are changed to store a pair of data fields, representing one key/value pair.

```
public class HashEntry {
    private Object key;
    private Object value;
    private HashEntry next;
    ...
}
```

Suppose a map is created with integers as the type for its keys and values, and the following pairs are added to it:

```
mymap.put(1, 37);
mymap.put(39, −2);
mymap.put(25, 44);
mymap.put(−5, 0);
```

Figure 18.12 shows the internal state of the hash table containing these pairs. Each index stores a list of `HashEntry` objects.

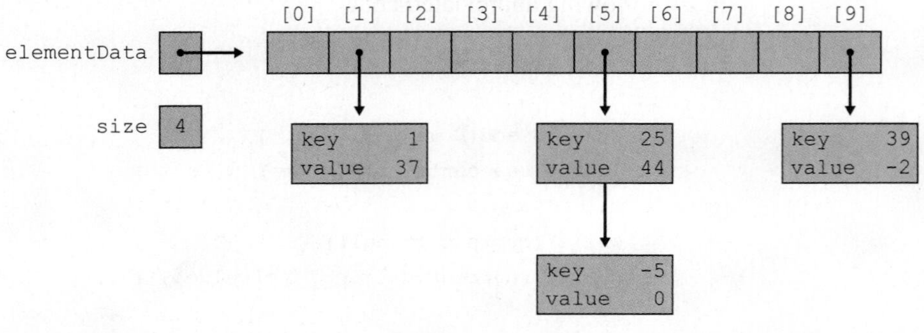

Figure 18.12 Hash map

To be able to accept any type of data for the keys and values, most hash map implementations are generic classes that accept a pair of type parameters, `K` for the key type and `V` for the value type. The hash map therefore has the following class header:

```
public class HashMap<K, V> {
    ...
    private class HashEntry {
        private K key;
        private V value;
        private HashEntry next;
        ...
    }
}
```

You can find complete code for the `HashSet` and `HashMap` classes on our web page at http://buildingjavaprograms.com.

18.2 Priority Queues and Heaps

In Chapter 14, you saw how queues are useful for storing data in First-In, First-Out (FIFO) order. There are other situations in which a queue-like structure is needed but with an ordering other than FIFO. In this section we will discuss a collection called a priority queue that is useful in these situations. We will also explore an underlying data structure called a heap that can be used to efficiently implement a priority queue.

Priority Queues

Consider the task of simulating the waiting line of patients at an emergency room. In general it seems that the patients should be served in the order in which they arrived. But some patients require urgent care and should be able to step in front of others in line. The primary consideration in the line's ordering is the importance of treating that particular patient.

A similar situation is the task of processing the set of customers waiting to purchase their goods at a food market. Again the customers naturally want to gather into lines, but real markets have found that they can serve more customers if they have "express lines" and other features to allow some customers to go ahead of others; in this case, customers with fewer items can skip ahead.

The general principle in situations like these is that of a queue, but organized by urgency or priority of each element rather than strictly on the order of insertion. There is a collection called a *priority queue* that is well suited to tasks like these. You can add elements to a priority queue in any order, but when you remove them, they will come out in order of priority or importance.

> **Priority Queue**
>
> A collection that associates each added element with a priority or importance and allows access or removal of the elements in order of priority.

Java's Collections Framework in `java.util` includes a class called `PriorityQueue` that arranges elements into their natural ordering from smallest to largest. For primitive values like integers and real numbers this means arranging the elements in ascending order.

The following example briefly illustrates the usage of a priority queue. Seven integers are added to the queue in no particular order. When the integers are removed from the queue, they come out in ascending order.

```
Queue<Integer> pq = new PriorityQueue<Integer>();
pq.add(42);
pq.add(17);
pq.add(9);
pq.add(42);
pq.add(35);
pq.add(−1);
pq.add(88);
while (!pq.isEmpty()) {
    System.out.print(pq.remove() + " "); // −1 9 17 35 42 42 88
}
```

For objects, the priority queue arranges the elements by the ordering of their `compareTo` method. If the elements of the queue are not `Comparable` (or if you would like to arrange them in an order other than their natural ordering), you can pass a `Comparator` to the queue's constructor to indicate the relative ordering to use. The most commonly desired reordering is to reverse the queue so that the elements come out in descending rather than ascending order. This can be done easily by calling `Collections.reverseOrder`, a method that returns a `Comparator` that reverses the natural ordering of any comparable class:

```
Queue<Integer> pq =
    new PriorityQueue<Integer>(Collections.reverseOrder());
...
while (!pq.isEmpty()) {
    System.out.print(pq.remove() + " "); // 88 42 42 35 17 9 −1
}
```

The useful methods of `PriorityQueue` objects are listed in Table 18.1.

A priority queue is a bit like a sorted list. You could achieve similar behavior to a priority queue by storing your data in an `ArrayList`, calling `Collections.sort`

Table 18.1 `PriorityQueue<E>` Methods

`PriorityQueue<E>()`	constructs a new empty priority queue
`PriorityQueue<E>(comparator)`	constructs a new empty priority queue, using the given `Comparator` to order its elements
`add(value)`	adds the given element to the queue
`clear()`	removes all elements from the queue
`isEmpty()`	returns `true` if there are no elements in the queue
`Iterator`	returns an `Iterator` over the queue's elements
`peek()`	returns the minimum element in the queue
`remove()`	removes and returns the minimum element in the queue; throws a `NoSuchElementException` if queue is empty
`size()`	returns number of elements in the queue
`toArray()`	returns an array containing the queue's elements
`toString()`	string representation of queue, such as `"[10, 20, 30]"`

after adding each element, and always removing the element from index 0 every time. One key difference with a priority queue compared to a sorted list is that it manages the ordering automatically without the need for the client to sort the elements manually. Another big advantage is that the priority queue implements this behavior in a much more efficient way. Sorting a list is a slow operation that requires O(N log N) time, and removing the first element from index 0 leads to bulky shifting of the elements, requiring O(N) time for each removal.

The priority queue, when implemented properly, can support its most common operations much more quickly than a sorted list. Adding and removing elements requires O(log N) time, and peeking at the minimum element requires constant O(1) time. The key to such an efficient implementation is a clever underlying data structure called a heap, which we will explore in the following sections.

Introduction to Heaps

A *heap* is a tree that arranges its elements with a vertical ordering. In a minimum heap or *min-heap*, child nodes always store values greater than or equal to the parent's value. In a maximum heap or *max-heap*, a parent node's value is always greater than or equal to those of its children. In other words, in a min-heap, the smallest element values are closer to the top (root) of the tree; in a max-heap, the largest element values are nearest to the root.

The fact that these elements are located at the top of the tree makes them easy to access and remove quickly and makes a heap an excellent structure to use to implement a priority queue. Since a priority queue is always finding and removing the smallest element, having that element at the very top of the tree makes finding it trivial. For this reason Java's `PriorityQueue` collection is implemented using a min-heap internally.

Heap

A tree that maintains a vertical ordering between parents and children, where parent nodes store smaller values than all of their children (min-heap) or parents store greater values than all of their children (max-heap).

Figure 18.13 shows an example of a min-heap. Notice how the smallest element value, `10`, is at the top of the tree. Larger elements are placed lower on the tree. You may be surprised initially by some of the ordering; `50` appears higher in the tree than `44`, and `90` is higher than `80` and `60`, and so on. But the key property of a heap is that a parent's value must be smaller than that of its children, and the nodes just listed are not in the same subtree as each other, so they share no direct parent–child relationship. Therefore, this example tree does satisfy the requirements to be a valid heap.

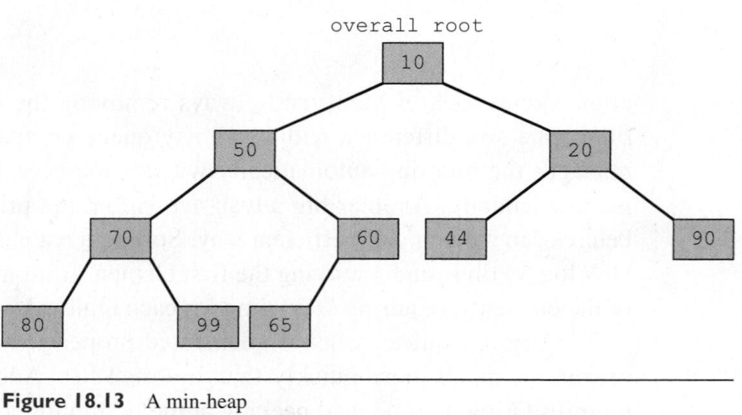

Figure 18.13 A min-heap

A heap can be implemented with nodes having any number of children, but as we did with trees in the previous chapter, we will focus on heaps whose nodes have at most two children, which are called *binary heaps*.

A heap is usually maintained as a *complete tree*, which is one where every level except possibly the lowest level is completely filled with all nodes having both children, and if the last level of the tree is not completely filled, all children are at the left-most edge of the tree. This minimizes the height of the tree relative to the number of elements; a wider and shorter tree is faster for traversing from the root to any given leaf.

Some people become confused about the difference between a priority queue and a heap. A priority queue is an abstract data type, a description of a set of operations that a collection should have. A heap is one possible efficient way of implementing those operations, but it is not the only way of doing so. The Java class libraries add to this confusion by naming their class `PriorityQueue` when it should probably be represented as an interface named `PriorityQueue` that is implemented by a class called `HeapPriorityQueue`, to match other pairs like `List/ArrayList` or `Set/TreeSet`.

The key operations for a priority queue are adding elements and finding/removing the minimum value. Let's explore how those operations can be implemented efficiently using a heap. Finding the minimum value (`peek`) is trivial since it is simply the data stored in the overall root element of the tree. So we'll focus on adding and removing values from a heap.

Removing from a Heap

Suppose we have the heap shown in Figure 18.13 and want to remove the minimum value, 10. We can't simply yank the node out of the tree because it leaves a hole at the tree's root that must be filled. When dealing with binary search trees with their left-to-right ordering, removal usually involves moving one of the removed element's children up to occupy its spot and rearranging the tree as necessary to ensure that the ordering is left intact. With a heap we employ a different algorithm that begins not with the removed element's children but with a leaf.

To remove the root of a heap, first we remove the rightmost leaf of the tree. Then we place this leaf's value into the tree at the root, replacing the previous root value. This is likely to place the tree in a temporarily invalid state, since the leaf is presumably one of the larger element values and therefore is not suitable as a new root. But we then repair this problem by pushing the invalid root down the tree by swapping it with its smallest child until it is in a legal location, a process called *bubbling* or *percolating* the element down the tree.

Bubble (Percolate)

Moving a heap element upward or downward until the heap's state satisfies the required vertical ordering.

The overall remove-min algorithm is described by the following pseudocode:

```
find and remove rightmost leaf node.
insert leaf's value into root node.
current node = root.
while (current node's value is not smaller than both children) {
    choose smaller of two children.
    swap current node's value with smaller child value.
    current node = smaller child node.
}
```

Figure 18.14 demonstrates the removal of the minimum value, `10`, from our previous heap. First the rightmost leaf, `65`, is inserted as the root. Then since `65` is not smaller than its children, it is swapped for its smaller child repeatedly until it is in proper order. The first swap is with `20`, because `20 < 80`. Then `65` is compared with

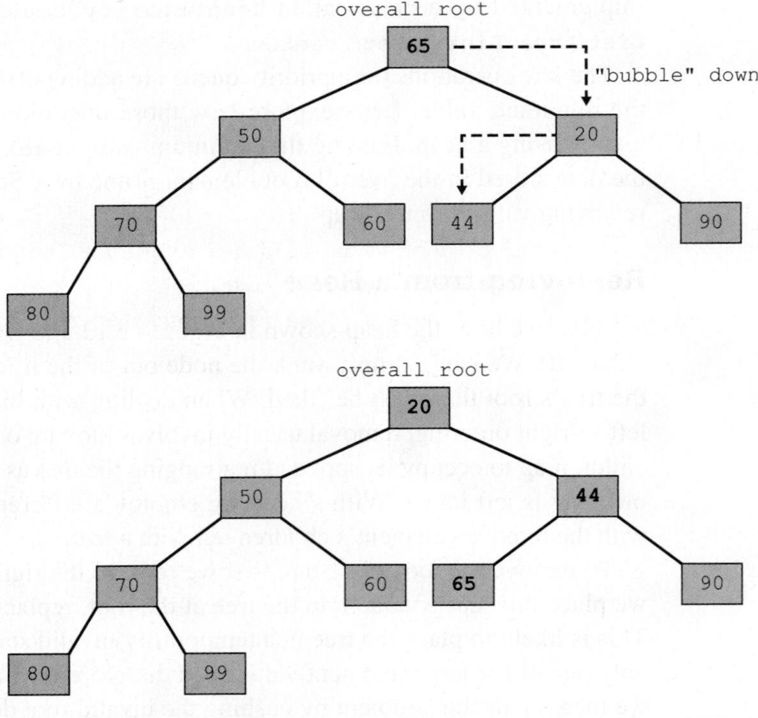

Figure 18.14 Removing from min-heap with bubble-down

its new children, 44 and 90. The 44 is smaller so the 65 is swapped there. Now the heap is back into proper order so the removal is complete.

The runtime of the remove-min operation is related to the number of swaps that occur as the new root is bubbled down to its proper location. Since our tree is a complete tree, it is as wide as possible for its height; the number of nodes in a tree of height H is roughly equal to 2^H. Thus, the height of a tree containing N elements is very close to $\log_2 N$. This means that the number of bubble-down swaps, and therefore the overall runtime of removing the minimum element from a heap, is $O(\log N)$.

Adding to a Heap

VideoNote

Adding a value to a heap is similar to removing the minimum element but in reverse. Suppose we have the heap shown in Figure 18.14 and want to add a new value, 37. The value needs to be placed properly to maintain the heap's overall ordering. The algorithm for adding an element to a heap begins at the bottom of the tree.

To add an element to a heap, we first insert it as a new rightmost leaf. (If the tree is completely full at its bottom level, the new value becomes the left child of the leftmost leaf, starting its own new level in the tree.) This is likely to place the tree in a temporarily invalid state, since the newly inserted leaf may not be larger than all of its parents and therefore not suitable to be placed there. We repair this problem by swapping the new value upward with its parents until it is in a suitable location, bubbling it upward much like we bubbled values downward upon a removal. The overall pseudocode for adding to a heap is the following:

```
insert new element value as a new rightmost leaf node.
current node = the new leaf node.
while (current node's value is not greater than its parent) {
    swap current node's value with parent's value.
    current node = parent node.
}
```

Figure 18.15 demonstrates adding the value `37` to our example heap from Figure 18.14. The value bubbles up twice, swapping with `60` and then with `50`, because those values are greater than `37`. It stops there because the next parent is `20`, which is smaller than `37` and should therefore remain higher in the tree.

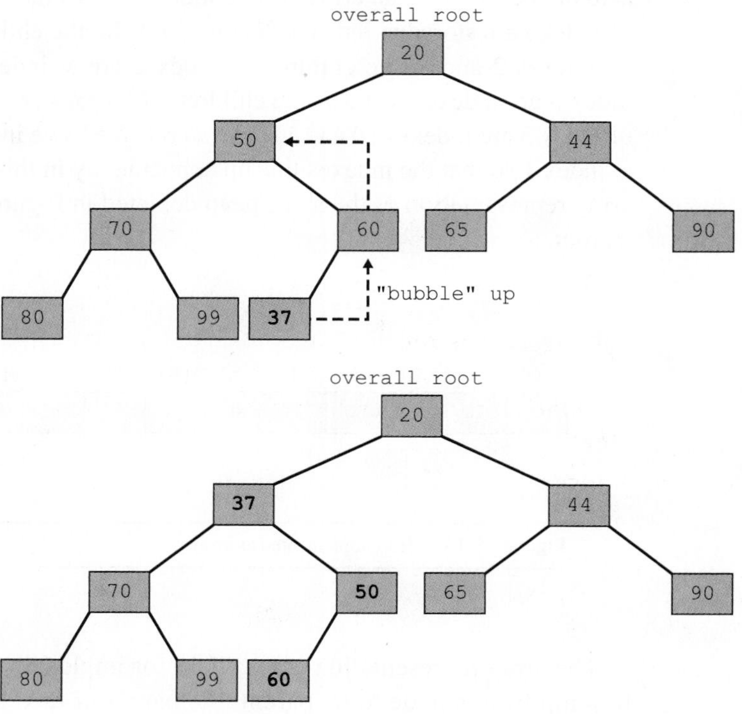

Figure 18.15 Adding to min-heap with bubble-up

The runtime complexity of adding to a heap is similar to that of removing the minimum element. In an ideal case, the newly added element will be larger than its parent and no upward bubbling will be required, which would yield a constant O(1) runtime. In the worst case, the newly added node is smaller than all of the values in the heap and must bubble all the way to the root. Since the height of a heap with *N* elements is almost exactly $\log_2 N$, the worst case for adding to the heap is O(log *N*). In general the newly added element must bubble itself some portion of the distance up the tree, so we say that the `add` operation has a O(log *N*) average runtime.

Array Heap Implementation

A heap can be implemented as a tree of linked node objects much like the binary trees implemented in the binary trees chapter. But a few of the operations we want to perform don't lend themselves well to the node implementation. For example, bubbling upward requires us to be able to reach a node's parent, and our tree implementation did not contain references from a node to its parent. Also, the add and remove operations both involve manipulating the rightmost leaf in the tree, which is not trivial to access in a tree implemented with nodes.

There is another clever implementation of heaps that provides great efficiency for the operations we want to implement. It turns out that any complete binary tree can actually be stored as an array, where index 1 stores the root element, and the children of index *i* are stored at indexes 2*i* and 2*i* + 1. So the children of index 1 (the root) are at indexes 2 and 3; the children of index 2 are at indexes 4 and 5; the children of index 3 are indexes 6 and 7; the children of index 4 are indexes 8 and 9; the children of index 5 are indexes 10 and 11; and so on. We leave index 0 blank and start our root at index 1 so that the indexes line up conveniently in this way. Figure 18.16 shows an array representation of the same heap depicted in Figure 18.13, with the value `10` as its root.

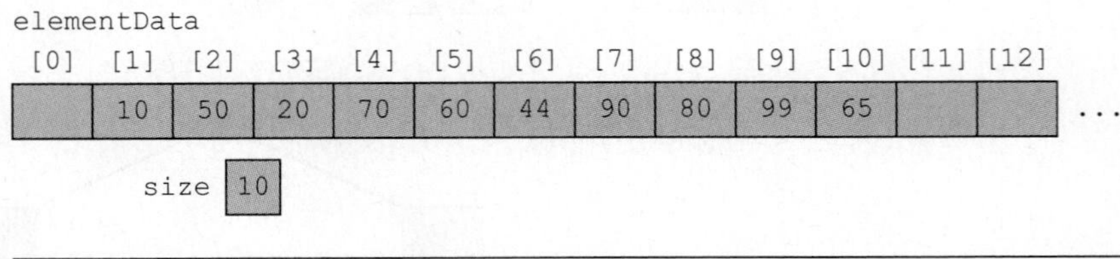

Figure 18.16 Heap implemented as array

The array representation is excellent for implementing a heap because it is easy to jump from a node to its parent; the parent of the element at index *i* is stored at index *i*/2. It is also trivial to find the rightmost child in the heap; the rightmost child is always located at index *size*, and any new rightmost child we want to insert should be inserted at index *size* + 1. For example, in the array heap shown in Figure 18.16, the rightmost leaf is `65`, stored in index 10, and a new leaf would be added at index 11.

Let's implement a skeletal version of a priority queue using a heap represented as an array.

```
public class HeapIntPriorityQueue {
    private int[] elementData;
    private int size;

    public HeapIntPriorityQueue() {
        elementData = new int[10];
        size = 0;
    }
    ...
```

To simplify the implementation of the add and remove operations, we'll introduce several short helper methods for navigating upward and downward in the tree from parents to children and vice versa, as well as a method to swap elements in the array, since swapping is used in bubbling.

```
// helpers for navigating indexes up/down the tree
private int parent(int index) {
    return index / 2;
}

private int leftChild(int index) {
    return index * 2;
}

private int rightChild(int index) {
    return index * 2 + 1;
}

private boolean hasParent(int index) {
    return index > 1;
}

private boolean hasLeftChild(int index) {
    return leftChild(index) <= size;
}

private boolean hasRightChild(int index) {
    return rightChild(index) <= size;
}
```

```
private void swap(int[] a, int index1, int index2) {
    int temp = a[index1];
    a[index1] = a[index2];
    a[index2] = temp;
}
```

First let's implement the add operation, since it is a bit simpler than removal. Figure 18.17 shows the adding of element value 37 to the heap. It bubbles upward as far as necessary until the value is not smaller than its parent value or until it reaches the root of the tree.

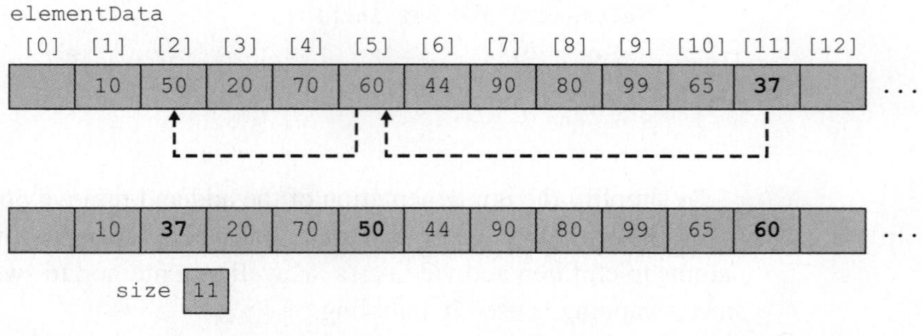

Figure 18.17 Array heap add operation

The following code implements the add operation on our min-heap. The code uses the helper methods defined previously such as parent and swap. Notice that the node is initially inserted at the end of the array (index *size* + 1) and then bubbled upward to parent indexes as long as the node's value is less than that of its parent.

```
// Adds the given element to this queue.
public void add(int value) {
    elementData[size + 1] = value; // add as rightmost leaf

    // "bubble up" as necessary to fix ordering
    int index = size + 1;
    boolean found = false;
    while (!found && hasParent(index)) {
        int parent = parent(index);
        if (elementData[index] < elementData[parent]) {
            swap(elementData, index, parent(index));
            index = parent(index);
        } else {
            found = true; // found proper location; stop the loop
        }
```

```
    }

    size++;
}
```

As with an array list or hash table, the array can run out of space. A proper `add` method should also check to make sure that the array has enough capacity to hold the element being added. The following code can be inserted at the start of the `add` method to handle this:

```
// resize if necessary
if (size + 1 >= elementData.length) {
    elementData = Arrays.copyOf(elementData, elementData.length * 2);
}
```

Now let's implement the remove-min operation. Figure 18.18 shows the removal of the root element value from the heap from Figure 18.17. The rightmost leaf, `60`, is moved to the root, then it is bubbled downward, swapping it with its smaller child as far as necessary until the value is not larger than either of its children (or until it is a leaf and has no children). In the example, `60` swaps with its right child, `20`, which is smaller than `37`; then it swaps with its left child, `44`, which is less than its right child, `90`.

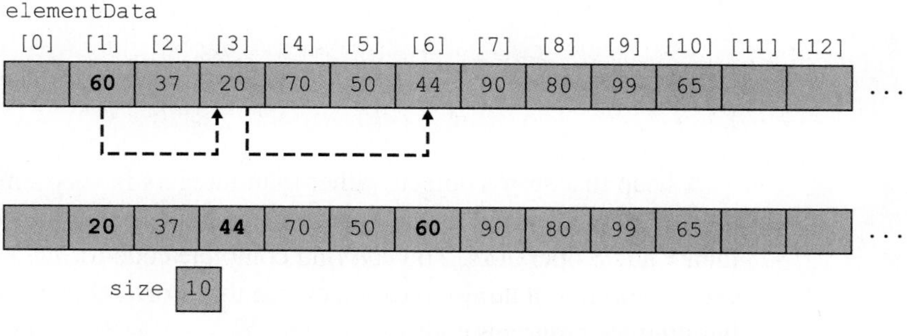

Figure 18.18 Array heap remove-min operation

The following code implements the remove-min operation on our min-heap. The code uses the helper methods defined previously, such as `leftChild` and `hasRightChild`. The code inside the loop initially chooses to swap with the left child, but if the right one is smaller than the left, the right one is chosen. The loop stops when the node has no children (when it becomes a leaf) or when it is not larger than its child and has therefore reached the correct position.

```
// Removes and returns the minimum value in the queue.
public int remove() {
    // move rightmost leaf to become new root
```

```
    int result = peek();
    elementData[1] = elementData[size];
    size--;

    // "bubble down" as necessary to fix ordering
    int index = 1;
    boolean found = false;
    while (!found && hasLeftChild(index)) {
        int left = leftChild(index);
        int right = rightChild(index);
        int child = left;
        if (hasRightChild(index) &&
                elementData[right] < elementData[left]) {
            child = right;
        }

        if (elementData[index] > elementData[child]) {
            swap(elementData, index, child);
            index = child;
        } else {
            found = true; // found proper location; stop the loop
        }
    }

    return result;
}
```

A heap that stores objects rather than integers is very similar to the code we have already shown, except that comparisons are made using the `compareTo` method rather than < and > operators. You can find complete code for the `HeapIntPriorityQueue` class, as well as a `HeapPriorityQueue` that stores objects, on our web page at http://buildingjavaprograms.com.

Heap Sort

In a previous chapter, we discussed details of several sorting algorithms, such as selection sort and merge sort. There is a simple algorithm for sorting called *heap sort* that takes advantage of the ordering of heaps to arrange data quickly. If you add all elements of an array to a priority queue and then remove them, they will come out in ascending (sorted) order. The heap sort algorithm can be described by the following pseudocode:

```
heapSort(A):
    H = create new heap.
```

```
for each element n in A:
    add n to H.
while (H not empty):
    remove element from H.
    add element back into A.
```

Here is a simple implementation of the heap sort for sorting an array of integers using a `PriorityQueue`:

```
public static void heapSort(int[] a) {
    Queue<Integer> pq = new PriorityQueue<Integer>();
    for (int n : a) {
        pq.add(n);
    }
    for (int i = 0; i < a.length; i++) {
        a[i] = pq.remove();
    }
}
```

When sorting an array of *N* elements, heap sort performs *N* add and *N* remove operations on a heap. Each add or remove has a O(log *N*) complexity, so the overall heap sort algorithm has O(*N* log *N*) complexity. Heap sort is a fairly efficient algorithm, certainly much faster than selection sort and with comparable performance to merge sort.

One drawback of the heap sort algorithm as shown is the memory required. To sort the array we must create another large data structure (the priority queue, and the array heap inside it) to temporarily store the data. For very large data sets this can be undesirable.

It is possible to implement heap sort "in-place" so that it uses the original array itself as the heap. The basic idea is to treat the array as an initially invalid heap and "repair" it into a proper heap by repeatedly bubbling elements into proper positions. Once the array represents a heap, performing `remove` operations repeatedly on the array and moving the removed elements to the end of the array end up fully sorting the array contents. The algorithm arranges the elements into ascending order if a max-heap is used and descending order if a min-heap such as our `HeapIntPriorityQueue` is used.

The in-place version of the heap sort algorithm would require a modified version of our `HeapIntPriorityQueue` implementation with a few tweaks. The details of implementing an in-place heap sort algorithm are outside the scope of this chapter, but a full implementation of the algorithm is posted on our web page at http://buildingjavaprograms.com.

Chapter Summary

Hashing is a technique for mapping between element values and integers representing array indexes at which to store those elements. Hashing allows for the implementation of sets and maps with extremely efficient O(1) runtime for adding, removing, and searching for elements.

A hash function is an algorithm that maps element values to array indexes. A common technique for integer data is to mod (`%`) the value by the array's length.

When multiple element values have the same hash function value, there is a collision. Collisions can be resolved by moving to another index (probing) or by storing a list of matched elements at each index (separate chaining).

Rehashing is the process of resizing a hash table, generally to enlarge it so that it can efficiently store more elements. The array cannot simply be enlarged; the elements must be readded because their hash function values may change in the new larger array.

Non-integer elements can be hashed by calling their `hashCode` method.

A priority queue allows elements to be inserted in any order and removed in ascending order.

A structure called a heap is often used to implement priority queues. A heap is a tree with a vertical ordering, where parents store smaller values than their children (min-heap) or larger values than their children (max-heap).

When adding a value to a heap, it is added as a leaf and then "bubbled" (swapped) up the tree until it is in a proper place in the vertical ordering. When removing a value from a heap, the heap's rightmost leaf is moved to the root and then "bubbled" down the tree until it is in a proper place in the vertical ordering.

Because of its complete structure, a heap can be implemented efficiently using an array, rather than as a linked tree of node objects.

Heaps can be used to help sort data, an algorithm called heap sort.

Self-Check Problems

Section 18.1: Hashing

1. What is hashing, and why is hashing a good way of implementing a set?
2. Which of the following statements about hash tables is true?
   a. A hash table has O(log *N*) average time to add and search for elements.
   b. The higher a hash table's load factor, the more quickly elements can be found.
   c. Once a hash table's load factor reaches 0.75, no more elements can be added.
   d. A hash function maps element values to integer indexes in the hash table.
   e. A good hash function returns the same value as much as possible for all data.
3. How do you know when a hash table has become "full"? At what point does it become impossible to add further elements to a hash table of a given size? Does it depend on the collision resolution strategy used?

4. The following statement is an incorrect attempt to resize a hash table to twice its current size. Why is this code incorrect? What is the proper way to enlarge a hash table?

```
elementData = Arrays.copyOf(elementData, 2 * elementData.length);
```

5. What is the final state of a hash table of size 10 after adding 35, 2, 15, 80, 42, 95, and 66? Assume that we are using the standard "mod" hash function shown in the chapter and linear probing for collision resolution. Do not perform any resizing or rehashing. Draw the entire array and the contents of each index.

6. If separate chaining is used for collision resolution, and the same elements from the previous problem (35, 2, 15, 80, 42, 95, and 66) are added to a hash table of size 10, what is the final state of the hash table? Do not perform any resizing or rehashing. Draw the entire array and the contents of each index.

7. Suppose we have a hash set that uses the standard "mod" hash function shown in the chapter and uses linear probing for collision resolution. The starting hash table length is 5, and the table chooses to rehash to twice its former size once the load factor reaches or exceeds 0.5. If we begin with an empty set, what will be the final state of the hash table after the following elements are added and removed? Draw the entire array and the contents of each index, including any resizing and rehashing necessary. Write "X" in any index in which an element is removed and not replaced by another element. Also write the size, capacity, and load factor of the final hash table.

```
HashIntSet set = new HashIntSet();
set.add(15);
set.add(5);
set.add(13);
set.add(24);
set.add(32);
set.remove(13);
set.add(17);
set.add(44);
set.remove(15);
set.add(47);
```

8. Suppose we have a hash set that uses the standard "mod" hash function shown in the chapter and uses linear probing for collision resolution. The starting hash table length is 11, and the table does not rehash during this problem. If we begin with an empty set, what will be the final state of the hash table after the following elements are added and removed? Draw the entire array and the contents of each index. Write "X" in any index in which an element is removed and not replaced by another element. Also write the size, capacity, and load factor of the final hash table.

```
set.add(4);
set.add(52);
set.add(50);
set.add(39);
set.add(29);
set.remove(4);
set.remove(52);
set.add(70);
set.add(82);
set.add(15);
set.add(18);
```

9. For each of the following possible `hashCode` implementations: Is the following a legal `hashCode` method for a `Point` class, according to the general contract of that method? Does it distribute the hash codes well between objects? Why or why not?

   a.
   ```
   public int hashCode() {
       return x * y;
   }
   ```
   b.
   ```
   public int hashCode() {
       return 42;
   }
   ```
   c.
   ```
   public int hashCode() {
       Random rand = new Random();
       return rand.nextInt();
   }
   ```

10. Write a `hashCode` method for a `Date` class, whose fields are a year, month, and day, as integers. Follow the general contract for the `hashCode` method.

11. Write a `hashCode` method for a `Student` class, whose fields are a name (a string), age (an integer), student ID number (an integer), and weight in pounds (a real number). Follow the general contract for the `hashCode` method.

12. Suppose we have a hash map that uses the standard "mod" hash function shown in the chapter and uses linear probing for collision resolution. The starting hash table length is 5, and the table chooses to rehash to twice its former size once the load factor reaches or exceeds 0.5. If we begin with an empty map, what will be the final state of the hash table after the following key/value pairs are added and removed? Draw the entire array and the contents of each index, including any resizing and rehashing necessary. Write "X" in any index in which an element is removed and not replaced by another element. Also write the size, capacity, and load factor of the final hash table.

```
HashMap<Integer, String> map = new HashMap<Integer, String>();
map.put(7, "Jessica");
map.put(34, "Tyler");
map.put(17, "Ryan");
map.put(15, "Tina");
map.put(84, "Saptarshi");
map.remove("Tyler");
map.put(7, "Meghan");
map.put(33, "Kona");
map.remove(17);
map.put(6, "Tina");
map.remove(84);
map.put(15, "Daisy");
```

Section 18.2: Priority Queues and Heaps

13. Which of the following statements about min-heaps is true?

   a. Smaller values are on the left and larger values are on the right.
   b. The smallest value is the root.
   c. The smallest value is one of the leaves.

d. Every value is smaller than all values at lower levels of the tree. For example, if there is a 25 at level 3, there will not be any elements with values less than 25 at levels 4 and beyond.

e. The `peek` operation returns the largest value in the heap.

14. If a binary heap has 26 nodes, what is its height? If it has 73 nodes, what is the height? How do you know for sure?

15. Which of the following are valid min-heaps? For the one(s) that are invalid, what makes them invalid?

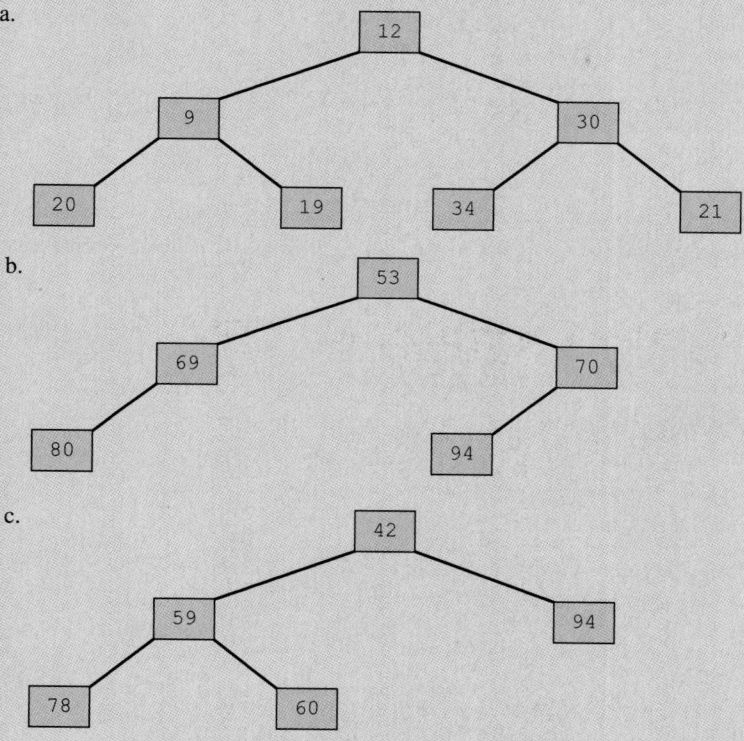

16. In an array heap as implemented in this section, for the element at index 8 of the array, what are the indexes of its left and right children? What is the index of its parent? If the element is at index 23, what are the indexes of its children and parent?

17. Simulate the adding of the value `21` to the following min-heap:

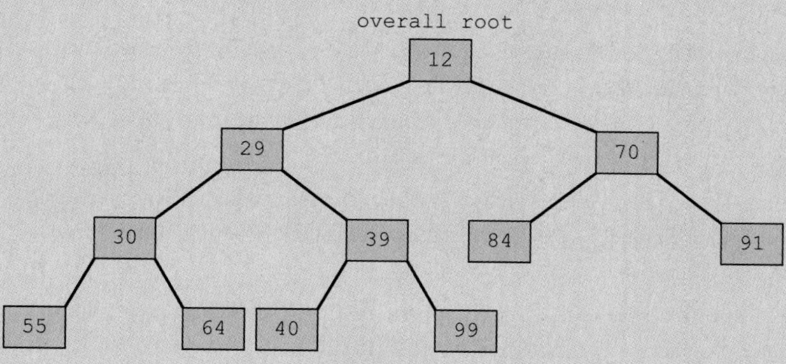

18. Simulate the adding of value `7` to the same heap from the previous problem, after the `21` has already been added.

19. Draw the tree for the binary min-heap that results from inserting 4, 9, 3, 7, 2, 5, 8, 6 in that order into an initially empty heap.

20. Perform 3 removals on the heap you drew in the previous problem. Show the complete state of the tree after each removal.

21. Draw the tree for the binary min-heap that results from inserting 11, 9, 12, 14, 3, 15, 7, 8, 1 in that order into an initially empty heap.

22. Perform 3 removals on the heap you drew in the previous problem. Show the complete state of the tree after each removal.

23. The following is an incorrect diagram of the array representations of the heap shown in Self-Check Problem 17 using the array representation described in this section of the chapter (before any adds or removals are made from it). What is wrong with the diagram? What changes must be made to fix it so that it accurately represents the given heap?

[0]	[1]	[2]	[3]	[4]	[5]	[6]	[7]	[8]	[9]	[10]	[11]	[12]	
12	29	30	39	40	55	64	70	84	91	99			...

24. Draw the min-heap being represented by the given array:

[0]	[1]	[2]	[3]	[4]	[5]	[6]	[7]	[8]	[9]
	29	41	30	55	68	37	41	80	

25. Draw the array representation of the heap you computed as your answer to Self-Check Problem 19 (after all of the elements are added to it).

26. Draw the array representation of the heap you computed as your answer to Self-Check Problem 21 (after all of the elements are added to it).

Exercises

1. Write a method in the `HashIntSet` class called `addAll` that accepts another hash set as a parameter and adds all of the elements from the other set into the current set. For example, if the set stores `[−5, 1, 2, 3]` and the method is passed `[2, 3, 6, 44, 79]`, your set would store `[−5, 1, 2, 3, 6, 44, 79]`.

2. Write a method in the `HashIntSet` class called `containsAll` that accepts another hash set as a parameter and returns `true` if your set contains every element from the other set. For example, if the set stores `[−2, 3, 5, 6, 8]` and the method is passed `[3, 6, 8]`, your method would return `true`. If the method were passed `[3, 6, 7, 8]`, your method would return `false` because your set does not contain the value `7`.

3. Write a method in the `HashIntSet` class called `equals` that accepts another hash set as a parameter and returns `true` if the two sets contain exactly the same elements. The internal hash table size and ordering of the elements does not matter, only the sets of elements themselves.

4. Write a method in the `HashIntSet` class called `removeAll` that accepts another hash set as a parameter and ensures that this set does not contain any of the elements from the other set. For example, if the set stores `[−2, 3, 5, 6, 8]` and the method is passed `[2, 3, 6, 8, 11]`, your set would store `[−2, 5]`.

5. Write a method in the `HashIntSet` class called `retainAll` that accepts another hash set as a parameter and removes all elements from this set that are not contained in the other set. For example, if the set stores `[−2, 3, 5, 6, 8]` and the method is passed `[2, 3, 6, 8, 11]`, your set would store `[3, 6, 8]`.

6. Write a method in the `HashIntSet` class called `toArray` that returns the elements of the set as a filled array. The order of the elements in the array is not important as long as all elements from the set are present in the array, with no extra empty slots before or afterward.

7. Write a method in the `HashIntSet` class called `toString` that returns a string representation of the elements in the set, such as `"[−2, 3, 5, 6, 8]"`. The order of the elements in the string does not matter as long as they are all present in the proper format. Do not list any empty or meaningless indexes in the string.

8. Write a method called `descending` that accepts an array of integers and rearranges the integers in the array to be in descending order using a `PriorityQueue` as a helper. For example, if the array passed stores `[42, 9, 22, 17, −3, 81]`, after the call the array should store `[81, 42, 22, 17, 9, −3]`.

9. Write a method called `kthSmallest` that accepts a `PriorityQueue` of integers and an integer *k* as parameters and returns the *k*th-smallest integer from the priority queue. For example, if the queue passed stores the integers `[42, 50, 45, 78, 61]` and *k* is 4, return the fourth-smallest integer, which is `61`. If *k* is 0 or negative or greater than the size of the queue, throw an `IllegalArgumentException`. If your method modifies the state of the queue during its computation, it should restore the queue before it returns. You may use one stack or queue as auxiliary storage.

10. Write a method called `isConsecutive` that accepts a `PriorityQueue` of integers as a parameter and returns `true` if the queue contains a sequence of consecutive integers starting from the front of the queue. Consecutive integers are integers that come one after the other, as in 5, 6, 7, 8, 9, etc., so if the queue stores `[7, 8, 9, 10, 11]`, your method should return `true`. If your method modifies the state of the queue during its computation, it should restore the queue before it returns. You may use one stack or queue as auxiliary storage.

11. Write a method called `removeDuplicates` that accepts a `PriorityQueue` of integers as a parameter and modifies the queue's state so that any element that is equal to another element in the queue is removed. For example, if the queue stores `[7, 7, 8, 8, 8, 10, 45, 45]`, your method should modify the queue to store `[7, 8, 10, 45]`. You may use one stack or queue as auxiliary storage.

12. Write a method called `stutter` that accepts a `PriorityQueue` of integers as a parameter and replaces every value in the queue with two occurrences of that value. For example, if the queue stores `[7, 8, 10, 45]`, your method should modify the queue to store `[7, 7, 8, 8, 10, 10, 45, 45]`. You may use one stack or queue as auxiliary storage.

13. Write a method in the `HeapIntPriorityQueue` class called `toArray` that returns the elements of the queue as a filled array. The order of the elements in the array is not important as long as all elements from the queue are present in the array, with no extra empty slots before or afterward.

14. Write a method in the `HeapIntPriorityQueue` class called `toString` that returns a string representation of the elements in the queue, such as `"[42, 50, 45, 78, 61]"`. The order of the elements in the string does not matter as long as they are all present in the proper format.

15. Write a method in the `HeapIntPriorityQueue` class called `merge` that accepts another `HeapIntPriorityQueue` as a parameter and adds all elements from the other queue into the current queue, maintaining proper heap order such that the elements will still come out in ascending order when they are removed. Your code should not modify the queue passed in as a parameter. (Recall that objects of the same class can access each other's private fields.)

Programming Projects

1. Add an iterator to the `HashSet` class written in this chapter. To do this you will need to write an inner class that can iterate over the elements of the set, remembering its position as it moves along. Also write a method in the `HashSet` class called `iterator` that returns such an iterator object.
2. In this chapter, we implemented a `HashSet` that used separate chaining to resolve collisions. Implement your own version of `HashSet` that uses linear probing to resolve collisions. Perform lazy removals, placing a special "removed" marker value into any bucket where an element is removed.
3. Modify the `HeapIntPriorityQueue` class written in this chapter to make it configurable in ways similar to Java's `PriorityQueue` class. Make it possible for the heap to be a min-heap or max-heap. (If you create a heap of objects, you could also modify it to accept a `Comparator` parameter to its constructor.)
4. Modify the `HeapIntPriorityQueue` class written in this chapter to make it into a three-heap. A three-heap is similar to a binary heap, except that each node is considered to have three children rather than two children. A three-heap is a wider tree though not as tall as a binary heap. The heap can still be represented as an array, but the algorithms for traversing it must be modified to consider all three children when bubbling as appropriate, etc. (Do you expect that a three-heap will be faster or slower than a binary heap for insertion, and for removal? Why? You can create a test to verify the performance of each operation.)
5. Write a program that implements the "Huffman coding" compression algorithm using priority queues and binary trees. Huffman coding is an algorithm devised by David A. Huffman of MIT in 1952 for compressing text data to make a file occupy a smaller number of bytes. Normally text data is stored in a standard format of 8 bits per character, commonly using an encoding called ASCII that maps every character to a binary integer value from 0–255. The idea of Huffman coding is to abandon the rigid 8-bits-per-character requirement and use different-length binary encodings for different characters. The advantage of doing this is that if a character occurs frequently in the file, such as the letter "e", it could be given a shorter encoding (fewer bits), making the file smaller.

   The steps involved in Huffman coding a given text source file into a destination compressed file are the following:

   a. Examine the source file's contents and count the number of occurrences of each character (consider using a map).
   b. Place each character and its frequency (count of occurrences) into a priority queue ordered in ascending order by character frequency.
   c. Convert the contents of this priority queue into a binary tree with a particular structure. Create this tree by repeatedly removing the two front elements from the priority queue (the two nodes with the lowest frequencies) and combining them into a new node with these two nodes as its children and the two nodes' combined frequencies as its frequency. Then reinsert this combined node back into the priority queue. Repeat until the priority queue contains just one single node.
   d. Traverse the tree to discover the binary encodings of each character. Each left branch represents a '0' in the character's encoding and each right branch represents a "1".
   e. Reexamine the source file's contents, and for each character, output the encoded binary version of that character to the destination file to compress it.

Chapter 19

Functional Programming with Java 8

Introduction

Every 10 to 15 years the computer science education community updates the suggested curriculum for computer science majors. In the most recent curriculum revision in 2013, the ACM/IEEE joint task force updated the suggestions for coverage of programming languages. As they explained in their introduction to that section:

> Software developers must understand the programming models underlying different languages and make informed design choices in languages supporting multiple complementary approaches. Computer scientists will often need to learn new languages and programming constructs, and must understand the principles underlying how programming language features are defined, composed, and implemented.

They went on to describe specific concepts from various programming paradigms that should be studied by every undergraduate computer science major. Two of the paradigms that they emphasize are the procedural and object-oriented paradigms that have been discussed thoroughly in this book. Java is a hybrid language that supports both approaches. We began the book by studying procedural programming with static methods that we used to decompose a large program into action-oriented components. Then starting in Chapter 8 we moved on to the object-oriented approach in which a large program is decomposed into a set of interacting objects each with their own class defining their state and behavior.

In this chapter, we will explore a third approach to programming that is known as *functional programming*. Java uses the term "method" for what many other languages call a "function," so in the discussion that follows, you can mentally substitute "method" for "function."

Functional Programming

A style of programming that emphasizes the use of functions (methods) to decompose a complex task into subtasks.

The Java community has spent years discussing how best to add functional features to the language, culminating with the release of Java 8 in 2014. The new features added to the language in this release allow Java programmers to take advantage of this different approach to programming. The new curriculum guidelines list five specific topics that undergraduates should study related to functional programming:

1. Effect-free programming
2. Processing structured data via functions
3. First-class functions
4. Function closures
5. Higher-order operations on collections

The first three are categorized as Core Tier-1 and items 4 and 5 are categorized as Core Tier-2. As the guidelines explain, "computer-science curricula should cover all the Core Tier-1 topics" and "all or almost all of the Core Tier-2 topics." Each of these concepts has its own section in this chapter, except for Item 2 which does not translate easily to Java. In addition, this chapter includes a separate section that discusses the central Java 8 concept of streams because much of the functional programming support is provided using that mechanism. This chapter ends with a short case study that picks up an additional Core Tier-1 concept of using concurrency to speed the execution of a complex computation. As we will see, the functional programming approach is particularly well suited to safe and reliable concurrency, which is becoming increasingly important in modern computing where the average PC now comes with multiple processors (sometimes described as "multi-core processing"). The terminology can sometimes be intimidating, but as we will see, these concepts are fairly straightforward to discuss using Java 8 constructs.

19.1 Effect-Free Programming

Consider the following line of code:

```
int result = f(x) + f(x);
```

This code computes a result by calling a function (a method) two different times and adding together the results. Offhand it seems that we would get the exact same behavior with this line of code:

```
int result = 2 * f(x);
```

Sometimes the two are equivalent and sometimes not. The question to consider is whether the function produces a *side effect.*

Side Effect

A change to the state of an object or program variable produced by a call on a function (i.e., a method).

As an example, consider the following program:

```
1  // This program demonstrates a method with a side effect.
2  // Each time f is called, the variable x's value changes.
3
4  public class SideEffect {
5      public static int x;
6
7      public static int f(int n) {
8          x = x * 2;
9          return x + n;
10     }
11
12     public static void main(String[] args) {
13         x = 5;
14         int result = f(x) + f(x);
15         System.out.println(result);
16     }
17 }
```

This confusing program begins with the declaration of a static variable called `x` that has the entire class as its scope. Such variables are called *global variables.* We have discouraged the use of global variables because they can lead to the kind of confusing code we have here.

The program begins by initializing the global variable `x` to the value 5. Then on line 14 the program calls the function `f` twice, passing it the value of `x` each time. But `f` doubles the value of `x` before returning the sum of the value passed as a parameter and `x`. If you find this all highly confusing, you're not alone. This style of programming is very bad.

On the first call to `f`, the variable `x` has the value 5. This is passed from `main` as the parameter called `n`. Inside function `f`, we first double `x`, which gives it the value 10. It then returns the sum of `x`, which is now 10, and `n`, which is 5. So it returns 15 for the first call. On the second call, it passes the current value of x, which is 10, to the function and uses this to initialize n to be 10. Then it doubles x from 10 to 20 and returns the sum of x and n, which are 20 and 10. So it returns the value 30 on the second call. The variable result is set to the sum of these two returns values, which is 15 plus 30, or 45.

What happens if we substitute our other line of code for setting result?

```
int result = 2 * f(x);
```

The first call on the function behaves as it did before, returning the value 15. We double that to 30 and set result to 30. So we end up with a program that has different behavior because the function f has a side effect.

Because functional programming focuses so much on individual functions, the community of programmers who use functional programming regularly have concluded that side effects should be avoided when possible, leading to the kind of "effect free" functions that serve as the title of this section.

The object-oriented community has been less wary of functions with side effects. A central idea of OOP is that objects have state that changes as methods are called. Recall from Chapter 8 that instance methods are classified as *accessors* that can be thought of as read-only operations accessing the object's state and *mutators* that can be thought of as read/write operations that often change the state of the object. Using the terminology from functional programming, we would say that accessors are usually effect-free functions while mutators are functions with a side effect. Even accessors can have side effects because they might change the state of other objects.

One of the simplest and most pervasive sources of side effects we have seen is the printing of values. Continuing our example of a function f that might be called once or twice, if the function includes a call on System.out.println, then it will produce more output when called twice than when it is called once. So even though the variable result in our example might be set to the same value, there is still a possible side effect caused by the function if it produces output.

As we will see in the case study at the end of this chapter, there are great advantages to writing code that is free of side effects. It is easier to take advantage of concurrency using such code and it is easier to prove formal properties of programs that are written using the effect-free approach.

Did You Know?

Functional Programming Influences on Java

One of the most successful functional programming languages is the Scheme language developed at MIT in the 1970s by Guy Steele and Gerry Sussman. Jim Gosling who designed the Java programming language was well aware of Scheme and it is clear that many of the ideas from Scheme influenced the design of Java.

Continued on next page

Continued from previous page

As mentioned in Chapter 3, objects of the `String` class are immutable, which means that all of their methods are free of side effects. This has greatly simplified the use of `String` objects. Consider, for example, a class with a field called name of type `String` and an accessor method for examining the value of that field:

```
public String getName() {
    return name;
}
```

In Java, you don't have to worry about the possibility that a client of this class might alter your string object. In other programming languages, you might make a defensive copy to give to the client to avoid any possible interference.

The idea of effect-free programming is also evident in the `Collections` class that has methods for constructing an "unmodifiable" version of a collection, such as `Collections.unmodifiableList`.

Another example of the influence of Scheme can be found in Java's concept of interning of strings (read the description of the method `String.intern` if you are curious). It is also worth noting that Guy Steele, the co-designer of Scheme, was hired by Sun Microsystems in 1994 to work on the Java team.

19.2 First-Class Functions

When you study any particular programming language, you will soon learn what the basic elements of the language are. For example, almost every programming language allows you to manipulate numbers as basic elements. You can store a number in a variable, you can pass a number as a parameter, you have various operations for manipulating numbers, and you can return a number from a method call. Strings are also basic elements of Java because they are easy to declare, store, and pass as parameters.

Not every data type is a first-class citizen of every language. For example, not every programming language allows you to manipulate Boolean values as basic elements the way Java does. For decades the C programming language did not have a proper type for storing Boolean values and programmers instead used the integer values 1 and 0 to represent true and false. Some languages consider collections like lists and maps to be first-class citizens, providing special syntax for declaring and manipulating them; in Java, arrays receive first-class treatment and special syntax, but the collection objects do not.

First-Class Citizen

An element of a programming language that is tightly integrated with the language and supports the full range of operations generally available to other entities in the language.

What would it mean to provide first-class status for functions? Let's begin with an example that points out the motivation. Consider the task of performing drill and practice with a user where you make up addition problems involving two numbers between 1 and 12 and you keep track of how many answers the user got right. Below is a typical interaction.

```
10 + 6 = 16
you got it right
9 + 6 = 15
you got it right
3 + 7 = 9
incorrect...the answer was 10
12 + 10 = 22
you got it right
9 + 12 = 20
incorrect...the answer was 21
3 of 5 correct
```

Suppose that the above quiz is represented as a method called `giveProblems` that is passed a `Scanner` that reads from the console and a number of problems to provide to the user, as in:

```
Scanner console = new Scanner(System.in);
giveProblems(console, 5);
```

This is a straightforward task to solve building on material from Chapters 1 through 5.

```
public static void giveProblems(Scanner console, int numProblems) {
    Random r = new Random();
    int numRight = 0;
    for (int i = 1; i <= numProblems; i++) {
        int x = r.nextInt(12) + 1;
        int y = r.nextInt(12) + 1;
        System.out.print(x + " + " + y + " = ");
        int answer = x + y;
        int response = console.nextInt();
```

```
            if (response == answer) {
                System.out.println("you got it right");
                numRight++;
            } else {
                System.out.println("incorrect...the answer was " + answer);
            }
        }
        System.out.println(numRight + " of " + numProblems + " correct");
    }
```

We now have a method that allows us to have a user practice addition problems. What if we wanted to also practice multiplication problems? Most of the code stays the same, but we would have to change the addition in these two lines of code:

```
System.out.print(x + " + " + y + " = ");
int answer = x + y;
```

to be multiplication:

```
System.out.print(x + " * " + y + " = ");
int answer = x * y;
```

In a sense, we want to replace the plus with an asterisk in both of these lines of code. If we want the code to work for both addition and multiplication, the first line of code is easier to generalize. The only part that needs to change is the text to be printed, and we have the ability to manipulate text as a basic element of Java using a `String`. We can change the method header to take a third parameter specifying the text to print:

```
public static void giveProblems(Scanner console, int numProblems,
                                String text) {
    ...
    System.out.print(x + " " + text + " " + y + " = ");
    ...
}
```

We can then make two calls on the method to have it use a plus the first time and an asterisk the second time:

```
giveProblems(console, 5, "+");
giveProblems(console, 5, "*");
```

So far so good. But now we run into the problem that the method is computing the right answer as the sum of the two numbers, even if an asterisk is passed as the text. That will make for a very frustrating experience on the second call where the console indicates to the user that the problem is a multiplication problem.

The question is how to change the computation of the right answer. It would be great if we could say:

```
int answer = x text y;
```

If Java somehow filled in "+" or "*" appropriately and then used the corresponding operator for the computation, then it would work. But Java doesn't work this way. The way that we usually get around this in Java is by introducing an `if/else` structure that tests whether the string is a plus or an asterisk. But then the code works for only those two operators, and additional branches must be added to the code later to make it support subtraction and other operations.

What we really want is the ability to pass an additional parameter that specifies the calculation to perform. We want to say, "Use the addition operation the first time and the multiplication operation the second time." A functional programmer would say that what we want to be able to do is to pass in a function. This is an example of what we mean by elevating functions to first class status in the language. We want to be able to introduce a fourth parameter that specifies the function to use for computing the right answer. That requires thinking of the function as a thing in the language that can be passed as a parameter.

Lambda Expressions

Java 8 provides a nice mechanism for doing exactly that. We can form a *lambda expression.*

Lambda Expression (Lambda)

An expression that describes a function by specifying its parameters and the value that it returns.

The term "lambda" was coined by a logician named Alonzo Church in the 1930s. The term is used consistently across many programming languages, so it is worth becoming familiar with it. The Python programming language, for example, uses "lambda" as a keyword for forming this type of anonymous function.

Lambda expressions are formed in Java by specifying the parameters of the function and an expression that represents the value to return separated by the special operator "->".

```
<parameters> -> <expression>
```

For example, we can use the following lambda expression to represent a function that adds together two arguments:

```
(int x, int y) -> x + y
```

Notice that the parameters are enclosed in parentheses. In reading this expression, we typically describe it as, "Given the parameters x and y of type int, we return x + y."

We can also write this as a method with a name, as in:

```
public static int sum(int x, int y) {
    return x + y;
}
```

Notice how the lambda expression takes the parenthesized parameter list from the method header and the expression used in the return statement to form a simple expression. Once you get used to reading lambda expressions, you will find that it is a concise way to read and reason about the underlying computation being performed.

It is also often possible to eliminate the types for the parameters because they can usually be inferred by the surrounding context. For our sample code, we will be able to use this lambda expression to describe addition:

```
(x, y) -> x + y
```

And this expression to describe multiplication:

```
(x, y) -> x * y
```

Given this new option, we can rewrite our client code as follows to perform 3 each of addition and multiplication problems.

```
Scanner console = new Scanner(System.in);
giveProblems(console, 3, "+", (x, y) -> x + y);
giveProblems(console, 3, "*", (x, y) -> x * y);
```

Below is a sample log of execution.

```
9 + 1 = 10
you got it right
4 + 4 = 8
you got it right
6 + 2 = 9
incorrect...the answer was 8
2 of 3 correct

10 * 11 = 110
you got it right
9 * 6 = 64
incorrect...the answer was 54
5 * 7 = 45
incorrect...the answer was 35
1 of 3 correct
```

This ability to pass a lambda expression as a parameter points out the benefit of treating functions as first-class elements of the language. Just as we can provide a different number of problems to perform or a different text to use for displaying the problems, we can also provide a different function for computing the right answer. This is a much more flexible approach than having to write tedious `if/else` constructs that say exactly what to do for each different possibility. Instead we provide a simple definition of the function we want to use and the function is stored in a parameter of the method.

It is more important that you learn how to become a client of these functional programming features of Java than to learn how to implement them yourself. But for those who are interested in seeing the implementation, the following is the revised method code:

```
public static void giveProblems(Scanner console, int numProblems,
                                String text, IntBinaryOperator operator) {
    Random r = new Random();
    int numRight = 0;
    for (int i = 1; i <= numProblems; i++) {
        int x = r.nextInt(12) + 1;
        int y = r.nextInt(12) + 1;
        System.out.print(x + " " + text + " " + y + " = ");
        int answer = operator.applyAsInt(x, y);
        int response = console.nextInt();
        if (response == answer) {
            System.out.println("you got it right");
            numRight++;
        } else {
            System.out.println("incorrect...the answer was " + answer);
        }
    }
    System.out.println(numRight + " of " + numProblems + " correct");
    System.out.println();
}
```

There are other variations on lambda expression syntax. For example, if a lambda expression accepts only a single parameter, the parentheses around it are not required. The following is a lambda expression that accepts an integer and returns that integer plus 1:

```
n -> n + 1
```

Another syntax variation is that if the computation is not a simple expression, you can include multiple statements enclosed in curly braces, such as:

```
x -> { int z = x * x; System.out.println(z); return z; }
```

Our discussion of first-class functions is a little generous to Java because it turns out that functions in Java 8 are not truly first-class. The language designers have done some fancy work behind the scenes to make it feel like Java has first-class functions, but they aren't really first-class because you can't do basic things like storing them directly in a variable. Instead Java takes advantage of interfaces that have a single abstract method in them (known as *functional interfaces*) and constructs an object for you that implements the interface's method using the elements of the lambda expression. As a result, Java's implementation of functional programming is more clunky and restrictive than in a true functional programming language. But for our purposes, the lambda expressions and functional interfaces act enough like first-class functions that we can explore the concept, even though it is a bit of an illusion.

19.3 Streams

You don't truly appreciate the benefits of functional programming in Java until you explore streams, which are the primary mechanism that Java provides for this style of programming. We have seen this concept before when we studied files in Chapter 6. We saw input streams that are a source of data and output streams that are a destination for results. The streams in this chapter are a generalization of that idea. Oracle describes a Java stream as a sequence of elements of data on which various functional programming operations can be performed.

> **Stream**
>
> A sequence of elements from a data source that supports aggregate operations.

Basic Idea

The best way to think about a stream is to visualize it as a flow of data from a source to a terminator with possible modifiers in between, as shown in Figure 19.1.

There is always one source and one terminator, but there can be any number of modifiers (including none) in between. As the diagram indicates, think of each modifier as transforming the stream in some way. One sequence of values flows in and a different sequence of values flows out. This way, we solve a complex programming task by identifying the source of the data to process, the final result we want to compute, and a series of transformations in between that move us closer to completing the task. Each of the modifiers will be specified by a function, which means that we

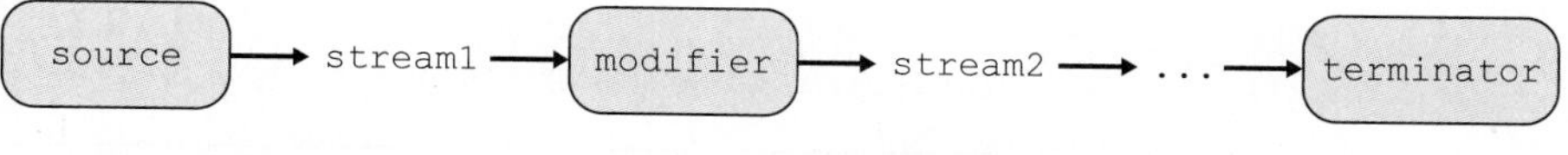

Figure 19.1 Streams

are decomposing the overall task into a series of subtasks that each involve a single transformation specified by a function.

As a first example, suppose we want to find the sum of the squares of the integers 1 through 5. We could use a classic cumulative sum to accomplish this:

```
// compute the sum of the squares of integers 1-5
int sum = 0;
for (int i = 1; i <= 5; i++) {
    sum = sum + i * i;
}
```

This code specifies exactly how to perform this computation, using a loop variable called `i` that varies from 1 to 5 and accumulating the final answer in a variable called `sum`. You will see that when we use streams, we describe more *what* we want computed instead of specifying *how* to compute it. This can make the coding itself simpler, but more importantly, it gives the computer more flexibility to decide how to implement the computation. As we will see in the case study at the end of this chapter, this can allow the computer to optimize the solution to run faster.

Using a stream approach, we first have to identify a source of data. We don't have a convenient source for the squares of the positive integers, but there is a static method called `IntStream.range` that produces a stream of sequential integers in a particular range. As with the `substring` method of the `String` class, the `range` method has a first parameter that is inclusive and a second parameter that is exclusive. So we will make the call `IntStream.range(1, 6)` to produce a stream with the integers [1, 2, 3, 4, 5]. There is a variation of the method called `rangeClosed` that would allow us to pass `(1, 5)` as parameters, but the `range` method uses the same convention we have studied in Java for substrings and it is also more commonly used in other programming languages. Python, for example, has a `range` function that works the same way.

We also need to pick an appropriate terminator. In this case Java provides one for us in the form of a method called `sum` that adds up the values in a stream of numbers. For now, let's just add up the integers and store the result in a variable. So we would write this line of code:

```
int sum = IntStream.range(1, 6).sum();
```

This sets the variable `sum` to 15 (1 + 2 + 3 + 4 + 5). In this case, we have the required source of data and the required terminator, but there are no modifications along the way. Figure 19.2 shows a diagram of what is going on.

```
IntStream.range(1, 6) -> [1, 2, 3, 4, 5] -> sum -> 15
```

Figure 19.2 Stream operations on range of integers

In our computation, the initial call to `IntStream.range` is the source, and `sum` is the terminator. The call on `range` produces a stream of five integers. This stream is fed into the `sum` method, which adds them up to produce the final result of 15. But recall that we want the sum of the first five squares, not the first five integers. We can accomplish that by introducing a modifier in between the range creation and the sum operation.

Using Map

Stream objects have a method called `map` that takes a function as a parameter. We can provide a function that squares a number. What `map` does is to produce a new stream that has the result of applying the given function to each element of the original stream. So if the original stream had five numbers, then the new stream will also have five numbers, but they will be new numbers obtained by calling the function passed as a parameter on each of the five elements in the stream. So our line of code becomes:

```
int sum = IntStream.range(1, 6).map(n -> n * n).sum();
```

There is a convention popular among Java programmers to list each step of this operation on a different line of code. The first line of code should have the source and the final line should have the terminator and any modifications should be listed as separate lines in between. So the code above becomes:

```
int sum = IntStream.range(1, 6)
    .map(n -> n * n)
    .sum();
```

This is just a formatting convention to make it easier to read the code. We would read this in a high-level way as, "To assign the variable `sum`, first form the given range of integers, then map the given function over those integers, and then find their sum." We can update our diagram as shown in Figure 19.3, again using the convention of including one step on each line.

As the diagram indicates, it is useful to think in terms of a flow of data. First the call on `range` produces the sequence [1, 2, 3, 4, 5]. This is then passed through the `map` modifier that changes the stream by applying the squaring function to each value, generating the new stream [1, 4, 9, 16, 25]. This new stream is then sent into the `sum` terminator that adds them up to produce the value 55.

```
IntStream.range -> [1, 2, 3, 4, 5]
        -> map -> [1, 4, 9, 16, 25]
        -> sum -> 55
```

Figure 19.3 Stream operations with `map`

This example has the classic structure of one source of data, one modification, and one terminator that computes a result. It is useful to keep in mind these three basic elements of a typical stream computation. But you can have more than one modification along the way, so let's look at an example that has many.

Using Filter

Suppose that instead of using sequential integers, we decide to work with the first 10 digits of *pi*. We can form a specific stream of integers by calling the method `IntStream.of` and listing the individual values, so let's use the same code as before but using those 10 digits:

```
int sum = IntStream.of(3, 1, 4, 1, 5, 9, 2, 6, 5, 3)
    .map(n -> n * n)
    .sum();
```

This sets `sum` to be 207, as indicated in Figure 19.4.

But suppose that we don't want to add up the squares of all of these digits. Suppose we are only interested in the odd digits. We could rewrite the function we used in `map` to return 0 for even numbers and the square of the number for odd numbers, but there is a better way. There is a modifier known as `filter` that can be used to restrict a stream to those values that pass some test. So while the `map` modifier gives you a stream of new values of the same length as the original, the `filter` modifier gives you a stream of unchanged values, but not necessarily of the same length because not all values pass the given test.

The `filter` method takes as its argument a Boolean-valued predicate. In our case, we will test that the remainder when divided by 2 is not 0.

```
int sum = IntStream.of(3, 1, 4, 1, 5, 9, 2, 6, 5, 3)
    .filter(n -> n % 2 != 0)
    .map(n -> n * n)
    .sum();
```

Updating our diagram for the flow of data we get the result shown in Figure 19.5.

We now have two different stream modifiers; let's throw in a third. Suppose that we don't want to include any given number more than once in computing this sum. That would normally require some kind of structure like a set to remember values that we have seen so as to eliminate duplicates. But Java provides a specific modifier for this known as `distinct`. The stream that it produces will have values from

```
IntStream.of -> [3, 1, 4, 1, 5, 9, 2, 6, 5, 3]
     -> map -> [9, 1, 16, 1, 25, 81, 4, 36, 25, 9]
     -> sum -> 207
```

Figure 19.4 Stream operations on digits of *pi*

```
IntStream.of -> [3, 1, 4, 1, 5, 9, 2, 6, 5, 3]
   -> filter -> [3, 1, 1, 5, 9, 5, 3]
   -> map    -> [9, 1, 1, 25, 81, 25, 9]
   -> sum    -> 151
```

Figure 19.5 Stream operations with `filter`

the original stream in the same order, but with all duplicates removed (only the first occurrence of each value will be included). So we can add this to our code to get:

```
int sum = IntStream.of(3, 1, 4, 1, 5, 9, 2, 6, 5, 3)
    .filter(n -> n % 2 != 0)
    .distinct()
    .map(n -> n * n)
    .sum();
```

Figure 19.6 shows an updated diagram of this new code.

```
IntStream.of -> [3, 1, 4, 1, 5, 9, 2, 6, 5, 3]
 -> filter   -> [3, 1, 1, 5, 9, 5, 3]
 -> distinct -> [3, 1, 5, 9]
 -> map      -> [9, 1, 25, 81]
 -> sum      -> 116
```

Figure 19.6 Stream operations with `distinct`

This is a fairly complex operation that we have described without saying much about how it is accomplished. We are requesting the sum of the squares of the odd numbers of this sequence after duplicate numbers have been removed. The stream mechanism and these individual modifiers take care of the rest of the work for us.

As another example, suppose we want to write a method to test whether a number *n* is prime. By definition a prime is a number that is divisible by 1 and itself but nothing else. Another way of saying that is that primes have exactly two factors. We can express that using streams by producing the values 1 through *n*, filtering on factors, and seeing whether there are exactly two of them.

```
public static boolean isPrime(int n) {
    return IntStream.range(1, n + 1)
        .filter(x -> n % x == 0)
        .count()
        == 2;
}
```

Remember that the second parameter to `range` is exclusive, which is why we use *n*+1 to have the stream go all the way up to and including *n*. It is worth considering the special case of 1. This method says that it is not prime, because there is only one value between 1 and 1 that is divisible by 1. That is the right answer because the value 1 is not considered a prime. This computation is inefficient because it only needs to test values up to the square root of *n*, but we will delay that discussion for the case study at the end of this chapter.

Using Reduce

Now let's consider the task of computing the factorial of an integer *n*, which is defined as the product of the integers 1 through *n*. This is a slightly different task and requires a slightly different approach. In this case, we want to take all of the integers in a stream and combine them into one integer using multiplication. There is a special stream terminator known as `reduce` that combines elements from a stream. Below is a method that computes the factorial using this approach.

```
public static int factorial(int n) {
    return IntStream.range(2, n + 1)
        .reduce(1, (a, b) -> a * b);
}
```

You will notice that the call on `reduce` begins with an extra parameter `1`. This is the starting value to use for the computation. Multiplying by 1 does not change the overall result and it allows the expression to guarantee that it returns a value even if the stream is empty. That means that 0 factorial is correctly reported as 1. It also means that negative factorials are reported as 1 which we could fix with a test that throws an exception in that case because the factorial is undefined for negatives.

There are many details we have left out about streams. For example, we have not yet discussed the problem that some computations do not produce a result. You can generally compute an average or a maximum or a minimum of a sequence of values, but not if the sequence is empty. Java has a notion of an option type that sometimes has a result and sometimes does not, which we will briefly explore in the next section. We will close with a simple variation of our computation on the first ten squares that uses a built-in terminator known as `summaryStatistics` in place of `sum`:

```
System.out.println(IntStream.range(1, 11)
    .map(n -> n * n)
    .summaryStatistics());
```

which produces the following output:

```
IntSummaryStatistics{count=10, sum=385, min=1, average=38.500000,
max=100}
```

Each of these statistics has a corresponding terminator, such as `average` and `max`. You can read more about them and the other modifiers and terminators in the documentation for the `IntStream` class.

Optional Results

Some of the provided stream terminators have a subtlety that merits investigation. For example, if you want to find and print the largest multiple of 10 in a certain group of integers, you might perform the following stream operations to filter out all the non-multiples of 10 and then print the largest of the remaining numbers:

```
// print largest multiple of 10 in list (does not compile)
int largest = IntStream.of(55, 20, 19, 31, 40, -2, 62, 30)
    .filter(n -> n % 10 == 0)
    .max();
System.out.println(largest);
```

But you'd find that the preceding code generates a compiler error such as the following:

```
incompatible types: OptionalInt cannot be converted to int
```

This is because the results of some stream terminators like `average`, `findFirst`, `max`, and `min` are undefined if the stream does not contain any data. What if there were no multiples of 10 after doing the filtering? There would be no maximum to return. The terminator could have chosen a default value like 0, but this is not guaranteed to be what the programmer would want.

For this reason, those terminators do not actually return the type of result you would expect, such as an `int` or `double`. The designers of the library needed a way to represent that the result might be undefined. So these terminators actually return values of types called `OptionalInt` and `OptionalDouble`. These "optional" types are small wrapper objects for storing a single `int` or `double` result respectively. Each type has a corresponding method called `getAsInt` and `getAsDouble` to extract the value. Those methods will throw a `NoSuchElementException` if the value is undefined. (There is also a more general optional type called `Optional<T>` that is outside the scope of this chapter.)

The following code properly stores the largest multiple of 10 as an integer:

```
// print largest multiple of 10 in list
int largest = IntStream.of(55, 20, 19, 31, 40, -2, 62, 30)
    .filter(n -> n % 10 == 0)
    .max()
    .getAsInt();
System.out.println(largest);
```

A full discussion of these optional types is outside the scope of this chapter, but you can read more about them in the Java 8 API documentation.

19.4 Function Closures

We have seen that Java has extensive rules about the scope of variables that guarantees that every reference to a variable will work out. Consider, for example, the following program that attempts to count how many factors of 10 there are.

```
// Attempts to count the factors of 10.
// Does not compile; not an example to follow.

public class BadScope {
    public static boolean isMultiple(int x) {
        return n % x == 0;
    }

    public static void main(String[] args) {
        int n = 10;
        int count = 0;
        for (int i = 1; i <= n; i++) {
            if (isMultiple(i)) {
                count++;
            }
        }
        System.out.println("count = " + count);
    }
}
```

This program does not compile. Java complains that the variable `n` referred to in the method `isMultiple` is not defined. You might argue that it is defined in the `main` method and is set up before the function is called. But as we have seen, Java has strict rules about this and requires that the variable `n` be visible in the scope of the method or in the outer class scope. Being available in the scope of a different method isn't good enough.

The usual fix is to pass `n` as a parameter:

```
// Counts the factors of 12.

public class GoodScope {
    // Returns true if n is a multiple of (is divisible by) x.
    public static boolean isMultiple(int x, int n) {
        return n % x == 0;
```

```
    }

    public static void main(String[] args) {
        int n = 10;
        int count = 0;
        for (int i = 1; i <= n; i++) {
            if (isMultiple(i, n)) {
                count++;
            }
        }
        System.out.println("count = " + count);
    }
}
```

This program now compiles and correctly reports that there are four factors of 10 (1, 2, 5, and 10). But consider the following code that uses a stream, a call on `filter`, and a call on the terminator `count` which returns a value of type `long`.

```
int n = 10;
long count = IntStream.range(1, n + 1)
    .filter(x -> n % x == 0)
    .count();
System.out.println("count = " + count);
```

It also correctly reports that there are four factors of 10. There is similar code used in the `isPrime` method included in the previous section. But how does it work? Think about the lambda expression being passed as a parameter to `filter`:

```
x -> n % x == 0
```

This is supposed to represent an independent function. In fact, it looks a lot like the `isMultiple` method from the `BadScope` class. It has a single parameter called `x` and it returns a `boolean` value based on whether the variable `n` is divisible by `x`. It has access to the variable `x` because it is the parameter, but how does it have access to the variable `n`?

You might say that you can see the variable `n` defined in the scope in which this lambda expression occurs and that is the key to understanding this, but it is important to recognize that something special is going on here. Remember that you are passing a function to the `filter` method that it will execute. That `filter` function is in a different class that doesn't have access to the variable `n` that is defined here. So somehow the value of `n` is being passed along with the code.

When you form a lambda expression, some of the variables you refer to will be included as parameters to the function. We call such references *bound variables* because they are each connected to a parameter. Any reference that is not to a parameter in a lambda expression is considered a *free variable*. Variables cannot be completely free of definition because then they would be undefined. But because a lambda expression occurs in the middle of code that potentially has variables defined, the lambda expression can refer to free variables that are defined in its outer scope.

Bound/Free Variable

In a lambda expression, parameters are bound variables while variables in the outer containing scope are free variables.

In our sample lambda expression, the outer code defines a local variable called `n`, which means that the reference to `n` in the lambda expression makes sense. But Java has to perform some work behind the scenes to include this variable definition along with the code. We refer to such a combination as a *closure*.

Function Closure

A block of code defining a function along with the definitions of any free variables that are defined in the containing scope.

Let's use another example that goes to an extreme to make the point. Suppose we have a method called `compute` that takes a function of two arguments as a parameter. We might call it like this:

```
compute((x, y) -> x + y);
```

This lambda expression refers to `x` and `y` which are both parameters, which means they are bound. There are no free variables in this expression. But suppose the code instead had been:

```
int min = 10;
int max = 50;
int multiplier = 3;
compute((x, y) -> Math.max(x, min) * Math.max(y, max) * multiplier);
```

This lambda expression has references to `x` and `y` just like the other one, but those aren't a problem because they are bound because they are parameters. But it also has references to variables called `min`, `max`, and `multiplier`, which are not parameters of the lambda expression, which means they are free variables. Java has to include those definitions along with the code in order for the compute method to be able to do its job.

For a visual representation, imagine that Java puts together the code of the lambda expression along with the definitions of the parameters and these three free variables into one big object, as shown in Figure 19.7.

```
parameters    : (x, y)
free variables: min = 10, max = 50, multiplier = 3
code          : Math.max(x, min) * Math.max(y, max) * multiplier
```

Figure 19.7 Diagram of a function closure

This object is the closure. It contains both the code and the relevant context in which the code occurs. The free variables `min`, `max`, and `multiplier` have been included so that the code can be executed. We say that they have been *captured* in forming this closure.

The word closure comes from mathematics (e.g., the concept of a transitive closure), but here is a way to think about it that might be helpful to remember the concept. We all seek closure in our lives, which means that we don't want any loose ends from our past left around to upset us. Free variables are loose ends in a lambda expression that would make it impossible to evaluate the code. By including their definition in the closure, we are tying up those loose ends so that there isn't anything left that is undecided. Once we've done that, we've reached a kind of closure with this computation.

We run into potential problems if any of the free variables included in a closure change in value. If the value of a free variable changes, then the computation isn't well defined. For example, it means that the order in which we perform the individual computations for a stream can change the overall result. This relates to the concept of effect-free programming described earlier in this chapter. We want to write code that does not have these potential sources of inconsistency.

Java requires that any free variable included in a lambda expression has to effectively be a constant. The easiest way to guarantee this is to use values that are defined with the keyword `final`. But the Java compiler will allow you to use ordinary variables as long as your code never assigns those variables a value more than once. This is a helpful restriction, but it still leaves open the possibility that you will have a reference to an object whose state changes. That leads to unpredictable results and should be avoided whenever possible.

19.5 Higher-Order Operations on Collections

You may have noticed that methods like `map`, `filter`, and `reduce` are functions that accept other functions as arguments. As a result, they are known as higher-order functions.

> **Higher-Order Function**
>
> A function that takes another function as an argument.

We have already discussed these higher-order functions previously with examples of streams composed of simple `int` values. In this section, we will explore how similar operations can be performed on arrays and other Java collections. This section also discusses stream terminators that collect stream elements into a collection.

Working with Arrays

Any array can serve as the source for a stream by passing it as a parameter to the method `Arrays.stream`. For example, suppose that you have an array of simple `int` values defined as follows:

```
int[] numbers = {3, -4, 8, 4, -2, 17, 9, -10, 14, 6, -12};
```

Suppose that we want to find the sum of the absolute values of the even integers in this list and we want to exclude any duplicates. That sounds a lot like what we were doing before and we can do it in the same way but using the array as the source of data.

```
int sum = Arrays.stream(numbers)
        .map(n -> Math.abs(n))
        .filter(n -> n % 2 == 0)
        .distinct()
        .sum();
```

We can once again use a diagram to explore what happens on each step of this computation, as shown in Figure 19.8.

Order can matter for these components that modify the stream. For example, if we call `distinct` before we use `map` to convert to the absolute value, then we would miss the fact that there is a −4 and a 4 in the original list. There is a minor efficiency improvement in performing the `filter` operation before the `distinct` operation because `distinct` is easier to perform on a shorter sequence, which is what `filter` provides.

One of these lambda expressions is of particular interest. We call map passing it an expression that converts a number to its absolute value:

```
        .map(n -> Math.abs(n))
```

Think about this expression. It describes a function that takes a value `n` as a parameter and that returns the value of `Math.abs(n)`. But isn't that exactly what `Math.abs` already does? In other words, `Math.abs` is the function we want to pass to `map`. We don't need to make a new function that is basically a second version

```
Arrays.stream -> [3, -4, 8, 4, -2, 17, 9, -10, 14, 6, -12]
  -> map      -> [3, 4, 8, 4, 2, 17, 9, 10, 14, 6, 12]
  -> filter   -> [4, 8, 4, 2, 10, 14, 6, 12]
  -> distinct -> [4, 8, 2, 10, 14, 6, 12]
  -> sum      -> 56
```

Figure 19.8 Stream operations on an array

of Math.abs. Java allows you to avoid this redundancy by directly referring to the Math.abs method. We use the name of the class followed by two colons followed by the name of the method. This syntax in Java is called a *method reference*. That means that our code can instead be written as:

```
int sum = Arrays.stream(numbers)
    .map(Math::abs)
    .filter(n -> n % 2 == 0)
    .distinct()
    .sum();
```

Things work slightly differently for arrays of objects, but we'll explore that in the next section on working with lists. Java cares about the values in a stream but not where those values come from. So a stream whose source is an array of objects would be manipulated in exactly the same way as a stream whose source is a list of objects.

It is also worth noting that the various stream classes have a special terminator called toArray that collects the stream contents into an array. For example, the following code:

```
int[] sublist = Arrays.stream(numbers)
    .map(Math::abs)
    .filter(n -> n % 2 == 0)
    .distinct()
    .toArray();
```

will set the variable sublist to the following array:

```
[4, 8, 2, 10, 14, 6, 12]
```

Working with Lists

As noted earlier, Java doesn't care what the source of a stream is. It only cares about the kind of data in the stream. But so far we have only looked at streams that contain simple int data. Lists store objects, so they tend to be manipulated in a slightly different way.

The List interface now includes a method called stream that can be used to create a stream of values from a list. For example, suppose that we want to process a list of words. We can use the Arrays.asList method to create a list of specific words to manipulate:

```
List<String> words = Arrays.asList("To", "be", "or", "Not", "to", "be");
```

Suppose that we simply want to print these words on a line of output. We could use a for-each loop to do so:

```
System.out.print("words:");
for (String s : words) {
   System.out.print(" " + s);
}
System.out.println();
```

This code produces the following output.

```
words: To be or Not to be
```

Think about what is going on here. We are using a for-each loop to go through every element of the list and to perform some specific task on each of those elements. We can accomplish the same effect by creating a stream from the list and calling the `forEach` method of the stream class to perform the same task expressed using a lambda expression. The stream method `forEach` accepts a lambda that, in turn, accepts a single element from the stream and performs some action on it.

```
System.out.print("words:");
words.stream()
   .forEach(s -> System.out.print(" " + s));
System.out.println();
```

It seems odd to use `forEach` instead of `map`. Isn't this a mapping operation? The answer is yes and this is one of the cases where Java is showing it's clunky implementation of functional programming. There are two reasons that we need to use `forEach` instead of `map`. Remember that `map` is a modifier that takes one stream and produces a new stream. We are calling the `System.out.print` method, which has a `void` return type. Because it doesn't return anything, it would not be an appropriate method to use for a `map` operation. More importantly, each stream needs a terminator. In this case, the application of the `print` method is the last thing we want to do with the stream, so we need a terminator rather than a modifier. It's not a bad idea to think of `forEach` as a variation of `map` that serves as a terminator rather than a modifier.

We can make this code a bit more functional by noticing that we are modifying each string to have a space in front of it and then applying the print method to each of those strings. We can describe this more clearly with a call on `map` that modifies each string and then a call on the `System.out.print` method that can be referred to directly using a method reference:

```
System.out.print("words:");
words.stream()
   .map(s -> " " + s)
```

```
    .forEach(System.out::print);
System.out.println();
```

As usual, we can add more modifiers to this stream computation. For example, we can apply the `toLowerCase` method to eliminate any differences in case, the `distinct` method to eliminate duplicates, and the `sorted` method to put the results into sorted order.

```
System.out.print("words:");
words.stream()
    .map(String::toLowerCase)
    .distinct()
    .sorted()
    .map(s -> " " + s)
    .forEach(System.out::print);
System.out.println();
```

This code produces the following output:

```
words: be not or to
```

There is enough going on here that a diagram is again helpful to understand each individual step. Figure 19.9 shows the various steps in the computation.

Let's explore one last example that shows one of the potential pitfalls that comes up when working with streams. Suppose we want to know the sum of the lengths of the strings in the original list. We can apply the `length` method of the `String` class to each of the strings and then ask for the sum of those values. This seems fairly straightforward:

```
int totalLength = words.stream()
    .map(String::length)
    .sum();
```

Unfortunately, this code does not compile. It says that there is no method called `sum` for the given stream. But doesn't the `length` method of the `String` class return an `int`? So wouldn't the call on `map` produce a stream of `int` values? If so, it should have the `sum` method we were using in the previous section.

```
words.stream -> ["To", "be", "or", "Not", "to", "be"]
 -> map      -> ["to", "be", "or", "not", "to", "be"]
 -> distinct -> ["to", "be", "or", "not"]
 -> sorted   -> ["be", "not", "or", "to"]
 -> map      -> [" be", " not", " or", " to"]
 -> forEach  -> prints: " be not or to"
```

Figure 19.9 Stream operations on a list of strings

The problem is that Java has different stream types and these types are preserved by modifying components unless you explicitly tell Java to change the stream type. The source is a stream of objects, so the `map` command will produce a stream of objects. In particular, it boxes each of the `int` values returned by the `length` method and gives you a stream of `Integer` objects. If you really want it to produce a stream of simple `int` values, you have to instead call the `mapToInt` method that changes the stream type:

```
int totalLength = words.stream()
    .mapToInt(String::length)
    .sum();
```

This version of the code works properly, setting the variable `totalLength` to `13`. Making a diagram is again helpful to consider exactly what is happening here, as shown in Figure 19.10.

Notice that the original stream contains strings, but after the call on `mapToInt`, we have a stream of `int` values. That stream can be terminated with a call on `sum`, as we did in the examples in the last section.

As noted earlier, this short chapter is not meant to cover all of the details of these Java 8 constructs. We are exploring the important concepts with a representative subset of these operations. But if you keep in mind the idea of streams changing their types, then you will probably understand why there are methods with names like `mapToInt`, `mapToDouble`, `mapToLong`, and `mapToObj` and why it is sometimes handy to call the modifier called `boxed` that converts a stream of primitive values into its corresponding wrapped objects.

We saw that you can collect the values in a stream into an array by using the terminator called `toArray`. There is a similar method called `collect` that allows you to collect the results in a collection. You need to construct an appropriate `Collectors` object by calling an appropriate method such as `toList` or `toSet`. For example, using our words example from before, we can convert all of the words to lowercase and collect the results in a set.

```
Set<String> words2 = words.stream()
    .map(String::toLowerCase)
    .collect(Collectors.toSet());
System.out.println("word set = " + words2);
```

```
words.stream -> ["To", "be", "or", "Not", "to", "be"]
 -> mapToInt -> [2, 2, 2, 3, 2, 2]
 -> sum      -> 13
```

Figure 19.10 Stream operations on a list of strings mapped to integers

This code produces the following output:

```
word set = [not, be, or, to]
```

If you want to specify exactly which type of collection to produce, you can do so with a call that passes in a reference to the constructor of the appropriate class. For example, if you want to guarantee that you get a `TreeSet` that keeps the keys in sorted order, you would instead say:

```
Set<String> words2 = words.stream()
    .map(String::toLowerCase)
    .collect(Collectors.toCollection(TreeSet::new));
System.out.println("word set = " + words2);
```

In which case the output becomes:

```
word set = [be, not, or, to]
```

As with the other examples, we are only scratching the surface here of the details of how all of this works, but these examples serve as good indicators of the kind of operations that can be performed using streams.

As you can see from the examples in this section, functional style programming is particularly helpful for processing of collections like arrays and lists. The trio of higher-order functions `map`, `filter`, and `reduce` provide a particularly powerful set of tools for solving a wide variety of computational tasks on collections.

Working with Files

Java 8 provides a new facility for reading the lines of a file into a stream of strings. Importing the package `java.nio.file` will give you access to the `Files` class, which contains a static method `lines` that returns a stream of the lines of a file. The syntax is the following:

```
Files.lines(Paths.get("<filename>"))
```

The `Files.lines` method throws an `IOException` if the file does not exist or cannot be read, so you must surround it with a `try/catch` block or use a throws clause in your method heading. For example, suppose we have a file in the current directory named `haiku.txt` that stores the following three lines of text:

```
haiku are funny
but sometimes they don't make sense
refrigerator
```

The `Files.lines` method would return the file's three lines as a stream containing three string elements. The following code would read and print every line of `haiku.txt` using a stream:

```
// print every line of the file
try {
    Files.lines(Paths.get("haiku.txt"))
        .forEach(System.out::println);
} catch (IOException ioe) {
    System.out.println("Could not read file: " + ioe);
}
```

If you want to process each line, the standard stream operations like `map`, `filter`, and `reduce` can be used on the strings in the stream. For example, the following code finds out the length of longest line in the file:

```
// find longest line in the file
int longest = Files.lines(Paths.get("haiku.txt"))
    .mapToInt(String::length)
    .max()
    .getAsInt();
```

Figure 19.11 summarizes the stream operations and their results. Recall that we need to use `getAsInt` at the end of our stream calls because the `max` terminator returns an `OptionalInt` to represent the possibility that there might be no lines in the file.

```
Files.lines -> ["haiku are funny",
                "but sometimes they don't make sense",
                "refrigerator"]
-> mapToInt -> [15, 35, 12]
-> max      -> 35
```

Figure 19.11 Stream operations on the lines of a file

19.6 Case Study: Perfect Numbers

To complete our exploration of functional programming, we will look at a classic problem from mathematics that is known to take a lot of computational power to solve. We are going to write a program that looks for perfect numbers. A perfect number is defined as one that is equal to the sum of its divisors other than itself. For example, the divisors of 6 are [1, 2, 3, 6]. If you exclude 6, the other divisors add up to 6 (1 + 2 + 3). In fact, 6 is the smallest perfect number. The next perfect number is 28 whose divisors are [1, 2, 4, 7, 14, 28].

If you search for "perfect number" in your web browser, you will find several web sites that chronicle the fascination that many people have had over the years with this concept. Some ancient Greeks believed that the world was created in 6 days because 6 is the first perfect number. St. Augustine repeats this claim in his writings. The ancient Greeks also believed that the moon completes an orbit every 28 days because 28 is the second perfect number.

The first four perfect numbers have been known since ancient times, but the earliest known references to the fifth perfect number date from the fifteenth century. In this section we will write a program to find the fifth perfect number. In doing so, we will be able to explore one of the biggest benefits of functional programming: that it can speed up the execution of programs that require a lot of computational power.

Computing Sums

This problem, as with many problems from mathematics, lends itself naturally to a functional approach. In this first version, let's write code that finds the sum of the divisors of a number not including the number itself and include debugging code that will allow us to have confidence that it is working correctly.

We can use `Intstream.range` to produce a stream of integers and filter it with a test for divisibility and then compute the sum. Let's put it into a method so that we can call it easily:

```
public static int sumDivisors(int n) {
    return IntStream.range(1, n)
        .filter(x -> n % x == 0)
        .sum();
}
```

Normally we would have range go up to `n+1` so that it will include `n`, but in this case we want to exclude `n` from the sum because we are looking for the sum of the divisors other than the number itself.

In the `main` method, we can compute the sums for the first 10 integers and print them out again using a call on `IntStream.range` and a call on `map` to apply our function:

```
IntStream.range(1, 11)
    .map(Perfect1::sumDivisors)
    .forEach(n -> System.out::println.print(n + " "));
System.out.println();
```

Notice that we terminate this stream with a call on `forEach` that prints each number with a space after it. This will produce an extraneous space at the end of the line, but that's not a problem for us at this stage in development. Also notice that the call on `map` takes a method reference to the function to be applied. We use the name of the class (the one we are writing) along with the double colon operator and the name of the method from this class that we want to call.

The code above produces the following output:

```
0 1 1 3 1 6 1 7 4 8
```

We could hand-check that these values are correct, but it is helpful to build some debugging code into our solution that will allow us to see more clearly exactly what is going on in this computation. Java provides a special method called `peek` that is particularly helpful for this kind of debugging. In some sense, the `peek` method has no effect on a stream at all. It produces as output the same stream that it is given as input. But it allows you to pass it a function to be executed on each value in the stream. In our case, we would like to do some printing of individual stream values. We see 10 numbers above and can figure out which one goes with each input value to the function, but we can use `peek` to confirm this more directly.

The code below includes a call on `peek` that prints the number and an equals sign before it maps that number to its divisor sum and prints it.

```
IntStream.range(1, 11)
    .peek(n -> System.out.print(n + "="))
    .map(Perfect1::sumDivisors)
    .forEach(n -> System.out.print(n + " "));
System.out.println();
```

It produces the following output.

```
1=0 2=1 3=1 4=3 5=1 6=6 7=1 8=7 9=4 10=8
```

This output indicates that the sum of divisors for 1 is 0, the sum of divisors for 2 is 1, the sum of divisors for 3 is 1, and so on. This sounds wrong, but remember that we are excluding the number itself from these divisors. We can make this even clearer by adding a call on `peek` to our stream that is computing divisors:

```
return IntStream.range(1, n)
    .filter(x -> n % x == 0)
    .peek(x -> System.out.print(x + ","))
    .sum();
}
```

This version of the code produces the following output:

```
1=0 2=1,1 3=1,1 4=1,2,3 5=1,1 6=1,2,3,6 7=1,1 8=1,2,4,7 9=1,3,4 10=1,2,5,8
```

This output is a little hard to read as well, but keep in mind what we have added. As the method that sums up the divisors encounters a new divisor, it prints it with a

```
IntStream.range -> [1, 2, 3, 4, 5, 6, 7, 8, 9]
      -> filter -> [1, 2, 5]
      -> peek   -> [1, 2, 5] with side effect of printing "1,2,5,"
      -> sum    -> 8
```

Figure 19.12 Stream operations to compute sum of divisors of 10

comma afterward. For example, when it is finding the divisors of 10 it finds the divisors 1, 2, and 5. So it produces the output "1,2,5," which includes an extra comma at the end. Then the code we have in `main` prints the actual result, which is 8. We can see that 1 + 2 + 5 is equal to 8, so we know that this output verifies that the code is working properly.

It is useful to look at a diagram for the specific computation of the divisors of 10. Figure 19.12 shows the steps of the stream computation.

As the diagram above indicates, the call on `peek` is producing a side effect. Normally we want to write code that is effect-free without such side effects, but in this case it is a useful way to make the computation more visible for debugging purposes.

Consider a similar diagram for the overall computation being performed by the `main` method. Figure 19.13 shows the stream operations.

Figure 19.13 is confusing. It implies that it prints all of the text from the call on `peek` before it calls `map` and only later prints all of the answers through the call on `forEach`. A diagram can only convey so much of a complex process like the processing of a stream. The diagram is showing the resulting stream on each step, but that is different from the order of operations. This can get very tricky to understand, but here is a brief explanation. Nothing happens until Java encounters the terminator. When it gets to the call on `forEach`, it works backward to get a value from the stream to process. It goes all the way back to the source which was the call on `range`. The `range` method sends out the value 1, which is given to `peek` to print "1=", and then it passes to `map` which converts it to 0, and then it makes it back to `forEach` that prints the 0. At this point in time we have as output "`1=0`". Then the `forEach` method asks for another value and we begin the process over again using the value 2, then 3, then 4, all the way up to 10. So the right way of thinking of this is that individual values of the stream pass through each of the different modifiers in sequence before the next value from the stream is processed.

```
IntStream.range -> [1, 2, 3, 4, 5, 6, 7, 8, 9, 10]
     -> peek    -> [1, 2, 3, 4, 5, 6, 7, 8, 9, 10]
                   with side effect of printing "1=2=3=4=5=6=7=8=9=10="
     -> map     -> [0, 1, 1, 3, 1, 6, 1, 7, 4, 8]
     -> forEach -> prints to System.out: "0 1 1 3 1 6 1 7 4 8"
```

Figure 19.13 Stream operations to compute sum of divisors of 10

There is a great moral of the story here. The main reason this is confusing is that the output generated by `peek` is mixed in with the output generated by the terminator in a surprising way. And that output generated by `peek` is a side effect. If we restrict ourselves to effect-free code that doesn't have side effects, then we rarely need to think about these issues of ordering.

Below is the complete code for this version that prints the sums for the numbers 1 through 10 including debugging information.

```
// Prints the sum of factors of the integers 1 - 10.
// Initial version.

import java.util.stream.*;

public class Perfect1 {
    public static void main(String[] args) {
        IntStream.range(1, 11)
            .peek(n -> System.out.print(n + "="))
            .map(Perfect1::sumDivisors)
            .forEach(n -> System.out.print(n + " "));
        System.out.println();
    }

    // returns the sum of the proper divisors of n
    public static int sumDivisors(int n) {
        return IntStream.range(1, n)
            .filter(x -> n % x == 0)
            .peek(x -> System.out.print(x + ","))
            .sum();
    }
}
```

Incorporating Square Root

It seems like we are almost done. We can modify `main` so that it looks at a lot of integers (say, up to 1 million) and filters on those that are equal to their sum of divisors. We can also use the `System.currentTimeMillis` method introduced in Chapter 13 to keep track of how much time we spend computing the result. We can temporarily turn off our debugging code by commenting it out and include the following code in `main`.

```
long start = System.currentTimeMillis();
IntStream.range(1, 1000001)
    .filter(n -> n == sumDivisors(n))
    .forEach(System.out::println);
double elapsed = (System.currentTimeMillis() - start) / 1000.0;
```

```
System.out.println();
System.out.println("time = " + elapsed);
```

When one of the authors ran this on his laptop computer, it reported taking 2260.112 seconds to complete, which is over 37 minutes. It correctly reported the first four perfect numbers, but it didn't manage to find the fifth. And it isn't going to find the fifth in a reasonable amount of time.

We need to improve the efficiency of our computation. The easiest way to do this is to notice that each divisor that is less than the square root of a number is paired with a divisor that is greater than the square root. If, for example, we are looking for the divisors of 100, we find that the divisor 1 is paired with 100, the divisor 2 is paired with 50, the divisor 4 is paired with 25, and so on. So instead of finding each divisor by checking all the way up to the number, we can instead find pairs of divisors by checking up to the square root. If you search for the divisors in this way, for each divisor x you find, you know that you have also found its pair, whose value is n / x; so our modified code contains an additional call to `map` that adds in each divisor's pair to our sum.

Remember that we want to exclude the number n itself from the sum. It is always paired with 1, so an easy way to do this is to start our search for divisors starting at 2 rather than 1. If we do that, however, then we have to remember to add 1 to the final result because 1 is supposed to be included in the sum. The code below implements this strategy and updates the call on `peek` to report the pairs of divisors.

```
// returns the sum of the proper divisors of n
// (optimized version that computes up to square root only)
public static int sumDivisors(int n) {
    int root = (int) Math.sqrt(n);
    int sum = IntStream.range(2, root + 1)
        .filter(x -> n % x == 0)
        .peek(x -> System.out.print(x + "-" + n / x + ","))
        .map(x -> x + n / x)
        .sum();
    return sum + 1;
}
```

We can go back to our old client code that shows output for the numbers 1 through 10, which produces the following output.

```
1=1 2=1 3=1 4=2-2,5 5=1 6=2-3,6 7=1 8=2-4,7 9=3-3,7 10=2-5,8
```

This output is different from before in that it doesn't include 1 at the beginning of each list of divisors. That's because we are handling 1 as a special case, as described previously. But there is something else to notice. It is getting the wrong answers for some of these values. In particular, it has the wrong answer for 1, 4, and 9. You might be able to notice what those three numbers have in common, but you can also figure this out by looking at one of them in detail. Let's take 4. Its divisors other than itself are 1 and 2, so that should add up to 3. Instead we are getting an indication that it has a pair of divisors 2 and 2 and that it adds up to 5 when you include the special case of 1.

The problem comes for numbers that are perfect squares. It is true that every divisor that is strictly less than the square root of a number has a different divisor that it is paired with that is strictly larger than the square root. But for numbers that are perfect squares, their square root isn't paired with another divisor. This is a special case that we can handle after the main computation of `sum` by adding the following code.

```
if (n == root * root) {
    sum = sum - root;
}
```

Below is the complete program that checks numbers up to 1 million. This new version takes only 4.493 seconds to run, which is quite a bit better than 37 minutes.

```
// Prints the sum of factors of the integers 1 - 1,000,000.
// Second version with optimizations to compute the sum of
// n's factors more quickly by examining only up to sqrt(n).
import java.util.stream.*;

public class Perfect2 {
    public static void main(String[] args) {
        long start = System.currentTimeMillis();
        IntStream.range(1, 1000001)
            .filter(n -> n == sumDivisors(n))
            .forEach(System.out::println);
        double elapsed = (System.currentTimeMillis() - start)
                         / 1000.0;
        System.out.println();
        System.out.println("time = " + elapsed);
    }

    // returns the sum of the proper divisors of n
    public static int sumDivisors(int n) {
        int root = (int) Math.sqrt(n);
        int sum = IntStream.range(2, root + 1)
            .filter(x -> n % x == 0)
            .map(x -> x + n / x)
            .sum();
        if (n == root * root) {
            sum = sum - root;
        }
        return sum + 1;
    }
}
```

Just Five and Leveraging Concurrency

We are basically ready to see if we can actually find the fifth perfect number. We have checked up to 1 million and didn't find it. We could try going up to 10 million or 100 million or some other large number. But Java provides a nice alternative.

We have been using a call on `IntStream.range` to specify a specific range of numbers to use. We can instead use the method `IntStream.iterate` to produce a stream containing all positive integers. The `iterate` method takes a starting value and an update function. So the source of our stream will be the following call.

```
IntStream.iterate(1, n -> n + 1)
```

This is potentially an infinite stream of numbers because we say to start at 1 and to update by replacing n with n+1, but we never say how it stops. When you work with a stream like this, you have to include a special modifier that limits how many values it produces. Not surprisingly, this modifier is called `limit`. The following code prints the first five integers that are equal to the sum of their divisors (in other words, the first five perfect numbers):

```
IntStream.iterate(1, n -> n + 1)
    .filter(n -> n == sumDivisors(n))
    .limit(5)
    .forEach(System.out::println);
```

This is another place where it is important to understand in general the order of operations. If you think of the call on `iterate` as producing all of its result before you ever get to the call on `filter`, then this code makes no sense. You have to understand this code in terms of individual values being generated by `iterate` and then passed to `filter`. When one of those values passes the test, it is passed on to `limit` and then to `forEach` which prints it. After the `limit` method has produced five values, it stops requesting new values to be checked from the `iterate` method.

We can throw in a call on the modifier `unordered` because it makes the `limit` method easier to optimize so that it potentially runs a bit faster. Combining all of this and running the program with the timing code, it ends up producing output like the following. The program finds the fifth perfect number and takes less than 11 minutes on one of the authors' laptops.

```
6
28
496
8128
33550336

time = 629.301
```

But we can do even better. Computer scientists have realized for a while now that speeding up a single processor cannot be achieved indefinitely and that eventually we will have to leverage the power of concurrency. It is typical now for laptops to be dual-core or quad-core or some other form of multi-core where there is more than one processor. But it isn't easy to take advantage of multiple processors.

The pitfalls of concurrency are beyond the scope of this discussion, but think about something as simple as preparing a meal to be served at a restaurant. It is easy to see how one chef would complete the task by doing everything. Adding additional chefs might be helpful if you can divide up the task somehow. For example, one might prepare an appetizer while another prepares the main dish and a third prepares a dessert. Even in this case the timing matters because if the dessert is completed quickly and the main dish comes out last, then it is possible that the dessert will spoil because the customer won't want to eat it until the end of the meal. And if you try to have a dozen cooks work on the meal you generally end up with the well-known disaster of "too many cooks in one kitchen."

When Google was faced with the problem of performing massive calculations over vast databases, they quickly turned to concurrency with multiple machines to speed things up. They realized that many computations can be decomposed into a mapping operation and a reducing operation similar to the approach we have described in this chapter. For example, if you want to count how many web pages have a particular search phrase, you can map a function over the pages that returns 0 or 1 depending on whether the search term appears in that particular page and then you can reduce all of those 0s and 1s using simple addition. They built a system that they call MapReduce that uses exactly this approach. Typical computations are executed with hundreds of processors working on each problem. An open source version of their system called Hadoop has also been popular for applying concurrency effectively to large-scale computations.

The increasing importance of concurrency has led many to realize that functional programming is a powerful way to take advantage of parallel computation. Its emphasis on effect-free programming allows it to avoid many of the common pitfalls of running code on multiple processors. The model of expressing a computation in terms of mapping, filtering, and reducing lends itself naturally to a concurrent solution because usually these operations can be performed in parallel without affecting the overall result.

Many people enjoy functional programming because they like to express problems in a functional manner. Others appreciate the fact that you can write short code that has a certain elegance to it because complex computations can be expressed very concisely. But in the world of modern computing, the truly compelling reason to study functional programming is that it provides a practical solution to the problem of taking advantage of concurrency. In other words, concurrency is the "killer app" for functional programming that convinced the IEEE/ACM joint task force among others that every undergraduate majoring in computer science needs to understand the basics of functional programming.

It is therefore fitting to end this chapter by noting that the final version of the program has one minor change. We insert a modifier called `parallel` in the block in `main` that is searching for perfect numbers:

```
IntStream.iterate(1, n -> n + 1)
    .parallel()
    .unordered()
    .filter(n -> n == sumDivisors(n))
    .limit(5)
    .forEach(System.out::println);
```

This extra call tells Java that it would be okay to perform this computation in parallel. It's okay for Java to use as many cooks as it has available to work on the individual problems. Imagine, for example, that a thousand different processors are working on this. There is no reason you can't say, "Processor #1, you figure out whether 1 is a perfect number while processor #2 figures out whether 2 is and processor #3 figures out whether 3 is, etc., etc."

Notice, again, that this style of programming is characterized by the lack of specificity of how it is to be accomplished. We describe the source of the numbers to examine, the test to perform, the fact that we want five answers, the fact that we want to print each one, and the fact that the computations can be performed in parallel. But we leave it up to the computer to figure out how best to optimize the actual computations. Many programmers resist this style because many of us are control freaks who want to say exactly how everything is done. It turns out that loosening the reins and allowing the computer to optimize it for us often leads to much better results if we have expressed what we want in a way that preserves flexibility for how to get there. That is one of the things that functional programming is best suited for.

When this final version was run on the same laptop, it produced the following output on one of the authors' computers.

```
6
28
496
8128
33550336

time = 170.636
```

This is 3.7 times faster than it was before. Not surprisingly, the author's laptop is a quad-core machine with four different processors. The final program appears below.

```
// This program searches for the first five perfect numbers.  It uses
// a functional programming approach including a specification that
// the computation can be performed in parallel to speed it up.
```

```

import java.util.stream.*;

public class Perfect {
    public static void main(String[] args) {
        long start = System.currentTimeMillis();
        IntStream.iterate(1, n -> n + 1)
            .parallel()
            .unordered()
            .filter(n -> n == sumDivisors(n))
            .limit(5)
            .forEach(System.out::println);
        double elapsed = (System.currentTimeMillis() - start)
                          / 1000.0;
        System.out.println();
        System.out.println("time = " + elapsed);
    }

    // pre : n >= 1
    // post: returns the sum of the proper divisors of n (i.e., not
    //       including n itself)
    public static int sumDivisors(int n) {
        int root = (int) Math.sqrt(n);
        int sum = IntStream.range(2, root + 1)
            .filter(x -> n % x == 0)
            .map(x -> x + n / x)
            .sum();
        if (n == root * root) {
            sum = sum - root;
        }
        return sum + 1;
    }
}
```

Chapter Summary

Functional programming is a style that emphasizes the use of functions or methods to decompose problems. Java 8 added new constructs to the language to support functional programming.

A side effect is a change made to the state of a program that occurs when a function or method is called, such as modifying a global variable or printing output. Functional programmers try to avoid side effects as much as possible.

A first-class function is one that can be treated like other types of data, such as being passed as a parameter or composed with other functions.

Java provides a shorthand syntax for defining anonymous functions called lambda expressions or lambdas for short.

A stream is a sequence of elements from a data source that supports aggregate operations. An array, collection, string, range of integers, or many other sources of data can be converted into a stream.

Typical operations performed on a stream include map (apply an operation to each element), filter (keep or remove some elements based on various criteria), and reduce (combine multiple elements into a single element).

A closure is a function definition along with the definitions of any variables declared outside the function ("free variables") that the function utilizes.

A higher-order function is one that accepts another function as an argument. Java supports a limited form of higher-order functions through a feature called method references.

Self-Check Problems

19.1 Effect-Free Programming

1. Why do functional programmers want to avoid side effects?
2. Why is calling `System.out.println` considered a side effect? Does this imply that calling `System.out.println` is a bad thing?
3. What side effect does the following function have? How could it be rewritten to avoid side effects?

```
// Doubles the values of all elements in an array.
public static void doubleAll(int[] a) {
    for (int i = 0; i < a.length; i++) {
        a[i] = 2 * a[i];
    }
}
```

4. Rewrite the `SideEffect` program from this section so that it does not contain any side effects. Rather than modifying a global variable, make the function accept the value of `x` to use as a parameter.

19.2 First-Class Functions

5. What change must be made to the math drilling program from this section for it to support subtraction problems?
6. Write a lambda expression that converts an integer into the square of that integer; for example, 4 would become 16.
7. Write a lambda expression that accepts two integers and chooses the larger of the two; for example, if given 4 and 11, it would return the 11.
8. Write a lambda expression that accepts two strings representing a first and last name and concatenates them together into a string in "Last, First" format. For example, if passed `"Cynthia"` and `"Lee"`, it would return `"Lee, Cynthia"`.

19.3 Streams

9. Is a stream the same as an array? How are they similar, and how are they different?

10. What value is stored into the variable `result` by the following code?

```
int result = IntStream.of(1, 2, 3, 4, 5, 6, 7)
    .map(n -> n / 2)
    .distinct()
    .count();
```

11. Write a piece of code that uses stream operations to compute the sum the negations of a stream of integers. For example, if the stream contains `{2, 4, -1, 8}`, the sum to compute is –2 + –4 + 1 + –8 = `-13`.

12. Write a piece of code that uses stream operations to count the number of even integers in a stream. For example, if the stream contains `{18, 1, 6, 8, 9, 2}`, there are 4 even integers.

13. What value is stored into the variable `result` by the following code?

```
int result = IntStream.of(3, -4, 8, -6, 1)
    .map(n -> Math.abs(n))
    .reduce(0, (a, b) -> a + 2 * b);
```

14. The following code does not compile. Why not? How must it be modified?

```
double avg = DoubleStream.of(3.1, -4.5, 8.9, -6.2, 1.0)
    .map(n -> Math.abs(n))
    .average();
```

19.4 Function Closures

15. What is the difference between a free variable and a bound variable?

16. What are the free variables and bound variables in the lambda function in the following code?

```
int a = 1;
int b = 2;
compute((c, d) -> c + b - a);
```

17. The following code does not compile. Why not? What is upsetting the compiler?

```
int a = 10;
int b = 20;
int sum = IntStream.of(1, 2, 3, 4, 5)
    .map(n -> n + b - (++a))
    .sum();
```

19.5 Higher-Order Operations on Collections

18. What is the output of the following code?

```
int[] a = {10, -28, 33, 28, -49, 56, 49};
Arrays.stream(a)
    .map(Math::abs)
    .forEach(System.out::println);
```

19. Modify the code from the previous problem so that it does not print any duplicate values.

20. Suppose you have an array of integers called `numbers`. Write a piece of code that uses stream operations to make a new array called `positives` that stores only the positive integers from `numbers`.

21. Suppose you have a list of strings declared as follows. Write code to use stream operations to print all of the four-letter words in the list.

```
List<String> list = Arrays.asList("four", "score", ..., "ago");
```

22. Write code to print all lines from the file `notes.txt` that are at least 40 characters long.

23. The following code contains four problems causing it to fail to compile. What are they?

```
public static int longestLineLength(String filename) {
    return Files.lines(filename)
        .map(String::length)
        .max();
}
```

Exercises

1. Write a method `printDoubled` that uses stream operations to print twice the value of each element of array of integers. For example, if the array passed is `{2, -1, 4, 16}`, print `4 -2 8 32`.

2. Write a method `sumAbsVals` that uses stream operations to compute the sum of the absolute values of an array of integers. For example, the sum of `{-1, 2, -4, 6, -9}` is `22`.

3. Write a method `largestEven` that uses stream operations to find and return the largest even number from an array of integers. For example, if the array is `{5, -1, 12, 10, 2, 8}`, your method should return `12`. You may assume that the array contains at least one even integer.

4. Write a method `totalCircleArea` that uses stream operations to compute and return the sum of the areas of a group of circles, rounded to the nearest whole number. Your function accepts an array of real numbers representing the radii of the circles. For example, if the array is `{3.0, 1.0, 7.2, 5.5}`, return `289.0`. Recall that the area of a circle of radius r is πr^2.

5. Write a method `countNegatives` that uses stream operations to count how many numbers in a given array of integers are negative. For example, if the array is `{5, -1, -3, 20, 47, -10, -8, -4, 0, -6, -6}`, return 7.

6. Write a method `pigLatin` that uses stream operations to convert a `String` parameter into its "Pig Latin" form. For this problem we'll use a simple definition of Pig Latin where the first letter should be moved to the end of the word and followed by "ay." For example, if the string passed is `"go seattle mariners"`, return `"o-gay eattle-say ariners-may"`.

7. Write a method `countVowels` that uses stream operations to count the number of vowels in a given string. A vowel is an A, E, I, O, or U, case-insensitive. For example, if the string is `"Soo beautiful"`, there are seven vowels.

8. Write a method `toSortedForm` that uses stream operations to convert a `String` parameter into a sorted form with its letters in alphabetical order. For example, if the string passed is `"tennessee"`, return `"eeeennsst"`.

9. Write a method `stdev` that computes the standard deviation of an array of real numbers. The formula for computing a standard deviation σ of N values is the following, where x_i represents each ith element and μ represents the arithmetic mean (average) of all the elements:

$$\sigma = \sqrt{\frac{1}{N}\sum_{i=1}^{N}(x_i - \mu)^2}$$

10. Write a method `glueReverse` that accepts a `List` of strings as its parameter and uses stream operations to return a single string consisting of the list's elements concatenated together in reverse order. For example, if the list stores `["the", "quick", "brown", "fox"]`, you should return `"foxbrownquickthe"`.

11. Write a method `theLines` that accepts a file name as a parameter and uses stream operations to return a count of the number of lines in the file that start with the word "The", case-insensitive.

12. Write a method `fourLetterWords` that accepts a file name as a parameter and returns a count of the number of unique lines in the file that are exactly four letters long. Assume that each line in the file contains a single word.

Programming Projects

1. Write a file searching program that uses streams to efficiently search a set of files for a given substring. Write two versions of the code, one that sequentially reads each file with a `Scanner` and checks each line to see if it contains the substring, and a second that uses streams to open all of the files and search the lines using stream operations. The most efficient version of the stream code will open all of the files in parallel. Test how much more efficient the streams are than the `Scanner` by using `System.currentTimeMillis` to measure the elapsed time for both versions of the code when run on a collection of large files, printing output such as the following:

```
Searching 15 files for "the" using Scanner:
there were 84530 total matching lines.
Took 546 ms.

Searching 15 files for "the" using streams:
there were 84530 total matching lines.
Took 160 ms.
```

2. Write a program that prompts the user for an integer value *n* and that reports the sum of the first *n* prime numbers, reporting a sum of 0 if the user enters a value less than 1. Structure your program to be similar to the case study, using an iterating function to produce the sequence 1, 2, 3, . . . , and filtering using the `isPrime` method that appears at the end of section 19.3. Don't include the `unordered` modifier because we want the first *n* primes, not some other combination of *n* primes. Include timing code and print how long it takes to compute the sum.

Once you have a working program, explore the following efficiency improvements and note how the time changes with each using a fairly large value of *n* such as 10,000:

- Modify `isPrime` to check only up to the square root, as in the case study (remember that 1 is not a prime).
- Modify the iterating function to examine only odd numbers and manually add 2 to the sum (because 2 is the only even prime).
- Modify the overall iteration to include the `parallel` modifier, as in the case study. Note that the benefits of parallel execution might not be evident for this computation because the problem size is fairly constrained (values of *n* greater than 20,043 will lead to integer overflow).

Appendix A
Java Summary

Java Keywords

abstract	continue	for	new	switch
assert	default	goto	package	synchronized
boolean	do	if	private	this
break	double	implements	protected	throw
byte	else	import	public	throws
case	enum	instanceof	return	transient
catch	extends	int	short	try
char	final	interface	static	void
class	finally	long	strictfp	volatile
const	float	native	super	while

Primitive Types

Type	Description	Examples
`int`	integers (whole numbers)	`42, –3, 18, 20493, 0`
`double`	real numbers	`7.35, 14.9, –19.834`
`char`	single characters	`'a', 'X', '!'`
`boolean`	logical values	`true, false`

Arithmetic Operators

Operator	Meaning	Example	Result
`+`	addition	`2 + 2`	`4`
`–`	subtraction	`53 – 18`	`35`
`*`	multiplication	`3 * 8`	`24`
`/`	division	`4.8 / 2.0`	`2.4`
`%`	remainder or mod	`19 % 5`	`4`

Relational Operators

Operator	Meaning	Example	Value
`==`	equal to	`2 + 2 == 4`	`true`
`!=`	not equal to	`3.2 != 4.1`	`true`
`<`	less than	`4 < 3`	`false`
`>`	greater than	`4 > 3`	`true`
`<=`	less than or equal to	`2 <= 0`	`false`
`>=`	greater than or equal to	`2.4 >= 1.6`	`true`

Logical Operators

Operator	Meaning	Example	Value
`&&`	AND (conjunction)	`(2 == 2) && (3 < 4)`	`true`
`||`	OR (disjunction)	`(1 < 2) || (2 == 3)`	`true`
`!`	NOT (negation)	`!(2 == 2)`	`false`

Operator Precedence

Description	Operators
unary operators	`!, ++, --, +, -`
multiplicative operators	`*, /, %`
additive operators	`+, -`
relational operators	`<, >, <=, >=`
equality operators	`==, !=`
logical AND	`&&`
logical OR	`||`
assignment operators	`=, +=, -=, *=, /=, %=, &&=, ||=`

Wrapper Classes

Primitive type	Wrapper class
`int`	`Integer`
`double`	`Double`
`char`	`Character`
`boolean`	`Boolean`

Syntax Templates

Variable declaration without initialization:

```
<type> <name>, <name>, <name>, . . . , <name>;
```

Variable declaration with initialization:

```
<type> <name> = <expression>;
```

Assignment:

```
<variable> = <expression>;
```

Constant declaration:

```
public static final <type> <name> = <expression>;
```

Static method definition:

```
public static <type> <name>(<type> <name>, . . . , <type> <name>) {
    <statement>;
    ...
    <statement>;
}
```

Call on static method:

```
<method name>(<expression>, <expression>, . . . , <expression>)
```

Call on instance method:

```
<variable>.<method>(<expression>, <expression>, . . . , <expression>)
```

Class definition:

```
public class <class name> {
    // fields
    private <type> <name>;
    private <type> <name>;
    ...

    // constructors
    public <class name>(<type> <name>, . . . , <type> <name>) {
        <statement>;
        ...
        <statement>;
    }
    ...

    // methods
    public <type> <name>(<type> <name>, . . . , <type> <name>) {
        <statement>;
        ...
        <statement>;
    }
    ...
}
```

Constructor calling another constructor:

```
this(<expression>, <expression>, . . . , <expression>);
```

Instance method calling superclass method:

```
super.<method>(<expression>, <expression>, . . . , <expression>)
```

Constructor calling superclass constructor:

```
super(<expression>, <expression>, . . . , <expression>);
```

Specifying an inheritance relationship:

```
public class <subclass name> extends <superclass name> {
    ...
}
```

Implementing an interface:

```
public class <name> implements <interface> {
    ...
}
```

Specifying inheritance relationship and implementing interfaces:

```
public class <name>  extends <superclass name>
    implements <interface name>, <interface name>, . . . , <interface name> {
    ...
}
```

Interface definition:

```
public interface <name> {
    public <type> <name>(<type> <name>, . . . , <type> <name>);
    ...
    public <type> <name>(<type> <name>, . . . , <type> <name>);
}
```

Abstract class:

```
public abstract class <name> {
    ...
}
```

Abstract method:

```
public abstract <type> <name>(<type> <name>, . . . , <type> <name>);
```

`return` statement:

```
return <expression>;
```

`throw` statement:

```
throw <exception>;
```

`assert` statement:

```
assert <boolean test>;
```

Array declaration:

```
<element type>[] <name> = new <element type>[<size>];
```

Array initialization:

```
<element type>[] <name> = {<value>, <value>, . . . , <value>};
```

Simple `if`:

```
if (<test>) {
    <statement>;
    ...
    <statement>;
}
```

`if/else`:

```
if (<test>) {
    <statement>;
    ...
    <statement>;
} else {
    <statement>;
    ...
    <statement>;
}
```

Nested `if/else` ending in test:

```
if (<test1>) {
    <statement1>;
} else if (<test2>) {
    <statement2>;
} else if (<test3>) {
    <statement3>;
}
```

Nested `if/else` ending in `else`:

```
if (<test1>) {
    <statement1>;
} else if (<test2>) {
    <statement2>;
} else {
    <statement3>;
}
```

for loop:

```
for (<initialization>; <continuation test>; <update>) {
    <statement>;
    ...
    <statement>;
}
```

For-each loop:

```
for (<type> <name> : <array or collection>) {
    <statement>;
    ...
    <statement>;
}
```

while loop:

```
while (<test>) {
    <statement>;
    ...
    <statement>;
}
```

do/while loop:

```
do {
    <statement>;
    ...
    <statement>;
} while (<test>);
```

try/catch statement:

```
try {
    <statement>;
    ...
    <statement>;
} catch (<type> <name>) {
    <statement>;
    ...
    <statement>;
}
```

Useful Methods of ArrayList Objects

Method	Description	ArrayList<String> example
`add(value)`	Adds the given value at the end of the list	`list.add("end");`
`add(index, value)`	Adds the given value at the given index, shifting subsequent values right	`list.add(1, "middle");`
`clear()`	Removes all elements from the list	`list.clear();`
`contains(value)`	Returns `true` if the given value appears in the list	`list.contains("hello")`
`get(index)`	Gets the value at the given index	`list.get(1)`
`indexOf(value)`	Returns the index of the first occurrence of the given value in the list (–1 if not found)	`list.indexOf("world")`
`lastIndexOf(value)`	Returns the index of the last occurrence of the given value in the list (–1 if not found)	`list.lastIndexOf("hello")`
`remove(index)`	Removes the value at the given index, shifting subsequent values left	`list.remove(1);`
`set(index, value)`	Replaces the given value at the given index with the given value	`list.set(2, "hello");`
`size()`	Returns the current number of elements in the list	`list.size()`

Useful Methods of the `Character` Class

Method	Description	Example
`getNumericValue(ch)`	Converts a character that looks like a number into that number	`Character.getNumericValue('6')` returns `6`
`isDigit(ch)`	Tests whether the character is one of the digits '0' through '9'	`Character.isDigit('X')` returns `false`
`isLetter(ch)`	Tests whether the character is in the range 'a' to 'z' or 'A' to 'Z'	`Character.isLetter('f')` returns `true`
`isLowerCase(ch)`	Tests whether the character is a lowercase letterø	`Character.isLowerCase('Q')` returns `false`
`isUpperCase(ch)`	Tests whether the character is an uppercase letter	`Character.isUpperCase('Q')` returns `true`
`toLowerCase(ch)`	Converts a character into the lowercase version of the given letter	`Character.toLowerCase('Q')` returns `'q'`
`toUpperCase(ch)`	Converts a character into the uppercase version of the given letter	`Character.toUpperCase('x')` returns `'X'`

Useful Methods of the `Collection` Interface

Method	Description
`add(element)`	Adds the specified element to this collection
`addAll(collection)`	Adds all elements from the given collection to this collection
`clear()`	Removes all elements from this collection
`contains(element)`	Returns `true` if this collection contains the given element
`containsAll(collection)`	Returns `true` if this collection contains all elements of the given collection
`isEmpty()`	Returns `true` if this collection contains no elements
`iterator()`	Returns an object that can be used to traverse the elements of this collection
`remove(element)`	Removes one occurrence of the specified element, if it is contained in this collection
`removeAll(collection)`	Removes all elements of the given collection from this collection
`retainAll(collection)`	Removes all elements not found in the given collection from this collection
`size()`	Returns the number of elements in this collection
`toArray()`	Returns an array containing the elements of this collection

Useful Methods of the `Collections` Class

Method	Description
`binarySearch(list, value)`	Searches a sorted list for a given element value and returns its index
`copy(destinationList, sourceList)`	Copies all elements from the source list to the destination list
`fill(list, value)`	Replaces every element in the given list with the given value
`max(list)`	Returns the element with the highest value
`min(list)`	Returns the element with the lowest value
`replaceAll(list, oldValue, newValue)`	Replaces all occurrences of the old value with the new value
`reverse(list)`	Reverses the order of the elements in the given list
`rotate(list, distance)`	Shifts each element to the right by the given number of indexes, moving the final elements to the front
`shuffle(list)`	Rearranges the elements into random order
`sort(list)`	Rearranges the elements into sorted (nondecreasing) order
`swap(list, index1, index2)`	Switches the element values at the given two indexes

Useful Methods of `DrawingPanel` Objects

Method	Description
`getGraphics()`	Returns a reference to the `Graphics` object that can be used to draw onto the panel
`setBackground(color)`	Sets the background color of the panel to the given color (the default is white)

Useful Methods of `File` Objects

Method	Description
`delete()`	Deletes the given file
`exists()`	Indicates whether this file exists on the system
`getAbsolutePath()`	Returns the full path specifying the location of this file
`getName()`	Returns the name of this file as a `String`, without any path attached
`isDirectory()`	Indicates whether this file represents a directory/folder on the system
`isFile()`	Indicates whether this file represents a file (nonfolder) on the system
`length()`	Returns the number of characters in this file
`mkdirs()`	Creates the directory represented by this file, if it does not exist
`renameTo(file)`	Changes this file's name to be the given file's name

Useful Methods of `Graphics` Objects

Method	Description
`drawLine(x1, y1, x2, y2)`	Draws a line between the points (`x1, y1`) and (`x2, y2`)
`drawOval(x, y, width, height)`	Draws the outline of the largest oval that fits within the specified rectangle
`drawRect(x, y, width, height)`	Draws the outline of the specified rectangle
`drawString(message, x, y)`	Draws the given text with its lower-left corner at (`x, y`)
`fillOval(x, y, width, height)`	Fills the largest oval that fits within the specified rectangle using the current color
`fillRect(x, y, width, height)`	Fills the specified rectangle using the current color
`setColor(color)`	Sets this graphics context's current color to the specified color (all subsequent graphics operations using this graphics context use this specified color)
`setFont(font)`	Sets this graphics context's current font to the specified font (all subsequent strings drawn using this graphics context use this specified font)

Useful Methods of `Iterator` Objects

Method	Description
`hasNext()`	Returns `true` if there are more elements to be examined
`next()`	Returns the next element from the list and advances the position of the iterator by one
`remove()`	Removes the element most recently returned by `next()`

Useful Methods of `Map` Objects

Method	Description
`clear()`	Removes all keys and values from a map
`containsKey(key)`	Returns `true` if the given key maps to some value in this map
`containsValue(value)`	Returns `true` if some key maps to the given value in this map
`get(key)`	Returns the value associated with this key, or `null` if not found
`isEmpty()`	Returns `true` if this collection contains no keys or values
`keySet()`	Returns a `Set` of all keys in this map
`put(key, value)`	Associates the given key with the given value
`putAll(map)`	Adds all key/value mappings from the given map to this map
`remove(key)`	Removes the given key and its associated value from this map
`size()`	Returns the number of key/value mappings in this map
`values()`	Returns a `Collection` of all values in this map

Constants and Useful Methods of the `Math` Class

Constant	Description
`E`	base used in natural logarithms (2.71828 . . .)
`PI`	ratio of circumference of a circle to its diameter (3.14159 . . .)

Method	Description	Example
`abs`	absolute value	`Math.abs(-308)` returns `308`
`ceil`	ceiling (rounds upward)	`Math.ceil(2.13)` returns `3.0`
`cos`	cosine (radians)	`Math.cos(Math.PI)` returns `-1.0`
`exp`	exponent base *e*	`Math.exp(1)` returns `2.7182818284590455`
`floor`	floor (rounds downward)	`Math.floor(2.93)` returns `2.0`
`log`	logarithm base *e*	`Math.log(Math.E)` returns `1.0`
`log10`	logarithm base 10	`Math.log10(1000)` returns `3.0`
`max`	maximum of two values	`Math.max(45, 207)` returns `207`
`min`	minimum of two values	`Math.min(3.8, 2.75)` returns `2.75`
`pow`	power (general exponentiation)	`Math.pow(3, 4)` returns `81.0`
`random`	random value	`Math.random()` returns a random double value k such that $0.0 \le k < 1.0$
`sin`	sine (radians)	`Math.sin(0)` returns `0.0`
`sqrt`	square root	`Math.sqrt(2)` returns `1.4142135623730951`
`toDegrees`	converts radian angles to degrees	`Math.toDegrees(Math.PI)` returns `180.0`
`toRadians`	converts degree angles to radians	`Math.toRadians(270.0)` returns `4.71238898038469`

Useful Methods of the `Object` Class

Method	Description
`clone()`	Creates and returns a copy of the object (not a public method)
`equals(obj)`	Indicates whether the other object is equal to this one
`finalize()`	Called automatically by Java when objects are destroyed (not a public method)
`getClass()`	Returns information about the type of the object
`hashCode()`	Returns a number associated with the object; used with certain data structures
`toString()`	Returns the state of the object as a `String`
`notify(), notifyAll(), wait()`	Advanced methods for multithreaded programming

Useful Methods of `Point` Objects

Method	Description
`distance(p2)`	Returns the distance from this `Point` to `p2`
`setLocation(x, y)`	Sets the coordinates to the given values
`translate(dx, dy)`	Translates the coordinates by the given amounts

Useful Methods of `Random` Objects

Method	Description
`nextBoolean()`	random logical value of `true` or `false`
`nextDouble()`	random real number between `0.0` (inclusive) and `1.0` (exclusive)
`nextInt()`	random integer between -2^{31} and $(2^{31} - 1)$
`nextInt(max)`	random integer between `0` and `(max - 1)`

Useful Methods of `Scanner` Objects

Method	Description
`next()`	Reads and returns the next token as a `String`
`nextDouble()`	Reads and returns a `double` value
`nextInt()`	Reads and returns an `int` value
`nextLine()`	Reads and returns the next line of input as a `String`
`hasNext()`	Returns `true` if there is another token to be read
`hasNextDouble()`	Returns `true` if there is another token to be read and if it can be interpreted as a `double`
`hasNextInt()`	Returns `true` if there is another token to be read and if it can be interpreted as an `int`
`hasNextLine()`	Returns `true` if there is another line of input to be read

Useful Methods of `String` Objects

Method	Description	Example (assuming `s` is `"hello"`)
`charAt(index)`	Returns character at a specific index	`s.charAt(1)` returns `'e'`
`endsWith(text)`	Tests whether the string ends with some text	`s.endsWith("llo")` returns `true`
`indexOf(text)`	Returns index of a particular character or `String` (–1 if not present)	`s.indexOf("o")` returns 4
`length()`	Returns number of characters in the string	`s.length()` returns 5
`replace(s1, s2)`	Replace all occurrences of one substring with another	`s.replace("l", "yy")` returns `"heyyyyo"`
`startsWith(text)`	Tests whether the string starts with some text	`s.startsWith("hi")` returns `false`
`substring(start, stop)`	Returns characters from start index to just before stop index	`s.substring(1, 3)` returns `"el"`
`toLowerCase()`	Returns a new string with all lowercase letters	`s.toLowerCase()` returns `"hello"`
`toUpperCase()`	Returns a new string with all uppercase letters	`s.toUpperCase()` returns `"HELLO"`

Appendix B
The Java API Specification and Javadoc Comments

The Java API Specification

Java's Application Programming Interface (API) Specification is a set of web pages that describe the classes, interfaces, and methods of the Java class libraries. You can use these pages to learn class and method names or to find details about a particular method. The API pages can be thought of as a contract between the authors of the class libraries and you, the client of those classes.

The API pages exemplify the idea of the public view of a class versus its private implementation. Each class has a set of constructors, constants, and methods that its clients can access and use. The class also has private fields, methods, and method bodies that are used to actually implement the behavior specified in the public interface. The main benefit of this separation is that you don't need to know the private implementation of the class libraries to be able to use them.

As of this writing, the current Java API Specification pages can be accessed from the following URL:

http://docs.oracle.com/javase/8/docs/api/

(Each new version of Java has a new specification, so this URL will change as new versions are released.) When you visit the API pages you'll see a screen that looks like Figure B.1.

The main frame of the page (on the right) shows information about classes that you can select using the frames on the left. The lower-left frame lists all of the classes and interfaces, and the upper-left frame lists all of the packages in the class libraries. Recall that packages are groups of related classes that you can use in your program by importing them. If you're looking for a class from a particular package, you can click that package's name in the top-left frame to filter the results in the bottom-left frame.

Once you click a class name in the bottom-left frame, information about that class appears in the main frame. At the start of the page you'll see a tree showing the names of any superclasses and any interfaces that it implements, the class's header, and a summary description of the class. The summary description gives general information about the purpose and usage of the class and may link to other relevant documentation or tutorials.

An ordered list of the contents of the class follows the summary. Listed first will be any public fields and class constants. Next will be the class's constructors, followed by its methods. Each field, method, and constructor has a line showing information such

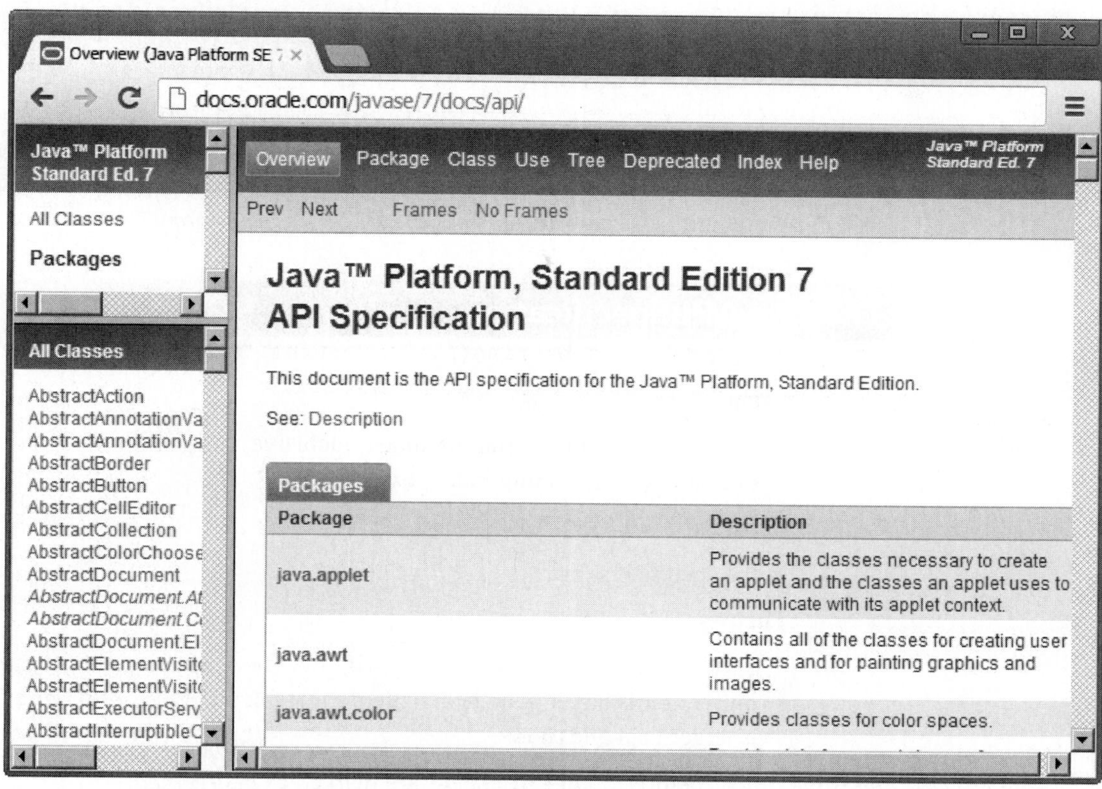

Figure B.1 The Java API Specification

as its name, parameters, and return type, followed by a one-sentence description. You can click the name of the item to see more details about it.

For example, the following is the summary information for the `Scanner` class's constructor to read input from a file:

Constructor Summary

`Scanner``(File source)`

Constructs a new `Scanner` that produces values scanned from the specified file.

Clicking on a method can provide useful details about how to use it, including a longer description, a detailed explanation of each parameter that the method requires, a description of what kind of value (if any) the method returns, and a listing of any exceptions the method may throw. These detail views allow you to learn the preconditions and postconditions of the method and to see examples of calls and their results.

For example, the following are the details about the `substring` method of the `String` class:

substring

```
public String substring(int beginIndex,
                        int endIndex)
```

Returns a new string that is a substring of this string. The substring begins at the specified `beginIndex` and extends to the character at index `endIndex - 1`. Thus the length of the substring is `endIndex - beginIndex`.

Examples:

```
"hamburger".substring(4, 8) returns "urge"
"smiles".substring(1, 5) returns "mile"
```

Parameters

`beginIndex`—the beginning index, inclusive
`endIndex`—the ending index, exclusive

Returns

the specified substring

Throws

`IndexOutOfBoundsException`—if the `beginIndex` is negative, if `endIndex` is larger than the length of this `String` object, or if `beginIndex` is larger than `endIndex`

Some of the methods in the API specs are marked as *deprecated.*

Deprecated
Discouraged from use.

Deprecated items are ones that Java's designers want to discourage you from using. Generally these are methods that Oracle has either renamed or decided shouldn't be called because they didn't behave correctly or safely. You might think that they should just remove these deprecated methods from Java, but doing so would break any older Java programs that call these methods. An example of a deprecated method is the `inside` method in the `Rectangle` class of the `java.awt` package:

`inside` `(int x, int y)`
Deprecated. As of *JDK version 1.1, replaced by* `contains(int, int)`.

Writing Javadoc Comments

If you write your comments in a special style called *Javadoc,* they can be used to automatically produce web pages like those in the API Specification. In fact, Oracle generates the API Specification by writing Javadoc comments in each class of the class libraries. The syntax to signify a Javadoc comment is to begin a multiline comment with `/**` rather than the usual `/*`:

```
/**
 *  This is a Javadoc comment.
 */
```

Javadoc comments may be added to class headers, methods, class constants, public fields, and any other visible members of a class.

Many Javadoc comments also specify additional information using special syntax called tags. A *tag* is an indicator for specific information such as a description of a parameter or return value, the author of a class, the version of a file, and so on. The information in a tag can include boundary conditions, acceptable parameter ranges, and examples.

The syntax for tags is to write an `@` sign and a tag name, followed by any additional information. Several common Javadoc tags are described in the following table:

Tag Name	Description
`@author <name>`	Name(s) of the author(s) who wrote this class
`@param <name> <description>`	Details about the given parameter to this method
`@return <description>`	Details about the value that is returned by this method
`@throws <type> <description>`	A type of exception that this method may throw and a description of the circumstances under which it will do so
`@version <number>`	Version or revision number of the file; may be a number such as 1.2.5 or a more complex string such as a date

The `@author` and `@version` tags are often used on class headers. For example, the following comment can precede the header for a `Point` class:

```
/**
 *  A Point object represents an ordered pair of
 *  (x, y) coordinates in the 2D Cartesian plane.
 *
 *  @author Marty Stepp (stepp@example.com)
 *  @version 1.2 (January 12, 2007)
 */
public class Point {
    ...
}
```

The `@param` and `@throws` tags are often used on methods and constructors. `Nonvoid` methods may also use the `@return` tag. It is best to use the three preceding tags if they supply valuable additional information that cannot be discerned from the method's header or overall comment header.

For example, the following comment can precede the header for the `distance` method of the `Point` class:

```
/**
 * Computes and returns the distance between this point
 * and the given other point.
 *
 * @param p the point to which the distance is computed
 * @return the distance, computed as the square root of
 *         the sums of the squares of the differences
 *         between the two points' x-coordinates (dx)
 *         and between their y-coordinates (dy)
 * @throws NullPointerException if p is null
 */
public double distance(Point p) {
    int dx = x - p.x;
    int dy = y - p.y;
    return Math.sqrt(dx * dx + dy * dy);
}
```

As we mentioned previously, Javadoc comments can be converted into web documentation pages. Some Java editing environments include this functionality; check your editor to see whether it is provided. If not, the JDK includes a command-line tool for generating the pages. To use it, open a terminal window to the directory of your source code files and type the following command:

```
javadoc *.java
```

The web page that is generated for the preceding `Point` class is shown in Figure B.2.

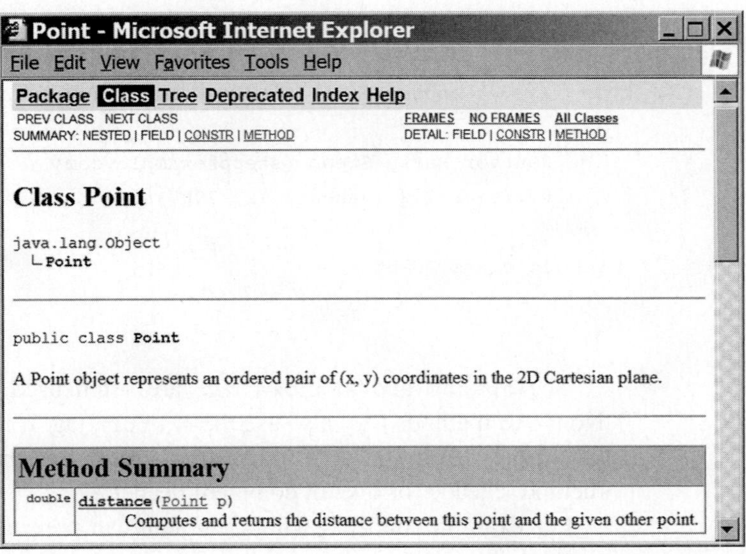

Figure B.2 Generated Javadoc pages for `Point` class

Clicking on the name of a method brings up the method's detail page, as in the API Specification. The web page that is generated for the preceding `distance` method looks like this:

Method Detail

distance

`public double` **`distance`**`(Point p)`

Computes and returns the distance between this point and the given other point.

Parameters:

`p` — the point to which the distance is computed

Returns:

the distance, computed as the square root of the sums of the squares of the differences between the two points' *x*-coordinates (`dx`) and between their *y*-coordinates (`dy`)

Throws:

`java.lang.NullPointerException` — if `p` is null

Because Javadoc comments are converted into HTML, they can contain HTML tags that will show up in any generated Javadoc pages. You may use these tags to format your comments.

Javadoc comments provide documentation to clients that lets them know how to use your class without needing to read its source code. However, they are lengthy and can take time to write. Writing Javadoc comments is most useful when you know that your class will be used by many clients.

Oracle maintains a web site with much more information about writing Javadoc comments at the following URL:

http://www.oracle.com/technetwork/java/javase/documentation/index-137868.html

Appendix C
Additional Java Syntax

This appendix briefly covers several features of Java that are not otherwise shown in the textbook. It is not intended to be a complete reference; see the Java Language Specification and Java Tutorial online for more detailed coverage of these language features.

Primitive Types: `byte`, `short`, `long`, `float`

In this textbook, we have focused our attention on four primitive data types: `int`, `double`, `char`, and `boolean`. Java has four additional primitive types that are used in certain special situations. Three of these additional types (`byte`, `short`, and `long`) are variants of `int` that use a different amount of memory, providing a tradeoff between memory consumption and the range of numbers that can be represented. The fourth, `float`, is a variant of `double` that uses half the memory. It can be useful in certain applications where reduced memory usage and faster computation is more important than extremely high numeric accuracy, such as in computer games.

Type	Description	Range	Usage
`byte`	8-bit (1-byte) integer	−128 to 127	Reading data from an input source one byte at a time
`short`	16-bit (2-byte) integer	−32,768 to 32,767	Saving memory when creating many integers
`long`	64-bit (8-byte) integer	-2^{63} to $(2^{63} - 1)$	Representing very large integers that may not fit into the range of `int`
`float`	32-bit (4-byte) real number	roughly −3.4E+38 to 3.4E+387	Saving memory when creating many real numbers

Many of the operators and much of the syntax that you have used with `int` and `double` work with these types. Two of these types use a suffix letter at the end of their literal values: `F` for float, and `L` for `long`. The following code declares a variable of each type:

```
byte var1 = 63;
short var2 = -16000;
long var3 = 1234567890123456L;
float var4 = 1.2345F;
```

Ternary Operator ? :

Java has a *ternary operator* that allows you to choose between two expressions based on the value of a `boolean` test. ("Ternary" means "having three sections.") Think of it as an abbreviated form of an `if/else` statement, except that an `if/else` chooses between two blocks of statements, while a ternary expression chooses between two expressions or values:

```
<test> ? <expression1> : <expression2>
```

A ternary expression is most useful when you want to assign a variable one of two values, or when you want to pass one of two values as a parameter or return value. For example:

```
// if d > 10.0, set x to 5;  else set x to 2
double d = ...;
int x = d > 10.0 ? 5 : 2;

// e.g. "I have 3 buddies" or "I have 1 buddy"
int pals = ...;
String msg = "I have " + pals + " " + (pals == 1 ? "buddy" :
                                          "buddies");

// Returns the larger of a and b
public static int max(int a, int b) {
    return (a > b) ? a : b;
}
```

Exiting a Loop: break and continue

Java has a statement called `break` that will immediately exit a `while`, `do/while`, or `for` loop. One common usage of `break` is to write a loop that performs its exit test in the middle of each iteration rather than at the start or end. The common template is to form what appears to be an infinite loop:

```
while (true) {
    <statement>;
    ...
    if (<test>) {
        break;
    }
    <statement>;
    ...
}
```

Because the `boolean` literal `true` always evaluates to `true`, this loop appears to execute indefinitely. But a test occurs in the middle of the loop. This technique is useful for solving fencepost and sentinel problems. For example, Chapter 5 examines a sentinel problem for summing numbers until −1. This problem can be elegantly solved with `break` as follows:

```
Scanner console = new Scanner(System.in);
int sum = 0;
while (true) {
    System.out.print("next integer (-1 to quit)?");
    int number = console.nextInt();
    if (number == -1) {
        break;
    }
    sum += number;
}
System.out.println("sum = " + sum);
```

The `continue` statement immediately ends the current iteration of a loop. The code execution will return to the loop's header, which will perform the loop's test again (along with the update step, if it is a `for` loop). The following loop uses `continue` to avoid negative integers:

```
for (int i = 0; i < 100; i++) {
    System.out.print("type a nonnegative integer:");
    int number = console.nextInt();
    if (number < 0) {
        continue; // skip this number
    }
    sum += number;
    ...
}
```

Many programmers discourage use of the `break` and `continue` statements because these statements cause the code execution to jump from one place to another, which some people find nonintuitive. Any solution that uses `break` or `continue` can be rewritten to work without them.

It is possible to label statements and to `break` or `continue` executing from a particular label. This can be useful for immediately exiting to particular levels from a set of nested loops. This syntax is outside the scope of this textbook.

The switch Statement

The `switch` statement is a control structure that is similar to the `if/else` statement. It chooses one of many paths ("cases") to execute on the basis of the value of a given variable or expression. It uses the following syntax:

```
switch (<expression>) {
     case <value>:
          <statements>;
          break;
     case <value>:
          <statements>;
          break;
     ...
     default:                    // optional
          <statements>;
          break;
}
```

The <expression> used in a `switch` statement must be an integral type (`byte`, `short`, `char`, or `int`) or an enumerated type (`enum`, discussed later in this appendix). In Java version 7 and up, you may also switch on a `String` value.

The benefit of the `switch` syntax is that you do not need to repeat the `else if` syntax or the variable's name for each path; you simply write `case` plus the next value to test. If the value does not match any of the cases, none of them is executed. The following code prints a runner's medal; if the runner was not in first through third place, no message is printed.

```
Scanner console = new Scanner(System.in);
System.out.print("In what place did you finish the race? ");
int place = console.nextInt();

switch (place) {
    case 1:
        System.out.println("You won the gold medal!!!");
        break;
    case 2:
        System.out.println("You earned a silver medal!");
        break;
    case 3:
        System.out.println("You got a bronze medal.");
        break;
}
```

The optional `default` case holds code to execute if the expression's value does not match any of the other cases, as shown in the code that follows.

The tricky part of `switch` is remembering to write a `break` statement at the end of each case. If you omit the `break` at the end of a case, the code "falls through" into the next case and also executes its code. A programmer may cause this to happen intentionally, as in the following code, but often it is done by accident and leads to bugs:

```
switch (place) {
    case 1:  // give the same response for values 1–3
```

```
    case 2:
    case 3:
        System.out.println("You won a medal!!!");
        break;
    default:
        System.out.println("You did not win a medal. Sorry.");
        break;
}
```

Many programmers avoid the `switch` statement because it is so easy to produce a bug such as that just described. In older programming languages the `switch` statement was a more efficient way to execute the `if/else` statement, but this benefit is not noticeable in Java.

The try/catch Statement

The `try/catch` statement "tries" to execute a given block of code (called the "`try` block"). The statement also specifies a second "`catch` block" of code that should be executed if any code in the "`try` block" generates an exception of a particular type. It uses the following syntax:

```
try {
    <statements>;
} catch (<type> <name>) {
    <statements>;
}
```

For example, the following code attempts to read an input file and prints an error message if the operation fails:

```
try {
    Scanner input = new Scanner(new File("input.txt"));
    while (input.hasNextLine()) {
        System.out.println(input.nextLine());
    }
} catch (FileNotFoundException e) {
    System.out.println("Error reading file: " + e);
}
```

If you wrap all potentially unsafe operations in a method with the `try/catch` syntax, you do not need to use a `throws` clause on that method's header. For example, you do not need to declare that your `main` method throws a `FileNotFoundException` if you handle it yourself using a `try/catch` block.

Some variations of the `try/catch` syntax are not shown here. It is possible to have multiple `catch` blocks for the same `try` block, to handle multiple kinds of exceptions. It is also possible to add another block called a "`finally` block" that contains code to execute in all cases, whether an error occurs or not. This technique can be useful to consolidate cleanup code that should be run after the `try` block finishes. These syntax variations are outside the scope of this textbook.

The assert Statement

In Chapters 4 and 5, we discussed preconditions, postconditions, and logical assertions. Sometimes programmers want to test logical assertions (Boolean expressions) as sanity checks in their own code. As the code runs, it will check each assertion that it reaches. If the assertion's expression is not true, the program will halt with an error.

Java supports the testing of assertions with its `assert` statement, which uses the following syntax:

```
assert <boolean test>;
```

For example, to test that a variable `x` is nonnegative, you could write the following line of code:

```
assert x >= 0;
```

In general, we expect these assertions to succeed. When an assertion fails, it signals a problem. It means that the program has a logic error that is preventing the assumptions from holding true.

Testing of assertions can be expensive, so Java lets you control whether this feature is enabled or disabled. You can enable assertion checking in your Java editor while you are developing and testing a program to make sure it works properly. Then you can disable it when you're fairly confident that the program works and you want to speed it up. By default, assertion checking is disabled.

Enumerations: enum

Since Chapter 2 we have seen the usefulness of class constants. Sometimes we want to create a type that has only a small number of predefined constant values. For example, suppose we are writing a program for a card game. Each card has a suit: Clubs, Diamonds, Hearts, or Spades. We could represent these values as integers (0 through 3) or strings, but these are clumsy solutions because the range of integers and strings is large, so it may be possible to slip in an invalid suit value.

In such situations, it can be useful to create an *enumerated type*, which is a simple type that has only a small number of constant values.

```
public enum <name> {
    <name>, <name>, ..., <name>
}
```

For example, to create an enumerated type for card suits, you could write the following code in a file named `Suit.java`:

```
public enum Suit {
    CLUBS, DIAMONDS, HEARTS, SPADES
}
```

The following client code uses the enumerated type:

```
// 9 of Diamonds
int myCardRank = 9;
Suit myCardSuit = Suit.DIAMONDS;
```

It would also be possible to create a `Card` class that has a field for the card's rank and a field of type `Suit` for the card's suit. This way an invalid suit can never be passed; it must be one of the four constants declared. You can test whether a variable of an enumerated type stores a particular value with the == and != operators:

```
if (myCardSuit == Suit.CLUBS) {
    // then this card is a Club
    ...
}
```

The `enum` concept is borrowed from past programming languages such as C, in which enumerated constants were actually represented as 0-based integers on the basis of the order in which they were declared. If you want to get an integer equivalent value for a Java `enum` value, call its `ordinal` method. For example, the call of `myCardSuit.ordinal()` returns 1 because `DIAMONDS` is the second constant declared. Every `enum` type also has a `values` method that returns all possible values in the enumeration as an array. For example, the call of `Suit.values()` returns the following array:

```
{Suit.CLUBS, Suit.DIAMONDS, Suit.HEARTS, Suit.SPADES}
```

Packages

Since Chapter 3 we have used the `import` statement to make use of classes from the Java class libraries. The classes in the libraries are organized into groups called *packages*. Packages are valuable when you are working with large numbers of classes. They give Java multiple *namespaces*, meaning that there may be two classes with the same name so long as they are in different packages. Packages also help physically separate your code files into different directories, which makes it easier to organize a large Java project.

Every Java class is part of a package. If the class does not specify which package it belongs to, it is part of a nameless default package. To specify that the class belongs to some other package, place a package declaration statement as the first statement at the top of the file, even before any `import` statements or the class's header. A package declaration has the following syntax:

```
package <name>;
```

For example, to specify that the class `CardGame` belongs to the `homework4` package, you would write the following statement at the top of the `CardGame.java` file:

```
package homework4;

import java.io.*;
import java.util.*;

// This class represents the main card game logic.
public class CardGame {
    ...
}
```

Packages may be nested, indicated by dots. The packages in the Java class libraries are nested at least two levels deep, such as `java.util` or `java.awt.event`. For example, to specify that a graphical user interface file for Homework 4 belongs to the `gui` subpackage within the `homework4` package, you would write the following statement:

```
package homework4.gui;
...
```

Packages are reflected by the directory structure of the files in your Java project. For example, if a file claims to belong to the `homework4` package, it must be placed in the `homework4/` directory relative to the root directory of your project. A file in the `homework.gui` package must be in the `homework4/gui` directory relative to the project's root.

If you write classes that are part of different packages and a class from one package wants to use a class from another, you must use an import statement for the compiler to find the classes. Remember that packages are not nested, so importing the `homework4` package does not automatically import `homework4.gui` and vice versa.

```
package general;

import homework4.*;
import homework4.gui.*;

...
```

Packages are generally not necessary for small projects, though some editors add them to the top of all files automatically. Users of basic Java IDEs or text editors often avoid packages because they can make it harder to compile the entire project successfully. More sophisticated Java editors such as Eclipse or NetBeans handle packages better and usually provide a one-click button for compiling and executing all of the packages of a project.

Protected and Default Access

In Chapter 8's discussion of encapsulation we learned about two kinds of access: `private` (visible only to one class) and `public` (visible to all classes). In general, you should follow the convention shown in this book of declaring all fields `private` and most methods `public` (other than internal helper methods). But Java has two other levels of access:

- `protected` access:

  Visible to this class and all of its subclasses, as well as to all classes in the same package as this class.
- default (package) access:

  Visible to all classes in the same package as this class.

Some programmers prefer to declare their fields as `protected` when writing classes that are part of an inheritance hierarchy. This declaration provides a relaxed level of encapsulation, because subclasses can directly access protected fields rather than having to go through accessor or mutator methods. For example, if a subclass `DividendStock` chose to extend the following `Stock` class, it would be able to directly get or set its `symbol` or `shares` field values:

```
public class Stock {
    protected String symbol;
    protected int shares;
    ...
}
```

The downside is that any class in the same package can also access the fields, which is generally discouraged. A compromise recommended by Joshua Bloch, author of *Effective Java*, is to give subclasses access to private data through protected methods instead of protected fields. This gives the class author the freedom to change the implementation of the class later if necessary.

Default access is given to a field when it has no access modifier in front of its declaration, such as in the initial versions of our `Point` class in Chapter 8 (prior to properly encapsulating it). A field or method with default access can be directly accessed by any class in the same package. We generally discourage the use of default access in most situations, since it can needlessly violate the encapsulation of the object.

Index

A

B

C

D

E

F

G

H

I

J

K

L

M

N

O

P

Q

R

S

T

U

V

W

Y

Z

Credits

Chapter 1

p. 2: Knuth, Donald E. "Computer Science and Its Relation to Mathematics." The American Mathematical Monthly. Vol. 81, No. 4 (Apr., 1974), pp. 323–343.
p. 3: By permission. From Merriam-Webster's Collegiate® Dictionary, 11th Edition © 2012 by Merriam-Webster, Inc. (www.merriam-webster.com)
p. 6: Buchholz, Werner. "Byte." IBM Corporation. 1956.
p. 14: Kernighan, Brian and Dennis Ritchie. "The C Programming Language." Prentice-Hall. 1988.
p. 24: Wilkes, Maurice V. Memoirs of a Computer Pioneer. MIT Press.1985.
p. 24: "Unfortunate that you rushed to face him . . . that incomplete was your training. Not ready for the burden were you." -Yoda. ™ & © Lucasfilm Ltd. All Rights reserved. Used under authorization.
p. 28: Kernighan, Brian and Dennis Ritchie. The C Programming Language. Prentice-Hall. 1988.
pp. 38–39: Raymond, Eric. "The New Hacker's Dictionary." MIT Press. 1996.
pp. 58–59: Taback, Simms. "There Was an Old Lady Who Swallowed a Fly." Scholastic, Inc.
pp. 59–60: "The Twelve Days of Christmas." Mirth Without Mischief. 1780.
p. 60: Orchard Halliwell, James. "This Is The House That Jack Built." The Nursery Rhymes of England: Collected Chiefly From Oral Tradition. 1846.
pp. 60–61: Copland, Aaron. "I Bought Me A Cat." Old American Songs, Volume 1. Boosey & Hawkes. 1950.

Chapter 3

p. 157: Baum, Frank L. "The Wonderful Wizard of Oz." 1900.
p. 158: Groening, Matt. "Springfield (or How I Learned to Stop Worrying and Love Legalized Gambling.)" The Simpsons. Season 5, Episode 10. December 16, 1993.

Supplement 3G

p. 211: Baum, L. Frank. 100th Anniversary Edition: The Wonderful Wizard of Oz. HarperCollins Publishers. 2000.
p. 236: Gregory, Richard. "Cafe Wall Illusion" Perception. Volume 8, Issue 4. pp. 365–380. Reproduced courtesy of Pion Ltd, London. Accessible at www.pion.co.uk and www.envplan.com

Chapter 4

p. 270: EBCDIC Programming Language. IBM Corporation. 1964.
p. 270: Okrand, Marc. Klingon. Stark Trek. CBS Entertainment, 2012.
p. 283: "SAT-Scoring" The College Board. 2012.

Chapter 5

p. 324: Wing, Jeannette. "Computational Thinking." CACM vol. 49, no. 3, March 2006,
p. 344: Pirsig, Robert. "Zen and the Art of Motorcycle Maintenance: An Inquiry into Values." 1984.

Chapter 6

p. 388: Twain, Mark. "Chapters From My Autobiography." North American Review, No. DXCVIII. September 7, 1906.
p. 389: Article 1, Section 2. The United States Constitution. 1788. Accessed at www.archives.gov
p. 389: 1790 Census. Census of Population and Housing. United States Census Bureau. Accessed at www.census.gov
p. 389: 'Herman Hollerith." History. United States Census Bureau. Accessed at www.census.org
p. 389: "The Punched Card Tabulator. Icons of Progress." IBM Corporation. July 12, 2011. Accessed at http://www-03.ibm.com/ibm/history/ibm100/us/en/icons/tabulator/
p. 410: St. Vincent-Millay, Edna. "First Fig" A Few Figs From Thistles: Poems and Four Sonnets. The Edna St. Vincent Millay Society. 1920.
p. 418: Lincoln, Abraham. "The Gettysburg Address." 1863.
p. 440: Carroll, Lewis. "Through the Looking-Glass and What Alice Found There." 1872.

Chapter 7

pp. 514–515: Vanderlinden, Ronald. "Sunspots." Royal Observatory of Belgium. August 28, 2003. Accessed at http://sidc.oma.be/html/sunspot.html
p. 527–528: Jung, Carl. "Myers-Briggs Type Indicator" from Psychological Types. Princeton University Press. 1921.

Chapter 8

p. 533: "Macintosh Computer (History)" Apple, Inc. 1984.
p. 569: Riel, Arthur. "Object-Oriented Design Heuristics." Addison-Wesley. April 30, 1996.

Chapter 9

p. 588: Brooks, Fred. "The Mythical Man-Month: Essays on Software Engineering." 1995.
p. 624: Vlissides, John. "Pattern Hatching: Design Patterns Applied" July 2, 1998.

Chapter 10

p. 695: "The Wheels on the Bus." Traditional American Folk Song.

Chapter 11

p. 753: Twain, Mark. "The Adventures of Tom Sawyer." 1876.

Chapter 12

p. 788: Mandelbrot, Benoit. "Les Objets Fractals: Forme, Hasard, et Dimension. 1e édition." Flammarion. 1995.

Chapter 16

p. 1016: Clancy, Mark. "Sliding Blocks Puzzle" (Windows and Regions) Nifty Assignments at Stanford University Computer Science Department. 2007.

Chapter 17

p. 1070: Huffman, David A. "A Method for the Construction of Minimum-Redundancy Codes," Proceedings of the I.R.E. September 1952. pp. 1098–1102.

Appendix B

pp. 1166–1171: "Java Platform, Standard Edition 7 API Specification." Oracle Corporation. 2012.